Children's Rights and the Developing Law

Jane Fortin LLB, Solicitor
Professor of Law, King's College, London

LexisNexis™ UK

Members of the LexisNexis Group worldwide

United Kingdom	LexisNexis UK, a Division of Reed Elsevier (UK) Ltd, Halsbury House, 35 Chancery Lane, LONDON, WC2A 1EL, and 4 Hill Street, EDINBURGH EH2 3JZ
Argentina	LexisNexis Argentina, BUENOS AIRES
Australia	LexisNexis Butterworths, CHATSWOOD, New South Wales
Austria	LexisNexis Verlag ARD Orac GmbH & Co KG, VIENNA
Canada	LexisNexis Butterworths, MARKHAM, Ontario
Chile	LexisNexis Chile Ltda, SANTIAGO DE CHILE
Czech Republic	Nakladatelství Orac sro, PRAGUE
France	Editions du Juris-Classeur SA, PARIS
Germany	LexisNexis Deutschland GmbH, FRANKFURT, MUNSTER
Hong Kong	LexisNexis Butterworths, HONG KONG
Hungary	HVG-Orac, BUDAPEST
India	LexisNexis Butterworths, NEW DELHI
Ireland	Butterworths (Ireland) Ltd, DUBLIN
Italy	Giuffrè Editore, MILAN
Malaysia	Malayan Law Journal Sdn Bhd, KUALA LUMPUR
New Zealand	LexisNexis Butterworths, WELLINGTON
Poland	Wydawnictwo Prawnicze LexisNexis, WARSAW
Singapore	LexisNexis Butterworths, SINGAPORE
South Africa	LexisNexis Butterworths, DURBAN
Switzerland	Stämpfli Verlag AG, BERNE
USA	LexisNexis, DAYTON, Ohio

Learning Resources Centre

12626082

© Reed Elsevier (UK) Ltd 2003

A CIP Catalogue record for this book is available from the British Library.

ISBN 0 406 93407 X

Typeset by Doyle & Co, Colchester

Printed by Hobbs the Printers Ltd, Totton, Hampshire.

Visit LexisNexis UK at www.lexisnexis.co.uk

Preface

Interest in the concept of children's rights has grown significantly since 1998 when the first edition of this work was published. Two factors appear to be driving a greatly heightened awareness of children as an important minority group with rights of their own. In the first place, there is an increasing appreciation, amongst lay people and lawyers, of the United Kingdom's obligations under the United Nations Convention on the Rights of the Child. Second, a greater rights consciousness was generated by the Human Rights Act 1998 being implemented, in October 2000. The fact that children are, like adults, entitled to claim the rights guaranteed by the European Convention on Human Rights and Fundamental Freedoms has had a dramatic impact on adults' perceptions of children's status. The cartoons conjuring up visions of children for ever consulting their solicitors about rises in their pocket money or ensuring a better brand of breakfast cereal, remain a source of amusement. Nevertheless, it is no longer a matter of dispute whether children are rights holders – the concept of children's rights has become a crucial aspect of our law.

Many of those who work with legal principles affecting children are fully committed to the notion that children have rights. Nevertheless, they may be unclear how to promote such a notion in a way that enhances children's lives at a practical level, rather than allowing it to remain a theoretical ideal. The law does not stand still and the purpose of this book is to consider the extent to which the emerging legal principles can be harnessed to achieve such a goal. Children, like other minority groups, are affected by various branches of law, all with their own distinctive character. Consequently, although there is a rapidly growing body of international human rights law, domestic case law and legislation, much of which can be utilised to promote children's rights, the principles are incoherent and inconsistent. Indeed, at times the developing law and policy in England and Wales are simultaneously promoting and undermining the rights of children. Certainly, there are many instances where they are failing to live up to the objectives of the Convention on the Rights of the Child. Some of this emerging law demonstrates a confusion about the extent to which our society is prepared to allow children certain basic freedoms, whilst at the same time protecting them from making mistakes.

The work considers the developing law in England and Wales within a traditional range of legal topics, which reflect children's own activities and the principles used by lawyers to assist them. The first part considers the theoretical sources of ideas about children's rights and the extent to which international activity in the field of human rights can inform the domestic law. The next and largest part of the book contains chapters all broadly considering the extent to which the law acknowledges the growing maturity of adolescents and their capacity for independent thought and action. These chapters review the extent to which the law encourages adults to consult adolescents and older children over decisions regarding their future and the scope they are given to reach legally binding decisions of their own. The work's third part assesses the way in which the law balances the rights of younger children who are incapable of making decisions for themselves, against parents' powers and responsibilities regarding their upbringing. It considers how the law's support for parental autonomy, at times, hampers the legal fulfillment of children's own rights in various contexts. The fourth part of the work contains chapters considering the manner in which the state fulfils children's rights to protection against parental abuse and the extent to which children are protected from abuse whilst in state care. It also considers the rights of young offenders to be protected against a society which continues to maintain savagely punitive attitudes towards those who offend against its rules. The last chapter assesses the dilemmas that the law poses and the ways in which children's rights could be enforced more effectively and coherently.

Placing the legal principles affecting children in a rights-based framework can achieve little when they lack practical relevance. This lack of relevance often occurs quite simply because adult assumptions about children's interests are entirely unrealistic. To redress this weakness, readers of this work will find that there are numerous references to the steadily growing body of research on children's real needs. This is used throughout the work to test and inform the legal principles under discussion. It should also be noted that a work of this nature cannot cover all the topics at a sufficient depth to do justice to the wealth of research and academic comment underpinning them. It is hoped that the many footnoted references to much of this material will provide signposts for those tempted to delve more deeply into some of the subject areas.

ACKNOWLEDGMENTS

As with the first edition, I am immensely grateful to numerous colleagues and practitioners who have assisted me when researching and writing this work. Amongst the countless busy people who responded to my queries with unfailing generosity, I would particularly like to thank Phil Bates, Tim Bateman, Kenneth Campbell, Carol Edwards, Neville Harris, Penney Lewis, Peter Newell, Peggy Ray, Richard White, Nigel Stone and Gary Vaux. Some of them even went so far as to provide me with detailed comments on drafts of chapters, and, more to the point, pointed out my mistakes. But the greatest support and help came from my husband. I am endlessly indebted to him not only for reading and commenting on huge chunks of draft material, but also for keeping me and himself sane whilst this work was in preparation. Our daughters, Abigail, Elizabeth and Katharine have again patiently suffered my lack of attention during its production and, as before, this book is dedicated to them.

Jane Fortin
March 2003

Contents

Table of statutes

References in the right-hand column are to page numbers. Where a page number is set out in **bold** this indicates that the statute is set out in part or in full.

Table of international instruments

References in the right-hand column are to page numbers. Where a page number is set out in **bold** this indicates that the instrument is set out in part or in full.

Table of cases

B

C

D

E

H

L

M

N

O

P

S

T

Part One

Theoretical perspectives and international sources

Chapter 1

Theoretical perspectives

(1) INTRODUCTION

The concept of children's rights has undoubtedly been strengthened by implementation of the Human Rights Act 1998. Nevertheless, the notion that children enjoy rights is not a new one – rather, it has been the topic of speculation and comment for over 30 years. Certain themes constantly recur. Indeed, although writers have often approached this field of thought from a variety of viewpoints, they have all identified common areas of concern, principally surrounding how to identify children's rights, how to balance one set of rights against another in the event of conflict between them, and how to mediate between children's rights and those of adults. Practitioners are wrong to assume that such a voluminous body of theoretical inquiry should be confined to the realm of intellectual speculation. If made more accessible, it might usefully inform their own attempts to apply legal principles to individual children in a way which promotes those children's moral and legal rights more effectively. Better still, when it can be demonstrated that existing legal principles clearly reflect such theoretical ideals, the law gains a greater intellectual validity.

This chapter sets out to identify these recurring themes and provide a brief summary of their treatment. It is divided broadly into two parts. The first analyses the contributions made by the 'children's liberationists', a group of authors whose radical claims provided the children's rights movement with a dramatic impetus. Although they over-emphasised the importance of children's rights to enjoy adult freedoms, they made an invaluable contribution to this field of thought. In particular they generated considerable interest in children's ability to take greater responsibility for their lives, which in turn led to a reassessment of the legal principles relating to children's capacity for decision-making. They also provoked considerable controversy and anxiety over how to balance children's rights to greater freedom against parents' rights to privacy from state interference.

The second part of the chapter analyses some of the more theoretical problems which have been the focus of philosophical and jurisprudential thought. The children's liberationists assumed that children, as a class, were rights-holders. In order to pre-empt suggestions that it is putting the cart before the horse to adopt the term 'children's rights' without attempting to justify the existence of such a concept per se, this part of the chapter briefly assesses the theoretical debates which have centred on the question of whether children, as a group, can be termed rights-holders at all. Many theorists have concentrated on finding an ideal theoretical model for the concept of children's rights and since debates on this will never be resolved, their contributions remain at the level of intellectual conjecture. Nevertheless, they are of considerable importance since they give the concept of children's rights a theoretical rigour that it might otherwise lack.

Even if it is established that children can be rights-holders, there are no clear methods of establishing what rights they may legitimately demand – perhaps explaining why claims are sometimes made for the recognition of a variety of children's 'rights' which seem spurious. The chapter proceeds to consider the partial solution to this problem which is met by classifying children's rights into categories. But even if the proposition that children are legitimate rights-holders is accepted, there is the further difficulty of balancing their rights against each other. Children, like adults, may have conflicting rights. In particular they may have the right to have their decision-making powers respected, whilst also having a right to be protected, so that they may live their lives to the full. A consideration of the extent to which children's decision-making rights can be overridden by paternalistic interventions, in the event of their making choices which might endanger their future lives, has been a constant source of commentary at a theoretical level. This may be utilised to assist practitioners who often confront this dilemma when attempting to apply the developing law to individual children.

(2) THE CHILDREN'S RIGHTS MOVEMENT AND THE CHILDREN'S LIBERATIONISTS

(A)   Children's liberation

The ideas of the 'children's liberationists' generated a wealth of valuable debate about the extent to which society should encourage children to develop their powers of self-determination. The American civil rights movement had encouraged, in the 1960s and early 1970s, a far more sympathetic attitude to the treatment of all minority groups, including children. In the long run, however, the early American children's liberationists may have done the concept of children's rights a disservice, in so far as they conveyed the misleading impression that it is almost wholly concerned with giving children adult freedoms. It was Foster and Freed, writing in the 1970s, who claimed that adults exploited their power over children and that children's inferior status should be radically reassessed. They argued that 'Children are persons and the law should recognize that fact, although it will take some doing. The status of minority is the last legal relic of feudalism …',[1] and they gathered inspiration from a series of decisions reached by the United States Supreme Court.[2] Most notable of these was the landmark decision of *Re Gault*[3] in which the court ruled that 'neither the Fourteenth Amendment nor the Bill of Rights is for adults alone'[4] and that as 'persons', children were entitled to claim the same procedural safeguards as those offered to adults by the United States Constitution. In their view, this case law indicated that there were now important checks on the way parents and the state exercised their authority over children under the guise of promoting their welfare.[5]

Adopting the views of writers such as Ariès[6] that childhood is a relatively recent Western social 'invention', Holt and Farson, the most well-known of the children's liberationists, argued that it was a form of oppressive and unwarranted discrimination

1   See H Foster and D Freed (1972) p 343.
2   Eg *Tinker v Des Moines Independent Community School District* 393 US 503 (1969) and *Goss v Lopez* 419 US 565 (1975).
3   387 US 1 (1967).
4   387 US 1 at 13 (1967).
5   See H Foster and D Freed (1972) p 345.
6   P Ariès (1962). The strength of his view has been undermined by later historical research. See eg L Pollock (1983).

to exclude children from the adult world. In their view, children had a far greater ability for self-determination than most societies cared to admit and there was little reason to exclude them from the freedoms granted by the state to adults.[7] Thus Holt argued that children of any age should have, amongst other things, the right to vote, to work for money, to own and sell property, to travel, to be paid a guaranteed minimum state income, to direct their own education, to use drugs and to control their own private sexual lives.[8] The fact that children might be too young to wish to exercise any of these rights was merely part of their freedom of choice; they could exercise them, when and if they chose, in precisely the same way as adults do. The publicity these radical views attracted led to the movement for children's rights becoming inextricably associated with giving adult rights to children.[9]

Not surprisingly, the liberationists' writings provoked considerable criticism. But their importance lies in the fact that they also generated a reassessment of children's capacity for autonomy and responsible action. There is now a fairly widespread view that it is wrong to underestimate children's abilities and moreover that they should be encouraged to develop their independence. A general interest in this notion continues to underlie much of what is written about children's rights today.

(B)   Children should be allowed to be 'children'

To modern readers the claims of writers like Holt and Farson for children to enjoy adult freedoms might seem not only unrealistic but reckless. The views of the child liberationists were, from the first, extremely controversial. Much of the criticism, both in the 1970s[10] and after,[11] has focused on a variety of relatively practical issues. Two main topics have been recurrent themes. The first is that there are obvious dangers in ignoring the slow rate of children's physical and mental development by giving them the same rights and responsibilities as fully mature adults. The second is the danger of interfering with the relationship between children and parents, including the potential damage to the family unit as a whole.

Many writers have voiced considerable concern over the liberationists' failure to accord sufficient attention to the physical and mental differences between childhood and adulthood.[12] Indeed, this is the most obvious weakness of the liberationists' ideas. They appeared to ignore the evidence on developmental growth through childhood, which establishes clearly that children are different from adults in development, behaviour, knowledge, skills and in their dependence on adults, most often their parents. Current research evidence becoming available since the 1970s reinforces the view that the liberationists' ideas were based on an unrealistic perception of children's capacities. It is obviously impossible to set a single age when all children can be deemed competent to reach any particular type of decision. It seems clear, however, that the relatively slow development of children's cognitive processes makes the *majority* of children unfit to take complete responsibility for their own lives by being granted adult freedoms before they reach mid-adolescence.[13] Moreover, as Fox

---

7   J Holt (1974). See also R Farson (1974).
8   J Holt (1974) p 18. Farson's list of rights was very similar to that set out by Holt. See also the list of rights proposed by H Foster and D Freed (1972) p 347.
9   The work of the children's liberationists is described by D Archard (1993) Part II.
10   See, inter alia, M Wald (1979) and B Hafen (1976).
11   See, inter alia, L Fox Harding (1997) ch 5. See also D Archard (1993) chs 4 and 5.
12   See particularly L Fox Harding (1997).
13   Discussed in chapter 3 below.

Harding cogently points out, a failure to regulate childhood would lead to more exploitation of children, rather than less.[14]

The child's gradual developmental state is also crucial to the relative importance of his or her capacity for autonomy. Children have a whole range of rights and many, such as the right to care and protection, have little to do with making decisions. Acknowledging these may, depending on their maturity, be much more important to young children than acknowledging any claimed right to autonomy. Nevertheless, they soon move out of dependence and into a developmental stage where their capacity for taking responsibility for their lives needs encouraging. A frequent source of comment is the difficulty of reconciling one phase with the next. Whilst there may be sympathy with the view that even quite young children should be groomed for future citizenship by adopting ever increasing responsibilities, there is also the fear that children may be encouraged to become increasingly sophisticated and, in particular, to develop greater powers of self-determination before they are ready to do so.

The need to protect children from being forced into adulthood before they are sufficiently mature is a common theme of those opposing the liberationists' calls for children to gain autonomy rights. Campbell points to the constant stress on children's adult-like competence to make rational decisions for themselves, which in his view is tantamount to claims to redraw the boundaries between childhood and adulthood. He urges that the current needs of the child *here and now*, should not be sacrificed to those of the future child. Children have a right to be children and not adults.[15] The frequency with which these arguments and counter-arguments are raised reinforces the notion that the same child may need both care for one purpose and autonomy or self-determination for another.[16]

The more recent proponents of the children's liberation school, such as Harris[17] and Franklin,[18] are less radical than the early writers. But they continue to promote their central premise, that even quite young children are capable of competent thought and of making informed choices, and some are far more competent to make decisions than many adults. Moreover, as they point out, arguments against children being entrusted with the capacity to make decisions apply equally to adults. Adults, like children, make mistakes; they too may be ignorant and lack education and experience. There is also the not unreasonable view that until quite young children are trusted with more decision-making, they are denied the opportunity of gaining experience in doing so and, more importantly, of developing any decision-making skills. Freeman wisely suggests that whilst the special treatment of children can be justified on the basis of the child's incapacity or immaturity, at the same time they should be brought 'to a capacity where they are able to take full responsibility as free, rational agents for their own system of ends'.[19]

The reassessment of children's capacities provoked by these views led to a more critical examination of the role of the law in its treatment of children. There has, for example, been condemnation of the arbitrary and inconsistent age limits determining

---

14   L Fox Harding (1997) p 134.
15   T Campbell (1992) p 20.
16   See M Minow (1986) p 14.
17   J Harris (1982).
18   B Franklin (1986), (1995) pp 10–14 and (2002).
19   M Freeman (1983 a) p 57.

children's competence to take part in various activities.[20] These exclude intelligent 17-year-olds from voting, whilst allowing incompetent adults to exercise such rights. The majority of the House of Lords in *Gillick v West Norfolk and Wisbech Area Health Authority*[21] obviously sympathised with the notion of adopting a more intelligent approach to assessing children's legal competence. Lord Scarman commented:

> 'If the law should impose on the process of "growing up" fixed limits where nature knows only a continuous process, the price would be artificiality and a lack of realism in an area where the law must be sensitive to human development and social change.'[22]

Indeed, the decision in *Gillick* reflects a more liberal view of the status of children in society and the ability of teenagers to take responsibility for important decisions regarding their health and their future generally.[23]

(C) Children's autonomy and the parental role

The ideas of the children's liberationists were particularly controversial in the way they affected the child-parent relationship. Nevertheless, in this context, they were more comprehensible when applied to adolescents. Indeed, the *Gillick* decision[24] translated the concept of a qualified form of teenage autonomy into new legal principles governing the boundaries between parents' rights and children's rights. It suggested that, in some circumstances, parents might have no power to interfere with the decisions taken by mature teenagers over a variety of matters relating to their own future lives. It also strongly promoted the idea that parents should stand back and allow their teenagers to take responsibility for their lives when capable of doing so. But if parents are not willing to do so, should the law make them? The more radical children's liberationists certainly considered parents incapable of giving children greater freedom without being forced to do so. They saw childhood as an oppressed state and parents as the chief oppressors. Rather than the family being a protective haven, it was the place where, at best, parents might exploit their children and treat them as a mixture of expensive nuisance, slave and 'Ideal Cute Child';[25] at worst a place where parents could abuse their children in private.

A fundamental weakness of the liberationists' assessment of the role of parents in the lives of their children is that they denied the realities of the younger child's physical dependence on his or her parents.[26] To be fair, some of the proponents of children's 'liberation' did not deny the ties between parent and child. Thus Foster and Freed listed as the first principle in their Bill of Rights for Children the need of a child for parental love and affection.[27] Writers like Holt, however, appeared to have

---

20 Eg whilst it is unlawful for a young person under the age of 16 to sell scrap metal (Scrap Metal Dealers Act 1964, s 5(1)), the same young person can be sentenced to long terms of detention for certain criminal offences (Powers of Criminal Courts (Sentencing) Act 2000, s 90, formerly Children and Young Persons Act 1933, s 53). Freeman calls for these age limits to be constantly re-examined and criticises the double standards applied to children by such arbitrary age limits. See M Freeman (1983 a) p 46 and M Freeman (1992) pp 34–36.
21 [1986] AC 112.
22 [1986] AC 112 at 186.
23 See J Eekelaar (1986) pp 177–182. Discussed in chapter 3 below.
24 [1986] AC 112.
25 J Holt (1974) p 126.
26 See particularly L Fox Harding (1997) ch 5.
27 See H Foster and D Freed (1972) p 347.

a distorted view of the parent-child relationship in the majority of modern homes. He failed to recognise that, although parents may once have treated their children like chattels, this is no longer the case. Furthermore, although a minority of parents abuse their children, most parents are, in reality, the adults who know and love their children best and are therefore rightly cast by the state in the caring role and in a position to exercise powers over their children.

If the privacy of family life does allow a minority of parents to undermine their children's self-confidence and capacity for self-determination, should the government intervene to promote a 'better' relationship between all parents and children? The prospect of government intervention in family life through legislation has traditionally provoked strong hostility, especially if such legislation threatens to interfere with the parent-child relationship. Fox Harding notes that nineteenth-century laws restricting child labour and introducing compulsory education were opposed on grounds that they constituted an unacceptable interference with family responsibility and parental rights.[28] Currently, anxieties about family privacy are often linked with the fear that if children's capacity for autonomy were promoted by the state, this would involve a much closer monitoring of the way parents bring up their children, with the consequent undermining of their authority. Goldstein, Freud and Solnit,[29] the most famous proponents of this argument, elaborated on three interrelated issues underlying it. First, there is the view that parents cannot carry out their child-rearing responsibilities with any confidence if they are subject to constant scrutiny. Underlying this is the conviction that privacy is essential to family life and that interference detracts from its value to its members. Second, there is the view that families operate most successfully if they are allowed to establish their own values and rules, and that therefore family autonomy is essential to a well-ordered community. Third, there is the view that the state has not the resources or the sensitivity to do a good job of parenting instead of parents.

There are obvious problems for the concept of children's rights of maintaining the importance of family privacy and autonomy. Goldstein, Freud and Solnit rather implausibly couched the concept of parental power and family autonomy in terms of children's rights rather than parents' rights. In their view it was the child who had a fundamental right to autonomous parents and family integrity. Moreover, they considered that:

> '... a child's need for continuity of care by autonomous parents requires acknowledging that parents should generally be entitled to raise their children as they think best, free from state interference. This conviction finds expression in our preference for *minimum state intervention* and prompts restraint in defining justifications for coercively intruding on family relationships.'[30]

These views have been strongly criticised as being far too extreme in relation to the need for family autonomy.[31] Historically, however, the law has adopted a similar 'laissez-faire'[32] approach in relation to parental care of their children. In many respects, the Children Act 1989 reflects an assumption that the child's interests are identical to those of its parents and that the parents will fulfil their parental obligations best if left alone to do so without undue interference. Despite an attempt to liberalise the parent-

28   L Fox Harding (1997) p 35.
29   J Goldstein, A Freud and A Solnit (1973) and J Goldstein, A Freud and A Solnit (1980).
30   J Goldstein, A Freud and A Solnit (1980) p 4.
31   Critics include, inter alia, B Dickens (1981) and M Freeman (1983 b).
32   L Fox Harding (1997). This author uses the terms 'laissez-faire' and 'minimalism' to describe the view that the role of the state in child care should be a minimal one, while the privacy and sanctity of the parent-child relationship should be respected.

child relationship by a change of language,[33] the 1989 Act adopts a non-interventionist approach to family life. The fact that, unlike Scottish parents, English parents are not obliged to consult their children aged over 12 about major decisions to do with their upbringing,[34] indicates an exaggerated legislative 'hands-off' approach to family democracy.[35]

The Children Act 1989 does not attempt to change the habits of the minority but keeps faith with the majority of parents who, it implicitly assumes, can be trusted not to treat their children as chattels but to exercise their parental powers in a loving fashion. It sees the average parents as fully aware of the requirements of society and assumes that their relationship with their children has changed considerably since Victorian times, when some clearly exercised their powers over their children in a tyrannical way. In this respect, it reflects the aims of article 8 of the European Convention for the Protection of Human Rights and Fundamental Freedoms (ECHR) by reinforcing the view that the state must respect family privacy. But although a degree of family privacy is obviously desirable, a hands-off presumption endangers the concept of children's rights by fostering the view that parental behaviour towards their children should largely be outside the scope of the law. The family may be likened to a state within a state; interference by the public state within family affairs is a grave matter, comparable to interference by one state with the internal affairs of another.[36] The consequence of such an approach is that children are doubly dependent. Not only are they themselves situated outside the sphere of a rights-bearing status, but they are also situated within the sphere of the private family, with parents standing between them and the state.[37]

Finally, there is also the rather more practical issue of the effect on parents of promoting children's decision-making rights. Requiring parents to promote their children's capacity for autonomy may result in a diminution of their own confidence and ability to bring up their children according to their family beliefs and values. These concerns are well expressed by O'Brien Steinfels:

> 'There is a deep contradiction between the political theory underlying our law with its impulse to protect individuals by an appeal to rights, and the biological and psychological requirements for successfully rearing children to participate as adults in such a polity. In effect, one of the most perplexing questions raised by these changes is whether the efforts to extend rights of citizens to minors will not inhibit and undermine the kind of parental authority and family autonomy necessary to foster the qualities and virtues adult citizens must possess and be able to exercise in our society.'[38]

There is a hint, in these words, that those promoting children's rights are wholly motivated by a concern to achieve recognition for children's right to autonomy, rather than any of their other rights. Although this is a false perception, such views are widely held and cause concern.[39] Indeed, some argue that giving children greater liberties risks rendering the parental role not only unworkable but quite untenable. Purdy considers that the more radical claims of the children's liberationists appear to

---

33   Ie using the term 'parental responsibilities' as opposed to 'parental rights'. But see A Bainham (1998 b), who (pp 4–5) considers that this change in language produces an unbalanced view of the child-parent relationship.

34   See Children (Scotland) Act 1995, s 6.

35   Discussed in more detail in chapter 3.

36   J Bigelow et al (1988) p 185.

37   M Minow (1986) p 18.

38   M O'Brien Steinfels (1982) p 232.

39   See, inter alia, M Wald (1979) and B Hafen (1976).

overlook the fact that the parenting role might eventually hold little attraction for many adults and points out that if children were free to leave home, so could parents.[40] She appeals to 'the common-sense view' that certain limits imposed especially on children are justifiable. Parents are right to require their children to go to school and to help around the house. Society is justified in requiring children to be educated and restricting them in various ways, such as limiting their working hours.[41] Clearly, she derives force for this approach from a belief that it is perfectly justifiable to restrict children's choices by paternalistic intervention.[42]

This continued preoccupation with children's autonomy, initially generated by the children's liberationists, has produced a surprising depth of conflict. At a practical level, it can be seen that the stress placed on children's rights to enjoy adult freedoms, at the expense of, or in addition to, a child's other rights causes deep disagreement.[43] Some writers even tend to identify a reluctance to acknowledge this category of rights with an attack on the concept of children's rights itself,[44] an approach which reflects a conviction that their other rights are somehow of lesser importance. Much of the controversy produced by these ideas may stem from a perceived need to reassess the nature of childhood and an uncertainty over what form of upbringing is most suitable for contemporary children.

(D)   The changing nature of childhood

The overriding emphasis placed by the children's liberationists on autonomy might not appear particularly important to many children in the world. Indeed, the right to basic sustenance is a far more urgent need for children in an under-developed country where starvation is endemic. In pragmatic terms, governments would achieve more by fulfilling the rights ensuring children's survival and good health than any claimed right to autonomy. Predictably, the United Nations Convention on the Rights of the Child (CRC)[45] reflects a wide range of rights. So whilst articles 12,[46] 13[47] and 14[48] promote the view that part of a good upbringing involves children being encouraged to develop a capacity for self-determination, many of the other articles concentrate on their rights to basic care and nurture.[49]

Ideas about children's rights undoubtedly reflect the nature of the society in which they are being brought up and the type of childhood they will experience. It is perhaps only when the general well-being of children is sufficiently guaranteed that attention can be shifted away from their basic needs to their need to develop their capacity for decision-making. The early children's liberationists were able to focus

---

40   L Purdy (1992) p 129.
41   L Purdy (1994) p 224.
42   The part to be played by paternalism when balancing children's rights against each other is a theme which is returned to in the second part of this chapter, in a more theoretical context.
43   See the dispute between L Purdy (1994), A McGillivray (1994) and T Campbell (1994).
44   See above n 43. This appears to be at the root of the disagreement between Purdy, who is sceptical about according to children adult autonomy, and McGillivray, who assumes from this a scepticism of the whole concept of children's rights.
45   Formally adopted by the United Nations General Assembly in 1989 and came into force in 1990.
46   The child's opinion.
47   Freedom of expression.
48   Freedom of thought, conscience and religion.
49   Eg art 3(2): the right to protection and care; art 6: the right to life; art 24: the right to health and health services.

on children's rights to self-determination, as opposed to the rights underpinning their survival, because American children enjoyed a relatively privileged childhood, compared with those growing up in under-developed nations. Rawls notes:

'... as the conditions of civilisation improve, the marginal significance for our good for further economic and social advantages diminishes relative to the interests of liberty ...'[50]

There is a growing view in wealthy nations that children should be provided with far greater opportunities for developing their decision-making capacities and their sense of responsibility, not only for their own sake, but also for the sake of the communities in which they live. Industrialised societies expect children to emerge from minority immediately ready to take their place as newly minted citizens. In truth, childhood is short and it is unrealistic to argue that a child who is protected throughout from responsibility and from participation in important decisions regarding his or her upbringing will become a confident teenager or indeed a responsible citizen.[51]

In this respect, contemporary parents must accept that an important parental task is to provide children with the conditions they need to develop into fully autonomous adults. In particular, parents are required to promote their children's capacity to reach all important decisions about their future for themselves. Children need to develop 'the ability to conceive, evaluate alternatives, and act on a life plan – to pursue, in other words, a self-given system of ends that has at least rough internal consistency'.[52] However mature, they will be unable to make a successful transition to adulthood unless they are given opportunities for practising their decision-making skills and are provided with 'a dry run' at adulthood.[53] Indeed, contemporary society may have contrived a situation whereby its children can only thrive if they are able to take on more responsibility for their own lives at an earlier age than before and in more complex situations. Whilst in Victorian times it might have suited society well to promote the idea that children should be seen and not heard and that parents could treat their children with some disdain, today such ideas have lost their appeal, quite simply because society needs more sophisticated children. As Gardner has said:

'We have remade childhood experience in a way which requires an earlier engagement with adult concerns, and hence an earlier submission to ideals of adulthood such as autonomy.'[54]

Despite a changing approach to the status of childhood, an admission of the need for children to develop their decision-making capacities does not lead to an admission that they have a *right* to autonomy. Furthermore, there is an obvious danger in admitting that children do have such a right; this is that they may not choose what adults consider is best for them. Indeed, many theorists are concerned with justifying paternalistic interventions to ensure that children's decisions do not cut them off from future opportunities. These themes will be returned to below. But whatever theoretical model of rights is accepted, controversies about the existence, significance and impact of children's right to autonomy often threaten to detract attention from promoting other rights, which are arguably of greater importance for large numbers of children.

50   J Rawls (1971) p 542.
51   See M de Winter (1997) p 26.
52   P Brown (1982) pp 210–212.
53   Acknowledgment to J Gardner for his 'dry run' idea.
54   J Gardner (1996) unpublished communications with author.

(3)   DO CHILDREN HAVE ANY RIGHTS AND, IF SO, WHICH ONES?

Practitioners and policy makers are more concerned with what rights children have or should have, than whether they have rights at all. Their concerns are with balancing one right against another in order to clarify measures for their enforcement. But on a more theoretical level, there has been a measure of speculation over whether children can be termed rights-holders at all.

(A)   International rights

Strength might be derived for the claim that children must be right-holders from the wealth of international material based on such an assumption. There appears to be a world-wide acceptance that children have rights to be protected.[55] The CRC, which was the latest of a list of international documents recognising children's rights, contains a list of 40 substantive rights. The fact that, excepting East Timor, the United States and Somalia, every country in the world has ratified it,[56] and that no other international human rights Convention has had more response,[57] suggests that the notion that children are as entitled as adults to demand recognition for their rights is widely accepted.

Nevertheless, international documents do not necessarily legitimise the belief that children do enjoy rights. Indeed, it is arguable that many of the economic, social and cultural rights included in international treaties are, in reality, social ideas rather than individual rights. Whilst some human needs are undoubtedly sufficiently fundamental to ground moral rights, some writers question the moral and legal reality of these social welfare rights.[58] In a similar vein, one might argue that some of the economic, social and cultural rights contained in the CRC are not rights at all but merely claims based on ideals regarding children's needs in a perfect world. These provisions describe how children should be treated and what they should be granted, were governments to take their rights seriously.[59] For example, despite its inclusion in a document which is binding on those countries who have ratified it, it is difficult to argue that article 27 of the CRC can ever be legally enforced, due to its extreme vagueness.[60]

Feinberg suggests that many of the rights contained in international documents are no more than 'manifesto' rights.[61] But he, like O'Neill,[62] sympathises with the manifesto writers who describe claims based on need and aspirations alone, as if they were rights already, considering it a powerful way of expressing the conviction that they ought to be recognised by states here and now as potential rights. He considers such language to be 'a valid exercise of rhetorical licence'.[63] Some writers are less sympathetic with such an approach, arguing that by transforming ambitions regarding children's welfare and autonomy into treaty rights, international documents let governments 'off the hook', by allowing them to couch their responses in formalistic terms, without achieving real progress towards promoting such rights.[64]

---

55   Discussed in chapter 2 below.
56   As of December 2002.
57   T Hammarberg (1995) p 15.
58   C Wellman (1999) esp pp 20–29 and 155ff.
59   See O O'Neill (1992) p 37.
60   The 'right of every child to a standard of living adequate for the child's physical, mental, spiritual, moral and social development'. This phrasing partially reflects the wording of art 25 of the Universal Declaration of Human Rights of 1948.
61   J Feinberg (1980) p 153.
62   See O O'Neill (1992) pp 37–40.
63   J Feinberg (1980) p 153.
64   See M King (1994) p 396.

It is also clear that the language of rights is often used very loosely in a domestic context, particularly by practitioners and the judiciary, to describe claims regarding children which, on reflection, they might find difficult to justify, even on intuitive grounds. For example, in the context of parental disputes over contact, the judiciary have often referred to a child's 'right' to contact with his or her father, even in cases where the father has a past record of violence towards the mother and the child does not desire to see him.[65] As Freeman has so rightly observed: 'Many references to children's rights turn out on inspection to be aspirations for the accomplishment of particular social or moral goals.'[66] The very assumption that children are rights-holders requires sound theoretical justification.

(B)   Children as rights-holders

An acceptance of the existence of the rights of the individual underlies most liberal political theories. Indeed, whilst there have been endless theoretical debates over the part to be played by the concept of rights in the social order and over how rights are to be defined, the premise central to rights theories is that moral rights do exist.[67] As discussed below, MacCormick's model of rights is an attractive one, in so far as it accommodates many of the problems involved in relating the concept of rights to children. First though, no assessment of children's rights would be complete without a brief reference to the philosophical and jurisprudential controversies over whether children can justifiably be described as rights-holders at all.[68] The main doubt over this issue stems from disagreements over the nature of rights themselves – which in turn are linked with a related controversy over the relevance of choice. There is the view that a person cannot be described as a rights-holder unless they are able to exercise a choice over the exercise of that right. The 'choice' or 'will'[69] theory of rights invests the importance of choice with such significance that it alone is capable of grounding all rights. Since the existence of a right is therefore dependent on the right-holder's interest in choosing and since the majority of children lack the competence to make choices, proponents argue they cannot be described as having any rights. Thus Hart considers the term 'rights' inappropriate for application to babies, or indeed to animals.[70]

The assertion that children, who are too young and incompetent to claim rights, therefore have no rights, has an unattractive logic. It negates the intuitive view that children must have rights because it would be wrong to deny such a proposition. Fortunately, theorists such as MacCormick,[71] Raz[72] and Campbell[73] provide a competing view that the concept of rights need not be confined only to those who

65   Discussed in chapter 14.
66   M Freeman (1983 a) p 37.
67   A usefully brief consideration of general rights theories can be found in J Waldron (1984).
68   M Freeman provides an exhaustive theoretical discussion of the concept of children's rights in M Freeman (1983 a) ch 2. See also A Bainham (1998 a) ch 3.
69   Alternatively sometimes described as the 'power' or 'claim' theory of rights. For proponents see, inter alia, H L A Hart (1984) and J Feinberg (1980).
70   H L A Hart (1984) p 82. In Hart's view the fact that it is considered *wrong* to ill-treat babies or animals does not justify utilising the expression 'rights' when describing such situations (emphasis supplied).
71   N MacCormick (1982) ch 8. MacCormick (pp 154–156) clearly sets out the basis for the two competing views on the importance of choice.
72   J Raz (1986) esp pp 165–192.
73   T Campbell (1992).

can lay claim to or waive them. They present an interest theory of rights which posits that a person has a right where his *interests* are protected in certain ways 'by the imposition of (legal or moral) normative constraints on the acts and activities of other people with respect to the object of one's interests'.[74] Children, like adults, have interests which require protecting in such a way and the use of this model avoids denying them moral and legal rights until they have acquired the capacity to reach reasoned decisions. Such a rights model fully accommodates the view that children are no less precious because of their lack of adult capacities.[75] MacCormick forcefully sets out the value of applying such a model to children:

> 'To argue, on the other hand,[76] that each and every child is a being whose needs and capacities command our respect, so that denial to any child of the wherewithal to meet his or her needs and to develop his or her capacities would be wrong in itself (at least in so far as it is physically possible to provide the wherewithal), and would be wrong regardless of the ulterior disadvantages or advantages to anyone else – so to argue, would be to put a case which is intelligible as a justification of the opinion that children have such rights.'[77]

MacCormick proceeds to criticise the proponents of the choice (or will) theory of rights for putting the cart before the horse in their insistence on there being a means of remedying a child's right, through the enforcement of someone else's correlative duty, before they can accept the existence of the right itself.[78] He considers this to be an obsession with the existence of remedies, *ubi remedium ibi ius*, rather than with rights themselves. By contrast, he maintains that it is *because* children have the right, for example, to care and nurture, that the imposition of legal provisions requiring others to provide that care and nurture is justified. In other words, the existence of the right presupposes the remedy, *ubi ius, ibi remedium.*

Before gratefully accepting these assurances that children are respectable rights-holders, brief attention should be paid to the theoretical concerns revolving around the difficulties involved in enforcing children's rights, in the light of their innate powerlessness. In the first place, children are often dependent on those very adults who are acting in breach of their rights, most commonly their parents, and, secondly, they may be too young to take steps to enforce their rights. O'Neill, who considers that adopting a rights-based approach for children suffers from many theoretical problems, including that of enforcement, would prefer to couch children's rights in terms of the obligations owed to them by others. Although the 'rhetoric of rights' has relevance for oppressed adults, she considers that an appeal to rights has little chance of empowering children. If they are too young they will be unable to respond to such an appeal, and if they are old enough to respond, they are well on their way to adulthood and freedom from dependence. Indeed, as she points out, the fundamental difference between children and groups of oppressed adults is that children emerge from their powerless state. This leads her to conclude that the main remedy for children's powerlessness 'is to grow up'.[79]

---

74   N MacCormick (1982) p 154. See also J Raz (1984 b) and J Raz (1986) esp pp 165–192.
75   T Campbell (1992) p 5.
76   Ie when countering the choice or will theory of rights.
77   N MacCormick (1982) p 160.
78   The choice model of rights is underpinned by Hohfeld's classification involving the existence of duties in others, correlative to the rights asserted. See W Hohfeld (1919).
79   O O'Neill (1992) pp 38–39.

Fortunately, not everyone agrees with O'Neill's diagnosis or remedy, which might, to children, appear to be a counsel of despair. According to MacCormick, neither problem prevents rights vesting in children. Indeed, in his view children may have moral rights *prior* to any correlative duties vesting in anyone to fulfil them or indeed without it being clear who is obliged to fulfil the right. He cites, by way of example, the child's right to be educated to the limit of his or her abilities. Although such a right exists, it may be unclear whose is the power to enforce it and whose the duty to provide it. But he nevertheless concedes the purely practical difficulty which attaches to the enforcement of children's rights and admits that it is the legal rights which are supported by private remedial rights and private powers of initiating proceedings which are of central concern in the practice of the law.[80] This concession supports those who argue that children's rights will not be adequately promoted and enforced within a broad range of contexts until they gain an official adult representative, preferably in the role of Children's Rights Commissioner.[81]

Ultimately, agreement over a universally acceptable theory of rights for dependent children may always prove elusive.[82] Nevertheless, MacCormick's description of a moral right as 'a good of such importance that it would be wrong to deny it to or withhold it from any member of C (a given class)'[83] has an arresting simplicity that many non-theorists may find attractive. Without underestimating the difficulties implicit in its generality, it provides a scheme of thought which promotes a compelling and flexible assessment of the concept of children's rights. Its drawback is that it provides little guidance over defining what interests may become translated into moral rights.

(C)   What rights do children have?

There are two questions that follow on from the adoption of MacCormick's interest model of rights. What interests can be translated into moral rights and what moral rights will be translated into legal rights? The second question is slightly easier to answer than the first. Most commentators accept that moral rights are translated into legal rights[84] if there is some recognition of their importance by the rest of society and consequently the imposition of correlative legal duties on others regarding the fulfilment of those rights.[85] The law thereby makes it unlawful to withhold a particular moral right from any one of a class of individuals. Meanwhile, unhappily, there appear to be no clear answers to the first question. Indeed, proponents of the interest theory of rights often tend to refer to children's interests rather than their rights, because of their uncertainty over whether there is sufficient unanimity over the

---

80   N MacCormick (1982) pp 162–166.
81   Discussed in chapter 19 below.
82   Some maintain that the theorists are striving to describe with the term 'rights' what are in truth totally different concepts. See J Harris (1980) p 86.
83   N MacCormick (1982) p 160.
84   See D Lyons (1984) who (pp 113–117) discusses Bentham's rejection of the concept of moral rights being an essential ingredient of legal rights. The extent to which Bentham's arguments undermine the concept of natural law is considered at length by J Finnis in his seminal work (1980).
85   See eg J Raz (1984 b) pp 13–14 who proposes that: 'a law creates a right if it is based on and expresses the view that someone has an interest which is sufficient ground for holding another to be subject to a duty ... His right is a legal right if it is recognized by law, that is if the law holds his interest to be sufficient ground to hold another to be subject to a duty.'

wrongness of denying any particular good for it to be translated into a moral right. Eekelaar's words reflect this dilemma:

'… whether these interests can also be said to be 'rights' depends on the extent to which it is generally believed that children have them and that they should be protected by law. If such beliefs were part of "official" ideology it might make sense to say that children had those rights. It is not claimed that such an ideology actually exists. But it could be put forward as a challenge. Should not our community behave towards its children as if they had rights? If so, are these not the rights which they should have?'[86]

Perhaps inevitably, a common criticism of the interest theory is that it is far too broad; the interests relevant to the justification of rights are without clear demarcation.[87] Adoption of MacCormick's description of a moral right as 'a good of such importance that it would be wrong to deny it to or withhold it from any member of C (a given class)' would inevitably lead to controversy over the 'wrongness' of denying the importance of many potential interests. There is considerable disagreement, for example, over the 'wrongness' of denying to children the right to autonomy or self-determination. MacCormick acknowledges that his description of a moral right will inevitably involve controversy over whether any particular denial or withholding would be wrong. He merely responds, a little unhelpfully, that 'rights belong to the class of essentially contested concepts'.[88] Campbell, who uses a description of moral rights not dissimilar to that adopted by MacCormick,[89] neither claims that all children's interests give rise to rights nor underestimates the difficulty of identifying and classifying the full range of the sometimes conflicting interests protected by rights. Indeed, he admits that it may be a weakness of the interest theory of rights that 'it leaves us with a very open ended basis for determining which interests are to serve as the ground of rights'.[90] Nevertheless, the extent of children's rights cannot be left in the realms of philosophical debate. An appreciation of this problem has led to various attempts to provide a more practical framework for children's rights, not by attempting to list them, but by classifying them into identifying groups.

In a seminal article, Eekelaar explores the type of children's interests that might deserve recognition and protection, before providing a threefold classification.[91] He notes that such an exercise is complicated by the conflicts arising between the interests of children and those of their parents. In order to prevent perceptions of children's interests being distorted by such conflicts, he suggests that interests should be conceived only in terms of 'those benefits which the subject himself or herself might plausibly claim in themselves'.[92] To meet the problem that children often lack the information or ability to appreciate what will serve them best, he proposes that the adult should 'make some kind of imaginative leap and guess what a child might retrospectively have wanted once it reaches a position of maturity'.[93]

---

86   J Eekelaar (1991) p 103.
87   See eg O O'Neill (1992). She criticises the whole concept of children having 'fundamental rights', considering that far more would be achieved by way of improving children's lives if a theoretical framework of obligations were adopted.
88   N MacCormick (1982) p 160.
89   'Moral rights may be regarded as those interests which are thought to be of such significance to the life of the human individual that they ought to be given priority in the organization of societal existence wherever possible.' T Campbell (1992) p 9.
90   T Campbell (1992) p 16. Also discussed at pp 6–7.
91   J Eekelaar (1986) p 166ff. He adopts an interest theory of moral rights similar to that set out by J Raz (1984 b).
92   J Eekelaar (1986) p 169.
93   J Eekelaar (1986) p 170.

Employing an adult's 'imaginative leap', Eekelaar suggests an ordering of children's interests into three groups: basic, developmental and autonomy interests.[94] Their 'basic' interests arise from children's claims regarding their immediate physical, emotional and intellectual care and well-being. Children's 'developmental' interests revolve round their claims on the wider community to maximise their potential. All children should have an equal opportunity to maximise the resources available to them during their childhood. A child's autonomy interests relate to 'the freedom to choose his own lifestyle and to enter social relations according to his own inclinations uncontrolled by the authority of the adult world, whether parents or institutions'.[95] In the event of a child's autonomy interest conflicting with his developmental or basic interest, Eekelaar suggests that the latter interests should prevail. This suggestion has obvious and far-reaching implications if applied to practical situations involving teenagers refusing to accept life-saving medical treatment.[96] He justifies this view by asserting that few adults would retrospectively approve of the exercise of their autonomy interest being allowed to prejudice their life-chances in adulthood.

Eekelaar's discussion is valuable in so far as it demonstrates how theories about the concept of rights can be applied in the more practical context of the developing law relating to children. It also demonstrates how children's rights may be ordered and delineated. Many other classifications of children's rights have been formulated. Freeman proposes four categories: welfare rights, protective rights, those grounded in social justice and those based on children's claims to more freedom from control and more autonomy over their lives.[97] This is similar to another fourfold classification of rights proposed by Wald, described as: 'Rights Against the World', 'Protection from Inadequate Care', 'Rights to an Adult Legal Status' and 'Rights Versus Parents'.[98] Campbell suggests a fourfold classification according to the minor's status as person, child, juvenile and future adult.[99] Bevan proposes a simpler scheme of children's rights with two broad categories: protective and self-assertive.[100]

On balance, Bevan's classification is to be preferred. Although such a twofold classification is essentially simplistic, in that it loses the fine-tuning available to those involving more categories, it is easier to use. It also reflects the fundamental conflict currently underlying the whole of child law as it is developing in practice – that is the conflict between the need to fulfil children's rights to protection and to promote their capacity for self-determination. Children's 'protective rights' arise from their innate dependence and vulnerability and an obvious need for nurture, love and care, both physical and psychological. These rights must include the right to protection from ill-treatment and the right to state intervention in order to achieve such protection. Bevan's term 'assertive rights' is usefully broad enough to include their claims to adult human rights,[101] such as the right to bodily integrity and to freedom of expression and thought, conscience and religion and to certain 'decision-making rights'. As case law illustrates, the courts are used to encountering situations where children's capacity for decision-making needs assessing in order to decide whether or not their decisions carry legal weight.

94   J Eekelaar (1986) pp 170–171.
95   J Eekelaar (1986) p 171.
96   See below.
97   M Freeman (1983 a) p 40.
98   M Wald (1979) p 260ff.
99   T Campbell (1992) p 22.
100 H Bevan (1989) p 11.
101 See discussion in chapter 2.

Whatever classification of rights is adopted, it does not and never can provide an authoritative list of the rights that children may or may not enjoy – indeed no such list would ever be free from controversy. The experience of those drafting the CRC proves that any attempt to bridge the gap between theory and practice with an authoritative list of children's rights will be endlessly controversial.[102] As commented above, some even deny that a number of 'rights' contained in the Convention merit such a description. Whilst many theorists currently accept that children can be rights-holders, there remains no clear test providing guidance over what rights they have or should have. Eekelaar's threefold classification, basic, developmental and autonomy interests, is posed in terms of the '*interests*' children have, rather than the rights that they have. His uncertainty over whether they can be correctly described as rights is emphasised by his words quoted above. Indeed, this comment highlights the doubt underlying the concept of children's rights. But, as Eekelaar's words suggest, perhaps strict theoretical justifications for the existence of moral rights do not matter so much as believing that children have rights. More pragmatically, the activity inspired by the CRC demonstrates that the language or rhetoric of rights is a politically useful tool to ensure the achievement of certain goals for children; it is after all the language in which political priorities are settled.[103]

In practice, the existence or extent of children's moral rights may often remain a matter of conjecture until dispelled by the law translating them into legal rights – at which point there is no longer room for argument.[104] Thus, for example, whilst few would cavil at accepting the existence of a child's moral right to physical care, or complain over the legislative translation of this into a legal right,[105] there might be less agreement over a child's moral right to autonomy and in turn, whether this should have the force of law. For example, whilst the decision in *Gillick v West Norfolk and Wisbech Area Health Authority*[106] gave the House of Lords a chance to translate certain aspects of children's moral right to make choices in their lives into legal principles, it left considerable uncertainty over the legal boundaries to these rights.

A growing body of literature reflects the controversies surrounding children's right to make choices, more often described as their right to autonomy. Some of these have already been dealt with when discussing the writings of the children's liberationists. At a theoretical level, there has been a detailed examination of the degree to which mature children's choices can be overridden, either by the state or by their parents, in order to fulfil their rights to protection. Indeed, the extent to which paternalistic restrictions can be imposed legitimately on children, without negating their autonomy rights, continues to generate philosophical thought. Although both these issues are returned to in more detail in the context of the developing law on children's decision-making rights, a brief assessment of some of this literature is provided below, since it can be utilised at a more practical level to inform the way in which the law should be developed as effectively as possible.

---

102   See chapter 2.
103   T Campbell (1992) p 7.
104   But see J Raz (1984 b) pp 15–21.
105   Eg Children and Young Persons Act 1933, s 1.
106   [1986] AC 112.

(D)   Children's capacity for autonomy and the role of paternalism

(i)   The concept of 'children's autonomy'

Claims that children have a right to autonomy are derived from liberal political philosophies which emphasise the need to promote as fully as possible an individual's freedom to make rational autonomous decisions. It is argued that children, as human beings, should, like adults, also be free to lead their own lives according to their own conception of a good or worthwhile life, provided that this does not illegitimately restrict the liberty of others to do the same.[107] The early children's liberationists saw the child's right to autonomy as of overriding importance. Farson made his views on this clear:

> '... the issue of self-determination is at the heart of children's liberation. It is in fact, the only issue, a definition of the entire concept. The acceptance of the child's right to self-determination is fundamental to all the rights to which children are entitled.'[108]

Although the more radical children's liberationists claimed most adult freedoms for all children, more recent proponents of children's liberation often demand a far less extensive portfolio of rights.[109] Indeed, it appears that few commentators today claim complete personal autonomy for all children, or even for all mature teenagers. Claims for more acknowledgment of 'children's rights to autonomy' on closer examination often constitute merely claims for children to acquire more extensive rights to self-determination than they are already allowed by the domestic law or by their parents. As Freeman has pointed out, it is a respect for the child's eventual *capacity* for autonomy, rather than autonomy itself, which is important.[110]

It should be noted at this point that confusion may sometimes be caused by a loose use of the term 'children's autonomy' by family lawyers, without further explanation of what is really intended. In most cases what is being referred to does not correspond to common conceptions of an adult's autonomy, which involves an adult's freedom to determine his destiny, so far as society permits adults to do. Nor does its use normally involve a reference to many of the rights selected by international human rights documents as being an essential component of moral autonomy, such as the right to freedom of assembly and of thought, conscience and religion. By contrast, family lawyers often use the term 'children's autonomy' or 'children's autonomy rights' as a short-hand to indicate a far more qualified form of autonomy embracing children's rights to reach decisions within the narrow confines of their immediate home and school, often in the context of medical decision-making.

A further point of confusion arises from a common failure to distinguish between children's rights to have their decisions fulfilled and their right to be *consulted*. It may not be appropriate for a child to choose where he or she is to live, but the child may have valuable views about the matter. In any event, these are not claims of precisely the same nature. Whilst society and parents may choose to protect younger children from self-determination over such matters to do with their upbringing, this does not preclude *consulting* them over such matters. Indeed, consultation may promote a child's capacity for eventual autonomy. But those arguing that the law should

---

107   R Lindley (1989) p 75.
108   R Farson (1974) p 27.
109   Eg J Harris (1982). He suggests (p 51) that the possession of firearms and the freedom to drive dangerously powerful or large motor vehicles should be made 'age-dependent'.
110   M Freeman (1983 a) pp 54–57.

provide greater recognition for children's decision-making abilities do not always make it entirely clear whether they are referring to children's rights to make choices of their own, or merely the right to participate in the decision-making process.

Article 12 of the CRC is sometimes misleadingly discussed by lawyers as if it provides an international recognition for the children's liberationists' approach to children's rights.[111] Nevertheless, article 12(1), which requires states to 'assure to the child who is capable of forming his or her own views the right to express those views freely in all matters affecting the child, the views of the child being given due weight in accordance with the age and maturity of the child', does not guarantee autonomy but refers to consultation and participation in decision-making. More specifically, article 12(2) deals with procedural issues by requiring states to provide the child with 'the opportunity to be heard in any judicial and administrative proceedings affecting the child, either directly or through a representative or an appropriate body, in a manner consistent with the procedural rules of national law'. These provisions may be influenced by the concepts of empowerment that inspired the child liberationists. But whilst they promote a child's capacity for self-determination and autonomy, they do not suggest that children possess the right to have their decisions implemented. In this work, the use of the term 'children's autonomy rights' is avoided since, arguably, it carries with it misleading connotations of adult freedoms. Instead, 'children's decision-making rights' is used to indicate children's right to have their capacity for autonomy promoted, though not necessarily acted upon,[112] and their right to be consulted.[113]

(ii)   Children's 'autonomy' and the role of paternalism

Few deny that mature children are often able to take much more responsibility than many adults give them credit for. However, the children's liberationists deplored any paternalistic restrictions on children's freedom. In their view it was a mistake to assume that children lacked the competence to exercise these freedoms. Nevertheless, the discussion above makes it clear that many contemporary writers are now chary of claiming for children a moral right to autonomy, identical to that claimed by adults. It would appear that they have good theoretical grounds for their reluctance to do so. It seems clear that few philosophers today consider that children have the competence for complete autonomy and the majority see paternalism as having an important role to play in restricting their powers of self-determination.

John Stuart Mill gave a classic exposition of the concept of an adult's right to autonomy[114] and other philosophers have constantly re-assessed it.[115] Despite the importance Mill attached to autonomy, he considered it self-evident that children are too immature to be autonomous. Since they lacked the capacity for autonomy, for them there was an obvious need for paternalism:

111   Eg S Toope (1996) p 42.
112   Bearing in mind the use of paternalistic interventions to override their choices, discussed below.
113   Thereby retaining an element of paternalism justifying adult refusal to implement decisions which are not 'in the child's best interests'. Discussed below.
114   J S Mill (1859).
115   See eg J Rawls (1971) pp 90–95 and 130–136. See also J Raz (1986) pp 245–250.

'It is, perhaps, hardly necessary to say that this doctrine is meant to apply only to human beings in the maturity of their faculties. We are not speaking of children, or of young persons below the age which the law may fix as that of manhood or womanhood. Those who are still in a state to require being taken care of by others, must be protected against their own actions as well as against external injury.'[116]

Mill considered that adults should make choices on behalf of children, mainly because children are not capable of rational autonomy. They have not yet developed the cognitive capacity to make intelligent decisions in the light of relevant information and their judgment is prone to be wild and variable under the influence of 'emotional inconstancy'.[117]

A variety of writers have subsequently discussed the concept of paternalism, in the context of children's decision-making powers.[118] It might appear, at first sight, that the varying theoretical models of rights place a different weight on the importance of children's autonomy. It is, for example, argued that adoption of the choice or will theory of rights leads to particular emphasis being placed on a child's capacity for rational choice, an obvious pre-requisite of autonomy.[119] Indeed, MacCormick attacks the choice (or will) theory of rights for carrying the presumption that people are the best judges of what is good for them when claiming enforcement of their rights.[120] Nevertheless, embracing an interest theory of rights does not involve rejecting the concept of children having an interest in making choices and therefore their interest in autonomy. Children may indeed have rights to self-determination based on their interest *in* choice, without having a right to complete autonomy.[121] Archard explores this point in some depth. He points to the fallacy of claiming that if one lacks rights to self-determination, then any choices one makes simply do not 'count'. The fact that some children lack the competence required to possess rights of self-determination does not mean that their views can be completely discounted. Furthermore, the weight to be accorded to their choices should reflect their competence to choose for their own good.[122]

Whilst such propositions make very good sense, some writers commenting on developments in family and child law appear to assume that acknowledging that children have an interest in choice rules out paternalistic interventions to safeguard their welfare. This leads to the view that it is difficult to justify the law preserving an ability to override children's wishes, because it thereby undermines their rights.[123] These commentators tend to utilise the terms 'welfarism', or 'utilitarianism'[124] or the 'welfare test', rather than 'paternalism'. So, it is argued, a commitment to promoting

---

116 J S Mill (1859) p 73.

117 Archard discusses Mill's approach in D Archard (1993) p 52.

118 Freeman discusses the paternalistic ideas of Hobbes, Locke and Mill relating to the dependence of children, in M Freeman (1983 a) pp 52–54. See also D Archard (1993) ch 1 for a discussion of Locke's approach to childhood.

119 T Campbell (1992) p 20.

120 N MacCormick (1982) p 166.

121 The author is grateful to J Gardner for his lucid explanation of this point.

122 D Archard (1993) p 87.

123 Inter alia: S Parker (1992) esp pp 319–325; J Dewar (1998) esp pp 471–472; J Eekelaar (1994 a) esp pp 301–302 and 326–327; J Roche (1999) p 56.

124 Parker employs the term 'utility' as a means of describing a 'welfare' dominated approach to family law debates, which he argues is inconsistent with a 'rights based' or 'justice' model. See S Parker (1992) p 321. But as Raz explains, it is logically perfectly possible to combine utilitarianism with a conception of prima facie rights, despite some people finding such a conclusion unacceptable: J Raz (1984 a) esp p 128.

children's rights, particularly their right to reach decisions for themselves, conflicts with attempts to promote their welfare. Eekelaar returns to this theme many times and argues that a welfarist relationship between A and B is inconsistent with the concept of B having rights against A, since:

> 'Although it might logically be held that B has the right that A should promote B's welfare in accordance with A's conception of that welfare, such a right is really no right at all. A person who surrenders to another the power to determine where his own welfare lies has in a real sense abdicated his personal autonomy.'[125]

The argument that there is a clash between a rights-based system of principles and one incorporating 'a relationship-based welfare approach' is revisited by Herring when considering the impact of the Human Rights Act 1998 on the principles of child law.[126]

Fortunately, many theorists see little need to rule out paternalistic interventions to restrict the actions of adults or children; indeed they consider them justified by reference to the rights of those constrained. On this basis, it is right to restrain or require activity simply because this will better promote that which the individual is interested in. Whatever their age, child or adult, their interests are not always achieved by letting them follow their own views on how to contribute to their achievement.[127] Children are obviously more prone than adults to limit their own future prospects by making unwise short-term choices. For example, a young child may not wish to go to school and may adversely affect his or her own potential development by refusing to do so. MacCormick explains his position persuasively:

> 'Children are not always or even usually the best judges of what is good for them, so much so that even the rights that are most important to their long-term well-being, such as the right to discipline or to a safe environment, they regularly perceive as being the reverse of rights or advantages …'[128]

But by utilising an interest model of rights he is –

> 'at once glad and regretful to discover that it is possible for me to acknowledge that my children have rights, without being thereby committed to the outrageous permissiveness to which my natural indolence inclines me.'[129]

Raz also points out that independence is not all or nothing. In his view, various reasons may justify coercion: it may be necessary to protect someone else, or to protect the coerced person's own long-term autonomy, or some other interest. He suggests that paternalistic coercion may be justified by the trust reposed in the coercer by the coerced person.[130] This idea is presented in the context of paternalistic coercion by government against its adult citizens, but it may similarly be applied to situations involving children. An unco-operative child may sufficiently trust parents, doctors, or indeed representatives of the education authority, to justify their adopting a degree of coercive paternalism, with a view to achieving school attendance, or compliance with medical advice or some other course of action. Despite providing sound support for the view that the use of paternalism is consistent with the concept of children's

---

125 J Eekelaar (1994 a) p 301.
126 J Herring (1999) esp pp 232–235. See also S Harris-Short (2002) p 337.
127 T Campbell (1992) p 15. Nevertheless, he concedes that there are risks involved in considering children's concerns from an adult-centred point of view.
128 N MacCormick (1982) p 166.
129 Above n 128.
130 J Raz (1996) p 121.

rights, these explanations do not sufficiently clarify *when* interventions to restrict children's choices could be fully justified – this question will be explored below.

(iii) Restricting paternalistic interventions

MacCormick, in his words quoted above, seems to assume that his paternalism, as a parent, will be 'good' for his children. Certainly, parents are those most obviously fitted to exercise paternalism in relation to children. In a successful family unit, parents are the adults who will know their children best and will, through their affection for them, seek to raise them in the best way possible, judged as objectively as possible. Society recognises this by imposing legal and moral duties on those who brought the children into the world, on the basis that they are the most likely to have their interests at heart.[131] Indeed, there is the view that paternalism, rather than being seen as 'an odious tyranny',[132] is essential to the relationship of parent and child and that an abandonment of parental authority would be 'an act of immorality, as well as a failure in nurturing'.[133]

Nevertheless, whilst one can argue that being made to go to school is necessary for maturation into a rational autonomous individual, and that therefore present compulsion is a precondition for subsequent choice, it is far less clear how much should be denied to children and the precise ends to be served by such denial.[134] Indeed, the prospect of unrestricted paternalism being applied to override children's choices leaves many writers with a sense of unease, particularly because powers of coercion are largely vested in parents. Whilst it may be possible to justify paternalistic coercion to ensure that children fulfil their potential for future choices, it should not unduly restrict their capacities for decision-making. The ability to exercise paternalism may be exploited by those in a position of power over children. Some suggest that paternalism comes in all shapes and sizes, and what Olsen describes as 'bad faith' or negative paternalism may oppress children just as much as it does some groups of adults.[135] Indeed, it was the abuse of parents' power over their children that in part influenced the children's liberationists to claim that the only remedy was to empower children against their parents.

In many of his papers, Eekelaar returns to his concern that adults, and particularly the judiciary, when subjecting children to coercive paternalism, may ignore their interest in making choices in their lives.[136] The paramountcy test embodied by the Children Act 1989, section 1 deliberately provides the courts with a paternalistic formula with which to justify their view of an outcome fulfilling the child's welfare. When courts reach decisions that are said to conform with the 'welfare' or 'best interests' principle, this formula is sufficiently indeterminate to take little account of the child's true views. As noted above, Eekelaar rejects what he describes as the 'welfarist' stance that a child may be described as having a 'right' to have performed for him or her what someone else considers to be in accordance with that child's

---

131 Gerald Dworkin gives these as reasons for society selecting parents as proxies for their children when reaching decisions, for example, decisions on health care. See G Dworkin (1982) p 204.
132 D Archard (1993) p 11.
133 W Gaylin (1982) pp 30–31.
134 D Archard (1993) pp 55–57.
135 See F Olsen (1992) pp 206–207.
136 See particularly, J Eekelaar (1986), (1992) and (1994 b).

welfare.[137] He also maintains that such an argument fails to give proper respect to the human worth of the child and argues that no assessment of how best to advance children's interests should take place without allowing them to exercise of any choices.[138] Though sometimes true, by stressing children's interest in choice so emphatically, this approach risks being seen as ignoring the need for a paternalistic or welfarist stance, even when a child's psychological immaturity undermines any ability to reach decisions without damaging his or her own future prospects. As Eekelaar perceives, the difficulty is to establish a set of clear principles which respect a child's choices as far as possible, whilst retaining the power to override those choices, as a last resort.

Eekelaar proposes various approaches to ensure that children's views are fully considered by adults. One method, when claiming rights on behalf of children too young to decide for themselves, is to guess what the child might retrospectively have wanted. Though ingenious, the use of the hypothetical retrospective judgment has not escaped criticism. Campbell has described it as a methodologically dubious 'device', its weakness being that it is very much adult-centred, since it is taken at the point at which childhood is over and adulthood is present. In his view:

> 'It is easy from this sort of hindsight position to welcome sacrifices that were made in the happiness of the child because of the advantages that are now involved … The method of retrospective substituted judgment does not play fair and equally with the interests of the child as they are manifest in the experiences of childhood.'[139]

Though this criticism has some justification, it is difficult to see how Campbell's own claim that greater weight should be given to what children are actually interested in, as current children and not future adults, can be freed of adult perceptions.[140]

Maintaining his concern to ensure that children's interest in choice should not be overlooked, Eekelaar subsequently develops a more sophisticated approach to promoting children's own views. He proposes a method of decision-making in the place of the best interests test, described as the concept of 'dynamic self-determinism' which is intended 'to bring a child to the threshold of adulthood with the maximum opportunities to form and pursue life-goals which reflect as closely as possible an autonomous choice'.[141] This constitutes helpful guidance. It should also be noted that crucially, in this paper, Eekelaar does not rule out paternalism. Indeed, he goes to some lengths to stress that this approach does not imply that decisions are being delegated to the child, merely that his or her wishes are a significant factor in the adult's decision.[142]

In summary, the claims of the children's liberationists that children should not be subjected to any paternalistic restrictions now command little support. Theorists are able to justify paternalistic coercion to restrict children's liberty, whilst accepting the need to promote their capacities for decision-making and responsibility. Nevertheless, the need to find an acceptable balance between respecting children's choices and retaining the power to override decisions which may destroy their future lives is a theme constantly returned to by commentators on children's rights, particularly when adolescents are concerned. The two Court of Appeal decisions, *Re R (a minor)*

137　J Eekelaar (1994 a) p 301.
138　See J Eekelaar (1992) pp 226–227.
139　T Campbell (1992) p 21.
140　But see also C Coady's critique (1992) p 50.
141　J Eekelaar (1994 b) p 53.
142　J Eekelaar (1994 b) p 54.

(wardship: medical treatment)[143] and *Re W (a minor) (medical treatment)*,[144] decided in the aftermath of *Gillick v West Norfolk and Wisbech Area Health Authority*,[145] made clear that this is an issue of considerable importance at both a practical and theoretical level. This, and later case law,[146] suggests that adolescents need protecting from reaching decisions which might restrict or endanger their future ability to live fulfilling and healthy lives. Though controversial, the outcome achieved by the judiciary in these cases is fully consistent with the model of rights advocated above. Nevertheless, the methods adopted by the courts for overriding the wishes of the adolescents are far more difficult to justify.[147]

(iv) Adolescents and paternalism

The case law referred to above involved adolescents nearing the age of legal maturity. Do the arguments regarding paternalistic interventions need adjusting in the light of an adolescent's relatively advanced age and maturity? The claims of the children's liberationists that children should be autonomous and free of paternalistic restraints become most cogent when applied to mature adolescents. Freeman points out, 'no one can seriously believe that there is a real distinction … between someone of 18 years and a day and someone of 17 years and 364 days'.[148] Although the argument that childhood is a social construct[149] is difficult to justify in relation to young children, the suggestion that adolescence, as a new stage after infancy and before adulthood, artificially prolongs the inferior status of childhood is rather more plausible. The increase in the compulsory school age to 16, together with legislation banning children from full-time employment until that age, artificially postpones the time when adolescents can start engaging in activities carrying fuller responsibility.

As commented earlier, adoption of MacCormick's description of a moral right as 'a good of such importance that it would be wrong to deny it to or withhold it from any member of C (a given class)' inevitably leads to controversy over the 'wrongness' of denying the importance of certain interests to certain groups. It is unlikely that there would be agreement over the wrongness of denying complete autonomy to all mature adolescents. Nevertheless, there seems little doubt that many adults would approve of the concept of mature adolescents having a degree of personal autonomy, by acknowledging their right to reach certain major decisions for themselves. Inevitably though, there would be disagreement over which decisions such adolescents should and should not have a right to determine. Gerald Dworkin considers that: 'Our self-esteem and sense of worth are bound up with the right to determine what shall be done to and with our bodies and minds.'[150] Whilst not underestimating the younger child's right to dignity and self-respect, these words are particularly apposite when applied to adolescents. This group of children need formal acknowledgment of their right to reach decisions for themselves over a variety of matters, particularly regarding their own bodily integrity. Accordingly, in *Gillick v West Norfolk and Wisbech Area*

143 [1992] Fam 11.
144 [1993] Fam 64.
145 [1986] AC 112.
146 Eg *Re L (medical treatment: Gillick competency)* [1999] 2 FCR 524 and *Re M (medical treatment: consent)* [1999] 2 FLR 1097.
147 Discussed more fully in chapters 3 and 5.
148 M Freeman (1992) p 35.
149 See P Ariès (1962).
150 G Dworkin (1982) p 203.

Health Authority[151] the House of Lords accepted that mature adolescents have the right to decide for themselves a variety of matters long before they reach legal maturity.[152]

But what if adolescents foreclose on their future opportunities by reaching decisions which adults consider unwise or ill-conceived? They may truant from school, take up smoking or drinking and, more dramatically, as subsequent cases like *Re W (a minor) (medical treatment)*[153] demonstrate, take risks with their health by refusing life-saving medical treatment. As stated above, many theorists would advocate paternalistic intervention to prevent adults harming themselves and the same must apply to adolescents. But the difficulty is to get the balance right between over-protection and allowing a dangerous freedom. Paternalistic restrictions should not deny adolescents all opportunity to take risks, for as Freeman states, 'We cannot treat persons as equals without also respecting their capacity to take risks and make mistakes'.[154] Moreover, a 'dry run' loses all credibility if it contains no risks.

Though adolescents are individuals nearing adulthood and respect for their views is arguably more important to their own self-respect than it is to a toddler, many writers are reluctant to allow them the freedom to make life-threatening mistakes. There seems general agreement over being prepared to grant more autonomy generally to adolescents, whilst still supporting a paternalistic role for the state in protecting them against foolish, self-destructive choices. This is variously described as a form of 'justified paternalism',[155] or 'liberal paternalism'.[156] Freeman considers that protection against a teenager reaching decisions which threaten death or serious physical or mental harm to him or her can be justified and suggests the following formula:

> 'The question we should ask ourselves is: what sorts of action or conduct would we wish, as children, to be shielded against on the assumption that we would want to mature to a rationally autonomous adulthood and be capable of deciding on our own system of ends as free and rational beings?'[157]

Similarly, Eekelaar's concept of 'dynamic self-determinism' also avoids the position whereby even 'competent'[158] adolescents are given complete powers of self-determination if their decisions are contrary to their self-interests, in terms of their physical and mental well-being.[159]

In summary, there appears therefore to be unanimity amongst many modern writers that whilst decision-making cannot be delegated to children whatever their age, paternalism should always be kept to a minimum and carefully justified, particularly when adults override children's own choices. Such an approach is particularly apposite when dealing with adolescents, whose decision-making powers should be encouraged and allowed increased respect. The difficulty lies in establishing a formula which

---

151   [1986] AC 112.
152   Discussed in more detail in chapters 3 and 5.
153   [1993] Fam 64. This case involved a dangerously anorexic girl of 16 who refused to undergo treatment for her condition. See also *Re E (a minor) (wardship: medical treatment)* [1993] 1 FLR 386, which involved a teenage boy, a Jehovah's Witness, who refused to undergo blood transfusions as part of his treatment for leukaemia. Both cases are considered in more detail in chapter 5.
154   M Freeman (1992) p 38.
155   R Macklin (1982) pp 293–294.
156   M Freeman (1983 a) p 57.
157   M Freeman (1983 a) p 57.
158   Eekelaar devotes some discussion to the significance of this term in (1994 b) pp 54–57. A child's legal competence to reach decisions is discussed in chapter 3.
159   J Eekelaar (1994 b) esp p 57.

authorises paternalistic interventions to protect adolescents from making life-threatening mistakes, but restrains autocratic and arbitrary adult restrictions on their potential for autonomy.

(4) CONCLUSION

The considerable wealth of scholarship discussed above reflects a common assumption that children's rights are of immense importance but that attempts to fulfil them require considerable care. The concerns expressed by the theorists often resurface in the conflicts involving children that practitioners tussle with on a day-to-day basis. There is, though, an unfortunate disjunction between theory and practice. Practitioners who deal with the here and now may not see any relevance in theories which have been developed for hypothetical children as a class. They perceive no clear and practical message which assists them when applying the law to individual children in situations involving considerable complexity. Even if sympathetic with the need to fulfil the individual child's rights, they may find it difficult to find a means of doing so, when the law is not developing in a rights-based framework. Furthermore, a child's rights may not only conflict with each other, but also with those of adults in his or her life, such as parents and other carers.

The ideas of the theorists can obviously be of more practical assistance if translated into a set of legal principles which provides clear guidance over the extent to which children's rights can be fulfilled. This sometimes occurs, but even when it does not, their theories should not be dismissed as having little practical impact. They may provide a sound intellectual basis for preferring one course of action to another. Despite the fact that this body of intellectual thought has not taken particular account of the needs of practitioners, it does provide a far better basis for translating the concept of children's rights into practice than mere intuition or prejudice.

BIBLIOGRAPHY

Archard D, *Children: Rights and Childhood* (1993) Routledge.

Ariès P, *Centuries of Childhood* (1962) Jonathan Cape.

Bainham A, *Children – The Modern Law* (1998 a) Family Law.

Bainham A, 'Changing families and changing concepts – reforming the language of family law' (1998 b) 10 Child and Family Law Quarterly 1.

Bevan H, *Child Law* (1989) Butterworths.

Bigelow J et al, 'Parental Autonomy' (1988) 5 Journal of Applied Philosophy 183.

Brown P, 'Human Independence and Parental Proxy' in W Gaylin and R Macklin (eds) *Who Speaks for the Child* (1982) Plenum Press.

Campbell T, 'The Rights of the Minor' in P Alston, S Parker and J Seymour (eds) *Children, Rights and the Law* (1992) Clarendon Press.

Campbell T, 'Really Equal Rights? Some philosophical comments on "Why children shouldn't have equal rights" by Laura Purdy' (1994) 2 International Journal of Children's Rights 259.

Coady C, 'Theory, Rights and Children: A Comment on O'Neill and Campbell' in P Alston, S Parker and J Seymour (eds) *Children, Rights and the Law* (1992) Clarendon Press.

Dewar J, 'The Normal Chaos of Family Law' (1998) 61 Modern Law Review 467.

Dickens B, 'The Modern Function and Limits of Parental Rights' (1981) 97 Law Quarterly Review 462.

Dworkin G, 'Consent, Representation and Proxy Consent' in W Gaylin and R Macklin (eds) *Who Speaks for the Child* (1982) Plenum Press.

Eekelaar J, 'The Emergence of Children's Rights' (1986) 6 Oxford Journal of Legal Studies 161.

Eekelaar J, *Regulating Divorce* (1991) Clarendon Press.

Eekelaar J, 'The Importance of Thinking that Children Have Rights' in P Alston, S Parker and J Seymour (eds) *Children, Rights and the Law* (1992) Clarendon Press.

Eekelaar J, 'Families and Children: From Welfarism to Rights' in C McCrudden and G Chambers *Individual Rights and Law in Britain* (1994 a) Clarendon Press.

Eekelaar J, 'The Interests of the Child and the Child's Wishes: The Role of Dynamic Self-Determinism' (1994 b) 8 International Journal of Law and the Family 42.

Ennew J, 'Outside childhood: street children's rights' in B Franklin (ed) *The Handbook of Children's Rights: Comparative Policy and Practice* (1995) Routledge.

Farson R, *Birthrights* (1974) Collier Macmillan.

Feinberg J, *Rights, Justice and the Bounds of Liberty* (1980) Princeton University Press.

Finnis J, *Natural Law and Natural Rights* (1980) Clarendon Press.

Foster H and Freed D, 'A Bill of Rights for Children' (1972) 6 Family Law Quarterly 343.

Fox Harding L, *Perspectives in Child Care Policy* (1997) Longman.

Franklin B (ed), *The Rights of Children* (1986) Blackwells.

Franklin B (ed), *The Handbook of Children's Rights: Comparative Policy and Practice* (1995) Routledge.

Franklin B (ed), *The New Handbook of Children's Rights: Comparative Policy and Practice* (2002) Routledge.

Freeman M, *The Rights and Wrongs of Children* (1983 a) Frances Pinter.

Freeman M, 'Freedom and the Welfare State: Child-Rearing, Parental Autonomy and State Intervention' (1983 b) Journal of Social Welfare Law 70.

Freeman M, 'The Limits of Children's Rights' in M Freeman and P Veerman (eds) *The Ideologies of Children's Rights* (1992) Martinus Nijhoff Publishers.

Gaylin W, 'Who Speaks for the Child?' in W Gaylin and R Macklin (eds) *Who Speaks for the Child* (1982) Plenum Press.

Goldstein J, Freud A and Solnit A, *Beyond the Best Interests of the Child* (1973) New York Free Press.

Goldstein J, Freud A and Solnit A, *Before the Best Interests of the Child* (1980) Burnett Books Ltd.

Hafen B, 'Children's Liberation and the New Egalitarianism: Some Reservations About Abandoning Youth to their "Rights"' (1976) Brigham Young University Law Review 605.

Hammarberg T, 'Children, Crime and Society: Perspectives of the UN Convention on the Rights of the Child' in *Child Offenders: UK and International Practice* (1995) The Howard League.

Harris J, *Legal Philosophies* (1980) Butterworths.

Harris J, 'The political status of children' in K Graham (ed) *Contemporary Political Philosophy* (1982) Cambridge University Press.

Harris-Short S, '*Re B (Adoption: Natural Parent)* Putting the child at the heart of adoption?' (2002) 14 Child and Family Law Quarterly 325.

Hart H L A, *Law, Liberty and Morality* (1963) Oxford University Press.

Hart H L A, 'Are There Any Natural Rights?' reproduced in J Waldron *Theories of Rights* (1984) Oxford University Press.

Herring J, 'The Human Rights Act and the welfare principle in family law – conflicting or complementary?' (1999) 11 Child and Family Law Quarterly 237.

Hohfeld W, *Fundamental Legal Conceptions as Applied in Judicial reasoning* (1919) Yale University Press.

Holt J, *Escape from Childhood: The Needs and Rights of Childhood* (1974) E P Dutton and Co Inc.

King M, 'Playing the Symbols – Custody and the Law Commission' (1987) Family Law 186.

King M, 'Children's Rights as Communication: Reflections on Autopoietic Theory and the United Nations Convention (1994) 57 Modern Law Review 385.

King M and Piper C, *How the Law Thinks About Children* (1995) Arena.

Lindley R, 'Teenagers and Other Children' in G Scarre (ed) *Children, Parents and Politics* (1989) Cambridge University Press.

Lyons D, 'Utility and Rights' in J Waldron (ed) *Theories of Rights* (1984) Oxford University Press.

MacCormick N, *Legal Right and Social Democracy: Essays in Legal and Political Philosophy* (1982) Clarendon Press.

McGillivray A, 'Why children do have equal rights: in reply to Laura Purdy' (1994) 2 International Journal of Children's Rights 243.

Macklin R, 'Return to the Best Interests of the Child' in W Gaylin and R Macklin (eds) *Who Speaks for the Child* (1982) Plenum Press.

Mill J S, *On Liberty* (1859) from H Acton (ed) *Utilitarianism, Liberty, Representative Government* (1972) Dent.

Minow M, 'Rights For the Next Generation: A Feminist Approach to Children's Rights' (1986) 9 Harvard Women's Law Journal 1.

Minow M, 'Interpreting Rights: An Essay for Robert Cover' (1987) 96 Yale Law Journal 1860.

O'Brien Steinfels M, 'Children's Rights, Parental Rights, Family Privacy, and Family Autonomy' in W Gaylin and R Macklin (eds) *Who Speaks for the Child* (1982) Plenum Press.

O'Neill O, 'Children's Rights and Children's Lives' in P Alston, S Parker and J Seymour (eds) *Children, Rights and the Law* (1992) Clarendon Press.

Olsen F, 'Children's Rights: Some Feminist Approaches to the United Nations Convention on the Rights of the Child' in P Alston, S Parker and J Seymour (eds) *Children, Rights and the Law* (1992) Clarendon Press.

Parker S, 'Rights and Utility in Anglo-Australian Family Law' (1992) 55 Modern Law Review 311.

Pollock L, *Forgotten Children: Parent-Child Relations from 1500-1900* (1983) Cambridge University Press.

Purdy L, *In Their Best Interest? The Case Against Equal Rights for Children* (1992) Cornell University Press.

Purdy L, 'Why children shouldn't have equal rights' (1994) 2 International Journal of Children's Rights 223.

Rawls J, *A Theory of Justice* (1971) Oxford University Press.

Raz J ,'Hart on Moral Rights and Legal Duties' (1984 a) 4 Oxford Journal of Legal Studies 123.

Raz J, 'Legal Rights' (1984 b) 4 Oxford Journal of Legal Studies 1.

Raz J, *The Morality of Freedom* (1986) Clarendon Press.

Raz J, 'Liberty and Trust' in R George (ed) *Natural Law, Liberalism and Morality* (1996) Oxford University Press.

Roche J, 'Children and Divorce: A Private Affair?' in S Day Sclater and C Piper *Undercurrents of Divorce* (1999) Dartmouth.

Toope S, 'The Convention on the Rights of the Child: Implications for Canada' in M Freeman (ed) *Children's Rights: A Comparative Perspective* (1996) Dartmouth.

Wald M, 'Children's Rights: A Framework for Analysis' (1979) 12 University of California Davis Law Review 255.

Waldron J (ed), *Theories of Rights* (1984) Oxford University Press.

Wellman C, *The Proliferation of Rights: Moral Progress or Empty Rhetoric?* (1999) Westview Press.

de Winter M, *Children as Fellow Citizens: Participation and Commitment* (1997) Radcliffe Medical Press Ltd.

Chapter 2

International children's rights

(1) INTRODUCTION

A large body of international human rights law exists today which can be used to inform the way that domestic law promotes children's rights in the United Kingdom. Indeed, the translation of ideas about children's rights into principles of English law was accelerated by the British government ratifying a series of international instruments prepared by the General Assembly of the United Nations and by the Council of Europe. The instrument of outstanding importance is the United Nations Convention on the Rights of the Child (CRC) ratified by the United Kingdom in 1991. This long and ambitious list of children's rights constitutes a painstaking attempt to define children's needs and aspirations and to commit ratifying states to their accomplishment. Although not part of English law as such, it currently exerts an increasingly powerful influence on the developing law and is often used as an international template against which to measure domestic standards.

Unlike the CRC, the European Convention on Human Rights and Fundamental Freedoms (hereafter ECHR) was not designed specifically to protect children as a group. But they, as human beings, are entitled to claim its protection and it too has influenced the way in which children's rights have been protected in this country. Indeed, ever since 1959, when the European Court of Human Rights was established to adjudicate complaints on breaches of the European Convention, practitioners in the United Kingdom knew that they might, as a last resort, seek its assistance to reinforce children's claims that their rights under the Convention were being infringed. The ECHR will undoubtedly provoke more dramatic changes in the future now that the rights it contains have been made part of domestic law. On 2 October 2000, the day on which the Human Rights Act 1998 was implemented, the rights listed in the ECHR left the international domain and formed part of the slowly accumulating layers of domestic case law and legislation. Despite its new status as part of the United Kingdom's domestic law, no chapter devoted to an assessment of children's rights from an international perspective would be complete without a discussion of the ECHR's significance in its own right, alongside the CRC.

The following chapter discusses the importance of these two international treaties and the manner in which they have been interpreted. It also considers briefly a variety of other international instruments produced by the United Nations and the Council of Europe which provide insight on international expectations regarding the treatment of children in various areas of activity. First, though, it devotes a short discussion to the links between theories about children's moral and legal rights and those underlying their international human rights.

(2)   RIGHTS THEORIES AND INTERNATIONAL HUMAN RIGHTS

The jurisprudential doubts underlying the existence and scope of children's rights[1] did not inhibit the efforts of those seeking to promote children's protection in an international context. Indeed, had it not been for the driving force of international human rights lawyers, ideas and theories about children's rights might have remained in the realms of intellectual speculation. At first sight, the academics and legal practitioners concerned with the field of international human rights appear to be interested in entirely different concepts from the pure rights theories which concern the moral philosophers and jurists. These differences are perhaps more apparent than real and are certainly exacerbated by the different language they employ. It was not until the aftermath of the Second World War that the term 'human rights' crept into common parlance as a way of describing the moral rights considered fundamental to civilised existence.[2] The draftsmen of the post-War international treaties adopted the new term in preference to the well-known phrase 'rights of man' favoured by natural law theorists. Thus the United Nations in its founding charter of 1945 stated that one of its primary purposes was to promote and encourage 'respect for human rights and for fundamental freedoms for all without distinction as to race, sex, language, or religion'. Only three years later, in 1948, the Universal Declaration of Human Rights, adopted by the United Nations General Assembly, contained a general statement guaranteeing 'the inherent dignity and ... equal and inalienable rights of all members of the human family'.

It was the civil and political rights selected for protection by the post-War treaties that were most clearly based on the ideas of the earlier natural law philosophers. They were derived from those inalienable rights of man that seventeenth-century theorists, like Hugo Grotius and John Locke, considered to be fundamental to human nature. Locke argued that, according to the laws of nature, each human being is entitled to the inalienable moral right to life, liberty and property.[3] These ideas had grounded the eighteenth-century bills of rights emanating from America and France – the American Declaration of Independence of 1776 and the French Declaration of the Rights of Man and of the Citizen of 1789. Although interest in natural rights theories waned during the nineteenth century, it revived in the 1940s in response to the manner in which totalitarian regimes, such as that of Nazi Germany, had been able to commit atrocities on a horrifying scale. As Feldman observes:

> '... the idea at the root of human rights thinking is that there are certain rights which are so fundamental to society's well-being and to people's chance of leading a fulfilling life that governments are obligated to respect them, and the international order has to protect them.'[4]

The ECHR 1950 and the International Covenant on Civil and Political Rights 1966 were both primarily concerned with fundamental liberties. The 'first generation human rights' they listed sought to protect the individual from oppressive interference by a nation state. Their provisions typically guarantee freedom from torture, from conviction without a fair trial, of expression and the right to peaceful assembly. By contrast, documents such as the Universal Declaration of Human Rights 1948[5] and the

1   See discussion in chapter 1.
2   Wellman succinctly describes the historical development of ideas about natural rights and their later translation into 'human rights', as set out in a series of international treaties. See C Wellman (1999) esp pp 13–21. See also G Van Bueren (1995) pp 1–9.
3   C Wellman (1999) esp pp 13–21.
4   See D Feldman (2002) pp 34–35.
5   See arts 22–29; cf arts 1–21 which embrace the traditional civil and political rights.

International Covenant on Economic, Social and Cultural Rights 1966, which contain a list of 'second generation rights', reflect a more developed theory of human rights.[6] These seek to ensure that the first generation of 'negative' liberties are complemented by requiring states to take positive action to promote the welfare of individual human beings. In an approach later echoed in the CRC, the International Covenant on Economic, Social and Cultural Rights reflects the view that it is not enough for human rights documents to identify certain liberties essential to individual autonomy, such as freedom of speech and assembly.[7] These rights may be of no value to those too poor or ill to benefit from them, whose time is taken up surviving from day to day.[8] Consequently, the Covenant obliges states to take a more active role. They are required to make resources available for certain additional social welfare rights; for example by guaranteeing the right to an adequate standard of living[9] and to the highest attainable standard of physical and mental health,[10] thereby enabling people to take advantage of their innate freedoms. Some international lawyers refuse to acknowledge that these social welfare rights can have the force of international law, because there is no obvious means of enforcing them.[11] Nevertheless, their inclusion in a variety of international documents, including the CRC, constantly reminds states of their wider obligations regarding their citizens.

The notion that children are, as human beings, entitled to human rights, was gradually accepted in an international and domestic context. Indeed, during the second half of the twentieth century it became widely acknowledged that children's human rights were theoretically no different from those of adults – they too were entitled to certain fundamental moral rights carrying the force of international law. This perception underpins the CRC. That document not only contains the civil and political rights derived from the inalienable 'rights of man', but also the second generation social welfare rights guaranteed by documents like the International Covenant on Economic, Social and Cultural Rights. So, in this way, the concept of children's rights has acquired a valuable international dimension which has encouraged all government ministries and agencies, including the courts, to promote it more wholeheartedly in a domestic context within the United Kingdom.

(3) THE UNITED NATIONS AND THE AFTERMATH OF THE SECOND WORLD WAR

The atrocities perpetrated before and during the Second World War led to a firm resolve to strengthen international unity. Indeed, the main spur to identify the human rights important to mankind, to include them in international treaties and to persuade governments to recognise them on a world-wide basis has always been some serious disregard for humanitarian values.[12] A determination to prevent such appalling events

6 A third generation of human rights is now emerging, these being 'solidarity rights' or the rights of normally vulnerable groups to protection, *as a group*, rather than as individuals. Eg, inter alia: the Convention on the Prevention of the Crime of Genocide 1948, which was motivated by the German attempts to destroy the Jewish race throughout Europe; the Convention on the Elimination of All Forms of Discrimination against Women 1979. See C Wellman (1999) pp 29–30.
7 This approach was also evident in arts 22–29 of the Universal Declaration of Human Rights.
8 See D Feldman (2002) pp 12–14.
9 Art 11 of the International Covenant on Economic, Social and Cultural Rights.
10 Art 12 of the International Covenant on Economic, Social and Cultural Rights.
11 These arguments are summarised by C Wellman (1999) pp 20–29.
12 D Feldman (2002) p 35.

occurring again was accompanied by the promulgation of a large number of human rights instruments setting out those rights deemed essential to civilised life. Attempts to strengthen international unity included establishing the United Nations, whose charter came into force in 1945.

This post-War activity was intended to strengthen human rights generally. Although children implicitly benefited from it, it did not aim to protect them as a group. This is clear from the wording of the charter of the United Nations, which seeks to promote and encourage the human rights and fundamental freedoms 'for all without distinction as to race, sex, language or religion'. Whilst it certainly does not exclude children from its ambit, it does not specifically refer to them.[13] Similarly, the Universal Declaration of Human Rights adopted in 1948 contains references to children[14] and guarantees the 'equal and inalienable rights of all members of the human family',[15] but makes no attempt to provide for a range of rights more suitable for children with needs of their own.

A wide variety of UN human rights instruments now exists which refer to children's rights in various different contexts,[16] but again their main emphasis is not on children specifically. Admittedly, some, like the twin covenants adopted by the General Assembly of the United Nations in 1966, the International Covenant on Civil and Political Rights and the International Covenant on Economic, Social and Cultural Rights, do refer specifically to children's special needs.[17] The former covenant provides particularly important safeguards for the religious rights of minority groups.[18] Nevertheless, these general human rights documents make no attempt to deal with the broad spectrum of children's needs, nor to make them their main focus of attention.[19] By contrast, the CRC, adopted by the General Assembly over 20 years later in 1989, achieves both aims outstandingly well. Indeed, it utilises many of the provisions contained in the earlier, more general, documents.

A second remarkable document is the Beijing Rules, whose official title is the United Nations Standard Minimum Rules for the Administration of Juvenile Justice. These were adopted by the General Assembly in 1985 and, like the CRC, relate only to children. They are, nevertheless, limited to a very narrow focus of their activities. They provide a complete and detailed framework for the operation of a national youth justice system.[20] Their weakness is that they are not binding per se. Despite this, they provide a complete and realistic coverage of what an ideal youth justice system should aim to achieve at every stage of the process for dealing with children caught up in youth crime. The Beijing Rules display an impressively thorough understanding of the whole area of youth crime and of the need to avoid dealing with

---

13   Art 55(c).
14   Art 25(2) refers to motherhood and childhood both requiring special care and assistance; see also Art 26, which concerns educational rights.
15   See the Preamble.
16   See generally, G Van Bueren (1995).
17   Eg art 10(3) of the International Covenant on Economic, Social and Cultural Rights seeks to protect children from economic and social exploitation, particularly in the work place, whilst art 13 enshrines the right of everyone to education. Similarly, art 10 of the International Covenant on Civil and Political Rights deals with the rights of juvenile offenders, whilst art 24 guarantees children's right to protection by his family, society and the state.
18   Art 27. See discussion in chapter 11.
19   It is, however, arguable that since these treaties are intended to protect all human beings, children automatically benefit from all rights therein listed. See D Hodgson (1992) pp 274–275.
20   See G Van Bueren (1995) pp 170–171.

young offenders in an over-aggressive and inhumane way. The extent to which English law measures up to their expectations is considered in the context of the discussion of the developing law in this area.[21]

(4)　THE UNITED NATIONS AND CHILDREN'S RIGHTS

Although the special vulnerability of children as a group had been recognised much earlier than the international human rights activity generated by the Second World War, little progress was made towards producing an instrument which had binding force, covering the full scope of their needs. The first important international document devoted entirely to protecting the rights of children was adopted by the Fifth Assembly of the League of Nations in 1924. This was the Declaration of the Rights of the Child, known as the Declaration of Geneva.[22] It contained only five basic principles, all of which were couched in forthright terms. Thus the first commenced with the words 'The child must be given the means requisite for its normal development, both materially and spiritually'. The second went on to state that 'The child that is hungry must be fed; the child that is sick must be nursed ...' The third was even more to the point, stating merely that 'The child must be the first to receive relief in times of distress'.

The Declaration of Geneva was brief and only aspirational, since it merely invited the member states to be 'guided by its principles in the work of child welfare'.[23] Of far greater importance for the promotion of children's rights was the Declaration of the Rights of the Child adopted in 1959 by the General Assembly of the United Nations. This was a longer document containing ten principles, but again, since it had the limited status of a declaration, it did not attempt to claim that the 'rights' listed constituted legal obligations. Instead, states were merely required to take note of the principles contained therein, on the basis that they were universally accepted as being applicable to all children.

Some of the principles set out in the 1959 Declaration now appear idealistic, others simply outdated. For example, parts of Principle 6 which refer to a child's need for 'love and understanding', and to grow up in an atmosphere of 'affection and of moral and material security', are extremely vague. Other parts reflect outmoded stereotyped ideas about the roles to be played by mothers and fathers in the lives of their children. Principle 6 also asserts that a 'child of tender years shall not, save in exceptional circumstances, be separated from his mother'. These latter aspects of the 1959 Declaration render it far too anachronistic to have any current domestic import. This was emphasised by Thorpe LJ, who trenchantly rejected a mother's claim that Principle 6 strengthened her application for a residence order. In his view:

> 'The relevance and value of the UN 1959 Declaration is most doubtful. In terms of relevant social policy it could be said to be almost antiquated since it is now nearly 40 years old and in terms of social development and in terms of understanding of child development and welfare that is an exceedingly long time.'[24]

Despite its outdated wording, the importance of the 1959 Declaration lies in the fact that it embodies the first serious attempt to describe in a reasonably detailed manner

21　Discussed in more detail in chapter 18.
22　See D Hodgson (1992) pp 260–261.
23　D Hodgson (1992) p 261.
24　*Re A (children: 1959 UN Declaration)* [1998] 1 FLR 354 at 358. There the Court of Appeal allowed the father's appeal against the grant of a residence order to the mother over their 3½-year-old son.

what constitutes children's overriding claims and entitlements. The phrasing of many of its principles are far too ill-defined to justify inclusion in any future document intended to carry the weight of international law. Nevertheless, some of the ideas it contains are surprisingly modern and reappear in an elaborated form in the CRC, introduced 30 years later in 1989. For example, it refers to the child's right to treatment without discrimination, to special protection, to material and spiritual development, to socio-economic rights, such as housing, medical care and food, and to rights to education and protection from exploitation, neglect and cruelty. It also includes a reference to the child's right to name and nationality.

Perhaps the generality of the 1959 Declaration, and the fact that it carries no legally binding obligations, led to a general tendency by many nations to continue ignoring the appalling conditions being suffered by large numbers of children. In particular, it contains no acknowledgment that children are entitled, like adults, to the first generation human rights, the freedoms from state oppression. Indeed, barring the reference to name and nationality, there is no mention of children's civil and political rights. The CRC was borne out of calls for a more systematic approach to protecting children's rights. By the 1970s, growing concern over the violations of children's rights throughout the world led finally to a move to establish an international document guaranteeing children's rights through the imposition of legal obligations.[25] In 1976, the United Nations General Assembly, fulfilling a request from the executive board of UNICEF, declared 1979 the International Year of the Child and urged governments to commemorate the year by making special contributions to improving the well-being of children. As its contribution to the year, the Polish government in 1978, submitted to the United Nations Commission on Human Rights a draft for a new CRC. It was virtually identical in format to the 1959 Declaration and it was hoped that it could be adopted by the United Nations the following year, as a legally binding international document. Such an optimistic timescale proved unrealistic. Although there was general agreement that a document of this nature should be created, it was considered that there was little point in repeating the mistakes of the 1959 Declaration. Governments would continue to ignore their obligations to children unless the provisions were sufficiently specific and realistic. Nearly ten years were to elapse before a final draft of the CRC was completed in 1988 and submitted to the Commission on Human Rights for approval in 1989. It was finally adopted by the General Assembly in November 1989, entering into force in 1990. It was ratified by the United Kingdom in 1991[26] and came into force in the United Kingdom in January 1992.

(5)   THE CONVENTION ON THE RIGHTS OF THE CHILD

(A)   Classifying the Convention rights

The Preamble to the CRC makes plain the enormity of the task taken on by its draftsmen and the conflicting ideals that required accommodation within a document commanding international respect. Whilst recognising the importance of the family as 'the fundamental group of society' and the child's need to 'grow up in a family environment' with love and understanding, it also asserts that 'a child should be fully

---

25   D Hodgson (1992) pp 275–276.
26   The UK's ratification was subject to reservations regarding the care of young offenders, immigration, employment regulations regarding over 16-year-olds, and children's hearings in Scotland. The latter two reservations have now been withdrawn.

prepared to live an individual life in society, and brought up in the spirit of the ideals proclaimed in the Charter of the United Nations, and in particular in the spirit of peace, dignity, tolerance, freedom, equality and solidarity'.[27] Despite these difficulties, the decade of drafting produced a document which, if fully complied with, would indeed achieve many of these aims.

The rights listed cover the broad spectrum of children's needs and aspirations. Its 54 articles, some 40 of which are concerned with substantive rights, cover civil, political, economic and social issues. Unlike other international human rights treaties, notably the International Covenant on Civil and Political Rights and the International Covenant on Economic, Social and Cultural Rights, the Convention contains both sets of rights in one single document. The Convention applies to 'every human being below the age of eighteen years',[28] and by including all the traditional civil and political rights, such as freedom of expression,[29] religion,[30] association and assembly,[31] it departs radically from the earlier international documents which primarily aimed to address children's immaturity and need for care. By including children's social welfare rights, the Convention also emphasises that states must not only protect children and safeguard their fundamental freedoms, but also devote resources to ensuring that they realise their potential for maturing into a healthy and happy adulthood.

The articles demonstrate a strange mixture of idealism and practical realism. Some, like article 28 on education, descend into the detailed aspects of schooling, such as ensuring regular attendance and 'the reduction of drop-out rates'.[32] Others, like article 12, assuring respect for the child's views, maintain a more philosophical approach to their capacity for autonomy. The substantive rights listed often overlap each other considerably in their aims and the wording of many reflects a compromise in the drafting sessions. When interpreting some of the more opaque provisions, valuable assistance can be derived from the research which has analysed the 'Concluding Observations'[33] of the Committee on the Rights of the Child.[34] This throws light on the Committee's view of the Convention's intentions.

Although the Committee has stressed that the articles of the Convention are interrelated and should be considered together, it has itself elevated articles 2,[35] 3,[36] 6[37] and 12[38] to the status of general principles.[39] Theoretically, none of these four principles is more important than any other; nevertheless article 3, requiring a commitment to the child's best interests, underpins all the other provisions. It should be noted, however, that unlike the Children Act 1989, section 1, which provides that the child's best interests are paramount,[40] article 3(1) only provides that 'the best

27   See Preamble to the CRC, para 7.
28   Unless the age of majority is attained earlier. See art 1.
29   Art 13.
30   Art 14.
31   Art 15.
32   Art 28(1)(e).
33   The 'Concluding Observations' of the Committee on the Rights of the Child, whose job it is to monitor compliance with the Convention, are the Committee's responses to the reports (both initial and periodic) from ratifying governments, describing their progress towards implementing the terms of the Convention. This process is discussed in more detail below.
34   Eg P Newell and R Hodgkin (1998) and C Price Cohen and S Kilbourne (1998).
35   Freedom from discrimination.
36   The child's best interests.
37   The right to life.
38   Respect for the child's views.
39   P Newell and R Hodgkin (1998) p 40.
40   See also Principle 2 of the 1959 Declaration of the Rights of the Child which made the child's interests paramount.

interests of the child shall be *a* primary consideration'.[41] This wording is attributable to the concerns of delegates that there might be other competing interests, for example, those of justice and society, at times making paramountcy inappropriate.[42] Although this might appear to be a rather grudging approach to a principle overriding an entirely child-centred document, it is comprehensible, given that the formula was intended to govern all the articles contained in the Convention, including those applicable to young offenders. Whilst a court might wish to balance the needs of the young offender against society's need for protection, it would be difficult to claim that the offender's needs should always be *paramount* to those of society.[43] Despite the 'best interests' formula not adopting a paramountcy criterion, the Committee on the Rights of the Child is keen not to allow it to be downplayed.[44] It has emphasised that, since article 3 underwrites article 4, it must be used as 'a guiding principle' when interpreting all Convention provisions.[45] In other words, *all* children's rights must be interpreted in accordance with their best interests.

The contents of the Convention have been classified in a variety of ways, none of which avoids overlap.[46] Although not ideal, LeBlanc's classification,[47] by including 'membership rights', emphasises the way in which the Convention addresses children's need for community. According to his arrangement, the rights are classified into 'survival rights', 'membership rights', 'protection rights' and 'empowerment rights'.[48] The survival rights include not only the right to life itself, but also the right to all those rights which sustain life, such as the rights to an adequate standard of living and to health care. Membership rights include those which treat the child as a member of his or her community and family. Protection rights guard the child against abuses of power by individuals and the state. Finally, empowerment rights secure a respect for children as effective members of the communities in which they live, through protecting their freedom of thought and conscience and encouraging their capacity for self-determination.[49]

Children's survival rights are obviously of primary importance. They include more than the rights necessary for bare survival. States must take positive steps to ensure that children enjoy a full life, with the potential for maturing into healthy adults. It is not enough for article 6 to protect children's right to life,[50] or for article 37 to bar the

---

41   Art 3(1): 'In all actions concerning children, whether undertaken by public or private social welfare institutions, courts of law, administrative authorities or legislative bodies, the best interests of the child shall be *a* primary consideration.' Emphasis supplied.

42   See R Barsh (1989) pp 143–144. See also D McGoldrick (1991) pp 135–137.

43   See Children and Young Persons Act 1933, s 44, which requires youth courts to reach decisions having 'regard to the welfare of the child'.

44   P Newell and R Hodgkin (1998) esp pp 39–43.

45   Eg Committee on the Rights of the Child (1995 a) para 24.

46   Eg T Hammarberg (1990) suggests a classification involving the four 'P's: the participation of children in decisions involving their own destiny; the protection of children against discrimination and all forms of neglect; the prevention of harm to children; and the provision of assistance for their basic needs.

47   Adapted from that proposed by J Donnelly and R Howard (1988).

48   L LeBlanc (1995) Pt Two.

49   L LeBlanc (1995) p xviii.

50   NB Although art 6 does not make it clear that the unborn child is protected, para 9 of the Preamble requires States Parties to bear in mind that 'the child, by reason of his physical and mental immaturity, needs special safeguards and care, including appropriate legal protection, *before as well as after birth*' (emphasis supplied). On ratification, the UK declared that it interprets the Convention as applying only following a live birth. This ensures that the right to life does not conflict with domestic abortion legislation.

death penalty for criminal acts,[51] children must also be provided with the resources to develop their full potential.[52] Consequently, the Convention ensures that children's social and economic rights are fully acknowledged. It recognises that a child cannot do so without a standard of living adequate for his or her 'physical, mental, spiritual, moral and social development',[53] social security benefits,[54] and the right to the 'highest attainable standard of health and to facilities for the treatment of illness and rehabilitation of health'.[55] Many of these rights require a considerable commitment of resources before being fully implemented. The wording of article 4 implicitly recognises that for some states, where resources are scarce, this may not be possible immediately, or even in the near future. Nevertheless, as the Committee on the Rights of the Child has repeatedly stressed, all states are required to take measures to promote children's economic, social, and cultural rights, *'to the maximum extent of their available resources ...'*[56]

The membership rights recognised by the Convention refer to a child's upbringing as a member of a family and also as a member of a larger community. Virtually all international instruments stress the need to promote equality between individuals. Making it clear that this aim is as appropriate for children as for adults, the Convention asserts the equality of all children and their freedom to enjoy all rights free of discrimination on the grounds of 'race, colour, sex, language, religion, political or other opinion, national, ethnic or social origin, property, disability, birth or other status'.[57] Children with disabilities are protected by a series of positive measures enabling them to become as fully integrated into the community as possible.[58] Furthermore, the right of children of minority groups to follow their own culture, religion and language is specifically protected.[59] The Convention also recognises that in order for children to gain membership of a community or state they must have a name and nationality,[60] and the right to preserve their identity.[61] Article 8 was introduced by the Argentinian representatives to prevent children being allowed to 'disappear', as they had during the reign of the Argentinian Junta between 1975 and 1983.[62] These rights are also particularly important to children caught up in the type of 'ethnic cleansings' which took place in the former Yugoslavia, who may become separated from their homes and communities.

Echoing the terms of the Preamble to the Convention, a number of articles recognise the importance to children of being members of a family unit. They set out to protect

---

51 See art 37(a)–(d) and discussion in chapter 18.
52 See art 6(2).
53 Art 27.
54 Art 26.
55 Art 24(1). Art 24(2)(a)–(f) provides considerable detail on implementation of this right. The inclusion of art 24(3) was particularly controversial at the drafting stage, since it directs states to abolish 'traditional practices prejudicial to the health of children', and was opposed by delegates from countries practising female circumcision. See discussion in chapter 10.
56 Emphasis supplied. See the Committee's successive criticisms of the United Kingdom's failure in this respect: Committee on the Rights of the Child (1995 a) para 9 and (2002) paras 10 and 11. For the Committee's responses to the efforts of other countries, see P Newell and R Hodgkin (1998) esp pp 63–65.
57 Art 2(1). This article was controversial for failing specifically to protect children born out of wedlock.
58 Art 23(1)–(4).
59 Art 30. See also art 29(1)(c) (aims of education).
60 Art 7.
61 Art 8.
62 See S Detrick (1992) pp 292–294.

and support the family, recognising that for most children, family life will provide them with the greatest chance of enjoying a happy and stable upbringing. Article 5 emphasises the importance of the parental role, requiring states to –

'... respect the responsibilities, rights and duties of parents ... to provide, in a manner consistent with the evolving capacities of the child, appropriate direction and guidance in the exercise by the child of the rights recognized in the present Convention.'

Article 18 directs states to achieve recognition for the principle that both parents have common responsibilities for the upbringing and development of their children. It also recognises that whilst parents will have the 'primary responsibility' for their children's upbringing, they may require assistance from the state in fulfilling their task.[63] Meanwhile, articles 9 and 10 require states to ensure that children will not be separated from their parents against their will and to promote family reunification. State care and substitute parenting should be provided for children deprived of an upbringing by their own parents.[64]

The Convention contains a lengthy list of 'protection rights', Le Blanc's third group of rights. These are an essential ingredient in any document seeking to protect children from abuse, exploitation and maltreatment in various different contexts. It is obviously essential to stamp out child prostitution and other forms of sexual exploitation,[65] whilst children must also be protected from economic exploitation and other harmful effects of child labour, such as interference with education and harm to health.[66] Moreover, states are specifically required to protect children from all forms of abuse, including physical, emotional, sexual abuse and ill-treatment and neglect, whilst in the care of their parents.[67] The Convention also seeks to protect children from various aspects of armed conflict, including from participating in the hostilities themselves below the age of 15[68] and to ensure that refugee children receive humanitarian assistance.[69] Procedures and penalties adopted by states for dealing with juvenile crime must be fair, humane and take account of their youth and their need for rehabilitation within the community.[70]

The empowerment rights listed by the Convention are the most remarkable given that many of the delegates involved in the drafting sessions were from Islamic countries whose conceptions of the role of children in families and the wider community were relatively narrow. The Convention recognises that children are active and creative and may need to struggle to shape their own lives. As such they must be assisted to develop their independence and ability to take responsibility for their future. In particular, by extending the traditional civil and political rights to children, the Convention indicates that all children, irrespective of age, have the same dignity and worth as adults.[71] In particular, they require the liberties essential to notions of adult

63   Art 18(2) and (3) (state child care services and additional facilities for working parents).
64   Art 20 (protection for children without families); art 21 (regulation of adoption).
65   Art 34.
66   Art 32. See also art 35 (prevention of the sale and trafficking in children); art 21 (the regulation of inter-country adoption); art 36 (protection from all forms of prejudicial exploitation).
67   Art 19. See also art 33 (protection from drug abuse); art 37(1) (protection from torture, cruel or other inhumane treatment or punishment).
68   Art 38.
69   Art 22.
70   Arts 37, 39 and 40.
71   See the second paragraph of the Preamble to the Convention, which reminds states that the UN Charter reaffirmed faith in 'fundamental human rights and in the dignity and worth of the human person ...'

autonomy if they are to develop their own capacity for autonomy and play an active part in society.

Article 12 is often singled out as being one of the most important in the Convention.[72] It assures to children capable of forming their own views, 'the right to express those views freely in all matters affecting (them), the views of the child being given due weight in accordance with the age and maturity of the child'.[73] Moreover, article 12(2) provides children with the procedural right to be heard in any judicial or administrative proceedings affecting them – this latter provision being crucially important to children who are the subject of parental disputes. When responding to each state's periodic reports on the progress made towards implementation, the Committee on the Rights of the Child has often stressed that the principles set out in article 12 should be given 'greater priority'; the implicit message being that it should be seen as a right and not merely a matter of discretion for individual governments.[74] Article 13, complementing article 12, secures the right to freedom of expression, including the right to seek, receive and impart information and ideas. The Convention also recognises that in order to form and express their own views, children need access to information and material from a variety of sources.[75] Even more fundamental, they are entitled to respect and dignity, as they mature to adulthood. States must secure their rights to freedom of thought, conscience and religion,[76] to privacy[77] and a freedom to meet and mix with others and share views.[78] Crucially, children cannot develop their views and critical thought without a right to education. This too is fully recognised, with detailed provisions regarding the practical aspects of providing schooling,[79] and additionally setting out the more philosophical aims of education, including the need to promote a respect for the child's parents and his or her cultural identity.[80]

(B) Internal inconsistencies

The aims of the Convention, as set out in the Preamble, are difficult to reconcile. In particular, it emphasises the need to promote children's capacity for eventual autonomy, whilst simultaneously supporting the traditional role of the family in society and the authority of parents over their children. Not surprisingly, this led to many disagreements during the drafting sessions. Conflicting views were expressed by the delegates from the Islamic countries, who were deeply opposed to giving children freedom from parental direction and religious teaching and by those from countries like the United States, who, influenced by their own constitutional history, strongly favoured the concept of children enjoying similar civil and political rights to adults.[81] Some delegates also feared that providing families with protection from

---

72 See, inter alia: C Price Cohen and S Kilbourne (1998) p 648 and appended tables; K Marshall (1997) esp pp 11–31; P Newell and R Hodgkin (1998) esp pp 148–164.
73 Art 12(1).
74 Eg see Committee on the Rights of the Child (1995 a) para 27. See K Marshall (1997) pp 29–31.
75 Art 17.
76 Art 14(1).
77 Art 16.
78 Art 15.
79 Art 28(1)(a)–(e).
80 Art 29.
81 L LeBlanc (1995) ch 1 and pp 112–117.

state interference would provide parents with arbitrary control over their children, thereby inhibiting children from being able to develop their own views. The compromises resulting from attempts to balance these differing approaches to the family are reflected in many of the articles. Thus article 3(2) stresses that: 'States Parties undertake to ensure the child such protection and care as is necessary for his or her well-being', but continues:

'taking into account the rights and duties of his or her parents, legal guardians, or other individuals legally responsible for him or her, and, to this end, shall take all appropriate legislative and administrative measures.'

There is also an obvious tension between the position adopted by article 5, which respects the parents' right to direct and guide their children, with that adopted by other provisions which promote a child's capacity for independence. As McGoldrick observes, the wording of article 5 itself is fraught with difficulty, since those obliged to fulfil it are the very individuals who may have a personal interest in ensuring that children do not exercise their rights.[82] Furthermore, neither article 12, which requires states to ensure that children's opinions are sought, nor article 13 regarding a child's right to freedom of expression, contains any qualifying phrase requiring states to take account of parental wishes. Indeed, article 12(1) makes it clear that *every* child who is capable of forming his or her own views should have the right to express them freely over all matters affecting him or her.[83] The fact that article 12(1) ends with the phrase 'the views of the child being given due weight *in accordance with the age and maturity of the child*'[84] provides some scope for a paternalistic restriction of the underlying aims of the article. Nevertheless, the Committee on the Rights of the Child has criticised attempts to exploit this phrase in a way which dilutes children's participation rights.[85]

The inclusion of the traditional human right to freedom of religion provoked considerable disagreement amongst those attending the drafting sessions. Islamic states were strongly opposed to any suggestion that the child should have complete freedom of religious choice.[86] It is notable that article 14, which respects children's 'freedom of thought, conscience and religion', does not, unlike its counterpart in the International Covenant on Civil and Political Rights, specifically set out a correlative right to 'have or adopt a religion or belief of his choice'.[87] This could imply that the CRC merely gives children the right to *practise* their own religion, rather than the freedom to 'choose' it, thereby maintaining the parental right to impose a 'choice' of religion on their children. Although such an interpretation might also be justified by reference to article 14(2), which stresses the parental right 'to provide direction to the child in the exercise of his or her right in a manner consistent with the evolving capacities of the child', it would undermine the obvious intentions of articles such as articles 12 and 13, both of which stress the child's right to form his or her own views on important matters.[88] The Committee on the Rights of the Child has itself stressed that limitations on this right can only be justified if they fall within the terms of

---

82   D McGoldrick (1991) pp 138–139.
83   G Van Bueren (1995) pp 136–141.
84   Emphasis supplied.
85   K Marshall (1997) p 17.
86   L LeBlanc (1995) pp 168–175. See also B Walsh (1991) pp 184–186.
87   International Convention on Civil and Political Rights, art 18(1).
88   P Newell and R Hodgkin (1998) pp 180–181.

article 14(3).[89] It is also difficult to reconcile the need to allow children their own independence, whilst supporting their cultural heritage. This conflict comes out most clearly in the context of the child's right to education.[90] Although the child's need for a broad education is recognised by article 29,[91] that provision also refers to the need for education to develop 'respect for the child's parents, his or her own cultural identity, language and values ...'[92]

It would be foolish to deny the existence of compromises and internal inconsistencies within the Convention. Indeed, like most domestic legal systems, including our own, it reflects an obvious ambivalence over the need to promote children's capacity for self-determination, whilst at the same time maintaining the traditional rights of parents to provide direction, support and discipline.[93] Inevitably, its drafting could, with hindsight, be improved upon, for example, to give greater attention to certain groups of children.[94] Like many other international Conventions, it contains little very practical or specific advice. Indeed, as King rightly says, it 'contains a wide range of rather vague political and economic rights and duties which require further precision and transformation at the national level if they are to become amenable to lawful/unlawful decisions'.[95] But for all its faults, the Convention remains a remarkable document, which provides a comprehensive set of standards against which ratifying states may measure the extent to which they fulfil children's rights.

(C)   Enforcement

The CRC had a startling success in so far as it was quickly ratified by every country in the world, bar the United States, Somalia and East Timor. The American opposition to ratifying the Convention is unfortunate, as it appears to be largely unfounded, based on an incorrect interpretation of its provisions and of its underlying aims. Contrary to the beliefs of some American parents, the Convention provides a framework for implementation through government policies and programmes, not through interference with individual families.[96] The Convention also attracts two more reasonable forms of criticism which require addressing, the first theoretical and the second practical.

The first has been discussed in the context of establishing a theoretical justification for the concept of children's rights.[97] Though acceptable as moral claims, many of the 'rights' listed by the Convention are far too vague to be translated into international or domestic law. Wellman persuasively argues that there is a danger that a 'proliferation of the language of rights' devalues its appeal.[98] It is arguable that by listing 40 substantive 'legal rights', the Convention certainly contributes to this process of rights devaluation. Indeed, amongst those 40, there are many that are, in reality, no more than aspirations regarding what *should* happen if governments were to take children's needs seriously. For example, it is unrealistic to argue that either article 24,

---

89   Eg Committee on the Rights of the Child (1995 b) para 17.
90   Recognised by art 28(1).
91   Art 29(1)(a).
92   Art 29(1)(c). This conflict is discussed in more depth in chapter 12.
93   J Fortin (2002) p 19.
94   See M Freeman (2000) pp 282–289.
95   M King (1994) p 395.
96   See S Kilbourne (1998).
97   See discussion in chapter 1.
98   See C Wellman (1999) esp ch 7.

which requires governments to recognise the child's right to 'enjoyment of the highest attainable standard of health and to facilities for the treatment of illness and rehabilitation of health', or article 27, which recognises 'the right of every child to a standard of living adequate for the child's physical, mental, spiritual, moral and social development', could ever be translated into genuine legal rights. These are no more than an insistence on certain ideals or goals. Furthermore, article 4 clearly acknowledges that the resource implications of such provisions may rule out their immediate or even long-term fulfilment. Its use of the future tense, when enlarging on states' obligations under these articles, emphasises this realism.[99] More seriously, as King observes, there is a danger that –

> 'the transformation into law of substantive demands for the promotion of children's welfare and autonomy lets governments off the hook by allowing them to couch their responses to the Convention in formalistic terms, void of any substantive improvements in children's lives.'[100]

Although these concerns are well founded, many authors consider that the 'rhetoric of rights' is justified if it gives them added credence – if fulfilled, they will enhance the lives of the 'rights' holders. It is a powerful way of expressing the conviction that they ought to be recognised by states here and now as potential rights and that they provide guides to present policies.[101] Minow persuasively argues that children, like adults, are entitled to use the language of rights to gain the community's attention.[102] In her view:

> '... rights represent articulations – public or private, formal or informal – of claims that people use to persuade others (and themselves) about how they should be treated and about what they should be granted.'[103]

Eekelaar is surely right to argue that the symbolism of the Convention is as important as its practical efficacy. In his view, '... to recognize people as having rights from the moment of their birth continuously into adulthood could turn out, politically, to be the most radical step of all'.[104]

A second more practical, and more fundamental, weakness is that the Convention has no direct method of formal enforcement, either available to the rights-holders themselves, or to the United Nations Commission. By contrast with the ECHR, there is no court which can assess claims that its terms have been infringed. Governments are merely directed to undertake 'all appropriate legislative, administrative and other measures' to implement the rights contained in the Convention.[105] The implementation mechanism is similar to that of other United Nations human rights treaties.[106] Thus the only body with responsibility for 'examining the progress made by States Parties in achieving the realisation of the obligations' contained therein is the Committee on the Rights of the Child, established under the auspices of the General Assembly of the United Nations. The Committee sits in Geneva and consists of ten experts elected from within the ranks of states parties who have ratified the

---

99   See also art 24(4), which directs states, regarding children's health rights, to 'promote and encourage international co-operation *with a view to achieving progressively* the full realization of the right recognized in the present article' (emphasis supplied).
100   M King (1994) p 396.
101   See J Feinberg (1980) p 153.
102   See M Minow (1987) p 1887.
103   M Minow (1987) p 1867.
104   J Eekelaar (1992) p 234.
105   Art 4.
106   C Price Cohen and S Kilbourne (1998) p 638.

Convention.[107] In the absence of any formal method for requiring governments to account for infringements of the Convention, the reporting mechanism is extremely important.[108] Two years after ratification, each government is expected to send an initial report to the Committee on the Rights of the Child, detailing the progress it has made in fulfilling its obligations and any difficulties experienced in doing so. Thereafter, it must submit periodic reports at five-year intervals. After receiving a report, the Committee will obtain additional information on the government's record on implementation from other UN organisations and domestic non-governmental organisations by inviting them to comment on the report itself. In advance of discussing the report with government representatives, the Committee will consider all this material and compile a list of issues requiring further explanation. In the formal discussion meeting and the Committee's final report, its 'Concluding Observations', the Committee may identify and criticise areas of non-compliance and make suggestions for remedy.

The popularity of the treaty soon led to problems for the Committee on the Rights of the Child. Over 80 governments produced initial reports within a very short time of the Convention itself having come into force. The Committee then faced the overwhelming task of considering their reports and producing detailed concluding observations on each. This enormous workload in turn led to an increasingly long backlog of reports awaiting review.[109] It also prevented the Committee immediately following the model of the Human Rights Committee responsible for monitoring the International Covenant on Civil and Political Rights, which produces series of 'General Comments' explaining how the Human Rights Committee interprets many of the articles of the Covenant.[110] Nevertheless, the Committee wields considerable influence in its interpretation of the Convention. Its Concluding Observations, which have gradually become more detailed and complex,[111] are read with considerable interest by human rights experts throughout the world. Researchers have been able to gain, from this growing body of jurisprudence, some insight into the way in which the Committee interprets the Convention and the relative importance it places on states' obligations thereunder.[112] This guidance is available for use by governments to inform their policies regarding implementation.

(D)   The reporting mechanism and the United Kingdom

Like many other countries, although the United Kingdom has ratified the CRC, it has not incorporated it into domestic law. Consequently, the Convention is of persuasive influence only. It was hoped that the need to produce periodic reports and the knowledge that they would be subjected to detailed consideration by the Committee, would encourage states to implement the provisions in the Convention effectively. Certainly the publication of the Committee's detailed observations on these reports

---

107   See art 43, which sets out the reporting mechanism and establishes the Committee on the Rights of the Child.
108   Discussed in detail by U Kilkelly (1996). See also C Price Cohen and S Kilbourne (1998) pp 640–642.
109   The UK's second report, Department of Health (1999), was submitted to the Committee on the Rights of the Child in September 1999, but did not receive full consideration until 2002.
110   See C Price Cohen and S Kilbourne (1998) p 642.
111   C Price Cohen and S Kilbourne (1998) p 646.
112   See, inter alia: C Price Cohen and S Kilbourne (1998) esp the appended tables; K Marshall (1997); P Newell and R Hodgkin (1998).

produces media attention and a heightened public awareness of the principles contained in the Convention as well as the extent to which governments are implementing its obligations. Indeed, media fury at the Committee's criticisms of the United Kingdom's record of implementation following its initial report led to such headlines as 'How dare the UN lecture us'.[113] Nevertheless, the reporting mechanism relies on governments to subject their implementation programme to an objective and critical analysis before compiling their reports. The absence of any supervision or coercion over this can lead to reports painting an over-optimistic and complacent picture of governmental achievements. This weakness in the reporting procedure was illustrated well by the United Kingdom's own performance when submitting to the Committee on the Rights of the Child its initial report in 1994[114] and its second report in 1999,[115] providing information about its progress towards full implementation of the Convention.

Although reports should indicate to the Committee 'factors and difficulties, if any, affecting the degree of fulfilment' of their obligations under the Convention,[116] the United Kingdom's initial report failed to identify any real difficulties over doing so. It was mainly descriptive, providing vague and superficial information about compliance with each right or groups of rights. Admittedly, its second report was far more detailed than the first.[117] It also specifically addressed some of the Committee's concerns contained in its response to the first.[118] Nevertheless, it was highly selective and curiously unbalanced in its coverage of the Convention's requirements.[119] Indeed, it is notable that in both reports, the government time and again fulfilled King's predictions and exploited the Convention's internal incoherence by choosing the policies which suited them and ignoring those that did not.[120] At times, it even distorted the aims of current legislation to justify spurious claims of compliance with the Convention's provisions. For example, in the initial report, the government claimed that article 14, which secures a child's freedom of religion, was not infringed by the provision of religious education and daily collective worship for all pupils in all state schools, because '*Parents* ... have the right to withdraw their children' from such activities.[121] This not only ignored the fact that article 14 secures the *child's* right to freedom of thought, conscience and religion and not the parents' right, but also that full compliance with article 12(1) would also ensure that the *child* has the right to decide whether or not to attend such classes.[122] Similarly, in the second report, the government claimed that changes made to the law on youth offending, notably the abolition of the presumption of doli incapax for accused children between the ages of 10 and 14,[123] would be beneficial. With astonishing insouciance, it

---

113   *Daily Mail*, 28 January 1995.
114   See Department of Health (1994).
115   Department of Health (1999).
116   Art 44(2).
117   Eg it included limited information about family poverty: Department of Health (1999) para 8.34.9.
118   Eg the Committee's concerns about teenage conception rates (expressed in Committee on the Rights of the Child (1995 a) para 15) were specifically addressed in Department of Health (1999) paras 8.21.1–8.24.1.
119   Eg Department of Health (1999) devoted three pages of comment to children's civil rights and freedoms (arts 7, 8, 13, 14, 15, 16 and 17) compared with 27 pages of comment to children's health and associated rights (arts 6, 18, 23 and 24).
120   M King (1994) p 397.
121   Department of Health (1994) para 4.20 (emphasis supplied).
122   This is discussed in more detail in chapter 6.
123   Crime and Disorder Act 1998, s 36.

even argued that such a change would promote children's rights, on the basis that it would –

> '... ensure that, if a child has begun to offend, he or she is entitled to the earliest possible intervention to address that offending behaviour and eliminate its causes. The changes will also have the result of putting all juveniles on the same footing as far as courts are concerned, and will contribute to the *right* of children appearing there to develop responsibility for themselves.'[124]

In making this claim, the United Kingdom disregarded the Committee's stated view that English law was already infringing the aims of the Convention by setting the age of criminal responsibility at the low level of 10 years of age.[125] Indeed, the government had not only ignored the Committee's earlier criticisms but, by abolishing the doli incapax presumption, had exacerbated the harshness of the existing law.[126]

As Kilkelly points out, a government's failure to participate in critical self-analysis undermines the value of the reporting mechanism.[127] It was only due to the well co-ordinated response of non-governmental organisations to the United Kingdom's first and second periodic reports, that the Committee on the Rights of the Child received a clear picture of the weaknesses in the government's implementation programme.[128] In particular, its relatively low spending on basic services for children, such as health, education, housing and social security, judged against other European countries, was clearly highlighted. It was easy to perceive from its responses[129] that the Committee had taken full note of the concerns documented by the non-governmental organisations. They enabled it to produce relatively hard-hitting sets of concluding observations. In its response to the United Kingdom's initial report, the Committee included candid criticisms regarding issues of continuing concern, together with clear recommendations for the steps to be taken by the government by way of improvement. When responding to its second report, the Committee noted with regret that –

> 'notwithstanding the legal obligations inherent to the ratification of the Convention, many of the concerns and recommendations (CRC/C/15/Add.34) it made upon consideration of the State party's initial report (CRC/C/11/Add.1) have been insufficiently addressed ...'[130]

Showing a degree of restraint, the Committee urged the United Kingdom 'to make every effort' to address those unimplemented recommendations, in addition to those contained in its current response to the second report.[131]

It is not intended to detail here the various ways in which the law in the United Kingdom still fails to comply with the aims of the Convention. Many of these will be discussed throughout this work, in the context of the developing principles of domestic law. In terms of overall progress towards implementation, the Committee on the Rights of the Child has made it reasonably plain that for a wealthy nation our record is relatively poor. It has voiced particular concern over the absence of any central mechanism for achieving a comprehensive and coherent children's rights policy.[132]

---

124 Department of Health (1999) para 10.30.1 (emphasis supplied).
125 Committee on the Rights of the Child (1995 a) paras 17 and 36.
126 This change is discussed in more detail in chapter 18.
127 U Kilkelly (1996) pp 119–120.
128 Children's Rights Development Unit (1994) and Children's Rights Alliance (2002).
129 See Committee on the Rights of the Child (1995 a) and (2002).
130 Committee on the Rights of the Child (2002) para 4.
131 Committee on the Rights of the Child (2002) para 5.
132 See Committee on the Rights of the Child (1995 a) para 23 and Committee on the Rights of the Child (2002) paras 12–15.

Indeed, in its response to the United Kingdom's second report, the Committee noted that devolution of powers to the regional governments has made this need more urgent.[133] Furthermore, it did not consider that this need had been addressed by the formation of the Children and Young People's Unit, which now operates across government departments.[134] Its call for the government to 'expedite the adoption and implementation of a comprehensive plan of action' for implementing the Convention in all parts of the United Kingdom should now be taken very seriously.[135]

(E)   More effective enforcement procedures

The overall impression created by the United Kingdom's first and second reports to the Committee on the Rights of the Child was that the government was relatively untroubled by fear of its criticism. This impression was reinforced by the government's failure to address the more obvious breaches in compliance noted by the Committee, before preparing its second report. A cynic might argue that a casual approach to the Convention will continue until there are improved enforcement procedures. One obvious problem is that the Committee lacks the power to impose sanctions on governments who ignore its recommendations. Its lack of teeth, in conjunction with the absence of any complaints system or mechanism whereby children have a right of individual petition regarding alleged breaches, means that in reality the Convention is legally unenforceable.

The impact of the CRC would be significantly strengthened were enforcement procedures to be grafted on to it – similar to those established in connection with the ECHR. Such procedures were not considered to be appropriate at the Convention's drafting stage because it was feared that it would discourage some developing nations from ratifying it.[136] Those opposing an individual petitioning system being provided for all children argue that it would be appropriate only for children's civil and political rights, rather than the economic, social and cultural rights, which require government resources. But such an argument seems to lack real credence, particularly when it is so difficult to distinguish logically between many of the rights.[137] As Van Bueren observes, the African Charter on the Rights and Welfare of the Child, which protects not only civil and political rights but also economic, social and cultural rights, incorporates the right of individual petition for all children.[138]

Doubts have also been voiced regarding the capacity of children to petition a court and the practicality of their doing so in the event of their complaints focusing on the behaviour of their own parents.[139] But these are not insurmountable problems. For example, although many complaints to the European Commission and Court of Human Rights have been taken by parents on their children's behalf, this is not always the case and it is possible for someone other than the child's parents to be sufficiently motivated to do so instead.[140] Establishing a system providing children

---

133 Committee on the Rights of the Child (2002) para 12.
134 Discussed in more detail in chapter 9.
135 Committee on the Rights of the Child (2002) para 15.
136 U Kilkelly (1996) p 117.
137 G Van Bueren (1995) p 411.
138 G Van Bueren (1995) p 411.
139 U Kilkelly (1996) pp 117–118.
140 Eg the Official Solicitor took a complaint to the European Commission and Court on Human Rights on behalf of the children involved in *X v Bedfordshire County Council* [1995] 3 All ER 353. See discussion in chapter 16.

with a right of individual petition would immediately strengthen the arguments in favour of creating a Children's Rights Commissioner in this country.[141] Numerous countries which have ratified the Convention have established such a post and many commissioners or ombudspersons assume the task of ensuring that infringements of children's rights are investigated and remedied. The Committee on the Rights of the Child recently noted with deep concern that despite the existence of an independent Children's Commissioner in Wales and there being plans in train for a similar post in Scotland and Northern Ireland, there was still no independent children's rights institution in England.[142] If a system of individual petition were to be created, an obviously important task for the Commissioner would be to petition the court on behalf of individual children claiming infringement of their rights.

(F) The practical influence of the CRC

The CRC has been enormously influential – indeed, to many it is regarded as the touchstone for children's rights throughout the world. It constitutes the most comprehensive list of human rights created for a specific group. International bodies refer to it with approval on the basis that it can be utilised to promote 'a change in the way children, as individuals with rights, are viewed and also to encourage their active and responsible participation within the family and society'.[143] The European Commission and Court of Human Rights have increasingly referred to its provisions as being of persuasive authority when reaching their decisions.[144] Many countries have been extremely active in fulfilling their duty under article 42 to make its principles widely known to adults and children alike.[145] Regrettably, the United Kingdom has signally failed to comply with its obligation to ensure that its children are aware of the Convention.[146] Nevertheless, despite the United Kingdom's rather poor record in this respect,[147] those working with children in this country are increasingly aware of the Convention's existence and their obligations thereunder.[148] Even the domestic courts, when dealing with children's cases, are more commonly drawing attention to its provisions.[149] The fact that the present government introduced and implemented the Human Rights Act 1998 suggests that it is committed to strengthening respect for human rights generally. Hopefully, by the time the United Kingdom's third report on implementation of the CRC is prepared, greater attention will have been given to promoting full compliance with its terms.

---

141 Discussed in chapter 19.
142 Committee on the Rights of the Child (2002) para 16.
143 Eg Council of Europe (1996) para 4.
144 Eg, inter alia: *Costello-Roberts v United Kingdom* [1994] 1 FCR 65 para 35; *A v United Kingdom (human rights: punishment of child)* [1998] 2 FLR 959 (para 22); *V v United Kingdom* (1999) 30 EHRR 121 (inter alia, paras 73, 76, 97).
145 Eg Spain, which, on implementing the Convention, launched a mass media campaign designed to ensure the aims of the Convention were widely known.
146 When asked whether they had been told in school about the CRC, 43.5% of children in Botswana, 53% in Zimbabwe and 68% in India were able to answer in the affirmative, whilst only 6% of children in Northern Ireland were able to do so: R Bourne et al (1998).
147 See comments and recommendations on this by the Committee on the Rights of the Child (1995 a) para 26.
148 See the examples of local good practice contained in V Combe (2002).
149 Eg *R v Secretary of State for the Home Department, ex p Venables; R v Secretary of State for the Home Department, ex p Thompson* [1997] 3 All ER 97, per Lord Browne-Wilkinson at 122–123 and Lord Hope at 151.

(6)   THE EUROPEAN CONVENTION ON HUMAN RIGHTS

(A)   The post-War background

On 2 October 2000, the Human Rights Act 1998 incorporated the ECHR into the domestic law of the United Kingdom – a dramatic event indeed. The importance of this change can only be fully appreciated if it is placed within the Convention's own historical context. The ECHR was a product of the late 1940s, a period when there was considerable enthusiasm for the concept of a united Europe – an enthusiasm provoked by the destructive havoc wreaked on European countries by the Second World War. Progress towards political union was, overall, slow. Indeed, Europe's severe post-War economic problems resulted in far greater headway being been made towards achieving co-operation on trade and other economic matters.[150] Nevertheless, the Statute on the Council of Europe, signed in 1949, provided for a Committee of Ministers and a Parliamentary Assembly. The Council of Europe initiated and became involved in many cultural, economic and scientific activities and in 1961 adopted the European Social Charter with a view to protecting economic and social rights.[151] Possibly its greatest achievement in the human rights field, however, was to adopt the ECHR, signed in 1950.

The ECHR reflected a revived interest, in the late 1940s, in the natural rights theories of an earlier generation of political philosophers.[152] Strongly influenced by the Universal Declaration of Human Rights 1948,[153] the intention was to guarantee certain inalienable freedoms, namely those first generation civil and political rights considered essential to life in a civilised society. Consequently, the Convention's aims are relatively limited. Its main focus is to prevent governments from interfering with certain fundamental but negative liberties, rather than obliging them to promote, in positive ways, people's civil, economic, social, and cultural rights.[154] Very broadly, the Convention aims to protect the individual's right to life itself,[155] the right to liberty[156] and the right to marry and found a family.[157] It also requires respect for the individual's own private and family life.[158] Like other human rights instruments, it secures the traditional freedoms: from slavery,[159] torture or inhuman or degrading treatment,[160] unfair trial[161] and punishment,[162] freedom of thought, conscience and religion,[163] freedom of expression[164] and peaceful assembly.[165] Article 14, which has no independent existence,[166] but which governs the interpretation of all the other

---

150   See P Craig and G de Burca (1998) ch 1.
151   This has achieved important protection for children in the context of regulating their employment. See discussion in chapter 4.
152   See discussion above.
153   Arts 1–21.
154   Art 2 of the First Protocol is a notable exception, in so far as it protects a social welfare right, the right to education.
155   Art 2.
156   Art 5.
157   Art 12.
158   Art 8.
159   Art 4.
160   Art 3.
161   Art 6.
162   Art 7.
163   Art 9.
164   Art 10.
165   Art 11.
166   An infringement of art 14 cannot be complained about discretely, it must instead be linked with one of the other articles.

rights, ensures that these rights are all secured 'without discrimination on any ground such as sex, race, colour, language, religion, political or other opinion, national or social origin, association with a national minority, property, birth or other status'.

The ECHR became immensely influential, largely because it was the first international instrument of its kind to provide a mechanism for its own interpretation and enforcement. Pursuant to this, it established a Commission on Human Rights to receive and examine complaints about infringements of the Convention by state parties and, in 1959, a Court of Human Rights was set up to adjudicate finally on those complaints, in the light of its authoritative interpretation of the Convention.[167] This special feature undoubtedly enhanced the Convention's reputation for being one of the world's foremost human rights instruments. The original procedure was a complicated one; petitions were first investigated by the Commission and if it did not find the petition irregular, or manifestly ill-founded it would attempt to effect a reconciliation between the opposing parties. Should this fail, the case was then referred to the Court of Human Rights to obtain a legal ruling. In the event of the Court finding a violation of the Convention, it could order adequate reparation, but in practice its most important function was often to bring it to the attention of the state in question, together with the need for a change in its domestic law. In 1998[168] the system was simplified and the part-time Commission and Court were replaced by a single full-time Court, which thereafter decided both on the admissibility and merits of each case.

(B) Incorporation of the European Convention on Human Rights into domestic law

Even before implementation of the Human Rights Act 1998, the list of rights embodied by the ECHR had already become a relatively familiar one to people living in the United Kingdom. This was partly because the domestic courts were entitled to assume, when interpreting domestic legislation, that the legislature had not intended it to be inconsistent with any of the United Kingdom's obligations under the Convention.[169] The Convention also gained a far more direct way of influencing English law when, in 1966, the British government made a declaration, under article 25, recognising the jurisdiction of the European Commission to consider individual petitions regarding any events occurring after that date. Consequently, from the mid-1960s, having exhausted the remedies offered by the domestic courts, United Kingdom residents were able to take alleged infringements of their human rights to the European Commission and Court in Strasbourg. They could argue that English law was violating the ECHR and should be amended. Indeed, despite its not being part of English law until 2000, the Convention's contents had considerable influence on the development of law here. English law was adjusted from time to time to take account of decisions of the Strasbourg institutions in cases where it concluded that the human rights of those living in the United Kingdom had been infringed.[170] Nevertheless, procedurally

---

167 See D Feldman (2002) pp 45–46.
168 The new system was implemented by the Eleventh Protocol of the ECHR, which came into force on 1 November 1998.
169 Eg *Re KD (a minor) (ward: termination of access)* [1988] 1 All ER 577, in which the House of Lords took full account of the need for all domestic legislation and case law to comply with the Convention's terms. See, particularly, Lord Oliver's attempts (at 587–589) to reconcile English law with the terms of art 8.
170 Eg *W (and R, O, B and H) v United Kingdom* (1987) 10 EHRR 29. This decision led to reform of the legislative methods whereby local authorities gained the authority to care for children.

such a system was so expensive and lengthy that only the most determined were prepared to utilise this remedy of last resort.[171]

Since October 2000, people of any age, including children, have been able to challenge the existing law in any domestic court anywhere in the United Kingdom, on the basis that it ignores their rights under the Convention. The government argued that this change, introduced by the Human Rights Act 1998, would produce a vastly improved system, both procedurally and substantively.[172] But incorporation of the ECHR into domestic law also marked a radical change of approach towards protecting the fundamental rights of those who live in the United Kingdom. The view was formerly that our innate freedoms were properly protected by a democratically elected Parliament and that they existed, unless and until they were expressly abrogated by common law or legislation. Furthermore, it was considered that to adopt a written constitution, as in France and the United States, would endanger our underlying liberties, since only those listed would gain recognition.[173] By enacting the Human Rights Act 1998, the government signalled the view that it was not enough to assert the theoretical existence of fundamental liberties, everyone's constitutional rights should now also have formal guarantees and direct modes of protection.[174]

(C)   The European Convention on Human Rights and children's claims

The ECHR guarantees the fundamental human rights of all people living within the boundaries of those states which ratified it, irrespective of age. From October 2000, as people, all children living in the United Kingdom have been able to complain to the domestic courts that their rights are being infringed. Since that date, all those involved in children's proceedings, practitioners and the judiciary alike, have been rapidly familiarising themselves with the decades of very technical case law produced in Strasbourg, illuminating the Convention's provisions.[175] Their task is not eased by the speed at which the newly streamlined procedure now allows the European Court of Human Rights to hear and decide cases, with increasing numbers devoted to disputes over children. But although the existing body of jurisprudence is extremely influential, the Convention is a 'living instrument' and its interpretation must keep abreast with changes in society's needs.[176] Therefore, despite its importance, the domestic courts are not obliged to follow the Strasbourg case law slavishly, if they can be persuaded that it is anachronistic.

If an infringement of a child's right stems from the terms of old legislation, a court may itself be able to interpret that legislation afresh to ensure compatibility.[177] If that

---

171   It took on average five years to get applications into the European Court of Human Rights and cost an average of £30,000: Home Office (1997) para 1.14.
172   Home Office (1997) esp paras 1.16–1.19.
173   See C Gearty (1997) who, at pp 65–83, provides a comprehensive discussion of the legal and political background to the campaign to incorporate the Convention.
174   Home Office (1997) esp paras 1.16–1.19.
175   See Human Rights Act 1998 (hereafter HRA), s 2, which directs the domestic courts, when considering any alleged infringement of Convention rights, to be guided by the way in which the Convention has been interpreted in the past by the European Commission and Court. The Strasbourg jurisprudence relevant to children is usefully covered by H Swindells, A Neaves, M Kushner and R Skilbeck (1999) and U Kilkelly (1999).
176   Eg *Cossey v United Kingdom* [1991] 2 FLR 492 at 501.
177   Under HRA, s 3(1), the courts must 'read' the terms of existing legislation deemed incompatible with Convention rights, 'so far as it is possible to do so' in accordance with the Convention's terms.

is impossible,[178] a court[179] may promote the legislation's speedy amendment by making a declaration of incompatibility.[180] The 1998 Act also forces government departments to review carefully any new draft legislation which directly or indirectly affects children in every context, to ensure its compatibility with their rights under the Convention.[181] But children may alternatively claim that it is the existing principles of the common law itself which infringe their Convention rights. A court finding in a child claimant's favour, must, as a 'public authority',[182] act compatibly with the Convention and adapt the principles of common law so that they secure his or her rights. In so doing, the court may feel obliged to override case law, irrespective of its age or the level of court from which it emanated. Despite the relative lack of enthusiasm with which the senior courts have embraced the new jurisprudence on behalf of children,[183] this change will gradually oblige them to re-cast many aspects of domestic law in a human rights mould. Indeed, neither the narrow scope of the ECHR itself, nor the cautious approach taken by the European Court of Human Rights to claims brought on behalf of children,[184] can disguise the importance of 2 October 1998 – it marked the point at which children came of age, in terms of rights enforcement.

(D)   The European Convention on Human Rights and its interpretation – strengths and weaknesses for children

(i)   Introduction

Because of its persuasive influence, the manner in which the European Commission and Court of Human Rights have applied the provisions of the Convention to children deserves close attention. When reviewing this body of case law, one is particularly aware of the Convention's defects so far as children are concerned. Its main weakness is that it was never designed to deal with children's claims, as such. Nevertheless, much credit is due to the European Commission and Court for their skilful and dynamic interpretation of the Convention's provisions. The last decade or so of Convention case law demonstrates the Strasbourg institutions responding to a variety of contemporary demands. It reflects their obvious determination to address some of the Convention's most obvious shortcomings regarding children. A short summary of some of the more notable developments in this case law will be set out below, drawing out the Convention's strengths and weaknesses regarding children's claims.

178 Eg *R v A (No 2)* [2001] UKHL 25, [2001] 3 All ER 1. But there is judicial disagreement over whether HRA, s 3 allows express statutory provisions to be given a strained or non-literal construction in order to comply with Convention demands. See *R v A (No 2)* [2001] UKHL 25, [2001] 3 All ER 1, per Lord Steyn at [44]–[45]; cf *R v Lambert* [2001] UKHL 37, [2001] 3 All ER 577, per Lord Hope at [80]–[81]; and *Re S (children: care plan); Re W (children: care plan)* [2002] UKHL 10, [2002] 2 All ER 192, per Lord Nicholls of Birkenhead at [37]–[39].
179 Only the House of Lords, Court of Appeal and High Court have jurisdiction to make a declaration of incompatibility. See HRA, s 4(2) and (5). It was intended that such declarations would lead to a fast track Parliamentary procedure being used to introduce amending legislation: see HRA, s 10 and Sch 2.
180 Eg *R (H) v London North and East Region Mental Health Review Tribunal (Secretary of State for Health Intervening)* [2001] EWCA Civ 415, [2002] QB 1.
181 According to HRA, s 19, any government minister introducing draft legislation in either House of Parliament must annex to it a written statement confirming that it is compatible with the terms of the European Convention.
182 HRA, s 6.
183 See discussion below.
184 Eg *Nielsen v Denmark* (1988) 11 EHRR 175, discussed below.

(ii)   The Convention's narrow focus

Prior to implementation of the Human Rights Act 1998, writers had voiced doubts about the ECHR's ability to promote children's rights very effectively.[185] A fundamental problem is its very limited scope, which prevents its addressing the wide variety of children's needs. With the exception of article 2 of the First Protocol, which protects the right to education, the Convention is principally concerned with civil and political rights – the basic freedoms deemed essential to individual autonomy and to privacy from state interference, such as freedom from torture and the right to a fair trial. Although these rights are available to all human beings, including children, they have a very adult focus. The narrow focus of the ECHR is brought into sharp relief when compared with the provisions of the CRC. The latter treaty not only provides children with the right to their basic civil and political freedoms but also aims to secure their social, economic and cultural rights. The adult orientation of the European Convention[186] is probably inevitable, given its history – it was intended to protect individuals from state interference with their lives. Nevertheless, these kinds of rights are usually far less important to children, who are brought up in the protected environment of the home, than to adults. This is borne out by the fact that, since the European Court of Human Rights was established, there have been relatively few applications testing the scope of children's right to enjoy some of the more traditional political and civil rights.

The few applications which might have involved children's civil and political rights, such as their freedom of expression, have been interpreted cautiously by the Strasbourg institutions. They have tended to interpret such rights in a manner erring on protecting children from offensive material, rather than favouring their freedom to obtain relevant information. Thus in *Handyside v United Kingdom*[187] the European Court accepted that the United Kingdom government's censorship of *The Little Red Schoolbook* was justified because it had contained obscene material aimed at adolescents. Accordingly, it was entitled to interfere with the publisher's freedom of expression under article 10, in order to protect children's moral development under article 10(2). It has been argued[188] that had the application in the *Handyside* case been brought by an adolescent, the European Court might have reached a different conclusion since it would have been forced to consider a child's own right to freedom of expression, including the right to receive information under article 10.[189]

(iii)   Distinguishing parents' claims from children's claims

The obvious practical difficulties inherent in children claiming the Convention's protection have serious implications. Applications which focus on children's rights will inevitably be brought on their behalf by adults, quite simply because children are too young to cope with the procedural complications of making claims themselves. The adults acting for children are often their parents, and the adult perspectives of the

---

185   See eg J Fortin (1999 a) esp pp 354 and 357–359; and J Herring (1999).
186   J Eekelaar and R Dingwall (1987) p 21.
187   (1976) 1 EHRR 737.
188   See G Van Bueren (1995) p 135. But see U Kilkelly (1999) pp 131–132, for a contrary view.
189   But see *Kelly v BBC* [2001] 1 All ER 323: per Munby J, an injunction prohibiting the BBC from publishing a recorded interview with a 16-year-old boy might infringe the media's freedom of expression under art 10 of the ECHR. But he made little mention of the potential infringement of the boy's own rights under art 10 to disseminate his views.

articles of the Convention may, at times, be exploited by parents to promote their own rights, at the expense of those of their children. In this respect, the Convention's terms are not helpful when it comes to delineating the boundaries between parents' powers and children's rights. Indeed, its wording is completely neutral on the relationship of parents with their children; it not only omits any reference to it, but it obviously was not a matter within the contemplation of the draftsmen. The wording of article 8, the article most often used for Convention challenges relating to children,[190] promotes the value of family privacy, but its emphasis appears to be on the adults' privacy rather than that of the children. Indeed, as noted elsewhere, it implicitly suggests that as long as families are protected from undue state interference, the regulation of family life can be safely left to its adult members.[191] Equally, article 2 of the First Protocol,[192] despite appearing to focus on children's rights to education, then proceeds to advise states, when carrying out their duties, to 'respect the right of *parents* to ensure such education and teaching in conformity with their own religious and philosophical convictions'. This provision, which reflects the post-War concerns about religious persecution, has led to a variety of claims which, although involving aspects of children's education, are, in reality, complaints about infringements of the parents' own strong philosophical convictions.[193]

When interpreting the Convention's provisions, the Commission and Court have sometimes adopted a very cautious approach to the notion of children having rights of their own, independent of those of their parents. The controversial decision in *Nielsen v Denmark*[194] was obviously partly motivated by a perceived need to prevent children's article 5 rights undermining parents' rights under article 8. Had it allowed children to use article 5 to challenge parents' decisions, the Court might have been accused of condoning an indirect form of state interference with family life. Alarmists might have rekindled memories of the Hitler Youth movement in Nazi Germany and the methods used there to suborn children to act against their parents. Nevertheless, to assert that the mother's actions were well within the normal exercise of parental authority was, even in the late 1980s, a surprisingly authoritarian interpretation of the parental role. It also displayed an inability to come to terms with the idea that adolescents, as independent individuals, may have rights of their own under article 5.

The *Nielsen* decision reinforces the view that the Convention is ill-equipped to help courts find an appropriate balance between parents' powers and children's rights.[195] This view is borne out by the European Commission's inconsistent approach to interpreting article 8 in cases involving children challenging their parents' rights to force them to live at home. It has had an obvious difficulty in accommodating a

190 Right to respect for private and family life.
191 J Fortin (1999 a) p 357.
192 Right to education.
193 Eg *Kjeldsen, Busk Madsen and Pedersen v Denmark* (1976) 1 EHRR 711: Danish parents failed to establish that the Danish government had violated their own rights under art 2 of the First Protocol by providing compulsory sex education in schools, since it had been conveyed in a balanced and objective manner, with no element of indoctrination.
194 (1988) 11 EHRR 175: a 12-year-old boy, not mentally ill but suffering from a 'nervous condition', was placed, at his mother's request, in the closed psychiatric ward of a state hospital for 5½ months. Despite the contrary views of the European Commission, and three dissenting judges of the European Court (all of whom considered that the boy's rights under art 5 had been infringed), the majority of the European Court decided that his rights under art 5 had not been infringed, because he was still at an age when it was normal for decisions to be made by a parent, even against his wishes. The implication was that, had he been older, this might not have been so reasonable (para 195). See discussion by U Kilkelly (1999) pp 34–38. See also G Van Bueren (1995) pp 73–74.
195 See J Fortin (2002) p 22.

child's own right to family privacy alongside his or her parents' right to run their household as they please.[196]

Subsequent decisions continue to reflect an innate reluctance to see children as individuals in their own right. Thus in *Valsamis v Greece*[197] the European Court saw no reason to consider a child's right to freedom of religion under article 9 separately from that of her parents.[198] Furthermore, it refused, in *Koniarska v United Kingdom*,[199] to consider particularly seriously a teenager's claims that a secure accommodation order infringed her rights under articles 3, 5 and 8.[200] As noted by Douglas and Lowe, this rather paternalistic approach is 'disappointing'. They suggest that the European Court has some way to go before it 'truly takes on board the increasing international recognition of the child's developing autonomy rights' and that it has not yet faced squarely how to balance out the competing interests of different family members.[201]

(iv)   No 'welfare or best interests' formula

A further concern about the format of the ECHR is the absence of any formula, in any of its provisions, directing states to consider children's welfare or best interests. A direction to courts considering disputes over children, to take account of such a factor, is common to most legal systems throughout the world. Its absence from any part of the Convention makes its application awkward in court proceedings involving children. Indeed, it particularly concerns the effectiveness of article 8, given that it is the provision most relevant to disputes over children, be they private disputes between parent and parent or child protection disputes between a child care agency and parents.

Concerns over the welfare principle being diluted in the face of parents' claims to protection of their own rights under article 8 were voiced in the late 1980s. These were provoked by the way in which the Strasbourg institutions were then dealing with parents' complaints about their children being removed from them by state welfare agencies. The European Commission and Court had stressed that the wording of article 8(2) required states to justify the interference with the parents' rights to private and family life by evidence of '*necessity*', rather than desirability.[202] Misgivings were expressed over the difficulties thereby created for welfare agencies attempting to address the danger children faced by removing them from their homes. Eekelaar and Dingwall criticised the structure of article 8 for characterising the initial

---

196   *X v Netherlands* (1974) Application No 6753/74 (1975–76) 1-3 DR 118: the European Commission dismissed the complaints of a 14-year-old Dutch runaway that her rights under art 8 had been infringed by the welfare authorities returning her home unwillingly. The Commission considered such action was justified to protect her health and morals under art 8(2). But see *X v Denmark* (1978) Application No 6854/74 (1977–78) 7-9 DR 81: the European Commission refused to accede that the Danish welfare authorities had infringed the parents' rights under art 8 by refusing to force their 14-year-old daughter to return home against her will.

197   (1996) 24 EHRR 294.

198   See U Kilkelly (1999) p 75.

199   12 October 2000, Application No 33670/96, Admissibility decision. See discussion in chapters 5 and 16 and by G Douglas and N Lowe (2002) p 19.

200   Her application was declared inadmissible. This decision was subsequently utilised by the Court of Appeal in *Re K (secure accommodation order: right to liberty)* [2001] 1 FLR 526 to justify rejecting a similar challenge in the domestic courts. But see *D G v Ireland* (Application no 39474/98) (16 May 2002, unreported): European Court of Human Rights upheld the complaint by a teenager that his detention under the equivalent of a secure accommodation order was of such a nature that it infringed his rights under art 5.

201   G Douglas and N Lowe (2002) p 19.

202   *Olsson v Sweden* (1988) 11 EHRR 259.

state intervention in such cases, as a breach of the parents' rights and therefore prima facie unlawful. In their view, the fact that the breach could only be justified by reference to the needs of a 'democratic society', and the rights and freedoms of 'others' under article 8(2) indicated that the 'minds of the drafters 'were not directed at the children within the family, but on the relationships between the adult members and the outside world'.[203] Indeed, in their view, '… When "respect for family life" is in issue under Article 8, it is almost always the family life of the parents, rather than of the children which is given dominance …'[204]

Just over a decade later, the implementation of the Human Rights Act 1998 provoked similar misgivings. Some suggested that, when incorporated into domestic law, the Convention would downgrade the strength of the 'paramountcy principle'[205] contained in the Children Act 1989, section 1.[206] It was argued that, whereas prior to implementation of the 1998 Act, a parental contact dispute hinged on the court's view of the child's best interests, now the courts could favour parents' claims regarding infringements of their own rights under article 8(1), at the expense of their children's best interests.[207] Similarly, child protection agencies might be hampered by their need to justify intervention infringing parents' article 8 rights, through satisfying the requirements of article 8(2).

A study of the more recent jurisprudence emerging from Strasbourg suggests that at least some of these concerns were exaggerated. By 2000, the European Commission and Court were, through a more flexible interpretation of article 8, already softening their approach. When dealing with parents' complaints about the actions of welfare agencies in removing children from their homes, the Strasbourg jurisprudence was reflecting a far more obvious appreciation of children's need for protection *against* their parents. Indeed, the Commission and Court were achieving a way of ensuring that the concluding phrase of article 8(2), 'for the protection of health or morals, or for the protection of the rights and freedoms of others', was interpreted taking full account of the welfare principle. First, the European Court was stressing that countries have a wide margin of appreciation[208] when assessing how 'necessary' it is to take a child into care, bearing in mind the need to reach a fair balance between the parents' interests and those of the child. Second, it was repeatedly referring to its decision in *Johansen v Norway*,[209] in which it stressed the crucial importance attached, in the balancing exercise –

'to the best interests of the child, which, depending on their nature and seriousness, may override those of the parent. In particular … the parent cannot be entitled under article 8 of the Convention to have such measures taken as would harm the child's health and development.'[210]

This approach placed the domestic courts in a reasonably good position to achieve an identical outcome to that obtained prior to October 2000, but with the reasoning and language used in their judgments complying with Convention requirements, in

203 J Eekelaar and R Dingwall (1987) p 17.
204 J Eekelaar and R Dingwall (1987) p 21.
205 Children Act 1989, s 1(1) states that 'When a court determines any question with regard to – (a) the upbringing of a child … the child's welfare shall be the court's paramount consideration'.
206 See H Swindells, A Neaves, M Kushner and R Skilbeck (1999) pp 90–93. See also J Herring (1999), who discusses the various approaches adopted by the Strasbourg institutions to the welfare principle.
207 See J Fortin (1999 b) pp 250–251.
208 For a detailed explanation of this concept, see K Starmer (1999) pp 187–189.
209 (1996) 23 EHRR 33.
210 (1996) 23 EHRR 33 (para 78). See also, inter alia: *EP v Italy* (Application No 31127/96) (1999, unreported) (para 62); *Scott v United Kingdom* [2000] 1 FLR 958 at 968; *K and T v Finland* [2001] 2 FLR 707 (para 154); *L v Finland* [2000] 2 FLR 118 at 118.

particular those of article 8(2). Thus the domestic courts must ensure that the parents' rights are balanced against those of their children and the intervention, which infringes their rights, must be proportionate to its legitimate aim.[211] Accordingly, whilst the exclusivity of children's rights has disappeared, the same result as before may often be achieved.[212]

When considering whether the state has made sufficient efforts to ensure the child is reintegrated into his or her family after being removed into care, the European Court has traditionally allowed state authorities less margin of appreciation. It has consistently claimed the right to scrutinise far more aggressively the decision-making processes of states, when considering parental claims that undue restrictions have been placed on their retaining contact with their children. State care must be seen as a temporary measure only, with real efforts at the child's integration being quickly made.[213] Nevertheless, even here, the Court has more clearly acknowledged the importance of considering a child's best interests when deciding on a possible return home. Thus in *Johansen v Norway,*[214] the Court stressed the importance of the balancing act. Although public care should be seen as a temporary measure, a fair balance has to be struck between the interests of the child in remaining in public care and those of the parents in being reunited with him or her. Furthermore, the Court has sympathised with the claims of welfare agencies that, when considering the child's best interests, they must fully consider the child's own wishes over such a step, as the CRC obliges them to do.[215]

Incorporating the welfare principle into private law disputes also proved relatively straightforward, up to a point. The European Court of Human Rights confirmed that since domestic courts were inevitably required to find a balance between the rights of the competing adults, it was perfectly appropriate for them to interpret article 8(2) flexibly, under their margin of appreciation. When doing so, the Court advised, they should consider '… the rights and freedoms of all concerned … and more particularly the best interests of the child and his or her rights under Article 8 of the Convention'.[216] A court order restricting the parents' rights can therefore be justified by reference to the child's best interests, as long as both parents have been fully and fairly involved

211   For a detailed explanation of the principle of proportionality, see K Starmer (1999) pp 169–176.
212   Eg *Re C and B (care order: future harm)* [2001] 1 FLR 611, per Hale LJ (paras 33 and 34).
213   Eg, inter alia: *Olsson v Sweden* (1989) 11 EHRR 259 (para 81); *Johansen v Norway* (1996) 23 EHRR 33 (para 64); *K and T v Finland* [2001] 2 FLR 707 (paras 155 and 178); *S and G v Italy* [2000] 2 FLR 771 (paras 174–181).
214   (1997) 23 EHRR 33.
215   Eg *L v Finland* [2000] 2 FLR 118: the interests of two girls, now aged 8 and 14, justified the state welfare agency reducing their father's access to them, given their own reluctance to see him and the evidence suggesting that they might have been sexually abused by him and their paternal grandfather.
216   *Hokkanen v Finland* (1994) 19 EHRR 139 (para 58) (custody dispute between father and maternal grandparents) a father's right to be reunited with his daughter (now aged 12) was not absolute, given her own strong desire to remain with her grandparents. See also, inter alia, *Hoffman v Austria* (1993) 17 EHRR 293 (custody dispute) 'the predominant consideration in this respect [for the domestic court] must be the best interest of the children, including the protection of their health and morals' (per European Commission of Human Rights (para 91)); *Yousef v Netherlands* [2002] 3 FCR 577 (dispute after the mother's death over residence and contact between the child's maternal relatives and the unmarried father), 'if there was any clash of art 8 rights between a child and its father, the interests of the child should always prevail' (per European Court of Human Rights (para 66)). *Hoppe v Germany* [2003] 1 FCR 176 (contact dispute) reduction of the father's rights of access based on a careful weighing of evidence on the child's best interests was 'sufficient' for the putposes of art 8(2) (per European Court of Human Rights (para 51)).

in the decision-making processes, the restriction is proportionate to its legitimate aim and a fair balance is struck between the competing interests of all concerned.[217]

The Strasbourg institutions have very obviously taken full account of the widespread commitment amongst European countries to the welfare principle. Their response has been to formulate a way of accommodating it within the terms of the Convention, more particularly article 8, thereby preserving that article's practical effectiveness. Accompanying this development is a growing awareness that disputes over children do not merely involve parent and parent or state authorities and parents, but also a third player, the child, and that an appropriate balance has to be found between them all. The European Commission and Court have also acknowledged the need to produce decisions in conformity with the provisions of the CRC. This in turn stemmed from European member states' own increasing concern to fulfil their duties, as required by that Convention.

This new approach cannot, however, disguise the problems underlying it. First, there are evidential differences between the requirements of article 8 and the paramountcy principle established by the Children Act 1989.[218] In a dispute between parents over a child, prior to implementation of the Human Rights Act 1998, the Children Act had enabled the court to identify, at the outset, an outcome indicated by the child's best interests and to make an order reflecting such a view. Now such a simplistic response is impossible when a parent argues that such an order will infringe his own rights to family life under article 8. Such an infringement may be justified by the court, but only by reference to article 8(2), supported by evidence regarding the child's own rights and issues revolving around his or her welfare. Although the outcome will often be the same, this is not always the case. For example, the European Court of Human Rights implicitly criticised the German domestic courts for assuming that because an order refusing a parent contact appeared to fulfil a child's best interests, it justified the claimant's loss of family life.[219] Indeed, a revival of outdated notions of parents' rights over their children may now undermine the Children Act's efforts to promote a more liberal approach to the parent child relationship by employing the term 'parental responsibilities'. Furthermore, the English courts' obvious relief at discovering that the Strasbourg jurisprudence incorporates the welfare principle, has led them largely to ignore the more technical demands of article 8(2). In particular, they apparently see no need to consider whether the infringement of the parent's rights is proportionate to the child's immediate needs.[220]

Second, and even more fundamentally, by subsuming the child's own interests within arguments relating to his or her welfare and the technical requirements of article 8(2), the Strasbourg institutions have largely failed to articulate the concept of children being independent players, with article 8 rights of their own. Adopting this technique, the domestic courts are similarly reluctant to focus on the child's own Convention rights.[221] Of all the rights listed by the Convention, none is more important

---

217 See above case law.

218 J Herring (1999) p 231. But see A Vine (2000), who concludes that the Strasbourg jurisprudence allows the best interests principle to prevail and H Swindells (2000) pp 62–65.

219 Eg *Elsholz v Germany* [2000] 2 FLR 486. See J Eekelaar (2002) p 241. See also *Sahin v Germany* [2002] 1 FLR 119. This case law is discussed in more detail in chapter 8.

220 Eg *Re B (a child) (adoption by one natural parent)* [2001] UKHL 70, [2002] 1 All ER 641, per Lord Nicholls of Birkenhead, esp at [31]. See also *Re H (contact order) (No 2)* [2002] 1 FLR 22, per Wall J (para 59). This case law is discussed further in chapter 9.

221 A Bainham (2002).

to children than article 8; a refusal to acknowledge that they have rights of their own within its purview may seriously weaken its ability to enhance their lives.

(v)   *Flexible interpretation of Convention provisions*

As discussed above, although problems remain, some of the more obvious weaknesses of the Convention have been addressed by the Strasbourg institutions by interpreting its provisions in a purposeful way. An imaginative treatment of the wording of the articles has also produced protection for children from articles which, although not particularly happily worded, have been interpreted to protect children's interests efficiently. For example, although many parents might find it difficult to accept that using physical punishment could, in some circumstances, be described as a form of 'torture' or even as 'inhuman or degrading treatment', article 3 has been pressed into service very effectively to protect children from such treatment.[222] Equally, it is unlikely that the draftsmen of the Convention ever considered the need to prevent parental child abuse. Nevertheless, through a combination of articles 2, 3 and 8, the Convention now imposes an obligation on welfare authorities to protect children from abusive treatment.[223]

As discussed above, the Convention is not particularly successful in encouraging adults, particularly parents, to treat children as independent individuals.[224] But this weakness is not so evident regarding the protection it offers young offenders. Indeed, it seems that when children's claims do not endanger their parents' rights, but are independent challenges to the criminal justice system itself, the Strasbourg institutions are willing to interpret their rights vigorously.[225] This approach has provided, mainly through applications made under article 6, a valuable impetus for improving the criminal justice system, as it applies to children and young people accused of criminal offences.[226] For example, the two killers of James Bulger successfully argued before the European Commission and Court that the form of their trial was unfair under article 6,[227] thereby forcing the government to adjust the procedures used for trying very young children accused of serious crimes.[228] Article 6 carries other equally potent forms of protection for children. It not only ensures that the procedures for dealing with parents involved in private and public law proceedings are fair,[229] but also that a litigant obtains a hearing

---

222   *A v United Kingdom (human rights: punishment of child)* [1998] 2 FLR 959. The School Standards and Framework Act 1998 finally abolished the use of all physical punishment in all schools in the United Kingdom. See discussion in chapter 9.
223   See *Z v United Kingdom* [2001] 2 FLR 612, esp paras 73–75. Whilst art 2 protects children from life threatening abuse, art 3 protects them from abusive treatment amounting to inhuman or degrading treatment and art 8 protects them from infringements of their physical integrity.
224   See *Nielsen v Denmark* (1988) 11 EHRR 175 and the discussion above.
225   Discussed in more detail in chapter 18. See also U Kilkelly (1999) ch 3.
226   *Hussain v United Kingdom* (1996) 22 EHRR 1: this decision secured a change in the arrangements made for the release of young offenders detained under the Children and Young Persons Act 1933, s 53.
227   *V and T v United Kingdom* (2000) 30 EHRR 121.
228   Discussed in chapter 18.
229   See *W (and R, O, B and H) v United Kingdom* (1987) 10 EHRR 29: the success of the parents' applications led to the statutory abolition of the power of local authorities to acquire parental responsibility over children by administrative resolution. It also provoked procedural changes giving parents far more involvement in local authority decision-making regarding children. Eg Children Act 1989, s 22(4). See also *McMichael v United Kingdom* (1995) 20 EHRR 205 and *Elsholz v Germany* [2000] 2 FLR 486.

within a reasonable time, without procedural delay producing a de facto determination of the issue before the court. Delay, of course, has a particular relevance to cases involving very young children.[230]

A broad interpretation of the concept of respect for a person's private and family life, as protected by article 8, has also borne fruit. Indeed, the concept of family life itself has been interpreted flexibly, so that it protects the relationships between children and unmarried, as well as married parents,[231] and their relationships with other members of de facto family groupings.[232] Furthermore, the absence of any specific reference to procedural fairness within its wording has not prevented the European Court asserting that article 8 guarantees fairness in any procedures infringing family life.[233] Perhaps more surprisingly, the right to respect for private life has even secured for children the right to obtain information about themselves held by any public agencies which enables them to know and understand their childhood and early development.[234] It has also been interpreted to include respect for private sexual life; consequently, a successful application to the European Commission, combining article 8 with 14, ensured that gay adolescents were provided with sexual freedom equal to that enjoyed by their heterosexual and lesbian counterparts.[235] Indeed, article 14 has a particular relevance to all children, in so far as it protects individuals from discriminatory treatment for any reason, including age. As long as it can be linked with another Convention right, the value of such a claim lies in the fact that article 14 prohibits all discriminatory treatment, unless it can be justified by arguing that children, because of their minority, require special measures to protect them.

(vi) Positive obligations

As discussed above, a flexible interpretation of the Convention by the European Commission and Court has extended the protection available to children in a surprisingly forceful way. The Convention's ability to promote children's rights has also been strengthened through the notion of positive obligations attaching to many of its provisions.[236] Thus the view has been taken by the European Commission and Court that certain parts of the Convention impose more onerous duties on member states than others. In other words, these provisions not only compel states to abstain from interfering with the rights they protect, they require them to take active steps to secure these rights effectively.[237] For example, it is not enough for states to refrain from the intentional and unlawful killing of a child under article 2, they must also

---

230 See *H v United Kingdom* (1987) 10 EHRR 95, esp para 85.

231 *Marckx v Belgium* (1979) 2 EHRR 330: the European Court of Human Rights stated that art 8 protects members of the 'illegitimate' family in the same ways as members of the traditional family.

232 Eg, inter alia: *X, Y and Z v United Kingdom* (1997) 2 FLR 892 (transsexual parent); *Marckx v Belgium* (1979) 2 EHRR 330 (grandparent); *Boyle v United Kingdom* (1994) 19 EHRR 179 (uncle).

233 *McMichael v United Kingdom* (1995) 20 EHRR 205; *W (and R, O, B and H) v United Kingdom* (1987) 10 EHRR 29.

234 *Gaskin v United Kingdom* (1989) 12 EHRR 36. This right was finally secured in the United Kingdom by the Data Protection Act 1998. Discussed in more detail in J Fortin (1999 a) pp 362–363.

235 *Sutherland v United Kingdom* (1997) 24 EHRR CD 22. This decision led to the introduction of the Sexual Offences (Amendment) Act 2000 which lowered the age of consent to homosexual activity from 18 years to 16 years.

236 See U Kilkelly (1999) esp pp 12–13.

237 See D Harris, M O'Boyle and C Warbrick (1995) pp 19–22 and K Starmer (1999) ch 5, for a general discussion of the positive obligations imposed by the Convention.

take appropriate steps to safeguard his or her life.[238] The force of such a principle is also seen when interpreting article 3. Social service departments must protect children effectively from abusive parental behaviour, in order to fulfil their positive obligations under article 3 to protect children against inhuman or degrading treatment. Accordingly, they must not stand back and allow abuse that they are aware of to continue, they must intervene to prevent its continuation.[239] Similarly, rather than merely refraining from interfering with a child's private life under article 8, a state must take appropriate steps to ensure that laws are in place to make such a right practical and effective,[240] including those safeguarding his or her right to physical integrity.[241]

It was through employing the concept of positive obligations when interpreting the Convention, that the Strasbourg institutions achieved a dramatic extension of its jurisdiction. The Convention is not confined to a 'vertical' application, whereby individuals are only protected from public agencies, but not against the behaviour of each other. A 'horizontal approach'[242] to interpreting the Convention extends its jurisdiction sideways from the public domain into the realm of private relationships and disputes. The European Court has ruled that states must prevent infringements occurring, irrespective of the circumstances, whether or not this involves interfering with private relationships between individuals. Such an approach has far-ranging implications, since it requires states to establish laws ensuring that private individuals behave towards each other in a way which does not infringe their rights under the articles in question. For example, the European Court has ruled that article 3 does not merely require public authorities like schools to refrain from punishing children in a way which infringes their right to freedom from inhuman or degrading treatment.[243] States must also ensure that children are protected from such behaviour in the privacy of their own homes, even when it is administered by their parents under the guise of physical punishment.[244] Similarly, whilst article 8 clearly protects individuals against arbitrary interference by public authorities, states are also under a positive obligation to adopt measures designed to ensure an effective respect for family life in the sphere of private relations between individuals.[245]

---

238 *Osman v United Kingdom* [1999] 1 FLR 193 (para 115).
239 See *Z v United Kingdom* [2001] 2 FLR 612 (paras 73–74).
240 Eg *Marckx v Belgium* (1979) 2 EHRR 330: by not recognising that a child born out of wedlock could be a member of the mother's family, Belgian law prevented mother and child from leading a normal family life.
241 Eg *X and Y v Netherlands* (1985) 8 EHRR 235: Dutch law had failed to ensure that a 16-year-old mentally disabled girl had a proper remedy, despite being the victim of a sexual assault. Criminal proceedings could not be brought without the victim making a complaint, and she was incapable of doing so.
242 For an explanation of the 'horizontal approach' to interpreting the Convention, see D Harris, M O'Boyle and C Warbrick (1995) pp 21–22. See also M Hunt (1998) pp 425 and 440–441. The Court of Appeal in *Douglas v Hello! Ltd* [2001] 2 All ER 289 confirmed that the terms of the Human Rights Act 1998 do not prevent the ECHR having a horizontal effect under domestic law.
243 The success of some applications to the European Court claiming infringements of art 3 led to new legislation abolishing the use of physical punishment in all schools. See Education Act 1996, ss 548–549. Discussed in more detail in chapter 10.
244 *A v United Kingdom (human rights: punishment of child)* [1998] 2 FLR 959.
245 *X and Y v Netherlands* (1985) 8 EHRR 235 (para 23): Dutch law should have adopted measures designed to secure that respect for private life was observed between private individuals.

(vii) Summary

Children in the United Kingdom, just like adults, can now complain to the domestic courts if any right listed in the ECHR is infringed by any public authority,[246] such as a hospital trust, a local education authority, or a department of social services. Similarly, they can complain if the state, through its laws, has failed to protect them adequately from the behaviour of some private individual – even a parent. They may obtain a remedy within the near future now that they are no longer subjected to the delays of getting a case before the European Court of Human Rights in Strasbourg.

As the analysis above demonstrates, by the time the Human Rights Act 1998 was implemented, the domestic courts were reasonably well armed by the more recent Strasbourg case law to ensure that the ECHR largely promoted, rather than undermined, children's rights. They had the wherewithal to ensure that they interpreted the Convention in an imaginative and child-centred way, as far as its narrow scope allows. Nevertheless, the European Court's disinclination to treat children as individuals, with rights of their own, unfortunately provided the domestic courts with a good excuse to do the same. Indeed, there is a risk of the Human Rights Act 1998 being exploited by parents pursuing their own rights under the Convention at the expense of those of their children. Furthermore, the domestic courts' reluctance to adapt their traditional ad hoc approach to children's cases, aided and abetted by the indeterminate welfare principle,[247] will undoubtedly hinder any creative attempts to subject the principles of child law to a rights-based approach.

(7) THE COUNCIL OF EUROPE AND CHILDREN'S RIGHTS

As noted above, perhaps the greatest achievement of the Council of Europe was to adopt the ECHR. This had no specific remit to protect children's rights; had it been designed with this purpose in mind, it could have done so far more efficiently. Nevertheless, the Council of Europe has also played a direct part in encouraging important reforms in the area of family law, many of which have promoted children's rights.[248] This has been achieved through the work of the European Ministers of Justice, the Parliamentary Assembly, and the Committee of Experts on Family Law. Whilst the Resolutions and Recommendations of the Parliamentary Assembly[249] and

---

246 HRA, s 6.
247 Eg, inter alia: *Re K (secure accommodation order: right to liberty* [2001] 1 FLR 526: the Court of Appeal rejected the claim that the Children Act 1989, s 25 is incompatible with art 5 of the Convention (discussed in chapter 16); *Re S (children: care plan), Re W (children: care plan)* [2002] UKHL 10, [2002] 2 All ER 192: the House of Lords rejected the Court of Appeal's purposeful approach to its obligations under the HRA regarding local authorities' duties to children in care (discussed in chapter 16); *Re B (a child) (adoption by one natural parent)* [2001] UKHL 70, [2002] 1 All ER 641: the House of Lords argued (per Lord Nicholls of Birkenhead) that the Children Act 1989, s 1 imposes identical demands on the courts to those imposed by art 8(2) of the ECHR (discussed in chapters 8 and 14); *Re H and A (paternity: blood tests)* [2002] EWCA Civ 383, [2002] 1 FLR 1145: children's rights under art 8 of the Convention to know the identity of their father escaped any mention by the Court of Appeal.
248 See Council of Europe (2000 a).
249 Eg, inter alia: Recommendation 1065 (1987) On the Traffic in Children and other Forms of Child Exploitation; Recommendation 1071 (1988) Providing Institutional Care for Infants and Children; Recommendation 1286 (1996) on a European Strategy for Children.

of the Committee of Ministers[250] only have persuasive influence, many reflect a clear and refreshingly forthright approach to the concept of children's rights and to the part children could play in Europe were they given appropriate encouragement.[251] Some of these recommendations have achieved concrete results, in so far as they have led to the preparation of international instruments whose specific aim is to harmonise the laws of European member states in order to promote children's welfare more effectively.[252] Many, for example, the European Convention on the Legal Status of Children Born Out of Wedlock, achieved improvements in domestic law.[253] It was the combination of the *Marckx* decision[254] and the United Kingdom's ratification of this Convention in 1981, which led the English Law Commission to recommend the widespread reform of the English law relating to children born out of wedlock.[255]

Though these developments have been of some significance, the Council of Europe has not initiated any reforms broad enough in scope to match the impact of the United Nation's CRC. Things might have turned out very differently. In 1979, the Parliamentary Assembly of the Council of Europe, in recognition of the International Year of the Child, recommended to the Committee of Ministers that a draft European Charter on the Rights of the Child should be prepared, embodying a detailed list of principles.[256] Had this been acted on, the ECHR might have been supplemented by a Convention designed specially for the protection of children's rights. This proposal remained in abeyance until, in 1990, the Parliamentary Assembly, recalling its earlier initiative, recommended a further list of steps now to be taken to promote children's rights, but omitting the preparation of a European Charter devoted to such a theme.[257] This omission implicitly acknowledged that there was now nothing to be gained by the Council of Europe attempting to create a European Charter on the Rights of the Child, since it could do little more than reproduce a list similar to that provided by the CRC. Instead, the proposals sought to build on the Convention by encouraging its implementation by member states and by seeking to promote its aims in as practical a way as possible.

---

250 Eg, inter alia: Recommendation (No R (84) 4) on Parental Responsibilities; Recommendation (No R (85) 4) on Violence in the Family; Recommendation (No R (87) 20) on Social Reactions to Juvenile Delinquency; Recommendation (No R (98) 8) on Children's Participation in Family and Social Life.

251 Eg the Committee of Ministers has emphasised the importance of enabling children to influence the conditions of their own lives through full and effective participation in family and society: see Council of Europe, Committee of Ministers, Recommendation (No R (98) 8) on Children's Participation in Family and Social Life.

252 Inter alia: the European Convention on the Adoption of Children 1967; the European Convention on the Legal Status of Children Born Out of Wedlock 1975; the European Convention on Recognition and Enforcement of Decisions Concerning Custody of Children and on Restoration of Custody of Children 1980; the European Convention on the Exercise of Children's Rights 1996; the European Convention for the Protection of Human Rights and Dignity of the Human Being with Regard to the Application of Biology and Medicine 1997; the European Convention on Contact Concerning Children 2002.

253 See also the European Convention on the Adoption of Children 1967 and the European Convention on Recognition and Enforcement of Decisions Concerning Custody of Children and on Restoration of Custody of Children 1980.

254 *Marckx v Belgium* (1979) 2 EHRR 330.

255 See Law Commission (1982) paras 4.11–4.12. The Family Law Reform Act 1987 enacted most of these recommendations for reform.

256 Parliamentary Assembly of the Council of Europe, Recommendation 874 (1979) on a European Charter on the Rights of the Child.

The recommendations set out by the 1990 Recommendation included the following: to appoint a special ombudsman for children who could, inter alia, take legal action on their behalf; to ratify and implement the CRC; to instruct the Steering Committee for Human Rights to consider elaborating an additional protocol to the ECHR concerning the rights of the child; and to convene a small group of experts to consider how children might better exercise their existing rights under the Convention. The Parliamentary Assembly of the Council of Europe made further recommendations designed to ensure that the aims of the Convention were more actively promoted by member states.[258] The document covered a number of issues. It suggested measures intended to encourage governments to fulfil children's social and economic rights through adopting well co-ordinated and child-focused policies at national and local levels.[259] It also recommended ways in which children's civil and political rights could be promoted; for example by encouraging them to assume responsibilities for themselves within the community, as a preparation for their future citizenship.[260]

An initiative directly emerging from the 1990 Recommendation was for the Committee of Experts on Family Law to prepare and introduce the European Convention on the Exercise of Children's Rights, opened for signature in 1996. The intention of this Convention was to supplement the CRC by assisting children to exercise their substantive rights set out in the Convention. It recognises that the most practical means for children to claim and enforce their rights is through legal proceedings. The European Convention on the Exercise of Children's Rights therefore confines itself to creating and strengthening procedural rights to be exercised by children when becoming involved in family proceedings.[261]

These proposals and initiatives illustrate that those involved in legal reform programmes in the Council of Europe are well aware of the need to promote the rights of children in member states. They are also aware of the restricted ability of the ECHR to achieve such a goal. Their implicit acknowledgment of the current futility of preparing a European charter to emulate the CRC is realistic – there is little point in attempting to reinvent the wheel. Nevertheless, it is disappointing that the proposal for producing an additional protocol to the ECHR concerning the rights of the child was never pursued. A specific reinterpretation of the Convention from the perspective of children's rather than adults' rights would have proved particularly beneficial for children living in the United Kingdom, since it could have been incorporated into domestic law alongside the ECHR. Meanwhile, the Council of Europe continues to pay special attention to its law reforming role. Through its Committee of Experts on Family Law, it identifies areas of law requiring reform and harmonisation with a view to improving the lives of children living in member states, both in their families and in their wider communities.[262]

---

257 Parliamentary Assembly of the Council of Europe, Recommendation 1121 (1990) on the Rights of the Child.

258 Parliamentary Assembly of the Council of Europe, Recommendation 1286 (1996) on a European Strategy for Children.

259 Parliamentary Assembly of the Council of Europe, Recommendation 1286 (1996) on a European Strategy for Children, para 7.

260 Discussed in more detail in chapter 19.

261 See Council of Europe (1997) p 18. Discussed in more detail in chapter 7. See also art 6 of the European Convention on Contact Concerning Children.

262 Eg Council of Europe (2000 b) and Council of Europe (2000 c).

(8)   CONCLUSION

The contribution made by international human rights law to promoting the rights of children has been of inestimable importance. Ratification of the CRC by nearly all countries throughout the world means that it has become an international treaty of major significance. Moreover, for children in this country the work of the Council of Europe, both in establishing the ECHR and through its reforming initiatives, has also had considerable impact. Even before implementation of the Human Rights Act 1998, these developments had combined to produce a practical rights-oriented consciousness amongst those dealing with legal problems affecting children on a day-to-day basis. It was also becoming increasingly common for domestic courts to justify their decisions on matters affecting children by reference to children's rights and to draw on both these treaties to substantiate such an approach. Now that the ECHR has become part of domestic law, it may achieve a far greater impact on the legal principles underpinning children's rights than the CRC, hampered as the latter treaty is by its weak enforcement mechanism. Be that as it may, a situation has already been achieved whereby practitioners and the judiciary are not only far more open to arguments based on children's rights, but also more willing to consider international instruments as an important source of guidance over the standards to be reached by domestic law.

BIBLIOGRAPHY

NB Some of these publications can be obtained on the relevant organisation's website.

Bainham A, 'Can We Protect Children and Protect their Rights?' (2002) Family Law 279.

Barsh R, 'The Convention on the Rights of the Child: a Re-assessment of the Final Text' (1989) 7 New York Law School 142.

Bourne R et al, *School based understanding of human rights in four countries* (1998) Department for International Development.

Children's Rights Alliance, *Report to the Pre-Sessional Working Group of the Committee on the Rights of the Child, preparing for examination of the UK's second report under the CRC*, (2002) (unpublished).

Children's Rights Development Unit, *UK Agenda for Children* (1994) Children's Rights Development Unit.

Combe V, *Up for it: Getting young people involved in local government* (2002) The National Youth Agency.

Committee on the Rights of the Child, *Concluding Observations of the Committee on the Rights of the Child: United Kingdom of Great Britain and Northern Ireland* CRC/C/15/Add 34 1995 (1995 a) Centre for Human Rights, Geneva.

Committee on the Rights of the Child, *Concluding Observations of the Committee on the Rights of the Child: China* CRC/C/15/Add 56 1995 (1995 b) Centre for Human Rights, Geneva.

Committee on the Rights of the Child, *Concluding Observations of the Committee on the Rights of the Child: United Kingdom of Great Britain and Northern Ireland* CRC/C/15/Add 188 2002 (2002) Centre for Human Rights, Geneva.

Council of Europe, *Report on a European Strategy for Children* Parliamentary Assembly of the Council of Europe, Recommendation 1286 (1996).

Council of Europe, *European Convention on the Exercise of Children's Rights and explanatory report* (1997) Council of Europe Publishing.

Council of Europe, *Council of Europe Achievements in the Field of Law: Family Law* DIR/JUR (2000) 8 (2000 a).

Council of Europe, *Report of the Working Party of the Committee of Experts on Family Law on Custody and Access* CJ-FA-GT1(2000) RAP11 (2000 b).

Council of Europe, *Report of the Working Party of the Committee of Experts on Family Law on the Legal Status of Children* CJ-FA-GT2 (2000) RAP6 (2000 c).

Craig P and de Burca G, *EU Law: Text, Cases and Materials* (1998) Oxford University Press.

Department of Health, *The UN Convention on the Rights of the Child: The UK's First Report to the UN Committee on the Rights of the Child* (1994) HMSO.

Department of Health, *United Nations Convention on the Rights of the Child: Second Report to the UN Committee by the United Kingdom 1999* (1999) The Stationery Office.

Detrick S (ed), *The United Nations Convention on the Rights of the Child: A Guide to the 'Travaux Préparatoires'* (1992) Martinus Nijhoff Publishers.

Donnelly J and Howard R, 'Assessing National Human Rights Performance: A Theoretical Framework' (1988) 10 Human Rights Quarterly 214.

Douglas G and Lowe N, 'Annual Review of International Family Law' in A Bainham (ed) *The International Survey of Family Law* (2002) Family Law.

Eekelaar J, 'The Importance of Thinking that Children Have Rights' in P Alston, S Parker and J Seymour (eds) *Children, Rights and the Law* (1992) Clarendon Press.

Eekelaar J, 'Beyond the welfare principle' (2002) 14 Child and Family Law Quarterly 237.

Eekelaar J and Dingwall R, *Human Rights: Report on the Replies of Governments to the Enquiry under Article 57 of the European Convention on Human Rights* (1987) Council of Europe.

Feinberg J, *Rights, Justice and the Bounds of Liberty* (1980) Princeton University Press.

Feldman D, *Civil Liberties and Human Rights in England and Wales* (2002) Oxford University Press.

Fortin J, 'Rights Brought Home for Children' (1999 a) 62 Modern Law Review 350.

Fortin J, 'The HRA's impact on litigation involving children and their families' (1999 b) 11 Child and Family Law Quarterly 237.

Fortin J, 'Children's Rights and the Impact of Two International Conventions: The UNCRC and the ECHR' in The Rt Hon L J Thorpe and C Cowton (eds) *Delight and Dole: The Children Act 10 years on* (2002) Jordan Publishing Ltd.

Freeman M, 'The Future of Children's Rights' (2000) 14 Children and Society 277.

Gearty C, 'The United Kingdom' in C Gearty (ed) *European Civil Liberties and the European Convention on Human Rights: A Comparative Study* (1997) The Hague.

Hammarberg T, 'The UN Convention on the Rights of the Child – and How to Make it Work' (1990) 12 Human Rights Quarterly 97.

Harris D, O'Boyle M and Warbrick C, *Law of the European Convention on Human Rights* (1995) Butterworths.

Herring J, 'The Human Rights Act and the Welfare Principle in Family Law – Conflicting or Complementary?' (1999) 11 Child and Family Law Quarterly 223.

Hodgson D, 'The Historical Development and "Internationalisation" of the Children's Rights Movement' (1992) 6 Australian Journal of Family Law 25.

Home Office, *Rights Brought Home: The Human Rights Bill* Cm 3782 (1997) HMSO.

Hunt M, 'The Horizontal Effect of the Human Rights Act' (1998) Public Law 423.

Kilbourne S, 'The wayward Americans – why the USA has not ratified the UN Convention on the Rights of the Child' (1998) 10 Child and Family Law Quarterly 243.

Kilkelly U, 'The UN Committee on the Rights of the Child – an evaluation in the light of the recent UK experience' (1996) 8 Child and Family Law Quarterly 105.

Kilkelly U, *The Child and the European Convention on Human Rights* (1999) Ashgate.

King M, 'Children's Rights as Communication: Reflections on Autopoietic Theory and the United Nations Convention' (1994) 57 Modern Law Review 385.

Law Commission, *Family Law Report on Illegitimacy* Law Com No 118 (1982) HMSO.

LeBlanc L, *The Convention on the Rights of the Child: United Nations Lawmaking on Human Rights* (1995) University of Nebraska Press.

McGoldrick D, 'The United Nations Convention on the Rights of the Child' (1991) 5 International Journal of Law and the Family 132.

Marshall K, *Children's Rights in the Balance: The Participation – Protection Debate* (1997) The Stationery Office.

Minow M, 'Interpreting Rights: An Essay for Robert Cover' (1987) 96 Yale Law Journal 1860.

Newell P and Hodgkin R (eds), *Implementation Handbook for the Convention on the Rights of the Child* (1998) UNICEF.

Price Cohen C and Kilbourne S, 'Jurisprudence of the Committee on the Rights of the Child: A Guide for Research and Analysis' (1998) 19 Michigan Journal of International Law 633.

Starmer K, *European Human Rights Law* (1999) Legal Action Group.

Swindells H, 'Crossing the Rubicon – Family Law Post The Human Rights Act 1998' in S Cretney (ed) *Family Law: Essays for the New Millenium* (2000) Jordans.

Swindells H, Neaves A, Kushner M and Skilbeck R, *Family Law and the Human Rights Act 1998* (1999) Family Law.

Van Bueren G, *The International Law on the Rights of the Child* (1995) Martinus Nijhoff Publishers.

Vine A, 'Is the paramountcy principle compatible with article 8?' (2000) Family Law 826.

Walsh B, 'The United Nations Convention on the Rights of the Child: A British View' (1991) 5 International Journal of Law and the Family 170.

Wellman C, *The Proliferation of Rights: Moral Progress or Empty Rhetoric?* (1999) Westview Press.

Part Two

Promoting consultation and decision-making

Chapter 3

Adolescent decision-making, *Gillick* and parents

(1) INTRODUCTION

Adolescents are fast approaching adulthood. They cannot be expected to make the transition from childhood to an adult legal status successfully unless they are assisted in this process. They should be encouraged to develop the skills they need for independent life in our relatively wealthy and technologically sophisticated society. Although parents have an essential part to play in this process, it is important for the law to assist, by ensuring that an adolescent's decisions are, as far as possible, respected. It is, however, unrealistic to expect children of any age to make decisions for themselves before they are developmentally ready to do so. Those who argue over the extent to which children should be allowed greater legal responsibilities seldom refer to the extensive body of research on children's mental processes and cognitive powers. This chapter briefly summarises some of this material with a view to clarifying for parents, lawyers and other practitioners the extent of children and adolescents' developmental capacity for decision-making.

The second part of the chapter considers, in general terms, the confused legal principles now governing disputes between adolescents and their parents.[1] In practice, adolescents' relationship with their parents are probably the most influential in their lives. Parents are the people who can most effectively encourage their children to develop a capacity for independence. Parents are, however, also in a good position to undermine their children's self-confidence so effectively that they emerge into adulthood quite unable to fend happily for themselves. The decision in *Gillick v West Norfolk and Wisbech Area Health Authority*[2] acknowledged this and demanded a great deal of parents. They were expected to stand back and allow their adolescents an increasing measure of freedom. Unfortunately, the later case law confused this approach, rendering it now impossible to give adolescents any very clear advice over their legal right to reach decisions for themselves in the event of family disputes.

---

1 More specific aspects of legal decision-making, eg medical decision-making, are dealt with in more depth in later chapters.
2 [1986] AC 112.

(2)   CHILD AND ADOLESCENT DEVELOPMENTAL CAPACITY FOR DECISION-MAKING – THE RESEARCH EVIDENCE

The early children's liberationists and their contemporary counterparts have criticised society's reluctance to give children greater freedom. But their claims should be tested against the research evidence on the developing abilities of children to handle different tasks, as they mature in age. Generalisations are, of course, always misleading. Ideally, a child's capacity for decision-making should always be considered on an individual case-by-case basis, since it will hinge largely on the type of decision, its context and the child's own personal circumstances.[3] Nevertheless, research does provide information about the cognitive skills of the majority of children, depending on their developmental growth and it clearly challenges the arguments of those advocating equal rights for children, irrespective of age.

In the first place, there are important developmental differences between children and adults which cannot be ignored. Although Piaget's ideas relating to the existence of discrete and successive stages of developmental growth have been largely discredited,[4] Rutter and Rutter maintain that it is impossible to discount the concept of stages altogether: 'No amount of training will cause, say, a four-month-old to walk or talk, or a six-year-old to learn differential calculus.'[5] Cognitive performance is dependent on the emergence of specific metacognitive skills which are simply not available to young children.[6] Accordingly, the claims of the early liberationists that it is wrong to exclude children from adult freedoms appear to have been based on a false premise regarding children's decision-making abilities.

Research on the way in which children and young people think and reason can take matters further than merely distinguishing between the thought processes of children and adults. Researchers broadly agree that there are fundamental differences between childhood thought, preoccupied as it is with practical issues to do with the here and now, and adolescent thinking which is much more sophisticated. Adolescents are increasingly able to cope with abstractions and to distinguish between the real and concrete and the abstract or possible. They can test hypotheses and think and plan about the future. They become aware of their own thought processes and become self-reflective, even introspective.[7] Their thinking is multi-dimensional, with a greater use of relative, rather than absolute, concepts.[8] This material suggests that the intellectual competence of young children aged up to about 11 to 12 is far less sophisticated than that of adolescents between the ages of 12 and 18.[9]

Researchers have not confined their attentions to the distinctions between the thought processes of children and adolescents. They have also noted significant changes in the cognitive and social development within both groups as they grow older. For example, the manner in which the older adolescent deals with moral dilemmas is significantly more sophisticated than that adopted by children between

3   M Rutter and M Rutter (1993) p 197.
4   Piaget's research and writings, which had considerable influence in the field of developmental psychology, spanned nearly 50 years from the early 1920s to the late 1970s. See, inter alia, J Piaget (1924). The main criticisms of Piaget's work are summarised by J Coleman and L Hendry (1999) pp 36–43.
5   M Rutter and M Rutter (1993) p 195.
6   M Rutter and M Rutter (1993) p 197.
7   Much of this material is summarised by T Gullotta et al (2000) pp 59–62.
8   M Rutter and M Rutter (1993) p 253.
9   M Rutter and M Rutter (1993) pp 6 and 7.

the ages of 8 and 12, which is, in turn, more sophisticated than that of children below the age of 8.[10] This material is reinforced by research on adolescents' ability to involve themselves in political thought and reasoning.[11] According to this research, there are important and subtle differences between the approach of a 12-year-old to political dilemmas, from that of the 14- or 15-year-old, and again from that of a 16-year-old. It shows that the typical adolescent of 12 or 13 years of age cannot appreciate that there may be more than one solution to a problem or that individual acts or political solutions are not necessarily absolutely right or wrong. Whereas the concept of moral relativism is not yet available for the 12-year-old, by the age of 14 or 15, the adolescent is able to think in a more critical and pragmatic way.[12] Interestingly, the growth in competence which takes place at around the age of 15 corresponds with the belief of many adolescents themselves that the age of 15 is an appropriate age for gaining the right to make major personal decisions.[13]

It is also during later adolescence that young people start understanding themselves and becoming aware of their own personalities.[14] Although Erikson's theory[15] that adolescents have to pass through a series of identity 'crises' to achieve a coherent sense of identity or self-concept has been much criticised,[16] it is nevertheless generally accepted that it is during the teenage years that young people establish a clearer sense of personal identity.[17] Indeed, in summary, it is the older adolescents' ability to conceptualise, to think about the meaning of their experiences and to establish concepts about themselves as distinctive persons that marks out adolescence from the earlier years of life.[18]

This research material suggests that the majority of older adolescents are equipped with developmental skills for relatively sophisticated decision-making.[19] Nevertheless, cognitive capacity to reach decisions does not necessarily correlate with 'mature' judgment. The adolescent years are also characterised by change and transition. Adolescents start questioning the belief-system with which they were brought up and discard their parents' values as they respond to influences outside the family. It is a time for experimenting with new ideas, clothes, sexual behaviour. They may engage in behaviour which endangers their health and well-being and that of society as a whole. Some indulge in alcohol abuse, drug abuse, unprotected sexual activity, dangerous driving and criminal activities.[20] Indeed, youthful recklessness, leading to self- and socially destructive behaviour is the topic of much speculation,

---

10   J Coleman and L Hendry (1999) pp 43–48.
11   J Coleman and L Hendry (1999) pp 194–196. Coleman and Hendry discuss the research of Adelson and O'Neill on this topic. See eg J Adelson and R O'Neill (1966).
12   J Coleman and L Hendry (1999) pp 195–196.
13   L Taylor et al (1984). See also L Taylor et al (1985).
14   J Coleman and L Hendry (1999) ch 4.
15   E Erikson (1968).
16   J Coleman and L Hendry (1999) pp 59–65.
17   M Rutter and M Rutter (1993) pp 253–254.
18   M Rutter and M Rutter (1993) p 252.
19   See L Mann et al (1989). These authors set out a list of the elements required for competent decision-making and assess the research evidence indicating how adolescents of varying ages 'score' on each category synthesised into the following nine 'C's: choice; comprehension; creativity; compromise; consequentiality; correctness; credibility; consistency; commitment.
20   Department of Health (1996) p 6. See also Communities that Care (2002) p 50. Around 40% of the 14- and 15-year-olds surveyed reported stealing or trying to steal at least once in their lives, with 28% of year 10 boys and 27% of year 10 girls saying that they had stolen from a shop in the past 12 months. Just over 30% of year 10 boys and girls said they had vandalised property. This is discussed in more detail in chapter 18.

both as to its causes and as to appropriate interventions.[21] Research suggests that those who become involved in such activities often do so because they feel obliged by peer pressure to gain esteem by joining the activities of others.[22] They also commonly believe that they are immune from their dangerous consequences; for example, that they will not become infected from sexually transmitted diseases as a result of unprotected sexual activity. They assume that they can control and prevent any damaging outcome.[23] Researchers also argue that risk-taking experimentation, particularly when it comes to taking health risks through alcohol and drug misuse, is an important educational element in the path to adulthood.[24]

Clearly the research on the thought processes of young children and adolescents cannot provide generalisations or 'rule of thumb' guidelines to assist with assessing an individual's capacity to reach decisions. Competence for decision-making will vary enormously, depending on a variety of factors, such as peer pressure and family environment. It not only depends on the maturity and social circumstances of the person reaching the decision but also on the content and context of the decision in question. Thus whilst a person of any age may need a variety of skills, and therefore a relatively sophisticated type of competence before being able, for example, to consent to surgery, they will require a much lower level of competence to activate a machine. Some of the relevant skills manifest earlier and there is a gradual increase in the ability, for example, to conceptualise, with decision-making depending on context and task. Nevertheless, whilst individual children will demonstrate different abilities, the average child will develop along similar lines to his or her contemporaries. Furthermore, it appears that before early adolescence, the *majority* of children do lack the cognitive abilities and judgmental skills to make major decisions that might seriously affect their lives. So although the significance given by society to chronological age is probably excessive, the relative youth of a child is very relevant to the reasonableness of the choices put to him or her.[25]

When considering children's capacity to reach decisions for themselves, writers, practitioners and the judiciary often use imprecise terms such as 'competence', 'maturity' and 'understanding'. It appears that these are essentially meaningless without much further refinement, preferably by reference to the body of psychological research on children's developmental processes discussed above.

(3)   CHILD AND ADOLESCENT CAPACITY FOR DECISION-MAKING – SHOULD THE LAW ON MINORITY BE LIBERALISED?

The children's liberationists have been exerting pressure on policy makers for many years to liberalise the law's recognition of children's ability for independence. One wonders whether they ever consider the import of the research on cognitive development in children and adolescents, discussed above. Had they done so, it seems doubtful that Holt and Farson would have called for virtually all important adult freedoms to be extended to any child wishing to exercise them.[26] Such views

---

21   See eg N Bell and R Bell (1993).
22   J Coleman and L Hendry (1999) esp p 121. See also J Graham and B Bowling (1995) pp 42–43.
23   A Benthin et al (1993) esp p 166. But see S Millstein (1993), who claims (p 55ff) that there is little or no empirical evidence supporting the concept of 'adolescent invulnerability'.
24   J Coleman and L Hendry (1999) p 135.
25   J Hughes (1989) p 38.
26   See J Holt (1974); R Farson (1974). Discussed in more detail in chapter 1.

continue to attract support. Like Holt and Farson, Harris claims that children should acquire full political status with the right, inter alia, to vote, work, initiate and defend legal proceedings, own property, write wills and enter into contracts.[27] He asserts:

'Bold quick, ingenious, forward and capable young people are by no means a rarity, neither, unfortunately, are dull-witted incompetent adults. If freedom from control and full political status are things that we qualify for by the acquisition of a range of capacities, then as soon as anyone possesses those capacities they qualify, and if they never acquire them they never qualify. So if it is supposed that it is the comprehensive possession by adults of capacities lacked equally comprehensively by children that sustains and justifies the political disabling of children and the rule of adults, the supposition is false. False because there are numerous children whom it would be implausible to regard as incompetent and numerous adults whom it would be implausible to regard as anything else.'[28]

Harris later deftly dilutes his remarkably liberal approach by emphasising that it is only children who are capable of making 'maximally autonomous' decisions who can be in control of their own destinies.[29] Only the children free from four types of defects (defects in their ability to control their desires or actions; defects in their reasoning; defects in the information available to them regarding the choices in hand; defects in the stability of their own desires) can be maximally autonomous.[30] These are onerous conditions. Indeed, the psychological research referred to above[31] suggests that relatively few children or adolescents would fulfil Harris's requirements. As Brazier and Bridge cogently comment, although adults suffer from defects in control, the 15-year-old is more likely to be heavily influenced by parental wishes than the 25-year-old. Similarly, adolescent impetuosity may defy reason.[32]

Other writers, although not making claims as apparently radical as Harris's, point out that Piaget's assumptions about the stages of children's cognitive ability can be refuted by the activities of children themselves and that the law should recognise and respect their decision-making abilities.[33] Like Harris, they criticise the traditional assumptions regarding adult and childhood intellectual and psychological capacities. They point to the many children under the age of 18 who care for ill or disabled parents with little or no help, the street children in the world's major cities who exhibit survival strategies equal to those of many adults, and the children who happily take on a responsible role in working parents' households, if properly involved in the division of labour.[34] Alderson's research with children in hospital led her to conclude:

'Many children exceed many adults in, for example, intelligence, ability, prudence, confidence, size, strength, and profound experience of certain aspects of life ... Differences between adults and children lie mainly in social beliefs about childhood and behaviours affected by those beliefs, rather than in children's actual abilities.'[35]

Alderson and Montgomery later draw on this research to justify their proposal for the introduction of a legal presumption that all 5-year-olds should be deemed competent

---

27   J Harris (1982) p 51.
28   J Harris (1982) p 37.
29   J Harris (1985) p 215.
30   J Harris (1985) pp 194–200.
31   See discussion at pp 72–74.
32   See M Brazier and C Bridge (1996) pp 91–92.
33   P Alderson and J Montgomery (1996) ch 2.
34   Eg A Solberg (1990) p 118ff.
35   P Alderson (1993) p 190.

to consent to all medical care.[36] Franklin used similar arguments to justify his claims for more extensive legal rights for children, including the right to vote at any age.[37] All these writers appear to overlook the research material on the cognitive development of the average child and adolescent. It is undeniable that there are significant and subtle differences between the thought processes of young children and adolescents and between younger and older adolescents. As noted above, younger children are far less able than adolescents to weigh up alternatives and cope rationally with major decisions. Although some children may prove competent to deal with the challenges that life throws up and able to make decisions in the face of pain, hardship and ill-health, this may be at considerable psychological cost. Maturity also depends on a number of other factors; for example, being good or even amazingly good at maths, does not indicate that a child knows enough about the working of a democratic society to vote,[38] or assess the implications of surgery.[39] Indeed, it is appropriate to shield the average child from making significant choices before acquiring the cognitive tools to do so adequately. Such an approach readily accords with the interest theory of rights which presupposes that although children may have an interest in making choices, they do not necessarily have a moral right to do so. Under MacCormick's test, an interest in choice could only be deemed a moral right if it is so important to the child that it would be wrong in itself to deny or withhold it from him or her.[40]

The slow rate of children's developmental growth indicates that far from being wrong to deny the younger child a choice, it may be wrong in itself to ask him or her to make a decision over a variety of matters, at least before reaching adolescence. In any event, children's interest in choice may be fulfilled by acknowledging their moral right to have their decision-making capacity *promoted*, rather than a right to have their choices respected. This would involve consulting them, rather than giving them complete responsibility for choice. Giving them the opportunity to participate in decisions over their future may be appropriate when they are capable of making a sensible contribution, but lack the maturity to reach a decision, given its context and seriousness. To argue otherwise is to overlook the fact that children have a variety of rights, all of which need fulfilling, in particular their right to protection. It is perfectly appropriate for society to protect children from being required to make significant choices if it considers that they may suffer unnecessarily from being involved in decision-making before they are sufficiently mature. Furthermore, if their decisions interfere with and restrict their ability for future choices, then they should be overborne.[41]

The research on the older adolescent's psychological development suggests that a different approach might be justified for those at the upper end of adolescence. It certainly lends some support for those who argue that the current law is too restrictive in its approach to recognising the decision-making capacity of older children. It does not, however, justify any radical changes. Some writers, like Lindley, argue in favour of a more sophisticated approach to children's liberation. In his view there are good

---

36   P Alderson and J Montgomery (1996) ch 5. Discussed in more detail in chapter 10.
37   B Franklin (1992) and (1986). But see his later view that children should be entitled to vote only at the age of 16. See B Franklin (1995) p 20.
38   J Hughes (1989) p 40.
39   See the research of N Kaser-Boyd et al (1985). This indicates that older adolescents identified more risks and benefits in therapy decisions than younger subjects.
40   N MacCormick (1982) p 160. Discussed in chapter 1.
41   N MacCormick (1982) p 166.

reasons for rejecting the claim that all children should have equal rights to self-determination because of the significant correlation between childhood and incompetence.[42] As he points out:

> '... it is clear that allowing five-year-olds to decide whether they will go to school and what they will learn would actually reduce their chances of *developing* autonomy. Furthermore, a lack of education is most likely to reduce a person's chances of the *exercise* of autonomy later.'[43]

Nevertheless, he considers it difficult to justify paternalistic restrictions on all adolescents under the age of 18, simply by reason of their minor status. He suggests that by the time children are 13, they are sufficiently stable and have sufficient conceptual competence to be able to have the objectives of a life plan. On that basis, he argues, there should be a liberalisation in the laws relating to the 13- to 16-year-old category. Citing the high rates of adolescent sexual activity below the age of 16, he criticises the laws which prevent girls under the age of 16 from consenting to sexual intercourse.[44] He also argues that the high levels of truancy in schools indicates that young people between the ages of 13 and 16 should not be forced to remain in full-time compulsory education, but should be allowed to take full-time employment instead. Furthermore, in his view, adolescents should be given political education in schools and allowed to vote.[45]

There appear to be flaws in Lindley's proposal. He does not take sufficient account of the fact that the development of maturity is a gradual process, and that adult maturity does not emerge suddenly on attaining adolescence, or indeed on a child's 13th birthday. The research indicating important differences between the thinking of younger and older adolescents suggests that it would be ill-judged to assume that the young adolescent should be given the same degree of independence as the older category of teenager. Indeed, the rates of truancy indicate that there is a good number of adolescents within this age group who would not appreciate the educational advantages of remaining at school beyond that age.[46]

Although it is sensible for adolescents to be allowed greater responsibility for taking decisions for themselves, as was decided by the House of Lords in *Gillick v West Norfolk and Wisbech Area Health Authority*,[47] the liberationists are rash to advocate the age governing the attainment of adult status being lowered. By leaving it at the age of 18, the older adolescents still prone to youthful recklessness gain a few extra years of legal protection. These may ensure that they attain sufficient maturity to emerge into adulthood with a degree of confidence. But this cautious approach should not be taken as signalling complete approval of the existing law. There are clear arguments in favour of giving 16-year-olds voting rights.[48] Furthermore, as discussed below, there is a need for considerably greater clarity in the legal principles applying to adolescents and for the law to maintain a better balance between allowing

---

42   R Lindley (1989) p 79.
43   R Lindley (1989) p 85.
44   See *R v K* [2001] UKHL 41, [2001] 3 All ER 897, per Lord Millett, who (at [44]) subscribes to a similar view. He considers that the age of consent 'has long since ceased to reflect ordinary life, and in this respect Parliament has signally failed to discharge its responsibility for keeping the criminal law in touch with the needs of society'.
45   R Lindley (1989) pp 88–92.
46   Discussed in more depth in chapter 6.
47   [1986] AC 112.
48   Discussed in chapter 4.

young people as much freedom as they have the capacity for, whilst restraining them from making choices which restrict their own future development.

(4)   ADOLESCENTS, PARENTS AND THE *GILLICK* HERITAGE

Although children mature at different rates, the law withholds the right to full adult autonomy from all adolescents until they attain the age of 18.[49] But on attaining that age, adolescents are expected to make an immediate successful transition from the legal status of childhood to responsible citizenship.[50] Giving them a 'dry run' at adulthood is therefore essential. Whether they get it depends enormously on their parents' willingness to encourage in their children a capacity to take responsibility for their own future.[51] Research provides practical support for the views of the theorists who argue that parents have a duty to encourage children to develop decision-making capacities from as early an age as possible. It suggests not only that family environment and family dynamics are major factors in adolescent psychological development,[52] but that parents help shape adolescents' capacity for reaching decisions competently and influence the extent to which they participate in decision-making.

Most parents agree that they have an important part to play in helping their children gain emotional independence, but this may not always be as easy as it sounds. Whilst many parents subscribe to the idea of the family becoming an increasingly democratic unit, they often find that life with teenagers 'presents fundamental contradictions between ideals and lived reality'.[53] The following words have a ring of truth for parents with teenage children:

> 'The teenage years herald a period of re-negotiation as budding adults take up the banner of freedom – freedom to make choices, such as what to wear, who to associate with or when to engage in sexual relations. On the other side, parents and carers wave the flag of responsibility, struggling to push recalcitrant adolescents towards maturity, sobriety, practical skills and "appropriate" behaviour.'[54]

Parents' proximity to their children may lead them to underestimate their children's maturity and abilities, particularly their ability to discuss sensibly decisions relating to their own future. They may effectively undermine their children's self-confidence and hamper their decision-making skills by involving them very little in family decisions.[55] In particular, many parents find it extremely difficult to allow even quite mature children to make up their own minds on major matters affecting their upbringing and future. Knowledgeable parents might argue that they are supported in such an approach by article 5 of the CRC. This requires governments to respect parents' rights and duties to provide 'appropriate direction and guidance in the exercise by the child of the rights recognised ...' Nevertheless, parents should not overlook the article's qualifying phrase, which emphasises that parental direction and guidance should only be provided 'in a manner consistent with the evolving capacities of the child'. Furthermore, articles 12, 13 and 14 of the Convention all emphasise the child's

---

49   Family Law Reform Act 1969, s 1.
50   See M de Winter (1997) p 26.
51   Discussed in chapter 1.
52   See J Coleman and L Hendry (1999) ch 5.
53   W Langford et al (2001) p 47.
54   Department of Health (1996) p 18.
55   Eg many divorcing parents fail to consult even quite mature children over their proposed arrangements for their children's future upbringing. See discussion in chapter 7.

right to develop a capacity for independent thought and action. Whilst article 12 guarantees the right of all children who are capable of forming their own views, the right to express those views over matters to do with their upbringing, articles 13 and 14 secure their freedom of expression and their freedom of thought, conscience and religion.

Although domestic legislation could usefully encourage changes in parental attitudes, the Children Act 1989 failed to seize the opportunity to do so. There is the admirable duty imposed on local authorities before reaching any decision relating to a child they are looking after or proposing to look after, to 'ascertain the wishes and feelings' of the child so far as is reasonably practicable[56] and then to take them into consideration when reaching a decision.[57] The failure to impose a similar duty on parents is disappointing, given the Law Commission's ambitions for that part of the statutory checklist requiring the courts to consider the child's views.[58] This was to ensure that it reflected 'the increasing recognition given both in practice and in law to the child's status as a human being in his own right, rather than the object of the rights of others ...'[59]

The absence of any principle of English law requiring parents to consult their children over important matters regarding their own future contrasts unfavourably with the Children (Scotland) Act 1995, section 6(1). This provision requires any parent when reaching 'any major decision' involving his child's upbringing to 'have regard so far as is practicable to the views (if he wishes to express them) of the child concerned ...'[60] The existence of such a direction to parents in Scotland has an important symbolic significance. As Bainham comments, it provides a statutory recognition for children's legitimate expectations that parents 'will behave democratically, and not dictatorially, when taking decisions affecting them'.[61] The draftsmen, on the recommendation of the Scottish Law Commission,[62] were also determined to prevent parents assuming that their children were always too immature to consult. They therefore inserted a legal presumption that a child of 12 years of age or more is 'of sufficient age and maturity to form a view' on such decisions.[63] Such a presumption has the obvious value of shifting the onus on to anyone ignoring it to justify reaching a decision without consulting a child over that age.[64] Interestingly, the Scottish Law Commission considered that the age limit of 12 was in line with psychological evidence on children's intellectual development, but recommended that the word 'maturity' was used, rather than 'understanding', to ensure that it is not

---

56   Children Act 1989, s 22(4)(a).
57   Children Act 1989, s 22(5)(a). Discussed in chapter 17.
58   Children Act 1989, s 1(3)(a).
59   Law Commission (1988) para 3.24.
60   Children (Scotland) Act 1995, s 6(1) provides: 'A person shall, in reaching any major decision which involves—
      (a) his fulfilling a parental responsibility or the responsibility mentioned in section 5(1) of this Act; or
      (b) his exercising a parental right or giving consent by virtue of that section,
      have regard so far as practicable to the views (if he wishes to express them) of the child concerned, taking account of the child's age and maturity, and to those of any other person who has parental responsibilities or parental rights in relation to the child (and wishes to express those views); and without prejudice to the generality of this subsection a child twelve years of age or more shall be presumed to be of sufficient age and maturity to form a view.'
61   A Bainham (1993) p 8.
62   Scottish Law Commission (1992) paras 2.63–2.65.
63   Scottish Law Commission (1992) paras 2.63–2.65.
64   See A Bainham (1993) p 8.

merely a child's cognitive development which is considered.[65] Although this recommendation was not supported by reference to any particularly weighty psychological research, such a view seems reasonably consistent with the research evidence discussed above.[66] Although, at the age of 12, the average child is probably too young to reach important decisions for him or herself, since children of such an age lack the ability to weigh up alternatives and conceptualise or plan, they do have the intellectual capacity to be involved in the decision-making process.

The imposition of a duty on Scottish parents to consult their children was prompted by the Scottish Law Commission's view that such a provision would emphasise 'that the child is a person in his or her own right and that his or her views are entitled to respect and consideration'.[67] It also noted that legislation incorporating such a provision would be consistent with article 12 of the CRC and that a number of other legal systems had introduced a similar provision, including Germany, Sweden, Norway and Finland. The Scottish Law Commission openly acknowledged the difficulties involved in introducing such a 'vague and unenforceable' provision, in particular the fact that there is no obvious sanction. It also admitted that it would not always be easy to distinguish 'major' decisions from 'minor' ones. Nevertheless, it considered the benefits of introducing such a provision outweighed the difficulties, particularly because it could influence behaviour.

The failure of the English Children Act 1989 to introduce a similar provision suggests to parents in England and Wales that there is no need for them to consult their children, whatever their age and irrespective of the importance of the decision. Its omission reflects the general tenor of the 1989 Act, which assumes that parents will duly comply with their parental responsibilities, with no guidance on how to do so. One might excuse the English legislation by pointing out that, unlike the Children (Scotland) Act 1995, the 1989 Act was drafted before the publication of the CRC; consequently its draftsmen were not privy to the terms of article 12, which was to become so influential throughout the world. But this excuse overlooks the implications of the decision in *Gillick v West Norfolk and Wisbech Area Health Authority*,[68] which was decided in 1985, well before the introduction of the 1989 Act. Although the *Gillick* decision clearly influenced some aspects of the Children Act, notably the inclusion in the 'welfare checklist' of the reference to the 'ascertainable wishes and feelings of the child concerned ...',[69] the legislation ignored its wider implications. Indeed, a more imaginative interpretation of its effect might have led to the inclusion in the Children Act 1989 of a term similar to that included in its Scottish counterpart.

Although the 1989 legislation made little attempt to liberalise the parent-child relationship, well-informed parents can learn a great deal from the House of Lords' decision in *Gillick v West Norfolk and Wisbech Area Health Authority*.[70] It shows that, by the mid-1980s, a far more enlightened approach to the parental role was emerging, compared with that of earlier generations. Indeed, the *Gillick* decision established new legal boundaries for parents' relationships with their adolescent children. It reflected the view that the law should encourage parents to stand back and permit their adolescents to reach important decisions with as little interference as

---

65   Scottish Law Commission (1992) paras 2.63–2.65.
66   See pp 72–74.
67   Scottish Law Commission (1992) para 2.62.
68   [1986] AC 112.
69   See Children Act 1989, s 1(3)(a).
70   [1986] AC 112.

possible. Lord Scarman was uncompromising regarding the position of parents. In his view:

'... [the] parental right yields to the child's right to make his own decisions when he reaches a sufficient understanding and intelligence to be capable of making up his own mind on the matter requiring decision.'[71]

These words indicate very plainly that he was concerned with the broad issue of potential conflicts between parent and child, in the light of teenagers' developing capacity for adult autonomy. There seemed little doubt in his mind that parents had no right to oppose their children once they had reached sufficient understanding and intelligence to make up their own minds on the matter in question. Lord Fraser's views were, in the main, restricted to the narrow confines of consenting to contraceptive treatment and advice. Nevertheless, he too made some general remarks about the need to encourage adolescents' capacity for independence:

'It is, in my view, contrary to the ordinary experience of mankind, at least in Western Europe in the present century, to say that a child or young person remains in fact under the complete control of his parents until he attains the definite age of majority ... In practice most wise parents relax their control gradually as the child develops and encourage him or her to become increasingly independent.'[72]

Such an approach was remarkably enlightened, particularly bearing in mind that their Lordships were dealing with the legal capacity of adolescents under the age of 16 to reach decisions for themselves. It was certainly in tune with the needs of a society which requires sexually active adolescents to take a responsible attitude to birth control. But it went much further and translated into law what their Lordships clearly perceived to be the moral right of adolescents to take responsibility for important decisions in their lives, when competent to do so. It also went considerably further than article 12 of the CRC, which merely requires participation in decision-making, not that children's choices should be complied with. At the most, article 12(1) requires a child's views to be given 'due weight', depending on his or her age and maturity. The *Gillick* decision sent a strong message to parents that their own rights of decision-making were constrained and that they had a duty to allow their adolescents to make a gradual transition into adulthood.

Would their Lordships have rejected Mrs Gillick's application so decisively had she delayed her attempt to prevent her daughters receiving contraceptive advice against her will until after implementation of the Human Rights Act 1998? It is arguable that the decision reached by the European Court of Human Rights in *Nielsen v Denmark*[73] provides a far more robust approach to the parental role within the family, as protected by article 8 of the ECHR, than that favoured by the House of Lords in *Gillick*. The fact that the restrictions placed on the boy in *Nielsen* were at his mother's request clearly suggested to the European Court of Human Rights that there was a potential conflict between the aims of article 5 and article 8.[74] The Court's decision that the boy's article 5 rights were not infringed was comprehensible, in so far as it tried to ensure that article 5 does not undermine the manner in which article 8 protects family life and parental autonomy from undue state interference. According

71   [1986] AC 112 at 186.
72   [1986] AC 112 at 171.
73   (1988) 11 EHRR 175: a 12-year-old boy was placed, at his mother's request, in the closed psychiatric ward of a state hospital for 5½ months. The majority of the European Court decided that his rights under art 5 had not been infringed. See discussion in chapter 2.
74   Art 5: right to liberty and security of person; art 8: respect for private and family life.

to the European Court, article 8 protects the right of parents to reach decisions over how their children spend their time:

> 'Family life in this sense, and especially the rights of parents to exercise parental authority over their children, having due regard to their corresponding responsibilities, is recognised and protected by the Convention, in particular by Article 8.'[75]

As the Court observed, family life necessarily involves parents making a variety of decisions regarding their children's upbringing, so long as they are for a 'proper purpose'.[76] The Court clearly considered that a proper purpose included parental decisions restricting children's freedom of movement, including where they should reside, whether they should go to an educational or recreational institution, or to hospital and whether they should receive medical treatment.[77]

The domestic courts are, however, quite entitled to reinterpret the thinking behind the *Gillick* decision in Convention-compatible terms. The ECHR is a living instrument and its interpretation must keep abreast of present-day conditions.[78] The Strasbourg judiciary were far from united in their treatment of the boy's application in *Nielsen*. The European Commission of Human Rights had, by a large majority, favoured his claim[79] and its approach was only overturned by a slim majority of the judges comprising the European Court of Human Rights.[80] In any event, the boy involved in that case was only 12 years old. Although the majority of the European Court decided that at such an age it was normal for decisions to be made by a parent, even against his wishes, the strong implication was that had he been older, they would not have considered this to be so reasonable.[81] Indeed, it is difficult to accept the Court's view that the lengthy restrictions placed on a nervous boy of 12, who was not mentally ill, were for 'a proper purpose'. To assert that the mother's action was well within the normal exercise of parental authority suggests an immoderate view of the parental role, given that a 12-year-old is normally quite old enough to have strong views.[82]

Article 8 of the Convention, alongside most domestic legal systems in the world, protects the right of parents to bring up their children without undue state interference. But, as the House of Lords themselves perceived in *Gillick*, parents' rights must be balanced against those of their children, especially as the latter mature in age and wisdom. Indeed, the balance between the rights of parents and children must gradually adjust in favour of a maturing adolescent's need to gain confidence and a sense of responsibility. Consequently, it is not a proper aspect of a parent's decision-making powers to impose his or her will arbitrarily on a mature adolescent, in a manner which is manifestly against the adolescent's best interests.

An interpretation of the law in these terms does not, however, provide clear guidance over the point at which adolescents reach a stage of maturity when they can reach decisions for themselves. Indeed, the weakness of the concept of *Gillick* competence is its uncertainty. The fact that an adolescent's legal capacity hinges on notions as debatable as understanding and maturity fundamentally hampers its effectiveness as

---

75   (1988) 11 EHRR 175 (para 61).
76   (1988) 11 EHRR 175 (paras 61 and 69).
77   (1988) 11 EHRR 175 (para 61).
78   See eg *Cossey v United Kingdom* [1991] 2 FLR 492 at 501.
79   The European Commission had concluded by 11 votes to one that there had been a violation of art 5(1) and by 10 votes to two that there was a violation of art 5(4).
80   The European Court of Human Rights concluded by only nine votes to seven that art 5 was inapplicable.
81   (1988) 11 EHRR 175 (para 72).
82   These arguments are developed in chapter 4.

a means of settling internal family conflicts. Parents struggling to impose restrictions on recalcitrant adolescents may find it impossible to retain their objectivity when deciding whether their offspring can comply with Lord Scarman's test of capacity. According to this, parents must decide whether their sons and daughters have reached 'a sufficient understanding and intelligence to be capable of making up their own mind on the matter requiring decision'. Many parents might assume that their offspring have no legal right to reach major decisions regarding their lives because they are not sufficiently mature to consent to take part in any one of a variety of dangerous activities. They might gain support for such a view from the research evidence discussed above, indicating that adolescents' ability to make wise decisions is fundamentally undermined by various factors, such as peer pressure. Indeed, the Scarman test contains no guidance over the extent to which an adjustment should be made for factors affecting the adolescent's understanding, such as peer pressure, drug and substance abuse, family stress, emotional disturbance, physical and mental illness. But attempts to produce a formula for determining competence, taking account of all the factors which might undermine an adolescent's judgment, risk producing unrealistically high criteria. In practice, a definitive ruling on a teenager's legal competence in various situations can only emerge through applying for the courts' assistance over the matter.

There is a temptation for the courts to conclude that the adolescent's capacity for decision-making should be judged by the outcome of the decision. Adolescents cannot be *Gillick* competent if their decisions risk their future safety. This enables the arbiter of competence to judge the teenager incapable of legal decision-making by virtue solely of the fact that the decision he or she is making is patently unwise, but by adult standards. Freeman appears to favour this 'outcome' approach, suggesting that the concept of 'liberal paternalism' enables the requirements for competence itself to be adjusted to exclude a teenager reaching *irrational* decisions which threaten death or serious physical or mental harm. He proposes choosing a definition of irrationality which would include actions leading to major, irreversible impairment of interests.[83] The courts have used this approach to justify overriding an adolescent's refusal to undergo life-saving medical treatment. It allows them to conclude that any adolescent prepared to contemplate death by refusing treatment cannot be competent to make the decision.[84] The case law regarding children's capacity to instruct their own solicitors also demonstrates this outcome approach being used in an extremely paternalistic way.[85] Its implicit danger is that it involves imposing overtly adult criteria of rationality on young people, whilst ignoring their own individual beliefs and characters, which might provide perfectly sound reasons for their decisions, but according to their own system of values.

(5) ADOLESCENTS AND PARENTS – PATERNALISTIC U-TURNS

What is the legal position of the parents, who, having struggled to apply the *Gillick* test, decide as objectively as possible that their adolescent son or daughter is *Gillick* competent, but their offspring nevertheless refuses to co-operate over any decisions

83   M Freeman (1992) pp 37–38.
84   Eg *Re E (a minor) (wardship: medical treatment)* [1993] 1 FLR 386, discussed in chapter 5.
85   Eg *Re S (a minor) (independent representation)* [1993] 3 All ER 36. See discussion in chapter 7.

they make regarding his or her upbringing?[86] According to the decision in *Gillick*,[87] parents lose all rights to influence their son or daughter regarding any decisions reached within his or her competence – or do they? This was a proposition unlikely to be embraced with enthusiasm by parents, or indeed, by a conventional and paternalistic judiciary. It is remarkable, however, that such a short time was to elapse between the *Gillick* decision and the case law involving the Court of Appeal comprehensively undermining that decision's attempt to ensure that parents respected their growing adolescent's capacity for autonomy. In a remarkable U-turn, the Court of Appeal in *Re R (a minor) (wardship: medical treatment)*[88] and *Re W (a minor) (medical treatment)*[89] radically undermined the liberal sentiments expressed only a few years earlier by the House of Lords. This case law was essential for a society intent on retaining a means of exercising a form of benevolent paternalism to prevent adolescents endangering their own lives. As discussed earlier, there is a sound theoretical justification for paternalistic interventions to override the wishes of children, however mature in age and intellect, if they are determined to make choices which will destroy their own opportunities for choice in the future.[90] Indeed, such an approach may be justified by reference to the rights of the children themselves – they have a right to be protected from the outcome of such choices. It is, though, imperative that if their wishes are to be overridden, appropriate methods should be adopted to constrain them – those utilised by the court to date require much improvement.

The Court of Appeal considered it essential to override the wishes of the two young patients in *Re R* and *Re W* only because they required life-saving treatment, albeit against their wishes.[91] This it did by exercising its powers under the inherent jurisdiction. Whether a court can still override the wishes of an adolescent using this method, without itself, as a public authority,[92] infringing his or her rights under the ECHR is discussed later in this work.[93] But a far more controversial aspect of this case law was the notion, coined by Lord Donaldson in *Re R* and fully developed in *Re W*, that parents were entitled to override their children's wishes. In the latter case, the Court of Appeal had gone much further than merely establishing the *court's* right to overturn the refusal of an adolescent to undergo life-saving treatment. It firmly established that the refusal of *Gillick* competent teenagers, under or over the age of 16, to undergo some procedure, such as medical treatment, need not hamper the action proposed. Instead, legal consent can be obtained from their parents, or indeed from anyone with parental responsibility. Accordingly, Lord Scarman's view in *Gillick* that 'the parental right *yields* to the child's right to make his own decisions when he reaches a sufficient understanding and intelligence to be capable of making up his own mind on the matter requiring decision',[94] has no effect on the parents' right to consent. Since their right to consent survives the child's achieving *Gillick* competence,[95] that phrase merely means that parents cannot veto *affirmative* decisions

---

86   Discussed in more detail by J Fortin (2001) pp 247–250.
87   [1986] AC 112.
88   [1991] 4 All ER 177.
89   [1992] 4 All ER 627.
90   See chapter 1 at pp 20–26.
91   This case law is discussed in more detail in chapter 5.
92   Human Rights Act 1998, s 6.
93   Discussed in the context of medical decision-making in chapter 5.
94   [1986] AC 112 at 186 (emphasis supplied).
95   Per Lord Donaldson MR in *Re R (a minor) (wardship: medical treatment)* [1991] 4 All ER 177 at 185 and *Re W (a minor) (medical treatment)* [1992] 4 All ER 627 at 633. See also Balcombe LJ in *Re W* [1992] 4 All ER 627 at 642–643.

reached by such a child. Consequently, whatever his or her age, parents cannot overrule an adolescent's consent to any procedure that he or she has the competence to comprehend fully. But, according to *Re W*, the parents can themselves consent to any procedure on behalf of an adolescent of any age or competence, as long as they consider it to be in his or her best interests, and even if the adolescent objects violently. In this respect, the law not only created inordinate confusion, but retreated significantly from *Gillick*. Predictably, this case law attracted a storm of criticism.[96]

Both Lord Donaldson and Balcombe LJ seemed clearly aware of the implications of undermining *Gillick* in this way and were keen in *Re W* to stress that the wishes of a mature teenager should always be given great weight. Lord Donaldson made this clear when he said:

> 'Adolescence is a period of progressive transition from childhood to adulthood and as experience of life is acquired and intelligence and understanding grow, so will the scope of the decision-making which should be left to the minor, for it is only by making decisions and experiencing the consequences that decision-making skills will be acquired ... "good parenting involves giving minors as much rope as they can handle without an unacceptable risk that they will hang themselves".'[97]

He and his colleagues in the Court of Appeal suggested that the courts would be extremely slow to overrule the decisions of adolescents who had already attained the age of 16. But they appeared to overlook the fact that such moderation in the hands of the judiciary is of little relevance to a teenager whose tyrannical and obsessive parents are endeavouring to force on him or her a wholly unwanted course of action. The legal limitation on the parents' activities is that their choices for their child must be consistent with the child's best interests. But the subjectivity of the best interests test may not provide a particularly effective deterrent in situations involving bullying parents who see only their own point of view. They might, for example, argue that it is in their daughter's best interests to be sent back to their country of origin to be married against her will to a man she has never met.[98]

Lord Donaldson and Balcombe LJ acknowledged in *Re W* that parents might endeavour to force adolescents to undergo procedures against their will. They only envisaged this happening in a medical context, more particularly in the context of a teenage girl being forced by her parents to have an abortion against her wishes. But by confining their discussion to medical issues, they were able to rely on the restraining influence of medical ethics. They considered it highly unlikely that adolescents would ever be bullied by parents, since doctors confronted with such a dispute would seek court approval before going ahead.[99] This overlooks the fact that the principle in *Re W* is not confined to medical matters and has a general application. More remarkably, the principle applies to all adolescents up to their 18th birthdays. As Douglas cogently pointed out, Lord Donaldson's interpretation of *Gillick* '... would have the result of destroying mature minors' capacities to say no to any decision a parent wanted to make for them'.[100]

96 See, inter alia: G Douglas (1992); J Montgomery (1992); J Masson (1993); M Freeman (1993); J Eekelaar (1993). Cf N Lowe and S Juss (1993). Discussed in more detail in chapter 5.
97 [1992] 4 All ER 627 at 637–638.
98 Eg *Re KR (a child) (abduction: forcible removal by parents)* [1999] 4 All ER 954.
99 [1992] 4 All ER 627 at 635 and 645. This issue is discussed in more detail in chapter 5.
100 G Douglas (1992) p 576.

Only a radical reassessment of the law can address the complete lack of coherence between the *Gillick* principle and that contained in the later case law. According to *Gillick*, adolescents of any age, and certainly those over the age of 16 should be allowed to consent legally to a variety of decisions, without parental supervision. According to the later case law, these same adolescents may have their refusal to fulfil their parents' wishes on a variety of topics overborne by their parents consenting on their behalf, until they attain the age of 18. In educative terms the later case law is disastrous. The *Gillick* decision contained a powerful message for parents intent on maintaining a repressive and authoritarian family regime. They should heed the law which acknowledges adolescents' increasing ability to make important decisions for themselves. The later decisions appear to be saying the opposite. The fact that a court would be unlikely to uphold the repressive decisions of domineering parents is neither here nor there. Unlike the exercise of paternalism by the judiciary, which is at least open to public scrutiny, parental paternalism is restrained only by the indeterminacy of the best interests test and hidden from view by the curtain of family privacy. Many adolescents are law abiding and will feel obliged to comply with their parents' wishes, if told that they are backed by the law.

Few would relish being a member of the judiciary confronted by an adolescent determined to deprive him- or herself of life-saving treatment. Nevertheless, it is regrettable that the Court of Appeal did not perceive the dangers of handing back to parents so much of the power removed from them by the House of Lords in *Gillick*.[101] There seem good grounds for arguing that the principle established by *Re W* should be reviewed judicially and that the ECHR might assist this process. It could, for example, be claimed that authoritarian parents are infringing their children's rights under articles 5 and 8 of the ECHR by forcing them to comply with parental demands against their will. Although, at first sight, such arguments would fail under the force of the decision of the European Court of Human Rights in *Nielsen v Denmark*,[102] as discussed above, a domestic court might take a different view.

A robust reassessment of the *Nielsen* decision is long overdue. The decision leaves the boundaries between what is acceptable parental behaviour and children's rights quite unclear.[103] The obiter remarks of Dame Elizabeth Butler-Sloss P and Judge LJ in *Re K (secure accommodation order: right to liberty)*[104] suggest that they may sympathise with such an argument. The President indicated that although she recognised the principles set out in *Nielsen*, 'There is a point, however, at which one has to stand back and say – is this within ordinary acceptable parental restrictions upon the movements of a child or does it require justification?'[105] According to Judge LJ, it is an easy matter to distinguish normal from abnormal family life, the former involving parents –

'... for example, putting young children into bed when they would rather be up, or "grounding" teenagers when they would prefer to be partying with their friends, or sending children to boarding schools, entrusting the schools with authority to restrict their movements. All this reflects the normal working of family life, in which parents are responsible for bringing up, teaching, enlightening and disciplining their children as necessary and appropriate, and into which the law and local authorities should only intervene when the parents' behaviour can fairly be stigmatised as cruel or abusive.'[106]

---

101   [1986] AC 112.
102   (1988) 11 EHRR 175. See discussion above at pp 81–82.
103   See discussion in chapter 4.
104   [2001] 1 FLR 526.
105   [2001] 1 FLR 526 (para 28).
106   [2001] 1 FLR 526 (para 99).

Admittedly these comments are ambiguous. What is an 'acceptable parental restriction' and what is the 'normal working of family life'? These uncertainties need clarification. Nevertheless, hopefully the courts will not condone parents behaving in an over-authoritative manner. After all, it would be entirely appropriate for a domestic court to maintain, as the House of Lords was effectively doing in *Gillick*, that the rights of adolescents who are sufficiently mature to understand the consequences of exercising Convention freedoms must take precedence over their parents' rights to control their upbringing. The rights to freedom from restraint,[107] freedom to lead a private personal life,[108] freedom of thought, conscience and religion,[109] freedom of expression[110] and of assembly[111] are all particularly prized aspects of adult autonomy. These rights are increasingly valued by adolescents as they grow older and as they start becoming more independent and preferring the company of their peers to that of their parents and siblings. A challenge brought under the Human Rights Act 1998 might establish that mature teenagers do, after all, have the right to say no to their parents.

(6) CONCLUSION

The research evidence discussed at the beginning of this chapter suggests that children should not be expected to reach decisions for themselves before entering adolescence. By then, however, although they have started developing the skills they need for independent life, they also need their parents' assistance to develop the confidence to exercise them. The House of Lords clearly perceived that the majority of adolescents are mature enough to reach sensible decisions for themselves without needing constant parental supervision. The *Gillick* decision acknowledged that adolescents' sense of responsibility and ability to take control of their own lives are qualities which should be developed. Most parents will happily, or grudgingly, promote the liberal principles it introduced. They will comply with the law's expectations and provide adolescents with an increasing measure of independence. Nevertheless, for those adolescents caught up in family disputes and crises, the law does not now provide an effective framework for dealing with their problems. The ad hoc decision-making of the Court of Appeal was intended to fill a gap left by the *Gillick* decision – how to ensure that medical care was provided for ill and incapacitated adolescents, even against their wishes. The pity is that, by going too far, it developed legal principles which are at odds with the ability of 'average' adolescents to judge for themselves what is in their own best interests. The result is that parents and the courts may now exercise a form of 'we know best' paternalism which takes little account of the need to respect adolescent capacity for independence.

107 Art 5.
108 Art 8.
109 Art 9.
110 Art 10.
111 Art 11.

BIBLIOGRAPHY

Adelson J and O'Neill R, 'The development of political thought in adolescence' (1966) 4 Journal of Personality and Social Psychology 295.

Alderson P, *Children's Consent to Surgery* (1993) Oxford University Press.

Alderson P and Montgomery J, *Health Care Decisions: Making decisions with children* (1996) IPPR.

Bainham A, 'Reforming Scottish children law – sense from north of the border' (1993) 5 Journal of Child Law 3.

Bell N and Bell R (eds), *Adolescent Risk Taking* (1993) Sage Publications.

Benthin A et al, 'A Psychiatric Study of Adolescent Risk Perception' (1993) 16 Journal of Adolescence 153.

Brazier M and Bridge C, 'Coercion or caring: analysing adolescent autonomy' (1996) 16 Legal Studies 84.

Coleman J and Hendry L, *The Nature of Adolescence* (1999) Routledge.

de Winter M, *Children as Fellow Citizens: Participation and Commitment* (1997) Radcliffe Medical Press Ltd.

Douglas G, 'The Retreat from Gillick' (1992) 55 Modern Law Review 569.

Department of Health, *Focus on Teenagers: Research into Practice* (1996) HMSO.

Eekelaar J, 'White Coats or Flak Jackets? Doctors, Children and the Courts – Again' (1993) 109 Law Quarterly Review 182.

Erikson E, *Identity, Youth and Crisis* (1968) Norton.

Farson R, *Birthrights* (1974) Collier Macmillan.

Fortin J ,'Children's rights and the use of physical force' (2001) 13 Child and Family Law Quarterly 243.

Franklin B, *The Rights of Children* (1986) Blackwells.

Franklin B , 'Votes for Children' (1992) 85 Childright 10.

Franklin B, 'The case for children's rights' in B Franklin (ed) *The Handbook of Children's Rights: Comparative Policy and Practice* (1995) Routledge.

Freeman M, 'The Limits of Children's Rights' in M Freeman and P Veerman (eds) *The Ideologies of Children's Rights* (1992) Martinus Nijhoff Publishers.

Freeman M, 'Removing rights from adolescents' (1993) 17 Adoption and Fostering.

Graham J and Bowling B, *Young People and Crime* Home Office Research Study 145 (1995) Home Office.

Gullotta T et al, *The Adolescent Experience* (2000) Academic Press.

Harris J, 'The political status of children' in K Graham (ed) *Contemporary Political Philosophy* (1982) Cambridge University Press.

Harris J, *'The Value of Life: An introduction to medical ethics* (1985) Routledge and Kegan Paul.

Holt J, *Escape from Childhood: The Needs and Rights of Children* (1974) E P Dutton and Co Ltd.

Hughes J, 'Thinking about Children' in G Scarre (ed) *Children, Parents and Politics* (1989) Cambridge University Press.

Kaser-Boyd N et al, 'Minors' ability to identify risks and benefits of therapy' (1985) 16 Professional Psychology 411.

Langford W et al, *Family understandings: closeness, authority and independence in families with teenagers* (2001) Joseph Rowntree Foundation.

Law Commission, *Family Law Review of Child Law, Guardianship and Custody* Law Com No 172 HC 594 (1988) HMSO.

Lindley R, 'Teenagers and Other Children' in G Scarre (ed) *Children, Parents and Politics* (1989) Cambridge University Press.

Lowe N and Juss S, 'Medical Treatment – Pragmatism and the Search for Principle' (1993) 56 Modern Law Review 865.

MacCormick N, *Legal Right and Social Democracy: Essays in Legal and Political Philosophy* (1982) Clarendon Press.

Mann L et al, 'Adolescent decision-making: the development of competence' (1989) 12 Journal of Adolescence 265.

Masson J, 'Re W: appealing from the golden cage' (1993) 5 Journal of Child Law 37.

Millstein S, 'Perceptual, Attributional, and Affective Processes in Perceptions of Vulnerability Through the Life Span' in N Bell and R Bell (eds) *Adolescent Risk Taking* (1993) Sage Publications.

Montgomery J, 'Parents and children in dispute: who has the final word?' (1992) 4 Journal of Child Law 85.

Piaget J, *The Language and Thought of the Child* (1924) Routledge.

Rutter M and Rutter M, *Developing Minds: Challenge and Continuity across the Life Span* (1993) Penguin.

Scottish Law Commission, *Report on Family Law* Scot Law Com No 135 (1992) HMSO.

Solberg A, 'Negotiating Childhood: Changing Constructions of Age for Norwegian Children' in A James and A Prout (eds) *Constructing and Reconstructing Childhood: Contemporary Issues in the Sociological Study of Childhood* (1990) Falmer Press.

Taylor L et al, 'Attitudes toward involving minors in decisions' (1984) 15 Professional Psychology: Research and Practice 436.

Taylor L et al, 'Minors' attitudes and competence toward participation in psycho-educational decisions' (1985) 16 Professional Psychology: Research and Practice 226.

Youth at risk? (2002) Communities that Care.

Chapter 4

Child runaways, emancipation and rights to support

(1) INTRODUCTION

One of the most emphatic ways in which children can assert their right to take responsibility for their own lives is by running away from home. This is a drastic step. Most children, particularly teenagers, sometimes find their parents' ideas outdated and their attempts to discipline them tedious. In turn, parents may be reluctant to allow their offspring greater independence before they consider them ready to cope with it. Nevertheless, in well-functioning families, negotiation and compromise will ensure that both 'sides' emerge relatively unscathed. Sadly, increasing numbers of children find life at home so unbearable that they vote with their feet and leave. The law presents them with a contradictory set of principles. There is confusion over whether they have the right to leave home at all, at what age they may do so, what rights they have on leaving and what rights their parents have to force their return.

The numbers of children running away from home are far greater than can be accurately estimated.[1] The research undertaken by the charities providing homeless children with assistance shows that they leave for a variety of reasons:[2] to escape physical, mental or sexual abuse, including inter-parental violence;[3] disputes with step-parents;[4] unhappiness in residential or foster care;[5] problems at school, including

---

1 But research indicates that as many as 11% teenagers under the age of 16 run away for one night or more on more than one occasion and that around 77,000 young people run away for the first time each year. See Safe on the Streets Research Team (1999) p 38. Similarly, 46% of homeless young people surveyed by Centrepoint had run away from home before they were 16: Centrepoint (2001 a).

2 Much of this research is summarised in Social Exclusion Unit (hereafter SEU) (2002) chs 1 and 2.

3 See, inter alia: Safe on the Streets Research Team (1999) pp 57–58 and pp 109–112; J Smith et al (1998) pp 30–31. 25% of this sample of homeless young people had suffered abuse before leaving. Similarly, of the runaways surveyed by Centrepoint, 25% gave physical violence as the reason for leaving: Centrepoint (2001 a).

4 21% of the young people surveyed living in step-families ran away, compared with 7% of children living in families with two birth parents. See Safe on the Streets Research Team (1999) p 51. See also pp 54–55 and 135. This trend is confirmed by other research, eg J Smith et al (1998) pp 26–28 and 32.

5 45% of young people currently living in foster or residential care are likely to run away, compared with only 9.5% of children living in families. See Safe on the Streets Research Team (1999) p 60. See also G Newiss (1999) p 5.

bullying and exclusions.[6] Surprisingly large numbers are quite simply told by their parents or step-parents to leave, or they feel forced to go.[7] Many teenagers leave home with nowhere to go and either end up sleeping rough or in unsafe accommodation.[8]

Although, outwardly, children who leave home demonstrate their capacity for independence, the fact that they do so does not necessarily indicate that they are sufficiently mature to look after themselves. Indeed, they are often at their most vulnerable and need considerable support. Despite the apparent liberality of the House of Lords' decision in *Gillick v West Norfolk and Wisbech Area Health Authority,*[9] the legal principles and policies governing children who leave home are quite inappropriate for a group of young people who often feel obliged to leave home. Official policy appears to have changed very little since the time, well over a decade ago, when it was stated in the House of Commons: 'Many of these people [the homeless] are children, and our first advice to them is, therefore, to go back to their parents.'[10] Such an attitude ignores the impact on young people of a rising divorce rate, family disruption and step-parenting.[11] It also absolves the government of an obligation to make adequate state provision for those children who, for a variety of reasons, consider it quite impossible to return home.

Admittedly, the current government has recognised that tackling the problems of young people requires a new approach, particularly regarding those with multiple disadvantages – the groups of 'socially excluded' young people, who through a combination of poverty, family conflict, poor educational opportunities and poor services, 'find themselves apparently destined for a life of underachievement and social exclusion'.[12] Various groups of young people, including young runaways,[13] have attracted the attention of the Social Exclusion Unit (SEU), whose reports have produced a range of valuable recommendations and initiatives.[14] Nevertheless, many policies, including the whole emphasis of the benefits system and the governments' initiatives on youth unemployment[15] remain firmly focused on relieving the hardships of young people between the ages of 18 and 25, rather than on those under that age. Indeed, there apparently remains a widely held official conviction, reflected by much of the law, that children under the age of 18 should be living at home and that, if they

6   Between 8–10% of children under 16 mentioned school-related issues as having contributed to their running away: Safe on the Streets Research Team (1999) p 48. See also: N Biehal et al (2000) esp ch 4; J Smith et al (1998) pp 40–41; SEU (1998) ch 1.
7   Research suggests that 19% of those children who run away overnight are forced to leave home and that around 14,000 young people in each school year cohort are forced to leave before the age of 16: Safe on the Streets Research Team (1999) pp 37–39, 41–45 and 114. See also figures indicating that 86% of homeless 16- and 17-year-olds leave home due to reasons beyond their control, such as eviction, physical violence, family conflicts. Centrepoint (2000).
8   See discussion below.
9   [1986] AC 116.
10   Michael Spicer, former housing minister, HC Deb Oral Answers, 24 January 1990, vol 165, col 881.
11   J Smith et al (1998) esp p 48.
12   Paul Boateng, SEU (2000) Foreword, p 1. The concept of 'social exclusion' is discussed in more detail in chapter 19.
13   SEU (2002).
14   Eg the Connexions service, aimed at keeping teenagers in school or training, was influenced by the SEU's report, SEU (1999 a), discussed in more detail in chapter 6.
15   Eg the 'New Deal for Young People' designed for those aged between 18 and 24.

are not, they only have themselves to blame. The following chapter considers the inconsistencies in the law and the extent to which it could be improved.

(2)   LEGAL AGE LIMITS AND LEGAL CONFUSION

The law reflects a sense of deep confusion regarding the point at which children should be allowed to take full responsibility for their activities. Some of the legislation governing what children can do, and when, broadly correlates with the research material regarding their cognitive abilities,[16] by making certain important freedoms available at the age of 16. Sixteen-year-olds are not only free to leave school and take full-time work, they may also consent to surgical, medical or dental treatment,[17] marry with the consent of their parents and consent to sexual intercourse.[18] But despite these freedoms, the Family Law Reform Act 1969, section 1 bars teenagers under the age of 18 from full legal 'emancipation'. As Bainham has pointed out, between the ages of 16 and 18, young people 'exist in a legal "Twilight Zone" between minority and adulthood'.[19] There are formal legal barriers which exclude them from voting, standing for Parliament, being a school governor, acquiring a legal estate in land or making a will. More fundamentally, as discussed below, those contemplating leaving home will find that there are further severe legal restrictions on their financial independence. They can claim only very limited social security benefits, and, with the exception of contracts for the supply of 'necessaries' and beneficial contracts of service, they cannot enter into any legally binding contract.[20]

   Meanwhile, no clear policy is discernable in the law governing teenagers aged between 16 and 18 seeking employment. By and large it treats them like adults, requiring them to pay national insurance contributions and taxes. But even at 16, they are far more vulnerable than adult employees and the Council of Europe is gradually forcing the British government to introduce further protective restrictions to take account of this age group's continuing need for employment protection.[21] Nevertheless, and despite international criticism,[22] 16-year-old employees are excluded from the protection of the minimum wage legislation. They neither gain the

---

16   See discussion in chapter 3.

17   See Family Law Reform Act 1969, s 8(1), discussed in more detail in chapter 5.

18   The Sexual Offences (Amendment) Act 2000 ensured that homosexual males finally acquired sexual parity with their heterosexual male and lesbian female counterparts. This legislation addressed the view of the European Commission of Human Rights in *Sutherland v United Kingdom* (1997) 24 EHRR CD 22 that English law, by fixing the age of 18 as the minimum age for lawful homosexual activities, rather than 16, infringed homosexuals' rights under arts 8 and 14 of the ECHR.

19   A Bainham (1988) p 63.

20   See discussion below.

21   See European Council Directive on the Protection of Young People at Work (94/33/EC), which requires strict regulation and protection of work done by 'adolescents' (those between minimum school leaving age and 18). See also the Health and Safety (Young Persons) Regulations 1997, SI 1997/135, which require employers to make a risk assessment of certain types of employment for employees between the ages of 16 and 18.

22   The UN Committee on Economic, Social and Cultural Rights criticised both the low level of the UK's national minimum wage and its failure to extend minimum wage protection to workers under the age of 18. The Committee considered the minimum wage scheme 'discriminatory on the basis of age', for protecting the younger age group at a lower rate. See Committee on Economic, Social and Cultural Rights (2002) paras 15 and 33. See also Committee on the Rights of the Child (2002) paras 53 and 54.

protection of the standard rate national minimum wage,[23] nor the lower rate, which applies to 18 to 21-year-olds.[24] Although the absence of any statutory minimum wage for employees aged between 16 and 18 does not necessarily imply an official indifference to their working conditions, it does leave this group vulnerable to exploitation at an age when they may find it extremely difficult to stand up to their employers.[25] The hourly wages that working children of all ages receive clearly indicate that they are not receiving the protection of article 32 of the CRC – namely freedom from economic exploitation.[26]

For teenagers under 16, a series of legislative provisions have, over the years, thrown up a collection of arbitrary age limits governing a range of activities, such as purchasing pets and liqueur chocolates.[27] These are more a source of amusement than of any practical utility. There is certainly little logical rationale for the age differences, the simple explanation for this legislative hotchpotch being that the qualifying ages were adopted on an ad hoc and piecemeal basis. Of more practical significance are the provisions of the criminal law making the age of 16 govern the point at which adolescents can agree to sexual intercourse[28] and of education law making full-time education compulsory for children under the age of 16.[29] Until they attain that age, they cannot gain financial independence by taking full-time employment. Unfortunately, the well-intentioned regulations designed to implement the Council of Europe's requirements[30] protecting children from being employed for over-long hours and in unsuitable conditions,[31] ensure that even fewer prospective employers than before understand the complicated laws limiting the part-time work of children under the age of 16. These now differ considerably, depending on a child's precise age and the type of work he or she is undertaking.[32] The confusing nature of the provisions restricting the hours and days of the week on which young people below 16 may work[33] enables them to be widely flouted,[34] not only by

23 Under the National Minimum Wage Act 1998, implemented on 1 April 1999, there is a general minimum wage level of £4.10 per hour for adults over 22 (as from October 2002).

24 The minimum level of wages for 18–21-year-olds is £3.50 per hour (as from October 2002). The UK's scheme compares most unfavourably with countries like The Netherlands, where 16-year-olds are included in protective wage scales.

25 See M Rahman et al (2000) p 43. These figures indicated that, in 2000, nearly one third of all young people aged between 16 and 24 years in employment were being paid less than half the male median hourly income.

26 See J Shropshire and S Middleton (1999) p 16 and Committee on the Rights of the Child (2002) para 53.

27 See C Hamilton and A Fiddy (2002).

28 See *R v K* [2001] UKHL 41, [2001] 3 All ER 897, per Lord Millett, who (at [44]) clearly considers that the age of 16 is far too high.

29 Discussed in more detail in chapter 6.

30 European Council Directive on the Protection of Young People at Work (94/33/EC).

31 Children (Protection at Work) Regulations 1998, SI 1998/276 and Children (Protection at Work) Regulations 2000, SI 2000/1333 and the Children (Protection at Work) (No 2) Regulations 2000, SI 2000/2548.

32 See Children and Young Persons Act 1933, s 18 (as amended), which regulates children's part-time work, regarding the hours they can work and the type of work they can undertake, depending on whether they are aged 13, 14 or 15.

33 Children and Young Persons Act 1933, ss 18–21 (as amended by the Children (Protection at Work) Regulations 1998–2000) *broadly* prohibit employers from employing children under 14 at all (unless employed by a parent or guardian in specified light work). Those between 14 and 16 cannot be employed before 7 am and after 7 pm on any day and on school days, they can only be employed for a maximum of two hours after the end of school. These provisions are all subject to the provisions of local byelaws, themselves amended to comply with EC Directive 94/33/EC.

34 Surprisingly high numbers of children (10% of 11–12-year-olds and 37% of 13-year-olds) work in excess of seven hours per week. See J Shropshire and S Middleton (1999) pp 13–16.

employers, but by local authorities who are responsible for their enforcement.[35] This is regrettable, since they are intended to protect the younger child's ability to attend school and do homework.

All activities not specifically covered by legislation are governed by the House of Lords' decision in *Gillick*.[36] Their Lordships rejected the proposition that fixed age limits could ever be a satisfactory method of determining a child's legal competence. For otherwise, Lord Scarman declared, the price would be 'artificiality and a lack of realism'.[37] In his view, the child has a right to make his own decisions, 'when he reaches a sufficient understanding and intelligence to be capable of making up his own mind on the matter requiring decision'.[38] Although liberal, such an approach fails to clarify a body of law fast lapsing into incoherence. On the one hand there is the variety of inflexible age limits, below which there is no capacity and above which there is total freedom to perform the activity in question. On the other hand, the *Gillick* principle superimposes further uncertainty, with capacity depending entirely on the individual circumstances of each case.

Greater clarity would undoubtedly be achieved by lowering the age of majority to 16 years. But despite the logical attraction of such a change, the existence of methods by which children over that age can be protected from danger up to the age of 18 justifies leaving the law as it is. A care order, once made, will endure until a child attains that age[39] and the High Court's inherent jurisdiction is available for providing protection regarding any child below that age. These are important safeguards which should not be jettisoned. A partial change in the law would, however, promote the enlightened approach adopted by the House of Lords in *Gillick*.[40] This would be to extend the right to vote in local and national elections to 16-year-olds. At 16, teenagers have as much ability to reach sensible decisions over the way their own country is run as the majority of adults. After all, if they are old enough to work full-time and pay taxes, they should be entitled to have some influence over which political party is to govern them.

(3)   LEGAL RIGHTS TO LEAVE HOME

'When can I leave home?' This is one of the most common questions the children's advice centres are asked by young people.[41] Unfortunately, there is no simple answer. It depends on two further questions: do their parents have a legal right to stop them leaving in the first place and can their parents force them to return home if they do leave?[42] In relation to the first question, there has always existed a principle of common law that parents have a power to control the person and property of their children, as long as such a right is exercised in accordance with the welfare principle. But, as Lord Scarman pointed out in *Gillick*,[43] the parental 'right or power' exists, but

---

35   For a more detailed assessment of the law governing children's employment, see A Bainham (1998) pp 530–535. See also B Pettitt (1998).
36   [1986] AC 112.
37   [1986] AC 112 at 186.
38   [1986] AC 112. Discussed in more detail in chapter 3.
39   See Children Act 1989, s 91(12). See also s 31(3): a care order can be made regarding a teenager up to the age of 17.
40   [1986] AC 112.
41   See C Hamilton (2002) p 40.
42   Discussed by J Fortin (2001) pp 247–250.
43   *Gillick v West Norfolk and Wisbech Area Health Authority* [1986] AC 112.

only does so 'primarily to enable the parent to discharge his duty of maintenance, protection, and education until he reaches such an age as to be able to look after himself and make his own decisions'.[44] His words also suggested that parents are not entitled to prevent a teenage son or daughter leaving home if they consider that he or she has reached 'a sufficient understanding and intelligence to be capable of making up his own mind on the matter requiring decision'.[45] But, of course, the point at which an adolescent reaches such an age is unclear. In any event, parents might be reluctant to acknowledge that their offspring had reached such maturity.

At first sight, one might have assumed that teenagers faced by authoritarian parents seeking to prevent their leaving would gain assistance from article 5 of the ECHR.[46] It appears to provide children with protection against deprivation of liberty. Nevertheless, the decision of the European Court of Human Rights in *Nielsen v Denmark*[47] creates confusion, since it suggests that all parental decisions reached for 'a proper purpose' over how their children spend their time are protected by article 8 and are therefore completely outside the ambit of article 5 of the ECHR.[48] The European Court did not clarify what they meant by such a phrase. Indeed, its failure to grasp the nettle and delineate more clearly what parental behaviour is authorised by article 8 left the Strasbourg jurisprudence in an unsatisfactory state.

The obiter remarks of Judge LJ and Dame Elizabeth Butler-Sloss P in *Re K (secure accommodation order: right to liberty)*[49] suggest that the domestic courts may withdraw article 8 protection from parents who behave in an outrageously over-authoritarian manner. But, as discussed earlier, their own approach needs clarification.[50] Judge LJ thought he could easily distinguish between parents disciplining their children 'as necessary and appropriate' and parents behaving in a cruel or abusive way.[51] Similarly, Dame Elizabeth Butler-Sloss P considered that a court's response should depend on whether the parent's actions were 'within ordinary acceptable parental restrictions upon the movements of a child'.[52] Rather surprisingly, she also considered that 'It might be permissible' for a parent to detain a child 'for a few days'.[53] One would have thought that 'ordinary acceptable parental restrictions' would exclude restricting the liberty of an older child for more than a few *hours*, or even over night. Fortunately, neither she nor Judge LJ considered that a parent would ever be able to justify restricting the liberty of a child for *more* than a few days.[54] On such an interpretation, even boosted by the decision in *Nielsen,* parents today might find it difficult to justify preventing, for more than a few days, a teenager from leaving home.

Once the teenager leaves the premises, the law remains confused over whether the parent can force him or her to return. The criminal law has, like the civil law, maintained

44   [1986] AC 112 at 185.
45   [1986] AC 112 at 186.
46   Art 8 might also assist, protecting the child's private life and physical integrity.
47   (1988) 11 EHRR 175.
48   (1988) 11 EHRR 175 (para 69). Discussed in more detail in chapter 3, pp 81–82.
49   [2001] 1 FLR 526.
50   See chapter 3.
51   [2001] 1 FLR 526 (para 99).
52   [2001] 1 FLR 526 (para 28).
53   [2001] 1 FLR 526 (para 29).
54   [2001] 1 FLR 526, per Butler-Sloss LJ (para 29) and per Judge LJ (para 101). Thorpe LJ (para 61) controversially appeared to consider that 'the deprivation of liberty was a necessary consequence of an exercise of parental responsibility for the protection and promotion of his welfare', and that therefore a parent has the authority to deprive a child of his or her liberty for longer than 72 hours, if necessary.

a disapproving attitude towards parents who attempt to enforce their right to control their children by force.[55] Such an approach is consistent with the eighteenth- and nineteenth-century case law when the courts refused to issue writs of habeas corpus ordering children to return home against their will once they had attained the age of discretion – 14 for boys and 16 for girls.[56] But there is no real clarity over the point at which parental behaviour changes from being a reasonable form of discipline to abusive behaviour amounting to false imprisonment.[57]

Whilst it is arguable that a teenager could claim the protection of the ECHR, there is little case law supporting such an approach. Indeed, the European Commission has responded inconsistently to runaway teenagers. As noted earlier,[58] the European Commission of Human Rights rejected the claim of a 14-year-old Dutch runaway that her rights under article 8 had been infringed by the actions taken by the welfare authorities to return her home. Any infringement of her rights was justified by their need to protect her health and morals under article 8(2).[59] But in a later decision, the European Commission rejected the parents' arguments that by refusing to force their 14-year-old daughter to return home against her will, the Danish welfare authorities had infringed their own rights under article 8.[60] Hopefully a domestic court would favour an adolescent's own right to respect for his or her private life under article 8, free from parental interference and to freedom from restraint under article 5.

The law's failure to clarify when teenagers acquire the right to legal independence from their parents may have contributed to a climate in which some parents even feel entitled to force their teenager daughters to marry against their will.[61] Indeed, the common law's lack of clarity probably explains why children are given such ambivalent advice about their right to leave home against their parents' wishes. This varies according to whether they are over or under the age of 16. Once over that age they may gain the false impression that parental responsibility has terminated and that they are legally 'emancipated' and can behave as adults. Nevertheless, it is quite incorrect to give teenagers such advice – the law is clear that they do not attain full legal independence until their 18th birthday. Until then parents retain parental responsibility and the adolescent, as a legal minor, is subject to all the confusing legal incapacities affecting his or her ability to follow an independent existence. Despite this, attaining the age of 16 does have considerable legal significance, so far

---

55   Eg *R v D* [1984] 2 All ER 449: the House of Lords confirmed that a parent could be charged with the common law offence of kidnapping if he 'stole and carried away' a child against that child's consent.

56   See Lord Scarman's summary of this old case law in *Gillick v West Norfolk and Wisbech Area Health Authority* [1986] AC 112 at 187–188. See also *Krishnan v London Borough of Sutton* [1970] Ch 181 for a contemporary version of the age of discretion cases. There the court refused to order the local authority to require a girl of nearly 18 to return to her father against her will, since, in practical terms, such an order could not be enforced.

57   Eg in *R v Rahman* (1985) 81 Cr App Rep 349, Lord Lane CJ disapproved of a father who had bundled his teenage daughter into a car against her will in order to return her to Bangladesh. Such behaviour could amount to false imprisonment if, as in this case, it was outside the realms of reasonable parental discipline. But such a qualification creates further uncertainty: what is 'reasonable parental discipline'? See discussion in chapter 9.

58   Discussed in chapter 2, pp 55–56.

59   *X v Netherlands* (Application No 6753/74) (1975–76) 1-3 DR 118.

60   *X v Denmark* (Application No 6854/74) (1977–78) 7-9 DR 81.

61   Eg *Re KR (a child) (abduction: forcible removal by parents)* [1999] 4 All ER 954.

as leaving home is concerned. The criminal provisions on 'harbouring'[62] and regarding a parent's duty not to neglect a child,[63] including the sanctions against failing to provide him or her with adequate food, clothing, medical aid or lodging,[64] drop away for children aged 16. Indeed, it appears that, for these reasons, some parents regard 16 as the point at which they can reasonably 'kick out' their offspring if they are causing trouble in the home.[65]

Conversely, parents who wish to persuade their teenagers over the age of 16 to return home will have an uphill battle. The courts have no general power to make any section 8 orders regarding children over 16.[66] Such a restriction reflects the realistic view that it is normally pointless for courts to make residence orders contrary to the wishes of teenagers over 16.[67] It is also unlikely that parents can force a 16-year-old to return home by involving the local authority. If the local authority considers him or her to be suffering significant harm, they can apply for a care order,[68] but it is unlikely they would contemplate seeking such an order against the wishes of an 'elderly' teenager, unless exceptional circumstances existed.[69] On the other hand, a child over the age of 16 who is opposed to returning home, might avoid doing so by persuading the local authority to provide him or her with accommodation, as the local authority is entitled to do,[70] even against his or her parents' wishes. That child's parents would then have no right to remove him or her from such accommodation.[71]

Large numbers of children who run away from home are under the age of 16.[72] Many children leave for very good reasons, such as abusive treatment.[73] But although returning such children to the source of their unhappiness solves nothing, the child care agencies often consider that they have very little alternative when dealing with these younger runaways. Indeed, the provisions of criminal law and those contained in the Children Act 1989 reflect a view of family life which is radically out of step with the reality experienced by many. In practice, due to family disruption and reconstitution, these children are often asked to leave or feel forced to do so. But the principles of the civil and criminal law implicitly assume that those assisting child runaways are breaking up happy family units – a situation which can be simply solved by the child's rapid return. The law therefore produces an immediate response from those dealing with this younger group, which is to advise them to return home.

Children's aid agencies advising runaways under the age of 16 are principally deterred from assisting them by the criminal law on 'harbouring'. The scope of section 2

---

62 Child Abduction Act 1984, s 2; see discussion below.
63 Children and Young Persons Act 1933, s 1(1).
64 Children and Young Persons Act 1933, s 1(2)(a).
65 J Smith et al (1998) p 48.
66 Unless the circumstances are exceptional, see Children Act 1989, s 9(6) and (7), or unless the order is in favour of a third party and the court so directs. See Children Act 1989, s 12(5), as inserted by Adoption and Children Act 2002, s 114.
67 Law Commission (1988) para 3.25.
68 Children Act 1989, s 31(3).
69 Eg *Re V (care or supervision order)* [1996] 1 FLR 776. Discussed in chapter 12.
70 See Children Act 1989, s 20(3), discussed further below.
71 Children Act 1989, s 20(11). See also *Krishnan v London Borough of Sutton* [1970] Ch 181.
72 See figures referred to above, in Introduction.
73 See discussion above.

of the Child Abduction Act 1984[74] is extremely wide. This provision, which replaces the old legislation relating to child-stealing, ensures that providing a child under the age of 16 with advice or assistance over running away from home could theoretically amount to an offence under the 1984 Act. Case law certainly bears out arguments favouring a broad interpretation.[75] But, as Bainham points out, it is questionable whether charges could lie against an adult who has provided a *Gillick* competent child with assistance over leaving home, since it would be impossible to argue that it had been offered 'without lawful authority or reasonable excuse'.[76] Furthermore, it is claimed that since this offence hinges on intention, a prosecution is unlikely to succeed if the adult has merely responded to a teenager's plea for support, rather than actively encouraging the teenager to run away.[77] Whatever its real scope, the 1984 Act has produced a situation in which child runaways under the age of 16 come under considerable pressure from aid workers and the police to return home,[78] often without any follow-up support to sort out the problems they ran from.[79] It was hoped, following implementation of the Children Act 1989, that as a last resort, runaways under the age of 16 could avoid being returned home by seeking accommodation at a 'child refuge'. A range of these were to be run by voluntary organisations who obtained authority to provide specialised assistance for child runaways under section 51 of the Children Act 1989.[80] Exempted from the harbouring laws, they are authorised to provide children with a place in a refuge if it appears that they are at risk of harm if not taken in.[81] Although immensely valuable, these establishments proved expensive and difficult to maintain.[82]

Very often the police simply return the child home, without matters being taken any further or the real reasons for their leaving being discovered.[83] Some children are

74   Child Abduction Act 1984, s 2(1) provides that a person unconnected with the child (ie not a parent or guardian) commits an offence – 'if, without lawful authority or reasonable excuse, he takes or detains a child under the age of 16—(a) so as to remove him from the lawful control of any person having lawful control of the child; or (b) so as to keep him out of the lawful control of any person entitled to lawful control of the child.'
       S 2(3) provides a statutory defence in the event of the person charged showing that he believed the child to have attained the age of 16 or in the case of a non-marital child, that he reasonably believed himself to the child's father.
       See also the Children Act 1989, s 49 which creates an offence for any person knowingly and without lawful authority or reasonable excuse, to take away and keep children or induce or incite them to stay away from those responsible for their care under a care or emergency protection order, or police protection.
75   Eg *R v Leather* [1993] 2 FLR 770: on separate occasions, the appellant persuaded small numbers of unsupervised children to leave activities authorised by their parents, to accompany him to places they had previously visited with their parents, but without parental consent. The appellant had not attempted to touch the children and they had felt free to leave him at any time. The Court of Appeal dismissed his appeal against conviction under the Child Abduction Act 1984, s 2.
76   See A Bainham (1994) p 129.
77   See C Hamilton (2002) p 41.
78   Safe on the Streets Research Team (1999) pp 9–10.
79   SEU (2002) para 6.5.
80   See G Brown and M Elks (1994) p 22. See also M Stein et al (1994) esp section Two.
81   A child can only stay for a maximum of 14 days. See the Refuges (Children's Homes and Foster Placement) Regulations 1991, SI 1991/1507.
82   See SEU (2002) paras 5.30–5.35. Regretting that only one children's refuge remains in being, the SEU calls for more community-based services of this kind.
83   G Newiss (1999) suggests (p 21) that 'welfare interviews' with missing persons being returned home 'may often amount to little more than a "word in the back of the car"'. Furthermore, these interviews often take place in the presence of the child's parents, in which case the child may be reluctant to disclose the cause of his or her unhappiness. See also SEU (2002) paras 6.10–6.13.

formally removed from the streets into police protection,[84] but the police are then unable to hold them under these provisions for more than 72 hours, and must inform the local authority and the child's parents of the steps taken.[85] In general terms, social services departments may show more concern over young people who go missing from local authority care, than over those who leave their own families.[86] Indeed, as the SEU observes, the latter type of runaway normally receives no support at all from departments of social services.[87] This inactivity partly reflects the legal principles governing child protection procedures. A local authority can respond to a child's reluctance to return home by investigating his or her home circumstances,[88] but would normally undertake such an investigation only if it appeared that very severe family problems existed, such as sexual and/or physical abuse. Many children are reluctant for this to happen, but in any event, they can then only remain away if there is sufficient evidence of parental ill-treatment to justify the local authority applying for a care order or emergency protection order,[89] or for the police to intervene. Even then, until the local authority acquires an order authorising them to care for the child, they are under no duty to accommodate him or her unless the child is orphaned, lost or abandoned, or his or her present carers are prevented from doing so themselves.[90] More to the point, they are powerless to do so against his or her parents' wishes.[91] Research indicates that local authorities are, in any case, reluctant to accommodate young people in all but the most extreme circumstances, even when parents of troublesome children indicate their intention of turning them out of the house.[92] This response is apparently often linked to a fear that 'accommodating a runaway, even for a short period of time, may lead to them having to take on longer-term responsibilities towards that young person'.[93] Indeed, the SEU observes that since young runaways do not clearly fall under the responsibility of any one organisation, they are currently falling through the gaps.[94]

Given the high numbers of children running away from home and the reasons for this happening, it is regrettable that the law constrains those providing them with assistance. It fails to acknowledge that even in the absence of serious abuse, a child may be so unhappy at home that if returned, he or she will simply run away again. Research indicates that although children may have very good reasons for not wanting to return home, if they come into contact with police officers or social workers, they may be forced to do so, with the inevitable result that there is a small group of children who run away from home or foster care on numerous occasions.[95] Nevertheless, being returned home or told to return may very easily increase such

84   Children Act 1989, s 46.
85   Children Act 1989, s 46(3)(a) and (4)(a).
86   G Newiss (1999) p 7.
87   SEU (2002) para 5.45.
88   Under the Children Act 1989, s 47(1). Discussed in more detail in chapter 16.
89   Children Act 1989, s 31 or s 44.
90   Children Act 1989, s 20(1).
91   Children Act 1989, s 20(7). See also s 20(8): the child's parents may remove him or her from local authority accommodation at any time.
92   N Biehal (2000) pp 27–28.
93   SEU (2002) para 5.45. Local authorities' reluctance to provide homeless teenagers with accommodation is discussed in more detail below.
94   SEU (2002) para 5.54.
95   Research indicates that 25% of the young people surveyed, under the age of 16, had run away twice, 12% had run away more than three times and 53% of these persistent runaways had started running away before the age of 11. See Safe on the Streets Research Team (1999) p 36.

children's feelings of despair and make it all the more likely that they will simply vote with their feet and take to the streets. Child runaways strongly resent this response, considering it quite inappropriate that they should be made to feel frightened of the police and social services, 'as if running away is a crime'.[96] Furthermore, a policy of automatic return avoids greater attention being given to investigating the reasons for the children leaving in the first place.

There is clearly a need for far greater liaison between the police and social services departments in cases of this kind.[97] Although, in some areas, the two agencies have developed joint protocols for dealing with runaways, these appear to be almost solely in the context of children going missing from local authority care.[98] Meanwhile, the legal provisions not only reflect notions of parental autonomy but also conveniently dovetail with current policies assuming that parents will happily take responsibility for their teenage children's financial support until they reach their early twenties.[99] Whilst in reality increasing numbers of children are leaving home or being forced to leave home at earlier ages, the law still reflects the view that home life is a haven and so provides little support for those who may justifiably wish to leave.

(4)   LEAVING HOME – STATE ASSISTANCE WITH FINANCIAL SUPPORT

The list of rights contained in the CRC reflects the view that it is not enough to identify certain liberties essential to a child's capacity for eventual autonomy, such as freedom of speech. These are of no value to those too poor or ill to benefit from them, particularly if their time is taken up surviving from day to day. These rights must therefore be complemented by more positive action on the part of the state to enable children to enjoy fully their basic liberties.[100] Articles 26 and 27 are consistent with this approach. Article 26 reserves the right of every child 'to benefit from social security, including social insurance' and article 27(1) states that governments should 'recognise the right of every child to a standard of living adequate for the child's physical, mental, spiritual, moral and social development'. The principles of English law fail to match up to both these international obligations when dealing with children who leave home.

Young people who leave their homes before attaining adulthood quickly discover that although the law may recognise their rights to express their views and to reach certain decisions, such rights may be of little value to them. Freedom from the restrictions of family life is often a bleak experience for those who have no correlative rights to financial help or accommodation. Homelessness and poverty combine to produce further practical difficulties, so that those without a home have no address and therefore no obvious credentials to offer prospective employers.[101] Teenagers who leave home hurriedly may have no formal identification documents with which to satisfy the demands of the benefit system. Those who are still under the age of 16 will find it particularly difficult to survive with no legal means of support. They should be in full-time school and so are not entitled to take full-time employment. They have no right to welfare benefits and are not entitled to work-based training

---

96   Safe on the Streets Research Team (1999) p 166.
97   See M Custerson (1997) p 19.
98   SEU (2002) paras 5.14–5.21.
99   See discussion below.
100   See discussion in chapter 2.
101   G Randall and S Brown (1999) p 17.

places. If they are determined to stay away from home and the local authority fails to assist them, they will have no alternative but to find friends and relatives to care for them, or take to the streets. Independent living, even for children over 16, often amounts to a struggle to survive. For many, the legal disqualifications which make them broadly incapable of entering into a legally binding contract, hold a legal estate in land, make a will, vote and marry without parental consent hold little practical relevance. Even if a teenager over 16 obtains employment,[102] the chances are that it will be far less well paid than adult work[103] and also less secure.[104] Statistics show rates of high unemployment,[105] homelessness[106] and poverty[107] for 16- and 17-year-olds living away from home. Indeed, some turn to theft, drugs[108] and/or prostitution[109] to survive.

Although the government has committed itself to improving the employment prospects of those who currently leave school at the age of 16,[110] many of the training opportunities are focused on those having attained the age of 18.[111] Official policy continues to categorise minors very differently, according to their situations. They are dependent children if living at home and in full-time education, in which case their parents are still entitled to child benefit. They are young adults if on training programmes, with their own training allowance. If unemployed and not in school they are neither.[112] Indeed, the benefits law continues to attract considerable criticism for the way that it discriminates against those under the age of 18, in so far as it clearly reflects government policy that children should live at home during their minority and those who refuse to do so are merely being perverse. It was the Social Security Act of 1986 which so controversially withdrew from most 16- and 17-year-olds entitlement to supplementary benefit, a prohibition maintained by successive governments since then.[113] The government assumes this age group either to be capable of supporting

102 See G Jones (2002), who notes (pp 7–8) that many of the jobs typically held by 16-year-old school leavers have reduced, with traditional craft apprenticeships for young men and clerical/secretarial jobs for young women being replaced by low paid, part-time sales occupations.
103 See discussion above.
104 See SEU (1999 a) paras 2.7–2.9.
105 Young people are far more likely to be unemployed than older people. In Spring 2001, 18% of economically active 16–17-year-old men (13% of women) were unemployed, compared with only 5% of men (2% of women) within 5 years of state pension age. The gap in rates between the highest and lowest age groups has increased over the last ten years. See Office for National Statistics (2002) p 80 and Table 4.20.
106 See research summarised in SEU (1999 a) para 6.15.
107 37% of the runaways surveyed who had left home under 16 had no income: Centrepoint (2001 a). In 1999, 23% of 16–18-year-olds not in education, training or work were living independently and, of those, only 15% were claiming benefit: see M Rahman et al (2000) p 44.
108 Drugs use by young people, and their involvement in crime to fund drug-taking, sometimes precipitates parents telling them to leave home. See J Smith et al (1998) pp 20–21. See also Safe on the Streets Research Team (1999) p 68.
109 Safe on the Streets Research Team (1999) pp 87 and 151. See also D Barrett (2000) p 32.
110 See the discussion of various government initiatives for this age group, such as the Connexions service, in chapter 6.
111 Eg the New Deal scheme, which relates only to those aged 18 and over. Nevertheless, 16- and 17-year-olds are guaranteed a training place through the 'Work-Based Training for Young People' scheme, which incorporates the 'Foundation Modern Apprenticeship' scheme. See B Chatrik (1999) Pt 2.
112 N Harris (1992) p 184.
113 Similar rules excluded this age group from claiming income support and jobseekers allowance, when supplementary benefit was replaced.

themselves through work or youth training or to be supported by their parents whilst remaining in full-time education. Accompanying these changes in benefits law was an undertaking to provide every young person with a place on a youth training scheme and payment of a training allowance if they decided not to stay on at school, or were unable to find a job.

The policy behind these changes was to persuade more young people to stay on at school or college to acquire better skills, to prevent a 'dependency culture' and to persuade families to support their children at home for longer.[114] Nevertheless, they caused immediate hardship,[115] increasing the obvious vulnerability of this group of teenagers. The removal of a general entitlement to benefits, combined with the inadequacy of successive youth training schemes[116] has led to considerable criticism over the years following this change. A continuing disincentive for young people to become involved in youth training schemes or to remain on them are the very low wages being provided. Many young people refer to the schemes as 'slave labour'.[117] Simply ensuring attendance on training courses, through the threat of benefit sanctions, is clearly not sufficient to encourage young people to 'engage productively with training'.[118] Nor did the withdrawal of income support from teenagers below the age of 18 have its desired effect, indeed, it merely led to an immediate and marked increase in youth homelessness.[119] The Committee on the Rights of the Child has noted that the rules preventing those aged 16 and 17 from claiming income support clearly contravenes the terms of the CRC.[120] In its response to the United Kingdom's first report on implementation of the Convention, the Committee suggested that the current benefits system may have contributed to the phenomenon of British children begging and sleeping on the streets.[121] Responding to the second, it urged the government to review its legislation and policies on benefits and social security allowances for 16- to 18-year-olds.[122] It has also emphasised its concern that the government is not fully implementing the Convention to the 'maximum extent of [its] available resources', as required by article 4, in order to provide benefits for unemployed school leavers.[123]

The hardship suffered by teenagers who leave home under the age of 18 has been exacerbated by the harsh and chaotic nature of the benefits system governing the 16- and 17-year-olds. A few remain entitled to income support, such as those still in education who are able to satisfy the Department of Work and Pensions that they are estranged from their parents.[124] But they are still paid a lower rate of benefit than

---

114   See R Horseman (1992) p 168.
115   See National Children's Homes (1993) p 3. Due to lack of money, one in three of young people living independently, in this survey, had eaten only one meal or no meals at all, during the previous 24 hours.
116   The Youth Training Scheme (YTS) has now been renamed 'Work-Based Training for Young People', encompassing the 'Foundation Modern Apprenticeships' scheme.
117   See, inter alia: J Smith et al (1998) p 42 and G Randall and S Brown (1999) p 24.
118   G Randall and S Brown (1999) p 25.
119   J McCluskey (1994) p 9ff.
120   See esp art 26.
121   Committee on the Rights of the Child (1995) para 15.
122   Committee on the Rights of the Child (2002) para 44.
123   Committee on the Rights of the Child (1995) paras 9 and 24. See also Committee on the Rights of the Child (2002) para 11.
124   Under the Income Support (General) Regulations 1987, SI 1987/1967, reg 42A and Sch 1B (as amended), claimants are, in exceptional circumstances, eligible for income support on the basis that they do not have to be available for work. These include, inter alia, if the claimant is a single parent, or pregnant, or is in full-time education but living away from home because of being estranged from his parents, or being in physical or moral danger, or

adults over the age of 25,[125] despite having precisely the same needs. Those claiming income support, on grounds of estrangement, or a discretionary severe hardship payment of jobseekers allowance from the job centre, face searching and sometimes, insensitive interviews,[126] carried out by complete strangers, about their personal lives.[127] Furthermore, the interrelationship between the various benefits is so confusing that young people often do not know what they are entitled to.[128] For this reason, those assisting homeless young people find that some young claimants never complete the process of claiming benefits and they conclude: 'For these, the young people in our society who are most at risk, social exclusion has already begun.'[129]

The SEU has criticised, increasingly vehemently, the benefits system's extreme anomalies and perversities, pointing out that money is paid through at least eight different routes by eight different agencies on behalf of two government departments.[130] Reaffirming its extreme dissatisfaction with the system it has stated:

'One of the most powerful messages that emerges from consulting young people is that the benefits system as it operates offers inadequate protection, particularly for those who have left home under 18. As described in the SEU's *Bridging the Gap* report, support for under-18s is delivered through a variety of benefits and allowances, administered by different agencies from different locations. The complexity of the system and the confusion over the terms and conditions prevent many young people getting the help they need.'[131]

This official acknowledgment that the present system of financial support for under 18-year-olds is unsatisfactory may lead to its reassessment.[132] The SEU has suggested, as a long-term objective, a complete overhaul of the wide range of benefits presently available, perhaps with the view of introducing a single youth allowance, as in Australia.[133] Root and branch reform is certainly long overdue.[134] One group of

at serious risk to his physical or mental health. Alternatively, unemployed young people aged 16 or 17 may, in certain circumstances, be eligible for jobseekers allowance on a temporary basis after leaving education if living away from home. Finally, 16–17-year-olds could qualify for discretionary severe hardship payments of jobseekers allowance under the Jobseekers Act 1995, s 16(1). These are usually paid on the grounds of homelessness or inadequate accommodation, parents' inability to support, lack of income or vulnerability. A 16- or 17-year-old who is in local authority care or who has left care since October 2001 will only be able to claim income support if a lone parent or if sick or disabled. See below.

125 The rates are also lower than those paid to the 18-plus age group.

126 SEU (2000) para 3.52.

127 Benefits agency staff may press for family or third party evidence of estrangement. See C Havell and I Nassor (1998) para 3.3. Similarly, the severe hardship interviewer will attempt to establish why the claimant is unable to live at home and will ask permission to contact his or her parents to confirm the reasons given. See B Chatrik (1999) pp 31–41, esp p 39.

128 SEU (2000) para 3.52. An extreme situation affects young people who are living independently when they leave school. Immediately after leaving school, if unemployed, they can claim income support; they may then qualify for job-seekers allowance during the 'child benefit extension period'; on its expiry, they may obtain a severe hardship payment. I am grateful to Gary Vaux, Head of Money Advice Unit, Herts County Council, for this example of three different payments, with three different qualifying criteria, applying to young people, within a period of four to five months, at a time in their lives when they are extremely vulnerable (personal communication).

129 C Havell and I Nassor (1998) para 3.4.

130 SEU (1999 a) paras 5.20–5.24.

131 SEU (2000) para 3.51.

132 SEU (1999 a) paras 5.19–5.24.

133 SEU (1999 a) para 9.4, Action 9. See also Annex F, which describes the working of the Australian Youth Allowance.

134 Reforms may emerge from a joint review of the systems of financial support for young people initiated in 2002 by the Department of Work and Pensions (DWP) and the Department for Education and Skills (DfES).

teenagers has already benefited from a more coherent approach to their financial support. Most 'looked after' children who are eligible for 'leaving care' support[135] have been removed from the present confusing benefits system altogether,[136] with all financial assistance being provided by social services departments, and none at all from the benefits system.[137]

Meanwhile, the key to higher wages for those 16- and 17-year-olds living independently from their parents is to obtain better qualifications. They will be entitled to the new Education Maintenance Allowance, if they can be persuaded to remain at school or college.[138] But it may require more than the provision of a relatively small weekly sum[139] to encourage homeless and unemployed young people to return to full-time school or take up training opportunities.

(5)   LEAVING HOME – ASSISTANCE WITH HOUSING

Many children who leave home are caught in a vicious spiral of no home, no address, no job prospects. The increasing homelessness of large numbers of children and young people continues to cause widespread problems.[140] Some homeless young people find accommodation with friends and relatives, but others inevitably end up living rough on the streets.[141] The Committee on the Rights of the Child has twice urged the government to improve its efforts to deal with the phenomenon of youth homelessness.[142]

Although the SEU's report on *Rough Sleeping*[143] did not pay special attention to the needs of young people, it led to various valuable initiatives on homelessness being introduced in the late 1990s.[144] Far more significantly, the homelessness legislation was finally strengthened, with the categories of priority need now including homeless 16- and 17-year-olds and care leavers aged between 18 and 21.[145] This

---

135 These obligations were introduced by the Children (Leaving Care) Act 2000, which amended the Children Act 1989, ss 22–24 and Sch 2, para 19, governing 'looked after children'.

136 But a 16- or 17-year-old who is in local authority care or who has left care since October 2001 will be able to claim income support if a lone parent or sick or disabled.

137 See Children (Leaving Care) Act 2000, s 6. Discussed below and in chapter 16.

138 Discussed in chapter 6.

139 Following piloting, the EMA will be introduced nationally from September 2004, paying a weekly sum (in addition to other welfare benefits) of up to £30 per week, plus a bonus.

140 Homelessness has increased significantly amongst young people since the 1970s. See research on this summarised in J Smith et al (1998) p 9.

141 The SEU maintains that very few homeless under the age of 18 are now amongst those who now sleep rough on the streets: SEU (1998) para 1.6. This, however, belies the experience of voluntary organisations assisting young homeless. See, inter alia: Safe on the Streets Research Team (1999), which (pp 92 and 149) reports that sleeping rough was resorted to by half those surveyed under 16 running away for the first time and over one third of 16- and 17-year-olds. It also indicates (p 92) that the homeless young people interviewed, aged under 16, resorted to sleeping on the streets, in derelict houses, bus and train stations, parks, back alleys and fields. Centrepoint's research indicates that 58% of the 16- and 17-year-olds surveyed had slept rough at some stage: see Centrepoint (2001 b).

142 See Committee on the Rights of the Child (1995) para 15 and (2002) para 44.

143 SEU (1998).

144 Eg in 1998 the Youth Homelessness Action Partnership (YHAP) was established under the auspices of the Department of the Environment, Transport and the Regions (DETR). See NCH Action for Children (1998) for a description of its organisation and programme, pp 99–100.

145 See Homelessness (Priority Need for Accommodation) (England) Order 2002, SI 2002/2051 and Office of the Deputy Prime Minister and Department of Health (2002) ch 8, esp paras 8.34–8.42. The guidance stresses (para 8.31) that there may be vulnerable and homeless

change ensures that housing authorities can no longer refuse to house homeless teenagers on the assumption that social services departments will eventually do so instead. It has the potential for dramatically reducing the number of homeless teenagers. Hopefully, the teenager who has left home and whose central problems revolve round money and homelessness, need no longer be involved in interdepartmental battles, being shuttled from social services department to housing and back again.[146] Young single homeless people, in the past, found it difficult to establish that they were 'in priority need' under the Housing Act 1996,[147] but instead might be offered poor quality bed and breakfast accommodation or places on young homeless projects. Alternatively, they might be sent back to the social services department.

If a homeless teenager is under 16, even if the social services department is prepared to assist, parental objections may prevent such a move.[148] Although the parents of the over 16-year-olds have no legal right to object to accommodation being provided, the Children Act 1989 makes it clear that these older teenagers have no legal right to insist on the social services department solving their accommodation problems.[149] Indeed, there is no easy way of forcing social services departments to accept that they have a duty to accommodate homeless 16- and 17-year-olds (unless they are care leavers).[150] Parents pleading with social workers to accommodate their teenage offspring whom they intend 'throwing out' are told of departmental 'policies' against such assistance, in order to 'keep young people within their families'.[151] Too often, in the past, this group have been sent back to the housing agencies, on the basis that departmental assistance would be provided under the Children Act 1989, section 27.[152]

The refusal of social services departments to accommodate homeless teenagers has usually been motivated by lack of social services accommodation and other pressures on their financial resources.[153] Long-term accommodation can be costly, since it may involve paying for residential care or a fostering allowance to foster carers. By refusing to accommodate a teenager under the 1989 Children Act, section 20, some social services departments obviously consider that they avoid incurring the more onerous legal obligations regarding 'looked after' children.[154] Instead, these

young people outside these specified categories who should also be assessed as being in priority need, for example, because they have been forced to leave home by violence or sexual abuse.

146 See D Cowan (1997) ch 3. See also N Biehal et al (2000) p 77.

147 Housing Act 1996, s 189.

148 See Children Act 1989, s 20 (7) and (8). See discussion above.

149 Children Act 1989, s 20(3) obliges local authorities to provide accommodation for children in need over the age of 16 only if their welfare is considered 'likely to be seriously prejudiced' without it.

150 See below.

151 N Biehal et al (2000) pp 27–28.

152 Children Act 1989, s 27 authorises the social services department to request the help of other authorities, such as a local housing authority, with the exercise of any of their functions. But the extent to which social services departments could persuade local housing departments to assist by providing housing for young people was substantially undermined by *R v Northavon District Council, ex p Smith* [1994] 2 AC 402: the House of Lords held that the Children Act 1989, s 27 merely requires housing departments to co-operate with social services and not to change their existing housing policies. See D Cowan and J Fionda (1995).

153 See SEU (2002) para 5.45.

154 See Children Act 1989, s 22(2), under which a child qualifies as a 'looked after child' as soon as he or she has been accommodated by the local authority for a continuous period for more than 24 hours. Prior to the implementation of the Children (Care Leaving) Act 2000, 'looked after' children were only entitled to advice and assistance until they attained the age of 21. See Children Act 1989, s 24. Now, local authority duties may be more onerous. See below.

authorities may place homeless young people in short-term bed and breakfast accommodation paid for out of the emergency resources they have available under section 17, recouping the rent via housing benefit.[155] The obvious disadvantage for young people is that emergency section 17 arrangements have no permanence.[156] Researchers observed that 'Policy decisions about the level of support they [homeless 16- and 17-year-olds] would receive appeared to be resource-driven rather than needs-led'.[157] This reluctance to provide accommodation has led some young people to make unplanned moves to ad hoc arrangements, such as staying with friends in uncertain circumstances.[158] With the imposition on social services departments of far more extensive duties towards some groups of looked after children,[159] social workers may show a similar reluctance to accommodate young children away from home under section 20, in order to avoid their qualifying for much more expensive assistance, on leaving care, when they are older.[160]

As noted above, through being defined as in priority need, a homeless teenager may now gain assistance from the housing authority and avoid involvement with the social services department altogether. The guidance makes it clear that housing authorities must not attempt to avoid providing accommodation by pressurising 16- to 17-year-olds into returning home. Before discussing such a possibility, they should first liaise with social services departments, to ensure that it is safe for the teenager to do so.[161] In any event, many homeless teenagers have needs that cannot simply be met by the provision of accommodation and money. They may require further assistance from other agencies, for example, from the social services department, on the basis that they are children in need.[162] There have been increasing calls for a far more co-ordinated housing strategy to address the needs of homeless young people, ensuring not only that the various agencies work better together,[163] but also that more suitable accommodation is made available. Addressing these, recent legislation has placed housing authorities under a statutory obligation to establish an over-arching homelessness strategy within their areas, with better co-ordination between the various official agencies tackling the problem.[164] Official guidance to local housing authorities now also stresses the need for far better collaborative working, with jointly agreed protocols, between housing authorities and departments of social services, to avoid young people being sent back and forth between departments without obtaining help from either.[165]

155 N Biehal et al (2000) pp 21–22 and 77–78.
156 But see *Re T (accommodation by local authority)* [1995] 1 FLR 159: on judicial review the court held that the local authority could not deny their duty under the Children Act 1989, s 20(3) to house the teenager concerned by arguing that s 17 assistance fulfilled her needs.
157 N Biehal et al (2000) p 78.
158 N Biehal et al (2000) p 84.
159 See Children Act 1989, ss 23A–E, 24, 24A–C and Sch 2, paras 19A–C, inserted by the Children (Care Leaving) Act 2000, discussed below and in more detail in chapter 16. In particular, under s 23B(8) the 'eligible child' (a child who has been provided with care by a local authority for at least 13 weeks after the age of 14), on leaving local authority care, becomes a 'relevant child' and thereby entitled to maintenance and suitable accommodation, at least until the age of 18. See discussion below.
160 Ie the new leaving care obligations may deter local authorities from 'looking after' a child over the age of 14 for more than 13 weeks, to prevent 'eligibility' arising.
161 Office of the Deputy Prime Minister and Department of Health (2002) para 8.38.
162 Ie under Children Act 1989, s 17.
163 See, inter alia: N Biehal et al (2000) pp 79–80; C Havell and I Nassor (1998) para 4.4.
164 See Homelessness Act 2002, ss 1–4; and Office of the Deputy Prime Minister and Department of Health (2002) ch 1 and Annexes 3, 4 and 7.
165 Office of the Deputy Prime Minister and Department of Health (2002) ch 1, paras 10–12. See also Department of Health (2001) p 23, para 25.

Despite these changes, the chance of all homeless young people finding suitable accommodation remains restricted. Affordable accommodation in the rented sector is scarce. In the first place, the single room rent restrictions put a ceiling on the amount of housing benefit for which they are eligible.[166] Furthermore, the little understood principle of property law barring teenagers under 18 from executing a legal lease on a flat greatly exacerbate the difficulties of homeless 16- and 17-year-olds seeking housing authority accommodation. A widespread misunderstanding of the law prevents this principle being avoided by relatively simple expedients.[167] For example, since a minor can hold an equitable tenancy in any property,[168] if a minor arranges to take a tenancy, it will operate as a contract for a lease,[169] binding on him or her, unless and until repudiated.[170] Nevertheless, housing authorities often refuse to offer tenancies to under 18-year-olds unless the social services department acts as guarantor, which they may not wish to do.[171]

Enabling teenagers to rent property may not be an appropriate solution for young people fending for themselves for the first time. Supported accommodation in hostels, lodgings and foyers, some of which also provide specialised training schemes, can offer a far better approach.[172] Nevertheless, hitherto there has been a lack of suitable accommodation for young people in a supported environment. Indeed, research indicates that too often vulnerable teenagers have been placed by social workers in a series of bed and breakfast hotels, until private sector tenancies can be found. Perhaps predictably, without ongoing support, these arrangements quickly break down.[173] The dangers involved in placing vulnerable teenagers in independent dwellings are now becoming much more widely recognised. The SEU, which painted a bleak picture of the poor conditions in which teenage mothers bring up their children, was particularly concerned by the effect on them of placing them in lone tenancies where their isolation is increased.[174] Hopefully this situation will improve, with local housing authorities being directed to recognise the special need of 16- and 17-year-olds, including young teenage parents, for supported accommodation.[175] New arrangements

---

166 Restrictions on housing benefit for rented accommodation for those under 25 have increased the difficulties of young people. The amount of benefit (based on the assumption that people under 25 do not need one-bedroom single flats) is limited to the average rent for a room in a shared house. See V White and D Levison (1999).

167 For a detailed exposition of the legal pitfalls and remedies regarding the grant of tenancies to underage tenants, see D Cowan and N Deardon (2002) pp 173–182.

168 Taking effect under the Trusts of Land and Appointment of Trustees Act 1996, Sch 2, para 2. See D Cowan and N Deardon (2002) pp 173–182 and J Morgan (2000).

169 Suitable accommodation for a minor will also inevitably be deemed 'a necessary'. But few understand the anachronistic rules of contract which ensure that minors can enter into binding contracts only for the supply of 'necessaries' and beneficial contracts of service. See G Treitel (1999) ch 13. See also A Bainham (1988) pp 522–528 for a damning critique of the confusing legal principles regarding a minor's contractual capacity.

170 See Hale J's explanation of a minor's position regarding leases of land in *Kingston upon Thames Borough Council v Prince* [1999] 1 FLR 593.

171 See N Biehal et al (2000) p 22.

172 See G Randall and S Brown (1999) esp chs 5 and 8.

173 N Biehal et al (2000) pp 21–22.

174 See SEU (1999 b), which recommended (para 11.15) that all under 18 teenage lone parents, who could not live with their own families or partners, should be placed in supervised semi-independent housing, with support.

175 Office of the Deputy Prime Minister and Department of Health (2002) paras 11.5–11.7. See also Department of Health (2001), which (p 23, para 26) urges local authorities to provide a broad range of accommodation for care leavers, including various forms of supported accommodation.

for providing additional supported accommodation for vulnerable people of all ages in the community may also ease the situation.[176]

Meanwhile, during the late 1990s, government attention focused on the overwhelming problems of care leavers, a very specific group of vulnerable teenagers, some of whom were also teenage mothers.[177] There were particular concerns about the plight of children leaving the care of local authorities with very poor life chances.[178] The SEU noted the increasing trend for local authorities to discharge young people from care early, largely for financial reasons, with the proportion leaving care at the age of 16 increasing from 33% in 1993, to 46% in 1998. This situation contrasted with the average for the population as a whole, where young people typically leave home at the age of 22.[179] Whilst some were supplied with suitable accommodation, others were provided with unsupported accommodation in unsafe or unsuitable areas.[180] Given their childhood histories, many of these teenagers were quite unable to cope with independent living, and inevitably this group became greatly over-represented amongst those who ended up sleeping rough.[181] The imposition of new statutory responsibilities on departments of social services[182] and on housing authorities[183] to provide appropriate accommodation for 16- and 17-year-olds and care leavers aged between 18 and 21 may well do much to transform the lives of many vulnerable young people.

Whilst special measures designed to alleviate the hardship suffered by these specific groups of teenagers are obviously welcome, there is a danger that resources will be targeted exclusively on them, to the detriment of other homeless young people with significant needs.[184] Indeed, there remain serious gaps in housing provision for those adolescents who, whilst not falling into any particularly disadvantaged category, have no option but to leave home without support. They too deserve government attention.

176 New 'Supporting People' budgets are to be established at local level, as from 2003, to fund sheltered/supported housing for vulnerable groups of people eg inter alia: people with long-term mental problems, young homeless people and victims of domestic violence. See Department of Environment Transport and Regions (2001).

177 See Department of Health (1999), which notes (para 2.1) a far higher risk of teenage pregnancy amongst those in local authority care and those who have left care. See also paras 8.23–8.25.

178 See, inter alia: Social Services Inspectorate (1997) para 1.2; W Utting (1997) pp 91–93; Nacro (1998); Department of Health (1999) para 2.6.

179 See Department of Health (1999) para 2.1.

180 Department of Health (1999) para 2.5.

181 All the research studies on children running away show that there is an over-representation of young people from local authority care. See particularly Centrepoint (2001 b), which records that 89% of care leavers surveyed had slept rough at some point. For a more detailed discussion of the quality of care provided by local authorities for children in state care, see chapter 16.

182 Social services departments must provide all 'relevant children' and 'former relevant children' (ie care leavers, who were previously 'eligible' children) with accommodation and maintenance, up to the age of 18, or 21, depending on their educational circumstances. See Children Act 1989, ss 23B(8) and 23C(9).

183 Discussed above.

184 N Biehal et al (2000) p 78.

(6)   CHILDREN 'DIVORCING' THEIR PARENTS

(A)   The child applicant

A child leaving home will often turn to friends or relations for accommodation and help. In such circumstances, obtaining a court order approving such an arrangement clarifies the carer's legal position. In the past, a situation of this kind could only have been formalised through wardship and then normally only on the initiative of the adult carer. Under current law, obtaining a section 8 order under the Children Act 1989 is a simpler way of obtaining a judicial stamp of approval for such an arrangement, and children may take the initiative and apply for such orders themselves.[185] A residence order confirming the new carer's parental responsibility for the child[186] not only avoids the risk of criminal charges under the Child Abduction Act 1984[187] and under the legislation designed to protect girls from sexual offences,[188] but also persuades schools and other agencies that the carer has authority to make decisions regarding the child.[189]

It is a remarkably liberal aspect of English law that the Children Act 1989, by permitting children to apply for section 8 orders, enables them to instruct their own solicitors and initiate proceedings, thereby forcing their parents into court to answer their claims. It in no way detracts from the liberality of these provisions that they do not guarantee that the outcome will necessarily be what these children want. The court may ultimately decide that an order complying with a child's own wishes would not be in his or her best interests. Despite this, embarking on litigation is, in itself, a dramatic way of taking independent action. The fact that a solicitor who considers a child competent to give instructions is able to respect that child's wishes on this and treat him or her as a client, indicates the extent to which English law currently acknowledges children's capacity for making important choices in their lives and taking the responsibility to pursue them.

It is unlikely that many solicitors would take instructions from a child very much below adolescence. Indeed, children face at least two procedural hurdles before the courts hear their applications for section 8 orders under the Children Act 1989. They must first convince their solicitors that they have sufficient understanding to instruct them without a guardian or next friend.[190] Next they must obtain leave under section 10(8), by convincing the court that they have 'sufficient understanding' to apply for the order. A solicitor considering that the child would pass this test may nevertheless suggest that the adult with whom the child intends to live makes the application instead, perhaps to avoid the child being closely involved in potentially unpleasant litigation. But this might have financial implications. Although a mature child, with no income of his or her own, will probably obtain public funding for the litigation, an adult in paid employment will not. The Legal Services Commission will, however,

---

185   Having first obtained leave to do so under Children Act 1989, s 10(8). See discussion below and in chapter 7, in the context of children instructing their own solicitors.

186   Children Act 1989, s 12(2).

187   Discussed above.

188   Eg the various offences under Sexual Offences Act 1956.

189   Eg *B v B (a minor) (residence order)* [1992] 2 FLR 327: the High Court agreed that although under the Children Act 1989, s 3(5) the child's grandmother could, as her carer, take decisions necessary to safeguard her welfare, a residence order would provide her granddaughter's school with legal confirmation of her authority to do so.

190   Both solicitor and court must be convinced on this score. Discussed in more detail in chapter 7.

normally scrutinise a child's application to ensure that it does not disguise an adult's attempt to obtain indirect public funding for his own cause. Moreover, since the checklist of factors to be complied with in order to obtain leave under section 10(9) is more rigorous than the qualifying formula applicable to a mature child under section 10(8), it is clear in some cases that the child is more likely to obtain leave to proceed than the adult.[191] The legal outcome will be no different, whether the child takes the initiative and obtains leave under the Children Act 1989, section 10(8) to apply for a residence order, or the third-party residential carer does so under section 10(9).[192] In each case the residence order will be in the adult's 'favour', in so far as it vests parental responsibility in the person with whom the child now wishes to live.[193]

(B)   Applying for leave

Children's applications for leave under the Children Act 1989, section 10(8) have received a rather mixed judicial response.[194] Indeed, this method of resolving family disputes very obviously challenges well-established perceptions about the appropriate roles of parent and child. Misgivings about children's ability to litigate in this fashion comes in numerous forms. A variety of practitioners has questioned the benefits of a process which, by allowing a child to play a prominent part in litigation, places him or her in a position of power in the family.[195] This can be particularly damaging if the child has become drawn into what is essentially a dispute between the child's own parents over the child's future care. The child's changed status may upset the psychodynamics between family members; children 'empowered' within family proceedings are given a false idea of their own importance, tending to play one parent off against another.[196] In the more typical running away scenario, where the child has fallen out with both parents,[197] the parents may argue that strangers to the family are unaware of the dangers of allowing a teenager's wishes to cloud adult perceptions of their safety.[198] Furthermore, case law also indicates that there may be an insufficient commitment made by departments of social services to providing the family with any assistance to help them overcome the corrosive effects of the litigation, through,

191   Eg *Re SC (a minor) (leave to seek residence order)* [1994] 1 FLR 96: the foster carer with whom the child wished to live had been considered and rejected by the local authority as a prospective foster-parent for S and so was unlikely to satisfy the test under s 10(9) for obtaining leave to apply for a residence order.

192   Eg *Re O (minors) (leave to seek residence order)* [1994] 1 FLR 172: a distant cousin of two boys aged 13 and 10 was persuaded by them to go to the magistrates' court to seek a residence order authorising them to stay with him rather than returning to their mother and their alcoholic step-father.

193   Per Booth J in *Re SC (a minor) (leave to seek residence order)* [1994] 1 FLR 96 at 100.

194   NB all children's applications for leave to apply for a s 8 order must be initiated in the High Court. See *Practice Direction* [1993] 1 All ER 820.

195   See S Bennett and S Armstrong Walsh (1994) p 93. See also C Sawyer (1995) p 192.

196   S Bennett and S Armstrong Walsh (1994) p 93.

197   Eg *Re CE (section 37 direction)* [1995] 1 FLR 26: CE, a girl of 14, ran away to live with her boyfriend and his parents, against the wishes of her own parents. Her parents applied for a residence order, to determine where she should live. Their application was countered by CE herself instructing a solicitor to do the same on her own behalf.

198   See W Utting (1997), who notes (paras 8.48–8.53) the concern of some parents over social workers listening to their children's views of unhappy home situations and ignoring their own, without the former apparently realising the dangers of exploitative adults weaning the children away from their parents.

for example, servicing a family assistance order, with the result that the child's relationship with his or her parents may become irrevocably damaged.[199]

Re C (a minor) (leave to seek section 8 orders)[200] was one of the first reported cases involving a minor seeking judicial authority to oppose her parents over various matters.[201] Johnson J clearly doubted the wisdom of allowing children to force their parents into court to answer their claims to independence – a view obviously shared by other members of the judiciary at the time.[202] Side-stepping the need to consider whether C was of sufficient understanding to make the application, as section 10(8) requires, he rejected her application, on the basis that it was not in her best interests for her disputes with her parents to be adjudicated in court.[203] But such an approach undermines the whole object of making section 8 orders available to children, which is to enable them to seek court assistance over problems that have proved beyond resolution by normal family discussion.

Admittedly, as noted earlier in this work,[204] there is the view that articulating the interests of family members in terms of rights merely polarises domestic disputes and undermines family relationships. Even so, Minow is surely correct to claim that if rights need asserting, serious conflict already exists. The process of enforcing the right gives it expression and provides a method of resolution which would not be arrived at otherwise.[205] Family disputes will not be resolved by simply closing the road to judicial scrutiny. Procedural restrictions are usually available far too late to protect many children claiming the right to pursue their own litigation. To attempt to protect them at this stage may achieve little more than shutting the stable door after the horse has bolted. Johnson J's refusal in *Re C (a minor) (leave to seek section 8 orders)*[206] to allow C's application for leave, when she had shown sufficient determination to commence proceedings against her parents, risked alienating her entirely. The statistics measuring the rising number of teenage runaways suggest that C might have responded to the decision by not only leaving home but also leaving the community and all those who knew her.

Johnson J's handling of *Re C*[207] hinged on his view that children's applications for leave under section 10(8) are governed by the paramountcy test under the Children Act 1989, section 1. This approach perhaps overlooked the fact that there was no need to pre-judge whether the outcome would be in the girl's best interests at the leave stage, since all matters regarding welfare could be dealt with by the court

---

199   Eg *Re C (family assistance order)* [1996] 1 FLR 424: Johnson J had hoped that the boy's poor relationship with his mother could be improved with the help of a family assistance order but the local authority explained to the court that they had insufficient resources to service such an order. The boy's relationship with his mother had been soured by his successful application for a residence order approving of his living with his uncle and aunt.

200   [1994] 1 FLR 26.

201   C sought leave under section 10(8) of the Children Act 1989 to apply for a specific issue order regarding a holiday in Bulgaria and a residence order to confirm the lawfulness of her living with her friend's family instead of her own.

202   See Thorpe J (1994), who expressed concerns that children's ability to make section 8 applications would be exploited by adults, such as solicitors and parents, for their own ends.

203   Johnson J thought that the matter could be better dealt with in discussion by C and her parents. Obviously hoping that a reconciliation might be effected between them, a court welfare officer had, on his instigation, already arranged a meeting between C and her parents.

204   See chapter 1, pp 7–10.

205   See M Minow (1987) p 1890.

206   [1994] 1 FLR 26.

207   [1994] 1 FLR 26.

hearing the full application for a section 8 order. Indeed, in *Re H (residence order: child's application for leave)*[208] Johnson J later acknowledged that he had been wrong in interpreting section 10(8) as being governed by the paramountcy criterion.[209] Nevertheless, his general concerns over the wisdom of allowing children's applications for section 8 orders continue to colour the way such cases are sometimes dealt with. For example, in *Re H*,[210] a highly intelligent 12-year-old boy, S, was caught up in his parents' dispute over where he and his sister should live. Nevertheless, he was refused leave to apply for his own residence order authorising him to live with his father. Despite concluding that S had 'sufficient understanding' for the purposes of the Children Act 1989, section 10(8),[211] Johnson J did not consider that S's evidence would add anything to the evidence provided by S's father in support of his own application. Although the court would take account of his wishes, there was 'no advantage to the court in making that difficult decision [where the boy and his sister were to live] or advantage to S himself in his being legally represented'.[212]

The decision to prevent the boy in *Re H*[213] proceeding with his application for a section 8 order is open to criticism on a number of fronts. Admittedly, the court would inevitably hear the evidence supporting each parent's contested application for residence orders over their children, whether or not the boy provided his own interpretation of the situation. Nevertheless, the legislative formula contained in section 10(8) does not obviously allow the judiciary to refuse leave merely because the child's parent is giving similar evidence. More seriously, such an approach discounted the boy's own perspectives. S was already fully involved in his parents' dispute and refusing him leave could not protect him from further damage. Nor could such a refusal enhance his respect for the judicial process when it appeared to ignore legislation which gave him a procedural right to give his side of the picture, once he had established sufficient maturity to do so. As Sawyer observes, Johnson J's approach now creates a series of obstacles for children seeking leave under section 10(8).[214] It is not enough merely to have sufficient understanding to apply. Their application must have some chance of success,[215] and their own case must be different from that of any other party in the dispute.

Not all section 10(8) applications brought by children are interpreted so restrictively. Stuart-White J approached a teenager's application for leave very differently in *Re C (residence: child's application for leave)*.[216] There, despite her father's claims that C lacked objectivity and insight, the court accepted evidence indicating that she had the understanding needed by section 10(8). She was aged 14, articulate, with very decided views of her own, and she was not content with these

---

208 [2000] 1 FLR 780.

209 [2000] 1 FLR 780 at 782. Johnson J now preferred the judicial interpretation adopted in *Re SC (a minor) (leave to seek residence order)* [1994] 1 FLR 96 and *Re C (residence: child's application for leave)* [1995] 1 FLR 927 that applications for leave under s 10(8) are not governed by the Children Act 1989, s 1(1).

210 [2000] 1 FLR 780.

211 Such a decision was predictable, bearing in mind that the boy had been placed by an educational psychologist in the 99th intelligence percentile.

212 [2000] 1 FLR 780 at 783.

213 [2000] 1 FLR 780.

214 C Sawyer (2001) p 205.

215 *Re C (residence: child's application for leave)* [1995] 1 FLR 927 at 931, per Stuart-White J. But Re J (leave to issue application for residence order) [2003] 1 FLR 114 suggests that the need for a prediction of 'success' may be an unjustifiable gloss on the specific requirements of s 10(8).

216 [1995] 1 FLR 927.

being presented for her by the court welfare officer. Stuart-White J appreciated that if he now refused her leave she would be unable to explain what her real views were.

(C) Effect of a residence order obtained on a child's application

Leave to apply for a section 8 order having been granted, the court must arbitrate between a child totally opposed to returning home and parents opposed to him or her staying away. But despite the media's predilection for the term, if the child is successful, the result achieved does not involve that child 'divorcing' his or her parents.[217] As Freeman points out, unlike the situation on divorce, which enables the parties to remarry with the possibility of an entirely new legal relationship, the child-parent legal relationship persists.[218] Indeed, the law has contrived an incoherent situation regarding children who obtain residence orders. By making section 8 orders available to them, it acknowledges their growing capacity for autonomy. The procedure enables them to force essentially private family disputes into the public arena, and provides them with an opportunity to ensure that their own viewpoint is heard. Their ability to initiate an application for a section 8 order to resolve a situation which has become unbearable, may prevent them from simply disappearing from view, in company with the many other young people who inhabit the streets of large cities.

In the event of a residence order being granted, its subject is left in a kind of legal limbo. Whilst the order remains in being,[219] responsibility for all major decisions remain within the purview of adults – the child's present carers, but shared with his or her natural parents. The child has no greater legal status than before and remains under his or her parents' tutelage, despite their having been rejected by the child and the court as suitable carers. This must appear incomprehensible to child applicants, since it is intrinsically unlikely that a court will willingly grant a residence order on their application, unless their home circumstances have deteriorated very seriously. The law's failure then to provide *them* with any legal acknowledgment of their changed situation seems unreasonable. The legal restrictions which continue to affect such children, despite their having successfully obtained residence orders authorising them to live apart from their parents, are particularly inappropriate in the context of their being unable to initiate proceedings against their parents for financial support.[220]

(7) CHILDREN'S RIGHT TO PARENTAL MONEY

The teenager who becomes estranged from his or her parents and leaves home under the age of 18 is in an anomalous position. Even those who, through a residence order, have gained judicial permission to live with someone other than their parents, have no means of gaining complete financial independence without considerable assistance from some well-meaning adult. As noted above, they have very limited entitlement to social security benefits and will therefore suffer severe poverty, unless they can obtain reasonably paid employment or financial support from their parents or other carers.

---

217 The effect of the Children Act 1989, ss 2(6) and 12(2) is that the adult acquiring a residence order shares parental responsibility for the child with the child's parents.

218 M Freeman (1996) p 159. See also H Houghton-James (1994).

219 Although such an order would normally come to an end on the child's 16th birthday, there is now power to extend its term in favour of a third-party carer (ie who is not the child's parent or guardian) until the child's 18th birthday. See Children Act 1989, s 12(5) and (6), as inserted by Adoption and Children Act 2003, s 114.

220 See below.

A teenager wishing to extract financial support from a parent will find that the legal principles governing the child-parent relationship produce a bizarre situation, even in the event of that parent being exceptionally wealthy. These principles reflect the assumption that if money is to be extracted, it should be done by an adult and not by the child. If parents are separated, it is, of course, perfectly feasible for one parent to apply for child maintenance for their son or daughter, from the other parent, through the Child Support Agency.[221] But a parent cannot do so unless the child has remained at home in the parent's care. So teenagers who refuse to live with either parent are in an anomalous position.[222] One might assume that a teenager could independently initiate maintenance proceedings against a parent, particularly if the parent is extremely wealthy and the teenager is living in impoverished circumstances. But unlike Scottish law, which allows any child having attained the age of 12 to initiate an application under the Child Support Act 1991,[223] children in England and Wales are not provided with any direct method of doing so.

The Child Support legislation allows such a step to be taken only by an adult providing the child with a home and day-to-day care.[224] If an adult with whom a teenager has taken refuge is prepared to take such a step, the child maintenance will obviously provide the teenager with much needed financial assistance. Furthermore, an adult who has first obtained a residence order authorising him or her to provide the child with a home, can then apply to the courts for an additional order, forcing the parents to assist even more generously with the child's maintenance.[225] Such a carer could, for example, apply to the courts to obtain an order against a child's wealthy parents for additional periodical payments by way of 'topping up payments'[226] and school fees.[227] But adults with whom a runaway takes refuge may simply decide that they do not want the unpleasantness of initiating either set of proceedings against the parents – in which case the child has no means at all of taking the matter into his or her own hands.

Only elderly 'children' over the age of 18 seem to attract legislative attention,[228] in so far as they can utilise the legislative methods available to separating parents[229] and divorcing parents[230] to force their parents to maintain them. But applicants must justify such claims by reference to their educational or other special needs,[231] and can

---

221   Obtaining child maintenance under the child support legislation is discussed in more detail in chapter 9.
222   See below.
223   Child Support Act 1991, s 7(1) enables children habitually resident in Scotland, having attained the age of 12 years to apply for a maintenance assessment under the Act.
224   Child Support Act 1991, s 3(3). The person with care does not need to be a parent of the child, as long as he usually provides day-to-day care for the child and the child has his home' with that person.
225   Ie under Children Act 1989, Sch 1, para 1, for an order outside the jurisdiction of the Child Support Agency, as authorised by Child Support Act 1991, s 8.
226   Child Support Act 1991, s 8(6). The courts might consider such an order appropriate against a wealthy parent, in cases where the maximum child maintenance assessment is already in force.
227   Child Support Act 1991, s 8(7).
228   See M Letts (2001) pp 840–843.
229   Children Act 1989, Sch 1, para 2(1). But under para 2(3) a child can only apply on attaining the age of 18 if a periodical payments order has not been in force with respect to him prior to his attaining the age of 16. The teenager who has been the subject of a periodical payments order prior to attaining 16, can himself apply for a variation of that order, on attaining that age. See N Lowe and G Douglas (1998) pp 764–772.
230   Matrimonial Causes Act 1973, s 23(1).
231   Children Act 1989, Sch 1 para 2(1).

only apply at all if their parents are already separated[232] or have instituted matrimonial proceedings against each other.[233] It seems unsupportable that despite children being able to 'divorce their parents', there is no obvious way for a child under the age of 18 to initiate maintenance proceedings against such parents, unless those parents divorce each other.[234] This gap in the law suggests that the legislation is not designed for teenagers trying to sort out financial disputes with their parents themselves.

The type of family conflict which results in parents refusing to support their offspring might continue beyond the grave. A wealthy parent may die leaving a will excluding his or her estranged son or daughter entirely. The terms of the will could, of course, be disputed by the disinherited teenager (assisted by an adult next friend) bringing an application for reasonable provision out of the parents' estate.[235] Although the success of such an application is by no means a forgone conclusion, since it will depend on the court's view of the merits of the teenager's case, it seems unlikely that the court would refuse such an application entirely.[236] The dearth of relevant case law suggests that these situations rarely occur. If the parent dies intestate, the principles of law governing the distribution of his or her estate ensure that there is often little or nothing left from the estate for any issue after the surviving widow or widower takes their share.[237] Well-established case law demonstrates the inequities that such rules can produce.[238]

(8) THE AMERICAN EXPERIENCE OF EMANCIPATION

It is arguable that many of the legal principles discussed above are anachronistic and inappropriate when applied to the teenager who leaves home under the age of 18 and establishes a degree of independence. Some of the principles of legal emancipation developed in the United States could be adopted for teenagers in this country,

---

232 Matrimonial Causes Act 1973, s 29; Children Act 1989, Sch 1, para 4.
233 Under the Family Proceedings Rules 1991, SI 1991/1247, r 2.54, a child (if under the age of 18, he or she would require the assistance of an adult, as next friend) may apply, after obtaining leave to intervene as party to the parents' divorce proceedings, for a maintenance order under the Matrimonial Causes Act 1973, s 23. Eg *Downing v Downing (Downing intervening)* [1976] Fam 288: a child over the age of 18 successfully obtained financial provision from her parents using this type of procedural route.
234 The *Downing* route does not appear to be confined to 'children' over the age of 18.
235 A child of married or unmarried parents can claim, under the Inheritance (Provision for Family and Dependants) Act 1975, a share in a deceased parent's estate on the basis that the will did not make reasonable provision for him or her. See N Lowe and G Douglas (1998) pp 886–896.
236 The Inheritance (Provision for Family and Dependants) Act 1975, s 3 sets out the factors relevant to such an application, such as the financial resources and needs of the applicant. The child's potential need for education and training would be particularly relevant.
237 The surviving spouse is treated very generously by the intestacy legislation. Thus, under the Administration of Estates Act 1925, the surviving spouse is entitled to a statutory legacy of the first £125,000 of the estate, and a life interest in half the residue. Although legally, the remaining half of the residue is held on trust for the children, the surviving spouse's statutory legacy may entirely drain the estate. See N Lowe and G Douglas (1998) pp 876–881.
238 Eg, inter alia: *Sivyer v Sivyer* [1967] 1 WLR 1482 (the intestate's entire estate went to his widow, who had been his second wife, with nothing left for his 13-year-old daughter by a previous marriage); *Re Collins (decd)* [1990] Fam 56 (the deceased died having obtained a decree nisi (but not a decree absolute) of divorce against her husband. Her husband was duly entitled to the whole of her estate on her intestacy, with nothing left for their son and her illegitimate daughter).

particularly in the event of their obtaining court approval for their present living arrangements through a residence order. Legislation has been widely introduced in many states of the United States, allowing children under 18 years of age to petition the courts for a declaration of emancipation. California's legislation is typical in this respect.[239] Its civil code allows children aged 14 and over to petition the court for emancipation on showing that the child lives apart from the parents with the parents' consent and is self-supporting. The court will require evidence that the child can manage his or her own financial affairs and take responsibility for housing, food and other bills. Evidence of employment will normally be required. The petition is granted if the court finds the information contained in it to be true and, having taken account of objections from third parties, including parents, that emancipation would not be contrary to the child's best interests. The procedure is intended to be simple enough to enable the teenager to complete it without a lawyer.

The declaration of emancipation has an immediate and dramatic effect. So far as the child's parents are concerned, they have no further obligation to provide moral or financial support of any kind. Children seeking advice on the procedure are therefore warned that the clean break achieved by emancipation does not allow them to expect continued parental support. The emancipated minor is considered to be an adult for a wide range of specified purposes. These include consenting to medical, dental or psychiatric care, enabling the minor to enter into binding contracts, to enrol in any school or college, to buy, sell, lease, or transfer real or personal property, to make a will, and giving him or her tortious liability.[240]

Although many emancipated young Americans find coping with the demands of independent living a daunting experience,[241] some of these features could be made available to the English courts. The courts could be given the power to grant to a child any of a list of specified rights currently only available to adults. These might include the right to marry without the consent of those with parental responsibility, to enter into any contract, to vote, to acquire real property and to apply for financial assistance from their parents. The courts might also have the further power, exercisable only in very exceptional circumstances, to grant a minor complete emancipation. This would involve a residence order, granted on a child's application, being accompanied by an order terminating the parents' own parental responsibility. It seems unlikely that the courts would wish to exercise this power without being sure that the child would be financially secure, since it is unrealistic to argue that parents deprived of their parental responsibility would also remain liable to support their son or daughter.

(9) CONCLUSION

Children living in well-functioning families are not particularly affected by the confused hotch-potch of legal principles governing their gradual attainment of legal autonomy. These principles, though bewildering, do not impinge greatly on their everyday life. In the event of family life going badly wrong, however, the law's

---

239 For a detailed history of California's emancipation laws, see C Sanger and E Willemsen (1992) pp 250–258.
240 Eg See California Family Code, ss 7000–7002.
241 C Sanger and E Willemsen (1992) pp 290–297.

apparent liberality, in terms of recognising legal competence to obtain a residence order, is not accompanied by its providing a financial safety net for those who feel obliged to leave home.

Children are not always sufficiently realistic to know that the prospect of gaining freedom from their parents is, in practice, often accompanied by considerable financial and emotional hardship. The destitution and despair experienced by children of all ages who run away from home shows the extent to which English law is failing to live up to its international obligations under the CRC. The law neither protects their wage-earning nor provides them with appropriate welfare benefits when out of work. Indeed, this group of children slip through the net at every turn and simply do not obtain the special protection and support that should attend the legal status of minority. Overall, it appears that the law is attempting to have its cake and eat it. On the one hand it withholds an adult legal status from all children under the age of 18, on the basis that they require special protection. But on the other hand, it also assumes that the source of this protection will be provided by parents and withholds it from those children who inconveniently refuse to fit into family life.

BIBLIOGRAPHY

NB many of these publications can be obtained on the relevant organisation's website.

Bainham A, *Children, Parents and the State* (1988) Sweet and Maxwell.

Bainham A, '"See you in court, Mum": children as litigants' (1994) 6 Journal of Child Law 127.

Barrett D (ed), *Youth Prostitution in the New Europe: The Growth in Sex Work* (2000) Russell House Publishing Ltd.

Bennett S and Armstrong Walsh S, 'The No Order Principle, Parental Responsibility and the Child's Wishes' (1994) Family Law 91.

Biehal N et al, *Home or Away?: Supporting young people and families* (2000) National Children's Bureau.

Brown G and Elks M, 'Runaway children: a new response to an old problem' (1994) 6 Journal of Child Law 22.

Centrepoint, *Centrepoint factsheet series: 16 and 17 year olds 1999/2000* (2000).

Centrepoint, *Centrepoint factsheet series: Runaways 2000/2001* (2001 a).

Centrepoint, *Centrepoint factsheet series 2000/2001 Key Findings* (2001 b).

Chatrik B, *Guide to Training and Benefits for Young People* (1999) Unemployment Unit and Youthaid.

Committee on Economic, Social and Cultural Rights, *Concluding Observations of the Committee on Economic, Social and Cultural Rights: United Kingdom of Great Britain and Northern Ireland – Dependent Territories 2002* E/C 12/1/Add 79 (2002) Centre for Human Rights, Geneva.

Committee on the Rights of the Child, *Concluding Observations of the Committee on the Rights of the Child: United Kingdom of Great Britain and Northern Ireland* CRC/C/15/Add 34 (1995) Centre for Human Rights, Geneva.

Committee on the Rights of the Child, *Concluding Observations of the Committee on the Rights of the Child: United Kingdom of Great Britain and Northern Ireland* CRC/C/15/Add 188 (2002) Centre for Human Rights, Geneva.

Cowan D, *Homelessness – The (In) Appropriate Applicant* (1997) Dartmouth.

Cowan D and Deardon N, 'The Minor as (a) Subject: The Case of Housing Law' in J Fionda (ed) *Legal Concepts of Childhood* (2002) Hart Publishing.

Cowan D and Fionda J, 'Housing homeless families – an update' (1995) 7 Child and Family Law Quarterly 66.

Custerson M, 'The police perspective' in *Young Runaways: Report of a National Seminar* (1997) Dartington Social Research Unit.

Department of Environment, Transport and Regions, *Supporting People: Policy into Practice* (2001) .

Department of Health, *Family Support, Day Care and Educational Provision for Young Children* Vol 2, Children Act 1989 Guidance and Regulations (1991 a) HMSO.

Department of Health, *Family Placements* Vol 3, Children Act 1989 Guidance and Regulations (1991 b) HMSO.

Department of Health, *Employment of Children* Consultation Paper (1995).

Department of Health, *Me Survive Out There?: New Arrangements for Young People Living in and Leaving Care* Consultation Paper (1999).

Department of Health, *Children (Leaving Care) Act 2000: Regulations and Guidance* (2001) .

Fortin J, 'Children's rights and the use of physical force' (2001) 13 Child and Family Law Quarterly 243.

Freeman M, 'Can Children Divorce Their Parents?' in M Freeman (ed) *Divorce – Where Next* (1996) Dartmouth.

Hamilton C, *Working With Young People: Legal responsibility and liability* (2002) The Children's Legal Centre.

Hamilton C and Fiddy A, *At what age can I …?: a guide to age-based legislation* (2002) Children's Legal Centre.

Harris N, 'Youth, Citizenship and Welfare' (1992) Journal of Social Welfare and Family Law 175.

Havell C and Nassor I, *The young face of homelessness* (1998) Centrepoint.

Horseman R, Head of Homelessness Policy Division, Department of the Environment, '"Homes for our Children": the Government's Perspective' (1992) 4 Journal of Child Law 167.

Houghton-James H, 'Children Divorcing their Parents' (1994) Journal of Social Welfare and Family Law 185.

Jones G, *The Youth Divide: Diverging paths to adulthood* (2002) Joseph Rowntree Foundation.

Law Commission, *Review of Child Law, Guardianship and Custody* Law Com No 172 (1988) HMSO.

Letts M, 'Children – The Continuing Duty to Maintain' (2001) Family Law 839.

Lowe N and Douglas G, *Bromley's Family Law* (1998) Butterworths.

McCluskey J, *Acting in Isolation: An evaluation of the effectiveness of the Children Act for young homeless people* (1994) CHAR.

Minow M, 'Interpreting Rights: An Essay for Robert Cover' (1987) 96 Yale Law Journal 1860.

Morgan J, *Kingston upon Thames Borough Council v Prince:* 'Children are people too' (2000) 12 Child and Family Law Quarterly 65.

Nacro, *Going Straight Home* (1998) Nacro.

NCH Action for Children, *factfile '99* (1998) NCH Action for Children.

National Children's Homes, *A Lost Generation: A Survey of the Problems Faced by Vulnerable Young People Living on their Own* (1993) NCH Action for Children.

Newiss G, *Missing presumed ...? The police response to missing persons* Police Research Series Paper 114 (1999) Home Office.

Office of the Deputy Prime Minister and Department of Health, *Homelessness: Code of Guidance for Local Authorities* (2002).

Office for National Statistics, *Social Trends No 32* (2002) The Stationery Office.

Pettitt B (ed), *Children and Work in the UK: Reassessing the Issues* (1998) CPAG.

Rahman M et al, *Monitoring poverty and social exclusion 2000* (2000) Joseph Rowntree Foundation.

Randall G and Brown S, *Ending Exclusion: Employment and training schemes for homeless young people* (1999) Joseph Rowntree Foundation.

Safe on the Streets Research Team, *Still Running: Children on the Streets in the UK* (1999) The Children's Society.

Sanger C and Willemsen E, 'Minor Changes: Emancipating Children in Modern Times' (1992) 25 University of Michigan Journal of Law Reform 239.

Sawyer C, 'The competence of children to participate in family proceedings' (1995) 7 Child and Family Law Quarterly 180.

Sawyer C, 'Applications by children: Still seen but not heard?' (2001) 117 Law Quarterly Review 203.

Shropshire J and Middleton S, *Small Expectations: Learning to be Poor?* (1999) Joseph Rowntree Foundation.

Smith J et al, *The family background of homeless young people* (1998) Family Policy Studies Centre.

Social Exclusion Unit (SEU), *Rough Sleeping – Report by the Social Exclusion Unit* Cm 4008 (1998).

Social Exclusion Unit (SEU), *Bridging the Gap: New Opportunities for 16 –18 Year Olds Not in Education, Employment or Training* Cm 4405 (1999 a).

Social Exclusion Unit (SEU), *Teenage Pregnancy* Cm 4342 (1999 b).

Social Exclusion Unit (SEU), *Report of Policy Action Team 12; Young People* (2000).

Social Exclusion Unit (SEU), *Young Runaways* (2002).

Social Services Inspectorate, '... When leaving home is also leaving care' (1997) Department of Health.

Stein M et al, *Running the Risk: Young People on the Streets of Britain Today* (1994) The Children's Society.

Thorpe J, 'Independent Representation for Children' (1994) Family Law 20.

Treitel G, *The Law of Contract* (1999) Sweet and Maxwell.

Utting W, *People Like Us: The Report of the Review of the Safeguards For Children Living Away From Home* (1997) The Stationery Office.

White V and Levison D, *Housing Benefit and the Private Rented Sector* (1999) Department of the Environment, Transport and the Regions.

Chapter 5

Adolescent decision-making and health care

INTRODUCTION

It is no accident that many of the boundaries to adolescent legal independence have been mapped out by the courts in the context of health care. Medical treatment often involves an invasion of bodily and personal privacy which would be intolerable if patients had no right to control its delivery. International human rights law recognises that an important aspect of an adult's right to self-determination includes the right to decide what should happen to his own body[1] and the common law is also in no doubt that adult patients enjoy such a right.[2] Precisely the same reasoning could be applied to children and adolescents; they too should have the right to make choices over their treatment, if competent to make them.

Until relatively recently, the traditional legal approach was to ignore children's capacity for choice and to assume that their parents were the appropriate people to determine what happened to their children's bodies when receiving medical treatment. Consequently, parents were automatically treated by the medical profession as proxy consent-givers. This was convenient, in so far as doctors could avoid asking their young patients their own views on the matter. But latterly, the needs of society have changed and the law has adapted its approach to adolescents. It now acknowledges that, as a group, they are approaching mental and physical maturity and that, before reaching legal adulthood, they must be encouraged to develop the capacity to take responsibility for their own lives. Consequently, the legal principles relating to medical decision-making gave way to more liberal attitudes towards adolescents' own powers of consent.[3] For example, the Family Law Reform Act 1969, section 8(1) established

---

1   In *X and Y v Netherlands* (1985) 8 EHRR 235, the European Court of Human Rights established that the right to private life, as protected by art 8 of the ECHR, includes the right to 'physical and moral integrity'.

2   See, inter alia: *Re F (mental patient: sterilisation)* [1990] 2 AC 1 at 72, per Lord Goff: There 'is the fundamental principle, long established, that every person's body is inviolate'; *Sidaway v Board of Governors of the Bethlem Royal Hospital and the Maudsley Hospital* [1985] AC 871 at 882, per Lord Scarman: 'The right of "self-determination" ... is vividly illustrated when the treatment recommended is surgery ... The existence of the patient's right to make his own decision, ... may be seen as a basic human right protected by the common law...'

3   The medical treatment of children too young to consent for themselves is discussed in chapter 10. Doctors relying on parental consent must obtain consent from either mother or father, if the child is born to married parents. The mother's consent is necessary if the child is born to unmarried parents, unless the unmarried father has acquired parental responsibility. See Children Act 1989, s 2(1), (2) and (7).

that, at the age of 16, adolescents could be assumed to have sufficient capacity to make choices over their own health care.[4]

To ignore the decision-making capacities of adolescents under the age of 16 might also be counter-productive, given the increase in sexual activity amongst young teenagers. The law should encourage younger adolescents to take a responsible attitude to their own sexuality by giving them the freedom to seek out and obtain confidential medical advice and treatment. The decision of the House of Lords in *Gillick v West Norfolk and Wisbech Area Health Authority*[5] was the trigger for a much more liberal approach to this younger age group. Although it specifically dealt with the issue of adolescent competence to consent to contraceptive advice and treatment, the principles it established have a general application to all forms of medical treatment and assistance. It introduced the idea that adolescents' rights over their own bodies grow with their competence to understand the implications of the procedure involved. As Feldman has pointed out, this approach is 'consistent with the theory that autonomy is the value at the root of the moral justification of freedom: the greater one's capacity to exercise a choice in an informed way, the stronger is one's claim to be free to exercise it'.[6]

Some might argue that the full implications of *Gillick* could never be realised in a society which values the health of its teenagers, since it appeared to give them the right to martyr themselves by refusing life-saving medical treatment. The judiciary found it impossible to stand aside and allow teenage patients to reach such dangerous choices and subsequent case law was developed, preserving the rights of society to override their more dangerous choices.[7] But as Gostin says, 'Nothing degrades a human being more than to have intrusive treatment thrust upon him despite his full understanding of its nature and purpose and his clear will to say "no"'.[8] Although case law has achieved a situation whereby those responsible for the health care of adolescents can ensure that they received essential treatment, the methods adopted enabling this to happen are often unnecessarily insensitive and ignore the basic human rights accorded to adults forced to undergo medical treatment against their will.

This chapter is divided into two sections. It first assesses the extent to which the general principles of law recognise an adolescent's capacity to consent to and refuse medical treatment. It then goes on to consider the application of these general principles in the context of two specific areas of decision-making which cause particular difficulties: the control of fertility and the treatment of mentally disturbed young people.

SECTION A   ADOLESCENT DECISION-MAKING – THE GENERAL PRINCIPLES

(1)   ADOLESCENTS' LEGAL RIGHTS TO CONSENT TO MEDICAL TREATMENT

(A)   Consent and adolescents under sixteen

English law is apparently very liberal in its approach to the capacity of adolescents under the age of 16 to consent to their own medical treatment. It accepts that such

4   Discussed below, p 126.
5   [1986] AC 112.
6   D Feldman (2002) p 287.
7   This issue is discussed at a more theoretical level in chapter 1, and more generally in chapter 3, regarding adolescents and their legal relationship with their parents.
8   L Gostin (1992) p 76.

minors have the right to consent on their own behalf to a variety of medical procedures, as long as they fully understand what is involved. The House of Lords in *Gillick v West Norfolk and Wisbech Area Health Authority*[9] rejected the concept of fixed age limits below which consent could not be given. Indeed, Lord Scarman and Lord Fraser poured scorn on Mrs Gillick's suggestion that minors under the age of 16 could not consent to any medical advice or treatment. According to Lord Fraser:

'It seems to me verging on the absurd to suggest that a girl or a boy aged 15 could not effectively consent, for example, to have a medical examination of some trivial injury to his body or even to have a broken arm set. Of course the consent of the parents should normally be asked, but they may not be immediately available. Provided the patient, whether a boy or a girl, is capable of understanding what is proposed, and of expressing his or her own wishes, I see no good reason for holding that he or she lacks the capacity to express them validly and effectively and to authorise the medical man to make the examination or give the treatment which he advises.'[10]

Similarly, Lord Scarman considered that parents lose the right to consent to medical procedures on behalf of their children at the point at which:

'... the child achieves a sufficient understanding and intelligence to enable him or her to understand fully what is proposed. It will be a question of fact whether a child seeking advice has sufficient understanding of what is involved to give a consent valid in law.'[11]

They strongly disagreed with the claim that the Family Law Reform Act 1969, section 8(1)[12] precluded adolescents under the age of 16 from giving a valid consent to medical treatment. Indeed, they asserted that under the existing principles of common law adolescents under that age have legal capacity to consent to certain procedures.[13] On the face of it, the decision in *Gillick* is not only extremely liberal, in so far as it appears to give adolescents considerable freedom regarding their own medical treatment, but it introduces a sophisticated approach to assessing capacity to consent to treatment. Indeed, Lord Scarman's *Gillick* competence formula, to all intents and purposes provides an excellent method whereby doctors can determine those teenage patients who are sufficiently mature to reach responsible decisions for themselves. It allows a doctor to adopt a far more intelligent approach to the concept of capacity than one merely relying on age or even on the research evidence on children's cognitive growth.[14] The test is a functional one – whether the minor has capacity to comprehend and therefore consent to the procedure depends on the gravity of what is proposed. Even so, the difficulty implicit in the test for assessing *Gillick* competence is its deceptive simplicity.[15] It fails to provide doctors with any clear guidelines over the circumstances in which they should accept that an adolescent may consent to a

---

9   [1986] AC 112.
10   [1986] AC 112 at 169.
11   [1986] AC 112 at 189.
12   Family Law Reform Act 1969, s 8(1): 'The consent of a minor who has attained the age of sixteen years to any surgical, medical or dental treatment which, in the absence of consent, would constitute a trespass to his person, shall be as effective as it would be if he were of full age; and where a minor has by virtue of this section given an effective consent to any treatment it shall not be necessary to obtain any consent for it from his parent or guardian.'
13   According to Lord Fraser ([1986] AC 112 at 167) and Lord Scarman ([1986] AC 112 at 182), the Family Law Reform Act 1969, s 8(3) leaves open the question whether adolescents under the age of 16 can, under the existing common law, consent to medical treatment themselves.
14   See discussion in chapter 3.
15   See discussion in chapter 3.

particular procedure without involving his or her parents.[16] Furthermore, doctors know that by treating adolescents without consulting their parents, they take a risk of being found liable in tort, in the event of parents successfully challenging their assessment of *Gillick* competence.

Some have claimed[17] that greater clarity would be achieved if a provision were introduced along the lines of the Age of Legal Capacity (Scotland) Act 1991, section 2(4), which provides:

> 'A person under the age of sixteen years shall have legal capacity to consent on his own behalf to any surgical, medical or dental procedure or treatment where, in the opinion of a qualified medical practitioner attending him, he is capable of understanding the nature and possible consequences of the procedure or treatment.'

But the enactment of such a provision would do no more than to re-state the present law, as set out by their Lordships in *Gillick*.[18] Rather than introducing any *presumption* that children under the age of 16 can consent to all medical procedures, the provision leaves it to the medical practitioner to determine legal capacity on the basis of the child's apparent understanding.[19]

Current professional guidance provided by the British Medical Association (BMA) for doctors is interesting, in so far as it attempts to elaborate upon the *Gillick* competence formula and provide a more practical test of competence. It stresses that:

> 'The nature and complexity of the decision or task, and the person's ability to understand, at the time the decision is made, the nature of the decision required and its implications, are all relevant. Thus the graver the impact of the decision, the commensurately graver the competence needed to make it.'[20]

This general advice is further expanded upon at some length.[21] Doctors should take account of the fact that children of the same age differ in their ability to participate in decision-making; that consent, like treatment, is a process and not a single event and that adequate time must be provided; that background information about the child or young person should be obtained. It suggests that older children should be given opportunities to discuss their treatment without their parents being present and that 'Conflicts between people involved in the decision can hinder a young patient's ability to make a free choice. Discussion and attempts at achieving a consensus can help'.[22]

The BMA's guidance provides doctors with a test of competence which, though admirable, is far removed from the simple test put forward by Lord Scarman in *Gillick*. In many respects, it appears to draw on the test of competence now routinely used for all adult patients.[23] According to this test, an adult patient should not only be able to

16   See M Brazier and C Bridge (1996) pp 91–92.
17   P Alderson and J Montgomery (1996) p 87.
18   [1986] AC 112.
19   P Alderson and J Montgomery appear to assume that the introduction into English law of a provision similar to the Age of Legal Capacity (Scotland) Act 1991, s 2(4) would introduce a presumption of competence. P Alderson and J Montgomery (1996) pp 87–88.
20   British Medical Association (hereafter BMA) (2001 a) p 94.
21   BMA (2001 a) pp 94–103. See also BMA (2001 b) p 39.
22   BMA (2001 a) p 97.
23   Established in *Re C (refusal of medical treatment)* [1994] 1 FLR 31, per Thorpe J (para 36). This test has been applied subsequently, eg in *Re B (adult: refusal of medical treatment)* [2002] EWHC 429 (Fam), [2002] 2 All ER 449.

comprehend and retain information about the treatment,[24] but be able to use it and weigh it in the balance as part of the process of arriving at a choice.[25] According to the BMA, children and young people should be given all information relevant to the proposed treatment to enable them to weigh up the full consequences of their decision. Indeed, it implicitly criticises those doctors who, in the past, have deliberately withheld information from adolescent patients on the basis that it would cause them distress.[26] The guidance also suggests that the doctor should consider whether the child or young person has an understanding of what the illness means and the treatment needed, an appreciation of what the treatment involves and the intended outcomes, and the implications of treatment and non-treatment, and the consequences.[27]

Although Lord Scarman's test for *Gillick* competence is certainly deficient, the BMA's guidance provokes some concerns. In particular, it suggests that a child or young person must be competent to reach a decision over treatment 'free from undue external influences'.[28] It proceeds to warn that young people can be strongly influenced by their parents over treatment options, and suggests that although parents will often be consulted by a child patient, it is important that the ultimate decision is the 'person's own independent choice'.[29] This is an important issue, and not one touched on by their Lordships in their *Gillick* decision. Nevertheless, this advice risks excluding from competence any children brought up by strongly religious parents, such as Jehovah's Witnesses, since they will inevitably adopt their parents' faith. It would be virtually impossible for such a child to adopt his or her 'own independent choice'. There are also practical objections to the guidance, in that a general practitioner consulted in his or her surgery by a teenager opposed to parental involvement will not find its demands particularly realistic. Whilst a hospital doctor treating a young patient already in hospital may know this amount of background information about the patient and family, few general practitioners could undertake such extensive investigations, before reaching a conclusion over the patient's competence to consent to treatment.

The BMA's guidance unwittingly emphasises the overriding problem posed by the *Gillick* decision for adolescent patients who want medical advice or treatment without involving their parents. It places them entirely in the hands of the medical profession. Indeed, the doctor holds considerable power over a minor seeking treatment. Not only must the adolescent convince the doctor that he or she is competent to agree to the procedure but the doctor also occupies a gate-keeping position, in so far as treatment is concerned. Adolescents, like adults, must rely on their doctors to decide whether the treatment is medically indicated. This must be decided on a case-by-case basis, according to the circumstances of each patient and each procedure.

---

24   Currently, a doctor may be found liable in tort if he does not give an adult patient sufficient information to understand the nature, purpose and effects of the proposed treatment, thereby enabling him or her to give valid consent. It will be the tort of battery, if there is no valid consent, and negligence, if the information was insufficient to make an informed decision: *Sidaway v Board of Governors of the Bethlem Royal Hospital and the Maudsley Hospital* [1985] AC 871.

25   See *Re MB (medical treatment)* [1997] 2 FLR 426 at 437, per Butler-Sloss LJ. This test has been used in some cases involving teenagers when assessing their competence to *refuse* treatment. See discussion below.

26   As in *Re L (medical treatment: Gillick competency)* [1999] 2 FCR 524: a 14-year-old had not been told the detailed consequences of her refusing treatment for her severe scalds. See BMA (2001 a) p 100.

27   BMA (2001 a) pp 95–96.

28   BMA (2001 a) p 93.

29   BMA (2001 a) p 94.

As discussed above, the difficulty about the law, as established by *Gillick*, is its uncertainty. A teenage girl may, for example, be desperately anxious to undergo extensive plastic surgery. If satisfied that the procedure is in her best medical interests and that she can adequately understand all the issues involved, in terms of length of treatment, pain and suffering and the success rate, the decision in *Gillick* allows the doctor to proceed with treatment without involving her parents at all. They have no legal right of veto and an adolescent, like any adult patient capable of giving consent to treatment, is normally entitled to medical confidentiality, unless she agrees to disclosure.[30] Theoretically, therefore, her parents might not discover the plans for the treatment until after it has occurred. If they then violently objected to the doctor's actions, they might challenge his or her assessment of their daughter's legal capacity to consent, by suing in tort. In principle, if the court disagreed with the doctor's assessment of the young patient's competence to consent, the doctor would be liable on an action in battery, although it is unlikely that the damages would be more than nominal.

The uncertainty of the *Gillick* test implicitly encourages doctors to refuse to go ahead with any treatment for an adolescent which is not trivial or life-saving, unless they can involve the parents. It may thereby reinforce an over-protective attitude towards adolescents, which might be appropriate if they are ill and incapable of comprehending the implications of the procedure under consideration, but quite inappropriate if they are perfectly capable of making up their own minds. Indeed, it may often be the threat of legal proceedings which undermines the liberality of the *Gillick* principle.

(B)   Consent and adolescents over sixteen

The research evidence on developmental growth suggests that the older adolescents, those aged from about 14 to 15, are far more able to deal with major decisions over their own health care than those who are younger. By this time they are more able to identify a range of risks and benefits, foresee the consequences of alternatives and gauge the credibility of information provided by experts.[31] The Family Law Reform Act 1969, section 8(1) recognises this by stating:

'The consent of a minor who has attained the age of sixteen years to any surgical, medical or dental treatment which, in the absence of consent, would constitute a trespass to his person, shall be as effective as it would be if he were of full age; and where a minor has by virtue of this section given an effective consent to any treatment it shall not be necessary to obtain any consent for it from his parent or guardian.'

The meaning of this provision is clear enough; on attaining the age of 16, teenagers gain the legal right to consent on their own behalf to 'any surgical, medical or dental treatment'. It reflects the view that 16 marks the age at which adolescents' decision-

---

30   Unless a doctor considers that there is a risk of 'serious harm', for example, in cases of child neglect or abuse, but he or she should try to persuade the patient to disclose information voluntarily first, and then inform the patient and others of the intention to disclose. BMA (1999). See also General Medical Council (2000) which states (para 18) that a doctor may disclose information 'in the public interest' without his patient's consent where the benefits to an individual or to society of the disclosure outweigh the public and the patient's interest in keeping the information confidential. For an assessment of the law relating to children's right to medical confidentiality, see J Montgomery (2003) pp 308–311.

31   See L Mann et al (1989) pp 271–272. See also the discussion in chapter 3, pp 72–74.

making rights should be recognised by the law in the context of their health care. Thus whilst the decision in *Gillick*[32] indicated that the law should recognise the decision-making rights of adolescents below that age, but on a case-by-case basis, section 8 introduces the presumption that all adolescents over that age are competent to consent for themselves.

The consent rights of the teenager over the age of 16 are more limited than those of an adult patient simply because the scope of section 8 is relatively narrow. As Lord Donaldson MR pointed out in *Re W (a minor) (medical treatment)*,[33] it only authorises adolescents over the age of 16 to consent to treatment and diagnostic procedures. There is, of course, nothing to prevent a teenager over that age consenting to any procedure outside the section's scope, as long as they are *Gillick* competent. But in those circumstances, the teenager's competence is not presumed and must be assessed, as for the under 16-year-old, on a case-by-case basis, depending on the seriousness of the procedure involved. Furthermore, the consent must be 'effective'. Therefore, if a 16-year-old is incapable of giving an effective consent due, for example, to severe learning impairment, then his or her parents' consent must be obtained instead.

Blood and organ donations were singled out by Lord Donaldson MR as being outside the scope of section 8. In his view, the donation of blood would not present problems, since '"a Gillick competent" minor of any age would be able to give consent [to giving blood] under the common law'.[34] But, Lord Donaldson MR warned, organ donations are quite different. They are not only excluded from the scope of section 8 but, in his view, it would be 'highly improbable' that a teenager under the age of 18 wishing to become an organ donor could be *Gillick* competent 'in the context of so serious a procedure which would not benefit the minor'.[35] That being the case, a doctor should not proceed with an organ transplant without securing the consent of a parent on the teenager's behalf.[36]

(2) ADOLESCENTS' LEGAL RIGHTS TO REFUSE MEDICAL TREATMENT

(A) Overriding an adolescent's refusal to be treated

It is difficult to provide adolescents with a clear explanation of their legal rights regarding their treatment before they enter hospital. As a matter of good practice, medical teams now try to involve all children in medical decisions and do not generally feel it appropriate to force treatment on unwilling patients, however young.[37] But in the event of an adolescent's health deteriorating dangerously, doctors may advise, as they did in *Re R (a minor) (wardship: medical treatment)*[38] and *Re W (a minor) (medical treatment)*,[39] that it is essential for their patient to receive the treatment offered. The Court of Appeal in *Re W* was at pains to emphasise that the courts would normally assume that it was:

---

32   [1986] AC 112.
33   [1992] 4 All ER 627.
34   [1992] 4 All ER 627 at 635.
35   [1992] 4 All ER 627 at 635.
36   Sterilisation procedures are also clearly outside the ambit of s 8. Furthermore, a doctor is unlikely to consider any adolescent between the ages of 16 and 18 sufficiently competent to consent to such a serious irreversible procedure.
37   See BMA (2001 a) p 111.
38   [1992] Fam 11.
39   [1993] Fam 64.

'... in the best interests of a child of sufficient age and understanding to make an informed decision that the court should respect its integrity as a human being and not lightly override its decision on such a personal matter as medical treatment, all the more so if that treatment is invasive.'[40]

Despite these sentiments, the Court of Appeal felt obliged to override the strong objections of the seriously ill teenage patients in *Re R* and *Re W*, to ensure that they received the treatment they needed. In *Re R*, the court authorised compulsory treatment for R, a 15-year-old, in the form of anti-psychotic drugs for her increasingly paranoid and disturbed behaviour. In *Re W*, the patient was so dangerously ill with anorexia that the court considered it essential to override her refusal of treatment, despite her being over 16 and apparently being of sufficient understanding to make an informed decision.[41]

These two Court of Appeal decisions contrived a situation whereby the legal principles apparently depend entirely on whether an adolescent refuses to undergo medical treatment, or consents, even if the proposed treatment is precisely the same. *Gillick v West Norfolk and Wisbech Area Health Authority*[42] must be read in conjunction with the principles established in *Re R* and *Re W*. According to *Gillick*, a teenager of any age can consent to treatment, without parental involvement and however dangerous that treatment may be, as long as he or she passes the *Gillick* competence test. But according to the principles first mooted by the Court of Appeal in *Re R*, and more fully developed in *Re W*, a teenager's refusal to undergo treatment can be overridden, if legal authorisation can be secured from his or her parents or from the court. As Brazier and Bridge comment, according to this case law 'the right to be wrong applies only where minors say yes to treatment'.[43]

The decisions in *Re R* and *Re W* provoked considerable criticism.[44] As Eekelaar commented, Lord Donaldson MR seemed more concerned, in *Re W*, to provide doctors with a legal 'flak jacket',[45] protecting them from actions in negligence, in the event of making a mistaken assessment of *Gillick* competence, than with protecting minors' personal integrity.[46] But this exercise in paternalism was surely predictable. It is inconceivable that any court whose task is to safeguard the best interests of children will willingly stand aside from an adolescent requiring treatment deemed essential to avoid death or severe permanent injury.[47] His or her minor status justifies a paternalistic approach; indeed, one can argue that seriously ill adolescents have a right to greater

---

40   *Re W (a minor) (medical treatment)* [1992] 4 All ER 627 at 643, per Balcombe LJ.

41   Lord Donaldson MR doubted that Thorpe J (at first instance) had been right to conclude that, despite her anorexic condition, W was sufficiently competent to reach an informed decision, but he emphasised that the courts' powers were sufficient to override her wishes irrespective of her age (she was over 16) and her competence to refuse treatment: [1992] 4 All ER 627 at 637. See also Balcombe LJ [1992] 4 All ER 627 at 640. The issue of competence is discussed below, at pp 132–135.

42   [1986] AC 112.

43   M Brazier and C Bridge (1996) p 88.

44   See, inter alia: G Douglas (1992); J Masson (1993); J Eekelaar (1993); I Kennedy and A Grubb (2000) pp 986–989.

45   In *Re W (a minor) (medical treatment)* [1992] 4 All ER 627 at 635 Lord Donaldson coined his legal 'flak jacket' analogy, in preference to the 'key holder' analogy he had used in *Re R (a minor) (wardship: medical treatment)* [1992] Fam 11.

46   J Eekelaar (1993) pp 184–185.

47   In *Re W (a minor) (medical treatment)* [1992] 4 All ER 627 at 643, Balcombe LJ emphasised that it was only justifiable to override an adolescent's objections to treatment in these two particular situations.

protection than adult patients. This approach, though remaining controversial,[48] is in tune with an interest theory of rights which affirms the part to be played by paternalism to protect future choice. Despite its outward appearance of illogicality, the distinction between consent to and refusal of treatment is sustainable, since doctors only recommend treatment which is necessary and in the patient's best interests. Lowe and Juss point out that it is perfectly reasonable for the law to facilitate treatment, by allowing the child to consent to it, whilst refusing parents the right to veto it. Equally, it is reasonable to withhold a child's right to veto treatment which is designed for his or her benefit, particularly if refusal would lead to death or permanent damage.[49] Refusal of medical treatment not only rejects the advice of qualified doctors who know more about treatment for disease than children, but closes down options, rather than opening them up, in such a way which may be regretted later.[50]

Despite the arguments favouring the outcome in *Re R* and *Re W*, these legal principles require urgent reassessment now that the Human Rights Act 1998 has heightened a general awareness of children's rights. In the first place, the most objectionable aspect of this case law is not that the *courts* are entitled to authorise treatment for dying or seriously ill adolescents, despite the patients' own objections, but that parents can, in consultation with their doctors.[51] Indeed, *Re R* and *Re W* not only undermine the *Gillick* decision, so far as teenagers and their parents are concerned, but also significantly enhance the power of doctors. Doctors are gate-keepers to treatment and they alone can restrain the inappropriate exercise of parents' legal powers in disputes over such a matter. Neither adolescents nor their parents can take the ultimate decision whether treatment should go ahead; it will depend entirely on whose views the doctor considers most consistent with his patient's welfare. As noted above, it is now widely acknowledged amongst the medical profession that medical treatment should only be forced on a young patient as a measure of last resort, in a 'situation [which] is truly life-threatening'.[52] Nevertheless, the law implicitly encourages thoroughly poor clinical practice. There is a risk that seriously ill teenagers experience their parents and medical teams ignoring their wishes entirely, in a desire to ensure that they receive the treatment recommended.

Perhaps the most cogent reason for reassessing the principle established in *Re R* and *Re W* is that overcoming refusal inevitably involves interfering with a person's bodily and intellectual autonomy.[53] Current guidance to doctors warns:

'In addition to being difficult to achieve in practice, imposing treatment on young people when they refuse could damage the young person's current and future relationships with health care providers, and undermine trust in the medical profession … If, after spending as much time as is practicable, it is impossible to persuade a child to cooperate with essential treatment, the clinician in charge of the patient's care may decide that restraint is appropriate.'[54]

There are those able to cite examples of teenage patients who are subsequently grateful to their doctors for physically forcing them to undergo the recommended

48   Eg R Huxtable (2000).
49   N Lowe and S Juss (1993) pp 871–872.
50   See J Mason, R McCall Smith and G Laurie (2002) p 329.
51   See discussion in chapter 3.
52   See BMA (2001 a) p 110.
53   G Douglas (1992) p 576.
54   BMA (2001 a) pp 113–114.

treatment.[55] Nevertheless, many doctors feel reluctant to force treatment on a well-grown adolescent and the BMA is clearly uncomfortable with the way in which current law enables them to do so.[56] Current case law indicates that such caution is sensible. The courts have emphasised that the protection provided by the common law and by the ECHR should be taken seriously by those responsible for treating adult patients.[57] Consequently, if a medical team seeks judicial authority to override the refusal of an adult patient to undergo allegedly 'essential treatment', they must carefully justify such an application, particularly the patient's incapacity to decide such matters for him or herself.[58] Even if the patient is mentally incompetent, the team's decision-making may undergo rigorous judicial review.[59] It is arguable that a court should adopt a similar attitude to cases where medical teams wish to treat teenagers against their consent.

An adolescent being forced to undergo treatment may find that articles 3 and 5 of the European Convention, perhaps in conjunction with article 14, offer the strongest vehicles for a successful challenge. Although, at first sight, article 8 might seem useful, since it guarantees the right to 'physical and moral integrity',[60] any infringement of a teenager's rights under article 8(1), by forcing treatment on him or her, might be justified by the medical team arguing that it is *necessary* to protect their young patient's health or morals.[61] Strasbourg jurisprudence indicates that an article 3 challenge might be more fruitful. Forcing an adult patient to undergo medical treatment can involve 'inhuman or degrading treatment', even if he or she is mentally incompetent, unless the treatment is perfectly orthodox medically and is deemed essential by the medical experts consulted.[62] Arguably, the same principle should apply to minors. Similarly, article 5 which protects the right to liberty and security of person, threatens the ability of the courts and doctors to force a teenager, as opposed to a younger child, to undergo treatment in any situation involving the need for significant restraint or detention. Depending on their degree and intensity, even very

---

55   See R Lansdown (1998). He describes (p 460) 'a very large fifteen-year-old' needle phobic patient, who having been counselled, but then held down to undergo a blood test, telling his doctor: 'That's better. Next time I have to have a needle you hold me down, forget all that psychological rubbish.'
56   See BMA (2001 b) p 42.
57   See, inter alia: *Re B (adult: refusal of medical treatment)* [2002] EWHC 429 (Fam), [2002] 2 All ER 449; *R (on the application of Wilkinson) v Broadmoor Hospital* [2001] EWCA Civ 1545, [2002] 1 WLR 419 and commentary in (2002) 10 Med LR 220.
58   See *Re B (adult: refusal of medical treatment)* [2002] EWHC 429 (Fam), [2002] 2 All ER 449, and commentary in (2002) 10 Med LR 203.
59   *R (on the application of Wilkinson) v Broadmoor Hospital* [2001] EWCA Civ 1545, [2002] 1 WLR 419; *R (on the application of John Wooder) v Dr Graham Feggetter and the Mental Health Act Commission* [2002] EWCA Civ 554, (2002) 10 Med LR 223.
60   *X and Y v Netherlands* (1985) 8 EHRR 235.
61   Ie under art 8(2). But such a stance must be carefully justified as being proportionate to the risks involved in the patient not receiving the treatment.
62   See *Herczegfalvy v Austria* (1992) 15 EHRR 437: a dangerously aggressive mental patient had been confined to a security bed and suffered the forcible administration of food and drugs whilst handcuffed and strapped by his ankles. The European Court of Human Rights, held (paras 82–86) that forcible treatment may infringe a psychiatric patient's rights under art 3, unless it amounts to 'a measure which is a therapeutic necessity' according to the 'psychiatric principles generally accepted at the time'. In this case, however, despite the worrying two-week duration of the treatment, there was no infringement because these measures had fulfilled both conditions.

short periods of restraint or detention have been held to infringe its terms.[63] Although the medical team might have a defence to infringing the article 5 rights of an unwilling teenager if they could argue that such a patient was of 'unsound mind',[64] such an argument becomes implausible in the context of a mentally *healthy* adolescent who refuses to undergo life saving treatment.

It is arguable that the *Nielsen* decision[65] would prevent article 5 being available in situations where a relatively young child's parent has consented to the treatment involved. The domestic courts might, however, be loath to accept such an argument when the child is older,[66] or where evidence shows that the medical team has, in effect, dictated its terms of treatment to the parents. In such circumstances, the principle established in *Re R* and *Re W* might be vulnerable to challenges brought under the Human Rights Act 1998, based on articles 3 and 5, combined with article 14, arguing that minors require similar protection from forcible treatment as do adult patients.

Would the courts then be forced to stand aside and allow teenage patients to refuse life-saving treatment? Article 2 of the ECHR offers a possible solution to a court confronted by such a situation. A court might argue that since a minor's rights under the Convention sometimes inevitably conflict, notably his or her rights under articles 2, 3 and 5, it must find an appropriate balance between them. Although a minor patient is entitled to basic freedoms under articles 3 and 5, these rights may be outweighed by the patient's right to life itself, given that article 2 imposes a positive obligation on all public authorities, including the courts, to take all reasonable steps to preserve life.[67] A court exercising its inherent jurisdiction may therefore argue that it cannot ignore its duty to save the life of a desperately ill adolescent, despite his or her strong opposition to treatment,[68] particularly if he or she is incapable of consenting or dissenting from treatment.[69] In reaching such a decision, the court might be particularly influenced by whether the teenager is legally capable of consenting to treatment – but, as discussed below, the law governing this issue lacks clarity and coherence.

---

63   See, inter alia: *X and Y v Sweden* (Application No 7376/76) (1977–78) 7 DR 123 (detention for only two hours prior to deportation could, in principle, amount to a breach of art 5); *X v Austria* (Application No 8278/78) (1979) 18 DR 154 (detention in order to subject the detainee to a blood test, though short, could, in principle, amount to a breach of art 5); *Guzzardi v Italy* (1980) 3 EHRR 333 (para 92) – whether there is an infringement depends on a range of criteria, including the type, duration, effects, and manner of implementation.

64   Ie the art 5(1)(e) exception: 'the lawful detention of persons for the prevention of the spreading of infectious diseases, of persons of unsound mind, alcoholics or drug addicts or vagrants.' See discussion below on treatment for mentally disturbed teenagers.

65   (1988) 11 EHRR 175. Discussed in more detail in chapter 3, pp 81–82.

66   The boy in the *Nielsen* case was 12.

67   *Osman v United Kingdom* [1999] 1 FLR 193 (paras 115–116). See also *R (on the application of Pretty) v Director of Public Prosecutions* [2001] UKHL 61, [2002] 1 All ER 1, per Lord Hope at [87].

68   Such an approach would be consistent *X v Germany* (Application No 10565/83) (1984) 7 EHRR 152, in which the European Commission of Human Rights held that although force feeding a prisoner might, in certain circumstances, amount to a breach of his rights under art 3, the state had a positive obligation under art 2 to preserve his life. The Convention provided no guidance on how to solve the conflict between the two obligations, and here, since the state had acted in the prisoner's best interests in taking action to save his life, rather than to respect his will not to accept nourishment, the complaint was ill-founded.

69   Unless it is a matter of withdrawing life-prolonging care no longer considered beneficial for a desperately ill patient, as in *NHS Trust A v M; NHS Trust B v H* [2001] 1 All ER 801, discussed below.

(B)   Legal capacity to refuse life-saving treatment

Lord Donaldson MR has stated that 'The right to decide one's own fate presupposes a capacity to do so'.[70] Nevertheless, under the existing law, the assessment of a teenager's capacity to refuse treatment has become somewhat of a hollow exercise. As Downie comments:

> '... the application of the principle in *Re W (a minor) (medical treatment)*[71] that the court can always override a refusal of consent even by a *Gillick* competent minor, means that the assessment of his competence is almost a pretence.'[72]

Nevertheless, if, as discussed above, articles 3 and 5 of the ECHR protect teenagers from being forced to have medical treatment against their will, assessing their competence to refuse consent may become far more relevant than hitherto. A court might hesitate before asserting its own duty to preserve the life of a resisting teenager, under article 2, if it considers that the teenager is legally capable of making up his or her own mind over the matter. On this basis, the case law analysing how an adolescent's competence to refuse treatment is of current interest.

Despite their willingness to override a refusal, the courts have explored, in two types of cases, what level of competence an adolescent *theoretically* requires in order to refuse treatment. The first group comprises those teenagers so mentally disturbed that they are unable to assess the costs and benefits of the treatment advised. The second group contains the mentally mature teenagers who oppose life saving treatment for religious reasons or for strongly held ethical views. In some ways, the former group poses less difficult ethical challenges than the latter, since it is easier to countenance overriding the wishes of a mentally disturbed adolescent to ensure that he or she gets the treatment needed, in the same manner as adult mental health patients. But a sense of unease is generated when a court overrides the wishes of a competent adolescent.

The difficulties involved in ascertaining the competence of mentally disturbed adolescents are dealt with later in this chapter.[73] Meanwhile, within the second group of teenagers are the Jehovah's Witness patients, who, regardless of age, normally refuse treatment involving the use of blood products. In these situations, doctors will always attempt to use 'bloodless' alternative procedures.[74] But in some situations this may not be possible, in which case doctors have the added difficulty that they cannot turn to parents for consent, since the whole family is normally of the same faith and equally opposed to blood treatment. In a series of cases, the courts have found it impossible to stand aside and allow teenage Jehovah's Witness patients to bring about their own deaths. So, instead, they simply decide that the adolescent involved has insufficient capacity to be *Gillick* competent, that therefore his or her refusal can be ignored and a decision substituted by the court, in the minor's best interests. *Re E (a minor) (wardship: medical treatment)*,[75] remains the most well known, possibly because of its tragic sequel.[76] Supported by his parents, a 16-year-

---

70   *Re T (an adult) (consent to medical treatment)* [1992] 2 FLR 458 at 470.
71   [1993] Fam 64.
72   A Downie (1999) p 819.
73   See discussed below, pp 151–153.
74   BMA (2001 a) p 109.
75   [1993] 1 FLR 386.
76   Although the teenage patient was forced to undergo treatment, tragically, when he reached the age of 18, he exercised his right as an adult to refuse treatment and died. This sequel to the decision was revealed in *Re S (a minor) (consent to medical treatment)* [1994] 2 FLR 1065.

old Jehovah's Witness refused the advised treatment for his leukaemia which involved the use of blood transfusions. The court was satisfied that although he was of sufficient intelligence to be able to take decisions about his own well-being, he was not *Gillick* competent because there was a range of decisions facing him outside his full comprehension. In particular, he did not have a full understanding of the implications of refusing treatment and the manner of his own death. The hospital authority, who had warded him, obtained the court's consent to override his objections.

Subsequent courts confronted by unco-operative Jehovah's Witness patients[77] have continued to maintain Ward J's approach in *Re E* that they 'should be very slow to allow an infant to martyr himself'.[78] This view obliges them to find a way to overrule a refusal to undergo treatment in such circumstances. A finding of *Gillick* incompetence is readily available, given that the patient must not only understand his or her impending death but also possess 'a greater understanding of the manner of the death and pain and the distress'.[79] Such an approach is controversial. In particular, the court's assessment of incompetence usually focuses on the patients' inability to comprehend the detailed manner of their death, despite information about this having been deliberately withheld from them by their doctors because of its distressing nature.[80] Indeed, case law establishes far less stringent requirements when assessing an adult patient's competence to refuse treatment.[81] Although few adults could comprehend the process of dying, the pain they would suffer, the fear they would undergo and relatives' distress in watching them die, neither doctors nor the courts are entitled to overrule their refusal to undergo treatment for similar reasons.

The courts are obviously aware of the dangers of appearing to discriminate against Jehovah's Witnesses as a sect, simply because of their unorthodox views over medical treatment. After all, their opposition to blood transfusions has proved only too well-founded, in the light of information indicating that contaminated blood has been used by hospitals throughout the world for transfusions. Lord Donaldson MR particularly has urged caution regarding the treatment of both adults and children. Thus in *Re T (an adult) (consent to medical treatment)*[82] he warned that the fact that an adult patient makes a choice which is 'contrary to what is to be expected of the vast majority of adults' is not alone sufficient for doubting his capacity to decide.[83] In *Re W (a minor) (medical treatment)*,[84] he adopted a similar approach to child patients:

---

77   *Re S (a minor) (consent to medical treatment)* [1994] 2 FLR 1065: a 15½-year-old Jehovah's Witness patient suffering from thalassaemia virtually since birth, was kept alive by monthly blood transfusions and daily injections. The court authorised continued treatment despite her expressed wish to the contrary. See also *Re L (medical treatment: Gillick competency)* [1999] 2 FCR 524: a deeply religious 14-year-old Jehovah's Witness patient suffered life-threatening scalds sustained whilst bathing. The court authorised blood transfusion treatment alongside the required surgical intervention, despite her strong opposition.

78   [1993] 1 FLR 386 at 394, per Ward J.

79   *Re S (a minor) (consent to medical treatment)* [1994] 2 FLR 1065 at 1076, per Johnson J.

80   As in *Re E (a minor) (wardship: medical treatment)* [1993] 1 FLR 386 and *Re L (Medical treatment: Gillick competency)* [1999] 2 FCR 524. See C McCafferty (1999).

81   Eg *Re C (refusal of medical treatment)* [1994] 1 FLR 31: the court respected the right of a paranoid schizophrenic to refuse an amputation of his leg to cure potentially fatal gangrene. There was no indication that he fully realised the implications which lay before him as to the process of dying.

82   [1992] 2 FLR 458.

83   [1992] 2 FLR 458 at 471.

84   [1993] Fam 64.

'I personally consider that religious or other beliefs which bar any medical treatment or treatment of particular kinds are irrational, but that does not make minors who hold those beliefs any the less "Gillick competent".'[85]

Eekelaar also considers it inappropriate to hold a child incompetent because his decision reflects socially tolerated views ingrained in his upbringing. As he points out, if this were to be the case, competence could hardly ever be achieved by anyone.[86] Whilst such views promote an admirable religious tolerance, one wonders, like Bridge, whether a child, like the young patient in *Re E*, brought up within the confines of a strong religious sect from birth, is ever capable of truly autonomous decision-making.[87]

Whether or not their opposition to treatment stems from religious convictions, it is theoretically justifiable to argue that seriously ill adolescents have a right to greater protection than adult patients. As commented above, this approach is in tune with an interest theory of rights which affirms the part to be played by paternalism to protect future choice. The crucial question is whether it is appropriate to adjust the levels of legal competence, simply to ensure that they receive it. Where an adolescent refuses to undergo life-saving treatment and parental consent is not available, it may be more honest to accept that the patient is *Gillick* competent, and then to override his or her wishes. The court can legitimately argue that society has an interest in protecting under-age minors, irrespective of competence, from their own dangerous mistakes until they attain their majority. This approach was adopted by Johnson J in *Re M (medical treatment: consent)*[88] when explaining to a 15-year-old girl why he considered it appropriate to override her objections to a life-saving heart transplant. This approach does not demean the minor by suggesting that his or her emotional maturity is fundamentally flawed.

Whatever approach is adopted, the real dilemma remains the same – physical force may be needed to ensure that life-saving treatment takes place.[89] By using articles 3, 5 and 14 of the ECHR to challenge the courts' ability to order them to undergo treatment involving physical restraint, teenage patients may provoke a reassessment of the case law discussed above. The courts may adopt the view that they have a duty, under article 2 of the Convention, to protect the minor patient's life and that this outweighs their duty not to infringe his or her rights under articles 3 and 5.[90] But, as many medical teams fully appreciate, enforced survival to adulthood may not, in every case, be in a child's best interests.[91] Some writers have urged that the courts should adopt a more critical approach to the assumption that minors, unlike adults,[92] must always be forced to live. Thus as Lewis argues:

85   [1992] 4 All ER 627 at 637.
86   J Eekelaar (1994) p 57. See also I Kennedy (1992 a) pp 56–57, in relation to adults.
87   C Bridge (1999) p 588.
88   [1999] 2 FLR 1097.
89   This was specifically acknowledged by Johnson J in *Re S (a minor) (consent to medical treatment)* [1994] 2 FLR 1065, who considered it 'extremely distastful' (at 1074) to envisage the use of force.
90   As noted above at p 131, n 68, such an approach would be consistent with *X v Germany* (Application No 10565/83) (1984) 7 EHRR 152, in which the European Commission of Human Rights made it clear that the state could choose which obligations to promote if there is an obvious conflict.
91   See R Lansdown (1998). This author cites examples of dying children refusing treatment which might extend their life-span for a period.
92   In *Re B (adult: refusal of medical treatment)* [2002] EWHC 429 (Fam), [2002] 2 All ER 449 the Court of Appeal emphasised a competent adult patient's right to refuse life-saving treatment. See also *NHS Trust A v M; NHS Trust B v H* [2001] 1 All ER 801, in which the Court of Appeal held that art 2 does not oblige medical teams to continue treating desperately ill patients (in that case two PVS patients) against their best interests.

'It may be that in a small minority of cases, an adolescent will be able to make a competent, maximally autonomous choice to refuse life-saving treatment. Respecting such a choice will be difficult, but it is preferable to arbitrary discrimination on the basis of age alone.'[93]

Such an approach might involve the courts questioning the value of forcing a teenager to undergo years of regular invasive treatment,[94] as opposed to a one-off blood transfusion or even major surgery. In Bridge's words, 'Surely there must come a time when a mature adolescent, like an adult suffering from chronic disability, can say "enough is enough" and reject treatment'.[95]

SECTION B ADOLESCENT DECISION-MAKING – THE DIFFICULT CASES

(1) THE CONTROL OF FERTILITY

(A) Contraception

It would have been perverse for the law to spurn adolescents prepared to brave the doctor's surgery or birth control clinic to seek contraceptive treatment and advice, by refusing to acknowledge their right to take control over an intimate aspect of their lives. The decision in *Gillick v West Norfolk and Wisbech Area Health Authority*[96] provided a legal affirmation of an adolescent's right to act responsibly by seeking support and help outside the privacy of her family, even if this is contrary to her parents' own convictions. It confirmed that doctors can provide contraceptive advice and treatment for *Gillick* competent girls under the age of 16 without informing or consulting their parents. Moreover, the House of Lords was unanimous that a doctor would not incur criminal liability by so doing, if the prescription of contraceptive treatment was medically indicated.[97] He clearly has a defence if it involves the bona fide exercise of his clinical judgment over what is best for his patient's health.[98]

Some might describe the decision in *Gillick* as a victory of realism over idealism; certainly it was an exercise in pragmatism. The decision would never have reached the House of Lords had not Mrs Gillick been so determined to prevent her adolescent daughters obtaining contraceptive advice and treatment without being consulted herself. It is unlikely that a mother with similar views to Mrs Gillick would be treated particularly sympathetically if she now argued that the *Gillick* principle infringes her rights under article 8 of the ECHR.[99] Indeed, drawing strength from the fact that the European Commission and Court have stressed that article 8 protects all intimate aspects of private life,[100] the domestic courts might prefer to protect an adolescent girl's own right to respect for her private sexual life, free from parental interference.

---

93 See P Lewis (2001) p 159.
94 In *Re S (a minor) (consent to medical treatment)* [1994] 2 FLR 1065, the 15-year-old sufferer of thalassaemia was to be forced to undergo monthly blood transfusions for a further two and a half years until, at the age of 18, she could refuse treatment.
95 C Bridge (1999) p 593.
96 [1986] AC 112.
97 Aiding and abetting unlawful intercourse with a girl under 16 under the Sexual Offences Act 1956, s 28.
98 [1986] AC 112, per Lord Scarman at 190–191 and Lord Fraser at 175.
99 See discussion of this point in chapter 3, pp 81–82.
100 Eg *Dudgeon v United Kingdom* (1981) 4 EHRR 149. See also *Sutherland v United Kingdom* (1997) 24 EHRR CD 22 (para 56).

Adults may find it unpalatable to come to terms with adolescent sexual activity. The high rate of teenage pregnancy in the United Kingdom is clear evidence that adolescents reach physical, if not psychological, maturity extremely rapidly.[101] Research indicates that the outcomes for teenagers who complete their pregnancies, and for their babies, are extremely poor, both in health and in socio-economic terms. Furthermore, the adverse outcomes pass to the next generation who, in turn, are more likely to become teenage mothers themselves, more likely to experience poverty, poor housing and nutrition and to live in a single parent family.[102]

It seems unlikely that teenagers can be persuaded that complete abstinence from sexual activity is the best way of forcing down the rate of teenage pregnancies. Since the statistics suggest that adolescents are starting intercourse at increasingly early ages,[103] the key must be better sex education in schools,[104] and an increased use of contraception.[105] The contraceptive pill continues to be a relatively safe and easy method for teenage girls to adopt; indeed, Lord Scarman noted that:

> '… women have obtained by the availability of the pill a choice of life-style with a degree of independence and of opportunity undreamed of until this generation … The law ignores these developments at its peril.'[106]

The decision in *Gillick* reflected acceptance of the common-sense advice from the Department of Health that to abandon the principle of confidentiality for adolescents under 16 receiving contraceptive advice might lead to increased pregnancy and sexually transmitted diseases. Many teenagers would prefer to risk sexual activity without using contraceptive measures at all, rather than involve their parents in such a decision. Indeed, Mrs Gillick was wrong to assume that good parents can, through sympathetic discussion, ensure that their children will understand the need for restraint in sexual activity. Even in the closest families, teenagers and parents in the United Kingdom often feel uncomfortable when talking about matters to do with sex and contraception.[107]

Despite the *Gillick* decision being regarded as the high-water mark for recognising adolescent decision-making rights, within its own context its demands are relatively rigorous. A teenage girl can neither demand contraceptive services from her doctor nor confidentiality, irrespective of her circumstances. Lord Fraser's judgment provided doctors with practical advice which became immediately influential. He considered

---

101   The UK has the highest teenage birth rate in Europe and the highest in the world, bar the USA. See Innocenti Research Centre (2001) for a wealth of detailed statistics and international comparisons, esp figs 1, 2 and 3. See also R Kane and K Wellings (1999) pp 3–10.

102   By the age of 33, those who became mothers in their teens have, inter alia, a higher likelihood of lacking any qualification, being on substantially lower income, and being more likely to be divorced or separated. See Social Exclusion Unit (hereafter SEU) (1999) paras 3.9–3.10. See also Innocenti Research Centre (2001) Figures 5 and 12.

103   The numbers of those sexually active by the age of 16 doubled between 1965 and 1991, with the greatest rise for girls. See SEU (1999) paras 6.1–6.4.

104   See discussion in chapter 6, pp 186–191. The incidence of sexually transmitted diseases amongst teenagers has increased, with a 45% increase of gonorrhoea between 1995 and 1997: SEU (1999) para 7.1.

105   Between 1975 and 1999-2000 the numbers of girls under 16 visiting family planning clinics only increased from 1% to 7%. See National Statistics (2001) p 51. Between one third and half of sexually active teenagers do not use contraception for their first act of intercourse. See SEU (1999) para 7.0.

106   [1986] AC 112 at 183.

107   Although children are much more likely to talk about sex and relationships with their mothers than with their fathers, these conversations are far less likely to occur at all in UK families, compared with families in the Netherlands. See SEU (1999) para 5.19. See also Innocenti Research Centre (2001) pp 21–23.

that a doctor should only provide a girl with treatment or advice without involving her parents, if fully satisfied over five rigorous requirements.[108] These are that the girl must understand his advice; she cannot be persuaded to inform her parents of the matter; she is likely to have sexual intercourse with or without contraceptive treatment; it is likely that her physical or mental health will suffer should she not receive the treatment; her best interests require her to receive the treatment without her parents' consent.[109] Lord Fraser's five requirements were adopted by the revised government guidance[110] and by the medical profession and are regarded as the rules governing those prescribing teenagers with contraceptive services.[111]

Despite adolescents gaining the right to obtain contraception against their parents' wishes, as noted above, the rate of teenage pregnancies continues to be disappointingly high,[112] with strong efforts being made to reduce it.[113] The present law is contributing to this situation through its failure to provide all teenage girls with a clear right to medical confidentiality in the event of their seeking advice. Indeed, the confused state of the law clearly deters many teenagers from seeking medical advice altogether.[114] No doubt exists if a doctor decides that a girl is mature enough to receive contraceptive treatment. He then has a duty to keep this matter confidential from her parents and outside agencies, unless she agrees to this being disclosed.[115] But the law is unclear over whether a girl not deemed sufficiently mature to appreciate the contraceptive advice or treatment is also entitled to confidentiality. The House of Lords in *Gillick* did not put their respective minds to the question of medical confidentiality in such circumstances. Current professional advice is ambivalent over this situation. The General Medical Council appears to assume that a doctor needs only to maintain medical confidentiality in relation to a patient who is competent to consent to treatment. Consequently, it advises that a doctor can divulge information to the parents of a *Gillick incompetent* patient, but it suggests that he should only do so if he is convinced that the disclosure is essential in the patient's medical interests and he must inform her of his intention before telling them.[116] This advice has been strongly justified by Kennedy on legal and ethical grounds.[117] He argues that in the event of a child being assessed as *Gillick* incompetent, the doctor should be able to ensure that parents intervene to protect their daughter from involvement in sexual activity, if he considers this to be in her best interests. He

---

108 [1986] AC 112 at 174.
109 Some argue, perhaps unrealistically, that the last requirement should not be confined to the girl's best *medical* interests, but should be extended to her *general* best interests. See, inter alia: I Kennedy (1992 b) pp 93-96; P Parkinson (1986) and J Eekelaar (1986) pp 6–7.
110 Department of Health (hereafter DH) (1986).
111 Royal College of General Practitioners and Brook (2000) p 10.
112 The Committee on the Rights of the Child (1995) para 30 and (2002) para 42, suggested that the government should make additional efforts to reduce the problem of teenage pregnancies.
113 Responding to the SEU's report (1999), the government established the cross-departmental Teenage Pregnancy Unit, responsible for delivering the Teenage Pregnancy Strategy, via local teenage pregnancy programmes. The programme of implementation, funded by £16 m, aims to reduce teenage pregnancy by 15% by 2004.
114 Research indicates that many sexually active teenagers think that their parents will be told if they try to obtain contraception or that it is illegal to obtain it under the age of 16. See SEU (1999) para 7.7.
115 Professional guidance indicates that breach of medical confidentiality is normally only justified if a doctor believes the patient to be a victim of sexual or other abuse. See p 126, n 30.
116 General Medical Council (2000) para 38.
117 I Kennedy (1992 b) pp 111–117.

asserts that a doctor cannot owe a duty of confidentiality to a child legally incapable of entering into a legal relationship with him and therefore incapable of demanding his secrecy. Such a view is controversial, since it means that teenagers cannot be guaranteed secrecy, despite the fact that most doctors consider it to be against a young patient's best interests to make such a disclosure without her consent.[118] Meanwhile, the BMA takes the view that the duty of confidentiality is owed to all patients, including mature and immature minors, whether or not they have capacity to consent to treatment.[119]

The current uncertainty in the law means that the adolescent will not know the outcome of the doctor's assessment of her competence and therefore whether he intends telling her parents until after her consultation. Guidance produced for a wide range of practitioners involved in providing family planning and contraception services reminds them that many young people are apprehensive about talking to doctors for fear that their confidentiality will not be respected. It strongly urges practitioners always to maintain confidentiality other than in the most exceptional circumstances, for example, where they believe that the child is being sexually exploited or abused.[120] It appears that such advice is widely followed.

Despite this residual uncertainty over an adolescent's right to medical confidentiality, the present law reflects a refreshingly liberal approach to adolescent sexuality and the need to promote adolescents' capacity for autonomy by legally recognising their decision-making powers.

(B)   Abortion

Despite the United Kingdom having the highest rate of teenage birth in Western Europe, the abortion rate amongst teenagers is comparatively low.[121] Indeed, it is surprising there are not more abortions carried out in this age group, given the high number of accidental pregnancies and the grave adverse consequences attending teenage pregnancies and birth.[122] Research indicates that teenagers who decide to keep their babies are completely unprepared for the amount of time and effort involved in looking after them,[123] and that considerable barriers deter them from getting back into education or work.[124] Why such relatively large numbers of teenage mothers

---

118 See J Montgomery, who strongly criticises Kennedy's view, in J Montgomery (2003) pp 308–311.
119 See BMA (1999) p 7. See also BMA (2001 a), which (p 82) stresses that even in the case of a child too immature to consent to treatment, confidentiality should still generally be maintained, and unless there are very convincing reasons to the contrary, parents should only be told about their child's request for treatment, medication or advice with the patient's permission.
120 Royal College of General Practitioners and Brook (2000) pp 10–13.
121 Approximately half the pregnancies amongst under 16-year-olds are terminated. Over one third of conceptions to under 20s end in abortion and this figure is rising. See SEU (1999) para 8.14. The United Kingdom has the fourth highest abortion rate in Europe (the highest in Western Europe). Nevertheless, the teenage abortion ratio (the number of abortions per 1,000 live births) is relatively low, indicating that the majority of conceptions to women under 20 are carried to term. See R Kane and K Wellings (1999) p10 and Innocenti Research Centre (2001) fig 13.
122 See discussion above.
123 See S Tabberer et al (2000) pp 44–45.
124 SEU (1999) ch 9.

decide to keep their babies is unclear. It appears that young people in more deprived areas disapprove strongly of abortion[125] and that whilst teenage pregnancy has become socially acceptable, abortion is not seen as a positive option, and is often not considered at all.[126] Indeed, disapproval of abortion expressed by their own close families, particularly by their own parents, and by the baby's father influences some teenagers to keep their babies.[127] Research suggests that more open discussion about abortion might encourage young people, their parents and their communities to see it as a positive, rather than a negative choice.[128]

Sometimes a pregnant teenager, knowing her parents' views and the baby's father's opposition to the concept of abortion,[129] feels obliged to seek a termination secretly. Does she have the right to proceed with such a procedure without involving her parents? Just as the decision in *Gillick*[130] established the right of a *Gillick* competent girl to consent on her own behalf to receive contraceptive advice and treatment, the same principle should also apply to her undergoing an abortion. There seems no reason why a pregnant girl, whether under or over 16, should not be sufficiently intelligent and mature to understand what is involved in undergoing an abortion, if she wishes to have her pregnancy terminated.[131] Those opposed to abortion per se, would, of course, oppose such a course for any pregnant woman, irrespective of age. But others would urge that a young girl has a moral right to have her choice respected over this, bearing in mind the consequences of denial. Indeed, more pragmatically, unless her choice over such a matter were legally acknowledged, she might be tempted to take the law into her own hands and obtain an abortion by unofficial routes.

But, again, the test for *Gillick* competence does not clarify the degree of maturity a doctor should expect from a girl before assessing her sufficiently competent to agree to such a procedure. It might be argued that any girl asking for an abortion should be deemed sufficiently competent to consent to such a procedure. Although this is perhaps an over-simplistic approach,[132] a decision to undergo an abortion is not one taken lightly. A doctor might argue that the ability to reach such a decision indicates sufficient maturity to justify the adolescent concerned being given complete freedom in this respect. The principles established in *Gillick* in relation to contraception certainly imply that if a doctor considers the girl to be sufficiently competent to consent to an abortion, and he considers that an abortion is medically advised, he should not insist on consulting her parents over the matter. Thus English law is much more liberal in this respect than American case law,[133] which has confirmed[134] that it is neither unconstitutional for state legislation to require doctors to notify the parents of teenage

---

125 SEU (1999) para 8.18.

126 See S Tabberer et al (2000) pp 19 and 44.

127 S Tabberer et al (2000) ch 5.

128 S Tabberer et al (2000) pp 44–45.

129 NB the father of an unborn child has no legal right to prevent the mother undergoing an abortion, as long as she and her medical advisers comply with the procedures established by the Abortion Act 1967. See *Paton v British Pregnancy Advisory Service Trustees* [1979] QB 276; *Kelly v Kelly* [1997] 2 FLR 828; *Paton v United Kingdom* (1980) 3 EHRR 408.

130 [1986] AC 112.

131 M Brazier (1992) p 338.

132 The American Supreme Court could find 'no logical relationship between the capacity to become pregnant and the capacity for mature judgment concerning the wisdom of an abortion': *HL v Matheson* 450 US 398 (1981) p 408. See discussion by R Hartman (2000) p 1355.

133 The American case law is usefully discussed by R Hartman (2000) pp 1344–1355.

134 Following the lead established by the Supreme Court in *Bellotti v Baird* 443 US 622 (1979).

patients before arranging for them to undergo an abortion,[135] nor for it to make parental or judicial consent a pre-condition to such an abortion.[136]

Despite its apparent liberality, English law is confused over what happens if the girl's parents wish to take legal steps to oppose her arrangements for an abortion. As noted above, research suggests that some teenagers' parents may exert considerable pressure on their daughters to keep their babies due to their own antipathy towards abortion.[137] Legally, although her parents are not entitled to veto any medical procedure a *Gillick* competent girl has consented to, this does not prevent them seeking the assistance of the courts to stop her going ahead with an abortion against their wishes.[138] The case law relevant to this issue suggests that the courts are not particularly receptive to such parental applications.[139] Nevertheless, depending on her age and maturity, an open disagreement between an adolescent and her parents over whether her pregnancy should be terminated may often make doctors reluctant to go ahead without obtaining prior court authorisation.[140]

Has a *Gillick* competent pregnant girl the right to resist the wishes of her parents who want her to undergo an abortion? In *Re W (a minor) (medical treatment)*[141] both Lord Donaldson MR and Balcombe LJ admitted that, according to their interpretation of the law, a teenage girl could be forced to undergo an abortion against her wishes, merely on the consent of her parents. Balcombe LJ, however, considered that such a situation was highly unlikely, mainly because medical ethics would not permit doctors to carry out such procedures in these circumstances without obtaining court authority.[142] Lord Donaldson MR was less sure, saying:

'Whilst this may be possible as a matter of law, I do not see any likelihood, taking account of medical ethics, unless the abortion was truly in the basic interests of the child. This is not to say that it could not happen.'[143]

Clearly the parents could themselves invoke the assistance of the courts by warding their daughter and seeking court authorisation for the abortion. Nevertheless, Balcombe LJ thought it difficult to conceive of a court ordering an abortion against the wishes of a mentally competent 16-year-old.[144] One can only agree. Whilst paternalistic interventions to override the wishes of children, however mature in age, can be justified if they are determined to make choices which will destroy their own opportunities for choice in the future, a court would find it very difficult to justify overriding a pregnant girl's wishes, unless her doctors advised that continuing with

135 *HL v Matheson* 450 US 398 (1981). See B Bridge (1982).
136 *Planned Parenthood of Southeastern Pennsylvania v Casey* 112 S Ct 2791 (1992). This case law undermines the teenager's right to confidentiality since it forces her to consult her parents or seek court authorisation.
137 See S Tabberer et al (2000) ch 5.
138 Ie by seeking the court's assistance through its inherent jurisdiction, or by seeking a specific issue order or prohibited steps order under the Children Act 1989, s 8.
139 *Re P (a minor)* [1986] 1 FLR 272: the court authorised a 15-year-old girl in local authority care to undergo an abortion despite her parents' opposition to this procedure.
140 Eg *Re B (wardship: abortion)* [1991] 2 FLR 426: B, a 12-year-old girl, was made a ward of court in order to obtain court approval for the proposed termination. It was doubtful that B was *Gillick* competent given that she appeared to be completely overpowered by her mother and grandmother. Her mother opposed her undergoing the abortion and her grandmother favoured it.
141 [1992] 4 All ER 627.
142 [1992] 4 All ER 627 at 645.
143 [1992] 4 All ER 627 at 635.
144 [1992] 4 All ER 627 at 645.

her pregnancy was likely to jeopardise her future survival. Such objections could now be buttressed by a claim that articles 3,[145] 5 and 8 of the ECHR would probably all protect her from undergoing an abortion against her will.

The dearth of case law relevant to this issue suggests that in practice these situations very rarely come before the courts. Pregnant teenagers are probably bullied by their families into bearing or not bearing babies, without any external restraint. Regrettably, current case law supports parents in taking such a stance, as long as they can justify their behaviour on the basis that they believe it to be in their daughter's best interests. Nevertheless, few would quarrel with the proposition that an adolescent has a right to have her choices respected over whether she carries her baby to term or not and that this right should be translated into clear legal principles.

(2)   TREATMENT FOR MENTALLY DISTURBED ADOLESCENTS

(A)   The background

Adolescence is a time when young people commonly experience mood swings, ranging from intense exhilaration to extreme depression. It is also an age when the frequency of many psycho-social disorders increases.[146] Although there is no general agreement over the overall prevalence rate for child and adolescent mental health problems, there seems to be a consensus that it has been rising in nearly all developed countries.[147] Suicidal or self-mutilating behaviour,[148] aggression and violence obviously need urgent treatment and may endanger others if left untreated. Furthermore, children clearly have a right to the 'highest attainable standard of health'.[149] Nevertheless, medical teams must also take account of their young patients' other rights: their right to freedom from arbitrary deprivation of liberty[150] and to protection from all forms of physical violence.[151] Indeed, a working party report prepared for the Council of Europe has maintained that protective measures for minors undergoing involuntary placement and treatment should be *more* stringent than for adult mental health patients.[152] Under domestic law in England and Wales, however, as the discussion below indicates, minors' liberty may be restricted for indeterminate lengths of time, with no independent safeguards. Consequently, an adolescent with mental health problems may quite reasonably fear voluntarily entering a unit where he or she knows that 'emergency' sedating medication is used as a means of control, rather than treatment.[153]

---

145   It is unlikely that the doctors could argue that performing an enforced abortion is a therapeutic necessity and in accordance with accepted medical practice, as required by *Herczegfalvy v Austria* (1992) 15 EHRR 437.
146   See Audit Commission (1999) ch 2 for an analysis of the age, sex and type of problem presented to the child and mental health services (CAMHS). By far the highest number of inpatients are girls between the ages of 15 and 18. But see H Meltzer and R Gatward (2000) p 27. Their survey of prevalence rates of mental disorder amongst a younger age group of children, viz those aged between 5 and 15, showed greater numbers of boys than girls being affected: 11% cf 8%.
147   Audit Commission (1999) ch 2. See the research summarised in para 1 and appendix 2.
148   See SEU (2000) research summarised in ch 1, on 'Mental health, including suicide'. This suggests that the rate of self-harm amongst young people has increased since the mid-1980s.
149   CRC, art 24(1).
150   CRC, art 37(b); ECHR, art 5.
151   See CRC, esp arts 19(a) and 37. See also ECHR, arts 3 and 8.
152   See Council of Europe (2000) para 8.1.
153   See below.

The case law shows the courts, parents, treatment units and local authorities using a bewildering variety of overlapping methods to authorise both admission, detention and treatment against a young patient's will. In truth, the legal principles governing the treatment of adolescents with mental health problems are extremely confusing. This is exacerbated by the fact that the principles governing the compulsory admission of an adolescent to a unit do not also carry legal authority to treat the patient against his or her wishes. The distinction between the two sets of legal principles is an important one. In many cases the admission itself is unproblematic, but the patient objects to the form of treatment. The quickest method for practitioners to obtain the necessary consents is to seek parental authority for 'informal admission' and then to treatment. In complex cases, however, clinical teams may prefer to seek the High Court's assistance under its inherent jurisdiction to authorise compulsory admission and/or treatment. Alternatively, a local authority may obtain a secure accommodation order under the Children Act 1989, section 25(1). Although such an order deals with admission and detention, it cannot govern treatment; consent to compulsory treatment must then be obtained by some other means, either from the teenager, the parent or from the court. Despite being available, many commentators suggest that none of these methods should be used in preference to the procedures available under the mental health legislation, which carefully regulates compulsory admission and treatment.

(B)   The mental health legislation

A seriously ill adolescent confronting compulsory admission for treatment might quite reasonably conclude that there are considerable advantages to being admitted to hospital under the mental health legislation, rather than under the common law. This legislation, which may soon undergo radical reform,[154] applies to all patients requiring compulsory treatment for mental disorders, irrespective of their age. It recognises that removing an individual's liberty in order to treat them on a compulsory basis is a drastic step and it contains a set of strict legislative safeguards which apply to all mental health patients. Many of its provisions are specifically intended to protect all such patients from arbitrary restrictions on their liberty and unsupervised treatment regimes.[155] Admission is strictly regulated,[156] and there are

154 See DH/Home Office (2000), DH (2002 a), DH (2002 b), DH (2002 c).
155 See P Bartlett and R Sandland (2000) esp ch 7. Safeguards under the Mental Health Act 1983 include, inter alia: restrictions on the use of certain types of treatment (ss 57 and 58); the right to information and explanations over admission and treatment (s 132); the right of patients to have their case heard by a mental health review tribunal within 14 days of admission if detained under s 2 and once every six months if detained under ss 3–66. Various restrictions on the form of treatment available include, inter alia: treatment without consent must be confined to treating the mental disorder from which the patient is suffering and does not extend to unrelated physical disorders (although this is widely interpreted) (s 63); some treatments such as ECT can only be given with consent or with independent medical opinion (s 58); some treatments, including psycho-surgery, can, unless life-saving, only be given with consent and a second opinion (s 57). Patients' relatives also have important rights relating to the patient's care. The government intends that these safeguards will be redesigned and, in the main, strengthened under new legislation presented to Parliament, after consultation.
156 An application can be made for compulsory admission for assessment under s 2, or for treatment under s 3 of the Mental Health Act 1983. The grounds for admission for assessment are that the patient is suffering from mental disorder of a nature or degree which warrants his detention in a hospital for assessment (or for assessment followed by medical treatment) and that he ought to be so detained in the interests of his own health or safety or with a view to

clear procedures for gaining an early discharge.[157] These safeguards are designed to compensate for the fact that a patient's competence to consent to or refuse treatment does not prevent treatment taking place. Detention and compulsory treatment can be authorised if it is necessary for the patient's health or safety, or for the protection of others,[158] whether or not the patient has the capacity to agree to or refuse treatment.[159]

Despite all its in-built safeguards, those treating mentally ill or behaviourally disturbed minors have, in the past, been reluctant to use the mental health legislation for their treatment.[160] The most common objection,[161] and the judiciary have appeared to accept this view, is the perceived stigma attached to the use of compulsory powers.[162] It is arguably disadvantageous in later life for it to become known that an individual was formerly treated under the mental health legislation. Furthermore, those wishing to ensure that adolescents obtain the treatment they need have been able to turn to other methods. By far the simplest route for a clinical team is to gain legal authority for treatment from the adolescent's parents under the principle established by the Court of Appeal in *Re R (a minor) (wardship: medical treatment)*[163] and *Re W (a minor) (medical treatment)*.[164] In the absence of parental consent, the clinical teams have been able to turn to the courts instead for judicial authorisation of compulsory admission and treatment. This might appear preferable, since a court order may be of some comfort to a clinical team faced with a complex case and the child normally obtains some form of independent representation.[165] In its current form, the mental health legislation provides neither of these advantages. In particular, there is no method whereby a minor patient can be independently represented in the decision-making procedures regarding his or her detention and treatment.[166]

the protection of other persons. The grounds for admission for treatment are that the patient is suffering from mental illness, severe mental impairment, psychopathic disorder or mental impairment, his mental disorder is of a nature or degree making it appropriate for him to receive medical treatment in a hospital, and in the case of psychopathic disorder or mental impairment, such treatment is likely to alleviate or prevent deterioration in his condition. It must also be shown that the treatment is necessary for the patient's health or safety or for the protection of other persons and it cannot be provided unless he is detained under this section. These grounds will be substantially redesigned by the proposed reforms. See n 154 above.

157 See P Bartlett and R Sandland (2000) ch 8.
158 Mental Health Act 1983, s 3(2).
159 Mental Health Act 1983, s 63.
160 BMA (2001 a) p 140.
161 BMA (2001 a) p 140.
162 Eg *Re W (a minor) (medical treatment)* [1992] 4 All ER 627 at 639, per Lord Donaldson MR. See also *Re K, W and H (minors) (medical treatment)* [1993] 1 FLR 854 at 857, per Thorpe J. He accepted without question that the hospital's support for 'Parental preference' explained its avoiding the mental health legislation to ensure treatment of one of the three girls involved in that case.
163 [1992] Fam 11.
164 [1993] Fam 64.
165 When the inherent jurisdiction is invoked, the child is normally represented by CAFCASS Legal. In the event of a secure accommodation order being sought under the Children Act 1998, s 25, the child is represented by a children's guardian. See chapter 7 for further details regarding the legal representation of children.
166 But the new mental health legislation may contain provisions providing 16–18-year-olds with independent representation. See discussion below.

It appears that attitudes to the use of the mental health legislation are changing and that, particularly when treating eating disorders in older children, practitioners are much more prepared to envisage its use.[167] They may soon have little choice when considering compulsory treatment for adolescents aged 16 and 17. The government clearly appreciates the deficiencies in the existing law and has, subject to consultation on these points, undertaken to –

'introduce safeguards to protect children and young people who could otherwise be treated against their wishes, but with their parents' consent. These provisions are intended to strike a fair balance between the rights of the child to liberty under Article 5 of the European Convention on Human Rights (ECHR) and the rights of parents to respect for family life under Article 8.'[168]

More specifically, it suggests that 16 and 17-year-olds should 'have a greater say in decisions which affect their lives …', with the new mental health legislation treating them as adults. Thus 'wherever compulsory powers are needed they will have access to the full protection offered by the legislation'.[169]

This intention to prohibit the use of compulsory powers outside the mental health regime for these older adolescents has obviously been provoked by concerns that they might successfully challenge their compulsory admission and treatment under the Human Rights Act 1998. The use of compulsory powers to restrain and treat a mental health patient would, in normal circumstances, infringe his or her rights under article 5 of the ECHR, unless it fits into the 'of unsound mind' exception.[170] Although Strasbourg case law indicates that that term is not susceptible to a definitive interpretation, there are certain rigorous criteria to be fulfilled.[171] The new mental health legislation is, through a range of new safeguards, designed to make its provisions fully Human Rights Act compliant.[172] Consequently, if the government's intentions

167 It has now become far more commonplace for psychiatrists to use the mental health legislation as a means of treating anorexia nervosa and other eating disorders in older children. See BMA (2001 a) p 144. The law supports this approach. See *Riverside Mental Health NHS Trust v Fox* [1994] 1 FLR 614, where the Court of Appeal was satisfied that anorexia nervosa was a mental disorder under the Mental Health Act 1983, s 63 and that force-feeding an adult sufferer was a form of medical treatment for such a disorder; per Sir Stephen Brown P [1994] 1 FLR 614 at 619.
168 See DH (2002 c) para 3.7.
169 See DH (2002 c) para 3.8. See also DH/Home Office (2000) paras 3.70–3.72.
170 Art 5(1)(e) allows 'the lawful detention of persons for the prevention of the spreading of infectious diseases, of persons of unsound mind, alcoholics or drug addicts or vagrants'.
171 According to *Winterwerp v Netherlands* (1979) 2 EHRR 387 (para 39), the medical disorder must exist, according to objective medical advice, must be sufficiently extreme to justify the detention and detention must last only as long as the disorder itself. According to *Ashingdane v United Kingdom* (1985) 7 EHRR 528, detention must take place within a hospital, clinic or other appropriate institution. But even if the treatment is article 5 compliant, it may infringe the patient's rights under article 3 and/or 8. See *R (on the application of Wilkinson) v Broadmoor Hospital* [2001] EWCA Civ 1545, [2002] 1 WLR 419, and especially Hale LJ's discussion of *Herczegfalvy v Austria* (1992) 15 EHRR 437 at [77]–[84].
172 Inter alia: a new independent tribunal, the Mental Health Tribunal, to determine all longer-term use of compulsory powers; no compulsory treatment lasting more than 28 days unless authorised by a care and treatment order made by the Mental Health Tribunal, that order incorporating a care plan drawn up for the patient; the patient's care plan prepared after consultation with the patient, or a nominated person, chosen by the patient to represent him or her; the right to free independent advocacy to challenge the use of compulsory powers; strict time limits on reviews. See DH (2002 a), DH (2002 b).

bear fruit, all these will be available for older teenage patients, just like adult patients requiring compulsory admission and treatment.

The recommended new provisions governing 16 and 17-year-olds would fulfil many of the suggestions made by the Council of Europe for all minor patients. Although in that body's view, protection measures for minors should ideally be *more* stringent than those for adults, '[T]he conditions and safeguards relating to involuntary placement and treatment of adults should also apply to minors to the same extent at the very least'.[173] Nevertheless, whilst the older age group may gain such protection, the government has given no clear commitment regarding compulsory treatment for those under 16. Presumably reflecting a concern not to undermine parental autonomy, it asserts that, under the new law, '[P]arents will, as now, be able to consent to treatment on behalf of their children'.[174] But if the child resists the treatment, the parents' authority will only operate for 28 days, after which, treatment must be authorised by the mental health tribunal.[175] The flaw in this suggestion is that the extra safeguards are triggered by the child's resistance. Under these recommendations, the child who is bullied by his or her parents into submission is left without any independent advice or representation. Such grudging changes would not fulfil the recommendations of the Council of Europe. That body has placed no age limits on its recommendations regarding minors. Furthermore, it has observed that since minor patients may not be able to defend their own interests, those facing involuntary placement should have a representative from the *beginning* of the procedure, and that this should only be a family member if there is no conflict of interest.[176]

It is obvious that the government clearly perceives the need to reform the current legal principles governing the compulsory treatment of mentally disordered children. As discussed below, the reasons are obvious. English minors currently have significantly less protection than adults. But whilst it appears that radical reform is only planned for the older age group, further changes may emerge even for the younger age group. In the first place, medical practitioners, particularly child and adolescent psychiatrists, will become more familiar with using the mental health legislation for the older age group and perhaps more prepared to countenance its use for their younger patients. Second, younger patients may use the Human Rights Act 1998 to challenge involuntary placements and treatment.[177]

(C) Parental authorisation for admission and treatment

(i) Admission

Although teenagers with behavioural disorders are troublesome for those responsible for them, it appears that many of them obligingly avoid the need for their compulsory admission into a secure treatment unit. They comply with their parents' arrangements

---

173 Council of Europe (2000) para 8.1.
174 See DH (2002 c) para 3.9.
175 A patient who obviously resists treatment during the initial 28-day period will gain independent representation and the right to challenge his or her treatment by applying to the mental health tribunal. DH (2002 c) para 3.9.
176 Council of Europe (2000) para 8.2.
177 See discussion below.

and voluntarily enter and stay in residence,[178] despite their objection to compulsory assessment and/or treatment.[179] Some specialised treatment units do not use formal detention methods, such as locking the patients in, and therefore escape the need to comply with the secure accommodation regulations.[180] But although the young patients are in theory treated on 'open' wards, they often feel unable to leave. In some cases, a regime of tranquillising medication might undermine a patient's ability for independent thought or action; in others less subtle methods are used to prevent their leaving. Indeed, the decision in *R v Kirklees Metropolitan Borough Council, ex p C*[181] demonstrates that the current law does little to ensure that an adolescent patient's entry into a specialised unit is properly supervised. If a similar situation were to occur again, the adolescent involved could undoubtedly claim that her rights under the ECHR had been grossly violated by the hospital authorities. Having become violent, disruptive, self-destructive and suicidal, the local authority consented to a highly disturbed 12-year-old girl being admitted to a psychiatric hospital for assessment, as 'a short-term response'.[182] By the time she absconded from the hospital, she had been there over two weeks, during which time she had been kept on an adult ward, in a hospital night-dress, with her daytime clothes locked in a locker. The Court of Appeal rejected her applications for judicial review of the local authority's decision to place her in the hospital and damages for false imprisonment. There was nothing in the common law to prevent the admission of a voluntary patient to hospital for assessment, as opposed to treatment,[183] as long as the admission has the patient's consent. Consent had been supplied by the local authority, on the child's behalf, it having gained parental responsibility over her through a care order.

Arguably, the situation in *Kirklees* should never have occurred – by failing to apply for a secure accommodation order the local authority had ignored the spirit of the guidance accompanying the use of the Children Act 1989, section 25(1) if not its actual wording.[184] Nevertheless, the Court of Appeal seemed surprisingly unworried by the lack of legal safeguards available for the girl involved. Informal admissions may be a convenient way of dealing with difficult cases, not least because of the absence of any real legal scrutiny of such decisions. They can amount to a form of 'back door admission' organised by those with parental responsibility in situations where the criteria for detention under the mental health legislation would not be met.[185] More generally, if local authorities can consent to a disturbed teenager being admitted to a psychiatric unit as a voluntary patient, so can parents.

The *Kirklees* decision suggests that the law does little to prevent children being 'volunteered' for admission to hospital by their parents or others, with no additional

---

178 Eg *Re C (detention: medical treatment)* [1997] 2 FLR 180: the director of the private eating disorders clinic indicated that most of their patients entered the clinic with the consent of their parents.

179 Eg *Re H (a minor) (care proceedings: child's wishes)* [1993] 1 FLR 440: a 15-year-old with an obsessive compulsive disorder was unhappy over his stay in the Maudsley Hospital. Despite this, he returned there on the local authority obtaining a care order, only registering his protest by intermittently refusing to eat.

180 Eg *Re C (detention: medical treatment)* [1997] 2 FLR 180: although the specialised eating disorders clinic did not lock its doors during the day, it wanted judicial authority to use reasonable force to prevent a 16-year-old severely anorexic girl from leaving.

181 [1993] 2 FLR 187.

182 [1993] 2 FLR 187 at 188, per Lloyd LJ.

183 Because she was not admitted for *treatment* for a mental disorder, she was not deemed to be a voluntary patient under the Mental Health Act 1983, s 131.

184 See discussion below.

185 M Ruegger (1993) p 30.

check, such as an automatic review by a mental health tribunal.[186] Caring for handicapped or mentally disturbed children can be extremely burdensome and, as Hoggett points out, parents may not find it easy to put their children's interests first all the time.[187] Indeed, parental fear that 'adolescent children are out of their control, mixing with the wrong crowd, or prone to crazy and unpredictable behaviour ... may reflect a generation gap rather than psychopathology'.[188] For example, parents might consent, on their child's behalf, to his or her voluntary admission to an expensive private psychiatric unit and they might consent, on their child's behalf, to the use of sedative medication.

The *Kirklees* decision demonstrates the woeful deficiencies in the common law; it provides no machinery for reviewing the methods used to persuade a young patient to enter a treatment unit and then to remain there. Today, such treatment could be challenged under the Human Rights Act 1998. A clinical team might justify infringing a patient's physical and moral integrity under article 8(1)[189] by arguing that it was *necessary* to protect his or her health or morals.[190] But confining a young patient on an adult ward in his or her night clothes might well amount to 'inhuman or degrading treatment' under article 3.[191] Furthermore, restricting a patient's liberty for two weeks would appear to be a clear breach of his or her rights under article 5, unless the domestic court decided to follow *Nielsen v Denmark*.[192] The majority of the European Court of Human Rights considered that the mother had been reasonable in deciding to have her son placed in the closed psychiatric ward of a state hospital for five and a half months, against his wishes, despite the fact that he was not even mentally ill, albeit he had a 'nervous condition'. Consequently, article 5 was not even available to the boy. But as argued earlier, a domestic court should now reconsider *Nielsen*.[193] It might be influenced by the minority view of the European Court of Human Rights in *Nielsen* that the boy's incarceration had clearly infringed his rights under article 5 and that the medical team, as an agent of the state, should not be allowed to shelter behind the mother's authority. For example, Judge Pettitt stated that:

> 'In a field as sensitive as that of psychiatric committal, within the framework of the European Convention, in particular under Article 5 thereof, unremitting vigilance is required to avoid the abuse of legislative systems and hospital structures.'[194]

A domestic court might now rule that article 5, linked with article 14, entitles a minor patient to the same legal safeguards as those available to older adolescents and to adult mental health patients. Such a ruling would terminate the use of parental consent

---

186   See B Hoggett (1996) pp 9 and 65. If the unit is a nursing home or mental nursing home, those running the home must notify the local authority of any child who is accommodated by them for more than three months. The local authority must then determine whether his welfare is being adequately safeguarded and promoted: Children Act 1989, s 86. But per P Bartlett and R Sandland (2000) p 89, '... such post facto investigation is not a substitute for admission standards'.

187   B Hoggett (1996) p 65.

188   B Dickens (1981) p 478.

189   *X and Y v Netherlands* (1985) 8 EHRR 235.

190   Ie under art 8(2). But such a stance must be carefully justified as being proportionate to the risks involved in the patient not receiving the treatment.

191   It is unlikely that such treatment could be justified as complying 'with generally accepted psychiatric principles'. See *Herczegfalvy v Austria* (1992) 15 EHRR 437 (para 83).

192   (1988) 11 EHRR 175.

193   See D Feldman (2002) pp 458–459, for a similar view.

194   (1988) 11 EHRR 175, at p 199, para 3.

to authorise compulsory detention to ensure assessment and/or treatment and would force clinical teams to use the mental health legislation.

As discussed above, the government obviously recognises that these legal principles require reform. It may become impossible for such a situation to occur at all in the case of an adolescent over the age of 16 who requires compulsory mental health treatment. Meanwhile, if the current recommendations bear fruit, anyone with parental responsibility for a child under the age of 16 will retain the right to authorise compulsory treatment for up to 28 days. A patient like the *Kirklees* girl, who obviously resists treatment during that time, will gain independent representation and the right to challenge her treatment by applying to the mental health tribunal.[195] Although such a change would improve matters, she should be provided with independent representation from the outset so that her true views on the proposed treatment are obtained.

(ii)   Treatment

Once in a specialised treatment unit, a young patient may vehemently object to the form of treatment being advised. The clinical team may have grave doubts over whether he or she fully understands either the treatment being proposed or the implications of refusing it. Nevertheless, case law indicates that *whether or not* such a patient is legally capable of refusing to consent, consent can instead be provided by the adolescent's parents, thereby effectively overruling his or her objections.[196] The practical convenience of such a principle for those treating patients with mental disorders is obvious; parental consent avoids the need to obtain judicial authority for compulsory treatment.

The decision in *Re K, W and H (minors) (medical treatment)*[197] demonstrates the dangerously vulnerable position adolescent mental health patients may be in now that a clinical team can obtain consent from any adult authorised to give it.[198] They have none of the legal safeguards available to adult mental health patients undergoing compulsory treatment.[199] As discussed above, the government has acknowledged that the current law is unsatisfactory regarding the older category of mental health patient aged between 16 and 18. For these patients, it will eventually be impossible for any treatment unit to avoid using the mental health legislation by seeking parental approval for treatment in circumstances where the patient refuses to co-operate. But the government's assumption that only the older adolescent requires the full panoply of special safeguards appears to overlook the fact that a younger patient has no independent representation and may feel quite unable to voice his or her opposition to treatment. Furthermore, parents may not pay proper attention to the rights of mentally disturbed adolescents; indeed, the interests of members of the family may

195 See DH (2002 c) para 3.9.
196 *Re R (a minor) (wardship: consent to treatment)* [1991] 4 All ER 177 and *Re W (a minor) (medical treatment)* [1993] Fam 64.
197 [1993] 1 FLR 854.
198 Thorpe J ([1993] 1 FLR 854 at 859), applying the principle in *Re R*, stated that the law was perfectly clear. It was unnecessary for a specialised treatment unit to gain specific issue orders to authorise 'emergency medication' against the wishes of three 15-year-olds, because their mothers had consented in writing to the treatment. They were too highly disturbed to be *Gillick* competent, but even if they had been competent, parental consent was sufficient to exempt the head of the unit from civil or criminal liability.
199 M Brazier and C Bridge (1996) p 102.

be at complete variance with those of the patient.[200] Some parents will feel obliged to consent to whatever treatment is suggested, fearing that otherwise the treatment unit will refuse to continue treatment and that they themselves will be obliged to resume caring for their severely disturbed son or daughter at home.

Leaving the law largely unchanged for the younger category of mental patient also fails to address concerns regarding the absence of controls over specialised units who provide treatment for disturbed adolescents, particularly when compulsory sedating medication is used. There is no systematic external form of official monitoring or scrutiny of the admission and treatment of all young adolescent patients outside the mental health legislation. The three girls involved in *Re K, W and H (minors) (medical treatment)*[201] were all under the age of 16 and their parents had consented to the use of 'emergency medication'. Well-run treatment units adopt their own regulations regarding its use, for example, restricting it to situations 'where the young person is at serious risk of self-harm and/or harming others, and other alternative approaches have been attempted and have failed to manage the difficulty'.[202] But although these regulations often include more rigorous restrictions on the types of treatment used than those imposed by the mental health legislation, there is no legal compulsion on units to adopt them. Moreover, there is the risk that 'emergency medication' becomes a means of control rather than treatment.[203] Of greater concern is the fact that parental consent can still authorise the use of special treatments, such as ECT,[204] without the checks and controls required by the mental health legislation for its use on older patients.[205]

The principle established in *Re R* and *Re W* may, of course, prove vulnerable to challenges brought under the Human Rights Act 1998. As suggested above, challenges might be based on articles 3, 5 and 8, combined with article 14 of the ECHR. An adolescent under the age of 16, forced to undergo emergency medication might argue that adults cannot be forced to undergo treatment without the correct mental health procedures being complied with. Accordingly, failure to provide him or her with similar safeguards cannot be justified by his or her minor status and is therefore discriminatory. The decision in *Nielsen* might be reviewed, on the basis that parents would be acting outside their parental authority by authorising the medical authorities to force treatment on their mentally disturbed adolescent offspring. It might rule that in order to avoid discriminating against adolescent mental health patients, compulsory medical treatment should be delivered to them in the same manner as to older adolescents and adults – by complying with the mental health procedures, including their independent safeguards.

---

200 See Council of Europe (2000) para 4.5.

201 [1993] 1 FLR 854.

202 Excerpt from the written guidance governing the use of emergency medication in the John Clare unit, part of St Andrews Hospital, Northampton, whose treatment programme was considered in *Re K, W and H (minors) (medical treatment)* [1993] 1 FLR 854.

203 See P Bates (1994) p 134.

204 The administration of ECT to a child is controversial and good practice guidance suggests that a third medical opinion should be provided by a consultant specialising in child and adolescent psychiatry. Furthermore, the BMA urges clinical teams to consider seeking prior court approval for its use for any child who is an 'informal patient'. See BMA (2001 a) p 149.

205 The Mental Health Act 1983 currently contains various restrictions on the form of treatment available. The new mental health legislation will contain similar restrictions on the use of specialised treatments, such as ECT, for adults and minors in the 16–18-year-old category. See DH (2002 a) Part 4.

(D)   The courts – gaining authority for admission and treatment

(i)   The inherent jurisdiction – admission and detention

Parents may find it impossible to persuade a mentally disturbed adolescent to enter a specialised treatment unit – indeed, they may have little or no control over their offspring. Instead, it is not uncommon for a local authority to take over responsibility for ensuring that emotionally disturbed adolescents obtain the treatment they need. Some local authorities apply for a secure accommodation order as a means of ensuring that a young person enters the unit and then does not abscond.[206] Others will consider applying for a care order, hoping that the adolescent will co-operate with their plans for admission. But even if they can persuade the potential patient to enter a unit, he or she may refuse to stay long enough to be treated, choosing to abscond home. So some local authorities and clinics have, in the past, invoked the High Court's inherent jurisdiction to force an adolescent to enter the unit and then to prevent him or her leaving. For example, in *South Glamorgan County Council v W and B*[207] a local authority[208] obtained judicial authority for the forcible removal of a highly disturbed 15-year-old girl from home and her transfer to a specialised psychiatric unit where she would be assessed and receive appropriate medical treatment.[209] The decision was controversial[210] since this use of the inherent jurisdiction undermines the clear intention of the Children Act 1989, which is to prevent *Gillick* competent children being forced to undergo examinations or assessments against their will in the course of protective litigation.[211]

Again, it is doubtful whether a decision like that in *South Glamorgan* could now survive a challenge under the Human Rights Act 1998. The order authorised the local authority to 'take all necessary steps'[212] to remove the girl from her home. Although no mention was made of the degree of force necessary to achieve such an object, it is arguable that the court was itself, as a public authority,[213] responsible for infringing her rights to freedom from restraint under articles 3 and 5. Indeed, more recent case law, such as *Re C (detention: medical treatment)*,[214] suggests that even before implementation of the Human Rights Act 1998, the judiciary were becoming far more aware of the need to respect the rights of young patients whose admission and treatment they are asked to authorise under the High Court's inherent jurisdiction.

---

206 Discussed below.
207 [1993] 1 FLR 574.
208 A local authority must first obtain court leave to make such an application under the Children Act 1989, s 100.
209 [1993] 1 FLR 574. The local authority had obtained an interim care order with a direction under the Children Act 1989, s 38(6) that the girl be psychiatrically examined and assessed. She refused to leave home and enter the specialist unit where the assessment was to take place. Although, per Douglas Brown J ([1993] 1 FLR 574 at 582), she was 'of sufficient understanding to make an informed decision' within the Children Act, s 38(6), he utilised the inherent jurisdiction to allow the local authority to override her wishes.
210 See T Lyons (1994) for a strong condemnation of this decision. See also M Brazier and C Bridge (1996), who criticise (p 98) the failure to utilise the mental health legislation to ensure that the girl was appropriately assessed and treated.
211 See the Children Act, s 38(6), which warns courts that although, when making an interim supervision order or an interim care order, they may include a direction for the child to undergo a medical or psychiatric examination or other assessment, a child who is 'of sufficient understanding to make an informed decision' may refuse to submit to it.
212 [1993] 1 FLR 574 at 584, per Douglas Brown J.
213 Human Rights Act 1998, s 6.
214 Eg *Re C (detention: medical treatment)* [1997] 2 FLR 180.

In *Re C* Wall J was satisfied that he possessed the power under the inherent jurisdiction to authorise the clinic to proceed with the regime it proposed for a severely anorexic girl, whether or not she had capacity to consent on her own behalf to the restrictions proposed.[215] But he acknowledged that detention against her will was a Draconian remedy and that there were no built-in safeguards under the inherent jurisdiction.[216] In the absence of alternative means being available to safeguard her liberty, Wall J decided instead to insert safeguards into the order, similar to those used in the secure accommodation regulations.[217] He limited the duration of her stay in the unit for a maximum of four months and directed that treatment should be provided in accordance with the views of her doctors but 'to ensure that (she) suffers the least distress and retains the greatest dignity'.[218]

Wall J's approach in *Re C* is welcome, in so far as he acknowledged the arguments on behalf of C that orders of the type required had profound consequences for her civil liberties. This led to his view that orders made under the inherent jurisdiction should always be time limited, with stringent safeguards built in.[219] Nevertheless, those included were less effective than those available to C had she been admitted, assessed and treated under the mental health legislation. Although the director of the hospital declared herself philosophically opposed to sectioning children under the mental health legislation, she persuaded the court to restrict C's liberty in a far more oppressive way.[220] Had C been two years older, there would have been no alternative but to find a clinic able to provide her with treatment under the mental health legislation or to leave her untreated.

It is questionable whether the judiciary could now justify making an order of the kind made by Wall J in *C*'s case. A court, as a public authority, must not itself infringe an adolescent's rights under the ECHR.[221] Whilst any order it makes regarding a mentally disturbed adolescent would not infringe the terms of articles 3 and 5 if it fulfilled the requirements of the Strasbourg jurisprudence,[222] as noted above, these are not easily satisfied.[223] Arguably, the courts should be far more critical of claims that the mental health legislation is inappropriate and refuse to allow the inherent jurisdiction to be used as a kind of magic wand to solve the problems of treatment units and local authorities.

(ii)   The inherent jurisdiction – a minor's capacity to refuse compulsory treatment

Sometimes mentally disordered adolescents enter and remain in a specialised treatment unit, either because they are too ill to object or sufficiently biddable to do what they are told. Alternatively, they may be ordered there by a court using the

---

215 Wall J ([1997] 2 FLR 180 at 196) did not consider that she was sufficiently competent to comply with the test of competence established by *Re C (Refusal of Treatment)* [1994] 1 FLR 31.
216 [1997] 2 FLR 180 at 190 and 198.
217 Since Wall J rejected the possibility of the hospital being deemed a secure accommodation unit, C's stay was not automatically safeguarded by the regulations governing such units.
218 [1997] 2 FLR 180 at 200.
219 [1997] 2 FLR 180 at 190.
220 See C Frantz (1997) p 20.
221 Human Rights Act 1998, s 6(1).
222 See especially *Herczegfalvy v Austria* (1992) 15 EHRR 437 and *Winterwerp v Netherlands* (1979) 2 EHRR 387.
223 Discussed above, in the context of utilising the mental health legislation.

inherent jurisdiction or by a secure accommodation order. But once in residence, they may object to treatment or the regime being offered. Mental health problems may undermine the capacity of a minor patient to give a valid consent to the treatment advised. In some cases, for example, a patient suffering from a severe mental illness may not believe him- or herself to be ill at all.[224] As noted, current case law indicates that *whether or not* such a young patient is legally capable of refusing to consent, consent can instead be provided by the court, thereby effectively overruling his or her objections.[225]

Despite their willingness to override a refusal, the courts have explored what level of competence an adolescent *theoretically* requires in order to refuse treatment. There seems, on the face of it, no reason why any adolescent patient should need a higher level of competence to refuse to undergo treatment than to consent to it. Current case law nevertheless indicates that the courts often require very high levels of competence from highly disturbed adolescents refusing medical treatment deemed to be essential to safeguard their health. They have simply adjusted the level of competence required, in the light of the implications of the minor's decision. The more dangerous the outcome, the higher the competence required. The outcome in *Re R (a minor) (wardship: medical treatment)*[226] was that, without treatment, R would again lapse into a dangerously psychotic state. In *Re W (a minor) (medical treatment)*,[227] if W did not receive treatment for her anorexia nervosa, she would probably die. In the former case, Lord Donaldson MR demanded –

> '… not merely an ability to understand the nature of the proposed treatment – … but a full understanding and appreciation of the consequences both of the treatment in terms of intended and possible side effects and, equally important, the anticipated consequences of a failure to treat.'[228]

This is higher than the competence required of mentally disordered adults, when the question is whether an adult patient should be able to comprehend and retain information about the treatment, believe it and weigh it in the balance to arrive at a choice.[229] Indeed, the courts are reluctant to assume that an adult lacks capacity to consent to medical treatment, despite his or her reasoning appearing bizarre or irrational.[230] Lord Donaldson's test of competence in *Re R* becomes even more onerous when combined with his other demand that *Gillick* competence must be a permanent aspect of an adolescent's development and not a form of competence which exists on some days and not on others. Since the teenager in *Re R* was subject to 'fluctuating mental disability', being not only *Gillick* 'incompetent', but 'sectionable' on some days,[231] she could not satisfy the requirements of *Gillick* competence.[232] Given that

224 BMA (2001 a) p 134.
225 *Re R (a minor) (wardship: medical treatment)* [1991] 4 All ER 177; *Re W (a minor) (medical treatment)* [1992] 4 All ER 627.
226 [1991] 4 All ER 177.
227 [1992] 4 All ER 627.
228 [1991] 4 All ER 177 at 187.
229 See *Re C (refusal of medical treatment)* [1994] 1 FLR 31.
230 See *Re JT (adult: refusal of medical treatment)* [1998] 1 FLR 48: the High Court refused to overrule a woman patient's refusal to undergo dialysis for renal failure, despite her mental disabilities involving learning difficulties and extremely severe behavioural disturbance – she was capable of refusing agreement to treatment under the test in *Re C (refusal of medical treatment)* [1994] 1 FLR 31.
231 Ie liable to compulsory admission under the Mental Health Act 1983, s 2 or s 3.
232 Per Lord Donaldson MR [1991] 4 All ER 177 at 187.

the state of mind of many mentally disturbed teenagers fluctuates from day to day, this requirement is particularly demanding.

A paternalistic adjustment of the level of competence for adolescents might be justified if it ensured that the treatment were provided in a way that most respects the patient's personal integrity. But this is not the case. As discussed below, invoking the inherent jurisdiction has usually resulted in the courts authorising unrestricted treatment. Consequently, many have suggested that teenagers like those involved in *Re R* and *Re W* would be better safeguarded under the mental health legislation, with their admission to hospital and subsequent treatment rigorously regulated and reviewed.[233]

(iii)   The inherent jurisdiction – authority for compulsory treatment

The case law indicates that the judiciary only countenance teenagers being forced to undergo treatment if it will safeguard their future mental and physical health, thereby protecting their ability to fulfil their potential. Paternalistic reasoning of this kind is not unreasonable when dealing with an adolescent who is refusing life saving treatment. As de Cruz has argued, 'in some cases, respecting adolescent autonomy may be simply too high a price to pay'.[234] Nevertheless, this approach may ignore the humiliation of being physically forced to undergo treatment.

As Hale LJ has observed in relation to adult mental health patients:

'... the degradation of an incapacitated person shames us all even if that person is unable to appreciate it, but in fact most people are able to appreciate that they are being forced to do something against their will even if they are not able to make the decision that it should or should not be done.'[235]

When authorising treatment under the inherent jurisdiction, the courts have not often included any restrictions over the methods of treatment adopted by the unit. As in *Re R* and *Re W*, they leave the medical practitioners to use whatever forms they consider appropriate,[236] whilst in others they have specifically authorised those administering treatment to use force.[237] Nevertheless, as Wall J acknowledged in *Re C (detention: medical treatment)*,[238] the patient's civil liberties would undoubtedly be protected better by the imposition of controls.[239] This adds credence to Hoggett's argument that the existence of safeguards provided by the mental health legislation justifies regarding all children in psychiatric hospitals or secure facilities as detained patients for the purposes of compulsorily treating them.[240] Again, it seems likely that adolescents may claim that the use of the inherent jurisdiction to authorise compulsory treatment infringes their rights under the Human Rights Act 1998. A successful claim would force the judiciary to relinquish their authority to the mental health tribunals.

---

233   Inter alia: J Masson (1993) pp 38–39; M Brazier and C Bridge (1996) pp 96–97.
234   P de Cruz (1999) p 604.
235   See *R (on the application of Wilkinson) v Broadmoor Hospital* [2001] EWCA Civ 1545, [2002] 1 WLR 419 at [79].
236   See also *A Metropolitan Borough Council v DB* [1997] 1 FLR 767, where Cazalet J (at 777) authorised the use 'reasonable force for the purpose of imposing intrusive necessary medical treatment' on a 17-year-old crack cocaine addict.
237   Eg *Re C (detention: medical treatment)* [1997] 2 FLR 180.
238   [1997] 2 FLR 180. Discussed by P de Cruz (1999).
239   [1997] 2 FLR 180 at 190.
240   See B Hoggett (1996) p 66.

Only when the mental disorder is truly life-threatening could the courts argue that infringing an adolescent's article 3 and 5 rights, when authorising compulsory treatment, is justified by their fulfilling their own duties to preserve his or her life under article 2.[241]

(iv)   Admission and restraint by secure accommodation orders

The Children Act 1989, section 25(1) limits local authorities' power to restrict children's liberty for more than 72 hours in any 28 days without obtaining a court order to that effect.[242] Government guidance makes it clear that the restriction of a child's liberty 'is a serious step which must be taken only when there is no genuine alternative which would be appropriate. The use of such an order must be a "last resort" in the sense that all else must first have been comprehensively considered and rejected ...'[243] Secure accommodation orders are often sought by local authorities wishing to restrict the liberty of children they are looking after,[244] not for medical reasons but to control their aggressive and violent behaviour, both for their own sake, and for the sake of the public. Such orders are made without any intention of ensuring that they receive specialised treatment,[245] though they may need it.[246] Less well known is the use of secure accommodation orders to ensure the admission to and detention of children in specialised secure psychiatric units. These units often make the use of security and enforced detention a part of the treatment regime to control, modify and eliminate dangerous behaviour.

An application for a secure accommodation order to authorise detention for treatment purposes normally involves arguing that the adolescent is likely to injure himself or herself or other persons,[247] without their liberty being restricted.[248] The scope of section 25 was extended by regulations to govern children being provided with accommodation by health authorities and in residential care homes, nursing homes and mental nursing homes.[249] A degree of judicial uncertainty has been expressed over whether a unit not normally designed or intended to provide secure

---

241   See *X v Germany* (Application No 10565/83) (1984) 7 EHRR 152, referred to above, p 131, n 68.
242   See Children Act 1989, s 25(1) 'Subject to the following provisions of this section, a child who is being looked after by a local authority may not be placed, and, if placed, may not be kept, in accommodation provided for the purpose of restricting liberty ["secure accommodation"] unless it appears—(a) that—(i) he has a history of absconding and is likely to abscond from any other description of accommodation; and (ii) if he absconds, he is likely to suffer significant harm; or (b) that if he is kept in any other description of accommodation he is likely to injure himself or other persons.' See also the Children (Secure Accommodation) Regulations 1991, SI 1991/1505, reg 10(1).
243   DH (1991 a) para 5.1.
244   A local authority may only apply for a secure accommodation order in relation to a child already being 'looked after' under the Children Act 1989, s 22.
245   Discussed in more detail in chapter 16.
246   See T O'Neill (2001) ch 10.
247   Ie under the Children Act, s 25(1)(b). In *Re D (secure accommodation order)* [1997] 1 FLR 197, Singer J confirmed that the grounds contained in s 25(1)(a) and (b) are disjunctive and not conjunctive. Consequently a secure accommodation order can be made under s 25(1)(b) in cases where there is no history of absconding, but there is clear evidence that if the child is kept in any other description of accommodation, he/she is likely to injure him/herself or other persons.
248   Eg *A Metropolitan Borough Council v DB* [1997] 1 FLR 767: the court accepted that a 17-year-old crack-cocaine addict who had just given birth to a baby would injure herself if allowed to discharge herself from the maternity unit.
249   The Children (Secure Accommodation) Regulations 1991, SI 1991/1505, reg 7(2) and (3).

accommodation, is governed by these regulations, if it prevents individual patients leaving the unit against their will.[250] Since their intention is to prevent children being locked up without supervision or restriction, it is arguable that the regulations should be interpreted as generously as possible.

These regulations clearly attempt to safeguard the liberty of all young people requiring compulsory treatment. They prevent the admission of a teenager to a unit intended to restrict his or her liberty unless *either* the mental health legislation is employed, or a secure accommodation order is obtained under the Children Act 1989, section 25. The two sets of legislation are intended to be exclusive, so that section 25 does not apply to any child who is detained under the mental health legislation.[251] So once the new mental health legislation is in force, local authorities will not be able to use secure accommodation as a means of ensuring the compulsory admission of teenagers over the age of 16.[252] In relation to those under that age, the restrictions imposed by the Children Act 1989 and the secure accommodation regulations are intended to protect children from being deprived of their liberty unjustifiably. A child should not be kept in accommodation 'provided for the purpose of restricting liberty', for more than the authorised 72 hours without this being authorised by a secure accommodation order. The statutory guidance suggests that this formula could include taking any measure to prevent a child leaving a room or building of his or her own free will.[253] It also makes it clear that any of the more obvious methods, such as locking the child in a room or in part of a building, amounts to 'restriction of liberty' and requires a secure accommodation order by way of justification. Consequently, keeping a minor in a locked ward without an order would obviously be a clear breach of the provisions. The guidance acknowledges that there are other practices which are 'not so clear cut'.[254] It is arguable that amongst these might be keeping a patient in a ward in her night clothes, as in the *Kirklees* case.[255]

The forcible detention of an adolescent patient in a psychiatric unit against his or her will is a Draconian measure. The need for a local authority to obtain a court order to do so reflects an awareness that such a practice must be regulated properly and strictly limited, even when it is to ensure that young people obtain essential treatment. The subject of the application must be given the opportunity of having legal representation[256] and a children's guardian will normally be appointed for him or her.[257] Controversially, the courts have decided that since applications for secure accommodation orders are not governed by section 1 of the Children Act 1989, the child's welfare is not the court's paramount consideration.[258] Furthermore, although

250 Eg in *A Metropolitan Borough Council v DB* [1997] 1 FLR 767 the maternity ward had security locks on the doors designed to prevent outsiders entering the unit. Cazalet J held that because DB had not been given a key or pass, the unit intended to restrict her liberty and therefore was governed by the secure accommodation regulations. But see Wall J in *Re C (detention: medical treatment)* [1997] 2 FLR 180 who considered (at 193) that secure accommodation should be 'designed for, or have as its primary purpose' the restriction of liberty.

251 The Children (Secure Accommodation) Regulations 1991, SI 1991/1505, reg 5(1).

252 Discussed above, pp 142–145.

253 DH (1991 b) para 8.10.

254 DH (1991 b) para 8.10.

255 Eg *R v Kirklees Metropolitan Borough Council, ex p C* [1993] 2 FLR 187, discussed above.

256 Children Act 1989, s 25(6).

257 Children Act 1989, s 41. See *Re AS (secure accommodation order)* [1999] 1 FLR 103: a secure accommodation order was quashed because it had been made without the boy in question receiving notice of the application, without his having instructed solicitors to act for him and without a guardian ad litem being appointed to represent him.

258 *Re M (secure accommodation order)* [1995] 1 FLR 418. See P Bates (1995).

case law indicates that the court may properly expect psychiatric evidence substantiating the need to admit a child for treatment in a psychiatric unit,[259] it is unclear how often this is insisted upon in practice.

Some had predicted that secure accommodation orders would not survive the implementation of the Human Rights Act 1998,[260] since they authorise depriving children of their liberty and thereby infringe their rights under article 5 of the ECHR. This argument was rejected by the Court of Appeal in *Re K (secure accommodation order: right to liberty).*[261] Relying on previous Strasbourg case law,[262] the Court of Appeal held that although a secure accommodation order is a deprivation of liberty within the meaning of article 5, it can be justified if it falls within the 'educational supervision' exception, which itself can be interpreted flexibly.[263] Consequently, there is no question of section 25 itself being incompatible with the terms of article 5 and each case has to be judged on its merits.[264] The decision in *Re K* was controversial.[265] Nevertheless, the survival of section 25 clearly enables local authorities to continue using secure accommodation orders to ensure that an adolescent enters and stays in a specialised treatment unit. But since Butler-Sloss LJ conceded that every secure accommodation order must now be judged on its merits,[266] the decision may ensure that the standard of educational facilities provided in such units is closely monitored.[267] A secure accommodation order authorising detention in a treatment unit providing wholly inadequate educational supervision can be challenged as being incompatible with article 5 of the Convention. This last point is in tune with the views of the Council of Europe Working Party. Their report stresses that every minor placed as an involuntary patient in a psychiatric establishment should be individually assessed and receive, if possible, an individualised educational or training programme, to be organised by the relevant education departments in consultation with the psychiatric establishment.[268]

The legal restrictions imposed by section 25 and its attendant regulations protect a mentally disturbed adolescent's liberty to a degree, in so far as it imposes legislative controls on the circumstances and duration of his or her confinement in the unit. It cannot, however, restrict the form of treatment nor provide authority for compulsory treatment. Consent to treatment will often be obtained from the parents, whose parental responsibility is unaffected by a secure accommodation order.[269] But since parents may not assess the child's real needs particularly objectively, the mental health legislation offers better protection for the rights of the patient once restrained within the unit itself.

259   *Oxfordshire County Council v R* [1992] 1 FLR 648 at 655–656, per Douglas Brown J.
260   See H Swindells, A Neaves, M Kushner and R Skilbeck (1999), who argue (pp 116–118) that secure accommodation orders infringe the requirements of art 5 of the European Convention.
261   [2001] 1 FLR 526.
262   The admissibility decision reached by the European Court of Human Rights in *Koniarska v United Kingdom* (Application No 33670/96) (12 October 2000, unreported).
263   See art 5(1)(d), which authorises 'the detention of a minor by lawful order for the purpose of educational supervision or his lawful detention for the purpose of bringing him before the competent legal authority'.
264   Since the child in *Re K*'s case was receiving carefully supervised education whilst in secure accommodation, the Court of Appeal held that the restrictions of his liberty could be justified under art 5(1)(d).
265   See J Masson (2002) and discussion in chapter 16.
266   [2001] 1 FLR 526, per Butler-Sloss LJ (para 43).
267   See T O'Neill (2001) who suggests (pp 180–181) that educational provision in many secure accommodation units is very poor.
268   See Council of Europe (2000) para 8.4.
269   Eg *Re K, W and H (minors) (medical treatment)* [1993] 1 FLR 854.

CONCLUSION

The law relating to adolescents' decision-making powers over their health is confusing and arbitrary. On the one hand, the principle of *Gillick* competence recognises their capacity for choice and encourages them to take a responsible attitude to such matters as contraception and other medical procedures that they wish to undergo. But, on the other hand, the law attempts to maintain the right to override their choice to refuse all treatment. Whilst it might be comprehensible for the law to refuse them the right to make life-threatening mistakes, it goes much further and enables parents and doctors to correct any decision they consider to be irrational or unreasonable, and not in the patient's best interests. Such provisions may come under fierce attack from adolescents objecting to their rights under the ECHR being infringed.

For those with behavioural problems, the common law offers few obvious safeguards to ensure that their rights to bodily integrity and liberty are fully respected. It appears that only the consistent use of the mental health legislation will ensure that compulsory restriction of liberty and compulsory forms of treatment are well regulated and subject to appropriate external scrutiny. A minority status should not deprive adolescents of a respect for the civil liberties currently available to all mental patients, irrespective of age. The law certainly no longer matches up to the promise implicit in Lord Scarman's judgment in *Gillick v West Norfolk and Wisbech Area Health Authority*[270] that teenagers had gained a degree of autonomy over their own bodies. Again, challenges brought under the Human Rights Act 1998 may provoke a fundamental reappraisal of the case law which currently allows minors to be detained and treated on a compulsory basis without the safeguards accorded to adult mental health patients.

270 [1986] AC 112.

BIBLIOGRAPHY

NB many of these publications can be obtained on the relevant organisation's website.

Alderson P and Montgomery J, *Health Care Decisions: Making decisions with children* (1996) IPPR.

Audit Commission, *Children in mind: child and adolescent mental health services* (1999) Audit Commission Publications.

Bartlett P and Sandland R, *Mental Health Law, Policy and Practice* (2000) Blackstone Press Ltd.

Bates P, 'Children in psychiatric units: *Re K, W and H* – "out of sight, out of mind"?' (1994) 6 Journal of Child Law 131.

Bates P, 'Secure accommodation orders – in whose interests?' (1995) 7 Child and Family Law Quarterly 70.

Brazier M, *Medicine, Patients and the Law* (1992) Penguin.

Brazier M and Bridge C, 'Coercion or caring: analysing adolescent autonomy' (1996) 16 Legal Studies 84.

Bridge B, 'Parent Versus Child: H.L. Matheson and the New Abortion Litigation' (1982) Wisconsin Law Review 75.

Bridge C, 'Religious Beliefs and Teenage Refusal of Medical Treatment' (1999) 62 Modern Law Review 585.

British Medical Association (BMA), *Confidentiality and disclosure of health information* (1999).

British Medical Association (BMA), *Consent, Rights and Choices in Health Care for Children and Young People* (2001 a) BMJ Books.

British Medical Association (BMA), *Withholding and Withdrawing Life-prolonging Medical Treatment* (2001 b) BMJ Books.

Committee on the Rights of the Child, *Concluding Observations of the Committee on the Rights of the Child: United Kingdom of Great Britain and Northern Ireland* CRC/C/15/Add 34 (1995) Centre for Human Rights, Geneva.

Committee on the Rights of the Child, *Concluding Observations of the Committee on the Rights of the Child: United Kingdom of Great Britain and Northern Ireland* CRC/C/15/Add 188 (2002) Centre for Human Rights, Geneva.

Council of Europe, *'White Paper' on the protection of the human rights and dignity of people suffering from mental disorder, especially those placed as involuntary patients in a psychiatric establishment* (2000) CM (2000) 23 Addendum.

de Cruz P, 'Adolescent Autonomy, Detention for Medical Treatment and *Re C*' (1999) 62 Modern Law Review 595.

Department of Health (DH), Circular HC (86) 1 (1986).

Department of Health (DH), *Court Orders, Volume 1 of The Children Act 1989 Guidance and Regulations* (1991 a) HMSO.

Department of Health (DH), *Residential Care, Volume 4 of The Children Act 1989 Guidance and Regulations* (1991 b) HMSO.

Department of Health (DH), Draft Mental Health Bill, Cm 5538-I (2002 a) The Stationery Office.

Department of Health (DH), *Draft Mental Health Bill: Explanatory Notes* Cm 5538-II (2002 b) The Stationery Office.

Department of Health (DH), *Mental Health Bill: Consultation Document* Cm 5538-III (2002 c) The Stationery Office.

DH/Home Office White Paper, *Reforming The Mental Health Act, Part 1: The new legal framework* Cm 5016-I (2000) The Stationery Office.

Dickens B, 'Function and Limits of Parental Rights' (1981) 97 Law Quarterly Review 462.

Douglas G, 'The Retreat from Gillick' (1992) 55 Modern Law Review 569.

Downie A, 'Consent to Medical Treatment – Whose View of Welfare?' (1999) Family Law 818.

Eekelaar J, 'The Eclipse of Parental Rights' (1986) 102 Law Quarterly Review 4.

Eekelaar J, 'White Coats or Flak Jackets? Doctors, Children and the Courts – Again' (1993) 109 Law Quarterly Review 182.

Eekelaar J, 'The Interests of the Child and the Child's Wishes: The Role of Dynamic Self-Determinism' (1994) 8 International Journal of Law and the Family 42.

Feldman D, *Civil Liberties and Human Rights in England and Wales* (2002) Oxford University Press.

Frantz C, 'Re C (A Minor) – Is Forcible Detention of a Young Person Through the Court's Common Law Inherent Jurisdiction Acceptable Action?' (1997) 136 Childright 18.

General Medical Council, *Confidentiality, Protecting and Providing Information* (June 2000).

Gostin L, 'Consent to Treatment: The Incapable Person' in C Dyer (ed) *Doctors, Patients and the Law* (1992) Blackwell Scientific Publications.

Hartman R, 'Adolescent Autonomy: Clarifying an Ageless Conundrum' (2000) 51 Hastings Law Journal 1265.

Hoggett B, *Mental Health Law* (1996) Sweet and Maxwell.

Huxtable R, *'Re M (Medical Treatment: Consent)* Time to remove the "flak jacket"?' (2000) 12 Child and Family Law Quarterly 83.

Innocenti Research Centre, *A League Table of Teenage Births in Rich Nations* Innocenti Report Card Issue No 3 July 2001 (2001) UNICEF.

Kane R and Wellings K, *Reducing the rate of teenage conceptions: An International review of the evidence: data from Europe* (1999) Health Education Authority.

Kennedy I, 'Consent to Treatment: The Capable Person' in C Dyer (ed) *Doctors, Patients and the Law* (1992 a) Blackwell Scientific Publications.

Kennedy I, *Treat Me Right: Essays in Medical Law and Ethics* (1992 b) Clarendon Press.

Kennedy I, and Grubb A *Medical Law* (2000) Butterworths.

Lansdown R, 'Listening to children: have we gone too far (or not far enough)?' (1998) 91 Journal of the Royal Society of Medicine 457.

Lewis P, 'The Medical Treatment of Children' in J Fionda (ed) *Legal Concepts of Childhood* (2001) Hart Publishing.

Lowe N and Juss S, 'Medical Treatment – Pragmatism and the Search for Principle' (1993) 56 Modern Law Review 865.

Lyons T, 'What's happened to the child's right to refuse? – *South Glamorgan County Council v W and B*' (1994) 6 Journal of Child Law 84.

McCafferty C, 'Won't Consent? Can't Consent! Refusal of Medical Treatment' (1999) Family Law 335.

Mann L et al, 'Adolescent decision-making: the development of competence' (1989) 12 Journal of Adolescence 265.

Mason J, McCall Smith R and Laurie G, *Law and Medical Ethics* (2002).

Masson J, 'Re W: appealing from the golden cage' (1993) 5 Journal of Child Law 37.

Masson J , '*Re K (A Child) (Secure Accommodation Order: Right to Liberty)* and *Re C (Secure Accommodation Order: Representation)* Securing human rights for children and young people in secure accommodation' (2002) 14 Child and Family Law Quarterly 77.

Meltzer H, and Gatward R *Mental health of children and adolescents in Great Britain* Office for National Statistics (2000) The Stationery Office.

Montgomery J, *Health Care Law* (2003) Oxford University Press.

National Statistics, *Social Trends No 31* (2001) The Stationery Office.

O'Neill T, *Children in Secure Accommodation: A Gendered Exploration of Locked Institutional Care for Children in Trouble* (2001) Jessica Kingsley Publishers.

Parkinson P, 'The Gillick Case – Just What Has It Decided?' (1986) 16 Family Law 11.

Royal College of General Practitioners and Brook, *Confidentiality and young people: Improving teenagers' uptake of sexual and other health advice, A Toolkit for General Practice, Primary Care Groups and Trusts* (2000) Royal College of General Practitioners and Brook.

Ruegger M, 'Children's Rights in relation to giving and withholding their consent to Treatment' (1993) 3 Journal of the National Association of GALROs.

Tabberer S et al, *Teenage pregnancy and choice, Abortion or motherhood: influences on the decision* (2000) Rowntree Foundation.

Social Exclusion Unit (SEU), *Teenage Pregnancy* Cm 4342 (1999) Social Exclusion Unit.

Social Exclusion Unit (SEU), *Young People*, Report of the Policy Action Team 12, Social Exclusion Unit (2000).

Swindells H, Neaves A, Kushner M and Skilbeck R, *Family Law and the Human Rights Act 1998* (1999) Family Law.

Chapter 6

Promoting consultation and decision-making in schools

(1) INTRODUCTION

Education clearly has a crucial part to play in encouraging pupils to develop a sense of social responsibility and a capacity for planning and achieving their own life goals.[1] According to the Warnock Committee, education is not an end in itself, but also a means to an end. It has dual aims: to enlarge the 'child's knowledge, experience and imaginative understanding, and thus his awareness of moral values and capacity for enjoyment' and also enable the child 'to enter the world after formal education is over as an active participant in society and a responsible contributor to it, capable of achieving as much independence in it as possible'.[2] School life may enable some children to escape from narrow and stultifying home environments and help them assess critically the ideologies with which they have been brought up. But the principles of education law currently show little appreciation of the maturing child's capacity for taking responsibility for his or her school life or for reaching important decisions over his or her education, without parental interference. Indeed, in some respects, education law seems to have become increasingly blinkered to such an ideal and currently treats children as adjuncts of their parents rather than as responsible agents in their own right.

This myopic approach is surprising given the events of the late 1960s and early 1970s, when the germs of a pupil's rights movement made a brief appearance in British schools.[3] Student militancy had spread from universities into the schools, leading to the establishment of the Schools' Action Union (SAU) and the National Union of School Students (NUSS). These and various other bodies started discussing and asserting a range of pupils' rights in schools, including the right to educational democracy through the establishment of school councils, the abolition of school uniform and physical punishment and the right to freedom of expression. For example, in 1970 the SAU handed in a letter to County Hall London,[4] demanding, amongst

---

1   See art 29 of the CRC, which asserts that education should be directed towards, inter alia, preparing the child 'for responsible life in a free society, in the spirit of understanding, peace, tolerance, equality of sexes, and friendship ...'
2   H M Warnock (1978) para 1.4.
3   Eg the National Council for Civil Liberties which in 1970–71 published a series of discussion papers on children's rights, and the Advisory Centre for Education (ACE) which in 1971 published a draft Charter of Children's Rights.
4   The headquarters of the now defunct Greater London Council.

other things, the right to publish school magazines without censorship, to organise student meetings during lunch breaks and after school on school premises, to join student unions and engage in political activity, including strikes.[5]

It is unclear why the children's rights movement in English schools ran out of steam so rapidly. Possibly it was because, unlike in the United States, the boundaries to children's rights could not be tested out, in a school setting, against the provisions of a written constitution. There, Supreme Court decisions like *Tinker v Des Moines Independent Community School District*[6] and *Goss v Lopez*[7] emphasised the right of school children to be treated with respect.[8] In *Tinker*, the Supreme Court found that the First Amendment rights of three students had been violated when school authorities suspended them from school for wearing black armbands to protest over the government's policy in Vietnam. The court explained that: 'Students in school as well as out of school are "persons" under our Constitution. They are possessed of fundamental rights which the State must respect ...'[9] In *Goss*, the Supreme Court held that students facing disciplinary action by school officials were entitled to due process protection, such as prior notice of the action and a chance to be heard before punishment. Meanwhile, in the United Kingdom, the House of Lords' decision in *Gillick v West Norfolk and Wisbech Area Health Authority*[10] had relatively little impact on education law. Schools were left virtually unaffected by the concept of according legal competence to adolescents in a variety of contexts. Certainly, there seems little likelihood of today's pupils striking to promote their rights in schools.

Education legislation could do far more to promote children's need to be treated as individuals and to reach responsible decisions over their own education, particularly as they reach adolescence. After briefly considering the concept of a right to education per se, this chapter devotes more detailed discussion to four further topics particularly relevant to adolescents. The first considers the law's response to the problem of children so disenchanted with school that they fail to attend; the second discusses the methods for dealing with disruptive children in school; the third assesses the extent to which children are involved in school policy and administration; and the fourth relates to the provision of sex education in schools. A possible fifth topic, concentrating on the legal principles governing the provision of religious education and collective worship in schools, is discussed elsewhere, in the context of the educational rights of minority children.[11]

(2) A RIGHT TO EDUCATION

The right to be educated is probably one of the most important of children's moral and legal rights; without it they may be unable to develop their 'personality, talents and mental and physical abilities to their fullest potential'.[12] Wringe even claims that:

---

5   In 1972, approximately 2,500 pupils absented themselves from school to attend a 'Schools Demo' in Trafalgar Square mounted by the SAU.

6   393 US 503 (1969).

7   419 US 565 (1975).

8   But see B Hafen (1976), who claims (p 646) that the decision in *Tinker* protected *parents'* rights to teach and influence their children against state claims that would limit them. The parents of the students involved had encouraged their children to wear the armbands and were obviously instrumental in bringing the litigation that ensued.

9   393 US 503 (1969) at 511.

10   [1986] AC 112.

11   See chapter 11.

12   Phrasing used in art 29(1)(a) of the CRC.

'Failure to receive education is not simply to be left with a restricted view and distorted understanding of the universe and our place in it. It is to have no understanding at all. It is also to have no possibility of independent existence among other human beings.'[13]

The notion that the right to education is a fundamental human right is embedded in many international documents, notably the International Covenant on Economic, Social and Cultural Rights, which requires all states parties to 'recognize the right of everyone to education',[14] before it expands on the ways in which this should be fulfilled.[15]

English education law is oddly perverse in the way it virtually ignores those who are the reason for its existence. Indeed, when exploring the extent to which the educational system in the United Kingdom promotes human rights in education, Tomaševski caustically observes of the domestic legislation:

'Statutory enactments relating to education do not use human rights language nor do they mention international human rights law. Where individual rights are mentioned, these relate to parents who have been allowed to challenge school admissions as of 1980.'[16]

She points out that whilst a great deal of jurisprudence has developed on interpreting parental challenges on admissions, conditions in schools, methods of teaching and discipline, this has developed in the narrow context of education law, rather than exploring the human right of education itself. The provision of schooling is seen as a relationship between school and parents, without children having a legal standing – 'children are thus absent as actors in this process although it is aimed at their learning'.[17]

Tomaševski is not the only commentator to have criticised the way in which English education law treats parents as the consumers of education, whilst entirely ignoring children or their rights.[18] This approach underwrites the whole of education law, which fails openly to acknowledge that children have 'rights' to education. For example, it refers instead to the duties imposed on every local education authority (LEA). Thus LEAs must secure that there are 'sufficient schools' in their area for providing full-time[19] primary and secondary education,[20] so that all pupils have the opportunity to gain an 'appropriate education'.[21] Although LEAs are not obliged to

13   See C Wringe (1981) p 145.
14   Art 13(1).
15   Art 13(2)(a)–(d) describes the system of primary, secondary and tertiary education which should be made equally accessible to all. These provisions are largely mirrored by art 28 of the CRC.
16   K Tomaševski (1999) para 29.
17   K Tomaševski (1999) para 31.
18   Inter alia: A Bainham (1996) p 30; M Freeman (1996) p 43; P Meredith (2001) esp pp 203–208.
19   See Education Act 1996, s 2(1)(2).
20   The schools must be sufficient in number, character and equipment: Education Act 1996, s 14(2).
21   Education Act 1996, s 14(2). The education available will only be deemed 'appropriate' if it offers such variety of instruction and training (including practical instruction and training appropriate to their different needs) as may be desirable in view of (a) the pupils' different ages, abilities and aptitudes and (b) the different periods for which pupils may be expected to remain in school. See s 14(3)(a) and (b).
22   See *R v Surrey County Council Education Committee, ex p H* (1984) 83 LGR 219. Slade LJ (at 235) emphasised that Parliament had not placed local education authorities under an obligation to provide a child with the best possible education and consequently: 'There is no duty on the authority to provide such a Utopian system, or to educate him to his maximum potential.'

provide a child with 'the best possible education',[22] the legislation does appear to impose on the state far more extensive and demanding duties than those contained in the international human rights treaties. But whilst these domestic legislative provisions suggest that all children have a right to free full-time and appropriate education, the courts have not, to date, maintained a consistent approach to their interpretation, particularly when a temporary lack of resources results in an insufficient number of school places being available.[23]

The Human Rights Act 1998 may now give these legislative duties more teeth. Although the right to education is normally conceived as falling within the social, economic and cultural group of human rights, as Bradley points out, its inclusion in the ECHR indicates that it also has an obvious civil and political relevance.[24] Its inclusion in that Convention was derived largely from a concern to protect parents' right to educate their children according to their own beliefs, free from interference by totalitarian regimes.[25] Despite the negative phraseology adopted by article 2 of the First Protocol of the ECHR, which states merely that 'No one shall be denied the right to education', the right of access to an effective form of education is fully recognised by the ECHR.[26] Indeed, as the domestic courts have recognised, such a right comprises four separate rights: the right of access to such educational establishments as exist; a right to effective (but not the most effective possible) education; the right to official recognition of academic qualifications; a standard of education reaching a minimum standard (thereby fulfilling the 'effective' requirement).[27] Nevertheless, the Convention goes no further than this, leaving states complete discretion to determine for themselves issues about resourcing and methods of delivering the educational system.[28]

Admittedly, unless the education provided is so grossly inadequate that it fails to reach a minimum standard, the ECHR offers little succour to those wishing to complain, for example, about the teaching in schools. Nevertheless, children who have not been provided with a school place could claim that the LEA's failure amounts to an infringement of their rights under article 2 of the first protocol of the ECHR. In such circumstances, the domestic courts might show little sympathy with an LEA's

---

23   See *Meade v London Borough of Haringey* [1979] 2 All ER 1016: the Court of Appeal showed little sympathy with the local authority's decision to close schools in sympathy with a trade union's demand for higher wages for its school caretakers. The court would have granted an injunction restraining further breach of statutory duty had the strike continued. But in *R v Inner London Education Authority, ex p Ali and Murshid* (1990) 2 Admin LR 822, the Divisional Court refused the remedy of judicial review to an applicant whose child, along with many others, had not been provided with a school place in the Tower Hamlets area due to shortage of staff. The court held that by requiring a LEA to provide 'sufficient' places, the Education Act 1944, s 8 (now Education Act 1996, s 14) only imposed a 'target' duty on the LEA and not an absolute duty. See discussion by N Harris (1990).

24   A Bradley (1999) p 396.

25   A Bradley (1999) p 397. Thus art 2 of the First Protocol refers to states' obligation to respect the 'right of parents to ensure such education and teaching in conformity with their own religious and philosophical convictions'.

26   *Belgian Linguistics Case (No 2)* (1968) 1 EHRR 252 at 281.

27   See judgment of the Court of Appeal in *Holub and Holub v Secretary of State for the Home Department* [2001] ELR 401 at [25]. The court rejected a claim that, by refusing her permission to remain in England, the immigration authorities were depriving a 14-year-old Polish girl of her right to education under Protocol 1, art 2 of the ECHR. She was returning to a country where there was an effective system of education.

28   See D Harris, M O'Boyle and C Warbrick (1995) p 543.

argument that it has not deliberately withheld educational places and that the lack of resources will only be temporary.[29] But, as discussed below, it seems doubtful that the Human Rights Act 1998 will also provoke the education legislation to focus more on children as the consumers of education, as opposed to their parents.

(3)   SCHOOL ATTENDANCE

If children attend school regularly, it will probably have a profound influence on their lives, since they will spend approximately 2,000 days there between the ages of 5 and 16. But in the United Kingdom large numbers of teenagers are thoroughly disenchanted with school, long before they reach school leaving age. There is a saying, 'You can take a horse to water, but you can't make it drink'. The same could be said of children and education. It may be difficult to convince all children that attending school will benefit them when they can think of far better ways to spend their time. A right to free state education is wasted on a child who refuses to attend school, so the law imposes a duty on parents to see that their children of compulsory school age[30] receive a full-time education. Not all are successful. Truancy in schools has, over the last decade, become an intractable problem.[31]

Ironically, those children who stay away from school because they consider that it has nothing to offer them may eventually be barred from attending altogether. This is because when disaffected pupils do attend they often behave so disruptively that they are permanently excluded. The report of the Social Exclusion Unit (SEU) reviewing the associated problems of truancy and school exclusions[32] suggested that the total number of children who were missing school for these reasons was much higher than official figures suggested.[33] It also called for truancy rates to be reduced dramatically within a relatively short time frame.[34]

Should the law attempt to make pupils stay at school if they decide that education is not for them? Children's liberationists such as Holt and Farson urged that children of all ages should have adult freedoms, including the right to decide whether they go to school and what lessons to attend.[35] Today such attitudes seem extreme and contemporary liberationists acknowledge that the state is entitled to behave paternalistically in respect of children's education rights. They acknowledge that

---

29   But note the reservation on art 2 of the First Protocol, that the government of the United Kingdom will observe it 'only in so far as it is compatible with the provision of efficient instruction and training and the avoidance of unreasonable public expenditure'. See Human Rights Act 1998, Sch 3, Pt II. So parents cannot demand the establishment of maintained denominational schools for their children; this is discussed in more detail in chapter 11.

30   Between the ages of 5 and 16 (but 16-year-olds must wait for the next 'school-leaving date' before they can leave school). See Education Act 1996, s 8.

31   Although unauthorised absences are gradually falling, they remain extremely high, thereby resisting the government's aim, in 1999, to reduce truancy by one-third by 2002 (DfEE Press release, 316/99). See DfES (2002 b) Schools, Absence and Exclusion, Chart B. This notes that the average number of half days missed due to unauthorised absence in maintained primary schools fell from 10.4 per absent pupil in 1995/6 to 8.8 per absent pupil in 2001/2 and that the average number of half days missed due to unauthorised absence in maintained secondary schools fell from 21.1 per absent pupil in 1995/6 to 17.2 per absent pupil in 2001/2.

32   SEU (1998 a).

33   With many pupils involved in 'post-registration truancy'. SEU (1998 a) para 1.3.

34   It recommended that efforts should be made to reduce truancy rates by one-third by 2002. SEU (1998 a) para 4.2.

35   See J Holt (1974) and R Farson (1978). The ideas of Holt and Farson are discussed in chapter 1.

allowing young children to choose whether they wish to attend school might actually reduce their chances of developing a capacity for autonomy later.[36] Nor do the international treaties attempt to accommodate children's wishes in the matter of school attendance. Thus the CRC requires states to make primary education 'compulsory and available free to all'[37] and to 'take measures to encourage regular attendance at schools and the reduction of drop-out rates'.[38]

Whilst such an approach might be reasonable for younger children, what of adolescents who are often too large to frog-march to school?[39] Some argue that compulsion for these older children is not only counterproductive but brings education and teaching into disrepute.[40] Lindley suggests that young people between the ages of 13 and 16 should not be forced to remain in full-time compulsory education, but should be allowed to take full-time employment instead.[41] Others urge that, just as the law allows adolescents to take legal responsibility for seeking contraceptive help, it should also allow them to decide whether to attend school, without involving their parents.[42] Indeed, the *Gillick* decision[43] has already led to the courts taking much greater account of mature children's views in parental disputes over their education.[44] Despite the plausibility of these arguments, the House of Lords in the *Gillick* decision had not intended to introduce a blanket liberality regarding a fundamental aspect of the lives of all teenagers over a specified age. It introduced the sophisticated and difficult notion of individual adolescents acquiring legal maturity on an incremental and case-by-case basis – a concept which would cause chaos if applied to an activity being made available to all adolescents on a national scale. Allowing 13-year-olds to decide for themselves whether to attend school would probably merely swell the numbers of truanting pupils who generally go home or go to friends' houses 'to do nothing in particular'.[45] For half of those who truant, 'doing nothing' involves becoming involved in crime.[46]

Maintaining a system of paternalistic coercion regarding school attendance is also justified by the research evidence predicting an extremely poor long-term employment future for the older pupils who underachieve, truant or are excluded from school. They are far more likely to be out of education, training or employment

---

36   Eg R Lindley (1989) p 85.
37   Art 28(1)(a). See also art 13(2)(a) of the International Covenant on Economic, Social and Cultural Rights.
38   Art 28(1)(e).
39   See DfES (2002 a), which show that unauthorised absences are more than twice as high in secondary schools than in primary schools.
40   See T Jeffs (2002) esp p 56.
41   See R Lindley (1989) pp 88–92.
42   See M Grenville (1988) p 18.
43   *Gillick v West Norfolk and Wisbech Area Health Authority* [1986] AC 112.
44   Eg in *Re P (a minor) (education)* [1992] 1 FLR 316 the Court of Appeal recognised that a mature child's decision over what school he wished to attend should be respected. The desire of a 'mature, sensible and intelligent' 14-year-old boy to go to the local day school near his father's home, rather than to boarding school, as his mother wished, tilted the balance in deciding the dispute in favour of the day school. The courts should listen to and pay respect to the wishes and views of older children, per Butler-Sloss LJ (at 321).
45   See Audit Commission (1996) p 68.
46   Research indicates that persistent truants are particularly likely to offend. See C Flood-Page et al (2000) indicating (p 37) that almost half of 12–16-year-old boys who were persistent truants were offenders, compared with around 10% of those who did not truant or truanted less. See also MORI (2002) ch 7.
47   SEU (1999 a) para 4.6. Being out of education, training or employment at 16 is also the single most powerful predictor for unemployment at the age of 21. SEU (1999 a) para 4.6.

once they have reached the ages of 16 to 18.[47] This dismal picture is reinforced by research showing that an unemployed status for this age group is not only likely to have long-term effects well into adulthood, but is also strongly associated with homelessness, crime,[48] drug use and teenage pregnancy.[49] Since an adolescent's ability to reach wise decisions over whether to attend school may be undermined by a variety of factors, ranging from parental illness to peer pressure or bullying, it seems entirely justifiable for the state to insist on their school attendance, at least until they attain the age of 16.

At present, the government is showing a strong commitment to tackling truancy, despite there being no general agreement on how to do so.[50] It is unlikely that the law can play a particularly constructive part in coercing physically mature teenagers into school, if they are determined not to attend. Nevertheless, an official determination to provide legal sanctions which bite has led to truancy becoming excessively criminalised, both for children and parents. As a last resort, LEAs have the option of prosecuting a truant's parents.[51] Education law imposes on parents an absolute duty to ensure that their children attend school regularly.[52] The law makes no concessions and simply expects them to overcome any reluctance on the child's part. Neither ignorance of a teenager's absences,[53] nor their inability to force him or her to attend school will be a defence to a criminal prosecution.

The fact that criminal sanctions against parents have become more Draconian[54] arises from the belief that some parents not only condone their children's truanting but actively encourage it.[55] It also reflects practitioners' frustration with the low level of fines magistrates commonly impose on parents.[56] The courts have the additional power to impose on any parent convicted of such an offence a parenting order for any period of up to 12 months. Such orders, which are designed to help parents control their children's behaviour generally, can require parents to escort their children to school every day and to attend counselling or guidance sessions for up to three

---

48 See C Flood-Page et al (2000) p 45, noting that the second most important predictor of serious or persistent offending amongst 18–30-year-old men was leaving school without any educational qualifications.

49 SEU (1999 a) paras 4.8–4.11.

50 See DfEE Press Notice, 9 October 2002. Education Minister Stephen Twigg 'stepped up the Government's battle against truancy' with a package of 'truancy-busting measures', including renewed truancy sweeps across the country and funding for electronic registration in secondary schools.

51 Education Act 1996, s 444(1): failure to ensure the child's regular attendance at school amounts to an offence. See also s 443(1): the offence of parental failure to comply with a school attendance order.

52 Education Act 1996, s 7. But note that since a child can receive suitable full-time education by regular attendance at school '*or otherwise*', parents may choose to educate their children at home. Nevertheless, they must provide education suitable to the child's age, ability and aptitude – a condition not satisfied if the child is allowed to choose what he or she learns. Eg *Baker v Earl* [1960] Crim LR 363: a mother with no educational qualifications left it to her children aged 10 and 14 to determine for themselves what subjects interested them.

53 *Crump v Gilmore* (1969) 113 Sol Jo 998.

54 Education Act 1996, s 444(8) was amended by the Criminal Justice and Courts Services Act 2000, s 72, increasing the maximum fine which can be imposed on a parent to £2,500 and/or three months' imprisonment. In May 2002 this latter sanction was used for the first time when a mother was imprisoned for 60 days for not ensuring that her daughter regularly attended school. See *Guardian*, Leader, 15 May 2002.

55 SEU (1998 a) para 1.8.

56 SEU (1998 a) at para 4.14. See also Audit Commission (1996) para 51.

57 See Crime and Disorder Act 1998, s 8(1)(d).

months.[57] The police are also now required to assist in reducing truancy, with powers to collect up children of compulsory school age whom they find in public places during school hours and take them to 'designated premises' or back to their schools.[58] They are entitled to use reasonable force to ensure that a child goes with the officer concerned.[59]

Utilising the criminal justice system to combat truancy may be counter-productive. The government's continuing determination to penalise the small proportion of parents whose attitudes are irresponsible[60] will not necessarily accomplish any change in the attitudes or habits of truants themselves.[61] Nor, indeed, is it likely to enhance their relationship with their parents, which may be extremely poor already – a factor which may itself underlie their disenchantment with school. Furthermore, it seems inappropriate for the law to ignore the practical difficulty that parents may have no physical or social control over a rebellious teenager.[62]

The civil law provides an alternative to instituting criminal proceedings against parents for their children's failure to attend school. This is for a LEA to apply to the family courts for an education supervision order. Indeed, they are required to consider the appropriateness of so doing before instituting criminal proceedings.[63] The education supervision order was created by the Children Act 1989 to replace the old method of applying for a care order regarding persistent truants. A LEA can apply for an education supervision order on the sole ground that 'the child is of compulsory school age and is not being properly educated',[64] but should only do so having first consulted the department of social services.[65] In practice, truancy may often be attributable to family difficulties. Such consultation should at least alert social services and enable them to establish whether work can be done to support the family and avoid criminal proceedings against the parents for their child's school absences, which may merely make matters worse. The education supervision order was intended to help parents who find it difficult to exercise a proper influence over their child, by giving court backing to the efforts of the supervising officer whilst working with the family and child.[66] The order involves the child being placed under the supervision of the 'designated authority'[67] for its duration[68] and a social worker or education welfare officer being appointed to 'advise, assist and befriend' the child and his or her parents and give them directions ensuring that the child is properly educated.[69] But

---

58   Crime and Disorder Act 1998, s 16.
59   Home Office (1999) para 4.16.
60   Eg the proposal of Tony Blair, the Prime Minister, in April 2002, to stop the payment of child benefit to the parents of persistent truants and young offenders. Discussed by R Arthur (2002). See also plans for the introduction of a new fast-track prosecution process for the parents of persistent truants who refuse to send their children to school: DfEE Press Notice, 9 October 2002.
61   Complaints about behaviour at school can often increase existing tension between young people and their parents, leading to further behavioural problems, such as running away or offending. See N Biehal et al (2000) p 23.
62   See S Cretney (1987). See also M Grenville (1988) pp 18–19.
63   Education Act 1996, s 447(1). See also s 447(2), which enables the court, when hearing charges against the parents, to direct the LEA to apply instead for an education supervision order.
64   Children Act 1989, s 36(3).
65   Children Act 1989, s 36(8).
66   See Department of Health (hereafter DH) (1991) para 3.9.
67   Children Act 1989, s 36(7).
68   Children Act 1989, Sch 3, para 15(1) – in the first place not more than one year, although it can be extended for a further three years.
69   Children Act 1989, Sch 3, para 12(1).

although its creation indicated a well-intentioned effort to ensure that the individual needs of the non-attending child were considered and addressed, the education supervision order has proved unpopular with LEAs.[70] This is probably because in most cases LEAs can try most strategies authorised thereunder without going to the trouble of applying for a court order.[71]

There is now a wide range of non-legal strategies being used to address the problem of truanting from school.[72] LEAs and schools are being encouraged to introduce more effective procedures for managing absences[73] and to improve attendance rates by meeting annual targets.[74] Government guidance to schools on dealing with problems associated with pupil disaffection, including truancy,[75] clearly reflects its concern over the fact that some parents connive at their children's absences from school. It expects schools to emphasise to pupils and their parents (through home-school agreements,[76] parents' evenings, newsletters etc) the seriousness of unauthorised absence.[77] Surprisingly, the guidance omits any clear and specific encouragement to teachers to take steps to discover why individual children truant. Given that some pupils truant to avoid bullying,[78] a school's *first* priority should surely be to discover the reasons for a child staying away from school, rather than castigating his or her parents.[79]

Many adolescents currently assume that qualifications are unimportant because they will not succeed anyway.[80] A bewildering variety of government initiatives has been established recently to tackle the obvious disaffection amongst these older

---

70 In 2000 only 208 education supervision orders were granted by all tiers of courts. The maximum number ever granted since implementation of the Children Act 1989 was 380 in 1996. Figures supplied by the Lord Chancellor's Department.

71 Eg *Re O (a minor) (care order: education: procedure)* [1992] 2 FLR 7: all that could be achieved by an education supervision order had already been attempted, unsuccessfully, to stop a 15-year-old girl truanting from school for over three years. The parents had been prosecuted and fined for not ensuring her attendance. The local authority eventually obtained a care order to require her to live in a children's home, from whence she would be escorted to school every day.

72 Eg electronic registration is sometimes combined with providing parents of pupils who truant with pagers. They are contacted as soon as a child goes missing and are expected to ensure that he or she attends. See Office for Standards in Education (Ofsted) (2001) para 51.

73 See Audit Commission (1999) ch 2.

74 School Standards and Framework Act 1998, s 63.

75 DfEE (1999 b). See also DfEE (1999 c).

76 Government guidance on the contents of 'home-school agreements' suggests that these documents should include a provision making it clear that parents are responsible for ensuring that their children attend school regularly. See DfEE (1998 a) para 20. See discussion below.

77 DfEE (1999 b) paras 4.2–4.5.

78 See N Biehal et al (2000) p 23.

79 See L Johnston et al (2000) p 24. This research indicates that truanting is often triggered by particular problems or events, such as undiagnosed dyslexia or family bereavement. Certain groups of children are more prone to truant than others. Eg 33% of young people with mental disorders are likely to truant, cf 9% of other children, with 44% of children with conduct disorders being likely to truant. See H Meltzer and R Gatward (2000) p 94 and Table 8.9.

80 SEU (1999 a) para 5.6.

81 Eg the New Start programme providing government support for local projects designed to encourage disaffected pupils back into learning, through vocational options and with 'motivation counselling'. Young people from low income families are also entitled to an Education Maintenance Allowance (EMA) ie a financial incentive to remain in full-time school or FE college. The Education Maintenance Allowance and School Access Funds (England) Grant Regulations 2001, SI 2001/797 govern funding for this allowance. The EMA, piloted from 1999, appears to have had striking success in some pilot areas. See L Johnston et al (2000) p 33.

pupils.[81] Undoubtedly, if they could be persuaded to stay in education or training, they would be more likely to gain the skills required to gain well-paid employment.[82] Most ambitious is the Connexions service, a support scheme designed to combat this attitude and encourage disadvantaged young people between the ages of 13 and 19 to remain in mainstream education.[83] It provides them with a network of 'dedicated personal advisers' for 'reaching out and bringing them back into learning'.[84] But underachievement has strong links with factors spanning generations, such as family disadvantage and poverty. If these educational initiatives, combined with urban renewal programmes designed to revive disadvantaged communities,[85] could break the cycle of second and third generation unemployment within the same families, it might also change the low aspirations of family members, who cannot presently conceive what relevance academic learning can have for them or their offspring.[86]

Since pupils' aversion to school may simply be attributable to poor teaching,[87] new initiatives designed to ensure they stay in school will be useless unless attending school can be made a rewarding experience. Truancy rates vary significantly between schools and, perhaps predictably, many schools with very high truancy also achieve lower exam passes.[88] Indeed, since few children who are truly inspired and interested by their education will willingly stay away from school, efforts to raise the overall standard of education in schools[89] may reduce truanting more effectively.[90] But there is also a growing view that the real problem underlying truancy relates to the form of education on offer, with an over-emphasis on traditional academic skills. A conventional academic curriculum, reinforced by the straitjacket imposed by the National Curriculum, does not suit large numbers of the 14 to 16 age group. Research indicates that many view the curriculum as 'lacking relevance, stimulus and variety.

82   SEU (1999 a) para 1.11.
83   Established by the Learning and Skills Act 2000, ss 114–129.
84   DfEE (1999 a) ch 6, esp para 6.7. The scheme of Personal Advisers established by the Connexions service may be combined with the system of Learning Mentors (school-based employees employed to help pupils of all ages overcome barriers to learning, such as difficulties at home, truancy, bullying, disaffection etc) recruited as part of the EiC (Excellence in Cities) standards raising programme: DfEE press release 24 January 2001.
85   See SEU (1998 b). These proposals for breaking the cycle of deprivation and disadvantage suffered by families in deprived neighbourhoods led to various initiatives for deprived communities, including, inter alia, the New Deal for Communities (NDC) and the Neighbourhood Renewal Fund.
86   SEU (1999 a) para 5.6.
87   See N Pearce and J Hillman (1998), who note (p 28) that the likelihood of truancy appears to be reduced in schools where more teachers are trained graduates, with low pupil-teacher ratios and low staff turnover. See also Ofsted (2001) esp chs 7 and 8, which provides considerable evidence that the quality of teaching and the approach of teachers generally has a great impact on pupils' attitudes to attendance and discipline.
88   See DfES (2001 a) p 5. See also Figure 3 and Table 6.
89   Inter alia: through reductions in class size (School Standards and Framework Act 1998, ss 1–4); through strengthening LEAs' duty to promote high standards in primary and secondary education (Education Act 1996, s 13 A), and requiring them to prepare and submit to the Secretary of State, Education Development Plans (School Standards and Framework Act 1998, ss 6–7); through the adoption of 'innovative approaches to tackling disadvantage and raising standards' in Education Action Zones established in areas experiencing social decline and low educational achievement (School Standards and Framework Act 1998, ss 10–12).
90   Although the percentage of 15-year-old pupils achieving no GCSE passes is steadily falling, in 2000/01, 6.5% of boys and 4.4% of girls were in this category. DfES (2002 b) Attainment and Outcome, Section 5.5, Chart D.
91   See inter alia: N Pearce and J Hillman (1998) p 26, and pp 25–27 for a useful summary of this area of research; L Johnston et al (2000) pp 32–33; Communities that Care (2002), which indicates (p 34) from self-referral data that 33% of year 11 'hated being in school'.

Boredom features prominently in pupils' replies ...'[91] Consequently, they simply decide that attending school has nothing to offer them,[92] or they behave so disruptively that they are permanently excluded from school.[93]

The government is very aware of the need to meet these criticisms. It has acknowledged that a further way of persuading pupils over 14 that formal education can be relevant to their lives is to enable them to study predominantly vocational programmes in school.[94] With far greater flexibility being introduced into the syllabus for the 14 to 16 age group,[95] it is hoped that these programmes, will become part of every day school life. The intention is that many, sometimes with financial support,[96] will develop craft and technical skills, thereby preparing them for progression to apprenticeships[97] at the age of 16. Whilst it is arguable that this new approach will create a two-tier system of education, it may at least address the needs of many teenage pupils by providing them with instruction in subjects they find interesting and relevant. To argue that school should no longer remain compulsory after the age of 13 or 14 smacks of a counsel of despair in an industrialised society which rewards qualifications and skills. Nevertheless, there must be greater emphasis on making school more relevant to the disaffected.

(4) PUPILS AND SCHOOL DISCIPLINE

(A) Schools' powers and duties

Bored children, who cannot see the point of classes, may either stay away or behave disruptively. 'The antipathy between school and the disruptive child is usually mutual, and disaffected young people who are not excluded often truant from school.'[98] Whatever the causes, schools are experiencing increasing difficulties over disciplining a small but growing minority of violent and aggressive pupils. Although all pupils have a right to education, those exhibiting aggressive and anti-social behaviour may intimidate class-mates and teachers alike.[99] Indeed, in some schools it is increasingly common for children to be subjected by their peers to physical assaults, intimidation, theft, verbal abuse, racial and sexual harassment, or harassment on other grounds, such as gender and religion.[100]

---

92 The SEU found plenty of evidence of this attitude when consulting young people over non-participation in school. See SEU (1999 a) para 5.6. See also J Smith et al (1998) pp 40–41.

93 See discussion below.

94 See DfES (2002 d) esp ch 3. The government intends to implement the main proposals contained in this Green Paper. See speech by David Miliband, Minister of State for School Standards, on 21 January 2003.

95 See Education Act 2002, s 86, which gives the Secretary of State power to alter, remove or impose requirements for this age group.

96 Some pupils are already entitled to the educational maintenance allowance being phased in through the country (see p 169, n 81 above) or a 'learning allowance': see Education Act 2002, ss 181–184.

97 New GCSEs in vocational subjects are being made available to all schools throughout the country, as from 2003. See DfES (2001 c) ch 4, esp para 4.6. See also the new system of Modern Apprenticeships described in DfES (2002 d) paras 3.45–3.48.

98 See Audit Commission (1996) p 67.

99 Violent incidents in schools are increasingly being reported by the press. Eg a woman teacher was kicked and punched to the floor by a boy responding to her request to leave the classroom: *Guardian*, 4 June 2002.

100 Headmaster Philip Lawrence was stabbed to death in December 1995, when trying to break up a fight outside his school in North London. Operation of the same school was suspended by Westminster education authority in February 2000 due to further outbreaks of pupil violence.

Children have a right to receive their education in a safe environment. A couple of violent ill-disciplined pupils in a class can create a highly charged and frightening atmosphere for their peers. Nevertheless, schools must find a balance between over-harsh discipline, which can be counter-productive, and a lax and inconsistent approach. The CRC recognises this and requires states to 'take all appropriate measures to ensure that school discipline is administered in a manner consistent with the child's human dignity ...'[101] Domestic law clearly requires schools to maintain discipline, in so far as it imposes a duty of care on schools and their staff, just as it does on parents. A failure to do so may be actionable in tort by a pupil if it has led to his or her physical or psychological injury. A teacher is required to show the same standard of care as that of 'a reasonably careful parent', taking into account the school context and number of pupils.[102] He is bound to take 'all reasonable and proper steps' to prevent pupils from, for example, being injured by inanimate objects or injuring each other, or a combination of the two.[103] Bullying in schools can blight a child's school days[104] and is being taken increasingly seriously, with both the civil law[105] and criminal law being utilised by way of sanctions.[106] Education law[107] and government guidance acknowledge that the duty to impose discipline on pupils includes a duty to prevent pupils bullying each other,[108] even if that means permanently excluding the perpetrators.[109]

Discipline is obviously essential in schools, not only to avoid actions in negligence but also to maintain an atmosphere conducive to learning for those who want to gain from their education. Nevertheless, the law relating to discipline in schools has become increasingly complex and controversial. Over the last 20 years, it has been the subject of various reports[110] and government circulars.[111] The use of sanctions by teachers is strictly regulated, with current law prohibiting physical punishment in all schools, maintained and private alike.[112] In the late 1990s, media publicity over the disruption

---

101   Art 28(2). The Committee on the Rights of the Child (2002) para 45, indicated its concern over the widespread bullying in schools.

102   *Van Oppen v Clerk to the Bedford Charity Trustees* [1989] 3 All ER 389 at 401, per Balcombe LJ.

103   *Beaumont v Surrey County Council* (1968) 66 LGR 580 at 580, per Geoffrey Lane J. A head teacher was held liable in negligence for a pupil suffering a severe eye injury due to another pupil playing, unsupervised, with heavy duty elastic rope.

104   Bullying is by far the most common reason for children telephoning Childline. See Childline (2001) p 4.

105   In *Bradford-Smart v West Sussex County Council* [2002] EW Civ 7, [2002] ELR 139: the Court of Appeal acknowledged the existence of a duty of care on schools to prevent bullying on the school premises and even, depending on the circumstances, outside the school premises. Nevertheless, in that particular case, the school had taken reasonable steps to address the problem.

106   Eg ten pupils in a Doncaster school were charged with a total of 35 offences, including blackmail, robbery, affray, assault and theft after a police investigation into school bullying. *Guardian*, 16 May 1997. Anti-social behaviour orders can also be obtained (under the Crime and Disorder Act 1998, s 1) against children over the age of 10.

107   School Standards and Framework Act 1998, s 61(4) requires the school governors and head teacher to establish discipline policies designed to promote good behaviour and 'in particular, preventing all forms of bullying among pupils'.

108   See DfEE (2000 a). See also DfEE (1999 b) paras 4.29–4.33. Much of the research on bullying is usefully summarised by P Smith (2000).

109   Official guidance refers to 'serious actual or threatened violence against another pupil or a member of staff' as justifying a pupil's permanent exclusion even if a 'one off' offence. See DfES (2003 a) Part 1, para 1.4.

110   Eg Elton Report (1989), discussed below.

111   DfEE (1999 b), DfEE (1999 c) and DfES (2003 a).

112   Education Act 1996, ss 548–549, as amended by School Standards and Framework Act 1998. Discussed in chapter 9.

in some schools led to legislation clarifying what measures could and could not be taken by teachers confronted by disruptive and aggressive pupils. Teachers were given the power to use 'such force as is reasonable in the circumstances', for example, to break up fights or to exclude badly behaved pupils from their classrooms.[113] The new provisions attracted criticism. Hamilton claimed that the 'reasonable force' formula was far too broad, enabling teachers to slip back into using physical punishment under the guise of physical restraint.[114] The official guidance accompanying the provisions attempts to address such concerns by stressing that the use of physical force must not be used to prevent a pupil committing a trivial misdemeanour, it must only be used as a last resort, and must always be very carefully justified. Above all, it should only be used as a means of *control*, as opposed to punishment.[115] Teachers following this guidance closely are unlikely to infringe children's rights under the ECHR.[116] Nevertheless, there clearly remains a grey area between justifiable restraint and unacceptable force.[117]

Successive governments have placed considerable store on schools gaining parents' support in their efforts to promote good behaviour and discipline in schools. Consequently, parents with children in maintained and city technology schools are required to sign 'home-school agreements' indicating their own commitment to ensuring that their children keep the rules on such matters as attendance, discipline and homework.[118] Some schools sensibly adopt a system whereby such agreements are drawn up between teachers and pupils after consultation together, with each child signing his or her part of the agreement. Ideally, it should become standard practice for all schools to encourage pupils to take responsibility for the way they behave, rather than implying that issues of discipline are part of an adult regime of coercion. Although this would have been one way of meeting the requirements of article 12 of the CRC, government guidance merely encourages this practice,[119] without the legislation making it obligatory.[120]

113 Education Act 1996, s 550A (inserted by Education Act 1997, s 4) enables a teacher to use 'such force as is reasonable in the circumstances' for the purpose of preventing a pupil committing any offence, causing personal injury to anyone or damaging the property belonging to anyone, or engaging in 'any behaviour prejudicial to the maintenance of good order and discipline' at the school or among any of its pupils, 'whether that behaviour occurs during a teaching session or otherwise'.
114 C Hamilton (1997) pp 215–220.
115 DfEE (1998 c) para 17. The guidance provides a list of clearly described factual examples of situations where force may be justified: see para 14.
116 Discussed in more detail by J Fortin (2001) pp 250–252.
117 Eg the case of Mrs Marjorie Evans, who was suspended for 18 months from her post as head of a Welsh village primary school, having been found guilty of slapping an unruly 10-year-old. She was eventually cleared of this charge on the basis that she had been restraining him from trying to punch and head-butt her. *Daily Telegraph*, 17 March 2001.
118 See School Standards and Framework Act 1998, ss 110–111. See also DfEE (1998 a). Nevertheless, schools are unable to make it a condition of offering parents a school place that they sign such agreements.
119 DfEE (1998 a) para 42.
120 See School Standards and Framework Act 1998, s 110(5). Schools 'may' but not 'must' invite pupils they consider to have 'a sufficient understanding' of the agreement to sign the parental declaration as well, to indicate that they acknowledge and accept the school's expectations of its pupils.

(B) Exclusions

(i) Patterns of exclusion

There was a variety of reasons for the soaring rates of permanent exclusions during the 1990s.[121] Teachers clearly cannot pick and choose which children they are prepared to teach and which they are not. Nevertheless, a disruptive child's right to be educated in a mainstream school may seriously undermine a studious child's right to receive instruction in an atmosphere conducive to learning. In cases of serious infringements of discipline, schools may feel that they have little option but to resort to excluding pupils they are unable to control. It became clear, however, that some schools were using the exclusion process to exclude pupils whose poor academic skills lowered their performance tables.[122] Researchers noted that schools were under pressure to adopt inclusive policies and raise academic standards, while at the same time being under financial restraints, leading to larger classes and a lack of resources. 'Market forces operating in education and the greater involvement of parents may have created a climate where it is perceived desirable to exclude pupils who interfere with the education of others.'[123]

Most exclusions are for short periods of a few days,[124] but the dramatic increase in the use of permanent exclusions provoked government alarm and a determination to achieve a reduction. As the SEU notes, the impact of permanent exclusions, on children, on their families, and on the community as a whole, is significant.[125] Although it is impossible to establish whether permanent exclusion is a cause of criminal behaviour, rather than a consequence of it, excluded children clearly have more time on their hands to associate with other excluded delinquent peers in the community.[126] Research indicates a marked correlation between truancy, exclusion and youth offending.[127] They are also at a greater risk of homelessness[128] and educational underachievement,[129] with a consequent risk of unemployment.[130]

---

121 From 1990/91, when the level of permanent exclusions was 2,910, the rate rose to a peak of 12,700 in 1997. It fell to 8,300 in 1999/00, only to rise again in 2000/01 to 9,210 (an increase of 11% over the previous year). Over 61% of permanently excluded pupils are aged between 13 and 15. DfES (2002 b) Schools, Absence and Exclusion, Section 3.4, Chart C. See also DFES (2002 e).

122 SEU (1998 a) para 2.15 and paras 5.11 and 5.12.

123 S Hallam and F Castle (1999).

124 Currently up to a maximum of 45 days in any one school year, this maximum has not been changed by the new regulations governing exclusions: Education (Pupil Exclusion and Appeals) (Maintained Schools) (England) Regulations, SI 2002/3178.

125 SEU (1998 a) paras 3.3–3.6. Discussed below.

126 D Berridge et al (2001) esp ch 5 and p 49.

127 42% of young offenders of school age sentenced in the juvenile courts have been excluded from school. See Audit Commission (1996) pp 66–67. See also C Flood-Page et al (2000) pp 37–38 and MORI (2002) ch 7.

128 See N Biehal et al (2000) pp 22–23.

129 Audit Commission (1999) ch 5. As discussed below, the level of educational provision for excluded children is usually poor. A large proportion of excluded pupils aged between 14 and 16 never returns to mainstream education at all (p 50).

130 SEU (1999 a) ch 4.

The government's efforts to reduce the rate of exclusions[131] bore fruit,[132] so much so that in 2001 government targets to cut exclusions were suspended.[133] Even so, it appears that some schools still use permanent exclusion inappropriately and that many children are being excluded who could be kept in mainstream education.[134] Indeed, research suggests that reductions in exclusion rates mask the increasing use of unofficial exclusions by some head teachers – sometimes being recorded as authorised absences, perhaps to disguise the real level of exclusion.[135]

A variety of factors is often associated with bad behaviour leading to exclusion. These include poor basic skills, limited aspirations, strained or traumatic home circumstances, and poor relationships with teachers and other pupils.[136] This partly explains why exclusion rates vary from school to school, both at secondary and primary level and from LEA to LEA. Secondary schools with the highest exclusion rates are those with high percentages of pupils eligible for free school meals and low levels of pupil attainment, as measured by GCSE attainment rates.[137] Particular groups of pupils remain at much greater risk of permanent exclusion than others.[138] These include black Afro-Caribbean pupils, children looked after by local authorities and those statemented as having special educational needs (SEN).[139] Particular concern has been expressed from a variety of sources over the high rates of permanently excluded black Afro-Caribbean boys,[140] often for 'challenging behaviour', compared with the discipline meted out to white pupils. Research indicates that some disruption is caused by black pupils responding to racist abuse and attacks.[141] Although Ofsted research shows both white and black pupils being excluded for violent behaviour, the length of fixed-term exclusions often varies considerably, despite the incidents appearing essentially similar. These researchers observe: 'While it does not follow that schools treated pupils differently because of their ethnicity, they certainly could leave both pupils and parents with the impression that they had done so'.[142]

---

131 Eg by complying with 'exclusion targets', schools and LEAs were expected to reduce the level of permanent exclusions to a local target, as recommended by the SEU in SEU (1998 a) paras 5.3–5.8.

132 These measures achieved a 22% reduction in the total number of permanent exclusions between 1996/97 and 1999/2000.

133 On 9 July 2001, Estelle Morris, Education and Skills Secretary announced that she would set no further targets to cut exclusions further following an estimated fall of nearly one-third over three years.

134 Eg one school inspected by Ofsted used permanent exclusions as a means of alerting parents and children of the seriousness of the situation, knowing that the governors often revoked the exclusion. See Ofsted (2001) para 81.

135 See A Osler et al (2001). The Committee on the Rights of the Child expressed concern about the still high exclusion rates mainly amongst certain groups of children and has called for them to be reduced. Committee on the Rights of the Child (2002) paras 45–46.

136 N Harris and K Eden, with A Blair (2000) pp 60–63. See also Ofsted (1996) esp Appendices.

137 See DfEE (2000 c) pp 20–21.

138 Discussed in N Harris and K Eden, with A Blair (2000) pp 60–63.

139 See DfES (2001 b) Table 7. In 1996/97, the overall number of permanently excluded children with SEN statements was eight times higher than that of other children. Since then, these overall numbers have dropped. See DfES (2002 e) p 19. But this reduction may be due to changes in the underlying data collection.

140 Official statistics indicate that the rate of exclusions for Black Caribbean pupils has dropped since 1995/6. Nevertheless, in 2000/01, these pupils remained three times more likely to be excluded than other pupils (38 in every 10,000 Black Caribbean pupils, cf 4 in every 10,000 Chinese pupils). See DfES (2002 b) Schools, Absence and Exclusion, Section 3.4 Chart D and DfES (2002 e) Table 5.

141 See Ofsted (1999) para 124.

142 Ofsted (2001) para 86.

(ii)   Prevention

Considerable effort is being made, through official regulation[143] and guidance,[144] to ensure that schools take adequate preventative measures to ensure that permanent exclusion is utilised only as a remedy of last resort. The guidance requires schools to institute formal in-school preventative procedures well in advance of using exclusion as a means of dealing with disruptive behaviour. They should identify pupils who are so badly behaved that they are at serious risk of permanent exclusion and, with the help of external services, establish for each a formal 'Pastoral Support Programme' or PSP.[145] Schools are sensibly urged to involve outside agencies, such as social services departments, to help resolve home problems, housing departments, who may help with family accommodation difficulties and ethnic minority community groups, who may provide schools with additional support. This greater liaison between public agencies over educational problems is long overdue.[146] Regrettably, the guidance on designing a PSP fails to suggest that the preliminary discussions between a variety of adults, including the parents, should include the child, or that the child, in addition to his or her parents, should agree the details of the programme. As with the guidance governing home-school agreements,[147] the government appears blind to the concept of involving children in decisions regarding their school life.

The official guidance also emphasises that schools should use preventative measures to avoid excluding certain groups of children whose difficult behaviour may stem from their home difficulties.[148] Considerable attention is paid to reducing the exclusion rates of children being looked after by local authorities.[149] Schools are also reminded that exclusion rates amongst Black-Caribbean pupils, especially boys, are significantly higher than those for other pupils. The guidance warns against racial prejudice, pointing out that 'an incident' may have been caused by racial harassment and also warns teachers to avoid any risk of stereotyping and to be alert to cultural differences in manner and demeanour.[150] It also stresses that exclusion should not be used as a sanction for minor incidents such as breaching school uniform policy.[151] Although the guidance draws schools' attention to their legal duties not to discriminate against pupils under the Race Relations Act 1976,[152] it makes no mention

143   See Education (Pupil Exclusions and Appeals) (Maintained Schools) (England) Regulations 2002, SI 2002/3178, which set out every stage of the exclusion procedure.
144   DfEE (1999 b), DfEE (1999 c) and DfES (2003 a).
145   A PSP, which must be agreed with parents and an LEA representative, requires the child to work towards 'precise and realistic behavioural outcomes', to remedy the situation, academically and socially. DfEE (1999 b) ch 5. Extra help may be provided in an in-school 'learning support unit', which helps reintegrate such pupils into mainstream classes as quickly as possible.
146   See N Biehals et al (2000). These researchers record (pp 82–84) the need for more co-ordination of effort between education services and social services departments when attempting to resolve the problems of young people in crisis.
147   Discussed above.
148   DfEE (1999 b) ch 3 and DfES (2003 a) Part 1, sections 13–16. Eg inter alia: SEN children; ethnic minority children; traveller children; pregnant schoolgirls.
149   See generally DfEE (2000 b) and DH (2000).
150   DfEE (1999 b) para 3.6. See also DfES (2003 a) Part 1, para 3.1(c) and section 15.
151   DfES (2003 a) Part 1, para 5.
152   See DfES (2003 a) Part 1, para 3.1(b). In *Mandla v Dowell Lee* [1983] 1 All ER 1062 the House of Lords ruled that it had amounted to unlawful discrimination under the Race Relations Act 1976 for a headmaster to refuse to admit a Sikh boy to the school, due only to the boy's insistence on wearing a turban.

of their rights under the ECHR or under the CRC. Pupils might claim, for example, that attempts to prevent their following particular styles of dress, which infringe school dress codes, are infringing their right to freedom of expression under articles 10 and 14 of the ECHR,[153] and article 13 of the CRC.[154]

As noted above, SEN children have a particularly high risk of being excluded for their bad behaviour. But research indicates that practice remains extremely varied on the extent to which schools pick up on their underlying problems.[155] It may gradually improve in response to the threat of negligence claims. The House of Lords confirmed that LEAs can be held vicariously liable in negligence if educational practitioners employed by them fail to exercise reasonable skill and care when diagnosing learning difficulties and when determining and delivering educational provision appropriate to address them.[156] Within this group are children whose disruptive and aggressive conduct stems from 'emotional and behavioural difficulties', or what is, in mental health terms, a 'conduct disorder'.[157] Now the most common of all childhood psychiatric disorders,[158] this condition is currently contributing greatly to the difficulties of maintaining discipline in schools. The government recognises that these children often have undetected educational needs which should be investigated and addressed, either by the school itself or by the LEA. Indeed, LEAs are under a legislative duty[159] to establish special arrangements for the education of all children within their areas with behavioural difficulties, publishing them in the form of behaviour support plans.[160]

(iii) The impact of exclusion

The impact on pupils and their families of permanent exclusion is considerable.[161] Researchers note that excluded children 'often enter an insular and isolating environment, feeling bored and frustrated – not just excluded from school, but also from society and the typical lifestyle of other children their age'.[162] The strain may also affect the excluded child's parents and siblings.[163] Overriding all other factors is

---

153   See claims of this kind noted in A Ruff (2001) p 68. But, depending on the circumstances, a domestic court might consider such dress codes to be justified under art 10(2), taking account of the needs of the school itself.

154   See M Freeman (2002) p 106. Freeman cites the American Supreme Court's decision in *Tinker v Des Moines Independent Community School District* 393 US 503 (1969), see disucssion above, in support of his contention that the right to freedom of expression includes the right to opt out of school uniform.

155   Ofsted (2001) para 136. Most of the pupils who caused concern on the grounds of their behaviour had not been assessed by special educational needs staff.

156   *Phelps v London Borough of Hillingdon* [2001] 2 AC 619. Discussed in more detail in chapter 12.

157   The high numbers of SEN children being excluded are swelled by children with emotional and behavioural difficulties (EBD) for whom there are significant gaps in provision. See Audit Commission (1999) p 17.

158   H Meltzer and R Gatward (2000) p 33, indicating that 8.6% of boys aged between 11 and 15 have conduct disorders, compared with 5.1% of emotional disorders.

159   Education Act 1996, s 527A.

160   Multi-agency behaviour support teams have been established under this initiative. DfEE (1998 b) and Supplementary Note 2000.

161   See N Harris and K Eden, with A Blair (2000) pp 63–68.

162   N Harris and K Eden, with A Blair (2000) pp 65–66.

163   N Harris and K Eden, with A Blair (2000) pp 67–68.

the educational impact of being out of full-time school for long periods,[164] during which time the education offered may be highly unsatisfactory or even virtually non-existent. Some LEAs have an extremely poor record of providing alternative education for excluded pupils outside school,[165] partly due to the high cost of providing education outside mainstream school, and partly to placements being scarce.[166]

LEAs now appreciate that they must not interpret their legal duties to provide 'suitable' and 'efficient' education outside mainstream school by reference to the funds they have available, rather than by reference to a child's own particular needs.[167] Furthermore, the government's demand that LEAs establish full-time educational provision for all excluded pupils is forcing them to meet the many gaps in this service.[168] Improvements are long overdue; in the past, excluded pupils might be given part-time home tuition or a place in a pupil referral unit (PRU)[169] and either way, the quality was variable.[170] Provision was particularly inadequate for the older group, with the hours often being extremely limited.[171] The government has funded more learning support units (LSUs) to be attached to mainstream schools themselves, where problem pupils can be assisted.[172] But these are not appropriate for the most disturbed children since they may involve schools coping with the continued presence on the school premises of a violent or drug abusing or dealing pupil.

Although most excluded pupils want to return to mainstream education as soon as possible, the difficulty lies in persuading mainstream schools to take them. The guidance stresses the need for excluded children to be reintegrated into mainstream schools rapidly and directs schools not to make 'subjective judgements as to the suitability of certain children for the school, and refuse admission for pupils because of their past disciplinary record, including any previous exclusions'.[173] The government seems keen to ensure that groups of local schools co-operate over sharing out excluded pupils to avoid disproportionate numbers being placed in any one school.[174] At present, many older pupils never return to mainstream education,[175] the problem being exacerbated by legislation which entitles maintained schools to refuse to admit children who, within the last two years, have been already excluded from

164   But in *R (on the application of B) v Head Teacher of Alperton Community School* [2001] EWHC Admin 229, [2001] ELR 359, Newman J (at [67]) rejected a pupil's claim that by permanently excluding him, his school was denying him the opportunity to develop his personality alongside his peers, thereby infringing his right to private life under art 8.

165   Termed 'education otherwise', LEAs must provide 'suitable full-time or part-time education at school or otherwise than at school ...': Education Act 1996, s 19(1).

166   Audit Commission (1999) pp 54–56.

167   *R v East Sussex County Council, ex p Tandy* [1998] 2 All ER 769.

168   The government target, for LEAs to provide full-time education for all permanently excluded pupils by September 2002, was expected to be met by 'virtually all' LEAs. See DfES (2002 e) p 7.

169   Education Act 1996, s 19(2).

170   The Audit Commission (1999) recommended (para 92) that the overall standard of education offered by PRUs might be improved by Ofsted assuming responsibility for monitoring it.

171   See Audit Commission (1999) describing the 'education otherwise' provided for the 15–16-year-olds as 'often perfunctory', para 103. See also DfES (2001 b) Chart 5, showing that 10% of Key Stage 4 excluded pupils were receiving *no* educational provision in March 2001 and approximately 14% were receiving less than five hours per week.

172   See S Hallam and F Castle (1999).

173   DfEE (1999 b) para 7.4.

174   DfES (2003 b) section entitled 'Collective ownership'.

175   Out of the four LEAs examined in detail, only one fifth of excluded pupils aged between 15 and 16 returned to education provided solely by mainstream schools: Audit Commission (1999) para 79.

two or more other schools.[176] Despite LEAs being responsible for finding children places quickly,[177] parents often receive no help from their LEA when themselves attempting to do so.[178] This situation is highly regrettable. Excluded pupils provided with little or no alternative education might claim compensation from their LEAs for infringing their right to effective education under the ECHR.[179]

(iv) The exclusion process

When it comes to regulating the exclusion process, the government has struggled to ensure that the law finds an appropriate balance between the rights of two groups of children – the well-behaved and the disaffected. Children who behave in an anti-social and disruptive way in school must expect their behaviour to be treated seriously. Indeed, they may find that they are deprived permanently of their right to education in a mainstream school. Given the inadequate teaching arrangements often provided for excluded pupils, this may effectively mark the end of their educational careers. Nevertheless, their more studious peers also have a right to be educated without fear of bullying and classroom violence. Meanwhile, teachers obviously have a difficult task in maintaining discipline in schools; but they may not always be fair over their reaction to disruptive behaviour or in selecting the right pupils to be disciplined.

The law and official guidance acknowledges the serious implications of exclusion and provides a carefully regulated procedure which must be complied with.[180] A decision to exclude a child should only be taken by a head teacher '(a) in response to serious breaches of a school's discipline policy; and (b) if allowing the pupil to remain in school would seriously harm the education or welfare of the pupil or others in the school'.[181] The guidance stresses that it should not normally be used to punish a 'first or "one off" offence'.[182] Legislative and judicial efforts have been made to ensure that the exclusion procedures themselves comply with basic notions of fairness.[183] The guidance directs the head teacher to 'allow the pupil to give his or her version of events'.[184] The appeals

---

176 School Standards and Framework Act 1998, s 87. The duty to admit such a pupil is suspended for a period of two years from the date of the last exclusion.

177 The Audit Commission recorded that the average time taken to return permanently excluded children to mainstream schools varies widely, from 8–18 weeks: Audit Commission (1999) para 73. Furthermore, only two thirds of LEAs knew where their permanently excluded children were six months after the end of the school year in which they were excluded: Audit Commission (1999) para 90.

178 Nearly 30% of LEAs give no significant support to parents' efforts to place their children back in mainstream education: Audit Commission (1999) para 80.

179 Ie under art 2 of Protocol One. Discussed above.

180 See Education Act 2002, s 52 and Education (Pupil Exclusion and Appeals) (Maintained School) (England) regulations, SI 2002/3178 and DfES (2003 a). See also N Harris and K Eden, with A Blair (2000) ch 5.

181 DfES (2003 a) Part 1, para 1.1.

182 DfES (2003 a) Part 1, para 1.4. This recent guidance expands on the exceptional circumstances in which permanent exclusion might be appropriate for a 'first or "one-off" offence'. Eg serious actual or threatened violence against another pupil or member of staff.

183 See N Harris and K Eden, with A Blair (2000) chs 5, 6 and 9.

184 DfES (2003 a) Part 1, para 3.1(c).

process[185] provides parents of excluded pupils with a valuable chance to query school decisions and the discipline committee is directed to 'allow the excluded pupil to attend the meeting and speak, if the parent requests this'.[186] Similarly, the independent appeal panel (IAP) is directed that an excluded pupil under the age of 18 'should normally be allowed to attend the hearing and to speak on his or her own behalf, if he or she wishes to do so and the parent agrees'.[187]

The domestic courts, at least for the time being, seem prepared to follow Strasbourg jurisprudence in a narrow interpretation of the scope of article 6 of the ECHR, thereby excluding educational appeal procedures from its ambit.[188] Despite this cautious approach,[189] they have repeatedly stressed that the appeal bodies must conform with the common law rules of natural justice.[190] Nevertheless, IAPs may experience considerable difficulty in establishing whether the offence underlying the exclusion occurred at all. Their task is not eased by the courts insisting that they should use the controversial test propounded by Lord Nicholls in *Re H (minors) (sexual abuse: standard of proof)*.[191] Thus whilst the standard of proof is the balance of probabilities, the seriousness of the offence must be taken account of, when deciding whether the offence occurred. Accordingly, the IAP must be 'more sure before finding serious allegations proved than when deciding less serious or trivial matters'.[192] Matters are

---

185 The parents can appeal on the pupil's behalf to the pupil discipline committee, established by the school governors to review all exclusions. Appeals from that body go to the independent appeal panel (IAP) set up by the LEA. In limited circumstances, it may be possible for an excluded pupil to seek judicial review of the discipline committee's decision to uphold an exclusion. Eg *R v Governors of W School and T Education Authority (Borough Council), ex p H* [2001] ELR 192.

186 DfES (2003 a) Part 3, para 2.2.

187 DfES (2003 a) Part 4, para 6.3.

188 Early Convention case law interpreted the phrase 'civil rights and obligations' in art 6 to mean only those rights pertaining to private rather than public law. Consequently, in *Simpson v United Kingdom* Application No 14688/89 (1989) 64 DR 188, the European Commission rejected a mother's claim that the procedures used to determine her son's special educational needs were in breach of art 6 – his right to education was not of a 'civil' nature, falling as it did within the domain of public law. But see D Harris, M O'Boyle and C Warbrick (1995) pp 180–186, for a discussion of the later Strasbourg authorities reflecting a more flexible approach to the public/private law distinction. These authors suggest that the European Court should reformulate its approach to interpreting the phrase 'civil rights and obligations'.

189 See the comments of Newman J in *R (on the application of B) v Head Teacher of Alperton Community School* [2001] EWHC Admin 229, [2001] ELR 359, who applied *Simpson* on this point. See also discussion by Scott Baker J in *R (on the application of S) v London Borough of Brent* [2001] EWHC Admin 384, [2002] ELR 57. But see the Court of Appeal's view in *S, T and P v London Borough of Brent* [2002] EWCA Civ 693, [2002] ELR 556 (at [30], that it was a 'perfectly tenable assumption' that domestic human rights law and, arguably, the jurisprudence of the European Court of Human Rights, would today regard the right not to be permanently excluded from school without good reason a civil right for article 6 purposes.

190 See inter alia: *R v Governors of Bacon's City Technology College, ex p W* [1998] ELR 488; *R v Headteacher and Independent Appeal Committee of Dunraven School, ex p B* [2000] ELR 156. This case law establishes that pupils facing possible expulsion have the right to know the nature of the accusation against them, disclosure of all evidence relied on by the discipline authorities, the opportunity to answer it, including the right to appear before the tribunal dealing with the matter.

191 [1996] 1 All ER 1. Discussed in more detail in chapter 15.

192 See *R v Headteacher and Independent Appeal Committee of Dunraven School, ex p B* [2000] ELR 156 at 204–205, per Brooke LJ. This legal test has been adopted in a series of subsequent decisions. See, inter alia: *R (on the application of B) v Head Teacher of Alperton Community*

further complicated if a criminal prosecution is pending, since further and more detailed evidence may emerge in the criminal proceedings.[193] IAPs can adjourn appeal hearings pending the outcome of any criminal trial arising from the same incident but government guidance urges them to consider the impact of the resulting delay on the complainant, the excluded pupil and the school.[194]

Over recent years, the controversy surrounding the extent to which permanent exclusion should be used as a sanction for breaches of discipline has been reflected in the constant revisions of official guidance on this.[195] Indeed, it has been observed that:

'few, if any, areas of educational guidance have been subjected to so frequent alteration as that relating to school exclusion and appeals, exacerbating the sense of uncertainty in what is already considered to be a legal minefield.'[196]

The government's nervousness has been exacerbated by the ability of the appeal bodies to overrule head teachers wishing to exclude pupils from their schools – a situation which has increasingly fomented friction between teachers, school governors and parents.[197] In the mid-1990s, the spiralling permanent exclusion statistics indicated that exclusions were being imposed too readily. Stricter guidelines, exclusion targets and league tables gradually addressed the problem. Meanwhile, the IAPs attempted to play their part in ensuring that head teachers' decisions to exclude ill-disciplined pupils were fair. Their decisions, however, to reinstate children expelled for offences as serious as assaults on pupils and staff or drug taking,[198] sometimes based merely on technical procedural errors made by the discipline committees, produced problems.[199] Such decisions had serious repercussions for head teachers struggling to enforce drugs policies and classroom discipline codes, with teaching unions threatening industrial action if their members were forced to teach reinstated

---

School [2001] EWHC Admin 229, [2001] ELR 359 and *R (on the application of S) v Head Teacher of C High School* [2001] EWHC Admin 513, [2002] ELR 73. The current guidance fails to draw this sophisticated legal test to the attention of head teachers or IAPs. See DfES (2003 a) Part 1, para 3.2 and Part 4, para 8.1.

193 See *R v Headteacher and Independent Appeal Committee of Dunraven School, ex p B* [2000] ELR 156, per Latham LJ in the Court of Appeal, a pupil discipline committee should not assume that the head teacher has acted reasonably but should establish the facts for itself, cf *R v Independent Appeal Panel of Sheffield City Council, ex p N* [2000] ELR 700, per Moses J, in the event of a criminal trial pending, an appeal panel should not attempt to establish the truth of the allegations, but should instead, decide whether it is in the best interests of the school, the 'victim' and the pupil charged, for the latter to be reinstated. Discussed by R Gold (2001).

194 See DfES (2003 a) Part 5, para 3.2.

195 The guidance on exclusions contained in DfEE (1999 b), having been amended four times in five years, was recently replaced by DfES (2003 a).

196 N Harris (2002).

197 See R Gold (2001) pp 206–208; I Sutherland (2002).

198 Eg *R v Independent Appeal Panel of Sheffield City Council, ex p N* [2000] ELR 700: the appeal panel had decided that a boy should be reinstated, despite a girl pupil's claims that he had sexually assaulted her. It considered that, pending a criminal trial, it should presume that the boy in question was innocent. See also *R v London Borough of Camden and Governors of the Hampstead School, ex p H* [1996] ELR 360.

199 NB the current regulations direct an appeal panel not to reinstate a pupil merely due to a procedural error made by the head teacher or discipline committee. See Education (Pupil Exclusions and Appeals) (Maintained Schools) (England) Regulations 2002, SI 2002/3178, reg 6(4).

pupils considered to be a threat to their safety. They provoked claims that 'The "rights" of a [excluded] child must no longer be placed ahead of the good of the school',[200] and 'If it [the educational system] is to function smoothly in future, head teachers must be given their heads'.[201]

Constant tweaking at the official guidance is unlikely to produce a perfect balance between the rights of the excluded child and those of the wider school community. The Court of Appeal's implicit warning to the government about the way its 'guidance' to IAPs could jeopardise their independence may have been heeded. The current guidance omits earlier advice over how the Secretary of State would 'normally' respond to examples of serious behaviour when considering reinstating an excluded child.[202]

Worryingly, however, the new guidance enables the IAPs to produce a decision which, whilst indicating that permanent exclusion should not have taken place, also acknolwledges that reinstatement in the excluding school 'is not a practical way forward in the best interests of all concerned'.[203] This new 'half-way house' might allow IAPs to bow to precisely the same pressure that produced the exclusion in the first place. As noted above, head teachers sometimes exclude children in response to the vociferous complaints of the teachers' unions who resent their members being forced to teach unruly pupils.[204] The new guidance, combined with the changed composition of the IPAs,[205] may provoke a complete lack of sympathy with the hurdles experienced by large numbers of excluded pupils when attempting to get back into mainstream education. Even the courts seem reluctant to prevent schools from interpreting a direction to 'reinstate' a child in a manner which totally undermines its

200 Editorial leader, *The Times*, 2 August 2000.
201 Editorial leader, *The Times*, 12 October 2002.
202 Compare DfEE (1999 b) Annex D, para 35 with DfES (2003 a) paras 8.2–8.3. In *S, T and P v London Borough of Brent* [2002] EWCA Civ 693, [2002] ELR 556 the Court of Appeal concluded (at [32]) that the Annex D guidance did not encroach on the IAPs' ability to reach an independent judgment. Nevertheless, it was plainly uneasy about its effect on IAPs (see esp at [15]). Surprisingly, the current guidance retains the phrase that produced the court's greatest misgivings (see at [20]). The fact that the IAP must still consider whether 'in their opinion   permanent exclusion was a reasonable response' (see DfES (2003 a) para 8.3) might restrict its ability to reject an exclusion with which it disagrees.
203 See DfES (2003 A) Part 4, para 10.4.
204 See A Ruff (2001) and I Sutherland (2002). See *R (on the application of W) v Governors of B School; R (on the application of L) v Governors of J School* [2001] EWCA Civ 1199, [2002] ELR 105: in each case the teaching unions had threatened industrial action if the pupils were reinstated. Per Laws LJ (at [32]) the teaching unions' position had troubled him. Eg the unions had not wished to know the detailed reasons for the appeal panel's decision to reinstate one of the pupils. See also *R v Governors of W School and T Education Authority (Borough Council), ex p H* [2001] ELR 192.
205 Presumably irritated by the IAPs' habit of reinstating permanently excluded pupils, the government declared its intention to change their composition to ensure that 'appeals panels properly reflect the challenges facing head teachers and the interests of the school community': DfES (2001 d). See now Education (Pupil Exclusions and Appeals) (Maintained Schools) (England) Regulations 2000, SI 2002/3178, Schedule, cl 2, which requires appeal panels to include at least one member (if the appeal panel numbers three, but at least two members if the appeal panel numbers five) who is a person who is or has been a head teacher of a maintained school, and a least one member (if the appeal panel number three, but at least two members if the appeal panel numbers five) who is a person who is or has been for 12 consecutive months within the last six years, a governor of a maintained school.

real objectives.[206] Children forced to sit regularly outside the head teacher's room as part of their standard educational provision might challenge this practice in the courts claiming an infringement of their right to an effective education under article 2 of the First Protocol of the ECHR.

Of overriding concern is the fact that the government has doggedly resisted amending the law to give children a formal right to attend the discipline committee or the independent appeal hearing. Currently, children have no party status in any of the exclusion procedures, except in the unlikely situation of their being aged 18 or over.[207] Despite being the focus of the proceedings, a child under 18 is not statutorily defined as the 'relevant person' for these purposes, his or her parents being named instead.[208] It is the latter, not the excluded child, who have a right to appeal against a permanent exclusion, attend the proceedings, be represented and offer written or oral submissions. The government remained unmoved by the view of the Committee on the Rights of the Child that this aspect of British law infringed article 12 of the CRC[209] and its suggestion that a child's right to appeal against exclusions should be secured.[210] The government did not wish to create the expectation, particularly in cases involving very young or immature children, that pupils should always be present. Rather than creating a legislative right, it considered it better to leave it to statutory guidance to direct schools to give children the opportunity to set out their version of the events before the decision to exclude was reached.[211]

It is difficult to sympathise with the government's position over the child's lack of legal status in the exclusion procedures. Giving parents the sole right of appeal to an appeal tribunal over such matters reflects a false assumption that children's interests are always identical with those of their parents. A child's inability to become involved in the appeal processes deprives him or her of an important procedural right. This is particularly unjust in cases where, for example, parents are too uninterested or nervous to pursue an appeal on their child's behalf, or where they are incapable of presenting the child's case satisfactorily or objectively. Pupils might now attempt to persuade the domestic courts that by excluding them from party status in the appeal process, English education law deprives them of 'a fair and public hearing' under article 6 of the ECHR.[212]

---

206 See *R v Governors of J School, ex p L* [2003] UKHL 9, (2003) Times, 6 March: the House of Lords (Lord Bingham dissenting) confirmed the decision of the Court of Appeal that 'reinstatement' does not necessarily involve full reintegration within the class. The appeal committee's decision that an excluded pupil should be 'reinstated' was fulfilled by the school arranging for L to be taught in a separate room from the rest of the pupils, from whom he was kept completely isolated throughout the school day. See I Sutherland (2001) p 211.

207 SEN children are similarly deprived of party status in statementing appeals. See chapter 12.

208 This position has not been changed by the regulations governing exclusion appeals. See Education (Pupil Exclusions and Appeals) (Maintained Schools) (England) Regulations 2002, SI 2002/3178.

209 Committee on the Rights of the Child (1995) para 14.

210 Committee on the Rights of the Child (1995) para 32. Responding to the United Kingdom's second report on implementation, the Committee again called for children to be given a right to appeal against exclusions: Committee on the Rights of the Child (2002) para 46.

211 See Lord Whitty, HL Debs, Hansard, 8 June 1998, col 706, during the debates on the School Standards and Framework Bill.

212 See n 188 above and *S T and P v London Borough of Brent* [2002] EWCA Civ 693, [2002] ELR 556, per Court of Appeal (at [30]), that it was a 'perfectly tenable assumption' to regard this issue as being within the ambit of article 6.

(5)   SCHOOL ADMINISTRATION

Too many children are being excluded and it appears that one remedy is being consistently ignored. Were all schools to capitalise on their own resources amongst the pupil population, they might find pupils working with them instead of against them. Schools are not harnessing the goodwill of the pupils themselves to prevent disruption. Indeed, in some respects, it is regrettable that the militancy demonstrated by school children during the late 1960s and early 1970s died out.[213] Had it continued, greater attention might have been paid much earlier to giving pupils more responsibility in their own schools. The Elton Report[214] was impressed by research indicating that discipline and school behaviour generally improves if pupils are treated responsibly.[215] It noted that punitive regimes seemed to be associated with worse rather than better standards of behaviour.[216] It suggested that mutual respect was a useful starting point for policy building and recommended that head teachers and teachers should give older pupils more opportunities for setting a good example for the rest of the school, by assuming responsibility and generally contributing to the improvement of school behaviour.[217] Interestingly, it did not consider that such opportunities should be confined to sixth form pupils but recommended that fourth and fifth form pupils should also take on more adult and responsible roles. It considered that this work could be promoted through the establishment of school councils, but only as long as their contribution was genuine and not tokenistic.

Despite these strong recommendations in 1989, the government failed to put this body of research to good use when further legislation governing discipline within schools was introduced in the late 1990s. At present, the law merely requires school governors to produce a written statement of policy regarding disciplinary measures and requires them, before doing so, to consult both the head teacher and the parents of pupils, but not the pupils themselves.[218] Similarly, despite the head teacher being required to determine measures to promote self-discipline amongst pupils, he has no obligation to consult the pupils.

A similarly negative approach to pupil participation underlies the law on school administration. Indeed, in some ways the education legislation took a step backwards from promoting the right of children to become involved in school administration. Thus the Education (No 2) Act 1986, by setting the minimum qualifying age for becoming a school governor at 18, effectively prevented pupils from becoming school governors. Nor does education law currently oblige schools to establish democratic processes involving older children in framing policies over everyday school matters, such as decisions on school meals, school uniforms, supervision in the playground and discipline.

The government claims that it sympathises with the concept of encouraging pupils to participate in school decision-making.[219] For example, Ofsted inspectors are now expected to seek the views of pupils in their official inspections.[220] Nevertheless, successive attempts have failed to persuade it to introduce legislation requiring

---

213   Discussed above.
214   Elton Report (1989).
215   Eg when secondary pupils were given more responsible positions, such as form captains, they achieved better standards of behaviour: M Rutter et al (1979). Similarly, primary school children were better behaved when required to manage their own work: P Mortimore et al (1988).
216   Elton Report (1989) p 99.
217   Elton Report (1989) pp 142–143.
218   School Standards and Framework Act 1998, s 61(3).
219   See DfES (2001 c) para 3.46. See also DfES (2002 c).
220   See Ofsted (2000) paras 83–84.

mandatory consultation with pupils over the running of their schools. Efforts were made, when debating the School Standards and Framework Bill 1998, to introduce mandatory school councils, along the lines of those introduced in other European countries, such as Spain, France[221] and Poland. Although such a change would promote the aims of article 12 of the CRC,[222] the government refused to introduce 'legally prescriptive' provisions,[223] considering it better to allow schools to learn from examples of good practice. Similarly, during the debates on the Education Bill 2002, the government again resisted attempts to make pupil consultation mandatory.[224] It merely undertook to introduce 'best practice guidance' providing schools with 'a flexible menu of options', which would encourage them to adopt 'the best-fit model of participation and adapt it over time as circumstances change'.[225] Thus the enigmatic phrasing of section 176 of the Education Act 2002 merely indicates that regulations providing 'guidance ... about consultation with pupils in connection with the taking of decisions affecting them', are be introduced.[226]

Guidance requiring pupil consultation on many aspects of school life would, if followed, undoubtedly promote a far more responsible attitude amongst pupils. Some schools have established school councils and the results achieved through these initiatives are impressive.[227] They often link such an approach with instructing their pupils on citizenship and local and national government structures.[228] Engaging children in the more practical aspects of running their school not only encourages a sense of responsibility for and pride in the institution, but also gives them experience of how democratic processes can work outside school, at a local and national level.

The Committee on the Rights of the Child, when making its observations, has been keen to encourage the United Kingdom to facilitate children's participation in decisions affecting them within the family, in schools and in the local community. It has suggested that children 'should be provided with the opportunity to express their views on the running of the schools in matters of concern to them'.[229] The Crick committee hoped that schools' new obligation to provide citizenship education[230]

---

221 In France, high school pupils in their last two years of school are represented at three levels of the French education system: on student councils, on educational district high school councils and, at a national level, on the Board of Education. A post of representative of high schools was established in the French Ministry of Education in 1992. See Committee on the Rights of the Child (1993) para 80.

222 Per Baroness David, HL Debs, Hansard 7 July 1998, col 1206. She made the same point during the debates on the Education Bill 2002, HL Debs, Hansard 26 June 2002, col 1463.

223 Per Lord McIntosh of Haringey, HL Debs, Hansard 7 July 1998, col 1207.

224 See the forceful arguments presented by Baroness David and Baroness Howe of Idlicote, HL Debs, Hansard 26 June 2002, cols 1462–1466. Baroness David described the government's refusal to make pupil consultation mandatory as 'timid and uncourageous'. HL Debs, Hansard 26 June 2002, col 1468.

225 Per Baroness Ashton of Upholland, HL Debs, Hansard 26 June 2002, col 1462.

226 Education Act 2002, s 176(1) and (2). The guidance will require pupils' views to be considered in the light of their age and understanding.

227 See examples of such initiatives described in B Crick (1998) pp 12, 29 and 37–39 and by T Alexander (2001) Pt 2. The establishment of effective school councils in some schools have achieved remarkable results in terms of improving behaviour and truancy. But see A Prout (2000), who suggests, p 309, that these schemes are 'fragile and experimental'.

228 B Crick (1998).

229 Committee on the Rights of the Child (1995) para 32. See also Committee on the Rights of the Child (2002) para 46.

230 Citizenship education was made, in September 2000, part of the Personal, Social and Health Education framework for primary schools (which became the PSHE and Citizenship programme). It became part of the national curriculum for secondary schools from September 2002.

would encourage more schools to explore ways of involving their pupils in operational matters. It suggested that all schools should consider how far their ethos, organisation and daily practices were consistent with the aims and purposes of citizenship education and recommended:

> 'In particular, schools should make every effort to engage pupils in discussion and consultation about all aspects of school life on which pupils might reasonably be expected to have a view, and wherever possible to give pupils responsibility and experience in helping to run parts of the school. This might include school facilities, organisation, rules, relationships and matters relating to teaching and learning. Such engagement can be through both formal structures such as school and class councils and informal channels in pupils' daily encounters with aspects of school life. To create a feeling that this is "our school" can increase pupil motivation to learn in all subjects.'[231]

These are wise words which will undoubtedly be followed by some schools. Nevertheless, it is regrettable that the government resists forcing all schools to become more democratic. Children are naturally impressionable and take their cues from adults. If schools and teachers indicate that they cannot be trusted to take responsibility and that their views are not valued, small wonder that some will become disenchanted with the education process, and later with society in general.

(6)   SEX EDUCATION IN SCHOOLS

The government's policy on the provision of sex education by schools is curiously ambivalent. On the one hand, it declares its determination to reduce the level of teenage pregnancies, through a raft of measures, including improving the provision of sex education in schools.[232] But, on the other hand, it refuses either to make sex education in primary schools compulsory or to dispense with parents' absolute right to withdraw their children from sex education classes.[233] The government's concern to reduce the level of teenage pregnancies is understandable, given that the United Kingdom currently has the highest level of teenage birth-rate in Europe; indeed, the second highest in the world.[234]

The SEU's extremely comprehensive report on teenage pregnancy paints a depressing picture of the way in which quite young teenagers 'drift into pregnancy'[235] and how parenthood severely restricts their future life chances.[236] Teenage pregnancy is associated with poor educational achievement, poor physical and mental health, social isolation, poverty and related factors. These dismal short-term outcomes for teenagers and their babies, both in health and in socio-economic terms, are attended by long-term outcomes for the next generation – they too are more likely to become teenage mothers themselves, to experience poverty, poor housing and nutrition and to live in a single parent family.[237] Perhaps predictably, the SEU found that ignorance

---

231 Crick Report (1998) p 36.
232 See DH (1999) paras 8.21.1–8.25.8.
233 Discussed below.
234 The problem of teenage pregnancy (including statistics on rates of teenage conception and abortion) is discussed in more detail in chapter 5.
235 SEU (1999 b) para 5.21.
236 SEU (1999 b) esp chs 8 and 9.
237 Discussed in chapter 5, pp 135–136.

about sex was a key risk factor in teenage pregnancy and that young people in this country were frequently ignorant or misinformed about sex and their own physical development, despite having received sex education in school.[238] Having reviewed the international research on this issue, the report confirmed the widely held view that good comprehensive sex education in schools can reduce teenage pregnancy.

The provision of high quality sex education in British schools and an increased use of contraception is essential, in view of the high level of sexual activity amongst teenage children.[239] The role of schools is particularly important given that British teenagers and their parents commonly find it extremely difficult to communicate over matters relating to sex and contraception.[240] Research indicates that teenagers provide each other with information about sex,[241] but that they are more likely to rely on school teaching as their major source.[242] Indeed, rather than encouraging young people to start sex young, there is evidence that a sound sex education helps them delay doing so and to use contraception when embarking on a sexual relationship.[243] This may explain why the countries in Western Europe with extremely well-developed sex education programmes, in both secondary and primary schools, have the lowest rates of teenage pregnancy.[244]

The SEU was not impressed by the overall standard of sex education, in the form of 'sex and relationships education' (SRE), provided in British schools. Indeed, it reported that the vast majority of the young people consulted considered that they had been told 'too little, too late',[245] with SRE falling far short of what they thought they needed for managing relationships as they matured.[246] Informed by the SEU's recommendations,[247] the current guidance to schools encourages far more open discussion about relationships than earlier had been thought appropriate.[248] Backed up by legislation,[249] it emphasises that each school's sex education should include full information about contraception and how it is to be accessed, including information about local services. Admittedly, the guidance is weakened by its failure to acknowledge that young people find sexual activity pleasurable; it constantly advises that they should learn the benefits of delaying sexual involvement.[250] Nevertheless, whereas teachers previously had been discouraged from ever giving individual pupils contraceptive advice without their parents' knowledge or consent,[251] the current guidance acknowledges that pupils under 16 may at times confide in their teachers and makes suggestions for handling this when it happens.[252] Considerable

238 SEU (1999 b) ch 5.
239 Statistics suggest that adolescents are starting intercourse at increasingly early ages. The numbers of those sexually active by the age of 16 doubled between 1965 and 1991, with the greatest rise for girls. See SEU (1999 b) paras 6.1–6.4.
240 See SEU (1999 b) para 5.19. See also Ofsted (2002) indicating (para 77 and Figure 2) that parents are less and less the pupils' main source of advice on sexual matters.
241 K Wellings (1995) p 418.
242 Ofsted (2002) paras 78–79.
243 R Jepson (2000).
244 Eg Denmark and The Netherlands. See Innocenti Research Centre (2001) pp 20–22 and R Kane and K Wellings (1999) pp 31–32 and 47.
245 SEU (1999 b) para 5.16
246 SEU (1999 b) para 5.6.
247 SEU (1999 b) Annex 4, which sets out a draft revision of DFE (1994).
248 DfEE (2000 d) replacing DFE (1994).
249 Learning and Skills Act 2000, s 148, amending Education Act 1996, s 403.
250 D Monk (2001) pp 278–279. See also P Meredith (2001) pp 210–220.
251 DFE Circular 5/94, para 39.
252 DfEE (2000 d) paras 2.11 and 7.11.

emphasis is now placed on children learning about the nature of marriage and its importance for family life and for bringing up children.[253]

An emphasis on the importance of marriage is controversial, in so far as its inclusion implicitly downgrades non-marital heterosexual and same-sex relationships. Indeed, the current guidance coyly avoids any specific mention of same-sex relationships,[254] although it does suggest, in a section headed 'Sexual identity and sexual orientation', that: 'It is up to schools to make sure that the needs of all pupils are met in their programmes. Young people, whatever their developing sexuality, need to feel that sex and relationship education is relevant to them and sensitive to their needs ...'[255]

The current call for schools to deal with 'homophobic bullying'[256] is obviously essential, given Ofsted's recent finding that homophobic attitudes among pupils are, in too many secondary schools, going unchallenged.[257] Meanwhile, many teachers still feel discouraged from including in SRE programmes any discussion of gay or lesbian relationships. Indeed, this, according to some pupils, appears to be one of the 'no-go areas' in SRE classes.[258] This is presumably because of the widespread publicity devoted to 'section 28',[259] which prohibits the 'promotion' by local authorities of homosexuality as 'a pretended family relationship'. Teachers wrongly assume that this provision effectively prevents them from including positive information about same-sex relationships. This incorrect interpretation is widely held and extremely damaging.[260] The current guidance on SRE pointedly refrains from discouraging teachers from discussing any aspect of human relationships that they consider relevant. Nevertheless, the slight relaxation in official attitudes to male homosexuality, as marked by the lowering of the age of consent to 16,[261] has not been matched by repeal of section 28.[262] Further reforms of this widely criticised legislation[263] may be prompted by the need to respect the rights of young male homosexuals to be free of discrimination under article 14 of the ECHR.

In two important respects, the SEU's report and the current guidance are particularly disappointing. The first relates to sex education for primary school children. A minority of children become sexually active at relatively early ages,[264] with the rates of births

---

253   DfEE (2000 d) para 1.21 and Education Act 1996, s 403(1A)(a). The guidance must ensure not only that sex education includes 'information about the nature of marriage and its importance for family life and the bringing up of children' but also that children are protected from teaching and materials inappropriate for their age and religious and cultural background.

254   D Monk (2001) pp 285–286.

255   DfEE (2000 d) para 1.30.

256   DfEE (2000 d) para 1.32.

257   Ofsted (2002) para 21.

258   Ofsted (2002) para 44.

259   The Local Government Act 1986, s 2A, commonly known as 'section 28', was inserted into the 1986 Act by the Local Government Act 1988, s 28.

260   See J Bridgeman (1996) pp 78–82.

261   16-year-old males were granted the right to consent to homosexual intercourse by the Sexual Offences (Amendment) Act 2000, which ensured that homosexual males finally acquired sexual parity with their heterosexual male and lesbian female counterparts. This legislation addressed the view of the European Commission of Human Rights in *Sutherland v United Kingdom* (1997) 24 EHRR CD 22 that English law, by fixing the age of 18 as the minimum age for lawful homosexual activities, rather than 16, infringed homosexuals' rights under arts 8 and 14 of the ECHR.

262   The House of Lords has rejected the government's proposals to repeal this provision.

263   The Committee on the Rights of the Child called for a repeal of s 28 of the Local Government Act 1986. See Committee on the Rights of the Child (2002) para 42.

264   SEU (1999 b) para 1.1. This notes that in 1997 there were 2,200 conceptions to girls aged 14 or under.

to girls under 16 rising significantly since 1993, to the highest level ever recorded in 1996.[265] The timing of educational programmes is important, in so far as they should be provided before young people become sexually active, since they are less likely to change their sexual and contraceptive behaviour once established.[266] Consequently, many consider that these programmes need to start in primary schools.[267] At present, however, primary schools are only required to have a 'policy on sex education', rather than being obliged to teach it. Whilst some primary schools provide detailed and extensive programmes from quite early ages, others do nothing, with the result that some girls start their periods with no idea what is happening to them and a few even become sexually active without having received any sex education at all.[268] Although the SEU and the official guidance make it clear that primary schools *should* establish sex education programmes, there is no suggestion anywhere of *obliging* primary schools to do so.[269] This omission emphasises the very conservative official mind-set that pervades this field of education.[270] Arguably, article 13 of the CRC and article 10 of the ECHR[271] should be taken far more seriously regarding the provision of information about an activity which has such profound long-term effects on the lives of quite young children and their offspring.

The second unsatisfactory aspect of the current law is the retention of parents' right to withdraw their children from all forms of sex education classes. Indeed, the assumption made by education legislation that the interests of parents and children are identical is nowhere more apparent than in this area of the law. In a change described by the media as a 'concession to fundamentalist religious groups',[272] parents were given the same absolute right to withdraw their children from sex education classes, as they have in relation to religious education, and this remains the law today.[273] It was introduced in 1993,[274] to address the needs of those objecting on religious grounds and of all parents with strongly held beliefs.[275] That this provision was introduced at all is surprising given the government's view, only a few years earlier, in 1985, that 'health and sex education, taught within a moral framework, are a necessary preparation for responsible parenthood'.[276]

Bradney carefully explains why some religious and ethnic minority parents might wish to exclude their children from school sex education classes. These include objections based on cultural notions of modesty and honour, and their concerns relating to the co-educational nature of some classes and the sex of the teacher.[277] The government was obviously aware of these, but also argued that the right of parental withdrawal was necessary in order to comply with article 2 of Protocol 1 of the

265 C Howarth et al (1998) pp 60–61.
266 See NHS Centre for Reviews and Dissemination (1997) p 4.
267 D Acheson (1998) p 43.
268 SEU (1999 b) para 5.13.
269 DfEE (2000 d) paras 1.12–1.16.
270 The current Personal Social and Health Education (PSHE) curriculum makes no provision for any formal sex education between school ages 5 and 11.
271 In both articles, freedom of expression includes the right to receive information and ideas.
272 *Guardian*, 22 June 1993.
273 See Education Act 1996, s 405.
274 Education Reform Act 1988, s 17A, as inserted by Education Act 1993, s 241(3). See now Education Act 1996, s 405.
275 Per Baroness Blatch, HL Debs, 1993 Vol 547, col 140.
276 DES (1985).
277 A Bradney (1996) pp 92–93.

ECHR,[278] which requires education to be in conformity with parents' own religious and philosophical convictions. In fact, government nervousness about infringing this international provision appears to have been misplaced. In *Kjeldsen, Busk Madsen and Pedersen v Denmark*,[279] the European Court of Human Rights decided that the Danish government had not violated that provision by providing compulsory sex education in schools, since it had been conveyed in a balanced and objective manner, with no element of indoctrination. The fact that the parents had no right to exempt their children from such education did not amount to a breach of article 2 of Protocol 1. Although the decision did not assert children's absolute rights to sex education, it clearly indicated that the British government could have introduced a similar compulsory sex education programme which imparted information 'in an objective, critical and pluralistic manner', with no parental right of withdrawal.

Today, the high level of teenage pregnancies must justify making sex education compulsory, as long as it includes advice on contraception and protection against HIV infection. Although little used,[280] the existence of a parental right to withdraw children from SRE creates serious anomalies in the law and it certainly attracted criticism from the Committee on the Rights of the Child.[281] In particular, it completely undermines the aims of the House of Lords in *Gillick v West Norfolk and Wisbech Area Health Authority*.[282] In that decision, their Lordships emphasised that the law should reflect the realities of modern living and the fact that adolescents need legal encouragement to take a responsible attitude to their sexual activity.[283] Consequently, teenagers under the age of 16, who understand the dangers of unprotected sex, can seek contraceptive advice without their parents' knowledge or consent. Meanwhile, education law also enables parents to leave their children in a state of ignorance over the implications of sexual activity, in a manner which is patently contrary to their best interests.[284]

The present law has produced a ludicrous situation wherein the only remedy available to a child wanting to obtain sex education in school against his or her parent's wishes, is to pursue the matter through the courts. A teenager might now argue that the parental right to withdraw a child from sex education classes infringes his or her rights under a variety of international human rights treaties. It not only ignores the right to be consulted,[285] but also the right to freedom of expression,[286] more particularly under article 10 of the ECHR. Such a challenge would undoubtedly force the domestic courts to reassess the decision in *Handyside v United Kingdom*.[287] The European Court accepted that although the actions of the British government had infringed a publisher's right to freedom of expression,[288] this had been justified in the circumstances because the book had endangered children's moral development.

278   See Baroness Blatch, HL Debs, 1993 Vol 547, col 1292.
279   (1976) 1 EHRR 711.
280   Ofsted (2002) records (p 6) that only about 4 in every 10,000 pupils are currently withdrawn from the non-statutory aspects of SRE.
281   Committee on the Rights of the Child (1995) para 14.
282   [1986] AC 112.
283   See discussion in chapters 3 and 5.
284   A Bainham (1996) p 32.
285   Art 12 of the CRC.
286   Art 13 of the CRC. See also art 17 of the CRC which recognises that children need access to information and material from a variety of sources.
287   (1976) 1 EHRR 737.
288   The police had seized and destroyed copies of a sex education book for children, entitled *The Little Red Schoolbook*.

An adolescent's challenge of the government's actions in the *Handyside* case might have provoked a consideration of the adolescent's own right to freedom of expression, including the right to receive information under article 10. It was arguable that a book of this kind provided children with essential information about maturing into adult society and that the government ban directly interfered with their rights as individuals.

Government caution about sex education in schools sets a poor example to a public whose attitudes on teenage sexuality remain ambivalent. Such ambivalence is demonstrated by the ease with which the media is able to blow up controversies about officially commissioned literature and school programmes on this topic.[289] Furthermore, the fact that large numbers of parents are unlikely to exercise the right to withdraw their children from sex education classes ignores an important point of principle. In an area involving children whose sexual activity may have long-term implications for themselves and others, through teenage pregnancy and HIV infection, it is wrong to treat them as appendages of their parents.

(7) CONCLUSION

Throughout the reforming activity of the 1980s, the education legislation consistently treated parents as the 'consumers' of education, and as their children's proxies or representatives when making educational choices. Since then, it has progressively increased parental powers over making choices, but without suggesting that children should be involved in the process. The legislation provides parents and not children with the right to select a school,[290] and parents, not their children, are entitled to sit on the board of governors. Parents, not children, have the right to appeal against exclusions.

As Bainham comments, education law contains many provisions enshrining *parents'* rights and he asks: 'And just what has happened to the rights of children at school?'[2921] Indeed, it seems perverse that the legislative framework governing such a significant and influential aspect of children's lives has ignored the very different approach taken by private law principles to adolescent decision-making. In *Gillick v West Norfolk and Wisbech Area Health Authority*[292] Lord Fraser stated that, in his view, it was 'contrary to the ordinary experience of mankind ... to say that a child or a young person remains in fact under the complete control of his parents until he attains the age of majority ...'[293] Despite this, the pervasive impression given by the huge body of education law indicates an assumption that children are and should remain under their parents' complete control.

289   Eg the Health Education Authority commissioned leaflet (1994) was withdrawn because it was deemed by the government to be 'smutty'. See N Harris (1996) p 18.
290   School Standards and Framework Act 1998, s 86.
291   See A Bainham (1996) p 30.
292   [1986] AC 112.
293   [1986] AC 112 at 171.

BIBLIOGRAPHY

NB many of these publications can be obtained on the relevant organisation's website.

Acheson D (Chairman), *Independent Inquiry into Inequalities in Health* (1998) The Stationery Office.

Alexander T, *Citizenship Schools: A practical guide to education for citizenship and personal development* (2001) Campaign for Learning.

Arthur R, 'Tackling Youth Crime: Supporting Families in Crisis' (2002) 14 Child and Family Law Quarterly 401.

Audit Commission, *Misspent Youth: Young People and Crime* (1996) Audit Commission Publications.

Audit Commission, *Missing Out* (1999) Audit Commission Publications.

Bainham A, 'Sex education: a family lawyer's perspective' in N Harris (ed) *Children, Sex Education and the Law: Examining the issues* (1996) National Children's Bureau.

Berridge D et al, *The independent effects of permanent exclusion from school on the offending careers of young people* RDS Occasional Paper no 71 (2001) Home Office.

Biehal N et al, *At Home or Away? Supporting young people and families* (2000) National Children's Bureau.

Bradley A, 'Scope for Review: The Convention Right to Education and the Human Rights Act 1998' (1999) European Human Rights Law Review 395.

Bradney A, 'Ethnicity, religion and sex education' in N Harris (ed) *Children, Sex Education and the Law* (1996) National Children's Bureau.

Bridgeman J, 'Don't tell the children: The Department's guidance on the provision of information about contraception to individual pupils' in N Harris (ed) *Children, Sex Education and the Law: Examining the issues* (1996) National Children's Bureau.

Childline, *Annual Review* (2001) Childline.

Committee on the Rights of the Child, *Addendum to Initial Report submitted by France to the Committee on the Rights of the Child* CRC/C/3/Add 15 (1993) Centre for Human Rights, Geneva.

Committee on the Rights of the Child, *Concluding Observations of the Committee on the Rights of the Child: United Kingdom of Great Britain and Northern Ireland* CRC/C/15/Add 34 (1995) Centre for Human Rights, Geneva.

Committee on the Rights of the Child, *Concluding Observations of the Committee on the Rights of the Child: United Kingdom of Great Britain and Northern Ireland* CRC/C/15/Add 188 (2002) Centre for Human Rights, Geneva.

Communities that Care, *Youth at Risk: A national survey of risk factors, protective factors and problem behaviour among young people in England, Scotland and Wales* (2002) Communities that Care.

Cretney S, Case critique (1987) Family Law 164.

Crick B (Chairman), *Education for citizenship and the teaching of democracy in schools, Final report of the Advisory Group on Citizenship* (1998) Qualifications and Curriculum Authority.

Department for Education (DFE), *Sex Education in Schools* Circular 5/94 (1994).

Department for Education and Employment (DfEE), *Home-School Agreements: Guidance for Schools* (1998 a).

Department for Education and Employment (DfEE), *LEA Behaviour Support Plans* Circular 1/98 (1998 b) and Supplementary Note 2000.

Department for Education and Employment (DfEE), *Section 550A of the Education Act 1996: The Use of Force to Control or Restrain Pupils* Circular 10/98 (1998 c).

Department for Education and Employment (DfEE), White Paper *Learning to Succeed: a new framework for post-16 learning* Cm 4392 (1999 a).

Department for Education and Employment (DfEE), *Social Inclusion: Pupil Support* Circular 10/99 (1999 b).

Department for Education and Employment (DfEE), *Social Inclusion: The LEA Role in Pupil Support* Circular 11/99 (1999 c).

Department for Education and Employment (DfEE), *Bullying: Don't Suffer in Silence – an anti-bullying pack for schools* (2000 a).

Department for Education and Employment (DfEE), *Guidance on the Education of Young People in Public Care* (2000 b).

Department for Education and Employment (DfEE), *Statistics of Education: Permanent Exclusions from Maintained Schools in England* Issue No 10/00 November 2000 (2000 c).

Department for Education and Employment (DfEE), *Sex and Relationship Education Guidance* 0116/2000 (2000 d).

Department for Education and Science (DES), White Paper *Better Schools* Cmnd 9469 (1985) HMSO.

Department for Education and Skills (DfES), *Statistics of Education: Pupil absence and truancy from schools in England, 2001/2* Issue No 13/01 December 2001 (2001 a).

Department for Education and Skills (DfES), *Statistics of Education: Permanent Exclusions from Maintained Schools in England* Issue No 10/01 November 2001 (2001 b).

Department for Education and Skills (DfES), White Paper *Schools: Achieving Success* Cm 5230 (2001 c) DfES.

Department for Education and Skills (DfES), *Consultation on Exclusion Appeal Panels* September 2001 (2001 d).

Department for Education and Skills (DfES), *Pupil Absence in Schools in England 2001/2 (Provisional Statistics)* SFR 30/2002 (2002 a).

Department for Education and Skills (DfES), *Trends in Education and Skills* (2002 b).

Department for Education and Skills (DfES), *Listen to Learn: An Action Plan for the Involvement of Children and Young People* (2002 c).

Department for Education and Skills (DfES), Green Paper *14–19: extending opportunities, raising standards* Cm 5342 (2002 d).

Department for Education and Skills (DfES), *Statistics of Education: Permanent Exclusions from Maintained Schools in England* Issue No 09/02 November 2002 (2002 e).

Department for Education and Skills (DfES), *Improving Behaviour and Attendance: Guidance on Exclusion from Schools and Pupil Referral Unit* (2003 a).

Department for Education and Skills (DfES), *Working together on exclusions: a discussion paper on the prevention, management and funding of school exclusions* (2003 b) DfES.

Department of Health (DH), *Guardians Ad Litem and other Court Related Issues* Vol 7 *Children Act 1989 Guidance and Regulations* (1991) HMS0.

Department of Health (DH), *The UK's Second Report to the UN Committee on the Rights of the Child 1999* (1999) The Stationery Office.

Department of Health (DH), *Guidance on the Education of Young People in Public Care* LAC (2000).

Elton Report, *Discipline in Schools* Report of the Committee of Enquiry into Discipline in Schools (1989) HMSO.

Farson R, *Birthrights* (1978) Penguin.

Flood-Page C et al, *Youth Crime: Findings from the 1998/99 Youth Lifestyles Survey* Home Office Research Study 209 (2000).

Fortin J ,'Children's rights and the use of physical force' (2001) 13 Child and Family Law Quarterly 243.

Freeman M, 'Children's Education: A Test Case for Best Interests and Autonomy' in R Davie and D Galloway (eds) *Listening to Children in Education* (1996) David Fulton Publishers.

Freeman M, 'Children's rights ten years after ratification' in B Franklin *The New Handbook of Children's Rights: Comparative Policy and Practice* (2002) Routledge.

Gold R, 'Conflicting Interests: Exclusion, the Individual and the School Community' (2001) 2 Education Law Journal 202.

Grenville M, 'Compulsory School Attendance and the Child's Wishes' (1988) Journal of Social Welfare Law 4.

Hafen B, 'Children's Liberation and the New Egalitarianism: Some Reservations About Abandoning Youth to Their "Rights"' (1976) Brigham Young University Law Review 605.

Hallam S and Castle F, *Evaluation of the Behaviour and Discipline Pilot Projects* (1996–1999) DfEE Research Brief No 163 (1999).

Hamilton C, 'Rights of the child: a right to education and a right in education' in C Bridge (ed) *Family law towards the millenium: essays for P M Bromley* (1997) Butterworths.

Harris D, O'Boyle M and Warbrick C, *Law of the European Convention on Human Rights* (1995) Butterworths.

Harris N, 'Education by Right? Breach of the Duty to Provide "Sufficient" Schools' (1990) 53 Modern Law Review 525.

Harris N, *Law and Education: Regulation, Consumerism and the Education System* (1993) Sweet and Maxwell.

Harris N (ed), *Children, Sex Education and the Law* (1996) National Children's Bureau.

Harris N, Editorial (2002) Education Law Journal 3.

Harris N and Eden K, with Blair A, *Challenges to School Exclusion* (2000) Routledge Falmer.

Health Education Authority, *Your Pocket Guide to Sex Education* (1994).

Home Office, *Power for the police to remove truants: Guidance* (1999).

Holt J, *Escape from Childhood: The Needs and Rights of Childhood* (1974) E P Dutton and Co.

Howarth C et al, *Monitoring poverty and social exclusion: Labour's inheritance* (1998) Joseph Rowntree Foundation.

Innocenti Research Centre, *A League Table of Teenage Births in Rich Nations* Innocenti Report Card Issue No 3 July 2001 (2001) UNICEF.

Jeffs T, 'Schooling, education and children's rights' in B Franklin (ed) *The New Handbook of Children's Rights: Comparative Policy and Practice* (2002) Routledge.

Jepson R, 'The effectiveness of interventions to change health-related behaviours: a review of reviews' MRC Social and Public Health Sciences Unit, Occasional paper 3 (2000) Medical Research Council.

Johnston L et al, *Snakes and Ladders: Young people, transitions and social exclusion* (2000) The Policy Press.

Kane R and Wellings K, *Reducing the rate of teenage conceptions: An International review of the evidence: data from Europe* (1999) Health Education Authority.

Lindley R, 'Teenagers and Other Children' in G Scarre (ed) *Children, Parents and Politics* (1989) Cambridge University Press.

Meltzer H and Gatward R, *Mental health of children and adolescents in Great Britain* (2000) The Stationery Office.

Meredith P, 'Children's Rights and Education' in J Fionda (ed) *Legal Concepts of Childhood* (2001) Hart Publishing.

Monk D, 'New guidance/old problems: recent developments in sex education' (2001) 23 Journal of Social Welfare and Family Law 271.

MORI, *Youth Survey 2002: Research Study Conducted for the Youth Justice Board* (2002) Youth Justice Board.

Mortimore P et al, *School Matters: the junior years* (1988) Open Books.

NHS Centre for Reviews and Dissemination, 'Preventing and reducing the adverse effects of unintended teenage pregnancies' (1997) 3 Effective Health Care 1.

Office for Standards in Education (Ofsted), *Exclusions from Secondary Schools 1995/ 96* A Report from the office of HM Chief Inspector of Schools (1996) HMSO.

Office for Standards in Education (Ofsted), *'Raising the attainment of minority ethnic pupils'* (1999).

Office for Standards in Education (Ofsted), *Inspecting Schools: Handbook for Inspecting Secondary Schools, with guidance on self-evaluation* (2000) The Stationery Office.

Office for Standards in Education (Ofsted), *Improving Attendance and Behaviour in Secondary Schools* (2001).

Office for Standards in Education (Ofsted), *Sex and Relationships* HMI 433 (2002).

Osler A et al, *Reasons for Exclusion from School* DfEE Research Brief No 244 (2001).

Pearce N and Hillman J, *Wasted Youth: raising achievement and tackling social exclusion* (1998) IPPR.

Prout A, 'Children's Participation: Control and Self-realisation in British Late Modernity' (2000) 14 Children and Society 304.

Ruff A, 'Newsline' (2001) 2 Education Law Journal 167.

Rutter M et al, *Fifteen Thousand Hours: secondary schools and their effects on pupils* (1979) Open Book.

Social Exclusion Unit (SEU), *Truancy and School Exclusion: Report by the Social Exclusion Unit* Cm 3957 (1998 a).

Social Exclusion Unit (SEU), *Bringing Britain Together: a national strategy for neighbourhood renewal* Cm 4045 (1998 b).

Social Exclusion Unit (SEU), *Bridging the Gap: New Opportunities for 16 –18 Year Olds Not in Education, Employment or Training* (1999 a).

Social Exclusion Unit (SEU), *Teenage Pregnancy* Cm 4342 (1999 b).

Smith J et al, *The family background of homeless young people* (1998) Family Policy Studies Centre.

Smith P, 'Bullying in schools' Highlight no 174 (2000) National Children's Bureau.

Sutherland I, 'Promoting Inclusion – A New Approach: The ACE Exclusions Project' (2001) 2 Education Law Journal 210.

Sutherland I, 'Advances in Exlusions Law?' (2002) 3 Education Law Journal 216.

Tomaševski K, 'Special Rapporteur on the right to education' *Addendum, Mission to the United Kingdom of Great Britain and Northern Ireland (England) 18–22 October 1999* Report to UN Commission on Human Rights E/CN.4/2000/6/Add 2 (1999).

Warnock H M (Chairman), *Special Educational Needs* Report of the Committee of Enquiry into the Education of Handicapped Children and Young People, Cmnd 7212 (1978) HMSO.

Wellings K, 'Provision of sex education and early sexual experience: the relation examined' (1995) 311 British Medical Journal 417.

Wringe C, *Children's Rights: A philosophical study* (1981) Routledge and Kegan Paul.

Chapter 7

Children's involvement in family proceedings – rights to representation

(1) INTRODUCTION

Children may have all sorts of substantive rights but they are of little value if they cannot enforce them. It is therefore immensely important for the law to provide children with procedural rights entitling them to challenge any infringements through the court process. At one end of the spectrum, children may initiate proceedings themselves, to enforce their own substantive rights. They may, for example, apply for an order under the Children Act 1989 relating to their own health care, or gain the right to live with some adult other than their parents.[1] Empowering children to bring their own proceedings is a liberal way for the law to acknowledge their capacity for taking responsibility for their own lives.

It is relatively unusual for children to initiate their own litigation. Far more are drawn into legal proceedings by being the subject of parents' applications regarding their upbringing. When this occurs, a sophisticated society such as our own should provide children with a system of representation which treats them as people, rather than the passive objects of parental disputes. They should always be provided with the opportunity to convey to the courts their own perceptions of these family disagreements. As the following assessment demonstrates, despite recent reforms, the systems available for this not only remain confused, but might appear unfair to the children involved. Provision is variable and arbitrary; whilst some children are enabled to convey their wishes to the courts, others are not, even for children caught up in similar circumstances. Depending on the way the litigation started, the courts receive information about some but not all children, with some children being separately represented and not others. The recent amalgamation of the personnel supporting children in court[2] appears to have been prompted, at least in part, by the government's hope to produce efficiency savings, rather than to fund an improved service for children. Indeed, a failure to give budgetary priority to children's representation may explain the continuation of a system which still requires considerable improvement.

---

1   By applying for an art 8 order under the Children Act 1989, see discussed in chapter 4.
2   Through the establishment, on 1 April 2001, of the Children and Family Court Advisory and Support Services (hereafter referred to as CAFCASS), discussed below.

This chapter, whose overall theme is children's involvement in civil proceedings,[3] is divided into three parts. The first considers the provisions of international law recognising children's rights to participate in legal proceedings over their future. The second assesses the extent to which children whose parents separate or divorce obtain external support from adult services. The third considers children's involvement in family proceedings. This third section is itself divided into three parts. The first provides a short assessment of the organisational reforms leading to the establishment of CAFCASS, the single support service for children and families involved in family proceedings. The second considers the methods used for ascertaining the views of children involved in private law disputes over their upbringing, including the procedures governing children wishing to instruct their own solicitors and litigate on their own behalf. The last section assesses the system of representation for children involved in public law proceedings.[4]

(2)   THE REQUIREMENTS OF INTERNATIONAL INSTRUMENTS

The provision made by English law for the separate representation of children in family proceedings has not matched up to international requirements, despite the recent organisational reforms. Fortunately, those urging further reform can use the provisions of international human rights law to clarify the defects in English procedures. Article 12 of the CRC is of overriding importance because of the way it affirms that children should not be seen as passive individuals but as fully-fledged people with rights to express their own views on all matters affecting them.
Article 12(1) requires governments to:

'… assure to the child who is capable of forming his or her own views the right to express those views freely in all matters affecting the child, the views of the child being given due weight in accordance with the age and maturity of the child.'

Article 12(2) further provides that for this purpose:

'… the child shall in particular be provided with the opportunity to be heard in any judicial and administrative proceedings affecting the child, either directly, or through a representative or an appropriate body, in a manner consistent with the procedural rules of national law.'

It should be noted that the phrasing of article 12 does not promise autonomy to children – indeed, neither paragraph promises that children's wishes are to be acceded to. The article is about consultation and participation and not about self-determination. The fact that English law reserves the final decision to the courts fully accords with this provision, but it should also provide children with an opportunity to be heard in *any* judicial and administrative proceedings affecting the child.

How children are to be heard is not clearly specified. Article 12(2) makes no promise that the child will be heard in person, or even by a representative designated to act for that child. It merely refers to the child's views being transmitted either directly or through 'a representative or an appropriate body'. This formula does not specifically rule out the child's own parent claiming to represent the child, despite the obvious conflict of interest in most family proceedings involving both child and parent. Furthermore, article 12 should be read subject to article 3 of the Convention,

---

3   The involvement of children in criminal proceedings is considered in chapter 17.
4   These issues are all considered in the context of applications brought under the Children Act 1989, since this is the litigation which most commonly affects children. The extent to which the courts take account of children's wishes and feelings is considered in chapter 8.

which directs that 'the best interests of the child shall be a primary consideration'. It is therefore justifiable for any system establishing opportunities for children to be heard in civil proceedings to take account of their best interests and avoid damaging them in the process. For example, it might be deemed inappropriate for a very young child to be present in court when his or her mother's criminal record and medical history is discussed.[5] On the other hand, the need to consider the child's best interests does not justify diluting the aims of article 12 by interpreting it in a way which suits parents or the state, for example, by imposing an age restriction on its application.[6] The article's overall message is that it requires *any* 'child who is capable of forming his or her own views' to have the right to express those views, due weight then being given to those views, in accordance with the child's age and maturity.

Although article 12 of the CRC is of considerable importance, its terms are relatively vague. By contrast, the European Convention on the Exercise of Children's Rights (ECECR)[7] is a much more practical document, in that it specifically applies itself to detailing children's procedural rights in legal proceedings. Indeed, the Council of Europe's Committee of Experts on Family Law[8] noted that a weakness of the CRC is that children may not be able to exercise their substantive rights without appropriate procedural measures to back them up. It therefore set out to create a document to redress that deficiency.[9] Article 1(2) explains that:

> 'The object of the present Convention is, in the best interests of children, to promote their rights, to grant them procedural rights and to facilitate the exercise of these rights by ensuring that children are, themselves or through other persons or bodies, informed and allowed to participate in proceedings affecting them before a judicial authority.'

The ECECR goes into some detail regarding the kind of provision children should have.[10] It confines its application to 'family proceedings, in particular those involving the exercise of parental responsibilities such as residence and access to children'.[11] Within this context, it secures for children involved in such proceedings[12] the right to be granted and indeed, entitles them to request certain specific rights: to receive all relevant information;[13] to be consulted and express their views;[14] to be informed of the possible consequences of compliance with these views and the possible consequences of any decision;[15] and the right to apply for the appointment of a special representative,[16] if those with parental responsibilities cannot represent the child due to a conflict of interest.[17] Moreover, the Convention details the extensive duties of such a representative,[18] and also those of any court dealing with proceedings relating to a child. The court is required, before reaching a decision, not only to

---

5   See K Marshall (1997) pp 76–81.
6   K Marshall (1997) p 101.
7   Adopted by the Council of Europe in 1995 and open to signature January 1996. The United Kingdom has not yet signed or ratified this instrument.
8   Discussed further in chapter 2.
9   See M Killerby (1995) p 127. See also Council of Europe (1997) pp 18–19.
10 For a detailed discussion of the Convention's provisions, see C Sawyer (1999).
11 Art 1(3).
12 But see the qualifying condition applying to certain rights, n 24 below.
13 Art 3(a).
14 Art 3(b).
15 Art 3(c).
16 Art 4(1).
17 Art 4(1).
18 Art 10.

consider whether it has adequate information,[19] but also to ensure that the child has received all relevant information,[20] to consult the child in person in appropriate cases,[21] to allow the child to express his or her views,[22] and to give due weight to those views.[23]

Although more detailed, in many respects, the ECECR back-pedals on the aims of article 12 of the CRC. Thus many of the rights secured only extend to those children who are 'considered by internal law as having sufficient understanding'.[24] This qualifying phrase deliberately invites states to distinguish between groups of children by specifying an age to be attained before their rights under the Convention apply.[25] Whilst in some ways sensible and practical, such a provision enables a state to adopt an arbitrary and extremely high qualifying age before children can be deemed of 'sufficient understanding', irrespective of the actual competence of children below it.[26] Furthermore, since most of the protective provisions apply only to those with 'sufficient understanding', the interests of those excluded are extremely weak, with no rights, inter alia, to information, to be consulted, or express their views.[27] Indeed, the phrase is substantially more restrictive than that used in article 12(1) of the Convention. By specifying that any 'child who is capable of forming his or her own views' is entitled to express those views, the latter provision restricts the abilities of states to escape from their obligations by adopting an unreasonably high age for capacity.

Of equal concern is that the child's right to the appointment of a special representative[28] only exists 'where internal law precludes the holders of parental responsibilities from representing the child as a result of a conflict of interest with the latter'. Consequently, children involved in proceedings where a conflict of interest is not formally recognised by internal law cannot demand separate representation. There might, for example, be a conflict of interest if either parent involved in a parental contact dispute attempted to convey their child's views to the court. Nevertheless, unless the ratifying country's internal law formally recognises this, the child is not entitled to demand separate representation under article 4. Where the internal law does admit a conflict of interest, the Convention fleshes out the way in which such representation should be provided.[29] Special representatives are, however, given worrying leeway in interpreting their duties. For example, they need not convey to the court the child's views if they consider this to be 'manifestly contrary to the best interests of the child'.[30] As Sawyer points out, there is no indication of what a young child can do if 'represented' by an adult with whom he or she disagrees when that officer's duties involves expressing an opinion on the child's welfare.[31] The

---

19   Art 6(a).
20   Art 6(b).
21   Art 6(b). If necessary in private or through some other person or body, in a manner appropriate to the child's understanding, unless against the child's best interests.
22   Art 6(b).
23   Art 6(c).
24   Ie the rights listed in arts 3, 6(b), 10(a) and (b) contain this qualification. States are also invited to limit the right to a special representative to those children considered by internal law to have sufficient understanding. See art 4(1) and (2).
25   See M Killerby (1995) p 130.
26   C Sawyer (1999) p 156.
27   C Sawyer (1999) pp 163–164.
28   Arts 4(1) and 9(1).
29   The duties of the child's representative are listed in art 10.
30   Art 10(1).

Convention certainly makes no provision for a system of representation similar to that provided for children involved in public law proceedings in this country, whereby the child's representative provides the court with an assessment of the child's best interests, whilst the child's solicitor takes instructions from the child.[32]

Although the ECECR represents an international commitment to ensuring that children are eventually provided with very full rights of representation in litigation affecting them,[33] it effectively undermines the objectives of article 12 of the CRC. Despite being less detailed than the ECHR, article 12 provides a far more generous acknowledgment of children's entitlement to participate in decisions affecting them. It recognises that children mature at different rates and that their ability to express their views should be respected, even if, due to their age and relative immaturity, those views are not eventually acceded to. Furthermore, unlike the ECECR, which until it is signed and ratified by the United Kingdom is of only persuasive interest, compliance with the CRC is not voluntary. None the less, until recently, those responsible for providing a uniform system of representation for children caught up in parental litigation appeared unaware of the government's obligation to fulfil the aims of article 12.

The Committee on the Rights of the Child[34] recently expressed its 'concern' about the defects in the present system regarding children's right to independent representation in legal proceedings.[35] It was obviously troubled by the stark contrast between the excellent system of representation provided for children involved in public law proceedings, and the inadequate system provided for children caught up in private law proceedings.[36] The Committee specifically recommended that the government should take further steps to ensure compliance with both paragraphs of article 12, through legislation governing court and administrative procedures, including divorce proceedings. It considered that these changes should ensure that children capable of forming their own views should have the right to express them and that they are given due weight.[37]

When considering calls for further reform, the government was doubtless also aware that children might use the Human Rights Act 1998 to challenge their inability to gain independent representation in private law disputes. At first sight, article 6, the right to a fair trial, might promote an improved system of representation for children. But although it encompasses a variety of rights revolving round a litigant's right to participate effectively in litigation, the case law is largely confined to a consideration of the rights of those involved in criminal proceedings. In this context, the European Court of Human Rights has stressed that very young children accused of crimes are as entitled to participate effectively in their trial as are adults. Consequently, their rights

31   C Sawyer (1999) p 155.
32   Discussed below.
33   See art 5, which suggests further improvements over and above the obligations specified, by inviting states to 'consider granting children additional procedural rights', such as the right to apply for a *legally qualified* separate representative.
34   Committee on the Rights of the Child (2002), responding to the United Kingdom's second report on implementation of the CRC.
35   Committee on the Rights of the Child (2002) para 29.
36   NB the term 'private law proceedings' is used to describe proceedings between private individuals (often parents) over children. The term 'public law proceedings' is used to describe litigation over children, involving the (often protective) intervention of a public agency, such as a social services department.
37   Committee on the Rights of the Child (2002) para 30.

are infringed if they cannot comprehend what is going on, or feel too intimidated to reach decisions or to instruct their lawyers adequately.[38] Whilst the right to participate effectively in legal proceedings clearly also applies to civil proceedings,[39] there is little relevant case law indicating whether children who are the subject of parents' disputes should be represented in court or be present themselves at the hearing.[40] Nevertheless, the overall demands of article 6(1), which requires all litigants to be treated fairly, have obviously provoked the domestic courts into considering whether children should be separately represented more often in private law proceedings.[41] It may also lead them to accede more often to a child's desire to be present in court in public law proceedings. The need to fulfil the demands of procedural fairness is particularly pressing in secure accommodation proceedings where the outcome involves the restriction of the child's liberty.[42] Children might also argue that, since the outcome of parental disputes will affect their own family lives, their procedural rights guaranteed by article 8[43] would be infringed were they not provided with any chance to influence the outcome directly.

As discussed below, the procedures governing children involved in private disputes between their parents, often occurring on divorce and separation, have not ensured that their views were always sought and considered. The fact that this group of children have clear rights to independent representation under international human rights law clearly influenced the government to produce further much needed reforms. It is unclear, however, how long it will be before these are activated by rules of court.[44]

(3)   CHILDREN WHOSE PARENTS SPLIT UP

(A)   The right to consultation

Disputes between parents over aspects of their children's upbringing may arise at any time during their children's lives, but are most likely to occur when their own relationship is breaking up. Some disputes arise in the course of divorce proceedings, which tend to polarise existing adult hostilities to such an extent that parents fight over their children as if they were items of property, to be parcelled out. Others arise when married or cohabiting parents first separate. Certainly, it is at this stage of family life that the conflict between children's rights and parents' rights is very obvious. Parents may claim the right to put an unhappy relationship behind them by

---

38   *V and T v United Kingdom* (1999) 30 EHRR 121 (paras 85–91).

39   *Dombo Beheer BV v Netherlands* (1994) 18 EHRR 213. See more particularly *McMichael v United Kingdom* (1995) 20 EHRR 205: the European Court of Human Rights upheld the right of all parties to disclosure of all documents in children's hearings in Scotland.

40   In *Elsholz v Germany* [2000] 2 FLR 486 and *Sahin v Germany* [2002] 1 FLR 119, the European Court of Human Rights criticised the German courts, for not hearing the respective children involved in the contact disputes, but did not mention the need for their separate representation.

41   See *Re A (contact: separate representation)* [2001] 1 FLR 715, per Dame Elizabeth Butler-Sloss P at [22]. See discussion below.

42   But see *Re C (secure accommodation order: representation)* [2001] EWCA Civ 458, [2001] 2 FLR 169, discussed below.

43   In *W (and R, O, B and H) v United Kingdom* (1987) 10 EHRR 29 and *McMichael v United Kingdom* (1995) 20 EHRR 205, the European Court of Human Rights confirmed that art 8 carries important procedural safeguards.

44   The vehicle for these changes was the Adoption and Children Act 2002, s 122. See discussion below, p 211–222.

severing all connections between each other. But children may require their attachments with each parent to be maintained. Admittedly, the concept of children's rights will probably have little influence over parents' plans for their own future lives. For example, the law could not prevent parents from separating because their children would prefer them to stay together. Nevertheless, a commitment to children's rights can play an important part in the various stages leading up to resolution, if cast in terms of children's rights to be involved, consulted, and later to be represented in any court proceedings, as emphasised by article 12 of the CRC.

Parents and professionals alike should remember that children could probably give them an extremely clear and insightful account of their own needs, if adults took the trouble to ask. Indeed, a greater appreciation of the aims of article 12 of the CRC might persuade them to do so. Nevertheless, there are those who argue that the notion of children's rights has a limited practical value in this context. King has suggested that children have a right to be protected from consultation, since it is damaging for them to feel obliged to make choices over which parent they wish to live with.[45] This, of course, is true. But the right to participate in a decision is not a right to make choices. Furthermore, it is unrealistic to expect children brought up in the United Kingdom today to react to family disputes in the same way as did their counterparts in Victorian England. In the nineteenth century, it might have been more reasonable for children to assume a passive role when their parents fought over their future upbringing. Today's children are encouraged to think for themselves and develop a capacity for independence and responsibility. Depending on their age, it insults their self-respect not to allow them to participate in arrangements being made for their future.

Children's wishes are often disregarded by adults who consider that they know what these wishes will be without any consultation. Indeed, a growing body of research consistently supports the view that a damaging aspect of parental separation for children is the considerable shock that they suffer on the break-up, often exacerbated by their parents' failure to prepare them adequately for it, or give them any proper explanation.[46] As has been observed: 'Children are amazingly perceptive about what is going on, and not talking to them about the changes in their lives only raises their anxieties.'[47] Research shows that few parents, whether they are married or unmarried, are particularly adept at breaking such news sensitively. Furthermore, they often delude themselves over the extent to which their children understand what they are being told regarding an impending separation and how they react to such news. Mitchell's research indicated that whilst less than one-third of the parents considered that their children had been upset by the break-up, two-thirds of the children said that they had been very distressed. Indeed, some continued to feel this way but hid it from their parents.[48] These research findings reinforce the need to consider adult disputes from a child's point of view. Regrettably, under English law, no child, whatever his or her age, has a legal *right* to be consulted over the arrangements to be made for their future. By way of contrast, in Scotland, the aims of article 12 of the CRC are taken extremely seriously. Scottish law obliges parents, depending on their children's age and maturity, to consult them over any 'major decision' within their parental

---

45   See M King (1987) p 190.
46   See, inter alia: A Mitchell (1985) esp ch 4; C Lyon et al (1998) ch 2; G Douglas et al (2001) p 374; J Dunn and K Deater-Deckard (2001) pp 9–11.
47   I Gee (1999) p 50.
48   A Mitchell (1985) esp ch 5.

responsibility.[49] Arguably, a decision of this kind includes making arrangements for a child's future care after separation or divorce. Indeed, such events probably have greater impact on children than any other,[50] thereby justifying the introduction of a similar legislative provision in England and Wales. A statutory obligation on parents to consult their children over all important matters might promote a family culture of participation which would continue to operate when the adults' own relationships run into difficulties.

Imposing on parents a legal obligation to consult their children might appear to be a tokenistic gesture, in so far as there is no practical means of enforcing it.[51] Nevertheless, it represents an important attempt to improve the lives of many children who are, in practice, outside the reach of the law. As discussed below, the children whose parents were married and who now intend to divorce, have a narrow advantage over the children of cohabiting couples who separate. The former group has a limited form of protection, in so far as their parents must comply with a paper exercise linked with their divorce proceedings, designed to ensure that they make appropriate plans for their children's future upbringing.[52] But, without marriage and divorce, there is no obvious 'trigger point' at which support could be offered to the children of unmarried parents who separate.[53] These parents are therefore free to decide for themselves the future arrangements for their children's care, without any encouragement to consult their children or warn them of what to expect. A limited, though unenforceable, means of improving this situation would be to amend the law along the lines of the Scottish legislation. Not only is it imperative for parents and professionals to consult all children early on and listen carefully to their views, but also, if a parental dispute is later translated into litigation, to give them a genuine voice through competent representation.

(B)   Support for children on separation and divorce

Over recent years, although the divorce rate has dropped since the early 1990s,[54] the United Kingdom has continued to have the highest divorce rate in the European Union.[55] In 2000, 142,457 children under the age of 16 were affected by parental divorce, a quarter being under 5.[56] There is, however, now far less likelihood that

49   Children (Scotland) Act 1995, s 6(1). There is a legal presumption that a child of 12 years of age or more is 'of sufficient age and maturity to form a view' on major decisions. Discussed further in chapter 3.

50   Research into the mental health of children aged between 5 and 15 indicates that 50% of children with a mental disorder had experienced the separation of their parents compared with 29% of the sample with no disorder. See H Meltzer and R Gatward (2000) p 102. See also A Buchanan et al (2001) pp 78–79 and 92. This research indicates that children with parents involved in family proceedings suffer significantly higher levels of emotional and behavioural difficulties than children in united families.

51   See chapter 3.

52   Ie the procedure under Matrimonial Causes Act 1973, s 41. See discussion below.

53   See G Douglas, M Murch and A Perry (1996). These authors suggest (p 132) that such children might be entitled to support from local authority social services if they were deemed to be children 'in need' under the Children Act 1989, s 17.

54   Office for National Statistics (2002) indicates that 141,135 divorces were granted in 2000, compared with 144,556 in 1999 and an overall peak of 165,018 in 1993.

55   Britain has 2.7 divorces per 1,000 population, compared with a European average of 1.8. See Eurostat (2001).

56   Office for National Statistics (2002).

parental disputes over children, arising in the context of divorce, will end up in the court room. The days are over when divorce was accompanied by a 'package' of court orders relating to property, maintenance and children. Today, many of these disputes are settled with the help of the couples' respective solicitors. Depending on the practice and arrangements in the local court, they may also be referred for 'conciliation'[57] to a child and family reporter (CFR),[58] or to an outside mediation agency[59] and again, the outcome may be a negotiated settlement. As discussed below, there is, however, a risk that these settlements are arrived at without proper reference to the children's wishes or interests. Indeed, it is arguable that the children whose parents refuse to settle and obtain a court order regarding their upbringing are better served by the law than those whose parents ultimately resolve their differences with the assistance of solicitors and mediators. The Children Act 1989 directs the courts, when determining any dispute over children's upbringing, to have regard to their ascertainable wishes and feelings.[60] But there is no law obliging other practitioners to do so at any stage of the dispute.

Research studies increasingly raise concerns over the obvious sense of isolation experienced by the children of divorcing couples and the lack of any obvious source of support for them.[61] They suggest that the majority of professionals, from whatever discipline, consider it inappropriate to address children's needs directly, leaving the parents to do so themselves. For example, solicitors feel uneasy about discussing any arrangements with the children, for fear of suggesting that they are involving the children in the decision-making processes.[62] Meanwhile, parents often baulk at undertaking such a responsibility. Indeed, as Richards points out:

> 'Because of the difference of interest at divorce and the dynamics of parent-child relationships, parents themselves cannot always do this effectively. It may be precisely the relationship with a parent that a child needs to talk about.'[63]

Many children feel quite unable to confide in anyone over their distress at their parents' breakup and over the future arrangements being made for their upbringing. Though reluctant to talk to their own parents about these matters,[64] they feel strongly that they should be involved in helping their parents decide arrangements for the future.[65] Once the divorce is finalised, children feel powerless to affect plans and decisions that their parents often present to them as already made.[66] Ideally, of course, divorcing parents should always talk to their children about their breakup *before* they apply for a divorce. But to date, the law does little to ensure that children are

---

57   The term 'conciliation' appears still to be favoured by the in-court services, with the term 'mediation' being preferred by the out-of-court family mediation services.

58   There are 'in-court' conciliation services operating up and down the country. A conciliation appointment with a CFR (who specialises in civil work and is employed by CAFCASS) is directed by the district judge when considering contested arrangements made for the children of divorcing parents or contested applications for residence or contact orders.

59   This may be a 'not-for-profit' organisation, eg the National Family Mediation, or a 'private sector' provider, most usually local solicitors with mediation training.

60   Children Act 1989, s 1(3)(a).

61   Many of these studies are usefully summarised by A O'Quigley (2000) esp pp 10–11.

62   See M Murch et al (1999) para 3.3.5. See also C Piper (1999 a) and C Piper (1999 b) esp pp 83–88.

63   M Richards (1997) p 556.

64   G Douglas et al (2001) pp 374–376; J Dunn and K Deater-Deckard (2001) pp 11–12.

65   Inter alia: C Lyon et al (1998) ch 2; G Douglas et al (2001) p 375; A Buchanan et al (2001) p 67.

66   C Lyon et al (1998) para 2.09.

consulted by their parents, or by anyone else, about their parents' future plans for their upbringing. One might have imagined that compliance with the 'section 41 procedure' would prompt parents into doing so. The fact that all divorcing couples with children under the age of 16 are obliged to complete and file a 'statement of arrangements'[67] suggests that the state has an interest in the future welfare of their children. But Cardiff researchers have found that the system is severely flawed.[68] For example, there is no mechanism for checking on the accuracy of the information included in the statement. More to the point, the procedure's requirements appear to have little real impact on many divorcing parents, relatively few of whom discuss the arrangements with their children.[69] This is probably because so few solicitors suggest to their clients that they should do so.[70] The section 41 procedure might be more effective if district judges were more prepared to withhold divorce decrees in cases where the statements disclose worrying information about the parents' plans for their children. But it is extremely unusual for them to do so; indeed, they only request further information about the arrangements disclosed in a very few cases.[71] The reason why district judges so seldom fail to take action of any kind appears to stem from their strong view that:

> 'there is no point in doing anything procedurally if it is not going to make a difference in the long-run: "I might be concerned about a proposed change of residence, but what am I going to do about it, stop them moving?"'[72]

The government appears sympathetic to the now widespread view that the section 41 procedure in its present form fails to exploit its potential usefulness, particularly so far as children are concerned. Through its improvement, the divorce process could operate in a far more constructive way, with families receiving appropriate advice, support and assistance over how to cope with relationship breakdown. It appears that the statement of arrangements forms should be redesigned to ensure that the courts receive far more information relevant to the children themselves and the extent to which they are coping with the parental breakup. Parents will themselves be provided with early information about how to support their children through the divorce. It is intended that CAFCASS will be involved in servicing these changes, and hopefully it will be provided with sufficient resources to do so.[73]

---

67 Matrimonial Causes Act 1973, s 41. The statement of arrangements details a divorcing couple's arrangements for their children's future upbringing and welfare. For a summary of the history and purpose of the procedure, see G Douglas et al (2000) pp 180–184.

68 M Murch et al (1999). This research into the working of the s 41 procedure was carried out in 1997.

69 See M Murch et al (1999) p 186. Only 34% of parent petitioners in this research study had discussed the arrangements with their children.

70 65% of solicitors indicated that they do not advise their clients to discuss the arrangements for their children with the children themselves: M Murch et al (1999) p 63. Nevertheless, parents who had received such advice, appear to have been influenced by it into doing so: M Murch et al (1999) p 187.

71 G Douglas et al (2000) pp 189–190.

72 G Douglas et al (2000) p 189.

73 Lord Chancellor's Department (2002). Facilitation/Enforcement Response (p 7 website document), responding to recommendations for reform of the s 41 procedure made by the Children Act Sub-Committee of the Advisory Board on Family Law (herafter CASC (2002)) paras 3.38–3.43.

Many divorcing parents will be sucked into state funded mediation at some stage of the divorce process if they desire public funding for the legal costs of their involvement in disputes over family matters.[74] Given the overriding principles governing divorce law,[75] privately funded clients may also be encouraged by their solicitors to consider mediation. In this current climate of opinion, which assumes that 'mediation is a good thing' and that settlement is desirable,[76] mediators are obviously contributing to the growing intense pressure on parents to settle their disputes, a pressure which has been commented on by a variety of authors.[77] As Davis and Pearce observe, in the context of parental disputes which become contested applications, since all practitioners assume that litigation is destructive and must be avoided, the 'agreements' emerging may be the result of 'highly pressured lawyer/ welfare officer negotiation'.[78] Furthermore, channelling parents into mediation sessions may not necessarily benefit their children.[79] Indeed, it may even increase children's sense of isolation. In any event, 'shot-gun' agreements,[80] particularly in contact disputes,[81] may not stand the test of time. More seriously, they may mask situations where the mother and or the children are the victims of abuse.[82]

A particular concern is that mediation sessions may not produce an outcome which takes account of the children's views. Not-for-profit mediation services have been ambivalent over whether mediators should consult children directly over parental disputes involving them. Some, like Richards, strongly oppose such a proposition. In his view, 'mediation is adult business'.[83] Since mediators do not act either for the child or the parents, using information that the child gives them risks their losing their 'neutral' role.[84] Many mediators consider that achieving parental agreement is their primary task and, rather than directly involving children in the mediation process, they therefore prefer to improve communications between divorcing parents and

74 Under the Family Law Act 1996, s 29, now replaced by the Access to Justice Act 1999, Funding Code s 11 and Code Procedures C27–29, those requiring public funding to assist with legal costs relating to private family disputes, will normally be required to attend an assessment meeting with a mediator to assess their suitability for mediation before public funding is granted. See G Davis et al (2001). See also C Bradley (2002) p 496.

75 Family Law Act 1996, s 1(b) requires courts and practitioners to note 'that the parties to a marriage which may have broken down are to be encouraged to take all practicable steps, whether by marriage counselling or otherwise, to save the marriage'; and '(c) that a marriage which has irretrievably broken down and is being brought to an end should be brought to an end—(i) with minimum distress to the parties and to the children affected; (ii) with questions dealt with in a manner designed to promote as good a continuing relationship between the parties and any children affected as is possible in the circumstances...'

76 R Bailey-Harris, J Barron and J Pearce (1999) p 54.

77 See, inter alia: G Davis and J Pearce (1999 a) p 147; G Davis and J Pearce (1999 c) pp 460–462; R Bailey-Harris, J Barron and J Pearce (1999) p 54.

78 See G Davis and J Pearce (1999 a) p 147.

79 See, inter alia: C Piper and S Day Sclater (1999) pp 247–249; C Smart et al (2001) pp 162–167.

80 B Cantwell and S Scott (1995) p 345.

81 Discussed in chapter 13.

82 See F Kaganas and C Piper (1999) p 191. See also D Greatbatch and R Dingwall (1999), whose research shows mediators 'sidelining' allegations of domestic violence in mediation sessions. These researchers question (esp p 187) whether the official policy of encouraging mediation will provide victims of domestic violence with effective protection if mediators fail to investigate such allegations more vigorously.

83 M Richards (1995) p 225.

84 M Richards (1995) p 225.

their children. In the past, although some family mediators clearly have offered children a much needed chance to talk to someone in private about their worries,[85] the majority have not considered it appropriate to address the child's needs by talking to them directly, but instead have encouraged the parents to do so themselves.[86] More recently, however, not-for-profit family mediators seem to have become more open to 'direct consultation', in situations where 'indirect consultation' with the children through their parents is not likely to produce any true dialogue.[87]

Rather than seeing an out-of-court family mediator, some litigating parents will be funnelled into the in-court conciliation work carried out by CFRs.[88] Indeed, with their help, many contested private disputes are resolved. Research shows that in pre-CAFCASS days,[89] CWOs considered that their main role was to prevent disputes over children going to trial by promoting parental agreement.[90] Few would consider it appropriate to 'see' the children themselves, even the older ones, if the parents seemed likely to reach an agreement.[91] Even when they did talk to the children, the time devoted to proper assessment of their needs was extremely restricted.[92]

Overall, as research demonstrates, no professional group considers it to be their 'job' to talk to the children of divorcing and separating parents. Accordingly, the Cardiff team observe that the aims of article 12 of the CRC are not being fully translated into procedure and practice:

> 'We have seen that mediators, solicitors and the district judges were all reluctant to see children brought directly into the [divorce] arena, considering it preferable that parents be trusted to take decisions in their children's best interests ... The general preference among the three groups was to see some other type of professional take on the task of talking to the child directly, which was recognised as valuable, especially with older children ... Parents too, considered that *someone* should do this.'[93]

Producing a better support system for children will not, however, be an easy matter. Improvements would be achieved if solicitors were more prepared to discover children's wishes before they finalise negotiated settlements with their clients.[94] As Buchanan et al observe, CFRs should develop their skills in assessing children's real wishes and be given the time to engage more effectively with them.[95] Similarly, some

---

85   I Gee (1999). See also A O'Quigley (2000) pp 20–22.
86   M Murch et al (1999). In 1997, nearly 90% of the mediators in this research project encouraged divorcing parents to consider their children's views over the arrangements being discussed in the mediation (para 7.4.1). Just under 40% 'always or very often' suggested to parents that they should 'consult' their children over the arrangements being discussed in the mediation, depending on age (para 7.4.2). Although just under half of the experienced mediators in the project seemed prepared to undertake 'direct' consultation work themselves with children (para 7.5.1), in practice, very few actually carried out direct consultation with the children, considering that it was inappropriate in the circumstances, often due to the mediator's lack of training (paras 7.5.1–7.5.5).
87   See UK College of Family Mediators (2002) for its careful and detailed guidance for family mediators contemplating consulting children directly. The list of 'Don'ts' of direct consultation (para 12) stresses, inter alia, that direct consultation should not be used where 'either parent or the child could be undermined', nor to 'put pressure on the child'.
88   Formerly called court welfare officers (hereafter CWOs).
89   The establishment of CAFCASS is discussed below.
90   See G Davis and J Pearce (1999 a) p 147.
91   See C Sawyer (2000 b) p 173. See also M Hester et al (1997) p 30.
92   See C Sawyer (2000 b) p 173 and A Buchanan et al (2001) p 86. Discussed in more detail below.
93   M Murch et al (1999) para 8.3.5.
94   See C Piper (1997) and C Piper (1999 a).

children may become more truly involved in parental negotiations now that family mediators seem more willing to do 'direct work' with children,[96] although it remains unlikely that a mediator will ever feel free to unpick an agreement simply because it does not appear to promote the children's own views.[97] An overriding problem, however, is that children's needs vary considerably according to their individual circumstances.[98] As Day Sclater and Piper observe, they cannot be 'treated as a homogenous group in relation to whether and how they wish to participate in decision-making'.[99] Although, as noted above, many children consider that they should be involved more in helping their parents sort out arrangements for their future, some would prefer not to participate at all.[100] Not all those who wish to participate welcome the same type of support. Whilst some would like an outside 'advocate', to listen to their concerns and even to be present in discussions over their future,[101] others consider it important to maintain family privacy.[102] Some children may greatly resent being 'made to' talk to outsiders[103] or become involved in therapeutic intervention[104] and feel unable to confide in anyone involved in the legal process,[105] because of the lack of confidentiality.[106]

A variety of remedies has been suggested: children being provided with far more good-quality information about divorce, for example, through age-appropriate leaflets, videos and CD-ROMs;[107] the establishment of divorce support programmes in schools, along similar lines to those working successfully in the United States;[108] a child counselling or support service established to work independently, or alongside mediators.[109] Whatever route is adopted, it must ensure that children are provided with support sufficiently early in the process of their parents' separation. The Cardiff researchers acknowledge that a weakness of their proposal, to identify parents and children requiring support through the statements of arrangements, is that such families only emerge relatively late in the divorce process.[110] A further problem is that this intervention can only be activated by adult gatekeepers – the parents. It is only their answers to questions posed by professionals which will alert practitioners

---

95 See A Buchanan et al (2001) pp 93–94. The welfare reporting process provided by CFRs is discussed in more detail below, p 215–218.
96 See above.
97 M Richards (1995) pp 224–226.
98 For a useful summary of the research on involving children, see A O'Quigley (2000) ch 3.
99 S Day Sclater and C Piper (2001) p 427.
100 A O'Quigley (2000) p 30.
101 A Buchanan et al (2001) p 67.
102 C Smart et al (2001) pp 160–161.
103 C Smart et al (2001) pp 163–164.
104 C Smart et al (2001) pp 161–162.
105 C Smart et al (2001) p 163. See also A O'Quigley (2000), who refers (p 28) to various research projects, all of which conclude that children need unconditional confidentiality before they feel sufficiently confident to confide in adults.
106 All practitioners who talk to children in a professional capacity must warn them that any information the children give them must be made available to the court, if and when, a parental dispute is litigated.
107 C Smart et al (2001) p 169.This suggestion, reiterated by CASC (2002) paras 4.5–4.8, has been accepted by the government, which is funding the development of age-appropriate leaflets, telephone assistance etc. See Lord Chancellor's Department (2002), Communication and Information, Response (pp 3–5 website document).
108 A Buchanan et al (2001) pp 98–99.
109 Eg M Richards (1997) p 556; G Douglas et al (2000), who propose (pp 194–196) that families identified through their statement of arrangements should receive support services provided by CWOs (now CFRs).
110 G Douglas et al (2000) p 196.

to the children's need for support. Parents seeking to avoid state interference will undoubtedly ensure that their answers disguise any distress their children are experiencing.

Although legal changes have produced little real support for the children of parents in the throes of breaking up, progress may be made by an informal government sponsored initiative. Those couples who use the '*Parenting Plan*'[111] to assist them work out detailed arrangements regarding their children's future will find it difficult to ignore this document's strong encouragement to involve their children in their discussions.[112] It also provides them with practical information and guidance on how to discuss any arrangements they make with their children.[113] Valuable though this initiative is, other ways must also be found to ensure that children are consulted and supported, even when their parents deny any need for such intervention, claiming to be acting responsibly. After all, these may be the very cases where parents are *not* acting in their children's best interests. Although parents do often know their children best, a respect for their autonomy should not be allowed to submerge professionals' need to consider their children as individuals.

(4) CHILDREN'S INVOLVEMENT IN FAMILY PROCEEDINGS

(A) The background

The system provided for representing children in family proceedings is extraordinarily complicated and is considered in some detail in the next three sections of this chapter. Meanwhile, a brief summary of its framework is provided below, together with an explanation of how CAFCASS, the new integrated family support service, came into being.

(i) Organisational change – the establishment of CAFCASS

For the children of parents who refuse to settle their disputes and insist on litigating, the organisational changes introduced in 2001 are extremely important. The Children and Family Court Advisory Support Service (CAFCASS) is a non-departmental public body responsible to the Lord Chancellor.[114] This new regional service brought together the old family court welfare service (provided by the probation service), the children's branch of the Official Solicitor's department and the guardian ad litem and reporting officer services. The court welfare service had provided in-court conciliation work for parents involved in private disputes over children. Its court welfare officers (CWOs)[115] also carried out 'the reporting function' by preparing welfare reports for

---

111 Developed by the National Council of Voluntary Childcare Organisations and launched in 2002. See National Council of Voluntary Childcare Organisations (2002). Solicitors advising divorcing and separating couples, CAFCASS officers, mediators and other family practitioners are all urged to give copies of this document to the parents they work with, and encourage them to use it.

112 National Council of Voluntary Childcare Organisations (2002) p 2 states: 'Children: Need to feel involved in planning for their future.' Parents are also reminded to involve their children in various specific arrangements, such as contact arrangements (p 3).

113 Eg it urges parents to 'Make time to talk to each child separately, as well as together'. National Council of Voluntary Childcare Organisations (2002) p 4.

114 Established by the Criminal Justice and Court Services Act 2000, Ch II and Sch 2.

115 Renamed 'child and family reporters', abbreviated in this discussion to CFRs.

the courts, if requested to do so.[116] The Official Solicitor (OS) normally acted for children in the few cases where the child required separate representation in parents' private disputes and other specialised cases.[117] Guardians ad litem[118] represented children in public law proceedings and in adoption proceedings. Unlike CWOs, who were full-time officers employed by the probation service, many guardians were self-employed.

There were various reasons for this massive organisational change, at least one being the government's wish to save costs.[119] These groups of practitioners were brought together following a government consultation paper[120] which produced universal endorsement of the need for a new integrated service. Under the old, highly criticised system, the methods provided for conveying children's wishes to the courts in family proceedings depended entirely on the way the litigation started. The courts received information about some, but not all children, compiled by a variety of officials with different aims, backgrounds and training. Many also felt that the Children Act 1989 had created an unsatisfactory contrast between the very good system of representation for children involved in public law proceedings and their lack of representation in private law proceedings, which could involve just as intensely fought battles over a child's future.

There were hopes that the new service would, in future, always ensure that the courts could fulfil their legislative duty to consider the child's wishes and feelings, bearing in mind his or her age and understanding.[121] This direction reflects the Law Commission's view that although children should not be forced to 'choose' between their parents, it is 'pointless to ignore the clearly expressed wishes of older children'.[122] Unfortunately, the new CAFCASS regime suggests that the methods provided whereby children's wishes are conveyed to the court are still extremely fragmented and arbitrary.

(ii)   Public law system of representation – the 'tandem system'

The system of representation in public law proceedings operates through the joint services of a solicitor and a children's guardian.[123] The children's guardian,[124] who appoints a solicitor[125] to represent the child, provides the court with an assessment of

---

116 See Children Act 1989, s 7.

117 The OS still acts for children in certain cases, eg where the child is bringing an application regarding another child eg *Re S (contact: application by sibling)* [1999] Fam 283. See generally *Practice Note (Official Solicitor: Appointment in family proceedings)* [2001] 2 FLR 155.

118 Now renamed 'children's guardians'.

119 See Department of Health et al (hereafter DH et al) (1998).

120 See DH et al (1998) paras 1.31 and 4.5.

121 Children Act 1989, s 1(3)(a) directs the court to have regard to 'the ascertainable wishes and feelings of the child concerned (considered in the light of his age and understanding)'.

122 Law Commission (1988) para 3.23.

123 See Children Act 1989, s 41(1) which establishes a presumption that the child involved (who automatically acquires full party status and public funding) will, regardless of age, receive separate representation in all 'specified proceedings'. These include (see s 41(6)) most local authority interventions to protect children.

124 Under the pre-CAFCASS system, a guardian ad litem in public law cases was usually qualified in social work or an associated field. He or she was experienced at working with children and was therefore able to provide the court with a detailed assessment of the needs of even very young children.

125 Private solicitors who wish to represent children must be members of the Law Society Children Panel, having acquired the required training and accreditation to deal with children's cases.

what outcome would be in the child's best interests. Meanwhile, the solicitor acts as the child's legal representative in court and treats the child as his client. The child's solicitor, although unable to assess the needs of the child, particularly if very young, has the legal skills necessary for representing the child in what are sometimes extremely complex legal hearings involving a number of parties.

The children's guardian, 'in tandem' with the child's solicitor,[126] will investigate the child's background in depth, often commissioning experts to assess his or her needs. The guardian's report to the court is a lengthy affair, taking account of the child's wishes and feelings, and every other item on the welfare checklist,[127] but ultimately recommending an outcome deemed to be in the child's best interests. If the child is older, the children's guardian may recommend an outcome with which the child disagrees. In such circumstances, if the child is deemed sufficiently mature, he or she should be allowed to instruct the solicitor directly, without the assistance of the guardian, and the guardian will then instruct another solicitor to represent him or her.[128]

(iii)   Private law system of representation

One of the reasons for establishing CAFCASS was a general acknowledgment that there was 'scope for improvement of the present arrangements in private proceedings'.[129] Nevertheless, despite the reorganisation, it still varies enormously how, if at all, the court discovers information about the children involved in private disputes. The 'ladder' of these children's involvement appears to have at least four rungs. On the ladder's bottom rung, children have no means of providing the court with any indication of their wishes regarding their parents' dispute. On the next rung up, an account of their views will be included in the CFR's report to the court (but such a report need not be called for). On the third rung up, children are provided with party status and separate representation (but the court may not consider this to be appropriate). On the top rung, children litigate on their own behalf, possibly even having initiated the proceedings themselves. Disappointingly, despite the reorganisation of the system for representing children in family proceedings, the rules governing these situations remain extremely complicated and defy straightforward explanation.[130]

The fact that the Children Act 1989 discriminated against children involved in private law proceedings has been a constant source of criticism. Unlike those who are the subject of public law proceedings, the legislation contains no presumption that these children will be separately represented. This feature of the system remains unchanged. The court can (but need not) ask for a welfare report to be prepared,[131] which will give it a great deal of background information about the child. But the court may decide not to call for such a report,[132] in which case it has no means of

---

126 This dual system of representation is often called the 'tandem system' of representation.
127 Ie Children Act 1989, s 1(3).
128 See discussion below.
129 DH et al (1998) para 1.8.
130 See C Johnston (2001). See also Solicitors Family Law Association (2002), which sets out the various meanings of the term 'guardian' for the purposes of litigation involving children (pp 4–5).
131 See Children Act 1989, s 7. This is prepared by a CFR, formerly a CWO. NB the 'welfare report' appears to have been renamed the 'CAFCASS report' by some courts.
132 Discussed below.

obtaining a true picture of the child's views regarding the outcome of his or her parents' dispute. Since the parents are unlikely to provide the court with a totally impartial account of the child's wishes, these children are on the bottom rung of the ladder. Depending on their age, their rights under article 12(2) of the CRC may be infringed by a failure to involve them in court proceedings focusing directly on their future. It could be argued that it would also infringe their rights to a fair trial under article 6 of the ECHR and, because the outcome will affect their family lives, their procedural rights under article 8.

Even if the court requests the preparation of a welfare report, from the child's perspective, the reporting process is greatly inferior to the type of representation available to children involved in public law proceedings.[133] This child has only reached the second rung of the ladder from the bottom. The function of a CFR is not to provide the child with separate representation in the litigation, nor does the welfare report fulfil the aims of a report prepared by a children's guardian in public law proceedings under the Children Act 1989. It seems unlikely that, under the CAFCASS regime, CFRs will adopt the role of the child's 'representative', as opposed to the court's reporting officer.

A child climbs to the ladder's third rung if he or she obtains separate representation and party status. In the past, this was an exceptional step for the courts to take. Nevertheless, the courts now appear far more receptive to the fact that even very young children may need separate representation in private disputes.[134] They obviously appreciate that to refuse children separate representation when they are the focus of parental litigation, may infringe a variety of their human rights. For these children, however, recent reforms have introduced further complication – with this rung of the ladder now having two subdivisions. There is the 'A group' of children, who will receive a superior type of separate representation, similar to the 'tandem system' available to children involved in public law proceedings. It appears that they will have a legal advocate acting for them, together with a children's guardian, representing their best interests. The 'B group' will normally be represented by a legal advocate, acting alone, sometimes with the assistance of experts commissioned to assess the child's background.

In rare situations, children climb to the top rung of the ladder; they instruct their own solicitors to represent them in private family proceedings, just as adults would.[135] This may occur if the court makes the child a party to his or her parents' proceedings and also considers that he or she is sufficiently mature to have an independent legal advocate. It also occurs when a child initiates litigation on his or her own behalf, for example, by applying for an order under the Children Act 1989, section 8. A child is unlikely to succeed in 'divorcing' his or her parents without instructing a solicitor to represent him or her in court.[136]

133 Discussed below.
134 Eg *Re A (contact: separate representation)* [2001] 1 FLR 715, discussed below.
135 Under Family Proceedings Rules (hereafter FPR) 1991, r 9.2A, discussed below.
136 Discussed in more detail in chapter 4.

(iv)   CAFCASS's future role

The problems besetting the new service[137] may ensure that, in the short term, it will, at the very most, merely replicate the work of the old services.[138] Nevertheless, the long-term plans for CAFCASS are obviously crucial. It was rather gloomily predicted that without extra funding, improvements in the representation of children in private disputes would not be possible under the new unified structure, without diverting resources from the public law work of the service.[139] Indeed, the notion of some kind of 'trade-off', with children in private law proceedings only obtaining a better service at the cost of those in public law proceedings, has been a constant fear of practitioners since the proposal for a unified service was first initiated.[140] At least for the present, the existing public law system whereby children are legally represented by independent solicitors is not being replaced by in-house CAFCASS legal representation, as had been aired.[141] Furthermore, the tandem model of representation available in public law proceedings, is not, apparently, under threat, as had been feared.[142] Indeed, it now appears that it may even be extended to some children involved in private law disputes.[143]

Given the very high level of distress that children experience when their parents are involved in private disputes over them,[144] it had become increasingly obvious that, at the very least, the court welfare service had to be improved. The reasons for this are discussed below. Meanwhile, it remains unclear what was intended by the government's statement that CAFCASS's remit 'could be extended to take on additional functions on behalf of children involved in family court proceedings and their families'.[145] It had been envisaged that, in addition to providing a strictly court-based service, CAFCASS would take on wider family support functions. It would 'be a service which, through its other responsibilities, makes a wider contribution to the welfare of families likely to be involved in family proceedings'.[146] Currently, however, there is no hint whether a new counselling or support service will be made available for the children of divorcing parents or how the present in-court conciliation arrangements fit into the new service. Until these details are clarified, it is obviously far too early to predict whether many children will benefit very much from the new arrangements. Furthermore, there is a risk that the funding difficulties which led to delays in employing more staff[147] and developing adequate training facilities for the

---

137   Eg *R (on the Application of National Association of Guardians ad Litem and Reporting Officers) v Children and Family Court Advisory and Support Service* [2001] EWHC Admin 693, [2002] 1 FLR 255: on judicial review, the organisation representing self-employed panel guardians ad litem successfully forced CAFCASS to renegotiate the terms of their future employment with CAFCASS. See also R White (2001 a), R White (2001 b) and S Gerlis (2002).
138   See R White, P Carr and N Lowe (2002) ch 10, for a detailed discussion of CAFCASS officers' duties.
139   J Hunt and J Lawson (1999) p 111.
140   J Hunt and J Lawson (1999) p 114.
141   See DH et al (1998) pp 47–49.
142   A Poyser (2001) p 142.
143   Discussed below.
144   A Buchanan et al (2001) pp 78–81.
145   LCD Press Release No 199-99, 27 July 1999.
146   Inter alia: DH et al (1998) para 3.3; CASC (2002) ch 6, suggesting various contributions that CAFCASS could make to facilitate contact arrangements; Wall J in *Re M (dislosure: children and family reporter)* [2002] EWCA Civ 19, [2002] 2 FLR 893 at [80], suggesting that CAFCASS should rapidly establish its identity and role.
147   See R White (2001 b) pp 1567–1568.

new service, will reduce its overall quality. More fundamentally, as was pointedly stated by an influential committee:

> 'The Government should recognise the importance of CAFCASS and the expanding role which it has to play in the Family Justice System. It should ensure that CAFCASS is properly funded to undertake both the role of reporting to the court in children's cases and the important functions it has to perform in its advisory and support service.'[148]

(B)   Private proceedings

(i)   The welfare reporting process – pre-CAFCASS

Despite its importance, CAFCASS took over, in 2001, a deeply flawed welfare reporting process. The most serious procedural weakness undermining the Children Act's direction to the courts to consider the child's wishes and feelings[149] is that there is no guarantee that the court will receive any evidence indicating what those wishes are. The most obvious way for information about this to be conveyed to the court is through a welfare report – but there is no obligation on the court to request one,[150] even in long-running, bitterly contested disputes involving older children.

The constant delays involved in the production of court welfare reports often deterred courts from calling for them.[151] There were also considerable concerns about the quality of the process itself. Many considered it unsatisfactory that CWOs failed to focus on the children of disputing parents, with children not being 'seen' at all in cases where settlements were expected.[152] In those cases where a court welfare report was being prepared, publication of national standards[153] produced an improved situation, with more CWOs talking to the children themselves.[154] Nevertheless, CWOs seldom had sufficient time to talk to children particularly effectively. Parents reported the 'interview' often being short and, in inner city areas, usually conducted in the officer's office.[155] Many considered that the time devoted to talking to the children and to investigating their family background was far too limited to assess properly the children's needs or the parents' real ability to meet them.[156] Equally, the children themselves were very ambivalent over the extent to which the CWOs understood

---

148   CASC (2002) para 6.12. See also p 3. The government's response was disappointingly ambivalent. See Lord Chancellor's Department (2002) pp 10–11 (website document).

149   Children Act 1989, s 1(3).

150   Children Act 1989, s 7.

151   See R Bailey-Harris, J Barron and J Pearce (1999), noting (p 58) that in 26% of cases the court welfare reports took up to three months to produce, with 13% of cases taking between three and six months to produce. Court welfare reports were only ordered in 49% of cases. See also S Gerlis (2002) p 144, stating that reports were, in 2001, taking between 12 weeks and 40 weeks.

152   See C Sawyer (2000 b) p 173.

153   Home Office (1994). These standards specified (para 4.17) that all children should be seen by CWOs carrying out a reporting function, unless strong reasons existed for not doing so.

154   See A Buchanan et al (2001) who record (pp 32–33) that 95% of parents indicated that their children had been seen at least once.

155   A Buchanan et al (2001) pp 33–36. This research indicated that despite the fact that the *National Standards* (Home Office (1994)) made it clear (para 4.17) that home visits should be considered, only 9% of inner city parents reported their children receiving a home visit.

156   A Buchanan et al (2001) ch 4, pp 85–86 and 94. A number of parents in this research study (pp 35–36) criticised the CWOs for not talking to their new partners or to grandparents.

their real wishes and felt inhibited in what they could confide in them.[157] Overall, there was considerable dissatisfaction with the way in which the CWOs conducted their inquiries and the contents of the welfare report itself.[158]

A more fundamental weakness of the reporting function, from a child's perspective, largely stemmed from the CWO's role itself. This did not involve acting as the child's representative, but providing the court with a report about the child's background. Research indicates that CWOs varied over the weight they gave to the child's own views, which in turn depended on their perceptions of the adults as the 'clients'. This produced a 'we know best' attitude[159] – particularly inappropriate for adolescents. Solicitors experienced in representing children in court were concerned that CWOs did not take the views and allegations of teenagers particularly seriously.[160] Such an approach was worrying, given that relatively mature children were unable to put their views to the courts, either personally or through their own representatives. Of greater concern was CWO practice in contact disputes. The strong commitment of CWOs to the concept of maintaining contact between child and non-residential parent sometimes led them to discount the children's own reluctance to do so.[161] Indeed, in the past, some CWOs were over ready to assume that when children opposed contact, this stemmed from parental alienation rather than perfectly valid reasons, such as their fear of a violent father.[162] Researchers also criticised the influence CWOs had over the courts, given the paucity of their training in the disciplines underlying child care, such as child psychological development or attachment theory.[163] Indeed, there were numerous calls for CWOs to be better trained.[164]

Children found it deeply frustrating to discover CWOs reinterpreting their own wishes to the court through the welfare report.[165] Such frustration would be enhanced if the CWO recommended to the court an outcome opposed by the child, due to the CWO's view that the child's wishes did not accord with his or her best interests. For example, in *Re M (family proceedings: affidavits)*,[166] the CWO indicated to the court that M, an able, intelligent and articulate 12-year-old with an attractive personality,[167] was being unrealistic in her wish to live with her father. The CWO 'had an instinct based upon her experience that in this case it would be better for the girl to remain, as

---

157 A Buchanan et al (2001) p 66. See also C Smart et al (2001) p 163.
158 A Buchanan et al (2001) p 42.
159 See M Hester et al (1997) p 31.
160 C Sawyer (1995 a) p 130.
161 See M Hester and L Radford (1996) pp 23–24.
162 See M Hester and L Radford (1996) pp 23–24, and C Sawyer (2000 b) p 174. See also *Re L (a child) (contact: domestic violence)* [2000] 4 All ER 609, per Dame Elizabeth Butler-Sloss P, who (at 624–625) criticised the CWO for indicating in her report, with no evidence to justify such an allegation, that the child, now aged 9, was suffering emotional abuse resulting from the mother's refusal to force him to see his father, against his wishes.
163 G Davis and J Pearce (1999 b) p 240 and (1999 d) p 552.
164 Eg Children Act Sub-Committee of the Advisory Board on Family Law (2000) (hereafter CASC (2000)) reported that: 'There was universal agreement that there should be more training for Family Court Welfare Officers...' (para 3.10.1).
165 See A Buchanan et al (2001), who records a child saying (p 65) that the CWO 'kept changing your words, messing your head. Changed your words to things that were not true ...'
166 [1995] 2 FLR 100.
167 [1995] 2 FLR 100 at 101, per Butler-Sloss LJ.

she had always lived, with the mother ...'[168] The court would not allow M to give affidavit evidence setting out her own views,[169] because –

> 'it is not fair on children that they should be dragged into the arena, that they should be asked specifically to choose between two parents, both of whom they love, and they ought not to be involved in the disputes of their parents.'[170]

Although well intentioned, such an approach seemed misguided, given that M was very obviously already fully involved in her parents' dispute. It was surely impossible to put the clock back and pretend that a child's own strong views, whether they had been influenced by one parent or the other, simply did not exist. This decision effectively denied M any voice over her own future, other than through the voice of a CWO, with whom she fundamentally disagreed. This over-protective approach contrasted strongly with the robust way in which the courts deal with witness summons directed at children with a view to their giving evidence in criminal trials involving adults.[171]

A child of M's age should, perhaps, have been advised to institute her own proceedings for a residence order under section 8 of the Children Act 1989.[172] This would have forced the court to consider her own perspectives of the situation, uncoloured by any adult interpretation. Today, however, the courts may be prepared to adopt a better solution, which is to give such children separate representation.[173] Indeed, a girl like M might argue that because the outcome of her parents' dispute will affect her family life, her procedural rights under article 8[174] of the ECHR would be infringed were she *not* provided with any chance to influence the outcome directly.

(ii) The welfare reporting process post-CAFCASS

In the absence of being provided with separate representation, will the CAFCASS welfare reporting service provide children with support more like that received by those involved in public law proceedings? The answer is almost certainly no. As before, the CFR's role is to provide the court with a welfare (or CAFCASS) report and not to represent the child. At the very least, it is obviously essential for CAFCASS

---

168   [1995] 2 FLR 100 at 102.
169   Although counsel for the father had withdrawn his application to adduce M's affidavit before the hearing, Butler-Sloss LJ took the opportunity to emphasise her disapproval of children giving such evidence.
170   [1995] 2 FLR 100 at 103, per Butler-Sloss LJ.
171   Eg *R v Highbury Corner Magistrates' Court, ex p Deering* [1997] 1 FLR 683. The magistrates' refusal to issue a witness summons directed to a 9-year-old child was quashed on judicial review. The child's evidence would be material to the assault charges against his father, brought by his former cohabitant. The risk of harm to the child's welfare had to be balanced against the possible harm suffered by the defendant through depriving the court of evidence. This was a decision for the trial court to determine when the moment for calling the child arose.
172   See discussion below and in chapter 4.
173   See the Family Proceedings Courts (Children Act 1989) Rules 1991, SI 1991/1395 (as amended) (hereafter FPC (CA 1989) R 1991), r 11B(5) and (6) and Family Proceedings Rules 1991, SI 1991/1247 (as amended) (hereafter FPR 1991), r 4.11B(5) and (6) which place the CFR under a specific duty to consider whether the child should be given party status and advise the court accordingly. See discussed below.
174   *McMichael v United Kingdom* (1995) 20 EHRR 205 and *W (and R, O, B and H) v United Kingdom* (1987) 10 EHRR 29.

to ensure, through better training, that all CFRs acquire the ability to interview children and obtain detailed assessments of their needs, with more time in which to do so.[175] But, as commented above, this depends on whether resources will be made available for this improvement to take place. Staff shortages are already leading to a delay in producing reports, causing problems in the courts with consequential timetabling delays.[175a] Meanwhile, the new rules provide CFRs with the ability to commission expert opinion on children who are the subject of their reports, in order to inform their own assessments.[176] This facility is a welcome development.[177] Hopefully, when CFRs are allowed to exercise this new function,[178] it will not be restricted, on grounds of economy, to the most complex and exceptional cases. The ability, for example, to obtain a psychiatric report, would enable CFRs to focus far more on the children, rather than on their parents and to adopt a more therapeutic, rather than purely investigative, approach. It might also obviate the need to order separate representation in some cases.[179]

CFRs now have a new obligation to explain to each child, depending on his or her age and understanding, what they are including in their report and the outcome that they are recommending, 'in a manner appropriate to his age and understanding'.[180] This too is welcome progress towards recognising that those who are the focus of the proceedings have a right to information about how the decision was reached. As Buchanan et al observe, children will not only learn what arrangements are being proposed by the CFR but also whether their views have been accurately represented.[181] CFRs must now consider very carefully how children will respond to their reports and the recommendations being made. A mature child who does not receive an explanation from the CFR about the contents of the report might argue that his or her rights have been infringed under article 6 of the ECHR. Indeed, as acknowledged in Scotland,[182] it is arguable that such children should receive complete copies of these reports. Whether or not some children learn about the contents of the CFRs' reports, of greater concern is the fact that few children will benefit from the new procedures, if, due to a shortage of CFRs and delays in producing welfare reports, the courts decide not to call for them at all.

175   Inter alia: A Buchanan et al (2001) p 86; Association of Lawyers for Children (1998 a) p 408; J Hunt and J Lawson (1999) pp 55, 58, 86 and 132; A O'Quigley (2000) pp 16 and 20; CASC (2002) paras 12.13–12.16.

175a In *M v A (contact: domestic violence)* [2002] 2 FLR 921 Judge Cryan (at para 15) referred to the difficulties caused by CAFCASS taking seven months to produce a report and stated: 'Such delays are clearly not acceptable.'

176   FPC (CA 1989) R 1991, r 4.11(2)(b) and FPR 1991, r 4.11(2)(b).

177   See , inter alia: J Hunt and J Lawson (1999), who reported (pp 54–55) that a facility of this kind was considered essential by many of the CWOs interviewed; DH et al (1998), which suggested (para 4.9) that such a power would give 'caseworkers a more proactive role'; Advisory Board on Family Law (1999) Annex D, which indicated (p 25) the importance it attached to the unified service having an 'in house budget' to purchase such specialised services.

178   A CAFCASS senior officer stated (personal communication to author – Autumn 2002) that this rule is not being utilised by CFRs and that, to date, there is no budget for them to do so.

179   See *Re N (residence: appointment of solicitor: placement with extended family)* [2001] 1 FLR 1028, per Hale LJ, commenting (at [20]) on the inability of CWOs to instruct experts, making it desirable to order separate representation instead.

180   FPC (CA 1989) R, r 4.11B(1)(a) and (b) and FPR 1991, r 4(11)B(1)(a) and (b).

181   A Buchanan et al (2001) p 93.

182   Responding to *McMichael v United Kingdom* (1995) 20 EHRR 205, the Scottish children's hearing system was amended, requiring all Reporters to give copies of all reports and papers relating to the proceedings, not only to the child's parents, but also to the child himself. See discussion in *S v Principal Reporter and Lord Advocate* [2001] UKHRR 514 at [28]–[29].

(iii) Separate representation

(a)   NO AUTOMATIC SEPARATE REPRESENTATION

A strong sense of unease is generated by cases like *Re M (a minor)*,[183] where an adolescent was not given the chance to refute the CWO's view that she did not know what was good for her. That case was reported in the early 1990s. The judiciary now seem far more sympathetic to the view that separate representation may be appropriate in private law proceedings. Hale LJ has indicated that:

> 'The evidence is now quite clear that children whose parents are separating, and especially if their parents are in conflict with one another, need a voice, someone who is able to listen to anything they wish to say and tell them what they need to know. Sometimes they need more than this and that is someone who is able to orchestrate an investigation of the case on their behalf.'[184]

One of the reasons for establishing CAFCASS was the view that large numbers of children were the subject of private law applications every year, whose wishes and views were not being conveyed to the courts in any way. Nevertheless, the amended court rules still fail to give automatic party status to children whose parents are fighting over them in private proceedings, despite the outcome materially affecting their future. Some improvement has been achieved for this group, in that the rules now oblige CFRs to advise the court in every case whether it 'is in the best interests of the child to be made a party to the proceedings'.[185] Since in many cases, the judiciary will rely on the CFR to alert them of the need to direct separate representation, rather than acting on its own initiative, it is essential that CFRs interpret this duty from the perspectives of the children involved, rather than in an adult-focused manner. If they assume that children only need separate representation in the most exceptional circumstances, they will effectively undermine the aim of this rule, which is to ensure that children are effectively involved in litigation affecting their future lives.

Before discussing the separate representation now available, it is worth considering the reasons for children in the private sector of children's proceedings being deprived of *automatic* separate representation. The controversy over this matter goes back to pre-Children Act 1989 days. Before the Children Act reforms, although sympathetic to the concept of children receiving separate representation in private proceedings, the Law Commission had provisionally concluded that there was no need for automatic separate representation, as in public proceedings.[186] Public proceedings were different because whilst 'children should not be asked to choose between their parents [as in private proceedings], they may feel a strong sense of injustice if they are not given some voice in the decision between their parents' and the local authority's plans'.[187] In private proceedings this was unnecessary because: 'In ordinary family disputes, there is much to be said for allowing both the child's interests and the child's views to emerge through the normal method of a welfare officer's report.'[188] The Law Commission thought

---

183 [1995] 2 FLR 100, discussed above.

184 *Re A (contact: separate representation)* [2001] 1 FLR 715 at [31].

185 See FPC (CA 1989) R 1991, r 11B(5) and (6) and FPR 1991, r 4.11B(5) and (6), which place the CFR under a specific duty to consider whether the child should be given party status and advise the court accordingly.

186 Law Commission (1988) para 6.26.

187 Law Commission (1988) para 6.28.

188 Law Commission (1988) para 6.26.

it important for all courts to have the power to make a child a party to private proceedings in appropriate cases, for example, where the child is over a certain age. The rules of court accompanying the Children Act duly enabled the superior courts to exercise such a power, and these rules remain unchanged today.[189]

A majority of those responding to the consultation on how to reform the system[190] adopted a similar view to that taken by the Law Commission over a decade before.[191] The proposition that all children should have a right to automatic representation, whatever the circumstances, was not, by then, commanding enthusiastic support, even from children themselves.[192] Nor was there general approval for the views of some[193] that certain categories of cases, such as children over a certain age, should receive automatic separate representation. A reluctance to promote automatic separate representation for all children in a certain category, for example, all those over the age of 12, perhaps stemmed from the view that such a system would be exorbitantly costly. Nevertheless, there were other reasons. Practitioners had already seen children experiencing the corrosive effects of being sucked into divisive litigation between their parents[194] and feared that more children would be similarly affected if separate representation was made widely available.

Severe reservations had been voiced about the wisdom of relatively young children becoming actively involved in their parents' disputes and being traumatised by the experience.[195] The case law reflected and continues to reflect the judiciary's concerns about the impact on children of this type of involvement.[196] Sawyer's research in the early 1990s, with solicitors experienced at taking instructions from children, also showed that they found a variety of features of this work particularly worrying. Although many cases never got to court, they saw children suffering unforeseeable damage and stress from their involvement in the preparation for litigation. As she commented: 'Involvement of the child as a *subject* in the proceedings is a considerable step from the involvement which comes through being merely their *object*.'[197] Indeed, by the late 1990s, as Piper observes, it had obviously become a widespread view that 'court is a bad place for children',[198] with the Advisory Board on Family Law maintaining that separate representation of children in divorce cases could 'drive a wedge between children and their parents, and make divorce proceedings more

---

189 FPR 1991, r 9.5, which only applies to the county courts and High Court. There is no equivalent provision enabling the family proceedings courts to order separate representation for the child.

190 DH et al (1998).

191 See Advisory Board on Family Law (1999) Annex D, for a summary of the responses to the Consultation paper (DH et al (1998)) esp p 27.

192 C Lyon et al (1998) pp 55–56 and 189.

193 Eg See J Hunt and J Lawson (1999), who reported (p 63) CWOs suggesting that party status and legal representation might be needed in a variety of situations, including inter alia: where there is deeply entrenched parental conflict; where the case is complex or controversial; where the child holds a different view from the CWO; where the child is older. See also Association of Lawyers for Children (1998 b), which recommended a presumption in favour of legal representation in certain categories of cases, eg where the child is 12 or over.

194 These occurred in the rare cases where the courts directed that children in private proceedings should have party status and separate representation in their parents' disputes. There were also the children given leave to apply for section 8 orders in their own right. See discussion below.

195 These concerns are summarised by C Smart et al (2001) p 166.

196 Discussed below.

197 C Sawyer (1995 a) p 153.

198 See C Piper (1999 a) p 396.

acrimonious rather than less'.[199] Doubtless this feedback from practitioners was useful to a government anxious to avoid the expense of extending separate representation to large numbers of children. The principle was therefore retained that the courts would order separate representation only for those children deemed to require it,[200] assisted by CFRs' advice on this question.[201]

(b)   A RESTRICTED FORM OF SEPARATE REPRESENTATION?

What sort of separate representation will children acquire when the CFR's advice on this matter is followed by the courts? It appears that, under recent reforms, the courts will acquire the power to ensure that at least some children involved in private law proceedings receive the same quality of representation as those involved in public law proceedings.[202] The complicating feature is that these changes will create two groups of children – an A group and a B group. Only those selected to receive the superior form of separate representation will gain the services of a solicitor and children's guardian.[203] The B group will presumably carry on as before.

The first point to note, when attempting to explain this arcane situation is that a child cannot become involved in any litigation, as a party to the proceedings, without an adult to represent him or her in court.[204] For the B group of children, an officer from the legal branch of CAFCASS[205] normally acts for them,[206] as their 'guardian ad litem'.[207] He then attempts to fulfil two roles at once. He carries out the welfare tasks normally associated with children's cases, similar to those performed by the children's guardian in public proceedings and for which he is not trained, together with the

---

199 Advisory Board on Family Law (1998) para 4.12. But see A O'Quigley (2000), who summarises (pp 17–18) the views of those who favoured extending the system of separate representation for children involved in private disputes.

200 Under FPR 1991, r 9(5).

201 FPC (CA 1989) R 1991, r 11B(5) and (6) and FPR 1991, r 4.11B(5) and (6).

202 See Children Act 1989, s 41(6A) (inserted by Adoption and Children Act 2002, s 122(1)(b)), enabling section 8 proceedings to be added to the list of 'specified proceedings' warranting the appointment of a children's guardian. This will only occur when rules of court are made under Children Act 1989, s 93(2)(bb) (inserted by Adoption and Children Act 2002, s 122(2)) adding this group of children to the list of those separately represented under s 41, in 'specified proceedings'. These amendments were introduced late in the Adoption and Children Bill's progress through Parliament.

203 Under FPR 1991, r 9(5).

204 Unless he is permitted to litigate on his own behalf under FPR r 9.2A (see below), a minor, as a litigant under a disability, needs an adult to represent him. That adult's title is the child's 'next friend', when the child is the applicant; cf the child's 'guardian ad litem', when the child is the respondent (more normally the case).

205 Ie CAFCASS Legal – the legal branch of CAFCASS which employs legally qualified officers to fulfil the legal tasks associated with the service. See *CAFCASS Practice Note (Officers of Legal Services and Special Casework: Appointment in Family Proceedings)* [2001] 2 FLR 151 at [12]. If CAFCASS Legal decline the appointment, a local solicitor from the Law Society Children Panel, may be invited to do so instead.

206 But in some parts of the country, particularly in the north of England, local courts have organised slightly different arrangements, often involving solicitors on the Law Society Children Panel becoming involved in the separate representation of children in private law proceedings.

207 See Solicitors Family Law Association (2002) pp 4–5 for an explanation of the way that the term 'guardian ad litem', is used in various different situations.

tasks of a legal advocate.[208] Admittedly, he will often commission expert evidence from child psychiatrists and psychologists to give him specialised advice on the child's needs.[209] Nevertheless, this does not address the lack of any real support for the child nor the difficulty in obtaining a very detailed assessment of the child's background. Thus for the B group, the lack of a specialist children's guardian, the most criticised feature of the pre-CAFCASS system of separate representation for children involved in private law proceedings, has been carried over into the new regime. The judiciary themselves had, in pre-CAFCASS days, emphasised the problems that this restricted form of separate representation caused for the child, the solicitor and for the courts.[210]

The new provisions, will, when activated by rules of court,[211] give the courts power to select children for a superior system of separate representation – the A group. By introducing these reforms, the government implicitly acknowledged that the CAFCASS arrangements, operational from early 2001, were totally inappropriate for many children caught up in parental disputes. The courts will, in appropriate cases, be able to ensure that children caught up in family litigation receive as good a system of representation as those involved in public proceedings. They will have the power to appoint a children's guardian to act alongside the child's legal advocate. The A group will thereby gain the assistance of a practitioner whose professional background will enable him to assess their needs, and provide them with much needed support. Hopefully, where a CFR has already worked on the case, when preparing a welfare report, that officer might be reappointed to act as the children's guardian. With his knowledge of the children's family background, he would be well placed to undertake the investigative and supportive work that children's guardians undertake in public law proceedings. It is unclear how long it will be before the necessary rules of court are produced activating these new provisions. It would be highly regrettable if the rules attempted to restrict this new, and potentially very expensive, power[212] in a manner undermining its objectives. This might be done, for example, by restricting separate representation to only the most exceptional and complex of cases, perhaps with a foreign element, leaving the majority of children with the old limited model.

---

208 Ie he attempts to fulfil the old 'hybrid role' fulfilled by the Official Solicitor (OS) in pre-CAFCASS days, when providing children with separate representation. The OS fulfilled the 'welfare role', investigating the child's background and reporting on his or her best interests, whilst taking instructions from the child, as his or her solicitor. The conflict of interest involved in the OS representing a child, whilst advocating a course not desired by his client, led some children to apply to 'sack the OS' and instruct an independent solicitor on their own behalf. Eg *Re S (a minor) (independent representation)* [1993] 3 All ER 36. See discussion below.

209 See *Re C (prohibition on further applications)* [2002] EWCA Civ 292, [2002] 1 FLR 1136, per Dame Elizabeth Butler-Sloss P at [13], suggesting that such steps should be taken.

210 See *Re K (replacement of guardian ad litem)* [2001] 1 FLR 663 at 670–671, per Munby J; *Re N (residence: appointment of solicitor: placement with extended family)* [2001] 1 FLR 1028 at [20]–[24], per Hale LJ. See also *Re CE (section 37 direction)* [1995] 1 FLR 26 at [44]–[45], per Wall J.

211 Made under Children Act 1989, s 93(2)(bb).

212 Presumably, the children's guardian will normally be funded by the Legal Services Commission.

(c)   WHICH CHILDREN WILL GAIN SEPARATE REPRESENTATION?

What sort of private disputes justify children gaining separate representation – with or without the additional services of a children's guardian? As Hale LJ's words quoted above make plain,[213] recent case law suggests that the senior judiciary are increasingly open to the notion of separate representation for children involved in private proceedings. This had become apparent prior to the CAFCASS changes.[214] Nevertheless, the guidance produced by CAFCASS Legal providing examples of the type of case it deemed suitable for its own officers to offer separate representation in private cases is oddly limited.[215] Surprisingly, the list of examples does not include a situation where the child will very obviously benefit from separate representation, namely where he or she is opposing the views of the CFR.[216] Nor does it mention disputed contact cases involving allegations of domestic violence.[217] Hopefully, this official guidance does not deter CFRs from advising the courts that separate representation is necessary in any situations falling outside the list. Fortunately, the judiciary appear to be ignoring the list and ordering separate representation in a far wider category of cases. The new provisions, will, when activated, enable them to ensure that children are also represented by children's guardians, may also provoke a greater judicial willingness to envisage children being made parties to legal proceedings, given that these children will now receive welfare support from a separate source.

Children might today argue that, in order to fulfil the demands of article 12 of the CRC and articles 6 and 8 of the ECHR, they should always receive separate representation in cases where their parents are fighting over them.[218] The judiciary are well aware of such arguments. In *Re A (contact: separate representation)*[219] Dame Elizabeth Butler-Sloss P indicated that the new need to comply with the ECHR might provoke an increased use of guardians in private law cases and she hoped that, with

---

213   See above, *Re A (contact: separate representation)* [2001] 1 FLR 715 at [31], per Hale LJ. CASC (2002) also reported 'a strong feeling that in difficult cases, children ought to be separately represented more often (para 127).

214   Eg in cases involving applications to recover abducted children under the Hague Convention on the Civil Aspects of International Child Abduction 1980. See discussion in chapter 8. See also disputed contact cases, eg inter alia: *Re M (contact order: committal)* [1999] 1 FLR 810 and *Re W (contact: parent's delusional beliefs)* [1999] 1 FLR 1263.

215   See *CAFCASS Practice Note (Officers of Legal Services and Special Casework: Appointment in Family Proceedings)* [2001] 2 FLR 151 at [4], which provides the following examples, where: (a) there is a significant foreign element; (b) there is need for expert medical or other evidence on behalf of the child where joint instruction by the parties is impossible; (c) a child was refused leave to instruct a solicitor direct under FPR 1991, r 9.2A; (d) an application is made for leave to seek contact with an adopted child; (e) there are exceptionally difficult, unusual or sensitive issues making it necessary for the child to be granted party status (when the case will be dealt with in the High Court). Special category medical cases, such as applications to authorise sterilisations and those involving disputed life-sustaining treatment would also be taken on.

216   As described in DH et al (1998) para 4.22.

217   See CASC (2000), stating (para 5.2(e)) that when disputed allegations of domestic violence are being made, subject to the seriousness of the allegations and the difficulty of the case, the court should always consider whether the children should be separately represented.

218   See discussion above.

219   [2001] 1 FLR 715: when dealing with a contact dispute, the Court of Appeal accepted that the 4½-year-old child should receive separate representation so that, inter alia, her guardian ad litem could remedy the absence of any 'proper investigation of the child's sexual abuse allegations' against her father: [2001] 1 FLR 715 at [17]–[20]. See also *Re H and A (paternity: blood tests)* [2002] EWCA Civ 383, [2002] 1 FLR 1145: CAFCASS Legal were invited to provide twins aged 4½ with separate representation.

the establishment of CAFCASS, 'it will be easier for children to be represented in suitable cases …'[220] The fact that separate representation was ordered in that case for a child of only 4½ suggests that the practice of confining such a service to cases involving older children with strong views of their own has disappeared. Indeed, it suggests perhaps that the courts should consider ordering separate representation in *any* case where there is a conflict between the caring parent's account of the child's wishes and the respondent's own evidence.[220a] The Court of Appeal was also willing to countenance an independent professional organisation being appointed as a child's guardian ad litem, providing separate representation.[221] This ability to turn to alternative sources of legal advocacy for children, in the event of the services of CAFCASS being too limited to provide separate representation for all the children deemed to need it, may ensure that far more children play an appropriate part in disputes over their future.

(iv)   Children applying for section 8 orders

(a)   THE BACKGROUND

The legal procedures enabling mature children to initiate Children Act proceedings on their own behalf, with the assistance of a solicitor, go considerably further than is required by article 12 of the CRC or, indeed, by the ECECR. They enable mature children to take some control over situations going badly wrong at home, by presenting their own views to the courts for judicial consideration. In particular, mature children's procedural ability to apply for section 8 orders reflects a legal acknowledgment of their capacity to make important choices in their lives and to take responsibility for certain aspects of their own upbringing. Nevertheless, these provisions all enable children to become actively involved in litigation – a particularly adult and stressful pastime. Whilst children may wish to sort out difficulties in their own lives, they also have a right to be protected from a damaging process.

Given their importance, it is astonishing that the provisions allowing children to instruct their own solicitors and, with their help, apply for section 8 orders, were introduced with little or no discussion, certainly with no official guidance or court rules on methods of interpretation. The full implications of the Law Commission's recommendation that children should be given the right to obtain section 8 orders[222] was probably not entirely appreciated. It certainly seems unlikely that the Law Commission or the draftsmen of the Children Bill realised that children would thereby be able to 'divorce' their parents. The only procedural safeguard is the Children Act 1989, section 10(8). But this does no more than direct the court to consider whether 'the child has sufficient understanding to make the proposed application for the

---

220 [2001] 1 FLR 715 at [22], per Dame Elizabeth Butler-Sloss P.

220a CASC (2002) indicated that it was 'very impressed' by information that in New Zealand, independent counsel is appointed for the child in every disputed residence or contact case (para 12.8).

221 Eg the National Youth Advocacy Service (NYAS), which makes available social work skills and legal advice and advocacy to children in a variety of situations: see NYAS (2001). In *Re A*, although NYAS was deemed suitable to act as the child's guardian ad litem, it had been sought out by the mother and was not considered by the husband to be completely impartial. The OS was invited to act instead.

222 Law Commission (1988) para 4.44.

section 8 order', the judiciary being left to work out for themselves what factors to apply when confronted by a child seeking leave to apply.[223]

Rule 9.2A of the Family Proceedings Rules 1991[224] was also introduced without anyone apparently realising its radical nature and significance.[225] It enables a minor to initiate proceedings without a next friend or guardian ad litem 'where a solicitor ... considers that the minor is able, having regard to his understanding, to give instructions in relation to the proceedings ...'[226] Additionally, the court can, on application of a child with party status in his parents' dispute, remove the child's next friend or guardian ad litem, thereby allowing him or her to proceed without such assistance.[227] But the court can only take such a step if it considers the child 'has sufficient understanding to participate as a party in the proceedings concerned without a next friend or guardian ad litem'.[228] Again, the rules contain no guidance over the interpretation of this term, even though instructing a solicitor is an essentially adult task.

Children deemed to have sufficient understanding to instruct their own solicitors will be served by an adult whose duties do not encompass those of a children's guardian in public proceedings. Indeed, a solicitor acting for a child in these circumstances is under no legal duty to provide his client with any emotional support, or to mediate between the child and his or her family. Moreover, since the child is treated as an adult client, the solicitor need not provide the court with any information about his perceptions of the child's best interests. Obvious judicial misgivings about these changes led to the senior judiciary ensuring that they maintained supervisory powers over children instituting legal proceedings. All applications for leave under the Children Act 1989, section 10(8) were swiftly confined, by practice direction, to determination in the High Court.[229] Case law also established that the courts have the final word over whether children are sufficiently competent to instruct a solicitor to initiate or carry out legal proceedings regarding their upbringing without the services of a guardian ad litem.[230] The judiciary then set about establishing what level of understanding a child requires, in order to instruct a solicitor, or dispense with the services of his or her guardian ad litem.

(b)   COMPETENCE OF CHILDREN TO INSTRUCT THEIR OWN SOLICITORS

The leading authorities establishing the competence required of children to instruct solicitors independently, without the services of a guardian ad litem, arose primarily in the context of a relatively unusual situation. In the past, children sometimes wanted to dispense with the services of the Official Solicitor (OS),[231] who had been appointed

---

223   Eg Department of Health (1991) contains no discussion of the Children Act 1989, s 10(8), other than to repeat its exact wording.
224   Introduced through amendments made to the Family Proceedings Rules 1991 in 1992.
225   See Thorpe J (1994) pp 20–21.
226   FPR 1991, r 9.2A(1)(b).
227   FPR 1991, r 9.2A(4) and (6). In which case the child will instruct his or her own solicitor, who will act for the child, thereby supplanting the guardian ad litem, who in pre-CAFCASS days would normally have been the OS. Ie the child would apply to 'sack' the OS.
228   FPR 1991, r 9.2A(6).
229   *Practice Direction* [1993] 1 All ER 820.
230   See *Re T (a minor) (child: representation)* [1993] 4 All ER 518 at 530, per Waite LJ.
231   Eg *Re S (a minor) (independent representation)* [1993] 3 All ER 36, discussed below. See also *Re K (replacement of guardian ad litem)* [2001] 1 FLR 663: the child applied to dispense with the services of a private solicitor, acting as guardian ad litem.

to represent them, as their guardian ad litem.[232] The courts were often reluctant to allow the child to proceed without the protection of the OS, because they suspected that the child had been manipulated by a forceful parent into making such an application. In the event of their 'sacking' the OS, as guardian ad litem, such children became involved in litigation on their own behalf. They would thereafter instruct a solicitor, without a guardian to shield them from the influence of a domineering parent or provide them with emotional support and advice. The court would also be deprived of the services of an officer who provided it with independent advice over the child's best interests, often assisted by a consultant child psychiatrist and other practitioners.

These factors probably explained the very restrictive judicial interpretation placed upon the child's 'understanding' in the early case law. Indeed, the judicial caution with which these procedural rights have been interpreted has, at times, undermined their objectives. The question at stake is whether the children seeking to exercise these rights have reached an appropriate level of understanding to do so and whether it is justifiable to restrict the definition of 'understanding',[233] in order to protect them from the harm of participating, like adults, in damaging disputes. In particular, there is obvious uncertainty over the extent to which questions regarding the child's intellectual capacity to instruct a solicitor should be detached from broader questions regarding the child's overall maturity and welfare. The difficulty is to find an appropriate balance between allowing independent action and an over-restrictive paternalism.

Some of this case law provides good examples of the judiciary adopting an 'outcome approach' to judge a child's legal capacity for taking on a particular task.[234] For example, in *Re S (a minor) (independent representation)*[235] Sir Thomas Bingham MR appeared to judge S's competence to litigate on his own behalf, by considering the risks involved in the outcome. If the outcome of a child litigating without an adult next friend or guardian ad litem would be damaging, the child was obviously legally incompetent to do so. When considering the wording of rule 9.2A, the Master of the Rolls adopted the concept of '*Gillick* competence', as a means of testing the sufficiency of the child's understanding under the 1991 rules.[236] But he gave that term a relatively restrictive interpretation, seeming reluctant to accede that a child, however old, would have the capacity to participate as a party without a next friend or guardian ad litem. In his view, 'understanding' is not an absolute concept, it has to be assessed relative to the issues involved in the proceedings. Where 'sound judgment on these issues calls for insight and imagination which only maturity and experience can bring, both the court and the solicitor will be slow to conclude that the child's understanding is sufficient'.[237] The Master of the Rolls justified his approach by referring to an observation made by Lord Scarman in his judgment in *Gillick v West Norfolk and Wisbech Area Health Authority*,[238] regarding old case law on a child's capacity to make 'wise' choices.[239] Nevertheless, this passing remark was taken out of

---

232 Ie under FPR 1991, r 9.5. Discussed above.
233 The term 'understanding' is used in FPR 1991, r 9.2A(1)(4) and (6). It is also used in the Children Act 1989, s 10(8).
234 Discussed in chapter 3.
235 [1993] 3 All ER 36.
236 [1993] 3 All ER 36 at 45–46.
237 [1993] 3 All ER 36 at 43–44.
238 [1986] AC 112.
239 [1986] AC 112 at 188. Lord Scarman was reviewing the old case law on the age at which children attained the age of discretion. This, in his view, reflected 'the attainment by a child of an age of sufficient discretion to exercise a *wise* choice in his or her own interests' (emphasis supplied).

context of the remainder of Lord Scarman's judgment; the ability to make wise choices did not feature at all in his test of *Gillick* competence.[240] Indeed, it would have been a startlingly paternalistic additional requirement had it done so.

Sir Thomas Bingham MR's following words indicate his appreciation of the need to promote children's capacity for independence by consulting them and respecting their wishes, but also his great concern to protect them from making damaging mistakes:

> 'First is the principle, to be honoured and respected, that children are human beings in their own right with individual minds and wills, views and emotions, which should command serious attention. A child's wishes are not to be discounted or dismissed simply because he is a child. He should be free to express them and decision-makers should listen. Second is the fact that a child is, after all, a child. The reason why the law is particularly solicitous in protecting the interests of children is because they are liable to be vulnerable and impressionable, lacking the maturity to weigh the longer term against the shorter, lacking the insight to know how they will react and the imagination to know how others will react in certain situations, lacking the experience to match the probable against the possible ...'[241]

These gently persuasive words have been referred to in many subsequent decisions. Indeed, in the light of such discernment, the court's final decision to refuse S's application to 'sack the OS' appeared entirely comprehensible. Here was an 11-year-old, so strongly influenced by his father that he obviously lacked sufficient understanding to participate without the services of a guardian ad litem in emotionally complex and highly fraught proceedings. But the apparent sagacity of this approach disguises a paternalism which makes the child's right to benefit from rule 9.2A entirely dependent on the courts' discretion, on a case-by-case basis, with little guidance over what criteria they will use. More importantly, paternalism should be justified by the need to protect children from dangerous choices, ones which will restrict their own capacity for choice in later life.[242] This was hardly the likely outcome of being given permission to litigate without the services of S's guardian ad litem, particularly as the final outcome would still be within the discretion of the court. More cogently, it is difficult to accept that the word 'understanding' in rule 9.2A carries such a restrictive meaning. This approach undermines its apparent intention, which is to provide intelligent children with a right to take independent action.

It is questionable how realistic it is to attempt to protect children like S from the stress of involvement in litigation when, as in his case, they have been the subject of acrimonious parental litigation for many years. It may undermine their faith in a legal system which appears to give rights with one hand but takes away with another.[243] For all these reasons it is arguable that the interpretation placed on rule 9.2A by Booth J in *Re H (a minor) (guardian ad litem: requirement)*[244] is preferable. It is surprisingly liberal, bearing in mind that H appeared to be in far more obvious need of protection than S. Though aged 15 and of high academic ability, H had come under

---

240 Ie a child gains 'the right to make his own decisions when he reaches a sufficient understanding and intelligence to be capable of making up his own mind on the matter requiring decision', per Lord Scarman, [1986] AC 112 at 186.
241 [1993] 3 All ER 36 at 46–47.
242 Discussed in chapter 1.
243 S's father indicated that, after the litigation, S took matters into his own hands, left his mother and went to live with his father. See H Stephens (1994) p 908.
244 [1994] 4 All ER 762.

the influence of a Mr R many years before, when he was only 6 and had, since then, become so dominated by him that he had totally rejected his parents. Mr R was now awaiting trial for serious sexual offences relating to another boy aged 14. As party to wardship proceedings, H was represented by the OS, acting as his guardian ad litem. H applied to rid himself of these services,[245] with a view to gaining his freedom to have unrestricted contact with Mr R.

Solicitors considering Booth J's judgment in *H*'s case will have a slightly clearer view of what skills to demand from children seeking to instruct them than the advice given by Sir Thomas Bingham MR in *S*'s case.[246] Booth J held that H had the understanding necessary to instruct his own legal adviser without the services of the OS, and her interpretation of rule 9.2A was a refreshingly pragmatic one. In her view, the test of whether a child has sufficient understanding for this should be judged in the light of all the circumstances of the case, past, present and future. Here, although H could not see the dangers posed by Mr R, he was not so much under his influence that his ability to think independently had been overborne by Mr R. He was over 15 and his progress at school indicated that he had a high academic ability. He had already been involved in the proceedings to a far greater extent than was desirable and it would be extremely artificial now to prevent him putting his own case to the court and testing the evidence.[247]

In Booth J's view, a child's capacity to litigate without the services of a guardian ad litem requires much more than the ability to instruct a solicitor regarding his or her own views on the desired outcome. The child must also have an ability to enter the court arena alongside the adult parties, to give evidence and be cross-examined. Furthermore, he or she must be capable of giving instructions on a variety of matters and making decisions, as and when the need arises.[248] Booth J's guidance over what skills children should have to instruct their solicitors was inevitably skewed by her experience of those few applications brought by children that get to court, rather than the many which do not. Solicitors experienced in representing children are more concerned with their ability to take part in preparing a case for a hearing than those regarding performance in court, giving evidence and dealing with cross-examination. It is perhaps unrealistic to insist on abilities that will probably never be necessary.[249]

This early case law provided relatively flimsy guidance to solicitors deciding whether to accept instructions from a child wishing to 'divorce his parents', or take out some other section 8 order.[250] Contrary to what some members of the judiciary assumed when these provisions were first introduced,[251] solicitors experienced in children's cases seem relatively conservative in their views regarding the competence of a child to instruct them. Sawyer's research suggests that their assessment of competence is based on a number of factors, including the child's ability to cope with

---

245 Under FPR 1991, r 9.2A(4) and (6).
246 [1993] 3 All ER 36.
247 [1994] 4 All ER 762 at 767.
248 [1994] 4 All ER 762 at 765.
249 C Sawyer (1995 a) p 177.
250 Discussed in chapter 4.
251 See Thorpe J (1994), who refers (p 21) to the solicitor 'whose ambition for success and acknowledgement is rampant ...' and who accepts instructions from a child client to gain local attention. See also Waite LJ in *Re T (a minor) (child: representation)* [1993] 4 All ER 518, who emphasised (at 529–530) that the courts were entitled to reject some 'maverick assessment' made by a solicitor who, despite acting sincerely, was taking an unreal or even absurd view of a child client's abilities to instruct him or her.

the tasks and emotional difficulties involved in litigation.[252] But by asserting a right to supervise solicitors' assessments of a child's 'understanding',[253] the courts force solicitors into adopting extreme caution when deciding whether or not to take instructions from a child client. Although caution may be entirely appropriate in such circumstances, solicitors are in an invidious position in so far as they are required to second-guess the courts' views on a child's capacity to instruct them. This is despite the judiciary's relative ignorance of the appropriate skills required from children seeking to instruct solicitors or of the reasons underpinning children's desire for their own advocates.

Subsequent case law appears to favour the approach taken by Booth J in *Re H*, with the courts taking a rather more relaxed approach, particularly in relation to the type of understanding required of children seeking leave to apply for section 8 orders.[254] It suggests that the judiciary have become more used to children litigating on their own behalf. Nevertheless, some still seem reluctant to acknowledge that protective restrictions may be too late for many of those claiming the right to pursue their own litigation. To attempt to protect them from pursuing litigation at the stage they get to court may achieve little more than shutting the stable door after the horse has bolted. For example, Johnson J's refusal to grant an intelligent 12-year-old leave to apply for a residence order because his evidence would be similar to that of his father, surely came too late to protect the boy from getting sucked into acrimonious litigation.[255] More cogently, the son's perspectives might well have been quite different from those of his father. Johnson J's decision suggests an inability to see children as independent individuals with litigation rights of their own. As Sawyer points out, a child gains far more from being made party to proceedings, than merely gaining the ability to inform the court of his wishes.[256] Overall, the manner in which section 10(8) has been interpreted suggests that serious consideration should be given to this provision being abolished entirely.[257] If it were abolished, further steps would be necessary to protect children from the emotional trauma of becoming involved in litigation with members of their own family. As suggested below, one possibility would be to introduce some form of compulsory mediation process for all children seeking to instruct their own solicitors.

252 See C Sawyer (1995 a). The solicitors interviewed (pp 114–122) were reluctant to accept instructions from children under 10. In their experience, the senior judiciary required children to be aged between 13 and 15, with the magistrates being prepared to accept competence in children from 10.

253 *Re T (a minor) (child: representation)* [1994] Fam 49.

254 Eg *Re C (residence: child's application for leave)* [1996] 1 FCR 461: a 14-year-old girl was granted leave under the Children Act 1989, s 10(8), despite her father's claim that she lacked objectivity and insight. See discussion in chapter 4. See also *Re S (contact: application by sibling)* [1999] Fam 283: Charles J accepted that a child aged 9 had sufficient understanding to apply (through her adoptive mother, as her next friend) for leave under the Children Act 1989, s 10(9) to proceed for a contact order so that she could visit her half-brother, now adopted.

255 *Re H (residence order: child's application for leave)* [2000] 1 FLR 780: the boy's father had also applied for a residence order, opposed by the mother. Per Johnson J (at 783) although the court would take account of the boy's views, neither the boy nor the court would benefit from his being separately represented in the case. See discussion in chapter 4, p 112.

256 C Sawyer (2001) p 205. Discussed in more detail in chapter 4.

257 See CASC (2002) para 12.6, referring to Dame Margaret Booth's strong view that children should not be required to seek the High Court's permission to commence proceedings because of the difficulties and delays such a process produces.

(C)   IS PRIVATE LITIGATION BAD FOR CHILDREN?

None of the provisions enabling children to conduct their own litigation gives them the ability to determine the outcome of legal disputes for themselves; this rests with the courts. Indeed, there is an important distinction between providing children with access to the courts and considering their wishes once there. Nevertheless, procedurally, the law has moved a long way towards reflecting the liberality of *Gillick v West Norfolk and Wisbech Area Health Authority*[258] by providing children with the means of forcing essentially private disputes into the public arena of the court. The dilemma is that involvement in the legal process, the giving of instructions and preparation for a hearing is a potentially hostile activity which may make a poor home situation much worse for the child. Consequently, the procedural rules enabling children to litigate on their own behalf remain controversial, with strong arguments for and against their retention, abolition or amendment.

Well-known academics who have written widely about the concept of children's rights appeared to approve of the methods whereby children gained a much wider access to the courts to resolve family disputes.[259] In their view this development was consistent with the general trend in the law, encouraged by the decision in *Gillick*, that children's growing capacity for eventual autonomy should be acknowledged and promoted. According to Bainham, children should be entitled to obtain some court affirmation of their own views on such matters in order 'to avoid the absolutism of parental authoritarianism or the extremes of child liberationism'.[260] Reinforcing Bainham's views, it could also be asserted that children in this country are expected to acquire education and skills that enable them to attain adult status at the age of 18 in an extremely sophisticated and technologically advanced society. It is impossible to reverse this trend; these same children naturally want active involvement in disputes that threaten to disrupt their lives fundamentally. Moreover, it seems reasonably self-apparent that litigation in itself is not the root of family dissension and that happy well-functioning families do not produce children willing to take part in legal proceedings. Children who wish to litigate are probably already suffering agonisingly unhappy situations. It may be far better for these children to end up in court applying for residence orders than running away from intolerable conditions.[261] They may gain enormously from the ability to take some measure of control over what happens to them.

There remain, however, considerable and well-reasoned doubts about allowing children to become involved in private proceedings. There is an overriding need to consider whether having a right to state an opinion is, in itself, sufficiently important to outweigh the risks of being involved in the process of litigation. The fact that children need to be heard in disputes, or even to initiate them, should not disguise the fact that the process of litigation may itself exacerbate relations at home and prevent existing rifts from healing over. As discussed above, Sawyer's research showed that the solicitors experienced in acting for children considered the whole process of litigation to be a damaging one. In their view, it inevitably reinforces existing tensions and polarises dissension, makes agreement impossible and undermines the ability of the family to function adequately in the future. Although many cases never get to

---

258   [1986] AC 112.
259   See, inter alia: M Freeman (1996); A Bainham (1994); J Roche (1995).
260   See A Bainham (1994) p 130.
261   See discussion in chapter 4.

court, the preparation for litigation may, in itself, be stressful. Solicitors must obtain instructions from their child clients on the evidence being given by the adults in the case and the ways in which they might be cross-examined on this evidence. Children may have to challenge their parents' veracity, or at least criticise them to an outsider and have their own views written down and presented to each parent.[262] By the time of the hearing, it is probably too late to protect the child from experiencing unpleasant evidence – the damage has already been done.[263] Even the most 'children's rightist' solicitors who had considerable experience in representing children in court had become ambivalent over the wisdom of allowing children to pursue private proceedings, in so far as they might have a corrosive effect on the whole structure of the family.[264]

The judiciary also express concerns that children litigating on their own behalf in private proceedings may end up traumatised by the experience. Such cases tend to arise in the context of bitter and long drawn out parental litigation. Parents sometimes try to exploit their children's capacity to litigate themselves, in order to improve their own position in their battle with the other parent. The child's application may be used to reopen issues already dealt with by an earlier order.[265] As in *Re HB (abduction: children's objections)*,[266] by dint of instructing a solicitor independently and then appealing against an earlier order obtained by one parent against the other, a child effectively takes over one side of a parental dispute. The impact of becoming involved in such acrimonious litigation can be immense. In that case, the court welfare officer considered that 11-year-old C was now 'much more burdened and sad about the legal contest, in which her parents, and now she herself, are engaged'.[267] Thorpe LJ observed that the 'case illustrates only too vividly the enormous price that is paid when children are permitted to litigate …'[268] Hale J later reconsidered whether C should return to Denmark, against her wishes and in the light of changed circumstances. She too expressed concern over C's active involvement in her parents' litigation and although she did not criticise C's solicitor for accepting instructions from C, she referred to the CWO's view that C was:

> 'not mature enough to be other than anecdotal in her taking up of a position. She is not capable of comparative analysis of her own life history or current circumstances. She is strongly influenced in her perception of right and wrong by very strong judgmental and monolithic feelings typical of a child of her age.'[269]

If CWOs assessed the maturity of many adults who litigate, they might reach similar conclusions. None the less, it would be wrong to discount these well-founded concerns over the existence of a procedural rule[270] which allows children like C to litigate without a guardian ad litem.

---

262 C Sawyer (1995 a) p 155.
263 C Sawyer (1995 a) pp 155 and 175.
264 C Sawyer (1995 a) p 162.
265 Eg *Re S (a minor) (independent representation* [1993] 3 All ER 36 and *Re K (replacement of guardian ad litem)* [2001] 1 FLR 663: in each case, the court considered that the child involved had been pressurised by his father into applying to dispense with the services of his guardian ad litem and reopen earlier issues.
266 Eg *Re HB (abduction: children's objections)* [1998] 1 FLR 422: Butler-Sloss LJ (at 429) criticised the father for allowing his 11-year-old daughter to fight his battles with her mother for him.
267 *Re HB (abduction: children's objections)* [1998] 1 FLR 422 at 427.
268 *Re HB (abduction: children's objections)* [1998] 1 FLR 422 at 427.
269 *Re HB (abduction: children's objections) (No 2)* [1998] 1 FLR 564 at 567.
270 FPR 1991, r 9.2A.

A right to be fully involved in legal proceedings may, in certain circumstances, be of sufficient importance to the child to outweigh the risks of being involved in the litigation process. Nevertheless, the concerns discussed above provide a useful warning about the dangers of assuming that by promoting children's 'rights' to have their say in court with a view to their achieving a measure of autonomy, their position will be improved. There is little comfort to be drawn from the knowledge that, once children get to court, their capacity for independence will depend on the court's own paternalistic perceptions of their best interests. Indeed, the situation reinforces the views of King and Piper that using the language of rights when dealing with disputes relating to children may result in them being treated like little adults without child-like characteristics.[271] Similarly, as Sawyer points out:

> 'The fundamental questions in family proceedings however are about the child's position *as a child*. They entail those questions about the child's relationship of dependency, especially emotional dependency, which are not scientific assessments of the separate psychological competence of the individual (assuming such a thing were possible) but are involved with considerations of the structure and the value of family life and how the child's life in the particular family may be affected by his very empowerment.'[272]

These concerns, which are also expressed by other practitioners,[273] do not necessarily indicate that children's rights to litigate should be withdrawn or, indeed, that the judiciary should restrict children's rights to instruct their own solicitors in a way that undermines the whole point of allowing children to litigate at all. Competent children have been given a procedural right to have their views advocated and the law has thereby accepted the importance of their being provided with separate representation. At the very least this process ensures that the child's views are taken seriously by his or her parents, leading to the possibility of a better mode of operating within the family. It is nevertheless immensely important to consider carefully whether sufficient effort is being made in the early stages of litigation to avoid children becoming involved in a damaging process before it is too late.

It has been suggested that an early referral to well-constructed child-centred mediation could provide a good means of protecting children, before the damaging process of preparation for litigation is started.[274] Despite the inherent dangers of looking on mediation as a universal panacea for all ills connected with litigation, it may avoid children becoming involved in a process which has a dangerous ability to polarise attitudes and reinforce hostility. But, as Sawyer points out, such a change should only be introduced with great care, to avoid children being thereby excluded from access to the courts. They might, for example, be threatened with the prospect of facilities for litigation being withdrawn, in the event of proving 'unco-operative' with the mediation process. A similar result might obtain in the event of a parent refusing to co-operate. Moreover, insufficient time devoted to investigating the child's wishes and feelings might lead to his or her being silenced entirely.

An improved fall-back position should be available for those cases where mediation fails and the child proceeds to litigation. A way of maintaining children's rights to have their views advocated, whilst ensuring that they do not become too damaged in the process, would be to provide all such children with the services of both a solicitor

271 M King and C Piper (1995) p 144.
272 C Sawyer (1995 b) p 193.
273 See chapter 4, p 110.
274 C Sawyer (1995 a) pp 180–182.

and children's guardian, as in the case of public law proceedings. The new legislative changes, discussed above, might allow such an appointment to be made.[275] A children's guardian would be able to provide the child with support throughout the course of the litigation and protect him or her from its most damaging aspects. It seems unlikely that there would be many cases of this kind emerging, since these children would have to overcome three obstacles before proceeding. They would be required to convince a solicitor of their competence to instruct him, complete the mediation process and, if still determined to litigate, obtain court leave under the Children Act 1989, section 10(8). The rare child emerging at the other end still wishing to proceed would assuredly require and deserve the services of both a children's guardian and solicitor.

(C) Public law proceedings

(i)   The tandem system of representation

The system established for the representation of children involved in public law proceedings is an impressive one and fully complies with the requirements of international instruments such as the CRC and the ECECR. The child is provided with full party status, automatic public funding and, regardless of age, will normally be provided with the services of a children's guardian,[276] in addition to those of a legal advocate. The former provides the court with an assessment of what outcome would be in the child's best interests, whilst the latter acts as the child's legal advocate in court and regards the child as his client. The children's guardian, who in pre-CAFCASS days was usually qualified in social work or an associated field, should be experienced at working with children and therefore able to provide the court with a detailed assessment of the needs of even very young children. The solicitor, whilst unable to assess the needs of the child, particularly if very young, has the legal skills necessary for representing the child in what are sometimes extremely complex legal hearings, involving a number of parties.

The children's guardian, 'in tandem' with the child's solicitor, will do a great deal of investigation work, often obtaining experts' assessments of the child's needs. The guardian's report to the court will provide information about the child's background, referring to the items on the welfare checklist,[277] and recommending an outcome deemed to be in the child's best interests. This system of representation, though excellent, conceals areas of practice indicating that neither the judiciary nor the children's' advisers always appreciate the importance to children of being able to present their own views and see for themselves the process by which a decision is reached. Problems have arisen where there is a conflict of opinion between an older and more articulate child and his or her children's guardian over the desired outcome of the proceedings. In such circumstances, if the child is deemed sufficiently mature, he or she should be allowed to instruct a solicitor independently and the children's

---

275 Ie under Children Act 1989, s 41(6A) and s 93(2)(bb) (as inserted by Adoption and Children Act 2002, s 122(1)–(2)).
276 See Children Act 1989, s 41(1), which creates a presumption that a children's guardian will be appointed in all 'specified proceedings', defined by s 41(6) as including all public law proceedings.
277 Ie Children Act 1989, s 1(3).

guardian will then instruct another solicitor to represent him or her. But perhaps because of a disagreement over the child's capacity to give such instructions,[278] this separation between child and guardian does not always occur.

Public law proceedings will often drastically disrupt children's lives. It is therefore understandable that they may wish to attend court and convey their views about the desired outcome; they may even wish to give evidence. Nevertheless, the extent to which children should be allowed to participate in public law proceedings is a controversial one. In theory, there is nothing to prevent the court hearing evidence directly from any child, as long as the court considers that he or she understands the duty to speak the truth and has sufficient understanding to give evidence.[279] In practice the courts have been extremely reluctant to allow a child, however old, to give evidence,[280] preferring to hear the child's account of what occurred to be relayed to them by adults under the relaxed hearsay rules.[281] This is because they almost always assume that for a child to appear in court and provide them with a first-hand account would be a damaging experience.[282]

Research shows that some, but not all,[283] children strongly favour being present at care or related proceedings,[284] quite reasonably arguing that, even if they cannot give evidence, they should at least be entitled to see and hear the process that determines their future.[285] Children have been automatic parties to public proceedings since 1975 and so, perhaps not unexpectedly, the rules appear to assume that they will attend.[286] Nevertheless, a decision whether to allow children to attend the hearing of their case is ultimately for the court, and case law in the early 1990s made clear the senior judiciary's scepticism of the merits of allowing children to attend public law proceedings.[287] This was closely followed by influential guidance indicating that

278 See discussion below.
279 Children Act 1989, s 96(1) and (2).
280 See *R v B County Council, ex p P* [1991] 1 WLR 221: the Court of Appeal approved the decision of the court below not to issue a witness summons requiring a 17-year-old girl to give evidence in care proceedings, so that she could be cross-examined by her father whom she had accused of sexually abusing her.
281 Children Act 1989, s 96(3)–(7) and Children (Admissibility of Hearsay Evidence) Order 1993, SI 1993/621.
282 Eg Ward J in *Nottinghamshire County Council v P* [1993] 1 FLR 514 at 519–520. He made clear his disapproval not only of the attendance in court of the two girls involved in the application but also of the local authority's intention of calling the eldest, aged 16, with learning difficulties, to give evidence in the proceedings, rather than relying on the guardian's account of her views.
283 Some children are strongly opposed to the idea of attending the court hearing. See J Masson and M Winn Oakley (1999) pp 114–115 and J McCausland (2000) pp 80 and 105.
284 Eg applications to discharge a care order.
285 See J Masson and M Winn Oakley (1999) p 115; M Ruegger (2001) pp 40–41; J McCausland (2000) pp 103–104.
286 FPR 1991, r 4.16(2)(a) and FPC (CA 1989) R 1991, r 16(2). Although the child is a party to the proceedings, the rules provide that the proceedings may take place in the absence of the child, if the court considers this to be in the child's best interests and the child is represented by a children's guardian or solicitor. The decision is for the court but the court will give the solicitor, children's guardian and the child, if of sufficient understanding, an opportunity to make representations on this.
287 Eg *Re C (a minor) (care: child's wishes)* [1993] 1 FLR 832: per Waite J (at 841) guardians should give the question 'very careful thought' before arranging for children to be present at appeals and should be 'prepared, if necessary, to explain their reasons to the judge.' See also *Re W (secure accommodation order: attendance at court)* [1994] 2 FLR 1092: per Ewbank J (at 1097), who suggested that courts should 'always bear in mind that attendance in court is likely to be harmful to the child', and should only allow it 'if satisfied that attendance is in the interests of the child'.

the child's attendance should, generally speaking, only be permitted 'where there is some clear benefit to the child', and that normally the guardian's presence would obviate such a need.[288] This had an immediate impact on practice. A growing body of research now indicates that many children who want to attend the court are not allowed to do so.[289]

Solicitors and guardians often prefer either not to consult the children at all over their possible attendance at court,[290] or to dissuade them from attending such a 'boring' occasion.[291] Their guardians may simply tell them that they are 'too young'.[292] Obviously such reluctance can be justified by appeals to the child's welfare. Children's guardians seem often to take a particularly cautious attitude to children's attendance, referring to such matters as the child's immaturity, the risks of the child being distressed by some of the evidence and by seeing parents, relatives and others, undergoing cross-examination, all of which may indicate non-attendance.[293] But a solicitor's reluctance to obtain a court direction permitting attendance may also be provoked by the knowledge that the local judiciary are generally opposed to it.[294] Some guardians and solicitors arrange to show the children round the empty courtroom instead, but perhaps, not surprisingly, the children do not often find such visits particularly helpful.[295]

The strict control exercised by the judiciary over children's attendance in public law proceedings stems from a well meaning concern to 'some of the most damaged and disadvantaged children in our community'.[296] But they perhaps overlook the fact that children who are the focus of public law proceedings know better than anyone what has happened to them and that it may be entirely appropriate for them to be present at the final stages of a process which will affect their lives fundamentally. It may be far too late to protect them from exposure to potentially damaging material. This over-protective approach seems anomalous, particularly when compared with the present practice of calling very young children of 4 or 5 to act as witnesses in criminal trials, whether they wish to do so or not.[297] It also reinforces the impression that in public law proceedings a child is often incidental to the main focus of the proceedings, which is a conflict between state and parents.[298]

It seems unlikely that this judicial attitude will survive for much longer, with solicitors becoming more aware of children's rights and the importance of their being involved in decision-making.[299] Children might claim that article 6 of the ECHR, with its demands for a fair trial, supports such a wish. Furthermore, they might argue

---

288 Children Act Advisory Committee (1994) p 45. See also Children Act Advisory Committee (1997) p 36, indicating that the magistrates' courts should follow suit on this.

289 See J Masson and M Winn Oakley (1999) pp 112–113; M Ruegger (2001) pp 40–41; J McCausland (2000) pp 103–104.

290 See J Masson and M Winn Oakley (1999) p 112 and J McCausland (2000) pp 79–80.

291 J Masson and M Winn Oakley (1999) p 112.

292 J McCausland (2000) p 104.

293 See J Masson and M Winn Oakley (1999) pp 110–111.

294 J Masson and M Winn Oakley (1999) p 112.

295 J Masson and M Winn Oakley (1999) p 110.

296 *Re W (secure accommodation order: attendance at court)* [1994] 2 FLR 1092: the OS explained to Ewbank J (at 1095) that children of this kind (those who were the subject of applications for care orders and secure accommodation orders), would not benefit from sitting through the proceedings to the end.

297 Discussed in chapter 17.

298 Discussed in chapter 15.

299 J Masson and M Winn Oakley (1999) p 111.

that since a care order removing them from their parents would materially affect their family life, their procedural rights under article 8[300] would be infringed were they not provided with any chance to influence the outcome directly. But if more children start attending public law proceedings, as McCausland correctly comments, the nature of public hearings, both in terms of waiting room environment and timing of cases, must become far more 'child-friendly'.[301]

In one area, it appears that judicial attitudes are already changing. In an increasingly rights-based culture, the old judicial approach to children's attendance at secure accommodation hearings seems astonishingly anachronistic. Children would be excluded because, unlike criminal proceedings, they did not have a right to be present because they did not need it. Whereas in criminal proceedings the child's liberty was being curtailed to punish him or her, the secure accommodation jurisdiction was, according to Ewbank J, a 'benign' one designed to 'protect the child'.[302] Since then, the judiciary seem far more aware that it is unrealistic to expect a child to see a secure accommodation order as anything other than a Draconian measure[303] designed to lock him or her up. They now stress that, since these orders deprive children of their liberty, there is a need to comply strictly with all the procedural requirements of the Children Act 1989, section 25, plus the rules of natural justice.[304] Children are now being allowed to attend such proceedings more routinely[305] and are provided with effective legal representation.[306] Today, the subject of secure accommodation proceedings could challenge any attempt to exclude him or her from court, on the basis this would infringe his or her rights under article 6 of the ECHR.

It is questionable whether present guardian practice relating to the contents of their reports[307] is entirely satisfactory. Although the child should always see copies of all reports in secure accommodation proceedings,[308] practice varies in other types of case. Most, but not all, guardians consider it appropriate to discuss with the children the part of their report devoted to the child's own wishes. Few, however, discuss the remainder of the report or show the whole report to the children, even if they are older,

---

300   *McMichael v United Kingdom* (1995) 20 EHRR 205 and *W (and R, O, B and H) v United Kingdom* (1987) 10 EHRR 29.
301   J McCausland (2000) p 105.
302   *Re W (secure accommodation order: attendance at court)* [1994] 2 FLR 1092 at 1096, per Ewbank J. He rejected a 10-year-old boy's appeal against being refused permission to attend the hearing of a local authority application for a secure accommodation order. Not only would it not benefit them to attend, but such children might disturb the court with their unruliness.
303   Per Booth J in *Re W (a minor) (secure accommodation order)* [1993] 1 FLR 692 at 696 and per Butler-Sloss LJ in *Re M (a minor)* [1995] 1 FLR 418 at 423.
304   Eg *Re AS (secure accommodation order)* [1999] 1 FLR 103: Bracewell J quashed an interim secure accommodation order because the stipendiary magistrate had made it, knowing that the 12-year-old boy had not himself received notice of the application, had not instructed his solicitor or counsel and had no guardian ad litem appointed to represent him. See also *LM v Essex County Council* [1999] 1 FLR 988.
305   See, inter alia: *Re C (secure accommodation order: representation)* [2001] EWCA Civ 458, [2001] 2 FLR 169: C attended the s 25 hearing and gave evidence in person; *Re K (a child) (secure accommodation order: right to liberty)* [2001] 1 FLR 526: K had been allowed, on appeal, to attend the s 25 hearings. Dame Elizabeth Butler-Sloss P acknowledged (at para 44) that it had been 'very beneficial' for him to b allowed to play a part and to have some understanding of the legal procedures depriving him of his liberty.
306   *Re AS (secure accommodation order)* [1999] 1 FLR 103. But see *Re C (secure accommodation order: representation)* [2001] EWCA Civ 458, [2001] 2 FLR 169, discussed below.
307   The report must be filed with the court and a copy served on all the parties. FPR 1991, r 4.11A(7) and FPCR 1991, r 11A(6).
308   See FPR r 4.25(e).

for fear of distressing them with its contents.[309] Some children know that the report will be seen by their parents, others only discover much later, to their great distress and anger, that information they gave the guardian, is now known to their parents, the latter having read a copy of the guardian's report themselves.[310] It is arguable that a guardian's failure to provide an older child with a copy of his or her report infringes the child's rights to a fair trial under article 6 of the ECHR, even in cases where the child's liberty is not in question.[311] Furthermore, as Masson and Oakley point out, if older children are left unaware of the contents of a guardian's report, they are also unaware of any potential conflict between their own wishes and the outcome being recommended by the guardian. Consequently, these children will not get the chance to give their solicitor independent instructions, as envisaged by the rules of court.[312]

(ii)   Children instructing their own solicitors in public law proceedings

(a)   COMPETENCE TO INSTRUCT A SOLICITOR

In public law proceedings, articulate and intelligent teenagers may have very firm views over the desired outcome of a local authority's application, but they may not accord with the perceptions of the children's guardian regarding their best interests. In such a conflict, a teenager might certainly expect, under the Family Proceedings Rules, to have the right to instruct a solicitor without the intervention of a guardian. Indeed, the children's guardian is expected to bring this matter to the attention of the court promptly,[313] and advise the court whether the child is capable of instructing his or her solicitor independently. But the child's solicitor can only take instructions if satisfied that the child is 'able, having regard to his understanding, to give such instructions on his own behalf in which case he shall conduct the proceedings in accordance with instructions received from the child'.[314] A clear divergence of views between a mature child and his or her guardian should trigger a discussion between the guardian and solicitor about the child's ability to instruct the latter independently, with the guardian then seeking his own legal assistance.

Clearly, public proceedings throw up rather different problems to those arising in private disputes[315] when it comes to assessing a child's competence to instruct a solicitor. Children are often the subject of applications by the local authority because of serious concerns about the level of their care at home. Abusive treatment may have produced disturbed behaviour which undermines the ability of adolescent children, however intelligent, to take part in such litigation. Thorpe J considered that the rules must be interpreted sensibly in such cases and that a child –

---

309   J Masson and M Winn Oakley (1999) pp 103–105 and J McCausland (2000) p 77.
310   M Ruegger (2001) p 37.
311   Responding to *McMichael v United Kingdom* (1995) 20 EHRR 205, the Scottish children's hearing system was amended, requiring all Reporters to give copies of all reports and papers relating to the proceedings, not only to the child's parents, but also to the child himself, except where it would cause him significant harm. See discussion in *S v Principal Reporter and Lord Advocate* [2001] UKHRR 514 at [28]–[29].
312   Discussed below.
313   Per Wall J in *Re M (minors) (care proceedings: child's wishes)* [1994] 1 FLR 749 at 753–754.
314   FPR 1991, r 4.12(1) and FPCR 1991, r 12(1).
315   Discussed above.

'must have sufficient rationality within the understanding to instruct a solicitor. It may well be that the level of emotional disturbance is such as to remove the necessary degree of rationality that leads to coherent and consistent instruction.'[316]

Nevertheless, emotional disturbance amongst clients is not confined to children, and solicitors are well able to take this factor into account when judging the capacity of a child client to give them instructions.

In practice, solicitors normally rely on the guardian to advise them on the child's competence to give legal instructions. Some consider that guardians adopt unduly 'protectionist' attitudes in this respect and influence solicitors, by suggesting that children are too 'disturbed' even to be interviewed by them.[317] Any disagreement between children's guardian and solicitor over the child's capacity to instruct a solicitor independently must be settled by the court.[318] If the court agrees with the guardian, it could conceivably refuse to allow the child to proceed with his or her solicitor, despite the solicitor's own view of the child's capacity to instruct him.[319]

(b)   THE CHILD'S RIGHT TO INSTRUCT A SOLICITOR DIRECTLY

Research suggests that mature children seldom instruct their solicitors directly, despite this being envisaged by the court rules.[320] There are various reasons for this. As noted above, the practice of restricting children's access to the guardian's report conceals possible conflicts between the children's guardian and child, since a young person who is unaware of what their guardian is saying, cannot agree or disagree with it.[321] Even in cases where a clear conflict has arisen between child and guardian, either the child's solicitor or guardian may seek to deter the child from seeking to instruct the solicitor directly, for fear of antagonising the court.[322] Research also suggests that some practitioners leave a decision over a conflict between child and guardian until the last minute, in the hope that the child will come round to agreeing with the guardian.[323] Case law bears this out.[324] There is also a reluctance to change the existing arrangements for fear of losing the fixture for the hearing.[325]

Appeals brought by older children on the basis that they should have been given a right to instruct their solicitor directly have not always been dealt with particularly sympathetically. Thus in *Re H (a minor) (care proceedings: child's wishes)*[326] Thorpe J showed little sympathy with the view that a mature child's right to instruct a solicitor

316   *Re H (a minor) (care proceedings: child's wishes)* [1993] 1 FLR 440 at 449.
317   See D Clark (1996) p 114.
318   Per Wall J in *Re M (minors) (care proceedings: child's wishes)* [1994] 1 FLR 749 at 754.
319   Eg *Re K, W and H (minors) (medical treatment)* [1993] 1 FLR 854. The guardians ad litem who represented the three girls in the original public law proceedings indicated that they lacked capacity to instruct a solicitor. Thorpe J preferred this advice to the view of their legal advisers that they were perfectly capable of giving legal instructions.
320   J Masson and M Winn Oakley (1999) p 77.
321   J Masson and M Winn Oakley (1999) pp 105–106.
322   J Masson and M Winn Oakley (1999) p 78. See also C Sawyer (2000 a) p 111.
323   C Sawyer (1995 a) p 152.
324   Eg *Re H (a minor) (care proceedings: child's wishes)* [1993] 1 FLR 440 and *Re M (minors) (care proceedings: child's wishes)* [1994] 1 FLR 749.
325   Eg *Re P (representation)* [1996] 1 FLR 486: an appeal was allowed against Douglas Brown J's refusal to allow a teenage girl separate representation from that of her six siblings. He had considered that acting on the application at such a late stage would abort the hearing.
326   [1993] 1 FLR 440.

directly has a value of its own and, if breached, should vitiate the outcome. He refused an appeal against a care order by an intelligent 16-year-old because there was plenty of evidence justifying the care order and so:

'It seems to me that to order a retrial would simply be to commit everybody to delay, expense, stress, uncertainty and anxiety – all in the aid of the apparent cause of removing S's sense of grievance and meeting Mrs Malcolm's [his counsel] objection that justice must be seen to be done.'[327]

Pragmatism and paternalism may be necessary to protect children from making dangerous mistakes, but here a retrial would merely have led to delay, not in itself as dangerous as losing the boy's co-operation with those trying to ensure his recovery.[328]

The Court of Appeal adopted a similarly negative attitude to the child's right to effective legal representation in *Re C (secure accommodation order: representation)*.[329] In that case, prior to the hearing of a secure accommodation application, C, a 15-year-old girl had had only two hours to instruct her solicitor, in a public area of the court building, on how to respond to a 14-page supporting statement from the local authority. Despite the Court of Appeal's obvious sympathy with her arguments that there had been procedural irregularities,[330] it confirmed the original secure accommodation order because it considered that her appeal would have resulted in such an order being made in any event. As Masson observes, this approach is regrettable, given that secure accommodation applications provide little opportunity for challenge.[331]

The Court of Appeal in *Re C* recognised that children's rights to a fair trial under article 6 of the ECHR are particularly important in cases involving applications for secure accommodation orders, where a deprivation of liberty is the outcome. It nevertheless made no mention of the Strasbourg jurisprudence interpreting this provision. Despite its view that secure accommodation proceedings do not qualify as criminal proceedings for the purposes of article 6, the court conceded that the rights accorded by article 6(3) to those charged with criminal offences should be applied, 'as a matter of procedural fairness' to young people involved in secure accommodation proceedings.[332] But, having made such a concession, the Court of Appeal failed to refer specifically to the requirement in article 6(3)(b) that the accused should have 'adequate time and facilities' to prepare his defence, nor to any case law supporting it.[333] Given the facts of the case, C might have complained that she had not been given 'adequate time and facilities'. But, in any event, since she had very little time to oppose a well-prepared application from her 'opponent' (in this instance, the local authority), it was arguable that her rights under article 6(1)[334] to 'equality of arms' were infringed. After all, as a party to litigation, she was at a substantial disadvantage to her opponent.[335] The Court of Appeal's response that the order should stand, since

---

327 [1993] 1 FLR 440 at 450.
328 But cf *Re P (representation)* [1996] 1 FLR 486 at 488: per Thorpe LJ: it was impossible for an advocate to support the local authority's care plan for some siblings, whilst at the same time mounting 'an all-out attack upon that care plan on behalf of the one dissenting child'.
329 [2001] EWCA Civ 458, [2001] 2 FLR 169.
330 [2001] EWCA Civ 458, [2001] 2 FLR 169: see particularly Brooke LJ at [38]–[41].
331 See J Masson (2002) p 90.
332 [2001] EWCA Civ 458, [2001] 2 FLR 169 per Brooke LJ at [34].
333 Eg *Goddi v Italy* (1984) 6 EHRR 457 (para 31).
334 Which applies to civil as well as criminal proceedings.
335 *Dombo v Beheer B V v Netherlands* (1993) 18 EHRR 213 (para 33).

a secure accommodation order would have been the outcome of any appeal, smacks of highhandedness. One wonders whether the Court of Appeal would have thought it appropriate to respond in this way to an adult making similar complaints.

(c)   A GOOD QUALITY SYSTEM OF REPRESENTATION?

No system is perfect and, as discussed above, problems arise in public law proceedings, particularly if children's solicitors, guardians and courts fail to respect the child's own important procedural rights. Indeed, in the view of Masson and Oakley, the children in their research project did not benefit sufficiently from their party status. They often only had limited access to their legal representatives and their guardians tended to discourage their active participation in the proceedings.[336] These researchers urge that a mature young person's party status should be made far more of a reality, by, for example, strengthening their relationship with their legal representatives, by reducing the guardian's tight control over matters and by reducing the court's discretion over attendance at hearings.[337]

Despite these criticisms, overall there is no doubt that the system of representation for children involved in public law proceedings is a good one. Indeed, it has been held up to European legal systems as 'one of the most successful legal reforms of all times'.[338] Though expensive, the virtually automatic appointment of a guardian and solicitor can be justified with little difficulty. The dispute is a three-cornered one between local authority, child and parents. The children involved have no choice over the initiation of the application, nor any control over the process, and the outcome will materially affect their way of life, if they are taken away from home or deprived of their liberty. The need for a children's guardian and a solicitor is borne out by the difficulties referred to above, in the context of private law proceedings, when such representation has not been available. In public law proceedings, the investigative and supportive tasks can safely be left to the guardian and this system of dual representation helps maintain a balance between the state's role as protector of the child and the autonomy of the family.

(D)   Children seeing the judge in private

One way of providing children with an assurance that their views over legal disputes are taken seriously is for the judiciary to see and talk to them in private. Although there is no practice direction or, indeed, any specific rules on the matter,[339] it is well established that High Court and county court judges are entitled to see children in the privacy of their chambers. Whether a judge should see a child in private is a personal matter to determine for himself,[340] but at one stage this practice appeared to

---

336   J Masson and M Winn Oakley (1999) p 117.
337   J Masson and M Winn Oakley (1999) p 117.
338   See Association of Lawyers for Children (1998 b) para 1.5, quoting from an unpublished paper by Professor L Salgo, commissioned by the German government, comparing the current systems for representing children throughout the world.
339   Per Booth J in *Re M (child)* [1993] 2 FLR 706 at 709.
340   Per Ormrod LJ in *D v D (custody of child)* (1981) 2 FLR 74.

be very common, favoured by many.[341] Some seem to consider that it is acceptable in public law proceedings[342] but are much more ambivalent about its desirability in private law proceedings, mainly because of the difficulties involved in having to pass on any relevant information to the parents themselves.[343] Some consider that little would be achieved by talking to the child, particularly when the chances are that the decision will not fulfil the child's wishes.[344] Whilst the senior judiciary can see children privately if they wish, there has been some doubt over whether magistrates should do so.[345] It is difficult to understand why the senior judiciary should maintain the right to talk to children, whilst asserting that magistrates should not.

Case law[346] and research[347] indicates that some children want to see the judiciary dealing with their case in order to put their views forward, and that they feel extremely frustrated if they are refused such an opportunity.[348] But there are real doubts about whether such an interview really benefits children. They may feel bullied by the judge voicing his own views. It may be difficult for members of the judiciary to pick up the nuances underlying children's expressed views in a very short interview, however sympathetically carried out. More fundamentally, since the adults involved in the dispute will not be privy to such a conversation, the rules of natural justice, as reflected in the requirements of article 6(1) of the ECHR, require the parents to be given this information and have an opportunity to address the judge on it.[349] But even then it is arguable that there is an element of unfairness, unless the information provided by the child can be tested subsequently in cross-examination.[350] Children

---

341 *H v H (child: judicial interview)* [1974] 1 All ER 1145: per Megaw LJ (at 1147) it was often most desirable that the judge hearing the case should see the children otherwise than in open court. But he warned that in doing so, a judge should never promise the children that anything disclosed to him would be kept secret, since this would hamper any appeal.

342 Eg *Re M (minors) (care proceedings: child's wishes)* [1994] 1 FLR 749: per Wall J (at 755) an intelligent and articulate 12-year-old with 'an excellent grasp of the issues' was 'entitled to see the judge who was to decide his future'. He had, however, explained to the boy that his wishes could not be followed if they were not considered to be in his best interests.

343 Eg *B v B (minors) (interviews and listing arrangements)* [1994] 2 FLR 489: per Wall J (at 495) there was an inherent contradiction in seeing the children for the purpose of ascertaining their wishes, whilst at the same time being obliged to report to the parents anything material they said.

344 Eg *Re R (a minor) (residence: religion)* [1993] 2 FLR 163: per Purchas LJ (at 174), who indicated that since the judge at first instance had been perfectly aware of the 9-year-old child's views, transmitted to the court by the court welfare officer, to interview him would have been 'totally counter-productive'.

345 *Re M (child)* [1993] 2 FLR 706: per Booth J (p 710) magistrates should only see the child 'in rare and exceptional cases', particularly if the court welfare officer or guardian ad litem has already done so and reported to the court on the child's wishes.

346 Eg *Re S (a minor) (independent representation)* [1993] 3 All ER 36 and *Re R (a minor) (residence: religion)* [1993] 2 FLR 163.

347 See M Ruegger (2001) p 41.

348 See H Stephens (1994) p 908. Stephens was S's father in *Re S (a minor) (independent representation)* [1993] 3 All ER 36. He criticised the trial judge's refusal to meet S to discuss his views and called for a practice direction requiring judges to interview all children who wish to speak to them

349 See *B v B (minors) (interviews and listing arrangements)* [1994] 2 FLR 489 at 496, per Wall J. NB in *McMichael v United Kingdom* (1995) 20 EHRR 205 the European Court of Human Rights emphasised that *all* information available to the children's hearing should also be available to the parents.

350 When discussing the draft court rules prepared under the Children Act 1989, the Home Office and the Department of Health voiced this concern.

informed by the judge of his obligation to pass relevant information on to the parents might well feel quite unable to provide the judge with any frank view of their wishes regarding which parent they most want to live with.[351] If the representation of children in private proceedings was improved, the practice whereby members of the judiciary see children in private could safely terminate altogether.

(5)   CONCLUSION

This chapter assesses the extent to which the legal system helps children cope with family disputes which may end up in court. The demands of article 12 of the CRC are relatively simple. Children should be consulted over decisions reached regarding their future upbringing. But the extent to which domestic law fulfils this ideal is extremely variable. Although we know that many children whose parents separate and divorce suffer considerable psychological distress, large numbers are left entirely to their own devices. Indeed, the pressure imposed on separating parents to settle their disputes out of court often reinforces their children's isolation, ensuring that outsiders are kept totally unaware of their unhappiness and helplessness, with plans for their upbringing being made over their heads. Meanwhile, the various groups of practitioners called in to assist parents sort out their affairs on separation and divorce all dodge responsibility for supporting and counselling the children whose futures are being decided. Whilst CAFCASS might have plugged this particular gap, its teething problems have been exacerbated by a government reluctant to give it sufficient resources to become well founded, far less to initiate a support service for the adults and children caught up in acrimonious battles.

For the children who become the focus of litigation of varying kinds, the contrast between provision for children involved in public law proceedings and those who are the subject of private parental litigation has started diminishing. Nevertheless, whilst the first group is served by a system of representation widely considered to be ideal, the second group remain lucky to be represented at all. Finally, at the other end of the spectrum, mature children are empowered to litigate on their own behalf, as if they were adults, irrespective of the damage that doing so may have on their relationships with members of their families. Overall, the incoherence in the law and procedures gives the impression that children's well being is not particularly high on the policy makers' agenda. Improvements have started to trickle into the system – hopefully these will carry sufficient government funding to make them effective.

351   Eg *B v B (minors) (interviews and listing arrangements)* [1994] 2 FLR 489.

BIBLIOGRAPHY

NB many of these publications can be obtained on the relevant organisation's website.

Advisory Board on Family Law, *First Annual Report* (1998) Lord Chancellor's Department.

Advisory Board on Family Law, *Second Annual Report* 1998/1999 (1999) Lord Chancellor's Department.

Association of Lawyers for Children, 'The Future of Representation for Children' (1998 a) Family Law 403.

Association of Lawyers for Children, *Response of the Association of Lawyers for Children to the Support Services in Family Proceedings – Future Organisation of Court Welfare Services* (1998 b).

Bailey-Harris R, Barron J and Pearce J, 'Settlement culture and the use of the "no order" principle under the Children Act 1989' (1999) 11 Child and Family Law Quarterly 53.

Bainham A, '"See you in court, Mum": children as litigants' (1994) 6 Journal of Child Law 127.

Bradley C, 'The Family Law Protocol – revolution or evolution?' (2002) New Law Journal 495.

Buchanan A et al, *Families in conflict: Perspectives of children and parents on the Family Court Welfare Service* (2001) The Policy Press.

Cantwell B and Scott S, 'Children's wishes, children's burdens' (1995) 17 Journal of Social Welfare and Family Law 337.

Children Act Advisory Committee, *Annual Report 1993/4* (1994) Lord Chancellor's Department.

Children Act Advisory Committee, *Final Report 1997* (1997) Lord Chancellor's Department.

Children Act Sub-Committee of the Advisory Board on Family Law (CASC), *A Report to the Lord Chancellor on the Question of Parental Contact with Children in Cases Where There is Domestic Violence* (2000) Lord Chancellor's Department.

Children Act Sub-Committee of the Advisory Board on Family Law (CASC), *Making Contact Work* Report of the Children Act Sub-Committee (2002) Lord Chancellor's Department.

Clark D, 'The older child in care proceedings' (1996) Family Law 113.

College of Family Mediators, *Practice Guidelines: The Consultation of Children and Young People in Family Mediation* (2002) UK.

Committee on the Rights of the Child, *Concluding Observations of the Committee on the Rights of the Child: United Kingdom of Great Britain and Northern Ireland* CRC/C/15/Add 188 (2002) Centre for Human Rights, Geneva.

Council of Europe, *Explanatory Report to the European Convention on the Exercise of Children's Rights* (1997) Council of Europe Publishing.

Davis G and Pearce J, 'On the Trail of the Welfare Principle' (1999 a) Family Law 144.

Davis G and Pearce J, 'The Welfare Principle in Action' (1999 b) Family Law 237.

Davis G and Pearce J, 'A View from the Trenches – Practice and Procedure in Section 8 Applications' (1999 c) Family Law 457.

Davis G and Pearce J, 'The Hybrid Practitioner' (1999 d) Family Law 547.

Davis G et al, 'Family Mediation – Where Do We Go From Here?' (2001) Family Law 265.

Day Sclater S and Piper C ,'Social Exclusion and the Welfare of the Child' (2001) Journal of Law and Society 409.

Department of Health (DH), *The Children Act 1989, Guidance and Regulations* Vol 1 *Court Orders* (1991) Department of Health.

Department of Health (DH), Home Office, Lord Chancellor's Department and the Welsh Office (DH et al), *Support Services in Family Proceedings – Future Organisation of Court Welfare Services* Consultation Paper, LASSL (98) 11 (1998) Department of Health Publications.

Douglas G, Murch M and Perry A, 'Supporting children when parents separate – a neglected family justice or mental health issue?' (1996) 8 Child and Family Law Quarterly 121.

Douglas G et al, 'Safeguarding Children's Welfare in Non-Contentious Divorce: Towards a New Conception of the Legal Process?' (2000) 63 Modern Law Review 177.

Douglas G et al, 'Children's perspectives and experience of the divorce process' (2001) Family Law 373.

Dunn J and Deater-Deckard K, *Children's views of their changing families* (2001) Joseph Rowntree Foundation.

Eurostat, *Eurostat Yearbook 2001* (2001) Eurostat.

Freeman M, 'Can Children Divorce Their Parents?' in M Freeman (ed) *Divorce Where Next* (1996) Dartmouth.

Gee I ,'Tales of the Unexpected – A Child's Perspective on a Family Breakup' (1999) Family Law 49.

Gerlis S, 'Cafcass – Twisted Knickers' (2002) Family Law 144.

Greatbatch D and Dingwall R, 'The Marginalization of Domestic Violence in Divorce Mediation' (1999) 13 International Journal of Law, Policy and the Family 174

Hester M and Radford L, *Domestic violence and child contact arrangements in England and Denmark* (1996) The Policy Press.

Hester M et al, *Domestic Violence: A national survey of court welfare and voluntary sector mediation practice* (1997) The Policy Press.

Home Office, *National Standards for Probation Service Family Court Welfare Work* (1994) Home Office.

Hunt J and Lawson J, *Crossing the Boundaries* (1999) National Council for Family Proceedings.

Johnston C, 'Litigants Who Lack Capacity' (2001) Family Law 515.

Kaganas F and Piper C, 'Divorce and Domestic Violence' in C Piper and S Day Sclater (eds) *Undercurrents of Divorce* (1999) Dartmouth.

Killerby M, Directorate of Legal Affairs, Council of Europe, 'The draft European Convention on the exercise of children's rights' (1995) 3 International Journal on Children's Rights 127.

King M, 'Playing the Symbols – Custody and the Law Commission' (1987) Family Law 186.

King M and Piper C, *How the Law Thinks About Children* (1995) Arena.

Law Commission, *Review of Child Law, Guardianship and Custody* Law Com No 172, HC 594 (1988) HMSO.

Law Society, *Guidance on Acting for Children in Private Law Proceedings under the Children Act 1989* (1994) The Law Society Legal Practice Directorate.

Lord Chancellor's Department, *The Children Act Advisory Committee Annual Report 1993/4* (1994) The Lord Chancellor's Department.

Lord Chancellor's Department, *Government's Response to the Report of the Children Act Sub-Committee of the Lord Chancellor's Advisory Board on Family Law 'Making Contact Work'* (2002).

Lyon C et al, *Effective Support Services for Children and Young People when Parental Relationships Break Down: A Child-Centred Approach* (1998) University of Liverpool.

McCausland J, *Guarding Children's Interests: The Contribution of Guardians ad Litem in Court Proceedings* (2000) The Children's Society.

Marshall K, *Children's Rights in the Balance: The Participation – Protection Debate* (1997) The Stationery Office.

Masson J and Winn Oakley M, *Out of Hearing: Representing Children in Care Proceedings* (1999) John Wiley and Sons.

Masson M, '*Re K (A Child) (Secure Accommodation Order: Right to Liberty) and Re C (Secure Accommodation Order: Representation)* Securing human rights for children and young people in secure accommodation' (2002) 14 Child and Family Law Quarterly 77.

Meltzer H and Gatward R, *Mental health of children and adolescents in Great Britain* (2000) The Stationery Office.

Mitchell A, *Children in the Middle: Living Through Divorce* (1985) Tavistock Publications Ltd.

Murch M et al, *Safeguarding Children's Welfare in Uncontentious Divorce: A Study of s 41 of the Matrimonial Causes Act 1973* Research Series No 7/99 (1999) Lord Chancellor's Department.

National Council of Voluntary Childcare Organisations, *The Parenting Plan* (2002) Lord Chancellor's Department.

National Youth Advocacy Service (NYAS), 'Newsline Extra' (2001) Family Law 235.

Office for National Statistics, *Marriage, divorce and adoption statistics* Series FM2 no 28 (2002) HMSO.

O'Quigley, A *Listening to children's views: The findings and recommendations of recent research* (2000) Joseph Rowntree Foundation.

Piper C, 'Ascertaining the Wishes and Feelings of the Child' (1997) Family Law 796.

Piper C, 'Barriers to Seeing and Hearing Children in Private Law Proceedings' (1999 a) Family Law 394.

Piper C, 'The Wishes and Feelings of the Child' in S Day Sclater and C Piper (eds) *Undercurrents of Divorce* (1999 b) Dartmouth.

Piper C and Day Sclater S, 'Changing Divorce' in C Piper and S Day Sclater (eds) *Undercurrents of Divorce* (1999) Dartmouth.

Poyser A, 'The Way Forward: CAFCASS and the Future for the Representation of Children in Family Proceedings' in M Ruegger (ed) *Hearing the Voice of the Child: The representation of children's interests in public law proceedings* (2001) Russell House Publishing.

Richards M, 'But what about the children? Some reflections on the divorce White Paper' (1995) 7 Child and Family Law Quarterly 223.

Richards M, 'The Interests of Children at Divorce' in M Meulders-Klein (ed) *Families and Justice* (1997) Bruylant.

Roche J, 'Children's rights: in the name of the child' (1995)17 Journal of Social Welfare and Family Law 281.

Ruegger M, 'Children's Experiences of the Guardian ad litem Service and Public Law Proceedings' in M Ruegger (ed) *Hearing the voice of the child: The representation of children's interests in public law proceedings* (2001) Russell House Publishing.

Sawyer C, *The Rise and Fall of the Third Party: Solicitors' Assessments of the Competence of Children to Participate in Family Proceedings* (1995 a) Centre for Socio-Legal Studies.

Sawyer C, 'The Competence of Children to Participate in Family Proceedings' (1995 b) 7 Child and Family Law Quarterly 180.

Sawyer C, 'One step forward, two steps back – the European Convention on the Exercise of Children's Rights' (1999) 11 Child and Family Law Quarterly 151.

Sawyer C, 'An Inside Story: Professional Practices in Public Law' (2000 a) Family Law 109.

Sawyer C, 'An Inside Story: Ascertaining the Child's Wishes and Feelings' (2000 b) Family Law 170.

Sawyer C, 'Applications by children: Still seen but not heard?' (2001) 117 Law Quarterly Review 203.

Smart C et al, *The Changing Experience of Childhood: Families and Divorce* (2001) Polity Press.

Solicitors Family Law Association, *Guide to Good Practice for Solicitors Acting For Children* (2002) SFLA.

Stephens H, 'Independent representation' (1994) 144 New Law Journal 907.

Thorpe J, 'Independent Representation for Children' (1994) Family Law 20.

UK College of Family Mediators, *Children and Young People and Family Mediation: Policy and Practice Guidelines* (2002).

White R, 'Family Practice' (2001 a) 151 New Law Journal 1399.

White R, 'Family Practice' (2001 b) 151 New Law Journal 1567.

White R, Carr P and Lowe N, *The Children Act in Practice* (2002) Butterworths.

Chapter 8

Children in court – their welfare, wishes and feelings

(1) INTRODUCTION

When deciding what is in a child's best interests, the courts are directed to have regard to 'the ascertainable wishes and feelings of the child concerned (considered in the light of his age and understanding)'.[1] But despite its importance, demonstrated by its foremost position in the 'welfare checklist',[2] the courts are expected to achieve a result which most accords with adult notions of children's best interests, whether or not it accords with their wishes. The overtly paternalistic welfare principle[3] clearly justifies a court discounting information about children's views if it considers that they lack insight over their own needs. It can rely on a wealth of other factors in the welfare checklist to substantiate its decision. Although totally at odds with the notion of self-determination advocated by the children's liberationists,[4] these principles are perfectly reasonable. Children have a minor status and the final decision quite rightly remains with the court, taking account not only of a child's interest in choice but also his or her right to protection from the risk of future harm. Consulting children is very different from delegating the decision-making process to them entirely before they reach adulthood. This is implicitly acknowledged by article 12(1) of the CRC.[5]

Despite these limitations, compliance with the direction to pay regard to a child's views would enable the courts to promote children's capacity for choice more effectively if it was generously complied with. In disputes where the final decision accords with children's own wishes, their self-respect is left intact. On the other hand, a child may feel confused and vulnerable if the court appears to ignore his or her strongly voiced views about the outcome. Children may even have a better grasp of their own needs than adults. Indeed, the direction promotes a diluted form of the notion of autonomy by implying that a mature child's best interests may be fulfilled

1   Children Act 1989, s 1(3)(a).
2   The term commonly used to describe the list of factors contained in the Children Act 1989, s 1(3).
3   'The child's welfare shall be the court's paramount consideration', Children Act 1989, s 1(1). The terms 'paramountcy principle', 'welfare principle' and 'best interests test' are often used interchangeably.
4   As discussed in chapter 1.
5   Art 12(1): child's right to express his or her views, those views being given 'due weight' in accordance with his or her age and maturity.

most effectively by the court acceding to his or her own wishes. Furthermore, its inclusion in the welfare checklist reflects a conviction that 'the increasing recognition given both in practice and in law to the child's status as a human being in his own right' should also be matched by the courts, when hearing disputes over children.[6]

The case law reflects little judicial clarity over the extent to which courts should take account of children's wishes. This is hardly surprising, in view of the doubts attending the interpretation of the welfare principle itself. Before considering the weight given to children's wishes and feelings in litigation concerning them, this chapter briefly assesses the efficacy of the welfare principle, given the need to comply with the demands of the ECHR. The case law is diffuse and so this chapter does not attempt to review the cases where the courts appear to take particular account of children's wishes or to ignore them. Instead, it proceeds to discuss the complex interplay between children's age, their capacity, the type of dispute and the risks involved in acceding to or ignoring their views. It then discusses briefly three problem areas involving particularly complex issues: child abduction, the role played by indoctrination, and child abuse.

(2)   THE WELFARE PRINCIPLE – A REASSESSMENT

Many authors have questioned the utility of the welfare principle. Whilst it is arguable that the principle's innate strength lies in its flexibility,[7] a constant source of criticism is its extreme indeterminacy.[8] Although the welfare checklist is designed to ensure a measure of consistency, as Eekelaar says:

> 'the heavily subjective nature of the power granted to the judge means that, so long as he does not claim to be applying it as a conclusive rule of law, a judge can consider almost any factor which could possibly have a bearing on a child's welfare and assign to it whatever weight he or she chooses.'[9]

A frequent criticism has been that the innate vagueness of the welfare principle allows the judiciary to dress up adult-related concerns under the guise of promoting children's welfare. Some critics point to the dangers of the parents' position being undermined by this slightly underhand process. Reece, for example, refers to the courts' denigration of homosexual parents' ability to care for their children, whilst asserting a concern for their children's welfare.[10] Others are more concerned by the way in which the courts dress up issues relating to adults' interests, claiming to fulfil the child's best interests. For example, the courts often uphold parents' rights against third parties, whilst maintaining that they are, in truth, promoting their children's welfare or even their rights.[11]

The Human Rights Act 1998 has provoked fresh calls to refine the welfare principle so that it accommodates the need to strike the required balance between individuals' rights and other legitimate interests under article 8. As Herring has pointed out, contrary to Lord Oliver's view in *Re KD (a minor) (ward: termination of access)*,[12] the demands of the Children Act 1989, section 1 are very different, in evidential terms,

6   Law Commission (1988) para 3.24.
7   See S Day Sclater and C Piper (2001) p 412.
8   Inter alia: R Mnookin (1975); M Fineman (1988); S Parker (1994); H Reece (1996); J Herring (1999 a); J Eekelaar (2002).
9   J Eekelaar (1991) p 125.
10   H Reece (1996) p 303.
11   J Fortin (1999 a).
12   [1988] AC 806.

from those of article 8 of the ECHR.[13] Under the Children Act, section 1, the court merely has to reach a decision which accords with the child's best interests. Under article 8 (1) the court must uphold a parent's rights *unless* it can justify not doing so by reference to the requirements of article 8(2), only one of which can accommodate the child's welfare.[14] Herring suggests that one way of managing this new approach is to reconceptualise the welfare principle so that it includes a greater emphasis on the interests of adults, as part and parcel of a consideration of the child's welfare.[15] Whilst his approach might conceivably produce a greater evenhandedness between adults, one wonders whether it would provoke much change. Since in private law disputes over children there is always an adult winner and loser, the courts are forced to favour the interests of one of the adults, as opposed to those of the other. In the past, they merely did so by reference to the welfare principle, incorporating concerns about the adults. Adopting Herring's approach, they would do so by reference to the need to balance one parent's rights against the other's, accommodating parental issues within an assessment of the child's welfare. Furthermore, as Eekelaar points out, such an approach provides no real guidance on *how* to balance the interests of one adult against those of the other and, more to the point, how *not* to. After all, the courts in Victorian England justified giving pre-eminence in the family to the married father by arguing that it was in the interests of his children that they should.[16]

Eekelaar's suggested solution is to analyse the degree of 'well-being' which might benefit each member of the family involved in a dispute if a particular outcome were reached, compared with the degree of 'detriment' each would suffer if the opposing outcome were adopted. Having calculated as accurately as possible the implications of reaching one decision rather than another, the court could then attempt to find a solution which reduces the detriment to each adult as much as possible, without actually harming the child. Whilst, unlike the welfare test, this would not necessarily produce an outcome enhancing the child's well-being in the best way possible, it would spread the detriment amongst all the players involved, including the child.[17] Eekelaar himself foresees that such an approach might be seen as too complex and unrealistic. Nevertheless, he urges that the judiciary cannot be allowed to retreat into vague assertions about what is best for the child:

> '… the very ease of the welfare test encourages a laziness and unwillingness to pay proper attention to all the interests that are at stake in these decisions and, possibly, also a tendency to abdicate responsibility for decision making to welfare professionals.'[18]

It is arguable that if the courts complied with the requirements of the ECHR sufficiently conscientiously, they might reach a conclusion similar to that reached using Eekelaar's approach. The need to justify infringing an adult's article 8 rights in disputes over children by reference to the demands of article 8(2), including the principle of proportionality, should promote a critical examination of claims that a particular outcome necessarily promotes a child's best interests. For example, when considering parental disputes over whether one parent should take a child abroad, the court might

---

13   J Herring (1999 b) p 231.
14   Art 8 (2) only allows an infringement of art 8 rights if it is 'in accordance with the law and is necessary in a democratic society … for the protection of health or morals, or for the protection of the rights and freedoms of others'.
15   J Herring (1999 a) pp 101–104 and J Herring (1999 b) pp 232–234.
16   J Eekelaar (2002) p 238.
17   J Eekelaar (2002) esp pp 243–244.
18   J Eekelaar (2002) p 248.

conclude that the child's best interests would be promoted by allowing the mother to emigrate with the child, against the father's wishes.[19] But reaching such a conclusion is no longer sufficient in itself if the father's Convention rights are infringed by allowing her to do so. The court should also consider whether the damage suffered by the child if the mother is forced to stay is proportionate to the interference with the father's right to enjoy a family life with his child in this country. Such conclusion may be justifiable, but careful reasoning is required before such interference can be justified.[20]

Unfortunately, as the decision of the House of Lords in *Re B (a child) (adoption by one natural parent)*[21] demonstrates, the domestic courts are keen show that the requirements of article 8(2) hardly need serious consideration. Indeed, that decision neatly rounds off the post-Human Rights Act 1998 case law utilised by the family courts to ensure that the welfare principle still pre-empts every other process in children's cases – in other words, status quo ante bellum.[22] According to Lord Nicholls of Birkenhead in *Re B*, the courts adopt precisely the same balancing exercise when deciding whether a particular outcome is in the child's best interests as they do when deciding whether an order is justified under article 8(2) of the ECHR. In his view, the court's conclusion in that case that an adoption order was in the child's best interests identified 'the pressing social need for adoption . . . and represents the court's considered view on proportionality'.[23] Such an approach leads inexorably to the assumption that the processes so carefully followed by the European Court of Human Rights when considering the demands of article 8(2) are almost otiose. In particular, as Harris-Short points out, it assumes that the principle of proportionality is automatically fulfilled.[24]

Lord Nicholls of Birkenhead's approach differed greatly to that taken by the court below when considering *Re B*.[25] As the Court of Appeal so clearly saw, the claim that a decision accords with the child's best interests does not automatically indicate that its infringement of the parent's rights is proportionate to the risk faced by the child if the parent's rights are left intact. Indeed, Lord Nicholls' interpretation promotes a profoundly uncritical approach to assertions made by adults that a preferred outcome will certainly fulfil the child's best interests. As the Court of Appeal appreciated, there are various ways in which a child's need for stability and certainty can be promoted. In that case, it was a matter of opinion which would promote the child's welfare better. One was to leave her with her father, protected by a residence order and an order restricting the mother's right to seek court orders regarding her daughter in the future.[26] The fact that the father claimed that adoption would promote the child's welfare better did not necessarily indicate that this was true. Indeed, it is impossible to calculate scientifically whether one reasonably sound option will ever be *better* for the child than another reasonably sound option. If, however, one option is less drastic in the way it infringes the parents' rights than the other, its outcome may, in

19   Eg *Payne v Payne* [2001] EWCA Civ 166, [2001] 1 FLR 1052.
20   But a careful assessment of art 8 requirements was not a feature of the Court of Appeal's judgment in *Payne v Payne* [2001] EWCA Civ 166, [2001] 1 FLR 1052. Discussed by A Bainham (2001).
21   [2001] UKHL 70, [2002] 1 All ER 641. See also discussion in chapter 14.
22   Eg *Payne v Payne* [2001] EWCA Civ 166, [2001] 1 FLR 1052.
23   [2001] UKHL 70, [2002] 1 All ER 641 at [31].
24   S Harris-Short (2002) p 338.
25   [2001] 1 FLR 589, esp per Hale LJ at [39]–[40].
26   Under Children Act 1989, s 91(14).

the end, promote the child's welfare more effectively than the other – but the different options must be scrutinised carefully. Consequently, as suggested above, if the requirements of the ECHR were followed more conscientiously, the result might approximate reasonably closely with Eekelaar's suggested approach.

Admittedly, as Eekelaar points out, the European Court of Human Rights has itself demonstrated that a strict adherence to the wording of article 8(2) risks placing the child's interests too low in the hierarchy of interests. There may be cases where, although the child's welfare clearly requires one outcome, on a narrow reading of the 'necessity' of so doing, the court feels unable to infringe the adult's rights in order to achieve that outcome.[27] As occurred in *Elsholz v Germany*,[28] the fact that parents' article 8 rights receive presumptive weight means that despite a child's welfare requiring an order which infringes those rights, the court may not consider it 'necessary in a democratic society' to produce that order. There are three ways of answering this problem. The first is to point out that there is plenty of Strasbourg case law where the child's best interests have been allowed to outweigh those of his or her parents.[29] The second is to stress that the European Court of Human Rights is not itself infallible and that *Elsholz* and three similar decisions[30] were controversial on a number of points, as demonstrated by their being accompanied by strong dissenting judgments.[31] The third is to adopt Bainham's suggested approach and start quantifying the child's position in terms of his or her own Convention rights, as opposed to his or her best interests.[32] As commented elsewhere,[33] the European Court of Human Rights has been noticeably reticent in the way it has considered the interplay between children's rights and parents' rights.[34] If it had been more willing to acknowledge that children themselves have rights of their own under article 8, the Court might not have produced decisions like *Elsholz*, which the dissenting judges considered endangered children's welfare.[35]

Since children are vital players in all disputes involving their upbringing, it might strengthen their position immeasurably to argue that the rights of the adults cannot be balanced against each other without considering them alongside those of the children themselves. There is, of course, a risk that since a child has a right to a good family life, many welfare arguments would simply become rephrased as arguments about the child's rights.[36] Nevertheless, a rights perspective might reveal the different dimensions sought by Eekelaar in his approach referred to above. Such an approach might also help address the gamesmanship involved in private disputes when adults vie to obtain the protection of the article 8 presumption. A mother can only, for example, resist a father's claim for contact by showing that it is 'necessary' for his right under article 8(1) to be infringed, bearing in mind the high threshold sometimes placed on 'necessary' by the European Court of Human Rights.[37] But a child might

27 J Eekelaar (2002) p 241.
28 [2000] 2 FLR 486.
29 See discussion in chapter 2, p 57–60.
30 See *Sahin v Germany; Sommerfeld v Germany; Hoffmann v Germany* [2002] 1 FLR 119, and at 136 and 151.
31 See discussion below.
32 A Bainham (2002).
33 J Fortin (1999 b) pp 357–358.
34 See also discussion in chapter 2, pp 54–56.
35 See discussion below. See also J Eekelaar (2002) p 241, discussing *Elsholz*.
36 Judicial decision-making in contact disputes demonstrates such a trend. See discussion in chapter 13.
37 As in *Elsholz v Germany* [2000] 2 FLR 486.

counter the father's claim by arguing that he or she has independent article 8 rights which cannot be fully enjoyed unless restrictions are placed on the father's right to contact. The presumption attaching to the child's rights should produce a situation where the court must balance the child's rights against those of the father, rather than fitting the welfare principle into a defence available only to the mother.

(3)   THE INTERPLAY BETWEEN WELFARE, WISHES AND FEELINGS AND AGE

(A)   Introduction

Mnookin has pointed out that it is often unclear to a judge what questions he should be posing when trying to determine the child's best interests. Should this be considered from a short- or long-term view point? Should he be primarily concerned with the child's happiness?[38] Similar questions could be posed when weighing the impact of a child's wishes and feelings. What precise purpose is the court considering this information for in the circumstances of this case? Is it merely to reinforce the court's own decision or to provide information that may swing a finely balanced case? Was the information extracted in circumstances that indicate that the information can be relied on in the short term or the long term? What risks are involved in taking account of the child's wishes and of ignoring them? How should the courts treat evidence that a mother has attempted to influence her child against her father?

It is universally accepted that in this field of decision-making there are no 'right' answers, but judicial discretion should not be an excuse for an arbitrary approach which suggests to children that the process of seeking their views is a meaningless exercise to be completed and then forgotten. The child psychiatrists who advised the Court of Appeal on the childhood implications of contact disputes involving domestic violence have clear views about the importance of the courts respecting all children's views.[39] They maintain that:

> 'it is damaging to a child to feel he or she is forced to do something against his or her will and against his or her judgment if the child cannot see the sense of it.'[40]

Eekelaar has expressed some concern over the risk of the judiciary, when subjecting children to coercive paternalism, ignoring their interest in making choices in their lives and has proposed various approaches to ensure that children's views are fully considered.[41] He favours the concept of 'dynamic self-determinism' which introduces a presumption in favour of complying with children's choices as closely as possible without restricting their capacity for fulfilling their future life-goals.[42] This suggestion is useful and, if followed, might ensure that the courts paid more attention to a child's interest in choice and fulfilled the need to treat the individual child with respect. It might also ensure that the judiciary retained a measure of flexibility when confronted by a child whose strong views conflict with their own ideas about the needs of children in general.

---

38   R Mnookin (1975) p 260.
39   See C Sturge and D Glaser (2000). Discussed in more detail below.
40   C Sturge and D Glaser (2000) p 621.
41   Eekelaar repeatedly returns to this theme in three papers: J Eekelaar (1986), (1992) and (1994).
42   J Eekelaar (1994) p 53.

(B)   Age and its interrelationship with context and risk

The weight to be attached to a child's wishes and feelings will vary considerably, depending on a number of interlocking factors, some so entangled with each other that they often defy clear identification. Central to all these is the child's age and maturity. The importance of this factor is acknowledged by the Children Act 1989, section 1(3)(a), which directs the courts 'to have regard to the *ascertainable* wishes and feelings of the child concerned (*considered in the light of his age and understanding*)'.[43] A court might therefore conclude, for example, that the wishes of an infant are either not reliably ascertainable or, if they are, they carry little weight because the child is too young to comprehend the issues. One might argue that, at the other end of the age spectrum, there is little point in making court orders against the wishes of children mature enough to have strong views of their own. The Children Act only cautiously maintains such an approach, indicating that no orders should be made regarding children over the age of 16, unless the circumstances are exceptional.[44] The policy makers obviously did not consider that the majority of younger children could be sufficiently mature to justify bringing that age limit down, and left the courts free to judge for themselves whether to make orders against the wishes of younger children.

Sturge and Glaser have clear views about the relevance of age, recommending that within the overall context of the child's wishes –

> 'the older the child the more seriously they should be viewed and the more insulting and discrediting to the child to have them ignored. As a rough rule we would see these as needing to be taken account of at any age; above 10 we see these as carrying considerable weight with 6–10 as an intermediate stage and at under 6 as often indistinguishable in many ways from the wishes of the main carer (assuming normal development).'[45]

Notably, these child psychiatrists did not recommend any formal age limit, similar to those adopted by some European legal systems. Thus in Finland, children over the age of 12 can veto court decisions concerning their custody and access, their having the right to be heard in most child welfare decisions and to appeal from these.[46] One might justify this approach by reference to the research evidence on cognitive development. This suggests that although there are no clear-cut rules over this and some children develop certain skills earlier than others, there are fundamental psychological differences between the competence of young children aged up to about 11 to 12 and that of adolescents between that age and the age of 18. But researchers in the field of cognitive development warn that, even at these ages, competence for decision-making will vary enormously, depending on a variety of factors, such as peer pressure and family environment.[47] The obvious disadvantage of giving children as young as 12 an absolute legal veto is that it places on their shoulders the responsibility for choice which they may not be ready for. Making choices requires very different skills and maturity from those required for taking part in a consultation process. Furthermore, the adults involved in family disputes have the protection of article 8 of the ECHR. Giving children from the age of 12 an *absolute*

---

43   Emphasis supplied.
44   See Children Act 1989, s 9(6) and (7).
45   See C Sturge and D Glaser (2000) p 624.
46   This information is noted by the European Court of Human Rights in *K and T v Finland* [2000] 2 FLR 79 at paras 88–89.
47   See chapter 3, pp 72–74.

veto over decisions relating to their upbringing takes little account of their parents' rights, or of the balancing process required of the courts when dealing with Convention challenges.

The research evidence on cognitive development indicates that the implications of the child's age are more far-reaching than merely indicating whether or not he or she has capacity to form views. Age and maturity must be considered in the context of the type of situation, in this case the type of dispute, which may, in turn, have a bearing on the relevance of a child's views. For example, parents' contact and residence disputes often focus on younger children. Similarly, younger children are normally the subject of disputes between birth parents and foster carers over whether children should return to the care of the former or stay with the latter. In all these situations there may be special concerns about young children's extreme impressionability and, because of the context of the dispute, their vulnerability to indoctrination by the adults caring for them.[48] An additional complication in such disputes is that a court order, for example, favouring a child's wishes to remain with or resist contact with one parent, is that the other parent will not achieve the relationship with the child that he or she had sought. Such a loss may be expressed in terms of an infringement of their article 8 Convention rights. In disputes between birth parents and third parties over residence or adoption, the stakes are even higher, with the effect on the birth parents of losing their fight to retain their child in their care being particularly severe. Meanwhile, the effect on the child of the court refusing to accede to his or her wishes over the identity of future carers may result in the child suffering severe psychological harm when a change in care is attended by disruption of primary attachments.[49]

Much of the unease over taking account of the views of very young children centres on private law disputes and the knowledge that a young child is not only more easily subjected to the influence of others,[50] but is also vulnerable to external factors which may only have a short-term impact.[51] Many also consider it essential to avoid making young children feel responsible for choosing between parents, arguing that they have a right to be protected from making decisions before they are ready – indeed, to be children. Choosing can be immensely damaging, given that some parents even reject their children on learning, by reading the court welfare report, of their children's strong criticisms of them.[52] Furthermore, children often blame themselves for parental separation and feel loyal to both parents.[53] There is also the risk of elevating the child's status within the family to a position of power. It may unnaturally skew the psychodynamics of the family and allow the child to play one parent off against the other.[54]

Practitioners who interview young children are frequently reminded of the risks involved in expecting them to express preferences regarding their parents.[55] Nevertheless, research indicates that however carefully practitioners consult children

---

48   Discussed below.
49   This type of dispute is discussed in more detail in chapter 14.
50   The risks of young children being indoctrinated by a residential parent are discussed below.
51   B Cantwell and S Scott (1995) pp 340–343.
52   See I Waite and H Stead (1998) p 45.
53   Eg *B v B (minors) (interviews and listing arrangements)* [1994] 2 FLR 489: the county court judge, who had interviewed in private three children aged 16, 14 and 12, found that due to their loyalty to each parent, none was prepared to express a preference and expressed great distress at being asked to do so.
54   S Bennett and S Armstrong Walsh (1994) p 93.
55   Eg A O'Quigley (2000) p 30.

without apparently asking them to choose, the children often consider that they *are* being asked to choose between their parents.[56] Indeed, many children seem keen to have some element of choice regarding the arrangements being made for their future and, at the very least, want some involvement in the decisions reached.[57] Importantly, the research evidence about children's cognitive abilities does not indicate that an inability to weigh up complex information in order to make *choices*, also presupposes an inability to provide good explanations for any expressed inclinations. These explanations may be of vital importance, particularly in cases where there is a risk that the child has been abused by one or both parents. In such cases, the strength of the child's views may reflect the importance of what he or she is saying and the risks involved in ignoring them.

In the case of adolescents, there appear to be few parental battles over teenagers old enough to vote with their feet. The dearth of case law involving this age group probably reflects legal practitioners' view that there is little point in taking such cases to court since few courts would make decisions ignoring teenagers' wishes. When adolescents are consulted in private law disputes, the judiciary generally operate on the presumption that the wishes of 'older children' should be respected, since to ignore them would be counter-productive. Butler-Sloss LJ made this plain in her following words:

> 'The courts, over the last few years, have become increasingly aware of the importance of listening to the views of older children and taking into account what children say, not necessarily agreeing with what they want nor, indeed, doing what they want, but paying proper respect to older children who are of an age and the maturity to make their minds up as to what they think is best for them, bearing in mind that older children very often have an appreciation of their own situation which is worthy of consideration by, and the respect of, the adults, and particularly including the courts.'[58]

Although, as these words of Butler-Sloss LJ make plain, the Court of Appeal in *Re P (a minor) (education)*[59] adopted a refreshingly liberal approach to the views of a 14-year-old boy, the decision was not a particularly adventurous one. Yielding to this boy's wish to attend a day school rather than an expensive boarding school did not endanger his health or restrict his future choices in life. The dangers involved in allowing his choice to determine the outcome were very low and there was little point in the court overriding his wishes. The decision in *Re P* suggests that the views of adolescents should be respected over matters carrying little risk. All the more surprising that applications to change of an adolescent's surname, despite involving far less dangerous outcomes, produce such idiosyncratic judicial responses. Admittedly, the order in *Re B (change of surname)*[60] did not prevent the children, aged 16, 14 and 12, *informally* adopting whatever surname they chose in their everyday lives.[61] But it did prevent their mother changing it formally to that of their step-father, as they wished. Such an outcome surely risked exacerbating the implacable hostility they

---

56   Eg see the comments of the children interviewed by A Buchanan et al (2001) pp 64–68.
57   C Smart et al (2001) pp 97–104. See also the discussion in chapter 7.
58   *Re P (a minor) (education)* [1992] 1 FLR 316 at 321.
59   [1992] 1 FLR 316.
60   [1996] 1 FLR 791.
61   [1996] 1 FLR 791 at 795, per Wilson J.

felt for their father.[62] To subject teenagers to minor restrictions governing their future lives may appear to them not only senseless, but unjust and oppressive.

The courts obviously experience far greater difficulties where physical illness or psychiatric disturbance undermines an adolescent's capacity to assess the complexities of the decision.[63] These are the cases where the courts may decide, for paternalistic reasons, to override adolescents' choices, often on the basis that they are not competent to reach them, or simply in order to save their lives, or at least to safeguard their future.[64] Nevertheless, even in these cases, judicial decision-making reflects an awareness of the implications of overriding an adolescent's strong views, including the indignity of suffering physical compulsion.[65] Indeed, the courts have a reasonably good record of paying considerable attention to the adolescent's views in cases where the outcome will seriously disrupt his or her life, whether they relate to undergoing medical treatment,[66] or going into local authority care.[67] The judiciary commonly provide detailed reasons in their judgments for failing to accede to them.[68] This case law shows the judiciary implicitly adopting a 'risk analysis approach' to information regarding the wishes of mature teenagers. If acceding to a teenager's wishes risks his or her death, as in some cases involving refusal of medical treatment, then the court may feel obliged to override them, whatever they think of the individual's competence to form firm and reliable views.[69]

Age must be considered not only in the context of the dispute itself, but also in the context of the long- and short-term risks involved in acceding to or ignoring the child's own wishes. Thus the risks involved in ignoring a young child's reluctance to visit his or her absent father are not particularly high in the short term, unless the child has been abused. They may, however, be more serious in the long term if they involve a loss of contact with him, because young children's memories are short. By contrast, although adolescents are, by definition, assumed to have a good ability to reach decisions about their own future, acceding to some of these may involve extremely high long-term risks, particularly if they are refusing to undergo medical treatment. But, on the other hand, in the short term, maturity may come from being allowed to make mistakes. Furthermore, adolescents may simply ignore judicial decisions which displease them. Court orders themselves may be time limited. For example, when dealing with applications to return children abducted from their home, the courts are influenced by the short duration of orders made under the Hague

---

62   See also *Re S (change of surname)* [1999] 1 FLR 672: the judge at first instance refused to authorise a 15-year-old girl to change her name from that of her father (against whom child sexual abuse allegations had been made by her elder sister) to that of her maternal uncle and aunt. Allowing her appeal, Thorpe LJ criticised him for not identifying the fact that she was *Gillick*-competent.

63   A child's competence to make decisions is discussed more fully in chapter 3. Adolescents' decision-making in the context of health care is discussed more fully in chapter 5.

64   Eg, inter alia: *Re E (a minor) (wardship: medical treatment)* [1993] 1 FLR 386; *Re W (a minor) (medical treatment)* [1993] Fam 64; *Re M (medical treatment: consent)* [1999] 2 FLR 1097.

65   See *Re S (a minor) (consent to medical treatment)* [1994] 2 FLR 1065, per Johnson J, who considered it 'extremely distasteful' (at 1074) to envisage using force on a 15-year-old patient who was refusing life-saving treatment.

66   Eg *Re E (a minor) (wardship: medical treatment)* [1993] 1 FLR 386.

67   Eg *Re H (a minor) (care proceedings: child's wishes)* [1993] 1 FLR 440.

68   Eg *Re C (a minor) (care: child's wishes)* [1993] 1 FLR 832 and *Re R (recovery orders)* [1998] 2 FLR 401.

69   Eg *Re W (a minor) (medical treatment)* [1993] Fam 64. Discussed in more detail in chapter 5.

Convention.[70] Thus a court may justify an apparently extremely harsh decision to return a child to the country from whence he or she has been removed, arguing that it is only a short-term solution, pending a full hearing by the courts of the country to which the child is being returned.

As this discussion indicates, a child's age and competence to form views cannot be assessed *in vacuo*, since the context of the dispute and the risk involved in ignoring or acceding to his or her views will always impinge on the decision-making process. An attempt to clarify the extent to which one aspect of this information influences another may lead to a more consistent judicial approach. Whatever the context, a child may not understand why, having expressed strong views one way or the other, the court has apparently ignored them. However young, the courts should consider always including a careful explanation of their decisions in circumstances where they feel unable to comply with a child's own wishes. When older, these children may wish to understand more about the legal process and discover the reasons underlying the present arrangements for their care. This is particularly important in child protection cases, where the decision may radically change a child's life.[71] The children involved do not necessarily resent the court for not fulfilling their wishes, as long as an adult, such as their children's guardian, explains to them the terms of the order and reasons for the decision.[72] Finally, it should not be forgotten that in some cases, the court is unable to comply with the direction in section 1 of the Children Act 1989 to consider the child's wishes and feelings. Regrettably, the court may have no clear idea of the child's views at all. If a welfare report has not been asked for,[73] the only source of information is the parents, who may disagree over how the child feels.[74]

(4)   A CHILD'S VIEWS – SOME PROBLEM AREAS

(A)   Abducted children

There is a growing body of Hague Convention[75] case law involving abducting parents who resist claims to return their children on the basis that the children themselves oppose such an action and are sufficiently mature to have their views taken seriously.[76] Unlike ordinary domestic disputes, in abduction cases the child's welfare is not paramount.[77] Indeed, a prima facie presumption underlies the Convention that a prompt return of all abducted children to the country of their habitual residence is always in their best interests,[78] since that country's own courts will fully assess what

---

70   Discussed below.

71   See C Sturge (1998) pp 24–25.

72   See J McCausland (2000) pp 102 and 105. See *Re C (a minor) (care: child's wishes)* [1993] 1 FLR 832: Waite J (at 840) hoped that the court's decision would be conveyed to the 13-year-old girl sympathetically.

73   The weaknesses involved in process of welfare reporting are discussed in chapter 7.

74   Eg *Re A (specific issue order: parental dispute)* [2001] 1 FLR 121: an 8-year-old girl's parents gave differing accounts of her views. Nevertheless, the Court of Appeal refused to attach any weight to the trial judge's refusal to ascertain her true wishes over a choice of school through obtaining a welfare report or by seeing her himself.

75   The Hague Convention on the Civil Aspects of International Child Abduction 1980, given force of law by the Child Abduction and Custody Act 1985.

76   Much of this case law is clearly summarised by J Caldwell (2001) pp 130–133.

77   See Hale J in *Re R (abduction: consent)* [1999] 1 FLR 828 at 836.

78   See J Caldwell (2001) esp pp 121–124.

happens to them.[79] But the duty to return the child is not absolute and article 13 authorises the court to refuse to make such an order if 'it finds that the child objects to being returned and has attained an age and degree of maturity at which it is appropriate to take account of its views'.[80] In most family proceedings involving children, the courts have plenty of scope for offsetting the weight attributed to the child's wishes by referring to the long list of other factors contained in the statutory checklist.[81] The terms of article 13 of the Hague Convention, however, allow attention to be focused solely on the child's objections and maturity. Consequently, a court should not reject a parent's claim based on this aspect of article 13 without carefully considering and commenting on the child's wishes and maturity.[82] Indeed, according to Ward LJ, the exception in article 13 reflects the aims of article 12 of the CRC, to enable children, depending on their maturity, to express their views and be heard, though not to give them self-determination. So once the court considers that children are of sufficient maturity to take their views into account, it may exercise its discretion and depart from the usual presumption imposed by the Convention.[83] In his view, whether a court should do so will depend, inter alia, on the strength and validity of the child's views, taking account of the child's own perspectives of his or her own interests, the reality and reasonableness of the reasons for objection, the extent to which they have been shaped by the abducting parent and the extent to which the objections might be mediated on return.[84]

The facts of abduction cases being infinitely variable, there can be little consistency in the courts' preparedness to be influenced by children's objections to return or in the ages of the children who manage to influence them. Nevertheless, the differences in approach are sometimes surprising. In some, the views of relatively young children have swayed the court,[85] in others similarly aged children fare less well, despite the background circumstances being apparently more worrying.[86] Whilst the courts

---

79   See *Re P (abduction: minor's views)* [1998] 2 FLR 825 at 827, per Butler-Sloss LJ.
80   This exception is sometimes combined with the abducting parent's claim under art 13(b) that there is a grave risk that the child's return would 'expose the child to physical or psychological harm or otherwise place the child in an intolerable situation'.
81   Children Act 1989, s 1(3)(a)–(g).
82   But the absconding parent cannot demand an adjournment in order to allow a detailed investigation of the child's views, the court itself must decide whether it has sufficient information on this matter. See *P v P (minors) (child abduction)* [1992] 1 FLR 155 at 158–159, per Waite J.
83   *Re T (abduction: child's objections to return)* [2000] 2 FLR 192 at 203–204, per Ward LJ.
84   [2000] 2 FLR 192 at 204, per Ward LJ.
85   Eg, inter alia: *Re S (a minor) (abduction)* [1993] 2 All ER 683: a girl of 9 was considered to be of sufficient age and maturity to justify taking account of her great reluctance (largely attributable to her considerable psychological and speech difficulties in a French school) to return to her father in France; *Ontario Court v M and M (abduction: children's objections)* [1997] 1 FLR 475: a 9-year-old girl was not to be separated from her parents and returned to her grandmother against her strong objections; *Re T (abduction: child's objections to return)* [2000] 2 FLR 192: a girl of 11 had sufficiently clear and reasoned objections to returning to the care of her alcoholic mother in Spain.
86   Eg *Re C (abduction: grave risk of psychological harm)* [1999] 1 FLR 1145: the objections of boys aged 9 and 7 who had suffered severe physical abuse at their father's hands, were discounted on the basis that they were not sufficiently mature. Nor did the court consider that their situation fitted the art 13(b) exception.

commonly give very serious credence to teenagers' objections,[87] sometimes, as in *TB v JB (abduction: grave risk of harm)*,[88] they do not. Variations in approach seem largely attributable to the courts' concern, albeit somewhat fluctuating, not to usurp the function of the courts of the 'returned to' country. Thus the astonishing decision in *TB v JB*[89] to override the objections of a 14 ½-year-old girl to returning to New Zealand, seems to have been largely based on the Court of Appeal's firm view that the courts of that country could protect the mother and children from their severely abusive step-father.[90]

Since the courts require convincing that the child is sufficiently mature for his or her objections to be considered seriously, it is important that his or her views are always elicited with the same degree of care in every case. Although the courts commonly rely on the advice of child and family reporters (formerly court welfare officers) on this question, it is unclear whether the time these officers spend ascertaining maturity always justifies their clear opinions one way or the other,[91] particularly if the children are relatively young.[92] Fortunately, the courts are showing a greater willingness to allow older children separate representation so that their views are properly ascertained and conveyed to the court.[93] Most regrettably, this is not always done, nor is there always up-to-date evidence on this matter.[94]

There is the further difficulty that children may not understand that a decision to return them is only a short-term decision and that their long-term future may soon be reconsidered by the domestic courts. In the absence of any formal follow up, in most cases it is only possible to speculate what impact these judicial decisions have on the children themselves, if the courts appear to ignore their own stated wishes. For this reason, the on-going litigation in *Re HB (abduction: children's objections)*[95] was

---

87   Eg *Re P (abduction: minor's views)* [1999] 1 FCR 739: appeal was allowed against a decision ordering the return of a 13-year-old boy to his father in the United States; his strong objections and extreme distress over this decision had led him to run away in London for a week. See also *Re L (abduction: child's objections to return)* [2002] EWHC 1864 (Fam), [2002] 2 FLR 1042: father failed to obtain an order returning his 14-year-old son to France, inter alia, due to the boy's own objections, combined with the delays involved.

88   [2001] 2 FLR 515.

89   [2001] 2 FLR 515. Hale LJ dissenting.

90   See also *Re S (abduction: return into care)* [1999] 1 FLR 843: the objections of a girl of 9½ to returning to her mother in Sweden were discounted because the Swedish authorities had undertaken to investigate her allegations of sexual abuse at the hands of her mother's boyfriend and protect her against him if necessary.

91   Eg *Re C (abduction: grave risk of psychological harm)* [1999] 1 FLR 1145: the court welfare officer, described (per Ward LJ, at 1157) as a 'man of vast experience', advised the court that the views of the boys aged 9 and 7 should be discounted because, despite being intelligent and articulate, they were 'not sufficiently mature for their objections to be determinative'.

92   *Re K (abduction: child's objections)* [1995] 1 FLR 977: the court welfare officer spoke to a 7-year-old girl for half an hour and the court concluded from this evidence that she was probably not sufficiently mature to justify the court taking account of her objections to returning to the United States.

93   Eg, inter alia: *Re S (abduction: children: separate representation)* [1997] 1 FLR 486; *Re T (abduction: appointment of guardian ad litem)* [1999] 2 FLR 796; *Re L (abduction: child's objections to return)* [2002] EWHC 1864 (Fam), [2002] 2 FLR 1042.

94   In *TB v JB (abduction: grave risk of harm)* [2001] 2 FLR 515, despite discounting the 14 ½-year-old girl's objections, Arden LJ observed (at 544) that there was no documentary evidence of her present wishes nor any independent assessment of them. Had the position 'been less clear', she would have considered whether the court should have some formal confirmation of the girl's current views.

95   *Re HB (abduction: children's objections)* [1997] 1 FLR 392; *Re HB (abduction: children's objections)* [1998] 1 FLR 422; *Re HB (abduction: children's objections) (No 2)* [1999] 1 FCR 331. See also discussion in chapter 7.

instructive. It chronicled attempts to impose a court order on two children, originally aged 11 and 13, who were totally out of sympathy with what the court was trying to achieve. The younger child refused to return to Denmark as ordered, and, staying in England, became embroiled in her father's litigation with her mother. The older child obeyed the order and returned to Denmark, but, as he himself had predicted, again reverted to delinquent behaviour and returned to a Danish children's residential home. The litigation highlights the ease with which children can sabotage court orders that they do not consider reflect their real needs.

(B)   Indoctrinated children

Indoctrination comes in many forms and is usually not deliberate, in so far as children simply absorb the views of those who care for them. Nevertheless, a court's willingness to reach a decision according with the child's wishes may be undermined by its knowledge that children are extremely suggestible and can be strongly influenced by the adults around them. As Eekelaar has observed, it is arguable that children lack competence to reach decisions for themselves, if the decision is really that of the parent and not the child.[96] Nevertheless, it may be difficult to deny a child's right to reach a decision for him or herself simply because, for example, the child holds the views of strongly religious parents or third parties.[97]

> 'If one is to hold a person incompetent because his decision reflects socially tolerated values ingrained in his upbringing, competence could hardly ever be achieved by anyone.'[98]

A court may, however, be loath to accord freedom of choice to a child it considers to have been subjected to religious indoctrination by his or her carers. But a decision overriding a child's strong religious views, by, for example, removing him from his present home,[99] might be countered by his arguing that he is entitled to religious freedom under article 9 of the ECHR. The court might respond by arguing that an infringement is necessary under article 9(2) to preserve the child's best interests.

Dealing with children who have apparently been indoctrinated by their parents is particularly problematic in contact disputes. The court may be convinced, when confronted with a child who is hysterically opposed to contact with his or her father, that the parent with day-to-day care (normally the mother), has imposed on a young and suggestible child unwarranted fears and anxieties about the father.[100] The courts have emphasised that 'implacably hostile' mothers should not be allowed to undermine their children's 'right to contact' by provoking in their minds groundless fears about their absent fathers.[101] There is no clear research evidence indicating that

---

96   J Eekelaar (1994) p 56.
97   But see *Re E (a minor) (wardship: medical treatment)* [1993] 1 FLR 386: the opposition of a 15½-year-old Jehovah's witness to blood transfusion treatment was overborne by court order.
98   J Eekelaar (1994) p 57.
99   Eg *Re R (a minor) (residence: religion)* [1993] 2 FLR 163: despite the vehement wish of a 9½-year-old boy to remain with members of the Exclusive Brethren sect, with whom he had lived for 4½ years, his care was transferred to his father.
100 Eg *Re F (contact: restraint order)* [1995] 1 FLR 956: the Court of Appeal considered that the adamant opposition of two girls aged 7 and 6 to any contact with their father stemmed from their mother's unfounded hostility.
101 The 'implacably hostile' mother is a term that the courts quite often use to describe a mother who without reasonabe grounds is strongly averse to the father having contact. See further in chapter 13.

children benefit from court imposed contact in circumstances poisoned by mutual parental antipathy[102] Nevertheless, from the early 1990s, the judicial approach has been dominated by the 'pro-contact presumption'. Well established case law has indicated that the upsets to the child caused by unwanted contact visits are usually minor and temporary and are outweighed by the long-term benefits of keeping in touch with an absent parent.[103] Indeed, the courts have felt justified in making contact orders against the wishes of the children involved, unless there is 'a serious risk of major emotional harm to the child'.[104] This guidance has been applied enthusiastically, with research indicating that district judges order contact even when children exhibit signs of considerable distress before, during or after contact.[105]

Clearly the reasons for children opposing contact are often extremely complex. They may simply relate to the present contact arrangements not adjusting to a growing child's changing life-style[106] or to a mixture of misplaced loyalties.[107] It may be acceptable for a court to override a child's opposition to contact if it stems solely from the residential parent's unfounded hostility, but not if it is fully justified by the child's own experiences. The courts' rather inflexible ideas about the child's long-term needs, which they assume that the children themselves do not appreciate, have sometimes led them to overlook the importance of what a child is saying about the other parent's behaviour *as a parent* and not as a protagonist in a parental dispute. Thus in *Re J (a minor) (contact)*,[108] although Balcombe LJ felt unable to reverse a decision refusing the father contact with his 10-year-old son, he clearly disapproved of it, suggesting that the courts should be very reluctant to allow one parent's implacable hostility to deter them from making a contact order. He predicted that, when in his teens, the boy might blame his mother for denying him contact with his father. This was despite the evidence regarding previous contact visits which appeared to provide a good explanation for the boy's own fears about visiting his father which were quite unconnected with his mother's hostility to the father.[109] All these factors could have combined to make enforced contact an extremely unhappy and stressful experience for a sensitive child.

This judicial faith in the overriding need to preserve children's relationships with absent parents has filtered down and infected the practice of court welfare officers and solicitors acting for mothers in contact disputes.[110] Research shows that when told by children whose mothers were victims of domestic violence of their opposition to contact, court welfare officers (now child and family reporters) have often taken the view that mothers should convince their children of the need to preserve the relationship with their fathers.[111] Similarly, McGee observes:

---

102   See chapter 13.
103   *Re H (minors) (access)* [1992] 1 FLR 148 at 153, per Balcombe LJ.
104   Eg *Re D (a minor) (contact: mother's hostility)* [1993] 2 FLR 1 at 8, per Waite LJ.
105   See R Bailey-Harris et al (1999) p 119.
106   See CASC (2002) paras 13.13–13.15.
107   See C Smart and B Neale (1999) pp 96–98.
108   [1994] 1 FLR 729.
109   This included evidence that the father had left the boy alone in the house with his disabled grandmother, had left him unattended at the gym and had smacked the boy and sworn at him.
110   M Hester, C Pearson and L Radford (1996) pp 23–24.
111   M Hester, C Pearson and L Radford (1996) p 24.

'women were rightly critical of solicitors who advised the woman from the man's point of view, that is, advising that he has a right to see the children, rather than from the children's point of view, namely, what do the children want and how can that be facilitated?'[112]

An overall judicial preparedness to consider more carefully the basis for children's hostility to the non-resident parent may now be emerging. This change of heart was provoked by recent case law and by the 'Experts' Report' commissioned by the Court of Appeal in *Re L (a child) (contact: domestic violence).*[113] Sturge and Glaser[114] not only stress the dangers of forcing children into continuing contact arrangements with violent fathers, but also strongly emphasise the importance of taking account of children's own views, depending on their age and the circumstances.[115]

The senior judiciary have emphasised the importance of this advice.[116] The cases dealt with in *Re L*[117] itself and subsequent case law reflect a far greater willingness to consider whether a child's opposition to contact stems from some valid reason, even if he or she is very young.[118] For example, in *Re S (contact: children's views),*[119] Judge Tyrer, having gone to considerable lengths to explore the children's own perspectives of the dispute, emphasised to the father that the children's reluctance to have further contact with him did not stem from their mother having 'poisoned her children's minds'.[120] The father had to appreciate that:

'These children [aged 16, 14 and 12] are not, in the end, children. V and JO in particular are young adults. They are ordinary teenagers and this kind of approach to them [the father's unceasing attempts to obtain increased contact] is invariably counter-productive. They might obey, perhaps they will obey an order of the court, but with what result? What would be the quality of what is being asked of them by me to do if I order them to do it? ... If young people are to be brought up to respect the law, then it seems to me that the law must respect them and their wishes, even to the extent of allowing them, as occasionally they do, to make mistakes.'[121]

If the courts are to understand the reasons behind a child's opposition to have more contact with the non-resident parent, they may need someone to investigate the background to the case more thoroughly. Consequently, the judiciary seem more

---

112   C McGee (2000) p 177.
113   [2000] 4 All ER 609.
114   See C Sturge and D Glaser (2000).
115   C Sturge and D Glaser (2000) p 624. See also Appendix 2, p 627, for a list of difficulties (contributed by J Eekelaar) which may hamper considering a child's wishes and feelings. These include, inter alia: the need to distinguish between wishes and deeper feelings; the need to separate out the incidental or transitory; pressure from disputing adults; the difficulties involved in explaining alternatives to children.
116   See *Re L (a child) (contact: domestic violence)* [2000] 4 All ER 609 at 612–614, per Dame Elizabeth Butler-Sloss P, quoting extensively from the experts' report. See also Dame Elizabeth Butler-Sloss P (2001).
117   [2000] 4 All ER 609. See *Re V (a child)* and *Re M (a child)*: each case involved a boy, now aged 9, strongly opposed to contact with his father. The Court of Appeal considered that the court at first instance had in each case been rightly influenced by the child's own opposition to contact.
118   Eg *Re G (domestic violence)* [2000] 2 FLR 865: the Court of Appeal rejected the father's claim that his 3-year-old daughter's wishes should be disregarded. Since the child been brought up experiencing severe domestic violence, culminating in her father killing the mother in a drunken brawl, her reluctance to see him and her fear of him should be looked at with care. See esp Dame Elizabeth Butler-Sloss P, at 874–876.
119   [2002] EWHC 540 (Fam), [2002] 1 FLR 1156.
120   [2002] EWHC 540 (Fam), [2002] 1 FLR 1156 at 1169.
121   [2002] EWHC 540 (Fam), [2002] 1 FLR 1156 at 1169 and 1171, per HHJ Tyrer.

willing to consider separate representation for children in difficult contact disputes,[122] with the further possibility of expert psychiatric advice being made available.[123] There is, though, a real danger that an increasing resort to '"psy" experts'[124] may lead to more non-resident fathers arguing that children who resist contact must be suffering from a mental disorder induced by Parental Alienation Syndrome (PAS), and that they therefore need skilled psychiatric or psychological assessment and therapy.[125] Indeed, claims that residential parents who seek to alienate their children against the other parent suffer from PAS, which requires prescribed intervention, have been fuelled by a growing acceptance of the syndrome in the United States.[126] Bruch strongly denounces this trend, stating:

> 'The degree to which PAS has been invoked by expert witnesses, attorneys, or judges in these cases and the almost total absence of inquiries into its scientific validity is profoundly disturbing.'[127]

Fortunately, following Sturge and Glasers' firm rejection of the syndrome's existence as a recognised mental disorder,[128] the Court of Appeal shows little sign of accepting such arguments here.[129] Nevertheless, despite there being no formal acceptance of the existence of PAS in this country, the problem of mothers who refuse to obey contact orders is becoming rapidly medicalised. Thus it has been recommended that the courts acquire powers to order recalcitrant parents to undergo counselling, to refer them to a psychiatrist or psychologist, or to place them on probation with treatment conditions.[130] There is an obvious danger that this medicalised approach may influence the domestic courts' methods of dealing with children who resist contact, with the view being taken that they too require psychotherapy to improve their behaviour.

The domestic courts should resist such an approach, despite a series of decisions emanating from the European Court of Human Rights which might appear to support it.[131] In these, by upholding their applications regarding the infringement of their article 8 rights, the Court appeared sympathetic to the claims by German fathers that

---

122 See Lord Chancellor's Department (2002) para 1(2)(e).
123 See *Re H (contact order) (No 2)* [2002] 1 FLR 22 at paras 51 and 52, per Wall J. Separate representation was not ordered in that case, largely because of the potential delays it would cause. See also *Re C (prohibition on further applications)* [2002] EWCA Civ 292, [2002] 1 FLR 1136 at [13], per Dame Elizabeth Butler-Sloss P.
124 See M King and C Piper (1995) p 58.
125 Eg *Appeal in Re M (a child)* in *Re L (a child) (contact: domestic violence) and other appeals* [2000] 4 All ER 609: the psychological expert in PAS had recommended, on the father's behalf, that the child undergo six sessions of therapy. See also *Re C (prohibition on further applications)* [2002] EWCA Civ 292, [2002] 1 FLR 1136: the father repeatedly applied for a mental health expert or a psychologist, expert in PAS, to be appointed to assess his daughter's state of mind, given her refusal to have contact with him.
126 See T Hobbs (2002 a), and T Hobbs (2002 b).
127 See C Bruch (2002) pp 387–388.
128 See C Sturge and D Glaser (2000) pp 622–623.
129 See *Re L (a child) (contact: domestic violence) and other appeals* [2000] 4 All ER 609 at 625–627, per Dame Elizabeth Butler-Sloss P, and *Re C (prohibition on further applications)* [2002] EWCA Civ 292, [2002] 1 FLR 1136 at [12]–[13], per Dame Elizabeth Butler-Sloss P. But see T Hobbs (2002 b), who claims (p 383) that the Court of Appeal in *Re C* acknowledged the existence of PAS and C Williams (2002), who rejects (p 411) such an interpretation of the decision.
130 See CASC (2002) para 14.55.
131 See *Elsholz v Germany* [2000] 2 FLR 486 and *Sahin v Germany; Sommerfeld v Germany; Hoffmann v Germany* [2002] 1 FLR 119, and at 136 and 151.

the mothers had indoctrinated their children against them.[132] In *Elsholz v Germany*[133] the European Court upheld the father's claim that he had been treated unfairly by the domestic courts when refusing him contact with his son, in so far as it had failed to investigate more closely the child's real state of mind. Unfortunately, when reaching its conclusions, the Court did not specifically comment on the father's claims that his son was a victim of PAS or on his statements regarding that syndrome's importance.[134] Such arguments may or may not have influenced its criticism of the German courts' reliance on the boy's own stated opposition (in oral hearings and two lengthy interviews) to his father's contact application.[135] The European Court held that the German court's refusal to obtain further psychological expert evidence to evaluate the boy's statements could not be justified by simply asserting that contact would be incompatible with the boy's well-being.[136] Similarly, in *Sahin v Germany*[137] the European Court criticised the German court for not hearing the 5-year-old child herself, relying instead on the expert psychologist's 'vague statements about the risks inherent in questioning the child …'[138] Furthermore, in *Sommerfeld v Germany*[139] it criticised the domestic court for being satisfied with the 11-year-old girl's own firm assertions that she wanted nothing to do with her father. The court should have obtained 'psychological expert evidence in order to evaluate the child's seemingly firm wishes'.[140]

These Convention decisions are controversial. Given the domestic courts' margin of appreciation when interpreting article 8(2), the European Court subjected the domestic courts' handling of the contact disputes to a surprisingly critical scrutiny. Arguably, it was over-stepping its purely supervisory role by substituting its own interpretation of the evidential requirements for that of the domestic courts.[141] The decisions not only appear to expect the domestic court to hear evidence from the child him or herself, but also to obtain a skilled psychological evaluation of the child's views, irrespective of the child's age. This last requirement seems particularly unrealistic in the case of teenage children who give strong indications of their wishes. Indeed, one wonders how the European Court thought the German court in *Sommerfeld* might have responded, in practical terms, had a psychologist reported that the girl's views were the product of her mothers' indoctrination. The German courts were surely

---

132   In *Elsholz* and *Sommerfeld* the European Court of Human Rights additionally upheld the fathers' claims that their procedural rights under art 6 had been infringed, due to the non-availability of the evidence requested. In *Sahin, Sommerfeld* and *Hoffmann*, the Court also held that the unmarried fathers had been discriminated against under art 14 since their claims would have been handled more favourably had they been married.

133   [2000] 2 FLR 486.

134   *Elsholz v Germany* [2000] 2 FLR 486 at paras 33–36. But see the claim made by T Hobbs (2002 a) p 187 that this decision indicates the European Court's support for the concept of PAS.

135   Now aged nearly 14, he had been aged between 5 and 6 when these took place.

136   [2000] 2 FLR 486 at para 52. But see the dissenting judgments, at 502–503.

137   [2002] 1 FLR 119.

138   [2002] 1 FLR 119 at para 47. But see the dissenting judgments, at 134–136.

139   [2002] 1 FLR 119.

140   [2002] 1 FLR 136 at para 43. But see the dissenting judgments, at 148–151. The European Court of Human Rights reverted to a less interventionist approach in *Yousef v Netherlands* [2002] 3 FCR 577 and *Hoppe v Germany* [2003] 1 FCR 176.

141   This point was made by the four dissenting judges in *Elsholz v Germany* [2000] 2 FLR 486 at 503 and by the two dissenting judges in *Sahin v Germany* [2002] 1 FLR 119 at 135 and by the dissenting judge in *Sommerfeld v Germany* [2002] 1 FLR 136 at 149.

realistic in thinking that, given her age, whatever the reason for her views, it was not now in her interests to be forced into contact with her father.[142] The European Court now stopped far short of suggesting that indoctrinated children should undergo therapy to achieve a complete change of heart, but the proponents of PAS clearly consider this to be essential.[143] Hopefully, the domestic courts here will resist arguments that, before making an order infringing a father's rights to his child's company under article 8(1), they must obtain an expert evaluation of his child's opposition to contact to establish whether it is a distorted feature of the child's personality and also prescribe a course of specialised therapy to rid him or her of such contaminated views.

(C)   Abused children

An abused child's right to be consulted may conflict with his or her right to be protected. Indeed, the wishes and feelings of abused children may be so extremely complex that they provide the court with some very mixed messages. As Schofield points out, abused children whose future is being determined by the courts may be so significantly harmed that they are confused about themselves and what has happened to them and therefore present a confusing picture to others:[144]

> 'Troubled children in crisis ... very often and very understandably present entirely conflicting evidence of their wishes and feelings. They may express hopes for the future which are incompatible with what professionals and the children themselves know to be reality; for example, the wish to be at home and to be safe, the wish to be with a parent but for that parent to change.'[145]

As she explains:

> 'This does not mean that we should therefore disregard those wishes and feelings but it does mean that the process of ascertaining, understanding and determining the weight to be attached to children's wishes and feelings is more problematic than it may appear from the simple words of the Act.'[146]

Children who are allegedly the victims of sexual abuse present special problems, both in private and public law proceedings. A sexually abused child's present views may be grossly distorted by his or her damaging relationship with the abuser.[147] Furthermore, the court may not be sure that the child is telling the truth. Although research indicates that sexually abused children are usually telling the truth when they say they have been abused,[148] it also indicates that many sexually abused children may be telling lies when they deny that this has happened.[149] Sexually abused children may not only deny or refuse to acknowledge that abuse has occurred, but also refuse

---

142 See esp *Sommerfeld v Germany* [2002] 1 FLR 136 at para 17 and the comments of the dissenting judge, at 149.
143 See *Appeal in Re M (a child)* in *Re L (a child) (contact: domestic violence) and other appeals* [2001] Fam 260: the psychological expert in PAS had recommended that the child undergo six sessions of therapy.
144 G Schofield (1998) p 365.
145 G Schofield (1998) p 364.
146 G Schofield (1998) p 364.
147 See E Jones and P Parkinson (1995) pp 68–75.
148 See, inter alia: D Jones and J McGraw (1987); N Thoenness and P Tjaden (1990); T Lyon (1999).
149 See the example provided by G Schofield (1998) p 374.

to co-operate with those trying to help them.[150] Those who do disclose the abuse sometimes later deny it, due to pressure from the abuser.[151]

In private law proceedings, a court may be reluctant to place a great deal of store on children's accounts of sexual abuse by a non-resident parent, especially if they are very young and if it suspects that they have been manipulated by the residential parent. These difficulties may be compounded if the practitioners involved used poor interviewing techniques, using leading questions and undue pressure to obtain disclosures of the abuse.[152] Nevertheless, despite the risks of the court making a false finding that sexual abuse has occurred, the notion of forcing a child who has, in truth, been abused to have contact with an abusive parent is a deeply unpleasant one.[153] Fortunately, there appears to be little sign of fathers in this country responding to allegations of child sexual abuse by asserting that the children must be victims of PAS.[154] To date, the domestic courts also appear to accept that it often pointless attempting to force older children to obey contact orders, particularly if they strongly argue that they have been abused and oppose all contact for that reason.[155]

The courts are well aware that abused children who are the subject of child protection proceedings often strongly desire to stay at home or return home,[156] however illogical this may appear.[157] They are obviously fully justified in overriding an abused child's objections to removal from home; indeed, they are under a duty to consider his or her 'physical, emotional and educational needs'.[158] Sometimes it is too dangerous for abused children ever to return home. The government envisages that increasing numbers of those who are the subject of care proceedings will be placed for adoption.[159] Given the impact of such a change on their lives, the views of the children involved should obviously be sought well before the adoption application is heard in court,[160] and certainly before any sudden modification in placement plans.[161] Nevertheless, since most children being placed for adoption from care are probably very vulnerable,

150 Eg *Nottinghamshire County Council v P; Re P (minors) (local authority: prohibited steps order)* [1993] 3 All ER 815: none of the teenage daughters was prepared to stay away from their sexually abusive father.

151 See E Jones and P Parkinson (1995) p 64.

152 Eg *Re N (a minor) (sexual abuse: video evidence)* [1996] 4 All ER 225 and *Re M (sexual abuse allegations: interviewing techniques)* [1999] 2 FLR 92.

153 Discussed further in chapter 13, p 409–411.

154 See C Bruch (2002), who describes (pp 387–388) the way that some American courts have accepted arguments of this kind in such a context.

155 Eg *Re M (sexual abuse allegations: interviewing techniques)* [1999] 2 FLR 92: children now aged 10 and 13 strongly opposed contact with their father who they alleged had sexually abused them when aged 2 and 5. The father's application for direct contact was refused despite the court making no finding on the truth of their allegations.

156 Per Thorpe LJ in *Re F (Mental Health Act: guardianship)* [2000] 1 FLR 192 at 198.

157 Eg, inter alia: *Re C (a minor) (care: child's wishes)* [1993] 1 FLR 832: a 13-year-old girl did not want to leave her father, who was a weak and inadequate individual, unable to protect her from her unsuitable acquaintances; *Re F (Mental Health Act: guardianship)* [2000] 1 FLR 192: a 17-year-old with severe learning difficulties was warded to prevent her returning home where she was at significant risk of further abuse.

158 Children Act 1989, s 1(3)(b).

159 Discussed more fully in chapters 15 and 17.

160 See the Department of Health (2001) Standard A 4 directing that: 'Every child will have his or her wishes and feelings listened to, recorded and taken into account.'

161 See *R v Devon County Council, ex p O (adoption)* [1997] 2 FLR 388: Scott-Baker J (at 396–397) deplored the fact that no one had consulted a 9-year-old boy over the plans to remove him from his prospective adopters and return him to previous foster carers.

it is arguable that they should not be given a legal right to veto any adoption application.[162] It would, however, be unrealistic for the courts to ignore a child's views on the matter, particularly if he or she is reluctant to be adopted.[163]

(5) CONCLUSION

Children involved in litigation cannot claim complete autonomy; they must recognise their dependence on the courts for decisions determining their future. But they may be the focus of judicial decisions which make no mention of considering their views and worse, which appear to ignore them entirely. It is difficult to justify such an approach to children who are being brought up in a society which constantly urges them to develop their powers of critical awareness and to act responsibly and independently.

A more systematic approach to the process of considering a child's wishes in each case might produce decisions which concentrated on this factor in the welfare checklist in a far less arbitrary way. As Eekelaar has suggested,[164] the courts should attempt to ensure that their decisions accord as fully as possible with children's own wishes, but without restricting their capacity for personal safety, health and fulfilment. Although this would not involve adopting a formal presumption in favour of complying with a child's wishes in every case, it would concentrate judicial attention on the child's particular perspective. The courts already implicitly adopt a risk-analysis approach in cases involving adolescents refusing life-saving medical treatment or treatment designed to ensure that mental health problems receive appropriate attention. A similar approach could be routinely adopted in all cases where information exists regarding the child's views over the outcome. It would improve matters were the courts always to provide an explanation for failing to comply with a child's clearly stated wishes, and when doing so, they should analyse and spell out the risks involved in fulfilling or ignoring those wishes, in the light of the child's age, capacity to form independent views and the special context of the dispute itself.

---

162 Despite the Department of Health (1993) para 4.3 recommending that the consent of children of 12 would be a pre-condition of an adoption order being made, this never became the law. The Adoption and Children Act 2002, s 1(4)(a) merely requires the court or adoption agency to have regard to 'the child's ascertainable wishes and feelings regarding the decision (considered in the light of the child's age and understanding)'. But see C Piper (2003) who criticises this omission.

163 Eg *Re M (adoption or residence order)* [1998] 1 FLR 570: the opposition of an emotionally disturbed and backward 11-year-old to being adopted by the prospective adopters, with whom she had lived for over two years, influenced the court's decision not to dispense with the mother's consent to adoption.

164 J Eekelaar (1994).

BIBLIOGRAPHY

NB many of these publications can be obtained on the relevant organisation's website.

Bailey-Harris R et al, 'From Utility to Rights? The Presumption of Contact in Practice' (1999) 13 International Journal of Law, Policy and the Family 111.

Bainham A, 'Can We Protect Children and Protect their Rights?' (2002) Family Law 279.

Bainham A, 'Taking Children Abroad: Human Rights, Welfare and the Courts' (2001) 60 Cambridge Law Journal 489.

Bennett S and Armstrong Walsh S, 'The No Order Principle, Parental Responsibility and the Child's Wishes' (1994) Family Law 91.

Bruch C, 'Parental Alienation Syndrome and alienated children – getting it wrong in child custody cases' (2002) 14 Child and Family Law Quarterly 381.

Buchanan A et al, *Families in conflict: Perspectives of children and parents on the Family Court Welfare Service* (2001) The Policy Press.

Butler-Sloss Dame Elizabeth P, 'Contact and Domestic Violence' (2001) Family Law 355.

Caldwell J, 'Child welfare defences in child abduction cases – some recent developments' (2001) 13 Child and Family Law Quarterly 121.

Cantwell B and Scott S, 'Children's wishes, children's burdens' (1995) 17 Journal of Social Welfare and Family Law 337.

Children Act Sub-Committee of the Advisory Board on Family Law (CASC), *Making Contact Work* Report of the Children Act Sub-Committee (2002) Lord Chancellor's Department.

Day Sclater S and Piper C, 'Social Exclusion and the Welfare of the Child' (2001) 28 Journal of Law and Society 409.

Department of Health White Paper, *Adoption: The Future* Cm 2288 (1993) HMSO.

Department of Health White Paper, *National Adoption Standards for England* (2001) Department of Health.

Eckelaar J, 'The Emergence of Children's Rights' (1986) 6 Oxford Journal of Legal Studies 161.

Eckelaar J, *Regulating Divorce* (1991) Clarendon Press.

Eckelaar J, 'The Importance of Thinking that Children Have Rights' in P Alston, S Parker and J Seymour (eds) *Children, Rights and the Law* (1992) Clarendon Press.

Eckelaar J, 'The Interests of the Child and the Child's Wishes: The Role of Dynamic Self-Determinism' (1994) 8 International Journal of Law and the Family 42.

Eckelaar J, 'Beyond the welfare principle' (2002) 14 Child and Family Law Quarterly 237.

Fineman M, 'Dominant Discourse, Professional Language and Legal Change in Child Custody Decision-Making' (1988) 101 Harvard Law Review 727.

Fortin J, '*Re D (Natural Parent Presumption)* Is blood really thicker than water?' (1999 a) 11 Child and Family Law Quarterly 435.

Fortin J, 'Rights Brought Home for Children' (1999 b) 62 Modern Law Review 350.

Harris-Short S, '*Re B (Adoption: Natural Parent)* Putting the child at the heart of adoption?' (2002) 14 Child and Family Law Quarterly 325.

Herring J, 'The Welfare Principle and Parents' Rights' in A Bainham, S Day Sclater and M Richards (eds*) What is a Parent? A Socio-Legal Analysis* (1999 a) Hart Publishing.

Herring J, 'The Human Rights Act and the Welfare Principle in Family Law – Conflicting or Complementary?' (1999 b) 11 Child and Family Law Quarterly 223.

Hester M, Pearson C and Radford L *Domestic Violence and Child Contact Arrangements in England and Denmark* (1996) The Policy Press.

Hobbs T, 'Parental Alienation Syndrome and UK Family Courts' (2002 a) Family Law 182.

Hobbs T, 'Parental Alienation Syndrome and UK Family Courts – The Dilemma' (2002 b) Family Law 381.

Jones D and McGraw J, 'Reliable and Fictitious Accounts of Sexual Abuse to Children' (1987) 2 Journal of Interpersonal Violence 27.

Jones E and Parkinson P, 'Child Sexual Abuse, Access and The Wishes of Children' (1995) 9 International Journal of Law and the Family 54.

King M and Piper C, *How the Law Thinks About Children* (1995) Ashgate Publishing Ltd.

Law Commission, *Review of Child Law, Guardianship and Custody* Law Com No 172 (1988) HMSO.

Lord Chancellor's Department, *Guidelines for Good Practice on Parental Contact in cases where there is Domestic Violence* (2002) Domestic Violence Guidelines.

Lyon T ,'The New Wave in Children's Suggestibility Research: A Critique' (1999) 84 Cornell Law Review 1004.

McCausland J, *Guarding Children's Interests: The Contributions of Guardians ad Litem in Court Proceedings* (2000) The Children's Society.

McGee C, *Childhood Experiences of Domestic Violence* (2000) Jessica Kingsley Publishers.

Mnookin R, 'Child-Custody Adjudication: Judicial Functions in the Face of Indeterminacy' (1975) 39 Law and Contemporary Problems 226.

O'Quigley A, *Listening to children's views: The findings and recommendations of recent research* (2000) Joseph Rowntree Foundation.

Parker S, 'The Best Interests of the Child – Principles and Problems' (1994) 8 International Journal of Law and the Family 26.

Piper C and Miakisher A, 'A Child's Right to a Veto in England and Russia: another welfare ploy?' (2003) 15 Child and Family Law Quarterly 57.

Reece H, 'The paramountcy principle: Consensus or Construct?' (1996) Current Legal Problems 267.

Schofield G, 'Making sense of the ascertainable wishes and feelings of insecurely attached children' (1998) 10 Child and Family Law Quarterly 363.

Smart C and Neale B, *Family Fragments?* (1999) Polity Press.

Smart C et al, *The Changing Experience of Childhood: Families and Divorce* (2001) Polity Press.

Sturge C, 'Medical input to care planning: The contribution of child and adolescent mental health services (CAMHS) to the care planning process' in Thorpe LJ and E Clarke (eds) *Divided Duties: Care planning for children within the family justice system* (1998) Family Law.

Sturge C and Glaser D, 'Contact and Domestic Violence – the Experts' Court Report' (2000) Family Law 615.

Thoenness N and Tjaden P, 'The Extent, Nature and Validity of Sexual Abuse Allegations in Custody/Visitation Disputes' (1990) 14 Child Abuse and Neglect 151.

Waite I and Stead H, 'Reporting the Wishes and Feelings of Children' (1998) Family Law 44.

Williams C, 'Parental Alienation Syndrome' (2002) Family Law 410.

Part Three

Children's rights and parents' powers

Chapter 9

Children's rights versus family privacy – physical punishment and financial support

(1) INTRODUCTION

Parents are best placed to protect and promote their children's rights and the vast majority of them do so very happily. Nevertheless, the privacy of family life ensures that parents can also tyrannise and abuse their children. Indeed, the physical dependence of young children makes an imbalance in power between them and their parents inevitable. It is clear that the law could do more to ensure that parents paid greater attention to their children's rights, if it took a more interventionist role. But social policy, strongly influenced by common assumptions about family privacy and parental autonomy, reflects a distinct lack of sympathy for the view that the law should attempt to interfere with family life.

This chapter starts by assessing the extent to which the assumption that the family should be free from legal regulation underlies current legislation. It then considers two areas where the law's reluctance to intervene in order to promote children's rights is particularly obvious. It assesses first the legal principles governing parents' right to control and discipline their children as they think fit. Second, it considers the law's treatment of the child's right to financial support and to be brought up with a reasonable standard of living. Both areas of law demonstrate how the concept of 'private ordering' dominates policies in this field.

(2) FAMILY PRIVACY AND THE ROLE OF THE LAW

Article 8 of the ECHR requires the state to respect family privacy and many legal systems operate on the assumption that family life should not be interfered with unless the circumstances are exceptional. As Minow states, the basic legal framework:

> '… rests on a sharp distinction between public and private responsibilities for children. Using this public/private distinction, the framework assigns child-care responsibilities to parents, and thereby avoids public responsibility for children. Public power becomes relevant only in exceptional circumstances, when parents default. The government is not supposed to "intervene" in the private realm of the family, where children's needs and interests are managed by their parents.'[1]

---

1   M Minow (1986) p 7.

This common attitude permeated the social policy culminating in the Children Act 1989. In maintaining this approach, however, the policy makers optimistically assume that parenting styles have been sufficiently influenced by the way the law relating to the parent child relationship has changed over the last century. Undoubtedly, the law has gradually encouraged parents to adopt a more egalitarian approach towards their children, certainly to show a greater regard for their welfare. Although just over a century ago fathers had absolute authority over their children, the nineteenth-century case law supporting such a principle is now 'remaindered to the history books'.[2] Twentieth-century legislation and case law firmly established the concept of the child's welfare being paramount;[3] more important even than their parents' rights.[4] Decisions such as *F v Wirral Metropolitan Borough Council*[5] confirm the view that parents are now unable to regard their children as part of their accumulated property and have no independent cause of action in tort allowing them to allege an interference with their parental rights. The modern legal approach is now that since parents' rights are only derived from their duties and exist only to secure the welfare of their children, they are better described as 'responsibilities'.[6] Indeed, Bainham argues that a constant repetition of the fact that parents do not have rights but only 'parental responsibility', together with an acceptance that children do have 'rights', is 'capable of creating an unbalanced view of the parent-child relationship'.[7]

Despite this changed approach, the fact that parents are only legally entitled to act towards their children in accordance with the welfare principle and can be challenged, even overridden, if they fail to do so,[8] may have little direct impact on many parents. Although the average parent inevitably brings up his children with the best of intentions, the essential subjectivity of the 'welfare' or 'best interests' test[9] does little to persuade repressive parents to adjust their parenting style to promote their children's rights more effectively. Even the parents who do attempt to abide by the welfare principle in a disinterested way may not promote their children's rights as fully as they could. Furthermore, and perhaps of more practical relevance, parents who never go near the courts give the judiciary little opportunity to urge on them a more liberal approach to the upbringing of their children.

For parents who avoid the judiciary's ambit, only well-publicised legislation which directly interferes with family life could have any real effect on their parenting styles. To date, however, the government has shown a distinct lack of enthusiasm for undertaking such a task, although there are signs that it acknowledges the important role played by parents in their children's development. Despite some attempt to

---

2   Per Lord Scarman in *Gillick v West Norfolk and Wisbech Area Health Authority* [1986] AC 112 at 183, when commenting on the decision in *Re Agar Ellis, Agar Ellis v Lascelles* (1883) 24 Ch D 317. See also Lord Denning's criticisms of the same case in *Hewer v Bryant* [1970] 1 QB 357 at 369.

3   See S Maidment (1984) for her comprehensive discussion of the history of this developing legislation and case law (ch 5).

4   Eg *J v C* [1970] AC 668.

5   [1991] Fam 69.

6   See Law Commission (1988) para 2.4.

7   A Bainham (1998) p 5.

8   Per Lord Scarman in *Gillick v West Norfolk and Wisbech Area Health Authority* [1986] AC 112 at 184.

9   See discussion in chapter 8.

ensure that parents obtain practical support and advice with their parenting role,[10] there has been little effort to influence the type of parenting styles parents adopt in relation to their children. Indeed, the state has colluded with and even encouraged the attitude underlying the well-known saying, 'An Englishman's home is his castle', perhaps partly because it is cheaper to allow parents to operate without major interference or financial support. Notable exceptions are the provisions governing state intervention to protect children from abuse,[11] and the legislative provisions directed at the parents of young offenders.[12] These apart, the state shows its respect for family privacy and autonomy, as it is required to do by article 8 of the ECHR, by trusting parents to bring up children with minimum state surveillance, by and large maintaining a laissez-faire approach to family life.

The most influential piece of legislation to emerge in recent years, which relates specifically to children, is the Children Act 1989. It gave official approval to the change of emphasis emerging through case law and legislation that parents were no longer to be seen as having 'rights' over their children, in the proprietorial sense, but instead were deemed to owe 'responsibilities' to them.[13] Nevertheless, in many respects it maintains the essential privacy of family life. Indeed, it deliberately adopts what has been described as a 'hands-off approach', on the basis that lawyers and litigation often do more harm than good.[14] The assumption seems to be that parents' interests are identical to those of their children. Consistent with this approach, the Children Act 1989 makes no attempt even to define what basic responsibilities parents owe to their children, leaving it for them to decide for themselves what responsibilities are most appropriate for children of varying ages.[15]

It is regrettable that although the 1989 Act contains detailed provisions about the duties owed by local authorities to children they look after[16] and the services they should provide for children in need,[17] it fails to set out a basic list of parental responsibilities, available to be consulted by child-care practitioners and parents alike. Although it is arguable that the average parent is unlikely to refer to legislation before adopting a particular regime, this underestimates the indirect influence that the law can have on family life. The ability, for example, of Scottish child-care practitioners to refer to legislative provisions to justify advice to parents about their behaviour may gradually influence public perceptions of the parenting role.[18] By contrast, the failure of the English Children Act 1989 to expand on its definition of

---

10 Eg recommendations on how to support families better in Home Office (1998) led, inter alia, to the establishment of: Sure Start, a programme aimed at improving the life chances of infants under the age of 4, through better family support, health services and early education, in deprived areas; the National Family and Parenting Institute, a charity devoted to developing and improving support for parents; Parentline Plus, a confidential 24-hour telephone advice line for parents.

11 Discussed in chapter 15.

12 Eg the parenting orders introduced by the Crime and Disorder Act 1998, ss 8–9. Discussed in more detail in chapter 18.

13 Now enshrined in the Children Act 1989, s 3.

14 B Hoggett (1994) p 10.

15 Children Act 1989, s 3(1) merely provides 'In this Act "parental responsibility" means all the rights, duties, powers and authority *which by law a parent of a child has* in relation to the child and his property' (emphasis supplied) with no explanation of what these rights might be.

16 Children Act 1989, ss 22–24 and the regulations made thereunder.

17 Children Act 1989, Sch 2 and the regulations made thereunder.

18 See the Children (Scotland) Act 1995, s 1(1) for a reasonably detailed list of parental responsibilities.

'parental responsibilities' suggests a misplaced complacency over the existing state of family values.

Bainham has convincingly argued that the Children Act 1989 re-emphasises the privacy of the family so that the child-rearing role is likely to be seen increasingly as a matter for private regulation.[19] It is perhaps surprising that the Act adopted this approach, in view of the strong criticisms levelled at the views of Goldstein, Freud and Solnit in the second of their influential works, *Before the Best Interests of the Child*.[20] They considered a laissez-faire approach essential in order to maintain family privacy. Commentators writing in the early 1980s strongly criticised these authors for their extreme views over the value of family autonomy.[21] Despite this, less than ten years later, the Children Act 1989 not only promoted the assumption that responsible parents would automatically protect their children's interests without legislative encouragement, but was also intent on reinforcing the privatisation of family life, by withdrawing the law from areas where it formerly had had some influence.[22] Indeed, by introducing what is sometimes known at 'the principle of non-intervention', the Children Act 1989[23] significantly reduced the extent to which the law has any contact with parents, thereby restricting the scope of the law's persuasive influence.[24] Furthermore, it made no attempt to change parenting styles in favour, for example, of encouraging more consultation between parents and children.[25]

(3)   THE CHILD'S RIGHT TO CARE AND CONTROL, THE PARENTS' RIGHT TO DISCIPLINE

(A)   Introduction

The extent to which parents should be allowed to discipline and punish their children as they think fit produces deeply polarised views over whether the use of physical punishment on children can be justified on practical and ethical grounds, and more generally, over the extent to which the state should interfere with parents' family privacy and autonomy. Children will, of course, be unable to develop the confidence to make decisions of their own if parents provide them with little opportunity to do so, by imposing on them an over-strict atmosphere of control and discipline. Nevertheless, some writers involved in the debate about children's rights are sceptical about the law's ability to persuade parents to relax their parenting methods sufficiently to promote children's decision-making capacities. Wald humorously suggests that it would be a waste of resources, for example, to introduce legislation allowing young

---

19   A Bainham (1990) p 208ff.
20   J Goldstein, A Freud, A Solnit (1980). Discussed in more detail in chapter 1.
21   Inter alia, B Dickens (1981) and M Freeman (1983).
22   Eg the Children Act 1989, Sch 12, para 31 scaled down the courts' role in the arrangements made by divorcing parents for their children's future upbringing under the Matrimonial Causes Act 1973, s 41.
23   Ie the 'no order' principle introduced by the Children Act 1989, s 1(5).
24   See B Hoggett (1994), who describes (p 10) the Children Act 1989, s 1(5) as being known as 'the principle of non-intervention'. See also Munby J in *Re X and Y (leave to remove from the jurisdiction: no order principle)* [2001] 2 FLR 118, who discusses (at 135–146) the significance of s 1 (5). But see A Bainham (1998), who criticises (pp 3–4) the way in which the 'no order' provision has acquired an unnecessary emphasis by being described as 'the principle of non-intervention' and as a 'presumption'.
25   See discussion in chapter 3, pp 79–80.

children the right to decide 'when to go to bed, when to bathe and what to eat', due to its obvious unenforceability. He asks rhetorically whether the parents would:

'... be forbidden from enforcing their request [to the child to go to bed] by cutting off allowance, setting a curfew, not buying Christmas presents, or giving the child a spanking? ... [the] concept of total independence is just unrealistic unless we are prepared to place an outside monitor in every home to eliminate the authority parents have stemming from their greater strength and economic power.'[26]

Implicit in this comment is the assumption that parental behaviour is beyond the reach of the law, an attitude which has contributed to the 'hands-off' approach underlying so many of the legal principles applied to children. It is this approach to family life which has consistently prevented any legislative attempt to regulate the way in which parents discipline their children.

The dilemma is that the law expects parents to exercise a degree of discipline in the household. Indeed, children are naturally high-spirited and mischievous and parents may be found to be in breach of their duty to care adequately for them if they fail to control them sufficiently to prevent accidents in the home occurring. Consequently, a parent or foster parent failing to maintain a standard of care which can be expected from a reasonably careful and prudent parent may be liable in tort to a child who suffers an injury as a result. In *Surtees v Kingston-upon-Thames Borough Council; Surtees v Hughes*[27] the Court of Appeal warned that the courts should be cautious and avoid imposing 'an impossibly high standard', in the light of the demands of family life:[28]

'We should be slow to characterise as negligent the care which ordinary loving and careful mothers are able to give to individual children, given the rough-and-tumble of home life.'[29]

Despite this call for flexibility, parents must impose some discipline to maintain a safe level of control on the household and this may lead to their using punishment of various kinds.

(B) The current law

For many parents, the dividing line between physical abuse, which society will not condone, and reasonable physical punishment, which it will, remains unclear. The law's continued failure to clarify the extent to which physical punishment is unacceptable means that practitioners have no clear answers either. For example, the mother who had punished her son by hitting him on the thigh with a wooden spoon considered that she was behaving perfectly normally.[30] When the woman police constable asked her 'Don't you think that was a little over the top?', the mother's reply was 'No, every woman corrects their child'.[31] The court refused the mother's application for judicial review of the decision to place her two children on the child protection register. Registration indicated that the local authority were, at the very least, concerned about her son's future safety. Nevertheless, no criminal charges were

---

26   M Wald (1979) p 272.
27   [1991] 2 FLR 559.
28   [1991] 2 FLR 559 at 571, per Stocker LJ.
29   [1991] 2 FLR 559 at 583–584, per Browne-Wilkinson VC.
30   *R v East Sussex County Council, ex p R* [1991] 2 FLR 358.
31   [1991] 2 FLR 358 at 360.

contemplated, nor indeed, was there any suggestion that her children were to be removed from home. The mother must have been left in some confusion about society's views of her style of parenting.

The case described above occurred over a decade ago. Since then, the law governing physical punishment has become far more confused. Indeed, a precocious child attempting to ascertain whether his or her parents are behaving lawfully in adopting a particular form of punishment will find that there are few clear answers. Parents will be equally puzzled. The criminal law ostensibly appears to offer children adequate protection from physical punishment since there is a variety of offences with which a parent might be charged. A form of punishment which could be defined as ill-treatment or wilful neglect causing the child unnecessary suffering or injury to health might well amount to an offence under the Children and Young Persons Act 1933, section 1.[32] More violent punishment could attract a charge of common assault, or assault occasioning actual bodily harm or even inflicting grievous bodily harm. But although school teachers might be charged with any of these offences if they use physical punishment on their pupils,[33] parents and others to whom they delegate their child's care are in a different category. The common law has for centuries maintained their freedom to administer reasonable punishment by way of discipline, without incurring criminal liability. Statutory confirmation of this defence was provided by the Children and Young Persons Act 1933, section 1(7) which states:

> 'Nothing in this section shall be construed as affecting the right of any parent, or (subject to section 548 of the Education Act 1996) any other person, having the lawful control or charge of a child or young person to administer punishment to him.'

This statutory provision, which fails to clarify what level or type of punishment the law allows parents to adopt, must be read in the light of Victorian case law establishing that those with lawful control of a child are entitled to administer physical punishment which is 'moderate and reasonable'.[34] A parent[35] might be unclear over the exact point at which physical punishment is too severe to be deemed 'moderate and reasonable', thereby leaving him or her without such a defence to a criminal charge. Many judges and juries have shown similar confusion in the past.[36]

Further bewilderment is in store. When interpreting the common law, courts must consider the demands of the Human Rights Act 1998. Thus judges and juries considering whether punishment is 'reasonable' and within the common law defence, must also take into account the considerations underpinning a child's right to

---

32   Children and Young Persons Act 1933, s 1(1) provides: 'If any person who has attained the age of 16 years and has responsibility for any child or young person under that age, wilfully assaults, ill-treats, neglects, abandons or exposes him or causes or procures him to be assaulted, ill-treated, neglected, abandoned or exposed, in a manner likely to cause him unnecessary suffering or injury to health (including injury to or loss of sight, or hearing, or limb or organ of the body, and any mental derangement), that person shall be guilty of [an offence] ...'

33   See Education Act 1996, ss 548–549, as amended by the School Standards and Framework Act 1998, s 131, which makes the use of physical punishment in schools unlawful not only for civil purposes but also for criminal purposes, unless there was an immediate danger of personal injury or an immediate danger to the property (see s 548(5)).

34   *R v Hopley* (1860) 2 F & F 202.

35   Or other person with lawful control over the child, such as a babysitter, or child-minder.

36   Eg *B v Harris* 1990 SLT 208: a Scottish mother was acquitted of assault for having beaten her 9-year-old daughter with a belt, leaving her thigh bruised; cf *Peebles v MacPhail* 1990 SLT 245: a Scottish mother was convicted of assault for having struck her 2-year-old on the side of his face hard enough to knock him over.

protection from torture or inhuman or degrading treatment or punishment under article 3 of the ECHR. According to the Court of Appeal in *R v H (assault of a child: reasonable chastisement),*[37] the defence will apply only if the punishment was reasonable, taking account of the following criteria: the nature and context of the defendant's behaviour; its duration; its physical and mental consequences for the child; the child's age and personal characteristics; the reasons given by the defendant for administering the punishment. As is discussed below, the inclusion of this last item in the list – the reasons for the punishment – renders this interpretation of Convention requirements inaccurate. Furthermore, the direction superimposed on the common law defence makes the law so confusing that it is extremely difficult for anyone to decide on the lawfulness of using physical punishment. Before discussing the decision in *R v H,* it is intended to consider briefly what factors contributed to the law developing in such an unsatisfactory manner.

(C)   Physical punishment – the historical background

The current confusion in the law regarding the legality of various forms of discipline would, of course, disappear if the parental right to use physical punishment was abolished altogether. There were considerable efforts to scrap the Children and Young Persons Act 1933, section 1(7) when the Children Act 1989 was still in Bill form, but none succeeded. A further opportunity for amending the law appeared when the government was required to respond to the landmark decision of the European Court of Human Rights in *A v United Kingdom (human rights: punishment of child).*[38] Nevertheless, its bizarre consultation over how to reform the law demonstrated the Department of Health's reluctance to influence or change parental practices. It maintained that it would be counter-productive to outlaw physical punishment. In a similar approach to that taken by Wald above, it saw any legislative attempt to do so as a 'heavy-handed intrusion into family life'.[39] Such laws would 'victimise parents unfairly and compromise public confidence in the legal system'.[40] This view underwrote its final decision not to change the law at all.[41]

As noted, the need to reconsider the law on physical punishment had been triggered by the decision in *A v United Kingdom.* An English boy successfully argued that his step-father's ability to beat him, when he was only 9, with a garden cane over the period of a week as a form of punishment, without any criminal sanction, infringed his rights under article 3 to freedom from torture or to inhuman or degrading treatment or punishment. The European Court of Human Rights held that the United Kingdom government had a positive obligation to provide children with practical and effective state protection against treatment or punishment contrary to article 3. This it had manifestly failed to do, since a jury had acquitted the step-father of assault occasioning actual bodily harm, despite his having treated his step-son with sufficient severity to infringe the boy's rights under article 3.[42] When ruling against the United Kingdom

---

37   [2001] EWCA Crim 1024, [2001] 2 FLR 431 at [31], per Rose LJ.
38   [1998] 2 FLR 959.
39   Department of Health (2000) para 2.4.
40   Department of Health (2000) para 2.14. See also Department of Health (2001) para 76.
41   See discussion below.
42   The jury had accepted that the step-father was entitled to a defence to the criminal charges, namely that his behaviour had amounted to 'reasonable chastisement' under Children and Young Persons Act 1933, s 1(7) and *R v Hopley* (1860) 2 F & F 202.

government, the Court pointed out the inadequacy of the protection offered children, in so far as the common law defence of reasonable chastisement imposes a burden of proof on the prosecution to establish beyond reasonable doubt that the assault went beyond the limits of lawful punishment.[43] The Court asserted that the United Kingdom government has a positive obligation to protect children against parental infringements of their article 3 rights.[44]

The impact of the decision in *A v United Kingdom* was restricted by the European Court's failure to suggest that physical punishment per se amounted to a violation of a child's rights under article 3. Indeed, it reasserted its earlier view that it depends on the circumstances of each case whether ill-treatment reaches the level of severity required to infringe article 3. 'Factors such as the nature and context of the punishment, the manner and method of its execution, its duration, its physical and mental effects and, in some instances, the sex, age and state of health of the victim must all be taken into account.'[45] This refusal to rule out all physical punishment allowed the government to downplay the decision in *A v United Kingdom* by arguing that it merely precluded parents from treating their children particularly harshly. The Health Minister claimed that the 'overwhelming majority of parents know the difference between smacking and beating'.[46] Nevertheless, reform of the law throughout the United Kingdom appeared to be inevitable since the government expressly conceded, in the course of arguing its case in *A v United Kingdom*, that domestic law currently failed to protect children adequately from violations of their article 3 rights and that it would require amending.

Before introducing changes in the law, the government embarked on its bizarre 'consultation exercise'.[47] Without proposing or discussing the possibility of prohibiting all forms of physical punishment, it declared at the outset its apparently unshakeable view that 'it would be quite unacceptable to outlaw all physical punishment of a child by a parent', and that since the majority of parents would not support such a measure, it did not intend to introduce a law which would be 'intrusive and incompatible with our aim of helping and encouraging parents in their role'.[48] Despite the European Court's disapproval of allowing parents to use the 'reasonable chastisement' defence to criminal charges, that defence was not to be abolished.[49] Instead, the Department of Health merely sought views on how to delineate the ambit of that defence. Such guidance might, for example, involve listing specific types of conduct which would never be deemed reasonable, such as injuries to the brain, eyes or ears.

The Department of Health's consultation document reflected its obvious reluctance to interfere with parents' own ideas about how to discipline their children. Its timidity had been reinforced by the results of an opinion poll commissioned by the government indicating that the majority of parents considered it acceptable to smack their children,

43   [1998] 2 FLR 959 at [23].
44   The decision emphasised that the ECHR's scope extends to protecting private individuals from members of their own family, thereby providing an excellent example of the Convention's 'horizontal effect'. Discussed in chapter 2, p 62.
45   *Costello-Roberts v United Kingdom* [1994] 1 FCR 65 at para 30. The European Court of Human Rights referred again to this guidance in *A v United Kingdom* [1998] 2 FLR 959 at [20].
46   'Health Minister welcomes "common sense decision"', Department of Health press release, 23 September 1998.
47   Department of Health (2000).
48   Department of Health (2000) para 2.14; see also para 1.5.
49   Department of Health (2000) para 5.1.

and that the law should tolerate their doing so.[50] The Department of Health has a poor record when it comes to standing up to parental views favouring physical punishment. It had, for example, in 1994, felt obliged to revise its guidelines to local authorities; these had formerly suggested that physical punishment should not be used by anyone working with children in a local authority context.[51] The amended guidance made it clear that an intending child-minder should not be refused registration merely because she wishes to smack the children she is caring for, as long as the child's parents agree with this.[52]

None of the arguments in favour of abolishing parents' legal right to punish their children physically were mentioned by the government's consultation paper. By contrast, Northern Ireland, which initiated a separate consultation exercise in 2001, produced a paper comprehensively setting out the arguments for and against prohibiting physical punishment in the home, in a detailed and even-handed way.[53] In particular, it reviewed the considerable and accumulating international pressure on all countries within the United Kingdom to bring their legal systems into line with those countries which had long since prohibited the physical punishment of children.[54]

The arguments favouring root and branch reform of English law are discussed briefly below.[55] Before considering these, however, it should be noted that the government eventually reneged on its commitment to amend English law to take account of the European Court of Human Rights' decision in *A v United Kingdom*.[56] Indeed, its response to the consultation exercise conducted by the Department of Health was to announce that it intended to make no changes to the law.[57] It argued that reforms had been rendered unnecessary because, by implementing the Human Rights Act 1998, the law already provided children with sufficient protection from infringements of their Convention rights.

The government's view that law reform was now unnecessary was influenced by the decision of the Court of Appeal in *R v H (assault of a child: reasonable chastisement)*.[58] As noted above, according to the Court of Appeal, in order to comply with the Human Rights Act 1998, the direction to a jury considering whether to accept a parent's defence to criminal charges,[59] should include additional advice on the meaning of 'reasonable chastisement', enabling it to determine whether the father's behaviour infringed article 3 of the ECHR.[60] There are serious doubts over the

---

50   In 1998, 88% of respondents to a National Statistics Survey agreed 'that it is sometimes necessary to smack a naughty child'; 8% disagreed and 85% of respondents agreed that parents should be allowed by law to do so. Department of Health (2000) Annex A, para 2.
51   Department of Health (1991) para 6.22.
52   The Children Act 1989 (LAC [94] 23) para 10. This new guidance responded to *Sutton London Borough Council v Davis* [1994] 1 FLR 737 deciding that a local authority should not have adopted the non-smacking guidance as a 'blanket' policy when assessing the suitability of child-minders for local authority registration, and should take account of the parents' wishes on the matter.
53   Northern Ireland Office of Law Reform (2001). See also Scottish Executive (2001).
54   See below, p 284 n 74.
55   See also summary and discussion in Northern Ireland Office of Law Reform (2001) chs 4–7 and esp pp 38–39.
56   [1998] 2 FLR 959.
57   See Department of Health, press release, 8 November 2001 and Department of Health (2001) para 76. See C Barton (2002).
58   [2001] EWCA Crim 1024, [2001] 2 FLR 431.
59   In that case, a father who had beaten his son with a belt pleaded not guilty to a charge of assault occasioning actual bodily harm.
60   [2001] EWCA Crim 1024, [2001] 2 FLR 431 at [31], per Rose LJ.

government's confidence that the changes in the law prompted by *R v H* are sufficient to bring the law into line with the requirements of the ECHR.[61] In the first place, Rose LJ's description of the correct direction to be given to the jury inaccurately summarises the European Court's own interpretation of article 3. The list of factors to be considered is firmly established by Strasbourg case law,[62] and does not include Rose LJ's fifth and last factor, namely the reasons given by the defendant for administering the punishment. According to Northern Ireland's consultation paper, 'the addition of the final factor in *R v H* places a gloss on the *A v United Kingdom* factors which changes their meaning'.[63] This observation is undoubtedly correct. The European Court of Human Rights has never indicated that such a factor has any bearing on the severity of a punishment for the purposes of article 3. The addition produces a significant change, given that a jury's view of the parent's behaviour might be strongly influenced by the reasons underlying the punishment.

Northern Ireland's consultation paper considered that the *R v H* reforms were too limited to bring the law into full compliance with its own international human rights obligations. Indeed, the paper observed that since the ECHR is a living document which must be interpreted in the light of evolving social conditions and other human rights documents: 'It should not be assumed that the limited reform in *R v H* will satisfy Convention standards indefinitely. Further action is still necessary.'[64] It is regrettable that the United Kingdom government did not reach a similar conclusion in relation to English law. As can be seen from the summary above, the present law is now unsatisfactorily confusing and provides parents with no comprehensible guidance over what type of physical punishment is lawful, and what type is punishable as a criminal offence. It seems unlikely that the government can ignore for long the mounting pressure to reform the law more radically.

(D)   Pressure for further reform

Perhaps the strongest argument in favour of finally banning the use of physical punishment entirely is that social attitudes have changed radically over the last century. Whereas in Victorian society the physical punishment of adult and child criminal offenders was routine and domestic violence in the home was condoned, society today considers both unacceptable. It is now difficult to justify the law protecting adults from assaulting each other, whilst allowing adults to assault their smaller and more vulnerable offspring. 'Children are the only people in the United Kingdom whose right to physical integrity – to protection from all forms of inter-personal violence – is not yet supported by the law and social attitudes.'[65] Furthermore, there are the practical arguments against its use. In particular, research indicates not only that physical punishment is less effective than other forms of discipline, but also that its use is associated with long-term negative psychological effects.[66] When

61   See Northern Ireland Office of Law Reform (2001) pp 40–41.
62   Inter alia, *Costello-Roberts v United Kingdom* [1994] 1 FCR 65 and *A v United Kingdom (human rights: punishment of child)* [1998] 2 FLR 959. See above.
63   Northern Ireland Office of Law Reform (2001) pp 40–41. NB the Human Rights Act 1998, s 2(1) directs the courts, when considering the requirements of the ECHR, to 'take into account' the decisions of the European Court of Human Rights. They are not permitted to present these decisions with a gloss on them.
64   Northern Ireland Office of Law Reform (2001) p 41.
65   See Commission on Children and Violence (1995) p 15.
66   E Gershoff (2002) pp 544–551.

parents use physical punishment as a form of discipline, they indicate to their children that violent and aggressive behaviour is an acceptable method of dealing with stressful situations, thereby reinforcing violent behaviour in society.[67]

Underlying the debate over physical punishment is some uncertainty over the role that the law should be playing. Arguably, the law should 'send out a clear message about what behaviour is unacceptable in families, or what we, as a society, feel about violence'.[68] As the experience of other European countries, notably Sweden,[69] demonstrates, the law can promote attitudinal changes in society. Indeed, prohibiting physical punishment may well produce a different approach to discipline.[70] By contrast, this government's inconsistent attitude towards promoting attitudinal change has produced a confused and incoherent body of legal principles regarding punishment. On the one hand, it has clearly indicated its disapproval of the use of physical punishment by practitioners working with children. Consequently, teachers,[71] foster carers and residential care workers[72] cannot physically punish children in their care. But on the other hand, the government is not prepared to interfere with parents' views on how to bring up their children. It is difficult to defend this narrow interpretation of the law's proper role in society. Nor can the government argue that such an approach is in conformity with the aims of article 8 of the ECHR, which ensures respect for family privacy. In 1982, the European Commission of Human Rights rejected an application by Swedish parents alleging that the Swedish ban on parental physical punishment infringed their rights to respect for family life. According to the Commission, Swedish law was praiseworthy since it now discouraged abuse and prevented violence against children.[73]

Until parental use of physical punishment is banned in England and Wales, the law will become increasingly out of step with the legal systems of many countries

67   See Commission on Children and Violence (1995) pp 46–55.

68   Northern Ireland Office of Law Reform (2001) p 42.

69   Sweden banned all physical punishment in 1979.

70   Whereas in a 1979 survey about 50% of Swedish parents reported that they spanked their children (9% even used spanking every or every other week), a 1996 survey indicated that roughly 30% of middle-school pupils and a higher proportion of adults reported having been physically punished by their parents before they reached their teen years. Statistics Sweden (1996) p 15.

71   See Education Act 1996, ss 548–549, as amended by School Standards and Framework Act 1998, s 131. See *R (on the application of Williamson) v Secretary of State for Education and Employment* [2001] EWHC Admin 960, [2002] 1 FLR 493: Elias J (QBD) rejected all the claims of headteachers, teachers and parents from certain Christian independent schools, inter alia, that the Education Act 1996, s 548 had not completely abolished the use of corporal punishment in independent schools and that the abolition of corporal punishment infringed their rights under arts 9 and 2 of Protocol 1 of the ECHR. See also discussion of the gradual reform of the law relating to physical punishment in schools in J Fortin (1998) pp 235–237.

72   See Children's Homes Regulations 1991, SI 1991/1506, reg 8(2) and Department of Health (1991) para 6.22. See discussion by J Fortin (2001) pp 250–257.

73   *Seven Individuals v Sweden* (Application No 8811/79, unreported) (1982) 29 CDR 104. See also *Philip Williamson v United Kingdom* (Application No 55211/00) (7 September 2000, unreported): the European Court of Human Rights rejected unanimously and without hearing a similar application brought by individuals associated with a group of Christian schools in the United Kingdom. They alleged that the ban on corporal punishment in private schools infringed parents' rights to freedom of religion and family life.

throughout the world.[74] The United Kingdom is also failing to comply with its international human rights obligations. An argument that the government has consistently used is that parents can distinguish between a beating, which is clearly prohibited by the ECHR as amounting to inhuman or degrading treatment or punishment, and an ordinary smack, administered by a loving parent.[75] Nevertheless, an ordinary smack by a loving mother, which does not infringe article 3, may quickly escalate into a vicious and systematic form of physical abuse, which does. This argument also ignores the government's obligation to comply with article 19 of the CRC. Whilst the terms of article 37 of the CRC are quite narrow, prohibiting torture or other cruel, inhuman or degrading treatment or punishment,[76] article 19 goes much further. It requires states to –

> 'take all appropriate legislative, administrative, social and educational measures to protect the child from all forms of physical or mental violence, injury or abuse … while in the care of parent(s), legal guardian(s) or any other person who has the care of the child.'

Its terms clearly rule out all forms of violence, ranging from a smack to a beating.

When responding to the United Kingdom's first and second periodic reports on the implementation of the Convention,[77] the Committee on the Rights of the Child has stressed that the government is failing to address its international obligation to protect children's physical integrity, notably under articles 19 and 37.[78] In particular, it is quite unable to accept the concept of a 'reasonable' standard of physical punishment. When responding to its first report, the Committee recommended that the United Kingdom should introduce legislation prohibiting the use of physical punishment, as in many other countries, and that a public education campaign be launched to emphasise the child's right to physical integrity.[79] By the time it considered the United Kingdom's second periodic report, no real progress had been made to ban parents from using physical punishment to discipline their children. In an uncharacteristically robust response, the Committee stated that it deeply regretted –

> '… that the State party persists in retaining the defence of "reasonable chastisement" and has taken no significant action towards prohibiting all corporal punishment of children in the family … governmental proposals to limit rather than to remove the "reasonable chastisement" defence do not comply with the principles and provisions of the Convention.'[80]

It recommended that the government should 'with urgency' adopt legislation removing the reasonable chastisement defence and also carry out 'public education

---

74   Legislation banning physical punishment by parents is in place in Austria, Croatia, Cyprus, Denmark, Finland, Germany, Latvia, Norway and Sweden. In 1996, Italy's Supreme Court declared all physical punishment to be unlawful and, in 2000, Israel's Supreme Court did the same. In 2002, draft legislation (Criminal Justice (Scotland) Bill) was introduced in Scotland, which, it appears, will, prohibit hitting children with implements and hitting them on the head or shaking them. Nevertheless, clauses banning all physical punishment for children up to the age of 3 were rejected. See Scottish Parliament (2002) Pt 7, paras 99–141.

75   See inter alia, Department of Health press release, 23 September 1998 and Department of Health (2000) para 1.5.

76   Ie similar to art 3 of the ECHR.

77   Discussed in chapter 2.

78   Committee on the Rights of the Child (1995) paras 16 and 31 and (2002) paras 35–36. See also T Hammarberg (1995) p 21.

79   Committee on the Rights of the Child (1995) paras 16 and 31.

80   Committee on the Rights of the Child (2002) para 35.

81   Committee on the Rights of the Child (2002) para 36. See also Committee on Economic, Social and Cultural Rights (2002) para 36, recommending that the physical punishment of children in families be prohibited.

programmes on the negative consequences of corporal punishment'.[81] The government's exaggerated concern not to offend parental opinion on this topic seems ill suited to a society containing parents whose abusive behaviour leads to significant numbers of children being removed annually from home into public care.

(4) PARENTAL DUTY TO SUPPORT THE CHILD

(A) The state's role of non-intervention

The CRC recognises children's right to be brought up and cared for and also to be provided with a standard of living, at least adequate for their reasonable survival. But its provisions are conservative and reflect the way child care is currently organised throughout most of the world. It accepts that children are brought up in family units and that governments should leave them in a degree of privacy, expecting the parents to provide for children out of their own resources. As Walsh has commented, this approach is reflected in article 18(1) of the Convention which requires states to 'use their best efforts to ensure recognition of the principle that both parents have common responsibilities for the upbringing and development of the child'. Article 18(2) acknowledges that some parents may not be able to fulfil their duties to their children and will need extra help. It therefore expects states to 'render appropriate assistance to parents and legal guardians in the performance of their child-rearing responsibilities', by providing extra support for the children in the community. But the terms of these articles make it clear that state support is to be a form of safety-net assistance only. There is no suggestion in these provisions that children are to be regarded as 'children of the state'.[82]

The Convention also fully recognises that extreme poverty will prevent children fulfilling their full potential in a variety of ways, particularly if it undermines their health. Article 27(1) states that governments should 'recognize the right of every child to a standard of living adequate for the child's physical, mental, spiritual, moral and social development'. Furthermore, article 4 requires governments to implement children's economic rights 'to the maximum extent of their available resources'. Despite these provisions indicating the need for a state commitment to ensuring that children have a reasonable standard of living, paragraph 2 of article 27 clarifies the Convention's cautious approach. It states that: 'The parent(s) or others responsible for the child have the primary responsibility to secure, within their abilities and financial capacities, the conditions of living necessary for the child's development.' Thus again the Convention makes it plain that parents and not the state have primary responsibility for providing children with an adequate standard of living. It merely acknowledges that some parents will need state assistance over this by requiring governments to 'take appropriate measures to assist parents and others responsible for the child to implement this right and shall in case of need provide material assistance and support programmes, particularly with regard to nutrition, clothing and housing'.[83] Article 26(1) amplifies this obligation more specifically, requiring states to ensure that children, or their carers on their behalf, receive financial support, in the form of social security or other benefits, taking into account the circumstances of the adults responsible for their care.

---

82   B Walsh (1991) p 173.
83   Art 27(3).

English law and policy also emphasises this conservative approach to children's upbringing. Section 1 of the Child Support Act 1991 firmly states that parents are responsible for maintaining their own children. Furthermore, those caring for children may also incur criminal liability if they ill-treat or neglect them,[84] and, more specifically, a parent is deemed to have criminally neglected a child by failing to provide him or her with adequate food, clothing, medical aid or lodging.[85] The government does, however, acknowledge, albeit grudgingly, that some parents may not be able to fulfil their duties to their children and will need extra help. It therefore goes some way towards complying with its obligations under articles 18(2), 26(1) and 27(3) of the Convention and makes available certain back-up services, in the form of benefits for those with no income, free health care, education, and subsidised housing. Furthermore, the continued availability of child benefit, a weekly sum of non-means tested child benefit payable to every adult responsible for any child under the age of 16,[86] retains a symbolic, if not practical importance.[87] The government also places a duty on local authorities to provide extra support for families with children in need,[88] and, in the last resort, the state may even intervene to protect children from neglect by seeking the court's authority to remove them into local authority care.[89]

Families with children obviously need considerably higher incomes to cover the additional costs of child-raising to reach a similar standard of living to those enjoyed by their childless counterparts.[90] Furthermore, the costs of rearing children can fall disproportionately on families on low income, with the combination of high costs and low income pushing some families into poverty.[91] In the event of parents having insufficient income to maintain themselves and their children, families may become entirely dependent on income-related state benefits, probably in the form of income support or child tax credit, depending on their circumstances.[92] But state support for children is provided on the clear understanding that the primary responsibility for maintaining them is on the parents, and the state is only doing so because the parents have failed in this respect. 'The government intervenes only as a "safety net" to guarantee a minimum income, when the family and the market fail.'[93] Indeed, since 1601,[94] the state has expected reimbursement from a parent, as the child's 'liable relative',[95] for any public support paid over for a child, who could and should have been maintained by him.

84   Children and Young Persons Act 1933, s 1(1).
85   The Children and Young Persons Act 1933, s 1(2)(a) imposes criminal liability on 'a parent or other person *legally liable to maintain* a child or young person'. Section 17 does not clarify whom the Act considers to be 'legally liable to maintain a child'. It is generally assumed that liability to maintain a child falls on both parents, if married, and on the mother, if unmarried.
86   Unless the child continues to receive full-time non-advanced education, in which case it is extended to the age of 19: see Child Benefit (General) Regulations 1976, SI 1976/965, reg 7.
87   See G Douglas (2000) pp 266–267.
88   See Children Act 1989, s 17(1) and (10).
89   See discussion in chapter 15.
90   It was calculated in 1997 that a child reaching his/her 17th birthday would have cost an average £50,000 to rear: S Middleton, K Ashworth and I Braithwaite (1997) p 69.
91   Child Poverty Action Group (CPAG) (2001) p 129.
92   See CPAG's annual *Welfare benefits handbook*, for an up-to-date analysis of benefits law and practice.
93   C Solera (2001) p 466.
94   The date when the Elizabethan Poor Law was established.
95   The child's parents are liable relatives, irrespective of their marital status. See G Douglas (2000) pp 271–275, for a discussion of the history and current application of the liable relative rule.

It might be acceptable for the state to maintain its existing attitude towards the costs of childrearing, were it not for the impact that such an approach produces. Although the CRC expects parents to take *primary* responsibility for their children, it also recognises children's right to enjoy an adequate standard of living,[96] and the state's duty to provide parents with appropriate assistance,[97] to the maximum extent of its resources.[98] The United Kingdom's obvious and increasing failure on all these counts has attracted international criticism.[99] Despite a modicum of state support being available for those in real need, by the late 1990s the rate of families living in poverty had risen spectacularly,[100] with the inequalities between high and low-income families also widening. More to the point, the number of children living in poverty had grown particularly fast, with the numbers of children living in households with below half average income tripling between 1968 and 1995/96.[101] Whatever measures of poverty are used,[102] the poverty statistics make depressing reading,[103] particularly in relation to children, with a third of all children living in poverty,[104] and staying in poverty for longer than in many other industrialised countries.[105] Large numbers of these children are being raised by lone parents, whose financial hardships are now greater than those suffered by pensioners and far greater than those of two parent families,[106] due primarily to the women heading them up being unemployed or on relatively low wages.[107] Indeed, lone mothers in the United Kingdom have a very low employment rate compared with married mothers and unmarried mothers in other

---

96   Art 27(1).
97   See arts 27(3) and 18(2).
98   Art 4.
99   See, inter alia: Committee on the Rights of the Child (1995) paras 9, 15, 24 and 25, referring to the increasing numbers of children living in poverty in this country and the need for the government to allocate more resources to address the problem; Committee on the Rights of the Child (2002) paras 43 and 44, referring again to the high proportion of children living in poverty and the need for more resources and a more effective and co-ordinated policy; Committee on Economic, Social and Cultural Rights (2002) para 18, referring to the increasing gap between rich and poor and to the high levels of child poverty.
100 Whilst in 1983 only 14% of households lacked three or more socially perceived necessities, by 1999, this percentage had risen to 24% of households, roughly one in four: CPAG (2001) p 30.
101 See P Gregg, S Harkness and S Machin (1999) pp 3–7.
102 There is considerable disagreement over how poverty should be measured. For useful discussions of alternative approaches, see, inter alia: D Gordon et al (2000) Appendices 1 and 2; Department for Work and Pensions (DWP) (2002 b); M Brewer et al (2002) ch 3.
103 Depending on what poverty measure is used as the poverty line (eg below 50% of median income after housing costs or 60% of median income after housing costs), between 13 and 14 million people were living in poverty in 1999/2000: CPAG (2001) p 30.
104 In 1999/2000, a higher proportion of children were living in poverty than the population as a whole. Whatever measure is used, well over 4 million children (well over 30%) were living in poverty in 1999/2000, compared with over 1 million children (between 10–13%) who were living in poverty in 1979: CPAG (2001) pp 39–40, esp figure 2.5. See also G Palmer et al (2002) p 37.
105 See S Jenkins, C Schulter and G Wagner (2001) pp 19–20 and Innocenti Research Centre (2000) p 5.
106 In 1999/2000, 35% of lone parents were living in household below 60% median income, compared with 17% of couples with children. See Office for National Statistics (2002) Table 5.18. See also DWP (2002 a) p 15, Table 1.1.
107 The absence of a second carer renders child-care costs particularly high compared with two-parent families: S Middleton, K Ashworth and I Braithwaite (1997) pp 34–39.

countries.[108] Overall, the United Kingdom's record of child poverty had become, by the mid-1990s, amongst the worst in the world, compared with other industrialised countries.[109]

The impact of growing up in poverty is considerable. Long periods spent dependent on income support is not a happy experience for many families.[110] Significant numbers of children go without items which the vast majority of parents believe to be necessary: 7% of children do not have new properly fitting shoes, 3% go without three meals a day, 10% go without celebrations on special occasions and 6% without a warm waterproof coat.[111] Low-income families have a higher incidence of low birth weight babies,[112] poor levels of nutrition and infant growth,[113] poor levels of psychological health[114] and slightly higher levels of accidental deaths.[115] The lower educational attainment of children in schools in deprived inner city areas, higher levels of school exclusions, teenage pregnancies,[116] delinquency, drug and alcohol abuse and high unemployment can be added to this list.[117] As Utting has observed:

> 'Living on low income in a run-down neighbourhood does not make it impossible to be the affectionate, authoritative parent of healthy, sociable children. But it does, undeniably, make it more difficult.'[118]

Of greater concern is the evidence indicating that the factors associated with growing up in poverty have a long-term impact, extending well into adult life – and worse, they also affect subsequent generations of children.[119] This may be partly attributable to children from lone-parent families or from families dependent on income support 'learning to be poor' and, for example, having lower career aspirations than other children. These children are more likely to want careers with shorter training and, on the whole, they aim for lower academic qualifications than children in two-parent or

---

108   A great deal of international research links poverty with one-parent families and unemployment. See, inter alia: C Solera (2001) p 474; B Bradbury and M Jäntti (1999) pp 26–28. NB the links between child poverty and lone parenthood are too complex to assume that reducing poverty amongst lone-parent families will automatically reduce child poverty significantly: see Innocenti Research Centre (2000) p 16.

109   There is a wealth of data recording international comparisons. For short summaries of international material, see CPAG (2001) ch 9. For more detailed source material see, inter alia: B Bradbury and M Jäntti (1999) esp table 3.3; Innocenti Research Centre (2000) esp Figure 1 showing the United Kingdom fourth from the bottom in the league table (amongst 23 OECD nations in the mid-1990s) for relative child poverty, and Figure 2 showing that it sixth from the bottom in the league table for absolute poverty; K Vleminckx and T Smeeding (2001) esp ch 1; S Jenkins, C Schulter and G Wagner (2001).

110   See CPAG (2001) pp 60–63. In May 2002, 2.5 million children (19.4% of all children in Great Britain) were living in families claiming a key benefit: DWP (2002 c).

111   See D Gordon et al (2000) p 34. The children of lone parents were most likely to be without necessities: D Gordon et al (2000) p 36. See also CPAG (2001) pp 60–62 and Office for National Statistics (2003) p 109.

112   See G Palmer et al (2002) pp 32 and 38.

113   E Dowler et al (2001).

114   H Meltzer and R Gatward (2000) p 29 and Table 4.8. The prevalence of any psychiatric disorder ranged from 16% amongst children of families with a gross weekly income of under £100 to 6% among children of families earning £500 per week or more.

115   G Palmer et al (2002) pp 31–32 and 39.

116   G Palmer et al (2002) pp 28–29.

117   See summary of research on the effects of growing up in poverty, CPAG (2001) pp 136–140.

118   D Utting (1995) p 40.

119   See short summary of research on the intergenerational factors associated with child poverty in DWP (2002 b) pp 10–11.

non-income support families.[120] There are obvious policy implications in the evidence indicating that –

> 'the children of parents who grew up in a socially disadvantaged situation during their own childhood have lower early-age cognitive abilities suggesting a potentially important cross-generational link that may well spill over to affect the subsequent economic fortunes of children of disadvantaged individuals.'[121]

In the late 1990s, the government indicated its commitment to tackle the country's dismal record. Indeed, since 1999, when the Prime Minister pledged to end child poverty within 20 years,[122] the government has worked hard to reverse these trends. For example, there have been a number of initiatives aimed at improving the services and resources for families and children living in deprived areas.[123] More importantly, a number of policy changes were designed to ensure that families with children received greater financial support from the state.[124] But whilst the government proclaimed that the 'fundamental principle of the welfare state should be to support families and children', it also warned that families must be helped to help themselves, through employment.[125] Indeed, a strong component of the anti-poverty strategy has been to get as many unemployed adults as possible back to work,[126] including parents. Consequently, much of the new financial assistance available for parents is targeted at supplementing wages,[127] not replacing them.[128] All parents are expected to work if they can, since:

> 'Having a parent in work provides children with an active, valuable role model. It helps provide the parent with self respect and a social network. And most important of all, a waged family is less likely to be poor and benefit-dependent than an unwaged one.'[129]

Consequently, all lone-parent claimants of income support, are 'helped' to improve their families' lives by being 'helped' to overcome barriers to work,[130] through advice, training and 'help' with finding a job.[131] But since many lone parents are young, often

---

120 J Shropshire and S Middleton (1999) p 39.
121 P Gregg and S Machin (2001) p 147. See also Innocenti Research Centre (2000) p 12 for evidence indicating similar trends throughout OECD countries.
122 See Tony Blair, the Prime Minister, speech at Toynbee Hall, 18 March 1999. See also the relevant Public Service Agreement targets, set out by G Palmer et al (2002) pp 33–35.
123 Eg, inter alia: the Sure Start programme, see p 275, n 10 above; the Children's Fund, worth £380m – an initiative assisting preventive local authority projects aimed at helping children in the 5–13 age group and also funding voluntary sector local groups working to eradicate child poverty; the National Childcare Strategy aimed at establishing good quality affordable childcare for children aged 0–14; the plans to establish Children's Centres in disadvantaged areas. The government's child-focused initiatives are summarised in DWP (2002 a) ch 4. See also G Palmer et al (2002) pp 33–35.
124 See, inter alia: the minimum wage; increases in benefit rates for children under 11 in means-tested benefits; increases in child benefit; an increase in the income support earnings disregard; the introduction of the child tax credit in 2003, integrating into one payment all means-tested income related support for children. See DWP (2002 a) pp 59–62.
125 DSS (1998 a) Preamble and ch 7, para 1. See also DWP (2002 a) ch 2.
126 Through the 'welfare-to-work programme'.
127 See M Brewer et al (2002) ch 4.
128 Eg, inter alia: by guaranteeing a minimum income to families in full-time work through the working families tax credit; the national insurance reforms; lower income tax starting rates and the introduction of the children's tax credit.
129 See DSS (1998 a) ch 7, para 5.
130 Through the New Deal for Lone Parents (NDLP) introduced in 1998.
131 Home Office (1998) para 2.17. All lone parents on income support with children aged 5 and over are required to attend a work-focused interview to 'help them' consider their options for work.

without good skills, and with high child-care costs,[132] despite government hopes,[133] it seems unrealistic to expect large numbers of them to return to employment or to do so in an economically viable fashion.[134]

What of those unable to work, for example, through ill-health or disability, or even of those who wish to stay at home to care for their children? They might be influenced by research controversially suggesting that longer periods of full-time work by mothers of pre-school children tend, amongst other things, to reduce the child's educational attainment, increase the risk of his or her future unemployment and increase the risk of psychological distress as a young adult.[135] There is an official acknowledgment that: 'Not all parents can work or wish to do so, and we support and value those parents who want to bring up their children full-time.'[136] But despite the subsequent increases in child benefit and the child allowances in income support,[137] the controversial cuts to lone parent benefits in 1998[138] signalled the government's relative lack of sympathy with those lone parents choosing not to work. Neverthless, a commitment to children's rights requires the government to set aside the reasons for parents not being able to provide their children with a decent standard of living and to comply with its own international obligations in this respect. As Agell argues, the state interferes too much with individuals' freedom of choice when it tries to prevent parents from taking care of their own children in their own homes.[139]

Although the government's efforts to reduce child poverty and its associated hardships are bearing fruit,[140] progress is slower that the government admits[141] and it seems highly unlikely that it will achieve its target of eliminating child poverty by 2020.[142] Furthermore, the pressure on lone parents to return to work may produce undesirable side effects, with some feeling obliged to place very young children in sub-standard day-care facilities. It is unclear how future generations of children will respond to such changes. The official assumption that all parents should be in work entirely ignores the potential impact such strategies will have on children's well-being. Reducing child poverty by forcing parents to become self-sufficient may produce unwelcome consequences.

---

132 S Middleton, K Ashworth and I Braithwaite (1997) pp 34–39. Hopefully, the problem of meeting child-care costs will diminish as the National Child Care strategy is expanded.

133 See discussion of the progress made by the New Deal for Lone Parents programme in DWP (2002 a) pp 30–31. Despite considerable efforts, the employment rate of lone parents has only increased from 45.6% in 1997 to 53.6% in 2002.

134 See, inter alia: Innocenti Research Centre (2000) p 14; D Piachaud and H Sutherland (2000) ss 5.2, 5.3 and 7.4.

135 J Ermisch and M Francesconi (2001) esp pp 42–43.

136 Home Office (1998) para 2.15.

137 See M Brewer et al (2002) Table 4.2.

138 The lone parent higher rate of child benefit was abolished for new claimants from 6 July 1998.

139 See A Agell (1998) p 134.

140 DWP (2002 a) Annex, pp 141–159. See also M Brewer et al (2002) pp 26–27.

141 The 'Household Below Average Income' statistics (published April 2002) indicated that the new Labour government had significantly failed to meet its target to lift 1.2 million children out of poverty in its first term. See M Brewer et al (2002) p 3.

142 See D Piachaud and H Sutherland (2000) s 7.4 and M Brewer et al (2002) pp 17, 27–28 and 37. See also G Palmer et al (2002) pp 30–31, who whilst acknowledging that the short-term target for 2004 may just be met, are sceptical about the 2020 target.

(B)   The private maintenance obligation and the role of the state

(i)   Introduction

An increasing emphasis on children's rights might have led to the state taking a greater interest in the extent to which parents who break up fulfil their obligation to maintain their children. But the law continues to adopt the view that, in the event of separation and divorce, it is entirely up to the individual parents to decide for themselves how to redistribute their resources between them. As Eekelaar and Maclean have observed:

> 'Western countries have been tenacious in retaining the ideology that a child should look first to its parents for the retention of its living standards, even after the collapse of the family unit. The state, it is true, has been ready to move in as an ultimate guarantor against an unacceptable level of poverty, but even in this situation assistance has frequently been conditional on the instigation of legal machinery by the child's caregiver to extract support from the other parent.'[143]

The maintenance obligation owed by parents to their children is deemed to be part of their private relationship with each other. The law's stance on this is unaffected by the Child Support Act 1991 (CSA 1991), section 1 which emphasises that each parent of a 'qualifying'[144] child 'is responsible for maintaining him'. With the sole exception of a parent who is dependent on income support,[145] it is up to the parents themselves to enforce this responsibility, if and when they consider it to be necessary. In other words, the law trusts parents to place their children's interests in the forefront when negotiating over a division of their assets and will not check whether the settlement reached will provide the children with an appropriate standard of living.

Because the legal principles underpinning the private child maintenance obligation focus solely on regulating parents' relationships, a detailed analysis of this area of law has little place in a work considering children's rights – quite simply because they have been largely unaffected by the concept of children being important rights-holders. Nevertheless, since this area of legal ordering is an outstanding example of the extent to which law and policy maintains a hands-off approach to family life, the section below contains a short appraisal of the state's disastrous attempts to establish an efficient state system for collecting children's maintenance.

(ii)   The child support background

The titles to the papers setting out the government's proposals for the child support system, using phrases such as '*Children Come First*'[146] and '*A new contract for welfare: Children's Rights ...*',[147] might suggest a real concern to improve children's financial support, perhaps by supplementing their provision with state subsidies, as envisaged by the Finer Committee, in the early 1970s.[148] Further reading soon dispels such notions. The introduction of the CSA 1991 was designed 'to ensure that parents

---

143   See J Eekelaar and M Maclean (1986) p 109.
144   Ie within the jurisdiction of the Child Support Agency. See discussion below.
145   See discussion below.
146   DSS (1990).
147   DSS (1999). See also DSS (1998 b).
148   DHSS (1974) Pt 5.

honour their legal and moral responsibility to maintain their own children whenever they can afford to do so'.[149] As Lewis observes, the introduction of the child support legislation reflected the Conservative government's desire to roll back public expenditure and its conviction that state benefits were actually enabling the formation of one-parent families.[150] The idea of reducing the benefits paid to lone mothers through boosting their income from other sources was attractive.[151] The other sources were threefold: the state, the labour market and men.[152] The first and third sources were interrelated, since the state only provides mothers with income support on the understanding that their children's fathers will, as liable relatives, reimburse the state for such payments. But the third source had, by the late 1980s, proved extremely unreliable, since only 30% of lone mothers were receiving regular maintenance payments, the remainder relying on state benefits.[153] Even those in receipt of maintenance were often paid too little to enable them to survive without further assistance.

It was largely the government's impatience with the courts for producing inconsistent maintenance orders, often for unrealistically low amounts, and often lower than could be afforded by 'absent parents',[154] which led to a new administrative system being established. The CSA 1991 created a single government agency, the Child Support Agency (CSA), to take over from the courts the job of assessing and then collecting maintenance payments from non-resident parents. The intention of the new legislation was to bring home to fathers their responsibility for maintaining their biological offspring.[155] Indeed, as Lewis observes, it reflected the philosophy of the Children Act 1989; it was as much about impressing on parents that it was *they*, and not the state, who had a responsibility for their offspring, as about enforcing their responsibility for their children.[156] The underlying motive of emphasising parental responsibility was, of course, to reduce state support. Fathers were cast in their traditional role, as a source of financial support, rather than care.[157] There was certainly no intention to improve the relationship between father and child. For example, the formula for calculating the maintenance to be paid took no account of a father's expenses incurred when visiting his children.[158] Nor was there any discussion of the Finer Committee's recommendation that single-parent families should receive an additional state subsidy, a Guaranteed Maintenance Allowance, designed to give single parents a genuine choice between staying at home with their children and going out to work.[159]

---

149 DSS (1990) vol I, p 5.
150 See J Lewis (2000) p 95.
151 See DSS (1990), which observed (para 1. 5) that more than 750,000 lone parents were dependent on income support, with the costs to the taxpayer of such benefits having increased from £1.4bn in 1981/82 to £3.2bn in 1988/89.
152 J Lewis (2000) p 95.
153 See DSS (1990) vol I, para 1.5.
154 DSS (1990) vol I, para 1.5. NB the term 'absent parent' was replaced by 'non-resident parent': Child Support, Pensions and Society Security Act 2000 (CSPASSA 2000), Sch 3, para 11(2). This change reflected the view that 'absent' implied that maintenance payers had dropped out of their children's lives.
155 Note that, for the purposes of this section, it is assumed that the potential payer of child maintenance is the father and that the recipient is the mother. In practice, of course, the reverse may be the case.
156 See J Lewis (2000) p 95.
157 J Lewis (2000) p 95.
158 This inflexibility was later relaxed by deductions being allowed from the non-resident parent's income regarding high travel expenses for contact visits.
159 DHSS (1974) Pt 5.

The new use of a fixed formula for calculating maintenance would, the government promised, 'produce maintenance payments which are realistically related to the costs of caring for a child'.[160] One might argue that, in so doing, the legislation was asserting the state's interest in ensuring that children received sufficient maintenance to enable them to live fulfilling lives. This, however, was not the case. The formula adopted income support rates as a basis for calculating the child's maintenance requirement. As noted above, these rates leave families at a standard of living which is barely above subsistence level. In reality, the new legislation merely established a complicated and inefficient procedure aimed at moving money from one parent to another, with an inflexible formula for calculating the sum to be passed over. Fathers were to be the sole source of the money – not the state. Nevertheless, the fact that a state agency using this formula largely replaced the courts' jurisdiction over children's maintenance meant that official views about the standard of living required by children inevitably started permeating private ordering.[161]

(iii)   The weaknesses of the child support formula

(a)   COMPLICATED AND PRONE TO ERROR

The child support legislation introduced a rigid statutory formula for calculating how much a non-resident parent should pay the 'person with care'[162] towards the upkeep of any 'qualifying child'.[163] The original formula,[164] now replaced by a far simpler one,[165] required a calculation of child maintenance involving five separate calculations:[166] the child's maintenance requirement;[167] the exempt income of the non-resident parent;[168] the parents' assessable income;[169] the proposed maintenance calculated from the previous three calculations;[170] the protected income calculation.[171] The arcane complication of the child support formula added considerably to the difficulties and unpopularity of the ill-fated CSA.[172] In the first place, considerable amounts of information from both parents were required by the agency before the non-resident parent's child support liability could be calculated – a problem

---

160 See DSS (1990) vol I, para 2.1.
161 Discussed below.
162 Ie the person with whom the child has his home and who usually provides day-to-day care for the child: CSA 1991, s 3(3). Any person with care of a qualifying child can apply for child maintenance.
163 Ie a child under the age of 16, or under 19 if in full-time non-advanced education (CSA 1991, s 55), in respect of whom one or both of the parents is non-resident.
164 As amended by a variety of regulations.
165 Introduced by CSPASSA 2000. Discussed below.
166 For details of the old assessment formula, see CPAG (2002) chs 7–12.
167 Broadly based on the child and mother's income support personal allowances.
168 The amount of his income that he was allowed to retain to cover his minimum day-to-day living expenses, including his housing expenses.
169 The combined sum of the net income of the parent with care and that of the non-resident parent (minus their exempt income).
170 The non-resident parent would be expected to pay 50% of his assessable income until he had met the child's maintenance requirement; out of any income he had left, payments of a reducing amount would be levied, depending on available funds, number of children and subject to an upper limit.
171 This ensured that the non-resident parent's remaining income would not be reduced by his maintenance liability to below 30% of his net income.
172 See summary in DSS (1999) pp 2–3.

contributing to the delays and mounting arrears of maintenance, which quickly became chronic. Second, the calculation itself was so prone to error that many appeals against assessments sprang from mistakes made by the CSA. The formula was also extremely difficult for parents to understand, making it hard for them to predict how much they should pay. Furthermore, since the child's maintenance requirement underwent frequent updating, due to changes in income support amounts, and as the parents' own circumstances changed, the assessments themselves underwent constant 'periodic reviews' by the CSA, again contributing to the persistent delays. By the late 1990s, the difficulties produced by the formula resulted in CSA staff spending 90% of their time making assessments, keeping them up to date and making initial payment arrangements. Consequently, only 10% of their resources was left for chasing up non-resident parents who were behind on their payments, with only 66% of maintenance due actually being paid.[173]

(b)   UNPOPULAR WITH MOTHERS

Part of the unpopularity of the child support legislation lay in the fact that the formula produced results which pleased neither the non-resident fathers nor the mothers. It would obviously have benefited mothers had the child support legislation, as promised by the government, forced non-resident parents to pay maintenance which represented the true costs of caring for a child. Nevertheless, the figures used in the child support assessment formula proved unreliable in this respect. Research indicated that the age differentials in the income support allowances used in the formula did not match actual spending requirements. There was, for example, the assumption that children under 11 cost only 61% of the cost of supporting a 16-year-old, when in fact average spending on this younger group of children was 86% of what was spent on the older children.[174] Furthermore, income support allowances provided only between 50% and 70% of the average spending on all children.[175] Despite increases in income support since this research was completed, considerable numbers of families on income support, particularly lone parents, still go without essentials such as food.[176] Maintenance determined by a formula founded on such faulty assumptions had no real ability to lift families out of poverty.

Most mothers on income support would prefer not to involve the fathers of their children in making any contribution. In some cases, it merely exacerbates the relationship between their parents and renders their fathers less ready to visit them.[177] In other cases, a mother's reluctance to involve the father is influenced by her knowledge that unless he is earning enough to provide her with sufficient income to lift her above income support levels, forcing him to contribute to the child's maintenance will seldom benefit the child financially. This is because, until recently, there has been no income support 'disregard', so that, in most cases, every pound recovered from the father has merely gone straight into the coffers of the Treasury, to reimburse the state for the weekly amount of income support that the mother has been

173   DSS (1999) p 3.
174   See S Middleton, K Ashworth and I Braithwaite (1997) pp 40–42.
175   Parents simply spent less on themselves.
176   See discussion above.
177   According to G Davis, N Wikeley and R Young (1998) p 192, in over 40% of cases in their
        study, one or both of the parents claimed that their relationship had suffered from CSA
        involvement.

receiving.[178] For many children in families dependent on income support, the intervention of the CSA has often made their lives worse. Research shows that the mothers whose ex-partners have been able to make maintenance payments just high enough to lift them off income support, have lost the 'passported benefits' available with income support, such as free school meals, prescriptions, eye and dental care. Indeed, sometimes as a result of the loss of these passported benefits, they have been actually worse off – a serious plight for a family living at just above subsistence level.[179]

Despite their reluctance to do so, many mothers are effectively forced to co-operate with the CSA over identifying and then requiring fathers to contribute to the maintenance of their children. The legislation effectively requires a parent with care, who is in receipt of income support or income-based jobseeker's allowance, to co-operate with the agency over tracing the father of her child, with a view to recouping from him, in the form of child maintenance, some of the money she has been receiving from the state.[180] Theoretically, a mother is not obliged to identify the father of her child, thereby enabling the agency to pursue him, but if she refuses to do so, she often suffers a punitive benefit penalty.[181] She can only escape such a penalty if she can establish that there are 'reasonable grounds for believing that ... there would be a risk of her or any child living with her, suffering harm or undue distress as a result'.[182] The Child Support Officer is obliged to consider very carefully the mother's reasons for refusing to divulge the father's identity, before making a reduced benefit direction. But, when deciding whether they constitute 'reasonable grounds' for refusal, according to CSA 1991, section 2(1) he need only 'have regard to the welfare of any child likely to be affected by his decision'. Although a Child Support Officer must obey this direction whenever he reaches a decision involving his discretion, the formula contained in section 2(1) notably does not make the child's welfare paramount. Indeed, as was pointed out in a Social Security Commissioner's decision:

'The overriding purpose of the CSA and the Regulations laid thereunder, is to ensure that the absent parent makes proper financial provision for his or her children, and the exercise of discretions cannot be circumscribed so as to impede that objective. The overall purpose cannot be undermined simply by the fact that under section 2 of the Act regard has to be paid to the welfare of children affected by a decision of the Secretary of State or a CSO.'[183]

A mother cannot justify her refusal to allow the CSA to seek contributions from her child's father by arguing merely that she fears such an approach might sour his relationship with the family, and that her overall income will not be improved by his involvement. Nevertheless, in practice, many mothers will attempt to avoid applying for child maintenance, to escape the fathers blaming them for assisting the CSA to

---

178 G Davis, N Wikeley and R Young (1998) pp 50–60. The government finally bowed to pressure and introduced an income support disregard in 2002: see below.
179 K Clarke, C Glendinning and G Craig (1994) ch 7.
180 CSA 1991, s 6(1)–(3) (as amended by CSPASSA 2000).
181 A reduced benefit direction made under CSA 1991, s 46(5) currently reduces the recipient's benefit by 40%, for up to three years.
182 CSA 1991, s 46(3).
183 CCS/11/94, para 8. (1997) 4 Journal of Social Security Law D23.

trace them. Indeed, suspected collusion between parents eventually led to the benefit penalty being increased to a swingeing 40% deduction in income support.[184]

The concentration of the child support formula on income rather than capital also produced unhelpful results for those mothers seeking contributions from non-resident fathers who were well off. The self-employed fathers able to indulge in creative accounting to ensure that their capital assets produced little apparent income could avoid liability almost completely. Furthermore, as Davis et al observed[185] the fact that the CSA showed little inclination to challenge such parents' accounts of their financial circumstances, was presumably because to do so would be expensive and time-consuming. Indeed, unless the mother in *Phillips v Peace*[186] had applied to the courts under the Children Act 1989[187] to obtain a lump sum from her millionaire ex-partner, the CSA's nil assessment might have gone unnoticed by anyone, except those involved in the case itself. The agency's calculation that the child's father could not afford to pay anything at all towards their daughter's maintenance must have caused the mother some astonishment, bearing in mind that he lived in a house worth £2.6m and owned three cars valued at £35,000, £54,000 and £100,000 respectively.[188] This case bore out the research evidence that, contrary to the claims of those initiating the scheme, and particularly when dealing with self-employed fathers, the child support formula sometimes led to far lower levels of child maintenance than might have been ordered by the courts.[189] Undoubtedly the father's claim in *Phillips v Peace*[190] that he had insufficient income to provide *any* child support for his daughter would have been treated far more robustly by the courts than it was by the CSA.[191]

(c)   UNPOPULAR WITH FATHERS

The child support system quickly attracted considerable hostility from non-resident fathers up and down the country.[192] Most vocal were the middle-class fathers required to pay far higher sums of child maintenance by the CSA than they had previously paid under court orders for their children's maintenance. Their indignation was fuelled by the fact that liability ran from the date that the non-resident parent was sent the form requiring details of his financial position. By the time fathers received their assessments, given the CSA's delays in making assessments, they were often in arrears before they started paying. Because the formula was too complicated for most to calculate their future liability, many fathers found these delays and inefficiencies

---

184   This change was introduced in 1996, increasing the deduction rate from 20%. The government claimed that by 1999, as many as 70% of lone parents were attempting to avoid applying for child support. See DSS (1999) p 17. These concerns produced CSA 1991, s 6(3) (as amended by CSPASSA 2000) whereby parents with care on benefit are assumed to have authorised the collection of child maintenance, with the result that they must object if they do not wish this to occur. Under the former scheme, their specific authorisation was always required. See N Wikeley (2000) p 891 for the predicted effect of this change.
185   G Davis, N Wikeley and R Young (1998) p 180.
186   [1996] 2 FLR 230.
187   Children Act 1989, Sch 1, para 1(1)(c). See discussion below.
188   The father's income was derived from dealing with shares through a business he owned and controlled.
189   See G Davis, N Wikeley and R Young (1998) pp 32–34.
190   [1996] 2 FLR 230.
191   As emphasised by Johnson J, [1996] 2 FLR 230 at 231. See discussion by J Priest (1997).
192   Summarised by G Douglas (2000) pp 277–278.

difficult to accept, given the CSA's frequent inability to provide them with intelligible information about their cases.[193] Furthermore, by the time the father's assessment was produced, his circumstances might have changed, in which case a review and reassessment would be required. Indeed, the child support appeal tribunals would commonly hear a series of appeals from the same father, relating to a series of CSA assessments, sometimes spanning several years.[194] The irritation produced by such situations often exacerbated fathers' poor relationships with mothers.[195] Fathers who were less well off also found it unjust to be required to pay a minimum amount of maintenance, even if they themselves were dependent on income support.

Of considerable controversy was the fact that the child support formula included, within the child's maintenance requirement, an allowance designed to cover the expenses of the adult carer, based on income support rates of personal allowance.[196] This indicated to many men that they were being required to maintain the child's mother, even if their relationship with her had been non-marital and essentially fleeting.[197] A further source of resentment was the fact that, despite a non-resident father being required to contribute to the expenses of the child's mother, his own obligations to any second family were only partially taken into account.[198] Many fathers also found it incomprehensible that the CSA could not include in their exempt income, 'many outgoings which form part of modern consumerism', such as hire-purchase debts, car expenses and credit card bills.[199] Controversially, but perhaps understandably, contact disputes often became exacerbated by parents making a link between paying child maintenance and contact arrangements with their children. Fathers would claim increased contact, as a quid quo pro for complying with their child maintenance obligation, and mothers would refuse contact in cases where a father was refusing to comply.[200]

Further fury was engendered by the situation highlighted in *Crozier v Crozier*.[201] The original legislation provided no means whereby the CSA could take account of any clean-break settlement agreed by a divorcing couple prior to the agency's involvement. These settlements would commonly involve a transfer of the father's share of the matrimonial home to the mother, in return for agreement that the father would only be liable for nominal maintenance for any children. The CSA's ability – indeed, its duty – in cases where the ex-wife subsequently became dependent on income support, to assess the father's liability for child maintenance without making any allowance for the loss of his share of the matrimonial home, seemed particularly unjust. Reform of this aspect of the child support system was introduced relatively early in the scheme.[202]

---

193   See G Davis, N Wikeley and R Young (1998) ch 5.
194   G Davis, N Wikeley and R Young (1998) p 228.
195   G Davis, N Wikeley and R Young (1998) ch 5.
196   This would be up to 100% of the income support personal allowance, depending on the child's age.
197   G Davis, N Wikeley and R Young (1998) p 219.
198   Ie although his exempt income would include an allowance for any biological children of his, now living with him, plus housing costs of his new family, any voluntary liability to step-children would not be included.
199   See G Douglas (2000) p 278.
200   See G Davis, N Wikeley and R Young (1998) pp 203–205. See *Re H (parental responsibility: maintenance)* [1996] 1 FLR 867 for an example of such a dispute.
201   [1994] Fam 114.
202   See below.

(iv)   Reforming the child support scheme

As Douglas observes, reform of the child support scheme underwent three phases.[203]
The first involved the introduction of regulations in 1995, which tinkered with the
way in which child maintenance was to be calculated. Accordingly, non-resident
parents could now include in their exempt income the high costs of particularly long
journeys to work.[204] Similarly, a 'broad brush' provision was introduced to address
the *Crozier v Crozier* scenario. This allowed the father to claim, as part of his exempt
income, an allowance calculated according to the value of a property or capital
previously transferred to the child's mother, thereby reducing the value of his
maintenance obligation.

Reforming legislation[205] introduced the second wave of reforms responding to
complaints that the child support formula was far too rigid and produced injustice in
individual cases.[206] The new legislation established a system whereby applicants and
non-resident parents alike could claim the benefit of exceptions, or 'departures' from
the formula, in certain well-defined circumstances.[207] The non-resident parent might,
for example, wish to claim that his assessable income should be reduced by various
special expenses, such as the expense of contact visits, of supporting a step-child and
of exceptionally high travel to work costs.[208] A parent with care was now given the
chance to challenge a low assessment in situations like that arising in *Phillips v
Peace*,[209] where a non-resident parent's lifestyle was quite inconsistent with the level
of income he had disclosed to the CSA.[210] The system of departures radically
undermined the assumption underpinning the original legislation, which was that a
formulaic approach could produce an appropriate result in all circumstances. The
new legislation acknowledged defeat on that score and, furthermore, interposed a
discretionary element into the decision-making process; a decision in favour of
departures could now only be made if it was considered 'just and equitable' to do
so.[211]

The third wave of reforms was designed to alleviate the continuing deep
unpopularity of the child support scheme. By the late 1990s, it was not only clear
that the CSA had still failed to get on top of its case load, but it had also become a
'byword for bureaucratic incompetence'.[212] One of the fundamental objectives of the
legislation had still not been attained. Overall, about one million families dependent
on income support were headed by lone parents, with only one in five of those
families receiving maintenance for their children.[213] But despite the intervening years

---

203 See G Douglas (2000) p 279.
204 Child Support (Maintenance Assessment and Special Cases) Regulations, Sch 3B, which
     allowed only journeys of more than 150 miles per week.
205 The CSA 1995 amended the CSA 1991.
206 These reforms followed publication of DSS (1995).
207 CSA 1991, Sch 4B.
208 See the complete list of special expenses which could be grounds for making a departure
     application in CPAG (2002) ch 15.
209 [1996] 2 FLR 230.
210 The parent with care might also claim a departure on the basis that the non-resident parent's
     assessable income had been rendered unjustifiably low by employing various strategies, eg
     diverting his income, claiming unreasonably high housing costs, or travel-to-work costs etc.
     See CPAG (2002) ch 15.
211 The old scheme of departures was abolished by CSPASSA 2000 and replaced by a greatly
     restricted scheme of 'variations'. See S Cretney, J Masson and R Bailey-Harris (2002) 15-014.
212 H Davies and H Joshi (2001) p 303.
213 DSS (1999) p 17.

between the Thatcher government initiating the child support scheme and the new Labour government reviewing its operation in 1999, their respective approaches to the problem were remarkably similar. Both governments' primary concern was to reduce public expenditure on income support, by forcing fathers to take financial responsibility for their children. The continuing poverty of one-parent families was met by a resolve to make the child support scheme more efficient, rather than to produce a more generous system of benefits for the children being brought up in such needy circumstances.

The Labour government decided that the CSA could not operate more efficiently unless the child support formula was simplified. The new child support formula departed radically from the old.[214] The aim of the original child support legislation was to produce child maintenance assessments which reflected real child-care costs.[215] As noted above, the child's maintenance requirement was firmly linked to income support rates of personal allowance, thereby producing relatively low sums, but indicating a level below which child maintenance should not fall. Arguably, the state was ensuring that children received just enough maintenance to live on. Under the new system, such arguments would be specious. Rather than attempting to link real child-care costs with the maintenance assessment, a greatly simplified formula now requires the non-resident parent to pay 15% of his net income for the first child, 20% for two and 25% for three or more, irrespective of the children's age.[216] Controversially, the income of the parent with care is completely ignored,[217] as is the income of the non-resident's current partner. Equally controversially, it was not initially intended to impose any cap on the upper limit of child maintenance, so that the liability of an extremely wealthy man would amount to 15% of his total net income for his first child, even if still a baby.[218] As a result of a late amendment, an upper limit was imposed, so that the non-resident parent's net income of over £2,000 per week is ignored.[219]

The new formula seems to have no philosophical basis. The government simply maintained that the proposed base rate of 15% of the payer's net income was 'roughly half the average that an intact two-parent family spends on a child',[220] the assumption being that this is what a non-resident parent *should* also pay. The White Paper omitted to acknowledge that when two-parent families spend 30% of their income on their children, fathers contribute far more to this total than mothers. To argue that non-resident fathers should only contribute half what two parents spend on their children is nonsensical, given that mothers' incomes, if they exist at all, are far lower than that of fathers. The 15% formula therefore appears to be completely arbitrary. There was certainly no attempt to argue that it would produce levels of maintenance matching actual child-care costs. Indeed, the White Paper admitted that average weekly maintenance liability would be less under the new legislation,[221] but countered this

---

214 The CSPASSA 2000 introduced the new formula by amending CSA 1991, Sch 1, Pt 1.

215 DSS (1990) vol I, para 2.1.

216 The new scheme introduced four rates: the basic rate, a reduced rate, a flat rate and a nil rate. See CSA 1991, Sch 1, Pt I. For a detailed explanation of the application of the new formula, see R Bird (2002), N Wikeley (2000), S Cretney, J Masson and R Bailey-Harris 15-013.

217 See N Mostyn (1999) pp 99–101.

218 N Mostyn (1999) pp 100–101.

219 CSA 1991, Sch 1, Pt I, para 10(3).

220 DSS (1999) p 9.

221 The average would fall from £38 per week to £30.50 per week.

by arguing that the new simpler rules and tougher sanctions[222] would persuade more non-resident parents to pay more child maintenance.[223] Nevertheless, it is clear that for fathers at the lower end of the income spectrum, the formula produces levels of child maintenance far too low to meet real child care costs.[224] As Douglas observes:

> 'This reduction [in the non-resident parent's child maintenance liability] represents an acceptance that absent parents *will not* pay sums they deem unacceptable for their children, no matter how unrealistic their views on the costs of bringing up a child may be.'[225]

The shortfall must be picked up by the state, through income support or through mothers' earnings. Admittedly, the reform package included an income support disregard, or 'child maintenance premium' enabling caring parents on income support (and income-based jobseeker's allowance), to keep the first £10 per week of maintenance recovered, in addition to their benefit entitlement.[226] To the cynical, such a concession seemed principally motivated by a desire to encourage lone parents to co-operate with the CSA, rather by a new generosity of spirit. Despite this reform being welcome, it fails to transform the benefits available to one-parent families in this country into the type of generous package available to lone parents in many other European countries[227] or envisaged by the Finer Committee.[228]

Such phrases as 'Every child has the right to the best start in life' and 'We believe that children should come first'[229] do not disguise the fact that the emphasis has remained firmly on reinforcing the privacy of the family, under the auspices of what the government hopes will be a more efficient state collection agency.

(v)   Children's rights to child support

On reaching greater maturity, some children might look back on their lives and decide that that their mothers did not try hard enough to extract maintenance out of their fathers. Like their peers, they would have liked to have nice clothes and go on school outings, rather than managing without luxuries of any kind. It is notable that children in England and Wales are still unable to seek the assistance of the CSA themselves. Unlike Scottish law, which allows any child having attained the age of 12 to initiate an application under the CSA 1991,[230] English and Welsh children cannot approach the CSA themselves to obtain child maintenance from either parent. Since this is a step which can only be taken by the adult providing the child with a home and day-to-day care,[231] whether they do so or not is outside the child's control. Equally, although a non-parent carer with a residence order may proceed against the

---

222 Eg much higher rates of interim and default measures and court ordered punitive sanctions, such as driving disqualifications for non resident parents who deliberately defy maintenance calculations. See N Wikeley (2000).
223 DSS (1999) p 13.
224 A non-resident parent is liable to pay a reduced rate of child maintenance where his net weekly income is between £100 and £200 per week.
225 G Douglas (2000) p 280 (footnotes omitted).
226 See DSS (1999) ch 3.
227 See H Immervoll, H Sutherland and K de Vos (2001).
228 DHSS (1974) Pt 5. See discussion above.
229 DSS (1999) pp 1 and 9.
230 Under CSA 1991, s 7(1) children habitually resident in Scotland, having attained the age of 12 years, may apply for a maintenance assessment under the Act.
231 CSA 1991, s 3(3).

child's parents under the Children Act 1989[232] to obtain from the courts various orders for financial provision which the CSA has no power to make,[233] this option is not available to the child, except in very limited circumstances.[234] The failure of the policy makers to consider reforming the child support legislation along the lines of the Scottish system is not surprising. Their sights have, from the start, been firmly set on reducing public expenditure and, later, on addressing the CSA's lamentable record for inefficiency, rather than fulfilling children's rights.

(C)   The private maintenance obligation and the role of the courts

As the preceding discussion demonstrates, the law relating to children's maintenance contains few, if any, principles that promote, or even acknowledge the concept of children being rights bearers. The legal principles governing the courts' role in this area of law are even more adult-focused than those underpinning the child support legislation. Although the courts undoubtedly take a far more robust approach to ascertaining the true state of a man's income, perhaps by making an order based on their view of what he could make available if he wished,[235] this does not reflect any judicial zeal to obtain the best for the child, *on behalf of the child*. The private nature of the maintenance obligation is reflected in the way disputes over financial provision focusing on children reach the courts – these are applications brought by adults against adults, and the choice is theirs, whether or not they bring them at all. Had the mother in *Phillips v Peace*[236] decided that she would accept the CSA's nil assessment and depend on state assistance to bring up her daughter, no one could have forced her to apply to the courts for any of the remedies remaining outside the powers of the agency.[237] The fact that the child could have enjoyed a far higher standard of living had the mother felt equal to proceeding against the father, would have been irrelevant.

The child support system is designed to exclude applicants' involvement with the courts in all cases involving the CSA's jurisdiction,[238] namely where a parent with care requires income from a non-resident parent for a qualifying child. In practice, however, affluent couples generally reach agreement over child maintenance liability, and will often have such agreements incorporated in the form of a consent order.[239] When advising on the terms of such agreements, legal advisers should obviously take account of the child support formula, when calculating the amount needed by the parent retaining day-to-day care of the children.[240] This is largely because the CSA can, at the mother's request, bypass any agreement she entered into with the father, particularly if she accepted a level of income for the children less than it would have arrived at itself using the formula.[241] The existence of the CSA formula should,

---

232   Children Act 1989, Sch I.
233   See discussion below.
234   Discussed in chapter 4, pp 113–115.
235   *Phillips v Peace* [1996] 2 FLR 230 at 232, per Johnson J.
236   [1996] 2 FLR 230 at 232, per Johnson J.
237   See below.
238   CSA 1991, s 8(3).
239   See R Bird (2002) pp 116–120, for a discussion of the interrelationship of the courts and the CSA, in cases where maintenance agreements and consent orders exist. See ch 10 generally, for a discussion of the residuary powers of the courts.
240   In *E v C (child maintenance)* [1996] 1 FLR 472, Douglas Brown J indicated that all the judiciary, including the magistrates, should take account of what would be the CSA maintenance assessment in any given case.
241   CSA 1991, s 9(3).

in this way, reduce the possibility of parents agreeing a figure below that approved of by the state. Nevertheless, research indicates that solicitors have not, in the past, been as expert in calculating a client's child support liability as one might expect and have given poor advice over what should and should not be agreed.[242]

Since the CSA legislation assists mothers to force fathers to share their income with their children, the courts, as a general rule, have no power to deal with any aspect of the child's needs which could be met by income payments. Nevertheless, the CSA legislation itself sets out a list of important exceptions to this rule. The courts therefore retain the power to supplement the CSA's assessments with topping-up orders,[243] orders for additional educational expenses[244] and orders for the expenses of disabled children.[245] Parents may, of course, feel obliged to use the courts to obtain maintenance in situations outside the CSA's jurisdiction entirely.[246] For example, since the child support legislation only imposes financial responsibility in relation to children up to the age of 16,[247] parents must obtain orders for older children from the courts under the matrimonial legislation[248] or the Children Act 1989.[249] Similarly, under the CSA 1991, parents' financial liability is confined to their biological children; consequently, maintenance for step-children can only be claimed through the courts.[250] Furthermore, because the CSA's jurisdiction is restricted to a division of income, mothers with children whose fathers are wealthy may consider turning to the courts to obtain capital and property transfers in favour of their children.[251] Although such orders are relatively rare, cases like *Phillips v Peace*[252] indicate that this can be an extremely effective means whereby unmarried mothers can extract sufficient capital from wealthy fathers to obtain relatively comfortable accommodation for their children and themselves, together with enough capital to equip it.[253]

(5)   CONCLUSION

The law could do much more to ensure that children are not treated like chattels if the policy makers were prepared to grasp the nettle and use it to mould parental opinion more effectively. The fact that it does not do so in the context of physical punishment reflects an ambivalence over the merits of outlawing actions which large numbers of the public consider perfectly acceptable. But if the law had always maintained a

---

242   See G Davies, N Wikeley and R Young (1998) pp 172–175.
243   CSA 1991, s 8(6). See R Bird (2002) ch 10.
244   CSA 1991, s 8(7).
245   CSA 1991, s 8(8). Eg *C v F (disabled child: maintenance order)* [1998] 2 FLR 1.
246   For a more detailed discussion of this area of law, see N Lowe and G Douglas (1998) pp 764–772.
247   Or 19, if in full-time secondary education.
248   Under the Matrimonial Causes Act 1973 or the Domestic Proceedings and Magistrates' Courts Act 1978. The position of older children is discussed further in chapter 4.
249   Children Act 1989, Sch I.
250   Ie on the basis that the child is a 'child of the family', under the Matrimonial Causes Act 1973 or the Domestic Proceedings and Magistrates' Courts Act 1978 or under the Children Act 1989, Sch I.
251   Divorcing mothers would use the Matrimonial Causes Act, ss 23 and 24; unmarried mothers would use the Children Act 1989, Sch I.
252   [1996] 2 FLR 230.
253   In *Phillips v Peace* [1996] 2 FLR 230 the father was ordered to pay approximately £90,000 to purchase a house for the child and mother to live in and a further £24,500 for furniture, equipment and clothing for the child. See also *T v S (financial provision for children)* [1994] 2 FLR 883 and *A v A (a minor: financial provision)* [1995] 1 FCR 309.

sensitivity to public opinion, hanging convicted criminals might still be a current form of punishment. Regarding the law's role relating to children's rights to financial support, this appears to be driven by concerns which have little to do with children's welfare. Undoubtedly, children would benefit from being brought up in financially secure circumstances, but the law's respect for family privacy is exploited by the state to save money. Furthermore, motivated by concerns about the public purse and by policies over encouraging parents to seek employment, the state maintains a safety-net approach to family support. Such short-term policies ignore the long-term impact on society of large numbers of children being brought up in severely impoverished conditions.

BIBLIOGRAPHY

NB many of these publications can be obtained on the relevant organisation's website.

Agell A, 'Should and Can Family Law Influence Social Behaviour?' in J Eekelaar and T Nlahpo (eds), *The Changing Family: International Perspectives on the Family and Family Law* (1998) Hart Publishing.

Bainham A, 'Privatisation of Public Interest in Children' (1990) 53 Modern Law Review 206.

Bainham A, 'Changing families and changing concepts – reforming the language of family law' (1998) 10 Child and Family Law Quarterly 1.

Barton C, 'Parental Hitting – The "Responses" to "Protecting Children, Supporting Parents"' (2002) Family Law 124.

Bird R, *Child Maintenance: The New Law* (2002) Family Law.

Bradbury B and Jäntti M, *Child Poverty across Industrialized Nations* Innocenti Occasional Papers, Economic and Social Policy Series No 71 (1999) UNICEF International Child Development Centre.

Brewer M et al, (2002) *The Government's Child Poverty Target: How Much Progress Has Been Made?* Commentary 87 (2002) Institute for Fiscal Studies.

Child Poverty Action Group (CPAG), *Poverty: the facts* (2001) CPAG.

Child Poverty Action Group (CPAG), *Child support handbook 2002/3* (2002) CPAG.

Clarke K, Glendinning C and Craig G, *Losing Support: Children and the Child Support Act* (1994) The Nuffield Press.

Commission on Children and Violence, *Children and Violence* (1995) Calouste Gulbenkian Foundation.

Committee on Economic, Social and Cultural Rights, *Concluding Observations of the Committee on Economic, Social and Cultural Rights: United Kingdom of Great Britain and Northern Ireland – Dependent Territories 2002* E/C 12/1/Add 79 (2002) Centre for Human Rights, Geneva.

Committee on the Rights of the Child, *Concluding Observations of the Committee on the Rights of the Child: United Kingdom of Great Britain and Northern Ireland* CRC/C/15/Add 34 (1995) Centre for Human Rights, Geneva.

Committee on the Rights of the Child, *Concluding Observations of the Committee on the Rights of the Child: United Kingdom of Great Britain and Northern Ireland* CRC/C/15/Add 188 (2002) Centre for Human Rights, Geneva.

Cretney S, Masson J and Bailey-Harris R, *Principles of Family Law* (2002) Sweet and Maxwell.

Davis G, Wikeley N and Young R, *Child Support in Action* (1998) Hart Publishing.

Davies H and Joshi H, 'Who has borne the cost of Britain's children in the 1990s?' in K Vleminckx and T Smeeding (eds) *Child Well-Being, Child Poverty and Child Policy in Modern Nations: What do we know?* (2001) The Policy Press.

Department for Health and Social Security (DHSS), *Report of the Committee on One-Parent Families* Cm 5629 (1974) HMSO.

Department for Social Security (DSS), *Children Come First* Vols 1 and II, Cm 1264 (1990) HMSO.

Department for Social Security (DSS), *Improving Child Support* Cm 2745 (1995) The Stationery Office.

Department for Social Security (DSS), Green Paper *New Ambitions for our Country: A new contract for welfare* Cm 3805 (1998 a) Department for Social Security.

Department for Social Security (DSS), White Paper *Children First: a new approach to child support* Cm 3992 (1998 b) The Stationery Office.

Department for Social Security (DSS), *A new contract for welfare: Children's Rights and Parents' Responsibilities* Cm 4349 (1999).

Department for Work and Pensions (DWP), *Opportunity for All: making progress* Fourth Annual Report 2002, Cm 5598 (2002 a) The Stationery Office.

Department for Work and Pensions (DWP), *Measuring Child Poverty: A consultation document* (2002 b).

Department for Work and Pensions (DWP), *Quarterly Bulletin on Families with Children on Key Benefits – May 2002* (2002 c).

Department of Health (DH), *The Children Act 1989 Guidance and Regulations* Vol 2 *Family Support, Day Care and Educational Provision for Young Children* (1991) HMSO.

Department of Health (DH), *Protecting Children, Supporting Parents: A Consultation Document on the Physical Punishment of Children* (2000).

Department of Health (DH), *Analysis of Responses to the 'Protecting Children, Supporting Parents' Consultation Document* (2001).

Dickens B, 'The Modern Function and Limits of Parental Rights' (1981) 97 Law Quarterly Review 462.

Douglas G , 'The Family, Gender, and Social Security' in N Harris (ed) *Social Security in Context* (2000) Oxford University Press.

Dowler E et al, *Poverty Bites: Food, health and poor families* (2001) CPAG.

Eekelaar J and Maclean M, *Maintenance after Divorce* (1986) Oxford University Press.

Ermisch J and Francesconi M, *The effects of parents' employment on children's lives* (2001) Family Policy Studies Centre and Joseph Rowntree Foundation.

Fortin J, *Children's Rights and the Developing Law* (1998) Butterworths.

Fortin J, 'Children's rights and the use of physical force' (2001) 13 Child and Family Law Quarterly 243.

Freeman M, 'Freedom and the Welfare State: Child-Rearing, Parental Autonomy and State Intervention' (1983) Journal of Social Welfare Law 70.

Gershoff E, 'Corporal Punishment by Parents and Associated Child Behaviours and Experiences: A Meta-Analytic and Theoretical Review' (2002) 128 Psychological Bulletin 539.

Goldstein J, Freud A and Solnit A, *Before the Best Interests of the Child* (1980) Burnett Books Limited.

Gordon D et al, *Poverty and Social Exclusion in Britain* (2000) Joseph Rowntree Foundation.

Gregg P, Harkness S and Machin S, *Child development and family income* (1999) Joseph Rowntree Foundation.

Gregg P and Machin S, 'Childhood experiences, educational attainment and adult labour market performance' in K Vleminckx and T Smeeding (eds) *Child Well-Being, Child Poverty and Child Policy in Modern Nations: What do we know?* (2001) The Policy Press.

Hammarberg T ,'Children, Crime and Society: Perspectives of the UN Convention on the Rights of the Child' in *Child Offenders: UK and International Practice* (1995) The Howard League.

Hoggett B, 'Joint parenting systems: the English experiment' (1994) 6 Journal of Child Law 8.

Home Office, *No More Excuses – A New Approach to Tackling Youth Crime in England and Wales* Cm 3809 (1997).

Home Office, *Supporting Families: A Consultation Document* (1998).

Immervoll H, Sutherland H and de Vos K, 'Reducing child poverty in the European Union: the role of child benefits' in K Vleminckx and T Smeeding (eds) *Child Well-Being, Child Poverty and Child Policy in Modern Nations: What do we know?* (2001) The Policy Press.

Innocenti Research Centre, *A League Table of Child Poverty in Rich Nations* Innocenti Report Card Issue No 1 June 2000 (2000) UNICEF.

Jenkins S, Schulter C and Wagner G, *Child Poverty in Britain and Germany* (2001) Anglo-German Foundation for the Study of Industrial Society.

Law Commission, *Review of Child Law, Guardianship and Custody* Law Com No 172, HC 594 (1988) HMSO.

Lewis J, 'Family Policy in the Post-war Period' in S Katz, J Eekelaar and M Maclean (eds) *Cross Currents: Family Law and Policy in the US and England* (2000) Oxford University Press.

Lowe N and Douglas G, *Bromley's Family Law* (1998) Butterworths.

Maidment S, *Child Custody and Divorce* (1984) Croom Helm.

Meltzer H and Gatward R, *The mental health of children and adolescents in Great Britain* ONS (2000) The Stationery Office.

Middleton S, Ashworth K and Braithwaite I, *Small fortunes: Spending on children, childhood poverty and parental sacrifice* (1997) Joseph Rowntree Foundation.

Minow M, 'Rights For the Next Generation: A Feminist Approach to Children's Rights' [1986] 9 Harvard Women's Law Journal 1.

Mostyn N, 'The Green Paper on Child Support – Children First: a new approach to child support' (1999) Family Law 95.

Northern Ireland Office of Law Reform, *Physical punishment in the home – thinking about the issues, looking at the evidence* A consultation paper for Northern Ireland (2001) Office of Law Reform.

Office for National Statistics, *Social Trends 32* (2002) The Stationery Office.

Office for National Statistics, *Social Trends 33* (2003) The Stationery Office.

Palmer G et al, *Monitoring poverty and social exclusion 2002* (2002) Joseph Rowntree Foundation.

Piachaud D and Sutherland H, *How Effective is the British Government's Attempt to Reduce Child Poverty?* Innocenti Working Paper No 77 (2000) UNICEF Innocenti Research Centre.

Priest J, 'Child support and the non-standard earner – pass the Heineken please! *Phillips v Peace*' (1997) 9 Child and Family Law Quarterly 63.

Scottish Executive, *The Physical Punishment of Children in Scotland*: *A Consultation* (2001).

Scottish Parliament, *Report of Justice 2 Committee on Criminal Justice (Scotland Bill)* 13 September 2002 (2002).

Shropshire J and Middleton S, *Small Expectations: Learning to be Poor?* (1999) Joseph Rowntree Foundation.

Social Exclusion Unit, *Report of Policy Action Team 12: Young People* (2000) Social Exclusion Unit.

Solera C, 'Income transfers and support for mothers' employment: the links to family poverty risks' in K Vleminckx and T Smeeding (eds) *Child Well-Being, Child Poverty and Child Policy in Modern Nations: What do we know?* (2001) The Policy Press.

Statistics Sweden, *Spanking and Other Forms of Physical Punishment: A study of adults' and middle school students' opinions, experience and knowledge* 1.2 Demography, the Family and Children (1996).

Utting D, *Family and Parenthood: Supporting families, preventing breakdown* (1995) Joseph Rowntree Foundation.

Vleminckx K and Smeeding T (eds), *Child Well-Being, Child Poverty and Child Policy in Modern Nations: What do we know?* (2001) The Policy Press.

Wald M, 'Children's Rights: A Framework for Analysis' (1979) 12 University of California Davis Law Review 225–282.

Walsh B, 'The United Nations Convention on the Rights of the Child' (1991) 5 International Journal of Law and the Family 170.

Wikeley N, 'Compliance, Enforcement and Child Support' (2000) Family Law 888.

Chapter 10

Parents' decisions and children's health rights

(1) INTRODUCTION

The CRC recognises that without good health, children have little hope of fulfilling their potential. Article 24 (1) requires states to:

> '... recognise the right of the child to the enjoyment of the highest attainable standard of health and to facilities for the treatment of illness and rehabilitation of health. States Parties shall strive to ensure that no child is deprived of his or her right of access to such health care services.'

This requirement should not be too onerous for the United Kingdom to fulfil, with its well-established health service and comparatively good hygiene and living conditions – better by far than those in many developing countries. Nevertheless, advances made by medical technology sometimes confront parents and doctors alike with difficult dilemmas over what is the appropriate decision to reach. Does a child, for example, have a right to life, whatever the cost? When considering questions like this, the medical profession wields considerable power and it is the doctors who may in reality decide how best to fulfil a child's rights. In the event of a dispute between parents and doctors, the courts may be asked to intervene. At that point, medical paternalism may be replaced by judicial paternalism, with the child's own perspectives slipping into second place.

This assessment of the law is divided broadly into two sections. The first deals with the extent to which children's right to life can be endangered by decisions relating to their health. The second deals with the extent to which children's rights are jeopardised by medical procedures, which though not life-threatening, may damage their health, to a lesser or greater extent. Before these, however, there is a brief assessment of the general principles which recur in much of the case law regarding children's medical care.

(2) GENERAL PRINCIPLES

(A) Children's rights to healthcare and the best interests test

Advances in medical technology, the availability of antibiotics and immunisation, together with a higher standard of living, have led to British children today enjoying far better general health[1] than did their counterparts a century ago.[2] In particular, the rate of infant deaths due to infectious diseases has reduced very significantly, with the downward trend in infant mortality projected to continue into the early part of the twenty-first century.[3] Despite this, there are considerable inequalities in child health,[4] with a far higher incidence of low birth weight babies,[5] poor levels of nutrition and infant growth,[6] poor levels of psychological health[7] and a higher level of accidental deaths,[8] amongst families on low income.[9] The extent to which children's health can be improved on a national level only partly depends on better financial support[10] and improved health resources for families with children. It also depends on parents being educated about their children's health needs and the state's willingness to subject parents to a measure of surveillance to ensure that these needs are met.

Under the current law, there is no legal compulsion on parents to allow health agencies to monitor their children's health. Indeed, the government assumes that parents are the best judges of their children's medical needs. A preference for persuasion, as opposed to compulsion, pervades its approach to child-health issues. For example, parents are not obliged to allow health visitors into their homes to examine their babies.[11] Furthermore, despite the periodic outbreaks of serious childhood diseases, there is no legislation compelling parents to comply with immunisation programmes.[12] Although blanket immunisation would prevent the considerable fluctuations in rates of immunisation,[13] the rare cases of vaccines producing damaging reactions in some children render it unlikely that the government will consider reintroducing any forms of compulsion. Any attempt to do so would be strenuously opposed by many parents. They would undoubtedly claim not only that such laws would infringe their own rights to respect for their family life under article 8 of the ECHR, but also their children's right to family life and bodily privacy and integrity.[14]

1   British Medical Association (1999) pp 17–18.
2   See J Fortin (2000) p 169.
3   Infant mortality fell from 48.8 deaths before the age of 1, per 1,000 live births in 1948, to 5.4 in 2001. See Office for National Statistics (2003) p 131.
4   See D Acheson (1998) esp Part 2.
5   See G Palmer et al (2002) pp 32 and 38.
6   E Dowler et al (2001).
7   H Meltzer and R Gatward (2000) p 29 and Table 4.8. The prevalence of any psychiatric disorder ranged from 16% amongst children of families with a gross weekly income of under £100 to 6% among children of families earning £500 per week or more.
8   G Palmer et al (2002) pp 31–32 and 39. Although the number of accidental deaths has halved over the last decade, children from manual social classes are one and a half times more likely to die in such accidents than children from non-manual social classes.
9   Discussed in more depth in chapter 9.
10   Targeted at parents and children.
11   See 'the liberal compromise' between state surveillance and non-intervention, discussed by R Dingwall, J Eekelaar and T Murray (1995) pp 218–221.
12   Cf the Compulsory Vaccination Acts 1853 and 1867, which compelled parents to have their children vaccinated against smallpox within the first years of their lives and imposed fines or imprisonment for default. This was so unpopular that the Anti-Vaccination League was founded in 1867 to spearhead opposition.
13   Eg the outbreak of measles in early 2002 was caused by parents refusing the MMR vaccination for their children due to their fear of its possible side-effects. The target immunisation rate of 95% dropped in some areas to 65%.
14   See *Wain v United Kingdom* (1987) 9 EHRR 122: the European Commission of Human Rights rejected a father's claims that his rights under art 8 had been infringed by the government's failure to provide parents with detailed information about the risks of particular

There is an obvious concern on the part of the government not to interfere with parents' own views regarding the medical treatment of their children. Nevertheless, as the criminal law recognises, inactivity regarding healthcare may endanger children's lives.[15] A parent is guilty of criminal neglect if he wilfully fails to provide the child with adequate medical aid.[16] Indeed, the criminal law has shown little sympathy with a parent's reasons for failing to ensure that his child receives medical attention[17] or for refusing to consent to what is deemed to be essential medical care.[18] Criminal sanctions may, however, be too late to protect the child's health. Furthermore, the House of Lords' strict interpretation of the wilful element of the offence of child neglect[19] has left children vulnerable to the 'stupidity or fecklessness' of their parents.[20] The child protection laws can probably achieve far more than the criminal law in terms of ensuring that a child's right to health care is fulfilled. Local authorities are legally obliged to ensure that they seek out and protect children who are suffering or are likely to suffer 'significant harm' for any reason, and this will obviously include a duty to investigate cases of ill-health due to parental inattention.[21] Young children, particularly babies, die very quickly if they become ill and are not provided with medical attention. Depending on the urgency of the situation, parental failure to seek medical attention could be dealt with by the local authority seeking a child assessment order[22] or an emergency protection order.[23] Alternatively, they may seek a specific issue order regarding the child's further assessment or treatment.[24]

vaccines. Despite his son's serious reaction to the diphtheria, tetanus and whooping cough vaccination, there was no breach because the vaccination scheme was voluntary. See also the European Commission of Human Rights' decision in *Association X v United Kingdom* (Application No 7154/75) (1978) 14 DR 31.

15   See Children and Young Persons Act 1933, s 1(1).

16   Children and Young Persons Act 1933, s 1(2)(a): a parent or other person legally liable to maintain a child or young person 'shall be deemed to have neglected [the child] in a manner likely to cause injury to his health if he has failed to provide adequate food, clothing, medical aid or lodging for him ...'

17   Eg *R v Senior* [1899] 1 QB 283: a member of a religious sect called the Peculiar People was convicted of the manslaughter of his infant son. He had deliberately refrained from calling a doctor because it would show his unwillingness to accept God's will in relation to his child.

18   Eg *Oakey v Jackson* [1914] 1 KB 216: father found liable under Children Act 1908, s 12(1) (later replaced by Children and Young Persons Act 1933, s 1) for refusing to agree to his 13-year-old daughter undergoing an operation to remove her adenoids.

19   See *R v Sheppard* [1981] AC 394: per the House of Lords (majority), Children and Young Persons Act 1933, s 1(1), which imposes liability on anyone who '*wilfully* assaults, ill-treats, neglects, abandons or exposes him ...' includes only parents able to appreciate the need to obtain medical care for their child and not parents who through stupidity, ignorance or personal inadequacy fail to do so.

20   [1981] AC 394. See Lord Fraser's dissenting judgment, at 913.

21   See Children Act 1989, s 47. See discussion in chapter 15.

22   Children Act 1989, s 43. A child assessment order would enable the local authority to establish whether the child needs medical attention and, if so, what form it should take. But such an order is inappropriate in emergencies, since it takes time to obtain because it can only be obtained on notice to the parents, and it does not confer parental responsibility on the local authority.

23   Children Act 1989, s 44. This order is more suitable for emergencies, since it can be obtained rapidly ex parte and confers on the holder parental responsibility, thereby entitling the local authority to consent to medical treatment.

24   Eg *Re C (HIV Test)* [1999] 2 FLR 1004: the local authority obtained a specific issue order authorising the testing for HIV of a baby against the wishes of both her parents.

Once a doctor is consulted, the human right to bodily integrity is central to the notion of autonomy and, for adults and children alike, it is protected by article 8 of the ECHR.[25] Any medical treatment of an adult without consent will normally, unless life-saving treatment is required in an emergency,[26] amount to a trespass to the person and to a criminal assault.[27] Both legislation[28] and case law[29] acknowledge that it is similarly unlawful for doctors to treat children without consent, unless it is to avoid serious harm or death, in an emergency.[30] In the case of a child too young and immature to be deemed *Gillick* competent, doctors will seek consent from the child's parents, as his or her proxies.[31] It is they who brought their child into the world and they are assumed to be the adults most likely to have his or her interests at heart.[32] Historically, a married father could sue a doctor in tort if his children were given medical treatment without his consent. Indeed, it was probably an aspect of the father's position as their legal guardian,[33] and of his proprietorial rights over his children,[34] that he could do so. The modern law has rejected the notion of parents' rights being proprietorial;[35] it emphasises that they are derived from parental duties and exist only so long as they are needed to protect the child. Since any adult with parental responsibility can consent to a child's medical treatment,[36] consent can now be obtained from either parent, if they are married,[37] and from the child's mother, if unmarried, or from anyone with whom she shares parental responsibility.[38]

Given that the law adopts a non-interventionist approach to family life, can parents be trusted to protect adequately their young children's right to bodily integrity and to good health? Even prior to the introduction of the Human Rights Act 1998, parents' rights to determine their children's healthcare were not unfettered. English common law requires parents to reach all decisions regarding their children's upbringing,

25   See *X and Y v Netherlands* (1986) 8 EHRR 235. The European Court of Human Rights held that the right to private life includes the right to 'physical and moral integrity'.

26   In which case, the medical treatment can be carried out under the doctrine of necessity. Per Lord Goff in *Re F (mental patient: sterilisation)* [1990] 2 AC 1 at 74.

27   See Lord Scarman in *Sidaway v Board of Governors of the Bethlem Royal Hospital and the Maudsley Hospital* [1985] AC 871 at 882. See discussion in the context of adolescent decision-making and health care in chapter 5.

28   Family Law Reform Act 1969, s 8(1). See discussion in chapter 5.

29   *Gillick v West Norfolk and Wisbech Area Health Authority* [1986] AC 112.

30   [1986] AC 112 at 189, per Lord Scarman.

31   [1986] AC 112. 'It is abundantly plain that the law recognises that there is a right and a duty of parents to determine whether or not to seek medical advice in respect of their child, and, having received advice, to give or withhold consent to medical treatment', per Lord Scarman (at 184).

32   See G Dworkin (1982) p 204.

33   [1986] AC 112 at 184, per Lord Scarman. The rule of law that a married father was the legal guardian of his children was abolished by the Children Act 1989, s 2(4).

34   See *F v Wirral Metropolitan Borough Council* [1991] 2 All ER 648 for a useful discussion of parents' proprietorial rights over their children (per Ralph Gibson LJ, at 676–682).

35   [1991] 2 All ER 648.

36   But note that under the Children Act 1989, s 3(5), any person with care of a child, but without parental responsibility, such as a child-minder or foster carer, can do 'what is reasonable in all the circumstances of the case for the purpose of safeguarding or promoting the child's welfare'. This might include consenting to therapeutic medical treatment.

37   Married parents share parental responsibility (Children Act 1989, s 2(1)) and either can exercise it unilaterally, without the other (s 2(7)).

38   Eg an unmarried father with parental responsibility through being named on the child's birth certificate or through entering a parental responsibility with the mother or by court order, see Children Act 1989, s 4(1)(a)–(c) (as amended by Adoption and Children Act 2002, s 111).

more particularly regarding medical care, in accordance with their best interests.[39] Any decisions reached which manifestly infringe such a principle, can be challenged, even overridden.[40] Nevertheless, case law demonstrates that the best interests test, as interpreted by parents, has not always adequately protected children's rights, without the intervention of doctors or the courts. The real difficulty is that most parents find it relatively easy to justify their decisions by reference to their children's best interests. Since it is virtually impossible to interpret such a term objectively, it is questionable whether it provides the child with adequate protection. Indeed, as Gerald Dworkin has observed, the personal views of individual parents may define the 'best interests' of their child in terms of their own best interests.[41] This is obvious when considering some of the choices parents make when obtaining medical attention for their children. Their decisions over blood transfusions or circumcisions may be coloured by their religious faith; those regarding a healthy child providing bone marrow may be influenced by their anxieties over a seriously ill sibling; and their decisions about sterilising a mentally handicapped daughter may be influenced by their worries over their ability to provide future care.[42] The need for parents to remember that medical treatment may infringe their child's right to bodily integrity under article 8(1) of the ECHR adds little to children's protection. Parents told of these additional legal requirements would simply claim that the treatment is justified under article 8(2), since in their view the harm avoided will be greater than that inflicted by the infringement.

If parents and doctors disagree over a child's medical treatment, the parents' views of what is in the child's best interests may be fundamentally different from those of the doctors. Indeed, some consider it inevitable that doctors and parents will determine whether or not a medical procedure is in a child's best interests from very different perspectives.[43] The doctors consider it in terms of the child patient's best *medical* interests, taking into account clinical issues. These include the treatment's chances of success, its advantages and disadvantages, in terms of suffering and risks to the patient, and the quality of life to be gained. The parent often considers the child's best interests in more general terms, taking into account not only the medical advice, but also the child's psychological needs, bearing in mind the views and mores of the whole family. Disagreements between doctors and parents may need judicial intervention to resolve[44] and some have to be dealt with urgently if the child's life is in danger. If judicial assistance is invoked to resolve the dilemma,[45] the judiciary may consider it perfectly reasonable for the parent, as a proxy for the child, to take into

---

39 It is arguable that, for essentially trivial non-therapeutic procedures, the test is the less rigorous 'not against the child's best interests'. See *S v S; W v Official Solicitor (or W)* [1972] AC 24.

40 *Gillick v West Norfolk and Wisbech Area Health Authority* [1986] AC 112 at 184, per Lord Scarman.

41 G Dworkin (1982) p 200.

42 See discussion below.

43 *R v Cambridge District Health Authority, ex p B* [1995] 1 FLR 1055 at 1062–1063 (QBD), per Laws J.

44 In *R v Portsmouth Hospital NHS Trust, ex p Glass* [1999] 2 FLR 905 at 910, Lord Woolf MR indicated that conflicts of a grave nature between parents and doctors over future treatment should be submitted to the courts to obtain a ruling on what is in the child's best interests.

45 By application to the High Court for a declaration under the inherent jurisdiction, or by application for a specific issue order under the Children Act 1989, s 8. Both applications will be governed by the best interests criterion.

account non-medical issues.[46] Alternatively, they may be unable to sympathise with a parent's own ideas and beliefs, particularly if, as in cases involving Jehovah's Witness parents, they appear unorthodox. But in the past, the indeterminacy of the best interests test has sometimes led the judiciary to consider matters from a particularly adult view point.[47]

Parents sometimes demand treatment which doctors are unwilling to provide, others object to the form of treatment being advised. Doctors traditionally wield considerable power in such situations, since ultimately it is they, as the gatekeepers to treatment resources, who decide what treatment, if any, is medically indicated. It seems unlikely that the requirements of the ECHR will change the balance of power between parents and doctors, in disputes over the best treatment for ill children. Where the dispute centres on the treatment of children whose lives are not immediately at risk, the Strasbourg case law delineating parents' rights is particularly relevant. Although in *Nielsen v Denmark*,[48] the mother was held to be entitled, under article 8, to decide whether her son should receive medical treatment and where,[49] she could only reach such decisions 'for a proper purpose'.[50] Clearly the parent cannot be entitled under article 8(1) to have any measures taken that would harm the child's health and development.[51] Furthermore, in situations where the child's life is at risk, the decision in *Nielsen v Denmark*[52] is counter-balanced by the obligation on the state and its agents, such as hospitals and doctors, to promote the child's right to life under article 2.[53] Contrarily, in cases where the parents disagree with the doctors' wish to withhold treatment, a domestic court might sympathise with the parents' claim that their child is entitled to life-sustaining treatment, unless it considers such treatment to be futile and against the child's best interests.[54]

(B)   Capacity to consent to medical treatment and the right to be consulted

When treating an older child, doctors will turn, in the first place, to the child for consent to treatment. Despite the legislative presumption that only those over the age of 16 can legally consent to treatment,[55] as the *Gillick*[56] principle acknowledges, many adolescents under that age may be legally capable of consenting for themselves.[57] Doctors will often assume that below adolescence they should seek consent from the child's parents, especially if the procedure has major health implications. This

---

46   See the discussion of the different approaches in *R v Cambridge District Health Authority, ex p B* [1995] 1 FLR 1055 at 1062–1063, per Laws J. See also *Re T (a minor) (wardship: medical treatment)* [1997] 1 All ER 906 at 914, per Butler-Sloss LJ.

47   See discussion below in the context of sterilisation procedures for mentally handicapped girls.

48   (1988) 11 EHRR 175.

49   The European Court of Human Rights therefore rejected the boy's claim that his rights to liberty under art 5 had been infringed by his restraint in a closed psychiatric ward on his mother's request. Discussed in more detail in chapter 3, pp 81–83.

50   (1988) 11 EHRR 175 (para 61).

51   See *Johansen v Norway* (1996) 23 EHRR 33 (para 78).

52   (1988) 11 EHRR 175.

53   *Osman v United Kingdom* [1999] 1 FLR 193 at para 115. But compare the decision reached in *Re T (a minor) (wardship: medical treatment)* [1997] 1 All ER 906. Discussed below.

54   Eg *Re C (medical treatment)* [1998] 1 FLR 384. Discussed below.

55   See Family Law Reform Act 1969, s 8(1).

56   *Gillick v West Norfolk and Wisbech Area Health Authority* [1986] AC 112.

57   Discussion in chapter 5.

approach is consistent with the research on children's cognitive development which suggests that before early adolescence, younger children may be far less able to weigh up alternatives and cope rationally with important decisions affecting their upbringing.[58] Their lack of capacity for abstract thought or ability to weigh up risks and benefits of various options also indicates that the majority of young children, particularly if they are very ill, will lack the cognitive abilities and judgmental skills to make decisions that might seriously affect their health care.

Some refute such an approach, arguing that even very young children are capable of making far-reaching decisions about their health.[59] In Alderson's research, medical staff considered that even some 3- and 4-year-old children were able to understand medical information, 'as well as the average adult' and that 'exceptional' 5- and 6-year-olds were thought able to make complex, wise decisions.[60] On the basis of this research, Alderson and Montgomery argued in favour of introducing a new code governing health care for children which incorporated a legal presumption that all 5-year-olds should be deemed competent to consent to all health care.[61]

Despite a legal presumption of the kind recommended by Alderson and Montgomery ostensibly promoting the aims of article 12 of the CRC, it risks forcing children into reaching important decisions about their health before they are ready to do so. Furthermore, article 12 does not expect children to be given the right to autonomy, only the right to be involved in decisions relating to their future. Indeed, Marshall points out that the Committee on the Rights of the Child was not impressed by Swedish law which allowed children aged 7 and over, to receive legal and medical counselling without parental consent or involvement. The Committee considered that such provisions risked very young children forming mistaken opinions owing to their immaturity and inexperience and reaching decisions contrary to their best interests. It therefore recommended that the Swedish government reassess the advisability of permitting such young children to receive counselling without their parents' consent.[62]

Alderson and Montgomery's proposal would be less problematic were it couched in terms of requiring children over 5 always to be *consulted* over medical procedures. Although children are often too immature to decide such matters, they may have important views over the costs and benefits to them of the proposed treatment. It insults their dignity and self-respect for parents and doctors to make decisions which infringe their right to bodily integrity, without consulting them. Children are right to feel resentful and angry as they grow older, having to accept medical decisions with which they had no involvement. By the same token, they will respond to medical treatment much better if they have been fully involved in it, understand it and have confidence in it. Current medical guidance acknowledges this and states:

> 'It is essential that children and young people are shown that their views are valued ... Young patients are individuals whose interests need to be considered in a broad manner that takes account of their physical needs, their own wishes and the circumstances of the case ... The

---

58   Discussed in chapter 3.
59   P Alderson and J Montgomery (1996) ch 2.
60   P Alderson (1993) p 193.
61   P Alderson and J Montgomery (1996) ch 5. The authors' proposed code of practice contained guidance on the factors to consider when attempting to rebut this presumption.
62   See Committee on the Rights of the Child (1993) para 11. See discussion by K Marshall (1997) pp 26–28.

health team has a duty to ensure that the patient's contribution is not overlooked and that he or she has the information necessary to form a view.'[63]

(3)   A CHILD'S RIGHT TO LIFE AND THE LEGAL IMPLICATIONS OF LIFE-THREATENING DECISIONS

(A)   A child's right to life – whom does it benefit?

There are no rights more important than the right to life and the vast majority of parents will do everything in their power to ensure that a sick child obtains the best medical attention available. Article 6 of the CRC unequivocally demands that states 'recognise that every child has the inherent right to life' and that they 'shall ensure to the maximum extent possible the survival and development of the child'. Equally, article 2 of the ECHR provides in more general terms:

> 'Everyone's right to life shall be protected by law. No one shall be deprived of his life intentionally save in the execution of a sentence of a court following his conviction of a crime for which this penalty is provided by law.'

Many would argue that the need to protect a child's right to life, as required by the Human Rights Act 1998 makes little difference to medical practice since the sanctity of life has always been an important principle underlying all medical law. Strasbourg jurisprudence has, however, stressed the strength of article 2 of the ECHR. State authorities must do 'all that could be reasonably expected of them to avoid a real and immediate risk to life of which they have or ought to have knowledge'.[64] As discussed below, this positive obligation, combined with recent domestic case law, may provoke a reassessment of the principles of common law which have governed the treatment of desperately ill and dying children.

Article 2 imposes a duty on the state to make adequate provision for the protection of human life.[65] Does this mean that the right to life attaches to all human beings, however malformed and psychologically impaired? Since the European Commission of Human Rights avoided deciding whether an unborn child can claim the protection of article 2,[66] it remains theoretically possible for a domestic court to extend the protection of the right to life to all foetuses. Such a decision is unlikely, since it would effectively prohibit legalised abortion. Nevertheless, this uncertainty provokes further questions about the extent to which the right to life attaches to 'incomplete' persons after birth.[67]

(B)   A child's right to life – withholding treatment from desperately ill children

Does even the most catastrophically impaired neonate have a 'right to life' and, if so, is a neonatal unit obliged to use all means at its disposal to keep him or her alive?

---

63   British Medical Association (BMA) (2001) pp 5–6.
64   *Osman v United Kingdom* [1999] 1 FLR 193 at para 116.
65   See D Harris, M O'Boyle and C Warbrick (1995) p 38.
66   *Paton v United Kingdom* (1980) 3 EHRR 408: the European Commission of Human Rights merely decided that an abortion of a 10-week-old foetus was not an infringement of art 2, since it had been carried out to protect the health of the mother. See also *Open-Door Counselling Ltd, Dublin Well Woman Centre Ltd v Ireland* (1992) 15 EHRR 244.
67   Discussed below.

Even with improved ante-natal care, neonates are still sometimes born with very low birth weight and so massively handicapped, both mentally and physically, that they have little chance of survival for more than a few days or weeks, without aggressive intervention. Nevertheless, the increasingly sophisticated technology available to neonatal intensive care units has transformed the chances of survival of some of these babies, thereby encouraging their parents to hope against hope that some treatment will be found to keep them alive or at least delay their deaths. At common law the right to life attaches to a legal person, who in turn, is created at the moment of being born alive and separate from its mother.[68] But according to Mason, McCall Smith and Laurie, the practice of 'selective non-treatment of the newborn' which, they allege, at times comes 'perilously close to breaking the law',[69] ensures that at least some of these neonates fail to survive who could be kept alive.[70] Few cases involving such situations reach court, perhaps because parents faced with medical advice that life-saving treatment should be withheld seldom disagree with their medical advisers.[71]

Prior to the decision of the Court of Appeal, particularly the judgment of Ward LJ, in *Re A (conjoined twins: medical treatment)*,[72] the law governing disputes over the treatment of desperately ill and dying neonates appeared to be relatively clear. In *Re C (a minor) (wardship: medical treatment)*[73] the Court of Appeal confirmed that a dying baby's life does not have to be extended by artificial means, irrespective of the circumstances. The utility of the treatment is to be judged by the child's best interests, which in turn depends on the quality of life which might be achieved for the child through the proposed treatment. Many would agree with such an approach, arguing that a dying child has a right to die with dignity.[74] Nevertheless, disputes can arise over the withholding of life-sustaining treatment for an infant who has survived for many months or even longer. On the one hand, the medical team may consider that parents who object to resuscitative treatment being withdrawn are being unrealistic. They urge the court that when a child is suffering a serious fatal condition, constant resuscitative intervention may not only be futile but cruel, since it will cause the child distress, not balanced by any *real* benefit, in terms of quality of life. On the other hand, parents of older babies argue that they have a warm and loving relationship with the child, who recognises them and gets pleasure from their presence and that this relationship contributes to a quality of life worth sustaining for as long as possible.

In disputes of this kind, case law suggests that the judiciary see no real need for an analysis of the cognitive capacity of such infants, or of their ability to relate to their parents, particularly when the medical teams advise that their lives cannot be extended in the long-term. Unless the circumstances are exceptional, the courts allow the views

---

68   The criminal law protects any child 'born alive' and capable of breathing and existing independently of its mother. See *Rance v Mid-Downs Health Authority* [1991] 1 All ER 801 at 817, per Brooks J.

69   J Mason, R McCall Smith and G Laurie (2002) p 476.

70   It was estimated that in the mid-1980s, anything up to 30% of deaths occurred in neonatal intensive care units due to the deliberate withdrawal of life support: J Mason, R McCall Smith and G Laurie (2002) p 476.

71   J Mason, R McCall Smith and G Laurie (2002) p 474.

72   [2001] 1 FLR 1.

73   [1990] Fam 26. C was a 4-month-old massively handicapped and terminally ill baby. The court directed that the medical staff were not obliged to administer antibiotics and use intravenous feeding in the event of C acquiring an infection or becoming unable to take feeds by mouth. They could care for her in a way which would relieve her suffering and allow her to die peacefully and with dignity.

74   See M Freeman (2001) p 277.

of the medical teams to prevail over those of parents, on the basis that since no form of treatment will save the child's life, it is inappropriate to require doctors to treat, if in the exercise of their professional judgment they are opposed to doing so.[75] But there are deficiencies in this rather broad-brush approach to dying babies.[76] There appear to be good ethical reasons for distinguishing between a 3-month-old dying baby with 'a very low awareness of anything, if at all',[77] and a 16-month-old baby who, despite slowly dying from spinal muscular atrophy, is conscious, able to recognise her parents and smile.[78] It is arguable that the courts should give greater weight to the views of parents of a baby with obvious cognitive capacity, than to those of a neonate with little or no discernable brain activity. Their babies may have a quality of life which makes the treatment available to keep them alive 'worthwhile', compared with the parents of a baby with no intellectual capacity of any kind. As the discussion below demonstrates, the former has a potential for 'personhood', the latter none at all.

In disputes of this kind the courts should, in any event, drop their reverential view of medical opinion.[79] A presumption which always favours doctors who wish to withhold life-sustaining treatment contradicts the approach dictated by article 2 of the ECHR. Arguably, the burden of proof should be on those wishing to cease supporting life, rather than on those wishing to continue it. Parents will only have full confidence in an open-minded judiciary who are entirely free to decide for themselves what is in the child's best interests, irrespective of the doctors' own views on this. There may, after all, be room for doubt over what is medically indicated. If the court decides to favour the parents' standpoint, it might always be possible to find another specialist who would take a more optimistic view.[80]

Though tragic, a baby whose life is undoubtedly drawing to a close presents less obvious dilemmas than one who is not yet dying but whose future, nevertheless, looks extremely bleak, even with medical intervention. As in *Re J (a minor) (wardship: medical treatment)*,[81] these desperately ill babies and infants sometimes suffer numerous episodes of respiratory failure requiring ventilation to keep them alive. The dilemma for the medical team is whether such an infant's sanctity of life requires

---

75   *Re J (a minor)* [1990] 3 All ER 930 at 934, per Lord Donaldson MR; *Re J (a minor) (wardship: medical treatment)* [1992] 4 All ER 614 at 622, per Lord Donaldson MR, and at 625, per Balcombe LJ; *Re R (a minor) (wardship: medical treatment)* [1991] 4 All ER 177 at 187, per Lord Donaldson MR; *Re C (Medical Treatment)* [1998] 1 FLR 384 at 389–390, per Sir Stephen Brown P.

76   See J Fortin (2000) p 173 and J Fortin (1998) p 416.

77   *Re C (a baby)* [1996] 2 FLR 43 at 44. See also *Re C (a minor) (wardship: medical treatment)* [1990] Fam 26 and *Royal Wolverhampton Hospitals NHS Trust v B* [2000] 1 FLR 953. These babies were all only a few months old and had severe brain abnormalities.

78   Eg *Re C (medical treatment)* [1998] 1 FLR 384: this baby's strongly religious orthodox Jewish parents vehemently opposed the withholding of resuscitative intervention. See also *A National Health Service Trust v D* [2000] 2 FLR 677, a case involving a baby aged 19 months, who, despite suffering from severe chronic disabilities and irreversible brain abnormality, nevertheless greeted familiar people, smiled at them and waved goodbye. The parents opposed the medical team's view that he should not receive intensive care.

79   See J Fortin (2000) pp 176–177. See also I Kennedy and A Grubb (2000) p 822.

80   As in *Re J (a minor) (wardship: medical treatment)* [1992] 4 All ER 614, where a third consultant was found who, unlike the current medical team, did not regard artificial ventilation as 'cruel treatment'.

81   [1990] 3 All ER 930: although not dying, J had been born very prematurely. Apart from severe and permanent brain damage at birth, he had other disabilities which suggested an extremely poor quality of life in the event of his surviving. His life expectancy was uncertain but might extend to his late teens. It was predicted that he was likely to develop paralysis in all his limbs, deafness, limited intellectual abilities and would be unable to speak.

them to continue such treatment, irrespective of his or her quality of life. In *Re J* the Court of Appeal held that the doctors were not obliged to resuscitate J again, having done so twice already, bearing in mind that resuscitation was an invasive process and would cause him distress.

The decision in *Re J* was important in so far as the Court of Appeal established that a child does not need to be actually dying before a medical team can contemplate withholding treatment. It emphasised that there is an important difference between taking no steps to extend artificially the child's life, which might be lawful and taking steps to terminate the child's life, which will never be lawful.[82] Nevertheless, the court rejected any absolute notion of the sanctity of life, in favour of an inquiry into the baby's future quality of life, as a means of determining his or her best interests.[83] Continued intervention is not essential if the quality of life available to him or her would be so poor that it would be against the child's best interests to strive to keep it alive. The question is whether the treatment would produce increased suffering and no commensurate benefit.[84] Thus the concept of 'medical futility' becomes bound up with quality of life predictions and the best interests test, in so far as the treatment is deemed to be futile and not in the child's best interests, in the face of an unacceptable quality of life.[85]

To what extent does this case law, more particularly *Re J*, remain unchanged, given the demands of article 2 of the ECHR and the Court of Appeal's decision in *Re A (conjoined twins: medical treatment)*?[86] The facts of this case are well known, involving as it did, conjoined twins, Mary and Jodie, only one of whom could survive separation surgery. All members of the Court of Appeal agreed that the immensely physically and mentally deformed Mary had a right to life. According to Ward LJ, although Mary had such major deformities[87] that if she had been born separate, she would have had no capacity for survival,[88] she had a right to life, equal to that enjoyed by her sister, 'Jodie'. Indeed, he said: 'What the sanctity of life doctrine compels me to accept is that each life has inherent value in itself and the right to life, being universal, is equal for all of us.'[89] Influenced by the writing of Keown,[90] and by Lord Goff's judgment in the *Bland* case,[91] Ward LJ was eager to reject the 'quality of life argument' in favour of the 'sanctity of life' doctrine, on the basis that the former involved 'discriminatory judgments'[92] based on arbitrary preconceptions regarding physical or mental disabilities. Preferring the sanctity of life doctrine, he concluded from its application to Mary's position:

'Given the international Conventions protecting "the right to life" ... I conclude that it is impermissible to deny that every life has an equal inherent value. Life is worthwhile in itself whatever the diminution in one's capacity to enjoy it and however gravely impaired some of

---

82   [1990] 3 All ER 930 at 943, per Taylor LJ.
83   See I Kennedy and A Grubb (2000) p 2173.
84   [1990] 3 All ER 930 at 938, per Lord Donaldson MR.
85   See J Mason, R McCall Smith and G Laurie (2002) pp 471–474 for a discussion of the concept of medical futility.
86   [2001] 1 FLR 1.
87   Ie a very poorly developed 'primitive' brain, a very poorly functioning heart and no functioning lung tissue.
88   [2001] 1 FLR 1 at 14, per Ward LJ.
89   [2001] 1 FLR 1 at 42.
90   J Keown (1997).
91   *Airdale NHS Trust v Bland* [1993] 1 All ER 821, esp at 869.
92   [2001] 1 FLR 1 at 44.

one's vital functions of speech, deliberation and choice may be … Mary's life, desperate as it is, still has its own ineliminable value and dignity.'[93]

Does the fact that Ward LJ rejected quality of life arguments in favour of the sanctity of life doctrine,[94] throw doubt on the decisions discussed above,[95] given that they were unashamedly based on the former type of reasoning? More particularly, do these sentiments indicate that neonatal intensive care units are now legally obliged to keep alive grossly deformed and severely brain damaged neonates?' Probably not, since Ward LJ did not consider that Mary's sanctity of life precluded an assessment of the 'worthwhileness of treatment', given –

> 'the actual condition of each twin and hence the actual balance sheet of advantage and disadvantage which flows from the performance or the non-performance of the proposed treatment. Here it is legitimate, as John Keown demonstrates, and as the cases show, to bear in mind the actual quality of life each child enjoys and may be able to enjoy …'[96]

Thus a subtle distinction emerges. Every child is entitled to the right to life, and it is not legitimate to reach judgments on a child's future treatment based on predictions about his or her quality of life, because this amounts to making judgments on the worthwhileness of his or her life. Nevertheless, it is legitimate to consider whether the treatment will produce any benefit, bearing in mind the child's existing quality of life and what might be achieved through treatment. It appears then, that Ward LJ was prepared to introduce quality of life predictions at the point of deciding the least detrimental of several burdensome treatment options. Such fine distinctions produce a sense of confusion, if not astonishment.[97]

The importance of the decision in *Re A* should not be underestimated, given the fact that this new emphasis on the right to life could influence medical neonatal practice, as occurred in the United States during the late 1980s. There, regulations were introduced indicating that it was morally unacceptable for doctors to reach quality of life judgments on neonates.[98] This led to terminally ill infants receiving 'overly aggressive and futile treatment for long periods at great cost, both human and financial'.[99] Here, the risk of such a change in practice occurring has probably been diminished by the Family Division's decision in *NHS Trust A v M; NHS Trust B v H*.[100] Dame Elizabeth Butler-Sloss P held that the positive obligation imposed by article 2 of the ECHR only obliges medical teams to keep a terminally ill patient[101] alive if, according to responsible medical opinion, this would be in the patient's best interests. It 'does not impose an absolute obligation to treat if such treatment would be futile'.[102] Although the issues applying to neonates and babies were not discussed in that decision, the same interpretation could be put on article 2, in the context of their treatment. One wonders, though, whether the courts will, when faced with a scenario

93 [2001] 1 FLR 1. See also Brooke LJ, at 71 and Walker LJ, at 119.
94 [2001] 1 FLR 1 at 41.
95 Inter alia: *Re C (a minor) (wardship: medical treatment)* [1990] Fam 26; *Re J (a minor) (wardship: medical treatment)* [1991] Fam 33.
96 [2001] 1 FLR 1 at 53–54.
97 See J Harris (2001) esp pp 225–226.
98 'The Baby Doe' regulations. See J Mason, R McCall Smith and G Laurie (2002) pp 493–495.
99 A Campbell and H McHaffie (1995) p 342.
100 [2001] 1 All ER 801.
101 Two hospital trusts had applied for judicial authority to withdraw life-sustaining treatment from two adult PVS patients.
102 [2001] 1 All ER 801 at para 37, per Dame Elizabeth Butler-Sloss P.

similar to that in *Re J (a minor) (wardship: medical treatment)*,[103] continue to use quality of life arguments to justify withholding resuscitative intervention.

The Court of Appeal's decision in *Re A*[104] should not be confined to its own extraordinary and well-known facts, since, as the discussion above demonstrates, it explores a number of important issues which cannot simply be relegated to history. It usefully demonstrates the considerable difficulties involved in assuming that every human person has a right to life under article 2, from the point of birth, irrespective of massive impairment and handicap. Society may be confronted with severe ethical dilemmas in the future, if and when advances in medical technology ensure that virtually all neonates, however massively deformed, could be kept alive. At that point, as has been suggested elsewhere,[105] it may become necessary for the law to clarify what attributes a neonate must have or acquire, in order to claim the right to life, as protected by article 2. Indeed, as Harris points out when discussing *Re A*, the judges resorted to 'convoluted and fallacious reasoning'[106] because they were committed to the idea that both Jodie and Mary were 'persons', and therefore as entitled to full legal protection as any other human being. But it is arguable that 'personhood' should be confined to those who possess 'the capacity to value existence', whereas 'non-persons' who lack such a capacity, cannot 'be deprived by death of something that they could coherently be said to value'.[107] If, as Harris suggests, personhood were withheld from 'zygotes and embryos, or individuals who are "brain-dead", anencephalic infants, or individuals with PVS' then compliance with article 2 would not carry difficulties for neonatal units caring for massively handicapped neonates.[108]

Harris argues that persons are beings with the capacity to value their own existence,[109] whilst Campbell and McHaffie refer to the importance of a neonate having the potential to 'reciprocate in human relationships'.[110] These too are the qualities which mark out the person from the non-person. Indeed, as Ward J (as he then was) himself remarked in an early decision, these are the 'functions of intellect which make human life distinguishable, perhaps, from other forms of life'.[111] Such an approach suggests that when medical teams give evidence to courts over the advisability of continuing resuscitative treatment, part of their quality of life assessment should always take into account whether a baby has any cognitive capacity, or meaningful brain activity. This might in turn improve the courts' decision-making in disputes over the withholding of treatment from dying children, as suggested above.

(C)   A child's right to life – treatment on demand?

A further difficulty sometimes confronts medical teams treating desperately ill children. Is a health authority behaving unreasonably if it refuses to fund treatment

---

103 [1990] 3 All ER 930. See n 81 above.
104 [2001] 1 FLR 1.
105 See J Fortin (2000) p 173.
106 See J Harris (2001) p 233.
107 J Harris (2001) p 234. See also J Harris (1985) pp 14–27.
108 See also C Wells (1989) pp 202–209. Wells argues that there should be greater clarity about the relevance of the concept of personhood in the context of treating handicapped newly born babies.
109 J Harris (2001) p 234. See also J Harris (1985) p 17.
110 A Campbell and H McHaffie (1995) p 340.
111 *Re C (a minor) (wardship: medical treatment)* [1990] Fam 26, per Ward J, at first instance, referred to by Lord Donaldson MR (CA) at 34.

for a desperately ill child which might give him or her a chance of life? This question was raised by *R v Cambridge District Health Authority, ex p B*.[112] The Court of Appeal refused to quash on judicial review a health authority's refusal to fund further treatment for B, a 10-year-old child, desperately ill with terminal leukaemia.[113] B and her father had been determined to obtain experimental treatment for her because it had a slight chance of extending or even saving her life. The health authority refused to provide it, inter alia, because: the chances of success were very slight; the treatment was of an experimental nature; the chemotherapy would cause considerable further suffering; and, finally, the treatment would involve substantial expenditure, which in the light of the small prospects of success, the authority did not consider was an effective use of resources.

Laws J, at first instance, adopted a novel approach to a judicial review application, which in some ways foreshadowed the demands of the Human Rights Act 1998. He noted that the right of life was a right so fundamental that it should now be recognised as part of the common law. The health authority had failed to satisfy him that there was a sufficient justification for refusing child B her chance of life. The Court of Appeal reversed his decision since they did not consider the health authority's decision to be 'unreasonable' for judicial review purposes. It considered that the reasonableness of the health authority's decision was supported by the evidence indicating that it would have been of dubious benefit to the child herself. It was likely to cause her distress and was also 'experimental', with no well-tried track record of success; indeed, it was described as being 'at the frontier of medical science'.[114]

Now that the Human Rights Act 1998 is in place, the judgment of Laws J serves as a warning to health authorities that a child's right to life under article 2 of the ECHR cannot be jeopardised without rigorously careful decision-making, including a clear explanation of 'the priorities that have led them to decline to fund the treatment'.[115] As Morgan observes, the 'right to health care becomes in fact a *right to transparency* about the tragic choices that are being negotiated'.[116] Today a health authority might urge, in the first place, that article 2 does not carry the right to a particular treatment which will, in the view of the experts, be futile and against the patient's best interests.[117] Furthermore, although article 2 imposes a positive obligation on them, as a public authority, to devote resources to saving a patient's life, they are only obliged to do so within the confines of their duty to balance the competing interests of all their patients. The right to life is not an absolute right and the positive obligations that article 2 carries must be interpreted 'in a way which does not impose an impossible or disproportionate burden on the authorities'.[118] In other words, '[t]here must be a limit even in Utopia – some principle of maximum societal benefit must be applied ...'[119] Confronted by claims brought under the Human Rights Act 1998, the courts are unlikely to substitute their decision-making for those of health authorities, by ordering

---

112 [1995] 1 FLR 1055.
113 Later identified as Jamee Bowen. Further treatment was funded privately; it apparently extended her life for a further year and she then died.
114 [1995] 1 FLR 1055 at 1072, per Sir Thomas Bingham MR (CA).
115 [1995] 1 FLR 1055 at 1065, per Laws J.
116 D Morgan (2001) p 58.
117 See *NHS Trust A v M; NHS Trust B v H* [2001] 1 All ER 801 at [37], per Dame Elizabeth Butler-Sloss P.
118 *Osman v United Kingdom* [1999] 1 FLR 193 at [116].
119 J Mason, R McCall Smith and G Laurie (2002) p 368.

the latter to provide expensive procedures, thereby diverting resources from other patients, who are just as needy.[120]

Ex p B illustrates the severe ethical dilemmas raised by parents who attempt to persuade reluctant doctors to utilise a variety of invasive treatments to extend slightly the life of their fatally ill child. It was complicated by the fact that B herself had a very strong determination to undergo the treatment, despite its likely risks and unpleasantness and she expressed her views very clearly. Whilst a dying child's right to a reasonable quality of life whilst alive should not be sacrificed to the parent's own need to avoid the grief of their child's early death, the child's own views must carry considerable weight in such situations.

(D) Should neonates or infants be denied the right to life?

(i) The limits to parents' powers and the relevance of mental handicap

As the discussion above indicates, difficult legal and ethical dilemmas are posed by desperately ill and dying infants, whose lives can only be sustained by medical technology. There is, however, another group of children whose lives also hang in the balance, not because they are ill or dying, but because their parents have rejected them. It is an unpleasant notion that some assume that mentally handicapped newborn babies have an inferior right to life.[121] Society often seems more tolerant of parents who reject children born with disabilities than of those who simply abandon perfectly healthy babies. There is also a risk that although social attitudes to mental handicap have become more liberal, they may still deter the use of medical technology to save the lives of babies who are predicted to develop into mentally handicapped adults. The terms of the current abortion legislation reflects an intolerance with imperfection. It authorises a termination right up to full term, as long as 'there is a substantial risk that if the child were born it would suffer from such physical or mental abnormalities as to be seriously handicapped'.[122] This provision implies that parents have a right to physical and mental 'normality' in their offspring. It may even lead some parents to consider that they also have the power of life or death over their handicapped children, once born.

The response of the doctors caring for two Down's syndrome babies in the early 1980s, indicates that considerable sympathy then existed for parents who rejected perfectly healthy babies on the grounds of their mental handicap alone. A reading of decisions like *Re B (a minor) (wardship: medical treatment)*[123] and of accounts of the

---

120 I Kennedy and A Grubb (2000) pp 11–27.
121 See J Fortin (2000) pp 169–172.
122 Abortion Act 1967, s 1(1)(d).
123 [1990] 3 All ER 927: apart from her Down's condition, child B had no handicaps, bar an intestinal blockage which urgently required uncomplicated surgery. If successful, she would have a life expectancy of 20 to 30 years. The parents refused consent, being of the view that it was kinder to allow her to die. The local authority sought, through wardship, the court's authorisation for surgery to remedy the blockage.

trial in *R v Arthur*[124] shows that such parental rejection was neither uncommon, nor considered surprising. There was the strong view that families were entitled to family privacy, with a right to raise their children as they saw fit, free from state intervention. The lives of mentally handicapped people were viewed as being poor in quality. It was felt that parents' lives were blighted by caring for mentally handicapped children and that society needed citizens who were healthy, both in mind and body. Interlaced with such ideas may have been the notion that babies, particularly mentally handicapped babies, lacked the characteristics and attributes commonly associated with 'personhood', thereby justifying a lower order of protection.[125]

These views were underpinned by the assumption that parents had the right to determine the fate of their handicapped babies. It was urged that the law is incapable of effectively managing the delicate and complex relationship between parent and child and that if parents refused routine, but life-saving treatment for their children, the doctors should comply with their wishes. In *Re B*, the surgeon who was to have performed straightforward but life-saving surgery on baby B, declined to do so when informed of her parents' objections. Even Ewbank J, at first instance, concluded that their wishes had to be respected and refused to authorise the procedure. The Court of Appeal's decision overruling the parents' views was itself criticised by members of the general public, who considered it unfair to foist on parents the care of mentally handicapped children against their wishes.[126]

These two cases established that parents do not have the power to dictate whether their children should live or die. The law prohibits healthy, though mentally handicapped, babies being allowed to die by doctors, through normal sustenance being withheld. Furthermore, parents' decisions to reject straightforward life-saving surgery may be overridden. Public opinion has obviously changed since the early 1980s. Although many parents still consider they have considerable power over their children's lives, attitudes towards mental handicap appear to have modified. Down's syndrome is no longer considered to be an unacceptable handicap for parents to cope with and the concept of children having rights to protection *from* their parents has now gathered pace. Indeed, it seems unlikely that today British parents would consider asking doctors to allow their mentally handicapped babies to die through 'nursing care only'[127] or, indeed, would refuse treatment in circumstances like those arising in *Re B (a minor) (wardship: medical treatment)*.[128] As a result, doctors and not parents are now the arbiters of questions regarding the provision or withdrawal of treatment. They will be well aware that a mentally handicapped child's right to life under article 2 of the ECHR must be protected just as effectively as that of a mentally fit child.

124 *R v Arthur* (1981) 12 BMLR 1. In response to the parents' rejection of their Down's syndrome baby, Dr Arthur, a well-known and respected paediatrician, established a regime described as 'nursing care only'. This involved the baby being given a large dose of a sedating drug to suppress his appetite and thereafter being kept comfortable, to see whether he would rally and live or whether 'nature would take its course'. The baby died soon after birth. The *Arthur* case was discussed at length by M Gunn and J Smith (1985).

125 C Wells (1989) pp 202–203. See also the discussion above of the concept of 'personhood'.

126 See letters to *The Times*, between 10 August and 17 August 1981, following the decision in *Re B (a minor) (wardship: medical treatment)* [1990] 3 All ER 927.

127 Eg *R v Arthur* (1981) 12 BMLR 1.

128 [1990] 3 All ER 927.

(ii) A child's right to life and parents' objections to life-saving treatment

Their horror of mental handicap led the parents of the Down's syndrome baby B[129] to refuse life-saving treatment on her behalf. No doubt they were sincere in thinking it better that she should die rather than go through life mentally disabled. In other cases, the parents may have equally strong convictions which leads them to refuse life-saving treatment for their children, even if their survival would not be attended by mental or physical handicap. The courts most commonly encounter cases of this kind where the parents' opposition to treatment stems from their religious convictions. Doctors may seek the assistance of the civil law in life and death situations where parents are desperately anxious to secure treatment for their sick child, but only in a way consistent with their religious beliefs. Conflicts may, for example, arise between doctors and Jehovah's Witness parents who oppose their child receiving blood transfusions, even though failure to transfuse the child may lead to his or her death. They conscientiously consider that it is in their child's best interests to die rather than receive blood. Doctors may find it difficult to sympathise with parents whose views, however sincerely held, endanger the lives of babies and infants, which could be saved by modern medical treatment. After all, these children are too young to have formed their own convictions. Although when they are older they might agree with their parents,[130] the outcome of their parents' decisions would prevent them living long enough to develop their own ideas. Justice Holmes in *Prince v Massachusetts*[131] put it well when he said:

> 'Parents may be free to become martyrs themselves. But it does not follow they are free, in identical circumstances, to make martyrs of their children before they have reached the age of full and legal discretion when they can make that choice for themselves.'[132]

Legally, of course, there is no need for medical staff to obtain judicial consent before giving emergency life-saving treatment to children against the wishes of their parents. Life-saving treatment can be justified under the common law principle of necessity, backed up by the need to promote a child's right to life under article 2 of the ECHR. Nevertheless, since the 'defence of necessity' is uncertain in scope[133] and medical authorities are traditionally cautious, they will probably seek judicial authority to provide emergency treatment overriding parental wishes.[134]

Case law indicates a general willingness on the part of the judiciary to accept medical evidence indicating that the treatment proposed is the only means of ensuring the survival of the sick child. They commonly authorise treatment on the basis that

---

129 [1990] 3 All ER 927.
130 Although *Gillick* competent children can consent on their own behalf, those born to Jehovah's Witness parents will commonly refuse blood transfusion treatment themselves, in which case their views may be overridden by the courts. See eg *Re E (a minor) (wardship: medical treatment)* [1993] 1 FLR 386 and *Re S (a minor) (medical treatment)* [1994] 2 FLR 1065 and discussion in chapter 5.
131 321 US 158 (1944).
132 321 US 158 at 165 (1944).
133 See Lord Goff in *Re F (mental patient: sterilisation)* [1990] 2 AC 1 at 74.
134 The hospital trust may seek leave from the court under the Children Act 1989, s 10 to apply for a specific issue order under the Children Act 1989, s 8. See *Re R (a minor) (medical treatment)* [1993] 2 FLR 757. Alternatively, and more commonly, they may seek a declaration under the inherent declaration, as in *Re O (a minor) (medical treatment)* [1993] 2 FLR 149.

children's lives are too precious to be sacrificed to their parents' religious faith.[135] The judiciary emphasise, however, that parents' profound and sincerely held wishes should be considered with great respect and that it is no easy matter to overrule them. Thus Thorpe J in *Re S (a minor) (medical treatment)*[136] made plain his view that the stark choice of transfusing the child or allowing him to die left the court with little choice but to authorise treatment, bearing in mind that it was governed by the welfare test. He posed the following hypothetical questions:

> '... are the religious convictions of the parents to deny their child a 50% chance of survival? Are those convictions to deny him that 50% chance and condemn him to inevitable and early death?'[137]

Such an approach is fully consistent with the state's positive obligation under article 2 of the ECHR, to preserve the life of a desperately ill child, as long as survival is not accompanied by considerable pain and impairment of his or her quality of life.[138] Such arguments would counter a parent's claim that, by overriding his wishes, the court is infringing his right to respect for his family life under article 8, freedom of religion under article 9 and freedom from discrimination, under article 14.[139]

A court confronted by a similar situation to that in *Re T (a minor) (wardship: medical treatment)*[140] might now find it far more difficult to refuse to authorise treatment in the light of its duties under the Human Rights Act 1998. Regrettably, the decision indicated that the courts could not always be relied upon to protect children against their parents' views. The Court of Appeal upheld a mother's[141] refusal to allow her 18-month-old son, C, to undergo a life-saving liver transplant. This was despite the unanimous opinion of three medical consultants specialising in this field of medicine that the prospects of success were good[142] and that it was in C's best medical interests for a transplant to be carried out. C's mother opposed his being subjected to the inevitable post-operative pain and suffering and to the complications which might set in later. Influenced by the failure of earlier surgery, she preferred to ensure that his surviving months should be happy and free of pain. One of the three consultants supported her; he opposed any parent being coerced into allowing her child to undergo such invasive treatment, because of the vital part she would have to play in providing post-operative care.

The decision was a deeply worrying one. First, the Court of Appeal maintained that although there was a strong presumption in favour of prolonging a child's life,

---

135 See *Re O (a minor) (medical treatment)* [1993] 2 FLR 149 (3-month-old very low weight premature baby) and *Re R (a minor) (medical treatment)* [1993] 2 FLR 757 (10-month-old baby suffering from leukaemia). In both cases the courts authorised the use of blood transfusions.

136 [1993] 1 FLR 376: S was a child aged 4½ suffering from leukaemia.

137 [1993] 1 FLR 376 at 380.

138 The question whether treatment should be used to extend a child's life, despite massive impairment of quality of life, is discussed above.

139 Such an approach could also be justified under arts 8(2) and 9(2) on the basis that such action is necessary to protect the child's health and is proportionate to the infringement.

140 [1997] 1 All ER 906. Discussed by S Michalowski (1997); M Fox and J McHale (1997); A Bainham (1997).

141 Although the father supported the mother in her opposition to the procedure, she alone had parental responsibility because they were unmarried. The couple were living abroad with the boy.

142 All three consultants were agreed that if the child underwent the transplant, there was a high prospect of success and that his future life would be healthy and treatment free, except for the need to receive immuno-suppressive drugs on a long-term basis.

this was not the court's sole objective. Although Butler-Sloss LJ maintained that case law supported such a proposition,[143] this principle was established in the altogether different context of withholding life-sustaining treatment for babies born with massive handicaps, through low weight and premature birth.[144] It had little direct relevance to C's situation, since it was predicted that his future health would be good.[145] Second, the best interests test was interpreted in the light of the mother's views. But to suggest that the child's future care should be 'left in the hands of his devoted parents',[146] that the welfare of a baby 'depends on his mother',[147] and that mother and child 'are one',[148] carries the underlying message that a mother may always have the upper hand in unusual cases like this, where the proposed surgery is invasive, the child very young and there is a need for intensive post-operative after-care.

The decision in *Re T* undermined the clear principle established by the case law discussed above indicating that parents have no absolute right to parental autonomy, nor the final say over whether their children should live or die. Incomprehensibly, the parents' views in *Re T* were treated more sympathetically than those of strongly religious parents, such as Jehovah's Witness parents who refuse to consent to life-saving treatment. Even if, as in *Re T*, the parents' opposition to life-saving surgery stems from medical experience gained through their work, the court should not assume that this automatically invests their ideas with greater weight. It seems unlikely that parents can ever be as objective over their children as medical professionals unconnected personally with the case. Admittedly the case law concerning Jehovah's Witness parents has not involved opposition to major invasive surgery, accompanied by the pain of recovery and the possibility of long-term post-operative complications.[149] Blood transfusions are relatively simple procedures. But in both situations the choice remains equally stark – treatment or death. The orthodox Jewish parents in *Re C (medical treatment)*[150] must have found it puzzling that the courts were apparently more prepared to override the views of strongly religious parents like themselves, who wanted to keep their child alive, than those of non-denominational parents who had rejected life-sustaining treatment.

Although Waite LJ in *Re T* considered it inappropriate 'even in an age preoccupied with "rights" – to talk of the rights of a child, or of a parent, or the rights of the court',[151] today a court would be obliged to do so. It would consider the child's right to life, under article 2 of the ECHR. It would weigh up whether the parents' right to respect to family life, under article 8, as supported by the European Court of Human Rights in *Nielsen v Denmark*,[152] could include the right to reject life-saving treatment for their child, taking account of its risks and potential side effects. Above all, the court would be obliged to acknowledge, more honestly than the Court of Appeal ever did in *Re T*, the outcome of a decision to abide by the parents' wishes. This was that death would be better than the post-operative pain and suffering and potential

143 [1997] 1 All ER 906 at 916.
144 Eg *Re J (a minor) (wardship: medical treatment)* [1991] Fam 33, discussed above.
145 But see Southall's anxiety about the long-term risks of immuno-suppressive medication: D Southall (1997).
146 [1997] 1 All ER 906 at 916, per Butler-Sloss LJ.
147 [1997] 1 All ER 906 at 915.
148 [1997] 1 All ER 906 at 914.
149 D Southall (1997).
150 [1998] 1 FLR 384. See discussion above.
151 [1997] 1 All ER 906 at 916.
152 (1988) 11 EHRR 175.

complications attending the procedure, bearing in mind the mother's own reluctance to cope with the child's post-operative care. If the treatment available holds a good prognosis for a child's future health, then the presumption should be in favour of the courts ensuring the child's survival and not the parents' peace of mind.

(4)   CARING FOR A CHILD'S HEALTH

(A)   Decisions about general healthcare

Although there is no compulsion on parents to use the health services available, most are aware of the dangers of leaving sick children without medical attention. As the case law discussed above demonstrates, once they are consulted, doctors may seek judicial authority to override parental wishes and provide children with life-saving treatment. Fortunately, circumstances like these are rare. Even in non-life threatening situations, however, doctors wield considerable power and it is often they who determine the manner in which the child's right to 'the highest attainable standard of health'[153] will be fulfilled. They may be the effective decision-makers, despite the theoretical right enjoyed by parents, as their children's proxies, to determine their children's health care. Thus in *C (HIV test)*[154] it was the mother's general practitioner who, on discovering that a mother was infected with HIV, set in motion steps aimed at ensuring that the baby should be tested for HIV, against the mother's own strong opposition. The courts, both at divisional and appellate level, stressed their concern to protect the baby's rights, as opposed to those of her parents.[155]

Doctors are less likely to interfere with parents' decisions when it comes to arranging for children to undergo relatively uncomplicated, non-therapeutic, procedures such as ear-piercing and minor cosmetic surgery. Although the proprietorial attitude of Victorian parents towards their children is objectionable to modern eyes, many of today's parents unconcernedly exhibit a similar approach. They quite commonly arrange for their young children to undergo procedures which infringe their children's right to bodily integrity under article 8 of the ECHR, without always considering whether this can be justified. Brazier questions whether parents are entitled to arrange for their children to undergo cosmetic surgery. Whilst she considers it would be wrong for a mother, for example, to put her son through painful surgery to advance his career as a male model, since it would not be in his best interests, she is more ambivalent over the quite common surgery on boys to redress their 'bat ears'.[156] She suggests that it is for the parents to balance the pain of the surgery against the child's misery over being taunted for his deformity. Clearly his own strong views regarding the social benefit he will gain from the procedure should be balanced against the dangers involved in surgery under a general anaesthetic.

(B)   Organ and tissue donation

The prospect of having to watch a child die is one that no parent would wish to contemplate. In some cases, a seriously ill child's life might be saved by the donation of an organ, tissue or bone marrow provided by a healthy living donor. The advantages

---

153   See art 24 of the CRC.
154   [1999] 2 FLR 1004.
155   [1999] 2 FLR 1004 at 1016 and 1021.
156   See M Brazier (1992) p 350.

of genetic compatibility may lead parents to consider arranging for one of their healthy children to act as donor for the dying child.[157] Most practitioners have very grave reservations about the use of children and young people being used as donors of non-regenerative organs, such as a kidney.[158] Indeed, Mason and McCall Smith note that practitioners have introduced their own informal regulation and have simply stopped accepting children as donors.[159]

There is no case law in this country testing the legality of using children as donors of bone-marrow or other regenerative tissue for seriously ill siblings. Despite this, such practices occur.[160] Parents and medical advisers obviously assume that, by virtue of their parental autonomy, parents are entitled to use their healthy child's body to save the life of the other.[161] Legally, parents can only consent to their healthy child being used as a donor if they can both fulfil the requirements of the common law and justify infringing the donor's right to bodily integrity under article 8 of the ECHR. They might argue that such an infringement is justified under article 8(2), because such a procedure is necessary, being both in the recipient's best interests and those of the donor. In particular, the psychological benefits to the donor of saving his or her sibling's life will out-balance the dangers involved.[162] Indeed, they might adopt Eekelaar's approach and claim that the potential donor, when mature, would have chosen retrospectively to save a dying sibling.[163] Furthermore, they might suggest that if they refused to allow their healthy child to be used as a donor, he or she might react very badly to being told, when older, that the sibling had died because of the absence of a suitable donor.

These arguments are all persuasive, but do they give sufficient weight to the rights of the healthy potential donor? To suggest that there are no medical or ethical problems involved because the tissue is regenerative is to over-simplify the issues. The procedure often involves some risk to the donor child. For example, he or she will undergo a general anaesthetic, which in itself carries risk, will be sore and bruised at the site where the tissue was removed[164] and will need hospitalising for up to two days,[165] where there are risks of contracting an infection. A donor child may gain little real psychological benefit from helping a dying sibling where he or she is too young to have established any emotional bond with the proposed recipient.[166] The research evidence is, in any case, ambivalent over the extent to which siblings truly benefit

157   See J Mason, R McCall Smith and G Laurie (2002) pp 429–432.
158   BMA (2001) pp 161 and 165.
159   See J Mason, R McCall Smith and G Laurie (2002) p 432, whose inquiries indicate that only one transplant involving an identical twin aged 17 has occurred in the last 15 years. There is, in any event, doubt whether minors are ever legally competent to consent to such a procedure. See discussion in chapter 5, p 127.
160   Eg the younger sister of the child involved in *R v Cambridge District Health Authority, ex p B* [1995] 1 FLR 1055 provided bone marrow to help save her sister's life.
161   The provisions of the Human Organs Transplant Act 1989 do not protect children from donating organs to siblings since it only seeks to prohibit donations between non-relatives: see s 2(2).
162   Discussed below.
163   J Eekelaar (1986) p 170. But note that the 'substituted judgment test' has been rejected as a means of providing an incompetent patient's consent. See *Airedale NHS Trust v Bland* [1993] 1 All ER 821 at 872, per Lord Goff and at 892, per Lord Mustill.
164   S Mumford (1998) p 135.
165   L Delaney (1995).
166   L Delaney (1995) p 373.

from acting as donors, particularly if the procedure does not save the ill child.[167]
Furthermore, whilst parents may tell the medical team that the sibling donor is anxious
to undergo the process, family pressure may have rendered their consent quite unreal.[168]

There is a dearth of domestic authority on the legality of incompetent donors
providing organs or tissue. The first reported English case, *Re Y (mental incapacity:
bone marrow transplant)*,[169] involved an adult donor. The High Court had little
difficulty in deciding that it would benefit Y, a severely mentally and physically
handicapped woman, to provide bone marrow for her sister who was suffering from a
potentially fatal degenerative bone marrow disorder. Connell J stressed that the
criterion governing the lawfulness of the procedure was the best interests test. He
accepted that the risks involved in Y providing regenerative tissue were very slight
and were more than counter-balanced by the benefits to her of being able to retain
close contact with her mother, given that this was a very closely-knit family. There
was a somewhat tenuous logical connection between Y's donation to her sister, and
retaining contact with their mother. The court, however, accepted the argument that,
if the sister died, the mother's state of health would deteriorate, making it unlikely
that she would be able to continue visiting Y in her residential home. To prevent Y
suffering the loss of her mother's visits, she should provide her sister with bone
marrow.

As Feenan points out, the decision in *Re Y* is problematic.[170] In particular, there was
no detailed analysis of the dangers involved in the harvesting procedure,[171] nor any
evidence regarding the real value to Y of continuing to have contact with her mother,
whom, it appeared, she did not know was her mother. The looseness of this judicial
reasoning would be alarming if the decision was used as guidance for use in children's
cases, particularly if the decision 'could be seen as giving a "green light" to support
donations by incompetent adults and children in future'.[172] In the absence of English
precedent, Connell J turned to American case law for assistance. This has demonstrated
varying judicial approaches regarding adult and child donors,[173] but the decision of
the Illinois Supreme Court in *Curran v Bosze*[174] is particularly useful. Although he
referred to it in his judgment in *Re Y*, the interpretation of the best interests test by
Connell J was far looser than that adopted by the Illinois court.

In *Curran v Bosze*, the potential donors were 3-year-old twins whose unmarried
father wanted them to donate bone marrow for transplant to their seriously ill half-
brother.[175] Relying on the best interests test to protect the rights of the potential
donors, the court insisted on three critical factors being fulfilled before it could
conclude that the best interests test was satisfied. First, the parent consenting on

---

167   See BMA (2001) p 159, for a short summary on the research evidence on this aspect of bone
      marrow donations.
168   BMA (2001) p 162. This guidance suggests that health professionals should talk privately to
      the prospective donor to ascertain his or her real views.
169   [1996] 2 FLR 787.
170   See D Feenan (1997) pp 309–310.
171   Connell J merely stated that the risks of a general anaesthetic were extremely low, being 1 per
      10,000: [1996] 2 FLR 787 at 793.
172   I Kennedy and A Grubb (2000) p 789.
173   See, inter alia: *Strunk v Strunk* 445 SW 2d 145 (Ky 1969); *Hart v Brown* 289 A 2d 386
      (1972) and *Little v Little* 576 SW 2d 493 (1979) (kidney transplants authorised); cf *Lausier
      v Pescinski* 226 NW 2d 180 (1975) and *In Re Richardson* 284 So 2d 185 (1973) (kidney
      transplants refused); *Curran v Bosze* 566 NE 2d 1319 (1990) (bone marrow transplant
      refused).
174   566 NE 2d 1319 (1990).
175   Ie the father's son by another woman.

behalf of the child donor must be fully informed of the risks and benefits of the procedure; second, emotional support should be available to the donor from a trusted carer; third, there must be an existing and close relationship between the donor and the recipient so that the donor may realistically gain a psychological benefit from the donation. These criteria were not met since the twins had only ever met their half-brother twice and their own mother was actively opposed to the donation. The court refused to direct the donation, given the risks involved.

There is a growing view that regulations should be introduced in this country curbing the freedom presently enjoyed by parents and their doctors to arrange for healthy children to be used as bone marrow donors.[176] Although one form of supervision would be to involve the courts in every case, this might lead to dangerous delays. Furthermore, the decision in *Re Y*[177] regarding the provision of bone marrow by a mentally handicapped adult suggests that a procedural change involving court intervention might not provide sufficient extra protection, unless the courts adopted a far more rigorous approach to child donors. As Mumford explains, various systems of non-judicial regulation have been introduced elsewhere.[178] For example, in France, a committee of experts, two of whom must be doctors,[179] must authorise all donations of any kind.[180] Arguably, the criteria set out in *Curran v Bosze* provide better protection for child donors than those contained in article 20 of the European Convention on Human Rights and Biomedicine, which makes no mention of the donor's need to gain psychological benefit from the procedure.[181] Indeed, a combination of the two sets of criteria might be appropriate, since any body required to regulate all provision of bone marrow by incompetent donors should adopt a rigorous approach. State interference in these tragic cases, which involve highly personal values, might provoke public resentment. Nevertheless, regulation would not prevent donations taking place, it would merely safeguard the rights of healthy children.

(C)   Parents' culture and children's bodies

Some parents obviously feel free to arrange for their children to undergo what Feldman describes as various forms of 'mutilation' carried out for religious or social reasons, such as ear piercing, circumcision and clitorectomy (or female circumcision), all of which, in his view, infringe their children's right to bodily integrity.[182] Feldman refutes the argument that religious tolerance should allow any of these practices to continue, asserting that the parents' religious beliefs cannot justify a breach of their children's rights. In his view: 'This is a classic example of a case where the parent's freedom

---

176   See D Feenan (1997) p 311; S Mumford (1998) pp 145–146; BMA (2001) p 164.
177   [1996] 2 FLR 787.
178   S Mumford (1998) pp 138–139.
179   One of whom must be of 20 year's standing.
180   S Mumford (1998) pp 138–139 and 146.
181   This Convention was introduced for signature in 1997, but is not yet signed or ratified by the United Kingdom. Article 20 indicates that the removal of regenerative tissue from an incompetent person should only be carried out 'exceptionally' and then only if: (i) no compatible donor is available with capacity to consent; (ii) the recipient is a sibling of the donor; (iii) the donation must potentially be life-saving; (iv) authorisation is given in writing legally prescribed and with the approval of the competent body; (v) the potential donor does not object.
182   D Feldman (2002) pp 270–272.

ends where the child's nose (or other anatomical protuberance) begins.'[183] He urges that circumcision and other irreversible forms of 'mutilation' conducted without the victim's real consent and for non-therapeutic purposes infringe children's rights under article 3 of the ECHR.[184]

There is widespread agreement with Feldman's opposition to female circumcision, a practice widely condemned in the Western world and one now carrying criminal sanctions in this country.[185] It involves girls in extreme pain and often carries long-term and serious side effects, which may even affect their future child-bearing capacity. Considered from a Western view point, there seems little doubt that girls have a right to protection from such an apparently barbaric practice. Nevertheless, the beliefs and traditions of minority groups deserve consideration. Female circumcision is not only a cultural tradition going back centuries and pre-dating Islam, but one which is still widely performed on women and children in various communities throughout Africa and the Middle East. Even in this country, some religious groups still consider it an essential sign of a girl's virginity and without it she has no chance of marriage, her only route to security and prosperity. Parents are unwilling to reject the customs of their own community if they consider that their daughters will suffer socially as a result.[186]

The tension between the rights of parents to bring their children up according to their own beliefs and the rights of children to protection is reflected in the CRC. The topic of female circumcision proved a controversial one at the drafting stage of the Convention, with delegates from the United Kingdom and the USA wanting an outright condemnation of the practice and delegates from countries such as Senegal, wanting a more general formula.[187] A compromise emerged. Although article 24(3) provides that states 'shall take all effective and appropriate measures with a view to abolishing traditional practices prejudicial to the health of children', there is no specific reference to the prohibition of female circumcision.

The Prohibition of Female Circumcision Act 1985 clearly attempts to stamp out the practice altogether in this country, but the legislation appears to be rarely used. Some consider that criminal sanctions may in any case be inappropriate.[188] The harm and suffering caused by back-street abortions during the period when abortion was illegal suggest that these writers may be correct to urge caution. This view is reinforced by indications that the legislation may have simply driven the practice underground, with some girls being sent to Africa for holidays, where the procedure is carried out.[189] Clearly, any attempt to persuade parents to abandon the practice must take account of community values and the social identity of ethnic minorities.[190] Many consider that the only way to eradicate the practice is to educate communities from within and to persuade them of its dangers.[191] Nevertheless, this does not preclude using criminal sanctions; indeed, children's rights to protection from such extreme practices need

---

183 D Feldman (2002) p 271.
184 D Feldman (2002) p 272.
185 Prohibition of Female Circumcision Act 1985, s 1(1) renders it an offence to carry out such a procedure unless [s 2(1)] it is necessary for the physical or mental health of the person on whom it is performed and is performed by a registered medical practitioner.
186 See News (2000) 321 BMJ 262 and P Abboud et al (2000).
187 L LeBlanc (1995) pp 85–89.
188 J Roche (1995). See also J Black and G Debelle (1995).
189 See P Abboud et al (2000).
190 See letter from C Scherf (2000) 320 BMJ 570, responding to P Abboud et al (2000).
191 Letter from C Scherf (2000) 320 BMJ 570.

the clear message of effective criminal prohibition. Freedman is right to argue that female circumcision infringes children's rights to freedom from inhuman treatment.[192] Prosecutions should be brought in this country to fulfil the state's positive obligation to protect their rights, both under article 3 of the ECHR, and under article 8.

Some writers urge that it is impossible to persuade mothers not to mutilate their daughters through female circumcision, whilst male circumcision is so widely tolerated, socially and legally.[193] Male circumcision appears to have escaped either the widespread condemnation attending the circumcision of females or any effort to regulate it more closely. To many, the differences between the procedures are obvious. Male circumcision is far less invasive and attended by less risk and pain. Whilst female circumcision offers no therapeutic benefit whatsoever, male circumcision does have some medical benefits for rare conditions,[194] quite apart from its being more widely practised, for religious and social reasons.[195] Medical opinion nevertheless seems divided over whether the practice is beneficial and, like any surgical procedure, it is certainly not risk free, even when carried out under medical conditions.[196] There are at least some adults who consider that they should never have been circumcised as children.[197] Lack of regulation is obviously attributable to the influence enjoyed by the followers of the Jewish and Muslim faiths in this country, who attach considerable importance to their religious freedom to have their male children circumcised.

Strangely, the legality of male circumcision had never been considered directly until Wall J was confronted by a dispute between a Muslim father and Christian mother over whether their 5-year-old son should be circumcised. In *Re J (specific issue orders: Muslim upbringing and circumcision)*[198] Wall J acknowledged that much of the medical literature to which he had been referred adopted the view that such a procedure without medical necessity was an assault on the child's bodily integrity.[199] His conclusion was that the procedure is lawful because 'there have, historically, been a number of medical justifications put forward for male circumcision' and because 'it is insisted on by Muslim and Jews', and further that it has 'over the years, become an accepted practice amongst a significant number of parents in England'.[200] One wonders whether such reasoning really suffices as a good legal justification. Popularity of a parental practice should not prevent the judiciary declaring it to be unlawful, if they consider it to be against children's best interests.

Although the court in *Re J* considered and rejected the father's claimed right under article 9 of the ECHR, to arrange for his son's circumcision according to the tenets of his religion, there was surprisingly little attention given to the child's own rights. The decision established that parents must now seek judicial consent before they

192   D Feldman (2002) p 272.
193   P Abboud et al (2000).
194   A Rickwood et al (2000).
195   See M Freeman (2002) p112.
196   See J Eason, M McDonnell and G Clark (1994); N Williams and L Kapila (1993); BMA (1996) p 2.
197   See letter (1996) 312 BMJ 377 (10 February) from a group of men arguing that they had been harmed by circumcision procedures carried out in their childhood.
198   [1999] 2 FLR 678. This decision was reaffirmed on appeal in a short judgment by the Court of Appeal: see *Re J (specific issue orders: children's religious upbringing and circumcision)* [2000] 1 FLR 571.
199   [1999] 2 FLR 678 at 690.
200   [1999] 2 FLR 678 at 690.

have their child circumcised, but this only applies to children whose parents disagree over the issue. This leaves the children of united parents unprotected. It might be difficult to argue that circumcision infringes a child's rights under article 3, if carried out under medical conditions, given the very high threshold of severity required before treatment constitutes a breach.[201] Nevertheless, it is clear that the procedure infringes the child's right to bodily integrity under article 8, whilst not necessarily promoting his health or morals under article 8(2). To claim that it promotes the child's own religious rights under article 9, combined with his rights to freedom from religious discrimination under article 14, might be more justifiable.[202] Indeed, Wall J accepted that a child might be at a severe social disadvantage being brought up as a member of a Muslim or Jewish community without having been circumcised.[203]

It seems unlikely that any government would contemplate attempting to prohibit male circumcision altogether, since the result would be widespread evasion of the criminal law. A compromise would be to introduce greater protection for children by passing strict regulations requiring the procedure to be performed only by the medically qualified.[204] In more general terms, there is a need to encourage parents to think more about their children's right to bodily integrity, rather than treating them like mere family appendages. They should avoid making any arrangements for their young children to undergo procedures, however apparently trivial, which may damage their health. Instead, they should respect their children's individuality and leave them to decide for themselves when older how to treat their own bodies.

(D)   Sterilising mentally handicapped adolescents

(i)   The dilemmas

The sterilisation of mentally handicapped girls[205] was an issue which became controversial during the late 1980s, particularly following the House of Lords' decision in *Re B (a minor) (wardship: sterilisation)*.[206] Today, few cases involving women or adolescents appear in the law reports. This may be because more effective methods of menstrual management and contraception are being used to deal with the problems which a decade ago would have led to radical surgery. The need for state agencies to comply with the demands of the ECHR may also be forcing parents and medical practitioners to consider more carefully the human rights of mentally handicapped people. An alternative explanation may be that most of the sterilisations now being performed are allegedly for 'therapeutic' purposes, thereby escaping judicial supervision.[207]

The arguments in favour of allowing sterilisation procedures should not be dismissed without proper consideration. Parents and other carers cannot supervise

---

201 *Costello-Roberts v United Kingdom* [1994] 1 FCR 65 at 74.
202 See I Katz (1999), who argues (p 91) that 'it may be wrong, and indeed abusive for a Jewish child not to be circumcised'.
203 In *Re J* itself, this was not the case, since the father was a non-practising Muslim.
204 Such a requirement might, however, infringe the religious requirements attending the circumcision process.
205 In *Re A (male sterilisation)* [2000] 1 FLR 549 a parent sought to have her adult mentally handicapped son sterilised. Nevertheless, although this application may be more common than the dearth of case law suggests, this discussion assumes that the subject for sterilisation is female.
206 [1988] AC 199.
207 See discussion below.

mentally handicapped teenagers every minute of the day and, in any case, to do so would inhibit their privacy intolerably. These adolescents are as entitled as other maturing children to lead as full and as unrestricted a life as possible and to enjoy relationships with members of the opposite sex. At some stage in the future they may wish to derive pleasure from sexual activity. Sterilised girls, by reason of their inability to become pregnant, can be allowed more freedom in mixed units and consequently their lives may become more fulfilled. Gaining a relative degree of social freedom and well-being may involve a compromise with their other rights, such as the right to bodily integrity, but maturity always involves balancing conflicting objectives.

The arguments against such procedures being arranged for purely contraceptive purposes are, however, more compelling. The plausible but distasteful eugenic reasons used to justify compulsory sterilisation programmes in various countries in the world at different times in history,[208] perhaps cloud an objective approach to this topic. Nevertheless, it must be a remedy of last resort to submit a girl to a major invasion of her bodily integrity, which may be irreversible, and which may have a significant psychological impact on an already fragile personality. An inability to become pregnant will safeguard the girl neither from sexual exploitation nor sexually transmitted diseases, from which she has a right to be protected. The need to protect her from pregnancy might be avoided with more sensitive care, combined with a reliable form of contraception.

(ii) Parents and sterilisations

The initiative for arranging the sterilisation of mentally handicapped girls has almost always come from their parents.[209] Parents are particularly concerned by the risk of unwanted pregnancies, considering, probably justifiably, that a mentally handicapped adolescent would be incapable of coping with pregnancy, birth or motherhood. Even daughters in residential care units return home from time to time and their care may be difficult once they start menstruating and becoming sexually aware. Parents may not, however, always fully appreciate their daughters' rights to bodily integrity and human dignity. Furthermore, parents' emotional involvement sometimes prevents them acknowledging their daughters' capacity for intellectual growth. As in *Re D (a minor) (wardship: sterilisation)*,[210] they may even disbelieve strong evidence indicating a girl's growing capacity to consent for herself to such a procedure when older.[211]

Re D[212] brought to the public's attention the fact that even very young children were being sterilised for non-therapeutic purposes. It also demonstrated the essentially arbitrary way in which only some cases were coming to the notice of the courts. Had

---

208 It is estimated that more than 70,000 mentally 'defective' people were compulsorily sterilised in the USA, from the time its legality was upheld by the Supreme Court in *Buck v Bell* 274 US 200, 47 S Ct 584 (1927), until the late 1970s, when the practice ended.

209 Eg *Re D (a minor) (wardship: sterilisation)* [1976] 1 All ER 326; *Re P (a minor) (wardship: sterilisation)* [1989] 1 FLR 182; *Re M (a minor) (wardship: sterilisation)* [1988] 2 FLR 497; *Re E (a minor) (medical treatment)* [1991] 2 FLR 585; *Re HG (specific issue order: sterilisation)* [1993] 1 FLR 587.

210 [1976] 1 All ER 326.

211 In *Re D* [1976] 1 All ER 326, Heilbron J accepted evidence, which the mother rejected, indicating that D might be able to consent on her own behalf to the procedure when she attained the age of 18.

212 [1976] 1 All ER 326.

it not been for an educational psychologist using the wardship jurisdiction to prevent this 12-year-old girl being sterilised, the procedure would have proceeded without interference. Other young girls were presumably undergoing similar surgery without intervention, on the assumption that parents had the right to consent on their behalf. Matters only changed when, in the late 1980s, obtaining prior judicial sanction through a declaration of lawfulness became an established procedural requirement for the sterilisation of all patients, adults and children alike.[213]

Through this essentially informal process it became accepted that, in practice, parents could no longer consent to their children being sterilised, if the procedure was to be performed for contraceptive purposes only. Nevertheless, the law remains confused because court authority is only required for sterilisations with a non-therapeutic purpose. Parents may still arrange for and consent to a sterilisation whose purpose is essentially *therapeutic*. Court sanction is unnecessary for therapeutic sterilisations,[214] but only if they are medically indicated, being the only practicable means of treating the condition.[215] Parents and their medical advisers must therefore distinguish between therapeutic and non-therapeutic sterilisations since, for this narrow procedural purpose, the distinction remains an important one.[216]

Lack of court supervision of therapeutic sterilisations might matter less if there was more unanimity over how to draw the line between therapeutic and non-therapeutic procedures.[217] A sterilisation operation which constitutes medically indicated treatment for a diseased organ is undoubtedly therapeutic and so requires no court authorisation. Consequently, few would argue that such a procedure infringes the patient's human rights in any way. Similarly, sterilisations for contraceptive purposes are clearly non-therapeutic and do require judicial sanction. Nevertheless, some operations do not fall clearly into either category and lawyers are forced to rely on the advice of the medical profession to inform them of the correct classification. Indeed, the Law Commission considered that the lack of clarity over the distinction between therapeutic and non-therapeutic sterilisations was being exploited. It observed that the need for 'menstrual management' could be too easily invoked with a view to avoiding the judicial supervision necessary for sterilisation operations carried out for contraceptive purposes.[218]

The Court of Appeal has acknowledged the fact that borderline cases involving sterilisations for 'therapeutic purposes' may be avoiding judicial scrutiny, and has

213 See *Practice Note, Official Solicitor: Sterilisation* [1989] 2 FLR 447. This followed closely the House of Lords' decision in *Re F (mental patient: sterilisation)* [1990] 2 AC 1, holding that court approval was necessary for sterilisations. See *Practice Note (Official Solicitor: declaratory proceedings: medical and welfare decisions for adults who lack capacity) and Appendix 1: Sterilisation Cases* [2001] 2 FLR 158, for the most recent guidance.

214 Eg *Re E (a minor) (medical treatment)* [1991] 2 FLR 585: the performance of a therapeutic hysterectomy on a 17-year-old mentally handicapped girl who suffered from serious menorrhagia required no judicial authority.

215 See *Re GF (medical treatment)* [1992] 1 FLR 293 regarding the therapeutic sterilisation of an *adult* patient. Per Sir Stephen Brown P (at 294) no application for leave to carry out a sterilisation is necessary if two medical practitioners are satisfied that: it is necessary for therapeutic purposes; it is in the patient's best interests; there is no practicable, less intrusive means of treatment.

216 Cf *Re B (a minor) (wardship: sterilisation)* [1988] AC 199 in which the House of Lords rejected the need to distinguish between therapeutic and non-therapeutic sterilisations; see discussion below.

217 See A Grubb and D Pearl (1987), who discuss the distinction at length in this context.

218 Law Commission (1995) para 6.4.

urged that any case 'lying near the boundary' should be referred to court.[219] Such judicial guidance should be followed. Although judicial supervision has not produced particularly effective regulation of non-therapeutic sterilisations,[220] it is undoubtedly better than none at all. Arguably, the rights of the mentally handicapped would be improved by the introduction of a formal requirement requiring judicial authority for *all* sterilisations on minors, not merely those defined as 'non-therapeutic'.

(iii) Sterilisations, best interests and the courts

As discussed above, authorisation for non-therapeutic sterilisations became the preserve of the courts, rather than being left to parents and doctors. But the best interests test, as judicially interpreted, produced relatively weak protection for the teenagers involved. As the decision of the House of Lords in *Re B (a minor) (wardship: sterilisation)*[221] demonstrates, the judiciary have often adopted a particularly adult-centred approach to the rights of mentally handicapped girls. In that case, the medical evidence favouring sterilisation appeared weighty,[222] but their Lordships paid cursory attention to the rights of Jeanette, the subject of the application, relying solely on the best interests test to justify authorising her sterilisation. Indeed, their discussion of her rights was almost wholly confined to 'a woman's right to reproduce', the authenticity of which is somewhat dubious. Arguably only a spurious right, it seems to have originated in Heilbron J's assertion in *Re D (a minor) (wardship: sterilisation)*[223] that sterilisation involves violating a woman's 'right to reproduce'. Despite having a certain emotional appeal, it lacks substance. As Grubb and Pearl point out, international human rights documents reflect a concern to protect individuals against attempts to prevent children being born for eugenic or population control reasons. Consequently, they protect a right to choose whether *or not* to reproduce, and do not provide an absolute right to do so.[224]

As the Australian High Court in *Secretary, Department of Health and Community Services (NT) v JWB and SMB*[225] appreciated, the danger involved in placing an emphasis on a right to reproduce, rather than on the right to bodily integrity, is that it is far easier to justify infringing it in the case of a mentally handicapped patient. Having considerable doubts about the existence of a right to reproduce or its usefulness, that court emphasised the fundamental right to bodily integrity. By contrast, in *Re B (a minor) (wardship: sterilisation)*,[226] their Lordships did not question the existence of a right to reproduce. However, they discounted its relevance to

---

219 *Re S (sterilisation: patient's best interests)* [2000] 2 FLR 389 at 405, per Thorpe LJ.
220 See below.
221 [1988] AC 199.
222 Jeanette, the subject of the application, was aged 17, with the intellectual ability of a child aged between 5 and 6. She was epileptic and subject to mood changes, at times becoming violent and aggressive. She could dress and bath herself, and cope with menstruation, but probably lacked the capacity to form a long-term adult relationship, or to have maternal feelings, or to cope with contraception.
223 [1976] 1 All ER 326 at 332. Similarly in *Re Eve* (1986) 31 DLR (4th) 1 at 436, La Forest J referred to 'the fundamental right to bear a child'.
224 In *R v Secretary of State for the Home Department, ex p Mellor* [2000] 2 FLR 951, Forbes J held that art 12 of the ECHR, which protects the right of men and women of marriageable age to marry and to found a family, does not provide a prisoner with a right of access to artificial insemination services for him and his wife.
225 (1992) 66 ALJR 300.
226 [1988] AC 199.

Jeanette. They argued that such a right could only be of any value if accompanied by an *ability to choose* to exercise that right or enjoy that privilege,[227] and assumed that she had no ability to make such a choice. Utilising this argument and excluding anyone who cannot choose to exercise the rights contained in the ECHR from its protection would be a surprisingly simple way of reducing its scope to a very small portion of the population.

The decision in *Re B* provoked a storm of protest, mainly because the indeterminate nature of the best interests test allowed the House of Lords to produce a judgment with very little attention to legal analysis.[228] Many critics were highly dissatisfied with their Lordships' emphasis on Jeanette's best interests and her right to reproduce, at the expense of a full consideration of what other rights might be affected by the proposed sterilisation.[229] Despite being concerned to protect her from future pregnancy, the judgments made no mention of her right to be protected from sexual exploitation. Indeed, there was little serious attempt to assess and weigh her various rights in order to achieve an appropriate balance between them. Their Lordships controversially rejected the approach of La Forest J in *Re Eve*,[230] who had considered it crucial to distinguish between 'therapeutic' and 'non-therapeutic' procedures.[231] In his view, because a non-therapeutic sterilisation is not ordinarily performed for the purpose of medical treatment, it could never benefit that person and therefore should never be authorised under the *parens patriae* jurisdiction.[232]

The critics of the decision in *Re B* were fully vindicated when its shortcomings fed through into later decision-making on sterilising adolescents. Subsequent advice issued by the Official Solicitor stressed that a sterilisation procedure should genuinely be a remedy of last resort.[233] Despite this, a body of case law became established which pays little attention to assessing the rights actually at stake or to analysing what the best interests of an adolescent really are in circumstances of this kind.[234] Bearing out Kennedy's criticisms, the judiciary has continued to be impressed by the opinions of medical experts[235] and still too ready to justify decisions to authorise

---

227   [1988] AC 199 at 219, per Lord Oliver of Aylmerton; see also Lord Hailsham (at 213) and Lord Bridge of Harwich (at 214).
228   See, inter alia: I Kennedy (1992) ch 20; M Freeman (1988); J Montgomery (1989). See also the 'disquiet' over this and subsequent case law voiced by M Brazier (1992) pp 346–350 and 388–392. But see J Mason, R McCall Smith and G Laurie (2002), who consider that *Re B (a minor) (wardship: sterilisation)* was relatively unobjectionable on *medical* grounds (pp 126–127).
229   See M Freeman (1988) p 76.
230   (1986) 31 DLR (4th) 1 Supreme Court of Canada.
231   See I Kennedy (1992), who (pp 406–413) greatly favours La Forest J's approach.
232   (1986) 31 DLR (4th) 1 at 30 and 32.
233   This gives practitioners guidance on the issues they should normally satisfy before seeking authorisation for such procedures. See the current guidance contained in the *Practice Note (Official Solicitor: declaratory proceedings: medical and welfare decisions for adults who lack capacity)*, esp *Appendix 1: Sterilisation Cases* [2001] 2 FLR 158.
234   Eg *Re M (a minor) (wardship: sterilisation)* [1988] 2 FLR 497 (general reference to the girl's need for freedom to move around in the community); *Re P (a minor) (wardship: sterilisation)* [1989] 1 FLR 182 (reference to the human right to reproduce).
235   Eg *Re P (a minor) (wardship: sterilisation)* [1989] 1 FLR 182: Eastham J was greatly influenced by the claims of the consultant obstetrician and gynaecologist that the form of sterilisation used was reversible in 95% of cases.

sterilisations by bare assertions referring to welfare.[236] Dire predictions of the 'disastrous' or 'catastrophic' results of pregnancy are also common.[237]

The case law suggests that judicial authority is now sought for non-therapeutic sterilisations only very occasionally and then only in relation to young adult women. Perhaps adolescents are being allowed to reach formal majority before such procedures are considered. Alternatively, adolescent sterilisations are perhaps being performed under the guise of therapeutic menstrual management, thereby escaping judicial supervision. Regarding the adult cases, some courts are still being persuaded that sterilisation, rather than uterine contraception, is the only practical means of ensuring a young mentally handicapped adult's future care.[238] Nevertheless, the rapid development of extremely reliable methods of contraception appears to be producing a more cautious response from medical experts asked to comment on parental requests for the sterilisation of their mentally handicapped offspring.[239] Some courts are also becoming more critical of requests to authorise the sterilisation of mentally handicapped adults, both female and male.[240] The words of Thorpe J are as relevant to cases involving adolescents as they were to the young woman involved:

> 'It can be argued ... that if there is a risk of pregnancy that cannot be eliminated by supervision, then it had better be eliminated by surgery. The contrary argument is that what would be immediately and profoundly damaging to L would be to experience again the trauma of indecent assault or worse. That is the evil against which she must be protected. Sterilisation would do nothing to protect her from that. Indeed, it might reduce the protection, either in the sense that at some level the carers would become less careful, or alternatively because the potential abuser would measure the consequences of sexual invasion as reduced ... I simply cannot in conscience conclude that it would be in her best interests to subject her to that as long as she is receiving the very specialist dedicated care that she is.'[241]

This critical approach more obviously satisfies the courts' duty to protect the human rights of mentally handicapped adolescents. Indeed, the Human Rights Act 1998 may finally have rescued mentally handicapped women and girls from the threat of sterilisation. Admittedly, an article 8 challenge[242] would not necessarily prevent a proposed sterilisation. The court may consider that the girl's ability to form relationships with members of the opposite sex is sufficiently important to her to justify the infringement, particularly if there is no method of reliable contraception available. In other words, a gross violation of the adolescent's body without her

---

236 Eg, per Eastham J in *Re P* [1989] 1 FLR 182 at 194: 'In those circumstances I believe that, notwithstanding the contrary argument advanced by the Official Solicitor, *her welfare dictates that she should have this operation ...*' (emphasis supplied).

237 Eg *Re HG (specific issue order: sterilisation)* [1993] 1 FLR 587 at 591, per Peter Singer QC and *Re P (a minor) (wardship: sterilisation)* [1989] 1 FLR 182 at 194, per Eastham J. See also *Re Z (medical treatment: hysterectomy)* [2000] 1 FLR 523 at 534, per Bennett J, regarding the proposed sterilisation of a 19-year-old girl.

238 Eg *Re Z (medical treatment: hysterectomy)* [2000] 1 FLR 523 and *Re S (sterilisation: patient's best interests)* [2000] 1 FLR 465 (later reversed on appeal [2000] 2 FLR 389).

239 Eg *Re Z (medical treatment: hysterectomy)* [2000] 1 FLR 523: the medical experts disagreed over whether contraception or sterilisation was appropriate. See also *Re S (sterilisation: patient's best interests)* [2000] 2 FLR 389: appeal allowed against a declaration authorising a sterilisation because the medical experts had favoured a contraceptive coil over a hysterectomy.

240 See *Re LC (medical treatment: sterilisation)* [1997] 2 FLR 258; *Re S (sterilisation: patient's best interests)* [2000] 2 FLR 389; *Re A (male sterilisation)* [2000] 1 FLR 549.

241 *Re LC (medical treatment: sterilisation)* [1997] 2 FLR 258 at 261–262.

242 Ie alleging that the sterilisation will infringe the girl's right to bodily integrity, under art 8 of the ECHR.

consent might be balanced against her right to live as full a life as possible without stultifying supervision.[243] In *Re A (male sterilisation)*[244] the Court of Appeal sympathised with the argument that a mentally handicapped man's best interests might require him to be sterilised, not for any medical reasons, but to prevent his freedom of movement being restricted and his quality of life diminished.[245] Nevertheless, an article 3 challenge under the ECHR would be far more difficult to answer. It is hard to conceive of a form of treatment which is more inhuman and degrading than removing the reproductive organs of a mentally handicapped woman or girl without her consent. Strasbourg jurisprudence clearly indicates that forcing a mentally incompetent patient to undergo treatment could infringe his or her rights under article 3, unless the measure 'is a therapeutic necessity' according to the 'psychiatric principles generally accepted at the time'.[246] It would be impossible to argue that a non-consensual non-therapeutic sterilisation fulfilled such a narrow criterion. La Forest J's words remain immensely persuasive:

> 'The grave intrusion on a person's rights and the certain physical damage that ensues from non-therapeutic sterilization without consent, when compared with the highly questionable advantages that can result from it, have persuaded me that it can never safely be determined that such a procedure is for the benefit of that person.'[247]

Meanwhile, it is essential that those caring for mentally handicapped adolescents resist sterilisation procedures being arranged under the guise of a form of menstrual management carried out for therapeutic purposes. Indeed, as suggested above, it is arguable that judicial authorisation should be made a prerequisite of all sterilisation procedures.

(5)   CONCLUSION

Doctors increasingly influence the extent to which children's rights are protected when decisions are made regarding their treatment. Although they have the expertise and training to protect children's medical rights, they are not necessarily in the best position to advise over other rights, such as children's right to bodily integrity and to be consulted and treated with respect. But whilst doctors are not always the best judges of what is in the child's best overall interests, nor are his or her parents, who not surprisingly may find it impossible to be objective over the decisions to be made. The courts too may lose sight of their duty to protect the child's own rights from being infringed by decisions which appear to be in a child's best interests but which may be more to do with those of his or her carers. Children's rights should not be lost somewhere in the middle, between parental, medical and judicial paternalism.

---

243   Ie the intervention is necessary and its results proportionate to the harm avoided, under art 8(2) ECHR.
244   [2000] 1 FLR 549.
245   Per Dame Elizabeth Butler-Sloss P, [2000] 1 FLR 549 at 557. But since the restrictions imposed on this adult were to remain the same, irrespective of a sterilisation taking place, the Court of Appeal refused authority for the sterilisation, considering it not in his best interests.
246   See *Herczegfalvy v Austria* (1992) 15 EHRR 437 (paras 82–86). See discussion by Hale LJ in *R (on the application of Wilkinson) v Broadmoor Hospital* [2001] EWCA Civ 1545, [2002] 1 WLR 419 at [79] in the context of subjecting mental health patients to compulsory treatment.
247   (1986) 31 DLR (4th) 1 at 33.

BIBLIOGRAPHY

NB many of these publications can be obtained on the relevant organisation's website.

Abboud P et al, Reviews: Personal Views 'Stronger campaign needed to end female genital mutilation' (2000) 320 British Medical Journal 262 at1153.

Acheson D (Chair), *Report of the Independent Inquiry into Inequalities in Health* (1998) The Stationery Office.

Alderson P, *Children's Consent to Surgery* (1993) Oxford University Press.

Alderson P and Montgomery J, *Health Care Decisions: Making decisions with children* (1996) IPPR.

Bainham A, 'Do Babies Have Rights?' (1997) Cambridge Law Journal 48.

Black J and Debelle G, 'Female genital mutilation in Britain (1995) 310 British Medical Journal 1590.

Brazier M, *Medicine, Patients and the Law* (1992) Penguin Books.

British Medical Association (BMA), *Circumcision of Male Infants: Guidance for Doctors* (1996).

British Medical Association (BMA), *Growing Up In Britain: Ensuring a healthy future for our children. A study of 0–5 year olds* (1999).

British Medical Association (BMA), *Consent, Rights and Choices in Health Care for Children and Young People* (2001) BMJ Books.

Campbell A and McHaffie H, 'Prolonging life and allowing death: infants' (1995) 21 Journal of Medical Ethics 339.

Committee on the Rights of the Child, *Concluding observations of the Committee on the Rights of the Child: Sweden* CRC/C/15/Add 2 (1993) Centre for Human Rights, Geneva.

Delaney L, 'Child Bone-Marrow Donors – Victims or Volunteers?' (1995) Family Law 372.

Department of Health, *The Children Act 1989 Guidance and Regulations* Vol 2 *Family Support, Day Care and Educational Provision for Young Children* (1991) HMSO.

Dingwall R, Eekelaar J and Murray T, *The Protection of Children* (1995) Avebury.

Dowler E et al, *Poverty Bites: Food, health and poor families* (2001) CPAG.

Dworkin G, 'Consent, Representation and Proxy Consent' in W Gaylin and R Macklin (eds) *Who Speaks for the Child* (1982) Plenum Press.

Eason J, McDonnell M and Clark G, 'Male ritual circumcision resulting in acute renal failure' (1994) 309 British Medical Journal 660.

Eekelaar J, 'The Emergence of Children's Rights' (1986) 6 Oxford Journal of Legal Studies 161.

Feenan D, 'A good harvest? *Re Y (mental incapacity: bone marrow transplant)*' (1997) 9 Child and Family Law Quarterly 305.

Feldman D, *Civil Liberties and Human Rights in England and Wales* (2002) Oxford University Press.

Fortin J, '*Re C (Medical Treatment)*: A baby's right to die' (1998) 10 Child and Family Law Quarterly 411.

Fortin J, 'Babies and the challenges of medical technology' in S Cretney (ed) *Family Law Essays for the new Millennium* (2000) Family Law.

Fox M and McHale J ,'In Whose Best Interests?' (1997) 60 Modern Law Review 700.

Freeman M, 'Sterilising the Mentally Handicapped' in M Freeman (ed) *Medicine, Ethics and Law* (1988) Stevens.

Freeman M, 'Whose life is it anyway?' (2001) 9 Medical Law Review 259.

Freeman M, 'Children's rights ten years after ratification' in B Franklin (ed) *The New Handbook of Children's Rights: Comparative policy and practice* (2002) Routledge.

Grubb A and Pearl D, 'Sterilisation and the Courts' (1987) Cambridge Law Journal 439.

Gunn M and Smith J, *'Arthur's* case and the Right to Life of a Down's Syndrome Child' (1985) Criminal Law Review 705.

Harris D, O'Boyle M and Warbrick C, *Law on the European Convention on Human Rights* (1995) Butterworths.

Harris J, *The Value of Life: An introduction to medical ethics (*1985) Routledge and Kegan Paul.

Harris J, 'Human Beings, Persons and Conjoined Twins: An Ethical Analysis of the Judgment in *Re A'* (2001) Medical Law Review 221.

Katz I, 'Is male circumcision morally defensible?' in M King (ed) *Moral Agendas for Children's Welfare* (1999) Routledge.

Kennedy I, *Treat Me Right: Essays in Medical Law and Ethics* (1992) Oxford University Press.

Kennedy I and Grubb A, *Medical Law* (2000) Butterworths.

Keown J, 'Restoring Moral and Intellectual Shape after Bland' (1997) 113 Law Quarterly Review 481.

Law Commission, *Mental Incapacity* Law Com No 231 (1995) HMSO.

LeBlanc L, *The Convention on the Rights of the Child: United Nations Lawmaking on Human Rights* (1995) University of Nebraska Press.

Marshall K, *Children's Rights in the Balance: The Participation – Protection Debate* (1997) The Stationery Office.

Mason J, McCall Smith R and Laurie G, *Law and Medical Ethics* (2002) Butterworths.

Meltzer H and Gatward R, *Mental health of children and adolescents in Great Britain* Office for National Statistics (2000) The Stationery Office.

Michalowski S, 'Is it in the best interests of a child to have a life-saving liver transplantation?: Re T (Wardship: Medical Treatment)' (1997) 9 Child and Family Law Quarterly 179.

Montgomery J, 'Rhetoric and Welfare' (1989) 9 Oxford Journal of Legal Studies 395.

Morgan D, *Issues in Medical Law and Ethics* (2001) Cavendish Publishing.

Mumford S ,'Bone Marrow Donation: the Law in Context' (1998) 10 Child and Family Law Quarterly 135.

Office of National Statistics, *Social Trends* No 33 (2003) The Stationery Office.

Palmer G et al, *Monitoring poverty and social exclusion 2002* (2002) Joseph Rowntree Foundation.

Rickwood A et al, 'Towards evidence based circumcision of English boys: survey of trends in practice' (2000) 321 British Medical Journal 792.

Roche J, 'Children's rights: in the name of the child' (1995) 17 Journal of Social Welfare and Family Law 281.

Southall D, 'The Best Interest of the Child: A Paediatrician's Perspective of the Re T Case' (1997) 133 Childright 6.

Wells C, '"Otherwise kill me": Marginal Children and Ethics at the Edges of Existence' in R Lee and D Morgan (eds) *Birthrights: Law and Ethics at the Beginnings of Life* (1989) Routledge.

Williams N and Kapila L, 'Complications of Circumcision' (1993) 80 British Journal of Surgery 1231.

Williams N and Kapila L, *Circumcision of Male Infants: Guidance for Doctors* (1996) British Medical Association.

Chapter 11

Educational rights for children in minority groups

(1) INTRODUCTION

Religious and ethnic minority groups[1] contribute to the richness of a pluralistic society. One of the most important rights for such a group is to preserve its separate identity. It cannot do so unless it maintains its continuity by educating its children to understand and respect its own customs, religion and culture. They can then mature into adult members of the group, with a commitment to its future preservation. Nevertheless, when the educational rights of the children of minority groups are considered, a number of competing considerations become apparent. Indeed, a familiar dilemma arises, although in this context it is even more acute, how to find a suitable means of ensuring that parents' rights do not override those of their children.

Overarching this discussion is a more fundamental question regarding minority groups' relationships with mainstream society. An acceptable compromise must always be found between the views of extreme pluralists who maintain the absolute right of minority groups to preserve all the elements of their cultural traditions, and those of assimilationists who expect minorities to be absorbed into the culture of the mainstream community.[2] As Poulter comments, the compromise adopted in Britain has been to promote a 'cultural pluralism within limits'.[3] This reflects the pervading view that a democratic pluralist society should support the cultures and lifestyles of its ethnic groups, whilst expecting all groups to accept a set of shared values distinctive of that society as a whole. In the field of education, this approach was embraced by the Swann Report in the 1980s, which argued that the education system should reflect the fact that a policy of pluralism must be limited by the need for a cohesive society founded on shared fundamental values.[4]

The concept of cultural pluralism within limits provides no clear answers over how to define the fundamental values around which limits should be set. For example,

---

1   Finding an acceptable definition of the term 'minority group' is fraught with difficulty. See P Thornberry (1991) esp pp 164–172. For the purposes of this work, it is assumed that a 'minority group' is numerically smaller than the majority, whose members possess ethnic, religious or linguistic characteristics different from the rest and who show a sense of solidarity directed towards preserving their culture, traditions, religion or language.
2   See S Poulter (1998) ch 1.
3   S Poulter (1998) p 21.
4   M Swann (1985) p 6.

should society acknowledge that all minority groups have an absolute right to educate their children as they wish, even if their schools adopt educational methods that the state considers to be inadequate and stultifyingly narrow? If children receive an education which is too restricted to enable them to leave their community and compete for a place outside its confines, then they may justifiably accuse the state of failing in its duty to ensure that they have equality of opportunity in the education they receive. Attempts by the state to interfere with the education of minority children may, however, become difficult to justify if the community's educational methods are based on their religious and racial beliefs. Members of minority groups may see any attempt to interfere with their freedom to educate their children according to their own beliefs, not only in terms of a threat to their own convictions, but amounting to religious persecution, thereby infringing their fundamental human rights, as secured by international instruments.

This chapter considers the interests of minority children and their parents from two educational perspectives. First, it questions the extent to which the state should mediate between the interests of parents and children, once ethnic or religious minority groups are given the freedom to establish independent schools, perhaps through supervising their educational methods. The state must be able to justify whatever criteria it uses to evaluate the education provided, if it intends to interfere in any way. Second, some minority parents may be content to keep their children within the state educational system. It is then important to consider the degree to which they should be permitted to influence the content of their children's education, particularly in those areas which most offend their own principles, notably collective worship and religious instruction.

(2) PROTECTION FOR SEPARATE EDUCATION

(A) International protection for the concept of separate education

Some extreme minority groups might claim the right to bring up their children in an unenlightened fashion and to educate them in a manner which the majority considers to be reactionary. International human rights treaties do not support governments very effectively in the event of their deciding to interfere with such a regime, since they tend to identify children's interests with those of their parents. Thus whilst these treaties recognise the rights of minorities to enjoy their own culture, religion and language,[5] minority children's educational rights are treated in a particularly adult-focused manner. Given that the religious and racial persecution before and during the Second World War is still recent history, these treaties emphasise the need to avoid educational institutions being used by states to indoctrinate children in ways that undermine their allegiance to their families and their own culture and religion.

Members of minorities benefit from the civil and political guarantees provided by many human rights instruments, such as freedom of thought, conscience and religion,[6]

---

5   See esp art 27 of the International Covenant on Civil and Political Rights. See also the Council of Europe's Framework Convention for the Protection of National Minorities (adopted 1995 and ratified by the UK in 1998) esp arts 4–11, developing these rights in more detail.
6   See art 9 of the ECHR, employing the formula used in art 18 of the Universal Declaration of Human Rights (adopted in 1948 by the General Assembly of the United Nations), also used by art 18(1) of the International Covenant on Civil and Political Rights.

without discrimination.[7] Nevertheless, securing freedom from religious and racial persecution is not enough; minority groups should also enjoy the right to bring up and inculcate their children in their own faith and traditions. Accordingly, many human rights treaties include educational provisions protecting parents' freedom to have their children educated according to their own beliefs. Article 2 of the First Protocol of the ECHR notably provides that: 'No person shall be denied the right to education' and proceeds to require states to 'respect the right of parents to ensure such education and teaching in conformity with their own religious and philosophical convictions'.[8]

When interpreting article 2 of the First Protocol,[9] the European Court of Human Rights obviously appreciates the need to maintain a balance between protecting pluralism and upholding the state's right to run an efficient education system which reflects society's shared values. Thus in *Kjeldsen, Busk and Pedersen v Denmark*[10] it upheld the Danish state's right to set the curriculum and to impart information or knowledge of 'a directly or indirectly religious or philosophical kind'. This, the Court considered, was acceptable, as long as the information was conveyed in an 'objective, critical and pluralistic manner', without attempting to indoctrinate pupils in a way which does not respect their parents' religious convictions.[11] Consequently, it decided that the inclusion of sex education in primary schools' curriculum does not infringe parents' rights under the First Protocol.[12]

The European Court also indicated in the *Belgian Linguistics Case (No 2)*[13] that article 2 of the First Protocol has clear limits when it comes to the provision of educational resources. Whilst it guarantees a right to education, including education in a national language, its scope is relatively narrow. Although in conjunction with article 14, the protocol clearly protects minority children from being *excluded* from mainstream publicly funded state schools, it does not guarantee parents the right to obtain an education which they consider best meets their children's needs, using, for example, the language of their choice. Indeed, although international human rights

---

7   Eg art 14 ECHR, ensuring that all rights are enjoyed without discrimination on grounds of 'sex, race, colour, language, religion, political or other opinion, national or social origin, association with a national minority, property, birth or other status'.

8   See also art 5(2) of the Declaration on the Elimination of All Forms of Intolerance and of Discrimination Based on Religion or Belief (adopted by the General Assembly of the United Nations in 1981) and art 18(4) of the International Covenant on Civil and Political Rights.

9   See A Bradley (1999) pp 398–402.

10   (1976) 1 EHRR 711.

11   (1976) 1 EHRR 711 (paras 53–54).

12   See also *Valsamis v Greece* (1996) 24 EHRR 294: the European Court of Human Rights rejected the claim of Jehovah's Witness parents and their 12-year-old daughter that their rights under art 2 of the First Protocol had been infringed by the school punishing her for refusing to take part in a school parade on a national holiday to commemorate the outbreak of war between Greece and Italy in 1941. Although minorities must be treated fairly, school discipline was an integral part of education and the punishment had been a limited one.

13   (1968) 1 EHRR 252: French-speaking parents succeeded in their claim that, by excluding their children from certain schools in six communes, Belgium was discriminating against them. But they failed in their claim that by refusing to establish French-speaking schools for their children near their own homes, Belgium was infringing their rights under art 2 of the First Protocol.

law secures the right of minority parents to establish their own separate schools,[14] it does not require states to finance such establishments.[15]

It is notable that the international human rights treaties discussed above promote freedom of thought and religion and the right to an education free from state indoctrination from an almost entirely adult perspective. For example, in *Valsamis v Greece*[16] the European Court decided that neither the parents' religious convictions under article 9 nor their pacifist views under article 2 of the First Protocol of the ECHR had been infringed when their daughter was disciplined for refusing to participate in a school parade. Having rejected the arguments focusing on the parents' religious rights under article 9, the Court thought it unnecessary to consider their daughter's own perspectives.[17] Furthermore, when interpreting article 2 of the First Protocol, the Strasbourg institutions appear to consider it perfectly appropriate to assume that a child's interests are identical to those of his or her parents. They overlook the fact that although parents' rights to withdraw their child from religious education classes accords with their own rights to have their religious convictions respected, it quite possibly infringes the child's own rights to his or her privacy.[18]

Even the CRC, which was intended to address the concept of rights from a child's perspective, reflects some underlying dilemmas and tensions when it comes to securing children's own freedom of thought, religion and education. Indeed, its provisions contain some important compromises in the way they balance children's rights against their parents' rights. For example, whilst article 14(1) directs states to respect the child's right to freedom of thought, conscience and religion, article 14(2) directs them to 'respect the rights and duties of the parents ... to provide direction to the child in the exercise of his or her right in a manner consistent with the evolving capacities of the child'. The failure of article 14(1) to secure for children freedom to *choose* their religion was attributable to the lack of consensus over this at the drafting stage of the Convention. Islamic states were not able to compromise one of the fundamental tenets of their religion which is that children must follow their fathers' religious faith.[19] Although it is true, as Hodgkin and Newell observe, that 'the wording of article 14 and the Convention's general principles certainly do not support the concept of children automatically following their parents' religion until the age of

---

14 See art 13(3) of the International Covenant on Economic, Social and Cultural Rights, which requires states to respect parents' liberty to choose 'for their children schools, other than those established by the public authorities, which conform to such minimum educational standards as may be laid down or approved by the State and to ensure the religious and moral education of their children in conformity with their own convictions'. See also the UN Convention against Discrimination in Education 1962, art 5(1)(b), which allows parents to ensure that their children are educated in accordance with their convictions and art 5(1)(c), which recognises the right of national minorities to have their own schools and to teach their own language.

15 Eg Framework Convention for the Protection of National Minorities, art 13(2), which recognises the rights of minorities to set up their own educational establishments, but specifies that its exercise 'shall not entail any financial obligation for the Parties'. See also the United Kingdom's reservation on art 2 of the First Protocol (repeating the formula in the Education Act 1944, s 76), stating that it only accepts its terms 'so far as it is compatible with the provision of efficient instruction and training, and the avoidance of unreasonable public expenditure'.

16 (1996) 24 EHRR 294.

17 See a critical analysis of this decision by U Kilkelly (1999) pp 73–75 and 134–135.

18 See discussion below.

19 See G Van Bueren (1995) pp 156–159.

18',[20] their right to 'freedom' of religion nevertheless appears to be over-identified with parents' religious rights.[21]

As with the right to religious freedom, the CRC contains compromises regarding a child's educational rights; these might endanger a child's ability to break away from his or her parents' narrow beliefs through receiving a liberal education. Education could have an extremely important part to play in ensuring that children develop their own views, free of any indoctrination from their parents or indeed, from the group into which they were born. It could also help them form an ability to express their views, as promoted by article 12. Nevertheless, children may never develop these capacities nor those required to exercise any freedom of thought, conscience or religion, as secured by article 14(1), unless the state intervenes to prevent their parents educating them in such a way that undermines their capacity for independent thought. But whilst article 29(1)(a) stresses the need for education to develop the child's personality, talents and abilities to their fullest potential, article 29(1)(c) asserts that the child's education should develop a respect for the child's parents and his or her own cultural identity, language and values. Article 30 also reinforces the community rights of minority groups, as groups, rather than of their child members, as individuals. It requires states to respect the right of any child member of an ethnic, religious or linguistic minority 'in community with other members of his or her group, to enjoy his or her own culture, to profess and practise his or her own religion, or to use his or her own language'. Again, these provisions underline parents' rights in education, rather than children's rights.

The contributions that are made to the cultural wealth of society by minority groups certainly should not be underestimated. Thornberry points out that most communities with any history have a complexity derived from their divisions:

> 'Ethnic, religious and linguistic differences within States may be of startling complexity: religions divide into sects and denominations, languages branch into dialects, cultures flourish in diverse forms. To describe diversity in terms of a tapestry, or a hundred banners, or a coat of many colours, does inadequate justice to its richness.'[22]

One might claim, however, that it is in the best interests of a united community for all its children to be educated in multi-cultural and multi-faith state schools. Such a system would undoubtedly enable children to learn about and respect the beliefs of others and equip them better to take their place in the outside world, as they grow older. Nevertheless, by refusing to allow the establishment of separate schools, the government would interfere blatantly with the freedom of minority groups, as secured by the human rights instruments referred to above. The present government is in no danger on this score; indeed, it is keen to encourage the creation of more 'faith' schools.[23] But this policy is a controversial one, opposed by some on the basis that it tends to make minority communities more exclusive, thereby leading to community fragmentation.[24] There is no doubt that an extension in the numbers of faith schools

---

20   R Hodgkin and P Newell (1998) p 180.
21   See the wording of arts 14(2), 20(3) and 30.
22   See P Thornberry (1991) p 2.
23   See DfES (2001) para 5.30.
24   See Press Notice issued, June 2001, by the Commission for Racial Equality, opposing 'segregated schools'. See also the House of Lords Debates on the Education Bill 2002, which were dominated by concerns about the government's policy to extend maintained faith schools. Eg Lord Baker of Dorking expressed his concern (quoting the views of Amartya Sen) that children sent to faith schools would lose their right to a broad education, together with their right to choose their own identity: HL Debs, Hansard, 11 March 2002, col 592.

will highlight the obvious dilemmas created by their existence. These dilemmas, in turn, are not necessarily assisted by the manner in which the international human rights instruments largely identify the interests of minority children with those of their parents. Such an approach may, at times, undermine attempts to fulfil the children's full educational rights. It is therefore fundamentally important for domestic law to adopt a confident stance when it comes to supervising the level of instruction provided by separate schools.

(B)   State supervision of separate schools

Parents who are members of minority groups may conclude that mainstream education is unsuitable for their children's needs. They may oppose its fundamental aims, perhaps because they offend deeply held views and traditions. They may also fear that the methods of instruction will develop their child's individuality and independence, at the expense of his or her family and community loyalties. Since they may also doubt the ability of mainstream education to instruct their children in their own beliefs and customs, some will conclude that the only form of education they could support would be that provided by separate schools designed to cater for their particular needs.

Although minority groups are not obstructed from establishing independent denominational or 'faith' schools, questions inevitably arise over the legitimacy of the state then intervening to ensure that their children obtain a well-balanced education. A minority group may strongly resist any state interference with the content of the education offered and the methods of instruction, if the school is entirely funded by the group itself. But if, for example, the education in a minority school does not ensure that the children receive instruction in the language used by society at large, the children may be inadequately prepared for adult life if they later choose to work outside their own community or even to leave it entirely. Less dramatically, the education offered may itself preclude equality of opportunity in other ways. For example, some would argue that the Muslim practice of segregating Muslim boys and girls and providing them with a different balance of subjects, undermines the girls' equality of opportunity. Moreover, the instruction in some independent schools may be undertaken by teachers without formal educational qualifications, although they may be well qualified to teach the children about the customs and belief of the community for whom the school was established.

International human rights law recognises the right of the state to impose 'minimum standards of education' on separate schools[25] and article 29(1) of the CRC also expects the education provided to develop the child's personality, talents and abilities to their fullest potential. It is obviously important for any liberal democracy to clarify the aims of its educational system, when laying down the 'minimum standards' it requires of the education provided. Otherwise, it could be accused of attempting to achieve an authoritarian standardisation, at the expense of the religious freedom of the group itself. Overarching these considerations is the common view that the state should not interfere with family autonomy and privacy. Matters to do with religion and education are often assumed to be within this family preserve and, as such, left to parents to determine. Such an argument is reinforced by the view that the state should not intrude into the personal lives of members of minority groups.[26]

---

25   See art 13(3) of the International Covenant on Economic, Social and Cultural Rights, n 14 above.

26   See S Poulter (1998) p 27.

Well-known American case law demonstrates these issues being debated by the American Supreme Court in relation to the education provided by some of their more powerful religious groups. Attempts by states to interfere with their children's schooling were seen as violations of the parents' rights to free exercise of religion, as guaranteed by the First Amendment of the American Constitution. By the time the State of Wisconsin challenged the right of the Amish community to deny education to their children beyond the eighth grade,[27] the American Supreme Court had already proclaimed its view that states had a right to interfere with parental authority over children, even in situations involving parents' religious convictions. Thus in the celebrated decision in *Prince v Massachusetts*[28] the Supreme Court made the following observations:

'On one side is the obviously earnest claim for freedom of conscience and religious practice. With it is allied the parent's claim to authority in her own household and in the rearing of her children. The parent's conflict with the state over control of the child and his training is serious enough when only secular matters are concerned. It becomes the more so when an element of religious conviction enters. Against these sacred private interests, basic in a democracy, stand the interests of society to protect the welfare of children, and the state's assertion of authority to that end … It is the interest of youth itself, and of the whole community, that children be both safeguarded from abuses and given opportunities for growth into free and independent well-developed men and citizens … neither rights of religion nor rights of parenthood are beyond limitation.'[29]

Despite this strong justification for state intervention to protect minority children against their parents' authority,[30] nearly 40 years later the Amish community finally gained the right to exempt their children from school after the eighth grade, contrary to Wisconsin state laws which imposed compulsory schooling up to the age of 16. In *Wisconsin v Yoder*[31] the Supreme Court accepted that although the state had a compelling interest in the education of all its children, in this instance the state's law infringed the free exercise of Amish parents' religion and culture. If their children attended school for two more years, instead of learning the skills and customs of the Amish community through farm and household tasks, the identity of the community would suffer. In a powerful dissenting judgment, Justice Douglas asserted that the state should be concerned with the children's religious freedoms and not those of their parents.[32] He was particularly concerned that these restrictions on an Amish child's education might damage his or her adult prospects in the outside world.

'It is the future of the student, not the future of the parents, that is imperilled by today's decision. If a parent keeps his child out of school beyond the grade school, then the child will be forever barred from entry into the new and amazing world of diversity that we have today. The child may decide that is the preferred course, or he may rebel … If he is harnessed to the Amish way of life by those in authority over him and if his education is truncated, his entire life may be stunted and deformed.'[33]

---

27   *Wisconsin v Yoder* 406 US 205 (1972).
28   321 US 158 (1944): the US Supreme Court upheld the validity of a conviction against a Jehovah's Witness mother for allowing her two children and her 9-year-old ward to help her distribute Jehovah's Witness literature on the streets, in violation of a state child labour law.
29   321 US 158 at 165–166 (1944).
30   Limiting previous case law such as *Meyer v Nebraska* 262 US 390 (1923) and *Pierce v Society of Sisters* 268 US 510 (1925), which had protected the right of parents to direct the religious upbringing of their children.
31   406 US 205 (1972).
32   406 US 205 at 242 (1972).
33   406 US 205 at 245–246 (1972).

Justice Douglas suggested that the answer was to consult these pupils themselves. He considered that 14- to 15-year-old teenagers were quite old enough to speak for themselves over whether they wished to attend high school, rather than their parents being allowed to speak for the entire family. Although superficially sensible, this suggestion overlooked the fact that children brought up in a strict and enclosed community may be too indoctrinated to have independent views, or to express them confidently.[34] Arguably, the *Yoder* decision in favour of the Amish parents reflected the fact that the Amish community was extremely well-established, prosperous, law-abiding and self-reliant, with a history stretching back over two hundred years.[35] Hamilton suggests that it is doubtful that similar tolerance would be extended to all closed communities in the USA.[36]

It seems unlikely that a religious group running an independent faith school in this country could exempt its children from the last two years of compulsory education. Indeed, the law empowers the state to supervise closely and, if necessary, interfere with the operation of all independent schools in the country, irrespective of their catering for a particular religious or ethnic group. Although such schools are not obliged to follow the National Curriculum, the standard of instruction they offer can be monitored closely by the government. Indeed, a notice of complaint may be served by the Secretary of State on the proprietor of any independent school[37] for failing to meet certain standards, in terms of instruction, accommodation and staff.[38] If the school fails to remedy the defects, it may eventually be struck off the register, thereby forcing its closure.[39]

A reading of the reports of past inspection teams[40] sent to monitor the standards of education offered by minority schools provokes fundamental questions over the state's proper role regarding its supervisory function.[41] As discussed above, despite the benefits of pursuing a policy of 'cultural pluralism within limits', doubts arise over where the limits fall.[42] More particularly, it may be difficult to determine the point at which minimum national standards are breached by a particularly traditional approach to education. For example, an HMI report commenting on the education provided by a Muslim girls' high school described it as offering a learning experience which was 'intellectually unchallenging and aesthetically limited'.[43] In some cases, lessons have been criticised for not challenging the pupils to think independently, particularly if the instruction involves undemanding formal exercises, with the pupils

34   See C Hamilton (1995) pp 265–271 for a discussion of the decision in *Wisconsin v Yoder*.
35   All arguments considered by the Supreme Court in the *Yoder* decision.
36   C Hamilton (1995) p 270.
37   Which must be registered on the register of independent schools by the Registrar of Independent Schools. See Education Act 2002, ss 158–161.
38   Education Act 2002, s 165. The grounds for complaint must relate to educational standards, as set out in regulations: see s 157.
39   Education Act 2002, s 165. The school may appeal to an independent tribunal: ss 166, 167.
40   Formal school inspections are now carried out by teams from the Office for Standards in Education (hereafter Ofsted). A separate system of inspection was set up for denominational schools, although this system is also organised by Ofsted.
41   See A Bradney (1987).
42   See S Poulter (1998) p 21.
43   A Bradney (1987) p 413.

not encouraged to exercise initiative or to use the materials provided as a basis for discussion.[44] But as Bradney comments, these criticisms are based on assumptions about the proper aims of a system of education which are fundamentally different from those pursued by the schools or the communities for whom they have been established.[45] In particular, there is an implicit assumption that education should enable the child to take an independent place in society, whereas the notion of individual independence is contrary to the deep-rooted culture and traditions of many minority groups. Indeed, some Sikh parents saw a potential benefit of separate schooling as being that it would correct the perceived tendency of mainstream state schools to inculcate girls with ideas of independence. Equally, the criticisms directed at the lack of formal teaching qualifications of some of the staff at such schools perhaps overlooks the fact that they are chosen for their ability to teach the children about the values of their community and not to prepare them for public examinations.[46]

If the state is to interfere with separate schooling, it is crucial for it to establish what it expects of the schools and the criteria by which it is judging them. As Cullen argues, education is one of the most important tools for promoting minority characteristics and identity. But it is important to be clear whether minority education rights are perceived as those of the individual child or the right of the community to maintain its collective identity.[47] When the education offered by faith schools is subjected to state scrutiny, it is fundamentally important for the inspectors to clarify whether they are judging the education by its ability to give children equality of opportunity, preparing them to compete with others in the wider community, or by its ability to enable them take their place within their own community fully inculcated in its traditions and beliefs. Cullen suggests that a distinction should be made between an evaluation based on equality of opportunity and equality of results or outcome. In her view, if the emphasis on outcome is removed, equality of opportunity leaves more space for the operation of the value of pluralism.[48]

If HMI operate on an assumption that separate education should be providing equality of outcome, rather than equality of opportunity, this would indicate a lack of sympathy with the aims of the education provided. The children emerging from these schools often cannot claim equal, or even similar skills or attainments to those who have gone through mainstream schools, quite simply because the education they receive is not intended to enable them to do so. The confusion over what criteria are used on inspection was particularly evident in *R v Secretary of State for Education and Science, ex p Talmud Torah Machzikei Haddass School Trust*.[49] A boys' school run by the Belz section of the orthodox Hasidic Jewish community in Hackney was inspected by HMI. The report criticised the inadequacy of the buildings, the narrowness of the curriculum, the lack of encouragement of imaginative work and the staff's inattention to the need to promote imaginative responses from the pupils to

---

44   See HMI's observations (Ofsted 2001 b) regarding pupils' classroom experience in the Talmud Torah Yetev Lev School. This was 'often uninspiring' when covering their secular curriculum (mathematics and English), as opposed to their religious studies, due to the teaching materials utilised and the teachers' 'narrow pedagogic skills'.
45   A Bradney (1987) p 414.
46   None of the teachers of secular subjects at the Talmud Torah Yetev Lev School had teaching qualifications. The HMI report (Ofsted 2001 b) suggested that much needed doing to improve the organisation and delivery of the secular curriculum.
47   H Cullen (1993) p 144.
48   H Cullen (1993) p 152.
49   (1985) Times, 12 April.

ensure a stimulating learning environment.[50] After inspection the Secretary of State served a complaint on the school,[51] thereby starting the procedure to de-register and close the school. Criticism of the secular education, as opposed to the religious education, provided by such small independent faith schools is probably predictable, given their very narrow aims.[52] What was unusual about the *Talmud Torah Machzikei Haddass* case is that the school not only appealed the matter to the Independent Schools Tribunal, but also applied for judicial review of the Secretary of State's actions in serving the initial complaint.

In the judicial review application the school challenged the competence of HMI to review their work, asserting that it could only be assessed in the context of the traditions the school served. Only one of the inspectors on the team understood Yiddish, the language in which many of the lessons were conducted, and even his grasp of the cultural traditions of the community the school served were insufficient for him to comprehend fully the significance of the pattern of the lessons. More fundamentally, the school argued that the standard by which it had been assessed had been wrong. On this point, counsel for the Department of Education made a notable concession. He accepted that the education provided by such a school would still be suitable if it primarily equips a child for life within the community of which he is a member, rather than for the way of life in the country as a whole. Nevertheless, he added the important qualification that the education would be suitable only as long as it did not foreclose the child's option in later years to adopt some other form of life if he wishes to do so. This echoes the concerns of Justice Douglas in the *Yoder* case,[53] that the Amish children might be barred from 'the new and amazing world of diversity' provided by society today.

Although the judicial review application failed, the decision in the *Talmud Torah Machzikei Haddass* case is an important one. The Secretary of State's concession indicated that separate schools need not be treated in precisely the same manner as maintained schools and non-denominational independent schools.[54] A similar approach was taken by HMI, nearly 20 years later, regarding the teaching provided by the Talmud Torah Yetev Lev primary school in Hackney.[55] The report clearly accepted that the school's aims were quite different to those of a mainstream school serving a mixed community. As it explained, this is –

> 'a school which offers a highly specialised, non-standard education. It serves a faith community which has firm ideas about the education of its children. It is primarily concerned with the transmission of particular religious ideals, values and culture, all of which have, in the recent past, been subject to the threat of extinction. For these reasons, the community that it serves is, to a large extent, inwardly focused and is committed to maintaining its traditional style of education.'[56]

From an orthodox educational perspective, the school had obvious shortcomings. The pupils' knowledge of English was poor (classes being held in Yiddish), they

---

50 See A Bradney (1987) for a full discussion of the HMI report on the Talmud Torah Machzikei Haddass School.

51 Under Education Act 1944, s 71, now Education Act 2002, s 165.

52 See HMI's observations (Ofsted 2001 b) regarding pupils' classroom experience in the Talmud Torah Yetev Lev School.

53 *Wisconsin v Yoder* 406 US 205 (1972).

54 A Bradney (1987) p 418.

55 Ofsted (2001 b).

56 Ofsted (2001 b), section entitled 'How good are the curricular and other opportunities offered to pupils or students?'.

underwent no standardised testing, the teaching of secular subjects was weak,[57] with none of the teachers of secular subjects having qualified teacher status. Nevertheless, there was no suggestion that the school should be closed down. Indeed, it was praised for the manner in which it served its community. From an adult viewpoint, such an approach is beneficial, in so far as it encourages a more tolerant assessment of the educational aspirations of minority groups. Nevertheless, as Hamilton argues, from the child's view point, the education provided should not be accepted as being 'suitable' if the school can only equip pupils for life within the sect's community. Such an assessment negates the concept of equality of opportunity, as protected by international human rights instruments.[58] Neither of the Jewish schools referred to above offered an education which equipped the children to fit easily into British society. Indeed, as relatively few lessons were in English, the children might not even learn to speak English very fluently. The education provided did not comply with the Secretary of State's own requirement that the education provided should not foreclose on the children's ability to leave the community and follow some other form of life. Hamilton asserts:

> 'Allowing a child to be educated within such an ideological, social and educational enclosure cannot amount to equality of opportunity, although it undoubtedly upholds the principle of pluralism. However, the concession towards pluralism and parents' religious values and beliefs is too great.'[59]

Official involvement in these two schools demonstrates the difficulty involved in achieving a balance between the rights of a minority community to maintain its identity and the rights of children to equality of opportunity. As Cullen argues, minority educational rights should be seen in an educational context, and not as minority cultural rights. Such an approach allows the question to be asked whether the education fulfils the child's individual potential, rather than whether it protects the minority characteristics.[60] Nevertheless, Cullen also claims that 'the individual right to education must be understood against the background of the collective right to maintain minority identity'.[61] Herein lies the conflict. Undoubtedly, minority groups must retain their freedom to run separate schools. But the years available to fulfil children's right to a broadly based and enlightened education are very short. Unless such groups can ensure that the education they provide does not foreclose on the child's option in later years to adopt some other form of life if he or she wishes to do so, the state has a clear duty to ensure that their schools adjust their methods appropriately, or cease operating.

Whatever academic standards they achieve, separate schools may find it easier than maintained schools to contribute to the lives of the ethnic minority communities which they serve, through teaching the children in an informed way about their culture and religion, placing it in a historical context, and giving them a sense of pride in their cultural heritage. This may explain the present government's enthusiasm

---

57   The only non-religious subjects taught were mathematics (without geometry or algebra) and English.
58   C Hamilton (1995) pp 259–263.
59   C Hamilton (1995) p 262.
60   H Cullen (1993) p 144.
61   H Cullen (1993) p 144.

for bringing more faith schools into the maintained sector.[62] Currently, the state does not serve all minority groups particularly well in non-denominational maintained schools, either in terms of the education it provides their children, or in the extent to which it promotes their cultural identities. Research indicates that some groups of pupils, such as African-Caribbean, Pakistani and Bangladeshi children, show significantly lower than average levels of achievement.[63] This may in part be attributable to low teacher expectations in some maintained primary schools regarding the abilities of some groups of pupils.[64] Some teachers also show a worrying ignorance of such pupils' potential career goals, and their family and community cultures.[65]

Influenced by this research evidence and the findings of the Macpherson Report,[66] the government introduced measures both to reduce racist attitudes within schools[67] and to improve the academic attainment of minority groups of children attending maintained schools.[68] Nevertheless, progress is extremely patchy, with some schools being reluctant to select programmes of study reflecting pupils' cultural background, for fear of patronising the groups concerned.[69] By comparison, separate schools can unashamedly provide such programmes, with the full support of the communities they were established to serve. Nevertheless, as the *Talmud Torah Machzikei Haddass* case demonstrates, a proliferation of faith schools with extremely narrow aims may create considerable dilemmas for those whose job it is to monitor the standard of education being offered.

(3)   COLLECTIVE WORSHIP AND RELIGIOUS EDUCATION

A fundamental aim of education should be to broaden the horizons of all pupils so that they understand the diversity of values and lifestyles now present in a multi-cultural society. It is difficult to deny that children's right to a broadly based and enlightened education will be fulfilled better by attending multi-cultural and multi-faith schools, than separate schools. Clearly, although religious convictions may be an important factor in parents' choice of school for their child,[70] membership of a

---

62   The number of faith schools entering the maintained sector in the United Kingdom has increased over recent years, the present government believing that they play an important role in catering for the diversity of society. See DfES (2001) para 5.30. The maintained sector now includes Sikh, Muslim and Greek Orthodox schools. Like other maintained schools, maintained faith schools must comply with the National Curriculum and appoint suitably qualified staff.

63   See Ofsted (1999) esp paras 8–38. See also D Gillborn and H Mirza (2000) esp pp 12–17.

64   See Ofsted (1999) para 64.

65   See Social Exclusion Unit (1999) para 5.8. See also paras 6.5–6.11.

66   W Macpherson (1999).

67   LEAs and schools have a duty to avoid discrimination on racial grounds, and to promote good race relations. See Race Relations Act 1976, Sch 1A, paras 46–47.

68   Eg, the Ethnic Minority Achievement Grant (EMAG) of £430m, introduced in 1999, assists schools address the under-achievement of minority groups. Schools must, inter alia, clarify aims more clearly (through a new obligation to monitor attainment by ethnicity) and provide specialist support staff. See these innovations discussed in Ofsted (2001 a) esp Introduction.

69   See Ofsted (1999) para 86.

70   See *R (on the application of K) v London Borough of Newham* [2002] EWHC 405 (Admin), [2002] ELR 390: a devout Muslim father was influenced in his choice of a single-sex school for his daughter, by his strong religious opposition to mixed schools. Per Collins J (at 398–399), art 2 of Protocol 1 of the ECHR requires LEAs not to discount any expressed parental preference for a particular school for a child without identifying and considering any religious convictions underlying that preference.

particular religious group does not rule out their choosing non-denominational schools for their children.[71] Some parents who are members of religious or ethnic minority groups may even decide to send their children to non-denominational maintained schools, in the hope that they will thereby learn society's shared values and traditions and develop a respect for the beliefs of others. The law against racial discrimination, reinforced by the provisions of the ECHR,[72] will protect minority children from unjustifiable requirements relating to school dress.[73] But some parents may be deterred from using the state system, not only by the lack of attention given by some schools to the beliefs and customs of the broad spectrum of religious and ethnic groups in the country, but also by the law's emphasis on Christian ideals.

One might argue that the education legislation is extremely outdated in its approach to the religious ethos of the country. Despite falling church rolls,[74] it obliges all maintained schools to promote the Christian religion, through a daily act of collective worship and by providing religious instruction in class. Whilst maintaining parents' legal right to withdraw their children from both activities,[75] the Education Reform Act 1988 reflected a deliberate desire to increase the Christian content of religious education in all state schools. It thereby reversed the practice of many schools to adopt a multi-faith approach, rather than concentrating on any one religion.[76] In relation to the act of collective worship,[77] the 1988 Act retained the need for every state school to arrange a daily assembly of pupils, but it was now to be 'wholly or mainly of a broadly Christian character'.[78] Although schools are entitled to interpret the 'broadly Christian' requirement quite loosely, to enable pupils of a non-Christian background to take part,[79] the act of corporate worship must contain some elements which can be related specifically to the traditions of Christian belief.[80]

---

71   But although some parents deliberately choose a denominational school not catering for their own faith because of it reputedly offers an excellent secular education, their faith may exclude their obtaining a place. See *Choudhury v Governors of Bishop Challoner Roman Catholic Comprehensive School* [1992] 3 All ER 277: per House of Lords, an over-subscribed Roman Catholic maintained school was entitled to apply an admissions policy using religious criteria and reject the applications of a Muslim parent and a Hindu parent for places for their daughters.

72   Eg arts 9 and 10 (freedom of religion and expression).

73   In *Mandla v Dowell Lee* [1983] 1 All ER 1062 the House of Lords ruled that it had amounted to unlawful discrimination under the Race Relations Act 1976 for a headmaster to refuse to admit a Sikh boy to the school, due only to the boy's insistence on wearing a turban.

74   Although in 2000, 55% of the population claimed to be Christian and a further 5% to belong to other faiths, half the adults aged over 18 had never attended a religious service. See Office for National Statistics (2002) p 220 and Table 13.19.

75   See School Standards and Framework Act 1998 (hereafter SSFA 1998), s 71(1), which gives parents the right to withdraw their children from receiving religious education and attending religious worship in school. See discussion below.

76   See C Hamilton (1995) pp 271–309, for a discussion of the background to the changes introduced by the Education Reform 1988.

77   See C Hamilton and B Watt (1996).

78   SSFA 1998, s 70 and Sch 20, para 3(2). Not *every* act of worship need comply with this requirement, providing that, taking any term as a whole, *most* do: Sch 20, para 3(4).

79   See *R v Secretary of State for Education, ex p R and D* [1994] ELR 495, esp at 501.

80   The headteacher of a school containing large numbers of non-Christian pupils may apply to the local Standing Council on Religious Education (SACRE) for permission to avoid the requirements of the legislation altogether or to provide a form of collective worship more appropriate to the pupils' family backgrounds. See SSFA 1998, Sch 20, para 4(1) and Education Act 1996, s 394.

The same features are present in the legal principles governing provision of religious education, which must be provided by all state-maintained schools.[81] As in the case of the provisions governing collective worship, the legislation shows a determination to include a clear religious ideology in the subject's content.[82] The provisions of the 1988 Act, surviving re-enactment, attempt to ensure that Christianity predominates, specifying that every agreed syllabus –

'shall reflect the fact that the religious traditions in Great Britain are in the main Christian whilst taking account of the teaching and practices of the other principal religions represented in Great Britain.'[83]

The objectives of that legislation may now seem anachronistic to a society which has perhaps, since the 1980s, become a little more tolerant of differences in faith and culture. These attitudinal changes appear to have produced extreme confusion over the required content of religious education classes in the maintained sector – so much so that the legislative intentions of the 1988 Act have been diluted. Indeed, the guidance given to Ofsted inspectors of religious education programmes at secondary level reflects a degree of uncertainty as to what form religious education should be taking in this country. This is surprising, given that Ofsted school assessments have considerable influence on the methods adopted by teachers up and down the country. The official guidance given to those conducting Ofsted inspections of religious education in primary schools correctly interprets the legislation on the required aims of religious education, indicating that inspectors should expect to see an emphasis on Christianity.[84] By contrast, the guidance to secondary school inspectors misleadingly states that whilst the provision of collective worship must be 'wholly or mainly of a Christian character', *'this is not the requirement for RE'*.[85] Such an interpretation distorts the legislative formula set out above. Indeed, the guidance appears to consider that a multi-faith approach should be demonstrated by teachers of religious education in secondary schools. Presumably to this end, inspectors are directed to focus on pupils' ability to, inter alia:

'demonstrate knowledge and understanding of religions and of what is distinctive to each, and explain in some depth what it means to be, for example, a Christian, a Muslim, or a Hindu; understand what religions have in common, how and why they differ ...; understand about faith communities and their teachings, and evaluate their contribution to personal, local, national and international life; ...'[86]

Despite misinterpreting the law, the religious education of the nature promoted by Ofsted at a secondary level may reflect the nature of our multi-cultural and multi-faith society far better than that intended by the draftsmen of the Education Reform Act 1988. It undoubtedly furthers the objectives of article 29(1)(d) of the CRC, which requires a child's education to prepare him or her for 'responsible life in a free

---

81 Education Act 2002, s 80 and SSFA 1998, s 69(1). It is therefore a compulsory subject, though the parent has a right to withdraw his or her child. But because it is not included in the National Curriculum, it is not subject to national assessment.
82 See C Hamilton (1995) pp 298–300.
83 See now Education Act 1996, s 375(3). See also DFE (1994).
84 See Ofsted (2001 c), which advises (p 54) inspectors of religious education to focus on the pupils' 'knowledge and awareness that the religious traditions in the United Kingdom are mainly Christian although other principal religions are represented'.
85 See Ofsted (2001 d) Annex 2. Emphasis supplied.
86 Ofsted (2001 d) p 9.

society, in the spirit of understanding ... among all peoples, ethnic, national and religious groups and persons of indigenous origin'. Nevertheless, the multi-faith approach to the teaching of religious education encouraged by Ofsted in secondary schools, obviously requires careful planning and a degree of skill and training. Government inspection data suggests that these qualities may not always be available and that, despite improvements, '[P]upils' achievements in religious education (RE) remain disappointingly low', with the quality of RE teaching still falling below that in other subjects.[87] The syllabus sometimes lacks continuity, with teaching moving from one faith to another, making it 'difficult for pupils to establish a firm basis of knowledge, let alone to develop their conceptual understanding of religions or religious ideas'.[88] Furthermore, due to a severe lack of specialist religious education staff, the subject is being taught by 'unwilling non-specialists' resulting in 'low expectations, lack of pupil involvement, and unexciting and undemanding work ...'.[89] What appears to be a relatively confused and unsuccessful approach to religious education suggests that the legislation and policy underpinning it requires radical revision. Once a formal multi-faith approach has been officially sanctioned by new legislation, a new syllabus could be designed which imposes realistic expectations on teachers and pupils alike.

A more fundamental objection to the education law in this field is the way that it wholly identifies parents' right to religious freedom with that of their children. The education legislation attempts to maintain an uneasy balance between contributing to children's social and moral development through religious instruction, whilst acknowledging parents' freedom to exempt their children from any religious indoctrination. Consequently, the law requiring schools to hold an act of collective worship and to provide religious instruction gives parents the right to withdraw their children from both.[90] The ECHR case law contains little to persuade the British government that the parental right of exemption is too adult-focused. Admittedly, religious education which is delivered in an objective, critical and pluralistic manner and makes no attempt to indoctrinate pupils does not infringe parents' or children's rights under article 9.[91] But the case law suggests that unless parents can exempt their child from such classes, their rights under article 2 of the First Protocol would be infringed.[92] The Strasbourg institutions have not considered what rights, if any, children might have if they disagreed with their parents regarding any decisions over religion. Indeed, the case law interpreting article 2 of Protocol 1 is not about children's rights under the ECHR, but about parents' rights.[93] It asserts that it is wrong to indoctrinate children because *parents* have the right to bring up their children as they think fit, free from state interference. This approach rests on the assumption that although the state must not indoctrinate children, their parents can.

87   Ofsted (2002) pp 1–2.
88   Ofsted (2002) pp 1-9. See also Ofsted (2001 d), which notes (p 3) that, despite improvements (p 1), there is an enormous variation in syllabuses (their being determined locally), with many adopting such a disjointed curriculum that pupils' contact with any religion except Christianity is 'highly fragmented' (p 4), resulting in long-term confusion and lack of retention.
89   Ofsted (2002) p 3.
90   See SSFA 1998, s 71(1).
91   See *Angelini v Sweden* (1988) 10 EHRR 123. In reaching this conclusion, the European Commission of Human Rights followed the European Court's approach regarding the provision of compulsory sex education in schools in *Kjeldsen, Busk Madsen and Pedersen v Denmark* (1976) 1 EHRR 711 (para 53).
92   See discussion by U Kilkelly (1999) pp 72–73.
93   See chapter 2, for a more detailed discussion of children's rights under the ECHR. See chapter 6 for a more detailed discussion of the treatment of sex education.

By maintaining parents' entitlement to withdraw their children from religious education, our education legislation ignores the fact that children should be encouraged to make up their own minds on such matters. Indeed, it implicitly suggests to children that their own views are unimportant. Withdrawing children from school activities participated in by the majority, potentially marginalises them from their contemporaries and makes them feel different. By entitling parents to withdraw them with no explanation, the law reinforces parents' perceptions that they have a right to dictate religious matters to their children.[94] There is also a greater risk of their children becoming forced further into the confines of the family and their parents' beliefs. Since decisions about a child's religious education could be described as 'a major decision' involving a parent fulfilling his parental responsibility for his child, it is arguable that Scottish parents are obliged to consult their children over such matters and that they should give particular credence to the views of those over the age of 12.[95] English law should be changed enabling children over the age of 12 to reach their own decisions about collective worship and religious education. Such a change would reflect a more realistic and liberal view of children's capacity for choice and their own ability to think seriously and responsibly about their own beliefs and values.

(4) CONCLUSION

The methods adopted by the state in maintaining the balance between parents' rights and children's rights should always be exercised with sensitivity. The law must respect the right of minority groups to run separate schools which instruct their children on their culture and traditions. But although aggressive interference with their educational methods can very easily be seen as religious persecution, minority children are entitled to equality of educational opportunity; indeed, to an education which broadens their horizons, rather than narrowing their potential. Doubt over what stance is appropriate should always be resolved in favour of promoting children's rights rather than those of their parents.

The same sensitive balance has to be found regarding the provision of collective worship and religious education in schools. The present law gives the overall impression of being particularly adult-centred. The legislative reforms introduced in 1988 reflected the aims of a government convinced of the value of all children gaining a knowledge of the Christian faith. By maintaining such an approach, alongside a parental right to withdraw their children from any Christian activities, the government risks minority children being deprived of the opportunity to compare their parents' faith with those of others and develop their capacity for independent and critical thought. But in this respect, as in so many other aspects of education law, parents' interests are implicitly assumed to be identical to those of their children. In other words, the law effectively ignores the child's own right to religious freedom.

94 See C Hamilton (1995) pp 303–309.
95 See Children (Scotland) Act 1995, s 6(1), discussed in chapter 3, pp 79–80.

BIBLIOGRAPHY

NB many of these publications can be obtained on the relevant organisation's website.

Bradney A, 'Separate Schools and Ethnic Minorities and the Law' (1987) 13 New Community 412.

Bradley A, 'Scope for Review: The Convention Right to Education and the Human Rights Act 1998' (1999) 4 European Human Rights Law Review 395.

Cullen H, 'Education Rights or Minority Rights?' (1993) 7 International Journal of Law and the Family 143.

Department for Education (DFE), *Religious Education and Collective Worship* DFE Circular 1/94 (1994).

Department for Education and Skills (DfES), White Paper *Schools: Achieving Success* Cm 5230 (2001) DfES.

Gillborn D and Mirza H, *Educational Inequality: Mapping Race, Class and Gender* (2000) Ofsted.

Hamilton C, *Family, Law and Religion* (1995) Sweet and Maxwell.

Hamilton C and Watt B, 'A discriminating education – collective worship in schools' (1996) 8 Child and Family Law Quarterly 28.

Hodgkin R and Newell P, *Implementation Handbook for the Convention on the Rights of the Child* (1998) Unicef.

Kilkelly U, *The Child and the European Convention on Human Rights* (1999) Ashgate.

Macpherson W, (Chairman) *The Stephen Lawrence Inquiry* (1999) Cm 4262-I (1999) The Stationery Office.

Office for National Statistics, *Social Trends No 32* (2002) The Stationery Office.

Office for Standards in Education (Ofsted), *Raising the attainment of minority ethnic pupils* HMI 170 (1999) Ofsted.

Office for Standards in Education (Ofsted), *Managing Support for the Attainment of Pupils from Minority Ethnic Groups* (2001 a).

Office for Standards in Education (Ofsted), *Independent school HMI report on the Talmud Torah Yetev Lev School* (2001 b).

Office for Standards in Education (Ofsted), *Inspecting Subjects 3–11: Guidance to OFSTED subject inspectors* (2001 c).

Office for Standards in Education (Ofsted), *Inspecting Religious Education 11–16 with guidance on self-evaluation* (2001 d).

Office for Standards in Education (Ofsted), *Primary Subject Reports 2000/01, Religious Education*, HMI 366 (2001 e).

Office for Standards in Education (Ofsted), *Secondary Subject Reports 2000/01: Religious Education* HMI 375, a report from Her Majesty's Chief Inspector of Schools in England (2002) ,Ofsted.

Poulter S, *Ethnicity, Law and Human Rights: The English Experience* (1998) Oxford University Press.

Social Exclusion Unit, *Bridging the Gap: New Opportunities for 16–18 Year Olds Not in Education, Employment or Training* (*Bridging the Gap*) (1999).

Swann M (Chairman), *Education for All* Report of the Committee of Inquiry into the Education of Children from Ethnic Minority Groups Cmnd 9453 (1985).

Thornberry P, *International Law and the Rights of Minorities* (1991) Clarendon Press.

Van Bueren G, *The International Law on the Rights of the Child* (1995) Martinus Nijhoff Publishers.

Chapter 12

Educational rights for children with disabilities

(1) INTRODUCTION

It is notoriously difficult to obtain accurate statistics on the prevalence and patterns of childhood disability in the United Kingdom.[1] Those currently collected serve very different purposes.[2] Furthermore, any statistics on disability are undermined by a lack of agreement over definitions of disability or even a common language amongst the agencies working with children in various capacities.[3] Such differences in approach will inevitably influence any statistics collected.[4] In any event, official figures will always be incomplete since there is probably a high incidence of undetected childhood disabilities of various kinds.[5] Whatever their true level, the range of childhood disabilities is considerable, but the extent to which they hamper children from being able to benefit from educational provision varies. On the one hand, a physically handicapped child may be extremely able intellectually, but have difficulty negotiating the stairs and corridors of a local mainstream school. On the other hand, a physically strong and fit child may have severe learning difficulties. Some children suffer a multiplicity of disabilities, with behavioural disorders accompanying physical disabilities. For all of them, education is a fundamental necessity.

As the Warnock Committee stressed, even the most severely disabled children have a right to be educated, for 'education as we conceive it, is a good, and a

---

[1] The most detailed analysis of disability was carried out by the Office of Population Censuses and Surveys in the late 1980s. See OPCS (1989) esp Report 3. See also D Gordon et al (2000) summarised in SSI (1998 a) ch 3.

[2] See, inter alia, the annual Children in Need census (CiN) compiled by the Department of Health. But these statistics are confined to disabled children in need who are in receipt of services – see DH (2001 b) ch 6 for a detailed analysis. The register of disabled children established and maintained by social services departments under the Children Act 1989, Sch 2, para 2 and their Quality Protects obligations – see DH (1998 a) sub-objective 6.1 – local authorities must 'arrive at a complete picture of the numbers and circumstances of disabled children by sharing information held by SSDs, Health and Education Authorities'.

[3] Particularly regarding children in need of mental health services, see discussion below. For a commentary on the prevalence of mental disorders amongst children aged between 5 and 16, see H Meltzer and R Gatward (2000) ch 4.

[4] See Council for Disabled Children (2000) paras 2.3–3.8, for an extremely critical assessment of local authority practice in complying with their QP obligation to obtain better statistical data on disabled children. This was considered to be attributable, at least in part, to the lack of a common definition of disability used by health, social services and education.

[5] See British Medical Association (1999) pp 98–99.

specifically human good, to which all human beings are entitled'.[6] Indeed, an enlightened education will enable them:

> '... to lead a life very little poorer in quality than that of the non-handicapped child, whereas without this kind of education they might face a life of dependence or even institutionalisation. Education in such cases makes the difference between a proper and enjoyable life and something less than we believe life should be.'[7]

The dual aims of education, being to enlarge the child's knowledge, experience and imaginative understanding and later to enable him or her to enter the world as an active and independent participant in society, clearly apply as much to the disabled as to the unimpaired.[8] It is not only fundamentally important for education law to address these needs, but also to prevent disabled children being marginalised and discriminated against, by reason only of their difference from the unimpaired. As the Warnock Report so clearly perceived, providing education is far more than merely filling children with information, irrespective of their surroundings. A strengthening commitment to the human rights of all disabled people, regardless of age, has reinforced a growing international acceptance[9] of the concept of 'inclusion' in education.[10] Those embracing inclusion reject the practice of isolating disabled children from the rest of the community through their education and assert their right to attend, as far as possible, mainstream schools.[11] In so doing, they can socialise with their non-disabled peers and participate in the whole range of opportunities and activities provided by the school for all its pupils.

The need to avoid marginalising children with mental or physical disabilities is recognised, at least up to a point, by international human rights law. Thus article 2 of the First Protocol of the ECHR, in conjunction with freedom from discrimination under article 14, ensures a right to an effective education.[12] Nevertheless, these provisions lack the ability to deliver educational resources to disabled children.[13] The more child-focused CRC recognises 'the right of the child to education',[14] and also requires governments to respect the rights of every child 'without discrimination of any kind, irrespective of the child's or his or her parent's or legal guardian's race, colour, sex ... disability, birth or other status'.[15] Furthermore, article 23(1) secures the

---

6   H M Warnock (1978) para 1.7.
7   H M Warnock (1978) para 1.8.
8   H M Warnock (1978) para 1.4.
9   Various international organisations are involved in the 'inclusion' movement, especially UNESCO. Its World Conference on Special Needs Education in Salamanca in 1994 produced the Salamanca Declaration and Framework for Action. This calls for an international commitment to inclusive education and for governments to give policy and budgetary priority to improving their education systems to render them accessible to children. See P Mittler (2000) ch 2.
10 There is voluminous literature about the concept of 'inclusion' which requires mainstream schools to adapt to the pupil cf the concept of 'integration', which expects such pupils to adapt to mainstream schools. See, inter alia, G Thomas et al (1998) ch 1 and P Mittler (2000) ch 1, esp p 10.
11 Despite inclusion being widely adopted, the terminology has differed. The term 'mainstreaming' has been used in the USA, 'normalisation' in Scandinavia and Canada. For an assessment of the international 'inclusive schooling movement', see J Jenkinson (1997) chs 1–3.
12 *Belgian Linguistics Case (No 2)* (1968) 1 EHRR 252.
13 Discussed below.
14 Art 28(1).
15 Art 2(1).

right of a mentally or physically disabled child 'to enjoy a full and decent life, in conditions which ensure dignity, promote self-reliance, and facilitate the child's active participation in the community'. More particularly, in the context of education, article 23(3) requires the disabled child to have effective access to –

> 'education, training, health care services, rehabilitation services, preparation for employment and recreation opportunities in a manner conducive to the child's achieving the fullest possible social integration and individual development, including his or her cultural and spiritual development.'

Article 28, which deals with a child's basic right to education, directs that it should be achieved 'on the basis of equal opportunity'. But, as Freeman points out, these articles contain no specific reference to the disabled child's right to be educated alongside his or her peers in a mainstream school, the concept of inclusion.[16] Despite this omission, the Committee on the Rights of the Child has stressed the need for states to recognise disabled children's rights to inclusion and to include in their reports to the Committee, information on how this goal is being fulfilled.[17]

On a domestic front, the notion of inclusion is not a new one,[18] and, as discussed below, the current legislation promotes it forcefully. Nevertheless, statistics indicate that despite official encouragement, the educational and employment prospects of disabled children and young people are relatively very poor. Children with disabilities report a variety of difficulties at mainstream schools, such as physical barriers to accessing educational facilities and low teacher expectations for them.[19] Statistics indicate that the rate of permanent exclusion for children with statements of special educational needs was, in 1999/2000, seven times higher than that for children without statements,[20] and that these children are far more likely than others to leave school with no qualifications.[21] About two fifths of disabled people of working age have no educational qualifications, compared with under one fifth of the non-disabled, with unemployment rates amongst disabled people being two and a half times higher than non-disabled.[22] Furthermore, 25% of the 18-year-olds with a health or disability problem surveyed in 1998, were either out of work, looking after home or family or 'doing something else', compared with only 12% of those with no such problems.[23]

These figures paint a gloomy picture of the educational plight of children with disabilities. Nonetheless, it must be acknowledged that the government has, in recent years, made considerable efforts to promote the right of disabled adults and children[24]

16   M Freeman (2000) p 283.
17   See R Hodgkin and P Newell (1998) pp 306–307.
18   The Education Act 1944, s 33(2) provided for less severely handicapped children to be catered for in mainstream schools.
19   See SEU (1999) para 6. 21.
20   See DfES (2001 b) Table 7. By 2000/01, the overall number of permanently excluded children with SEN statements had dropped to only three times higher than that for other children. Despite this apparently dramatic improvement, the DfES indicates that due to changes in the underlying data collection, these latest figures may not 'be directly comparable with those for earlier years'. See DfES (2002 b) p 18.
21   See SEU (1999) para 6.19.
22   Of those reporting a disability or health problem, 11% were not in education, employment or training in Spring 1998, following completion of schooling, compared with 6% of those not reporting such problems. See SEU (1999) para 6.20.
23   SEU (1999) para 6.20.
24   See Children Act 1989, Sch 2, para 6, which requires social services departments to provide services to minimise the effect of disabled children's disabilities and give them the opportunity to live lives 'as normal as possible'. For a general appraisal of the law relating to disabled children, see J Read and L Clements (2001).

to participate fully in society and to access appropriate services[25] – thereby giving them the right to do 'those ordinary things' like going to the swimming pool or cinema.[26] Changes in education law reflect these efforts; notably, disabled pupils have recently been brought under the protection of the disability discrimination legislation.[27] The following chapter assesses first the development of ideas about equal access to education, free from discrimination, as applied to children with 'special educational needs' or SEN.[28] It then proceeds to consider three specific areas where particular problems currently arise in promoting their rights to an appropriate and fulfilling education.[29] The first relates to children's need for their learning difficulties to be identified and diagnosed as early and accurately as possible. The second involves their right to be educated in mainstream schools alongside their unimpaired colleagues. The third relates to maintaining a balance between involving parents of children with learning difficulties in their children's educational provision and recognising the individuality and independence of their children.

(2)   EQUAL ACCESS TO EDUCATION FREE FROM DISCRIMINATION

(A)   A new approach

The Warnock Committee was intent on preventing children's educational needs being determined by virtue of their disability or disorder, rather than by virtue of their special educational needs. Its report pointed out that there were many children, indeed, as many as one in five, who might, at some time in their educational careers, need special educational provision due to learning difficulties and it assumed that much of this could be provided within mainstream schools.[30] It was therefore not appropriate or even necessary to distinguish between the 'handicapped and non-handicapped'.[31] Careful and specialised assessments might disclose that in a small category of these cases there would be severe and complex needs requiring much longer-term support, documented by a record or 'statement' of special educational needs, recording the local education authorities' (LEAs) special obligations towards that child. Whichever was the case, children with special educational needs should not be marginalised and

25   See, inter alia: the Disability and Discrimination Act 1995 (hereafter DDA 1995), gives disabled people the right to a range of services and protection from discrimination in employment; the Disability Rights Commission established under the Disability Rights Commission Act 1999 to work towards eliminating discrimination against disabled persons and to promote equality of opportunities for such persons; the Valuing People programme established (as recommended by the White Paper, DH (2001 a)) inter alia, to promote the rights of those with learning disabilities; see also the Learning Disability Development Fund and the Learning Disability Task Force.

26   See DH (2001 a) para 2.2.

27   The DDA 1995 was extended to every aspect of education by Pt 2 of the Special Educational Needs and Disability Act 2001 (hereafter SENDA 2001). See discussion below.

28   Now governed by the Education Act 1996 (hereafter EA 1996), Pt IV. For a more detailed assessment of the law relating to children with special educational needs, see, inter alia: J Ford, M Hughes and D Ruebain (1999) ch 9; N Harris (1997) pp 6–13 and ch 10; and N Harris (2002).

29   NB some disabled pupils have no special educational needs (thereby falling outside the SEN framework, but within the protection of the DDA 1995). This chapter concentrates on those with SEN, by virtue of their disabilities affecting their access to education, either through mental or physical impairment. For a detailed assessment of the SENDA 2001, see A Blair and A Lawson (2003).

30   Warnock Report (1978) para 3.17.

31   Warnock Report (1978) para 3.6.

every effort possible should be made to ensure that they be educated in ordinary mainstream schools, rather than in special schools. Furthermore, parents should be brought into partnership with those seeking to ensure that their children's educational needs were met.

The Warnock Report was enormously influential. The Education Act 1981 implemented many of its recommendations and introduced a fundamentally new approach. It was intent on ensuring that disabled children should not be singled out by their handicaps but assessed simply as children requiring education. Moreover by using non-stigmatising terms such as 'learning difficulties' and 'special educational needs', it made it clear that these children were no different from any other. The Education Act 1981 contained certain fundamental objectives.[32] These were that all children with learning difficulties would have their educational needs fully assessed; that they would be provided with extra educational support; that the majority would be educated in ordinary schools; that parents' views would be taken into account by LEAs when assessing their children's needs; that pupils with statements[33] would be subject to regular review.

(B)   Difficulties of interpretation

Although the philosophy underpinning the Education Act 1981 has stood the test of time, the methods adopted for achieving its aims needed considerable adjustment. Numerous difficulties were experienced by those using the legislation, namely LEAs, schools and parents alike.[34] Indeed, many continue to cause problems today. The Warnock Committee had envisaged that there would be a distinction between two groups of children. It was central to its thinking that the majority of SEN children would only require special educational provision for short periods, at various stages of their school career and that there should be flexibility within mainstream education to provide for their needs quickly.[35] This first category encompasses the majority of children whose needs can be determined and met by ordinary schools, without specialised help from the LEA. The second group, the minority,[36] have exceptional needs, beyond the skills or resources of mainstream schools, at least without additional help from the LEA. The LEAs are under a clear duty to identify the latter group of children and take responsibility for fulfilling their educational needs, having assessed and recorded them in a statement. Nevertheless, under the original legislative scheme, there was no adequate guidance to LEAs and schools over the division between their respective duties towards the two groups of children in question. Consequently, it was not clear what level of need schools could be expected to meet, before reaching the point at which the LEA was obliged to take over the responsibility for the child's education by issuing a statement.[37]

---

32   Summarised in Audit Commission and HMI (1992) pp 51–52.
33   Ie records documenting the LEA's assessment of the child's needs and its obligations to meet them.
34   Summarised in Audit Commission and HMI (1992) pp 51–65.
35   See H M Warnock (1978) paras 3.16–3.17.
36   Warnock expected the first group to number approximately 2% of the school population and the second, 20%. These were underestimates, with both groups turning out to be larger: see DfES (2001 a).
37   Audit Commission and HMI (1992) pp 13–16.

Matters were improved somewhat by later legislation and guidance. Although this did not clarify the circuitous definition of the term 'special educational needs',[38] it ironed out some of the difficulties implicit in the scheme envisaged by Warnock. For example, a code of practice now provides clear guidance explaining the fundamental principles of the legislation and its practical application.[39] The assessment and statementing procedure was improved, together with the introduction of a vastly improved appeals procedure,[40] enabling parents to appeal against most aspects of the statementing process to an independent tribunal, the Special Educational Needs and Disability Tribunal (SENDIST).[41]

Though welcome, none of these changes addressed the considerable doubt over the threshold of need that warrants the issuing of a statement. The duty of LEAs to intervene with detailed arrangements for the educational needs of a child with learning difficulties remains a completely discretionary one.[42] Consequently, the distinction between the two categories of children with special educational needs, as described above, remains a fundamental feature of the SEN system.[43] The official guidance certainly provides useful pointers and suggests that, when deciding whether it is necessary to statutorily assess a child, LEAs should consider the child's particular requirements and whether these can be met from existing resources in mainstream maintained schools, through school-based intervention.[44] Similarly, an LEA should draw up a statement 'when it considers that the special educational provision necessary to meet the child's needs cannot reasonably be provided within the resources normally available to mainstream schools ...'[45] But, as case law confirms, LEAs remain free to determine for themselves the extent to which schools have sufficient funding and teaching skills to provide for the educational needs of children with learning difficulties, without extra assistance out of LEA funds, through the statementing process.[46]

---

38   See EA 1996, s 312(1) and (2):
   '(1) A child is deemed to have 'special educational needs' if he 'has a learning difficulty which calls for special educational provision to be made for him'. He is deemed to have a 'learning difficulty' 'if: (2)(a) he has a significantly greater difficulty in learning than the majority of children of his age, (b) he has a disability which either prevents or hinders him from making use of educational facilities of a kind generally provided for children of his age in schools within the area of the local education authority, or (c) he is under the age of five and is, or would be if special educational provision were not made for him, likely to fall within paragraph (a) or (b) when of or over that age.'
39   DfES (2001 c) (hereafter *SEN Code of Practice*) replacing DFE (1994).
40   See discussion below.
41   The Special Educational Needs Tribunal (SENT) was renamed when its jurisdiction was extended to include jurisdiction over complaints of disability discrimination by schools and LEAs. See SENDA 2001, Sch 8, para 2. The history of the Special Educational Needs Tribunal is discussed by N Harris (1997) ch 2.
42   This discretion survived the amendments of the Education Act 1993. Under EA 1996, ss 329 and 329A the LEA need only statutorily assess a child if it is 'necessary' so to do. Similarly under EA 1996, s 324, the LEA need only make and maintain a statement if it is 'necessary' so to do.
43   See L Lundy (1998) pp 40–44.
44   See *SEN Code of Practice*, para 7.54.
45   *SEN Code of Practice*, para 8.2. Chapter 8 of the code provides detailed guidance on when a statement should be made.
46   Eg *R v Secretary of State for Education and Science, ex p Lashford* [1988] 1 FLR 72 and *R v Isle of Wight County Council, ex p RS; R v Isle of Wight County Council, ex p AS* [1993] 1 FLR 634 (discretion over whether to draw up a statement). See also *H v Kent County Council and the Special Educational Needs Tribunal* [2000] ELR 660 (discretion over whether to statutorily assess a child).

From the inception of the Warnock scheme, there were very large variations in the extent to which LEAs statemented children[47] and these continue.[48] Parents will inevitably see an inequity in the fact that in some areas pupils with lesser needs receive extra help, while those in their own, with greater needs do not. Indeed, although statements are often seen by parents as the only gateway to the resources needed by the child, some LEAs may refuse to assess or statement a child, in order to avoid the financial consequences of doing so, with the legality of this practice being unclear.[49] Parents may find that they are caught in a buck-passing exercise between the LEA and the local mainstream school. Mainstream schools receive funds to meet special needs and LEAs may therefore refuse to statutorily assess or statement a child for this reason, considering that the local school has sufficient funds to provide for his or her needs.[50] But these funds are not ring-fenced or earmarked to the specific child; nor is there sufficient supervision of how they are spent.[51] Furthermore, the governors of the school which the child attends are merely required only to 'use their best endeavours, ... to secure that, if any registered pupil has special educational needs, the special educational provision which his learning difficulty calls for is made'.[52] Consequently although parents may claim that their child's needs are not being met by the local school, the LEA may still refuse to accept responsibility through the statementing process. Parents whose child is without a statement also find that no formal procedure exists whereby they can challenge a school for failing to follow LEA advice[53] over how to meet their child's educational needs,[54] or for failing to design an effective programme of measures to address his or her problem.[55]

Challenging an LEA or school for failing to address a child's learning difficulties adequately is no easy task. The complicated requirements of the law of tort make actions in negligence problematic[56] and judicial review applications are expensive

---

47 See DfEE (1997) pp 38–39.
48 See Audit Commission (2002 a) pp 26–30, discussing the considerable variations in statementing practice amongst LEAs, ranging from 1% of pupils to 5%.
49 See M Richards (1998), J Robinson (1998) and D Ruebain (1999). These authors discuss the impact of *R v East Sussex County Council, ex p Tandy* [1998] 2 All ER 769 and *R v Gloucestershire County Council and another, ex p Barry* [1997] 2 All ER 1, on SEN law.
50 Audit Commission (2002 b) para 89.
51 There is often poor overall control of the money spent on SEN pupils with in-school provision, with schools receiving delegated SEN funds from the LEA. See, inter alia: Ofsted (2002) paras 9, 15, 29 and 32; J Marks (2000) pp 17–20; M McLaughlin and M Rouse (2000) pp 173–174. Per Audit Commission (2002 b) (para 13) the overall cost of providing for the needs of SEN children is becoming considerable. Local authorities in England and Wales spent £3.6bn on SEN provision in 2001/2.
52 EA 1996, s 317(1)(a).
53 The LEA may accompany its formal refusal to statement a child with a 'note in lieu' explaining the reasons for its decision and setting out suitable strategies which might be taken by the school to meet the child's needs. See *SEN Code of Practice*, paras 8.15–8.20. Sometimes the note in lieu is not particularly detailed or specific. Eg *O v London Borough of Harrow and Sherwin* [2001] EWCA Civ 2046, [2002] ELR 195: the SENT allowed the parents' appeal against the LEA's refusal to statement their child, largely because the note in lieu was inadequate.
54 They might raise with the Secretary of State, under EA 1996, s 496, the LEA or school's failure to perform their statutory duties. The lack of accountability regarding unstatemented children is discussed by L Lundy (1998) esp pp 47–49.
55 Such a school-based programme should be drawn up by the school's special educational needs co-ordinator (SENCO) in the form of an individual education plan (IEP). The plan, inter alia, sets out the pupil's short-term targets, the teaching strategies to be followed and the provision to be made. See *SEN Code of Practice*, paras 6.58–6.60.
56 Discussed below.

and cumbersome. The SEN appeal process is infinitely preferable[57] and statistics show that parents are reasonably successful when they use it.[58] Nevertheless, it too carries difficulties. Only if the child's needs are beyond the resources 'normally available in ordinary schools in the area',[59] do parents have a good basis for appealing to the SENDIST against the LEA's refusal to assess the child's needs or to draw up a statement. Furthermore, a challenge under the Human Rights Act 1998 is unlikely to improve their chances. The case law interpreting article 2 of the First Protocol of the ECHR suggests that, as long as a child is not being entirely denied 'effective' education, detailed operational decisions over how it is delivered, within the resources available, are within the discretion of the state's educational authorities.[60]

Meanwhile, the government disapproves of large numbers of SEN children being statemented unnecessarily, when their needs are not complex and are well within the scope of school-based intervention.[61] Not only is the statementing process enormously expensive, but it also carries risks, including extreme delays in producing additional resources, a sometimes unnecessary 'labelling' of the child and enormous stress for parents.[62] The government considers that LEAs should promote parents' confidence in the ability of mainstream schools to provide effectively for this larger group of SEN children without statements. Furthermore, alarmed at the rising number of appeals going to the SENDIST,[63] it has established a new informal dispute resolution procedure, serviced by LEAs.[64] This is intended to defuse disagreements over statementing and other SEN issues, before parents resort to the SENDIST. Nevertheless, it is surely over-optimistic to expect parents to feel more confident with SEN provision for unstatemented children. In Ofsted's view:

> 'Schools cannot be held accountable for provision when it is unclear to them that they have the necessary resources, or where there is good reason to doubt that the resources are adequate.'[65]

Few schools or LEAs are even particularly clear what difference their provision makes to the attainment and progress of SEN pupils, with inadequate or no monitoring

---

57   See *O v London Borough of Harrow and Sherwin* [2001] EWCA Civ 2046, [2002] ELR 195 at [19], per Simon Brown LJ, stating that parents should not be forced to use judicial review, if appealing to the SENT is possible instead.

58   See DfEE (2001 a) p 8. Currently 67% of appeals against refusal to assess a child (these appeals constitute 31.8% of the total) and 70% of appeals against refusal to make a statement (these appeals constitute 8.4% of the total) are upheld.

59   *R v Secretary of State for Education and Science, ex p Lashford* [1988] 1 FLR 72 at 78, per Dillon J.

60   See *Belgian Linguistics Case (No 2)* (1968) 1 EHRR 252, *Simpson v United Kingdom* (Application No 14688/89) (1989) 64 DR 188 and other case law discussed by U Kilkelly (1999) pp 68–69 and 80–81. See *H v Kent County Council and the Special Educational Needs Tribunal* [2000] ELR 660 at 672, per Grigson J who, applying this case law, rejected a parents' claim that the LEA's refusal to assess a child was a breach of his rights under art 2 of Protocol 1 of the ECHR.

61   See DfEE (1997) esp p 36. Numbers of children being statemented steadily increased from 1994, but the number of those being statemented for the first time has just begun to fall. See DfES (2002 a) Schools, section 3.5.

62   See Audit Commission (2002 a) paras 58–63.

63   See DfEE (2001 a) p 6. The number of appeals received annually by the Special Educational Needs Tribunal doubled between 1994 (when it was established) and 2000/01.

64   LEAs must establish parent partnership services which ensure that parents receive suitable information about their children's special educational needs and have access to an 'Independent Parental Supporter', to act as a facilitator in resolving disagreements between parents and LEAs. See *SEN Code of Practice*, paras 2.16–2.30 and EA 1996, s 332A and B.

65   Ofsted (2002) para 32.

mechanisms in place.[66] Indeed, parental confidence might seem absurd whilst education law condones the confused division of responsibilities between schools and LEAs and when there is so little accountability for the use of SEN funds throughout the system.

(3) EARLY DIAGNOSIS

(A) No common approach

Children with learning difficulties will suffer unnecessarily if they are forced to cope with an educational system that takes little account of their problems. Inattentiveness and general disruption in the class, all problems with which mainstream schools are becoming increasingly familiar,[67] may stem from pupils' learning difficulties. Indeed, SEN children have a high risk of being excluded for their bad behaviour,[68] especially those with 'emotional and behavioural difficulties' (EBD). Government guidance recognises this and stresses that pupils' special educational needs should be identified and diagnosed as soon as possible, so that they can be dealt with effectively.[69] Indeed, LEAs are under a legal duty to identify a SEN child[70] for whom they are responsible.[71] Nevertheless, the special educational needs which often underlie a child's more obvious problems, such as being the victim of bullying, may remain undetected by some schools and LEAs.[72] A mid-1990s Ofsted report indicated that schools were particularly poor at detecting disruptive pupils' underlying problems and were failing to detect reasonably straightforward learning difficulties, such as an inability to read, which might be simpler to remedy with extra help than other problems.[73] By the late 1990s, practice was improving, but patchily, with parents continuing to report lengthy delays in persuading schools of the need for early specialist intervention.[74]

It appears that children with mental health problems are a particularly vulnerable group, in so far as their problems still go unidentified more often than other types of learning difficulties. Matters are exacerbated by practitioners' inability to agree a common approach, with a different terminology being used to describe the young people they are working with. As the Audit Commission points out, whilst a child psychiatrist may categorise certain symptoms in a child as 'conduct disorder',[75] an

---

66 Ofsted (2002) para 15 and Audit Commission (2002 b) paras 104–121.
67 See discussion in chapter 6.
68 See n 20 above.
69 See *SEN Code of Practice*, paras 5.11–5.14, regarding primary school children and paras 6.10–6.13, regarding secondary school children.
70 EA 1996, s 321(1).
71 EA 1996, s 321(3). An LEA is responsible for any SEN child who is already registered at a school in its area, or if the child is over 2 years old and has been brought to the attention of the LEA as having or probably having special educational needs.
72 Eg see *South Gloucestershire Council and The Former Avon County Council* – 99/B/04049 and 00/B/17234, summarised by A Blair (2001) p 233.
73 See Ofsted (1996) p 20. 58 of the 112 pupils whose case-histories were studied had literacy difficulties which were often undetected, detected too late or not deemed sufficiently severe to warrant allocation of scarce additional support.
74 Ofsted (1999) esp paras 46 and 76.
75 A conduct disorder is now the most common of all childhood psychiatric disorders: see H Meltzer and R Gatward (2000) p 33.

educational psychologist seeing the same symptoms in the school room, might describe them as 'emotional and behavioural difficulties', which, if hampering the child from benefiting from education, could also be defined as special educational needs. Meanwhile, a social worker might describe the same child as having 'challenging behaviour', with concerns about his or her 'emotional development'.[76] The Social Exclusion Unit also notes the tendency for these young people to fall through both psychiatric and social work nets, and to be deemed 'troublesome, unmanageable and unhelpful'.[77] The failure to diagnose the learning difficulties of children with mental disorders is particularly regrettable, given the significant relationship between mental health and educational problems. Indeed, research shows that children with mental disorders are five times more likely to have had special educational needs than those without.[78]

(B)   A lack of inter-agency collaboration

Progress towards identifying children who require specialised educational help, diagnosing their difficulties and ensuring that they obtain the support they need has been hampered over the last decade by a lack of effective collaboration between public agencies. The impact of this failure to work together is not confined to education; it affects every aspect of a disabled child's life, and that of his or her family. Parents and children with multiple needs experience considerable difficulty in accessing services from more than one agency, with each agency having different statutory responsibilities. The government recognises this and a plethora of reports and guidance documents urge local agencies, education, social services and health, to co-ordinate the manner in which they identify and remedy the special needs of children with complex problems. Emphasising that the needs of vulnerable groups should not be sacrificed to 'sterile arguments about boundaries',[79] these encourage a far more effective collaboration between agencies.[80] Detailed guidance has been produced over how to improve collaborative practice through 'packages of care' for disabled children, with groups of professionals working together in multi-disciplinary teams, on pooled budgets,[81] with formal directives for putting them into operation.[82] But although a co-ordinated approach is being developed in some areas, particularly in relation to very young children,[83] there appears to be considerable resistance to

76   Audit Commission (1999) p 54.
77   SEU (1999) para 6.24.
78   H Meltzer and R Gatward (2000) para 8.2. These researchers also note (para 8.3) that among children with specific learning difficulties, 22% had a mental disorder.
79   DH (1998 b) p 3.
80   See, inter alia: DH (1998 b) esp ch 4; SSI (1998 a) esp chs 5–7; SSI (1998 b) paras 3.23–3.30 and ch 4; Audit Commission (1999) esp p 78.
81   See, inter alia: DH (1998 b) ch 4; National Children's Bureau (1999) esp ch 3.
82   See, inter alia: DH and DfEE (1996) requires social services departments to produce children's services plans, designed to co-ordinate with planning by other agencies; Health Act 1999, s 31 provides for 'partnership arrangements' between health authorities, NHS trusts, primary care trusts and LAs, involving powers to pool funds and delegate functions between agencies; SSDs are obliged to ensure that all agencies providing services for children and families maximise their resources for doing so through proper planning. See DH (1998 a) sub-objective 8.1.
83   See Council for Disabled Children (2000) ch 5.

joint working and, in many areas, services for disabled children remain very poorly co-ordinated.[84]

In the educational context, the needs of individual children are still sacrificed to inter-agency arguments about funding.[85] Various government reports have recognised the special need for agency co-operation over provision, given the high correlation between home circumstances, educational difficulties and mental disorders. The government's commitment to multi-agency working is particularly emphasised by the special duties imposed on LEAs in relation to EBD children.[86] Although welcome, it is surprising that the legislative emphasis on a multi-agency approach is confined to a particular group of children with special educational needs. In contrast, the SEN Code of Practice emphasises that all children with special educational needs have a range of difficulties requiring 'a concerted approach' from healthcare professionals, social services departments, and other providers of support services. These agencies should provide an integrated service which is perceived by parents and pupils as being 'seamless'.[87] This laudable aim seems far from being realised, with few authorities exploiting their ability to establish pooled budgets,[88] and considerable shortages of health services for SEN children, particularly speech and language therapy.[89] Meanwhile, it is difficult to see how joint working can become more effective whilst the legislative formula enabling LEAs to seek specialised assistance from other service agencies is so weakly phrased.[90] This allows other local agencies to refuse such a request on an ad hoc basis, purely on the grounds of lack of resources,[91] and prevents greater clarity being established in the longer term over the limits to their statutory responsibilities. The Audit Commission recommends that health and social services should 'be held to account for their part in meeting children's SEN' and it acknowledges that this may require a change in the primary legislation.[92]

84　See inter alia: Council for Disabled Children (2000), para 20.2; DH (2001 b) paras 6.35–6.37; DH (2002) para 6.6; Mencap (2000) paras 5.1–5.2. In July 2002, Health Minister, Jacqui Smith, announced plans to pilot new organisational models for the delivery of children's services. Eg 'children's trusts will bring together health, social care and education services, with a view to achieving joint planning, commissioning and financing of children's services. See also HM Treasury (2002) para 28.5.

85　See D Abbott, J Morris and L Ward (2001): decisions over whether disabled children should be sent to special residential schools were often delayed by a lack of inter-agency co-ordination and by inter-agency disagreements, pp 37–42.

86　See EA 1996, s 527A, the Local Education Authority (Behaviour Support Plans) Regulations 1998 (SI 1998/644) and DfEE (1998 a). LEAs are required to establish effective services for all EBD children, having consulted with other agencies over the contributions required to address their needs, and how these are to be co-ordinated, and then publishing the arrangements in the form of behaviour support plans.

87　See *SEN Code of Practice*, para 5.27. See also paras 1.7–1.13, 5.28–5.29 and 6.29–6.31.

88　Audit Commission (2002 b) para 82.

89　Audit Commission (2002 a) paras 46–49.

90　Under EA 1996, s 322(3) LEAs may request the help of other agencies such as health, who should comply unless, in the case of health, 'that authority consider that, having regard to the resources available to them for the purpose of the exercise of their functions ... it is not reasonable for them to comply with the request ...'

91　See eg *R v Brent Health Authority, ex p Harrow London Borough Council* [1997] 3 FCR 765: the High Court refused to quash on judicial review the district health authority's refusal to provide more than half the speech, language and occupational therapy sessions required for a child suffering from cerebral palsy. The DHA was entitled (under Education Act 1993, now EA 1996, s 322) to ration its scarce resources by prioritising and categorising the level of need required, by assessing the requirements of every client on an individual basis and by tailoring the child's needs to the resources available.

92　Audit Commission (2002 b) para 84.

(C)   Legal accountability

The law of negligence reinforces the official guidance urging early identification of a child's learning difficulties. Indeed, it indicates that schools and LEAs who fail to take appropriate action to diagnose and properly assess children's learning difficulties, or provide appropriate educational assistance, may be liable in damages to the children concerned. The old legal principle that it was against public policy to impose tortious liability on education authorities was effectively rejected by the House of Lords in *Phelps v Hillingdon London Borough Council*,[93] along with the argument that recognising such liability would lead to a flood of claims and to defensive practices. 'On the contrary it may have the healthy effect of securing that high standards are sought and secured.'[94] The decision, confirming earlier authority,[95] clearly establishes that teachers and other educational specialists, such as educational psychologists, owe a duty of care to their pupils and must exercise reasonable professional skill in responding to their special educational needs.[96] LEAs can therefore be held vicariously liable in negligence if educational practitioners employed by them fail to exercise reasonable skill and care when diagnosing learning difficulties and when determining and delivering educational provision appropriate to address them. Their Lordships were undecided whether LEAs could also be found directly liable in negligence for their own actions. Whether an LEA would, for example, be liable in negligence, in the event of its employing an educational psychologist without sufficient qualifications or competence, is therefore unclear.[97] But the issue has little practical importance, since vicarious liability could lie in all but the most exceptional circumstances.

For SEN children, the *Phelps* decision produces the right to sue schools and LEAs in tort if their learning difficulties are not properly diagnosed and provided for. Liability may lie in a variety of situations, including the following: an educational psychologist fails to diagnose dyslexia and so fails to ensure that the pupil obtains specialised teaching; an educational psychologist diagnoses a learning difficulty that the pupil does not have and so the LEA provides inappropriate provision, such as special schooling; the headteacher, knowing of a child's learning problems, does nothing about them; the LEA, knowing of a child's learning problems, fails to address them in the way recommended by the educational psychologist.[98] The House of Lords was keen, however, to emphasise that their decision does not justify children bringing 'generalised "educational malpractice" claims'.[99] A claim cannot be brought based simply on poor quality of teaching, as opposed to the sort of cases where the diagnosis is hopelessly wrong.[100] In any event, it will not be easy for a child to

93   Full name *Phelps v Hillingdon London Borough Council, Anderton v Clwyd County Council, Jarvis v Hampshire County Council, Re G (a minor)* [2000] 4 All ER 504.

94   [2000] 4 All ER 504 at 535, Lord Clyde. See also Lord Slynn of Hadley (at 519), and Lord Nicholls of Birkenhead (at 530).

95   Particularly the judgment of Lord Browne-Wilkinson in *X (minors) v Bedfordshire County Council; M (a minor) v Newham London Borough Council; E (a minor) v Dorset ounty Council* [1995] 3 All ER 353.

96   Ie they must comply with the *Bolam* test, as established in *Bolam v Friern Hospital Management Committee* [1957] 2 All ER 118.

97   Example given by Lord Slynn of Hadley [2000] 4 All ER 504 at 522. See Lord Nicholls of Birkenhead (at 531) and Lord Clyde (at 538), both of whom also expressed doubt over the direct liability of LEAs.

98   All these scenarios are broadly similar to the cases dealt with in *Phelps*, [2000] 4 All ER 504.

99   Per Lord Jauncey of Tullichettle [2000] 4 All ER 504 at 528.

100   Per Lord Nicholls of Birkenhead [2000] 4 All ER 504 at 531.

establish all the requirements for negligence. It may be particularly difficult to show a direct link or 'causal connection' between the disability or suffering now experienced and the failure of the educational authorities in the first place.[101] Whilst some deplore the decision in *Phelps*, arguing that negligence actions are an extremely expensive and inefficient way of improving educational standards,[102] it should ensure that a particularly vulnerable section of the school population gains appropriate attention and financial compensation. SEN children are entitled to expect that their needs are diagnosed in a careful and professional manner and dealt with as early as possible.

(4)   DISABLED CHILDREN AND THEIR RIGHT TO INCLUSION WITHIN MAINSTREAM SCHOOLS

Like any other child, a child with special educational needs[103] should be given the opportunity to enjoy an 'appropriate education'.[104] As discussed above, the concept of inclusion is based on the belief that disabled adults and children have an equal right to share the opportunities for self-fulfilment enjoyed by the unimpaired. It is entirely consistent with the Warnock Committee's view that disabled and unimpaired children should not be treated for educational purposes as falling into distinctive medicalised groups.[105] The needs of children with learning difficulties should, as far as possible, be met in mainstream schools with extra support, rather than in special schools.[106] This policy remains a central tenet of the legislation applying to children with special educational needs.

The present government disapproves of SEN children being segregated in special schools, as often occurred in the past,[107] maintaining that 'there are strong educational, as well as social and moral grounds for educating children with SEN with their peers'.[108] Both its Green Paper and implementation programme[109] strongly emphasise the view that mainstream schools should be encouraged to become far more accessible to disabled pupils and that changes in attitude are required to make the policy of inclusion work effectively. Domestic education legislation reflects this determination to ensure

---

101   See T Birtwistle (2002).
102   See, inter alia: A Mullis (2001) p 338; M Harris (2001) p 27.
103   See EA 1996, s 312(1) and (2). See n 38 above. There is voluminous case law interpreting what is and is not an 'educational' need, summarised by N Harris (2002) pp 144–166.
104   See EA 1996, s 14, which obliges LEAs to provide sufficient schools to give all pupils the opportunity of appropriate education. It will only be 'appropriate' (s 14(3)) if the LEA offers 'such variety of instruction and training as may be desirable in view of (a) the pupils' different ages, abilities and aptitudes'. In exercising these duties, it must have regard to (s 14(6)(b)) the need to secure special educational provision for SEN pupils.
105   H M Warnock (1978) esp ch 7.
106   A 'special school' is one 'specially organised to make special educational provision for pupils with special educational needs and is for the time being approved by the Secretary of State': EA 1996, s 337.
107   The total number of children attending special schools has for many years been consistently small and is very gradually decreasing – currently 1.1% of the total school population. The total number of special schools has decreased quite rapidly, as LEAs have embraced the concept of inclusion and closed many special schools. See DfES (2001 a) Tables 13 and 14. Nevertheless, 34% of children with statements of SEN attend special schools in England. See Audit Commission (2002 b) para 41.
108   See DfEE (1997) p 43.
109   DfEE (1998 b) esp ch 4.

that SEN children will normally be educated in mainstream schools. There is a clear legal obligation on LEAs to educate all SEN children in a mainstream school,[110] unless, in the case of a statemented child, his or her parents object or if it would be incompatible with the efficient education of other children.[111] But whilst parents may be keen on sending their SEN child to a local mainstream school, some schools are very unwilling to take children with special needs,[112] for fear of them 'dragging down' their position in the league tables of school performance.[113]

Despite the advantages of educational inclusion, the Warnock Committee acknowledged that it would be impossible to educate all disabled children in mainstream schools. Pupils with very severe physical and/or mental handicaps often pose specialised difficulties that ordinary schools are unable or reluctant to deal with.[114] The fact that legislation now aims to eradicate discrimination against disabled children by schools and LEAs,[115] may eventually ensure that the concept of inclusion is fully embraced, rather than merely flirted with. Although schools must ensure that disabled pupils are not substantially disadvantaged by any educational services they provide their pupils,[116] they are not immediately required to adapt their school premises to accommodate severely handicapped children.[117] Nevertheless, LEAs must, over time, improve mainstream schools' physical environment to increase their accessibility to disabled pupils. LEAs and parents will thereby eventually gain more choice when it comes to finding a mainstream placement for a severely physically disabled child.[118]

Education legislation implicitly accepts that parents are not always as enthusiastic about the concept of inclusion as are educationalists; indeed, parents may be convinced that their handicapped child needs the more sheltered environment of a special school. Consequently, as noted above, the LEA's duty to provide a mainstream place for an SEN child is suspended when parents disagree with such a choice.[119] Furthermore, if

---

110 EA 1996, s 316 (as amended by SENDA 2001, s 1). All SEN children *without* statements must be educated in mainstream schools: EA 1996, s 316(2). The duty regarding those with statements is qualified, see below.

111 EA 1996, s 316(3). Eg if the pupil's severe challenging behaviour would significantly disrupt other pupil's learning or safety. But this exception only applies if the LEA can show (s 316A(5) and (6)) that there are no reasonable steps available to prevent such incompatibility.

112 See Audit Commission (2002 b) paras 42–46.

113 Audit Commission (2002 b) para 122.

114 See Mencap (2000) for a description of the difficulties involved in persuading mainstream schools to provide for children requiring specialised medication. Refusal to take 'reasonable steps' to provide such medication might now infringe a school's statutory obligations under DDA 1995, s 28 C. See examples in Disability Rights Commission (2002).

115 Governing bodies of schools must not unjustifiably treat a disabled pupil or prospective pupil less favourably than others, due to his or her disability. See DDA 1995, s 28A and B. They must also take reasonable steps to ensure that such pupils are not placed at a substantial disadvantage compared with non-disabled pupils, in relation to the school's admission procedures and educational services. DDA 1995, s 28C. The obligations imposed by the new legislation are discussed by T Linden (2002) and A Blair and A Lawson (2003). See also Disability Rights Commission (2002). NB pupils may either have a disability or special educational needs, or both. A pupil with only a disability may be protected by the DDA 1995, but not by the SEN legislation, and vice versa.

116 See DDA 1995, s 28C(1).

117 DDA 1995, s 28C(2)(a).

118 See DDA 1995, s 28D. The Schools Access Initiative funds projects in mainstream schools to adapt their buildings to improve access to disabled pupils.

119 But the LEA's choice of school must be determined by its own assessment of the appropriateness of the education offered, and not by the parents' wishes on the matter. See below.

the parents favour a special school in the maintained sector, there is a presumption in favour of the LEA naming that school in a child's SEN statement.[120] Sometimes, however, parents want their child to attend an expensive independent school, believing the resources offered there to be far preferable to those in any mainstream school. There is nothing to prevent parents paying for such education themselves,[121] but they may fail to induce the LEA to fund a private school's fees. The LEA is entitled to refuse to follow the parents' preferences if it can ensure that the child would obtain 'appropriate' education[122] in a maintained school, thereby avoiding unreasonable public expenditure.[123] When disputes over such decisions reach the SENDIST, the tribunal will balance the inevitable arguments about cost and resources with educational considerations.[124]

Educationalists' enthusiasm for inclusion may, so far as parents are concerned, undermine their ability to appreciate fully the arguments favouring severely handicapped children attending more specialised institutions. A disabled child will not necessarily fit in happily into the mainstream school specified as being appropriate for him by the LEA, especially if it is large and involves long journeys to and from school. Some feel more isolated, rather than less, by their handicaps, particularly when attending a busy school, despite its physical facilities having been adapted to suit his or her disabilities.[125] They may find it difficult to make friends with their non-disabled peers,[126] and need more specialised help with the social and practical skills that non-disabled children learn routinely as they grow up.[127] Furthermore, ongoing concern has been expressed that the learning support assistants, on which mainstream schools rely so heavily for help with SEN pupils, often lack training, with their duties being inadequately planned or co-ordinated with class teachers.[128] Indeed, some argue that this reliance 'could become a new form of segregation within mainstream schools whereby pupils with SEN were taught by the least qualified staff'.[129]

Parents sometimes claim that the LEA does not sympathise with their child's unhappiness in a mainstream school or support parents' wish to find suitable alternatives.[130] They feel frustrated at the LEA's reluctance to find a place for their

---

120   See EA 1996, Sch 27, para 3. The parents' choice must be adopted, unless the LEA considers such a choice to be unsuitable to the child's age, ability or aptitude or to his special educational needs, or the child's attendance would be incompatible with the efficient education of the other pupils with whom he or she would be educated or with the efficient use of resources. EA 1996, Sch 27, para 3(3)(a) and (b).

121   EA 1996, s 316A(1).

122   See *C v Buckingham County Council and the Special Educational Needs Tribunal* [1999] ELR 179 at 189, per Thorpe LJ. See also *R v London Borough of Brent and Vassie (Chairman of the Special Educational Needs Tribunal), ex p AF* [2000] ELR 550.

123   If the parents favour an independent school, the LEA's obligation under s 316 to place the child in a mainstream school is suspended. Nevertheless, it must specify a school in his or her statement which would be 'appropriate for the child' (s 324(4)), bearing in mind its duty under s 9, to take account of the parents' wishes, but only 'so far as that is compatible with the provision of efficient instruction and training and the avoidance of unreasonable public expenditure'. See *L v Worcestershire County Council and Hughes* [2000] ELR 674 at 678–684, per Hale LJ, for a clear explanation of this tortuous statutory guidance.

124   See N Harris (2002) pp 153–155 for an assessment of the case law on this topic.

125   See D Abbott, J Morris and L Ward (2001) ch 2.

126   D Abbott, J Morris and L Ward (2001) pp 15–17. See also P Murray (2002) pp 27–28.

127   D Abbott, J Morris and L Ward (2001) p 19.

128   See Mencap (1999) pp 22 and 35–36.

129   M Ainscow et al (1999) p 3.

130   D Abbott, J Morris and L Ward (2001) esp pp 27–37.

child at a maintained special school or to fund an independent school placement.[131] Despite their strong convictions, any claim that the LEA is infringing their rights under article 2 of the First Protocol of the ECHR to have their child educated according to their 'religious and philosophical convictions' is unlikely to succeed. The absence of any relevant case law indicating that a parents' views about where his or her disabled child should be educated falls within the ambit of philosophical convictions,[132] has enabled the domestic courts to side-step such arguments.[133] Indeed, according to the Strasbourg jurisprudence, as long as the child has been properly assessed, and the educational provision is consistent with that assessment, decisions over how a child's education is to be delivered can be left to the discretion of the state's own education authorities.[134]

(5)   THE DISABLED CHILD'S RIGHT TO INDIVIDUALITY AND EDUCATIONAL INDEPENDENCE

Depending on the severity of their children's handicaps, the parents of disabled children often play an exceptionally important part in their upbringing and education. Case law shows the tenacity with which such parents are prepared to fight to ensure that their children obtain the best education possible.[135] Current legislation fulfils the recommendations of the Warnock Committee that parents should be fully involved at the various stages of determining their child's educational needs and provision.[136] Thus they are entitled to request the LEA to carry out an assessment[137] and must themselves also be involved in the assessment and statementing process.[138] The legislation not only ensures that parents can veto the LEA's obligation to place their SEN child in a mainstream school, but gives them considerable influence over the choice of school when drawing up a statement.[139]

Clearly then, the education legislation has made considerable progress in ensuring that the parents of children with learning difficulties are very fully involved at all stages of deciding on appropriate educational support for them. But it is doubtful whether education law maintains a satisfactory balance between protecting parents' rights to be involved and children's rights to be treated as distinct individuals. Undoubtedly, in the majority of cases it will be perfectly appropriate for parents to be involved in planning for their disabled children's education, since they have a more specialised knowledge of their needs than anyone else. Nevertheless, the risks of

---

131   Eg *L v Hereford and Worcester County Council and Hughes* [2000] ELR 375.
132   See U Kilkelly (1999) p 79.
133   *L v Hereford and Worcester County Council and Hughes* [2000] ELR 375 at 384, per Carnworth J: although the mother's opposition to mainstream education for her daughter related to sincere and practical concerns about her schooling, they were nothing to do with her religious or philosophical convictions under art 2 of the First Protocol of the ECHR. See also *T v Special Educational Needs Tribunal and Wiltshire County Council* [2002] EWHC 1474 (Admin) at [39], per Richards J, for a similar approach.
134   See *Belgian Linguistics Case (No 2)* (1968) 1 EHRR 252 and *Simpson v United Kingdom*, Application No 14688/89) (1989) 64 DR 188 and other case law discussed by U Kilkelly (1999) pp 80–81 and see also pp 68–69.
135   Eg the mother's ongoing legal battle against Worcester County Council, culminating in *L v Worcestershire County Council and Hughes* [2000] ELR 674.
136   See Warnock Report (1978) esp ch 9.
137   EA 1996, s 329.
138   EA 1996, Sch 27.
139   Discussed above.

identifying parents' interests with those of their children, as the education legislation tends to do, are greater for disabled children, than for the unimpaired. Severely disabled children may be wholly dependent on their parents and their parents often shoulder overwhelming burdens in terms of the care and attention which they provide. But in such circumstances, parental attitudes are extremely important and may not always be as helpful to their children as might be desired. Indeed, their anxieties may undermine their child's self-confidence and ability to deal with demanding situations. In particular, they may be unable to assess objectively their child's intellectual, physical and social abilities and these attitudes may influence a child's ability to settle happily into a mainstream school. Moreover, there is disturbing evidence that some disabled children are particularly vulnerable to physical and sexual abuse by their carers, be they parents or staff of residential homes and schools.[140] This evidence reinforces the need to consider the disabled child as a person in his or her own right, rather than accepting the parent's view of where and how the child should be educated.

The facts of *Re V (care or supervision order)*[141] illustrate vividly that parents may sometimes be incapable of assessing impartially their disabled child's real needs. A boy, S, aged 17, suffered from cerebral palsy, spastic quadriplegia, and had speech and learning difficulties. His mother's fiercely over-protective attitude towards him as he grew up led her to control every aspect of his life, finding excuses for not allowing him to attend a special school as a weekly boarder and making it impossible for him to have any social life. Mrs V, who had overriding power over her son, would leave him on a sofa all day, without physical or intellectual stimulation and refused to act on professional advice urging her to change her ways. The local authority eventually obtained a care order over him on the evidence that she was preventing his developing his full potential, physically, socially, emotionally or educationally.[142] Such circumstances are obviously extreme but the case provides a salutary reminder that disabled children must be regarded as individuals in their own right.

It is important to maintain a balance between utilising parents' special knowledge of their disabled child's needs and respecting the child's own individuality. The government literature for parents of SEN children stresses parents' special place in the process of finding a suitable school for their child: 'Remember – you know your child better than anyone.'[143] Nevertheless, the Code of Practice encourages an important change of approach by educational practitioners, in favour of involving SEN children far more in decisions over their education. Indeed, by devoting a complete chapter to 'Pupil Participation', it emphasises this more strongly than any other form of educational guidance. The chapter starts with the assertion:

> 'All children and young people have rights. Most references to rights are about what is due to children from others, particularly from their parents and the state and its agencies. This chapter is about the right of children with special educational needs to be involved in making decisions and exercising choices.

---

140 See the body of research evidence summarised and discussed by W Utting (1997) paras 8.8– 8.19.

141 [1996] 1 FLR 776.

142 See also *Re V (declaration against parents)* [1995] 2 FLR 1003. The Official Solicitor, on S's behalf, obtained declarations against his parents that, on attaining 18, he had a right to choose where he lived and associate with whom he wished, and injunctions restraining them from interfering with his right to do so when he visited home. Less than one year later, the Court of Appeal discharged the injunctions against S's parents. See *The Times*, 3 February 1996.

143 See DfEE (2001 b) p 7 and see also p 17.

Children and young people with special educational needs have a unique knowledge of their own needs and circumstances and their own views about what sort of help they would like to help them make the most of their education ...'[144]

The risk of parents failing to perceive their children as individuals in their own right is tackled firmly:

'Some parents may need support in seeing their children as partners in education; they may be reluctant to involve their child in education decision-making perhaps considering them ill-equipped to grasp all the relevant factors. If the parents' experience of working with professionals has been disappointing, or they perceive their views as being marginalised, they may suspect that professionals may give undue weight to the views of their children. LEAs, schools and settings should show sensitivity, honesty and mutual respect in encouraging pupils to share concerns, discuss strategies and see themselves as equal partners with the school ...'[145]

And it goes on to state that:

'All children should be involved in making decisions where possible right from the start of their education. The ways in which children are encouraged to participate should reflect the child's evolving maturity ...'[146]

Unfortunately, this enlightened approach is not reflected in the legislation and regulations underpinning the SEN appeals process. Many aspects of decision-making over an SEN child can be appealed to the SENDIST,[147] but the legislative provisions and accompanying official documentation governing these appeals[148] emphasise that it is parents who are entitled to go through the appeals process and not their child. Indeed, the child is not expected to play any formal part in the proceedings, being provided with no independent representation or party status.[149] Consequently, SEN children have no right to initiate appeals themselves and so cannot do so in circumstances where they are on bad terms with their parents or the latter are not interested in their education. For example, an intelligent physically handicapped adolescent living in residential school on a 52-week placement would have no right to appeal against the LEA if it decided to change the named school in his or her statement. By assuming that there is no need for the child to be made a party to appeals to the SENDIST, the legislation seems to ignore the possibility of parents appealing against decisions over educational provision because they want to retain control over their child.[150] Even more pertinently, the regulations undermine the intentions of the SEN Code of Practice itself. As discussed above, the Code directs LEAs to involve the child very fully in all the decision-making processes and to take account of his or her separate interests.

---

144   *SEN Code of Practice*, paras 3.1–3.2.
145   *SEN Code of Practice*, para 3.5.
146   *SEN Code of Practice*, para 3.6.
147   Under EA 1996, parents can appeal against, inter alia: refusal to assess the child (ss 329 and 329A); refusal to reassess a statemented child (s 328) refusal to make a statement (s 325); the contents of the statement (s 326); refusal to name the parent's choice of school in the statement (Sch 27, para 8); amend the contents of a statement (Sch 27, para 10); cease to maintain a statement (Sch 27, para 11).
148   EA 1996 and the Special Educational Needs Tribunal Regulations 2001, SI 2001/600.
149   *S (a minor) v Special Educational Needs Tribunal* [1996] 2 All ER 286.
150   Eg *Re V (care or supervision order)* [1996] 1 FLR 776, discussed above.

The fact that a child is not a party to the proceedings makes it all the more important that the tribunal is fully conversant with the child's own views regarding an appeal. The current regulations governing SENDISTs contain no provisions like those contained in the Children Act 1989, either directing the tribunal to consider the child's welfare as being paramount or, indeed, requiring it to take account of the child's wishes and feelings, so far as they are ascertainable. Admittedly, there is a fleeting acknowledgment of the child's existence as an independent player in the proceedings. The regulations oblige the LEA to discover and state to the tribunal the views of the child on the matter being appealed, or explain why it has not ascertained the child's views.[151] Furthermore, the child is entitled to attend the hearing[152] and although the tribunal is not obliged to hear the child's views at the hearing, it can do so if it wishes.[153] Nevertheless, research carried out in the mid-1990s indicated that children rarely attended SENT hearings.[154] Furthermore, extreme ambivalence was expressed by those involved in the SENT over whether children should attend and, if so, whether they should be allowed to address the tribunal regarding their wishes. Their concerns were that if children did attend they might hear demoralising evidence regarding their academic ability; they might also find the proceedings lengthy and tedious. But as Harris observes, if the tribunal was obliged by law to consider the child's independent views and perspectives, it might focus more on the child's own interests and become less bogged down by issues revolving around resources and technicalities.[155] Further research would be useful in this area. It might establish, for example, the extent to which a child's attendance and oral views influence the tribunal and the extent to which the experience of attending and giving oral evidence distresses the child.

Unless the domestic courts can be persuaded to interpret the rights of SEN children under article 6 of the ECHR relatively vigorously, it seems unlikely that the current failure to provide children with party status can be rectified by international human rights law. Although ostensibly such failure infringes the child's rights to a fair trial under article 6, Strasbourg case law suggests that procedures relating to the right to education are not within the scope of that article, because the right to state education is not a 'civil right', as it requires.[156] Nevertheless, as observed by the Committee on the Rights of the Child regarding the general state of the United Kingdom's education law, to deny children the right to express their own opinions on a variety of educational matters fails to give sufficient attention to the importance of article 12 of the CRC.[157] Legislation fully acknowledging that children are the focus of proceedings considering their educational future is long overdue.

(6) CONCLUSION

It is difficult to deny the good intentions underlying the education legislation in this field of law. It goes to great lengths to fulfil the enlightened objectives of the Warnock

---

151 Special Educational Needs Tribunal Regulations 2001, SI 2001/600, reg 13(2)(e).
152 Special Educational Needs Tribunal Regulations 2001, SI 2001/600, reg 30(2)(a).
153 Special Educational Needs Tribunal Regulations 2001, SI 2001/600, reg 30(7).
154 N Harris (1997) pp 146–151. During the currency of this author's research, children were not entitled to attend hearings of the Special Educational Needs Tribunal (as the tribunal was then named) hearings, but could do so at the tribunal's discretion.
155 N Harris (1997) p 149.
156 See *Simpson v United Kingdom* (Application No 14688/89) (1989) 64 DR 188.
157 Committee on the Rights of the Child (1995) para 14.

Report and to ensure that the rights of SEN children in England and Wales to a good education are fulfilled. Nevertheless, it is arguable that further legal reforms will not solve the fundamental problems undermining the entire SEN system. Its enormously cumbersome structure involves so many different agencies and workers within agencies that children and families suffer inordinate delays at every stage of decision-making over their educational provision. During the assessment and statementing processes some children with severe learning difficulties are left many months, and sometimes longer, without adequate educational support.[158] Blair points out that the many cases of administrative blunders relating to SEN children are compounded by –

> 'an incapacity on the part of those involved to recognise, and address with urgency, the extreme hardship and frustration that some of these parents and young people have suffered. In several of these cases this looks more like a failure of human sympathy ...'[159]

Meanwhile, the general weakness shared by the large body of legislation governing the education of all children results in the legal provisions governing SEN children consistently identifying their interests with those of their parents. They are not viewed as individuals with personalities and rights of their own. Unless disabled children, some of whom are wholly dependent on adults for many things, are treated with respect by the legislation governing their educational rights, those involved in their education will not be encouraged to do the same.

158   See D Abbott, J Morris and L Ward (2001) pp 31–32. This research indicates that decisions sometimes took more than a year, and (pp 37–46) that delays were exacerbated by inter-agency disputes.
159   See A Blair (2000) p 246.

BIBLIOGRAPHY

NB many of these publications can be obtained on the relevant organisation's website.

Abbott D, Morris J and Ward L, *The best place to be? Policy, practice and the experiences of residential school placements for disabled children* (2001) Joseph Rowntree Foundation.

Ainscow M et al, *Effective Practice in Inclusion, and in Special and Mainstream Schools Working Together* Research Brief No 91 (1999) DfEE.

Audit Commission, *Children in mind: child and adolescent mental health services* (1999).

Audit Commission, *Statutory Assessment and Statements of SEN: In Need of Review?* (2002 a).

Audit Commission, *Special Educational Needs: A Mainstream Issue* (2002 b).

Audit Commission and HMI, *Getting in on the Act – Provision for Pupils with Special Educational Needs: the National Picture* (1992) HMSO.

Birtwistle T, 'Liability for "educational malpractice"' (2002) Education Law Journal 95.

Blair A, 'Local Government Ombudsmen Reports' (2000) 1 Education Law Review 243.

Blair A, 'Local Government Ombudsmen Reports' (2001) 2 Education Law Journal 232.

Blair A and Lawson A, 'Disability discrimination reforms in education – could do better? (2002) 15 Child and Family Law Quarterly 41.

British Medical Association, *Growing up in Britain: Ensuring a healthy future for our children: A study of 0–5 year olds* (1999) BMJ Books.

Committee on the Rights of the Child, *Concluding Observations of the Committee on the Rights of the Child: United Kingdom of Great Britain and Northern Ireland* CRC/C/15/Add 34 (1995) Centre for Human Rights, Geneva.

Council for Disabled Children, *Second Analysis of the Quality Protects Management Action Plans: Services for Disabled Children and their Families* (2000)

Department for Education (DFE), *Code of Practice on the Identification and Assessment of Special Educational Needs* (1994) DFE.

Department for Education and Employment (DfEE), Green Paper *Excellence for all Children: Meeting Special Educational Needs* Cm 3785 (1997) DfEE.

Department for Education and Employment (DfEE), *LEA Behaviour Support Plans* DfEE Circular 1/98 (and Supplementary Note 2000) (1998 a).

Department for Education and Employment (DfEE), *Meeting Special Educational Needs: A programme of action* (1998 b).

Department for Education and Employment (DfEE), *Special Educational Needs Tribunal: Annual Report 2000–2001* (2001 a) DfEE Publications.

Department for Education and Employment (DfEE), *Special Educational Needs (SEN): A Guide for Parents and Carers* (2001 b).

Department for Education and Skills (DfES), *Statistics for Education: Special Educational Needs in England* January 2001, Issue No 12/01 (2001 a) DfES.

Department for Education and Skills (DfES), *Statistics for Education: Permanent Exclusions from Maintained Schools in England* Issue No 10/01 (2001 b).

Department for Education and Skills (DfES) *Special Educational Needs: Code of Practice* DfES/581/2001 (2001 c) DfES.

Department for Education and Skills (DfES), *Trends in Education and Skills* (2002 a).

Department for Education and Skills (DfES), *Statistics for Education: Permanent Exclusions from Maintained Schools in England* Issue No 09/02 (2002 b).

Department of Health (DH), *Quality Protects Programme: Transforming Children's Services* LAC (98)28 (1998 a).

Department of Health (DH), *Partnership in Action (New Opportunities for Joint Working between Health and Social Services) A Discussion Document* (1998 b) DH.

Department of Health (DH), White Paper *Valuing People: A New Strategy for Learning Disability for the 21st Century, Cm 5086* (2001 a) The Stationery Office.

Department of Health (DH), *Children Act Report 2000* (2001 b) DH.

Department of Health (DH), *Children Act Report 2001* (2002) DH.

Department of Health and DfEE *Children's Services Planning Guidance* LAC 96(10) (1996) DOH.

Disability Rights Commission, *Disability Discrimination Act 1995 Part 4: Code of Practice for Schools* (2002).

Ford J, Hughes M and Ruebain D, *Education Law and Practice* (1999) LAG.

Freeman M, 'The Future of Children's Rights' (2000) 14 Children and Society 277.

Gordon D et al, *Disabled Children: a Re-analysis of the OPCS Disability Survey* (2000) The Stationery Office.

H M Treasury 2002, *Spending Review: New Public Spending Plans 2003–2006* CM 5570 (2002) The Stationery Office.

Harris M, 'Education and Local Authorities' (2001) 117 Law Quarterly Review 25.

Harris N, *Special Educational Needs and Access to Justice* (1997) Jordans.

Harris N, 'Special Educational Needs: The Role of the Courts' (2002) 14 Child and Family Law Quarterly 137.

Hodgkin R and Newell P, *Implementation Handbook for the Convention on the Rights of the Child* (1998) Unicef.

Jenkinson J, *Mainstream or Special? Educating students with disabilities* (1997) Routledge.

Kilkelly U, *The Child and the European Convention on Human Rights* (1999) Ashgate Publishing.

Linden T, 'Disability Discrimination in Education: The New Law' (2002) Education Law Journal 82.

Lundy L, 'Stating a case for the "unstatemented" – children with special educational needs in mainstream schools' (1998) 10 Child and Family Law Quarterly 39.

McLaughlin M and Rouse M (eds), *Special Education and School Reform in the United States and Britain* (2000) Routledge.

Marks J, *What Are Special Educational Needs? An Analysis of a New Growth Industry* (2000) Centre for Policy Studies.

Meltzer H and Gatward R, *Mental health of children and adolescents in Great Britain, Office for National Statistics* (2000) The Stationery Office.

Mencap, *On a Wing and a Prayer: Inclusion and Children with Severe Learning Difficulties* (1999) MENCAP.

Mencap, *Don't count me out: The exclusion of children with learning disability from education because of health needs* (2000) MENCAP.

Mittler P, *Working Towards Inclusive Education: Social Contexts* (2000) David Fulton Publishers.

Mullis A, '*Phelps and Hillingdon London Borough Council*: A rod for the hunch-backed teacher?' (2001) 13 Child and Family Law Quarterly 331.

Murray P, *Hello! Are you listening? Disabled teenagers' experience of access to inclusive education* (2002) Joseph Rowntree Foundation.

National Children's Bureau, *Making it work Together: Advice on joint initiatives between education and social services departments* (1999) NCB.

Office of Public Censuses and Surveys, *Surveys of Disability in Great Britain* Reports 1–6 (1989) HMSO.

Office for Standards in Education (Ofsted), *Exclusions from Secondary Schools 1995/ 96, A Report from the office of HM Chief Inspector of Schools* (1996) HMSO.

Office for Standards in Education (Ofsted), *Pupils with specific learning difficulties in mainstream schools* (1999) Ofsted.

Office for Standards in Education (Ofsted), *LEA Strategy for the Inclusion of Pupils with Special Educational Needs* HMI 737 (2002) Ofsted.

Read J and Clements L, *Disabled Children and the Law: Research and Good Practice* (2001) Jessica Kingsley Publishers.

Richards M, 'Resources, rights and special educational needs' (1998) 3(2) Education, Public Law and the Individual 24,

Robinson J, 'Beth Tandy's case – resources and the ratio' (1998) 3(3) Education, Public Law and the Individual 42.

Ruebain D, 'Can Local education authorities take their available resources into account in determining a child's special educational provision?' (1999) 4(1) Education, Public Law and the Individual 5.

Social Exclusion Unit (SEU), *Bridging the Gap: New Opportunities for 16 –18 Year Olds Not in Education, Employment or Training* (1999).

Social Services Inspectorate (SSI), *Disabled Children: Directions for Their Future Care* (1998 a) DH Publications.

Social Services Inspectorate (SSI), *Removing Barriers for Disabled Children: Inspection of Services to Disabled Children and Their Families* (1998 b) DH Publications.

Thomas G et al *The Making of the Inclusive School* (1998) Routledge.

Utting W, *People Like Us: The Report of the Review of the Safeguards for Children Living Away from Home* (1997) The Stationery Office.

Warnock H M (Chairman), *Special Educational Needs, Report of the Committee of Enquiry into the Education of Handicapped Children and Young People* Cmnd 7212 (1978) HMSO.

Chapter 13

Children's right to know their parents – the significance of the blood tie

(1)   INTRODUCTION

It is increasingly common for children to be brought up in families differing greatly from the traditional unit formed by a married couple and their children. Today, society accepts that parent-child relationships can be created through adoption, fostering, reproductive technology, unmarried birth, family breakdown and family re-creation. A child born to a couple through infertility treatment may be completely unrelated to them biologically.[1] Indeed, the law acknowledges that adults caring for children may have a social relationship with them which is far more important to the children themselves than any link with their biological progenitors.[2] There nevertheless remains great ambivalence over what significance to attach to the biological tie between a child and birth parents. Does the tie's existence, in itself, justify the creation of a social relationship between them where none existed before, or is it enough for the child to be given accurate information about the identity of an absent parent?

There is a considerable and diverse body of research which may inform this dilemma, but there are no clear answers. In the first place, research indicates that it is of immense importance for children to have accurate information about their birth parents in order to link their present selves with their biological origins. Indeed, society increasingly sympathises with those who feel psychologically deficient without this information.[3] There is also the body of research on the damage suffered by the children of divorcing parents through losing their relationships with now

---

1   The Human Fertilisation and Embryology Act 1990, ss 27 and 28, ignores the biological link between the donor of donated gametes and the child. The woman who gives birth is deemed to be the child's legal mother, despite conceiving with donor gametes (s 27). For a child conceived through artificial insemination, the married mother's husband is deemed the legal father (s 28(2)) if he consented to the donation. For the child of an unmarried mother, the legal father is the man with whom the mother received 'treatment together' in a licensed clinic (s 28(3)). See S Bridge (1999).

2   See Children Act 1989, s 12(2), which enables a person unrelated to the child to acquire parental responsibilities over him or her through obtaining a residence order.

3   See *Rose v Secretary of State for Health and Human Embryology Authority* [2002] EWHC 1593 (Admin), [2002] 2 FLR 962 at [7], for the reasons underlying the adult applicant's request for information regarding the identity and characteristics of her sperm donor father. Per Scott Baker J (at [47]), the need for AID children to know about their origins 'was entirely understandable'. Discussed below.

absent parents. But should the circle be squared between them, by arguing that a child always has a right to a social relationship with an absent parent, whether or not one ever existed between them in the past?

It is unclear from the research evidence whether establishing a social relationship between birth parent and child benefits the child as much as it does his or her birth parents. The assumption that the birth tie automatically guarantees a beneficial in-built affinity between parent and child is surely naive. Certainly cloaking claims of these kinds in the language of international children's rights has a dubious merit. As O'Donovan has so wisely observed in the context of adoption, the search for identity does not exist in a vacuum: 'It is produced by legal and social structures which attach value to concepts of identity linked to genitors.'[4] This chapter reflects on the extent to which the law should contribute to a situation where children and parents consider that the biological link must always be consummated by a social relationship to achieve any semblance of 'normality'.[5] In so doing, it explores areas of law where the notion of children's rights appears to be utilised to support arguments about promoting contact between children and their birth parents which perhaps have more to do with adults' rights than those of their children.

(2) THE LESSONS FROM ADOPTION

(A) Knowledge of origins

Research carried out in the context of adoption practice suggests that adopted children have a psychological need to know the true identity of those who brought them into the world. There are two reasons why such information should be provided early in life. First, information about children's origins gives them the ability to place themselves in a social context. They gain a continuity with the past and a complete and consistent biography.[6] Second, concealment and secrecy contribute to children's sense of bewilderment if told later that they have been brought up in the incorrect belief that their present carers are their birth parents. It may often be very damaging for adoptees to discover the truth when older if they have been deceived over this by those who brought them up and in whom they have always trusted.[7]

The Houghton Committee's recommendations for greater openness in adoption[8] responded to the research describing the shock felt by some adopted people when discovering by accident that they had been adopted. Legislation implementing the committee's recommendations was introduced giving adoptees a procedural right to discover the identity of their birth relatives.[9] Despite Triseliotis' view that adopted

---

4   See K O'Donovan (1990) p 102.
5   See also chapter 14, which considers the same issue from a different viewpoint.
6   See E Haimes (1987) p 363.
7   See J Triseliotis (1973), who found (p 20) that those adoptees aged between 4 and 8 years when told of their adoption experienced the greatest satisfaction. Those told in adolescence and adult life experienced the greatest distress and shock.
8   W Houghton (1972) paras 299–301.
9   See Adoption Act 1976, s 51, which enabled adopted persons over the age of 18 to obtain access to their birth records by obtaining from the Registrar General a copy of their original birth certificates. Permission could be refused in exceptional circumstances, eg *R v Registrar General, ex p Smith* [1991] 2 QB 393. See also s 51A establishing an Adoption Contact Register assisting adoptees and their birth relatives to contact each other through registering their names and addresses. This system was replaced by a far more complicated and prescriptive system for obtaining information by the Adoption and Children Act 2002, ss 56–65.

children should discover the truth as early as possible, the right to check the adoption records is confined to those aged over 18.[10] Nevertheless, few adoptees have to wait until they reach adulthood to obtain such information, since it is now well-established national policy for all adoption agencies to obtain from couples selected to become adoptive parents a commitment to tell their adopted children about the circumstances of their adoption. Adoption agencies are required to compile detailed case records to be given to adopters regarding the child and his or her background.[11] They should give the adopted person 'as much information as possible about his social and personal history and the reasons for the adoption'.[12] Adopters, on receiving this file, are advised that they should make this information available to the child when appropriate, but no later than his or her 18th birthday.[13]

Adoptees who want to discover more about their birth family may ask the adoption agency who handled their adoptions to disclose to them all the documents in their adoption files.[14] An agency refusing to provide an adoptee with all relevant documents runs the risk of infringing his or her rights under article 8 of the ECHR. Respect for private life includes the concept of personal identity and carries the right to clarify details about a person's past, through obtaining officially held information.[15] Nevertheless, such a right is not absolute. The adoption agency may be entitled to withhold information about third parties, such as birth parents and adoptive parents; but only if it properly weighs up the adoptee's need for information and balances it against third parties' own rights to confidentiality and privacy.[16]

Precisely how many adoptees search for information about their birth parents is difficult to establish. Judging by those who seek counselling before making contact, the numbers have steadily risen.[17] But their desire to seek information about their parentage is not always associated with an additional need to establish a social relationship with their birth parents. Some adoptees simply wish to obtain information

---

10 Adoption and Children Act 2002, s 60.
11 See, inter alia: reg 7(2)(a) of the Adoption Agencies Regulations 1983, SI 1983/1964 (to be replaced by regulations made under the Adoption and Children Act 2002, s 64) (requires agencies to compile a case record for every child for whom adoption is planned, for adoptees who later wish to learn about the circumstances of their adoption); Social Services Inspectorate (hereafter SSI) (1996) Appendix C (recommends the inclusion of 28 items in an adopted child's 'case record', including, inter alia: basic non-identifying details of the child's and family's medical history; information about the child's family and social background; the circumstances of and reasons for the adoption; any letters, photographs, or other material provided by the birth parents); Department of Health (hereafter DH) (2002 a) and DH (2002 b) standard 18 (requires agencies to ensure that birth parents can provide their adopted child with up-to-date information about his or her birth and early life); and standard 20 (requires agencies to keep comprehensive and accurate records for the child and adopters).
12 See DH (1997) para 58.
13 The Adoption Agencies Regulations 1983 SI 1983/1964, reg 13A (to be replaced by regulations made under the Adoption and Children Act 2002). Most agencies provide a counselling service giving adoptees advice over contacting birth parents.
14 Adoption agencies have a discretion to do so under Adoption Agencies Regulations 1983, SI 1983/1964, reg 15(2).
15 *Gaskin v United Kingdom* (1989) 12 EHRR 36. Discussed in more detail by J Fortin (1999 a) pp 362–363.
16 See *Gunn-Rosso v Nugent Care Society and Secretary of State for Health* [2001] EWHC Admin 566, [2002] 1 FLR 1: the adoption agency's refusal to disclose confidential documents relating to third parties could not be justified since it had not assessed carefully the merits of disclosing each document to the applicant.
17 See D Howe and J Feast (2000) p 14. The true numbers may be higher since it is possible to search without involving any authorities and without applying for counselling.

about them, for example, through obtaining copies of their original birth certificates or background medical information. Others want to meet their birth relatives to establish their physical appearance, without wishing to develop a relationship with them.[18] Research suggests that even those adults who search, with a view to forming a relationship with their birth parents, encounter difficulties in maintaining such relationships.[19] Certainly an adoptee's need for knowledge, but not for a relationship, fits in well with the research on attachment and Goldstein et al's concept of the 'psychological parent':

> 'Whether any adult becomes the psychological parent of a child is based thus on day-to-day interaction, companionship, and shared experiences. The role can be fulfilled either by a biological parent or by an adoptive parent or by any other caring adult – but never by an absent, inactive adult, whatever his biological or legal relationship to the child may be.'[20]

If such an approach is accepted, it becomes easily comprehensible that whilst adopted children experience a psychological need to complete the details of their biological history, their need for a loving child-parent relationship is usually satisfied by their adoptive parents. Nevertheless, as discussed below, such an approach may be inappropriate for older children adopted at an age when they have fully established relationships with birth parents, siblings and other relatives.

The lessons gained from adoption research can, of course, be applied more generally. As Scott Baker J indicated in *Rose v Secretary of State for Health and Human Embryology Authority*,[21] adopted children are clearly not alone in their need for information about their origins.[22] The continued secrecy surrounding the birth of children conceived through sperm donation and other methods of assisted conception is becoming increasingly objectionable,[23] given our more open society and the increasing numbers of children conceived in such a way.[24] Many have argued in favour of a system giving all children conceived through infertility treatments the right to discover the full identity of their biological parents.[25] There are, of course, purely practical reasons for enabling them to do so. For example, they may need to

18   D Howe and J Feast (2000) pp 14–15 and ch 5.
19   D Howe and J Feast (2000) p 127. This research showed a significant fall-off in contact between 'searching' adoptees and their birth mothers after initial contact – after five years, 69% remained in contact, 31% had lost contact. After eight + years, these figures had changed to 57% and 43% respectively.
20   J Goldstein, A Freud and A Solnit (1973) p 19.
21   [2002] EWHC 1593 (Admin), [2002] 2 FLR 962.
22   [2002] EWHC 1593 (Admin), [2002] 2 FLR 962 at [47].
23   Under the Human Fertilisation and Embryology Act 1990, s 31(3) and (4), an adult only has right to apply to the Human Fertilisation and Embryology Authority for information contained on its register indicating whether someone other than the applicant's 'parents' are his biological parents and if so information relating to his biological background and whether or not the person he intends marrying is biologically related to him. Section 31(5) precludes the applicant obtaining information identifying his biological parents. An applicant under the age of 18 can only apply for information if he or she intends getting married and the information sought must be confined to indicating whether he or she is related biologically to the intended spouse (s 31(6) and (7)).
24   Figures provided by the Human Fertilisation and Embryology Authority indicate that 18,000 babies have been born using assisted conception methods since 1991, when the authority was established. The overall numbers are probably far larger.
25   See, inter alia: M Freeman (1996) pp 283–291; A McWhinnie (1998); J Feast (2000).

discover whether they have inherited a genetic disorder, before starting a family of their own.[26]

International human rights law clearly supports claims that the current law is deficient in the way it withholds information about the biological heritage of children born by assisted conception methods. The Committee on the Rights of the Child expressed concern that, contrary to the terms of article 7 of the CRC, such children have no right, so far as possible, to know the identity of their parents. It recommended reforms enabling them to obtain this information.[27] Similarly, in *Rose v Secretary of State for Health and Human Embryology Authority*,[28] Scott Baker J accepted that Strasbourg case law establishes that the concept of respect for a person's private and family life is sufficiently broad to entitle a person to establish details of his or her identity.[29] Consequently, he considered, without finally determining the issue, that the current law may well be infringing the rights of children born by assisted conception methods, under article 8 of the ECHR.[30] The government seems prepared to reform the law in some way.[31] Nevertheless, since under the present system, sperm donors were recruited on the basis of complete anonymity, new legislation giving children full identifying information of their biological parents could not operate retrospectively.[32] A compromise might be to amend the law ensuring that future donors will be identified, but that only a limited amount of non-identifying information would be made available on past donors.[33]

(B)   Adoptees' contact with birth parents

Adoption law addresses adopted children's need for information about their biological heritage. But, whilst doing so, it implicitly acknowledges that a child's right to identify his or her biological parents is entirely detached from issues regarding the existence of a social relationship between them. It makes no attempt, for example, to set up any direct contact between adoptees and their birth parents. Indeed, the law seeks to protect adoptees and adopters from being traced by birth parents against their wishes.[34] Nevertheless, since the late 1970s, when major adoption reforms were introduced,[35] adoption practice has changed radically, with extensive 'openness' in adoption often being promoted by adoption agencies. This approach reflects the

---

26   Eg *Re H (adoption: disclosure of information)* [1995] 1 FLR 236: the High Court allowed
     information from a sibling to be passed on to an adopted adult, alerting him to the danger of
     having inherited a biological disorder.
27   Committee on the Rights of the Child (2002) paras 31 and 32.
28   [2002] EWHC 1593 (Admin), [2002] 2 FLR 962.
29   See *Mikulic v Croatia* [2002] 1 FCR 720 at [54]. See also *Gaskin v United Kingdom* (1989)
     12 EHRR 36.
30   Per Scott-Baker J, applications brought for non-identifying information about the sperm
     donors who had fathered the applicants engaged art 8 ECHR. Depending on further evidence,
     the applicants might therefore obtain a declaration of incompatibility regarding the failure of
     the Human Fertilisation and Embryology Authority to introduce regulations allowing this.
31   See the recent consultation on this topic: DH (2002 c).
32   DH (2002 c) para 2.14.
33   DH (2002 c) paras 2.16–2.22.
34   *D v Registrar General* [1996] 1 FLR 707: the High Court confirmed that the Registrar
     General was unable to pass information about an adoptee to her birth mother, because the
     adoptee had not registered herself in the Adopted Contact Register: see discussion above. See
     now Adoption and Children Act 2002, ss 56–65.
35   Ie the Adoption Act 1976. NB this Act was not fully implemented until 1988.

changing profile of adopted children. The traditional model of adoption involved a baby being placed with adopters who assumed the guise of the child's birth parents, often in circumstances of extreme secrecy. Since these children had no memories of their birth parents, adoptive parents felt free to hide the circumstances of their adoptees' birth, and under no obligation to arrange for them to remain in contact with their birth families. Today, however, few babies are available for adoption and the vast majority of adoptees come from the ranks of children looked after by local authorities.[36] These children know very well who their birth parents are and have established relationships with them.

Adoption practitioners increasingly pursue the concept of openness for many of these 'older' children.[37] This involves them commonly arranging some form of continuing contact, either direct or indirect 'letter-box' contact with their birth parents, and/or siblings and other relatives.[38] The courts' approach to adoption proceedings does not accord with the increasing amounts of direct and indirect contact being arranged between adopted children and their birth families. Rather, they follow the traditional legal model of adoption, which involves a complete legal break between adoptees and their birth parents.[39] Consequently, although the courts are empowered to accompany an adoption order with a contact order in favour of birth parents, they commonly maintain that such an order should not be imposed on reluctant adopters, except in the most exceptional circumstances.[40]

The Adoption and Children Act 2002 omits any provision obliging the courts to consider making a contact order alongside any adoption order.[41] This may disappoint those who favour an increasing degree of openness in adoption. Indeed, the law has been criticised for failing to promote an ongoing social relationship between adoptees and their birth parents. Previous efforts to reform the adoption law[42] have often been accompanied by calls to introduce laws obliging the courts to consider accompanying adoption orders with contact orders in favour of birth parents, even in contested

36　In 1977, approximately 3,000 babies were adopted; cf in 1991, fewer than 900 babies were adopted. See DH (1993) paras 3.2–3.3.

37　But see DH (2001) Figure A, indicating that the average age of children adopted currently has decreased from 5 years 5 months, to 4 years 3 months between 1996/97 and 2000/01 and that during that period the percentage of children adopted, aged 1 to 4, has increased from 48% to 60% of all adoptees. Since then, the average age has slightly risen. See DH (2002 e) para 6.

38　See DH (1999 a) ch 5, esp p 47. See also N Lowe and M Murch et al (1999) whose research (pp 280 and 295–308) showed that 77% of the families with adopted children had some kind of contact with the birth families. But note that these children were all over 5 when adopted, so the rate of contact was probably higher than the norm for children adopted at a younger age.

39　See Adoption and Children Act 2002, ss 46 and 67 (formerly Adoption Act 1976, ss 12 and 39), discussed by N Lowe (1997 a).

40　See, inter alia: *Re C (a minor) (adoption order: conditions)* [1989] AC 1; *Re S (a minor) (blood transfusion: adoption order condition)* [1994] 2 FLR 416; *Re T (adoption: contact)* [1995] 2 FLR 251. But cf, inter alia: *Re A (a minor) (adoption: contact order)* [1993] 2 FLR 645; *Re T (adopted children: contact)* [1996] Fam 34. See discussion by C Smith and J Logan (2002) pp 286–289.

41　Although a court might consider it appropriate to do so, given that the Adoption and Children Act 2002, s 1(4) requires it to consider (c) the likely effect on the child of ceasing to be a member of his birth family and (f) the child's relationships with his relatives, including (i) the likelihood of any of these continuing and the value to the child of its doing so. See also s 26(2)(b) in the context of making placement orders.

42　Various official papers and reports marked efforts to reform the Adoption Act 1997: DH and Welsh Office (1993); DH (1996); Performance and Innovation Unit Report (2000); DH (2000).

cases.[43] Critics consider that the courts' refusal to impose contact orders on adopters reluctant to be bound by such arrangements compares unfavourably with their preparedness to force contact arrangements on recalcitrant mothers in private contact disputes.[44] Indeed, Casey and Gibberd claim that the legal profession has adopted an 'entrenched position' regarding post-adoption contact.[45]

Such claims seem to assume that it is natural for the biological tie between children and birth parents to be promoted by a social relationship and that the law is remiss for not promoting this. Ryburn uses the language of children's rights to support his claims, arguing that there is no difference between adopted children and those children who are involved in domestic contact disputes. He argues that since the latter have rights under the CRC, notably articles 8 and 9, to maintain contact with absent parents, the former should also have a right to contact with their birth parents. In his view:

'… there is no reason to assume that the moral imperative of the Convention should apply less equally in adoption matters than in other private family law cases.'[46]

It is implausible to use articles 8 and 9 to support the contention that adopted children have a 'right' to a relationship with their birth parents. Those provisions were, in any case, clearly intended to cover very different situations. Article 8 responded to the abuses committed by the military regime in Argentina, during which babies were abducted from their mothers at birth, before their births could be registered, and illegally given to childless couples associated with the armed forces and police.[47] Article 9 was intended to bar children being removed from their parents by the state, except in situations of abuse or neglect. Neither the Convention's background nor its later interpretation by the Committee on the Rights of the Child[48] suggest that these provisions demand adoption or fostering laws to provide birth parents with a presumptive right to contact with their adopted children.

Those who favour more openness in adoption also call on an impressively large body of research to substantiate their views.[49] Adopted children may derive benefit from knowing that they have not been rejected and any anxieties about the well-being of their birth parents and siblings can be relieved by direct contact.[50] Research suggests that children can make multiple attachments and therefore attachments with their adoptive parents need not be threatened by 'secondary attachments' with their birth parents.[51] Furthermore, for those children placed for adoption at an age when they already have established relationships with birth families, direct contact arrangements may actually enhance their new attachments with their adoptive parents.[52]

43　See, inter alia: M Ryburn (1997); M Ryburn (1998); B Lindley (1997); Adoption Law Reform Group (2000); D Casey and A Gibberd (2001); S Harris-Short (2001) pp 416–419.

44　See discussion below.

45　D Casey and A Gibberd (2001) p 40.

46　M Ryburn (1997) p 29.

47　S Detrick (1992) pp 292–294.

48　See R Hodgkin and P Newell (1998) pp 104–107, for a discussion of the interpretation of these articles by the Committee on the Rights of the Child.

49　See M Ryburn (1998) pp 57–61.

50　See inter alia: C Macaskill (2002) pp 56–58; C Thomas et al (1999) ch 8. See also D Howe and J Feast (2000) pp 37–39, recording adult adoptees' reasons and expectations regarding the desired direct contact with birth parents.

51　See O Stevenson (1998) p 47 and H Schaffer (1998) pp 164–168.

52　J Fratter (1996).

This research material does not, however, substantiate claims that adopted children, as opposed to their birth parents, would benefit from a change of legal policy in contested adoptions. Contact is not always beneficial, especially for previously abused children. Indeed, adopters sometimes claim that social workers' enthusiasm for promoting direct contact derives from their sympathy with birth parents who regret the need for adoption, and that this attitude clouds their perceptions of the adoptee's own best interests.[53] At times, social workers fail to acknowledge that contact with birth parents can not only upset children, but actually harm them emotionally.[54] Adopters then feel angry at being expected to continue arranging contact which they strongly believe is harming their adopted children.[55] Nor is there unanimity amongst the children themselves who have no contact with their birth parents, over whether they want it or not – some do, but others are content with matters as they are.[56] Their reasons for not wanting contact include the fact that they were adopted at too young an age to remember their birth parents and anxiety or fear over what contact might entail.[57] Case law bears out the fact that some older children have very clear perceptions of their real needs and may be emphatically opposed to contact with birth parents.[58]

Critics argue that the concept of openness, as initiated in New Zealand in the early 1980s,[59] has been taken up by practitioners here with 'almost missionary zeal' not merited by research on long-term outcomes.[60] Quinton et al have exhaustively reviewed the research evidence on the outcome of contact arrangements for fostered and adopted children. They point to a variety of methodological weaknesses in many of the research projects used by those advocating the benefits of contact between adopted and long-term foster children and their birth parents.[61] For example, the research does not always provide information about the age of the children considered, nor analyse the types of contact arranged, nor the quality of the children's existing relationships with their birth parents, prior to adoption. There is therefore no way of assessing what caused the improvement in the children's well-being, if any, after adoption (or fostering) with contact. Moreover, some research projects were conducted with self-selected adoptive parents who were therefore probably wholly committed to the value of establishing contact with birth parents. Quinton et al argue that far more research needs to be done before confident claims can be made on behalf of children, birth parents and adopters regarding the benefits of post-adoption contact.[62]

The detailed assessment of the research evidence carried out by Quinton et al suggests that claims that adopted children have a right, not only to know about their origins, but also to establish a social relationship with their birth parents should be

---

53   See N Lowe and M Murch et al (1999) pp 282–283 and 313–314.
54   See C Macaskill (2002) pp 58–61, describing the dangers involved in direct contact for formerly abused children.
55   N Lowe and M Murch et al (1999) pp 282–283.
56   C Thomas et al (1999) ch 8.
57   DH (1999 a) pp 45–46.
58   Eg *Re B (adoption: father's objections)* [1999] 2 FLR 215: the birth father's consent to his son's adoption was dispensed with largely because his son, a boy of 12, strongly supported his step-father's application to adopt him and rejected the birth father's argument that he should retain his links with his birth father's family.
59   See A McWhinnie (1994) pp 12–15, for a history of the New Zealand use of openness.
60   A McWhinnie (1994) p 15.
61   See D Quinton et al (1997) and D Quinton et al (1998).
62   See D Quinton et al (1997) p 411 and (1998) p 361. But see M Ryburn (1998), who strongly rebuts the arguments used by D Quinton et al.

treated with extreme caution. The existence of a biological tie between an adopted child and his or her birth parents does not, in itself, merit the creation of a social relationship between them. To move from the premise that some birth parents and children do benefit from contact to the proposition that the law should therefore introduce the presumption of adoption orders being accompanied by contact orders, appears insupportable.[63] Nor is it strengthened by appeals to international children's rights law. Until further research establishes that contact with birth parents would benefit the *majority* of adopted children as much as their birth parents, there seems little to justify these arguments being couched in terms of children's rights. In any event, in cases where adoption is not appropriate because of the child's close bonds with his or her birth parents,[64] a special guardianship order might be a better option.[65]

(3)   UNMARRIED FATHERS

The law's response to the biological relationship between the unmarried father and his child is of obvious relevance to a discussion of the extent to which the law should reinforce the link between a child and his or her biological parents. The question whether the biological tie between unmarried fathers and their children should be legally recognised in precisely the same way as that between married parents and their children continues to provoke disagreement. Meanwhile, the declining popularity of marriage and corresponding growth in unmarried cohabitation has been accompanied by increasing rates of children born outside marriage,[66] many of whom are born to cohabiting couples who jointly register their children's birth.[67] There are well-known reasons for the Family Law Reform Act 1987 not matching these attitudinal changes by automatically granting all unmarried fathers an equal status to that enjoyed by their married counterparts.[68] The confused messages regarding the importance of the relationship between non-marital children and their fathers have been reinforced by the recent legislative reform giving automatic parental responsibility only to those unmarried fathers whose names appear on their children's birth certificates.[69]

The piecemeal nature of this reform has produced a complex picture, with three groups of children enjoying subtly different legal relationships with their parents.[70] The first are the marital children, the second, the non-marital, but with 'birth certificate fathers', and the third, the non-marital children whose fathers are not identified on their birth certificates. One could argue that because the new legislation is not retrospective, a fourth group has also been created. Those children born before the reforms are, despite their fathers' names appearing on their birth certificates, treated

---

63   See N Lowe and M Murch et al (1999) who argue (pp 323–325) that various conditions predicate post-adoption contact arrangements benefiting adoptees.
64   Eg *Re B (adoption order)* [2001] EWCA Civ 347, [2001] 2 FLR 26.
65   See Children Act 1989, ss 14A–G, introduced by Adoption and Children Act 2002, s 115. Discussed in chapter 14.
66   In 2001, approximately 40% of live births were outside marriage: Office for National Statistics (2003) p 50.
67   In 2000, about four fifths of births outside marriage were jointly registered by both parents and three quarters of these births were to parents living at the same address. Office for National Statistics (2002) p 47.
68   See N Lowe (1997 b) pp 198–201, describing the various attempts to reform this area of the law.
69   See Children Act 1989, s 4(1)(a), introduced by Adoption and Children Act 2002, s 111. Discussed in chapter 14.
70   See J Eekelaar (2001) pp 426–428.

in an identical manner to those in the third group. The first group, the marital children, are the most secure.[71] Unlike the second, their father's parental responsibility cannot be terminated by court order.[72] Only the last group (together with the fourth) will have no one with parental responsibility over them in the event of their mothers dying.

The recent changes in the law were obviously partly fuelled by the ease with which the paternal link can now be accurately proved by DNA testing. The secrecy which, in the past, often shrouded a non-marital child's birth and the identity of his or her father, is untenable today, partly due to the Child Support Agency's ability to identify him and pursue him for child support. But perhaps the greatest factor influencing the recent reforms was the government's recognition that many unmarried parents were ignorant of the way in which the law discriminated against unmarried fathers.[73] Despite the growing numbers of children born outside marriage, relatively few unmarried fathers availed themselves of the legal procedures whereby they could acquire parental responsibility, probably because they did not appreciate the need to apply.[74] Indeed, unmarried fathers commonly assume that, because they have lived with their partners for some years and have undertaken financial responsibility for their children, they automatically enjoy parental responsibility for them.[75]

The assumption that the biological link between parent and child should *normally* carry a social and legal relationship clearly underlies the widespread view that the law should not discriminate between married and unmarried fathers.[76] This assumption was implicit in the words of Ward LJ, who explained that the effect of a parental responsibility order is to confer 'upon a committed father the status of parenthood for which nature has already ordained that he must bear responsibility'.[77] Some, like Deech, strongly disagreed with this stance, believing that such arguments concentrated on father's rights, without considering their children's own perspectives.[78] In Deech's view, the biological tie between child and parent was not as important to a child as the care and love he or she received on a day-to-day basis. Nevertheless, this approach perhaps overlooked the law's failure to cater adequately for non-marital families breaking up. The children of married parents automatically enjoy a legal relationship with their fathers, come what may, whether or not their parents separate, or die, or abandon them. Prior to the recent reforms, if an unmarried mother died without entering into a parental responsibility agreement with her unmarried partner, the latter had no parental responsibility for their children, despite his having cohabited with her and jointly parented them throughout their lives. In such a situation, the children might

---

71   See Children Act 1989, s 2(1): both parents have automatic parental responsibility.
72   Children Act 1989, s 4(3): an unmarried father's parental responsibility can be terminated by court order on application by anyone with parental responsibility or by the child with court leave.
73   Lord Chancellor's Department (1998) paras 51–56.
74   Lord Chancellor's Department (1998) para 53.
75   See R Pickford (1999 a) pp 145–152. See also R Pickford (1999 b) for a full account of this research project which found that 75% of the fathers who knew that they were financially responsible for their non-marital children were unaware that they lacked parental responsibility.
76   See, inter alia: A Bainham (1989); N Lowe (1997 b); H Conway (1996); J Eekelaar (2001).
77   *Re S (parental responsibility)* [1995] 2 FLR 648 at 657. See also *F v S (wardship: jurisdiction)* [1991] 2 FLR 349, in which Ward J criticised English law for 'the considerable disadvantage' an unmarried father finds himself in if his child is abducted abroad.
78   R Deech (1992) p 3. See also J Fortin (1995) pp 163–166.

be pawns in a dispute between relatives and their father over who might care for them in future[79] – an unthinkable dispute in the event of a married woman dying.

Now, the children whose parents are alert enough to ensure that both their names appear on their birth certificates, like marital children, have two parents with automatic parental responsibility over them. From birth, however, the third group of non-marital children lack two parents with a legal relationship with them, since only their mothers gain such legal recognition.[80] Their fathers have no legal status relating to their children. Nevertheless, the law goes out of its way to ease their position. Firstly, by virtue of the Family Law Reform Act 1987, section 1, references to 'parent' in legislation like the Children Act 1989[81] and the Child Support Act 1991,[82] must be interpreted as if the difference in legal status between all married and unmarried fathers is irrelevant. Secondly, although the non-birth certificate unmarried fathers must still take steps to acquire parental responsibility,[83] the case law shows that it is usually[84] a relatively simple task for them to satisfy the requisite 'attachment and commitment to the child' test to obtain a parental responsibility order.[85] But the very existence of a procedure apparently allowing the courts to distinguish between the meritorious and unmeritorious,[86] must create an expectation amongst mothers that fathers, whom they claim to be unmeritorious, will fail to obtain a parental responsibility order. It must be confusing for them to be told that because the order merely confers parental status, rather than giving the father a right to interfere with the day-to-day management of the child's life,[87] an assessment of merit is unnecessary. Is it realistic to expect the woman struggling to bring up her child free from the violent attentions of the father,[88] or without his financial help,[89] to think 'calmly' about a law providing him with parental responsibility, because it merely carries the status of parenthood?[90] Meanwhile, overarching the recent reforms, there remain the principles of law still maintaining the traditional view that all children of unmarried parents have no legal relationship with their fathers, irrespective of the state of their

79   Eg *Re S (custody: habitual residence)* [1998] 1 FLR 122.
80   Children Act 1989, s 2(2).
81   Eg *Re B (care proceedings: notification of father without parental responsibility)* [1999] 2 FLR 408: care order was set aside because the child's unmarried father was not served with notice of the care proceedings.
82   Child Support Act 1991, s 1 imposes liability on the non-residential parent irrespective of legal status.
83   Children Act 1989, s 4(1)(b) and (c), which enable an unmarried father to enter into a parental responsibility agreement with the mother or to apply for a parental responsibility order.
84   See S Gilmore (2003) for a detailed consideration of the case law on parental responsibility orders, together with its inconsistencies.
85   *Re H (minors) (local authority: parental rights) (No 3)* [1991] Fam 151. The court must consider the unmarried father's degree of commitment to the child, the degree of attachment existing between him and the child, and his reasons for applying for the order. Complying with the test is not difficult, eg, inter alia: *Re B J (a child) (non-molestation order: power of arrest)* [2001] 1 All ER 235 (an unmarried and violent father obtained a parental responsibility order despite its being accompanied by a non-molestation order and power of arrest to protect his daughter and her mother from his further harassment); *Re H (parental responsibility: maintenance)* [1996] 1 FLR 867 (an unmarried father obtained a parental responsibility order despite his refusing to pay any maintenance for his children).
86   See discussion by S Gilmore (2003) of this case law.
87   *Re P (a minor) (parental responsibility order)* [1994] 1 FLR 578 at 585, per Wilson J.
88   Eg *Re B J (a child) (non-molestation order: power of arrest)* [2001] 1 All ER 235.
89   Eg *Re H (parental responsibility: maintenance)* [1996] 1 FLR 867.
90   *Re S (parental responsibility)* [1995] 2 FLR 648 at 657, per Ward LJ. See F Kaganas (1996) for a critical discussion of this decision.

birth certificates. Consequently, no such child can claim British nationality from his or her father by descent[91] or inherit a peerage or other dignity.[92]

As is apparent, an extraordinarily inconsistent set of principles now apply to the children whose birth certificates omit their fathers' names. Of greatest concern is the fact that their mothers' death may still deprive them of the only adult with parental responsibility over them. Despite this source of discrimination, it does not appear that European human rights law will provoke further reform. Article 8 of the ECHR does indeed impose a positive obligation on states to provide legal safeguards enabling the child to be integrated within his or her marital and non-marital family from the moment of birth.[93] Furthermore, article 8 protects various forms of de facto family,[94] and, together with article 14, prohibits legal provisions which prevent unmarried parents from forming a family with their children, merely by virtue of their unmarried status.[95] Consequently, the domestic courts are rightly anxious to protect the procedural rights of unmarried fathers.[96] Nevertheless, the European Court of Human Rights has rejected claims that unmarried fathers' relationships with their children must always be recognised. Thus their rights under articles 8 and 14 of the ECHR are not infringed by English law denying them automatic parental responsibility.[97] The fact that the relationship between unmarried fathers and their children 'varies from ignorance and indifference to a close stable relationship indistinguishable from the conventional family-based unit' justifies the difference in treatment between them and married fathers.[98] Nor does an unmarried father have an absolute right to have his family ties with his non-marital child recognised legally even after the mother's death.[99]

The European Court's approach to the position of unmarried fathers reflects Deech's views. It clearly doubts the sense of providing all unmarried fathers with parental responsibility, irrespective of their relationship with the child or mother. Nonetheless, until English law is changed again, there remains a small group of children, who, through no fault of their own, have no legal relationship with their fathers. The fact

91 See S Cretney, J Masson and R Bailey-Harris (2002) pp 519–520. See *R (on the application of Montana) v Secretary of State for the Home Department* [2001] 1 FLR 449: the Court of Appeal rejected the claim that by barring a non-marital child from inheriting British citizenship, the British law of nationality infringes the rights of such children under arts 8 and 14 of the ECHR.

92 S Cretney, J Masson and R Bailey-Harris (2002) pp 519–520.

93 *Marckx v Belgium* (1979) 2 EHRR 330 (para 31).

94 Eg *Johnston v Ireland* (1986) 9 EHRR 203: the European Court held that the child of a cohabiting couple was entitled to protection of her family life under arts 8 and 14 of the ECHR and *X, Y and Z v United Kingdom* [1997] 2 FLR 892: the European Court held that the family unit existing between a transsexual, his partner and child, was a de facto family warranting the protection of art 8.

95 *Keegan v Ireland* (1994) 18 EHRR 342: the European Court held that Irish law had infringed an unmarried father's rights under arts 8 and 14 by denying him a right to challenge his child's adoption. See also *Kroon v Netherlands* (1995) 19 EHRR 263.

96 Eg *Re H: Re G (adoption: consultation of unmarried fathers)* [2001] 1 FLR 646: per Court of Appeal, to place a child for adoption without the unmarried father being given notice of pending adoption proceedings would be a prima facie breach of his rights under arts 8 and 6 of the ECHR.

97 *B v United Kingdom* [2000] 1 FLR 1.

98 *B v United Kingdom* [2000] 1 FLR 1 at 5.

99 See *Yousef v Netherlands* [2002] 3 FCR 577: the infringement of the father's rights (under art 8) to have his family ties between him and his daughter recognised was justified (under art 8(2)) by the domestic court's view that this would be against her best interests.

that few unmarried couples realise this will doubtless provoke further reforms conferring automatic parental responsibility on all unmarried fathers.[100]

(4)   PATERNAL IDENTITY DISPUTES

In the past, the 'gooseberry bush approach' was not that unusual, if a child was born whose father's identity was doubtful.[101] Aided and abetted by the courts,[102] the view was that as long as the child had a stable home, it did not much matter who he or she called 'Daddy'. Indeed, 'least said, soonest mended' often appeared to be the order of the day. It may be a deepening knowledge of genetics that is now fuelling our current preoccupation with biological origins. The ease with which DNA testing can now establish biological parentage with complete accuracy means that for the vast majority of children there is little reason to deny them this information. Nevertheless, the adults involved in a child's life may not always agree over the importance of its either being obtained or divulged. Their disagreement is often wholly attributable to the assumption that biological parentage automatically carries a right to enjoy a social relationship with the child and that, once established, the court will assist in promoting such a right through court-ordered contact. Indeed, it seems clear that it is only in the context of adoption that a child's right to obtain information about the identity of his or her biological parents is normally kept separate from any issue over whether there should be a social relationship between them. This is because the law ensures that the adoptive relationship displaces the claims of the natural parents to a social relationship. In other contexts, the confusion between these two logically unrelated issues, namely the child's right to identify both natural parents and the value to the child of creating a social relationship between them, becomes very obvious.

The most common situation where these two issues can become inextricably entwined is where, despite the mother's assertions to the contrary, either of two men could have fathered the child and there is a dispute between her and one of them, over whether he should have a social relationship with the child.[103] Often in such cases, the mother refuses to acknowledge the existence of doubt over the identity of her child's father, refuses to tell the child who his or her real father might be and does all she can to keep the man out of the child's life. Meanwhile, the putative father does all he can to achieve a social relationship with the child through obtaining contact. But a vital first step is for him to establish his biological links with the child by asking the court to make a direction for blood or DNA testing.[104]

It may not be too cynical to suggest that these disputes are entirely adult-centred and that the adults concerned do not, by seeking directions for blood or DNA tests, want to fulfil the child's right to know the true identity of his or her father, as a right with an intrinsic value of its own. They are motivated by the assumption that the biological tie should always be accompanied by a social relationship and vice versa. The impetus for the putative father's application for paternity testing is his desire to

---

100 N Lowe (1997 b) p 208. See also J Eekelaar (2001) p 430.
101 See J Fortin (1994), commenting on *Re F (a minor) (paternity test)* [1993] 1 FLR 598.
102 Eg *Re F (a minor) (paternity test)* [1993] 1 FLR 598.
103 Eg, inter alia: *Re F (a minor) (paternity test)* [1993] 1 FLR 598; *Re G (a minor) (blood test)* [1994] 1 FLR 495; *Re H (paternity: blood test)* [1996] 2 FLR 65; *Re G (parentage: blood sample)* [1997] 1 FLR 360; *Re T (paternity: ordering blood tests)* [2001] 2 FLR 1190; *Re H and A (paternity: blood tests)* [2002] EWCA Civ 383, [2002] 1 FLR 1145.
104 Under Family Law Reform Act 1969, s 20(1).

follow this up with an application for a contact order. Equally, the mother's desire to stop him is motivated by her fear that if he establishes his paternity, the courts will force her to allow him contact. Alternatively, the mother herself seeks a direction for paternity testing, hoping that it will show that a particular man is not the father and that she can *therefore* oppose his contact application, on the basis that there is no biological tie between them and consequently no merit in granting a contact order.[105]

The need to comply with the Human Rights Act 1998 has highlighted the way in which these disputes involve a complex web of conflicting rights. As Bodey J made clear in *Re T (paternity: ordering blood tests)*,[106] on the one hand, the child enjoys a right to knowledge of the identity of his or her father, as protected by article 8 of the ECHR, a right which can only be established by paternity testing. But he also has the right to stability in his present family. On the other hand, the child's mother and her new partner have a right to respect for their private and family life, free from interference from the man claiming to the child's real father. Such a right might be protected by refusing to direct blood tests. Equally, the claimant himself may have a right to family life with his child, if he is proved to be the child's father, which should be protected by a contact order.[107]

In purely practical terms, a mother is probably fully justified in opposing blood tests in such situations. She recognises this from the case law surrounding women who know the true identity of their children's father, but who bring their children up to think of their step-fathers as 'Daddy'. If the man's paternity is clearly established, the courts will disapprove of any attempt on her part either to keep this information from the child or to prevent the father from having contact with the child.[108] Perhaps influenced by the research relating to adopted children,[109] the courts have referred to the dangers of a child discovering the true facts by accident:

> 'To do and say nothing now is in truth storing up a potential bombshell for the future, which might be very damaging for J to learn and might indeed seriously undermine his sense of trust in his mother ...'[110]

In *Re R (a minor) (contact)*,[111] Butler-Sloss LJ even indicated to the mother that if she could not tell her daughter the truth herself, a child psychiatrist instructed by the Official Solicitor, who was acting as guardian ad litem for the child, might do so instead.[112] It is notable that the judiciary, in these cases, clearly consider that knowledge of identity alone is not enough. These mothers are not only expected to identify the child's real father, but also introduce him to the child through gradually increasing contact. Indeed, these disputes over whether a child should be informed of the real identity of his or her father are almost inevitably underpinned by the courts' assumption that the father should also have contact with the child, albeit only indirect contact in some cases. This is not surprising since the courts are, in all these cases, being presented with claims which, despite appearing to fulfil the child's right to

---

105 See *O v L (blood tests)* [1995] 2 FLR 930 and *Re G (parentage: blood sample)* [1997] 1 FLR 360.

106 [2001] 2 FLR 1190.

107 Bodey J was doubtful over the strength of this argument, see below.

108 Eg, inter alia: *Re R (a minor) (contact)* [1993] 2 FLR 762; *A v L (contact)* [1998] 1 FLR 361; *Re K (specific issue order)* [1999] 2 FLR 280.

109 Discussed above.

110 *A v L (contact)* [1998] 1 FLR 361 at 366, per Holman J.

111 [1993] 2 FLR 762.

112 [1993] 2 FLR 762 at 768.

knowledge of the identity of the child's father, in fact are aiming for nothing of the sort. They are merely an essential step on the road to claiming contact with the child.

In cases where there is some genuine doubt about the identity of the child's father, the mother will be confronted by a man seeking to establish his paternity by obtaining a direction for blood or DNA testing which must be ancillary to an application for some other order regarding the child's parentage.[113] The most obvious route for a putative father to use is to combine his application for a direction for paternity testing with one for a contact order and/or a parental responsibility order. This form of litigation immediately brings him into direct conflict with the child's mother, if she is reluctant to allow him to develop a relationship with the child. Now that the scope of the declarations of paternity procedure has been widened, a man claiming to be the father of a child could instead apply for a direction for paternity testing, appended to an application for a declaration that he is the father of that child.[114] Theoretically, such an application might appear less threatening to a mother wishing to keep him out of the lives of herself and her child, than the former more obvious route, since it does not claim involvement in the child's life. But even if he chooses this more neutral strategy, it seems unlikely that a mother who is on bad terms with him will believe that he merely wants to establish the child's parentage. She will probably resolutely oppose such an application, fearing his next step.

Today, when dealing with these strongly opposed applications for paternity testing, the courts seem fully aware of the child's need to know the truth about his or her origins and the way in which this need is protected by human rights law. Confirming older case law,[115] the Court of Appeal has stressed that it is normally in children's best interests for the truth of their parentage to be established speedily. Indeed, referring to article 7 of the CRC in support, Ward LJ maintained that 'every child has a right to know the truth unless his welfare clearly justifies the cover-up'[116] and that '… if [the child] grows up knowing the truth, that will not undermine his attachment to his father-figure, and he will cope with knowing that he has two fathers. Better that than a time bomb ticking away'.[117] More recently, Bodey J stated in *Re T (paternity: ordering blood tests)*[118] that the child in question had a right to respect for his private life under article 8 of the ECHR 'in the sense of having knowledge of his identity, which encompasses his true paternity …'[119]

This approach represents a welcome break with past case law in which the judiciary made relatively little attempt to consider the merits of an application for blood tests independently from the possible outcome of the application for other orders, such as

---

113   Under s 20(1) of the Family Law Reform Act 1969, the courts are *only* able to make a direction for blood tests in the course of 'any civil proceedings in which the parentage of any person falls to be determined'. Eg in *Re E (parental responsibility: blood tests)* [1995] 1 FLR 392, Balcombe LJ explained (at 400) that the court had no power to deal with a free-standing application for blood tests.

114   See Family Law Act 1986, s 55A, which makes it clear that, subject to restrictions (see sub-s (3)–(5)), anyone can apply for a declaration of parentage regarding another person. This replaces the procedure formerly available under s 56(1)(a) (now repealed) whereby only a child (or his or her representative) could apply for a declaration of parentage.

115   *S v S; W v Official Solicitor (or W)* [1972] AC 24.

116   *Re H (paternity: blood test)* [1996] 2 FLR 65 at 80.

117   [1996] 2 FLR 65 at 82.

118   [2001] 2 FLR 1190.

119   [2001] 2 FLR 1190 at 1197. See also *Re H and A (paternity: blood tests)* [2002] EWCA Civ 383, [2002] 1 FLR 1145 at [21], per Thorpe LJ, voicing concerns over 'the risks of perpetuating a sense of uncertainty that breeds gossip and rumour', and the danger of the children discovering the true identity of their father.

contact. Perceiving that an applicant seeking a direction for blood tests was also intent on gaining contact with the child in question, the courts allowed one issue to determine the other. If the court was convinced that fulfilling the applicant's wish for contact with the child would be against the child's best interests, it would refuse to grant the direction for blood tests,[120] and vice versa.[121] There appeared to be little appreciation that the child might one day feel cheated by the court's refusal to clarify the identity of his or her father.[122] More recently, the senior judiciary seem keen to deal with the issue of biological parentage as a preliminary issue, detached from the question whether the applicant should in future be allowed to acquire a psychological or social relationship with the child.[123] Thus Ward LJ has pointed out that if the blood test excludes the applicant from paternity, this does not necessarily prevent a future contact application succeeding; he might then convince the court that the child would benefit from continued contact with a devoted step-father.[124] Equally, Bodey J in *Re T*, emphasised that in the event of blood tests confirming the putative father's claims, it would not automatically follow that he would then succeed in obtaining a contact order or a parental responsibility order.[125]

Few mothers involved in these disputes seem to acknowledge that their children have a right to a knowledge of their origins. Indeed, in the past, mothers' opposition to blood testing caused problems, with the courts showing a reluctance to override their refusal to allow their children to be tested.[126] Today, mothers can no longer prevent their children discovering the true identity of their fathers by simply ignoring a court's direction for paternity testing.[127] Nevertheless, the court obviously cannot override the mother's views without taking full account of the complexity of these disputes. As discussed above, *Re T (paternity: ordering blood tests)*[128] demonstrates well that the child is not the sole player. The mother and her husband may claim a right to live a life free of the putative father's interference in the child's life. Equally, the putative father may claim rights to a family life with his child, if blood testing establishes his paternity.[129] In *Re T*, Bodey J concluded that when finding a balance between the competing rights, weight should be given to the child's rights under article 8 of the European Convention, including his right to security with his present de facto family, but with greatest weight being given to his right to know 'perhaps with certainty, his true roots and identity'.[130] Consequently, any interference with the

---

120 Eg *Re F (a minor) (paternity test)* [1993] 1 FLR 598; see discussion by J Fortin (1994).

121 Eg *Re G (a minor) (blood test)* [1994] 1 FLR 495.

122 J Fortin (1994) pp 297–300.

123 *Re H (paternity: blood test)* [1996] 2 FLR 65 at 82, per Ward LJ. But see *Re H and A (paternity: blood tests)* [2002] EWCA Civ 383 [2002] 1 FLR 1145: the trial judge's approach was similar to that of the Court of Appeal in *Re F (a minor) (paternity test)* [1993] 1 FLR 598. His refusal to order blood testing was reversed on appeal.

124 *Re G (parentage: blood sample)* [1997] 1 FLR 360 at 366, per Ward LJ.

125 [2001] 2 FLR 1190 at 1196, per Bodey J.

126 Eg *Re F (a minor) (paternity test)* [1993] 1 FLR 598 and *Re O and J (paternity: blood tests)* [2000] 1 FLR 418.

127 Responding to the gap in the law disclosed by *Re O and J* [2000] 1 FLR 418, the Family Law Reform Act 1969, s 21(3)(b) (as amended) gives the courts power to direct paternity testing on the child, if it 'considers that it would be in [the child's] best interests for the sample to be given', irrespective of his or her carer's lack of consent.

128 [2001] 2 FLR 1190.

129 But in *Re T* [2001] 2 FLR 1190 at 1198–1199, Bodey J doubted the strength of the unmarried father's claim that he too enjoyed art 8 rights, since the absence of any contact between him and the child undermined his claim to 'family life'. See also U Kilkelly (1999) pp 89–95 and 191–193, for a discussion of the Strasbourg jurisprudence on this point.

130 [2001] 2 FLR 1190 at 1198.

rights of the mother and her husband was justified under article 8 (2) of the Convention, as being proportionate to the legitimate aim of furthering T's right to certainty as to his real paternity.

Current case law suggests that putative fathers will have little difficulty in obtaining directions for blood or DNA tests and that children will normally have their right to discover their biological origins fulfilled by the courts. But the child's right to know the identity of his or her father is not the only right of any importance in such cases. As Bodey J pointed out in *Re T*,[131] a child also has a right to security in his or her present family unit. It was the risk of losing this security that worried the trial judge in *Re H and A (paternity: blood tests)*.[132] He considered that it would be disastrous for the mother's husband to be excluded from paternity because twin little girls would lose their 'psychological father'. The Court of Appeal disagreed, considering that the uncertainty over their father's identity would cause greater damage. Achieving an appropriate balance between the two sets of rights may not be easy. One also wonders whether the courts will always manage to keep the two issues, that of knowledge of origins and a social relationship between putative parent and child, entirely separate. Children have a right to be protected from distressing information about their parentage.[133] How would the courts deal, for example, with an application from a rapist wishing to establish his paternity of the child his victim gave birth to? The court's preparedness to sympathise with the mother's claim that it would be damaging for the child to know that his or her father is a rapist might be influenced by its knowledge that any future contact application will surely fail. Such an example is an extreme one. Nevertheless, the courts' approach to all these disputes is undoubtedly complicated by society's assumption that biological ties *should* always carry social relationships, despite the growing evidence provided by family disruption and reproductive technology that this is not always appropriate.

(5)   IDENTITY AND NAMES

When describing the practice whereby married parents give a child the father's surname, Lord Jauncey of Tullichettle suggested that this was a way of –

> 'demonstrating its relationship to him. The surname is thus a biological label which tells the world at large that the blood of the name flows in its veins.'[134]

Views like this regarding the importance of maintaining the blood tie between child and father through their surnames may still be common. Indeed, they may be shared by many women, perhaps explaining women's predilection for ensuring that their children carry their partners' surnames whilst the relationship lasts. Hale LJ, however, provides a very different approach:

> 'It is also a matter of great sadness to me that it is so often assumed, and even sometimes argued, that fathers need that outward and visible link [through surnames] in order to retain their relationship with, and commitment to, their child. That should not be the case ... After all,

---

131   [2001] 2 FLR 1190 at 1198.
132   [2002] EWCA Civ 383, [2002] 1 FLR 1145.
133   See A Bainham (2002) pp 282–284.
134   *Dawson v Wearmouth* [1999] 2 All ER 353 at 361. See discussed by M Hayes (1999).

that is a privilege which is not enjoyed by many mothers ... They have to rely on other more substantial things.'[135]

Children's surnames carry a practical as well as symbolic importance. When children are named they are identified, given membership of their family group and provided with a link to their cultural background. It is important that children's existence is recognised in this way, as soon after birth as possible, for otherwise they could be abandoned or kidnapped with relative impunity. Articles 7 and 8 of the CRC recognise this. Article 7 requires children to be registered immediately after birth and from birth, to have the right to a name and nationality. Article 8 requires states to respect a child's right 'to preserve his or her identity, including nationality, name and family relations as recognised by law without unlawful interference'.

Neither of these articles seems particularly relevant to the type of parental dispute over children's names that are becoming increasingly commonplace in this country today. Instead, they reflect concerns about the dangers that children encounter on a global scale, such as losing their parents when caught up in mass movements of refugees from country to country. Thus article 7 principally aims to ensure that children are immediately registered and named on birth, so that following war, abandonment or abduction, they know their age, race and parentage.[136] As observed above, the principal aim of article 8 was to prevent a reoccurrence of the atrocities in the late 1970s and 1980s in Argentina when large numbers of babies and children disappeared, some to be killed, others to be adopted by childless couples linked to the official regime. Article 8 ensures that babies are not only identified on birth but that their right to preserve their identities is respected.

In this country, parental litigation over children's surnames[137] is not a new phenomenon. Indeed, the law reports spanning more than 20 years contain accounts of such disputes.[138] Most of these arise over whether a child should now adopt a different surname, reflecting the residential parents' own change of circumstances. Disagreements over the child's initial surname are uncommon, probably because a child's birth usually marks a time when the parents are still happy together. In any event, the law gives no indication what surname the child should take on birth,[139] merely indicating who should register it and when.[140] The initial selection of a surname for children is strongly influenced by the now outdated customs of a patriarchal society. Women on marriage took their husbands' surnames. Furthermore, by habitually giving their children the husband's name, married couples publicly indicated that their children were legitimate, with inheritance rights and membership of their father's

---

135 *Re R (surname: using both parents')* [2001] EWCA Civ 1344, [2001] 2 FLR 1358 at [18]. See also Hale LJ's clear view (at [13]) that Lord Jauncey's views in *Dawson v Wearmouth* [1999] 2 All ER 353, do not accord with the modern law.

136 See R Hodgkin and P Newell (1998) p 99.

137 Disputes over children's names normally involve disputes over surnames. More recently disputes over 'forenames', 'Christian' names or 'given' names are becoming more common. Eg *Re H (child's name: first name)* [2002] EWCA Civ 190, [2002] 1 FLR 973.

138 Eg *D v B (otherwise D) (child: surname)* [1979] 1 All ER 92 and *Re R (surname: using both parents')* [2001] EWCA Civ 1344, [2001] 2 FLR 1358.

139 The Registration of Births and Deaths Regulations 1987, SI 1987/2088, reg 9(3) merely state that the surname to be entered 'shall be the surname by which at the date of the registration of birth it is intended that the child shall be known'.

140 The Births and Deaths Registration Act 1953, s 2, requires the child's birth to be registered within 42 days of its birth and if the parents are married, either should do so. If the parents are unmarried, the duty is on the mother to do so.

extended family. Historically, an unmarried woman usually retained her own surname, since she would not normally live openly with her partner. Her 'illegitimate child', as a filius nullius, was not entitled to any acknowledgment from his father and commonly took his mother's surname. Today, despite a rising divorce rate and ever increasing rates of cohabitation outside marriage, these customs still seem to influence the initial choice of surnames by married couples. Furthermore, rather than retaining their own surnames, many unmarried women now also adopt their partners' surnames on entering cohabitation. Later when they have children, although they are entitled to choose what surname they please for their children,[141] unmarried women often agree to the child taking the father's surname, rather than their own.[142] This rather anachronistic approach seems at odds with cohabiting mothers' rejection of marriage. Indeed, they obviously think it appropriate to copy their married counterparts in this respect. Perhaps they also agree with Lord Jauncey's outdated views referred to above.[143]

On separation, a mother commonly decides to mark her changed way of life by shedding her ex-partner's surname. She then decides that her child should carry the same name as she does now – which may be that of her new partner.[144] A non-resident father may see such a change, often combined with new registration details with all official agencies, such as schools and doctors,[145] as an attempt to cut his links with his children. When the dispute ends up in court, the judiciary's response to the mother's application to change the child's name[146] is variable. Incidentally, it is unclear how the courts obtain any authority to be involved in such disputes at all. The legislation clearly allows a parent with parental responsibility to meet his or her responsibilities regarding the child unilaterally, without consulting the other,[147] and certainly without obtaining court permission.[148] Nevertheless, through a series of decisions, the courts have laid down the proposition that if parents, married and unmarried alike, cannot agree whether to change their child's surname, they must seek judicial authority first.[149]

Changing a child's surname can only be justified if it is in the child's best interests.[150] When the courts hear applications for permission to do so, the essential subjectivity of the best interests test is demonstrated only too clearly. Some courts consider that a child's surname is a matter of fundamental importance because it may break the

---

141   *Dawson v Wearmouth* [1999] 2 All ER 353. See discussion by M Hayes (1999).
142   Eg *Re C (change of surname)* [1998] 2 FLR 656: dispute between an unmarried couple over whether the mother should be made to change their daughter's surname back to that of the father, which appeared on her birth certificate. The mother had changed the child's surname to her own soon after the couple separated.
143   *Dawson v Wearmouth* [1999] 2 All ER 353 at 361.
144   Eg *Re PC (change of surname)* [1997] 2 FLR 730: a divorced mother, having remarried, sought unsuccessfully to force her children's school to re-register the children under her new surname, having persuaded her family doctor to do the same.
145   *Re PC (change of surname)* [1997] 2 FLR 730.
146   Alternatively, the father may apply to force her to change the child's name back, she having made the change already, eg *Re C (change of surname)* [1998] 2 FLR 656.
147   Children Act 1989, s 2(7) states: 'Where more than one person has parental responsibility for a child, each of them may act alone and without the other (or others) in meeting that responsibility ...'
148   See J Eekelaar (1998) and J Eekelaar (2001) pp 428–429.
149   *Re PC (change of surname)* [1997] 2 FLR 730; *Re C (change of surname)* [1998] 2 FLR 656; *Dawson v Wearmouth* [1999] 2 All ER 353.
150   *Dawson v Wearmouth* [1999] 2 All ER 353 at 359, per Lord Mackay. See also *Re W, Re A; Re B (change of name)* [1999] 2 FLR 930 at 933, per Butler-Sloss LJ.

child's link with his or her non-resident father.[151] Others consider that surnames are relatively trivial matters and that children should not be embarrassed by being forced to retain a different name to that of their mothers. That being so, the courts should therefore concentrate on fostering the father's actual links with the child through good contact arrangements.[152] Hale LJ sums up the two different approaches:

> 'Generally, therefore, what the court is doing is balancing the long-term interests of a child in retaining an outward link with the parent with whom that child is not living against what are often shorter-term benefits of lack of confusion, convenience, lack of embarrassment and the like.'[153]

This ad hoc approach provides parents with little clear guidance. Fortunately, the courts are gradually taking more account of children's own views about what names they should carry.[154] Nevertheless, these bitter disputes will continue until parents adopt a more pragmatic approach, like that suggested by Hale and Thorpe LJJ in *Re R (surname: using both parents')*.[155] This was for the child to carry both parents' surnames on separation. Although such a solution does not prevent parents disagreeing over which surname should be listed first, it does overcome sexist assumptions about children bearing their fathers' names. Meanwhile, we need more research on the extent to which children's own sense of identity is bound up with the names they become familiar with in their early years. This will help us clarify whether these names are the ones they should carry for the rest of their lives.

(6)   PARENTAL CONTACT DISPUTES

(A)   A child's 'right' to contact

Contact disputes very obviously reflect the need experienced by parents and children to spend time together and also an assumption that it is their right to do so, by virtue of the biological link between them. Although most parents who fall out seem able to agree who is to be the main carer of their children,[156] they increasingly disagree over the contact arrangements to be enjoyed by the non-resident parent.[157] As Buchanan et al observe, these disputes provoke profound debates within our society – in particular,

---

151 Eg *W v A (child: surname)* [1981] Fam 14 and *Re C (a child) (change of surname)* [1999] 1 FCR 318. Such a view may be strengthened by circumstances in which changing a child's surname would risk his losing his links with his racial and religious identity. Eg *Re S (change of names: cultural factors)* [2001] 2 FLR 1005.

152 Eg *D v B (otherwise D) (child: surname)* [1979] 1 All ER 92 and *Y v Y (child's surname)* [1999] 2 FLR 5. See also *Yousef v Netherlands* [2002] 3 FCR 577: the European Court of Human Rights implicitly approved of the Dutch court's view that the child might be harmed by the automatic assumption of her father's surname were he allowed formally to recognise her as his daughter. She was being brought up by her mother's family under their surname and a different surname might set her apart from them.

153 *Re R (surname: using both parents')* [2001] EWCA Civ 1344, [2001] 2 FLR 1358 at [15].

154 Eg *Re M, T, P, K and B (care: change of name)* [2000] 2 FLR 645; cf *Re B (change of surname)* [1996] 1 FLR 791. Discussed in more detail in chapter 8.

155 [2001] EWCA Civ 1344, [2001] 2 FLR 1358.

156 In the rare event of residence being fought over, the court will normally grant a residence order (under Children Act 1989, s 8(1)) to the parent deemed most suitable to offer day to day care. Despite the work of fathers' pressure groups, the English courts seem reluctant to make shared residence orders under s 11(4), although the decision in *D v D (shared residence order)* [2001] 1 FLR 495 marks a less restrictive attitude to such orders.

157 In 2001, 29,546 residence orders were made cf 55,030 contact orders. See DH (2002 d) p 45.

there is the question whether a biological tie entitles a parent to an ongoing relationship with his child or whether the role of parent has to be earned.[158]

Few doubt that it is *normally* in children's best interests to remain in contact with the parent who leaves the home when a couple separate. International human rights law recognises this. Both the CRC[159] and the European Convention on Contact Concerning Children[160] emphasise the need for the child to maintain direct and regular contact, except in circumstances where this would be against the child's best interests. A concern to ensure that the father[161] should retain his links with his children carries obvious sense when they have enjoyed a valuable relationship together and if this can be promoted without causing the child psychological harm. For many years, the judiciary have assumed that it will 'almost always' benefit children to have as much contact with their non-resident fathers as possible.[162] They have little patience with the 'implacably hostile mother' who has no acceptable reasons[163] for refusing to co-operate over contact.[164] In a leading case, Sir Thomas Bingham MR explained very firmly:

> 'Neither parent should be encouraged or permitted to think that the more intransigent, the more unreasonable, the more obdurate and the more un-cooperative they are, the more likely they are to get their own way.'[165]

By the mid-1990s, the extent to which the rebuttable presumption of contact had become official policy was evident in the now defunct Family Law Act 1996, section 11(4).[166] The judiciary stressed to mothers that contact was for the child's sake, rather than for the father.[167] They consistently employed the language of children's rights to justify decisions fulfilling fathers' claims to contact,[168] without paying much attention to the quality of the relationships between father and child or between the parents. Furthermore, the courts commonly attributed the child's own reluctance to comply with contact arrangements to their being indoctrinated by their mothers.[169]

Plainly the contact presumption was intended to deter mothers from subtly alienating their children against their absent fathers for no good reason.[170] Meanwhile, by the end of the 1990s, a rising tide of criticism focused on the courts' approach to contact disputes involving domestic violence. This bore fruit, leading to important changes in judicial practice.[171] But what of the other cases – those involving mothers

---

158   See A Buchanan et al (2001) p 1.
159   See CRC, art 9(3).
160   Adopted and opened for signature in 2002. See especially art 1.
161   NB this section is written on the basis that the father is the non-resident parent, reflecting the fact that contact disputes normally involve father applicants and mother respondents.
162   See especially *Re O (contact: imposition of conditions)* [1995] 2 FLR 124 and *Re P (contact: supervision)* [1996] 2 FLR 314.
163   Such as domestic violence or child abuse. Discussed below.
164   See *Re J (a minor) (contact)* [1994] 1 FLR 729 at 736, per Balcombe LJ.
165   *Re O (contact: imposition of conditions)* [1995] 2 FLR 124 at 129–130.
166   When considering divorcing parents' statements of arrangements regarding their children's upbringing post-divorce, the courts should pay regard to 'the general principle that, in the absence of evidence to the contrary, the welfare of the child will be best served by – (i) his having regular contact with those who have parental responsibility for him ...'
167   See R Bailey-Harris et al (1999) pp 114–118, for a historical assessment of the contact presumption.
168   See, inter alia: *Re S (minors) (access)* [1990] 2 FLR 166 at 170, per Balcombe LJ; *Re R (a minor) (contact)* [1993] 2 FLR 762 at 767, per Butler-Sloss LJ; *Re F (contact: restraint order)* [1995] 1 FLR 956 at 963, per Waite LJ; *Re A (contact: domestic violence)* [1998] 2 FLR 171 at 174, per Connell J; *A v Y (child's surname)* [1999] 2 FLR 5 at 8, per Judge Tyrer.
169   Eg *Re J (a minor) (contact)* [1994] 1 FLR 729. See discussion in chapter 8.
170   S Maidment (1998). But note the controversy over the existence of parental alienation syndrome (PAS), discussed in chapter 8.
171   Discussed below.

whose 'rooted objection stands on no objective foundation'?[172] Thorpe LJ in *Re L (a child) (contact: domestic violence) and other appeals*[173] made it clear that he now favoured a change of legal language. He not only disliked the language of rights being used to buttress judicial reasoning in such disputes, but also the use of the word 'presumption', preferring 'assumption'.[174] Nevertheless, despite a change of language masking its strength, the presumption itself appears to be impregnable,[175] with the approach adopted in the earlier case law being fully endorsed.[176] Indeed, the Court of Appeal apparently consider that there is sufficient scientific knowledge to justify the courts 'assuming' that contact with a father is beneficial for the children in all other cases[177] – other, that is, than those involving domestic violence or situations involving proved harm or risk of harm to the child.[178]

Many would question the Court of Appeal's view that there is sufficient research evidence to justify retaining the presumption (or 'assumption') of contact in ordinary contact disputes. Davis and Pearce describe lawyers and the courts adopting 'the pro-contact presumption with a zeal hardly justified by evidence derived from the social scientific world',[179] with a self-referencing body of case law being built up, supported by little other than judicial pronouncements. This, combined with a 'settlement culture', leads to couples, especially mothers, coming under considerable pressure to settle their disputes out of court.[180] There is indeed a large body of research literature indicating not only that divorce and separation has a long-term psychological impact on many children, but also that this can be mitigated by both parents remaining easily accessible to the child and involved in the parenting role.[181] If contact can occur happily, it will provide the child with many benefits, including reinforcing the child's sense of identity and knowledge of origins.[182] But, as critics point out, assuming from such research that contact will always be beneficial does not accord with the complexities of contact disputes.[183]

The research evidence on the effects of maintaining contact between a child and non-resident parent in *less* than happy circumstances is extremely ambiguous.[184] Longitudinal studies suggest that it is impossible to generalise over what is best for children after parental separation, since this will depend on the diversity of experiences and family processes. In particular, the benefits of the non-resident father's involvement are linked with the quality of the relationship and the degree of on-going conflict between the parents.[185] Despite the paucity of the research evidence, it

172 *Re H (a child) (contact: mother's opposition)* [2001] 1 FCR 59 at [32], per Thorpe LJ.
173 [2000] 4 All ER 609.
174 [2000] 4 All ER 609 at 637–638.
175 See F Kaganas (2000) pp 315–316.
176 [2000] 4 All ER 609 at 617–618, per Dame Elizabeth Butler-Sloss P, confirming the approach adopted in previous case law regarding the presumption of contact, described notably by Bingham MR in *Re O (contact: imposition of conditions)* [1996] 1 FCR 317.
177 [2000] 4 All ER 609 at [38], per Thorpe LJ.
178 [2000] 4 All ER 609 at 616, per Dame Elizabeth Butler-Sloss P.
179 See G Davis and J Pearce (1999 a) p 145.
180 G Davis and J Pearce (1999 a) p 147. See also G Davis and J Pearce (1999 b) pp 239–240 and R Bailey-Harris et al (1999) p 124.
181 See B Rogers and J Pryor (1998) esp pp 42–43, for a summary of the research on this topic. See also P Amato and J Gilbreth (1999) esp pp 13–14 (of Internet version) and J Kelly (2000) p 9 (of Internet version).
182 See C Sturge and D Glaser (2000) pp 616–617 and 627.
183 See, inter alia: G Davis and J Pearce (1999 a); G Davis and J Pearce (1999 b); B Cantwell et al (1999); R Bailey-Harris et al (1999).
184 See M Maclean and J Eekelaar (1997) pp 53–59. See also J Eekelaar (2002) pp 271–272.
185 See J Kelly (2000). See also A Buchanan et al (2001) pp 4–5 for a useful summary of recent research on this topic.

appears that court enforced contact arrangements may actually damage children psychologically, given that it provides further opportunities for conflict between the parents.[186] Indeed, although many children would often like to have more contact with non-resident parents, they would prefer there to be no contact at all, if it means an end to arguments.[187] Perhaps more ominously, some adults who, as children, were subjected to inflexibly enforced court orders, deeply resented their experiences, found them damaging and considered that the orders fulfilled only their parents' needs rather than their own.[188] There is also a growing view that many contact orders are far too inflexible to accommodate children's own developmental and practical needs[189] and that children also want to be far more involved in the decision-making process.[190]

Despite the absence of any clear research evidence favouring the contact presumption, the courts seemingly favour its retention where the mother, without any good reason, is implacably hostile to contact.[191] It seems unlikely, however, that this fast moving field of case law will stand still. The courts could, in future, adopt one of two approaches. One is to rein back the contact presumption and follow the direction in the Children Act 1989, section 1. This, as the Scottish House of Lords has stated,[192] clearly places the onus on the father claiming contact to show that this would be in the child's best interests. In other words, a father must earn his contact by satisfying the court that it is in the child's best interests for him to have it. As noted above, Thorpe LJ hints at being attracted by such an approach. He clearly feels uncomfortable with the present presumption, backed, as it is, by the language of children's rights, preferring to describe it as 'an assumption'.[193] Nevertheless, whilst this moderate approach could be squared with the requirements of article 8(1) of the ECHR, it requires a degree of care. Indeed, fulfilling these Convention requirements may, instead, provoke a second approach – a far more unashamed adoption of a 'fathers' rights' approach to contact disputes.[194]

Recent Strasbourg case law certainly indicates a sympathy with the best interests criterion and suggests how the concluding phrase of article 8(2)[195] can be interpreted

---

186   J Dunn and K Deater-Deckard (2001) p 19.

187   A Buchanan et al (2001) p 71. One third of the small group of children interviewed indicated such views.

188   See J Wallerstein and J Lewis (1998) pp 375–377.

189   Many research projects find that fitting in children's extracurricular commitments round contact arrangements are a constant source of stress. See A Buchanan et al (2001) esp pp 18 and 97. This problem was acknowledged by CASC (2002) paras 13.13–13.15.

190   Inter alia: C Smart et al (1999) pp 372–375; A Buchanan et al (2001) ch 7; C Lyon et al (1998) ch 4.

191   See above.

192   See *S v M (access order)* [1997] 1 FLR 980 at 987, per Lord Hope, when commenting on a provision in the Scottish legislation identical to the Children Act 1989, s 1. See also Munby J's view in *Re X and Y (leave to remove from the jurisdiction: no order principle)* [2001] 2 FLR 118, that all presumptions in family proceedings are ruled out by the Children Act 1989, s 1(5).

193   *Re L (a child) (contact: domestic violence) and other appeals* [2000] 4 All ER 609 at 637–638.

194   See J Fortin (1999 b) pp 250–251 and J Fortin (2002) p 22.

195   Which emphasises that art 8 rights can be infringed if this is 'necessary … for the protection •
of health or morals, or for the protection of the rights and freedoms of others'.

in contact disputes, taking full account of its formulation.[196] Nevertheless, such an approach should be adopted with some care since article 8(1) does not strictly allow the court to identify, at the outset, an outcome indicated by the child's best interests.[197] To be Convention compliant, a court order restricting a parent's contact rights can only be justified by reference to the child's best interests, as long as it fulfils certain requirements: both parents have been fully and fairly involved in the decision-making processes; the restriction is proportionate to its legitimate aim; a fair balance is struck between the competing interests of all concerned; the parent has not been discriminated against.[198]

The domestic courts may, of course, attempt to back two horses at once, so to speak. They will refuse the father his order, on the basis that although it infringes his rights to family life, it is necessary to do so, *because* it promotes the child's best interests.[199] Alternatively, they will reinforce the strength of the 'presumption' or 'assumption' of contact, in cases where they do not consider the mother is justified in opposing it, arguing that this promotes the father's rights to contact under article 8(1), whilst maintaining that such an outcome complies with the child's best interests. The danger is that by reverting to a parents' rights agenda the courts can favour fathers' claims regarding infringements of their own rights to contact under article 8(1), without giving sufficient weight to their children's best interests. As recent Strasbourg case law so clearly demonstrates,[200] although refusing the father contact can clearly favour the child's best interests, the court may conclude that it is not 'necessary' to produce such an order, and that it would not be a proportionate response to its legitimate aim.

Meanwhile, the courts continue to seek ways of enforcing contact orders against mothers who refuse to comply with them. Do their efforts fulfil children's rights? The judiciary have, in the past, been strongly criticised for their assumption that firm enforcement of contact orders, with imprisonment as an ultimate sanction,[201] can magically transform parental relationships or benefit their children,[202] even in disputes involving domestic violence.[203] Fortunately, case law now suggests that a child's 'right to contact' should not be promoted by imprisoning his or her mother, except in the most exceptional circumstances.[204] Instead, more subtle means are

---

196 See discussion at pp 58–60 and *Hoppe v Germany* [2003] 1 FCR 176, for a recent example of this approach.
197 J Herring (1999) p 231.
198 On discrimination see, inter alia: *Hoffman v Austria* (1993) 17 EHRR 293: the custody order to the father was primarily motivated by the mother's membership of the Jehovah's witness sect and so infringed the mother's rights under arts 8 and 14; *Sahin v Germany* [2002] 1 FLR 119: the German courts' refusal of unmarried fathers' applications for custody and contact had been influenced by their unmarried status and therefore infringed their rights under arts 8 and 14.
199 Eg, inter alia: *Payne v Payne* [2001] EWCA Civ 166, [2001] 1 FLR 1052 at [35]–[37], per Thorpe LJ and at [82], per Dame Elizabeth Butler-Sloss P; *Re H (contact order) (No 2)* [2002] 1 FLR 22 at [59], per Wall J. This approach is discussed in chapter 8.
200 See *Elsholz v Germany* [2000] 2 FLR 486 and *Sahin v Germany*; *Sommerfeld v Germany*; *Hoffman v Germany* [2002] 1 FLR 119. Discussed in more detail in chapter 8.
201 Eg, *F v F (contact: committal)* [1999] 2 FCR 42.
202 Inter alia: B Cantwell et al (1999) p 231; C Smart and B Neale (1999) esp p 189.
203 Eg *A v N (committal: refusal of contact)* [1997] 1 FLR 533.
204 *Re M (contact order: committal)* [1999] 1 FLR 810 at 825, per Ward LJ.

adopted, such as directing family therapy[205] or inviting a child psychiatrist to work with all members of the family.[206] Nevertheless, a recent report exposes a rather chilly authoritarianism, perhaps reflecting a greater concern to prevent judicial orders being scoffed at, than to fulfil children's interests. It shows a growing inclination to medicalise the problem, recommending that the courts acquire powers to order disobedient mothers to undergo counselling, to refer them to a psychiatrist or psychologist, or to place them on probation, with treatment conditions.[207] Community service orders and fines should also be available.[208] As Eekelaar notes, these recommendations 'signal a significant increase in legal coercion over family matters'.[209] This might be justified if there was good research evidence indicating that court enforced contact is clearly beneficial to the child – but in the absence of such evidence, such heavy-handed intervention seems quite inappropriate. Indeed, international experience indicates that an authoritarian approach to the enforcement of contact orders produces judicial decision-making that sometimes endangers children's safety.[210] Given that the Strasbourg case law is not particularly consistent in its approach to the non-enforcement of contact orders,[211] it would be regrettable if this approach were adopted here.

(B) The exceptional cases

(i) Domestic violence

The strength of the contact presumption led to the courts rejecting mothers' explanations for their hostility to contact in all but the most exceptional of cases. By labelling a mother reluctant to allow contact as 'implacably hostile' and by maintaining that contact was the child's right and therefore would always benefit the child, the courts were able to discount her reasons on the basis that she did not appreciate her child's needs.[212] Indeed, women were actively discouraged by their

---

205 *Re M (contact: committal)* [1999] 1 FLR 810 at 825, per Ward LJ.
206 Eg *Re H (a child) (contact: mother's opposition)* [2001] 1 FCR 59 at [25].
207 See CASC (2002) para 14.55.
208 CASC (2002) para 14.55.
209 J Eekelaar (2002) p 272.
210 See M Harrison (2002), H Rhoades (2002), M Hester (2002).
211 See particularly *Ignaccolo-Zenide v Romania* (2001) 31 EHRR 7; cf *Nuutinen v Finland* (2002) 34 EHRR 15. In *Nuutinen*, the child's opposition to contact with the father largely explained the Court's view that the father's art 8 rights had not been infringed by the non-enforcement of his contact rights cf *Ignaccole*, similar evidence had little impact. See also *Hokkanen v Finland* [1994] 19 EHRR 139; cf *Glaser v United Kingdom* [2001] 1 FLR 153.
212 Eg, inter alia: *Re F (minors) (contact: mother's anxiety)* [1993] 2 FLR 830: for the court to refuse contact was, per Balcombe LJ (at 834) 'Draconian', despite the violent husband having been convicted of assaulting his wife occasioning actual bodily harm; *Re P (a minor) (contact)* [1994] 2 FLR 374: contact order awarded an unmarried father who had treated the mother 'with quite unjustifiable and reprehensible violence' and despite her doctor's evidence that renewed contact would significantly endanger her poor mental health; *A v N (committal: refusal of contact)* [1997] 1 FLR 533: the father's mental stability was questionable, he had a history of violence, including assaults against the mother and a very serious assault against his first wife for which he had been imprisoned. Mother committed to six months' imprisonment for refusing to comply with contact orders because, per Ward LJ (at 541) she had only 'flimsy objections to contact taking place'.

legal advisers and by the courts from attempting to justify their opposition to contact by giving accounts of their partners' past conduct, on the basis that this was backward looking and irrelevant to the present dispute.[213] Some mediators would ignore or minimise mothers' reports of violent acts[214] and court welfare officers suggested that they were themselves abusing their children by denying contact with the non-resident parent.[215] Moreover, the children's own reluctance to comply with contact arrangements would be attributed to their being indoctrinated by their mothers against their fathers.[216]

Influenced by a growing body of criticism,[217] and by the government's own determination to ensure that public authorities took adequate steps to protect women from domestic abuse,[218] the senior judiciary started adjusting their approach to contact disputes involving domestic violence. The Court of Appeal became more chary of using the label 'implacably hostile mother' to buttress the contact presumption, especially in disputes involving domestic violence.[219] Furthermore, new case law emerged suggesting that when considering contact applications involving violent fathers, the courts should transfer their attention from the mother's shortcomings, to the father's. They should consider the impact on the mother and the children of the father's behaviour and the need for him to demonstrate a change in attitude and establish his fitness to exercise contact.[220] This judicial activity culminated with the Court of Appeal's decision in *Re L (a child) (contact: domestic violence)*,[221] together with the CASC Report[222] setting out guidelines for the judiciary and family court welfare service on the correct approach to such contact disputes in future.[223]

In *Re L*, the Court of Appeal acknowledged that the judicial approach to cases involving allegations of domestic violence needed adjusting and strongly emphasised that the courts should, in future, take proper account of the impact of the father's violence on the family and the psychological dangers to children of ordering contact in such cases.[224] This strong judicial lead,[225] combined with the CASC guidance to those involved in the family justice system may, in time, achieve much needed changes in the manner in which mothers opposing contact arrangements are treated. Rather than dismissing the mother's explanations for her resistance to contact as being irrelevant, the courts are now expected to make proper and earlier findings of fact in all cases where domestic violence is alleged.[226] If domestic violence is established, the courts should also take full account of its impact on the children and the reasons

213 R Bailey-Harris et al (1999) pp 123–124.
214 See D Greatbach and R Dingwall (1999) p 177ff.
215 Eg *Re L (a child) (contact: domestic violence)* [2000] 4 All ER 609: the court welfare officer's report in the *Appeal in Re M (a child)* claimed that the mother's failure to implement the contact arrangements had resulted in the child suffering serious emotional abuse.
216 Discussed in more detail in chapter 8.
217 See, inter alia: M Kaye (1996); P Parkinson and C Humphreys (1998); R Bailey-Harris et al (1999); C Humphreys (1999).
218 See, inter alia: Cabinet Office/Home Office (1999); DH (1999 b).
219 *Re D (contact: reasons for refusal)* [1997] 2 FLR 48 at 53, per Hale J.
220 Eg *Re M (contact: violent parent)* [1999] 2 FLR 321 and *Re K (contact: mother's anxiety)* [1999] 2 FLR 703. See also *Re R (abduction: consent)* [1999] 1 FLR 828, esp at 834–835.
221 [2000] 4 All ER 609.
222 CASC (2000).
223 See republished in Lord Chancellor's Department (hereafter LCD) (2002).
224 [2000] 4 All ER 609 at 616, per Dame Elizabeth Butler-Sloss P and at 642–643, per Thorpe LJ. See also Dame Elizabeth Butler-Sloss P (2001) and Wall J (2000).
225 See also the case law following *Re L*, adopting a similar approach, eg *Re G (domestic violence: direct contact)* [2000] 2 FLR 865.
226 LCD (2002) paras 1.5–1. 6. This echoes a similar suggestion made by Hale J (1999) p 384.

for contact being sought by the violent partner. They should consider whether the children should be separately represented and above all, ensure that any contact orders they make, including any interim orders,[227] do not involve the mother and children in any danger.[228]

A change of judicial direction is timely. It may deflect the mounting criticism that the judiciary have ignored the large body of research showing that children who witness their mothers being abused suffer severe and long-term psychological damage similar to the effects of abuse perpetrated on themselves.[229] Domestic violence between divorcing and separating couples is much higher than many family practitioners suspect.[230] More to the point, the high correlation between spousal violence and child abuse suggests that the courts are naive to think that a man who has seriously abused his partner will not also abuse his children.[231] Since abusers commonly continue abusing their victims after separation if they can find them,[232] court orders imposing contact arrangements on mothers who have been the victims of sustained domestic violence may endanger not only the women but the children in further incidents of intimidation and abuse.[233] Furthermore, women have often felt coerced into agreeing to unsafe contact arrangements by court welfare officers and even by their own solicitors, in order to appear 'reasonable'.[234]

Controversially, the Court of Appeal in *Re L*[235] refused to accept the experts' suggestion[236] that there should be an assumption against contact in cases involving domestic violence.[237] The CASC report similarly rejected calls for the law to be amended along the lines adopted by some other legal systems, such as New Zealand,[238] where findings of domestic violence create a presumption against contact being granted to the perpetrator.[239] It was felt that attention to the new guidelines[240] would be sufficient to produce a change of approach. Nonetheless, without a specific legislative change of this kind, it may be hard to change the habits of the local family practitioners – the district judges, magistrates, solicitors and children and family reporters, whose 'contact at (almost) any cost' approach is so embedded in their every day work.[241] Hopefully, the fact that all references to 'harm' in the Children Act 1989 must now be read as including the mental and psychological harm caused by children seeing or hearing domestic violence,[242] will produce a less blinkered approach.

227　See *Re M (interim contact: domestic violence)* [2000] 2 FLR 377.
228　LCD (2002) esp paras 1.4–1.5.
229　See M Hester et al (2000) ch 3 for a useful summary of much of the research material. See also C McGee (2000) chs 4 and 5.
230　A Buchanan et al's research indicates that 56% of the parents interviewed reported physical violence and 78% reported fear at some point: A Buchanan et al (2001) p 15. Dissatisfaction was expressed by some mothers over the family court welfare officer's handling of this issue. A Buchanan et al (2001) pp 49–50.
231　See the research summarised by M Hester et al (2000) pp 30–32.
232　M Hester et al (2000) pp 19–20.
233　C McGee (2000) pp 177–178.
234　C McGee (2000) pp 175–176, whose research showed that solicitors often failed to recognise the dangers involved in advising mothers to enter into contact arrangements with violent ex-partners.
235　[2000] 4 All ER 609.
236　C Sturge and D Glaser (2000) p 623.
237　[2000] 4 All ER 609 at 616, per Thorpe LJ, and at 643, per Dame Elizabeth Butler-Sloss P.
238　See discussion by M Kaye (1996) pp 289–291.
239　CASC (2000) section 3.5ff.
240　LCD (2002).
241　R Bailey-Harris et al (1999) p 122.
242　See Children Act 1989, s 31(10), as amended by Adoption and Children Act 2002, s 120. Thus the reference to 'harm' in Children Act 1989, s 1(3)(e), must be interpreted, taking account of this type of harm.

Perhaps of greatest concern is the courts' continued preparedness to assume that when direct contact is inappropriate, supervised or indirect contact (letter-box contact) should be ordered instead.[243] A continued faith in indirect contact as a last resort has survived the Court of Appeal's 'new approach' to contact disputes involving domestic violence,[244] with an order for supervised or supported contact at a contact centre being a preferred option. Furniss refers to the worrying propensity of practitioners at every level to resort to contact centres as a remedy for patently unsuitable cases and to their ignorance of the true facilities offered.[245] Not only are such centres in short supply,[246] but few who accept families with adult safety or child sexual abuse concerns have staff trained to deal with complex cases. Nor do many provide close supervision of contact, or even safe 'handover' arrangements, such as separate entrances.[247] Whether the appeals to the government to fund additional more specialised contact centres will bear fruit remains to be seen.[248]

(ii) Child sexual abuse

As noted above, the presumption of contact appears to have survived intact for all cases, other than those involving domestic violence or situations involving proved harm or risk of harm to the child.[249] Although it apparently no longer applies to disputes involving allegations of child sexual abuse,[250] mothers will continue to encounter considerable difficulties if they refuse to agree to contact due to such fears. As Hale J (as she then was) pointed out, the mother who truly believes that her child has been sexually abused is in a difficult position. If she does nothing, she may be criticised for failing to protect the child. If she resists contact, she 'may be regarded as a wicked woman who has made it up to get rid of him [the father claiming contact].'[250a] Such a mother already faces an immensely hard task in satisfying the court that sexual abuse has occurred, since she must comply with the standard of proof established by *Re H (minors) (sexual abuse: standard of proof)*.[251] Consequently, merely showing that there is 'a substantial risk that abuse has occurred' is not enough;

---

243 Eg *Re G (domestic violence: direct contact)* [2001] 2 FCR 134: indirect contact ordered (cards and presents at Christmas and birthdays) despite the fact that the father had murdered the mother, had no understanding of his child's needs and despite the fact that the child was frightened of him and reluctant to see him.

244 Indirect contact orders were confirmed by the Court of Appeal in *Re L (a child) (contact: domestic violence) and other appeals* [2000] 4 All ER 609 in all four cases considered. See also *Re L (contact: genuine fear)* [2002] 1 FLR 621.

245 See C Furniss (2000). She points out (p 275) that Ward LJ in *Re M (contact: supervision)* [1998] 1 FLR 727, was (at 730) obviously confused over the distinction between 'supervised contact' and 'supported contact'. See also R Aris et al (2002) Section 4.

246 Cabinet Office/Home Office (1999) p 40.

247 C Furniss (1998) pp 5 and 8. See also R Aris et al (2002), who strongly criticise the lack of adequate safety arrangements at many contact centres and the paucity of well-trained staff. See esp Sections 4, 5, 9 and 10.

248 CASC (2002) ch 8, esp para 8.35.

249 *Re L (a child) (contact: domestic violence) and other appeals* [2000] 4 All ER 609 at 616, per Dame Elizabeth Butler-Sloss P.

250 [2000] 4 All ER 609 at 643, per Thorpe LJ.

250a See Hale J (1999) p 385.

251 [1996] 1 All ER 1. According to *Re M and R (child abuse: evidence)* [1996] 2 FLR 195, courts can only justify refusing contact by reference to Children Act 1989, s 1(3)(e) (harm or risk of harm) if they are satisfied *on the balance of probabilities* that a child has suffered or is likely to suffer harm. Discussed more fully in chapter 15.

she must go further and establish that it occurred on the balance of probabilities.[252] The mother who fails to produce sufficient evidence of what is an essentially private and pernicious form of child abuse[253] will not find the advice to her and her family to 'try to put the allegations of sexual abuse behind them' particularly convincing or helpful.[254]

Sometimes a mother, fearing that she has insufficient evidence of sexual abuse, is persuaded to settle the contact dispute on agreed terms with her children's father. As in *Re M (sexual abuse allegations: interviewing techniques)*,[255] such a decision may backfire when, many years later, the father, unencumbered by any finding of fact regarding the occurrence of child sexual abuse, reapplies for contact. Despite being supported by the children's own vehement protestations that they had been sexually abused by their father, the mother was unable to prove their allegations to the required standard of proof.[256] This situation suggests that the new practice guidelines for contact disputes involving allegations of domestic violence should also apply to those involving other damaging circumstances, most particularly those involving child sexual abuse. The courts should make findings of fact as early as possible, whenever disputed and damaging allegations are made in contact disputes.[257]

The mother who, against all odds, manages to prove her allegations of child sexual abuse to the required standard of proof, may find that the court is keen to award the father supervised or indirect contact.[258] The research on the relationship between sex abusers and their young victims indicates that the courts' faith in supervised contact as a means of keeping alive the link between father and child can be extremely dangerous. The lack of trained staff at most contact centres prevents such arrangements protecting children from re-abuse. Indeed, as Furniss caustically observes, 'One wonders, for example, just how the court thought referral to a contact centre in the case of *Re P (Parental Responsibility)*[259] would prevent the paedophilic father "grooming" his child, given that conversations are not generally monitored'.[260] The abuser may not only use contact sessions to revive the sexual relationship between him and the child,[261] but also to bring pressure to bear on the victim to retract his or her story.[262] It is urged:

---

252 Eg *Re P (sexual abuse: standard of proof)* [1996] 2 FLR 333: since the trial judge's view that there was a 'substantial risk that sexual abuse had occurred' was insufficient, the Court of Appeal allowed the husband's appeal against a refusal of an order for unsupervised contact. The mother had not shown that children might undergo future harm under Children Act 1989, s 1(3)(e) to the required standard of proof – the balance of probabilities.

253 She must produce evidence of child sexual abuse through a properly conducted investigative interview, carried out by a police officer and a social worker. See *Re B (sexual abuse: expert's report)* [2000] 1 FLR 871 at 873, per Thorpe LJ.

254 *Re P (sexual abuse: standard of proof)* [1996] 2 FLR 333 at 345, per Wall J.

255 [1999] 2 FLR 92.

256 Swayed by the children's (aged 14 and 11) vehement opposition to contact, the court awarded the father only indirect contact, involving his sending the children cards and receiving school reports and photographs.

257 See *Re S (contact: evidence)* [1998] 1 FLR 798: Hale J (at 801–802) criticised the trial judge for failing to make clear findings of fact regarding allegations of child sexual abuse in a contact dispute.

258 See R Bailey-Harris et al (1999) pp 125–126.

259 [1998] 2 FLR 96.

260 See C Furniss (2000) p 258.

261 See C Macaskill (2002) p 60, for a chilling description of supervised contact visits between a sexually abusive father and his 5-year-old daughter.

262 See E Jones and P Parkinson (1995).

'The argument for the continuity of the child's relationship with the absent parent through regular contact assumes an altogether different complexion when set against this background of a history of a distorted and abusive relationship with that same parent. Far from ensuring continuity of the parent-child relationship, it may foster the continuance of a relationship which is aberrant and emotionally damaging to the child.'[263]

The old practice of resorting to indirect contact, as a kind of consolation prize for the abusive father refused direct contact,[264] also appears to continue. Indeed, research indicates that the pro-contact approach of solicitors and judges is little affected by cases involving the sexual abuse of children. They acknowledge that this might be a reason for refusing direct contact, but are reluctant to countenance contact being refused altogether.[265] The courts' preparedness to order indirect contact in such cases is astonishing, given the large body of research evidence indicating that victims of child sexual abuse commonly suffer serious and very long-term psychological damage and that sexual abuse is addictive behaviour.[266] It is arguable that contact orders for indirect contact in such circumstances merely promote a notion of fathers' rights, based on the existence of a dangerous blood tie. The Court of Appeal should take a stronger lead and convince family practitioners and local judiciary that it may sometimes be appropriate to refuse all contact, of any kind.[267]

(C) The blood tie – promoting or creating attachments through contact?

There is an additional reason for arguing that there is often little connection between the concept of children's rights and the presumption in favour of contact. This is that a blanket presumption fails to distinguish between two quite separate types of situations in which contact disputes arise. There is the more common case where the parents lived together after the child's birth and a good relationship existed between the father and child. In these cases, court ordered contact may, depending on the circumstances, be justified to keep the relationship alive and to promote the child's existing attachments with the absent parent. There is also the very different type of case where the child and father have never known each other, perhaps due to the parental relationship ceasing before or soon after the child's birth, and the child being brought up by the mother alone, or with a new partner acting as a substitute father.

In the second situation, the child is sometimes being brought up to believe that the mother's partner is the child's real father.[268] Research indicates that the judiciary often have an unquestioning belief in the value of contact, even in cases where the

---

263 E Jones and P Parkinson (1995) p 77.

264 Eg *Re H (minors) (access: appeals)* [1989] 2 FLR 174; *H v H (child abuse: access)* [1989] 1 FLR 212; *L v L (child abuse: access)* [1989] 2 FLR 16.

265 R Bailey-Harris et al (1999) pp 125–126.

266 See D Jones and P Ramchandani (1999).

267 Eg *Re M and B (children) (contact: domestic violence)* [2001] 1 FCR 116: an order for indirect contact was replaced, on appeal, by an order for no contact and a moratorium (under Children Act 1989, s 91(14)) on the violent father reapplying for contact within two years without court leave. Thorpe LJ criticised the trial judge for failing to consider the impact of indirect contact on the mother's mental health, she having been subjected to six years of serious domestic violence culminating in the father's imprisonment.

268 Inter alia: *Re R (a minor) (contact)* [1993] 2 FLR 762; *Re W (a minor) (contact)* [1994] 2 FLR 441; *A v L (contact)* [1998] 1 FLR 361; *Re K (specific issue order)* [1999] 2 FLR 280; *Re T (paternity: ordering blood tests)* [2001] 2 FLR 1190.

child is too young to have had any relationship with his or her father.[269] This approach follows established case law indicating that the 'temporary upset' caused by reintroducing children to a father with whom they have lost contact for a prolonged period should be balanced against the long-term benefits which are expected to accrue to them.[270] Many judges clearly consider that a child who is 'being deprived of knowledge of his real father',[271] is also being deprived of a fundamental 'right' to contact.[272]

Regrettably, some mothers behave in this fashion with no reasonable excuse. Nevertheless, the courts' confidence that contact will be beneficial in such circumstances is puzzling, given the absence of any obvious research supporting it. As noted above, a large body of research suggests that separation and divorce can have adverse consequences on children due to the loss of a parent with whom they have developed attachment bonds. There is also good research literature developed in the context of work with adopted and fostered children, showing that children need information about their origins. But until research is produced squaring the circle between these two bodies of research, there currently appears to be little basis for arguing that children need a *social* relationship with a parent whose existence they have been unaware of. Forcing contact on the mother's new family may seriously disrupt a stable family unit.[273] It seems particularly inappropriate for the courts to use heavy-handed methods of coercion on mothers who refuse to comply with contact orders in such circumstances.[274]

Notably, the experts who advised the Court of Appeal on the benefits of contact to children, emphasised that although the absence of any relationship already existing between the child and non-resident parent does not preclude trying to establish one, 'other considerations may come into play'. They suggested that in such cases the courts should consider the child's existing emotional investments, for example, with a step-parent, and what the new relationship would specifically add to the child's life and well-being. Furthermore, in cases where there is 'no meaningful relationship between the child and non-residential parent' and an established history of domestic violence between the parents, there would have to be very good reasons to embark on building up a relationship.[275] Obviously influenced by these comments, Thorpe LJ in *Re L*[276] suggested that the judiciary had, in the past, made insufficient distinction between contact orders sought to maintain an existing relationship, to revive a dormant relationship and those to create a non-existent relationship. In his view:

> 'The judicial assumption that to order contact would be to promote welfare should surely wane across that spectrum. I would not assume the benefit with unquestioning confidence where a child has developed over its early years without any knowledge of its father, particularly if over those crucially formative years a psychological attachment to an alternative father has been achieved.'[277]

---

269 R Bailey-Harris et al (1999) p 119.
270 Per Balcombe LJ in *Re H (minors) (access)* [1992] 1 FLR 148 at 153.
271 Per Sir Stephen Brown P in *Re W (a minor) (contact)* [1994] 2 FLR 441 at 447.
272 See Holman J in *A v L (contact)* [1998] 1 FLR 361 at 365.
273 See B Cantwell et al (1999) esp p 230.
274 See J Eekelaar (2002) p 273.
275 C Sturge and D Glaser (2000) p 622.
276 [2000] 4 All ER 609.
277 [2000] 4 All ER 609 at 637. See also *Re M and B (children) (contact: domestic violence)* [2001] 1 FCR 116, per Thorpe LJ, who (at [25]) emphasised that this father was seeking to establish and not continue a relationship with his daughter, she having had no contact with him for five years since she was 4 years old.

These words may usher in a more thoughtful approach to the benefits of contact in cases where no existing relationship exists between father and child. The assumption that the blood tie between parent and child has magical properties which, if enhanced by physical proximity, will inevitably produce a happy and long-term relationship seems misguided. Children clearly have a protective right to psychological health and happiness and it is desirable for the courts to promote conditions supporting such a situation. But it seems foolish to argue that to fulfil a child's rights, the caring parent must undergo serious unhappiness, merely to nurture a blood tie that has no real significance for the child. Blood, in such circumstances, may be far thinner than water.

(7) CONCLUSION

Considerable confusion is generated by society's assumption that children have a right to 'know' both their birth parents through a social relationship and that their childhood will be defective if no such relationship exists. A loving relationship between parents and children is of inestimable value and its loss is always tragic for all concerned. But its essence and value does not depend on the act of procreation or on their genetic links. Indeed, there are many parent-child relationships where no blood ties exist, which are none the worse for their absence. Children's psychological need to know about their biological origins does not imply that their relationship with their present carers is defective or needs to be replaced by a social relationship with their birth parents and it may be positively harmful to assume that this should occur.

More research is required considering the costs and benefits to children of being the subject of enforced contact arrangements, both in the context of adoption and private parental disputes. Until this is available, far greater emphasis should be placed on a child's right to protection from psychological harm. Children's need for information about their origins could be promoted by indirect contact arrangements, involving the transfer of letters and presents, perhaps to box office addresses. In some cases, particularly those involving serious domestic violence or child abuse, no contact may be the appropriate legal response. Respecting children's own individuality involves paying far greater attention to information about their own reluctance to comply with contact arrangements, as urged by Sturge and Glaser.[278] Finally, the judiciary should suspend what appears to be a naive belief in the power of court orders to transform stressful situations into ones which will automatically benefit the child.

278 See C Sturge and D Glaser (2000) pp 621, 624 and 627. The extent to which children's wishes should affect such situations is considered in chapter 8.

BIBLIOGRAPHY

NB many of these publications can be obtained on the relevant organisation's website.

Adoption Law Reform Group, *Reforming Adoption Law in England and Wales* (2000) British Agencies for Adoption and Fostering.

Amato P and Gilbreth J, 'Nonresident fathers and children's well-being: A meta-analysis' (1999) 61 Journal of Marriage and the Family 557.

Aris R et al, *Safety and Child Contact: An Analysis of the Role of Child Contact Centres in the Context of Domestic Violence and Child Welfare Concerns* Research Series No 10/02 (2002) Lord Chancellor's Department.

Bailey-Harris R et al, 'From Utility to Rights? The Presumption of Contact in Practice' (1999) International Journal of Law, Policy and the Family 111.

Bainham A, 'When is a parent not a parent? Reflections on the unmarried father and his child in English law' (1989) 3 International Journal of Law, Policy and the Family 208.

Bainham A, 'Can we protect children and protect their rights?' (2002) Family Law 279.

Bridge S, 'Assisted Reproduction and the Legal Definition of Parentage' in A Bainham et al (eds) *What is a Parent?: A Socio-Legal Analysis* (1999) Hart Publishing.

Buchanan A et al, *Families in Conflict: Perspectives of children and parents on the Family Court Welfare Service* (2001) The Policy Press.

Butler-Sloss, Dame Elizabeth P, 'Contact and Domestic Violence' (2001) Family Law 355.

Cabinet Office/Home Office, *Living Without Fear: An integrated approach to tackling violence against women* (1999).

Cantwell B et al, 'Presumption of Contact in Private Law – An Interdisciplinary Issue' (1999) Family Law 226.

Casey D and Gibberd A, 'Adoption and Contact' (2001) Family Law 39.

Children Act Sub-Committee of the Advisory Board on Family Law (CASC), *A Report to the Lord Chancellor on the Question of Parental Contact with Children in Cases Where There is Domestic Violence* (2000).

Children Act Sub-Committee of the Advisory Board on Family Law (CASC), *Making Contact Work* Report of the Children Act Sub-Committee (2002).

Committee on the Rights of the Child, *Concluding Observations of the Committee on the Rights of the Child: United Kingdom of Great Britain and Northern Ireland* CRC/C/15/Add 188 (2002) Centre for Human Rights, Geneva.

Conway H, 'Parental responsibility and the unmarried father' (1996) 146 New Law Journal 782.

Cretney S, Masson J and Bailey-Harris R, *Principles of Family Law* (2002) Sweet and Maxwell.

Davis G and Pearce J, 'On the Trail of the Welfare Principle' (1999 a) Family Law 144.

Davis G and Pearce J, 'The Welfare Principle in Action' (1999 b) Family Law 237.

Deech R, 'The unmarried father and human rights' (1992) 4 Journal of Child Law 3.

Department of Health (DH), *Adoption – A Service for Children* (1996).

Department of Health (DH), *Local Authority Circular* LAC (97) 13 (1997).

Department of Health (DH), *Adoption Now: Messages from Research* (1999 a) John Wiley and Sons Ltd.

Department of Health (DH), *The Family Law Act 1996: Domestic Violence Survey Report on Local Authority Implementation of Part IV* (1999 b) DoH.

Department of Health (DH), *Adoption: A New Approach* Cm 5017 (2000) HMSO.

Department of Health (DH), *Children Adopted from Care in England: 2000/1* DH Statistical Bulletin 2001/25 (2001).

Department of Health (DH), *National Minimum Standards and Regulations Local Authority Adoption Services in England – Consultation Document* (2002 a) DH Publications.

Department of Health (DH), *National Minimum Standards and Regulations Voluntary Adoption Agencies England and Wales – Consultation Document* (2002 b) DH Publications.

Department of Health (DH), *Donor Information Consultation: Providing Information about Gamete or Embryo Donors* (2002 c) DH.

Department of Health (DH), *The Children Act Report 2001* (2002 d) DH Publications.

Department of Health (DH), *Children Adopted from Care in England: 2001/2* DH Statistical Bulletin 2002/24 (2002 e).

Department of Health (DH) and Welsh Office, *Adoption: The Future* Cm 2288 (1993) HMSO.

Detrick S (ed), *The United Nations Convention on the Rights of the Child: A Guide to the 'Travaux Préparatoires'* (1992) Martinus Nijhoff Publishers.

Dunn J and Deater-Deckard K, *Children's views of their changing families* (2001) Joseph Rowntree Foundation.

Eekelaar J, 'Do Parents have a Duty to Consult?' (1998) 114 Law Quarterly Review 337.

Eekelaar J, 'Rethinking parental responsibility' (2001) Family Law 426.

Eekelaar J, 'Contact – Over the Limit' (2002) Family Law 271.

Feast J, 'Embryological secrecy syndrome' (2000) Family Law 897.

Fortin J, 'Re F: The Gooseberry Bush Approach' (1994) 57 Modern Law Review 296.

Fortin J, 'Parenthood in Child Law – What is its Real Significance?' in D Pearl and R Pickford (eds) *Frontiers of Family Law* Part II (1995) Wiley.

Fortin J, 'Rights Brought Home for Children' (1999 a) 62 Modern Law Review 350.

Fortin J, 'The HRA's impact on litigation involving children and their families' (1999 b) 11 Child and Family Law Quarterly 237.

Fortin J, 'Children's rights and the impact of two international conventions: the UNCRC and the ECHR' in Thorpe LJ and C Cowton (eds) *Delight and Dole: The Children Act 10 years on* (2002) Family Law.

Fratter J, *Adoption With Contact: Implications for Policy and Practice* (1996) British Agencies for Adoption and Fostering.

Freeman M, 'The new birth right?: Identity and the child of the reproductive revolution' (1996) International Journal of Children's Rights 273.

Furniss C, *Family Contact Centres: The Position in England, Wales and Scotland* (1998) Centre for Research on Family, Kinship and Childhood.

Furniss C, 'The process of referral to a family contact centre: policies and practice' (2000) 12 Child and Family Law Quarterly 255.

Gilmore S, 'Parental responsibility and the unmarried father – a new dimension to the debate' (2003) 15 Child and Family Law Quarterly 21.

Greatbach D and Dingwall R, 'The Marginalization of Domestic Violence in Divorce Mediation' (1999) International Journal of Law, Policy and the Family 174.

Goldstein J, Freud A and Solnit A, *Beyond the Best Interests of the Child* (1973) Collier Macmillan.

Haimes E, '"Now I know who I really am": Identity change and redefinitions of the self in adoption' in T Honess and K Yardley (eds) *Self and Identity* (1987) Routledge and Kegan Paul.

Hale J, 'The View from Court 45' (1999) 11 Child and Family Law Quarterly 377.

Harris-Short S, 'The Adoption and Children Bill – a fast track to failure?' (2001) 13 Child and Family Law Quarterly 405.

Harrison M, 'Australia's Family Law Act: the First Twenty Five Years' (2002) 16 International Journal of Law, Policy and the Family 1.

Hayes M, '*Dawson v Wearmouth* "What's in a name?" A child by any other name is surely just as sweet?' (1999) 11 Child and Family Law Quarterly 423.

Herring J, 'The Human Rights Act and the Welfare Principle in Family Law – Conflicting or Complementary?' (1999) 11 Child and Family Law Quarterly 223.

Hester M et al, *Making an Impact: Children and Domestic Violence, A Reader* (2000) Jessica Kingsley Publishers.

Hester M, 'One step forward and three steps back? Children, abuse and parental contact in Denmark' (2002) 14 Child and Family Law Quarterly 267.

Hodgkin R and Newell P, *Implementation Handbook for the Convention on the Rights of the Child* (1998) Unicef.

Houghton W (Chairman), *Report of the Departmental Committee on the Adoption of Children* Cmnd 5107 (1972) HMSO.

Howe D and Feast J, *Adoption, Search and Reunion: The Long Term Experience of Adopted Adults* (2000) The Children's Society.

Humphreys C, 'Judicial Alienation Syndrome – Failures to Respond to Post-separation Violence' (1999) Family Law 313.

Jones D and Ramchandani P, *Child Sexual Abuse* (1999) Radcliffe Medical Press.

Jones E and Parkinson P, 'Child Sexual Abuse, Access and The Wishes of Children' (1995) 9 International Journal of Law, Policy and the Family 54.

Kaganas F, 'Responsible or feckless fathers? – *Re S (Parental Responsibility)*' (1996) 8 Child and Family Law Quarterly 165.

Kaganas F, '*Re L (Contact Domestic Violence); Re V (Contact Domestic Violence); Re M (Contact Domestic Violence); Re H (Contact Domestic Violence);* Contact and domestic violence' (2000) 12 Child and Family Law Quarterly 311.

Kaye M, 'Domestic violence, residence and contact' (1996) 8 Child and Family Law Quarterly 285.

Kelly J, 'Children's Adjustment in Conflicted Marriage and Divorce: A Decade Review of Research' (2000) 39 Journal of the American Academy of Child and Adolescent Psychiatry 936.

Kilkelly U, *The Child and the European Convention on Human Rights* (1999) Ashgate Publishing.

Lindley B, 'Open adoption – is the door ajar?' (1997) 9 Child and Family Law Quarterly 115.

Lord Chancellor's Department (LCD), *Procedures for The Determination of Paternity and on The Law on Parental Responsibility for Unmarried Fathers: A Lord Chancellor's Department Consultation Paper* (1998).

Lord Chancellor's Department (LCD), *Guidelines for Good Practice on Parental Contact in cases where there is Domestic Violence* prepared by the Children Act Sub-Committee of the Lord Chancellor's Advisory Board on Family Law (2002).

Lowe N, 'The changing face of adoption – the gift/donation model versus the contract/ services model' (1997 a) 9 Child and Family Law Quarterly 371.

Lowe N, 'The Meaning and Allocation of Parental Responsibility – A Common Lawyer's Perspective' (1997 b) International Journal of Law, Policy and the Family 192.

Lowe N and Murch M et al, *Supporting Adoption: Reframing the approach* (1999) British Agencies for Adoption and Fostering.

Lyon C et al, *Effective Support Services for Children and Young People when Parental Relationships Break Down – A Child-Centred Approach* (1998) University of Liverpool.

Macaskill C, *Safe Contact? Children in permanent placement and contact with their birth relatives* (2002) Russell House Publishing.

Maclean M and Eekelaar J, *The Parental Obligation: A study of parenthood across households* (1997) Hart Publishing.

McGee C, *Childhood Experiences of Domestic Violence* (2000) Jessica Kingsley Publishers.

McWhinnie A, 'The Concept of "Open Adoption" – How Valid is It?' in A McWhinnie and J Smith (eds) *Current Human Dilemmas in Adoption* (1994) University of Dundee.

McWhinnie A, 'Ethical dilemmas in the use of donor gametes' (1998) 17 Medical Law 311.

Maidment S, 'Parental Alienation Syndrome – A Judicial Response?' (1998) Family Law 264.

O'Donovan K, 'What shall we tell the children?' in R Lee and D Morgan (eds) *Birthrights* (1990) Routledge.

Office for National Statistics, *Social Trends No 33* (2003) The Stationery Office.

Parkinson P and Humphreys C, 'Children who witness domestic violence – the implications for child protection' (1998) 10 Child and Family Law Quarterly 147.

Performance and Innovation, Unit *Prime Minister's Review of Adoption* (2000) Cabinet Office.

Pickford R, 'Unmarried Fathers and the Law' in A Bainham, S Day Sclater and M Richards (eds) *What is a Parent?: A Socio–Legal Analysis* (1999 a) Hart Publishing.

Pickford R, *Fathers, Marriage and the Law* (1999 b) Family Policy Studies Centre.

Quinton D et al, 'Contact between Children Placed away from Home and their Birth Parents: Research Issues and Evidence' (1997) 2 Journal of Clinical Child Psychology and Psychiatry 393.

Quinton D, 'Contact with birth parents in adoption – a response to Ryburn' (1998) 10 Child and Family Law Quarterly 349.

Rhoades H, 'The "No-Contact Mother": Reconstructions of Motherhood in the Era of the "New Father"' (2002) 16 International Journal of Law, Policy and the Family 71.

Rogers B and Pryor J, *Divorce and separation: The outcomes for children* (1998) Joseph Rowntree Foundation.

Ryburn M, 'Welfare and Justice in Post-Adoption Contact' (1997) 27 Family Law 28.

Ryburn M, 'In whose best interests: post adoption contact with the birth family' (1998) 10 Child and Family Law Quarterly 53.

Schaffer H, *Making Decisions About Children* (1998) Blackwell Publishers.

Smart C and Neale B, *Family Fragments?* (1999) Polity Press.

Smart C et al, 'Objects of concern? – children and divorce' (1999) 11 Child and Family Law Quarterly 365.

Smith C and Logan J, 'Adoptive parenthood as a "legal fiction" – its consequences for direct post-adoption contact' (2002) 14 Child and Family Law Quarterly 281.

Social Services Inspectorate, *For Children's Sake: An SSI Inspection of Local Authority Adoption Services* (1996) DH.

Stevenson O, 'Recent Research in Child Welfare: Implications for Policy and Practice' in the Rt Hon LJ Thorpe and E Clarke (eds) *Divided Duties: Care planning for children within the family justice system* (1998).

Sturge C and Glaser D, 'Contact and domestic violence – the experts' court report' (2000) Family Law 615.

Thomas C et al, *Adopted Children Speaking* (1999) British Agencies for Adoption and Fostering.

Triseliotis J, *In Search of Origins* (1973) Routledge and Kegan Paul.

Wall J, 'Domestic Violence at the Millenium – Contact between Children and Violent Parents' in S Cretney (ed) *Family Law Essays for the new Millennium* (2000) Family Law.

Wallerstein J and Lewis J, 'The Long-Term Impact of Divorce on Children: A First Report from a 25-Year Study' (1998) 36 Family and Conciliation Courts Review 368.

Chapter 14

Children's right to know and be brought up by their parents

(1) INTRODUCTION

As Wall J observed:

> 'The case thus raises as a central issue the classic dilemma sadly so often found in children's cases. B has become attached to people who are not her natural parents. To break that attachment will undoubtedly cause her harm. Does the harm that will be caused outweigh the benefit which B will otherwise derive from being brought up by her parents in the cultural heritage and traditions into which she was born?'[1]

These words encapsulate very well the difficulties confronting the courts when dealing with disputes over children who form attachments with those who care for them and love them on a day-to-day basis, but who are not their birth parents. Schaffer warns against assuming that these affectionate ties are somehow less important to the child:

> 'The widespread belief in the blood bond is based on the notion that there is a natural affinity between child and biological parents which makes the latter more fit to be responsible for the child's care and upbringing than any outsider. Such fitness is assumed to be due to the common heredity found in parent-child pairs; whatever experiences a child may share with some other adult and whatever affectionate ties then develop between them are considered to be of secondary importance to the blood bond which is said to exist from the moment of conception.'[2]

Having summarised the well-documented research showing only too clearly the way in which children can form positive attachments with adopters and other carers,[3] Schaffer concludes:

> 'It is a history of social interaction, not kinship, that breeds attachment, and to break these bonds cannot be done lightheartedly – certainly not on the basis of a myth, namely a psychological blood bond.'[4]

Very similar views led Goldstein et al to coin their concept of the child's 'psychological parent'.[5] Schaffer's words make clear his disapproval of those who assume that the bonds between a child and his or her attachment figures can be broken simply because

---

1   *Re B (adoption: child's welfare)* [1995] 1 FLR 895 at 896.
2   H Schaffer (1998) p 51.
3   See also the research summarised by I Weyland (1997) pp 175–178.
4   H Schaffer (1998) p 62.
5   J Goldstein, A Freud and A Solnit (1973) p 19.

they are not linked to each other by ties of blood. Children suffer severe psychological trauma when separated from such carers,[6] whether or not they are biologically related. Against this view has to be balanced the importance society places on the blood tie between children and birth parents and a feeling of unease generated by laws which might allow foster parents or adoptive parents to keep children in their care despite the birth parents' strong opposition. Most societies assume that 'normal' families comprise birth parents and their children and that the genetic tie between parent and child is not merely a symbolic one. The law recognises the special role that parents play in their children's lives, by giving them an initial and presumptive right to bring up their children themselves. As Eekelaar has pointed out:

> 'It would surely be legally wrong for a hospital to hand a child over to a stranger rather than to its mother, not simply because the child would (or might) do better with the mother, but because the mother is entitled to her child unless deprived of this right through proper legal procedures ... It is surely not a matter of embarrassment to hold that parents have a prima facie right to possess their children. This must be fundamental to our social ordering.'[7]

It is impossible to quarrel with this comment or with the commonly held view that, unless circumstances are exceptional, children have a corresponding right to be brought up by their birth parents. This is reflected in articles 7, 8 and 9 of the CRC, all of which emphasise the importance to children of retaining membership of their own families. Similarly, article 8 of the ECHR stresses the value of family life, with the Strasbourg case law emphasising the obligation on national authorities to ensure that separated family members are reunited as soon as possible.[8]

Whilst such an approach is irrefutable so far as a newborn baby is concerned, it may not be appropriate to suggest, as some of the domestic case law does, that the child's 'right' to be brought up by his or her birth parents survives any disruption in that child's care, and even in the event of the child forming stronger emotional ties with other carers. Furthermore, some children have been removed from their birth parents, having been abused in their care. To them the blood tie may be of little value; indeed, they may need a fresh start with a new family who can provide them with security and long-term happiness.

This chapter is divided into two parts. It first traces the historical development of the legal principles now applied to disputes between birth parents and private foster carers. These disputes usually arise in situations developing, almost by accident, through birth parents making informal fostering arrangements for their children to be cared for temporarily. The birth parents probably had no intention of leaving their children for long, but by the time they seek their return, the children have become so attached to their foster carers, and vice versa, that the foster carers refuse to return them. This area of case law is interesting in so far as it demonstrates the varying ways in which the judiciary respond to arguments based on the value of the blood tie between child and birth parents. The chapter proceeds to consider the extent to which the courts adjust their respect for the blood tie in disputes involving applications to adopt the child.

---

6   See H Schaffer (1998) pp 90–111.
7   See J Eekelaar (1991) p 388.
8   See discussion below.

(2)   DISPUTES BETWEEN BIRTH PARENTS AND PRIVATE FOSTER CARERS

(A)   Differences in approach

Despite their legal obligations,[9] local authorities often find it difficult to exercise any real control over the placement or welfare of privately fostered children, simply because birth parents and foster families fail to notify them of the arrangements that they make.[10] When a dispute arises, in the majority of cases, the court will be faced with a single issue, whether to allow the foster parents to continue caring for the child or to order the child's return to his or her birth parents. In principle, there is nothing to prevent the birth parents visiting the foster carers in person, demanding that their child be handed over to them there and then. Unless they have already taken legal steps to protect their continued care of the child,[11] foster carers confronted by birth parents in this way have no legal authority to retain the child. In practice, the disputes which reach the courts are probably those involving birth parents who are too timid to take the law into their own hands in such a way.

These disputes are governed by the paramountcy principle.[12] Nevertheless, over the last three decades there have been three different judicial approaches to its interpretation. Though subtle, these differences would have crucially affected the legal advice given to foster carers over the likelihood of their successfully opposing the birth parents' claim to retrieve the fostered child. In particular, they have materially affected the manner in which the courts have handled evidence indicating that the child might suffer significant psychological harm by being returned to his or her birth parents – more to the point, the weight attached to the evidence presented by the foster parents wishing to retain the child. Some of the case law illustrates the notion of children's rights being distorted to mask concerns regarding the rights of birth parents being deprived of their children's care. Indeed, the child's right to protection from psychological harm has, at times, been sacrificed to promoting the biological tie between children and their birth parents.

(B)   No presumption favouring the birth parents

J v C[13] remains one of the best factual examples of a dispute between birth parents and foster carers arising out of an informal fostering arrangement. The House of Lords considered it to be against the best interests of a 10-year-old boy to return him to his Spanish parents in Spain, after seven years in the care of English foster parents. The decision established that all the evidence relating to where the child should live should be weighed together, with no presumption favouring his birth parents. Indeed,

---

9   See Children Act 1989, Pt IX and Children (Private Arrangements for Fostering) Regulations 1991, SI 1991/2050.
10   Regulations require private foster carers to notify the local authority of their fostering arrangements. See Children Act 1989, Sch 8, para 7. See Social Services Inspectorate (hereafter SSI) (2002), indicating (para 5.1) that most private foster carers are unaware of the need to register with social services departments.
11   In the past, foster carers often utilised the wardship jurisdiction to gain authority for continued care of a foster child. Today they might apply under the High Court's inherent jurisdiction for such an order or for a residence order under the Children Act 1989, s 8.
12   See Children Act 1989, s 1. Alternatively referred to as the best interests or welfare principle.
13   [1970] AC 668.

Lord MacDermott quoted with approval the words of Wilberforce J in an earlier adoption decision:

> 'The tie ... between the child and his natural father (or any other relative) may properly be regarded in this connexion, not on the basis that the person concerned has a claim which he has a right to have satisfied, but, only if, and to the extent that, the conclusion can be drawn that the child will benefit from the recognition of this tie.'[14]

In evidential terms, the birth parents in *J v C* were not deemed to occupy a more favourable position to retrieve their son than the foster carers. The decision established that although the claims of birth parents would often have great weight and cogency, they had to be 'assessed and weighed in their bearing on the welfare of the child in conjunction with all other factors relevant to that issue'.[15] The nearest that Lord MacDermott went to suggesting that birth parents occupied a special position in such disputes, was to comment:

> 'While there is now no rule of law that the rights and wishes of unimpeachable parents must prevail over other considerations, such rights and wishes, recognised as they are by nature and society, can be capable of ministering to the total welfare of the child in a special way, and must therefore preponderate in many cases.'[16]

The decision in *J v C* was controversial for a number of reasons. In particular, it suggested that the special relationship and tie between parents and children carried no significant weight.[17] Consequently, in disputes of this kind, there was no onus on the foster parents to overturn a legal presumption favouring continuation of the birth parents' care, rather it was the job of the court to assess which course of action would promote the child's best interests. As Eekelaar commented, 'parental claims have no independent weight but are relevant only as evidence as to what course is best for the child'.[18] *J v C* was subsequently applied to other disputes of this kind, with birth parents being denied special treatment. The courts considered it perfectly appropriate not only to consider the disruption that children suffered when being uprooted from their homes with their foster carers after some years, but also to compare the advantages of family life offered by the foster carers, with the natural care and affection that birth parents were able to offer.[19] Indeed, case law indicated the judiciary placing the blood tie between a child and his or her birth parents in the context of a variety of other factors.[20]

(C)   The child's 'prima facie right' to an upbringing by a surviving birth parent

The unemotional way in which the judiciary considered the value of maintaining the blood tie between parent and child was soon to give way to a rather different approach.

14   *Re Adoption Application No 41/61 (No 2)* [1963] 2 All ER 1082 at 1085.
15   [1970] AC 668 at 713, per Lord MacDermott.
16   [1970] AC 668 at 715.
17   See J Eekelaar (1973) p 217.
18   J Eekelaar (1973) p 216.
19   Eg *Re H (a minor) (custody)* [1990] 1 FLR 51: a boy, now aged 8, born to an English father and Indian mother, was brought to England from India by his father and placed in the care of his paternal uncle and aunt. His mother failed in her application to recover his care, because by then he had been settled happily with his English foster carers for two and a half years and a change would be disruptive. Moreover, the home and education he was presently enjoying was more secure than any his mother could presently offer.
20   Eg *Re M (a minor) (custody appeal)* [1990] 1 FLR 291: a dispute involving an adoption application. See this type of dispute discussed below.

This utilised the concept of children's rights to promote what, in reality, appeared to be concerns about parents' rights. Indeed, the Court of Appeal now seemed to see the child-parent tie in an entirely different light, carrying a far greater significance. It produced an evidential formula which considerably favoured birth parents. In a new line of cases, starting with *Re K (a minor) (ward: care and control)*,[21] the judiciary made it clear that it was wrong for courts to weigh up the evidence relevant to the child's future life with one family rather than the other, before deciding whether to order the child's return to his or her birth parents:

'The question was not: where would R get the better home? The question was: was it demonstrated that the welfare of the child positively demanded the displacement of the parental right? The word "right" is not really accurate in so far as it might connote something in the nature of a property right (which it is not) but it will serve for present purposes. The "right", if there is one, is perhaps more that of the child.'[22]

This mysterious change of attitude may have been influenced by the developing adoption law.[23] The judiciary's anxiety to avoid accusations of 'social engineering', when considering evidence relating to a child's future well-being with prospective adopters,[24] may have coloured their approach to similar disputes between foster carers and birth parents. It also appears that the then recent decision of the House of Lords in *Re KD (a minor) (ward: termination of access)*[25] had a powerful impact on judicial decision-making. Their Lordships voiced some stirring views about the concept of parenthood.[26] Indeed, it was probably Lord Templeman's eminently quotable and emotive phrases that invoked a new willingness to give the blood-tie between child and parent a far greater significance:

'The best person to bring up a child is the natural parent. It matters not whether the parent is wise or foolish, rich or poor, educated or illiterate, provided the child's moral and physical health are not endangered.'[27]

Lord Oliver also said:

'Parenthood, in most civilised societies, is generally conceived of as conferring on parents the exclusive privilege of ordering, within the family, the upbringing of children of tender age, with all that that entails. That is a privilege which, if interfered with without authority, would be protected by the courts ...'[28]

Despite this recognition of the privileges of parenthood, Lord Oliver stressed, contrary to the mother's claims in *Re KD*, that no provision in the ECHR required a reassessment of the principles established by *J v C*[29] regarding parents' 'rights'. Indeed, he made it

---

21 [1990] 3 All ER 795: after his mother's suicide, a boy, now aged 4½ years had been placed by his father with his maternal aunt and uncle. After he had been in their care for one year, the foster parents refused to return him to his father.
22 [1990] 3 All ER 795 at 798, per Fox LJ.
23 See discussion by J Fortin (1999) pp 436–439.
24 See Butler-Sloss LJ, in *Re K (a minor) (wardship: adoption)* [1991] 1 FLR 57 at 62 and *Re O (a minor) (custody: adoption)* [1992] 1 FLR 77 at 79.
25 [1988] AC 806.
26 The case involved an application in wardship by a mother claiming that the local authority was acting in breach of her parental 'right' to visit her baby whilst in local authority care.
27 [1988] AC 806 at 812.
28 [1988] AC 806 at 825. He then qualified this statement with the following words: '... but it is a privilege circumscribed by many limitations imposed both by the general law and, where the circumstances demand, by the courts or by the authorities on whom the legislature has imposed the duty of supervising the welfare of children and young persons.'
29 [1970] AC 668.

plain that the mother was to be given no special preference when it came to weighing the evidence regarding her claimed 'right' to access to her child. This would be determined by the child's welfare.[30] As Eekelaar comments of this outcome: 'Neither party, it seems, starts with an inherent *legal* advantage. If he or she is to "win", the erstwhile "right-holder", as much as the challenger, must establish that his or her proposals are better for the child than the competing set.'[31] Lord Oliver's confidence that this approach was consistent with article 8 of the ECHR is difficult to accept, since the article creates an initial presumption in favour of upholding parents' rights, which must then be rebutted by evidence relating to the child's welfare.[32] Be that as it may, *Re KD* clearly influenced the future treatment of disputes between birth parents and foster carers.

Their Lordships' remarks in *Re KD* were later enthusiastically utilised by the Court of Appeal in *Re K (a minor) (ward: care and control).*[33] They were taken to mean that the court should not oppose the claims of a birth parent, unless there was some evidence relating to the child's welfare which positively required that the parental rights should be suspended or superseded. The assumption was that the child had a 'prima facie right' to an upbringing by his or her birth parents and this right survived any subsequent changes in the child's care. This subtly down-graded the principle in *J v C*, since foster carers were now required to produce evidence showing that the child's best interests required the *displacement* of the parent's prior claims. The court's job was not to assess the child's potential happiness in the two households, since the onus was on the foster carers to provide the court with evidence that there were 'compelling factors which required him [the learned judge] to override the prima facie right of this child to an upbringing by its surviving natural parent'.[34]

It was unfortunate that the evidential presumption favouring the birth parents was concealed behind the language of children's rights, given that its effect was to endanger children's right to protection from psychological harm. Obviously in many cases the most crucial evidence for the foster parents to produce would relate to the psychological risks to the child of being uprooted from a home with them. The birth parents, on the other hand, would attempt to persuade the court of their love for their child and their child's love for them. They would also invite the court to bear in mind that society assumes it 'normal' and advantageous for children to be brought up by their birth parents. But the new presumption encouraged the courts to give far less serious consideration to the dangers of psychological damage being caused by removing the child from his or her present home, than to the benefits of being brought up by birth parents.[35] Indeed, as Weyland points out, in most cases, no expert evidence was produced to show that the natural parent was intrinsically better suited than the child's psychological parent to bring him or her up.[36]

Thus in *Re K (a minor) (ward: care and control)* itself[37] there was no evaluation of the relationship between father and child, although the court took account of the fact

30   [1988] AC 806 at 827.
31   J Eekelaar (1988) p 632.
32   See discussion in chapters 2 and 8 below.
33   [1990] 3 All ER 795. See also *Re K (a minor) (wardship: adoption)* [1991] 1 FLR 57.
34   [1990] 3 All ER 795 at 800, per Waite J.
35   See J Fortin (1999) pp 439–440 and I Weyland (1997) pp 180–184.
36   I Weyland (1997) p 178.
37   [1990] 3 All ER 795.

that the father had regularly visited his son.[38] By refusing to compare the homes being offered by the birth and foster parents, the courts not only failed to apply the Children Act 1989, section 1(3) correctly,[39] but also risked endangering the child's psychological health by investing the blood tie between child and parents with undue importance. Hayes and Williams suggest that to adopt the notion of children's rights in disputes of this kind actually inhibits the decision-making process. They observe:

> 'A child's right to family life is separate and independent of that of his parents, and the child may, or may not, agree with the characterisation of his right to family life as the "right to be brought up by the parents who gave birth to him". The child's views are likely to be coloured by the strength of his attachment to his "natural" parents and the strength of his attachment to those who have been caring for him as substitute parents ... He certainly may not regard it as his "right" to be brought up by his parents, who, to him may be the strangers, rather than his substitute parents whom he regards as his family.'[40]

It is difficult to justify the ties of affection between the child and foster parents being automatically out-weighed by concerns focusing on the blood tie and the rights of the birth parents. In such circumstances, a child has as much of a 'right' to continue being cared for by the foster carers, as he or she had to being cared for initially by birth parents.

(D)   The 'other things being equal' formula

Judicial unease over the direction being taken by the case law regarding disputes between birth parents and foster parents marked a further change in approach. Lord Donaldson MR admitted that he was:

> '... slightly apprehensive that *Re K (a minor) (ward: care and control)*[41] may be misconstrued ... it is not a case of parental right opposed to the interests of the child, with an assumption that parental right prevails unless there are strong reasons in terms of the interests of the child ... all that *Re K* is saying, as I understand it, is that of course there is a strong supposition that, *other things being equal* , it is in the interests of the child that it shall remain with its natural parents. But that has to give way to particular needs in particular situations ...'[42]

Although in a number of subsequent decisions these words were adopted with approval,[43] it is unclear whether their real import was fully appreciated. What are the practical implications of Lord Donaldson's words? A strict reading suggests that a court should not assume that other things are equal, until it has made a proper comparison of the two homes available, in order to decide which would better fulfil the child's welfare. In order to make this comparison, the court might consider a number of factors, including the strength and quality of the child's relationships with his or her natural parents, comparing them with those formed with the foster parents. Indeed, Lord Donaldson's 'other things being equal' formula suggests that the value

---

38 For a similar approach in disputes involving adoption applications, see *Re K (a minor) (wardship: adoption)* [1991] 1 FLR 57. These disputes are discussed in more detail below.
39 I Weyland (1997) p 178.
40 See M Hayes and C Williams (1999) pp 287–288.
41 [1990] 3 All ER 795.
42 *Re H (a minor) (custody: interim care and control)* [1991] 2 FLR 109 at 112–113, per Lord Donaldson MR (emphasis supplied).
43 Eg *Re W (a minor) (residence order)* [1993] 2 FLR 625; *Re B (adoption: child's welfare)* [1995] 1 FLR 895; *Re M (child's upbringing)* [1996] 2 FLR 441.

of the blood tie between parent and child should be fully assessed, in terms of the benefit to be derived by the child from the recognition of that tie. This approach would appear to be fully consistent with the intention underlying the Children Act 1989, section 1. The courts should consider what course would best promote the child's welfare, bearing in mind all the factors in the checklist in section 1(3), including not only any harm or risk of harm to the child through uprooting him or her from the present carers, but also the birth parents' ability for parenting.

These expectations regarding the interpretation of the 'other things being equal' formula were not borne out by the case law utilising it. Indeed, whilst avowedly taking full account of Lord Donaldson's words, the courts' attitude to foster carers' evidential burden remained very much the same as before. In evidential terms, the formula appeared to achieve precisely the same result as that advocated by Fox LJ in *Re K (a minor) (ward: care and control).*[44] Furthermore, the line of cases applying this approach stretches from the early 1990s to the present day. The courts remain unshaken in their assumption that a change in the child's care makes little or no difference to the child's 'right' to be brought up by the birth parents. Consequently, there is a marked reluctance to assess and weigh all the evidence from each 'side', in order to decide what course of action would be in the child's best interests.

Re W (a minor) (residence order)[45] is a case in point. The decision at first instance to uproot a 7-year-old boy from his home with his grandparents with whom he had lived for over three years, demonstrates very clearly the dangers of giving a presumptive weight to a birth parent's claims. Despite the court welfare officer's view that there were considerable psychological risks in changing the status quo against the little boy's own wishes, the trial judge was not persuaded that this change presented 'a risk of harm that is sufficient to displace his *right* to be brought up by his father'.[46] Balcombe and Waite LJJ wholeheartedly approved of the 'other things being equal' formula adopted by the trial judge when reaching his decision. Neither, however, indicated how, in practice, a court should decide whether other things *were* equal. There was no suggestion that the formula might allow a comparison of the relative merits of the two homes available for the child, as in much earlier case law.[47] There was no reference to the quality of relationship existing between the father and son, despite the evidence indicating the child's obvious happiness with his grandparents and his desire to stay with them. The use of the concept of children's rights to justify sending the boy back to his father was particularly unfortunate. The decision not only placed little weight on the boy's own distress at the thought of leaving his grandparents,[48] but appeared to discount the way his grandparents had turned him from a disturbed child into a settled and happy little boy. Given the Court of Appeal's full approval of the decision at first instance, the boy would have been handed over to his father, were it not for the grandparents' fortuitous discovery of fresh evidence regarding the father's alleged ill-treatment of a step-son.[49] Only in the light of that evidence was the case sent for rehearing. Thanks to the grandparents' perseverance, the boy was given a second chance.

44   [1990] 3 All ER 795.
45   [1993] 2 FLR 625.
46   [1993] 2 FLR 625 at 630, emphasis supplied.
47   Eg *Re H (a minor: custody)* [1990] 1 FLR 51. See above.
48   The weight to be placed on children's own wishes is discussed more fully in chapter 9.
49   The father had admitted to the police that he sometimes hit his step-sons playfully but maybe on occasions a little too hard. His 13-year-old step-son had run away from home to live with his grandparents, and now apparently had no contact with either his step-father or his own mother.

(E)   Current legal incoherence and compliance with the ECHR

With subsequent case law failing to clarify the practical effect of the 'other things being equal' formula, the presumption in favour of birth parents has retained its strength, in most, but not all, cases involving disputes of this kind. It has been adopted in the context of adoption law[50] and with disastrous consequences by the Court of Appeal in *Re M (child's upbringing)*.[51] Thus despite the 10-year-old Zulu boy's own strong opposition to such a step,[52] Neill LJ stated '... he has the *right* to be reunited with his Zulu parents and with his extended family in South Africa'.[53] The Court of Appeal ignored the psychiatrist's warnings that the damage to the boy's emotional well-being, by being forced to return to his birth parents, might wholly undermine his ability to benefit from his renewed links with his Zulu heritage. Unfortunately, court orders cannot magically transform children's affections. The boy's unhappiness in South Africa forced his parents to admit defeat and to return him to his foster mother's care in England.

The approach in *Re K (a minor) (ward: care and control)*[54] clearly leaves just enough flexibility for the courts to investigate any factors providing reasons why a child should not return to his or her natural parent.[55] But it more obviously justifies their refusing to do so and undermines the legal respectability of any decision which fails to follow it.[56] For example, in *Re D (care: natural parent presumption)*,[57] it led the Court of Appeal to approve of a social work placement motivated solely by a belief that the blood tie between father and child would make up for the absence of any relationship between them and any flaws in the father's character. The local authority explained that they had started on the basis that 'wherever possible you place the child with the natural side of the family'.[58] This approach conveniently saved the local authority the task of undertaking a detailed assessment of the qualities offered by the two possible carers, the father and the grandmother.[59] Short cuts of this kind bear out research findings indicating that the circumstances of potential carers are not always adequately investigated by social services when making 'kinship placements', nor is the long-term viability of such placements always adequately assessed.[60]

---

50   Eg *Re B (adoption: child's welfare)* [1995] 1 FLR 895. See discussion below.

51   [1996] 2 FLR 441.

52   Discussed in chapter 9.

53   [1996] 2 FLR 441 at 454 (emphasis supplied).

54   [1990] 3 All ER 795.

55   Eg *Re D (residence: natural parent)* [1999] 2 FLR 1023: per Johnson J, although the magistrates should not have balanced the advantages of a 13-year-old boy staying with his aunt, against the disadvantages of returning to his mother, here there were enough criticisms of the mother's household to warrant further investigation. Case sent back for rehearing.

56   Eg *Re N (residence: appointment of solicitor: placement with extended family)* [2001] 1 FLR 1028: Court of Appeal allowed the father's appeal (and ordered a rehearing) against an order allowing the maternal aunt and her husband to retain the care of a boy now aged 5 who had lived with them for four years from the time his mother died in a car accident. The trial judge should have applied the 'other things being equal' formula and considered the possible medium- and long-term advantages of an upbringing in the father's family.

57   [1999] 1 FLR 134.

58   [1999] 1 FLR 134 at 144. The father, who had a history of abusing drugs, had had very little contact with his son since his birth. He and his third wife wanted to care for his son, together with their new baby and step-daughter. The boy's maternal grandmother, who was already caring for his two half-brothers, wanted to take over the boy's care herself.

59   Discussed by J Fortin (1999).

60   See J Hunt and A Macleod (1999) p 182.

This insouciant approach on the part of social services was reinforced by the courts' own failure to scrutinise the respective homes on offer. Indeed, according to the Court of Appeal, the principle established by *Re K (a minor) (ward: care and control)*[61] should have prevented the trial judge comparing the child's prospects with the two protagonists, given that one was a parent, and the other only a grandmother. Despite the fact that the father had no well-established relationship with his son, the court should have considered whether there were any compelling factors to override the child's prima facie 'right' to live with his father.[62] Indeed, the Court of Appeal criticised the trial judge for carrying out a 'balancing exercise' in which he compared the benefits the boy would enjoy in his grandmother's household with those in his father's.[63]

Those familiar with case law relating to children know that there will always be the odd unaccountable exception to any apparently consistent line of decisions. Despite the approach established so firmly by the Court of Appeal in *Re K (a minor) (ward: care and control)*[64] and in subsequent cases like *Re D,*[65] the courts now and again do not refer to it at all when reaching decisions allowing children to remain with their long-term foster carers. Most of these cases involve children who have become so very strongly attached to their present carers that there is weighty evidence indicating that a return to their birth parents will cause them immense psychological damage. The courts' ability to jettison the concept of a parental presumption in such circumstances is comprehensible, since presumptions can always be rebutted. Nevertheless, in these cases, the presumption is not mentioned and, more to the point, they vary very little factually from those like *Re W (a minor) (residence order)*[66] and *Re M (child's upbringing),*[67] where there were similar risks of the children concerned undergoing very grave psychological harm by being uprooted from their foster carers on the court's direction.

The decisions where a reference to *Re K (a minor) (ward: care and control)*[68] is omitted entirely often involve the concept of the 'psychological parent' being used to justify the child staying with foster carers to whom he or she is strongly attached. Thus, according to Thorpe LJ, the Court of Appeal 'fell into error' in *Re M (child's upbringing),*[69] through placing such weight on the biological attachment and ordering the boy's return to his birth mother in South Africa.[70] Indeed, in his view that decision should not now be cited at all to justify removing children against their wishes from their 'psychological parent',[71] in order to return them to their birth parents.[72] Similarly,

---

61   [1990] 3 All ER 795.
62   [1999] 1 FLR 134 at 141.
63   In favouring the grandmother over the father, the trial judge had been influenced by the fact that the boy would remain with his half-brothers if he lived with her.
64   [1990] 3 All ER 795.
65   [1999] 2 FLR 1023, discussed above.
66   [1993] 2 FLR 625.
67   [1996] 2 FLR 441.
68   [1990] 3 All ER 795.
69   [1996] 2 FLR 441.
70   Note: *Re O (family appeals: management)* [1998] 1 FLR 431n at 431n and *Re B (residence order: leave to appeal)* [1998] 1 FLR 520 at 521.
71   It should be noted that the distinction made by Thorpe J (when hearing *Re M* at High Court level), between M's 'psychological' parent and his 'biological' parent, was rejected by Ward LJ and Neill LJ in the Court of Appeal, as being 'unhelpful'. See *Re M (child's upbringing)* [1996] 2 FLR 441 at 453 and 455.
72   See also *Re K (adoption and wardship)* [1997] 2 FLR 230 (Fam D): no mention of the 'right' of E, an orphaned Bosnian child, now aged nearly 5, to live with her birth relatives in Switzerland, despite the loss of her cultural ties through remaining with her adoptive English parents who had become her 'primary psychological parents', per Sir Stephen Brown P (at 248).

it was because an 8-year-old Down's syndrome girl considered her devoted foster carers to be her 'real' parents that led the Court of Appeal to refuse her orthodox Jewish birth parents' application to recover her care.[73] The court accepted that she would suffer considerable psychological damage if removed from those who had cared for her almost from birth,[74] but it provided virtually no explanation for its failure even to consider the principle in *Re K (a minor) (ward: care and control)*.[75] Butler-Sloss LJ merely asserted that an application for an order to *vary* an existing court order must be dealt with differently to one applying de novo, and that therefore there was no presumptive right that the girl's orthodox Jewish 'natural parents should be favoured to the foster parents'.[76] But, as commented elsewhere, this seems an inadequate explanation for the absence of any discussion of such a well-established principle of law.[77]

It remains to be seen how this body of case law will be affected by the domestic courts' duty to respect the birth parents' family life under article 8 of the ECHR when dealing with disputes of this kind. Since its phrasing suggests that the interests of parents and children are united, the courts may feel under no obligation to dress up orders fulfilling parents' rights to look like orders fulfilling children's rights. As the birth parents' presumption now seems fully justified, there is a danger that the principle in *Re K (a minor) (ward: care and control)*[78] will be promoted even more aggressively than before. The judiciary should, however, take account of the Strasbourg case law, which supports a flexible approach to such disputes. The European Court of Human Rights in *Hokkanen v Finland*[79] stated that, by failing to take effective measures to overcome the grandparents' opposition and reunite a father with his daughter, the Finnish authorities had infringed the father's right to respect for family life under article 8 of the Convention.[80] Nevertheless, it also emphasised that the state's obligation in this respect is not absolute and that there comes a time when the child has been living so long with other people (in that case, her grandparents) that such a reunion between parent and child may not be feasible. Indeed, the state's duty to reconcile them may have to give way to the child's own interests under article 8(2).[81]

Foster carers who have, as in many of these disputes, cared for a child virtually since his or her birth, might also support their claim by arguing that they have de facto family ties with their foster child which need protecting under article 8 by an order protecting their future care of the child and providing it with a degree of permanence.[82] They are also entitled to be treated fairly by the courts, when attempting to justify their retaining the child's care against the parents' wishes. Indeed, they

---

73 *Re P (a child) (residence order: restriction order)* [2000] Fam 15.
74 She was now aged 8.
75 [1990] 3 All ER 795.
76 [1990] 3 All ER 795 at 746. The birth parents had applied to vary a residence order made four years before in favour of the foster carers.
77 See discussion by J Fortin (1999) pp 441–442.
78 [1990] 3 All ER 795.
79 (1994) 19 EHRR 139.
80 (1994) 19 EHRR 139 (para 62).
81 (1994) 19 EHRR 139 (para 64). See also *Johansen v Norway* (1996) 23 EHRR 33 (para 80).
82 Eg *Söderbäck v Sweden* [1999] 1 FLR 250: the European Court of Human Rights (paras 33–34) accepted that the need to formalise the de facto family ties between a child and her step-father by granting him an adoption order justified the infringement of the birth father's family ties with his daughter under art 8.

might argue that a refusal to weigh their evidence in an even-handed way against that of the birth parents infringes their rights to procedural fairness under articles 6 and 8 of the ECHR.[83] However the arguments are presented, the courts should not ignore the fact that a court order is unable to put the clock back on a child's changed affections. It would be regrettable in the extreme if the ECHR were utilised to justify an outmoded myth about 'a psychological blood bond'.[84]

(3)   THE BLOOD TIE, PRIVATE FOSTER CARERS AND ADOPTION

A long-term fostering arrangement arranged privately by birth parents with friends or acquaintances may work perfectly well for many years but suddenly turn sour when the parents demand the child's return against the foster carers' wishes. The foster carers' response may be to apply to adopt the child. Alternatively, the dispute may have been triggered by the foster parents' plans to adopt the child in question.[85] Since an adoption order terminates the child's legal ties with his or her birth parents altogether,[86] there is far more at stake for them than merely losing the right to care for their child for the time being.[87] Indeed, at the mere mention by the foster parents of the possibility of adoption, the birth parents may attempt to retrieve their child before matters go any further. The question then becomes a simple one – whether the foster carers can retain the child's care, with the backing of a court order, against the wishes of the child's birth parents. Refusal of an adoption order need not necessarily involve the foster parents handing the child back to the natural parents. The court may instead allow them to retain him or her in their care, on the authority of a residence order[88] or a special guardianship order,[89] whilst nurturing the ties with the child's biological parents by court ordered contact.[90]

Faced with an opposed adoption application, the court must be convinced that an adoption order fits the circumstances, and, under the new adoption law, giving paramount, as opposed to first, consideration to the child's welfare.[91] It can only dispense with the birth parents' consent if it considers that the child's welfare so requires.[92] A court may be reluctant to accept that an adoption order is an appropriate order to make in favour of informal foster carers, even in circumstances where the child is well settled in his or her foster home. Unlike foster carers who have been

---

83   See *Elsholz v Germany* [2000] 2 FLR 486: in the context of a parental contact dispute, the European Court of Human Rights held that the domestic court's refusal to obtain an expert psychological opinion on the child's state of mind infringed the father's rights under art 6.

84   See this approach criticised by H Schaffer (1998) p 62.

85   Eg, inter alia: *Re K (a minor) (wardship: adoption)* [1991] 1 FLR 57; *Re O (a minor) (custody: adoption)* [1992] 1 FLR 77; *Re B (adoption: child's welfare)* [1995] 1 FLR 895; *Re M (child's upbringing)* [1996] 2 FLR 441.

86   Adoption and Children Act 2002, s 46(2).

87   See *Re B (adoption: child's welfare)* [1995] 1 FLR 895 at 897–899, per Wall J.

88   Children Act 1989, s 8.

89   Children Act 1989, ss 14A–14G, as inserted by Adoption and Children Act 2002, s 115. These provisions may not be fully implemented until 2004.

90   Eg *Re O (transracial adoption: contact)* [1996] 1 FCR 540.

91   Adoption and Children Act, s 1(2), replacing Adoption Act 1976, s 6, which formerly required the courts to give only *first* consideration to the child's welfare.

92   Adoption and Children Act 2002, s 52(1)(b).

picked for the task by adoption agencies,[93] private foster carers are chosen by parents who have no experience of gauging a person's suitability for child care. Since the initial arrangement did not envisage that the foster carers would adopt the child, the foster carers were not chosen with this purpose in mind.[94] Indeed, the law prohibits private adoption placements in order specifically to prevent children being placed with adults who would make totally unsuitable adopters.[95] The grant of an adoption order would be a radical method of legally securing the foster carers' care of the child, since its effect is to replace the child's birth parents with the adoptive parents, the latter becoming in law the child's 'real' parents.[96] It involves a complete legal break between the child and the birth parents.[97] Adopted children may even lose all touch with their birth families if the adopters are reluctant to allow direct contact and if the court refuses to accompany the adoption order with a contact order in favour of the birth parents.[98]

Adoption case law shows the courts using the approach established in *Re K (a minor) (ward: care and control)*[99] to justify the birth parents being permitted to retrieve their children in this type of dispute.[100] Thus in *Re K (a minor) (wardship: adoption)*[101] the Court of Appeal authorised the return of a baby to her mother after a year with prospective adopters – she had been in their care since the age of six weeks. According to Butler-Sloss LJ, the birth parent 'must be shown to be entirely unsuitable before another family can be considered, otherwise we are in grave danger of slipping into social engineering'.[102] She was plainly concerned by the way in which the mother had privately arranged the adoption placement with a couple that an official adoption agency would probably have deemed unsuitable.[103] In the circumstances, the social workers' plan to rehabilitate the baby with her mother was considered reasonable, despite posing considerable risks. After all, if this had been an officially arranged adoption, a mother's change of mind in such circumstances might well have provoked an attempt to rehabilitate the child with her.[104]

The Court of Appeal's disapproval of the informal way in which the baby's placement had been arranged, and the lack of social work support available for the mother when she first changed her mind about the adoption, clearly influenced their decision. One wonders, however, whether the court would have considered the evidence in quite the same way had they not been so convinced, on the authority of

93   See N Lowe, M Murch et al (1999) ch 10.
94   Eg in *Re M (child's upbringing)* [1996] 2 FLR 441, the white South African foster carer of the Zulu boy had gained his parents' permission to bring him to England with her and her family when they left South Africa, without disclosing her intention to adopt him.
95   Under the Adoption and Children Act 2002, ss 92–93 (formerly Adoption Act 1976, s 11) it is a criminal offence to arrange a private adoption placement and to receive a child unlawfully placed for adoption, unless the child was initially received on a fostering basis and not for adoption. Eg *Gatehouse v R* [1986] 1 WLR 18.
96   See Adoption and Children Act 2002, ss 46 and 67, replacing Adoption Act 1976, ss 12 and 39.
97   See discussion by N Lowe (1997).
98   See the discussion of open adoption involving contact with birth parents in chapter 13.
99   [1990] 3 All ER 795. Discussed above.
100 See discussion by I Weyland (1997) pp 181–182.
101 [1991] 1 FLR 57.
102 [1991] 1 FLR 57 at 62, per Butler-Sloss LJ.
103 The adopters were childless Greek Cypriots aged 55 (husband) and 47 (wife). The birth mother, who was Irish, had met them in a Greek restaurant when eating there with her children.
104 [1991] 1 FLR 57 at 62, per Butler-Sloss LJ.

Re K (a minor) (ward: care and control),[105] that this baby had a 'right' to be brought up by her birth parents.[106] The court considered it wrong to weigh up what the foster parents' family could offer the child unless it was shown that the birth parents were 'entirely unsuitable'.[107] Surprisingly, this unsuitability was not apparent to the Court of Appeal, despite the trial judge's fears, inter alia, about the mother's history of drug addiction, an unstable marriage and a husband with a criminal record, who was addicted to gambling.[108] As Eekelaar points out, Butler-Sloss LJ's use of the term 'social engineering' in a pejorative way in situations like this[109] reflects her assumption that 'natural' parenthood is far preferable to the social parenthood contrived by fostering and adoption.[110] The danger of being accused of social engineering would certainly deter any court tempted to compare a child's prospects in the two households on offer. But, as commented above, the danger is that by refusing to do so the courts risk placing an undue value on the blood tie between child and parent, at the expense of the child's psychological health.

Claims that children have a 'right' to be brought up by their birth parents can obviously be strengthened in cases like *Re B (adoption: child's welfare),*[111] where their foster carers are of a different racial and cultural background to themselves. The courts may well consider that the weight to be given to the child's '"heritage" or "birthright"' in such cases is sufficiently strong to outweigh evidence regarding the child's attachments to his or her foster carers.[112] To a certain extent, it is surprising that there are not more cases of this kind reaching the courts. No one knows the exact number of children from ethnic minorities who are privately fostered, since many foster families fail to notify their local authorities of arrangements made for private foster care.[113] Some of these children are refugees from conflict, some are fostered to allow their parents to study or work here, others come for informal visits and stay on.[114] The early 1970s saw a considerable growth in the numbers of West African children, in particular, Nigerian children, being placed in private foster care.[115] More

---

105 [1990] 3 All ER 795.
106 [1991] 1 FLR 57 at 62, per Butler-Sloss LJ.
107 [1991] 1 FLR 57 at 62, per Butler-Sloss LJ.
108 The trial judge had considered that 'it would be a gamble with long odds against', to attempt rehabilitating the child with her family. She was worried by the birth mother's lack of commitment in visiting the child and her apparent lack of warmth and affection for her. [1991] 1 FLR 57 at 61–62, per Butler-Sloss LJ.
109 The same phrase was used in *Re O (a minor) (custody: adoption)* [1992] 1 FLR 77 at 79, per Butler-Sloss LJ. See discussion below.
110 J Eekelaar (1994) pp 80–82.
111 [1995] 1 FLR 895: Gambian birth parents successfully opposed a European couple's application to adopt their child, now aged 4. Although the birth parents had allowed the couple to take their daughter to England for a 'long holiday' lasting up to six months, she had remained with them for 18 months and had become strongly attached to them and they to her.
112 [1995] 1 FLR 895 at 902, per Wall J. But see *Re O (transracial adoption: contact)* [1996] 1 FCR 540 and *Re N (a minor) (adoption)* [1990] 1 FLR 58.
113 See Save the Children (1997) p 5 and SSI (2002) para 1.20.
114 For a discussion of the dangers children undergo in private fostering arrangements, see, inter alia: W Utting (1997) pp 43–46; B Holman (2002); T Philpot (2001); SSI (2002) paras 1.16 and 6.4. Lord Laming recommended that the government should review the law regarding the registration of private foster carers. H Laming (2003), Recommendation 11, General recommendations.
115 By the early 1990s, it was estimated that there were probably at least 6,000 children of West African origin privately fostered in the UK. Save the Children (1997) p 1. Victoria Climbié was a recent example; she was fostered by her great aunt and brought to England from the Ivory Coast in 1999. In 2001, the great aunt and boyfriend were convicted of Victoria's murder and child cruelty.

recently, it appears that there have been increasing numbers from other parts of Africa and from Eastern European countries, such as Bosnia.[116] Whatever their total, it is clear that large numbers of white foster carers foster children of a different racial and cultural origin, whose birth parents are abroad and therefore unable to be actively involved in their children's upbringing or the type of care being provided.

It appears that the majority of privately fostered children eventually returns to their birth parents, but 'the consequences of their returning to a culture, religion and language that is alien to them, and perhaps seen as inferior by them because of experiences they have had in their placements, are plain'.[117] In a minority of cases, the ties of affection between these children and their foster parents strengthen over time, to such an extent that their reluctance to return the child to their birth parents culminates in litigation.[118] Today, it seems unlikely that the birth parents would clothe their arguments in the language of children's rights. They might instead refer to their own rights under the ECHR, not only to have their child restored to their family under article 8, but also to ensure that their right to bring up their child in their own religion under article 9 is fully respected. It would be the foster carers' task to convince the court that the harm that the child would suffer psychologically through being uprooted from a home with them justifies infringing the birth parents' own rights, through the grant of an adoption order.

The Strasbourg jurisprudence acknowledges that there may come a time when the child's need for a permanent home, combined with his or her own reluctance to return to the birth family, justifies the domestic courts allowing an adoption order in favour of foster carers.[119] Nevertheless, it also stresses that measures depriving a birth parent of his or her family life with their child should only be adopted in exceptional circumstances 'motivated by an overriding requirement pertaining to the child's best interests'.[120] Clearly an adoption order must meet a pressing social need and this may be the child's need for security and stability with his or her present carers. Nevertheless, an adoption order has a drastic effect on the child's relationship with his or her birth parents and may not be a proportionate response to the situation if there are less radical methods of strengthening the foster carers' legal position.

Hopefully, the House of Lords' decision in *Re B (a child) (adoption by one natural parent)*[121] will not deter the domestic courts from assessing the options carefully in this type of dispute. Lord Nicholls of Birkenhead's view was that by deciding that an adoption order fulfils the child's best interest, the court is automatically identifying the pressing social need required to be fulfilled by the order and at the same time ensuring that the order is a proportionate response to the present circumstances.[122] Unfortunately, this approach does not encourage a critical response to arguments that an adoption order is the only measure that can provide the foster carers and the child with security and stability together, and that therefore only such an order could fulfil

---

116 Save the Children (1997) p 12.
117 Save the Children (1997) p 38.
118 Eg *Re B (adoption: child's welfare)* [1995] 1 FLR 895.
119 See *Bronda v Italy* (2001) 33 EHRR 4 (paras 61–62) and *Scott v United Kingdom* [2000] 1 FLR 958 at 970–971.
120 *Johansen v Norway* (1996) 23 EHRR 33 (para 78) and *Gnahore v France* (2002) 34 EHRR 38 (para 59).
121 [2001] UKHL 70, [2002] 1 All ER 641.
122 [2001] UKHL 70, [2002] 1 All ER 641 at [31]. See S Harris-Short (2002) p 338 for a critical assessment of this approach.

the child's best interests. Given the radical effect of an adoption order, the domestic courts should instead be encouraged to consider whether there are alternative ways of dealing with such a dispute. It might be more appropriate to grant the foster carers a residence order, with contact to the birth parents, buttressed by an order restraining the birth parents from constantly litigating to get their child returned.[123] This would fulfil the child's best interests by preserving the birth parents' status as parents, whilst admitting that the foster carers are the right people to provide him or her with a home for the time being.[124] Alternatively, the grant of a special guardianship order to the foster carers might be considered.[125] These orders were created to 'provide permanence for those children for whom adoption is not appropriate, and where the court decides that it [special guardianship] is in the best interests of the child or young person'.[126] Although a special guardianship order would not confer on the foster carers the legal status of parenthood, they would thereby obtain parental responsibility, and could reach decisions regarding the child's upbringing without consulting the birth parents.[127] Meanwhile, they would also gain automatic protection from the birth parents attempting to harass them through constantly applying to have their status reviewed.[128]

(4)   THE BLOOD TIE, BIRTH PARENTS AND ADOPTION PLACEMENTS

(A)   Parents who place their children for adoption

(i)   The background

According to conventional wisdom, children do best if they are brought up by their own parents. Nevertheless, adopted children often go to adoptive parents who are emotionally secure, better off and able to maintain an environment superior to that of their birth parents. This probably explains the research literature suggesting not only that adopted children usually form good attachments with their adoptive parents, but also that adoptive homes can produce considerable benefits for them. This does not, of course, indicate that the state should remove children from 'inadequate' parents and place them with meritorious childless couples.[129] Nevertheless, it does suggest

---

123 Eg *Re P (a child) (residence order: restriction order)* [2000] Fam 15: the Court of Appeal considered that an order made under the Children Act 1989, s 91(14) prohibiting Jewish orthodox birth parents from applying for any court order regarding their 8-year-old Down's syndrome daughter would provide her foster carers with a period of peace and stability.

124 Eg *Re B (adoption order)* [2001] EWCA Civ 347, [2001] 2 FLR 26: the Court of Appeal considered that a residence order to the child's foster carer (backed by an order under Children Act 1989, s 91(14) restraining the father applying himself for a residence order without leave of the court) might be a more proportionate response to the child's need for a permanent home than an adoption order, given the foster carer's willingness to continue caring for him on such a basis. Father's appeal against the adoption order granted.

125 Under Children Act 1989, ss 14A–G, as inserted by Adoption and Children Act 2002, s 115. Applicants for special guardianship orders need court leave to apply for such an order under the Children Act 1989, s 9(3), unless they can comply with the requirements of s 10(5)(b) or (c) in which case they can apply as of right. See Children Act 1989, s 14A(4) and (5).

126 See Department of Health (hereafter DH) (2000) para 5.10.

127 Children Act 1989, s 14C(1)(b).

128 The birth parents cannot apply to have the special guardianship order varied or discharged without obtaining prior court leave: Children Act 1989, s 14D(3).

129 See H Schaffer (1998) pp 60–62.

that if birth parents arrange adoptions for their children, the law should pay considerable attention to the strength of the attachments their children then form with the prospective adopters, before acceding to the demands of birth parents who change their minds and subsequently want to retrieve their child.

The unequivocal effect of an adoption order is that it finally and completely removes the status of parenthood from a birth parent. The law protects birth parents by giving them a final veto over the adoption order.[130] If the adoption agency is convinced that, despite the parents now refusing to agree to an adoption, it is in the child's best interests to be adopted, it may ask the court to dispense with the parents' consent. Under the old adoption law, if a child had already formed ties of affection with prospective adopters, the court would consider dispensing with the birth parents' consent on the basis that they were withholding it unreasonably.[131] But the courts found it extremely difficult to decide how reasonable parents would behave in such circumstances, particularly the extent to which they would take account of their child's best interests when deciding whether to agree to the adoption. The famous formula established by Lord Hailsham illustrates the logical gymnastics the judiciary adopted when interpreting this particular ground.[132] The courts were required to remember that –

'the test is reasonableness and not anything else ... It is reasonableness, and reasonableness in the context of the totality of the circumstances. But, although welfare per se is not the test, the fact that a reasonable parent does pay regard to the welfare of his child must enter into the question of reasonableness as a relevant factor.'[133]

But, as many pointed out, the concept of the reasonable parent was a fiction designed to find an appropriate balance between the child's welfare and the parents' own wishes and concerns:

'The law conjures the imaginary parent into existence to give expression to what it considers that justice requires as between the welfare of the child as perceived by the judge on the one hand and the legitimate views and interests of the natural parents on the other.'[134]

Indeed, the ability of any parent to behave reasonably when opposing an adoption order was doubtful, particularly when struggling with his or her own personal problems.[135]

This aspect of adoption law has changed; indeed, the most controversial aspect of the new adoption legislation is the way it aligns all adoption decision-making with the paramountcy (or welfare) principle set out in the Children Act 1989, section 1. Before, the courts were required to ask whether –

---

130 Both parents must consent to the making of an adoption order if they are married, or if the unmarried father has parental responsibility. See Adoption and Children Act 2002, ss 47(2) and 52(6). An unmarried father who lacks parental responsibility nevertheless normally be joined in the adoption proceedings. See discussion below.

131 Adoption Act 1976, s 16(2)(b). The other grounds (the parent could not be found; was incapable of signing the agreement; had abandoned or neglected the child; or had persistently or seriously ill-treated the child) were very seldom used.

132 *Re W (an infant)* [1971] 2 All ER 49: a mother agreed to her son being adopted. The foster carers who took over his care when he was eight days old, later applied to adopt him, the mother signing the consent form. She withdrew her consent just before the hearing, by which time the child was aged 16 months.

133 [1971] 2 All ER 49 at 55, per Lord Hailsham. See the case law interpreting this test discussed by N Lowe and G Douglas (1998) pp 638–647.

134 *Re C (a minor) (adoption: parental agreement: contact)* [1993] 2 FLR 260 at 272, per Steyn and Hoffmann LJJ.

135 See *Re S (an infant)* [1973] 3 All ER 88 at 91, per Davies LJ.

'the advantages of adoption for A appear sufficiently strong to justify overriding the views and interests of the objecting parent or parents.'[136]

Under the new adoption law, unless the parent cannot be found or is incapable of consenting to the adoption,[137] the courts must ask a simple question when deciding whether a parent's consent should be dispensed with. Does the child's welfare require the adoption order to be made, taking account of the various factors set out in the welfare checklist?[138] This change, which had been mooted for some years, may have a drastic effect on the way in which the courts deal with parents who finally oppose their child's adoption. Indeed, the introduction of a simple welfare formula as a basis for dispensing with parental consent attracted considerable opposition when reforming the adoption law was first mooted.[139] Thus the 1992 Review of Adoption Law indicated its strong view that considerations of the child's welfare should not be allowed to determine whether an adoption order should be made against the parents' wishes.[140] It argued that any new legislation should achieve a balance between the interests of the child, adopters and birth parents, and suggested that a court should ask whether –

'the advantages to a child of becoming part of a new family and having a new legal status are so significantly greater than the advantages to the child of any alternative option as to justify overriding the wishes of a parent.'[141]

As critics point out, the new law theoretically enables the judiciary to dispense with parental consent, having interpreted what is in the child's best interests in such a subjective way that adoption will be a forgone conclusion.[142] They also argue that the new formula does not reflect the complexities of adoption. Although an adoption order often ostensibly benefits a child, it deprives the child and his or her birth parents of a unique relationship in a family, which can never be retrieved.[143] These concerns perhaps carry greater cogency when considered in relation to children placed for adoption by local authorities, having been removed from their parents compulsorily,[144] but they are also relevant in any situation where the birth parents now oppose an adoption order. Whilst there is nothing to prevent the courts, when deciding whether to dispense with the parents' consent, to take full account of the parents' perspectives, they are free not to do so. The factors listed in the welfare checklist certainly give the courts plenty of scope to consider the strength of the child's links with his or her birth family.[145] Furthermore, the new law, freed from the unreasonable parent formula, is certainly clearer and more logical. But whether, when using the new criterion, the courts will promote children's rights better, in so far as the child's welfare is unequivocally placed centre stage, remains to be seen.

Returning to the type of dispute under consideration, the traditional scenario is the young unmarried mother who, feeling unable to care for her child herself, and

136 *Re F (adoption: freeing order)* [2000] 2 FLR 505 at [22], per Thorpe LJ.
137 Adoption and Children Act 2002, s 52(1)(a).
138 Adoption and Children Act 2002, ss 52(1)(b) and 1(2) and (4).
139 See summarised and discussed by S Harris-Short (2001) pp 419–421.
140 Interdepartmental Working Group (1992) para 7.1.
141 Interdepartmental Working Group (1992) para 12.6.
142 See B Lindley and N Wyld (1996) esp pp 330–331.
143 E Cooke (1997) p 263.
144 See discussion below.
145 See Adoption and Children Act 2002, s 1(4)(c) and (f). Under s 1(4)(a) the child's own wishes and feelings regarding the adoption must also be considered; for a further discussion of this factor, see chapter 8.

wanting to ensure a better future for him or her in adoptive care, places her baby for adoption. As Lowe points out, here the '"gift" mindset' may be apposite; this sees adoption as a process whereby the mother makes a 'gift' of her baby to the prospective adopters whom the adoption agency has carefully selected to become the baby's 'real' parents in her place.[146] But if the mother later changes her mind about the adoption, the baby may, by then, have formed strong attachments with the prospective adopters and they with the baby. A second scenario arises when an unmarried father discovers that his child has been placed for adoption without his knowledge and opposes the adoption proceedings on the basis that he wants to bring up the child himself. In both situations, the courts are obliged to reflect on the long-term value to the child of being brought up by a birth parent whom the child probably no longer remembers, rather than by the prospective adopters, who may have become his or her 'real parents' through attachment.

(ii) Vacillating mothers

The response of the courts to applications from one or other of the birth parents to stop the adoption process reflects a variety of judicial views regarding the importance of the blood tie between parent and child. The young mother who agrees to the child being placed for adoption, but later changes her mind, creates a particularly distressing situation for everyone involved. Unlike the father opposing an adoption, she is the one who instigated the adoption process and she may have done so extremely early in the baby's life, at a time when neither she nor the baby had formed any attachments with each other. By the time she agreed to the adoption she should have been sure that this was the appropriate course of action. The law not only insists on her having a period of reflection after the baby's birth before she provides any formal consent,[147] but it also attempts to ensure that she agrees to the adoption unconditionally and with a full understanding of what is involved.[148] But even with support and counselling, a mother may remain uncertain about her decision and her continuing vacillations may be very damaging if the child has meanwhile been placed for adoption and has already formed very strong attachments with the prospective adopters. In such a situation, under the old law, the court would normally consider dispensing with the mother's consent, on the basis that she was withholding it unreasonably.[149] As Ormrod LJ pointed out:

'Although it is easy to understand the difficulties of the mother as a young woman, it is equally easy to be over-indulgent in approaching her problems because, once she takes the step of initiating adoption proceedings, she starts a chain reaction which can only be stopped with great damage to some people.'[150]

146 See N Lowe (1997) esp pp 371 and 382.
147 A mother cannot consent to her child's adoption within six weeks of the child's birth: see Adoption and Children Act 2002, s 52(3) replacing Adoption Act 1976, s 18(4).
148 Adoption and Children Act 2002, s 52(5), replacing Adoption Act 1976, s 16(1)(b). See *Re A (adoption: agreement: procedure)* [2001] 2 FLR 455: the Court of Appeal stressed the need for the authorities to check prior to the court hearing that a parent fully understands the import of having consented to an adoption order. There a 15-year-old rape victim from Kosovo had signed a consent to a freeing for adoption order over her baby without appreciating the full import of such an action.
149 Adoption Act 1997, s 16(2)(b). See discussion above.
150 *Re W (adoption: parental agreement)* (1981) 3 FLR 75 at 81. See a discussion of the case law on 'vacillating mothers' by N Lowe and G Douglas (1998) pp 641–642.

Meanwhile, as in *Re A (adoption: mother's objections)*,[151] the mother may support her opposition to the adoption by arguing that her child has a right to be brought up by his or her birth mother, rather than by strangers.[152] Such a claim would find support in case law such as *Re K (a minor) (ward: care and control)*.[153] But if, as there, the child was moved from his mother at the age of three days and placed with foster carers and then with prospective adopters at two months, the birth tie between him and his mother has little real significance – at least for the child. The decision in *Re A* to dispense with the mother's consent to the adoption shows the courts' clear perception in this type of dispute that the dangers of uprooting a child left at a very early age with prospective adopters more than outweigh the long-term value of the blood tie between mother and child.[154] It seems unlikely that the courts' new ability to dispense with a mother's consent to her child's adoption, if the child's welfare requires it, will greatly affect the outcome of such decisions in future.

(iii) Unmarried fathers

Perhaps the greatest swings in judicial opinion relating to the long-term value to the child of the parental blood tie can be seen in the cases involving unmarried fathers who endeavour to save their children from adoption by seeking permission to take over their care themselves. Although an unmarried father without parental responsibility has no right to veto his child's adoption proceedings,[155] he should be notified of them. Indeed, the need to respect an unmarried father's right to family life under article 8 of the ECHR and to ensure that the adoption proceedings fairly involve him, as required by article 6,[156] makes his early involvement increasingly common. The courts have stressed that a mother's desire for secrecy when she places her child for adoption should only be observed in exceptional circumstances.[157] In most cases, despite the mother's opposition, the father should be identified and joined as a party to the adoption proceedings,[158] and the social worker advising the mother should warn her of this possibility as early as possible in the adoption proceedings.[159]

The remarkable differences in approach to an unmarried father's claim to bring up his child himself can be seen from a brief comparison of two cases involving very similar facts but divided by over 30 years. Thus, in the mid-1960s, Russell LJ approved of an unmarried father and his wife gaining custody of his small 17-month-old son whom the father had never met. He explained:

---

151 [2000] 1 FLR 665.
152 [2000] 1 FLR 665 at 691.
153 [1990] 3 All ER 795. See also *Re K (a minor) (wardship: adoption)* [1991] 1 FLR 57, discussed above.
154 The Court of Appeal held that at the age of nearly a year, the baby boy's attachment to prospective adopters was too deep and secure to disrupt, he having lived with them from the age of two months.
155 Adoption and Children Act 2002, s 52(6).
156 See *Keegan v Ireland* (1994) 18 EHRR 342.
157 Eg *Re M (adoption: rights of natural father)* [2001] 1 FLR 745: the father's right to respect for his family life under art 8 (if it existed here, given the fact that he had never lived with the mother and the child was conceived mistakenly) and to be fairly involved in the adoption proceedings under art 6, were not absolute and here were qualified by the need to protect the mother and her children from his extreme violence.
158 See *Re H; Re G (adoption: consultation of unmarried fathers)* [2001] 1 FLR 646, for a review of the law on this point. See also A Bainham (2002) pp 280–284.
159 [2001] 1 FLR 646 at 661–662, per Dame Elizabeth Butler-Sloss P.

'I myself do attach great weight to the blood tie. If a father (as distinct from a stranger in blood) can bring up his own son as his own son, so much the better for both of them, whether or not by the accident of events the legitimate relationship exists.'[160]

Russell LJ clearly considered that the value of the blood tie between father and son more than counter-balanced the medical evidence spelling out the risks of uprooting this child from his home with the prospective adopters who had cared for him for 15 months, from the age of two months. The child psychiatrist had indicated that to move the child would 'take an unjustifiable risk with his future'.[161] Nevertheless, the majority of the Court of Appeal[162] was surprisingly confident that the 'instinctual tie' between child and father and the qualities of the father's wife would protect the child from the dangers of severe psychological damage.

In the years intervening between that decision and *Re O (adoption: withholding agreement)*,[163] the line of decisions commencing with *Re K (a minor) (ward: care and control)*,[164] establishing a child's 'right' to be brought up by his or her birth parents, had become well known. Lord Templeman had made his rousing assertion in *Re KD (a minor) (ward: termination of access)*[165] that the 'best person to bring up a child is the natural parent ...'[166] Judicial anxieties had also emerged about 'social engineering',[167] in the event of a birth parent being compared harshly with 'idealised perfect adopters'.[168] Nevertheless, in *Re O (adoption: withholding agreement)*[169] the Court of Appeal adopted an entirely different approach to that taken by Russell LJ, more than 30 years before. It considered that, despite the presumption that it is a child's right to be brought up by his natural family, the trial judge's decision refusing the father a residence order had been fully justified. He had quite rightly taken full account of the psychological evidence indicating the severe risks of uprooting this 18-month-old child, who had never met his birth father, from his home with prospective adopters where he had been since he was two months old. Since the child's bonds of affection with the prospective adopters could not be broken without adversely affecting his personality and security, his welfare would not be promoted by his father gaining his care.[170]

It should be noted that *Re O* was complicated by the fact that, although unmarried, the father had acquired a parental responsibility order, and so could effectively veto the adoption proceedings, unless the court could dispense with his consent to the adoption. This meant that the court's logical difficulties when applying two different criteria in the same case were very obvious. The father's application for a residence order relating to his child was governed by the child's best interests, according to the

---

160 *Re C (MA) (an infant)* [1966] 1 All ER 838 at 863, per Russell LJ.
161 [1966] 1 All ER 838, at 855.
162 Willmer LJ dissented, partly because he considered that the benefits to be derived by the child from being brought up by his own father were 'rather shadowy and conjectural'. [1966] 1 All ER 838 at 856.
163 [1999] 1 FLR 451.
164 [1990] 3 All ER 795.
165 [1988] AC 806.
166 [1988] AC 806 at 812.
167 *Re O (a minor) (custody: adoption)* [1992] 1 FLR 77.
168 [1992] 1 FLR 77 at 79, per Butler-Sloss LJ.
169 [1999] 1 FLR 451.
170 See also *Re M (a minor) (custody appeal)* [1990] 1 FLR 291 at 297, per Purchas LJ, who indicated his lack of sympathy with arguments based on the blood tie between a young unmarried father and his baby daughter. This did not justify the father obtaining the child's custody, thereby preventing her obtaining a stable adoptive home.

Children Act 1989, section 1. But, having refused this application, the court proceeded to consider whether to dispense with his consent to the adoption. Although under the new adoption law the best interests test governs both applications, here, governed as it was by the old law, the criterion had to shift to the reasonable parent test. Swinton Thomas LJ, having acknowledged the unreality created by the concept of the hypothetical reasonable father, upheld the trial judge's finding that the father was unreasonable in withholding his consent to the adoption. The court clearly rejected the notion that the blood tie between the child and his father could make up for the child's loss of attachments with adults who, despite being biological strangers, had become his 'real' parents. The decision is welcome because it acknowledges that it may be too late to repair a parent's sense of injustice at being deprived of the chance to have a relationship with his own 'flesh and blood', without endangering the child's own emotional stability.[171]

(B)   Children adopted from care

Since many of the situations discussed above were put in train by the birth parents themselves, one can assert that they only had themselves to blame when their children became so firmly attached to their present carers that the courts decided to leave them where they were. But the parents whose children are compulsorily removed from them into the care of local authorities and who then feel unable to consent to their children's adoption are in a very different position. Furthermore, here the opposing parties are not two sets of private litigants but the birth parents and the state – the latter acting on behalf of the child to protect him or her from the parents.

Again, one can argue that most of these parents brought the situation on themselves by treating their children so badly that the state was forced to intervene. For some seriously abused children, the blood tie certainly carries very little significance. Nevertheless, matters are not always that simple. Some parents, with more social work support, might be able to provide a good home for their children.[172] Moreover, many of the 'older' children,[173] despite having been removed from home because of their parents' abusive behaviour, will retain strong ties of affection for their parents. Their relationships, albeit flawed by the child's abusive experiences, may have a value for child and parent alike. Indeed, these children may be difficult to place if adoptive parents cannot contemplate an open form of adoption involving direct contact.[174] The law therefore has to tread a tightrope between protecting the valuable aspects of the relationships between children in care and their birth families, and ensuring that as many as possible obtain a fresh start in a new family without undue delay. This, of course, is behind the government's aggressive campaign to ensure that more children are adopted from care more rapidly.

Meanwhile, critics consider that the recent reforms of the adoption law ensuring that the child's welfare governs all aspects of the adoption process may affect this

---

171   [1999] 1 FLR 451: the father felt a deep sense of injustice that the local authority had not informed him of the existence of his child until the hearing of the adoption application.

172   Eg *Re D (grant of care order: refusal of freeing order)* [2001] 1 FLR 862: the trial judge considered that the child's parents, who abused alcohol and heroin, might, if they availed themselves of local substance abuse services, be able to take over their baby son's care.

173   But see DH (2001 a) Figure A. The average age of children adopted currently has decreased from 5 years 5 months, to 4 years 3 months between 1996/97 and 2000/01. During that period the percentage of children adopted, aged 1 to 4, has increased from 48% to 60%.

174   See discussed in chapter 14.

parent group particularly harshly. In many cases involving abused children who have been the subject of care proceedings, the courts will be in little doubt that their welfare requires them to be adopted. Nevertheless, some abusive parents love their children and refuse to agree to their adoption. A request from the local authority to dispense with the parents' consent was, under the old adoption law, dealt with on the basis that the parents were withholding their consent unreasonably. As discussed above, the courts found the concept of the reasonable parent difficult to apply in practice and a large body of case law indicates that this difficulty did not abate in relation to parents whose abusive behaviour had led to the child being removed from home.[175] The judiciary were very aware that dispensing with parental consent would not only deprive the parents of their parenthood, but also leave them bearing the stigma of unreasonableness. Sometimes, as in *Re D (grant of care order: refusal of freeing order)*,[176] a court's excessive sympathy with parents' personal difficulties undermined its ability to reach a finding of 'unreasonableness'. Although humane, a refusal to dispense with parental consent to adoption might mean that a seriously abused child's chances of gaining a permanent home with prospective adopters were delayed whilst unrealistic attempts at supporting his or her parents were attempted yet again. As Thorpe LJ slightly caustically stated:

'Of course in an uncertain world almost anything can be said to be possible, but in evaluating the hypothetical reasonable parent test and in applying it, it is not open to a judge to give prominence to theoretical possibility unless the possibility has a quantifiable and realistic content. It is simply irrelevant to the judicial exercise ...'[177]

Meanwhile, as discussed above, despite the obvious artificiality involved in the test of unreasonableness, many organisations involved in adoption practice opposed the courts being given the power to dispense with their consent whenever 'the welfare of the child requires the consent to be dispensed with'.[178] This, they argued, would mean that children could be removed from their families and have the legal relationship with their parents irrevocably severed 'simply because an adoption agency and court are satisfied that another family could do a better job ...'[179] Critics claimed that this 'could lead to social engineering of the worst kind'.[180]

These fears should be seen in the context of the government's efforts to overhaul the whole adoption system. The government had been extremely critical of the extent to which large numbers of children being looked after by local authorities were 'drifting in care'.[181] The 'solution' was to ensure that far more children gained permanent adoptive families who would give them safety, stability and lifelong support.[182] By introducing a new, highly regulated adoption service, with adoption

---

175 See the case law discussed by N Lowe and G Douglas (1998) pp 642–647 and by M Hayes and C Williams (1999) pp 362–368.
176 [2001] 1 FLR 862: the trial judge refused to find parents who abused heroin and alcohol unreasonable in refusing to consent to their child's adoption. If they would only take up offers of help from local substance misuse teams, one of them might be able to care for him in future. Nevertheless, their inadequacies as parents justified the grant of a care order.
177 [2001] 1 FLR 862 at [31].
178 Adoption and Children Act 2002, s 52(1)(b).
179 British Association of Social Workers (2001) para 1.
180 National Organisation for the Counselling of Adoptees and Parents (2001) Summary.
181 Discussed in more detail in chapter 16.
182 Performance and Innovation Unit Report (2000) para 4.9.

targets,[183] and standards,[184] and by amending the law to introduce a more efficient and rapid legal process, the government hoped that more children could be adopted faster. In particular, the new legislation ensures that applications for care orders in relation to abused children will often be combined with applications for adoption placement orders.[185] These reforms were, however, accompanied by severe misgivings on the part of adoption practitioners who questioned whether more and quicker adoptions would necessarily benefit large numbers of children entering the care system.[186] Children with an abusive background have extremely complex needs and finding the 'right' adoptive parents for them may not be easy, appropriate or even practicable.[187] Furthermore, the new adoption targets, combined with legislation making it easier to dispense with parental consent to adoption, were seen as a threat to disadvantaged and impoverished parents, who with more social work support, might eventually manage to provide a stable home for their children.[188]

Many of the critics argued that the adoption reforms would infringe not only the parents' rights to respect for their family life under article 8 of the ECHR, but also their children's rights to remain in their birth families if at all possible.[189] These concerns have some cogency. The European Court of Human Rights has constantly emphasised that in order to comply with article 8 of the Convention, welfare agencies who remove children from their parents into care should treat such a measure as a temporary one only. They should take all steps which could reasonably be expected of them to re-establish the parent-child relationship as soon as possible.[190] To deprive parents entirely of their family life with the child by placing the child for adoption is only justifiable in the most exceptional circumstances motivated by an overriding need to protect the child's best interests.[191] The Court recently criticised the way that care proceedings had been allied with freeing a child for adoption, thereby decreasing the possibility of exploring future rehabilitation and reunification.[192] Nevertheless, the Strasbourg jurisprudence also acknowledges that an adoption order may eventually be an appropriate means of giving a child security, rather than leaving

---

183   New national targets for adoption were, in 2001, incorporated into the DH's Public Service Agreement (PSA) – by 2004–05 to increase by 40% the number of looked after children adopted in 1999/2000 (but from 2001–02, calculated as a percentage of those looked after for six months or more), and aim to exceed this by achieving a 50% increase; to increase to 95% the proportion of looked after children placed for adoption within 12 months of the decision that adoption is in the child's best interests: DH (2001 b). The number of looked after children adopted increased by just under 55% between 1998/9 and 2001/2002. See DH (2002) p 82.

184   See DH (2001 c). The National Care Standards Commission was established to improve standards and to monitor practice, together with the Adoption and Permanence Taskforce, established to work alongside local authorities to improve local authority adoption practice. The establishment of an Adoption Register also enables adoption agencies to match children waiting for adopters with approved adoptive families: see DH (2001 d).

185   See discussion in chapter 16. Note the six-month optimum period between the care proceedings and the 'panel approved [adoption] "match"': DH (2001 c) Standard A3(b).

186   See S Harris-Short (2001) pp 417–420 and 421.

187   See Family Policy Studies Centre (2000) pp 2–3.

188   See British Agencies for Adoption and Fostering (2001) para 11.3.

189   British Agencies for Adoption and Fostering (2001) para 11.3.

190   See, inter alia: *Johansen v Norway* (1996) 23 EHRR 33 (esp para 78); *EP v Italy* (2001) 31 EHRR 17 (esp para 62). See also *Olsson v Sweden* (1988) 11 EHRR 259; *K and T v Finland* [2001] 2 FLR 707; *S and G v Italy* [2000] 2 FLR 771.

191   *Johansen v Norway* (1996) 23 EHRR 33 (para 78).

192   *P, C and S v United Kingdom* [2002] 2 FLR 631 at [98] and [104].

him or her in a state of uncertainty in temporary placements with foster carers.[193] This Convention case law indicates that local authorities have a difficult path to tread. Whilst they must take all appropriate steps to attempt a rehabilitation between parent and child removed into care, they must also protect the child's best interests and ensure that the child's sense of uncertainty is terminated without undue delay. Doubtless the government would argue that by following its twin-track planning guidance, local authorities will correctly balance these two objectives. This requires local authorities to work towards rehabilitating the child with his or her family, whilst arranging an adoptive placement in the event of the rehabilitation failing.[194]

Meanwhile, the domestic courts must themselves also negotiate the tightrope designed by the Strasbourg jurisprudence. They acknowledge, on the one hand, that children cannot be expected to wait for new families indefinitely. Local authorities must therefore take adequate steps to secure for a child who has been deprived of family life with his birth family, 'a life with a new family who can become his new "family for life" to make up for what he has lost'.[195] Nevertheless, on the other hand, the court should consider carefully whether an adoption order is a proportionate response to the child's need for permanency, given that an adoption order is the most radical form of interference with family life.[196] As discussed above, it would be regrettable if the House of Lords' decision in *Re B (a child) (adoption by one natural parent)*[197] deterred practitioners and the domestic courts from assessing all the options carefully. Lord Nicholls of Birkenhead's view that as long as an adoption order is in the child's best interests, it is a proportionate response to the present situation,[198] should not prevent the local authority and court from considering whether there are alternative ways of dealing with the child's needs. For example, a special guardianship order might provide foster carers with an adequate degree of security in their care of the child.[199] Overall, social services departments will probably conclude that the law and government policy currently provide them with a series of inconsistent and contradictory messages. In one respect, however, the law is reasonably clear – parents who have treated their children so badly that they have been removed into care have forfeited the right to argue that their ties of blood justify rehabilitative measures being attempted indefinitely.

(5) CONCLUSION

In cases outside the child protection arena, there appear to be three features common to the judicial treatment of disputes between parents and informal foster carers over a child's future. First, the courts tend to invest the blood tie between child and birth parents with considerable significance long after their relationship has been disrupted.

---

193   See *Bronda v Italy* (2001) 33 EHRR 4 (paras 61–62) and *Scott v United Kingdom* [2000] 1 FLR 958 at 970–971.

194   Discussed in chapter 16.

195   Per Hale LJ, in *Re W and B; Re W (care plan)* [2001] EWCA Civ 757, [2001] 2 FLR 582 at [55]. Although this decision was reversed by the House of Lords in *Re S (children: care plan); Re W (children: care plan)* [2002] 2 All ER 192, Hale LJ's views, in this respect, remain relevant.

196   *Re B (adoption by one natural parent to exclusion of other)* [2001] 1 FLR 589, per Hale LJ at para 37. This decision was reversed by the House of Lords, but the principle referred to by Hale LJ remains an important one.

197   [2001] UKHL 70, [2002] 1 All ER 641.

198   [2001] UKHL 70, [2002] 1 All ER 641 at [31].

199   Children Act 1989, ss 14A–G.

Second, the courts appear to assume that the same set of principles should apply to disputes involving the child awaiting a fostering or adoption placement, who has not yet formed bonds of attachment with foster carers, as to the child happily settled in a foster home. Whilst it may be more appropriate for the courts to presume that the child awaiting placement should be brought up by his or her birth parents, unless there are strong and positive reasons for this not occurring, this is not necessarily the case for the child already placed in a foster home. Third, the courts have exploited the language of children's rights to support what are often, in truth, claims to adults' rights to resume caring for their children. Ironically, when adopting this approach, the courts appear more likely to neglect making a proper assessment of the child's psychological needs or rights, than in cases where this 'rights language' is not used. Birth parents' ability to appeal to their rights under the ECHR may strengthen their hand in disputes of this kind.

The discretionary nature of judicial decision-making in this area of child law masks a lack of clarity over the issues at stake and a failure to establish a well-defined evidential approach. A well-founded children's rights framework for decision-making might lead to a more beneficial outcome for the children who are the subject of these disputes. Paying attention to children's right to protection would concentrate attention on their potential safety and care and a more reasoned approach to their real needs, rather than those of their birth parents. There would be no reason to discount special factors, such as a disrupted early childhood and a child's new-found happiness and security with foster carers, particularly if they were able to offer a level of care much higher than that available from the birth parent. When attempting to reach a decision, it is perfectly appropriate for the courts to place some weight on the common assumption that 'normal' family life involves children being brought up by their birth parents. Nevertheless, fulfilling the child's protective rights would also require careful consideration of the strength of the ties of attachment formed by children with their foster carers. The court should weigh the risks caused by breaking those ties against the benefits to be gained by being brought up by their birth parents, particularly if this maintains their links with their cultural and racial heritage.

Even greater complexities are involved in disputes over whether a child should be adopted by foster carers or prospective adopters. Here the issue is not merely whether the child should remain with the carers to whom he or she may have become firmly attached, despite their lack of kinship ties. It also involves the courts deciding whether an adoption order is the appropriate means of providing the child with security in his or her new home, given that it finally and irrevocably terminates the legal relationship between birth parents and child, irrespective of their blood ties. The law cannot provide detailed guidance on professional practice. Nevertheless, the combination of government policy and Strasbourg jurisprudence has produced, in this context, a worryingly incoherent set of aims and principles.

BIBLIOGRAPHY

NB many of these publications can be obtained on the relevant organisation's website.

Bainham A , 'Can We Protect Children and Protect their Rights?' (2002) Family Law 279.

British Agencies for Adoption and Fostering, *Memorandum of Evidence submitted to the House of Commons Special Select Committee on the Adoption and Children Bill* (April 2001).

British Association of Social Workers, *Memorandum of Evidence submitted to the House of Commons Special Select Committee on the Adoption and Children Bill* (April 2001).

Cooke E, 'Dispensing with parental consent to adoption – a choice of welfare tests' (1997) 9 Child and Family Law Quarterly 259.

Department of Health (DH), White Paper *Adoption: a new approach* Cm 5017 (2000) HMSO.

Department of Health (DH), *Children Adopted from Care in England: 2000/1* DH Statistical Bulletin 2001/25 (2001 a).

Department of Health (DH), *Adoption* LAC (2001) 33 (2001 b).

Department of Health (DH), *National Adoption Standards for England* (2001 c).

Department of Health (DH), *Paving the Way – the 'Catch up' Exercise for the Adoption Register* LAC (2001) 21 (2001 d).

Department of Health (DH), *Social Service Performance Assessment Framework Indicators, 2001– 2002* (2002) Government Statistical Service and DH.

Department of Health (DH) and Welsh Office, *Adoption: The Future* Cm 2288 (1993) HMSO.

Eekelaar J, 'What are Parental Rights?' (1973) 89 Law Quarterly Review 210.

Eekelaar J, 'Access Rights and Children's Welfare' (1988) 51 Modern Law Review 629.

Eekelaar J, 'The Wardship Jurisdiction, Children's Welfare and Parents' Rights' (1991) 107 Law Quarterly Review 386.

Eekelaar J, 'Parenthood, Social Engineering and Rights' in D Morgan and G Douglas (eds) *Constituting Families: A Study in Governance* (1994) Steiner.

Family Policy Studies Centre, *Families and Adoption* Family Briefing Paper 14 (2000) Family Policy Studies Centre.

Fortin J, '*Re D (Care: Natural Parent Presumption)*' (1999) 11 Child and Family Law Quarterly 435.

Goldstein J, Freud A and Solnit A, *Beyond the Best Interests of the Child* (1973) Free Press.

Harris-Short S, 'The Adoption and Children Bill – a fast track to failure?' (2001) 13 Child and Family Law Quarterly 405.

Harris-Short S, '*Re B (Adoption: Natural Parent)* Putting the child at the heart of adoption?' (2002) 14 Child and Family Law Quarterly 325.

Hayes M and Williams C, *Family Law: Principles, Policy and Practice* (1999) Butterworths.

Holman B, *The unknown fostering: a study of private fostering* (2002) Russell House Publishing.

Hunt J and Macleod A, *The Best-Laid Plans: Outcomes of Judicial Decisions in Child Protection Proceedings* (1999) The Stationery Office.

Interdepartmental Working Group, *Review of Adoption Law* A Consultative Document (1992) HMSO.

Laming H, *The Victoria Climbié Inquiry: Report of an Inquiry by Lord Laming* Cm 5730 (2003) The Stationery Office.

Lindley B and Wyld N, 'The Children Act and the draft Adoption Bill – diverging principles' (1996) 8 Child and Family Law Quarterly 327.

Lowe N, 'The changing face of adoption – the gift/donation model versus the contract/services model' (1997) 9 Child and Family Law Quarterly 371.

Lowe N and Douglas G, *Bromley's Family Law* (1998) Butterworths.

Lowe N, Murch M et al, *Supporting Adoption: Reframing the approach* (1999) British Agencies for Adoption and Fostering.

National Organisation for the Counselling of Adoptees and Parents, *Memorandum of Evidence submitted to the House of Commons Special Select Committee on the Adoption and Children Bill* (May 2001).

Performance and Innovation Unit Report, *The Prime Minister's Review of Adoption* (2000) Cabinet Office.

Philpot T, *A very private practice: an investigation into private fostering* (2001) British Agencies for Adoption and Fostering.

Save the Children, *Private fostering: Development of policy and practice in three English local authorities* (1997) Save the Children.

Schaffer H, *Making Decisions about Children* (1998) Blackwell.

Social Services Inspectorate (SSI), *By Private Arrangement: Inspection of Arrangements for Supervising Children in Private Foster Care* (2002) DH Publications.

Utting W, *People Like Us: The Report Of The Review Of The Safeguards For Children Living Away From Home* (1997) DH/Welsh Office, HMSO.

Weyland I, 'The blood tie: raised to the status of a presumption' (1997) 19 Journal of Social Welfare and Family Law 173.

Chapter 15

An abused child's right to state protection

(1) INTRODUCTION

The state assumes that, because parents brought their children into the world, they will care for them and protect them from harm; indeed, it trusts them to do so. The vast majority of parents fulfil these state expectations conscientiously. They not only fulfil their children's right to protection, but bring them up in an atmosphere of love and security. Unfortunately, the children's liberationists' view of childhood as an oppressed state and parents as the chief oppressors, with the freedom to abuse their children in private, is not entirely ill-conceived. Some parents do exploit their privacy and their children's vulnerability to abuse.

The dilemma is that the degree of state surveillance and control necessary to prevent all ill-treatment would involve an unacceptable interference with the upbringing of many thousands of children, the majority of whom are perfectly well cared for by loving parents. This presents the law with the need to find a satisfactory compromise between an unacceptable level of authoritarian state interference and a passive assumption that it is impossible to prevent a tiny minority of children suffering in the privacy of their homes. Indeed, the overriding problem dogging the enforcement of children's rights to protection is to ensure that the majority of parents continue to fulfil their parenting role on behalf of the state, without undermining their willingness or ability to do so by undue intervention.

This chapter considers first the background to this problem and proceeds to discuss the lack of clarity over what children need protecting from. It then assesses how efforts to fulfil children's rights to state protection could be improved by better support from the law.

(2) THE BACKGROUND

The reports of inquiries into child deaths make overwhelmingly depressing reading.[1] The Beckford Report commenting on society's resistance to acknowledging the existence of child abuse stated:

---

1   See Department of Health and Social Security (hereafter DHSS) (1982), which reviewed 18 reports published during the late 1970s. See also Department of Health (hereafter DH) (1991 a) which reviewed 19 reports published during the 1980s. The inquiry into the death of Victoria Climbié, chaired by Lord Laming, joined the lengthening list of inquiries into child deaths.

'Some parents abuse, even kill their children. Throughout history, they always have, and they always will. What is new about child abuse has been the increased and still increasing public awareness of this socially unpalatable, endemic phenomenon. Realisation that the deliberate abuse of children not only occurs but is also by no means a rare occurrence is profoundly shocking both to the individual and to the body politic.'[2]

Whilst the early reports into child deaths had focused on physical abuse, or 'non-accidental injuries', as they are euphemistically referred to, towards the end of the 1980s, the Cleveland crisis confronted the public with the unpleasant notion that child sexual abuse might be even more common.[3] Information of this kind makes it hard for anyone to deny that children have a basic right to protection from ill-treatment and that the state must ensure that they receive it, even if it means removing them from their parents' care. Governments are unlikely to cavil at the terms of international instruments reminding them of their duties in this respect.[4]

Thus far, there is little scope for disagreement. English criminal law certainly acknowledges children's rights to protection from ill-treatment by setting a line below which parents may not descend, without risking criminal charges. The criminal process is, however, somewhat of a blunt instrument, in so far as it can only punish adults for past abuse which should never have happened. Indeed, criminal proceedings may not improve a child victim's life and may even exacerbate the effects of the abuse if the child is called as a witness at the offender's trial.[5] The principles of civil law acknowledge the fact that children need protecting from abuse, if possible before it starts, or at least before it becomes very serious. But the fundamental difficulty is that the type of ill-treatment meted out to abused children occurs behind the closed doors of perfectly normal looking houses.

The law over the last century has reflected an underlying uncertainty experienced by policy makers over finding an appropriate compromise between obliging the state to find and protect every child who is being abused and maintaining family privacy. As Fox Harding has so clearly argued,[6] it is possible to perceive four broad theoretical perspectives underlying the development of child-care policies and all four maintain distinctive positions on the state's duty to protect children from harm. There is the 'laissez-faire' and patriarchal approach, typified by case law in the late nineteenth century, which broadly took the view that power in the family should not be disturbed except in very extreme circumstances and the role of the state should be a minimal one. Writers such as Goldstein, Freud and Solnit[7] later adopted a similar position, maintaining that parents fulfil the nurturing role better than anyone else and need family privacy and autonomy in order to bring their children up without undue interference from the state.

The second and third theoretical perspectives both assume state intervention is desirable, but with differing emphasis placed on the degree of authoritarianism accompanying it. The second perspective considers it justifiable to attribute an essentially paternalistic role to the state, by pointing to the innate vulnerability and dependence of children. The state is thereby obliged to protect them, even if it involves an authoritarian stance which undermines the biological ties between children and

2   London Borough of Brent (1985) p 9.
3   Butler-Sloss LJ (1988).
4   See esp arts 19 and 37(a) of the CRC and art 3 of the ECHR.
5   Discussed in chapter 17.
6   See L Fox Harding (1997) ch 1.
7   See J Goldstein, A Freud and A Solnit (1973) and (1980).

their parents. The third perspective defends the birth family and parents' rights. It legitimises state intervention to protect children, but also sees the dangers of targeting poorer and socially deprived parents who are thereby seen as the victims of heavy-handed state authoritarianism. State intervention should therefore support families and assist them in the difficult task of bringing up children in inadequate home circumstances.

The first three perspectives appear to assume that because the state intervenes on behalf of the child there is no special need to emphasise the child's individual position. Thus when finding a balance between over-authoritarianism and laissez-faire, the contest is between parents and state. It is assumed that once an appropriate balance is found, the state will automatically adopt the protective role for children. The last and fourth approach, that maintained by the children's liberationists, differs fundamentally from the others, in so far as it alone concentrates on the child's own position, seeing the contest as one between children and parents. They consider that children should be treated as independent persons in their own right with a right to adult freedoms, in order to release them from parental domination. The negative aspects of family life are used to substantiate their claim that children should be freed from adult oppression. These are exemplified by parents' ability to exploit their position of power within the family and abuse their children. This last perspective, which focuses almost exclusively on the liberationists' claims regarding children's autonomy, seems to assume that once emancipated, children will be able to achieve their own physical protection. This emphasis during the 1980s led to the establishment of agencies which set out to 'empower' abused children to help themselves. Childline and the Children's Legal Centre were established and encouraged children to seek help on their own behalf, rather than waiting for the state to assist with their protection.

Of the four approaches, the last is perhaps the weakest. As Fox Harding points out, it is certainly unrealistic to assume that such an approach is sufficient in itself. Very young children who, by reason of their size are particularly vulnerable to abuse, are quite unable either to cope with adult freedoms or to protect themselves physically against adult abuse.[8] Older children might be expected to make choices in abusive situations and often do so, but these may be strongly influenced by their past experiences. As in so many other fields of law involving the older child, the difficulty is to find an appropriate balance between the exercise of paternalism to fulfil the child's right to protection and respecting his or her capacity for choice. Arguing that abused children's choices should be respected by the state[9] overlooks the distorted relationships that abused children often have with their abusers. In this context, the need to recognise a child's interest in choice has less obvious relevance than his or her need for protection, bearing in mind that abused children's choices may be strongly influenced by their psychological dependence on parent abusers.[10]

These very different approaches are all discernible in the violent swings in child-care policy during the last century and they are all reflected, to a lesser or greater extent, by provisions of the Children Act 1989 itself. Indeed, the Act adopts an uneasy compromise between emphasising parents' rights to autonomy and privacy and fulfilling children's rights to protection. It clearly reflects the 'moral panics' arising from the child abuse inquiries of the 1970s and 1980s which led to demands for the government to 'do something about child abuse'. There is a clear commitment

8   See L Fox Harding (1997) p 136.
9   Eg, see the views of F Olsen (1992) pp 210–213.
10   Discussed in chapter 9 and below.

to ensuring that local authorities have sufficient powers to intervene to protect children when essential. By providing relatively broad grounds for intervention through the 'significant harm' formula,[11] by strengthening the emergency powers to seek and find a child whose safety is believed to be at risk[12] and by creating the child assessment order,[13] local authorities gained relatively straightforward methods for protecting children against abusive and unco-operative parents. The legislation also flirts briefly, although not particularly convincingly with the concept of respecting children's decision-making rights.[14]

The Children Act 1989 gives state agencies wide powers to protect children effectively. Nevertheless, one of its important objectives was to respond to the public fears generated by the Cleveland crisis, during which very large numbers of children were taken into state care on a suspicion of being victims of child sexual abuse.[15] This crisis led, in the late 1980s, to a widely held perception that laws and policies then existed allowing social workers to adopt an over-authoritarian approach to families and a marked lack of respect for parents' own rights. Consequently, the 1989 Act takes care to ensure that parents' own family rights are promoted, with clear boundaries demarcated between the family and the state. It stresses that although the state has an important part to play, it is to be residual and supportive – the primary responsibility for bringing up children remains with their parents. Since parents are those best fitted to care for their children, in the event of their children being considered to be 'in need',[16] the legislation empowers local authorities to provide parents with considerable state support if they desire it, to assist them keep the family together.[17] But local authority services can only be provided for the family on a voluntary basis in partnership with parents.[18] In the event of disagreement between parents and local authority over whether the parents are providing appropriate care for the child, state intervention against the parents' wishes is possible, but only with court authority, and then only by establishing clear statutory grounds for intervention.[19] The 'significant harm' criterion for intervention is intended to flag up the fact that children can only be removed from their parents as a measure of last resort, in order to protect children in severe risk and potentially dangerous situations.[20] Parents retain their parental responsibilities, even in the event of their child being removed from them on the authority of a care order.[21]

One of the aims of the Children Act 1989 was to reassure the public that the traditional privacy and autonomy of parents should not be undermined by over-zealous state intervention. This was very much in tune with the intentions of article 8

11   See, in particular, Children Act 1989, s 31(2) and (9). Discussed below.
12   Children Act 1989, s 48(3).
13   Children Act 1989, s 43.
14   Eg Children Act 1989, ss 38(6), 43(8), 44(7) and Sch 3, paras 4(4) and 5(5). Discussed below.
15   Butler-Sloss LJ (1988).
16   Children Act 1989, s 17(10). Discussed below.
17   The range of family support services envisaged for families containing children in need is very wide.
18   See Children Act 1989, s 20(7): accommodation cannot be provided against the wishes of anyone with parental responsibility. Eg *R v Tameside Metropolitan Borough Council, ex p J* [2000] 1 FLR 942. See also s 20(8) entitling anyone with parental responsibility to remove the child at any time. Children over 16 are exempt from this parental veto: see s 20(11).
19   Local authorities are prohibited from using the wardship jurisdiction as a way of obtaining judicial authority for removing children from their parents. See Children Act 1989, s 100.
20   Children Act 1989, s 31.
21   Children Act 1989, s 33(3)(b).

of the ECHR, which reflects the post-War objectives of the Convention's draftsmen, namely to protect private individuals, including parents, from authoritarian regimes. Its phrasing suggests that, as long as families are adequately protected from undue state interference, the regulation of family life can be entrusted to its adult members.[22] The 1989 Act responded to early decisions reached by the European Commission and Court in favour of parents claiming that their rights to family privacy under article 8 of the ECHR had been infringed by state intervention to protect their children.[23] But whilst such an approach certainly strengthens family autonomy and also prevents children being taken away from their parents unnecessarily, it does not so obviously promote an abused child's *own* rights to a happy upbringing free from parental abuse.[24] Whilst later Strasbourg case law demonstrates that the ECHR can be used extremely effectively to protect abused children,[25] like the Children Act itself, these decisions reflect the tensions in this field of practice. Indeed, when considering parental complaints over state intervention to protect their children, the European Court of Human Rights has repeatedly emphasised the need to maintain an appropriate balance between infringing the parents' rights and protecting those of their child.[26]

The Children Act 1989 makes valiant efforts to maintain this balance, but there is now an accumulating body of government-commissioned research[27] which makes one doubt whether an appropriate equilibrium between children's interests and those of their parents can ever be found. Overall, it suggests that matters have not changed greatly since the early 1980s when Dingwall et al described the child protection system as one reflecting 'a liberal compromise'. Now, as then, 'The result is a system which is fully effective neither in preventing mistreatment nor in respecting family privacy but lurches unevenly between these two poles'.[28] This is probably inevitable since no system will ever achieve perfection. But, more worryingly, for many children the protective process may do more harm than good.

(3)   THE CHILD PROTECTION PROCESS – WHAT CRITERIA SHOULD BE USED?

Whilst there is little doubt that children must be protected from serious physical abuse which threatens their lives, a growing body of research evidence has clarified the long-term effects of a variety of other types of ill-treatment, such as emotional abuse and neglect.[29] Studies have produced a particularly bleak picture regarding the

---

22   See J Fortin (1999) pp 357–359.
23   Eg *W (and R, O, B and H) v United Kingdom* (1987) 10 EHRR 29. The success of these parents' applications led to the abolition of the power of local authorities to acquire parental responsibility over children by administrative resolution. They also provoked the Children Act 1989, s 34 giving parents a right to apply for contact with their children whilst in state care.
24   J Fortin (1999) pp 357–359.
25   Eg, inter alia: *Johansen v Norway* (1996) 23 EHRR 33; *K and T v Finland* [2001] 2 FLR 707; *Z v United Kingdom* [2001] 2 FLR 612. See discussion in chapter 2, pp 57–58.
26   See, inter alia: *Olsson v Sweden (No 2)* (1992) 17 EHRR 134; *Johansen v Norway* (1996) 23 EHRR 33; *Scott v United Kingdom* [2000] 1 FLR 958.
27   See, inter alia, the research summarised in DH (1995) and DH (2001 a).
28   R Dingwall, J Eekelaar and T Murray (1983) p 219.
29   See, inter alia: M Lynch and J Roberts (1982); D Cicchetti and V Carlson (1989); D Wolfe (1987); C Hobbs, H Hanks and J Wynne (1999).

effects of child sexual abuse, with victims demonstrating a relatively high level of psychological and behavioural problems lasting well into adulthood.[30] Research also shows the damaging effects on children of living in households where domestic violence is commonplace,[31] and with parents who suffer from mental illness or who abuse drugs or alcohol.[32] Overall, there is general agreement that:

> 'The sustained abuse or neglect of children physically, emotionally or sexually can have major long-term effects on all aspects of a child's health, development and well-being. Sustained abuse is likely to have a deep impact on the child's self-image and self-esteem, and his or her future life.'[33]

An appreciation of the damaging outcomes of abuse in general may itself encourage practitioners to intervene whenever confronted with abusive behaviour, on the basis that, unless it is stopped, these outcomes will inevitably ensue. At one point, research indicated that child protection practitioners were demanding higher standards from parents, '... the threshold beyond which child abuse is considered to occur is gradually being lowered. This is happening for a variety of reasons, including an emphasis on the rights of children as individuals ...'[34]

Just over seven years later, however, matters had apparently changed radically. In Lord Laming's view, the suffering and death of Victoria Climbié was not only 'a gross failure of the system and was inexcusable' but 'the agencies with responsibility for Victoria gave a low priority to the task of protecting children'.[35] Similarly, the Chief Inspectors of eight public agencies involved in child protection work stated:

> 'The level at which social services operated its thresholds for responding to child welfare concerns was a major concern in almost all the areas. The view was strongly held that social services were only responding to the highest level of child welfare concerns where evidence of abuse or neglect was very apparent. Lower level concerns that other agencies felt warranted follow-up were too often not accepted for a response or a service by social services.'[36]

Both reports noted the fact that many social services departments were experiencing serious staffing difficulties,[37] and were under intense pressure, due to the high number of child protection referrals being received.[38] In other words, this apparent U-turn, in terms of social work perceptions, may simply reflect the grim reality that child protection work is gravely under-resourced. Nonetheless, it is obviously important for social workers to be reasonably clear what, in an ideal world, children should be protected *from*. Clarity is particularly desirable, given that families subjected to child protection investigations find the process extremely distressing and that it also alienates them against further contact with local authorities.[39] To the lawyer, the answer to the question 'which children need the attentions of a child protection service?'[40] seems reasonably straightforward. It is those children who are suffering or

---

30   See, inter alia: D Jones and P Ramchandani (1999); C Woodward and D Fortune (1999).
31   See C McGee (2000) ch 2. See also the international research literature summarised by M Hester et al (2000) ch 2.
32   H Cleaver et al (1999) esp part 4.
33   DH, Home Office and Department for Education and Employment (hereafter DH et al) (1999) para 2.8.
34   DH (1995) p 15.
35   H Laming (2003) para 1.18.
36   DH (2002 a) para 6.10.
37   DH (2002 a) para 6.8 and H Laming (2003) esp paras 5.188–5.193.
38   DH (2002 a) para 6.15 and H Laming (2003) at para 17.102.
39   See J Thoburn, A Lewis and D Shemmings (1995) pp 53–64.
40   See a similar question posed by C Wattam (1997) pp 110–111.

at risk of suffering significant harm; this is the formula used for establishing the threshold criteria for making a care or supervision order.[41] But there are also the demands of articles 2 and 3 of the ECHR. Consequently, the social worker who stands back and fails to prevent a child from suffering from significant harm which amounts to ill-treatment and neglect so serious that it results in the child's death[42] or amounts to 'torture, or inhuman or degrading treatment', is not only ignoring his powers under the Children Act 1989,[43] but also risks infringing the child's rights under articles 2 or 3 of the Convention.[44] Thus the legal framework provides the social worker with a metaphorical bottom line below which parental behaviour should not sink without child protection intervention being contemplated.

Few would argue over children requiring protection from significant harm sufficiently serious to fall within the ambit of article 3 of the ECHR.[45] It is the less obviously abusive behaviour that causes disagreement. Indeed, even with the assistance of legal definitions,[46] lawyers, in common with social workers, are often very ambivalent over what amounts to 'normal' and 'abnormal' parental behaviour. The fact that we have no official agreement over what constitutes child abuse in our time and our culture[47] was reflected in the dramatically different reactions of three sets of judiciary to information from a father that a mother and her new partner walked around nude at home in front of her two children, aged 9 and 6, and may even have bathed with the children.[48] Whilst one of the judges who had dealt with the case clearly considered this information reasonably innocuous, another not only found it alarming but considered that it raised child protection issues warranting investigation by the local department of social services. Butler-Sloss LJ considered the latter reaction to be extreme but pointed out:

'A balance has to be struck between the behaviour within families which is seen by them as natural and with which that family is comfortable and the sincerely held views of others who are shocked by it. Nudity is an obvious example ... Communal family bathing is another example. This is often entirely innocent. In other families abuse may lie behind it.'[49]

41 See the 'significant harm' formula used in the Children Act 1989, ss 31(2) and 47.
42 In *Osman v United Kingdom* [1999] 1 FLR 193, the European Court of Human Rights ruled (at [116]) that a child's rights under art 2 will be infringed if the authority fail to do all that could be reasonably expected of them to avoid a real and immediate risk to life of which they have or ought to have knowledge.
43 Ie to apply for a care order under Children Act 1989, s 31.
44 In *Z v United Kingdom* [2001] 2 FLR 612, the European Court of Human Rights (at [70]–[73]) held that state agencies must take reasonable steps to prevent children being subjected to ill-treatment amounting to torture or inhuman or degrading treatment in situations where they had or ought to have had knowledge of that ill-treatment. See also *TP and KM v United Kingdom* [2001] 2 FLR 549.
45 See *A v United Kingdom (human rights: punishment of child)* [1998] 2 FLR 959. The European Court of Human Rights (at [20]) stressed that ill-treatment must attain a minimum level of severity before falling within art 3. The assessment of this minimum is relative and depends on all the circumstances of the case, including the nature and context of the treatment, its duration, its physical and mental effects, and in some circumstances, the sex, age and state of health of the victim.
46 See Children Act 1989, s 31(9), which provides the following definitions which clarify the term 'significant harm': '"harm" means ill-treatment or the impairment of health or development including, for example, impairment suffered from seeing or hearing the ill-treatment of another; "development" means physical, intellectual, emotional, social or behavioural development; "health" means physical or mental health; and "ill-treatment" includes sexual abuse and forms of ill-treatment which are not physical.'
47 C Wattam (1997) p 110.
48 *Re W (residence order)* [1999] 1 FLR 869.
49 [1999] 1 FLR 869 at 873.

Agreement over what is abusive and what is not may always be elusive.[50] Nevertheless, the Department of Health has, over recent years, striven to clarify the type of situation meriting child protection intervention. A major official reappraisal of the assumptions underlying such intervention was provoked, in the mid-1990s, by several publications all reaching a remarkably similar conclusion. This was that social workers were mounting child protection investigations in situations not meriting such a heavy-handed response, whilst also failing to detect the children whose treatment did justify intervention.[51] A summary of research commissioned by the Department of Health at the time the Children Act 1989 was first implemented (*Messages from Research*),[52] indicated that very large numbers of children were being sucked into the child protection process, with little ultimate benefit accruing to the vast majority of them.[53] Many involved in inquiries were then filtered out of the system on the basis that there was no cause for serious concern.[54] This approach led to the system becoming overloaded, with a less thorough investigation of the small proportion of truly dangerous cases.[55] Even the children identified and retained in the child protection net, by being registered on the child protection register, did not necessarily get the services they needed.[56] The focus remained on their physical safety rather than on their developmental needs. Consequently, the outcome for children removed into state care was not always any better than if they were left at home.[57]

The current guidance, *Working Together*,[58] not only goes to some length to define such terms as 'physical abuse', 'emotional abuse', 'sexual abuse' and 'neglect', together with their impact on children,[59] but also endeavours to introduce greater clarity over when intervention is essential. It emphasises that practitioners should concentrate on the outcomes for the child of the parents' current behaviour, when it builds up to provide a persistent pattern. Echoing *Messages from Research*,[60] which stresses that it is *long-term* low warmth and high criticism which is particularly damaging, official guidance emphasises that all abuse must be seen in the context of the family[61] and that although single abusive events can be dangerous, 'it is the corrosiveness of *long-term* emotional, physical or sexual abuse that causes impairment to the extent of constituting significant harm'.[62] It is this pattern of behaviour which should alert practitioners to consider some action on behalf of the child.

This guidance also reflects research findings that social workers had developed an over-narrow concentration on short-term measures, such as identifying children at risk of serious physical abuse, rather than ensuring that children's long-term

50   Eg see the considerable variation in the numbers of children being placed on child protection registers: Social Services Inspectorate (hereafter SSI) (1999) Table 11.

51   Audit Commission (1994); W Rose (1994); DH (1995).

52   DH (1995).

53   In some circumstances, their outcomes were exacerbated by involvement in the child protection system. See E Farmer (1999) pp 160–161.

54   See J Gibbons, S Conroy and C Bell (1995) reporting (p 55) that 67% of the cases investigated were filtered out of the system without a case conference. See also later research by M Brandon et al (1999) reaching similar conclusions.

55   J Gibbons, S Conroy and C Bell (1995) pp 84–85.

56   See C Hallett (1995) pp 338–339.

57   DH (1995) esp p 50. See also E Farmer (1999) p 160.

58   DH et al (1999).

59   DH et al (1999) paras 2.3–2.7 and 2.11–2.15.

60   DH (1995) p 54.

61   DH et al (1999) paras 2.8–2.18. See also DH, Home Office, Department of Education and Employment (hereafter DH et al) (2000) esp paras 2.9–2.25.

62   DH et al (1999) para 2.17.

developmental problems were addressed.[63] The format of the legislation may have contributed to this problem. The 'significant harm' formula may itself encourage a superficial and legalistic approach to child protection work. Its adoption in the Children Act 1989, section 47, the linchpin of the child protection process, forces practitioners to focus on the severity of particular incidents and the child's immediate safety. Inquiries must be made regarding any child that local authorities reasonably suspect to be suffering 'significant harm' or at risk of such harm in the future.[64] The current *Working Together*, when providing official guidance on the investigation process, attempts to broaden the focus of a child protection investigation or 's 47 enquiry'. It stresses the need to consider the child's situation in the context of a number of interrelating family factors.[65] This can only be done by assessing the child's circumstances as thoroughly as possible, prior to arranging a child protection conference.[66] It emphasises that it is the likelihood of continuing risk which is important, rather than a backwards look at what triggered the initial investigation. Consequently, child protection conferences should concentrate on securing good outcomes for children in the future through effective child protection plans, rather than merely deciding whether to place their names on the child protection register.[67] The government was also alarmed at the steady rise in number of children being re-registered on child protection registers, implying that registration itself had not secured an effective and lasting child protection plan. The fact that social services departments are now meeting the official target[68] to reduce these re-registrations[69] may suggest that they are indeed securing the children's safety, or merely that they are not registering them in the first place.[70]

The Children Act 1989, section 47 only requires a local authority to 'make, or cause to be made, such enquiries as they consider necessary to enable them to decide whether they should take any action to safeguard or promote the child's welfare'. Thus, according to the law, the threshold for intervention through investigation, is relatively low.[71] Nevertheless, as noted above, due to staff shortages and the deployment of inexperienced and poorly supervised members of staff,[72] social services are often reluctant to undertake section 47 inquiries, and in cases where they do,

63   DH (1995) pp 47–48.
64   Children Act 1989, s 47(1) directs that a local authority where: '(a) informed that a child who lives, or is found, in their area—(i) is the subject of an emergency protection order; or (ii) is in police protection; or (iii) has contravened a ban imposed by a curfew notice within the meaning of Chapter 1 of Part I of the Crime and Disorder Act 1998; or (b) have reasonable cause to suspect that a child who lives, or is found in their area is suffering, or is likely to suffer, significant harm, the local authority shall make, or cause to be made, such enquiries as they consider necessary to enable them to decide whether they should take any action to safeguard or promote the child's welfare.'
65   DH et al (1999) para 2.18.
66   DH et al (1999) ch 5.
67   DH et al (1999) paras 5.67–5.69.
68   Ie Social Services Performance Assessment Framework (PAF) Indicator A3 – target set to reduce the number of children re-registered on the child protection register by 10% between 1997 and 2002.
69   See DH (2002 b) para 2.5, noting the fourth year running that re-registrations had fallen.
70   DH (2002 b) para 2.2 recording the dramatic reduction in the number of children being registered on the child protection register. See discussion below.
71   See *Re S (sexual abuse allegations: local authority response)* [2001] EWHC Admin 334 [2001] 2 FLR 776: per Scott Baker J (at [36]) a local authority does not have to be satisfied on the balance of probabilities that a person is an abuser before intervention under s 47 is justified.
72   DH (2002 a) para 6.8. Lord Laming also strongly criticised the relevant social services departments for not ensuring that social workers involved in child protection work were adequately trained and supervised. See H Laming (2003) esp chs 5 and 6.

reluctant to convene child protection conferences'.[73] Furthermore, child protection referrals are often only being responded to if they involve what appear to be 'the highest levels of child welfare concerns',[74] resulting in some external agencies no longer reporting concerns due to lack of confidence that social workers would respond positively.[75] This suggests that the dramatic reduction in the number of children being registered on the child protection register[76] may not be attributable to social workers following the advice of *Working Together* and assessing more carefully the likelihood of future harm, but to the fact that they are too inexperienced and hard-pressed to respond adequately.[77]

According to *Working Together*, the agencies involved in child protection work should co-operate sufficiently to enable them to identify and support those children requiring protection. Sadly, as the report into Victoria Climbié's death makes clear, this still does not always happen.[78] For those children who are identified as being at risk, social services departments have all the legal powers they need to intervene and protect them. Even then, however, perhaps because of their concentration on dangerous incidents of physical abuse, social workers often appear indecisive in their later handling of cases involving long-term chronic parental neglect and inadequate parenting.[79] For example, when considering a case involving five seriously neglected children who had been receiving social work attention spanning over 20 years, Bracewell J commented:

> 'In my experience in cases of neglect, abuse and failure to thrive it is quite common to find that children have been left to deteriorate in inadequate homes year upon year with no effective action. Intervention which may be described as sticking plaster does not address the fundamental issues and social workers often appear unwilling to make crucial decisions in favour of intervention and they tolerate wholly inappropriate parenting, even when faced with serious evidence of concern and lack of parental co-operation with professionals, so that the children drift, become more damaged and vulnerable.'[80]

As the joint Chief Inspectors' Report makes plain,[81] Bracewell J is not alone in maintaining such views. Reports of official inspections continue to provide clear evidence that some social services departments are failing to protect children known to be at risk.[82] They note the delays over social services departments intervening decisively to safeguard children in some very dysfunctional families where there are longstanding and well-documented concerns about the adequacy of parenting over an extended

---

73   DH (2002 a) para 6.18 and H Laming (2003) para 17.110.
74   DH (2002 a) para 6.10.
75   DH (2002 a) para 6.9 and H Laming (2003) para 17.102.
76   See DH (2002 b) para 2.3.
77   DH (2002 a) para 6.8.
78   Lord Laming, who was extremely critical of the failure of the various agencies to respond jointly to clear evidence that Victoria needed protection, recommended that *Working Together* should be rewritten and clarified. See H Laming (2003) esp para 17.111. See also DH (2002 a) ch 5 for strong criticism of 'working together' arrangments.
79   Eg in *Z v United Kingdom* [2001] 2 FLR 612, despite the local authority receiving numerous reports from other agencies that five children were being subjected to appalling abuse and neglect over a period of five years, it failed to intervene to protect them.
80   See *Re E (care proceedings: social work practice)* [2000] 2 FLR 254 at 256, per Bracewell J.
81   DH (2002 a), ch 6.
82   See, inter alia: SSI (2001 a) noting (para 3.10) that although the majority of children who were the subject of child protection inquiries were well safeguarded, in 6% of cases this was not the case and in a further 26% there were aspects of children's protection which had not been fully considered; SSI (2002), noting (para 2.57) that the welfare of children was adequately protected in only 21 out of 32 councils and that staff recruitment was 'insufficiently robust to ensure adequate safeguards'; DH (2002 a) ch 6, noting a catalogue of concerns.

period of time. [83] These reports and the continuing deaths of abused children, [84] reflect ongoing failures in the child protection system, despite the assistance of the revised *Working Together* and the *Quality Protects* programme. The latter was designed to improve the management and delivery of children's services, [85] strengthened by the need to meet a long list of carefully defined objectives. [86]

One way of ensuring more decisive child protection work would be to strengthen the wording of section 47, to ensure that the state's obligations to fulfil children's rights under the Human Rights Act 1998 are fully complied with. The provision might, for example, state that having investigated a referral, 'a local authority *shall* take such steps as are reasonably practical to secure the child's safety unless they are satisfied that such action is not necessary to safeguard or promote the child's welfare'. [87] Similarly, *Working Together* should contain a stronger emphasis on local authorities intervening to secure the child's safety through some further positive action, such as taking care proceedings. [88] The introduction of such provisions might be an appropriate response to the risk of local authorities being sued by children in damages for failing to intervene to protect them from abuse soon enough, thereby infringing their Convention rights under article 3 of the ECHR. [89] Such a provision might, on the other hand, promote a more 'trigger happy' approach on the part of local authorities, which might then undermine the aims of article 8 of the Convention. Indeed, the demands of the Convention jurisprudence will doubtless reinforce social workers' perception that in child protection work, they 'are damned if they do and damned if they don't'. As noted above, article 3 requires vigilance and a preparedness to intervene to prevent serious abuse continuing, but article 8 requires a cautious approach to interfering with family life, combined with procedural fairness. [90] Consequently, any decisive intervention, such as an application for an emergency protection order, [91] should only be contemplated if it is a proportionate response to the danger that the child is considered to be in and the procedure used must also be as fair as possible, in the circumstances. [92]

83   SSI (2001 a) para 3.9.
84   Eg suspicions about the ill-treatment of Victoria Climbié, who died in 2000, and of Lauren Wright, who died in 2001, had been referred to the relevant authorities well before the two children died from the abusive behaviour of their carers.
85   DH (1998 a).
86   DH (1998 a) Annex 1. See the *Quality Protects* objectives for children's social services, together with a range of measurable performance indicators and targets. See esp objective 2.0, 'To ensure that children are protected from emotional, physical and sexual abuse and neglect (significant harm)'.
87   Emphasis supplied. This is similar to the formula contained in Children Act 1989, s 47(4).
88   See R White (2000). See also M Hayes (1998) p 128, for a similar suggestion.
89   In *Z v United Kingdom* [2001] 2 FLR 612 and *TP and KM v United Kingdom* [2001] 2 FLR 549, the European Court of Human Rights awarded relatively high sums in damages against the local authority responsible for infringing the children's rights. The domestic courts may feel obliged to do the same under the Human Rights Act 1998, s 8.
90   Ie the procedures used to interfere in parents' family life must be fair to all parties affected. Eg *W (and R, O, B and H) v United Kingdom* (1987) 10 EHRR 29; *McMichael v United Kingdom* (1995) 20 EHRR 205; *P, C and S v United Kingdom* [2002] 2 FLR 631.
91   Under Children Act 1989, s 44.
92   An ex parte application for an emergency protection order, as opposed to an inter partes application on notice to the parents, could not be justified as being 'necessary' under art 8(2) of the ECHR, unless it was feared that the child was in extreme danger. Using an emergency protection order to remove a new-born baby from its mother could only be justified by 'the most extraordinarily compelling reasons': *K and T v Finland* [2001] 2 FLR 707 at [168], per Grand Chamber of the European Court of Human Rights. But see *P, C and S v United Kingdom* [2002] 2 FLR 631 at paras 150–153 per the European Court of Human Rights, the special circumsntances of the case justified the decision to obtain an ex parte emergency protection order to prevent the mother removing the baby from hospital but did not justify removing the baby from her mother shortly after birth.

One wonders whether any official guidance, however well crafted, will help social workers find the right balance in their child protection work. Research suggests that it is difficult to persuade social workers to concentrate less on short-term issues, such as identifying and safeguarding children at risk, and more on considering their long-term developmental needs. [93] This is surely inevitable, given a lack of staff resources, [94] together with the mixed messages from official sources and the public over what their principal concerns should be. Social workers will inevitably focus on children in danger from abusive incidents since they are only too aware of the tragedies involving children who die from parental abuse. These emphasise the risks involved in allowing children to remain with truly dangerous parents. As researchers point out: 'It is not surprising that the question which causes much anxiety to social workers in child protection work is: "Does this family contain the potential for inflicting death or life-limiting injury to the child, and how will I know?".' [95] The distress of the social workers involved in such cases is compounded by the media's criticism. [96] Furthermore, as critics point out, neither the government commissioned research projects [97] nor the current guidance takes full account of the impact of the public inquiries into child deaths on the child protection system. [98] They have played a crucial part in producing a more legalistic and proceduralised way of operating, [99] with an emphasis on keeping children alive in the short term. [100] Although *Working Together* stresses that processes and procedures are never ends in themselves, but only a means of bringing about better outcomes for children, [101] English social workers see their own child protection system as 'heavily proceduralised', compared with those in other European countries. They voice a general concern over the emphasis placed, in this country, on following the right procedures and the anxiety it produces in their practice. [102] The present procedures certainly have not prevented a widespread confusion existing in the minds of social workers as to the scope of their powers regarding child protection work; indeed, it may have contributed to it. [103]

Meanwhile, as Littlechild comments, there has been no real attempt to assist social workers over deciding when to stop supporting families in order to move into a controlling situation. According to him, if we are to take seriously children's rights to be free from abuse, this 'inevitably means encroaching on the idea of an "Englishman's home is his castle"'. [104] Nevertheless, it may be genuinely impossible to answer questions such as 'What are the circumstances in which removal [of a child from home] should be voluntary or compulsory?'. [105] This, in the end, is a matter of professional judgment, which will only emerge with good staff management, accountability and training. [106]

93   DH (2001 a) pp 44–47.
94   See DH (2002 b) para 6.8.
95   M Brandon et al (1999) p 63.
96   English social workers involved in a comparative research project saw themselves as more open to media attention and criticism than their European colleagues. See R Hetherington et al (1997) pp 94–95.
97   DH (1995) and DH (2001 a).
98   See, inter alia: N Parton (1997) pp 16–17, B Littlechild (1998).
99   N Parton (1997) p 13.
100 E Farmer (1997) p 161.
101 DH et al (1999) Preface.
102 See R Hetherington et al (1997) p 94.
103 See H Laming (2003) at para 17.100ff. He considered that this confusion should be remedied by the official guidance being rewritten.
104 B Littlechild (1998) p 126.
105 DH (2001 a) p 42.
106 H Laming (2003) esp Pt 5.

(4)   PREVENTION AND AVOIDANCE OF PROTECTIVE LITIGATION

Despite all the exhortations of the government in the guidance accompanying the Children Act 1989, [107] one of the main objectives of Part III of the Children Act 1989 still remains inadequately complied with. This is that social services will, through their support work with families, help prevent parents losing their children into state care. [108] Each local authority has a general duty to safeguard and promote the welfare of children within its area who are in need [109] and, so far as is consistent with that duty, to promote their upbringing by their own families. [110] It should also avoid the need to remove the child into care through public law proceedings. [111] But official assessments of social work practice in the years following implementation of the Act indicated that social services departments were prioritising their work with children at risk of suffering abuse, at the expense of providing long-term family support to families with children in need. Once cases were labelled 'child protection' cases, the need to investigate overcame notions of prevention and family support. [112]

Practitioners are now exhorted not to think only in terms of child protection *or* family support, without also attempting to assess the child's overall welfare and the need to work in partnership with his or her family. [113] Successive research projects, however, show social workers resisting these official efforts to adjust the balance between their child protection work and family support work:

'In spite of long-standing cumulative research that associates children's physical environment with severe health and social problems, [114] there remained a remarkable unwillingness to equate need with anything other than identification of serious child maltreatment.' [115]

Children are still being registered on the child protection register, as a means of ensuring that they receive the section 17 resources not made available to families merely 'in need'. [116] Meanwhile, the present distinctions being made by social workers between child protection referrals under the Children Act 1989, section 47 and cases categorised as section 17 cases are producing unacceptably poor working practices. [117]

---

107   Eg DH (1991 b).
108   See DHSS et al (1987) esp ch 2.
109   Children Act 1989, s 17(10): 'For the purposes of this Part [of the Act] a child shall be taken to be in need if—(a) he is unlikely to achieve or maintain, or to have the opportunity of achieving or maintaining, a reasonable standard of health or development without the provision for him of services by a local authority under this Part; (b) his health or development is likely to be significantly impaired, or further impaired without the provision for him of such services; or (c) he is disabled . . .'
110   A wide range of family support services is envisaged for families containing children in need, including, inter alia: day care (s 18); accommodation if the child's parents are prevented from providing it (s 20); occupational, social, cultural or recreational activities; home help; holiday provision; day centre facilities etc. See Children Act 1989, Sch 2.
111   Children Act 1989, Sch 2, para 7.
112   See, inter alia: DH (1995) pp 54–55; W Rose (1996) p 6; Audit Commission (1994) p 58.
113   See DH et al (1999) paras 1.9 and 5.15–5.17 and DH et al (2000) paras 1.11–1.38 and 3.15–3.16.
114   Footnoted references omitted.
115   DH (2001 a) p 45. But see DH (2001 b) which claims (para 3.21) that child protection work no longer dominates social services departments' work and that policies to refocus away from concentrating on risk towards assessing and responding to need are working.
116   See M Brandon et al (1999) esp p 96, whose findings match those reached earlier by E Farmer and M Owen (1995) p 87.
117   See H Laming (2003) paras 17.000–17.111.

Clearly the law can do little to influence the changes needed in the professional responses to child protection referrals, particularly at a time when child protection work continues to carry a much higher profile than organising services to families containing children in need. In any case, neither system will work effectively if undermined by a shortage of resources. Despite some very good practice, in terms of family support, [118] if the jam is too thinly spread to start with, attempts to re-spread it will not solve the problem. With regional variations, there are considerable shortages of social workers, [119] day care, homemakers, family aides, substitute carers, treatment resources for sexually abused children [120] and mental health support for those with behavioural problems. [121] It seems unrealistic for the government to assume that a reallocation of resources from child protection to child support will cure the general lack of funds available to departments of social services for children's services. [122] Recent spending plans aiming to put more investment into Children's Social Services, including Children and Adolescent Mental Health services, were welcome and overdue. [123] Furthermore, although the Children Act 1989 and subsequent guidance envisages a multi-agency response to the provision of children's services, [124] research continues to show a lack of good co-operation between all local agencies. [125] Indeed, there still appears to be little recognition that a child's health, education and social problems are often all connected and should not be considered or dealt with in isolation. [126] Efforts to ensure the provision of jointly co-ordinated services for children in need still have a long way to go. [127]

Arguably, the growing proliferation of government-commissioned research, analysis [128] and guidance will achieve little if it fails to take full account of the way in which child abuse springs from its socio-economic context, of poverty and social

118   SSI (1999) ch 4. See also J Tunstill and J Aldgate (2000), who note (ch 8) a high level of satisfaction amongst the families provided with services.
119   See DH (2001 b) paras 3.39 and 11.29. The best functioning London services reported 20% vacancy levels of social workers, with some with rates of 40%, or more. See also DH (2002 a) para 6.8.
120   See E Farmer and S Pollock (1998).
121   DH (2001 b) para 3.50.
122   See the great regional variation in spending on children in need, noted in SSI (1999) Table 12. This variation may be due to local authorities' failure to allocate sufficient government funds to their children and families services. See Lord Laming's criticism of Ealing, Brent and Haringey for starving these services of available funds, with consequent staff shortages, poor supervision and low morale. See H Laming (2003) para 1.51.
123   HM Treasury (2002) para 28.8.
124   Under Children Act 1989, s 27, departments of social services may request other agencies to help in the exercise of their functions under Pt III. See also DH et al (2000) ch 5.
125   Despite being urged on by the introduction of Children's Services Planning in 1996, which aims to ensure that the relevant agencies plan a co-ordinated system of children's services and support each other in their delivery. See DH and Department for Education and Employment (1996).
126   J Tunstill and J Aldgate (2000) ch 9, esp p 151.
127   SSI (1999) ch 4, which refers to the poor joint working arrangements between agencies, such as social services departments and health trusts. See also DH (2001 a) ch 6. In July 2002, the Health Minister, Jacqui Smith, announced plans to pilot new organisational models for the delivery of children's services. Eg, children's trusts will bring together health, social care and education services, with a view to achieving joint planning, commissioning and financing of children's services. See also HM Treasury (2002) para 28.5.
128   20 research studies are summarised in DH (1995), 13 in DH (1998 b), and a further 24 in DH (2001 a).

deprivation. [129] As Parton observes, despite re-labelling procedures and modifying operational perspectives, 'We may be in danger of expecting social workers and social services departments to resolve problems that are well beyond their remit and responsibility'. [130]

(5)   REMOVING THE ABUSER AND NOT THE CHILD

The state should fulfil a child's right to protection by the best means available. In many cases abused children love their parents and will not want to leave home; often they do not want the abuser to leave either, they simply want the abuse to stop. Indeed, they may even withdraw allegations of abuse if they fear that either result will be the outcome. This is a particular risk in the case of victims of child sexual abuse, whose psychological suffering is often exacerbated by removal. Farmer and Owen observed:

'For these young people the experience of abuse and of being rejected by their families became closely interwoven. Some felt that placement away from home was a punishment for telling about the abuse, and others that they had not been believed or had been held to blame for what had happened. For all of them it was hard to feel that telling had been the right thing to do when it had had such dire consequences ... The distress experienced by the children who were excluded from the family after disclosing abuse was evident from the suicide attempts made by two of them and the high scores on the depression inventory for all of them ... The depression scores reduced dramatically for those who later returned home ...' [131]

These findings indicate that, rather than removing abused children and later instituting care proceedings, greater efforts should be made to keep them at home, whilst protecting them from re-abuse. Such an approach complies with the demands of article 8 of the ECHR, which requires a proportionate response to the danger that the child is in. [132]

One of the most effective means of protecting the child is to ensure that the abuser leaves. Nevertheless, it appears that local authorities tend to react rapidly when alerted to suspicions of child sexual abuse and often remove the child from home at the start of their intervention. Fortunately, it is now very seldom considered appropriate to remove these children from home late at night, as was done in Cleveland, [133] although in a real emergency, an emergency protection order can be obtained extremely rapidly on an ex parte basis. [134] In families where physical abuse, neglect or emotional abuse has occurred, abused children are more likely to be left at home. But once the abuse has been identified, social workers and the police often expect mothers to protect their children from their abusing fathers. [135] This may be unrealistic, given the high correlation between child abuse of all kinds and adult domestic violence. [136] The damaging psychological effects suffered by children witnessing their mothers being

---

129   DH (2001 a) pp 26–32 notes research indicating that large numbers of families with children at risk of significant harm or impairment suffer multiple problems, including poverty and ill-health. See also J Tunstill and J Aldgate (2000) p 147, noting that many families' problems were defined by social workers as deriving from lack of material support, rather than family functioning problems.
130   N Parton (1997) p 11.
131   See E Farmer and M Owen (1995) p 205.
132   See Hale LJ in *Re C and B (care order: future harm)* [2001] 1 FLR 611 at [33]–[35].
133   Butler-Sloss LJ (1999) p 19.
134   Children Act 1989, s 44.
135   M Hester et al (2000) pp 121–124.
136   See SSI (1995) and C McGee (2000) pp 48–59.

subjected to domestic violence is now being taken far more seriously than hitherto. [137] Nonetheless, practitioners do not appear to appreciate that when abusive behaviour relating to children is identified, the mothers may themselves be the victims of domestic violence and unable to protect them adequately. Indeed, mothers of abused children often feel obliged to conceal the violence they themselves have been suffering at the hands of violent fathers. [138] Meanwhile, many mothers who are the victims of domestic violence are reluctant to ask social services departments for help for fear that they will lose their children into state care. They believe they will be blamed for the man's violence and be viewed as a bad mother. [139] Some, having asked for help, receive a very positive social work response. [140] Others, however, complain that their children are merely registered on the child protection register, with no follow-up support being provided. [141] They are expected to protect their children, without extra assistance or steps being taken by the local authority itself to exclude the abuser. [142]

Removing an abuser from the child's home may be well nigh impossible in cases where there is very little evidence substantiating suspicions of his identity. Nevertheless, in some cases the evidence identifying the mother's partner may be strong. She may freely admit that her partner physically abuses her; indeed, the police may have been called to the house to protect her and the children. He may be a Schedule 1 offender, [143] or there may be a clear finding of fact in previous care proceedings that he has abused one of her children. [144] It is questionable, however, whether the law provides local authorities or mothers with sufficient assistance in cases of this kind. Often the local authority will institute care proceedings but may also attempt to persuade parents that the only way of avoiding the child being removed from home under a care order is for the alleged abuser to withdraw voluntarily himself. [145] The Children Act 1989 enables the local authority to encourage a suspected abuser to move out by helping him obtain alternative accommodation, [146] but the extent to which this provision is utilised is unclear.

An alternative approach is to persuade the child's mother to apply for an order protecting the children under the Family Law Act 1996. She, or indeed, the child, [147] could apply for a non-molestation order. But the child would be much safer if the suspected abuser were forced to leave home. If the mother is an 'entitled person', [148]

---

137 See C McGee (2000) esp ch 2. See also the international research literature summarised by P Parkinson and C Humphreys (1998) and by M Hester et al (2000) ch 2. See also *Re K (supervision orders)* [1999] 2 FLR 303: the mother's preparedness, inter alia, to expose her children to witnessing domestic violence in the future indicated that there was a likelihood of their suffering significant harm, thereby fulfilling the requirements of the Children Act 1989, s 31.

138 E Farmer (1999) p 157.

139 C McGee (2000) pp 210–211 and 216.

140 C McGee (2000) pp 116–117 and 125–126.

141 C McGee (2000) pp 117–125.

142 C McGee (2000) and E Farmer and M Owen (1995) esp ch 13.

143 Ie he has committed an offence listed in the Children and Young Persons Act 1933, Sch 1; eg *Devon County Council v S* [1995] 1 All ER 243.

144 Eg *Re S (minors) (inherent jurisdiction: ouster)* [1994] 1 FLR 623.

145 Eg *Re FS (child abuse: evidence)* [1996] 2 FLR 158.

146 See Children Act 1989, Sch 2, para 5(1).

147 Although a child can apply for such a remedy (see Family Law Act 1996, ss 42(2)(a), 62(3) and 63), a child under the age of 16 must obtain court leave to do so, after satisfying the court that he/ she has 'a sufficient understanding to make the proposed application ...' See s 43(1) and (2).

148 An applicant is 'entitled' if she is married to the respondent or if she has some proprietary entitlement to occupy the property. A 'non-entitled' applicant may also in certain circumstances obtain such an order. See generally N Lowe and G Douglas (1999) pp 202–203, or S Cretney, J Masson and R Bailey-Harris (2002) pp 238–264.

she [149]can apply under the 1996 Act for an occupation order excluding the abuser from the home. [150] The clear intention of the legislation is to impose a duty on the courts to exclude an abuser from his home, or otherwise regulate his occupation, if they consider that the applicant or child is likely to suffer significant harm attributable to the abuser's conduct and such an order would secure the child's safety. [151] Indeed, it is notable that the 1996 Act adopts the same 'likelihood of significant harm' [152] formula as that used in section 31 of the Children Act 1989 as the threshold criterion for granting care orders. The courts therefore appear to have an interchangeable remedy – removing the abuser or removing the child under a care order. Unfortunately, these powers have been interpreted very restrictively, thereby undermining their usefulness to victims of domestic violence. [153] Matters are also greatly confused by the labyrinthine 'balance of harm' test, [154] which the courts must apply first and which qualifies their duty to regulate the other's occupation of the home. [155]

There is both a specific and general objection to this 'balance of harm' formula. Specifically, it is over-complex and may thereby fail to protect a child adequately. At first sight, it poses few problems in cases where there is plenty of evidence indicating that a child is suffering serious abuse at the hands of the respondent. It is inconceivable that a court presented with such evidence would ever conclude that the harm suffered by the abuser on being made homeless would be greater than the harm to the child from continued abuse. [156] But real difficulty could arise in cases where the abuse is less serious or where there is less clear evidence regarding the respondent's responsibility for it. In cases like this, the Law Commission's faith that the test would

149 Although children of any age can theoretically apply for an occupation order, they are unlikely to fulfil the 'entitled' or 'non-entitled' requirements for doing so. Ie they are unlikely to have a proprietary interest in the house, or qualify as the respondent's cohabitant or ex-cohabitant. See Family Law Act 1996, ss 35(1) and 36(1). A qualifying child under the age of 16 must obtain court leave to apply: see s 43.

150 Family Law Act 1996, s 33(3)(f).

151 See Family Law Act 1996, s 33(7) which states that: 'If it appears to the court that the applicant or any relevant child is likely to suffer significant harm attributable to conduct of the respondent if an order [excluding the respondent] ... is not made, the court *shall* make the order ...' (emphasis supplied).

152 See Family Law Act 1996, s 63(1), which employs a similar meaning of the term 'harm' as that used by Children Act 1989, s 31(9).

153 Eg see Thorpe LJ in *Chalmers v Johns* [1999] 1 FLR 392 at 397, who stated that an order requiring a respondent to leave the family home remains 'Draconian', only justified 'in exceptional circumstances'.

154 A 'balance of harm test' was recommended by the Law Commission (1992) paras 4.32–4.34.

155 See Family Law Act 1996, s 33(7)(a) and (b). This test applies whenever the applicant is an entitled applicant ie being either married to the respondent or having an estate or interest in the dwelling house in question. The statutory preumption (see s 33(7)) in favour of the court making an order protecting the applicant and/or child (eg by exluding the respondent) is negated if it considers that (a) the respondent or any relevant child is likely to suffer significant harm if the order is made and (b) the harm likely to be suffered by the respondent or child if the provision is included is as great as or greater than the harm attributable to the conduct of the respondent which is likely to be suffered by the applicant or child if the provision is not included. In the event of the applicant merely being an unentitled cohabitant or ex-cohabitant of the respondent, (see n 148 above) s 36(7) (unlike s 33(7)) includes no presumption in favour of the court excluding the respondent, although s 36(8) requires the court, before making such an order, to consider in s 36(8)(a) and (b) identical factors to those set out in s 36(5)(a) and (b). For further explanation of this complex area of law, see S Cretney, J Masson and R Bailey-Harris (2002) at 242–245.

156 Unless, as in *B v B (occupation order)* [1999] 1 FLR 715, the respondent himself has a child who would suffer greater harm if excluded from the home with his respondent father than that suffered by the applicant and her own child, in the event of the respondent not being excluded. See F Kaganas (1999).

not involve the courts having to *choose* between the interests of the child and adult may be misplaced. [157] It may be impossible for a court to decide who will suffer more, the suspected abuser or the child, without reaching some value judgment about the relative merits of leaving either in the home.

Unfortunately, in many cases the powers contained in the Family Law Act 1996 enabling mothers to apply for orders excluding their partners from home are of academic interest only. Cases like *Re S (minors) (inherent jurisdiction: ouster)* [158] and *Nottinghamshire County Council v P* [159] reflect the findings of research that an abused child's mother may be psychologically quite unable to take the initiative against her partner. [160] She may refuse to accept that he has abused the child or consider that even if he has, he is no longer a danger. Alternatively, she may be the victim of serious domestic violence at his hands herself. The stress involved in such a woman taking action herself could be avoided if the Family Law Act 1996, section 60 became operational. This allows a third person to apply for a non-molestation order or occupation order 'on behalf of another', but the provision still awaits the introduction of rules of court to activate it. [161] The Law Commission's suggestion that the police should have this power [162] was controversial with women's organisations, who feared loss of control over domestic situations. [163] The notion of a person acting on behalf of a woman might be more acceptable if the power to apply for protective orders were made available to local authorities rather than the police. Indeed, in such a form, section 60 would greatly assist local authorities wishing to protect abused children within their own homes – enabling them to take the initiative and obtain permanent exclusion orders on behalf of women.

Meanwhile, what assistance does the law give local authorities wishing to ensure that an abuser leaves the home rather than the child, in the event of the mother being reluctant to take steps herself? The *Nottinghamshire* decision [164] ruled out a local authority obtaining a prohibited steps order in order to oust a sexually abusive father from the household, [165] and its strong message was that if the local authority cannot trust the mother to exclude him herself, they have a duty to remove the child into care. [166] Some local authorities certainly assume that a mother should be forced to choose between safeguarding her children and taking steps to oust the man herself. Social workers often feel little sympathy with such a woman's refusal to oust him,

157 Law Commission (1992) para 4.34.
158 [1994] 1 FLR 623.
159 [1993] 3 All ER 815; full name *Nottinghamshire County Council v P, Re P (minors) (local authority: prohibited steps order)*. The factual background to this case is described in greater detail by Ward J in the High Court, reported at [1993] 1 FLR 514.
160 See K Rose and A Savage (2000) pp 116–117.
161 Research on the potential benefits of implementing s 60 by rules of court is under consideration by the Lord Chancellor's Department. See Written Answer (HC Deb) by Ms Rosie Winterton, 18 March 2002.
162 Law Commission (1992) paras 5.18–5.23.
163 See C Humphreys and M Kaye (1997). But see C McGee (2000), indicating (pp 131–132) that some women would prefer the police to take the initiative.
164 [1993] 3 All ER 815.
165 The court was barred from making such an order by the Children Act 1989, s 9(5). But see *Re H (prohibited steps order)* [1995] 1 FLR 638, which indicates that a parent applicant may obtain a prohibited steps order to keep someone without parental responsibility and not living in the house away from a child. The court treated the mother and guardian ad litem as the applicants for a prohibited steps order.
166 *Nottinghamshire County Council v P; Re P (minors) (local authority: prohibited steps order)* [1993] 3 All ER 815 at 825 and 828, per Sir Stephen Brown P.

assuming that it indicates collusion with the abuser over the abuse itself, [167] thereby justifying the institution of care proceedings to remove the child from home. [168] But such a response over-simplifies matters. Mothers may have such a low self-esteem that hostility from practitioners may strengthen their emotional dependence on their partners. [169] Furthermore, they may simply continue their relationships on a clandestine basis if pressurised into ending them. [170] Certainly they may be quite unable to contemplate the abuser leaving unless responsibility for making him go is removed from their shoulders.

Local authorities have powers to take the initiative themselves to exclude a suspected abuser in certain circumstances, but these are so limited that they do not greatly assist in situations of this kind. [171] A local authority may request the court to annex an exclusion requirement to interim care orders or emergency protection orders, thereby removing any person living in the same dwelling house as a child, if they consider that its effect would prevent the child continuing to suffer significant harm. The usefulness of these provisions is undermined by their short duration, so that even when annexed to an interim care order, [172] they may only postpone the need to find the child an alternative home. Furthermore, the local authority must not only show that there is someone able to care for the child in the household, but also that that person *consents* to the exclusion requirement being included in the order. Although the mother in the *Nottinghamshire* case might have been prepared to *acquiesce* in an application being made by the local authority for such an order, *consent* might have been another matter. To victims of domestic violence, the psychological difference between the two could be crucial. Nonetheless, these provisions represent some effort to protect abused children more effectively. The courts' ability to attach a power of arrest to the exclusion requirement [173] can be particularly useful in situations where the local authority suspects that a woman is not fulfilling an informal undertaking to keep her partner away from the home. [174] Although the police are unlikely to 'stake out' the house in order to detect him entering or leaving, such a power enables them to take action if they discover him breaking the terms of the order.

What is the remedy for the abused child whose mother steadfastly refuses either to oust her abusive partner herself or to consent to care for the child in the event of the local authority obtaining an exclusion requirement? In the *Nottinghamshire* case, [175] the Court of Appeal's refusal to grant a prohibited steps order excluding the paedophile father from the family home seemed partly motivated by its view that the local authority should have applied for care orders to protect his daughters from his attentions. [176] But it is questionable whether the grant of a care order is in the child's best interests, or indeed, whether it is a neccesary or a proportionate response to such

---

167 See K Rose and A Savage (2000) p 117.
168 Eg *Re S (care or supervision order)* [1996] 1 FLR 753.
169 K Rose and A Savage (2000) pp 116–119. These women may also be financially dependent on such partners.
170 K Rose and A Savage (2000) p 117.
171 Children Act 1989, ss 38A and 38B and ss 44A and 44B. See amendments set out by Family Law Act 1996, Sch 6.
172 An interim care order initially only lasts for a maximum of eight weeks, before being renewed. See Children Act 1989, s 38(4).
173 See *President's Direction (Children Act 1989: Exclusion Requirement)* [1998] 1 FLR 495.
174 Eg *Re S (minors) (inherent jurisdiction: ouster)* [1994] 1 FLR 623.
175 [1993] 3 All ER 815.
176 See Sir Simon Brown P, [1993] 3 All ER 815 at 824.

a situation, given that removing the children from home infringes the mothers' own rights under article 8 of the ECHR. [177] Greater use of supervision orders, [178] in the place of care orders, would more obviously comply with the principle of proportionality. [179] Such orders are, however, deeply unpopular, not only because the local authority gains no real control over the case, [180] but also because of they have no effective sanction in the event of a parent disobeying any directions the order contains. [181] Furthermore, in many situations, a local authority may quite justifiably doubt the mother's sincerity when she undertakes to protect her child at home and exclude her abusive partner. [182] A supervision order alone cannot protect the child unless the abuser also stays away.

Decisions like *Devon County Council v S* [183] and *Re S (minors) (inherent jurisdiction: ouster)* [184] demonstrate that the inherent jurisdiction may be invoked by the local authority to exclude an abuser if all else fails. In both these cases, the court was persuaded that the general aim of the Children Act 1989, section 100, which is to prevent local authorities invoking the inherent jurisdiction, did not apply since the desired outcome could not be achieved through conventional orders available elsewhere in the Act. [185] In each, the court accepted that although there might be evidence justifying the grant of care orders, these were not appropriate since the mother's care could not be faulted in either case. This use of the inherent jurisdiction fulfils the child's interests far better than by removing him or her into the care of strangers, as long as the mother can be trusted to protect the child in future. It not only avoids obtaining the mother's active co-operation, but, unlike the statutory powers to annex exclusion requirements to interim care orders and emergency protection orders, it enables orders to be made excluding the man indefinitely, rather than only for a limited period. [186]

If abused children are to stay at home, particularly in the case of those who have been the victim of sexual abuse, a great deal of therapeutic work must be done with the mothers to ensure that they believe their children and that they learn to support and protect them. [187] A growing range of research studies shows, however, that social workers too often concentrate a great deal of effort on investigation and short-term protection, at the expense of providing follow-up services in the form of treatment and family support programmes for either mothers or children. [188] Nevertheless, research also clearly shows that abused children would benefit if the option of

---

177   See the views of Hale LJ in *Re C and B (care order: future harm)* [2001] 1 FLR 611 at paras 33–35.
178   To obtain a supervision order under the Children Act 1989, s 35, the local authority must satisfy the same threshold criteria as those applying to care orders: see s 31.
179   See Hale J, in *Oxfordshire County Council v L (care or supervision order)* [1998] 1 FLR 70 at 76–78 and *Re O (supervision order)* [2001] EWCA Civ 16, [2001] 1 FLR 923 at [18]–[28].
180   It is *only* by obtaining a care order that the local authority acquire parental responsibility over the child, which they share with his or her parents. See Children Act 1989, s 33(3).
181   See J Hunt and A Macleod (1999) pp 213, 217–218 and 237–238.
182   Eg *Re J (expert evidence: hearsay)* [1999] 2 FLR 661: the mother had deliberately deceived the local authority into thinking she was having no contact with her child's father, who had a criminal record of indecent assaults on children. Nevertheless, per Cazalet J, a supervision order was not plainly wrong, as opposed to a care order.
183   [1995] 1 All ER 243.
184   [1994] 1 FLR 623.
185   See particularly, Children Act 1989, s 100(4).
186   See *C v K (inherent powers: exclusion order)* [1996] 2 FLR 506 at 523, per Wall J.
187   See K Rose and A Savage (2000) pp 119–122.
188   See, inter alia: J Hunt and A Macleod (1999) pp 155–157 and C McGee (2000) pp 118–124.

removing the abuser from home were considered more often. Farmer and Owen found that the children who were most troubled were those who left home as a consequence of disclosing sexual abuse. 'They had to try to come to terms with the double pain of telling about the abuse and of losing their place in the family in consequence.' [189]

Local authorities obviously have a difficult task if they decide to leave an abused child at home with his or her mother. Monitoring the child's safety at home may be undermined by mothers, who, as in *S*'s case above, deliberately deceive social workers into believing that they are fulfilling undertakings to exclude the abuser from home. [190] Matters are made worse when abused children display indiscriminate sexualised behaviour rendering them particularly vulnerable to re-abuse. [191] Unfortunately, no amount of tinkering with the law will achieve a situation whereby the children of mothers like those in the cases discussed above can be provided with assured protection.

(6) PROOF OF SIGNIFICANT HARM – CHILDREN'S RIGHTS OR JUSTICE FOR PARENTS?

(A) The evidence

The search for evidence to substantiate allegations of abuse and to assign responsibility for it is a powerful driving force in the initial stages of much child protection work. Nevertheless, a great deal of professional time and energy is devoted to collecting evidence to substantiate child protection applications which may never be made and criminal charges which may never be brought. [192] The vast majority of children who are the subject of child protection inquiries are never made the subject of legal proceedings of any kind, quite simply because local authority protection is provided in co-operation with the parents. Few of those whose names are registered on child protection registers leave home, even when they are deemed to be in potentially dangerous situations. [193] Many who do leave, do so only for a short time and, with the agreement of their parents, are provided with accommodation under short-term fostering arrangements or with relatives. [194]

Applications for care or supervision orders often never reach a final hearing. It is ironic, in view of the relatively few cases that get to court, that the entire child protection process seems geared to dealing with those that do involve confrontation and conflict – the battle lines are very readily drawn between the parents and the state. When battle commences, the parents and their advisers, the local authority social workers and even the judiciary themselves, take up such formalised positions that the child at the centre is treated very much as a passive pawn. Unfortunately, there is often a misguided assumption that as long as the court, as umpire between parents and state, ensures 'fair play', the outcome will automatically protect the child's best interests. But at this stage, the law's role in maintaining a balance between parents' rights to family privacy and children's rights to protection is put to a severe

---

189 E Farmer and M Owen (1995) p 77.
190 K Rose and A Savage (2000) p 117.
191 E Farmer and M Owen (1995) p 207.
192 Discussed in more depth in chapter 17.
193 See M Brandon et al (1999) chs 4 and 8 and p 203.
194 Ie under Children Act 1989, s 20. See DH (2001 b), which notes (para 1.21) the increased use of accommodation as a child protection measure, as opposed to a source of family support.

test. When comparing the child protection practice of English social workers with that of their colleagues in other European countries, researchers observe:

> 'Arrangements to secure the child's right to protection, and the due process of law protecting parents' rights against arbitrary bureaucratic interference can sometimes have the effect of cancelling each other out. English social workers in our study frequently expressed frustration about this sort of impasse ... The pre-eminent role of the law as protector of individual rights was ever present in the minds of the English social workers' discussion of the hypothetical case. Frequently, any action they contemplated was checked for its legality ... The possibility of using their "professional authority" (ie that deriving from their own expertise) was less apparent in their discussions.' [195]

Furthermore, driven by considerations of fairness to the parents, the courts have allowed a strict legalism to creep into the 'proof' stage of care proceedings, at the expense of the child. In particular, the case law increasingly suggests that the current law is more concerned with protecting parents from false accusations of child abuse than fulfilling children's rights to state protection.

There are a number of factors underlying this development. It is perfectly possible to obtain a care or supervision order by satisfying a court that the child 'is suffering significant harm' under the Children Act 1989, section 31, simply because he or she is being physically or sexually abused by *somebody*, despite there being insufficient evidence to identify the abuser. [196] Unlike the criminal law, which seeks to identify and punish the abuser, civil proceedings, with a lower standard of proof and a different aim, have a far greater chance of providing the child with a safe environment. But, in practice, even in civil proceedings, suspicions about abuse are often inextricably linked with the abuser's identity. First, the social workers carrying out the child protection investigation may be working alongside police officers who wish to identify the abuser in order to lay criminal charges. [197] Furthermore, local authorities often use specialised treatment and assessment units to assess the parenting qualities of parents of children considered the victims of abuse. These units place considerable emphasis on the need for parents to take responsibility and blame for suspected abuse. Faced with parental denial, they may not recommend that the child is safe either to return to them or to remain with them. [198] But if the parents are innocent of the abuse, they will refuse to take responsibility for it. Even if they are guilty, they may deny it, fearing a criminal prosecution. [199] The local authority will then consider it impossible to trust them sufficiently to contemplate their continuing to care for their child, particularly if the child is very young. [200]

A complete stalemate between parents and local authority may have to be resolved by care proceedings, with the court reaching a finding of fact one way or the other. This may be through conducting a split hearing to resolve a single disputed issue of fact, as a preliminary issue; for example, the identity of the abuser. Such a hearing may assist in situations where it is clear that a child has been injured, or even killed, by somebody

195   See R Hetherington et al (1997) p 119.
196   See *Lancashire County Council v A (a child)* [2000] 2 All ER 97, discussed below.
197   Discussed in chapter 17.
198   See D Jones (1998) pp 106–108.
199   Children Act 1989, s 98(2) provides little real protection to a parent who makes an admission in civil proceedings if the police later investigate the case. See *Re EC (disclosure of material)* [1996] 2 FLR 725 and *Re L (care: confidentiality)* [1999] 1 FLR 165.
200   Eg *Re FS (child abuse: evidence)* [1996] 2 FLR 158: the mother claimed that unless she stated to the local authority that she believed that her husband had abused one of their children, which she denied, she would not be trusted to continue caring for them.

very close to him, such as one or both of his parents, [201] a parent or child-minder, [202] a mother and/or boyfriend, [203] but no one will admit to responsibility for any or all the injuries. [204] Armed with a finding identifying the abuser, the local authority can justify intervening to protect future children born into a household in which he or she still resides. Unfortunately, it is often impossible to reach a clear view as to the abuser's exact identity, particularly when only one of two people could have been responsible, but neither admits responsibility. According to the House of Lords, [205] the court may then simply find that the child has suffered serious injuries at the hands of one or both of the carers, but in the absence of evidence indicating conclusively who it is, ruling out neither. [206] Such a finding allows the local authority to mount protective measures to protect future children being cared for by any of these potential abusers, despite the possibility that one or other is wholly innocent. Whilst such an approach can be justified in child protection terms, it undoubtedly places parents under a cloud of suspicion for unlimited periods. An exaggerated concern to protect a mother from such a position led the Court of Appeal, in *Re O and N (care: preliminary hearing)*, [207] to ignore earlier authority. It directed the local authority to treat the mother for the future as if she was not an abuser, since they could not establish to the requisite standard of proof that she was. [208] Hayes and Hayes rightly criticise this decision for allowing arguments about fairness to adults to outweigh efforts to safeguard children's rights. [209]

The courts' concerns about protecting adults from unfairness may be greatest in cases involving sexual abuse, which is notoriously difficult to prove. There may be little or no medical evidence indicating whether or not the child has been abused; often only the child and the abuser know the truth. As Hayes has pointed out, a problematic aspect of care proceedings is that the child's evidence will usually be in the form of hearsay evidence. [210] Since children are not normally called to give evidence in person in care proceedings, their words and behaviour will be conveyed to the court by their adult interviewers or in the form of video-taped evidence. [211] Although hearsay evidence is admissible, [212] it does not carry as much weight as evidence provided by a witness directly, mainly because the court cannot test its weight and credibility through cross-examination. Despite the obvious risk of relying only upon a child's hearsay evidence when identifying an adult as an abuser, a child's hearsay account can nevertheless be highly prejudicial to the parents. [213]

---

201   Eg *Re CB and JB (care proceedings: guidelines)* [1998] 2 FLR 211; *Re B (split hearing: jurisdiction)* [2000] 1 FLR 334; *Re O and N (non-accidental injury: burden of proof)* [2002] EWCA Civ 1271, [2002] 2 FLR 1167.

202   Eg *Lancashire County Council v A (a child)* [2000] 2 All ER 97.

203   Eg *Re B (non-accidental injury: compelling medical evidence)* [2002] EWCA Civ 902, [2002] 2 FLR 599.

204   In *Re O and N (care: preliminary hearing)* [2002] EWCA Civ 1271, [2002] 2 FLR 1167 the father admitted responsibility for some of the child's injuries, but the mother denied responsibility for the others.

205   *Lancashire County Council v A (a child)* [2000] 2 All ER 97.

206   [2000] 2 All ER 97 at 104, per Lord Nicholls of Birkenhead (at [38]–[43]). See also *Re B (non-accidental injury: compelling medical evidence)* [2002] EWCA Civ 902, [2002] 2 FLR 599 at [38]–[43], per Thorpe LJ.

207   [2002] EWCA Civ 1271, [2002] 2 FLR 1167.

208   [2002] EWCA Civ 1271, [2002] 2 FLR 1167 at [26], per Ward LJ.

209   See J Hayes and M Hayes (2002) esp p 828.

210   M Hayes (1997) pp 5–6.

211   Discussed in chapter 17.

212   Children Act 1989, s 96(3)–(7) and Children (Admissibility of Hearsay Evidence) Order 1993, SI 1993/621. See also *R v B County Council, ex p P* [1991] 1 WLR 221.

213   See *Re W (minors) (wardship: evidence)* [1990] 1 FLR 203 at [214], per Butler-Sloss LJ.

Expert psychiatrists and psychologists may be able to help the courts decide whether a child has been sexually abused or whether his or her allegations of abuse made in interviews are credible. Indeed, according to the Civil Evidence Act 1972,[214] the courts are fully entitled to take account of expert evidence on such matters, whenever they consider it to be relevant to the issues.[215] Some children are reluctant to provide any details of what has occurred and interviewers may then be unable to avoid questioning them without using leading questions and encouragement, thereby undermining the value of any evidence obtained. In the past, the courts often criticised some of the interviewing techniques used.[216] These are gradually improving now that the official guidance on this[217] is commonly complied with. Furthermore, if victims of poor interviewing techniques successfully sue local authorities and police authorities in negligence, this will doubtless provoke better training for all interviewers.[218] Nevertheless, interviewers are not obliged to follow the official guidance, indeed, it may be inappropriate to do so in cases not involving criminal proceedings.[219] As the *Newham* case demonstrates, even good interviewing techniques may produce extremely misleading evidence regarding the identity of a child's abuser.[220]

The courts are well aware that, for parents whose children are the subject of care proceedings, the stakes are very high indeed. They may lose their children into state care and there is not only the risk of criminal charges being brought against them, but future local authority surveillance may be mounted over any other children they have.[221] A man who is labelled a sex abuser risks losing his job[222] and also the right to visit his children unsupervised.[223] The stakes are also high for the child who has a

214 Civil Evidence Act 1972, s 3(1) indicates that if a person is called as an expert witness in any civil proceedings, 'his opinion on any relevant matter on which he is qualified to give expert evidence shall be admissible in evidence'. Discussed at length by Butler-Sloss LJ in *Re M and R (minors) (sexual abuse: expert evidence)* [1996] 4 All ER 239 at 249–254.

215 See Wall J (2000) para 5.3.

216 Eg *Re E (a minor) (child abuse: evidence)* [1991] 1 FLR 420; and *Re N (a minor) (sexual abuse: video evidence)* [1996] 4 All ER 225.

217 Home Office (1992), now replaced by Home Office et al (2002).

218 In *L and P v Reading Borough Council and Chief Constable of Thames Valley Police* [2001] EWCA Civ 346, [2001] 2 FLR 50 the Court of Appeal refused to strike out negligence claims brought by a father and his child against the local authority and police authority alleging that interviews jointly conducted by a social worker and police officer in 1990 were improper, incompetent and conducted in a manner grossly unfair to the child's father. No criminal proceedings had been brought against him and he had been finally exonerated of any abusive behaviour in the public law proceedings.

219 Discussed in chapter 17.

220 See eg *X (minors) v Bedfordshire County Council*; *M (a minor) v Newham Borough Council*; *E (a minor) v Dorset County Council* [1995] 3 All ER 353. In the *Newham* case, a child psychiatrist interviewed a 4-year-old child and mistook the identity of the man who the child alleged had sexually abused her. Relying on this information, the local authority kept the child away from home under a care order made in wardship for nearly a year. In *TP and KM v United Kingdom* [2001] 2 FLR 549 (a claim involving the same case) the European Court of Human Rights considered that the local authority's failure to disclose to the mother the contents of the video of the interview or transcript deprived her of proper involvement in the decision-making process, thereby infringing mother and daughter's art 8 rights.

221 Eg *Re S (care or supervision order)* [1996] 1 FLR 753: the mother ignored a warning by the local authority that if she moved to set up home with the man they suspected was a sex abuser, they would apply for a care order regarding her new baby. Care proceedings were duly commenced.

222 *A County Council v W (disclosure)* [1997] 1 FLR 574: a registered medical practitioner was found in care proceedings to have sexually abused his daughter and lost his job. The General Medical Council successfully obtained disclosure of the case documents in order to consider whether to bring disciplinary proceedings against him.

223 Eg *Re P (sexual abuse: standard of proof)* [1996] 2 FLR 333.

right to remain with loving parents, particularly if, as in the *Newham* case, they have been unjustly accused of abuse. [224]

These factors rightly concern the judiciary. Parents are entitled to complain that their rights under articles 6 and 8 of the ECHR have been infringed by care proceedings which treated them unfairly. [225] Some judges appear particularly concerned by the special risk of a man being unfairly accused of child sexual abuse. [226] Morritt LJ stresses: 'The accused man – because it is usually a man, whether the father or not – does not have the protection of the high standard of proof or corroborative evidence, which would be his right if he were charged with the equivalent criminal offence.' [227] Nonetheless, as the case law discussed below indicates, the pendulum is in danger of swinging too far the other way, resulting in the child's own right to protection being compromised. There is also a danger that the need to protect parents' rights, at the expense of those of their children, will become even more of a driving force, with parents turning to claims under the Human Rights Act 1998 as a popular means of opposing care proceedings.

(B)   The standard of proof

In an anxiety to be fair to parents, the courts at times, allow the child's own rights to protection to slip into second place, particularly if their ability to interpret the law flexibly is undermined. Current case law on the standard of proof required to establish that a child 'is suffering, or is likely to suffer, significant harm' under section 31 of the Children Act 1989, may give local authorities the impression, particularly in cases involving children's allegations of child sexual abuse, that it is futile mounting care proceedings, simply because they will be unable to satisfy the present unrealistically high standard of proof.

After some uncertainty, the House of Lords in *Re H (minors) (sexual abuse: standard of proof)* [228] tackled what had been a continuing controversy over the correct standard of proof for establishing significant harm. Lord Browne-Wilkinson who delivered a strong dissenting judgment made clear his verdict of its conclusion in the following words:

> 'My Lords, I am anxious that the decision of the House in this case may establish the law in an unworkable form to the detriment of many children at risk ... Take the present case ... After a long hearing a judge has reached the conclusion on evidence that there is a "real possibility" that her [229] evidence is true, ie that she has in fact been gravely abused. Can Parliament really have intended that neither the court nor anyone else should have jurisdiction to intervene so as to protect (her) from any abuse which she may well have been enduring? I venture to think not.' [230]

---

224 *X (minors) v Bedfordshire County Council; M (a minor) v Newham Borough Council; E (a minor) v Dorset County Council* [1995] 3 All ER 353.

225 See *P, C and S v United Kingdom* [2002] 2 FLR 631. See also *Re L (care: assessment: fair trial)* [2002] EWHC 1379 (Fam), [2002] 2 FLR 730.

226 Eg *Re FS (child abuse: evidence)* [1996] 2 FLR 158: Morritt LJ indicated concern at the local authority's attitude. They maintained that because the father had resolutely denied having sexually abused the child, he was untrustworthy and they would remove the child from the mother's care if he attempted to return home.

227 [1996] 2 FLR 158 at 168.

228 [1996] 1 All ER 1.

229 This was a reference to the older sister of the children who were the subject of care proceedings.

230 [1996] 1 All ER 1 at 4–5.

The majority disagreed with him. In fact, the decision in this case dealt with two interrelated questions. First, what standard of proof is required to satisfy the court that a child has suffered significant harm in the past?[231] Second, if the court finds the evidence insufficient to indicate that significant harm has occurred in the past, can the same evidence be used to establish the likelihood of significant harm in the future?[232]

On the first question, according to Lord Nicholls of Birkenhead, who delivered the majority opinion, the correct standard of proof required for proving that significant harm had occurred in the past, is the balance of probabilities. Accordingly, the court should be able to reach a finding that 'on the evidence, the occurrence of the event was more likely than not'.[233] On the face of it, this assessment of the law seems quite straightforward. In particular, Lord Nicholls appeared to reject conclusively the more sophisticated approach to the standard of proof adopted by previous case law. This had required evidence commensurate with the seriousness of the allegation: 'the more serious the allegation the more convincing was the evidence required to tip the balance in respect of it.'[234] According to Lord Nicholls, this approach was wrong – the standard of proof was *not* higher in cases involving serious allegations. This apparent clarity was, however, fundamentally undermined by his warning that:

> 'When assessing the probabilities the court will have in mind as a factor ... that the more serious the allegation the less likely it is that the event occurred and, hence, the stronger should be the evidence before the court concludes that the allegation is established on the balance of probability ... Deliberate physical injury is usually less likely than accidental physical injury. A stepfather is usually less likely to have repeatedly raped and had non-consensual oral sex with his under age stepdaughter than on some occasion to have lost his temper and slapped her ... The more improbable the event, the stronger must be the evidence that it did occur before, on the balance of probability, its occurrence will be established.'[235]

In the light of these words, it is difficult to accept Lord Nicholls' view that, when adopting his approach, despite the result being 'much the same, this does not mean that where a serious allegation is in issue the standard of proof required is higher'.[236] His claim that the test remains the balance of probabilities, whilst at the same time maintaining the need for a degree of increasing scepticism the more serious the alleged behaviour, bears the hallmarks of casuistry. Indeed, in different contexts, senior members of the judiciary routinely interpret his advice as establishing a *higher* standard of proof for cases involving serious allegations.[237] Furthermore, Lord Nicholls of Birkenhead's view that intrinsically unlikely events should require stronger evidence appears to overlook the fact that local authorities only ever bring care

231 This question arose in relation to allegations of child sexual abuse made by the 15-year-old sister of three younger girls, against their step-father.

232 The local authority wished to use the same evidence, despite its being too weak to show on the balance of probabilities that the older girl had been abused by the step-father, to show that her three younger siblings were not safe with him in the future.

233 Per Lord Nicholls of Birkenhead, [1996] 1 All ER 1 at 16.

234 Per Waite LJ in *Re M (a minor) (appeal) (No 2)* [1994] 1 FLR 59 at 67. See also *Re W (minors) (sexual abuse: standard of proof)* [1994] 1 FLR 419.

235 [1996] 1 All ER 1 at 16–17.

236 [1996] 1 All ER 1 at 17.

237 See, inter alia: *R v Headteacher and Independent Appeal Committee of Dunraven School, ex p B* [2002] ELR 156 at 204–205, per Brooke LJ; *Clingham (formerly C (a minor)) v Royal Borough of Kensington and Chelsea* [2002] UKHRR 1286 at [37], per Lord Steyn; *Re B (non-accidental injury: compelling medical evidence)* [2002] EWCA Civ 902, [2002] 2 FLR 599 at [38], per Thorpe LJ.

proceedings in circumstances which, by their very nature, are unlikely to occur in normal households. Since allegations regarding ill-treatment of children serious enough to amount to significant harm always relate to rare events, this suggests that the courts must always require stronger evidence than the courts would normally require to establish that their occurrence was more likely than not. [238]

The result in *Re H* was that the local authority was unable to use the evidence regarding the sexual abuse of C, now aged 15 and in foster-care, to show that her three younger siblings were also at risk from her step-father's attentions in the future. The judge below had considered 'that there was a real possibility' that the step-father had sexually abused C, as she claimed. Indeed, in his view there was a considerable amount of evidence substantiating 'a classic unfolding revelation of progressively worse abuse'. [239] Nevertheless, he could not be satisfied 'on the balance of probabilities' that C had suffered significant harm in the past. The House of Lords considered his approach was correct; more was required than suspicion, however reasonably based. Lord Browne-Wilkinson's words set out above make clear his own deep disagreement with the majority judgment in *Re H*. He and Lord Lloyd both delivered strong dissenting opinions, considering that the county court judge had incorrectly applied a higher than ordinary standard of proof. Indeed, in Lord Lloyd's view, there was a strong general argument in favour of making the threshold criteria *lower*, rather than higher, in serious cases where the anticipated danger to the child is greater. [240]

The House of Lords' decision effectively brings the law round in a full circle. The courts must pay lip service to Lord Nicholls of Birkenhead's assertion that the courts need not require a higher standard of proof 'commensurate with the seriousness of the allegation' for more serious allegations. But, in truth, they will continue to require more cogent evidence because they must be sceptical over any events deemed intrinsically unlikely. Thus, according to the civil law, 'the worse danger the child is in, the less likely the courts are to remove her from it'. [241] As critics point out, such an approach might be sensible in criminal cases, where the more serious the allegations, the greater the injustice to an innocent person for being seriously punished for an offence he did not commit. But its use by the civil law is surely indefensible. The consequence for parents of a false finding that they nearly killed their child is that she is removed from them, whilst those for the child of being returned to parents who in truth did nearly kill him or her, are infinitely more dangerous. [242]

The first part of the decision in *Re H* regarding the standard of proof required to establish significant harm in the past materially affected the way in which the second question was interpreted. Evidence which is insufficiently weighty to indicate on the balance of probabilities that significant harm occurred in the past, cannot be used to indicate a likelihood of harm in the future. [243] This is despite Lord Nicholls of Birkenhead's view that 'likely' merely requires the court be satisfied that there is 'a real possibility' of the event occurring in the future, as opposed to being more likely than not. [244] In the majority's view, the court could not conclude from the fact that there was a real possibility of C having been abused in the past that there was also a real possibility that her sisters would be abused in the future. Again, Lord Browne-

---

238   See I Hemingway and C Williams (1997) pp 741–742.
239   She alleged that the abuse had started when she was 7 or 8, culminating in four acts of rape.
240   [1996] 1 All ER 1 at 8.
241   J Spencer (1994) p 161. See also R White (1995).
242   J Spencer (1994) p 161.
243   See Children Act 1989, s 31(2)(a).
244   [1996] 1 All ER 1 at 15–16.

Wilkinson and Lord Lloyd disagreed strongly. Neither accepted that because the court is unable to find on the balance of probabilities that a child had been abused in the past, it is barred from using that same evidence to consider, as a separate issue, that there is risk of that child or another child being abused in the future.

Re H has created an evidential straight-jacket for local authorities. Admittedly, if they wish to protect children from the risk of future harm, it will only cause insurmountable problems where no clear evidence exists of any *other* worrying features in the parents' past record of care, which could justify applying for a care order. Such cases are unusual but do occur. [245] Furthermore, the law now obliges local authorities to adopt what is essentially a diversionary tactic in cases where there is only 'a strong possibility' that the abuse of central concern has occurred in the past. Rather than basing their care application on it, they will exploit less serious but more certain aspects of the case to substantiate their fears of the children being at risk of abuse in the future. [246] The surer evidence of peripheral abuse will be used merely as a peg on which to hang a finding of significant harm under section 31. [247] The disadvantage of such a course of action is that it prevents the local authority obtaining a finding of fact regarding the events which are the true focus of its concerns. Without such a specific finding, the local authority may, for example, find it difficult to resist the suspected abuser claiming the right to future contact with his victim.

In explaining his conclusions in *Re H*, Lord Nicholls of Birkinhead referred by analogy to negligence claims in car accidents and goods being sold under deception. This reflects a scholarly approach to the law, but one detached from the ugly realities of serious child abuse. The House of Lords' decision not only undermines the civil law's ability to protect children from abuse, but produces an exaggerated fairness to alleged abusers who already avoid criminal prosecution with too great an ease. As Hemingway and Williams comment: 'Intuitively one feels a sense of unease towards the thesis to which Lord Nicholls, perhaps unwittingly, subscribes: namely that there is a positive correlation between the severity of the abuse alleged and the probability that the child has lied.' [248] When the court finds the child's allegations to be well-founded, the local authority gain a solid foundation for their work, but the implications are stark when, instead, the court fails to confirm the child's version of events. The result may not only be seen as a message that the child has lied, but also as a vindication of the alleged perpetrator, possibly even as an encouragement to the abuser to repeat the abuse. [249] Worst of all, if a mistake has been made, the unprotected child is not only returned to an abuser who believes himself to be beyond the law, but he or she will almost certainly suffer severe psychological damage as a result of not being believed. [250]

---

245 Eg *Re P (a minor) (care: evidence)* [1994] 2 FLR 751: a baby had died in circumstances attributable by the doctors attending him to non-accidental injury. There was no other evidence substantiating the local authorities' concerns regarding his surviving 2-year-old brother.

246 Eg *Re M and R (minors) (sexual abuse: expert evidence)* [1996] 4 All ER 239. Despite the view of three child psychiatrists that the children's allegations of child sexual abuse by their mother and two men in the family were true, since this only indicated 'a strong possibility' that sexual abuse had occurred in the past, it could not be used to justify fears about the likelihood of future sexual abuse. Care orders were obtained instead based on other evidence establishing on the balance of probabilities that all four children had been emotionally abused by their mother.

247 Eg *Re G and R (child sexual abuse: standard of proof)* [1995] 2 FLR 867.

248 See I Hemingway and C Williams (1997) p 742.

249 M King and J Trowell (1992) pp 118–119.

250 See E Sharland et al (1996) esp p 184.

The case law discussed above demonstrates the extreme difficulties confronting local authorities when attempting to satisfy the courts that on the balance of probabilities child abuse has occurred. The decision in *Re H* led Ward LJ to adopt a similarly narrow approach in *Re O and N (care: preliminary hearing)*[251] to the problem involving a child severely abused or killed by one of two parents, neither of whom will admit responsibility.[252] This over-restrictive approach to the interpretation of the standard of proof required to establish the threshold criteria is in strong contrast to the courts' efforts in other contexts to interpret the provisions of the Children Act 1989 as effectively as possible. For example, the local authority is not bound by the *Re H* straight-jacket during the investigative stage of the intervention.[253] Indeed, the House of Lords in *Re M (a minor) (care order: threshold conditions)*[254] rejected a restrictive interpretation of the present tense 'is suffering' as used in section 31. The use of the present tense does not mean that if a child was suffering significant harm and was rescued by the local authority from such conditions, a care order cannot later be made, merely because it can no longer then be said that the child 'is suffering' significant harm. The statute should be construed 'in accordance with the spirit rather than the letter of the Act'.[255] This flexible interpretation of section 31 enables care applications to be brought in cases where the child was suffering significant harm at the time of the local authority's initial application, despite the local authority later having worked towards establishing other arrangements for his or her care prior to the court hearing.[256]

Efforts have also been made to ease the rules of evidence so that the courts can be provided with all the information which may be relevant to children's cases. Case law has promoted the notion that once proceedings have commenced, the welfare of the children concerned overrides the strict rules of evidence common to adversarial proceedings.[257] Indeed, the judiciary are often at pains to stress the non-adversarial nature of cases involving children.[258] In particular, expert evidence commissioned by a parent in the course of legal proceedings is not protected from disclosure by legal professional privilege and may be made available to the court even if it is unfavourable to the adult concerned.[259] Tapper suggests that the whole thrust of the evidential changes in modern legal procedure is to promote a system in which litigation is conducted 'not only with all the cards on the table, but face-up for all to see ...' and that it is entirely right that such changes have occurred in children's cases.[260]

---

251 [2002] EWCA Civ 1271, [2002] 2 FLR 1167. Discussed above.
252 Discussed above.
253 *Re S (sexual abuse allegations: local authority response)* [2001] EWHC Admin 334, [2001] 2 FLR 776: per Scott Baker J, the *Re H* standard of proof does not apply to the local authority's duty to investigate under s 47, whether or not a child is likely to suffer significant harm.
254 [1994] 3 All ER 298. This decision is discussed at length by M Hayes and C Williams (1999) pp 200–204.
255 Per Lord Templeman, [1994] 3 All ER 298 at 309.
256 See Lord Mackay's explanation, [1994] 3 All ER 298 at 305.
257 Discussed by C Tapper (1997).
258 See Sir Stephen Brown P in *Oxfordshire County Council v M* [1994] 2 All ER 269 at 278. See also Wall J (2000) para 2.1.
259 *Oxfordshire County Council v M* [1994] 2 All ER 269. Confirmed by the House of Lords in *Re L (a minor) (police investigation: privilege)* [1997] AC 16. See also *L v United Kingdom* [2000] 2 FLR 322: according to the European Court of Human Rights, a parent's obligation to disclose to the court in care proceedings an incriminating expert's report is not an infringement of his or her rights under arts 6 or 8 of the ECHR.
260 C Tapper (1997) p 16.

Despite these developments, the principle established by *Re H* undermines the courts' ability to make sensible use of the evidence thus available. They are certainly unable to fulfil a child's right to protection as effectively as they can assist an adult to clear himself of false suspicions. Meanwhile, a desire to respect parents' rights under articles 6 and 8 of the ECHR need not inhibit a local authority from instituting care proceedings to protect a child, as long as their dealings with the parents are procedurally fair,[260a] and the intervention is both 'necessary in a democtratic society' to pretect the child's rights[261] and a proportionate response to the dangers that the child is in.[262] The local authority must also ensure that the intervention is seen, initially at least, as being only temporary, since their actions must be consistent with the ultimate aim of re-uniting parent and child as soon as practicable.[263] Nevertheless, the need for judges to demonstrate their awareness of parents' rights under article 8, as well as to comply with the Children Act 1989, section 31, may reinforce the approach established in *Re H*, producing domestic case law weighting the scales even further in favour of adults' rights, as opposed to children's rights.

(7)   THE CHILD'S OWN PERSPECTIVES

The children's liberationists stress the importance of empowering children to free themselves of parental abuse. This is often unrealistic given the behavioural problems and depression commonly experienced by abused children; these affect their school lives and friendships, with many worrying intensely about various aspects of their own and their parents' lives.[264] Despite this, the liberationists' message has proved useful. The establishment of Childline and initiatives involving teaching young children in schools about acceptable and unacceptable adult familiarity do appear to have encouraged more children to tell adults about ongoing abuse.[265] Nonetheless, many children who have experienced abuse often feel alone and confused, either having no one to confide in or feeling very reluctant to do so. This reluctance may stem from a fear of the consequences, particularly in the case of children who have suffered from child sexual abuse[266] or who experience domestic violence.[267]

Sadly, abused children often regret disclosing their abuse, feeling ignored and 'walked over' by those who try to protect them.[268] The victim of abuse is too often treated as 'an object of concern', rather than a person with a right to be involved and consulted.[269] Although child protection practitioners are keen to listen to children in order to discover what happened to them, they may not be so enthusiastic to consult them over the outcome of protective intervention. Indeed, this area of practice reflects an assumption that the state acts in the best interests of the child, on behalf of the child. In many respects, this paternalistic stance is realistic and reasonable. A child's right to protection should override his or her right to make choices if those choices will foreclose on a happy and fulfilled maturity. Article 12 of the CRC requires those

---

260a See *Re L (care: assessment: fair trial)* [2002] EWHC 1379 (Fam), [2002] 2 FLR 730.
261 Ie thereby complying with the requirements of art 8(2). See eg *L v Finland* [2000] 2 FLR 118 and *Scott v United Kingdom* [2000] 1 FLR 958.
262 See Hale LJ in *Re C and B (care order: future harm)* [2001] 1 FLR 611 at [33]–[35].
263 *Olsson v Sweden (No 1)* (1988) 11 EHRR 259 (para 81).
264 See M Brandon et al (1999) ch 5.
265 See M Macleod (1999) esp at 143–144.
266 C Wattam (1999).
267 C McGee (2000) pp 206–212.
268 B Smedley (1999) p 115.
269 Butler-Sloss LJ (1998) p 245.

working with children to allow them to express their views on 'all matters affecting the child', but it only requires those views to be given 'due weight in accordance with the age and maturity of the child'. Schofield points out the temptation of assuming that because a child wants to go home or wants more parental contact, the relationship and parenting cannot be as damaging as the otherwise overwhelming evidence would suggest. [270] But, as she observes, one should not ignore the psychological factors underlying the relationship between an abused child and his or her parents:

> 'Troubled children in crisis, as those subject to care proceedings invariably are, very often and very understandably present entirely conflicting evidence of their wishes and feelings. They may express hopes for the future which are incompatible with what professionals and the children themselves know to be reality; for example, the wish to be at home and to be safe, the wish to be with a parent but for that parent to change.' [271]

Since many abused children may be incapable of making real choices, it is arguable that their right to protection by the state overrides any right to self-determination. Indeed, child protection practitioners are aware, when dealing with an abused child, that any suggestion that he or she may have to leave home to be protected may lead to the child denying the abuse altogether. Consistent with this approach, the law maintains the view that the child's need for protection overrides claims to confidentiality. Practitioners, such as social workers [272] and doctors, [273] confided in by a child (or adult) with information indicating that a child is being abused should not promise to keep this to themselves. Indeed, they should warn the child that this information will normally be passed on to the relevant authorities and may eventually be used in court in the event of child protection proceedings commencing. Even solicitors consulted by children may feel obliged to infringe their confidentiality in the event of receiving information indicating that a child client is being abused. [274] The child should be warned that such information may eventually have to be disclosed to the court in the event of public law proceedings being brought. [275] The controversial result is that an abused child may feel unable to confide safely in any adult. Some feel strongly that since abused children will simply deny abuse because of their fear of the consequences, their choices should be respected. [276] But, as noted above, the dilemma is that an abused child's perceptions may be distorted by the abuse and adults therefore need the freedom to override their wishes and protect them.

A practical reason for the child's own position in child protection work being overlooked is the speed with which decisions to intervene are sometimes taken in the

---

270 G Schofield (1998) p 366.

271 G Schofield (1998) p 364.

272 See *Re M and N (minors) (wardship: freedom of publication)* [1990] 1 All ER 205 at 213, per Butler-Sloss LJ. See also *Re M (minors) (disclosure of evidence)* [1994] 1 FLR 760; *Re D (minors) (adoption reports: confidentiality)* [1996] AC 59; cf *Re C (disclosure)* [1996] 1 FLR 797.

273 If a doctor considers that there is a risk of 'serious harm', eg, in cases of child neglect or abuse, he should first try to persuade the patient to disclose information voluntarily, but should, in any event, pass this on to the relevant authorities, having informed the patient and others of the intention to disclose: British Medical Association (1999). See also General Medical Council (2000), which states (para 18) that a doctor may disclose information 'in the public interest' without his patient's consent where the benefits to an individual or to society of the disclosure outweigh the public and the patient's interest in keeping the information confidential.

274 Solicitors Family Law Association (2002) p 13.

275 The solicitor may be subpoenaed and ordered to disclose documentation or divulge information.

276 Eg F Olsen (1992) pp 210–213.

early stages, leaving practitioners feeling that they have no time to provide the child with explanations. Contrarily, the child may be taken aback by the speed with which child protection practitioners respond to a disclosure, sometimes with no preparation or discussion. [277] Suspicions of serious physical abuse will normally trigger considerable professional anxiety, particularly if a very young child is concerned, quite simply because of the fear that non-intervention may risk the child's death. A local authority may also consider it essential to take immediate steps to protect sexually abused children, particularly if a suspected abuser refuses to take responsibility for the abuse and there are fears that the child may come under pressure to withdraw his or her allegations if left at home. Lady Butler-Sloss nevertheless stressed the need for children to be given a proper explanation of what is going on, why they are being taken away from home and some idea of what will happen to them in the future. [278] But despite guidance urging practitioners to help children understand 'how child protection processes work, how they can be involved …', [279] this does not always occur and there is little legal impetus to ensure that it does. [280] Official inspections indicate that 'children's wishes and feelings were generally not sought and when they were, they were not recorded'; [281] that direct work was not being done with children even when the need to do so was clear, [282] and that social workers did not have sufficient or good enough skills to do such direct work. [283] If children are to be involved in the child protection process, the methods used for doing so should be sympathetic to their particular situation. For example, the growing practice of inviting children to the initial child protection conference may be damaging, particularly if their abusive parents attend as well and if the parents then behave in an aggressive and deeply hostile manner. [284]

Once protective litigation is commenced, for some children their children's guardian may be the first person available to really listen to them [285] and with whom to confide their hopes and fears regarding the outcome of the proceedings. But the guardian may be in a dilemma if, despite the child's opposition, the local authority indicates that, at the interim stage of the care proceedings, they intend to apply for a direction for him or her to undergo a medical or psychiatric examination or assessment. In practice most medical practitioners would be reluctant to examine or assess grown adolescents against their wishes. But the child's guardian may feel obliged to warn a mature child who is 'of sufficient understanding to make an informed decision' that, despite the Children Act 1989 appearing to give him or her a right to refuse to undergo such an assessment, [286] the local authority may obtain a court order overruling

277   See A Wade and H Westcott (1997) p 34.
278   Butler-Sloss LJ (1988) p 245.
279   DH et al (1999) para 7.12.
280   Under Children Act 1989, s 46(3)(c) police officers must inform any child (who appears capable of understanding) of the steps taken to remove him or her into police protection and the reasons for doing so; cf s 44, which imposes no similar obligation on social workers who remove children from home under emergency protection orders. But s 22(4) and (5) require local authorities 'to ascertain the wishes and feelings' of any child they are looking after or proposing to look after, 'so far as is reasonably practicable' and then to give 'due consideration' to such wishes before reaching any decision.
281   SSI (1997) para 3.10. See also SSI (2001 a) para 4.7.
282   SSI (1997) para 3.9.
283   SSI (1997) para 3.6.
284   DH (2002 a) paras 7.17–7.18.
285   J McCausland (2000) p 97. Nevertheless, some children were angry that their guardians appeared to ignore their views (pp 97–98).
286   Children Act, s 38(6) warns courts that although, when making an interim supervision order or an interim care order, they may include a direction for the child to undergo a medical or psychiatric examination or other assessment, a child who is 'of sufficient understanding to make an informed decision' may refuse to submit to it.

such objections. The controversial decision in *South Glamorgan County Council v W and B* [287] demonstrates how the courts' statutory duty to respect a mature adolescent's decision-making abilities regarding assessments can be ignored. There the High Court, exercising its inherent jurisdiction, authorised the forcible removal of an apparently mature 15-year-old from home and her transfer to a specialised psychiatric unit for assessment and appropriate medical treatment. [288] As Lyons rightly observes, the *South Glamorgan* decision conveys to children 'the message that they cannot trust that the clearly expressed "rights" given by Parliament will be safe in the hands of the judges'. [289] The express intention of the Children Act 1989 should surely have been obeyed, leaving the local authority to utilise the mental health legislation to ensure she was assessed and treated. [290]

Chid protection proceedings themselves leave practitioners and judiciary ambivalent over the desirability of the child's real involvement. Masson and Winn Oakley found that many of the adolescents in their research sample [291] only had limited access to their legal representatives and their guardians tended to discourage their active participation in the proceedings. [292] Although in theory, there is nothing to prevent the child attending court and giving evidence in person, [293] in practice this seldom occurs and the child's account of what happened will be relayed to the court by adults under the relaxed hearsay rules. [294] Although some children may want to attend the court hearing to understand better how their future lives are being determined, research suggests that many county court judges and children's guardians are opposed to the idea of their doing so. They assume, perhaps over-paternalistically, that children do not realise what a damaging experience this will be. [295]

Professionals involved in child protection work are all strongly motivated by their common goal – that of ensuring the child's protection and future safety. But even teenagers old enough to comprehend explanations very often experience a sense of complete bewilderment over the speed with which steps are taken to protect them, without any real effort to involve them in the arrangements being made for their care. [296] Research indicates that '[T]his uncertainty and loss of control could serve to magnify the sense of powerlessness which was already a central experience for abused children'. [297] Regrettably, children may end up feeling treated like pawns in an adult game. Consulting children over the steps being taken to protect them need not involve complying with their stated wishes, nor does it undermine the protective intervention itself, it merely involves treating children with respect and sensitivity.

287 [1993] 1 FLR 574.
288 The local authority had been granted an interim care order under the Children Act 1989, s 38(6), including a direction for the girl to undergo a psychiatric examination and assessment, but she refused to leave home and enter the specialist unit where the assessment was to take place. Despite his view that she did not lack *Gillick* competence, Douglas Brown J ([1993] 1 FLR 574 at 584) authorised the local authority 'to take all necessary steps to bring the child to the doctors so that she may be assessed and treated'.
289 T Lyons (1994) p 87.
290 Discussed in more depth in chapter 5.
291 20 children and young people aged between 8 and 18.
292 J Masson and M Winn Oakley (1999) p 117.
293 Children Act 1989, s 96(1) and (2).
294 Children Act 1989, s 96(3)–(7) and Children (Admissibility of Hearsay Evidence) Order 1993, SI 1993/621.
295 Discussed in more detail in chapter 7.
296 See E Farmer and M Owen (1995) pp 73–74.
297 E Farmer and M Owen (1995) p 72.

(8) CONCLUSION

The Children Act Now: Messages from Research observes:

> 'Simultaneously safeguarding and promoting children's welfare has been difficult to achieve. It is clear that, on the one hand, some children have not been made the subject of care proceedings soon enough. In other cases, the operation of a high threshold has led to insufficient emphasis on intervention at an early stage.' [298]

Recent reports, notably the Climbié report [299] and that of the joint Chief Inspectors', [300] suggest that this observation gravely understates the true state of affairs – indeed, it appears that large numbers of abused children are probably going undetected and unprotected. Arguably, many of the most unsatisfactory features of the child protection process are attributable to lack of resources and poor practice and not to the legislation itself. Nevertheless, the courts themselves cannot be acquitted of the charge that the legislation is being undermined by an excessive legalism. In such a climate of opinion, it is hardly surprising that child protection intervention tends to polarise hostility between parents and state, with the child's own perspectives being forgotten. When practitioners' efforts are concentrated on an over-technical court process, it is also understandable that protection is too often seen as a means to an end, with insufficient attention being given to dealing with children's ongoing needs, for example, for follow-up services in the form of treatment and therapy. [301] Overall, the Children Act 1989 contrives reasonably well to ensure that the state's role in fulfilling children's rights to protection is promoted with some sensitivity. Finding the ideal balance between undue state interference which impinges on parents and children alike and an approach which so respects family privacy that parents are free to abuse their children in private is probably as remote as finding the Holy Grail.

298 DH (2001 a) p 143.
299 H Laming (2003).
300 DH (2002 a).
301 E Farmer (1997) pp 161–162.

BIBLIOGRAPHY

NB many of these publications can be obtained on the relevant organisation's website.

Audit Commission, *Seen But Not Heard: Co-ordinating Community Child Health and Social Services for Children in Need* (1994) Audit Commission, HMSO.

Butler-Sloss LJ (Chairman), *Report of the Inquiry into Child Abuse in Cleveland 1987* Cm 412 (1988) Her Majesty's Stationery Office.

British Medical Association, *Confidentiality and disclosure of health information* (1999) BMA.

Brandon M et al, *Safeguarding Children with the Children Act 1989* (1999) The Stationery Office.

Cicchetti D and Carlson V (eds), *Child Maltreatment: Theory and research on the causes and consequences of child abuse and neglect* (1989) Cambridge University Press.

Cleaver H et al, *Children's Needs – Parenting Capacity: The impact of parental mental illness, problem alcohol and drug use, and domestic violence on children's development* (1999) The Stationery Office.

Cretney C, Masson J, Bailey-Harris R, *Principles of Family Law* (2002) Sweet and Maxwell.

Department of Health (DH), *Child Abuse: A Study of Inquiry Reports 1980–1989* (1991 a) HMSO.

Department of Health (DH), *The Children Act 1989 Guidance and Regulations* Vols 1 and 2 (1991 b) HMSO.

Department of Health (DH), *Child Protection: Messages from Research* (1995) HMSO.

Department of Health (DH), *Quality Protects Circular: Transforming Children's Services* DH (LAC (98) 28) (1998 a) DoH.

Department of Health (DH), *Caring for Children Away from Home: Messages from Research* (1998 b) John Wiley and Sons.

Department of Health (DH), *The Children Act Now: Messages from Research* (2001 a) The Stationery Office.

Department of Health (DH), *The Children Act Report 2000* (2001 b) DH Publications.

Department of Health (DH), *Safeguarding Children: A joint Chief Inspectors' Report on Arrangements to Safeguard Children* (2002 a) DH Publications.

Department of Health (DH), *The Children Act Report 2001* (2002 b) DH Publications.

Department of Health (DH), and Department for Education and Employment *Children's Services Planning Guidance* (1996).

Department of Health (DH), Home Office and Department for Education and Employment (DH et al) *Working Together to Safeguard Children: A guide to inter-agency working to safeguard and promote the welfare of children* (1999) The Stationery Office.

Department of Health (DH), Home Office and Department for Education and Employment (DH et al) *Framework for the Assessment of Children in Need and their Families* (2000) The Stationery Office.

Department of Health and Social Security (DHSS), *Child Abuse: A Study of Inquiry Reports 1973–1981* (1982) HMSO.

Department of Health and Social Security (DHSS), et al *The Law on Child Care and Family Services* Cm 62 (1987) HMSO.

Dingwall R, Eekelaar J and Murray T, *The Protection of Children: State Intervention and Family Life* (1983) Blackwell.

Farmer E, 'Protection and child welfare: Striking the balance' in N Parton (ed) *Child Protection and Family Support: Tensions, contradictions and possibilities* (1997) Routledge.

Farmer E and Owen M, *Child Protection Practice: Private Risks and Public Remedies* (1995) HMSO.

Farmer E and Pollock S, *Sexually Abused and Abusing Children in Substitute Care* (1998) Wiley.

Fortin J, 'Rights Brought Home for Children' (1999) 62 Modern Law Review 350.

Fox Harding L, *Perspectives in Child Care Policy* (1997) Longman.

General Medical Council, *Confidentiality, Protecting and Providing Information* (2000) GMC.

Gibbons J, Conroy S and Bell C, *Operating the Child Protection System* (1995) HMSO.

Goldstein J, Freud A and Solnit A, *Beyond the Best Interests of the Child* (1973) New York Free Press.

Goldstein J, Freud A and Solnit A, *Before the Best Interests of the Child* (1980) Burnett Books Ltd.

Hallett C, *Interagency Co-ordination in Child Protection* (1995) HMSO.

Hayes J and Hayes M, 'Child Protection in the Court of Appeal' (2002) Family Law 817.

Hayes M, 'Reconciling protection of children with justice for parents in cases of alleged child abuse' (1997) 17 Legal Studies 1.

Hayes M, 'Child protection – from principles and policies to practice' (1998) 10 Child and Family Law Quarterly 119.

Hayes M and Williams C, *Family Law: Principles, Policy and Practice* (1999) Butterworths.

Hemingway I and Williams C, '*Re M and R: Re H and R*' (1997) Family Law 740.

HM Treasury, *Spending Review: New Public Spending Plans 2003 – 2006, Opportunity and Security for all: Investing in an enterprising, fairer Britain* Cm 5570 (2002) The Stationery Office.

Hester M et al, *Making an Impact: Children and Domestic Violence, A Reader* (2000) Jessica Kingsley Publishers.

Hetherington R et al, *Protecting Children: Messages from Europe* (1997) Russell House Publishing.

Hobbs C, Hanks H and Wynne J, *Child Abuse and Neglect: A Clinician's Handbook* (1999) Churchill Livingstone.

Home Office, with DH, *Memorandum of Good Practice on Video Recorded Interviews with Child Witnesses for Criminal Proceedings* (1992) HMSO.

Home Office et al *Achieving Best Evidence in Criminal Proceedings: Guidance for Vulnerable or Intimidated Witnesses, Including Children* (2002) Home Office Communication Directorate.

Humphreys C and Kaye M, 'Third party applications for protection orders: opportunities, ambiguities and traps' (1997) 19 Journal of Social Welfare and Family Law 403.

Hunt J, 'A moving target – care proceedings as a dynamic process' (1998) 10 Child and Family Law Quarterly 281.

Hunt J and Macleod A, *The Best-Laid Plans: Outcomes of Judicial Decisions in Child Protection Proceedings* (1999) The Stationery Office.

Jones D, 'The effectiveness of Intervention' in M Adcock and R White (eds) *Significant Harm: its management and outcome* (1998) Significant Publications.

Jones D and Ramchandani P, *Child Sexual Abuse* (1999) Radcliffe Medical Press.

Kaganas F, '*B v B (Occupation Order)* and *Chalmers v Johns* Occupation orders under the Family Law Act 1996' (1999) 11 Child and Family Law Quarterly 193.

King M and Trowell J, *Children's Welfare and the Law: The Limits of Legal Intervention* (1992) Sage.

Laming H, *The Victoria Climbié Inquiry: Report on an Inquiry by Lord Laming* Cm 5730 (2003) HMSO.

Law Commission, *Domestic Violence and Occupation of the Family Home* Law Com No 207 (1992) The Stationery Office.

Littlechild B, 'Does Family Support Ensure the Protection of Children?' (1998) 7 Child Abuse Review 116.

London Borough of Brent, *'A Child in Trust'. The report of the panel of inquiry into the circumstances surrounding the death of Jasmine Beckford* (1985).

Lowe N and Douglas G, *Bromley's Family Law* (1999) Butterworths.

Lynch M and Roberts J, *Consequences of Child Abuse* (1982) Academic Press.

Lyons T ,'What's happened to the child's "right" to refuse? – South Glamorgan County Council v W & B' (1994) 6 Journal of Child Law 84.

McCausland J, *Guarding Children's Interests: The Contributions of Guardians ad Litem in Court Proceedings* (2000) The Children's Society.

Macleod M, '"Don't Just Do It": Children's Access to Help and Protection' in N Parton and C Wattam (eds) *Child Sexual Abuse: Responding to the Experiences of Children* (1999) John Wiley and Sons.

McGee C, *Childhood Experiences of Domestic Violence* (2000) Jessica Kingsley Publishers.

Masson J and Winn Oakley M, *Out of Hearing: Representing Children in Care Proceedings* (1999) John Wiley and Sons.

Olsen F, 'Children's Rights: Some Feminist Approaches to the United Nations Convention on the Rights of the Child' in P Alston, S Parker and J Seymour (eds) *Children, Rights and the Law* (1992) Clarendon Press.

Parkinson P and Humphreys C, 'Children who witness domestic violence: the implications for child protection' (1998) 9 Child and Family Law Quarterly 147.

Parton N, 'Child Protection and Family Support: Current debates and future prospects' in N Parton (ed) *Child Protection and Family Support: Tensions, contradictions and possibilities* (1999) Routledge.

Rose W, 'An Overview of the Developments of Services – the Relationship between Protection and Family Support and the Intentions of the Children Act 1989' (1994) DH Paper for Sieff Conference.

Rose W, 'Working Together – 10 Years On' (1996) 7 Children Act Services News Supplement.

Schofield G, 'Making sense of the ascertainable wishes and feelings of insecurely attached children' (1998) 10 Child and Family Law Quarterly 363.

Sharland E et al, *Professional Intervention in Child Sexual Abuse* (1996) HMSO.

Smedley B, 'Child Protection: Facing up to fear' in P Milner and B Carolin (eds) *Time to listen to children: Personal and professional communication* (1999) Routledge.

Social Services Inspectorate (SSI), *Domestic Violence and Social Care* (1995) DH Publications.

Social Services Inspectorate (SSI), *Responding to Families in Need: Inspection of Assessment, Planning and Decision-Making in Family Support Services* (1997) DH Publications.

Social Services Inspectorate (SSI), *Getting Family Support Right: Inspection of the Delivery of Family Support Services* (1999) DH Publications.

Social Services Inspectorate (SSI), *Developing quality to protect children: SSI Inspection of Children's Services* (2001 a) DH Publications.

Social Services Inspectorate (SSI), *Modern Social Services: a commitment to deliver, The 10th Annual Report of the Chief Inspector of Social Services, 2000/2001* (2001 b) DH Publications.

Social Services Inspectorate (SSI), *Modern Social Services: a commitment to reform, The 11th Annual Report of the Chief Inspector of Social Services, 2001/2002* (2002) DH Publications.

Solicitors Family Law Association, *Solicitors Family Law Association Guide to Good Practice for Solicitors Acting for Children* (2002) SFLA.

Spencer J, 'Evidence in child abuse cases – too high a price for too high a standard? *Re M (a minor) (appeal) (No 2)*' (1994) 6 Journal of Child Law 160.

Tapper C, 'Evidential privilege in cases involving children' (1997) 9 Child and Family Law Quarterly 1.

Thoburn J, Lewis A and Shemmings D, *Paternalism or Partnership? Family Involvement in the Child Protection Process* (1995) HMSO.

Tunstill J and Aldgate J, *Services for Families in Need: From Policy to Practice* (2000) The Stationery Office.

Wade A and Westcott H, 'No easy answers: children's perspectives on investigative interviews' in H Westcott and J Jones (eds) *Perspectives on the Memorandum* (1997) Ashgate.

Wall J, with Hamilton I, *A Handbook for Expert Witnesses in Children Act Cases* (2000) Family Law.

Wattam C, 'Can filtering processes be rationalised?' in N Parton (ed) *Child Protection and Family Support: Tensions, contradictions and possibilities* (1997) Routledge.

Wattam C, 'Confidentiality and the Social Organisation of Telling' in N Parton and C Wattam (eds) *Child Sexual Abuse: Responding to the Experiences of Children* (1999) John Wiley and Sons.

White R, 'Family Practice' (1995) 145 New Law Journal 187.

White R, 'Family Practice' (2000) 150 New Law Journal 193.

Wolfe D, *Child Abuse: Implications for child development and psychopathology* (1987) Sage.

Woodward C and Fortune D, 'Coping, Surviving and Healing from Child Sexual Abuse', in N Parton and C Wattam (eds) *Child Sexual Abuse: Responding to the Experiences of Children* (1999) Wiley.

Chapter 16

Right to protection in state care and to state accountability

(1) INTRODUCTION

Society expects parents to fulfil their children's rights to care, protection, optimum health and a good education. Parents should also promote their children's capacity for independence and take an interest in their future careers. Theoretically, when a local authority obtains a care order over a child, it is deemed to share parental responsibilities with his or her parents.[1] In practice, the sharing is nominal, since parents cannot demand a right to influence events, even though they should be consulted over decisions regarding their child's future care.[2] Consequently, the state effectively takes over the parenting role and should fulfil the same duties as birth parents. Indeed, the 'no order' principle[3] emphasises that by authorising an abused child's removal from home under a care order, the court is expecting the state to do a better job than the parents. But as case law and research indicates, the assumption that intervention to protect abused children will achieve a real improvement in their lives is all too often over-optimistic. Indeed, as in *Re F; F v Lambeth London Borough Council*,[4] the state sometime makes matters a great deal worse. In that case, as a result of the local authority's long-term neglect of two boys whilst in care, both suffered 'significant educational, emotional, psychological, social and behavioural harm'.[5] As Munby J observed:

'... it is a matter of gravity when the State's failure relates to its duties in relation to children and their families. It becomes a matter of the utmost gravity when the failure, as here, follows the intervention of the State in removing children against their parents' wishes from the parental home.'[6]

---

1   Children Act 1989, s 33(3) and (5).
2   Children Act 1989, ss 33(3)(b) and 22(4) and (5).
3   Children Act 1989, s 1(5).
4   [2002] 1 FLR 217: two boys aged 8 and 4, having been removed from home under care orders, were left without adequate care plans for eight years. Munby J found (at para 30(6)) that the local authority had not only failed to comply with their duty to safeguard the boys' welfare under the Children Act 1989, s 22(3)(a), but also to arrange reasonable parental contact under s 34(1)(a) and with their extended family under Sch 2, para 15(1).
5   [2002] 1 FLR 217 at para 30(4).
6   [2002] 1 FLR 217 at para 42.

The state's record as parent has been a disastrously poor one for many years. The late 1990s saw a mounting chorus of disapproval. The scathingly critical Utting Report[7] was followed by further damning indictments of the standard of care provided for children looked after by the state.[8] The Health Minister acknowledged:

> 'Too many children taken into care to protect and help them have received neither protection nor help. Instead they have been abused and molested. Many more have been let down, ignored, shifted from place to place, school to school and often simply turned out to fend for themselves when they turned 16.'[9]

Despite the measures introduced to improve the standard of children's care services[10] and the new need to fulfil the government's objectives regarding children receiving state care,[11] too many children still receive an inadequate service from social services departments. Planning for their future care is often poor or non-existent,[12] too many experience numerous foster placements[13] and the overall standard of physical and mental[14] health[15] and education[16] of 'looked after' children[17] continues to compare

7   W Utting (1997).

8   Inter alia: Social Services Inspectorate (hereafter SSI) (1998); House of Commons Health Committee (1998); Department of Health (hereafter DH) (1998 a).

9   DH Press Release 1998/0494. Statement in the House of Commons by Frank Dobson, Health Secretary, 5 November 1998.

10 See inter alia: the Quality Protects programme introduced in 1998, initially for three years, later extended to five years, and backed by £885m, DH (1998 b). Children's social services are required to meet a range of measurable performance indicators and targets for delivery of care, and to submit to the Department of Health 'annual quality protects management action plans' (MAPs) and progress reports; the establishment of the National Standards Commission to supervise and improve, through registration and inspection, the standard of residential care offered by all local agencies, public and private alike, including children's homes (see Care Standards Act 2000, ss 6–7). Within the Commission, a dedicated officer, the Children's Rights Director, is concerned solely with children's services; the reorganisation and improvement of the training and work practices of all social care staff, by the General Social Care Council (established by Pt IV of the Care Standards Act 2000); an improved system for preventing unsuitable people working with children, established, inter alia, by the Child Protection Act 1999.

11 See esp Quality Protects objectives for local authorities: C4.0 – looked after children to 'gain maximum life chance benefits from educational opportunities, health care and social care; C1.2 – to reduce the number of changes of placements for children looked after; C3.1 – to help improve the educational attainment of children in need; C3.2 – to ensure that children in need have the opportunity to enjoy a standard of health and development as good as that which can be expected for the general population ...'

12 Discussed below.

13 The government's aim was to reduce to no more than 16%, by 2001, the number of looked after children with three or more placements in one year. Nevertheless, many councils' fostering practice continues to show long-term instability in foster placements. See SSI (2002 b) ch 4: only two out of seven councils inspected had provided more than 50% of their children in long-term foster care (ie more than four years continuously in foster care) with at least two years in the same foster home. In the remainder, only 40% or less of children received this rate of stability. See also N Lowe and M Murch (2002) pp 99–105.

14 Large numbers of looked after children have mental health problems. See DH (2000 a) para 2.4, citing 67%.

15 Of a sample of looked after children from four local authorities in 1997/98, 21% had an ongoing physical health condition or disability and 12% had not visited a dentist during a year. See DH (2000 b) Table 5.2, p 53. See also the research and statistics summarised in S Howell (2001).

16 Large numbers of looked after children aged between 14 and 16 do not attend school regularly and many are excluded. See DH (2000 a) citing 25% (para 2.4). LEAs and social service departments must now comply with extensive guidance on the education of children in care. See Department for Education and Employment/DH (2000).

17 Discussed below.

very unfavourably with children brought up at home. Furthermore, many of the government targets seem over optimistic.[18]

Some local authorities are failing to comply with their clear statutory duties regarding vulnerable children in a way which has been described as 'scandalous'.[19] Such derelictions of duty not only infringe domestic law but the state's international obligations towards children removed into state care.[20] Indeed, the state's poor record lends some support to the laissez-faire views of Goldstein, Freud and Solnit. They pointed out that the state cannot always offer abused children anything better or, indeed, compensate them for what they have missed in their own home. 'By its intrusion the state may make a bad situation worse; indeed, it may turn a tolerable or even a good situation into a bad one.'[21]

This chapter assesses the extent to which the law encourages the state to make a bad situation better. Many more children are placed with foster carers than in residential homes; nevertheless, the latter service has been selected for special consideration due to the many reports highlighting the dangers of children suffering re-abuse whilst in residential care. The chapter considers the problems of 'control' experienced by residential establishments and the child's own perspectives whilst in state care and on leaving care. It then proceeds to consider the extent to which abused children can bring the state to account for failing to protect them at all or adequately.

(2) THE COURTS AND LOCAL AUTHORITY PLANNING FOR LOOKED AFTER CHILDREN

(A) The background

By the end of the 1990s, research was indicating that considerable improvements were necessary in local authority planning for the long-term care of all 'looked after children'.[22] These children fall broadly into two groups: those who are considered in sufficient danger to warrant the local authority formally assuming their care with the assistance of care orders,[23] and those who are accommodated with foster carers, or in residential homes, under voluntary arrangements with their parents.[24] Mounting criticism of local authorities' failure to plan properly for the future upbringing of all children being accommodated away from home was reinforced by the public outcry

---

18   The official targets for the educational attainment of looked after children required by 2001, 50% and by 2003, 75% of children leaving care at 16 to have gained at least one GCSE or GNVQ equivalent. 94% of 16-year-olds in the general population achieve such qualifications. By 2001/02, only 40% of children leaving care had achieved such a result and official statistics indicate that the significant improvements necessary to achieve the 75% target will not be achieved. See DH (2002 a) pp 27–28.
19   See Munby J in *Re F; F v Lambeth London Borough Council* [2002] 1 FLR 217 at 231.
20   See art 20 of the CRC entitling children removed from home into state care 'to special protection and assistance'.
21   J Goldstein, A Freud and A Solnit (1980) p 13.
22   Under Children Act 1989, s 22(1) and (2) a 'looked after child' is either a child who is the subject of a care order or a child being provided with accommodation under s 20 for a continuous period of more than 24 hours. Under s 22(3)(a), a local authority must 'safeguard and promote the welfare' of any looked after child.
23   The local authority thereby acquires parental responsibility, which is shared with the parents. See Children Act 1989, s 33(3) and (5).
24   Under Children Act 1989, s 20(1). Since the local authority lacks parental responsibility over these children, accommodation can only be provided with the parents' agreement. See s 20(7) and (8) and *R v Tameside Metropolitan Borough Council, ex p J* [2000] 1 FLR 942.

over the publication of the Waterhouse Report.[25] This suggested that too many children looked after by the state were being placed in residential care, only to be severely abused. Indeed, the radical reform of the adoption law was born largely out of two interlinking resolves.[26] The first was to reduce the delays and ineffective planning undermining this area of social work practice. The second was to ensure that far more looked after children were provided with adoptive families, rather than being left to 'drift in care', at risk of abuse by unsuitable carers.

These resolves were mapped out by the *Prime Minister's Review of Adoption* (PIU report),[27] and then reiterated in the White Paper on adoption.[28] The government considered that too many children were waiting far too long for permanent homes and that adoption should be seen as the solution. It clearly sympathised with critics like Bracewell J, who stated forcefully:

> 'For too long there has been a culture in which adoption has been regarded as the equivalent of failure and therefore a procedure to be considered only as a last resort when all else has been tried and has not succeeded.'[29]

Local authorities were castigated for traditionally exhausting the possibility of rehabilitation before adoption was even considered. This produced considerable delays in formulating plans for the child in the event of rehabilitation later proving impossible.[30] Such policies were being pursued, despite the government's Quality Protects programme encouraging a greater use of adoption as a means of providing looked after children with permanent families.[31]

(B)   Accommodated children

Local authorities were running into difficulties with children being accommodated on a voluntary basis, particularly those children who had been rejected by their parents.[32] Despite not wishing to take their children home, these parents were often unable to put their children's interests first. In such circumstances, foster carers and social workers felt uncertain about their legal powers and their role because of their awareness that the parents retained parental responsibility.[33] Social services departments often doubted their ability to obtain care orders in circumstances where the child had been away from home for long periods.[34] They also commonly rejected adoption on the basis that there would be no parental co-operation. But, as the PIU report commented, it is 'all too easy, however, where there is no court process driving the development of the Care Plan for accommodated children to wait for long periods with no active planning for their future or consideration of whether care proceedings should be instituted'.[35]

---

25   R Waterhouse (2000).
26   See also discussion in chapter 14.
27   Performance and Innovation Unit (hereafter PIU) (2000).
28   DH (2000 a) ch 2.
29   *Re D and K (care plan: twin track planning)* [1999] 2 FLR 872 at 874.
30   PIU (2000) ch 3, esp pp 25–26 and para 6.9.
31   See Quality Protects, Sub-objective C1.3: 'To maximise the contribution adoption can make to providing permanent families for children in appropriate cases.'
32   See G Schofield (2000 a) esp pp 354–359. See also G Schofield et al (2000 b).
33   See above.
34   G Schofield (2000 a) p 357. See also PIU (2000) para 3.32.
35   PIU (2000) para 3.30.

Through its new highly regulated adoption service, accompanied by adoption targets, standards and guidance,[36] the government hopes that: 'Achieving permanence for the child will be a key consideration from the day that they become looked after.'[37] Indeed, social services departments are now obliged to apply for adoption placement orders in relation to children they are looking after, if they consider that such children *should* be adopted and if the threshold criteria for a care order can be made out.[38] Furthermore, children in long-term foster care, for whom adoption is considered inappropriate, will gain far greater stability in their placements under the new 'special guardianship' orders.[39] Foster carers, with the support of the local authority,[40] will thereby obtain parental responsibility for their charges. Their ability to make decisions relating to the children's upbringing without parental interference,[41] will immeasurably strengthen foster carers' position and status, particularly vis-à-vis unco-operative parents.

(C) Children removed into care

The changes in the law are not, of course, confined to children being accommodated by local authorities under voluntary arrangements with their parents. The comment made by the PIU report, noted above, regarding the lack of planning for accommodated children, implied that for those who were the subject of care proceedings, things were different, and better. For these children, drift and delay were avoided – because the local authority would concentrate on developing comprehensive plans for the child's future upbringing. Unfortunately, research published in the late 1990s, suggested that such optimism was misplaced. Indeed, care proceedings seemed often to be used primarily to ensure that assessments were done and pressure was put on parents during the preparatory period prior to litigation, with many cases not ending in a care order and less than half of the children involved going into substitute care.[42] Given the expense, financial and emotional, of court proceedings, there was some irony in researchers concluding that 'it would probably have been possible to achieve the same result, with less stress to all concerned, without making an order'.[43]

Even the increased numbers of children for whom care orders were apparently fully justified[44] faced a gloomy prospect in the decade following implementation of the Children Act 1989. Researchers, government inspection teams and case law recorded the same message, that many of these children's lives were not being improved

---

36 See discussion in chapter 14, pp 441–442.
37 DH (2001 c) p 12, para 10.
38 See Adoption and Children Act 2002, ss 22(1)(c) and (d) and 21(2)(b). Eg parents who undermine the stability of their child's long-term foster placement by their behaviour towards him/her might thereby fulfil the threshold criteria under the Children Act 1989, s 31, so triggering the local authority's duty to place him/her for adoption.
39 DH (2000 a) paras 5.10–5.11.
40 Under Children Act 1989, ss 10(5)(c), 10(5A) and 14A(5)(d), a foster carer can apply for a special guardianship order if the local authority consents or if they have been caring for the child for at least one year.
41 Children Act 1989, s 14C(1)(b).
42 J Hunt (1998) p 287.
43 See M Brandon et al (1999) p 151, regarding 46% of the 28 cases in which an interim or full care order had been obtained.
44 Between 1995/6 and 2000, there was a 23% increase in care orders and a 13% decrease in s 20 placements. The volume of care provided under care orders increased by 25% and that provided under s 20 reduced by 2%. See DH (2001 a) para 1.18.

by state intervention, despite the no order principle[45] indicating that care orders should not be made unless they could produce improvements. According to Hunt and Macleod, at the end of court proceedings –

'it is natural to hope that the placement plan which has been formulated will be achieved, that this will be accomplished expeditiously and without unnecessary disruption, that the placement will be stable and that the child will do well.'[46]

These researchers found that only a minority of children were so fortunate.[47] Substantial numbers of children waited for between six and 18 months before adoptive or long-term foster placements, with a small proportion remaining unplaced several years after proceedings were over.[48] The unplaced children did particularly badly, with the care experience doing little to ameliorate their problems and, for some, even exacerbating them.[49] Extrapolating from their own data, they concluded:

'In national terms this means that every year nearly 4,000 children, already vulnerable by virtue of their experiences at home, and then through their involvement in the legal process, are subject to further vicissitudes once that process is over.'[50]

The government's own inspection teams reached similar conclusions, indicating that individual care plans were paying too much attention to short-term solutions rather than long-term outcomes for children. Social workers working with children who had come into care under such orders were 'often' even unclear over what the objectives of their intervention had been.[51] Furthermore, plans were not reviewed frequently and too many children were allowed to 'drift in care' due to too little managerial oversight of social workers' work.[52] This drift tended to undermine any long-term plans for the child to be adopted, which in turn were often hampered by delays and compromised by –

'… an inability to make decisions or clarify early enough what was the desired outcome for the child. Poor planning, lack of clear thinking, limited placement choice, restricted budgets, delay in widening the net to find an appropriate placement all had real costs for the child.'[53]

This depressing picture was reinforced by case law, with the courts criticising local authorities for failing to plan properly for the future of children received into care or to deal adequately with their health and education needs.[54]

Delays in finding permanent homes for children who were the subject of care proceedings were again being caused, at least in part, by social workers' reluctance to consider adoption until all chances of rehabilitation were explored and exhausted. The government guidance now urges local authorities to consider adoption far earlier. This is reinforced by the local authorities' new obligation to apply for placement

---

45   Children Act 1989, s 1(5).
46   J Hunt and A Macleod (1999) p 189.
47   J Hunt and A Macleod (1999). Furthermore, one third of the children in their research sample had to cope with the insecurity and/or disappointment of changed or unfulfilled plans (p 186).
48   J Hunt and A Macleod (1999) pp 188–189.
49   J Hunt and A Macleod (1999) p 166.
50   J Hunt and A Macleod (1999) p 189. This research was carried out in the early 1990s, but subsequent research provides similar results, see J Harwin and M Owen (2002) pp 67–72 and J Harwin and M Owen (2003).
51   See SSI (1999 a) para 6.25.
52   See SSI (1999 a) para 6.28.
53   SSI (1999 b) para 12.5. See also SSI (2000) para 3.20, indicating that whilst babies were being placed with adoptive families within six months of being looked after, one in five of the older children were waiting over three years.
54   See Munby J in *Re F; F v Lambeth London Borough Council* [2002] 1 FLR 217 at para 32.

orders in relation to a variety of children: those already under care orders, or the subject of care applications; those accommodated children in relation to whom the local authority considers that the threshold criteria for a care order can be made out, *and* are satisfied 'ought to be placed for adoption'.[55] Consequently far more applications for care orders will be accompanied by applications for placement orders or by care plans involving the child being placed for adoption quite rapidly.[56] The guidance also addresses the difficulties posed by the children for whom rehabilitation with their own family is considered still possible, but whose parents are deemed unlikely to make or sustain the necessary changes in their parenting. In such cases, alongside plans for their rehabilitation, the care plan must also contain detailed plans for the child to be provided with a permanent home through placement with the extended family or through adoption, without further delay.[57]

(D)   Care planning – the role of the courts?

Clearly the choice between rehabilitation, adoption or fostering will, in practice, depend on a number of interrelating factors, such as the child's age, background, degree of contact with birth parents and extended birth family, and even the extent to which the local authority favours adoption.[58] Nevertheless, Lowe and Murch refer to the fact that, in terms of planning for children, and compared with adoption, long-term fostering has become 'something of a "Cinderella option"'.[59] Furthermore, despite not having found any evidence of misuse of adoption, they refer to the danger that –

> 'authorities, keen to meet their percentage target for adoption, may too hastily rule out rehabilitation with the birth parents or wider family, particularly for young children who are likely to be thought more adoptable.'[60]

This new pressure on local authorities to find adoptive homes for children received into care also presents the courts with a dilemma – one which was ignored by the PIU report when it criticised some courts for hampering adoption plans by giving birth parents 'the benefit of the doubt' and insisting on repeat attempts at rehabilitation.[61] Indeed, social services departments and the courts are now expected to walk a tightrope. On the one hand, there is the need to meet the government's targets for providing the child with an alternative permanent home in the event of rehabilitation failing. But on the other hand, they must fulfil their obligation, under article 8 of the ECHR, to allow parents and children to enjoy their family life together without undue state

---

55   See Adoption and Children Act 2002, s 22(1)(d).
56   Ie, if adoption is included in the care plan, a match should be approved with suitable adopters within six months of the care order being obtained. See DH (2001 d) Standard A3(b).
57   Ie, the local authority should be pursuing 'contingency planning'. There are two kinds: 'concurrent planning', whereby the child is placed with foster carers who will not only support the parents in their attempts to fulfil the rehabilitation plan, but also, if such a plan fails, take over the child's care permanently. Alternatively, 'parallel or twin track planning' may be used. This involves the child remaining with his or her birth parents under a rehabilitation plan, alongside a detailed plan for alternative permanent placement, in the event of this failing. See DH (2001 c) p 13. See also *Re D and K (care plan: twin track planning)* [1999] 2 FLR 872, per Bracewell J, at 874 and *Re R (child of a teenage mother)* [2000] 2 FLR 660, per Bracewell J, at 662. See also N Lowe and M Murch (2002) pp 8–9.
58   See N Lowe and M Murch (2002) pp 141–143.
59   N Lowe and M Murch (2002) p 147.
60   N Lowe and M Murch (2002) p 149.
61   PIU (2000) para 3.62. See *Re D (grant of care order: refusal of freeing order)* [2001] 1 FLR 862, for an example of such judicial optimism, at first instance.

interference. When deciding whether state interference with parents' family life is 'necessary',[62] the reasons for the intervention must be sufficient and the intervention itself proportionate to the aim of protecting the child in question.[63]

The domestic courts may not be satisfied that the initial decision to remove a child from home was a proportionate response to an abusive situation.[64] But even if all agree that the child's need for protection fully justified the local authority's interference with the parents' family life, the courts must consider the Strasbourg jurisprudence interpreting the states' duties regarding the children removed from home. As noted earlier, the European Court of Human Rights has consistently stressed that such interference must be seen as a temporary measure only and that efforts should always be made to reintegrate the child at home as soon as possible.[65] The way in which care proceedings had been allied with freeing a child for adoption was recently criticised by the Court because this had decreased the possibility of exploring future rehabilitation and reunification.[66] This suggests that, despite local authorities coming under increasing government pressure to ensure that more children are adopted from care and more quickly, care plans envisaging adoption should be critically scrutinised. Since imposing an adoption order on parents against their wishes is a drastic form of state interference with their family life,[67] the domestic courts should always consider whether the child's need for security could be promoted by some less radical arrangement.[68]

Hopefully, the House of Lords' decision in *Re B (a child) (adoption by one natural parent)*[69] will not suggest to the lower courts that there is no need to question the local authority's view that adoption is the best option for the child.[70] The adoption and fostering team may not have weighed up all the alternatives before reaching such a conclusion. For example, turning a long-term fostering arrangement into one of adoption with generous contact may not be a proportionate response to the child's need for permanency when he or she has a strong relationship with his or her birth parents.[71] In such circumstances, a special guardianship order might be a good way of strengthening the foster carers' position.[72] Although not entirely risk free, local authorities might also start making greater efforts to promote 'kinship care',[73]

---

62   Ie under art 8(2) of the ECHR.
63   Eg *Scott v United Kingdom* [2000] 1 FLR 958 at 971 and *K and T v Finland* [2001] 2 FLR 707 at para 168.
64   See Hale LJ in *Re C and B (care order: future harm)* [2001] 1 FLR 611 at paras 33–35.
65   Eg, inter alia: *Olsson v Sweden* (1988) 11 EHRR 259; *Johansen v Norway* (1996) 23 EHRR 33; *K and T v Finland* [2001] 2 FLR 707; *S and G v Italy* [2000] 2 FLR 771; *EP v Italy* (2001) 31 EHRR 17. See discussion in chapter 14, pp 442–443.
66   *P, C and S v United Kingdom* [2002] 2 FLR 631 at paras 98 and 104.
67   *Re B (adoption by one natural parent to exclusion of other)* [2001] 1 FLR 589, per Hale LJ at para 37. This decision was reversed by the House of Lords, but the principle referred to by Hale LJ remains an important one.
68   See also discussion in chapter 14.
69   [2001] UKHL 70, [2002] 1 All ER 641, esp per Lord Nicholls of Birkenhead at [31].
70   Discussed in chapter 14.
71   See *Re B (adoption order)* [2001] EWCA Civ 347, [2001] 2 FLR 26: the Court of Appeal considered that a residence order in favour of the child's foster carer was preferable to an adoption order. It would preserve the birth father's art 8 rights and was a more proportionate response to the child's need for a permanent home, given his strong relationship with his birth father and his foster carer's willingness to continue caring for him on such a basis.
72   Foster carers thereby acquire parental responsibility to the exclusion of the birth parents. See Children Act 1989, s 14C(1)(a) and (b). Alternatively, foster carers or relatives might apply for a residence order combined with an order made under the Children Act 1989, s 91(14) restraining the birth parents from applying for any further court orders without court leave.
73   See J Hunt (2001).

involving care by members of the child's extended family, perhaps with the security of a residence order.[74]

(E) Care proceedings – at home or away?

Social workers may decide that some abused children are very obviously not candidates for adoption because there are good chances of their being able to return home in the near future. Indeed, local authorities may sometimes consider that abused children, who are in no immediate danger, can be left at home with their parents. But they nevertheless apply for a care order, so that in the event of the home situation deteriorating, the children can be quickly removed, without going back to court.[75] The courts are increasingly encouraging local authorities to seek supervision orders in such situations,[76] in order to comply with the principle of proportionality.[77] Nonetheless, supervision orders remain extremely unpopular with many practitioners, being seen as 'a complete waste of time' and 'toothless'.[78] They carry less control than care orders;[79] furthermore, local authorities have no real sanction when parents or relatives fail to comply with the directions they contain.[80]

In some situations, the boot may be on the other foot, so to speak.[81] Whilst the court may agree with the local authority's wish to obtain a care order, considering the parents to be extremely dangerous, it may doubt the wisdom of the local authority's plan to return the abused child home, once the care order has been made. The local authority might argue that such a strategy would promote both the legislation's aim to encourage social services departments to work in partnership with parents,[82] even with abusive parents, and the Strasbourg case law indicating that state care should be viewed as being a short-term measure. Nevertheless, accumulating research indicates that children left with abusive parents may suffer some further form of abuse in the aftermath of protective intervention.[83] In the light of this, the court may quite

---

74 Children Act 1989, s 23(6) directs the local authority to make arrangements to enable the child to live with: (a) a parent or other person who previously had parental responsibility for him; or (b) a relative, friend or other person connected with him, 'unless that would not be reasonably practicable or consistent with his welfare and subject to the Placement of Children with Parents etc Regulations 1991, SI 1991/893'. There is now a far greater emphasis on utilising members of the extended family to comply with this statutory provision.

75 Between 1996 and 2000, the number of children on care orders placed with parents at any time during the year increased by 35% and the number of days they were spending at home had increased by 42%. Some remain at home under care orders for several years. See DH (2001 a) para 1.28.

76 To obtain a supervision order under Children Act 1989, s 35, the local authority must satisfy the same threshold criteria as those applying to care orders: see s 31.

77 See Hale J, in *Oxfordshire County Council v L (care or supervision order)* [1998] 1 FLR 70 at 76–78 and *Re O (supervision order)* [2001] EWCA Civ 16, [2001] 1 FLR 923 at [18]–[28]. See also Hale LJ in *Re C and B (care order: future harm)* [2001] 1 FLR 611 at paras 33–35.

78 See J Hunt and A Macleod (1999) p 237. See also ch 8 generally and pp 217–218.

79 It is *only* by obtaining a care order that the local authority acquire parental responsibility over the child, which they share with his or her parents. See Children Act 1989, s 33(3).

80 See J Hunt and A Macleod (1999) pp 213, 217–218 and 237.

81 A metaphor used by Wall J to describe this situation. See Wall J (1998) p 6.

82 See also Children Act 1989, s 23(6).

83 See, inter alia: E Farmer and R Parker (1991); E Farmer and M Owen (1995); J Hunt and A Macleod (1999) p 199; M Brandon et al (1999), indicating that 40% of the children in this sample suffered some form of maltreatment in the 12 months following protective intervention, with 15% suffering serious maltreatment in the form of emotional neglect or abuse (pp 200–201). See also research summarised and discussed by E Farmer (2001).

justifiably consider that there is insufficient evidence to indicate that the parents have changed sufficiently to make it safe for the child to be returned home.[84] Nevertheless, a court is powerless in such a situation, its role in care proceedings being only 'adjudicative', rather than 'participative'.[85] It can certainly insist on making a care order, rather than the supervision order requested by the local authority, if it considers that the latter will not offer the child sufficient protection.[86] But where the local authority has applied for a care order, all the court can do is decide whether the threshold criteria are made out and, if so, whether or not to make it.[87]

If the court is extremely unhappy about the local authority's plans for rehabilitation, it might instead, make an interim care order, in order to await the outcome of a parental assessment.[88] It may even direct the local authority to undertake a residential assessment of the parents, to obtain further evidence regarding the situation.[89] Indeed, a greater use of interim care orders, whilst the details of care plans are being finalised, may be the outcome of *Re S (children: care plan); Re W (children: care plan).*[90] But if there is no further information to be gained from such an assessment, the court must reach a decision, one way or the other.[91] As Balcombe LJ has observed, the judge may be faced with choosing between the lesser of two evils; if he makes a care order, the local authority may implement a care plan he strongly disapproves of, but if he makes no order he may be leaving children in the care of an irresponsible or wholly inappropriate parent.[92] The latter approach is 'a potentially high-risk strategy if it means the child receives inadequate protection through the intransigence of the local authority on the one hand and of the court on the other'.[93] Indeed, the judiciary have expressed a degree of frustration over their inability to influence how the local authority provides for the child once in care. For example, they cannot prevent the child being rehabilitated with his or her parents, if that is the local authority's intention, even if they consider the parents to be inherently dangerous.[94] Perhaps even more unsatisfactory is the absence of any judicial power to supervise the delivery of a care plan, or any procedure whereby local authorities can be called to account in cases where they wholly fail to implement such plans.[95]

(3)   PROTECTING CHILDREN IN RESIDENTIAL CARE

(A)   The risk of abuse

The state's intervention to protect children from abusive parents must not lead the children into more danger than before. For the child who can neither return home, nor live with anyone in the extended family, residential care is normally rejected in

---

84   Eg *Kent County Council v C* [1993] 1 FLR 308.
85   See J Dewar (1995) p 16.
86   Eg *Re D (a minor) (care or supervision order)* [1993] 2 FLR 423.
87   *Re T (a minor) (care order: conditions)* [1994] 2 FLR 423 at 429, per Nourse J.
88   Eg *C v Solihull Metropolitan Borough Council* [1993] 1 FLR 290.
89   See *Re C (a minor) (interim care order: residential assessment)* [1997] AC 489.
90   [2002] UKHL 10, [2002] 2 All ER 192, discussed below.
91   [2002] UKHL 10, [2002] 2 All ER 192 at [94]–[95], per Lord Nicholls of Birkenhead.
92   *Re S and D (children: powers of court)* [1995] 2 FLR 456 at 464.
93   See J Dewar (1995) p 21.
94   *Re W and B; Re W (care plan)* [2001] EWCA Civ 757, [2001] 2 FLR 582 at [18], per Thorpe LJ. (NB House of Lords' decision is reported sub nom *Re S (children: care plan), Re W (children: care plan)* [2002] UKHL 10, [2002] 2 All ER 192.)
95   Discussed below.

favour of the more natural family life provided by long-term foster carers or adoptive parents.[96] Admittedly there are now growing concerns that a small minority of children are abused whilst in foster care,[97] particularly those who are privately fostered.[98] Despite this, the mounting number of investigations into child abuse in children's homes gives the impression that an abused child may be much safer with foster parents than in residential care.[99] Indeed, the Prime Minister's response to the Waterhouse Report[100] prompted the review of adoption policy to ensure that far more children looked after by local authorities were provided with adoptive parents.[101] But there are large numbers of children for whom adoption, or even long-term foster care, would be quite unsuitable. Some children do not want a family placement, perhaps because they have had repeated bad experiences of foster care; others have complex personal and social difficulties with a need for expert treatment in a residential setting; some are a danger to themselves or others and require secure accommodation; and there are those whose abusive experiences makes it undesirable to place them in another family.[102] These are the children who need care in children's homes. Despite this, residential child care is expensive and the closure of many children's homes makes it difficult to find appropriate placements for children who would benefit from this type of specialised care.[103]

Some of the closures may have been precipitated by the numerous inquiries into abuse in residential care in the late 1980s and 1990s, recording the systematic abuse of children by members of staff. These drew attention to the poor management, recruitment and selection procedures of care staff, which allowed small groups of paedophiles to gain access to vulnerable children. Some of the abuse uncovered had occurred years before the introduction of the Children Act 1989, with its detailed guidance and regulations regarding the management of residential homes.[104] A further

---

96   In 2001, 38,400 children were in foster placements, whilst 7,900 children were in children's homes, hostels and residential schools: see SSI (2002 a) p 101, Table 1.2. Between 1996 and 2000, there was a 15% increase in the use of foster care, with a 7% reduction in the number of children living in children's homes: DH (2001 a) para 1.24.

97   See SSI (2002 b) (para 5.4): unsatisfactory level of checks on foster carers, with insufficient thoroughness over checks of some identity and employment histories. In two councils, care leavers had felt unsafe in their foster homes (para 5.11). See also *S v Gloucestershire County Council; Tower Hamlets London Borough Council and Having London Borough Council* [2001] Fam 313: two 'children', now adults, brought actions in negligence against their respective local authorities for having placed them, during their childhood, with foster carers who allegedly sexually abused them and were convicted of sexual offences against other children.

98   See T Philpot (2001) and discussion in chapter 14.

99   See, inter alia: W Hughes (1985) (the 'Kincora' report) sexual abuse in Northern Ireland boys' hostels; G Williams and J Macreadie (1992) (the Ty Mawr report) ill treatment of children in the home leading to incidents of suicide and self-harm; A Levy and B Kahan (1991) (The Pindown report) regime adopted in some Staffordshire residential homes involving isolation, humiliation and confrontation of the children in their care; R Waterhouse (2000) sexual abuse of children in children's homes in North Wales. See also the literature review by B Gallagher (1999).

100 R Waterhouse (2000).

101 PIU (2000). See discussion above.

102 D Berridge and I Brodie (1998) p 90ff.

103 J Morris (2000) pp 10–11.

104 Children Act 1989, Sch 4 and DH (1991). See also the Children's Homes Regulations 1991, SI 1991/1506; the Disqualification for Caring for Children Regulations 1991, SI 1991/2094; the Children (Protection from Offenders) (Miscellaneous Amendments) Regulations 1997, SI 1997/2308; the Children (Protection from Offenders) (Amendment) Regulations 1999, SI 1999/2768.

tranche of statutory measures designed to prevent unsuitable people working with children,[105] together with greater regulation of the standard of care offered in children's homes[106] should improve children's chances in residential care. Nevertheless, as the Utting report chillingly pointed out:

> 'Persistent sexual abusers are a scourge of childhood ... sexual terrorists whose success depends, paradoxically, on their capacity to ingratiate themselves with adults and children. An outstanding characteristic is their ability to establish themselves in roles in which they are trusted to excess as friend, colleague or employee. Their subsequent activities are concealed by suborning, blackmailing and threatening their victims.'[107]

Detection may be hampered because the emotional needs of many children in residential homes make them particularly vulnerable 'to the flattering attention of improperly motivated adults'.[108] Their disturbed behaviour may itself lead other staff to dismiss their complaints as fantasy or lies. Although over-vigilance can lead to a poisoned atmosphere, staff must be prepared to complain about their colleagues' behaviour.[109] Managers should maintain a far more heightened awareness of the risks posed, not only by adults in such settings, but also by other child residents.[110] Too many children are 'rescued' from parental abuse, only to be bullied and abused by their peers,[111] or by residential care staff, and sometimes by both.[112]

(B)   The problems linked with 'control'

The need to maintain control in residential homes is a consistent theme in any commentary on residential establishments.[113] This is understandable, given the volatile mix of residents being cared for, often by young and inexperienced residential care staff. 'Some homes today have many violent, abused, abusing and self-mutilating children, rather than the orphans and truants of a bygone era and popular perception.'[114]

---

105   Inter alia: the Protection of Children Act 1999, which establishes a statutory list of people considered unsuitable to work with children and imposes a duty on agencies employing people in such a position to check the list before doing so; the Criminal Justice Court Services Act 2000, which disqualifies certain categories of people from working with children and makes it a criminal offence for any to apply for such work or carry it out; the Disqualification for Caring for Children (England) Regulations, SI 2002/635 and the Disqualification for Caring for Children (Wales) Regulations, SI 2002/896, overhauling the previous regulations preventing unsuitable people from acting as private foster carers.

106   By the National Care Standards Commission. All agencies seeking registration of a children's home must comply with the minimum standards and regulations. The Commission is also seeking to increase and improve the training and competence of residential care staff.

107   W Utting (1997) paras 9.1–9.2.

108   W Utting (1997) para 8.36. See also R Waterhouse (2000) para 29.33.

109   Junior staff must feel able to 'blow the whistle' on harmful practices by senior staff. See W Utting (1997) paras 15.25–15.37 and R Waterhouse (2000) para 29.57.

110   See E Farmer and S Pollock (1998), summarised in E Farmer and S Pollock (1999) p 377ff. This research indicates that a small but significant number of sexually abused residents in children's homes (just under one in five) go on to sexually abuse other child residents.

111   Eg *Re O (care: discharge of care order)* [1999] 2 FLR 119: three sisters were abused in residential care and one was severely bullied.

112   Eg *C v Flintshire County Council* [2001] ECWA Civ 302, [2001] 2 FLR 33: a girl, now adult, had been placed in care because of her parents' physical and emotional abuse, only to be bullied in one children's home and sexually abused by staff in the next.

113   See, inter alia: N Warner (1992) p 41; W Utting (1997) paras 11.11–11.28; DH (1998 a) p 28; D Berridge and I Brodie (1998) p 99ff.

114   N Warner (1992) p 7.

If these highly disturbed and difficult children get 'out of control', they can be a danger to themselves, each other, the staff and those living in the vicinity of the home. Indeed, many children in children's homes suffer bullying, physical abuse and theft at the hands of other residents.[115]

The methods of control used in some Staffordshire residential homes in the 1980s[116] were clearly completely unacceptable and blatantly infringed the residents' rights under the ECHR[117] and under the CRC.[118] The publication of the 'Pindown Report'[119] was soon followed by regulations[120] ruling out the various types of degrading punishments devised by the staff, including corporal punishment, depriving children of food and drink and requiring them to wear special clothes.[121] Measures were introduced designed to prevent punitive regimes of this kind operating in children's homes without detection.[122] Although this official response was overdue, as Utting pointed out, staff in children's homes have to maintain a sensitive balance. Whilst methods of control can very easily become abusive, in homes accommodating volatile and disturbed children, the staff and young people may themselves feel unsafe unless reasonable control is maintained. Indeed, issues of safety and control are inextricably interlinked.[123] Furthermore, staff may often be confronted by rebellious and disturbed children intent on absenting themselves at night.[124] They may be fully aware that some children, too immature to resist the blandishments of pimps and paedophiles, are leaving their residential units to take part in prostitution and crime.[125]

The Department of Health's inconsistent attempts to address these dilemmas have confused staff over what forms of discipline they can use. In the early 1990s, the guidance stressed the rights of children living in residential care to be treated with respect, emphasising that physical restraint or coercion should only be resorted to in an emergency.[126] This undermined the confidence of residential care staff when confronting residents intent on going out at night in risky situations.[127] Later 'clarification' of this guidance responded to adverse publicity about residential staff feeling powerless to prevent children absenting themselves to become involved in criminal activities. This now emphasised that the need to support children's rights did not prevent residential staff exercising their powers under the Children Act 1989, section 3(5) to safeguard and promote the children's welfare. Staff were urged to show

115 W Utting (1997) para 7.5.
116 A Levy and B Kahan (1991) esp ch 11.
117 Art 3 (freedom from torture or inhuman or degrading treatment) and art 5 (freedom from restraint).
118 Art 19(1) (freedom from physical or mental violence and other forms of abuse while in the care of any adult) and art 37(a) (freedom from torture or other cruel, or inhuman or degrading treatment or punishment).
119 A Levy and B Kahan (1991).
120 See Children and Young Persons, Children's Homes Regulations 1991, SI 1991/1506, reg 8; DH (1991) pp 15–19.
121 The regimes known as 'Total Pindown' or 'Sympathetic Pindown' involved subjecting children to isolation, humiliation and confrontation of varying degrees, in order to discipline them and deter them from absconding repeatedly.
122 Local authorities were required to establish complaints procedures in their children's homes, a system of unannounced monthly visits to all residential homes by local authority representatives, and of independent visitors for all children being looked after. See DH (1991) chs 5 and 6.
123 W Utting (1997) paras 11.12–11.17.
124 D Berridge and I Brodie (1998) p 100.
125 See T Lenihan and P Dean (2000) pp 36–37.
126 DH (1993) para 5.
127 D Berridge and I Brodie (1998) pp 99 and 134.

effective parenting and prevent children leaving children's homes at inappropriate hours, by using reasonable physical restraint or by bolting doors, to restrict the child's exit, when there were grounds for believing that they are putting themselves or others at risk or were likely seriously to damage property.[128] Further guidance later retreated from this position, emphasising that physical restraint can only be used to prevent 'likely injury to the child concerned or to others, or likely serious damage to property'.[129]

This retreat signals to residential care staff that they have no power to prevent highly disturbed children from involving themselves in dangerous situations. Nevertheless, it might be difficult for a children's home to defend a challenge brought by a child, who had been locked in at night, arguing that such restraint infringed his or her rights under article 5 of the ECHR.[130] Were such homes to obtain written authority from the parents of children they accommodate, specifically authorising such detention, the decision in *Nielsen v Denmark*[131] would probably provide them with a defence to such a claim.[132] After all, children not only have a right to be treated with respect but to be protected from their own lack of judgment.

(C)   Control through secure accommodation orders

The punitive regime known as 'Pindown' in some Staffordshire residential homes was adopted largely to control runaways or 'absconders' and break their habit of refusing to comply with rules and regulations about returning at night by set hours. A significant proportion of children run away from local authority care,[133] but it appears that large numbers of these children first went missing from their family home. Indeed, for many, running away may be only one aspect of a general picture of instability in their lives, with a likelihood of their also being non-attenders at school, through truanting or exclusion, and involved in offending behaviour, including substance misuse.[134] Some local authorities are said to resort to secure accommodation orders, simply to cure the absconding 'habit' of the children they are looking after.[135] Nevertheless, the official guidance on the Children Act 1989 emphasises that locking

---

128   See letter of 20 February 1997 from Sir Herbert Laming to all Directors of Social Services (CI (97) 6) clarifying DH (1993).

129   DH (2002 c) para 22.7.

130   *Guzzardi v Italy* (1980) 3 EHRR 333: it depends on the type, duration, effects and manner of implementation, whether art 5 is infringed by a restriction. Nevertheless, short periods of restraint may infringe its terms. See *X and Y v Sweden* (1977–78) 7 DR 123: detention for only two hours prior to deportation could in principle amount to a breach. Discussed in more detail by J Fortin (2001) pp 252–257.

131   (1988) 11 EHRR 175.

132   (1988) 11 EHRR 175 (para 61), the European Court of Human Rights considered it legitimate for parents to authorise others to impose various restrictions on children's lives, such as schools or recreational establishments, without infringing art 5. For further discussion of this issue, see J Fortin (2001) pp 252–257.

133   See J Wade, N Biehal et al (1998), indicating that 43% of 11–16-year-olds accommodated in residential units went missing at least once during a 12-month period, but with considerable variations between authorities and units.

134   Discussed in more depth in chapter 4.

135   See T O'Neill (2001) pp 192–193, 268 and 285. NB A secure accommodation order can only be obtained over a child who is already being looked after by the local authority under the Children Act 1989, s 22. For a more detailed consideration of the relationship between Children Act 1989, ss 20, 22 and 25, see J Fortin (2001) pp 255–257.

any child up is a major infringement of his or her right to liberty and should only be used as a last resort.[136] The law also makes it clear that secure accommodation orders can *only* be obtained to secure an 'an absconder' if he or she is likely to abscond from unsecure accommodation and in the event of doing so is likely to suffer significant harm.[137] But local authorities may argue that the grounds for the order are fulfilled because the child has a history of absconding and is likely to suffer significant harm, simply by *virtue* of absconding again. The circularity of this argument is obvious: 'runaways are at risk because they run away'.[138] Professionals working in secure units commonly encounter children being sent to secure accommodation, without the staff in their residential units having ever satisfactorily discovered either why they were absconding in the first place,[139] or whether and how secure accommodation would address their difficulties.[140]

The application for a secure accommodation order should be fully justified, not only in terms of what the order is seeking to achieve, but also in terms of the duration requested.[141] There is a risk that children will become institutionalised if they remain in secure units for many months.[142] As the grounds of the order make clear, restricting the child's liberty may be to protect the public, not the child. Consequently, case law has established that, although relevant, the welfare principle does not govern applications for secure accommodation orders.[143] This interpretation of the wording of section 25[144] seems unduly restrictive, bearing in mind, as the courts themselves have acknowledged, they are Draconian orders to make.[145] Nevertheless, in *Re K (secure accommodation order: right to liberty)*,[146] the Court of Appeal rejected the widely held view[147] that the Children Act 1989, section 25 is too widely drafted to fall within any of the exemptions to article 5 of the ECHR and is therefore incompatible with its terms. Strongly influenced by a confused admissibility decision reached by

---

136 See DH (1991) para 8.5.
137 Children Act 1989, s 25(1) provides that a secure accommodation order may not be made regarding a child who is being looked after by a local authority unless it appears that: (a) he has a history of absconding and he is likely to abscond from any other description of accommodation, and if he absconds, he is likely to suffer significant harm; or (b) that if he is kept in any other description of accommodation, he is likely to injure himself or other persons. The interpretation of these grounds is discussed in chapter 5, pp 154–156ff. See also M Parry (2000) and J Fortin (2001) pp 257–260.
138 National Children's Bureau (1995) p 28.
139 Eg R Waterhouse (2000) observes (para 29.59) that despite the high level of absconding from several of the children's homes in North Wales, and the frequent involvement of social workers and the police, little attempt was made to ascertain the true reasons for the absconders' leaving; they were merely punished for leaving.
140 National Children's Bureau (1995) ch 4. But see DH (2002 c) para 19.4, which requires the child's social worker or a person independent of the home to consider the reasons for the child's absence without authority.
141 Eg *Re W (a minor) (secure accommodation order)* [1993] 1 FLR 692.
142 See J Masson and M Winn Oakley (1999) p 133.
143 *Re M (secure accommodation order)* [1995] 1 FLR 418. Discussed by P Bates (1995).
144 Children Act 1989, s 25(4) directs the court that, if it 'determines that any such criteria (the grounds set out by s 25(3)) are satisfied, it *shall* make an order authorising the child to be kept in secure accommodation and specify the maximum period for which he may be so kept' (emphasis supplied).
145 Per Booth J in *Re W (a minor) (secure accommodation order)* [1993] 1 FLR 692 at 696 and per Butler-Sloss LJ in *Re M (secure accommodation order)* [1995] 1 FLR 418 at 423.
146 [2001] 1 FLR 526.
147 See H Swindells et al (1999) pp 116–118.

the European Court of Human Rights,[148] the Court of Appeal ruled that as long as the secure unit to which the particular child is sent provides properly supervised educational facilities, a secure accommodation order is exempted from infringing article 5, under the article 5(1)(d) exemption.[149] It clearly considered that the domestic courts could simply prevent article 5 being infringed, on a purely ad hoc basis. Thus, by disallowing those secure accommodation orders which failed to ensure that there were educational facilities available for a child, the courts could avoid declaring the Children Act 1989, section 25 incompatible with the Convention. Such a decision is disappointing,[150] not least because it appears to reflect a judicial determination to restrict the impact of the ECHR as far as possible.

In this context, the Court of Appeal's obvious anxiety to uphold a well-established legislative provision led them to ignore the central question: 'whether section 25 – as drafted – is sufficiently precise to have the quality of law which the Convention requires.'[151] As drafted, section 25 plainly fails to prevent the grant of an order falling outside the boundaries of the article 5(1)(d) exemption, since there is nothing in its wording which insists on every secure accommodation order being made for the purposes of educational supervision.[152] But *Re K* establishes that as long as educational facilities are provided by the secure unit to which the child is sent, whatever the quantity and quality, a secure accommodation order is impervious to challenges under the Human Rights Act 1998. Contrarily, an order not ensuring such provision, does prima facie infringe the child's rights under article 5 and can be challenged.[153] Although regrettable, at the very least, the decision may focus official attention on the poor standard of educational facilities offered by many secure accommodation units.[154]

The courts have repeatedly stressed that the official guidance on the use of secure accommodation orders should be followed closely.[155] They should never be used 'because the child is simply being a nuisance or runs away from his accommodation and is not likely to suffer significant harm in doing so, and never as a form of punishment'.[156] Clearly, there may be little alternative for some highly disturbed adolescents[157] and some make considerable progress in secure units.[158] Nevertheless,

---

148 *Koniarska v United Kingdom* (Application No 33670/96) (12 October 2000, unreported): declaring inadmissible complaints by a teenager that her detention under a secure acc, unreported ommodation order infringed her Convention rights under arts 5, 3 and 8. The European Court of Human Rights stated that the art 5(1)(d) exemption could be interpreted flexibly cf the Court's much stricter approach to interpreting art 5(1)(d) in *Bouamar v Belgium* (1988) 11 EHRR 1. But see *D G v Ireland* (Application No 39474/98) (16 May 2002, unreported): declaring admissible complaints by a teenager that his detention under a secure accommodation order was of such a nature that it infringed his rights under arts 3, 5, 8 and 14.

149 Ie covering cases where liberty is restrained 'for the purpose of educational supervision'.

150 See J Masson (2002).

151 See AIRE Centre (2001) pp 4–5.

152 According to Strasbourg jurisprudence, eg *Huvig v France* (1990) 12 EHRR 528, this is an insufficient delineation of legal discretion. See AIRE Centre (2001) p 5.

153 *Re K (secure accommodation order: right to liberty)* [2001] 1 FLR 526 at paras 42–43, per Dame Elizabeth Butler-Sloss P.

154 See T O'Neill (2001) pp 180–181 and 224: many social workers interviewed were extremely dissatisfied with the educational provision in the secure units reviewed.

155 *Re K (secure accommodation order: right to liberty)* [2001] 1 FLR 526 at para 93, per Judge LJ.

156 See DH (1991) para 8.5.

157 Eg *Re G (secure accommodation order)* [2001] 1 FLR 884: Munby J considered that a secure accommodation order was fully justified regarding a girl, now aged 15, who had been involved in prostitution and drug taking since the age of 13, and who had absconded repeatedly from local authority accommodation.

158 See R Bullock et al (1998).

there is a view that far too many secure accommodation orders are obtained quite unnecessarily.[159] They are sometimes used to ensure that emotionally disturbed children receive medical treatment in secure treatment units, when the mental health legislation might be a better vehicle for ensuring that adolescents undergo compulsory treatment.[160] Furthermore, magistrates' courts have not always treated applications for secure accommodation orders sufficiently critically.[161] This is regrettable, since such orders can have a potentially devastating effect on the children involved. Indeed, the current practice of mixing, within the same units, the 'welfare secures'[162] with young offenders, clearly infringes the rights of young people needing protection. Staff in such units describe –

> 'the absurdity of seeing young people deprived of their liberty to protect them from perpetrators of abuse, sitting across the table from other young people convicted of abuse or violent offences.'[163]

(4)   THE CHILD'S OWN PERSPECTIVES

(A)   Consulting children

As article 12 of the CRC makes clear, children should be consulted on all matters affecting them, and due weight should be given to their views, in accordance with their age and maturity. Most parents recognise the sense of this guidance. The local authority, like any other good parent, should respect the children in their care and consult them over their future upbringing. Nevertheless, the lives of children cared for by the state are marked by continual instability. Placements break down causing further unhappiness and, when faced with moves in accommodation, often with little notice, many feel helpless and powerless:

> 'I've been moved about six times, in about three years. It would be nice if they'd ask you what sort of place you'd like, not sort of say you'll go there. Ask you what things you like, what you like doing. They don't even give you the option, they just ship you off somewhere. And it's what they think, not what you think ... I did actually run to my social worker ... and she just put me in a place I didn't want to be. Because she reckoned there wasn't enough room in any other places. I had to run away from there, just for people to listen to me. (John Dalley)'[164]

This quotation suggests that at least some children who run away from local authority care do so because they are unhappy with decisions being made about them. They may even have been abused, but feel that no one will listen to them.[165] The Children Act 1989 acknowledges this and encourages social workers to treat children as individuals and persuade them to participate in the decision-making process.[166]

---

159   National Children's Bureau (1995) esp ch 8. See also C Smith and P Gardner (1996).
160   Discussed in more depth in chapter 5.
161   Eg *Re W (a minor) (secure accommodation order)* [1993] 1 FLR 692: Booth J criticised the magistrates for making a secure accommodation order lasting three months without clarifying why this was better than a five-week order, as recommended by the guardian ad litem.
162   See A Pack (2001) p 140.
163   T O'Neill (2001) p 152.
164   Quoted in J Morris (2000) pp 9 and 11.
165   See Safe on the Streets Research Team (1999) pp 110–111. See also W Utting (1997) para 7.4.
166   Children Act 1989, s 22(4) and (5). See also Quality Protects Objective C8.0, particularly sub-objective C8.1, which requires local authorities: 'To demonstrate that the views of children and families are actively sought and used in the planning, delivery and review of services.'

Although there have been some improvements,[167] effective compliance with this duty is still extremely patchy.[168] The government is keen to promote better practice in this respect.[169] The guidance on assessing children in need urges social workers, when assessing families, to communicate with the children themselves and, in so doing, talk to them. It acknowledges that 'although this may seem an obvious part of communicating with children, it is clear from research that this is often not done at all or not done well ... Children themselves are particularly sensitive to how and when professionals talk to them and consult them. Their views must be sought before key meetings'.[170]

A common theme of commentaries on the shortcomings of state care is the fact that looked after children lack the individual attention of an adult committed to them. They need a consistent person to act as their 'champion' or mentor, to ensure that their views are heard and that agreed decisions are implemented.[171] Regrettably, it is only the older children, due to leave local authority care,[172] who gain the assistance of a 'personal adviser' provided by the local authority.[173] The provision of a champion for *every* child in state care might support the efforts being made to address their educational and other problems, and might even improve their future employment prospects, and indeed, their sense of security.

(B)   Making complaints

Children received into residential care are particularly vulnerable to abuse because of their inability to get their complaints taken seriously. Since residential care is largely a service for adolescents,[174] one might assume that they are old enough to complain vociferously if they are ill-treated by members of staff or bullied by other residents. But although all children in local authority children's homes are informed about the way to use both the home's own complaints procedure and the statutory complaints procedure,[175] the assumption that they will feel able to do so underestimates the hurdles that they confront.[176] Children lacking mobility by virtue of physical disabilities, or because the homes are geographically remote, may feel cut off from the outside world and, being totally dependent on the staff,

---

167   See DH (2001 e) ch 5, Part I.
168   See, inter alia: SSI (2002 b) para 5.7, children were not confident that their views were listened to; DH (2002 b) paras 7.22–7.23, some children were uncomfortable in review meetings and some in residential and foster care considered that they had insufficient contact with their social workers; *R v Devon County Council, ex p O (adoption)* [1997] 2 FLR 388, in which Scott Baker J (at 396–397) criticised the local authority for failing to discover the views of a child of 9 about its plans to remove him from his foster carers with whom he had lived for two and a half years. See also J Morris (2000) esp pp 1–19, for a useful summary and discussion of much of the research and practice in this area.
169   Children and Young People's Unit (2001).
170   DH et al (2000) para 3.42.
171   See, inter alia, DH (1996) p 31 and DH (1998 c) pp 26–27.
172   Although those who stay on at school may gain the support of a Personal Adviser provided by the Connexions service. Discussed in chapter 6.
173   Under the 'Leaving Care' legislation, discussed below.
174   DH (1998 a) p 22.
175   Children Act 1989, s 26(3). See DH (1991) ch 5, Part I.
176   According to estimates, only about 20% of complaints come from children or young people themselves. See DH (2000 c) para 5.2. See also SSI (2002 b): some young people were ignorant of the complaints procedure's existence (para 5.10); SSI (2002 c): concern was expressed about 'the unrealistically low numbers of formal complaints' being made by looked after children; those who had complained often felt that their complaints had not been taken seriously (para 5.26).

unable to complain.[177] Many have emotional and/or behavioural difficulties, and a significant proportion may have been sexually abused.[178] But countless inquiry reports find that, when re-abused in a residential setting, few children complain, fearing that complaints will go unheeded and that they may be victimised by members of staff loyal to the abuser.[179] The children in North Wales who did have the courage to complain found that either they or the member of staff involved were moved from the home, but –

'otherwise the complaint would be stifled or lost in the mists of bureaucracy. There was compelling evidence that a number of those in positions of authority did all they could to ensure that complaints did not get out of the system or at least outside the confines of the home.'[180]

Once improvements are made to the complaints procedure,[181] more children might feel prepared to use it, but many need independent adult assistance before doing so. Increasing numbers of local authorities have appointed children's rights officers, whose task is to promote good practice amongst those working with children looked after by the local authority. Part of their job is to ensure that children know what rights they have, how to use the statutory complaints procedure, to help them express their views over decisions they object to and provide formal advocacy if required. Not all children would, however, feel able to trust anyone who was a local authority employee with disclosures about members of that local authority's staff. At first sight, a promising alternative source of independent assistance might be the child's 'independent visitor' who is an unpaid volunteer, with no standing within the local authority, and whose role it is to visit, advise and befriend him or her. But since the local authority is not obliged to make such an appointment in every case,[182] a child in residential care may not have the services of such a person,[183] and in any case the official guidance stresses that an independent visitor is not expected to play the part of an advocate, particularly in situations where the child is alleging abuse.[184]

Providing all children wishing to complain with an advocate to assist them[185] is an important step in the right direction.[186] When operational, such a scheme may gradually encourage all children in state care to believe that their concerns will be taken seriously. Meanwhile, some children gain the assistance of a variety of independent organisations established to ensure that they have some external channel of communication.[187]

---

177 See W Utting (1997) paras 8.3–8.35 for a useful discussion of the research evidence on the special vulnerability of disabled children to abusive treatment.

178 DH (1998 a) p 21.

179 Staff may be tempted to 'turn a blind eye' to what is happening or to minimise or rationalise it. See W Utting (1997) para 18.10; R Waterhouse (2000) para 29.50.

180 See E Ryder (2000) p 408. See also R Waterhouse (2000) para 29.50

181 The government intends to improve the procedure in a variety of ways, eg by ensuring a more rigorous adherence to the set time limits and the need for independent scrutiny. See DH (2000 c) esp paras 6.1–6.11. But see C Williams (2002) who (pp 29–32) criticises the present time limits.

182 Children Act 1989, Sch 2, para 17(1) and (2). The obligation only arises if communications between the child and his or her parents have become infrequent or the parents have not visited the child for more than one year and if the appointment is deemed to be in the child's best interests.

183 See SSI (1998) para 8.15, which records that some local authorities were totally unaware of their duty to appoint such a person and SSI (2002 c) recording that out of over 11,000 children (being looked after by 32 councils) only 165 had independend visitors (para 5.22).

184 See DH (1991) para 6.47.

185 See Children Act 1989, s 26A(1)(b), as inserted by Adoption and Children Act 2002, s 119.

186 As recommended by W Utting (1997) para 10.12.

187 Eg the Direct Advocacy Service provided by the Voice for the Child in Care (VCC). See also the National Youth Advocacy Service (NYAS), which provides advice, representation and advocacy for all children, whatever their circumstances.

(C)   Leaving care

For many children, the defects in the 'parenting' provided by the state are brought home most clearly at the point at which they leave care. Some of the problems that care leavers experience are obviously attributable to their disturbed home lives, rather than what occurs whilst in care. Nevertheless, during the late 1990s, there were mounting concerns about the plight of children leaving the care of local authorities with far poorer life chances than those of the average teenager.[188] Particularly unforgivable, given their extreme vulnerability, was the increasing trend for local authorities to discharge young people from care early, largely for financial reasons.[189] Whilst some were supplied with suitable accommodation, others were being provided with unsupported accommodation in unsafe or unsuitable areas.[190] Their childhood histories undermined the ability of these teenagers to cope with independent living, and inevitably this group became greatly over-represented amongst those who ended up sleeping rough.[191] The overriding message concerned care leavers' loneliness and depression coping alone, with very little support.[192]

Legislation now aims to ensure that young people who have been looked after by social services departments move from care into living independently, in a way that they can cope with. Indeed, the aim is to provide them with the sort of support that an average child might expect from his or her own parents, including the provision of suitable accommodation and financial support.[193] An important task for the local authority is to assess the young person's needs and prepare a 'pathway plan' covering his or her future education, training, accommodation and financial support on leaving care. Each care leaver has a personal adviser,[194] whose prime role is to enable the young person to 'identify someone as committed to their well-being and development on a long term basis',[195] and to provide him or her with advice and support. This support will last until the care leaver attains the age of 21.[196] The personal adviser should also assist with the preparation of the care leaver's pathway plan and supervise its proper implementation. Personal advisers, who are expected to form a 'constructive

---

188   See, inter alia: SSI (1997) esp para 1.2; W Utting (1997) pp 91–93; DH (1999 a) para 2.6. See also DH (2000 a) para 2.4. These all refer, inter alia, to care leavers' low educational qualifications, low employment prospects, poor physical and mental health, and high levels of homelessness.

189   The proportion leaving care at the age of 16 increased from 33% in 1993, to 46% in 1998. This situation contrasted with the average for the population as a whole, where young people typically leave home at the age of 22: DH (1999 a) para 2.1

190   DH (1999 a) para 2.5. See also J Vernon (2000) pp 86–88.

191   All the research studies on children running away show that there is an over-representation of young people from local authority care. For a more detailed discussion of the problem of children running away and sleeping rough due to lack of accommodation, see chapter 4.

192   See J Vernon (2000) p 114.

193   Local authorities were previously only obliged to advise and befriend a care leaver, with *power* to assist him or her: Children Act 1989, s 24. They must now assess and then meet the needs of an eligible child (only a child now aged at least 16, who has been provided with care by a local authority for at least 13 weeks after the age of 14) through a package of support up to the age of 18, and then on to the age of 21, if in full-time further education. See Children Act 1989, ss 23A–E, 24, 24A–D, and Sch 2, paras 19A–C, inserted by the Children (Leaving Care) Act 2000. See also DH (2001 f). For a more detailed discussion of the provisions relating to the financial support of care leavers, see chapter 4.

194   Children Act 1989, s 23D.

195   See DH (2001 f) p 47.

196   The local authority's duties last until the care leaver attains the age of 24, if in further education or training.

relationship' with the young person,[197] may help care leavers manage the demands of what often appears to be a hostile adult community. If departments of social services fulfil these obligations adequately, whilst reaching the government's targets for looked after children, the lives of many vulnerable young people will be greatly improved.[198]

(5) STATE ACCOUNTABILITY TO CHILDREN?

(A) The background

Hindsight is a wonderful thing. Social workers, police officers, children's guardians and even the courts would all benefit enormously from having a crystal ball when faced with taking decisions over protecting children. Often such decisions have to be reached rapidly and in harrowing circumstances. Like those of practitioners in any field of work, some are sensible and others turn out to be unwise or plain stupid, but these decisions materially affect a child's future. Departments of social services are alone obliged by legislation to carry out section 47 investigations and, under the Children Act 1989, section 17(1)(a), to safeguard and promote the welfare of children within their area who are in need.[199] Ultimately, it is for them to decide whether or not to initiate steps to remove children from their parents and case law makes it plain that sometimes decisions are taken far too late to avert a great deal of suffering.[200] Indeed, Munby J in *Re F; F v Lambeth London Borough Council*[201] described Lambeth London Borough Council's failure to comply with their statutory duties regarding two boys in their care as 'scandalous', 'shaming' and 'indefensible'.[202]

(B) Can children sue local authorities?

By the time the European Court of Human Rights reviewed the legal principles[203] established by the House of Lords in *X v Bedfordshire County Council*,[204] the legal landscape had changed fundamentally, principally because the Human Rights Act

---

197 See DH (1999 a) para 3.43ff.
198 See the government's Quality Protects Objective C5.0: 'To ensure that young people leaving care, as they enter adulthood, are not isolated and participate socially and economically as citizens.' See also sub-objectives C5.1, 2 and 3, which aim to maximise the number of young people over 16 who are in education, training or employment at 19; and to maximise the number of young people leaving care over 16 who are still in contact with social services at 19 and those who have suitable accommodation at 19.
199 See discussion in chapter 14.
200 Inter alia: *X (minors) v Bedfordshire County Council; M (a minor) v Newham Borough Council; E (a minor) v Dorset County Council* [1995] 3 All ER 353: although fully aware of the appalling abuse and neglect they were suffering, Bedfordshire County Council failed for five years to intervene to protect five children from further harm at the hands of their parents; *Re E (care proceedings: social work practice)* [2000] 2 FLR 254: there was ineffectual social work intervention spanning a period of 20 years during which four children were emotionally, physically and sexually abused; *Re F, F v Lambeth London Borough Council* [2002] 1 FLR 217, discussed above.
201 [2002] 1 FLR 217.
202 [2002] 1 FLR 217 at para 33.
203 *TP and KM v United Kingdom* [2001] 2 FLR 549 and *Z v United Kingdom* [2001] 2 FLR 612. These applications were made to the European Court of Human Rights by the Official Solicitor, on behalf of the children involved in the *Bedfordshire* case [1995] 3 All ER 353.
204 Full title: *X (minors) v Bedfordshire County Council; M (a minor) v Newham Borough Council; E (a minor) v Dorset County Council* [1995] 3 All ER 353.

1998 had been implemented. Furthermore, by then, as Bailey-Harris and Harris observe, 'the political and social climate appears far more receptive to increased accountability of local authorities ...'[205] Nevertheless, for a time, the *Bedfordshire* decision indicated that children could not call local authorities to account for failing to protect them when they should have done, or for intervening unnecessarily and without sufficient care.[206] Their Lordships had decided that a local authority's failure to intervene to protect a child was not a justiciable matter, since it was not just and reasonable for the common law to impose a duty of care in such circumstances. Consequently, authorities could not be sued in negligence by any children they failed to protect, nor could they be sued for breach of their statutory duties. Predictably, the decision in *Bedfordshire* was controversial.[207] Had the children's claims against the local authorities concerned been allowed to stand, there was no guarantee that they would have been able to establish all the elements of negligence. But by striking their claims out altogether, the children were deprived of the chance to try. Indeed, Sir Thomas Bingham MR's argument in the Court of Appeal 'that wrongs should be remedied'[208] appeared to carry little weight in the House of Lords. Furthermore, the decision gave the unfortunate impression that the whole child protection process had become largely unaccountable.

This gap in local authority accountability was eventually partly filled by the combined effect of Strasbourg case law[209] and the Human Rights Act 1998, the latter providing domestic remedies for infringements of children's human rights.[210] But by then, heeding the European Court's rejection of the notion of public agencies being immune to liability in negligence,[211] the scope of the *Bedfordshire* decision had already been dramatically reduced. First, the domestic courts had become chary of striking out any negligence claim against a statutory agency, for fear of infringing article 6 of the ECHR. Current law shows this approach continuing, with the domestic courts only allowing claims to be struck out in the very clearest case, where the applicant has no reasonable prospect of establishing a case against the authority in question.[212] Secondly, Lord Browne-Wilkinson's reasons for rejecting common law liability in *Bedfordshire* obviously seemed less convincing to other members of the judiciary, who later rejected them in only slightly different contexts. He had referred, amongst other things, to the multi-disciplinary nature of child protection work, to its extremely sensitive nature, to the need to avert over-defensive social work practice and to the existence of other remedies, such as the complaints procedure.[213] But local

---

205 Discussed by R Bailey-Harris and M Harris (2002) p 118.
206 In the *Newham* case, the local authority's inaccurate identification of the child's sexual abuser as her mother's boyfriend led to their removing the child unnecessarily from home for almost a year.
207 See S Bailey and M Bowman (2000) for a spirited criticism of the *Bedfordshire* decision.
208 See Court of Appeal decision reported under name of *M (a minor) v Newham Borough Council; X (minors) v Bedfordshire County Council* [1994] 4 All ER 602 at 619.
209 *TP and KM v United Kingdom* [2001] 2 FLR 549 and *Z v United Kingdom* [2001] 2 FLR 612.
210 Ie under the Human Rights Act 1998, ss 7 and 8.
211 See *Osman v United Kingdom* [1999] 1 FLR 193: the concept of police immunity from negligence claims was deemed by the European Court of Human Rights to infringe art 6, in so far as it obliged courts to strike out statements of claim, rather than dealing with them on their merits. NB the European Court of Human Rights later reneged on this approach in *Z v United Kingdom* [2001] 2 FLR 612: see n 221 below.
212 See, inter alia: *W v Essex County Council* [2000] 1 FLR 657; *S v Gloucestershire County Council; Tower Hamlets London Borough Council and Having London Borough Council* [2000] 1 FLR 825; *L and P v Reading Borough Council and Chief Constable of Thames Valley Police* [2001] EWCA Civ 346, [2001] 2 FLR 50.
213 Per Lord Browne-Wilkinson, [1995] 3 All ER 353 at 381–382.

authorities looking after children *already* in care were later held unable to escape tortious liability, despite this area of work being only slightly less sensitive than the situation where the local authority is considering whether to intervene at all.[214] Furthermore, the multi-disciplinary nature of some educational practice did not exclude public liability in an educational context, since it was considered perfectly possible to 'disentangle the relevant parts played by particular individuals and identify where the alleged negligence occurred'.[215] Nor would the imposition of liability inspire a defensive attitude on the part of teachers and other educationalists. 'On the contrary it may have the healthy effect of securing that high standards are sought and secured.'[216] Additionally, the fact that there were alternative remedies[217] did not justify the exclusion of tortious liability, since the other remedies were not as efficacious as the award of damages following a finding of liability at common law.[218]

Notwithstanding the scope of the *Bedfordshire* decision having been restricted, enabling children to sue local authorities for allowing them to be mistreated once in local authority care,[219] the principle it established remained intact. Children could not sue a local authority in negligence for failing to protect them in the first place. In *Z v United Kingdom*,[220] despite disapproving of its own decision in *Osman v United Kingdom*,[221] the European Court of Human Rights was in no doubt that the neglect and abuse suffered by the children in the *Bedfordshire* case amounted to an infringement of their rights under article 3.[222] It stressed the positive obligation on state agencies to take measures to ensure that children do not suffer abuse of such a severity that it infringes their rights under article 3 or, indeed, under article 2. If they fail to do so, as occurred here, the children must be provided with an effective remedy. Because the domestic law of tort excludes liability, the inability of the children to obtain redress against the local authority, in the form of an award of compensation, constituted a breach of their right to an effective remedy.[223] The Court considered that it was for the United Kingdom to decide what remedy should be made available in such circumstances.

By the time *Z v United Kingdom* was published, the introduction of the Human Rights Act 1998 had already fulfilled the government's obligation to establish an effective remedy for children involved in similar abusive situations in the future.

---

214 See *Barrett v Enfield London Borough Council* [1999] 3 All ER 193 at 208, per Lord Slynn.
215 *Phelps v Hillingdon London Borough Council, Anderton v Clwyd County Council; Jarvis v Hampshire County Council; Re G (a minor)* [2000] 4 All ER 504 at 537, per Lord Clyde. Discussed in chapter 12.
216 [2000] 4 All ER 504 at 535.
217 Eg using the complaints procedure.
218 See *Barrett v Enfield London Borough Council* [1999] 3 All ER 193 at 208, per Lord Slynn, and at 228, per Lord Hutton.
219 Eg *Barrett v Enfield London Borough Council* [1999] 3 All ER 193, and *C v Flintshire County Council* [2001] EWCA Civ 302, [2001] 2 FLR 33.
220 [2001] 2 FLR 612.
221 [1999] 1 FLR 193: the European Court of Human Rights held that the *Bedfordshire* decision had infringed the children's rights under art 6 of the ECHR by striking out the children's claims instead of allowing them to proceed to trial. In *Z v United Kingdom* [2001] 2 FLR 612 (at paras 91–103) the European Court considered that *Osman*, on the ambit of art 6, was incorrect and had sprung from a misunderstanding of the principles of English law of negligence. In this context, the Court clearly agreed with *Osman*'s many critics. See, inter alia: *Barrett v Enfield London Borough Council* [1999] 3 All ER 193 at 198–199, per Lord Browne-Wilkinson; L Hoffman (1999); C Gearty (2001).
222 This was conceded by the United Kingdom government.
223 Under art 13 of the ECHR.

Consequently, as observed by Cornwath, 'although failures of local authorities in the welfare field will not give rise to claims of damages under domestic law (whether for breach of statutory duty or negligence), they may, if the suffering is sufficiently serious, give rise to a claim under the Human Rights Act for breach of article 3'.[224] Nevertheless, *Z v United Kingdom* leaves a number of loose ends. In the first place, there is some doubt over the extent of the positive obligation attaching to article 3. Arguably it is an absolute one, enabling an abused child to claim an infringement of his or her rights under article 3, whenever the local authority, knowing of abuse of such severity, fails to intervene to prevent further harm.[225] Some, however, argue that when interpreting the positive obligation attaching to article 3, local authorities are not obliged to assume that there is an unlimited supply of funds available for child protection purposes.[226] Such an approach would be regrettable, given that local authorities' resources are always limited. Children's rights to protection would be greatly undermined were the domestic courts to restrict the ambit of article 3 in such a way.

Perhaps of greater concern are the important gaps in accountability, even in situations where a local authority has not intervened to protect a child from abusive conduct of which it is aware. Children suffering abuse many years before the implementation of the Human Rights Act 1998 are denied a remedy thereunder.[227] Still governed by the decision in *Bedfordshire*, they cannot establish tortious liability against their local authority, despite their rights being infringed under article 3. It is regrettable that, unless the domestic courts are prepared to reconsider the justiciability of local authority incompetence, these claimants can still only obtain an effective remedy by taking their case to Strasbourg.[228] The reverse of the coin involves children within the ambit of the Human Rights Act 1998, but who may not be able to establish the 'threshold of severity' for satisfying article 3. This is very high.[229] Consequently, abusive conduct which justifies the grant of a care order,[230] does not necessarily also infringe a child's rights under article 3 of the ECHR. Article 8 may be available in such situations, since it could protect a child from any abuse which infringes his or her moral and physical integrity, even if the abuse did not reach the high threshold of severity required for article 3.[231] There is, however, very little Strasbourg case law to guide the domestic courts when addressing such a claim.[232] Hopefully, they will interpret article 8 as widely as possible, together with the positive obligations attaching to it.

224 R Cornwath (2001) p 476.
225 See N Mole (2001) p 668.
226 See J Miles (2001) pp 437–440.
227 See Human Rights Act 1998, s 22(4). Discussed by R Bailey-Harris and M Harris (2002) pp 123–125.
228 Eg *E v United Kingdom* [2002] 3 FCR 700. See also *DP and JC v United Kingdom* [2003] 1 FLR 50.
229 See *Costello-Roberts v United Kingdom* (1995) 19 EHRR 112 (para 30). It depends on all the circumstances of the case, such as the nature and context of the treatment, its duration, its physical and mental effects and, in some instances, the sex, age and state of health of the victim.
230 Under Children Act 1989, s 31.
231 N Mole (2001) p 668.
232 See *X and Y v Netherlands* (1985) 8 EHRR 235: a 16-year-old mentally disabled girl was entitled to an effective remedy for her rights under art 8 being infringed by a sexual assault.

(C)   Calling local authorities to account for failing to implement care plans

As the discussion above shows, the *Bedfordshire* decision gave the impression that the child protection process was a largely unaccountable one and that children who suffered in the process should not be allowed to sue their local authorities who were undertaking sensitive work as best they could. Such an approach was controversial and becomes even more so when combined with a system which prevents the courts, or any other outside body, from monitoring the way local authorities care for children. Indeed, the *Bedfordshire* decision merely reinforced an approach already adopted by the Children Act 1989, in the context of child protection proceedings. One wonders whether, if that decision had reached the House of Lords before 1989, the draftsmen of the new legislation would have promoted such a strict separation of power between the local authorities and the courts. It was their deliberate intention to ensure that local authorities should not be accountable to the courts for decisions over the manner they choose to protect children. It is a controversial aspect of the statutory scheme that the courts have very little scope to initiate local authority intervention, or to override or circumscribe the exercise by local authorities of their statutory powers.[233] The courts are not only barred from using the inherent jurisdiction to order a child into the care of the local authority,[234] but they have no supervisory powers, similar to those formerly exercised by the courts over children taken into care under the wardship jurisdiction.

It must be acknowledged that the Children Act 1989 is not entirely consistent in its attempts to ensure that the courts, when dealing with local authority applications for orders to protect children from harm, must always adopt what Dewar describes as an 'adjudicative' role rather than a 'participative' one.[235] In particular, case law established the courts' entitlement under the Children Act 1989, section 34 to force the local authority to reassess the extent of contact it allows a parent to have with a child in care.[236] They also, under the Children Act 1989, section 38(6), have the power to direct a local authority to arrange for the child and family to undergo a residential assessment, despite the local authority's strong opposition to such a course of action.[237] Furthermore, the courts can force the local authority's hand, but only to a very limited extent, by making a section 37 direction,[238] together with an interim care or supervision order pending the outcome of the local authority's investigation.[239] Nonetheless, the decision in *Nottinghamshire County Council v P*[240] demonstrated only too clearly the toothlessness of this power. At both levels, the courts made clear their intense frustration with the local authority for merely complying with a section 37 direction, but refusing to apply for a care order to protect two sexually abused girls from their father.[241]

---

233   Applying the principle established in *A v Liverpool City Council* [1982] AC 363.

234   Children Act 1989, s 100(1) and (2).

235   See J Dewar (1995) p 16.

236   *Re B (minors) (termination of contact: paramount consideration)* [1993] 3 All ER 524: the courts can make a contact order regarding a child in care, despite the fact that the order will interfere with the long-term plans of the local authority.

237   *Re C (a minor) (interim care order: residential assessment)* [1997] AC 489.

238   Children Act 1989, s 37(1).

239   Children Act 1989, s 38(1)(a).

240   [1993] 3 All ER 815; full name *Nottinghamshire County Council v P; Re P (minors) (local authority: prohibited steps order)*.

241   See Sir Simon Brown P, [1993] 3 All ER 815 at 828.

These exceptions apart, the statutory regime devised by the Children Act 1989[242] ensures that the local authorities are free to decide whether to intervene and, if so, to choose the type of protection and care to offer the children they are willing to protect. In other words, the policy aspects of child protection are entirely within the local authority's purview, adhering to the principle that they are better placed to ascertain how and when to protect children than are the courts. Some, like Hayes, consider this to be a realistic approach. Indeed, she maintains that, as a general principle, the notion of local authority independence from court supervision and interference in child protection work should be reinforced.[243] After implementation of the Children Act 1989, the courts conscientiously emphasised the fact that their former powers in wardship now removed, they had no ability to maintain control over children after making a care order.[244] Nevertheless, a sense of unease had been created by the courts' inability either to persuade local authorities to intervene in the first place, or to control how local authorities exercised their parental responsibilities over the children, once ordered into their care. A legislative scheme of this nature, with a clear division of powers, can only work well if the courts are satisfied that local authorities can invariably improve a child's life. But it radically undermines the courts' ability to satisfy the no order principle if they cannot be confident either that the details of the care plan will remain substantially unchanged or that they will be fully complied with.

The absence of any system for calling local authorities to account for failing to comply with care plans was causing judicial concern[245] well before *Re S (children: care plan), Re W (children: care plan)* (hereafter *Re S and Re W*)[246] reached the House of Lords. Practitioners were also frustrated by their inability either to monitor what happened to children under care orders, or to ensure that their care plans were complied with.[247] Furthermore, despite official attempts to improve the quality of local authority care plans,[248] case law,[249] and research[250] indicated considerable deficiencies in the

---

242   But this approach to such a strict separation of powers pre-dated the Children Act 1989, being established by the House of Lords in *A v Liverpool City Council* [1982] AC 363.
243   M Hayes (1996) p 216.
244   See, inter alia: *Re T (a minor) (care order: conditions)* [1994] 2 FLR 423: the courts have no power to impose conditions in a care order; *Re J (minors) (care: care plan)* [1994] 1 FLR 253: interim care orders should not be used to resurrect the supervisory role enjoyed by the wardship court.
245   See Wall J (1998) esp p 8. See also *Re W and B; Re W (care plan)* [2001] EWCA Civ 757, [2001] 2 FLR 582 at [18]–[21], per Thorpe LJ, setting out the historical background to these concerns.
246   [2002] UKHL 10, [2002] 2 All ER 192, reported at CA level sub nom *Re W and B; Re W (care plan)* [2001] EWCA Civ 757, [2001] 2 FLR 582.
247   J Hunt and A Macleod (1999) ch 9.
248   DH (1999 b).
249   Eg *Re O (care: discharge of care order)* [1999] 2 FLR 119: care orders (over three girls aged 13, 12, and almost 11) were discharged and supervision orders substituted, mainly because the care plan had not been fulfilled. It had involved therapy work with all three girls and their residing for part of the time with foster carers. No therapy took place; furthermore all three were abused in residential care and one was severely bullied. See also *Re L (care: assessment: fair trial)* [2002] EWHC 1379 (Fam), [2002] 2 FLR 730: Munby J strongly criticised the local authority regarding the changes made to the original care plan because its details had not been discussed with the local authority's family placement team leader (at [275]–[278]).
250   See J Hunt and A Macleod (1999) chs 7–9. This research indicated that one third of the children in the research sample had to cope with the insecurity and/or disappointment occasioned by changed or unfulfilled care plans. Nationally, this grossed up to around 2,000 children per annum (p 186). See also J Harwin and M Owen (2002) pp 67–70 and J Harwin and M Owen (2003).

care planning processes. These included relatively low quality care plans,[251] with a lack of appropriate detail,[252] and, more seriously, an apparent inability to deliver the services set out in the plans themselves.[253] Furthermore, compliance with the statutory review process, under which care plans should be regularly reviewed,[254] was patchy in the extreme.[255] Children were understandably upset and bewildered both by the courts' inability to influence placements[256] and by planned placements not materialising and promised contact with relatives not being arranged.[257]

As the judiciary themselves fully appreciate,[258] there may be any number of reasons for local authorities failing to comply with care plans, including the difficulty of complying with a child's very complex needs, and a lack of resources, particularly the availability of suitable long-term placements.[259] Nevertheless, children suffer greatly when local authorities fail to make proper provision for their care. Indeed, to remove a child from his or her home in the first place constitutes a breach of the child's own rights to family life which must be very carefully justified. The Court of Appeal, when hearing *Re S and Re W*,[260] considered that the courts should not simply overlook a local authority's failure then to fulfil a child's care plan. Indeed, such failure might constitute a breach of the local authority's positive obligations under article 8 to fulfil the child's rights thereunder, by providing him or her with a substitute family, or by reuniting him or her with the birth parents.[261] But the problem confronting the judiciary was the absence of any formal mechanism for bringing care cases back to court – more to the point, there was no systematic procedure available for calling local authorities to account for failing to comply with the care plans upon which the courts had relied when making the original care orders.

Theoretically, when care plans are radically changed or left unfulfilled, the parents can apply for a discharge of the care order itself.[262] Although the existence of such a remedy impressed the European Court of Human Rights,[263] in practice it is more apparent than real. Few parents make discharge applications, presumably because they have little faith that the courts will consider them fit to have their children returned to them.[264] In some cases, the courts may discover the local authority's failure to comply with a care plan only when, as in *Re F; F v Lambeth Borough Council*,[265] the parents apply for increased contact,[266] thereby providing the courts

251 SSI (2000) para 5.7.
252 J Harwin and M Owen (2003).
253 As in *Re S (children: care plan); Re W (children: care plan)* [2002] UKHL 10, [2002] 2 All ER 192 and *Re F; F v Lambeth London Borough Council* [2002] 1 FLR 217.
254 Under Children Act 1989, s 26(1) and (2) and the Review of Children's Cases Regulations 1991, SI 1991/895.
255 Discussed below.
256 M Ruegger (2001) p 143.
257 J Masson and M Winn Oakley (1999) ch 8 and J Hunt and A Macleod (1999) esp p 186.
258 *Re W and B; Re W (care plan)* [2001] EWCA Civ 757, [2001] 2 FLR 582 at [60], per Hale LJ.
259 J Hunt and A Macleod (1999) pp 229–236 and J Harwin and M Owen (2002) p 71.
260 [2001] EWCA Civ 757, [2001] 2 FLR 582, reported sub nom *Re W and B; Re W (care plan)*.
261 [2001] EWCA Civ 757, [2001] 2 FLR 582, see esp Hale LJ at [52]–[59].
262 Children Act 1989, s 39.
263 *Scott v United Kingdom* [2000] 1 FLR 958: the European Court of Human Rights considered that the availability of a discharge application negated the mother's argument that when a local authority abandoned the care plan to reunite the child with her, and placed the child for adoption, it had infringed the mother's rights under art 8, leaving her without an effective remedy.
264 J Hunt and A Macleod (1999) p 197.
265 [2002] 1 FLR 217.
266 Under Children Act 1989, s 34(3).

with an opportunity to review what has occurred since the initial care orders were made. But inadequate parents may be reluctant to take such a step. Furthermore, although older children may use the complaints system[267] or, with the help of advocacy services,[268] take their own case back to court,[269] as Thorpe LJ pointed out in *Re S and Re W*, 'the children who are most vulnerable to breakdown and delay are the very young whose healthy future development may depend on forming a sound psychological attachment in time ...'[270] Since the duties of the children's guardian terminate on the completion of the care proceedings, there is then no independent official whose job it is to ensure that the child's future care is adequately promoted, in accordance with the local authority's undertakings in the care plan.[271]

In *Re S and Re W*,[272] the House of Lords, perhaps predictably, rejected the Court of Appeal's radical solution to these problems. This was simply to read into the Children Act 1989 a means of supervising the implementation of the fundamental elements of care plans in selected cases.[273] But, as Lord Nicholls of Birkenhead pointed out, reinterpreting the Children Act 1989 in a way which undermines one of its cardinal principles – the separation of powers between the courts and local authorities – goes far beyond the scope of the Human Rights Act 1998, section 3.[274] Nevertheless, a different outcome could still have been justified. An inability to reinterpret the Children Act 1989 to provide a starring procedure, as envisaged by the Court of Appeal, does not rule out a child in care being provided with a remedy under the Human Rights Act 1998, in circumstances where the care plan has remained unfulfilled. Indeed, as Mole asserts, there is plenty of Strasbourg jurisprudence indicating that the right to a court hearing under article 6 would be illusory if a crucial aspect of a judicial decision were simply allowed to remain inoperative.[275] As she persuasively argues, the real weakness in Lord Nicholls' judgment was that he failed to ask or answer a crucial question:

> 'Does the care plan – considered in detail and approved by the court when making the care order in conformity with Article 8 – form such an integral part of the court's decision that the failure by the local authority to implement it is inconsistent with Article 6?'[276]

Hopefully, the House of Lords' 'bizarre' failure to answer this key question[277] will be remedied by the European Court of Human Rights itself.[278] Meanwhile, their Lordships, in *Re S and Re W*,[279] made plain their agreement with the Court of Appeal that a system which allows local authorities to fail children with impunity is quite

---

267 Ie under Children Act 1989, s 26. But see the defects in this procedure, especially the delays, discussed by C Williams (2002).
268 Discussed above.
269 Eg by applying for a discharge of the care order under Children Act 1989, s 39 or for increased contact with their parents under s 34(3).
270 [2001] EWCA Civ 757, [2001] 2 FLR 582 at [24], reported sub nom *Re W and B; Re W (care plan)*.
271 The new role of the officer responsible for carrying out statutory reviews is discussed below.
272 [2002] UKHL 10, [2002] 2 All ER 192.
273 These elements or 'milestones' were to be 'starred', with an obligation imposed on the local authority to report to the court or to the children's guardian on failure to implement any of them, thereby triggering an application by the children's guardian to apply for a discharge of the care order.
274 [2002] UKHL 10, [2002] 2 All ER 192 at [34]–[44]. The Human Rights Act 1998, s 3 directs that primary and subordinate legislation 'so far as it is possible to do so ... must be read and given effect in a way which is compatible with the Convention rights'.
275 N Mole (2002) pp 457–460.
276 N Mole (2002) p 459.
277 N Mole (2002) p 460.
278 A complaint has been taken to the European Court of Human Rights on behalf of the children involved in *Re S and Re W*.
279 [2002] UKHL 10, [2002] 2 All ER 192.

unsatisfactory and requires official review.[280] The government's legislative response to this judicial criticism was twofold. First, local authorities are now statutorily obliged to present to courts considering care applications, detailed and properly revised care plans.[281] Second, it endeavoured to produce a system whereunder once children have been received into care, their care plans are regularly and carefully reviewed, and revised when necessary.[282] The system for reviewing plans for children has been deficient for many years, mainly because the procedures are not properly complied with.[283] The obvious weakness of the new scheme is that it depends on local authority appointees[284] detecting cases where their own authority has behaved in an unsatisfactory manner. Time will tell whether it achieves its aims. For the time being, doubtless the courts will, with the implicit approval of the House of Lords, make far greater use of interim care orders, as a temporary 'holding measure',[285] until the details of care plans are fully clarified.[286]

For many children, interim care orders are out of the question – the care order is already in place, the care plan has not been implemented or has been changed quite radically, and for the worse. In such circumstances, parents who have not been adequately involved in the local authority's decision to change radically their child's care plan may force the local authority to reconsider, on the basis that their procedural rights under article 8 of the ECHR have been infringed.[287] Children whose experiences in care have produced grave physical and/or psychological damage, may now be able to sue local authorities in negligence for their failings.[288] Alternatively, they may seek compensation under the Human Rights Act 1998.[289] In all these situations, compensation comes after the event, far too late to prevent the child's suffering; but such litigation may provoke improvements in social work practice. Unless a formal and very effective mechanism is put in place to supervise the manner in which local authorities implement the care plans they agree to, the lives of children who are 'rescued' from parental abuse will continue to be damaged even further by their experiences in state care.

---

280   [2002] UKHL 10, [2002] 2 All ER 192 at [29]–[30] and [106], per Lord Nicholls and at [110], per Lord Mackay.

281   See Children Act 1989, s 31A, as inserted by Adoption and Children Act 2002, s 121, strengthening and clarifying the duties previously set out in DH (1999 b).

282   See Children Act 1989, s 26, as extensively amended by Adoption and Children Act 2002, s 118. The new procedure seeks to ensure that a local authority appointee, whose role is to chair statutory reviews for children in care, detects those cases where a child's care plan is not being adequately implemented and notifies the Children and Family Court Advisory and Support Service (CAFCASS). A children's guardian will then be appointed with a view to applying on behalf of the child for some further court order, such as a discharge of the care order.

283   See, inter alia: SSI (2000) (pp 26–28): reviews normally occurring at least at six-month intervals, nearly one fifth were only being held at 7- to 12-month intervals, and 3% were held at over 12-monthly intervals; SSI (2002 b) (para 6.8): 'most councils' failing to convene statutory child care reviews within statutory timescales, 3 councils only met timescales in 50% of cases, and in 1 of these there were 'weaknesses in completing the tasks laid out in the care plan.'

284   See Children Act 1989, s 26(2)(k).

285   [2002] UKHL 10, [2002] 2 All ER 192 at [91], per Lord Nicholls.

286   [2002] UKHL 10, [2002] 2 All ER 192 at [92]–[102].

287   Eg *Re M (care: challenging decisions by local authority)* [2001] 2 FLR 1300 and *C v Bury Metropolitan Borough Council* [2002] EWHC 1438 (Fam), [2002] 2 FLR 868.

288   Eg *Barrett v Enfield London Borough Council* [2001] 2 AC 550 and *C v Flintshire County Council* [2001] EWCA Civ 302, [2001] 2 FLR 33.

289   Under Human Rights Act 1998, ss 7 and 8.

(6)   CONCLUSION

Child protection work is undoubtedly delicate and difficult, but if local authorities set themselves up as being able to carry out the parenting role better than children's own parents, the children have a right to a professional service. It is clear that this is not always delivered, particularly when they are placed in residential care. Many of the children coming into state care are already emotionally disturbed and extremely vulnerable. Even making allowances for this, the experience of being looked after by the state is not always a particularly beneficial one. Because children are more vulnerable to abuse than adults, intervention to protect them should be more efficient and more open to scrutiny. By ensuring that local authorities are often unaccountable to the children they are responsible for, the law condones lax and careless practice. One way or another, the state must improve its record regarding the children it removes from abusive birth parents.

BIBLIOGRAPHY

NB many of these publications can be obtained on the relevant organisation's website.

AIRE Centre, *Secure Accommodation Orders, Police Protection "Orders", Curfews from the Convention perspective* (2001) AIRE Centre Family Law and European Convention on Human Rights Website Materials.

Bailey S and Bowman M, 'Public Authority Negligence Revisited' (2000) 59 Cambridge Law Journal 85.

Bailey-Harris R and Harris M, 'Local authorities and child protection – the mosaic of accountability' (2002) 14 Child and Family Law Quarterly 117.

Bates P, 'Secure accommodation orders – in whose interests?' (1995) 7(2) Child and Family Law Quarterly 70.

Berridge D and Brodie I, *Children's Home Revisited* (1998) Jessica Kingsley.

Brandon M et al, *Safeguarding Children with the Children Act 1989* (1999) The Stationery Office.

Bullock R et al, *Secure Treatment Outcomes: The care careers of very difficult adolescents* (1998) Aldershot.

Children and Young People's Unit, *Learning to Listen: Core Principles for the Involvement of Children and Young People* (2001) DfES.

Cornwath R, 'Welfare services – liabilities in tort after the HRA – Postscript' (2001) Public Law 475.

Department for Education and Employment (DfEE) and DH, *Guidance on the Education of Children and Young People in Public Care* LAC (2000) 13 (2000).

Department of Health (DH), *The Children Act 1989 Guidance and Regulations* Vol 4 *Residential Care* (1991) HMSO.

Department of Health (DH), *Guidance on Permissible Forms of Control for Children in Residential Care* LAC (93) 13 (1993).

Department of Health (DH), *Focus on Teenagers: Research into Practice* (1996) HMSO.

Department of Health (DH), *Caring for Children Away from Home: Messages from Research* (1998 a) Wiley.

Department of Health (DH), *Quality Protects Circular: Transforming Children's Services* LAC (98) 28 (1998 b).

Department of Health (DH), *Children Looked After by Local Authorities: Government Response to the Second Report of the Health Committee on Children Looked After by Local Authorities: Session 1997–98* Cm 4175 (1998 c) The Stationery Office.

Department of Health (DH), *Me Survive Out There? New Arrangements for Young People Living in and Leaving Care* (1999 a).

Department of Health (DH), *Care Plans and Care Proceedings under the Children Act 1989* LAC (99) 29 (1999 b) .

Department of Health (DH), White Paper *Adoption: a new approach* Cm 5017 (2000 a) The Stationery Office.

Department of Health (DH), *The Children Act Report 1995–99* Cm 4579 (2000 b) The Stationery Office.

Department of Health (DH), *Listening to People: A Consultation on Improving Social Services Complaints Procedures* (2000 c).

Department of Health (DH), *The Children Act Report 2000* (2001 a) DH Publications.

Department of Health (DH), *Adoption* LAC (2001) 33 (2001 b).

Department of Health (DH), *Draft Practice Guidance to Support the National Adoption Standards for England* (2001 c).

Department of Health (DH), *National Adoption Standards for England* (2001 d) DH Publications.

Department of Health (DH), *The Children Act Now: Messages from Research* (2001 e) The Stationery Office.

Department of Health (DH), *Children (Leaving Care) Act Guidance* 2001 (2001 f).

Department of Health (DH), *Social Service Performance Assessment Framework Indicators, 2001– 2002* (2002 a) Government Statistical Service and DH.

Department of Health (DH), *Safeguarding Children: A joint Chief Inspectors' Report on Arrangements to Safeguard Children* (2002 b) DH Publications.

Department of Health (DH), *Children's Homes, National Minimum Standards, Children's Homes Regulations* (2002 c) The Stationery Office.

Department of Health (DH et al), *Framework for the Assessment of Children in Need and their Families* (2000) The Stationery Office.

Dewar J, 'The courts and local authority autonomy' (1995) 7(2) Child and Family Law Quarterly 15.

Farmer E, 'Children Reunited with their Parents: A Review of Research Findings' in B Broad (ed) *Kinship Care: The placement choice for children and young people* (2001) Russell House Publishing.

Farmer E and Owen M, *Child Protection Practice: Private Risks and Public Remedies* (1995) HMSO.

Farmer E and Parker R, *Trials and Tribulations: Returning Children from Local Authority Care to their Families* (1991) HMSO.

Farmer E and Pollock S, *Sexually Abused and Abusing Children in Substitute Care* (1998) Wiley.

Farmer E and Pollock S, 'Mix and Match: Planning to Keep Looked After Children Safe' (1999) 8 Child Abuse Review 377.

Fortin J, 'Children's rights and the use of physical force' (2001) 13 Child and Family Law Quarterly 243.

Gallagher B, 'The Abuse of Children in Public Care' (1999) 8 Child Abuse Review 357.

Gearty L, 'Unravelling Osman' (2001) 64 Modern Law Review 159.

Goldstein J, Freud A and Solnit A, *Before the Best Interests of the Child* (1980) Burnett Books Limited.

Harwin J and Owen M, 'A Study of Care Plans and their Implementation and Relevance for *Re W and B and Re W (care plan)*' in Thorpe LJ and C Cowton (eds) *Delight and Dole: The Children Act 10 Years On* (2002) Family Law.

Harwin J and Owen M, 'The implementation of care plans and its relationship to children's welfare' (2003) 15 Child and Family Law Quarterly 71.

Hayes M, 'The proper role of courts in child care cases' (1996) 8 Child and Family Law Quarterly 201.

Hoffmann R H L, 'Human Rights and the House of Lords' (1999) 62 Modern Law Review 159.

House of Commons Health Committee, *Children looked after by local authorities: second report from the Health Committee* HC 319; session 1997–98, vol II (1998) The Stationery Office.

Howell S, *The health of looked after children* NCB highlight no 184 (2001) National Children's Bureau.

Hughes W (Chairman), *Report of the Committee of Inquiry into Children's Homes and Hostels* (1985) HMSO.

Hunt J, 'A moving target – care proceedings as a dynamic process' (1998) 10 Child and Family Law Quarterly 281.

Hunt J, 'Kinship Care, Child Protection and the Courts' in B Broad (ed) *Kinship Care: The placement choice for children and young people* (2001) Russell House Publishing.

Hunt J and Macleod A, *The Best-Laid Plans: Outcomes of Judicial Decisions in Child Protection Proceedings* (1999) The Stationery Office.

Lenihan T and Dean P, 'Child Prostitution in England' in D Barrett (ed) *Youth Prostitution in the New Europe: The Growth in Sex Work* (2000) Russell House Publishing.

Levy A and Kahan B (Chairmen), *The Pindown Experience and the Protection of Children* (1991) The Report of the Staffordshire Child Care Inquiry, 1990, Staffordshire County Council.

Lowe N and Murch M, *The plan for the child: Adoption or long-term fostering* (2002) BAAF.

Masson J, '*Re K (A Child) (Secure Accommodation Order: Right to Liberty)* and *Re C (Secure Accommodation Order: Representation)*' (2002) 14 Child and Family Law Quarterly 77.

Masson J and Winn Oakley M, *Out of Hearing: Representing Children in Care Proceedings* (1999) Wiley.

Miles J, '*Z and Others v United Kingdom; TP and KM v United Kingdom* – Human rights and child protection' (2001) 13 Child and Family Law Quarterly 431.

Mole N, 'Local Authorities and the European Court' (2001) Family Law 667.

Mole N, '*Re W and B; Re W (Care Plan) and Re S (Minors) (Care Order: Implementation of Care Plan); Re W (Minors) (Care Order: Adequacy of Care Plan)*: A note on the judgment from the perspective of the European Convention for the Protection of Human Rights and Fundamental Freedoms 1950' (2002) 14 Child and Family Law Quarterly 447.

Morris J, *Having Someone Who Cares? Barriers to change in the public care of children* (2000) National Children's Bureau and Joseph Rowntree.

National Children's Bureau, *Safe to be Let Out?: The current and future use of secure accommodation for children and young people* (1995) National Children's Bureau.

O'Neill T, *Children in Secure Accommodation: A Gendered Exploration of Locked Institutional Care for Children in Trouble* (2001) Jessica Kingsley Publishers.

Pack A, '"Sweet and Tender Hooligans" – Secure Accommodation and Human Rights' (2001) Family Law 140.

Parry M, 'Secure accommodation – the Cinderalla of family law' (2000) 12 Child and Family Law Quarterly 101.

Performance and Innovation Unit (PIU), *The Prime Minister's Review of Adoption* (2000) Cabinet Office.

Philpot T, *A Very Private Practice* (2001) BAAF.

Ruegger M, 'Seen and Heard but How Well Informed? Children's Perceptions of the Guardian Ad Litem Service' (2001) 15 Children and Society 133.

Ryder E, '" Lost and Found" – Looking to the Future After North Wales' (2000) Family Law 406.

Safe on the Streets Research Team, *Still Running: Children on the Streets in the UK* (1999) Children's Society.

Schofield G, 'Parental responsibility and parenting – the needs of accommodated children in long-term foster care' (2000 a) 12 Child and Family Law Quarterly 345.

Schofield G et al, *Growing up in Foster Care* (2000 b) BAAF.

Smith C and Gardner P, 'Secure accommodation under the Children Act 1989: legislative confusion and social ambivalence' (1996) 18 Journal of Social Welfare and Family Law 173.

Social Services Inspectorate (SSI), '... *When leaving home is also leaving care'* (1997) DH Publications.

Social Services Inspectorate (SSI), *Someone Else's Children: Inspections of Planning and Decision Making for Children Looked After and The Safety of Children Looked After* (1998) DH Publications.

Social Services Inspectorate (SSI), *Modern Social Services – A Commitment to Improve, The 8th Annual Report of the Chief Inspector of Social Services 1998/99* (1999 a) DH Publications

Social Services Inspectorate (SSI), *Meeting the challenges of adoption* (1999 b) DH Publications.

Social Services Inspectorate (SSI), *Adopting Changes* (2000) DH Publications.

Social Services Inspectorate (SSI), *Developing quality to protect children, SSI Inspection of Children's Services* (2001 a) DH Publications.

Social Services Inspectorate (SSI), *Modern Social Services: a commitment to deliver, The 10th Annual Report of the Chief Inspector of Social Services* (2001 b) DH Publications.

Social Services Inspectorate (SSI), *Modern Social Services: a commitment to reform, The 11th Annual Report of the Chief Inspector of Social Services* (2002 a) DH Publications.

Social Services Inspectorate (SSI), *Fostering for the Future: Inspection of Foster Care Services* (2002 b) DH Publications.

Social Services Inspectorate (SSI), *Delivering Quality Children's Services* (2002 c) DH Publications.

Swindells H et al, *Family Law and the Human Rights Act 1998* (1999) Family Law.

Utting W (Chairman), *People Like Us: The Report Of The Review Of The Safeguards For Children Living Away From Home* (1997) DH/The Welsh Office, HMSO.

Vernon J, *Audit and Assessment of Leaving Care Services in London* (2000) National Children's Bureau/Department of Health.

Wade J, Biehal N et al, *Going Missing: Young people absent from care* (1998) Wiley.

Wall J, 'Care Plans: A Judicial Perspective' in Thorpe LJ and E Clarke (eds) *Divided Duties: Care planning for children within the family justice system* (1998) Family Law.

Warner N (Chairman), *Choosing with Care: Report of the Committee of Inquiry into the Selection, Development and Management of Staff in Children's Homes* (1992) HMSO.

Waterhouse R (Chairman), *Lost in Care: Report of the Tribunal of Inquiry into the Abuse of Children in Care in the former County Council Areas of Gwynedd and Clwyd since 1974* (2000) The Stationery Office.

Williams C ,'The Practical Operation of the Children Act Complaints Procedure (2002) 14 Child and Family Law Quarterly 25.

Williams G and Macreadie J (Chairmen), *Ty Mawr Community Home Inquiry* (1992) Gwent County Council.

Chapter 17

The right of abused children to protection by the criminal law

(1) INTRODUCTION

Children obviously have as much right to protection by the criminal law as adults and its use on their behalf clearly indicates that society will not condone their ill-treatment. Behaviour which leads to a child being made the subject of care proceedings under the Children Act 1989, section 31 may also result in the perpetrator facing criminal charges. Consequently, throughout a child protection investigation there should often be close collaboration between social workers and the police with a view to using both the civil and criminal law. Despite this, the criminal justice system, in many ways, casts a blight over the child protection system. There is a widespread perception amongst child care practitioners that, as presently organised, the criminal justice system does not promote the welfare of children caught up in its processes and that its use may even victimise them over again. At every stage of the child protection process, efforts to help the child recover from the effects of abuse may be undermined by the prospect of criminal proceedings against the abuser. Sometimes the drive to obtain a conviction may prevail over the needs of the child victim.

If children as a class substantially benefited from criminal proceedings being brought against the perpetrators of abuse, this might justify individual children suffering in the process. The conviction rates do not, however, bear this out. It is notoriously difficult to obtain accurate statistics regarding the number of offences recorded against children, since they are compiled by type of offence and offender, often with no details regarding victim.[1] Recent legislative efforts to avoid child witnesses giving evidence against their alleged abusers in open court may eventually improve the rate of criminal prosecutions. Meanwhile, it is clear that the extent of child abuse is far higher than the number of offences reported to the police[2] and higher again than the number of adults convicted for such offences.[3] Indeed, despite

---

1   See D Grubin (1998), who discusses (pp 3–12) the difficulty of obtaining reliable statistics and prevalence rates relating to the sexual abuse of children. Grubin's research indicates that the rate of sexual abuse of children is far higher than official crime statistics would suggest and that the majority of sex offenders target only girls and sexually assault children known to them, in the homes of the victims or perpetrator. See also C Cobley (2000) pp 30–39.

2   Many crimes involving very young and/or mentally handicapped children may never get reported to the police at all because of difficulties in communicating their experiences to adults or because they do not recognise that they are being abused.

3   The investigation of 500 complaints of physical or sexual abuse in North Wales children's homes in the 1980s, led to only eight prosecutions and six convictions: R Waterhouse (2000) pp 7 and 20.

all the efforts of child protection practitioners to adapt their work practices to suit the requirements of the criminal justice system, only a tiny proportion of abusers is convicted, compared with the number of criminal offences actually committed against children in the form of abuse.[4] To many of those involved in child protection work this not only seems a waste of resources, when so few convictions are secured, but also diverts attention from establishing whether the families involved are eligible for family support services and protection. This chapter examines the features of the criminal justice system which most undermine efforts to promote children's rights to protection through the civil law.

(2) BACKGROUND

There is no offence of 'child abuse' as such, and it would be difficult to design one which was broad enough to cover all its features. Nevertheless, there is a wide range of criminal offences which protect children against what most would describe as 'abusive' behaviour.[5] Their existence clearly acknowledges a child's right to criminal protection from such ill-treatment. Physical assaults on children and adults are covered by identical offences. Consequently, as long as an assault cannot be justified as being a form of legitimate discipline,[6] physical abuse may result in a variety of criminal charges, ranging from common assault through to actual bodily harm, to grievous bodily harm, to murder and manslaughter. Regrettably, however, police child protection teams do not always devote the same resources or time and energy to investigating serious assults against children as they would assaults against adults.[7]

The law recognises that there are also certain types of ill-treatment which are often directed at children alone. Acknowledging that children can be as damaged by acts of omission as of commission, nineteenth-century legislation created offences regarding their neglect and cruelty; this legislation was later replaced by Part 1 of the Children and Young Persons Act 1933.[8] Many of these provisions are technical and outdated, but it is in the context of paedophilia that the inadequacies of the present law appear most obvious. Long before the Cleveland crisis in the late 1980s, concern about the sexual abuse of children had resulted in a series of criminal offences intended to protect them from various kinds of sexual activity.[9] Some of these are couched in extremely broad language; for example, it is an offence, to take or permit to be taken any 'indecent' photograph of a child or to possess such a photograph with a view to its being distributed or 'shown' by himself or others.[10] Nevertheless, as we discover

---

4   Eg although in 1995 there were 3,957 offenders throughout England and Wales cautioned or convicted for sexual offences against children, police crime reports suggest that as many as 72,600 cases a year of indecent assault and rape involving children may actually occur. See D Grubin (1998) pp 5 and 12.

5   Usefully set out in table form in Home Office (hereafter HO) (1992).

6   Discussed in chapter 9.

7   See H Laming (2003), who at paras 13.20–13.24 and 14.14–14.15, strongly criticised Brent and Haringey police child protection teams for treating the investigation of crimes against children as less important than other forms of serious crime. He called for such an approach to be eradicated: see Police Recommendation 92.

8   See esp Children and Young Persons Act 1933, s 1: this renders criminal all forms of wilful violent and non-violent neglect and ill-treatment which is 'likely to cause him unnecessary suffering or injury to health (including injury to or loss of sight, or hearing, or limb, or organ of the body, and any mental derangement) ...'

9   Eg Punishment of Incest Act 1908. See now Sexual Offences Act 1956, ss 10–11.

10   Protection of Children Act 1978, s 1. See *R v Land* [1999] QB 65.

more about the habits of paedophiles, the present law's inadequacies become increasingly evident. Children have a right to better protection, both from those outside their families and from those within. The government is intent on creating a new raft of offences designed to punish sex abusers who exploit children's innocence and find various ways of gaining their trust and confidence. There will, for example, be a new offence of sexual grooming, designed to prevent paedophiles befriending children with a view to eventually engaging them in sexual activities.[11] The new scheme of offences will ensure that sex offenders can be punished, whether or not children ostensibly consent to sexual activity.[12] Given the 'looser structure of modern families',[13] there will also be new offences to replace and extend the present offences of incest, prohibiting sexual relations between children and people who are in positions of trust, including wider family members, such as step-parents and foster-parents.[14]

Hopefully, there will be few types of abusive treatment of children that cannot be slotted into a criminal offence of some kind. Furthermore, the easing of the rules of evidence in criminal trials has made it feasible for younger children to give evidence as witnesses, thereby making it possible to bring more child abusers to trial.[15] There are, however, certain aspects of the criminal justice system which undermine its suitability for protecting individual children from abuse. These make it difficult for those involved in civil child protection work, such as social workers, to appreciate the approach adopted by police officers and prosecutors when dealing with child protection referrals. In many ways their objectives are not only very different but, at times, there are direct conflicts. First, the criminal law focuses on protecting society and children as a class, not on the interests of the individual child victim. Indeed, there is the assumption that by catching and punishing the offender, the victim's welfare will automatically be fulfilled. Second, since the focus of criminal intervention is on punishing the wrongdoer, there is considerable emphasis, not on the rights of the victim to comfort and support, but on those of the alleged perpetrator who may, after all, be innocent. Considerable effort is devoted to collecting evidence proving beyond reasonable doubt both that an offence has actually occurred and that the right person has been identified as the perpetrator.

If all the practitioners involved in a child abuse referral are eventually satisfied that an offence has been committed and by a correctly identified individual, the criminal justice system is geared to ensuring a conviction, possibly even at the expense of the victim. The decision to prosecute a defendant may be taken 'in the public interest',[16] even if those making such a decision are well aware that the proceedings will hinge on the child's evidence and that the experience of acting as a witness in a criminal trial may reinforce the distress and trauma suffered by the child already. But even if a conviction is secured, child care practitioners, intent on fulfilling the child's right to protection, often consider it particularly ironic that criminal sanctions for child abusers rarely ensure that they do not re-offend. Indeed, in the case of sex offenders, a prison sentence may reinforce their addiction. Not all civil

11 Eg through the use of internet chatrooms. See Home Office (hereafter HO) (2002 a) para 54 and Sexual Offences Bill 2003.
12 Inter alia: the offence of 'adult sexual activity with a child'; three new criminal offences designed to criminalise sexual activity with those who do not fully understand the implications of what is occurring, through mental disability. See HO (2002 a) ch 4 and Sexual Offences Bill 2003, Part I.
13 See HO (2000) chs 3 and 5, esp para 5.5.6.
14 See HO (2002 a) ch 4.
15 Discussed below.
16 Crown Prosecution Service (hereafter CPS) (2000) section 6.

child protection referrals march hand-in-hand with criminal investigations and trials. When they do, child care practitioners find it difficult to reconcile themselves to these features of the criminal justice system and the way it curtails their own freedom to deal with the case as they think most appropriate.

(3)   JOINT INTERVIEWING AND THE SEARCH FOR EVIDENCE IN THE INVESTIGATIVE STAGES

The civil child protection system, as presently organised, places considerable importance on referrals being jointly investigated by social services[17] and the police in those cases where a criminal offence has occurred and there is a possibility of bringing the perpetrator to trial. This will not be the objective in all cases. Current guidance, *Working Together*[18] states that there are three main questions governing the decision whether criminal proceedings should be initiated: whether or not there is sufficient evidence to prosecute; whether or not it is in the public interest for proceedings to be instigated against the particular offender; whether or not the institution of proceedings is in the child victim's best interests.[19] In those cases where it is clear from the start that the circumstances do not warrant a criminal prosecution, a joint investigation is unnecessary. But since this will not always be clear until well into the investigation process, it is regrettable that there is an apparent reluctance to consult the police over potential section 47 inquiries.[20] Fortunately, once they are consulted, it appears that there are good working relationships normally exist between the two agencies when responding to a child's need for protection.[21] Nevertheless, social workers' hostility towards police officers involved in child protection work sometimes hampers good working relationships between the two agencies, certainly in the initial stages of a referral.[22]

Official guidance stresses the need for the police and social services to work 'in partnership' when investigating any child protection referral involving a criminal offence.[23] Nevertheless, the police may often be cast in a central role during the investigation stage of a child protection referral.[24] The impetus for often involving the police in child protection referrals came in the late 1980s, when it was realised that far larger numbers of children were the victims of sexual abuse than had formerly been imagined. The Cleveland Report encouraged greater co-operation between social services and the police to avoid victims of child sexual abuse being repeatedly examined and interviewed by a variety of practitioners, all for slightly different purposes.[25] The involvement of the police in child protection work was accelerated by legislation permitting the admission of video-recorded interviews with child witnesses in criminal trials.[26] New procedures involving the police and social workers

---

17   Ie under Children Act 1989, s 47. Discussed in more detail in chapter 15.
18   Department of Health (hereafter DH) et al (1999).
19   DH et al (1999) para 3.62.
20   DH (2002 a) para 6.18.
21   DH (2002 a) para 6.27.
22   Relations between Haringey Social Services Department and the police child protection team were hampered by social work hostility. See H Laming (2003), paras 14.17–14.31.
23   DH et al (1999) para 5.8.
24   See E Farmer and M Owen (1995) p 326.
25   Butler-Sloss LJ (1988) pp 248–251.
26   Criminal Justice Act 1988 (hereafter CJA 1988), s 32A (as inserted by the Criminal Justice Act 1991). CJA 1988, s 32 had previously merely allowed children to give evidence at criminal trials by a live closed-circuit television link outside the court room itself.

jointly interviewing victims of child sexual abuse using video-recording equipment quickly became standard practice.

These legislative changes implemented some, but not all, of the Pigot Committee's recommendations.[27] That committee had been concerned to discover how few perpetrators of sexual offences against children were tried and convicted. It concluded that the strict rules of evidence, particularly the hearsay rule, made it extremely difficult for criminal courts to hear the accounts of the child victims themselves. Because they were often too young to give evidence in person, offenders were being left free to molest their very young victims in private.[28] Had all Pigot's recommendations been implemented immediately, many child witnesses would have been spared appearing in court altogether. Instead, an unsatisfactory compromise, 'half Pigot', was introduced whereby a video-recording of an investigative interview with a child became admissible to the court, taking the place of his or her evidence-in-chief.[29] But the rule that the child should be available for an oral cross-examination was left unchanged until over a decade later.[30]

Most social workers and police officers consider that using video-recorded investigative interviews as children's evidence-in-chief in criminal trials is a far more efficient process than taking written statements. It also enables children to provide their evidence in reasonably relaxed conditions.[31] Nevertheless, children themselves often find the interviews far more stressful than practitioners suppose, with insufficient time being devoted to explaining the process to them or involving them in the arrangements being made.[32] Furthermore, the new system introduced in the early 1990s clearly undermined the uneasy balance between the civil child protection system and the criminal justice system.[33] All practitioners are only too aware of the considerable body of psychological research indicating that children seldom lie, and that they provide accurate evidence of abuse if asked the right questions in an appropriate format.[34] Consequently, they are tempted to believe a child who says that he or she has been abused. But the training of those involved in the criminal justice system, such as police officers and lawyers from the Crown Prosecution Service (CPS), will force them to probe a child's version of events and seek evidence corroborating this. Social workers more naturally approach child protection work from the perspective of the child's right to present and future protection. Whilst they may wish to comfort and support a child when seeking evidence identifying the abuser, police officers and lawyers will wish to avoid suggestions that the child was encouraged, coached or bullied into identifying a defendant falsely. Those familiar with the criminal justice system are also aware that children are suggestible and may respond to leading questions.[35] The original official guidance[36] (the *Memorandum*) on conducting video-recorded interviews reinforced their approach. The courts often treated the *Memorandum* as an inflexible code, which could not be deviated from if interviewers

27   T Pigot (1989).
28   T Pigot (1989) ch 5.
29   CJA 1988, s 32A, subject to certain age limits depending on the nature of the offence.
30   Further changes were introduced by the Youth Justice and Criminal Evidence Act 1999 (hereafter YJCEA 1999), discussed below.
31   G Davies et al (1995); M Aldridge and J Wood (2000) p 172.
32   See A Wade and H Westcott (1997) pp 55–58.
33   J Brownlow and B Waller (1997) pp 18–21.
34   See the research evidence on children's powers of recall summarised in G Davies and H Westcott (1999) pp 8–10.
35   G Davies and H Westcott (1999) pp 9–10.
36   HO (1992). This was replaced by extended guidance in 2002: see below.

were to ensure that the child's evidence complied with the evidential requirements of a criminal trial.[37]

Admittedly, compliance with the *Memorandum*[38] ensured that children became less often subjected to the flawed interviewing techniques criticised in the Cleveland Report,[39] and by the judiciary in later child protection cases.[40] As Butler-Sloss LJ has pointed out, even civil court proceedings require the interviewers to be clear about the difference between interviewing children to ascertain the facts and interviewing them for therapeutic purposes to help them unburden their worries. When the interview is for the former purpose, although the interviewers need not adhere rigidly to official guidance, its underlying principles are equally applicable.[41] Nevertheless, the *Memorandum* soon attracted considerable criticism, due to the straight-jacket it imposed on the interviewing process.[42] Criticisms included: the recommended duration of one hour was unrealistically short; a neutral interviewing style, despite avoiding claims that the child had been led or coached, was incompatible with the child's need for support and reassurance; insufficient account was taken of the special needs of very young,[43] disabled[44] and black children;[45] there was insufficient emphasis on preparing the child for the interview.[46]

Some felt that the interviewing techniques promoted by the *Memorandum*[47] actually inhibited children and prevented them from giving the information necessary to protect them in the civil courts.[48] Interviewers often decided to follow the guidance, even when child protection procedures were inevitable and criminal proceedings highly unlikely – quite simply because compliance with the guidance ensured that the interview served both purposes. But by doing so, they precluded any ability to encourage the child to produce evidence which might not otherwise be forthcoming. There was also a view that the greater involvement of the police in child protection work, combined with the manner in which the interviews must be conducted, had a deleterious effect on social work practice.[49] The need to follow its requirements often led to police officers taking the lead in joint interviews, sometimes giving social workers the impression that they had greater concern for the perpetrator than for the child.[50] Particularly during the early

---

37 See *G v DPP* [1997] 2 All ER 755. Phillips LJ (at 761) stressed that courts have a discretion to admit interview evidence which does not comply with the *Memorandum*. Nevertheless, he warned that it was of great importance for the guidance to be followed; failure to do so might mean the child's evidence being excluded.
38 HO (1992).
39 Butler-Sloss LJ (1988) esp ch 12
40 Eg *Re E (a minor) (child abuse: evidence)* [1991] 1 FLR 420 and *L and P v Reading Borough Council and Chief Constable of Thames Valley Police* [2001] EWCA Civ 346, [2001] 2 FLR 50.
41 *Re D (child abuse: interviews)* [1998] 2 FLR 10 at 18.
42 Inter alia: Social Services Inspectorate (hereafter SSI) (1994) pp 16–19; see also summary in G Davies and H Westcott (1999) pp 3–5.
43 M Aldridge and J Wood (2000) p 174.
44 R Marchant and M Page (1997).
45 A Gupta (1997).
46 G Davies and H Westcott (1999) p 15.
47 HO (1992).
48 SSI (1994) p 50.
49 See C Wattam (1997 a) p 111.
50 See SSI (1994) p 48 and J Brownlow and B Waller (1997) p 20. This practice continues today, with police officers still, 'in almost all cases' taking the lead when interviewing children. See DH (2002 a) para 6.28. This is despite the current guidance (HO et al (2002)) stressing (paras 2.72–2.73) that that there should be no hard and fast rule over which of the two interviewers should take the lead, but that the lead interviewer should be a person with an ability to establish a rapport with the child and an ability to communicate effectively with him or her.

1990s, there were growing concerns over the large numbers of video-recorded interviews which, despite attempts to comply with the *Memorandum*, were never shown in court.[51] This suggested that children were suffering the worst of both worlds. They were being interviewed by methods that did not necessarily extract the truth, but were then being required to give evidence-in-chief orally in court because their video-recorded interview evidence was rejected. Subsequent studies suggest that a higher proportion of video-recorded interviews is now being admitted in criminal trials.[52] The more sophisticated recording equipment now available to interviewing teams has also reduced the number of interviews rejected due to poor technical quality.[53]

The *Memorandum* was finally replaced, in 2002, by *Achieving Best Evidence in Criminal Proceedings* (hereafter *ABE*),[54] a revised and expanded volume of official guidance on video-recorded interviewing methods. The current guidance attempts to address the criticisms of the old. It encourages interviewers to take proper account of the individual child's developmental needs and background, both in terms of the interview's style and duration. There is greater flexibility over the interview's duration.[55] It emphasises the need to involve the child fully in the whole process – to prepare him or her properly for the interview with adequate explanations,[56] and the need for interviewers to build a rapport with the child.[57] Overall, its style is less dogmatic than that of the *Memorandum* and it fully acknowledges the difficulties of interviewing children reluctant to speak freely about abuse without encouragement.[58]

A child victim's need for therapy was another issue which became increasingly controversial in the context of preparing children for a criminal trial. Social workers resented the needs of the criminal justice system overriding those of the abused child when it came to deciding whether therapy could be provided for a potential child witness. Indeed, it seemed ironic that the introduction of a scheme intended to improve the ways in which the criminal justice system treated child witnesses immediately led to less support being given to seriously abused children in the early stages of investigations, for fear of contaminating their evidence. In the past, the *Memorandum*[59] and the CPS, at a national level, maintained that children whose interviews had already been video-recorded could then receive therapy after the interview, but before the trial. Despite this, local CPS officers and prosecuting lawyers often took the view that it would contaminate the child's evidence.[60] This approach led to severely abused and traumatised children being deprived of urgently needed therapeutic support in the interim, in order to promote the aims of the criminal justice system, without any guarantee that the trial would eventually go ahead or, indeed, produce a conviction.

---

51 G Davies et al (1995). Between 1992 and 1993, only 24% of nearly 15,000 video-taped interviews were submitted to the CPS. Some were discarded by the CPS, with only 470 eventually obtaining permission from the courts for their showing.
52 See G Davis et al (1999) p 57 and Crown Prosecution Service Inspectorate (hereafter CPSI) (1998) pp 31–32.
53 CPSI (1998) pp 31–32.
54 HO et al (2002). This implemented the recommendations of HO (1998). Its introduction was timed to coincide with the implementation of YJCEA 1999, Pt II: see discussion below.
55 HO et al (2002) para 2.98.
56 HO et al (2002) paras 2.65–2.66.
57 HO et al (2002) esp paras 2.73 and 2.100.
58 HO et al (2002) paras 2.108–2.111.
59 HO (1992) para 3.44. See also *R v K* [1993] Crim LR 281: the court held that therapy which avoids reference to the specific allegations is not prejudicial to the criminal trial and is therefore not disclosable.
60 See J Brownlow and B Waller (1997) pp 20–21.

Such a policy inevitably produced strong criticism[61] and eventually proved unsustainable. Current inter-agency guidance emphasises that the child's best interests must govern such decisions, which are not the preserve of the police or the CPS, but which must be taken by all the agencies responsible for the child's welfare.[62] Furthermore, it stresses that if the child's need for immediate therapy overrides the need for him or her to appear as a credible witness in a criminal case, then this must be arranged, even at the cost of abandoning the criminal proceedings.[63] It also points out that there are ways in which the child may receive therapy without its undermining the strength of the prosecution's case.[64] Although such unambiguous guidance is welcome, matters are not always so clear cut. Child protection practitioners are fully aware that the more serious the alleged offence, the greater the need to prosecute the offender and they therefore may not wish to risk jeopardising the evidential requirements by supporting the child, in a way which could be exploited by the defence.

Overall, one wonders whether any official initiatives can overcome all the difficulties imposed by a system which, as observed by Davis et al, requires the video-recorded interview to serve three very conflicting purposes, namely: the initial step in a child protection investigation to ascertain whether an offence has been committed and by whom; an inquiry into whether the child needs protection; the examination-in-chief of the child at the criminal trial, with a need to comply with strict rules of evidence. These researchers conclude that the three purposes are so difficult to reconcile that unrealistic demands are being imposed on interviewers.[65] Nevertheless, the new official guidance on interviewing techniques, combined with greater flexibility over allowing child witnesses to receive therapy, may at least redress social work perceptions of the interviewing process as one which is legalistic, unhelpful and unsympathetic to children.

(4)   THE DECISION TO PROSECUTE

In cases where a joint investigation proceeds and the team is satisfied that a child has been abused, that the abuse amounts to a criminal offence and that the abuser has been accurately identified, a decision must be taken whether criminal proceedings are appropriate. The guidance provided by *Working Together*, which broadly reflects CPS guidance,[66] states that this question depends on whether there is enough evidence to prosecute, whether it is in the public interest to prosecute and whether this would be in the child victim's best interests.[67] It appears, however, that decisions over whether jointly investigated cases should go forward for prosecution are often reached in an unsatisfactorily idiosyncratic manner. Although the final responsibility for deciding on prosecution rests with the CPS, the decision whether to initiate criminal proceedings at all is taken by the police, although they should consult social services about what is in the child's best interests.[68] Research indicates that the police often

---

61   See S Nelson (1997) who described (p 159) such an approach as 'immoral and unsustainable'.
62   CPS et al (2001) para 4.5.
63   CPS et al (2001) paras 4.3–4.5.
64   CPS et al (2001) chs 5 and 6.
65   G Davis et al (1999) p ix. See also S Nelson (1997).
66   CPS (2000) sections 5 and 6.
67   DH et al (1999) para 3.62. But there is no specific reference to the child's best interests in the CPS code.
68   DH et al (1999).

operate on a number of undefined and arbitrary assumptions over the types of behaviour involving children which warrant prosecution.[69] Sometimes the police fail to identify cases as justifying CPS advice on this; they may even fail to define cases as warranting special protective measures for child witnesses, with the result that a child may not undergo a video-recorded interview.[70] The reasons are not only arbitrary, but vary from force to force. In some forces, the case is excluded if the child has only witnessed abusive behaviour, rather than being involved as a victim, or if the offence involved an adolescent perpetrator victimising another child.[71] Incidents of physical abuse are also less likely to be regarded by the police as sufficiently 'serious' to warrant prosecution in cases where the child has behaved badly prior to the incident, thereby warranting 'reasonable parental chastisement'[72] – it may then be assumed that the assault was 'provoked', especially if the child is older.[73]

Certain cases, such as sexual abuse, very obviously warrant CPS attention, but again, research indicates that the police and the CPS operate on a variety of assumptions about the 'seriousness' of an offence, which in turn are influenced by seemingly arbitrary preconceptions.[74] Thus, although it is common for sexual abuse to be regarded as very serious, a decision whether to prosecute may be influenced by such factors as the time lapse between the alleged assault and the child's complaint. There is, for example, the curious view that a 'genuine' complainant would not delay in reporting a sexual assault, when, in practice, the delay may be understandable if the victim is a child and the perpetrator lives in the same house.[75] Davis et al suggest that 'it would be helpful if, across the board, the yardsticks by which the police and the CPS determine whether child abusers should be prosecuted were to be reviewed and more clearly articulated'.[76]

When deciding whether to prosecute, the CPS must first assess whether there is sufficient evidence to provide a 'realistic prospect of conviction'.[77] This part of the Crown prosecutors' task has been greatly eased by their ability to assess the weight of evidence, together with the child's general demeanour, by viewing his or her video-recorded interview. The CPS will also view this to gauge the child's ability to stand up to the experience of cross-examination,[78] which is an essential part of the criminal trial, irrespective of the 'special measures' which may be adopted to protect the child witness in the process.[79] The second question, whether it is in the public interest to proceed, is interrelated with the first, and will obviously include a consideration of such matters as the effect of a prosecution on the victim's physical or mental health, including his or her interests and views. Having considered such matters, the CPS are entitled to decide not to prosecute, despite there being sufficient evidence to obtain a conviction.[80] CPS officers rely on the police to provide them with information

69   See C Keenan and L Maitland (1999).
70   CPSI (1998) pp 10–12. This research showed that 42% of cases reviewed were not 'flagged' by the police as being 'child witness' cases.
71   CPSI (1998).
72   Discussed in more detail in chapter 9.
73   G Davis et al (1999) pp 41–42 and Appendix C. See also C Keenan and L Maitland (1999) pp 402–403.
74   G Davis et al (1999) pp 41–42 and Appendix C.
75   G Davis et al (1999) p 85.
76   G Davis et al (1999) p 83.
77   CPS (2000) para 5.1.
78   G Davis et al (1999) ch IV.
79   Ie the special measures available under the YJCEA 1999, Pt II, which can avoid some children appearing in court at any stage of the criminal trial. See discussion below.
80   CPS (2000) para 6.3.

about the child witness and his or her family, and some child protection police officers do consult a variety of sources, including social services, for information about the child's welfare, before compiling a report for the CPS.[81] Nevertheless, CPS lawyers often reach a decision whether to prosecute in child abuse cases with insufficient background information about the child.[82]

Many social workers and the police wish to see higher rates of prosecution than are achieved, particularly in cases involving child sexual abuse. They sometimes express considerable frustration over decisions not to prosecute reached by the CPS.[83] Such a stance is understandable. In the first place, a prosecution offers the most powerful way of registering society's disapproval of the sexual abuse of children. Not only do children as a group have a right to be protected from a suspected abuser, but society as a whole also has an interest in his conviction. Indeed, the heightened public awareness of the evils of child abuse, particularly child sexual abuse, has led to a greater concern that so many child sex abusers are escaping conviction. Linked to this is the fact that instigating a prosecution demonstrates to the child that he or she is believed and has support from outside the family. It may also relieve children's sense of guilt by indicating that they were not responsible for what occurred and that guilt lies with the abuser.[84] In practical terms, imprisonment may provide other children and the child victim with a period of safety, during which the perpetrator is out of circulation. Prosecution may also stop sex abusers denying their offending behaviour and the harm it has caused. By contrast, a decision not to prosecute may indicate to the abuser that, so far as the community is concerned, he did not commit the offence, in turn making it far more difficult for social workers to work with the family and secure the child's safety.[85]

Research with children also tends to favour prosecuting abusers. It indicates that children often feel very let down by a failure or a delay in doing so. Sharland et al report that children who have been encouraged by child protection practitioners to tell them about the abuse, feel confused and frightened if no action is taken to prosecute their abuser:[86]

'… many parents and children were left disappointed, confused, betrayed and afraid, with, for instance, the perpetrator still living nearby and "laughing", having "got away with it".'[87]

Too often, the children and their families receive no proper explanation from the police for a case being discontinued.[88] More worryingly, the children whose abusers go unprosecuted show more clinically significant symptoms of depression than those whose abusers are taken to court. Indeed, it appeared to Sharland et al that failure to bring prosecutions left significant numbers of children both abused and, in their opinion, unsafe.[89] The children's own perceptions were in some respects different according to whether the abuser was inside or outside the family, in so far as they were more prepared to acknowledge the abuse and co-operate if the abuser was an outsider.

---

81   G Davis et al (1999) p 31.
82   CPSI (1998) pp 15–20. In 70.6% of cases the police had failed to provide the CPS with details of the wishes of the child, family or carer.
83   C Hallett (1995) pp 131–145.
84   See J Morgan and L Zedner (1992) p 115. NB the knowledge that a court has made findings of sexual abuse in care proceedings may have an equally cathartic effect on children: eg *Re X (disclosure of information)* [2001] 2 FLR 440 at [10]–[15]. See discussion below.
85   See C Hallett (1995) p 138.
86   See E Sharland et al (1996) pp 140–141.
87   E Sharland et al (1996) p 140. See also T Pigot (1989) para 2.15 and Childline (1996) pp 21–23.
88   CPSI (1998) p 24.
89   E Sharland et al (1996) p 183.

It is unclear from Sharland's research whether the children whose abusers had been prosecuted had appeared as witnesses at their criminal trials and had undergone cross-examination by defence counsel. Such an experience might have changed fundamentally their views on the merits of prosecution. Indeed, despite all the arguments in favour of prosecuting sex abusers, there are important factors favouring caution. Although children want the abuse to stop, they may feel guilty and upset if charges are brought against a member of their own families. But until very recently, the most fundamental problem was that giving evidence against the abuser at a criminal trial could be deeply traumatic and might eventually achieve nothing, if the defendant escaped conviction. Hopefully, research will tell us the extent to which the new legislative measures manage to shield child witnesses from being cross-examined on their evidence in open court.[90]

(5) COMPELLABILITY OF CHILD WITNESSES IN CRIMINAL TRIALS

Children become very worried and apprehensive over appearing as witnesses in criminal trials. Although giving evidence can be harrowing, there are no special rules protecting them from being required to do so; like any adult, a child witness is compellable.[91] No matter how young, children are presumed competent to give evidence in a criminal trial, unless they cannot understand questions put to them in court or answer them in a way which can be understood.[92] Nevertheless, when considering children's competence, the court must bear in mind the various special measures which can help them comprehend the process. These legislative provisions clearly enable the courts to take evidence even from very young children, assisted by video-recorded interviews and television-link technology.[93]

The civil courts have, in the past, robustly emphasised children's duty to act as witnesses in criminal trials; even children who are wards of court have no special privileges in this respect:

> 'Children, whether wards of court or not, are citizens owing duties to society as a whole (including other children), which are appropriate to their years and understanding ... it is not for the wardship court, whatever the theoretical scope of its jurisdiction, to use that jurisdiction to interfere with the performance by the criminal courts of their lawful duties.'[94]

Clearly, the interests of the child witness cannot be allowed to prevail over the needs of society, more particularly those of other children, for protection against criminals.[95] The principle is clear, whether or not criminal proceedings will be distressing for children,[96] it is up to the CPS and the trial judge to decide whether to call them.[97] In

---

90   YJCEA 1999, Pt II, discussed below.

91   See discussion by J Spencer and R Flin (1993) pp 70–73.

92   YJCEA 1999, s 53(1) and (3).

93   Eg *DPP v M* [1998] QB 913: a 5-year-old was considered potentially capable of giving intelligible evidence.

94   *Re R (minors) (wardship: criminal proceedings)* [1991] 2 All ER 193 at 198, per Lord Donaldson MR.

95   See *Re S (minors) (wardship: disclosure of material)* [1988] 1 FLR 1 at 5, per Booth J.

96   Eg *Re K (minors) (wardship: criminal proceedings)* [1988] 1 All ER 214: Waterhouse J held that there was no need for him to give leave for four wards of court aged 11, 9, 7 and 6 to be called as witnesses at their parents' trial for alleged indecent assault on them.

97   See *R v Highbury Corner Magistrates' Court, ex p D* [1997] 1 FLR 683: the High Court quashed on judicial review the magistrates' refusal to issue a witness summons requiring a 9-year-old to give evidence at the criminal trial of his father being tried for assault against his ex-partner. The final decision whether to call the child to give evidence should be left to the judge presiding over the criminal trial.

this respect, it is curious that the law is so inconsistent in its treatment of children's competence to give evidence of various kinds. An extreme paternalism is shown by the courts when deciding whether children should be allowed to give evidence in care proceedings and parental disputes.[98] In private law proceedings, notions about protection reinforce judicial concerns to keep children out of what are perceived to be adult conflicts.[99] The courts are also reluctant to allow quite mature children to give oral evidence in public law proceedings,[100] even in the event of their wishing to do so and even if they are deemed sufficiently competent to instruct their own solicitors. But this approach is not always matched by a similar concern to protect a child victim from the trauma of giving evidence at the criminal trial of a possible child abuser, even when it is known that this experience may well prove distressing. So far as criminal proceedings are concerned, it is convenient for society to utilise the capacity of even very young children to recall criminal acts which have affected them.

As indicated above, the final decision over whether to prosecute a child abuser is taken by the CPS and the child victim's interests may take second place to the interests of society and its need for protection. Indeed, whilst some CPS lawyers are concerned to spare very young children the ordeal of a court appearance, others, particularly when considering cases of child sexual abuse, operate on a presumption that it is in the public interest to prosecute all such cases, evidence permitting.[101] The Pigot Committee disapproved of compelling children to give evidence and recommended that no child should ever be required to do so against his or her wishes, whether in open court or protected by screens or closed circuit television.[102] It considered that it was essential to establish this principle, both for the children's welfare and to overcome the reluctance of children and their parents to assist the authorities.

It appears that CPS lawyers do take account of children's wishes, their reluctance to give evidence being the most common reason for terminating cases being prepared for trial.[103] The *ABE*[104] implicitly counsels a sympathetic approach to reluctant child witnesses, pointing out that whether or nor a witness is competent and compellable, the CPS is not obliged to insist on every witness giving evidence. It also states that the CPS will take into account the wishes of the witness, 'although they will not necessarily defer to them'.[105] It indicates that 'Reports to the Crown Prosecution Service should always include clear information about the wishes of the witness, and his or her parents or carers, about going to court'.[106] Despite this, in future the CPS

---

98   Discussed in more depth in chapter 7.
99   Eg *Re M (family proceedings: affidavits)* [1995] 2 FLR 100: Butler-Sloss LJ disapproved of a father procuring affidavit evidence from his 13-year-old daughter regarding her wish to live with him.
100 Eg *R v B County Council, ex p P* [1991] 1 WLR 221: the Court of Appeal approved the decision of the juvenile court not to issue a witness summons requiring a 17-year-old girl to give evidence in care proceedings, so that she could be cross-examined by her father who she had accused of sexually abusing her. See also *Re P (witness summons)* [1997] 2 FLR 447: the Court of Appeal approved the county court's refusal to issue a witness summons against a 12-year-old girl in care proceedings.
101 G Davis et al (1999) p 31.
102 T Pigot (1989) para 2.26.
103 CPSI (1998) pp 23–24.
104 HO et al (2002).
105 HO et al (2002) para 2.23.
106 HO et al (2002) para 2.23. But this may not be possible. In 70.6% of cases, the police had failed to provide the CPS with details of the wishes of the child, family or carer: CPSI (1998) pp 15–20.

may become more, rather than less, prepared to pressurise children into giving evidence if they can guarantee that child witnesses will be entitled to a range of special measures protecting them from appearing in open court. Such a development could be detrimental, since many children will still find it a stressful ordeal to rehearse painful and intimate experiences, albeit during a video-recorded interview and cross-examination, rather than in open court.

It is arguable that older children would be far more willing to give evidence in criminal trials if they were more fully involved in decisions over how they give evidence, for example, whether this should be by video-link or in person.[107] Australian research evidence on the use of closed-circuit television for children giving evidence in criminal trials lends pragmatic support for adopting such an approach. This research,[108] which showed that that if children's wishes are respected over *how* they wish to give evidence, their performance as witnesses will materially improve in quality, encouraged the introduction of legislation giving children far more control over the way in which their evidence is presented to court.[109] In comparison, although the current legislation very briefly flirts with the notion that giving children more control brings its own rewards, there is little real acknowledgment that children should be fully involved in the procedural arrangements regarding the way they give evidence.[110]

Children's apprehension about giving evidence at a criminal trial is often exacerbated by the long wait between the time of the initial investigation and the trial itself. The Pigot Report stated that 'one of the most substantial difficulties faced by children ... is the extraordinary and, in our view, quite unacceptable delay which they must often endure before cases come to court'.[111] Since then, the criminal justice system has shown a regrettable and continuing inability to 'fast-track' criminal trials involving children. Ironically, research suggests that the 'fast-tracking' schemes seem to exacerbate the 'normal' delays.[112] According to Davis et al, the absence of any co-ordination between the agencies involved in child protection investigations and prosecutions means that there is often no-one with overall responsibility for expediting child abuse cases. Cases become 'bogged down without anyone noticing'.[113] For trials involving children giving evidence in person, perhaps because the video-recorded interview is rejected for lack of fluency,[114] these delays cause major problems, such as children's recollections fading between the offence and the trial itself. The delays are also problematic for those children whose video-recorded interview constitutes their evidence-in-chief. The time-lag may result in a child giving replies, on cross-examination, which are inconsistent with his or her original evidence. Even

---

107 CPSI (1998) p 33.

108 J Cashmore and N De Haas (1992).

109 G Davis et al (1999) pp 73–74.

110 Under YJCEA 1999, s 21(7)(b) a witness may reject the option of undergoing cross-examination by a pre-recording, but the right to make such a choice is restricted to this specific 'special measure'. See discussion below.

111 T Pigot (1989) para 1.20.

112 J Plotnikoff and R Woolfson (1995) ch 5. This research indicated that some cases were taking over ten months to complete. Some years later, G Davis et al (1999) found (pp 51–54) that, on average, cases were now taking just under 58 weeks from investigation to the first day of trial, with many children bound up in the criminal process for 14 months.

113 G Davis et al (1999) p 53.

114 See A Wade et al (1998) who gives examples (p 184) of video-recorded interview evidence that can damage the prosecution's case rather than improve it. In some such cases, the video-recording is not used and the child is required to give evidence in person, perhaps by live video-link. See discussion below.

their appearance, as recorded by the video, may have changed between the initial interview and the trial itself.[115] There is the added factor that, until the trial begins, some child witnesses are under constant fear for their safety because the defendant has been left in the community, perhaps on bail with insufficient restrictions.[116] The strain suffered by the child and family whilst awaiting the trial may be exacerbated by cases being rescheduled at the very last minute, creating further unexpected delays. Even when the trial starts, some children required to attend court for cross-examination may be kept waiting for long periods spanning more than a day.[117] Since the special measures introduced by the new legislation[118] cannot ensure that all child witnesses undergo a pre-trial video-recorded cross-examination, these delays will continue to undermine attempts to improve the way that the criminal justice system deals with child witnesses.

(6)   PROTECTING CHILD WITNESSES IN CRIMINAL TRIALS

It is now widely recognised that children's fear over attending court can be alleviated by being familiarised with the courts and what will be required of them. Considerable efforts have been made to develop age-related leaflets, witness information packs, pre-trial visits and the services of court liaison officers, all of which may help them overcome some of their apprehension during their wait for the trial.[119] Unfortunately, these schemes do not wholly prepare children for the experience of actually appearing in open court and confronting the defendant. This can be so distressing that, in the past, some criminal trials which hinged on a child's evidence had to be abandoned. The Pigot Committee was critical of a system allowing children to suffer the trauma of giving evidence in open court and being cross-examined by defence counsel whose aim was systematically to discredit them.[120] Under the full Pigot scheme, most child witnesses would have avoided attending court entirely – both their main evidence and the cross-examination would take place in advance of the trial, in a video-recorded form. Instead, the compromise, or 'half Pigot', introduced in the early 1990s, only allowed the video-recorded interview to be shown in court in substitution for the child appearing in person to provide evidence-in-chief.[121] It retained the right of the defence to cross-examine all witnesses for the prosecution, irrespective of their youth. Even half Pigot should have ensured that most children were spared the experience of giving their evidence-in-chief in open court, but in practice this did not happen.[122] As noted above, many video-recorded interviews were never shown in court, some because

115   G Davis et al (1999) pp 53–54.
116   See E Sharland et al (1996) pp 140–141.
117   G Davis et al (1999) p 56. See also CPSI (1998) pp 38–39.
118   Discussed below.
119   See NSPCC (1993) and NSPCC (1998).
120   T Pigot (1989) paras 2.10 and 2.12.
121   CJA 1988, s 32A, subject to certain age limits depending on the nature of the offence.
122   CJA 1988, s 32A(3) introduced a presumption that the court should admit a video-recorded interview as the child's evidence-in-chief unless: (a) the child was unavailable for cross-examination, (b) there were failures regarding disclosure of the video-recording, or (c) if in the interests of justice the recording should not be admitted, having regard to all the circumstances of the case. But see *R (on the application of the DPP) v Redbridge Youth Court; R (on the application of L) v Bicester Youth Court* [2001] EWHC Admin 209, [2001] 4 All ER 411 at 420–422, per Latham LJ: this presumption could be rebutted by the defendant showing that there was no real risk that the quality of a child witness's evidence would be affected by refusal to admit his or her video-recorded interview.

the interviewers failed to obtain from the child a clear account of the offence, or because they were of poor technical quality.[123] Many children therefore still ended up being required to give their evidence in person, though increasingly often protected by a screen or in a separate room, linked to the court by video-link.[124] Practice also varied enormously regarding the preparedness of barristers and the judiciary[125] to accept the advantages of the new technology,[126] with many barristers and CPS lawyers maintaining that juries were more convinced by the child's evidence given live in court,[127] particularly if the child showed emotion and tears.[128] The view that the distress of a child witness can be justified because his or her presence secures a conviction is not borne out by the research evidence. Indeed, research findings are ambivalent over the extent to which juries are impressed by children giving evidence in person, compared with other means.[129]

The government rejected the Pigot Committee's[130] efforts to free child witnesses from the duty to be available at the trial for cross-examination and this duty will remain in being until all the special measures introduced by recent legislation become freely available.[131] Consequently, even very young children can be cross-examined on aspects of their evidence-in-chief, which has been provided sometimes more than a year before. Predictably, they may then produce answers apparently inconsistent with earlier evidence.[132] Despite calls for the judiciary to take greater control of criminal trials involving child witnesses, in some cases children continue to undergo the type of cross-examination techniques that adult witnesses would find harrowing, with defence barristers using an intimidating or even aggressive approach.[133] Not surprisingly, even those allowed to undergo cross-examination by video-link or behind screens show signs of stress.[134]

The problems created by the half Pigot scheme became increasingly controversial. The judiciary's right to exclude children's video-recorded evidence 'in the interests of justice' and to refuse applications to permit children to give evidence by video-link or behind screens, created uncertainty which influenced the whole tenor of child

123 See SSI (1994) para 2.3. Although the interviewing skills and technical quality of children's interviews is said to have steadily improved (see CPSI (1998) p 31), this is not always the case, particularly if the police officer leading the interview is inexperienced, not being from a specialist child protection team: see DH (2002 b) para 6.29. NB a failure to conduct an interview appropriately may lead to a negligence suit: eg *L and P v Reading Borough Council and Chief Constable of Thames Valley Police* [2001] EWCA Civ 346, [2001] 2 FLR 50: a father and his child sued the local authority and police authority in negligence alleging that interviews jointly conducted by a social worker and police officer in 1990 were improper, incompetent and conducted in a manner grossly unfair to the child's father.
124 Under CJA 1988, s 32, there was no presumption that a court should permit a child witness to give evidence by live link, so it could only make a direction for this to occur if there was some good reason for departure from the norm. See *R (on the application of the DPP) v Redbridge Youth Court; R (on the application of L) v Bicester Youth Court* [2001] EWHC Admin 209, [2001] 4 All ER 411 at 421, per Latham LJ.
125 CJA 1988, s 32.
126 See J Plotnikoff and R Woolfson (1995) p 97.
127 See G Davis et al (1999) pp 59–60.
128 J Plotnikoff and R Woolfson (1995) pp 55–59.
129 G Davis et al (1999) p 59.
130 T Pigot (1989).
131 Most of the changes introduced by the YJCEA 1999, Pt II were introduced in 2002; others, such as pre-trial cross-examinations and the use of intermediaries, are not expected to be introduced before 2003/04, after completion of piloting.
132 See G Davies and E Noon (1991) pp 55–66.
133 Although such instances are becoming rarer, they still occur. See G Davis et al (1999) p 61.
134 G Davis et al (1999) p 68.

abuse investigations.[135] Furthermore, child protection practitioners found it difficult to condone a situation whereby the *Memorandum* forced them to interview children using techniques that did not suit children's emotional state, only to find that, once children got into the witness box: 'The defence lawyers blow the children apart …'[136] The government finally accepted that the many flaws inherent in the existing 'half Pigot' scheme[137] dictated reform. The mounting calls to implement the full Pigot scheme,[138] reinforced by the recommendations of an interdepartmental working group,[139] led, at last, to new legislation enabling at least some child witnesses to give evidence without being involved in any court appearance.[140]

Ideally, the new legislation would have ensured, first, that *all* child witnesses involved in criminal trials automatically gained the benefit of being able to give their video evidence-in-chief in the form of a pre-recorded interview, and also to undergo a pre-trial video-recorded cross-examination, thereby escaping the ordeal of attending court. Secondly, it would have contained a formula for countering the inevitable resistance to technical change from some members of the judiciary. Regrettably, the reality is very different. To take the second point first, although more liberal members of the judiciary are entirely free to ensure that a child witness gains virtually any form of protection available,[141] their traditional freedom to regulate the procedural aspects of the trial survives intact, undermined only by 'a primary rule' or presumption available to *some* child witnesses.[142] This cautious approach was apparently adopted to prevent defendants successfully arguing that their rights to a fair trial under article 6 of the ECHR had been infringed by a form of blanket protection available to all child witnesses.[143] This approach may have been over cautious, given that the European Court of Human Rights accepts that:

> 'Organising criminal proceedings in such a way as to protect the interests of juvenile witnesses, in particular in trial proceedings involving sexual offences, is a relevant consideration, to be taken into account for the purposes of Article 6.'[144]

Meanwhile, the statutory encouragement to the courts to make the 'special measures' available to child witnesses is qualified in so many ways that
's comment that in some instances it produces 'an unhappy compromise' is somewhat of an understatement.[145]

---

135   G Davis et al (1999) p 67.
136   SSI (1994) p 24.
137   Summarised by L Hoyano (2000) pp 252–256.
138   Eg W Utting (1997) pp 192–196.
139   HO (1998).
140   YJCEA 1999, Pt II, which also extended protection to many adult witnesses, on the grounds of their vulnerability, see ss 16–17.
141   The court must make a special measures direction in relation to an eligible witness if it is of the opinion that such measure/s would 'be likely to improve the quality of evidence given by the witness': YJCEA 1999, s 19(2).
142   Discussed below.
143   See L Hoyano (2000) p 261.
144   *PS v Germany* (Application No 33900/96) [2002] Crim LR 312 (para 28). But despite this concession, the European Court of Human Rights upheld the defendant's claim that his rights under art 6 of the ECHR had been violated because he had been convicted of sexual abuse against a young girl, on the basis of her hearsay evidence only. See also the Strasbourg case law discussed by P Bates (1999) pp 300–302.
145   L Hoyano (2000) p 261.

Regarding the first point mentioned above, not all child witnesses gain full protection under the 1999 legislation.[146] Only child witnesses[147] in cases involving sexual offences[148] or offences of kidnapping, physical violence and neglect[149] benefit from a presumption or 'primary rule' that the court will make a 'special measures direction' requiring their evidence-in-chief to be admitted in the form of a video-recording.[150] One might have assumed that all these child witnesses would gain a similar presumption that their cross-examination would also be admitted by the court, in the form of a pre-trial video-recording.[151] This is not the case; such a presumption only applies to child witnesses to sexual offences[152] and not to those in the latter group. For children who are involved in offences of kidnapping, physical violence and neglect,[153] the primary rule is that their evidence-in-chief will be admitted in the form of a video-recording;[154] it is *not* presumed that they should also be allowed to undergo a pre-recorded cross-examination. Admittedly, the trial judge may make a direction allowing them to be cross-examined in this way if he considers that it is likely to improve the quality of their evidence, but the absence of a presumption provides an excellent excuse for not doing so.[155]

Many practitioners consider that perpetrators who target very young or mentally handicapped children are still evading prosecution because of the difficulties of obtaining clear evidence from their victims.[156] Some of the new provisions, such as dispensing with the wearing of wigs and gowns whilst the child gives evidence,[157] and enabling a child to give evidence through 'an intermediary'[158] may particularly benefit witnesses of this kind. Nevertheless, these measures presuppose that such children are deemed capable of attending court in person to give evidence, presumably by live link or behind screens. The 1999 legislation may eventually save these child witnesses from the ordeal of attending court altogether by allowing them to undergo pre-trial video-recorded cross-examination, since it is clear that even giving evidence by video-link is stressful. Hopefully, the availability of such forms of protection will

---

146 For a more detailed explanation of the special measures available, see L Hoyano (2000) pp 260–273. See also P Bates (1999) and D Birch (2000) pp 244–246.

147 Ie a child under the age of 17: YJCEA 1999, s 16(1). Child witnesses can benefit from the special measures, whether they were victims of an assault themselves or witnesses to an offence involving another person.

148 YJCEA 1999, s 35(3)(a).

149 YJCEA 1999, s 35(3)(b)–(d).

150 YJCEA 1999, s 21(3). Unless the court decides under s 27(2) 'in the interests of justice' to exclude the whole or any part of it. Since this formula is identical to that used in CJA 1988, s 32A(c), it may take little to justify excluding video-recorded evidence, as in *R (on the application of the DPP) v Redbridge Youth Court; R (on the application of L) v Bicester Youth Court* [2001] EWHC Admin 209, [2001] 4 All ER 411. See above.

151 But see L Hoyano's (2000) discussion of the disadvantages and concerns relating to the use of pre-trial video-recorded cross-examinations (pp 267–271).

152 YJCEA 1999, s 21(6). Even these children may not benefit from such a direction, in the event of the video-recording of their evidence-in-chief being excluded by the court under s 27(2). See n 150 above.

153 Ie those listed by s 35(3)(b)–(d).

154 YJCEA 1999, s 21(3).

155 Ie under s 19(2)(a) and (b).

156 See M Aldridge and J Wood (2000) p 178. See also *Re D (evidence: facilitated communication)* [2001] 1 FLR 148: Butler-Sloss P warned of the risks involved in using potentially unreliable and controversial communication processes for extracting evidence apparently indicating child sexual abuse from profoundly mentally handicapped children.

157 This informal practice had already become established in some courts, but was given legislative form by YJCEA 1999, s 26.

158 YJCEA 1999, s 29. Discussed by L Hoyano (2000) pp 271–272.

persuade the police and CPS to contemplate criminal prosecutions far more readily when dealing with these particularly vulnerable victims of child abuse.

Overall, it is particularly regrettable that the new legislation is so extraordinarily complex that those preparing child witnesses for their role find it extremely difficult to establish what form of protection they are entitled to and when.[159] The recommendation of Davis et al, that any new legislation should stipulate 'clear statutory criteria to guide the exercise of judicial discretion' in determining whether any special pre-trial procedures for receiving the child's evidence should be used, fell well clear of the mark.[160] It remains unclear whether the criminal justice system can now protect child witnesses, who, by definition, have already suffered serious abuse, from what the Pigot Committee described as 'a harmful, oppressive and often traumatic experience' and a form of 'secondary victimisation', through giving evidence in criminal trials.[161]

(7)   OUTCOMES FOR CHILDREN IF THE ABUSER IS CONVICTED

The discussion above indicates that there is a long list of problems involved in using the criminal justice system, so far as the child victim is concerned, at least until the methods for obtaining and using his or her evidence can be greatly improved. Even in the event of the abuser being tried and convicted, the outcome for the child may not always be a happy one. Despite the child's relief at the abuse being stopped, his or her sense of guilt will be exacerbated if a father or other close relative is sent to prison, and the family may suffer further financial hardship through loss of the breadwinner. There is the added drawback that the current methods used to punish child abusers do not necessarily reduce the chance of their re-offending, particularly when sex abusers are concerned. The traditional sanction is to imprison them for long periods, depending, of course, on the severity of the abuse.[162] Indeed, the public response to well-publicised offences by highly deviant sex offenders is to demand more incarceration, rather than less. For example, the trial of Sarah Payne's murderer, in 2001, led to demands for indeterminate sentences for paedophiles, with release delayed until there was no further prospect of re-offending.[163] Some urged that the mental health legislation should be amended to allow paedophiles to be detained compulsorily, alongside others with serious personality disorders.[164] But there are obvious civil rights objections to both suggestions. For example, it might often be impossible to predict that an offender had reformed sufficiently for there to be no risk of re-offending.[165] Furthermore, it would be difficult to defend a system which legitimises detaining people without trial who have not offended and who are not 'ill'.

---

159   See the flowcharts providing some guidance on this, created by L Hoyano (2000) pp 257–258.
160   G Davis et al (1999) p 85.
161   T Pigot (1989) paras 2.10 and 2.15.
162   See C Cobley (2000) ch 4 for a detailed discussion of sentencing policies regarding sex offenders.
163   See leading article, *Guardian*, 16 December 2001. The government has accepted these demands. See HO (2002 b) para 5.41 and Criminal Justice Bill 2002, cls 205–206.
164   Senior police officers responded to Sarah Payne's murder by demanding such changes: *Observer*, 16 December 2001. The controversy surrounding the government's proposals to make it possible to detain dangerous people with severe personality disorders through the use of mental health orders (see DH/HO (2000) and DH (2002 b) Part 3, ch 2) appears to have delayed the introduction of a mental health bill incorporating such provisions.
165   See D Grubin (1998) p 42.

The advantage of sentencing child abusers to long periods in prison is that during their removal from circulation their child victims are securely protected. Long sentences also enable prisoners to be supervised on licence in the community on their release, which, as Cobley observes, is a particularly apt way of managing sex offenders.[166] The government is currently determined to increase the probability that sex offenders deemed to be dangerous to the public are locked up for longer and supervised more closely on release.[167] Nevertheless, these 'lock them up' sentencing policies clearly fail to tackle abusing behaviour and the attitudes underlying it. The prison experience may cause the perpetrator himself to feel victimised and, more crucially, in the case of sex abusers, if they receive no treatment, prison may increase the likelihood of their re-offending, by allowing them time to rehearse their sexual fantasies about children.[168] Furthermore, if perpetrators know that imprisonment will be the probable outcome of admitting abuse, they are deterred from seeking help for controlling or changing their abusive behaviour. The difficulty for society, however, is that it remains unclear what other methods, if any, would achieve absolute prevention. The research on the effectiveness of treatment programmes for sex offenders, which are still relatively new, indicates that they can reduce the risk of re-offending, but not dramatically, and only if they are extremely well designed with extended after-care.[169] In any event, a far greater investment in treatment programmes is needed before they can provide adequately for the numbers of offenders allocated to them.[170] But as Grubin observes:

'Unless society is prepared simply to lock up for many years all those convicted of sexual offences, decisions are going to have to be made about returning these individuals to the community, about the amount of risk that will be tolerated, and the most effective way of managing that risk.'[171]

On the assumption that many child abusers, more particularly sex offenders, will remain in the community, improved strategies are needed to protect children more efficiently from their attentions. The 1990s saw a plethora of legislative initiatives. The establishment of the sex offender register[172] was introduced to ensure that police could keep track of sex offenders. This measure was controversial from the start.[173] In the first place, the legislation was not retrospective, so although current sex offenders have complied well with the requirement to register their names and addresses, and any changes in such details,[174] large numbers escaped its scope.[175] Furthermore, it appears that few police forces make best use of the information gained, for example,

---

166 See C Cobley (2000) p 203.
167 See HO (2002 b) paras 5.39–5.44 and Criminal Justice Bill 2002, Ch 5.
168 During his previous term of imprisonment, for kidnapping and indecently assaulting another child, Roy Whiting, Sarah Payne's murderer, had refused the psychiatric treatment on offer.
169 See D Grubin (1998) pp 40–41 for a short summary of the existing research on this topic. See also C Hedderman and D Sugg (1996).
170 In 2000, 1,020 offenders were allocated to treatment programmes offering only 786 places. Home Office Statistics.
171 D Grubin (1998) pp 42–43.
172 Established by the Sex Offenders Act 1997.
173 C Cobley (2000) pp 323–329.
174 One year after the Act was implemented, there was a national rate of compliance of 94.7%. See J Plotnikoff and R Woolfson (2000) p v. The Home Office reports that compliance is now up to 97%: see HO (2002 a) para 19.
175 Estimates are that at least 100,000 additional sex offenders would have been required to register had the legislation been retrospective: see C Cobley (2000) p 325.

by using it to prevent and investigate crime.[176] They even seem unclear whether the information should be made accessible to local officers.[177] The debate over whether information on the register, such as the identity and whereabouts of sex offenders, should be made available to the public intensified after the trial of the murderer of Sarah Payne.[178] There were increased calls from the media and parents' groups for the public to be notified of sex offenders moving into their area – the introduction of a so-called 'Sarah's Law'.[179] There is little evidence to substantiate claims that the American community notification schemes have enhanced children's safety there.[180] Although it intends to increase the register's effectiveness,[181] the English government has consistently resisted allowing uncontrolled access to the sex offenders' register.[182] It fears an increase in vigilante attacks on those identified as paedophiles[183] and an undermining of the register's objectives. If sex offenders expect to be hounded from place to place, they will simply disappear, rather than registering with the police.[184] Furthermore, as Lovell observes, there is a risk that 'offenders may use more force to silence the victim, target children less able to communicate details of the attack, or feel that they have nothing to lose by committing a more serious crime'.[185] The courts have also strongly maintained the need for caution over disclosing information; there is a need to maintain a balance between the interests of the individual and his right to privacy under article 8 of the ECHR, and the needs of the community. Disclosure should only be made if there is 'a pressing need for that disclosure'.[186]

A raft of legislation and regulations already exists, all aiming to control the activities of sex offenders,[187] and to prevent them from working with children.[188] Many initiatives

---

176   See J Plotnikoff and R Woolfson (2000). They observed (p 42) that only 23% of forces had used register information in investigations.

177   J Plotnikoff and R Woolfson (2000) pp 32–33. See also DH (2002 a) indicating (para 9.23) that information available at the time of sentencing was not made accessible to local police managing the offender in the community under the MAPPA arrangements, see discussed below.

178   The details of Roy Whiting, her murderer, had already been registered on the sex offender register, due to an earlier offence relating to a child.

179   A campaign was started by the *News of the World* in 2000, after the murder of Sarah Payne, to introduce a scheme, similar to 'Megan's Law' established in the US in the aftermath of the murder of Megan Kanka, whereby the public have access to information about sex offenders.

180   See E Lovell (2001) p 35.

181   Eg by tightening up on the time limits for the notification requirements. See HO (2002 a) ch 1 and Sexual Offences Bill 2003, Part 2.

182   See Home Office press release, 15 September 2000 and HO (2002 a) para 19.

183   The *News of the World*'s 'naming and shaming' campaign encouraging the public to identify paedophiles, led to attacks on some men wrongly suspected of abusing children. It also disrupted ongoing work with sex offenders. See Association of Chief Officers of Probation (1998).

184   HO (2002 a) para 19. Most police forces have a community notification policy for managing disclosure of information about offenders to local agencies, through the multi-agency public protection panels (MAPPPs). See below.

185   See E Lovell (2001) p 23.

186   Per Lord Woolf MR in *R v Chief Constable of North Wales Police, ex p Thorpe* [1999] QB 396 at 428.

187   Eg, under a sex offender order (see Crime and Disorder Act 1998, s 2), a sex offender can be prohibited, for example, from entering the vicinity of a school or playground. Although the order itself is civil in form, its breach amounts to a criminal act. For details, see C Cobley (2000) pp 332–339. See also the 'restraining order', whereby a court sentencing a sex offender can prohibit him from a variety of actions, such as attempting to communicate with his victim. Criminal Justice Act 2000, Sch 5, para 6, inserting Sex Offenders Act 1997, s 5A.

188   Inter alia: the Protection of Children Act 1999, establishing a statutory list of people considered unsuitable to work with children and imposing a duty on agencies employing people in such a position to check the list before doing so; the Criminal Justice Court Services Act 2000,

simply ensure that the presence of convicted sex offenders is more visible in the community and controlled. Amongst these, the government places particular store on the MAPPA scheme, through which the police and probation services operate local multi-agency public protection arrangements.[189] With the assistance of multi-disciplinary public protection panels (MAPPPs), they organise the risk assessment and management of sexual and violent offenders within the community.[190] Although potentially valuable, these schemes appear to be experiencing serious teething problems.[191]

Given that most sex offences are not reported and most perpetrators not apprehended,[192] a far greater threat comes from those who, for various reasons, are suspected of having sexually abused children, but against whom there are no convictions, often because they have never been brought to trial. Many child protection referrals involve situations of this kind and public agencies are forced to deal with a confused and inconsistent body of case law governing the extent to which they can share their concerns with each other. It seems reasonably clear that both social services departments and the police may disclose to third parties, such as schools and other agencies, allegations of sexual abuse of children, if they 'genuinely and reasonably believe that it is desirable to do so in the interests of protecting children and preventing crime'.[193] Nevertheless, when reaching such a decision, the agency must demonstrate that it has considered the need to maintain a balance between the public interest in protecting children and the individual's right to a private life, which should only be infringed if there is a pressing need to do so.[194] It may be difficult to justify such a decision if the agencies' suspicions arise from uncorroborated allegations of sexual abuse.[195]

An inability to bring a sex abuser to trial does not, of course, prevent child protection practitioners intervening on the basis that a child's allegations were true. Even if an alleged abuser is brought to trial and then acquitted of all criminal charges, this –

disqualifying certain categories of people from working with children and making it a criminal offence for them to apply for or fulfil such work; the Children (Protection from Offenders) (Miscellaneous Amendments) Regulations 1997, SI 1997/2308; the Children (Protection from Offenders) (Amendment) Regulations 1999, SI 1999/2768; the Disqualification for Caring for Children (England) Regulations SI 2002/635 and the Disqualification for Caring for Children (Wales) Regulations SI 2002/896, overhauling the previous regulations preventing unsuitable people from acting as private foster carers.

189 See Criminal Justice and Courts Act 2000, s 67: the police and probation services must establish local Multi-Agency Public Protection Arrangements (MAPPAs), for assessing and managing the risk posed by offenders convicted of sexual or violent offences in the community.

190 These panels have powers to disclose information about offenders to schools, voluntary groups and other local agencies. See HO (2002 a) p14.

191 See DH (2002 a) paras 9.11–9.32. Inter alia: records of meetings lacked detail; failures in monitoring MAPPP referrals; only 66% of the cases considered had been initially screened or assessed for risk of harm to children and then only 73% of screenings were of a satisfactory standard; discussions regarding arrangements for the offender, eg his accommodation, often focused on the offender and not on his potential victims; little or no supervision or monitoring of medium- to low-risk offenders.

192 See D Grubin (1998) pp 3–12.

193 Per Dyson J in *R v Local Authority and Police Authority in the Midlands, ex p LM* [2000] 1 FLR 612 at 619.

194 [2000] 1 FLR 612 at 622–626. Ie the 'pressing need' test, as established in *R v Chief Constable of North Wales Police, ex p Thorpe* [1999] QB 396.

195 As in *R v Local Authority and Police Authority in the Midlands, ex p LM* [2000] 1 FLR 612.

'... does not mean in absolute terms he has not committed the acts alleged against him. Acquittal in criminal sexual abuse proceedings does not mean that a local authority is thereby absolved from further responsibility to protect the child who made the allegations or any other children who may in some way be at risk.'[196]

If care proceedings succeed, with findings of fact made against a named abuser, practitioners may consider that the child victims should be told the details of the court's judgment, to appreciate fully that they have been believed and to make a better psychological recovery in the light of that knowledge. In *Re X (disclosure of information)*,[197] Munby J accepted this view and showed little sympathy with a sex abuser's attempt to prevent findings regarding his sexual abuse of the children in question being disclosed to his victims. Although such a disclosure would infringe the abuser's rights to privacy under article 8 of the ECHR, Munby J held[198] that his rights were clearly outweighed by the children's own rights under article 8 to understand fully their childhood and history.[199]

The disclosure of details of care proceedings to his immediate child victims, as in *Re X*, will not prevent the abuser from seeking out other children in the future. One might have assumed that findings reached in care proceedings could also be passed over to any third-party agency involved in working with children in any capacity. Such a disclosure would appear to fulfil the 'pressing need' test since, armed with this knowledge, the agencies could protect the children in their areas from the abusers' attentions. Nevertheless, in *Re V (sexual abuse: disclosure); Re L (sexual abuse: disclosure)*,[200] the Court of Appeal allowed an appeal against directions made by two previous courts for their findings to be disclosed to local agencies. According to Butler-Sloss LJ, disclosure should not be made if there is no *immediate*[201] need for co-operation between the agencies. Disclosure could only be justified when agencies were actually investigating matters to do with a particular child, or children who could be identified, and whose welfare would now be protected through such disclosures, rather than a more generalised future need regarding children in the community.[202] The decision in *Re V* has been strongly criticised.[203] Smith points out that there can be no 'immediate' need for co-operation *before* disclosure, because logically there is nothing for the agencies to co-operate about until such disclosure occurs. He described it as 'a crushing blow to child protection ...'[204] Although the decision does not prevent one local authority responding to a request for information from another, it does prevent the information being volunteered by one authority to the other, with the court's permission. Its impact is particularly obvious in cases

---

196 *Re S (sexual abuse allegations: local authority response)* [2001] EWHC Admin 334, [2001] 2 FLR 776 at [37], per Scott Baker J.
197 [2001] 2 FLR 440 at [10]–[15].
198 [2001] 2 FLR 440 at [34].
199 As established by *Gaskin v United Kingdom* (1989) 12 EHRR 36.
200 [1999] 1 FLR 267: in *Re V*, permission had been given for findings of sexual impropriety by W, including an indecent assault on an 8-year-old boy, and a finding that he posed a significant risk to two boys in a household in which he lived, to be disclosed to the new local authority in which W was now living; in *Re L*, permission had been given for findings that L had sexually abused three children in his care and that he posed a significant threat to children in the area where he lived, to be given to the football authorities covering the junior football clubs with which he was actively involved.
201 Emphasis supplied.
202 [1999] 1 FLR 267 at 271.
203 See V Smith (1999); T Shawkat (2001) pp 50–57.
204 V Smith (1999) p 251.

'where abusers flit between social services' areas'.[205] Furthermore, this narrow interpretation of the need for inter-agency co-operation sits uneasily with Butler-Sloss LJ's own endorsement of the importance of '... the free exchange of information between agencies in order to facilitate that work and the protection of children'.[206]

It appears that *Re V* can be distinguished in cases which, in addition to complying with the 'pressing need' test, appear to be sufficiently 'exceptional' to justify so doing.[207] Although welcome, this ad hoc method of side-stepping *Re V* only further confuses an already incoherent body of case law. The government's efforts to increase the effectiveness of agency surveillance of paedophiles living in the community requires the courts to give far clearer guidance to agencies responsible for children's safety.

(8) CONCLUSION

Until relatively recently, few child care practitioners considered that the rights of abused children were being adequately protected by the criminal justice system. Great efforts have been made over the last few years to ensure that the criminal law now supports, rather than seriously undermines, their work. Full implementation of the Pigot scheme took too long, but it was a good start. Nevertheless, most child care practitioners will still take some convincing that children's involvement in criminal trials can benefit them. Were it not for the risk of giving child abusers implicit permission to re-abuse with impunity, there might be some basis for arguing that a child's rights to protection would be better served by the civil law alone, without involving the criminal justice system. Time and again, commentators note the low level of convictions and the cost to the child victims of child protection workers attempting to assist in preparing cases for trials which may never occur or later collapse due to the distress of the children themselves. As Farmer and Owen point out, the search for evidence can be a powerful driving force in determining what happens at the investigative stage and may adversely affect what happens thereafter.[208]

Many involved in the child protection process will agree with Wattam's comment:

'Protection through prosecution ... directs practices, frames intervention, and defines the kind of service that children and their families receive if they are referred as a result of an allegation of child harm or injury. Like many myths it is rarely challenged. However, it is neither achieved nor achievable, except in a tiny minority of cases. Furthermore, pursuit of it can be damaging and traumatising to children.'[209]

205 V Smith (1999) p 252.
206 *Re W (disclosure to the police)* [1998] 2 FLR 135 at 141. Leave was given by the Court of Appeal for the disclosure of an assessment report filed with the court in preparation for care proceedings. See also *Re G (a minor)* [1996] 2 All ER 65 at 68, per Butler-Sloss LJ and *Re M (disclosure: children and family reporter)* [2002] EWCA Civ 1199, [2002] 2 FLR 893, per Thorpe LJ at [31].
207 See *Re C (disclosure: sexual abuse findings)* [2002] EWHC 234 (Fam), [2002] 2 FLR 375 at [120], per Bodey J. He held that there was a pressing need for findings in care proceedings (that a sexual abuser was a considerable risk to children) to be disclosed to the housing association owning the flat in which the abuser lived, to avoid its accommodating families with young children near him. This information could not be disclosed to any other landlords to whom he might apply for accommodation in the future.
208 See E Farmer and M Owen (1995) p 62.
209 See C Wattam (1997 b) p 105.

BIBLIOGRAPHY

NB many of these publications can be obtained on the relevant organisation's website.

Association of Chief Officers of Probation, *Recent cases of public disorders around sex offenders which have impeded surveillance and supervision* (1998).

Aldridge M and Wood J, 'Interviewing Child Witnesses with Memorandum Guidelines' (2000) 14 Children and Society 168.

Bates P, 'The Youth Justice and Criminal Evidence Act – the evidence of children and vulnerable adults' (1999) 11 Child and Family Law Quarterly 289.

Birch D, 'A Better Deal for Vulnerable Witnesses' (2000) Criminal Law Review 223.

Brownlow J and Waller B, 'The Memorandum: a social services perspective' in H Westcott and J Jones (eds) *Perspectives on the Memorandum: Policy, practice and research in investigative interviewing* (1997) Ashgate.

Butler-Sloss LJ (Chairman), *Report of the Inquiry into Child Abuse in Cleveland 1987* Cm 412 (1988) HMSO.

Cashmore J and De Haas N, *The Use of Closed-circuit Television for Child Witnesses in the Act* Research Paper 1 (1992) Australian Law Reform Commission.

Childline, *Going to court: child witnesses in their own words, A Childline Study* (1996) Childline.

Cobley C, *Sex Offenders: Law, Policy and Practice* (2000) Jordans.

Crown Prosecution Service (CPS), *Code for Crown Prosecutors* (2000) CPS.

Crown Prosecution Service (CPS) et al, *Provision of Therapy for Child Witnesses Prior to a Criminal Trial: Practice Guidance* (2001) CPS Communications Branch.

Crown Prosecution Service Inspectorate (CPSI), *The Inspectorate's Report on Cases Involving Child Witnesses, Thematic Report* (1998) CPSI.

Davies G and Noon E, *An Evaluation of the Live Link for Child Witnesses* (1991) Home Office.

Davies G and Westcott H, *Interviewing Child Witnesses under the Memorandum of Good Practice: A research review* (1999) Police Research Series Paper 115 (1999) Home Office.

Davies G et al, *Videotaping Children's Evidence: An Evaluation* (1995) Home Office.

Davis G et al, *An Assessment of the Admissibility and Sufficiency of Evidence in Child Abuse Proceedings* (1999) Home Office.

Department of Health (DH), *Safeguarding Children: A joint Chief Inspectors' Report on Arrangements to Safeguard Children* (2002 a) DH Publications.

Department of Health (DH), *Draft Mental Health Bill* Cm 5538-I (2002 b) The Stationery Office.

Department of Health (DH) and Home Office (HO), White Paper *Reforming The Mental Health Act, Part II: High risk patients* Cm 5016-I (2000) The Stationery Office.

Department of Health (DH) et al, *Working Together to Safeguard Children: A guide to inter-agency working to safeguard and promote the welfare of children* (1999) The Stationery Office.

Farmer E and Owen M, *Child Protection Practice: Private Risks and Public Remedies* (1995) HMSO.

Grubin D, *Sex Offending Against Children: Understanding the Risk* Police Research Series Paper 99 (1998).

Gupta A, 'Black Children and the Memorandum' in H Westcott and J Jones (eds) *Perspectives on the Memorandum: Policy, practice and research in investigative interviewing* (1997) Ashgate.

Hallett C, *Interagency Co-ordination in Child Protection* (1995) HMSO.

Hedderman C and Sugg D, *Does Treating Sex Offenders Reduce Reoffending?* Home Office Research Findings No 45 (1996) Home Office.

Home Office (HO), *Memorandum of Good Practice on Video Recorded Interviews with Child Witnesses for Criminal Proceedings* (1992) HMSO.

Home Office (HO), *Speaking Up for Justice: Report of the Interdepartmental Working Group on the treatment of Vulnerable or Intimidated Witnesses in the Criminal Justice System* (1998) HO.

Home Office (HO), *Setting the Boundaries: Reforming the law on sex offences* (2000) Home Office.

Home Office (HO), *Protecting the Public: Strengthening protection against sex offenders and reforming the law on sexual offences* Cm 5668 (2002 a) The Stationery Office.

Home Office (HO), *Justice for All* Cm 5536 (2002 b) The Stationery Office.

Home Office (HO) et al, *Achieving Best Evidence in Criminal Proceedings: Guidance for Vulnerable or Intimidated Witnesses, including Children* (2002) Home Office Communication Directorate.

Hoyano L, 'Variations on a Theme by Pigot: Special Measures Directions for Child Witnesses' (2000) Criminal Law Review 250.

Keenan C and Maitland L, '"There ought to be a law against it" – police evaluation of the efficacy of prosecution in a case of child abuse' (1999) 11 Child and Family Law Quarterly 397.

Laming H, *The Victoria Climbié Inquiry: Report of an Inquiry by Lord Laming* Cm 5730 (2003) The Stationery Office.

Lovell E, *Megan's Law: Does it protect children?* (2001) NSPCC.

Marchant R and Page M, 'The Memorandum and disabled children' in H Westcott and J Jones (eds) *Perspectives on the Memorandum: Policy, practice and research in investigative interviewing* (1997) Ashgate.

Morgan J and Zedner L, *Child Victims: Crime, Impact and Criminal Justice* (1992) Clarendon Press.

Nelson S, 'The Memorandum: quest for the impossible?' in H Westcott and J Jones (eds) *Perspectives on the Memorandum: Policy, practice and research in investigative interviewing* (1997) Ashgate.

NSPCC, *Child Witness Pack* (1993) NSPCC.

NSPCC, *Young Witness Pack* (1998) NSPCC.

Pigot T, *Report of the Advisory Group on Video Evidence* (1989) Home Office.

Plotnikoff J and Woolfson R, *Prosecuting Child Abuse: an Evaluation of the Government's Speedy Progress Policy* (1995) Blackstone Press.

Plotnikoff J and Woolfson R, *Where Are They Now?: An evaluation of sex offender registration in England and Wales* Police Research Series Paper 126 (2000).

Sharland E et al, *Professional Intervention in Child Sexual Abuse* (1996) HMSO.

Shawkat T, 'Passing on Information about Suspected Child Sexual Abusers: Striking the balance between protecting children and the privacy of the individual' (2001) Unpublished paper.

Smith V, 'Passing on Child Abuse Findings – *Re V and Re L*' (1999) Family Law 249.

Social Services Inspectorate (SSI), *The Child, The Court and the Video: A study of the implementation of the Memorandum of Good Practice on video interviewing of child witnesses* (1994) DH Publications.

Spencer J and Flin R, *The Evidence of Children: The Law and the Psychology* (1993) Blackstone Press.

Utting W (Chairman), *People Like Us: The Report Of The Review Of The Safeguards For Children Living Away From Home* (1997) HMSO.

Wade A and Westcott H, 'No easy answers: children's perspectives on investigative interviews' in H Westcott and J Jones (eds) *Perspectives on the Memorandum: Policy, practice and research in investigative interviewing* (1997) Ashgate.

Wade A et al, 'Stories in court – video-taped interviews and the production of children's testimony' (1998) 10 Child and Family Law Quarterly 179.

Waterhouse R (Chairman), *Lost in Care: Report of the Tribunal of Inquiry into the Abuse of Children in Care in the former County Council Areas of Gwynedd and Clwyd since 1974* (2000) The Stationery Office.

Wattam C, 'Can filtering processes be rationalised?' in N Parton (ed) *Child Protection and Family Support: Tensions, contradictions and possibilities* (1997 a) Routledge.

Wattam C, 'Is the Criminalisation of Child Harm and Injury in the Interests of the Child?' (1997 b) 11 Children and Society 97.

Chapter 18

Protecting the rights of young offenders

(1) INTRODUCTION

Children[1] who become involved in crime do not thereby lose their right to be treated as children. Indeed, as the Ingleby Committee so wisely observed, although they are 'often an appalling nuisance', young offenders are of less immediate danger to society than adult law-breakers, they are less responsible for their actions, and are more amenable to training and education.[2] The law should undoubtedly protect children from the full rigours of the criminal justice system until they are old enough to take full personal responsibility for their actions. These concepts might appear to be truisms; indeed, they inspired many of the provisions of the Children Act 1908. Nevertheless, English law is now increasingly becoming the focus of international criticism for its harsh treatment of young offenders. Since the early 1990s, successive Home Secretaries have responded to a fear of juvenile lawlessness with increasingly tough measures designed to crack down on youth crime. The measures introduced by the Crime and Disorder Act 1998 reflect this approach. Consequently, the government of England and Wales is currently infringing international instruments designed to safeguard the rights of children who offend, including their right to a form of trial adjusted to their juvenile status and to humane treatment once convicted. Those aspects of the youth justice system which are currently the subject of the most stringent criticism are discussed below. First, though, there is a brief assessment of the reasons for the current and increasingly punitive response to the problem of youth crime and the apparent lack of concern for the rights of young people in an adult society.

(2) CHILDREN'S RIGHTS VERSUS SOCIETY'S RIGHT TO PROTECTION

The CRC stresses the need for legal systems to respond to youth crime by respecting the legal status of juveniles and promoting their overall welfare.[3] Similarly, the United Nations Standard Minimum Rules for the Administration of Juvenile Justice 1985 (the Beijing Rules), which provide a complete and detailed framework for the

---

1   English criminal law uses the term 'children' to describe those under the age of 14 and 'young persons' to describe those under the age of 18.
2   Home Office (hereafter HO) (1960) para 106.
3   See particularly art 40, discussed in more detail below.

operation of a national juvenile justice system, continually emphasise the importance of dealing with juvenile offenders fairly and humanely. Although not binding per se, these provide a blueprint for the various processes which should be applied to children caught up in youth crime. The overall aim of these two international instruments is to ensure that young offenders are themselves protected from harm, treated justly and diverted from imprisonment and punishment into treatment and rehabilitation.[4] Additionally, the Human Rights Act 1998 now reinforces the need to comply with the provisions of the ECHR, a Convention which has already achieved important reforms in the law relating to young offenders.[5]

Had the policies developed in this country during the 1960s been implemented, these international instruments would have been fully complied with by English law. During this period, the 'welfare approach' to juvenile crime attracted increasing support. The Ingleby Committee wanted the age of criminal responsibility raised to 12.[6] Soon afterwards, the White Paper, *The Child, the Family and the Young Offender*[7] recommended keeping young offenders out of court as far as possible, through family councils and family courts. This was quickly followed by *Children in Trouble*,[8] which emphasised that juvenile delinquency is, in most cases, no more than a phase in a child's normal development, which needs checking in a way that will not merely reinforce his or her criminal tendencies:[9]

'The social consequences of juvenile delinquency range from minor nuisance to considerable damage and suffering for the community. An important object of the criminal law is to protect society against such consequences: but the community also recognises the importance of caring for those who are too young to protect themselves. Over recent years these two quite distinct grounds for action by society in relation to young people have been moving steadily together ... The aims of protecting society from juvenile delinquency, and of helping children in trouble to grow up into mature and law-abiding persons, are complementary and not contradictory.'[10]

The welfare approach lost momentum and the Children and Young Persons Act 1969, designed to introduce many of its ingredients, was never fully implemented. Even in the 1960s, an approach which saw children as the product of society, requiring 'treatment' to remedy their behaviour was a controversial one. Since then, it has been in almost continuous conflict with the 'justice model'.[11] The latter considers young offenders not as needing protection but as being personally responsible for their actions and therefore deserving punishment.[12]

Swings between the welfare and justice models have undermined policy makers' ability to develop any coherent youth crime strategy. The 1980s and early 1990s saw concerted efforts being made to divert young people from the criminal justice system[13] and to find alternatives to custodial responses, particularly for the younger children.[14]

---

4   See also the International Covenant on Civil and Political Rights, arts 10(2)(b) and 14(4).
5   Discussed below and in chapter 2.
6   HO (1960). See below.
7   HO (1965).
8   HO (1968).
9   HO (1968) para 6.
10   HO (1968) para 7.
11   See A Morris and H Giller (1987) esp ch 8.
12   L Gelsthorpe and A Morris (1994) pp 971–973.
13   Ie through the extensive use of cautions.
14   Ie through the use of intermediate treatment schemes. The Criminal Justice Act 1991 also abolished the use of custodial remands and sentences for 14-year-olds. See T Newburn (2002) pp 553–555.

But by 1993, the year that 2-year-old James Bulger was murdered by two 10-year-old boys, a far more punitive approach was emerging.[15] Today, the view that the type of measures appropriate for young offenders are similar to those appropriate for abused children has not only lost favour, but the justice model appears to have been embraced wholeheartedly. Indeed, partly in response to public opinion, the last 20 years have seen the development of an increasingly punitive approach to young people who offend, particularly the very young ones.[16] A series of measures has been introduced which clearly contravene the international provisions designed to protect the rights of young offenders. In 1994, more restrictive guidelines on cautioning undermined the previous presumption in favour of diverting young people from the courts. The Criminal Justice and Public Order Act 1994 introduced the new secure training order for 12- to 14-year-olds. It also reduced the minimum age for the detention of very serious offenders from 14 to 10, extended the maximum sentence for 15- to 17-year-olds from 12 to 24 months in a young offenders institution (hereafter YOI) and introduced secure remands for children aged between 12 and 14.[17]

Further developments reinforced this punitive approach. The numbers of young people sentenced to prison rose spectacularly during the 1990s.[18] Meanwhile, there was a steady increase in the number of teenage boys held in prisons awaiting trial in England and Wales. A new government then came to power in 1997. Greatly influenced by the Audit Commission's report, *Misspent Youth*,[19] it resolved to reform a youth justice system considered to be slow, inefficient, expensive and achieving little, in terms of addressing offending behaviour and preventing its reoccurrence.[20] With the assistance of the newly established Youth Justice Board to monitor the operation of the new system and provide policy guidance, an ambitious package of measures was introduced, designed to provide a clearer focus on tackling youth crime at national and local levels.[21] The new system of youth justice[22] comprises a strange blend of authoritarianism and liberalism – indeed, it is permeated with contradictions and tensions. Considerable faith is now placed in the abilities of the locally based and organised multi-agency youth offending teams (YOTs).[23] These organise and provide local community intervention programmes aimed at 'nipping crime in the bud',[24] thereby keeping more young offenders out of the courts and preventing today's young offenders too easily becoming 'tomorrow's hardened criminals'.[25] The youth courts also gained a bewildering armoury of orders,[26] some involving an element of restorative justice aimed at making the offender take responsibility for his behaviour.[27]

15   T Newburn (2002) pp 555–557.
16   See below.
17   See S Moore (2000) pp 116–118.
18   P White and J Woodbridge (1998) pp 5–6.
19   See Audit Commission (1996).
20   See T Newburn (2002) pp 557–559.
21   HO (1997 c) para 1. See also (1997 a) Introduction.
22   The youth justice system was largely reorganised by the Crime and Disorder Act 1998 (hereafter CDA 1998), the Youth Justice and Criminal Evidence Act 1999 and the Powers of Criminal Courts (Sentencing) Act 2000 (hereafter PCC(S)A 2000). See generally C Ball, K McCormac and N Stone (2001) Part I.
23   These local teams include probation officers, social workers, police officers, education and health authority staff.
24   HO (1997 a) Introduction.
25   HO (1997 a) Introduction.
26   See G Monaghan (2000) p 150, discussed in more depth below.
27   Discussed below.

Some of the organisational changes introduced by the new legislation, particularly the multi-agency approach to youth justice, seem sensible. Giving the YOTs the task of co-ordinating the work of various agencies, all of whom probably already deal with the same child, but in differing contexts, was a much-needed initiative.[28] Nevertheless, the new legislation had a darker side – as the language employed throughout the 1997 White Paper made clear.[29] Underlying it were the same intolerant ideas about punishment and retribution which had dominated the previous administration's approach to youth justice. As discussed in more detail below, a determination to protect the public and prevent young people 'drifting into crime' led to an aggressively authoritarian attempt to control children and their families. The already low age of criminal responsibility was made even harsher by the abolition of the presumption of doli incapax.[30] Local authorities acquired powers to impose local child curfews to keep children under 10 off the streets in the evenings.[31] The already restricted cautioning system was placed in a legislative strait-jacket, leading to widespread predictions that more young offenders would be dealt with by the courts than ever before.[32] Existing concerns about an increasing use of custodial sentencing for children were not addressed. Indeed, youth court magistrates acquired greater powers to lock up young offenders for longer than their colleagues have in relation to adult offenders,[33] together with the foundation of 'a new generation of penal institutions for children as young as 12'.[34] This harsh approach risks alienating large numbers of young people who will inevitably judge adult society by its apparently punitive attitudes.

It is undeniable that society is entitled to protect itself from young offenders. A disproportionate amount of crime is committed by young people,[35] and public spending on those aspects of the criminal justice system is very large.[36] The peak ages for offending behaviour appear to be around 18 for boys and 14 for girls[37] and, not surprisingly, the same young people who are responsible for anti-social behaviour in homes and schools[38] are those most likely to commit criminal offences. A growing body of research evidence supports the view that a young offender is more likely to

---

28   The Audit Commission had criticised the absence of local forums to co-ordinate the work of the various local agencies involved in youth offending work. See Audit Commission (1996) pp 98–99. See also J Fionda (1999) p 40.

29   HO (1997 a).

30   See below.

31   See below.

32   See B Goldson (2000) ch 3.

33   G Monaghan (2000) pp 150–159.

34   A Rutherford (2002) p 102.

35   In 1997, 11% of all known offenders were aged between 10 and 17: J Mattinson and C Mirrlees-Black (2000) p 11. See also Communities that Care (2002), indicating (pp 50–51) from self-referral material, relatively high levels of involvement in crime and anti-social activities, with one in ten boys in year 7 (rising to nearly one in five in year 11) saying that they had carried a weapon to school or in their neighbourhood and nearly one in five in year 11 saying that they had attacked someone in the last year intending to hurt them seriously. These figures are not dissimilar to those provided by Mori (2002) ch 2.

36   See Audit Commission (1996) pp 5–7.

37   C Flood-Page et al (2000) p 10.

38   See particularly Mori (2002) ch 7, for the links between truancy, school exclusion and youth crime. See also C Flood-Page et al (2000), indicating (pp 37–38) that almost half of 12- to 16-year-old boys who were persistent truants were offenders, compared with around 10% of those who did not truant or truanted less and also that almost 25% of boys, who had been excluded, were offenders.

be male, display aggressive and hyperactive behaviour in early childhood, prone to drug and alcohol abuse, with poor relationships with family, friends and relatives, involved with the police and is someone who truants or is excluded from school.[39] There is also a strong likelihood of a young offender having suffered from a childhood mental disorder.[40]

This depressing picture of marginalised young people should, however, be kept in perspective. An increasingly harsh youth justice system seems largely attributable to successive Home Secretaries playing to the populist vote and seeking to gain the law and order 'high ground'.[41] Whipped up by media portrayals of persistent young offenders, combined with memories of the James Bulger murder, the public has exaggerated fears of increasing youth crime, which are not supported by the criminal statistics.[42] Despite youth crime being relatively minor, mainly involving criminal damage and shoplifting,[43] it is much more visible than much adult crime. Public anxiety often concentrates on essentially non-criminal or relatively trivial criminal behaviour, such as hanging around on the streets, vandalism, graffiti and deliberate damage to property.[44] Pearson questions whether if the official criminal statistics included common adult crimes, such as theft from the work place and driving under the influence of alcohol, there would still be such a discrepancy between adult and youth crime.[45] Moreover, it is not often noted that young people themselves are more likely to be victims of personal crime than adults, with older teenagers having the highest risk of being assaulted.[46] Adolescents are more likely to suffer harassment than adults and, as the murders of Stephen Lawrence and Damilola Taylor indicate, they may be at a greater risk if they are members of ethnic minority groups.[47] Similarly, whilst few young people bring this harassment to the attention of the police, they are, themselves, more likely than adults to come into contact with the police, through being stopped and searched[48] and being 'moved on'.[49] Furthermore, black juveniles are more likely to be stopped by the police than white people or Asians[50] and are more likely to be prosecuted than cautioned.[51] Ethnic minority young people certainly believe the police behave less fairly towards them than towards white people.[52]

Despite these factors which indicate that there may be almost as many young people being sinned against as are sinners, politicians continue to curry favour with

---

39   See, inter alia: D Farrington (1996) ch 1; J Graham and B Bowling (1995) esp ch 4; C Flood-Page et al (2000) esp ch 3.

40   See H Meltzer and R Gatward (2000) p 85 and Tables 7.6 and 7.7. See also D Lader et al (2000).

41   See T Newburn (2002) pp 555–557.

42   J Mattinson and C Mirrlees-Black (2000) ch 3.

43   J Mattinson and C Mirrlees-Black (2000) p 11 and Mori (2002) ch 2.

44   J Mattinson and C Mirrlees-Black (2000) p 12. But see T Newburn (2002) pp 542–543, who points out the significant rise in violent offending by male juveniles in the last decade.

45   See G Pearson (1994) p 1193.

46   See T Newburn (2002) pp 546–547 and the sources quoted therein. See also Audit Commission (1996) p 9.

47   Mori (2002) p 38. But these figures indicate that the numbers of racial attacks against school children are still very low.

48   C Flood-Page et al (2000) pp 47–54.

49   T Newburn (2002) p 547.

50   C Flood-Page et al (2000) p 50. See also C Phillips and B Bowling (2002) pp 594–595, regarding black people, as a group (age unspecified).

51   See Nacro (2001 a) p 3. This summarises current statistics indicating that Black/Black British are over-represented at all stages of the youth justice system.

52   C Flood-Page et al (2000) p 54 and Mori (2002) p 33.

the public by playing on its fears. Indeed, certain aspects of the current youth justice system regarding the processing and treatment of young offenders reflect an implicit assumption that by becoming involved in offending behaviour, children forfeit most of their rights to a protected legal status. This might be justifiable if the methods used to correct young offenders achieved material benefits, either in ensuring their rehabilitation or in protecting society and deterring others from similar actions. It appears, though, that few forms of dealing with this group reduce the chances of their re-offending; indeed, many methods used achieve the reverse at enormous financial expense, given the cost of custody in YOIs.

(3)   THE AGE OF CRIMINAL RESPONSIBILITY

(A)   The international context

A crucial element in any youth justice system is the age at which offenders are obliged to take responsibility for their criminal actions. If this is too high, there is a risk that the law will be widely flouted and brought into disrepute; too low and the law risks being savagely harsh. International instruments recognise the importance of adopting an appropriate age for criminal responsibility, without being particularly helpful about what this should be. Article 40 of the CRC, which requires governments to establish special laws and procedures regarding children accused of or convicted of criminal offences, requires 'the establishment of a minimum age below which children shall be presumed not to have the capacity to infringe the penal law'. Rule 4.1 of the Beijing Rules states that: 'In those legal systems recognising the concept of the age of criminal responsibility for juveniles, the beginning of that age shall not be fixed at too low an age level, bearing in mind the facts of emotional, mental and intellectual maturity.' This rule is accompanied by the explanation that:

> 'The modern approach would be to consider whether a child can live up to the moral and psychological components of criminal responsibility; that is, whether a child, by virtue of her or his individual discernment and understanding, can be held responsible for essentially anti-social behaviour ... In general, there is a close relationship between the notion of responsibility for delinquent or criminal behaviour and other social rights and responsibilities (such as marital status, civil majority etc).'[53]

These measures give no specific guidance as to what might be an internationally acceptable age limit below which prosecution should be impossible.

It is undeniably difficult to define the age at which it is appropriate to expect children to take responsibility for actions which, if committed by adults, would be punishable under the criminal law. Although whatever age selected must be an essentially arbitrary one, the English government is coming under increasing international pressure to review the relatively low age of 10 presently marking the point at which children in England and Wales assume criminal responsibility.[54] Few European countries have lower ages[55] and most have adopted far higher ages.[56] The

---

53   Official Commentary to r 4.
54   The age of criminal responsibility has been 10 since 1963. See Children and Young Persons Act 1933, s 50, as amended by Children and Young Persons Act 1963, s 16.
55   Only three: Cyprus, Switzerland and Liechtenstein (7); Scotland (8).
56   Eg France (13); Germany, Austria, Italy and most eastern European countries (14); Scandinavian countries (15); Spain, Portugal and Andorra (16); Belgium and Luxembourg (18). See listed in Nacro (2002 a) Appendix 3.

European Court of Human Rights was influenced by the lack of uniformity on this matter throughout Europe. It therefore rejected the claim made by the child killers of James Bulger that, by attributing criminal responsibility to them as 10-year-old children, the United Kingdom had infringed their rights under article 3 of the ECHR.[57] Nevertheless, a strong minority rejected this view,[58] pointing to the vast majority of member states with far higher ages of criminal responsibility.[59] Hammarberg, the Vice-chair of the Committee on the Rights of the Child, commenting on English law, also noted that despite the CRC failing to say precisely what age governments should adopt, it was the Committee's view that the age of 10 is 'too young and not in the spirit of the Convention'.[60] The Committee itself recommended in its response to the United Kingdom's first report on implementation of the Convention that 'serious consideration be given to raising the age of criminal responsibility throughout the areas of the United Kingdom'.[61] In its response to the second report, it was more robust in its criticism, noting with 'serious concern' that the situation since the initial report had worsened,[62] with the age of criminal responsibility remaining at 10 (and 8 in Scotland).[63] It recommended that the government 'considerably raise the minimum age for criminal responsibility'.[64]

(B)   A source of controversy

The question whether the age of criminal responsibility should be raised has been a source of controversy in this country for many years. Although there is general agreement that society has a right to protect itself from youth crime, it is obviously inhumane and of little practical value to hold very young children responsible for breaking the law. At first sight, fixing an appropriate age for criminal responsibility might appear relevant only to the question whether a child should be found guilty of behaviour which would be criminal, if above the age selected. But the age of criminal responsibility has far greater influence than this. It governs every aspect of the youth justice system. Thus, for example, there is less obvious need for children to be protected from making incriminating admissions when being interviewed about their responsibility for certain actions if, by virtue of age, these actions cannot be defined as a criminal offence at all. An admission of guilt will not then constitute part of that child's criminal record. Equally, the type of hearing and evidential rules adopted for determining a child's responsibility for certain behaviour will be influenced by whether the behaviour could be described as criminal, which in turn depends on age.

The effectiveness of the criminal law would be undermined fundamentally by the introduction of a varying age which attempted to accommodate individual maturity, as employed by the concept of *Gillick* competence in civil law contexts.[65] There is, nevertheless, a stark contrast between the civil and criminal law regarding children's capacity for taking responsibility for the way they behave. Thus the rather punitive

57   *V and T v United Kingdom* (1999) 30 EHRR 121 (para 98).
58   A minority of five judges.
59   Para 1, joint partly dissenting opinion.
60   See T Hammarberg (1995) p 19.
61   See Committee on the Rights of the Child (1995) para 36.
62   Ie in relation to the abolition of the doli incapax presumption, see below.
63   Committee on the Rights of the Child (2002) para 59.
64   Committee on the Rights of the Child (2002) para 62(a).
65   Discussed in chapter 3.

approach of the criminal law regarding a young offender's ability to be held criminally responsible at the age of 10 compares unfavourably with the civil law's overtly paternalistic approach to a child's legal competence for decision-making. Whilst the civil courts take great care to ensure that adolescents do not obtain legal capacity to reach decisions before being deemed sufficiently mature to comprehend their implications, the criminal law imposes criminal responsibility on juveniles at an extremely early age, presumably to protect society from their evident lawlessness.

It is often suggested that an appropriate way of determining the age of criminal responsibility is to adopt the age at which children are commonly able to distinguish right from wrong. But as the Ingleby Committee pointed out many years ago, a capacity to do this does not necessarily indicate an ability to take personal responsibility equivalent to that in an adult.[66] Indeed, an ability to distinguish right from wrong may develop long before the child becomes sufficiently independent to take permanent personal responsibility for his or her actions, in the same way as an adult.[67] Research indicates that children are the product of their upbringing and are extremely vulnerable to influence from their environment and the climate of opinion in their immediate family and the group with which they mix. This suggests that although, for example, children of 11 may be perfectly able to distinguish right from wrong, they remain so much under the influence of a group of friends, that they feel obliged to join whatever criminal activity they are involved in.[68]

The ability to take personal responsibility for actions would suggest the need to understand their implications. Research evidence indicates that, in cognitive terms, important developmental changes occur during the teenage years.[69] It is only during the onset of early adolescence that young people become competent to think in abstract terms. With this comes the capacity to feel guilt and shame, linked with an awareness of the implications for others of the offender's wrongful actions.[70] This would appear to reinforce the view that –

> 'Older children are able to use internal justice principles and have concern for victims of wrong acts, whereas younger children tend to be more governed by fear of punishment after detection … Children and adolescents therefore have a diminished capacity, as compared with adults to think in terms of the long term consequences of their actions, to reflect about their behaviour and its effects on others, and to experience enduring feelings of guilt. This argues for a different approach to the application of criminal responsibility concepts, which recognises the special nature of childhood.'[71]

This evidence suggests the need for a considerable increase in the current age set by English law.

One of the factors hampering such an increase is the fact that the age of criminal responsibility cannot be viewed in isolation from broader considerations regarding how to deal with juvenile wrong-doing below the age chosen, and this itself has been a matter of considerable dispute. If the perception is that a child below the age specified will necessarily escape any attempt to improve his or her behaviour, despite having committed an 'offence', then the temptation will be to adopt a low age to

---

66   HO (1960) para 81.
67   HO (1960) para 81.
68   See D Farrington (1996) p 26; J Graham and B Bowling (1995) pp 42–43; and C Flood-Page et al (2000) pp 34–35. The two latter studies showed that having friends who were in trouble with the police strongly correlated with adolescents' own offending behaviour.
69   Discussed in chapter 3.
70   See N Tutt (1996) para 3.10.
71   See N Tutt (1996) paras 3.10 and 3.13.

ensure that society is able to protect itself against infant hooligans. But when the system provides a means of ensuring that children below the age of criminal responsibility can be dealt with by appropriate non-criminal methods, then there is far less need to keep it low. The Ingleby Committee discussed this issue and recommended that the age of criminal responsibility be raised to 12, with the possibility of it being raised again to 14.[72] The report nevertheless stressed that such a change would not allow children below such an age to 'get off', since it was to be combined with providing the civil courts with wide powers to deal with them by other means.[73] The later White Paper, *The Child, the Family and the Young Offender*[74] more radically recommended raising the age of criminal responsibility to the age of 16 and abolishing the juvenile court. By way of a compromise, the Children and Young Persons Act 1969 eventually provided for the age of criminal responsibility to be raised to 14, with the retention of the juvenile court. This higher age was, however, part of the controversial package of provisions recommended by the White Paper, *Children in Trouble*[75] and was never implemented.

Subsequently, there seems to have been less sympathy for the argument that the age of criminal responsibility is too high. In a 1990 White Paper, the government indicated its satisfaction that the present legal arrangements made proper allowance for the fact that children's understanding, knowledge and ability to reason were still developing.[76] Moreover, the 1993 Home Affairs Committee took the view that 'juveniles who commit the most serious crimes must remain subject to the jurisdiction of the criminal courts in order to reassure the public that justice is done'.[77] Furthermore, ideas about reducing the age of criminal responsibility have been frequently inextricably bound up with arguments about the value of the doli incapax presumption.

(C)   Abolishing the doli incapax presumption

In the past, opponents to reducing the age of criminal responsibility were often influenced by the argument that the low age of 10 years was mediated by the doli incapax presumption, which provided an important additional safeguard for younger children. Until the presumption was abolished by the Crime and Disorder Act 1998,[78] children under the age of 14 and above 10 were presumed incapable of knowing that what they had done was wrong and therefore not criminally responsible for whatever offence they might have committed. On the face of it, the presumption appeared to inject into the law a benign recognition that it was wrong to use criminal penalties to punish children under 14 who did not appreciate the wrongfulness of their actions. But it could be rebutted by the prosecution satisfying the court, not only that the child had committed the offence, but also that he or she knew that it was 'seriously wrong', as opposed to being 'merely naughty'. In practice, as the Bulger trial demonstrated, the presumption was rebutted relatively easily, particularly in

---

72   HO (1960) para 93.
73   Eg by authorising the removal of a child who needed care and protection from home into the care of a local authority or an approved school.
74   HO (1965).
75   HO (1968).
76   HO (1990 b) para 8.4.
77   See House of Commons Home Affairs Committee (1993) para 101.
78   S 34.

circumstances where the offence was very serious. This was illogical, since the most serious crimes are often committed by extremely emotionally disturbed children – indeed, they are the ones *least* likely to understand notions of culpability and the moral dimensions of taking responsibility for wrong-doing.[79] Despite its failure to protect these most serious wrongdoers, as Gelsthorpe and Morris point out, the importance of the presumption lay in its symbolism, 'it was a statement about the nature of childhood' and the vulnerability of children.[80]

On coming to power in 1997, the new government was clearly intent on abolishing the doli incapax presumption.[81] It instituted this change only three years after the Committee on the Rights of the Child had suggested that the United Kingdom should consider raising the age of criminal responsibility. The reform, which abolished a principle which had existed for over 800 years, met with a storm of critical comment.[82] Nevertheless, the Home Office drew strength from the fact that the Divisional Court had, in 1994, simply decided that the presumption was an anachronism and no longer remained part of English common law.[83] The House of Lords had, soon afterwards, rapidly reinstated the presumption,[84] but the Divisional Court's views provided ammunition for the suggested reform. Thus the government asserted that whilst such a presumption might have been justified before the days of compulsory education from the age of 5, today children grew up far more quickly, mentally and physically, and therefore knew right from wrong earlier.[85] The spuriousness of this argument is obvious. Children's ability to take complete responsibility for the criminality of their actions has little to do with formal education in primary school. Developmentally, children can have changed very little; they remain as much a product of their home background and as prone to influence from others as they were in the nineteenth century. Indeed, the vast majority of European countries consider that this type of maturity is not present in children under the ages of 13 or 14.[86]

The government also argued that children no longer needed this form of special protection from adult punishments because the reformed law would 'strengthen the capacity of the system to deal with child offenders in the most focused way, taking full account of their development' and ensuring that sentences were made age-appropriate.[87] This assertion ignores a number of issues. In particular, very young children can start being convicted for criminal offences from the age of 10, thus acquiring a criminal record – a factor which may have serious implications for them in later years. Furthermore, children over the age of 10 accused of very serious crimes may undergo a form of trial only marginally adapted to take account of their youth[88] and, if found guilty, may receive a relatively long period in

79   See G Boswell (1995) pp 30–31. Discussed below.
80   L Gelsthorpe and A Morris (1999) p 213.
81   See HO (1997 b) paras 6–13.
82   See, inter alia: L Gelsthorpe and A Morris (1999); J Fionda (1999) pp 38–40; S Bandalli (2000) ch 5; A Ashford (1998).
83   *C v DPP* [1994] 3 All ER 190.
84   *C v DPP* [1996] AC 1.
85   *C v DPP* [1994] 3 All ER 190 at 196, per Laws J and HO (1997 b) para 8.
86   See the views of the five dissenting judges in *V v United Kingdom (and T v United Kingdom)* (2000) 30 EHRR 121. In their view, through the combination of attributing criminal responsibility to two 10-year-olds (an age far lower than that set by 37 other European states), their mode of trial in an adult court and the imposition on them of an indeterminate sentence, English law had infringed their art 3 rights under the ECHR. Discussed in more detail below.
87   HO (1997 b) para 16.
88   Discussed below.

detention.[89] The combination of these factors, without the softening effect of the doli incapax presumption, produces a harshly punitive system automatically applying to all children once they attain the age of 10. It is therefore astonishing to read the government's assertion, in its second report on implementing the CRC, that this change in the law benefits children. Indeed, the report states that the government had abolished the presumption of doli incapax, together with the right of silence in the dock,[90] both having been rights formerly available to children aged between 10 and 14, because –

> 'if a child has begun to offend, he or she is entitled to the earliest possible intervention to address that offending behaviour and eliminate its causes. The changes will also have the result of putting all juveniles on the same footing as far as courts are concerned, and will contribute to the *right* of children appearing there to develop responsibility for themselves.'[91]

As Bandalli trenchantly asserts:

> 'The wording of this statement is profoundly disingenuous and distorted. The increasing extent to which legal safeguards are being removed and children are being held responsible in criminal law is presented here as a courtesy to children's rights, child development and justice.'[92]

(D)   Reappraising the age of criminal responsibility

The government had clearly considered the doli incapax presumption to be a hindrance, because it had prevented child offenders undergoing the measures required to teach them to mend their ways – it stopped some children, who ought to be prosecuted, from ever appearing in court.[93] Such a situation certainly needed reviewing, since it was an obvious by-product of a low age of criminal responsibility, combined with a protective feature that ensured that children 'got off' entirely. Only a conviction could ensure that a child with criminal tendencies obtained corrective 'treatment', whereas an acquittal meant that no action at all could be taken, certainly by the criminal law. The Children Act 1989, by abolishing the old 'criminal care order'[94] and by making care or supervision orders hinge on proving that the child in question is suffering 'significant harm', or is 'beyond parental control',[95] had made it more difficult to deal with young offenders by civil measures. Indeed, it had contributed to a situation whereby a young offender protected by the doli incapax presumption might not normally receive any attention from the civil or criminal law. But a far more fundamental remedy should have been attempted than merely abolishing the doli incapax presumption and leaving the age of criminal responsibility at 10. A more sophisticated approach would have been to select a far higher age of criminal responsibility, combined with well-designed civil powers to deal with child 'offenders' under that age, as proposed by the reformers in the 1960s.

---

89   Discussed below.
90   CDA 1998, s 35.
91   Department of Health (hereafter DH) (1999 a) para 10.30.1. Emphasis supplied.
92   S Bandalli (2000) p 89.
93   HO (1997 b) para 16.
94   Under Children and Young Persons Act 1969, s 7(7).
95   Children Act 1989, s 31.

Lord Jauncey and Lord Lowry in *C v DPP*[96] quite clearly appreciated that the removal of the doli incapax presumption had fundamental implications for the remainder of the youth justice system. Although they appreciated the principle's imperfections, in so far as it was illogical in its effect and conceptually obscure in meaning, they considered its value lay in its benevolent intentions. They drew attention to the wider implications of abolishing it, which would involve exposing children to the full criminal process at an earlier age than in most West European countries. They considered that such a step should be taken by Parliament and not the courts, as part of a larger review of the appropriate methods for dealing with youthful offenders. In the words of Lord Lowry:

> 'Whatever change is made, it should come only after collating and considering the evidence and after taking account of the effect which a change would have on the whole law relating to children's anti-social behaviour. This is a classic case for Parliamentary investigation, deliberation and legislation.'[97]

It is certainly not clear that those advocating the presumption's abolition, without at the same time raising the age of criminal responsibility, appreciated the *overall* effect of the age of criminal responsibility being left at its present low age.[98] The whole edifice of the criminal justice system is constructed on the basis that all child offenders are within its scope. The procedures for bringing them to trial are designed to fulfil criminal justice, rather than welfare requirements.[99] As noted above, the courts have very substantial criminal penalties at their disposal for younger children in the 10- to 14-year-old category, in the event of their being charged with serious offences. Even those offenders diverted from court appearances, through the reprimand and final warning system, have been involved in a criminal process. Although the existence of either, in a child's past, does not strictly amount to a criminal record, it has serious implications if he or she breaks the law again.[100]

(E)   Criminalising young children's behaviour – widening the net

The Crime and Disorder Act 1998 (CDA 1998) not only abolished the doli incapax presumption, it effectively reduced the age of criminal responsibility. Indeed, the reforms of the late 1990s reflected extraordinarily narrow views about how the young children who cannot conform and who behave in an anti-social way inevitably 'drift into a life of crime'.[101] Far from considering children as being vulnerable and in need of protection from adverse circumstances, as portrayed by the Children Act 1989,[102] the new legislation adopted an authoritarian approach which effectively criminalises the misbehaviour of very young children. The measures introduced by the Crime and Disorder Act 1998 were grounded on ideas about young children's need for discipline and control. Powers now exist to subdue their innate criminal tendencies before it is

---

96   *C v DPP* [1995] 2 All ER 43.
97   [1995] 2 All ER 43 at 64, per Lord Lowry.
98   HO (1997 b). This point was not mentioned in the discussion of the doli incapax presumption (paras 6–19).
99   Despite the requirement that courts sentencing young offenders are required to have 'regard to the welfare of the child', under Children and Young Persons Act 1933, s 44. Discussed below.
100   Discussed below.
101   HO (1997 a) Introduction.
102   See C Piper (1999) pp 402–403.

too late. The child safety order,[103] introduced to prevent children under 10 'slipping into the crime habit',[104] combined with local child curfew orders,[105] can effectively clear the streets of unsupervised young children in the late evenings.[106] Despite the local child curfew orders being particularly controversial and similar schemes producing negative results in the USA,[107] their scope was later extended to teenagers up to the age of 16.[108] Such orders very obviously pander to the public's misconceptions about high levels of crime being committed by children hanging about on the streets.[109] As critics have pointed out,[110] such measures not only have the capacity to exacerbate these fears, but also penalise children living in deprived areas, with poor home facilities, from carrying out essentially innocent activities, such as congregating in groups.[111] Indeed, as Walsh suggests, such restrictions might well infringe a variety of their rights under the ECHR, notably the right to freedom of assembly under article 11 and from discrimination under article14.[112] The government would find it difficult to argue, particularly in relation to a 10-year-old, that such restrictions are either 'necessary' for the public safety or for the prevention of disorder or crime, or that they are proportionate to the risk posed.[113]

The child safety orders have also been strongly criticised for bringing very young children within the perimeter of the criminal justice system.[114] Whilst being ostensibly civil in nature, in so far as they are only available on the application of social services departments of local authorities, the grounds are nevertheless strongly criminal in nature.[115] Very young children are certainly unlikely to appreciate that such proceedings are civil and therefore not punitive, particularly when they realise that their parents are being coerced into enforcing the conditions attached, through a parenting order.[116] Although the court is governed by the welfare principle when deciding whether a child safety order is justified, there is no obligation to consider a welfare checklist.[117] The order places the child under the supervision of a responsible officer,[118] to ensure that the child 'receives appropriate care, protection and support

103 CDA 1998, s 11.
104 See HO (1997 b) para 102.
105 CDA 1998, s 14.
106 As originally designed, these orders allowed local councils to ban children under 10 from public places during specified hours between 9pm and 6am, unless under the supervision of a responsible adult.
107 See C Walsh (2002) p 78.
108 Criminal Justice and Police Act 2001, s 48. See also s 49, which enabled the police to initiate these schemes, in addition to local authorities.
109 J Mattinson and C Mirrlees-Black (2000) pp 15–16.
110 See, inter alia: L Gelsthorpe and A Morris (1999) pp 214–217; S Bandalli (2000) pp 92–94; C Walsh (1999) and (2002).
111 CDA 1998, s 14 was amended by the Criminal Justice and Police Act 2001, ss 48–49.
112 C Walsh (2002) pp 74–77.
113 Ie under art 11(2) of the ECHR.
114 See, inter alia: L Gelsthorpe and A Morris (1999) pp 214–217; M Hayes and C Williams (1999); C Piper (1999) pp 405–407.
115 See CDA 1998, s 11(3). Such an order can be made if a child under the age of 10 commits what would be an offence if above that age, or if their behaviour suggests that they are likely to do so, or they have breached a local child curfew, or their behaviour is alarming, distressing or harassing to local residents.
116 CDA 1998, s 8. A parenting order can be made whenever a child safety order is made. See discussion below.
117 As set out in the Children Act 1989, s 1(3). The court must instead obtain information about the child's family circumstances and the likely effect of the order on those circumstances. CDA 1998, s 12(1).
118 A social worker, a member of a YOT, or of an LEA.

and is subject to proper control'.[119] It can, in practice, operate as a highly interventionist form of social control.[120] The conditions imposed may restrict the behaviour of a young child very radically; for example, he or she may be ordered to attend a local youth programme for up to one year.[121] Despite these features, the child is neither party to the proceedings nor entitled to separate representation in court. Arguably, a child maintaining that such failure infringes his or her rights to a fair trial under article 6 of the ECHR has a good chance of succeeding. Such an argument is strengthened by the Scottish Court of Session's decision that the failure to provide free legal representation for all children appearing before children's hearings in Scotland infringes their rights under article 6, despite those proceedings being civil, and not criminal, in nature.[122] A further source of concern is that a court can deal with a child's failure to comply with the terms of a child safety order by substituting a care order in its place, without satisfying the grounds for such an order specified by section 31 of the Children Act 1989.[123] As Gelsthorpe and Morris maintain:

> 'Through the child safety order, the age of criminal responsibility becomes meaningless, despite the Government's claim that it had no plans to change it: children under 10 who have committed, or might commit, offences will be penalised. The value of allowing children to grow out of crime and of minimum intervention ... is abandoned.'[124]

(F)   Alternative approaches

The various youth justice systems throughout the world reflect differing ideas about the age of criminal responsibility. Retaining a low age need not necessarily go hand-in-hand with a strongly punitive approach to young offenders. Indeed, as Lord Jauncey pointed out, although in Scotland criminal responsibility attaches to children aged 8 and over, the system of children's hearings avoids many children being dealt with by the criminal courts until they reach the age of 16.[125] By contrast, in most European legal systems, a much higher age of criminal responsibility, combined with a welfare approach, makes it quite impossible for children under that age to be dealt with through the criminal justice system, however serious the offence with which they are charged. Thus a child under the age of criminal responsibility who is charged with homicide, must normally be dealt with by specialised children's judges or by social welfare agencies.

There is considerable truth in the following comment regarding the English system:

---

119   CDA 1998, s 11(5). The anti-social behaviour orders, obtained under CDA 1998, s 19, are, like the child safety orders, civil in nature and were clearly designed with juvenile 'anti-social behaviour' in mind. See T Newburn (2002) p 563.
120   S Bandalli (2000) pp 92–93.
121   Although the normal maximum duration of a child safety order is three months, in exceptional circumstances it can be made for 12 months. CDA 1998, s 11(4).
122   *S v Principal Reporter and the Lord Advocate* [2001] UKHRR 514.
123   CDA 1998, s 12(6)(a). M Hayes and C Williams (1999) pp 318–319.
124   L Gelsthorpe and A Morris (1999) p 214, footnotes omitted.
125   *C v DPP* [1995] 2 All ER 43 at 45–46, per Lord Jauncey. NB children over the age of 8 accused of serious offences such as murder or rape in Scotland may be dealt with by the criminal courts. Nevertheless, prosecution in court is not inevitable, even for the commission of very serious offences (by those under 16). In 1996, just over 28,000 children were referred to a children's hearing, whilst only 47 (under 16 years) were sentenced to detention by criminal courts. See DH (1999 a) para 2.11.1.

'... having a low age of criminal responsibility gives the basic shape to society's response to crime by children, however the penal consequences are modified. At a time when the Government's criminal justice policy has one overriding aim – the protection of the public – it is impossible to meet all the special considerations of childhood within the framework of the criminal law.'[126]

These are wise words and require careful consideration. There is a clear need for a thorough review of English law with an overall objective of increasing the age of criminal responsibility. Such a review should obviously encompass a consideration of what system to put in place for child 'offenders' falling below that increased age. In particular, the arguments considered in the 1960s for and against a 'welfare approach' to juvenile offending, need reassessment. It is worth, for example, reconsidering how the Children and Young Persons Act 1969 would have worked had it been fully implemented.[127] In the countries which have adopted and retained the welfare model, whether it is presented in the form of a 'children's hearing', as in Scotland, or a 'family group conference', as in Australia and New Zealand,[128] the important benefit is that children are not labelled criminals by entering the system at a relatively early age. It prevents them acquiring a record of criminal offences long before they have developed a more responsible approach. Furthermore, a relatively informal procedure and non-legal style may be a far more appropriate method of dealing with children, many of whom are extremely disturbed, than a formal legal procedure. Indeed, such an approach might ensure that mentally disturbed children obtain the mental health services they often need so urgently, rather than attention being focused primarily on their offending behaviour.[129]

Admittedly, the welfare approach has not been universally acclaimed in its practical application. In the United States, by the late 1960s, serious concerns were emerging over its efficacy and the informality of the procedures accompanying its use.[130] These doubts were reinforced by the United States Supreme Court decision in *Re Gault*,[131] which condemned a system whereby juveniles could be subjected to long periods of detention in various forms of institution, without rights to 'due process'. These are the rights to counsel, rights against self-incrimination and the other procedural protections automatically accorded to adult defendants in criminal trials. The formal procedural system in England and Wales largely reflects such assumptions. Thus the present safeguards provided for children by the PACE Codes of Practice[132] are based on the view that juveniles in England and Wales should have at least as many due process rights as adults, when it comes to the police investigating a crime.[133] Nevertheless, a more sceptical attitude to children's due process rights reasserted itself in the Crime and Disorder Act 1998. As noted above, the right of those between

126 Nacro (1997) p 21.
127 See T Newburn (2002) p 551.
128 See Justice (2000) for a useful summary of the systems applying in Scotland, New Zealand, New South Wales and Austria.
129 See British Medical Association (2001) pp 150–151 and D Hindle and R Leheup (1998).
130 A Morris and H Giller (1987) pp 251–255.
131 387 US 1 (1967).
132 The Police and Criminal Evidence Act 1984 (PACE) and accompanying codes provide comprehensive regulations governing arrest and interrogation.
133 Eg children have a right to information about their rights; to contact a solicitor and receive free legal advice; to an appropriate adult to accompany them to interviews and the right to make a telephone call. See C Ball, K McCormac and N Stone (2001) ch 3.

10 and 14 to remain silent in court was abolished,[134] thereby infringing international standards.[135]

It must also be acknowledged that in those countries where the welfare approach has been retained, the procedures adopted for receiving children into a child-care system, by virtue of being essentially non-criminal and informal, risk undermining their civil liberties. There is a danger that adults dominate an unstructured and unregulated system and that the child's own voice is lost without legal representation.[136] The Scottish children's hearing system[137] has provided examples of these dangers. Failure to provide the parties with copies of all the documents relating to the hearing was held by the European Court of Human Rights to infringe their rights to a fair trial under article 6 of the ECHR.[138] Similarly, the Scottish authorities were forced to drop their opposition to providing children with free legal representation, despite considering this to be fundamentally inconsistent with the informal nature of the children's hearing. The Scottish Court of Session held that without representation, very young children would be unable to read the relevant documents or participate effectively in the proceedings, so their right to a fair trial was infringed under article 6.[139]

In systems adopting the welfare approach, decisions regarding the type of institution in which the child is accommodated and the length of stay, are usually taken by and at the discretion of the social welfare agencies.[140] Furthermore, it enables an equally intrusive intervention into a child's life to that allowed under the justice model, in so far as a child may be removed from his or her family for indeterminate lengths of time. To children, the orders may appear quite out of proportion to the seriousness of the wrongful act. Children may have little understanding of the official diagnosis that they are the product of seriously disturbed homes and that a substantial interference with their lives is required, perhaps involving removal from home for a long period. Any proposals for dealing with children below an increased age of criminal responsibility would have to take account of all these concerns. But until a full-ranging review is undertaken, the criminal law will continue to reflect harsh and unrealistic ideas about the capacity of very young children to take responsibility for their actions.

(4) DIVERSION FROM COURT

International instruments stress the importance of diverting young offenders out of the courts, whenever possible, without resorting to formal trial.[141] They aim to ensure that youth justice systems should not only take account of society's need for protection from juvenile lawlessness, but also a child's capacity for change. Children have not

---

134 CDA 1998, s 35. Like older children, this age group now risk adverse inferences being drawn if they do not enter the dock or answer questions during cross-examination.

135 Rule 7 of the Beijing Rules guarantees the right to remain silent at all stages of proceedings.

136 See M Henaghan (1996) pp 180–181.

137 The Scottish children's hearing system is briefly described in Justice (2000) ch 3.

138 *McMichael v United Kingdom* (1995) 20 EHRR 205.

139 *S v Principal Reporter and the Lord Advocate* [2001] UKHRR 514. The court made a declaration of incompatibility regarding the existing statutory framework governing the children's hearing system, despite the existence of draft legislation introducing such a change into the law.

140 See R du Bois (1996) p 133. See also Justice (2000) ch 6, for an account of the Austrian system which involves many cases being sent to mediation between offender and victim.

141 See art 40(3)(b) of the CRC and the Beijing Rules, rr 11.1–11.4, together with the commentary.

yet completed their growth and development. With appropriate education, training or psychological treatment, those involved in criminal acts may be helped to grow into law-abiding citizens, without the stigma of criminality attaching to them. Technical and formalistic legal procedures are ill-equipped to take account of these special factors applying to young offenders.

Such ideas are well established in this country. A growing body of research indicates that those children who enter the criminal justice system are unlikely to emerge reformed characters, particularly if they receive institutional care or custody.[142] Indeed, since hardly any form of sentence ensures a young offender's rehabilitation,[143] the fewer who enter the criminal justice system the better. Throughout the 1980s and early 1990s, the high rate of cautioning for young offenders indicated that, at least for a time, these lessons had been well learnt. Considerable care was taken to ensure that as many young people were diverted out of the courts as possible. With the active encouragement of the Home Office,[144] by providing increasing numbers of formal cautions and informal warnings, the police dramatically reduced the number of juveniles entering the criminal justice system.[145]

The advantages of the widespread use of cautions during this period seemed clear. Nevertheless, little was being achieved by a system involving young offenders, in some areas, receiving several cautions without any steps being taken to address their behaviour.[146] In 1994, the Home Office issued controversial new guidance discouraging the use of more than one caution before criminal proceedings were contemplated.[147] This policy change seemed to be the harbinger of an overall loss of faith in a system which allowed the police considerable discretion over how to avoid criminal justice proceedings for many young offenders. The statutory system of police reprimands and final warnings later introduced by the Crime and Disorder Act 1998[148] was intended to avoid '[I]nconsistent, repeated and ineffective cautioning [which] has allowed some children and young people to feel that they can offend with impunity'.[149] It replaced the old system of cautions with an inflexible straight-jacket which ensures that young offenders move through a structured system allowing a police reprimand to be given only for a first offence,[150] with subsequent offences warranting a final warning[151] or criminal charges, prosecution and conviction. But, despite its restricted nature, a welcome feature of the scheme is the way it seeks to ensure that a warning is combined with 'a rehabilitation programme' provided through the multi-agency local YOTs.[152] This effectively places on a legislative footing the 'caution plus' schemes so praised by the Audit Commission, which had already operated in some parts of the country.[153] The programme is aimed at addressing the

---

142 See Social Exclusion Unit (hereafter SEU) (2002) p 155: 84% of 14- to 17-year-olds discharged from prison in 1997, were reconvicted within two years. See also p 574, n 262 below.
143 See Audit Commission (1996) pp 42–43 and Appendix 1.
144 HO Circulars 14/85 and 59/90.
145 See L Gelsthorpe and A Morris (1999), who note (p 210) that in 1993, 90% of boys and 97% of girls were diverted from court through police cautioning. See also B Goldson (2000) pp 35–36.
146 See Audit Commission (1996) pp 22–23.
147 HO Circular 18/94. As the Home Secretary, Michael Howard, explained, the new approach meant 'From now on your first chance is your last chance': *The Times*, 16 March 1994. See R Evans (1994).
148 CDA 1998, ss 65, 66.
149 HO (1997 a) para 5. 10.
150 Unless the officer considers that a first offence is so serious that it warrants a warning. CDA 1998, s 65(4).
151 CDA 1998, ss 65–66.
152 CDA 1998, s 66(1)–(3).
153 See Audit Commission (1996) pp 46–47.

offender's behaviour and may involve compensating the victim. Indeed, the warning may be linked with 'a restorative conference' enabling the young offender to comprehend the impact of his or her behaviour through a meeting with the victim.[154] Many quite reasonably question the government's faith in restorative justice.[155] Nevertheless, requiring an offender to take part in a community programme may well achieve some improvement in his or her behaviour.

There are, however, major concerns about the system of reprimands and final warnings.[156] It effectively gives young offenders only two chances before appearing in the local youth court, and thereby risks undermining attempts to divert large numbers of young people from the criminal justice system. Indeed, some argue that this kind of early intervention for very minor offences prematurely launches children into criminal justice proceedings, in the event of community programmes failing to achieve an 'improvement' in their behaviour.[157] The decision whether to administer a reprimand or final warning, combined with a referral to the YOT, is entirely in the hands of the police, who may adopt variable attitudes to certain groups of young people, such as young women.[158] Furthermore, there are grave concerns about the fairness of the procedure.[159] In the first place, an offender may be tempted into admitting an offence without legal advice, merely to stay out of court and second, neither the offender nor his parents can object to warnings or reprimands being given.[160]

The absence of any need for the recipient's (or parents') consent or any formal conviction regarding the offence in question before a warning is given, becomes particularly objectionable, considering its impact on the recipient. The warning may be cited in subsequent criminal proceedings involving him or her.[161] Furthermore, any court faced with a young offender charged with an offence within two years of receiving a warning, is unable to make a conditional discharge, unless it considers the circumstances to be exceptional.[162] Instead, the young person will receive a penalty, probably in the form of a referral order, thereby progressing down the road to acquiring a serious criminal record. As Goldson asserts,[163] such a response to what may be an essentially trivial offence infringes the concept of proportionality, as established by international human rights documents. Deciding that it is a breach of a young person's rights under article 6 of the ECHR to be given a warning regarding a sexual assault, without being warned that an admission of guilt will result in his or her name being recorded on the sex offender's register, Latham J acknowledged that precisely the same arguments might apply whenever a young person is given a warning or

---

154   See C Ball, K McCormac and N Stone (2001) pp 53–54. See also C Hoyle et al (2002) for an assessment of the Thames Valley Police restorative cautioning scheme. But see R Evans and K Puech (2001) indicating (p 801) that there was no attempt to involve the offenders receiving warnings in any element of restorative justice in their research area.

155   Discussed in more detail below.

156   See B Goldson (2000) pp 37–42.

157   B Goldson (2000) pp 42–45.

158   B Goldson (2000) p 38. See also R Evans and K Puech (2001), whose research (pp 798–799) showed considerable inconsistency in the gravity of cases considered by police to warrant a warning.

159   Many of the young people and YOT workers considered the warning system to be arbitrary, disproportionate and unfair. R Evans and K Puech (2001) p 804.

160   R Evans and K Puech (2001) found (p 799) that some young people were given warnings after denying the offence or after making damaging admissions falling short of full admissions.

161   CDA 1998, s 66(5). It is also kept on police records for a minimum of five years until the offender reaches the age of 18, whichever is the sooner.

162   CDA 1998, s 66(4). See B Goldson (2000) pp 40–41.

163   B Goldson (2000) pp 48–49.

reprimand.[164] Because its receipt can so seriously affect the young person's future treatment by the police and courts, it potentially infringes his or her rights under article 6 – that is unless he or she has given informed consent to the procedure being adopted.[165] This decision suggests that existing police practice must change whereunder young people are given warnings or reprimands without an extremely full explanation of their possible impact.

(5)   SEPARATE COURTS AND SEPARATE PRACTICE

One of the overriding objectives of the nineteenth-century reformatory movement was to ensure that young offenders were kept separate from adult criminals in the courts. The Children Act 1908 established a system of separate magistrates' courts to deal with most criminal proceedings against young offenders under the age of 16. These were to have their own informal procedures and specialised magistracy and had a duty when reaching decisions to 'have regard to the welfare of the child'.[166] Although the youth court panels are not without their critics,[167] they retain their specialised nature and are closed to the public. They are undoubtedly sufficiently separate from the adult courts at least to comply with article 40 of the CRC.[168] Furthermore, the Criminal Justice Act 1991, by extending the jurisdiction of the youth courts to 17-year-olds, complied with the requirements of international instruments which require *all* young offenders to be dealt with by specialised authorities.

Despite this twentieth-century progress towards establishing a rather more enlightened approach to dealing with all young offenders under the age of 18, there remain extremely worrying features in the English system. Children over the age of 10 who have committed offences serious enough to warrant a long term of imprisonment may be committed for trial by jury to a Crown Court, rather than being dealt with by a youth court.[169] The lengthy and formal trial in 1993, of the two 11-year-olds,[170] Venables and Thompson,

---

164   *R(U) v Comr of Metropolitan Police; R(U) v Chief Constable of Durham Constabulary* [2002] EWCA 2486 (Admin), [2002] All ER (D) 445 Nov. Admissions regarding sexual assaults of young women had led to two young men aged 15 being given formal warnings. Per Latham LJ (QBD) at [36] their rights under article 6 ECHR had been infringed since the warnings had led to their names being recorded on the sex offenders' register, thereby public pronouncing their guilt of the sexual assaults by administrative process without formal trial.

165   *R(U) v Comr of Metropolitan Police: R(U) v Chief Constable of Durham Constabulary* [2002] EWCA 2486 (Admin), [2002] All ER (D) 445 Nov at [37]–[38]. Latham J suggested (at [39]) that informed consent need not be given specifically in every case but could be inferred from circumstances involving the young person being given a full explanation of the consequences of the procedure.

166   Children and Young Persons Act 1933, s 44.

167   See C Ball (1995) pp 202–205.

168   See esp art 40(2)(b)(iii) and (3).

169   Since detention under PCC(S)A 2000, ss 90 and 91 (formerly Children and Young Persons Act 1933, s 53) can only be imposed on conviction on indictment, the youth court may decline jurisdiction and commit a young offender charged with an indictable 'grave crime' (normally one punishable by imprisonment for at least 14 years) to the Crown Court. See C Ball, K McCormac and N Stone (2001) pp 442–443. But see also N Stone (2002) who (pp 47–49) discusses the case law (eg *D v Manchester City Youth Court* [2001] EWHC Admin 860 [2002] 1 Cr App R(S) 573) in which the Divisional Court has disapproved of some youth courts declining jurisdiction in such cases not warranting long sentences. NB some 5,000 young defendants currently go to the Crown Court for trial each year. See HO (2002) para 4.35.

170   By the time of the trial, they had both attained the age of 11.

for the murder of James Bulger, was conducted in the full glare of publicity. Their procedural rights under a variety of international documents were thereby clearly infringed.[171] Furthermore, the decision after conviction to lift reporting restrictions meant that the names of the offenders and their photographs were widely publicised. This feature of their trial also infringed international human rights law,[172] making their eventual rehabilitation much more problematic and even potentially dangerous.[173]

The European Court of Human Rights, in common with many international critics, considered this process entirely inappropriate for such young children.[174] Although the majority of the European Court rejected the claim that the trial process had subjected Venables and Thompson to inhuman or degrading treatment under article 3 of the Convention, it agreed that their right to a fair trial under article 6 had been infringed. Despite the modifications made to the trial procedure,[175] and the fact that they had been represented by skilled lawyers, the Court considered that the formality and ritual of the trial, which took place over a period of three weeks, would have seemed incomprehensible and intimidating to such young children. Given these conditions and their immaturity and disturbed emotional state,[176] they had been unable to participate effectively in the proceedings, and had therefore been denied a fair trial.

The European Court's ruling led to Crown Court trials being adapted to take greater account of the youth of the accused.[177] Defendants must now be protected from intimidation, humiliation or distress and all possible steps taken to ensure that they understand and participate in the proceedings. The trial room should, if possible, be arranged so that defendants are on the same level as other participants and able to sit with their family, in a place where they can have easy contact with their legal advisors. The defendants must be given constant explanations of the trial processes, which should be conducted in language which they can understand. The day must be shortened and breaks taken to take account of defendants' short attention span. Robes and wigs should not be worn and attendance by the public and press at the trial can be restricted. But do these changes really go far enough? It is questionable whether anything of real value was achieved by the process undergone by Thompson and Venables, given that the case took many months to get to trial, and in the interim, the accused children were denied any therapy or counselling.[178] Today, despite the greater

---

171 Art 40(1) of the CRC requires child offenders 'to be treated in a manner consistent with the promotion of the child's sense of dignity and worth ... and which takes into account the child's age ...' See also r 14.2 of the Beijing Rules, which requires the proceedings to be conducive to the juvenile's best interests and to 'be conducted in an atmosphere of understanding, which shall allow the juvenile to participate therein and to express herself or himself freely'.

172 See art 40(2)(b)(vii) of the CRC and r 8 of the Beijing Rules, both of which require the juvenile's privacy to be respected at all stages of the proceedings.

173 In *Venables v News Group Newspapers Ltd* [2001] 1 All ER 908 the Court of Appeal reviewed considerable evidence indicating not only that the press were determined to hound Thompson and Venables mercilessly, once they were released, but also that they would be in danger for their lives if identified by the public. The Court of Appeal granted injunctions designed to protect their anonymity on release.

174 *V and T v United Kingdom* (2000) 30 EHRR 121 (paras 87–91).

175 Eg explanations of the trial were given to them and the hearing times were shortened.

176 Expert psychiatric evidence indicated that the boys' emotional state prevented their understanding the import of the proceedings and instructing their lawyers in an informed manner.

177 *Practice Note (trial of children and young persons: procedure)* [2000] 2 All ER 285.

178 There was a nine-month gap between the offence and the trial, during which period the defendants received no treatment, in case it prejudiced their pleas.

informality, children are still required to sit in a dock, stared at by the jury, and cross-examined by barristers. Indeed, all those tried by the Crown Courts are considered to be capable of instructing their lawyers and comprehending the proceedings. This reflects the stark contrast between the stance taken by the criminal law and that of the civil law in the treatment of the child's capacity to instruct a legal adviser. Whilst in the context of civil law litigation, considerable care is taken to prevent children from instructing solicitors on their own behalf before being sufficiently competent to do so,[179] the criminal law simply assumes that any child above the age of criminal responsibility automatically has this capacity.

Despite the often horrifying circumstances, it seems entirely inappropriate for children charged with very serious crimes to bear the full force of the criminal law, with so few concessions being made to their youth. The research information on the type of children responsible for most serious crimes throws considerable doubt on their capacity to comprehend notions of culpability or indeed the objectives of formal criminal proceedings.[180] These aspects of the Bulger trial substantiate the widespread criticism of this branch of the law. Predictably, the Committee on the Rights of the Child has expressed concern over some children being tried in adult courts and their names being published, and has recommended that both practices should stop.[181] Pointing out that trials of this kind would be impossible in many European countries, mainly because the age of criminal responsibility is so much higher,[182] critics suggest that children under the age of 14 should be excluded from trial in adult criminal courts, irrespective of the severity of the charges.[183] Cases involving very serious crimes should instead be heard in private, by a judge, assisted by youth justices, all having first undergone special training fitting them for these cases. The government appears to sympathise with at least some of these suggestions, asserting its intention to provide 'strengthened youth courts' to deal with young offenders accused of serious crime, presided over by a judge with two 'experienced lay magistrates' in support.[184] It would, of course, be desirable for the government to combine a review of the benefits of introducing more informal procedures for trying young children accused of very serious crimes, with a reassessment of the low age of criminal responsibility.

The implications of the decision of the European Court of Human Rights in relation to the Bulger trial were not restricted to the Crown Courts. The procedures adopted by the youth courts, which deal with children who have committed less serious offences, must also ensure that such offenders receive a fair trial. Research has demonstrated that young offenders respond well to changes involving greater informality in the layout of the courtroom and the procedures used.[185] Building on this research, Home Office guidance was issued to all youth courts directing them to adopt a number of changes.[186] These include ensuring that youth court magistrates engage young offenders more directly, by talking and listening to them, by using plain language and by ensuring that the layout of the court is reorganised to assist

---

179 Discussed in chapter 7.
180 G Boswell (1995).
181 Committee on the Rights of the Child (2002) paras 60 and 62.
182 For a usefully brief assessment of other European systems, see Nacro (2002 a) pp 30–33. See also J Muncie (2002) pp 30–33.
183 See, inter alia: R Allen and P Cavadino (2000) pp 17–18; N Tutt (1996) Appendix 2; Nacro (2002 a) pp 33–36.
184 HO (2002) para 4.36.
185 C Allen et al (2000).
186 HO (2001).

such a process.[187] Hopefully this more open and informal system ensures that young offenders no longer feel alienated by impersonal and formal hearings which might have appeared to lack humanity and understanding.[188]

(6)   SEPARATE DISPOSITIONS

(A)   Underlying concepts

The CRC stresses the need for legal systems to respond to youth crime by meeting the welfare needs of young offenders, by avoiding depriving them of their liberty, except as a last resort,[189] and by promoting their rehabilitation through reintegration in society.[190] These principles are matched by the Beijing Rules, which not only promote the idea of welfare, but also the principle of 'proportionality' in sentencing, which takes account of the offender's personal circumstances, rather than imposing punitive sanctions designed to ensure that the offender receives his 'just deserts'.[191] Like the Convention, these rules also stress the need to avoid restricting a juvenile's personal liberty through the use of alternative forms of sanction, such as community rehabilitation orders and community punishment orders.[192] The overall aim of these international instruments is to ensure that young offenders are treated justly and diverted from punishment combined with imprisonment, into treatment and rehabilitation.

It is not appropriate here to discuss in depth the various sentences available under English law for dealing with children who break the law nor the theories underlying them. These justify detailed study in their own right.[193] Nevertheless, a consideration of the methods adopted provokes serious doubts that the rights referred to above are currently being adequately observed. Although, since the beginning of the twentieth century, the sentencing procedures applied to young offenders have differed from those for adults, there is little consensus over the extent to which the aims of sentencing adults should be adapted to the special needs of juveniles. An adult's sentence normally seeks to punish the offender, to ensure that he does not re-offend, to deter other potential offenders from committing similar criminal acts, to provide a public condemnation of the crime and to protect the public from harm by removing from circulation the most dangerous offenders. The extent to which these objectives can be achieved when responding to youth crime is controversial, particularly when considering the extent to which it should aim to punish the offender.

---

187   Eg by moving magistrates from their raised bench into the well of the court so that they are on the same level as the defendants. HO (2001) para 4.2.
188   Research showed that some of the offenders and their parents appreciated the chance to speak directly to magistrates. C Allen et al (2000) esp pp 19–22.
189   Art 37(b). Art 40(4) requires a variety of dispositions to be available as alternatives to institutional care, such as, inter alia, care, guidance and supervision orders; probation; vocational training programmes.
190   Art 39 requires measures to be taken to promote physical and psychological recovery and social reintegration of any child undergoing any form of punishment.
191   Rule 5.1 of the Beijing rules states: 'The juvenile justice system shall emphasise the well-being of the juvenile and shall ensure that any reaction to juvenile offenders shall always be in proportion to the circumstances of both the offenders and the offence.'
192   Rules 5, 17 and 18 and the commentary to these rules. See also the International Covenant on Civil and Political Rights, art 14(4).
193   See eg C Ball, K McCormac and N Stone (2001) ch 11.

There are certain fundamental aspects of childhood which clearly establish that it would be unjust to punish juvenile offenders as severely as adults. First, it is unjust to *blame* children for their actions when the correlation between an inadequate home background and offending is so clear. As Farrington observes, research literature provides considerable information about this:

'Among the main risk factors for offending are socio-economic deprivation, poverty, poor housing, and living in social housing in disorganised, inner-city communities. They also include poor parental child-rearing techniques, inadequate supervision, harsh or erratic discipline, parental conflict and separation from a biological parent. In addition, research has identified important individual factors as high impulsivity and low intelligence.'[194]

Furthermore, children have the ability to change and grow into law-abiding adults. Consequently, the form of correction selected should ensure a successful rehabilitation of the offender into society. Above all, it should not reinforce their delinquent tendencies by enabling them to come under the influence of older criminals. Whatever measures are taken against them, they should be kept separate from adult offenders. Although many acknowledge the importance of all these principles, there is considerable disagreement over the extent to which sentencing policies should make concessions to them in practice.

It appears that sentencing policies relating to young offenders have been undermined by the knee-jerk responses of successive Home Secretaries to public fears of juvenile lawlessness, fears which are only too easily exploited by the right-wing 'law and order' lobby. To a certain extent, there is a circularity in these responses, which is difficult to break. The media is keen to exploit the newsworthiness of annual crime figures by whipping up public anxiety about the dangers of urban life, particularly the criminal behaviour of young people. Consequently, the public have grossly inaccurate perceptions of crime statistics, many considering that young offenders are responsible for 'most crime', and most considering that there are increasing levels of youth crime, when in fact the statistics show the opposite.[195] In turn, the government responds with statements which indicate that it is 'taking a tough stance', and with policy documents making strong assertions, such as '[T]he commission of crime by young people cannot be tolerated'.[196]

Efforts to achieve a more enlightened approach to sentencing young offenders in this country have also been undermined by the unresolved dilemma over whether sentencing should promote the child's welfare or aim to punish the child – a question which has dogged youth justice systems across the world. Indeed, the commentary to the Beijing Rules expands on this dilemma by pointing out that when it comes to adjudicating on young people, there is a number of unresolved conflicts underlying a variety of objectives: rehabilitation versus just deserts; assistance versus repression and punishment; responses meeting the needs of the individual versus a reaction protecting society in general; deterrence versus individual incapacitation.[197] Unlike many European countries, where sentencing tends to give 'a clear priority to rehabilitative measures over punitive ones',[198] in England and Wales, a punitive response, delivered through 'the justice model' has, since the 1960s, broadly been in

194 D Farrington (1996) p 26.
195 C Flood-Page et al (2000) ch 3.
196 HO (1997 d) p 3.
197 Beijing Rules, Commentary to r 17 governing adjudication and disposition.
198 Nacro (2002 a) p 32.

the ascendant. It considers the young offender to be personally responsible for his or her actions and therefore deserving punishment, which itself, should be designed to reflect the seriousness of the offence to the victim and to protect society from juvenile lawlessness. Such an approach is, of course, more politically expedient since, with enthusiastic media assistance, it is more comprehensible to the public. The results are more immediately visible, as opposed to the possible achievements of a welfare approach, which must inevitably be more long term.[199]

Broadly, the Criminal Justice Act 1991 introduced a sentencing framework which remains substantially in existence today.[200] The 1991 Act established the principle of 'proportionality' in sentencing, which ensures that the sentence or punishment must be 'commensurate with the seriousness of the offence'. Since punishment is normally measured by the degree of restriction on the offender's liberty, a custodial sentence occupies the top of the scale, with a range of community orders occupying the middle, and financial penalties at the bottom.[201] One might assume that the principle of proportionality, which, as noted above, also carries the full authority of international human rights law,[202] would ensure that a young offender is always dealt with humanely. But this will not occur if the court's assessment of the seriousness of the child's offence is divorced from all considerations of the child's personal circumstances. Indeed, as Ball, McCormack and Stone point out, there is no guidance in this sentencing framework on the need to incorporate the welfare direction contained in the Children and Young Persons Act 1933, section 44.[203] Although research indicates that many young offenders have significant welfare needs, the case law reflects a deep ambivalence on the part of the courts over the idea of departing from commensurability in sentence, in favour of a less onerous sentence, on welfare grounds.[204]

(B)   Incarcerating children

(i)   The background

This country is the subject of increasing international criticism for the extent to which it imprisons young people,[205] compared with the rest of Europe.[206] Article 37

---

199   I am grateful to Julia Fionda for making this point.

200   Now replaced by PCC(S)A 2000.

201   These scales or 'sentencing bands' or 'thresholds' are used according to the court's assessment of the offence's seriousness. See generally, A Ashworth (2000) chs 3 and 4. See also Nacro (2000 a) for a usefully brief and clear summary. NB the government intends to standardise sentencing for adults through the introduction of formal sentencing guidelines, see HO (2002) ch 5 and Criminal Justice Bill 2002, Pt 12, Ch 1. These changes may have an impact on the youth justice system, see Nacro (2002 b) pp 6–9.

202   See r 5 of the Beijing Rules above. The principle of 'proportionality' is also an important concept underlying the interpretation of the ECHR ie any infringements of rights must be proportionate to the intended objective.

203   See C Ball, K McCormac and N Stone (2001) pp 143–146.

204   C Ball, K McCormac and N Stone (2001) pp 144–145, for an analysis of this case law.

205   At the end of September 2002, a total of 3,133 young offenders under the age of 17 were detained. Of these, 2,917 were boys and 216 were girls; 2,670 were held in young offender institutions (YOIs), 322 in local authority secure units and 141 in secure training centres. Statistics kindly provided by Nacro Youth Crime.

206   The countries of the United Kingdom send a vastly greater proportion of young people to prison than any other EU country. See Nacro (2002 a) pp 13–14 and J Muncie (2002) pp 30–33.

of the CRC states that the 'arrest, detention or imprisonment of a child shall be in conformity with the law and shall be used only as a measure of last resort and for the shortest appropriate period of time'. Similarly, rule 17(1)(c) of the Beijing Rules opposes the deprivation of liberty, except as a sanction for serious acts of violence and then, only if there is no other appropriate response. Furthermore, rule 19(1) emphasises that it should 'always be a disposition of last resort and for the minimum necessary period'. But the fact that young offenders who are locked up in this country are euphemistically described as being 'detained' in YOIs, as opposed to being 'imprisoned',[207] does not disguise the fact that young people constitute a significant percentage of the increase in the prison population.[208] Indeed, as Ashworth has commented regarding the reforms of the late 1990s: 'Probably the most worrying elements in the new system are its confirmation of the regular use of custody for young (especially very young) offenders …'[209]

Hammarberg, Vice-Chair of the Committee on the Rights of the Child, made no secret of his disapproval of the United Kingdom for its present practices. As he pointed out: 'Basically, the message of the Convention is that children should not be in prison. The burden of proof is heavy on a government or a governmental system which has a policy to put children in detention.'[210] The Committee on the Rights of the Child has robustly criticised the government for the increasingly high numbers of children in custody, at earlier ages, for lesser offences and for longer sentences. Considering that the UK is violating the terms of article 37(b) of the CRC, in so far as custody is not being used only as a measure of last resort and only for the shortest period of time, it has strongly recommended that all these matters be remedied.[211]

One might be more tempted to acquiesce in this country imprisoning large numbers of young people under the age of 18 if the conditions in YOIs were humane. This is far from the case. Indeed, despite efforts to raise the standards of care provided,[212] the recent Chief Inspectors' report stated:

> 'We identified the safeguarding of young people in Young Offender Institutions (YOIs) as a major concern. Previous inspections have highlighted the very serious nature of the risks many young people face in these institutions and the extent of self-harming behaviour. This contrasts with the reported good quality of care and protection of young people, including young offenders placed in secure accommodation provided by social services.'[213]

---

207   In magistrates' courts, the use of the term 'imprisonment' is only considered appropriate for those aged 21 and over. See C Piper (2001) for an entertaining discussion of the euphemisms now employed in the field of 'youth' crime.

208   See Nacro (2001 b) p 3. The overall numbers of children aged between 15 and 17 in prison doubled between 1993 and 2000, despite the level of detected youth crime having fallen during this period. Between 1996 and 1997 alone, the number of males sentenced to detention aged 15–17 increased by 32%. Between 1992 and 1998, the number of girls sentenced to detention rose by 382%, despite the number of female juvenile offenders falling. See Howard League (2000) and Nacro (2001 d). See also Youth Justice Board (2002) expressing 'concern at the significant increase' in the use of custodial sentences since January 2002 and the overcrowding in custodial establishments (pp 6 and 19).

209   A Ashworth (2000) p 332.

210   T Hammarberg (1995) p 20.

211   Committee on the Rights of the Child (2002) paras 59–62.

212   New standards were laid down by Prison Service Order (PSO) No 4950, *Regimes for Prisoners Under 18 Years Old*, PSI Ref No 49/99 and *Regimes for Young Women under 18*, PSI Ref No 09/2000. See below.

213   DH (2002) para 8.1 and generally chapter 8.

The appalling conditions still existing in some YOIs, as highlighted by this report and by reports compiled by HM Chief Inspector of Prisons,[214] were recently brought to the attention of the courts.[215] Munby J was clearly shocked by the evidence[216] indicating the extent to which the prison service's own policies[217] are not being complied with. Pointing out that detained young people are protected by articles 3 and 8 of the ECHR,[218] Munby J issued a stark warning to the prison service:

> '… if it really be the case that children are still being subjected to the degrading, offensive and totally unacceptable treatment described and excoriated by the Chief Inspector [of HM Prisons] … then it can only be a matter of time, as it seems to me, before an action is brought under the Human Rights Act 1998 by or on behalf of a child detained in a YOI and in circumstances where, to judge from what the Chief Inspector is saying, such an action will very likely succeed.'[219]

(ii)   Custodial remands

One of the most objectionable aspects of the practice of locking children up relates to the detention of young offenders awaiting trial. The conditions of juveniles refused bail and remanded into prison custody[220] are normally worse,[221] and their regimes far more restricted, than those for sentenced young offenders. In particular, their educational facilities and recreational activities are often severely limited,[222] due mainly to the lack of any official policy establishing a coherent regime for unsentenced young people.[223] Criticisms are mounting regarding the inadequate arrangements made for girls on remand, largely due to the shortage of appropriate accommodation for them.[224] There are obvious dangers in treating any young person

214 See discussion below.

215 *R (Howard League for Penal Reform) v Secretary of State for the Home Department* [2002] EWHC 2497 (Admin), [2003] 1 FLR 484.

216 In the form of the Chief Inspectors' report (DH (2002) ch 8) and various recent reports carried out by the Chief Inspector of Prisons, see detailed more fully below.

217 Principally set out in Prison Service Order (PSO) 4950.

218 See below.

219 [2002] EWHC 2497 (Admin), [2003] 1 FLR 484 at [173].

220 Boys aged between 10 and 14 and girls between 10 and 16 can be remanded into local authority secure accommodation. Boys aged between 15 and 16 can be remanded into local authority secure accommodation or remand centres or prisons. See Children and Young Persons Act 1969, s 23. Defendants aged 17 can only be remanded into prison service custody under Magistrates' Courts Act 1980, s 128. C Ball, K McCormac and N Stone (2001) pp 109–120. But note that there is a grave shortage of local authority secure accommodation.

221 Particularly if they were unlucky enough to be sent to Feltham YOI. See eg HM Chief Inspector of Prisons (1999), reporting that young remand prisoners were locked up for 22 hours each day in dilapidated, dirty and cold cells, often with no blankets, and often sharing cells with adult remand prisoners. Since then, conditions at Feltham YOI have improved considerably: see HM Chief Inspector of Prisons (2002 a).

222 See, inter alia: D Ramsbotham (2001) p 18; HM Inspectorate of Prisons for England and Wales (2001) esp p 21; HM Chief Inspector of Prisons (2001 a) indicating (para 5.35) that the young people on remand in Onley only had an average of access to education one half-day per week and, on days without education, they spent almost 20 hours per day in their cells, where they also took their meals.

223 See HM Chief Inspector of Prisons (2002 a) paras 1.65–1.74, esp para 1.73 and HM Inspectorate of Prisons for England and Wales (2001) pp 21–23.

224 Children's Rights Alliance for England (hereafter CRAE) (2002) section 5 and p 35. See also HM Chief Inspector of Prisons (2001 b), reporting that the girls under 18 averaged just over 15 hours per week of 'purposeful activity', with the remainder of their time spent in their cells (para 3.11). The staff's 'overriding priority was to prevent further suicides' (para 3.13).

in such a manner. They may have been removed from home for the first time and their sense of isolation and vulnerability will be increased if they are harassed and bullied on arrival.[225] Ties with home are difficult to maintain if travel arrangements for family visits are awkward and if the visitors' facilities are poor.[226] Some resort to self-harm and suicide.[227] Furthermore, they are not always separated from criminally sophisticated young adults aged between 18 and 20,[228] a practice condemned by the Committee on the Rights of the Child.[229] It infringes not only article 37 of the Convention on the Rights of the Child,[230] but also rule 13 of the Beijing Rules.

Throughout the 1990s, the government was constantly criticised for not phasing out the practice of remanding juveniles to prison.[231] As Judge Tumin asserted: 'No right minded person wishes to see such very young children whose guilt is yet unproven sent into prison and often into contact with hardened criminals.'[232] This was in 1995, at a time when attention was being brought to the dramatic rise in 15- and 16-year-old male offenders being held in prisons awaiting trial in England and Wales. Two years later, the Utting Report stated unequivocally: 'Prison is no place for children, especially for unconvicted children.' It criticised the fact that the provisions on the statute book since 1991,[233] designed to prevent those under 17 being remanded to prison, had not been implemented, due to there being insufficient local authority secure accommodation.[234] This, Utting asserted, represented a serious failure in public policy which required putting right as soon as possible.[235] Part of the problem is that the need for secure accommodation is itself constantly escalating, mainly because more younger children are now being remanded into the already scarce local authority secure accommodation places, leaving none free for the older age group.[236]

Regrettably, there seemed little official interest in Utting's strictures or in eliminating the power of the courts to remand young children into custody; quite the reverse. With an avowed intention of dealing with young 'bail bandits' who commit medium-level offences,[237] further legislation reduced the restrictions on the courts' powers to remand into secure accommodation or custody the 12- to 16-year-old age

---

225 See HM Chief Inspector of Prisons (2000 b) pp 51–52. Large numbers of young prisoners at Brinsford were bullied, intimidated and harassed on arrival.

226 See HM Chief Inspector of Prisons (2001 b), reporting (p 4) that there was little public transport to Eastwood, that visitors had nowhere to sit whilst waiting outside the gates, and were denied the use of any toilet facilities during visits.

227 Between January 1998 and January 2002, 12 boys under the age of 18 committed suicide in YOIs. There were also 1,111 incidents of self-harm. See discussion by CRAE (2002) pp 64–70.

228 Eg the common practice at Holloway Prison of holding unsentenced 15-year-old girls with much older sentenced offenders. See D Ramsbotham (2001) p 18.

229 Committee on the Rights of the Child (2002) para 59.

230 When ratifying the CRC, the United Kingdom government entered a reservation on art 37(c), entitling it to mix adult and child young offenders, in situations where there is a lack of suitable accommodation to keep them separate.

231 Eg, inter alia; ACOP/Nacro (1995); Penal Affairs Consortium (1996).

232 Nacro News Release, 'Call to End Juvenile Remands to Prisons' 1995, p 3.

233 Criminal Justice Act 1991, s 60.

234 W Utting (1997) para 5.9.

235 W Utting (1997) para 5.10.

236 Most critics of the use of prison for children consider that local authority secure units are preferable for children needing security. They are smaller, and, being governed by the Children Act 1989, have far higher standards of care and education.

237 HO Press Release, 27 February 2001.

group.[238] This policy, the government asserts, sends 'a clear message that young people can no longer walk away from courts and return to previous habits of offending without consequence'.[239] The present government clearly sees nothing objectionable in sending increasing numbers of unconvicted young people to prison, as opposed to the more protected secure accommodation regimes run by local authorities. Further work on developing bail support programmes, often relying heavily on electronic 'tagging',[240] co-ordinated through the local YOTs,[241] may help convince courts that custodial remands are unnecessary. Meanwhile, it is indefensible for a developed country to ignore so blatantly the right of all juveniles to have their best interests promoted whilst awaiting trial.

(iii) Detaining convicted young offenders

As in the case of remand detainees, the conditions suffered by many convicted young offenders whilst in custody are appalling, exacerbated by the current overcrowding in YOIs.[242] At present, children under the age of 15 cannot be held in YOIs, and are placed instead in local authority secure accommodation units or privately run secure training centres. Until more places are established in secure accommodation units, vulnerable 14-year-olds are decanted into YOIs on attaining 15, to make room for the younger age group. Meanwhile, there has been an ongoing controversy over the use of custodial sentences for young offenders; indeed, government policy has itself undergone a complete reversal on this issue since the early 1990s.[243] Underlying this controversy are two interrelated and unresolved questions. First, there is the question whether it is ever appropriate to use forms of community sentence to 'punish' young offenders for very serious offences. The public may find it difficult to accept that any measure can truly punish unless it deprives the offender of his or her liberty by being taken out of circulation altogether. During the last decade, it became increasingly clear that, unless they were dealing with essentially trivial offences, many youth court justices lacked faith in community programmes and considered that only custodial sentences could 'work'.[244] Hopefully, a greater confidence in the new community orders involving principles of restorative justice may reverse this trend.[245] In any event, the second more fundamental question is whether it is ever ethical to lock up young offenders, particularly those in the younger age range, and given that the Children and Young Persons Act 1933, section 44 requires every court, when dealing with children brought before them, to 'have regard to the welfare of the child or young person ...'

In 1990, the White Paper, *Crime, Justice and Protecting the Public*,[246] confirmed that the deprivation of liberty through a custodial sentence is the most severe penalty

---

238   See Criminal Justice and Police Act 2001, s 130, which extends the powers of the youth courts to remand into custody young people charged with a range of less serious offences, including car theft and burglary.

239   HO (2002) para 3.40. But see the Youth Justice Board's criticism of the over-use of secure remands: Youth Justice Board (2002) p 19.

240   See Nacro (2002 d) and (2002 e).

241   CDA 1998, s 38.

242   Discussed below.

243   For a usefully brief history of the trends in custodial sentencing regarding young offenders, see S Moore (2000).

244   See C Ball (1995) pp 204–205.

245   Youth Justice Board (2002) p 6.

246   HO (1990 b).

available to the courts and that, so far as possible, it should be avoided for young offenders, since it merely confirms them in their criminal career. The Criminal Justice Act 1991 appeared to accept the view that imprisoning children should be restricted, in so far as it abolished the power to put 14-year-olds in prison. But this more enlightened approach soon underwent a reversal, with the maximum length of sentence in a YOI for defendants in the 15- to 17-year-old age category being doubled, in 1994, from one year to two years.[247] Furthermore, a more aggressive policy was adopted for dealing with a small 'hard core' of younger offenders whose repeated offending, the government claimed, made them 'a menace to the community'.[248] Ignoring a storm of protest from a variety of quarters, including all the children's charities, the government introduced the new secure training order,[249] which gave the youth courts and the Crown Courts the power to order into detention children aged from 12 to 14, for a minimum length of six months and a maximum of two years. The critics' opposition appeared fully vindicated when evidence emerged indicating that the first secure training centre had run into severe difficulties,[250] and was achieving little, in terms of preventing re-offending.[251] The Committee on the Rights of the Child was in no doubt that the United Kingdom was acting in breach of the Convention by empowering the courts to make secure training orders on children as young as 12, and criticised the emphasis being placed on imprisonment and punishment.[252]

Whilst the Crime and Disorder Act 1998 emphasised the need for better crime prevention and stronger co-ordination of services, it did nothing to change penal policies regarding young offenders. This was despite constant criticisms of the practice of locking up young people in this country as a form of punishment. The youth justice system introduced by the Crime and Disorder Act 1998 wholly endorsed the use of detention as a means of punishing young offenders. Making no fundamental change to the existing sentencing framework, the detention and training order[253] replaced the power of the youth courts to sentence those aged 15 or over to a YOI, and to make secure training orders for the 12- to 14-year-olds.[254] Armed with this order, some youth courts[255] are detaining young people in increasing numbers, particularly

---

247   Criminal Justice and Public Order Act 1994.
248   Kenneth Clarke, Home Secretary, HC Deb, 2 March 1993, col 139.
249   Introduced by the Criminal Justice and Public Order Act 1994, s 1. The first contract for a Secure Training Centre was signed by the Home Secretary in March 1997.
250   Social Services Inspectorate (1999). See also DH (1999 b). The first of these reports was particularly critical of the regime operating in Medway.
251   A Hagell, N Hazel and C Shaw (2000). See also C Ball, K McCormac and N Stone (2001) pp 154–155.
252   See Committee on the Rights of the Child (1995) paras 18 and 36.
253   CDA 1998, ss 73–79, now governed by PCC(S)A 2000, ss 100–107. Such an order (which is divided into two halves, the first, the custodial element being spent in custody and the second, in the community, under supervision) directs a young offender, depending on age and circumstances, into a secure training centre, a YOI or local authority secure accommodation. See C Ball, K McCormac and N Stone (2001) ch 28.
254   Detention and training orders cannot be imposed on those aged under 15 unless they are 'persistent offenders'. See PCC(S)A 2000, s 100(2)(a). For the meaning of this term, see C Ball, K McCormac and N Stone (2001) pp 419–420. NB although PCC(S)A 2000, s 100(2)(b) refers to the availability of detention and training orders for defendants under the age of 12, the power to make such orders has not been implemented.
255   There are considerable regional variations in youth court practice regarding the use of custody, not explained by differences in the overall seriousness of offending. These suggest that some youth courts have a more punitive or interventionist approach than others. See T Bateman and C Stanley (2002) chs 2 and 3.

those in the 15- to 17-year-old age group.[256] This trend may be attributable, at least in part, to the fact that the youth courts are now dealing with more serious cases. But the youth justices are infringing international human rights law which requires them to regard detention as a sanction of last resort for convicted young offenders.[257] There also seems to be a lack of interest in the ability of many other European countries to achieve its aims by detaining only very small numbers of young offenders.[258]

The massive increase in the use of custodial sentencing over the last decade[259] demonstrates the courts' continuing conviction that prison is an appropriate sanction for children who break the law. Indeed, the zeal with which some youth courts are resorting to custodial sentences is causing a crisis, with YOIs filled to capacity.[260] In so doing, they ignore the decrease in the number of serious offences being committed by teenagers.[261] They also ignore the increasing volume of research evidence indicating that imprisonment achieves little and certainly does not act as a deterrent, given the extremely high reconviction rates.[262] Custodial sentences disrupt young peoples' lives, isolate them from the outside community and prevent them from growing up in a normal way, by gaining independence through employment and having families. These factors may actually prevent young offenders growing out of crime, as many do, eventually.[263]

Whatever the rights or wrongs of imprisoning young people under 18, they should not be required to endure the dreadful conditions existing in many YOIs. Countless reports have deplored the conditions suffered by young offenders sentenced to custody.[264] The Howard League's damning exposé of the juvenile prison system[265] was followed by a series of highly critical inspection reports compiled by the Chief Inspector of Prisons.[266] The inspections of YOIs, such as Feltham,[267] demonstrated that many young people were being locked in their cells for long periods in dirty squalid conditions. The efforts of the Prison Service to improve the regime applying

---

256 See n 208 above.
257 Eg art 37 of the CRC and r 19.1 of the Beijing Rules.
258 See Nacro (2002 a), providing (pp 13–14) a detailed comparison of the rates of custody for juveniles across Europe, with England and Wales top of the 'league table'.
259 Not only are more young offenders being given custodial sentences, but sentences are longer than a decade ago. See Nacro (2002 a) pp 10–13.
260 See Youth Justice Board Press Release, 22 August 2001. This referred to Lord Warner's letter to all youth courts and YOTs in which he expressed concern over the rise of the use of custodial sentences and the geographical disparity in sentencing practice. He called for a reduction in the use of short custodial sentences. See also the concern expressed in Youth Justice Board (2002) at the 'significant increase' since January 2002 and the overcrowding in custodial establishments (pp 6 and 19).
261 See Nacro (2000 b) p 11.
262 See, inter alia: SEU (2002) p 155 (some 84% of 14- to 17-year-olds discharged from prison in 1997 were reconvicted within two years); A Hagell, N Hazel and C Shaw (2000) found that 33% of children released from Medway Secure Training Centre in 1998/9 committed criminal offences within one month of their release and 67% had offended before their secure training order had expired at 20 weeks; N Hazel et al (2002) found (see esp Figure 7.3, p 91) that 50% of the supervising officers indicated that trainees on detention and training orders had breached the conditions of their supervision during the community period, with 10% having done so within the first week and just over 42% having done so before the end of the community period.
263 Nacro (2001 c) pp 8–9.
264 See esp CRAE (2002) section 3.
265 See Howard League (1995).
266 Summarised in C Ball, K McCormac and N Stone (2001) pp 158–161. See also CRAE (2002).
267 See HM Chief Inspector of Prisons (1999).

to juveniles in YOIs,[268] have made some impression[269] – but to a system with extraordinarily low standards at the outset. As noted above, YOIs still fail to meet the Prison Service's own minimum standards of care,[270] with new arrivals at one establishment being provided with 'mattresses in appalling conditions – torn and dirty', often with no pillows, inadequately thin blankets, poor food, and little or no access to fresh air or exercise.[271] The official inspection reports indicate that, whilst bullying amongst young offenders remains endemic in many YOIs,[272] some prison officers themselves bully the young prisoners, using informal punishments and frequent use of control and restraint techniques.[273]

The dangerously inadequate provision for inmates' health, particularly their mental health needs,[274] is a constant theme of many of the inspection reports.[275] This is particularly worrying, in view of the high level of health problems suffered by young offenders on their arrival in such institutions.[276] Mental health problems can be

268 All YOIs are now governed by Prison Service Order No 4950, *Regimes for Prisoners Under 18 Years Old*, PSI Ref No 49/99, introduced in 1999. These detail the ways in which young offenders are entitled to distinctive treatment, specifying various requirements regarding their regime, such as their spending ten hours per day outside their cells, and 30 hours per week in 'purposeful activities'. See also *Regimes for Young Women under 18*, PSI Ref No 09/2000 and C Ball, K McCormac and N Stone (2001) pp 429–430.

269 Eg HM Chief Inspector of Prisons (2002 a) p 3 commended Feltham YOI for the significant improvements made since previous inspections. See also HM Chief Inspector of Prisons (2002 b), commending Werrington YOI for the 'high levels of caring and sensitivity to the needs of the young people' (p 3).

270 See CRAE (2002) section 6 and various HM Inspection reports, inter alia: HM Chief Inspector of Prisons (2001 a) reported (p 59) that Onley YOI was 'falling very far short' of providing 30 hours of purposeful activity per week, with 'an unacceptably large number of young people locked up all day with nothing to do'; HM Chief Inspector of Prisons (2001 b) reported (p 83) that at Eastwood Park Prison, many of the girls neither had sufficient 'purposeful activity' each week, nor sufficient hours out of their cells, as required.

271 Summary by HM Chief Inspector of Prisons (2001 c) (pp 36–37) of the conditions met by arrivals at Huntercombe YOI. Nor did Huntercombe ((2001 c) esp p 23) or Onley ((2001 a) esp pp 4 and 66), provide 'a safe environment for young people', with high levels of bullying, intimidating behaviour and fights, and with no effective anti-bullying strategies.

272 CRAE (2002) pp 70–79. See also HM Chief Inspector of Prisons (2000 b) reporting on Brinsford YOI (where there had been five suicides in one year), noting that the 'whole life of young prisoners and juveniles was dominated by intimidation, abuse and violence' (p 52).

273 HM Chief Inspector of Prisons (2001 a) p 14. See also Howard League (2002) p 13, reporting that between April 2000 and January 2002, there were 3,620 recorded incidents of force by staff, resulting in injuries to 296 children and solitary confinement in segregation cells was used 4,437 times.

274 See, inter alia: HM Chief Inspector of Prisons (2001 b), reporting (pp 82–83) the inspectors' concern that despite 'the profound personality disturbance and mental health problems that many [girls] presented' the support from mental health specialists 'seemed wholly inadequate'; HM Chief Inspector of Prisons (2001 c), referring (paras 4.01–4.34) to the severe inadequacies of primary health care and mental health provision, with no access to an adequately resourced specialist mental health service, and with young offenders' mental health needs not being assessed or responded to adequately. The Inspector concluded (para 4.34) that this was a problem 'across the whole juvenile estate' and urged the Youth Justice Board to explore means of providing for the needs of young offenders with mental health problems.

275 See CRAE (2002) pp 55–58 and SEU (2002) pp 168–169. See particularly HM Chief Inspector of Prisons (2001 c).

276 Many young prisoners enter prison already damaged by a background of child abuse, mental health, alcohol and drug abuse problems, all of which could be mediated by expert assistance. HM Chief Inspector of Prisons (1997) ch 3. See also D Lader et al (2000), recording a high level of mental health problems amongst young offenders.

exacerbated by their inability to leave their cells and take part in recreation/or sports facilities.[277] This gloomy picture of life in YOIs is accentuated by the numerous reports criticising the extraordinarily low level of education provided by secure establishments.[278] Despite efforts to improve,[279] most YOIs experience great difficulty in providing good educational facilities, exacerbated by the large numbers in custody for short periods on detention and training orders.[280] Given the very low levels of literacy and numeracy of many of those in custody,[281] the failure to meet their special educational needs is particularly worrying.[282] Clearly, education and training can and should play an important part in efforts to rehabilitate young offenders and the Youth Justice Board recognises that it is vital to improve matters.[283]

Overall, it is of little surprise that the Committee on the Rights of the Child censured the conditions in YOIs in this country, including the high levels of bullying, self-harm and suicides and the inadequate rehabilitative opportunities.[284] It recommended that the government should –

> 'take all necessary measures, as a matter of urgency, to review the conditions of detention and ensure that all children deprived of their liberty have statutory rights to education, health, and child protection equal to those of other children.'[285]

Hopefully, this message will not fall on deaf ears. The government has shown little sign of reassessing the concept of imprisonment as a sanction for youth crime, although under the supervision of the Youth Justice Board, conditions in the YOIs are gradually improving.[286] Although government funding restrictions may delay plans to provide more secure accommodation to address YOI overcrowding,[287] improvements may come. Whilst holding that the Children Act 1989 does not apply to the Prison Service or to its establishments, Munby J nevertheless stated that children detained in YOIs are within the scope of local authorities' duties under sections 17 and 47 of that legislation – but 'subject to the necessary requirements of imprisonment'.[288] Since YOIs contain large numbers of young people at serious risk of significant harm, social services departments might now consider taking action to protect them from some of the more extreme forms of treatment meted out by YOI staff. Better links

---

277 Eg Werrington YOI (HM Chief Inspector of Prisons (2002 b)), which still fails to provide any exercise in the fresh air – 'a mandatory requirement that has eluded Werrington for some time' (p 100).

278 See, inter alia: SEU (1999) paras 6.28–6.33 and 11.14–11.17; ECOTEC (2002); Howard League (2001); HM Inspectorate of Prisons for England and Wales (2001); CRAE (2002) pp 108–111.

279 Prison Service Order No 4950, *Regimes for Prisoners Under 18 Years Old*, requires YOIs to ensure that the 30 hours per week of 'purposeful activity' per week, includes 15 hours of educational provision for those under school-leaving age.

280 See ECOTEC (2001) esp chs 5 and 7.

281 ECOTEC (2001) ch 4.

282 ECOTEC (2001) pp 44–46.

283 ECOTEC (2001) Forward. The Youth Justice Board is investing £40m over three years to 2004 into education and training provision in the secure estate. See SEU (2002) p 162, para D18 and see Youth Justice Board (2002) p 16.

284 Committee on the Rights of the Child (2002) para 59.

285 Committee on the Rights of the Child (2002) para 62(g).

286 The Youth Justice Board acquired responsibility for supervising the juvenile secure estate in April 2000.

287 See *Guardian*, 9 September 2002, reporting 'negotiations' between the Home Office and the Treasury over budget allocation for planned new secure training centres, to relax pressure on the YOIs.

288 *R (Howard League for Penal Reform) v Secretary of State for the Home Department* [2002] EWHC 2497 (Admin), [2003] 1 FLR 484.

should also be established between YOIs, Area Child Protection Committees (ACPCs) and YOTs, primarily in order to address child protection issues.[289] Meanwhile, as the ex-Chief Inspector of Prisons has rightly said:

> 'It is a national disgrace that the United Kingdom, the fourth richest country in the world, a nation known for the civilisation it has spread round so much of the world, should have remained silent when confronted with the evidence of how its children are treated in prison.'[290]

(iv)   Alternative approaches

Not surprisingly, many conclude that prison is not suitable for children under the age of 18,[291] and urge the government to consider reforming the law.[292] There is also a widespread view that custodial sentences can be avoided through greater efforts at preventing crime and by a far greater use of community programmes. During the 1980s, the powers of the courts to sentence young people to custody were moderated by the increased use of cautions and by alternatives to custody being used by the courts, in the form of intermediate treatment programmes, fines, compensation, and community service.[293] The White Paper *Crime, Justice and Protecting the Public*[294] was at pains to stress that community penalties should not be seen as being unduly lenient alternatives to real punishment. It was followed by the Criminal Justice Act of 1991, which placed community sentences on a more structured statutory footing.

The New Labour government came to power focusing on a slightly different approach to keeping children out of custody. It was clearly determined to force parents to take greater responsibility for their children's behaviour.[295] Whilst this is not a new approach, with parents having been regarded as a source of control for many years,[296] the parenting orders introduced by the Crime and Disorder Act 1998[297] reflect a new 'climate of blame' directed at parents of thoroughly anti-social children.[298] Critics not only doubt the practical value of requiring parents to undergo training and guidance sessions, but also question whether they do more harm than good.[299] Relationships between parents and recalcitrant teenagers are often difficult enough, without being further soured. In any event, many parents make great efforts to stop their offspring getting into trouble.[300] Furthermore, there is the risk that increasing

---

289   As recommended by DH (2002) pp 71–72.

290   Per Sir David Ramsbotham in CRAE (2002) p 4.

291   HM Chief Inspector of Prisons (1997) p 6. See also W Utting (1997), who, p 3, stated 'Prison is not a safe environment'.

292   B Goldson and E Peters (2000). This report (p 27) calls for the complete abolition of imprisonment for all children and young people under the age of 18.

293   See T Newburn (2002) pp 553–555.

294   HO (1990 b).

295   See HO (1997 a) paras 1.4–1.6 and 4.6.

296   See M Drakeford and K McCarthy (2000) p 98. Eg the introduction, by the Criminal Justice Act 1991 (extended by the Criminal Justice and Public Order Act 1994), of the power to bind over parents to exercise proper care and control over their children.

297   CDA 1998, s 8. A parenting order can be made against any parent whose child is the subject of: a child safety order, an anti-social behaviour order, a sex offender order, or any criminal conviction.

298   See M Drakeford and K McCarthy (2000) p 101.

299   L Gelsthorpe and A Morris (1999) esp pp 218–219 and M Drakeford and K McCarthy (2000).

300   See J Lyon, C Dennison and A Wilson (2000) pp 7–10 and B Goldson and J Jamieson (2002) pp 92–93.

numbers of parents will avoid such orders by simply forcing their difficult offspring to leave home, thereby swelling the increasing ranks of young homeless.[301] Although preliminary research suggests that these concerns may have been exaggerated,[302] some parents clearly bitterly resent the stigmatising effect of such orders.[303] Nevertheless, the government's commitment to parenting orders is clear from its intention to extend their use.[304]

Without greater efforts to promote community regeneration, punitive attitudes towards apparently feckless parents merely divert attention from the socio-economic background to youth offending and the need to pursue wider social policies to prevent its increase.[305] Indeed, research with young offenders indicates that the best way of preventing crime would be to: 'Clean up the estates and improve poor living conditions, where violence, drug dealing and crime are just part of everyday life.'[306] The government recognises this and has initiated various community programmes in deprived high-crime areas throughout the country.[307] Meanwhile, the legislation itself emphasises that crime prevention is the basis for an overall strategy on youth justice.[308] But in practice, prevention is interpreted as crime reduction, rather than prevention in absolute terms. With the assistance of community sentences and supervison programmes delivered through the YOTs (in liaison with education, health, probation and the police), the government's primary aim is to prevent first time offenders returning to the courts. Indeed, a confusing range of new orders was introduced by the new legislation,[309] some overlapping with dispositions already existing under the pre-1998 system,[310] and many involving a considerable restriction of the offender's liberty.[311]

301 See discussion in chapter 4.
302 See D Ghate and M Ramella (2002) ch 3, indicating that parents largely found the parenting programmes very helpful, even those who had been initially hostile. Nevertheless, there was little evidence indicating any measurable impact on their children's behaviour.
303 B Goldson and J Jamieson (2002) p 94.
304 See Criminal Justice Bill 2002, Sch 23.
305 See R Arthur (2002), who (pp 405–406) reviews the links between youth crime and economic deprivation.
306 J Lyon, C Dennison and A Wilson (2000) pp 76 and 10–11.
307 Inter alia: 'On Track', a Home Office project directed at primary school children and their families to prevent offending; the Youth Justice Board's 'Youth Inclusion Programmes' (YIPs) providing structured and supervised activities for young people living on particularly deprived estates; the 'holiday Splash Schemes' providing similar facilities to similar groups during the summer holidays (see Youth Justice Board (2002) p 10). See R Arthur (2002) pp 406–408, who discusses a wide range of community-based programmes, which by supporting parents and families may prevent youth crime.
308 See HO (1997 a) Introduction and esp para 3.1. See also CDA 1998, s 37(1), which states: 'It shall be the principal aim of the youth justice system to prevent offending by children and young persons.'
309 G Monaghan (2000) (p 150) lists 18 different disposal methods including, inter alia: referral orders, absolute or conditional discharges, fines, compensation orders, reparation orders, attendance centre orders, drug treatment and testing orders, action plan orders, supervision orders, community service orders, probation orders, detention and training orders. The exclusion order and the drug abstinence order were later introduced by the Criminal Justice and Court Services Act 2000, ss 46, 47.
310 Eg as noted by J Fionda (1999) p 44, all the features of an action plan order (see CDA 1998, s 69) could be reproduced by a supervision order (see CDA 1998, s 71).
311 Eg a community rehabilitation order can impose requirements of residence in an approved hostel, together with curfew requirements. Similarly, supervision orders can involve intensive supervision, backed by electronic tagging. The Youth Justice Board also established a network of intensive supervision and surveillance programmes (ISSPs), see Nacro (2002 c).

Many of the new orders created at the end of the 1990s reflect the government's commitment to the concept of 'restorative justice' which, in other countries, often involves techniques of mediation between offender and victim, through reparation and conferencing, as in the New Zealand 'family group conferencing' system. Dignan summarises the aims of such an approach: first, to engage with offenders to try to bring home the consequences of their actions and their impact on their victims; to encourage and facilitate the provision of appropriate forms of reparation for the offence; to seek reconciliation between victim and offender.[312] Some of these methods had already been developed, on an ad hoc and trial basis, during the 1980s and 1990s, in some parts of England and Wales.[313] Today, young offenders may be involved in a programme devised by the local YOT, involving some, or all of these elements, very early on in their criminal careers, on receiving a final warning from the police.[314] But the principles of restorative justice most obviously underlie the reparation orders,[315] the action plan orders[316] and the schemes associated with the referral orders. All may involve offenders apologising to the victim in person and carrying out acts of recompense, intended to bring home to them the implications of their offence.

The extent to which the reparation orders and action plan orders are utilised by the youth courts depends on the extent to which local magistrates become convinced that restorative justice can work as well as more punitive methods. But the referral order scheme introduced by the Youth Justice and Criminal Evidence Act 1999, Part I is very different. By making the referral order mandatory for all 10- to 17-year-olds pleading guilty and convicted of a first offence, the scheme ensures that such offenders are automatically referred to local youth offender panels (YOPs). The local panel works with each young offender to devise a programme of behaviour, based largely on principles of restorative justice, which the offender can agree to and sign – 'a youth offender contract'. After some experience of the new orders, some magistrates and their clerks are concerned over the way the youth courts are by-passed, effectively leaving the disposal to the YOPs.[317] These anxieties aside, referral orders appear to have been quickly accepted by all those working in the youth justice system, with the informality of the panel meetings producing encouraging levels of satisfaction for offenders and their parents.[318]

Many concerns were voiced about the way in which the new youth justice system attempts to absorb some, but not all, of the principles of restorative justice, in a peculiarly unbalanced way. The YOTs and YOPs have the power to produce programmes for young offenders that are far more intrusive and punitive than may be merited, thereby infringing the proportionality principle. Furthermore, the rights of the victim may be allowed to assume greater importance than those of an often extremely damaged offender, whose background may undermine his or her ability to feel empathy or remorse.[319] It is also unclear how well the principles of restorative justice can work when merely spliced on to a formal court system. Elsewhere, where they have succeeded – for example, the children's hearing system in Scotland and the family group conference in New Zealand – these arrangements are substitutes for court appearances,

---

312   J Dignan (1999) p 48.
313   Eg the Thames Valley project. See Justice (2000) ch 7.
314   Discussed above.
315   CDA 1998, s 67.
316   CDA 1998, s 69.
317   T Newburn et al (2002) pp 20–21.
318   T Newburn et al (2002) esp ch 7 and p 62.
319   See Justice (2000) p 64. See also K Haines (2000) pp 67 and 72.

not additional adjuncts.[320] Indeed, as critics point out, restorative justice requires co-operation and not coercion.

Many of these concerns are particularly relevant to the system established by referral orders.[321] Nevertheless, research on the piloted areas using these orders indicates that some of the criticisms may have been exaggerated. Despite the low level of victim involvement undermining the researchers' ability to gain a complete picture of the new scheme's overall efficacy,[322] worries that young offenders would feel coerced into agreeing programmes of behaviour designed by the YOPs have not, to date, been borne out.[323] Furthermore, most young people and their parents consider that the YOPs are fairer, treat them with more respect and give them a greater opportunity to explain their side of things, than do the youth courts.[324] The government's refusal to allow young offenders legal representation before the YOPs, on the grounds that this would undermine the informality of the proceedings, may also have been vindicated. The research suggests that young people feel far more able to participate fully in the YOP meetings than in the youth court hearings,[325] presumably because of the informality of the former. Nevertheless, Wonnacott's claim that such a refusal infringes the offenders' rights under article 6 of the ECHR[326] is borne out by the decision of the Scottish Court of Session that the failure to provide children with automatic representation in the children's hearings infringes their rights under article 6.[327] Meanwhile, it is obviously far too early to reach any general conclusions on the success of such a variety of ambitious measures.

(7)   CHILDREN WHO KILL

The ability of international human rights law to promote children's rights forcefully, even the rights of child murderers, was demonstrated during the last decade when the British government was forced to amend some of the most punitive aspects of the law applying to this small group of young offenders. Fortunately, the number of children involved in serious crime is low and very few are found guilty of homicide.[328] Research evidence indicates that there is an extremely high likelihood of children and adolescents who make homicidal assaults on others 'having themselves been the victims of childhood trauma in the form of abuse and/or loss and frequently both'.[329] Indeed, some go further and argue that there is a high probability of their suffering from some conduct disorder or neurological abnormality.[330] As noted above, the adult style of trial by jury used to establish their guilt or innocence is particularly inappropriate for such highly disturbed children. This remains the case, even taking account of the minor procedural adjustments[331] adopted after the ruling by the European Court of Human

320 See C Ball (2000) p 217.
321 For a devastating criticism of referral orders, see C Wonnacott (1999).
322 T Newburn et al (2002) ch 8.
323 T Newburn et al (2002) pp 39–40.
324 T Newburn et al (2002) pp 37–40.
325 T Newburn et al (2002) p 37, Table 7.1.
326 C Wonnacott (1999) p 285.
327 *S v Principal Reporter and the Lord Advocate* [2001] UKHRR 514.
328 The combined annual number of children and young people convicted of murder or manslaughter was 38 in 1989 and remained below that number annually for the next 11 years. See Nacro (2002 a) p 18 and charts on pp 18–19.
329 G Boswell (1995) p 34. This research showed that of one third of the mid-1993 section 53 population, 72% had experienced abuse, 57% had experienced significant loss, 35% had experienced both phenomena and 94% had experienced one or both.
330 S Bailey (1996) p 26.
331 *Practice Note (trial of children and young persons: procedure)* [2000] 2 All ER 285.

Rights in favour of Thompson and Venables, the two boys convicted of murdering James Bulger.[332] There is, though, a further aspect of the law governing child murderers which has been the subject of strong international criticism. Children and young persons convicted of murder face a mandatory sentence of indeterminate detention,[333] said to be 'during Her Majesty's Pleasure'.[334]

The indeterminate sentence governing child murderers was originally adopted by the Children Act 1908, to replace the death penalty for murder. Its intention was to protect child murderers from adult sentences and also to introduce a less severe form of sentence than a sentence for life.[335] Its indeterminacy was designed to enable improvements in behaviour to be reflected in the length and structure of the detention, this being regularly reviewed with a view to earlier release. In later years, however, administrative procedures were introduced, significantly increasing the punitive element of the indeterminate sentence, by introducing a minimum 'tariff' period to be served at the outset. This was to reflect the need for punishment, deterrence and retribution, irrespective of the child's progress or development. It was followed by a second, post-tariff, stage, during which time periodic assessments would be made to determine whether the detainee continued to present a risk to the public, thereby justifying further detention. The duration of both tariff and post-tariff periods was ultimately decided by the Home Secretary, not by the courts, nor by the Parole Board.

The most punitive aspects of this system have been gradually amended to take account of challenges successfully taken to the European Court of Human Rights. First to be amended was the post-tariff period of the indeterminate sentence. The European Court decided that English law infringed article 5(4) of the ECHR, in so far as it denied these serious offenders a judicial hearing of their applications for release during the post-tariff period of detention.[336] The United Kingdom was consequently forced to change its law by giving the Parole Board, rather than the Home Secretary, responsibility for deciding on the timing of the final release of these offenders.[337] Later, the procedure applying to the initial tariff period also underwent amendment. The particularly unjust features of this procedure had been highlighted by the decision of the Home Secretary to increase to 15 years the tariff recommended by the Lord Chief Justice for Thompson and Venables.[338] When quashing this decision on judicial review, the House of Lords considered that the length of any child's detention must be determined in a very different way from that adopted for adults.[339] Referring, inter alia, to the requirements of articles 3 and 40(1) of the CRC, the House of Lords[340] stressed that when deciding on a provisional basis how long they should remain in

332 *V and T v United Kingdom* (2000) 30 EHRR 121, discussed above.

333 Under PCC(S)A 2000, s 90 (formerly Children and Young Persons Act 1933, s 53).

334 This should be compared with the law governing a child who is convicted of a lesser but nevertheless, very serious crime. He or she will almost certainly be sentenced to a long term of detention under PCC(S)A, s 91, but the judge has complete discretion over its length. It should also be compared with the discretionary detention for life under PCC(S)A 2000, s 80. See C Ball, K McCormac and N Stone (2001) ch 29.

335 Per Lord Steyn in *R v Secretary of State for the Home Department, ex p Venables; R v Secretary of State for the Home Department, ex p Thompson* [1997] 3 All ER 97 at 143.

336 *Hussain v United Kingdom* (1996) 22 EHRR 1. See M Grewcock (1996).

337 Crime (Sentences) Act 1997, s 28.

338 The trial judge had recommended eight years for the initial tariff. This was increased by the Lord Chief Justice to ten years and increased by the Home Secretary to 15 years, meaning that there would be no review of their sentences until they attained the age of 23.

339 *R v Secretary of State for the Home Department, ex p Venables; R v Secretary of State for the Home Department, ex p Thompson* [1997] 3 All ER 97.

340 Per Lord Browne-Wilkinson and Lord Hope [1997] 3 All ER 97 at 123 and 151, respectively.

detention, the Home Secretary should have considered the boys' welfare, as well as the need to punish them. These considerations made it essential for the length of the boys' detention to be flexible and to be reviewed from time to time, taking account of their special ability to progress and develop throughout their detention.

Despite not ending the Home Secretary's involvement in the procedure for determining the initial tariff, the House of Lords' decision ensured that a system was established for reviewing the tariff half-way through its duration.[341] The government's continued determination to keep the process under the overall control of the Home Secretary was finally frustrated when the European Court of Human Rights upheld the article 6 claims of Thompson and Venables in this context as well. It held that their rights under article 6 of the ECHR had been infringed when the Home Secretary, who was patently not independent of the executive, rather than a court, had set the initial tariff. The government's response was, however, to introduce a less, rather than more, humane system than before. Legislation now ensures that tariffs[342] are set by the trial judge in open court, using the system for those aged over 18 who receive life sentences.[343] Thus judges, when sentencing child murderers, operate on a presumption, or 'starting point' in favour of a tariff of 12 years, to be increased or reduced for mitigating circumstances, such as age.[344] Consequently, and bizarrely, child offenders, however young, now merit no specially designed sentencing guidelines. They must rely instead on the judge being prepared to mitigate a 12-year 'starting point', by reference to their extreme youth.[345] Meanwhile, the government jettisoned the system for regularly reviewing the detainee's progress during the tariff period. Tariffs can be appealed against for being too harsh, but will not be reviewed.[346] In this way, the single humane element in the whole process, which had ensured that account could be taken of a young offender's growing maturity and progress whilst in custody, was thereby abolished.[347]

For the future, it appears that the concept of the tariff will be retained as a means of arriving at an initial period of minimum detention for the offender, and that the duration of the post-tariff period will remain the responsibility of the parole board. Meanwhile, a fundamental reassessment of the whole concept of indeterminate sentences for young children is long overdue, as recommended by the Committee on the Rights of the Child,[348] and by many other bodies.[349] This form of sentence is in obvious breach of articles 37(d) and 40(1) of the CRC. Indeed, it is notable that a

---

341   The government announced that the tariff would be set initially by the Home Secretary, on advice from the trial judge and the Lord Chief Justice. It would then be reviewed, half-way through, again by the Home Secretary, taking account of annual reviews of detainees' progress commissioned by the HO. See C Ball, K McCormac and N Stone (2001) p 470.
342   Officially renamed 'minimum terms': see *Practice Statement* [2002] 3 All ER 412 at para 2.
343   Criminal Justice and Court Services Act 2000, s 60.
344   *Practice Statement* [2002] 3 All ER 412 at paras 20–27, esp 24. Lord Woolf CJ suggests that there should be a reduction of about one year for every year that the offender's age is below 18.
345   C Ball, K McCormac and N Stone (2001) pp 471–472.
346   See *R v McBean* [2001] Crim LR 839.
347   In *Re Thompson (tariff recommendations)* [2001] 1 All ER 737, Lord Woolf (at paras 8–12) was impressed, when reviewing the tariff set for Thompson and Venables, by the way that they had responded to their punishment and the striking progress they had made whilst detained. He set their tariff at less than eight years. Reviews of this kind will no longer now take place with the Parole Board only able to consider the offender's progress at the end of the minimum term. See *Practice Statement* [2002] 3 All ER 412 at para 27.
348   See Committee on the Rights of the Child (1995) para 36.
349   See Nacro (2002 a) pp 36–37.

minority of the European Court of Human Rights stated their strong view that the indeterminate nature of detention 'during Her Majesty's Pleasure', had amounted to inhuman treatment of Thompson and Venables, under article 3 of the Convention. In their view, the uncertainty and anxiety suffered by very young vulnerable children when receiving a sentence of indefinite length could not be ignored.[350]

This aspect of English law currently reflects views about punishment and retribution which have little meaning for the offenders themselves, who are amongst the most disturbed in the country. As the public's continuing response to the Bulger murder so graphically demonstrates, large numbers currently label children who kill as 'evil', wishing to make them pay for their crimes indefinitely.[351] Some of these offenders will indeed spend long periods in institutions of various kinds. They normally spend their first few years of detention in local authority secure accommodation, transferring to a young offender institution between the age of 16 and 18, and then on to adult prison at the age of 21. When recommending a tariff ensuring the freedom of Thompson and Venables before such a transfer became necessary, Lord Woolf pointed out that a transfer to a young offender institution would undo much of the good work already achieved for them. They would be unable to cope with 'the corrosive atmosphere' in such an institution.[352] Clearly the current law is inadequate if it cannot ensure that these children receive sufficient ongoing help to understand the reasons for their offence and how to avoid it in future. International law may assist by gradually forcing the United Kingdom to adopt a more tolerant position regarding young offenders who commit serious crimes. This, in turn, may set a better example to a savagely intolerant public.

(8) CONCLUSION

There is a wealth of research material which suggests that it is not only unjust but unrealistic to deny that child offenders are the product of their upbringing and environment. They may also mature and grow out of their offending behaviour. Certainly there seems little point in ignoring this information when attempting to deal with their wrongdoing. Although the present government's determination to overhaul the youth justice system was laudable, the measures they introduced now enable the police and the courts to impose authoritarian restrictions on young people which may do little to make them sympathise with the aims of adult society. The criminal justice system currently neglects the rights of young offenders in a variety of ways and there are aspects of it, regarding their processing and treatment, which need urgent reform. These continue to provide depressing evidence that the progress made by the enlightened reformers early in the twentieth century has been reversed in recent years.

---

350 *V and T v United Kingdom* (2000) 30 EHRR 121. Two judges considered that the indeterminate sentence alone infringed the boys' art 3 rights. Five judges considered that the combination of the low age of criminal responsibility, the adult nature of the trial and the indeterminate sentence were sufficiently serious together to infringe their art 3 rights.

351 See *Venables v News Group Newspapers Ltd* [2001] 1 All ER 908: The Court of Appeal granted injunctions designed to protect the anonymity of Thompson and Venables on release, to protect them from harassment and attempts on their lives.

352 *Re Thompson (tariff recommendations)* [2001] 1 All ER 737 at para 13.

BIBLIOGRAPHY

NB many of these publications can be obtained on the relevant organisation's website.

ACOP/Nacro, *A Crisis in Custody: Findings from a survey of juveniles in prison awaiting trial* (1995).

Allen C et al, *Evaluation of the Youth Court Demonstration Project* Home Office Research Study 214 (2000) Home Office.

Allen R and Cavadino, P 'Children Who Kill – Trends, Reasons and Procedures' in G Boswell (ed) *Violent Children and Adolescents: asking the question why* (2000) Whurr Publishers.

Arthur R, 'Tackling youth crime – supporting families in crisis' (2002) 14 Child and Family Law Quarterly 401.

Ashford A, 'Making criminals out of children: abolishing the presumption of doli incapax' (1998) 16 Criminal Justice 16.

Ashworth A, *Sentencing and Criminal Justice* (2000) Butterworths.

Audit Commission, *Misspent Youth ... Young People and Crime* (1996) The Audit Commission.

Bailey S, 'Sadistic and Violent Acts by Children and Young People' in P Cavadino (ed) *Children Who Kill* (1996) Waterside Press.

Ball C, 'Youth justice and the youth court – the end of a separate system?' (1995) 7 Child and Family Law Quarterly196.

Ball C, 'The Youth Justice and Criminal Evidence Act 1999 Part I: a significant move towards restorative justice, or a recipe for unintended consequences' (2000) Criminal Law Review 211.

Ball C, McCormac K and Stone N, *Young Offenders: Law Policy and Practice* (2001) Sweet and Maxwell.

Bandalli S, 'Children, Responsibility and the New Youth Justice' in B Goldson (ed) *The New Youth Justice* (2000) Russell House Publishing.

Bateman T and Stanley C, *Patterns of Sentencing: Differential sentencing across England and Wales* (2002) Youth Justice Board.

du Bois R, 'The German System' in P Cavadino (ed) *Children Who Kill* (1996) Waterside Press.

Boswell G, *Violent Victims: The prevalence of abuse and loss in the lives of Section 53 offenders* (1995) The Prince's Trust.

British Medical Association, *Consent, Rights and Choices in Health Care for Children and Young People* (2001) BMJ Books.

Children's Rights Alliance for England (CRAE), *Rethinking Child Imprisonment* (2002) CRAE.

Committee on the Rights of the Child, *Concluding Observations of the Committee on the Rights of the Child: United Kingdom of Great Britain and Northern Ireland* CRC/C/15/Add 34 (1995) Centre for Human Rights, Geneva.

Committee on the Rights of the Child, *Concluding Observations of the Committee on the Rights of the Child: United Kingdom of Great Britain and Northern Ireland* CRC/C/15/Add 188 (2002) Centre for Human Rights, Geneva.

Communities that Care, *Youth at Risk: A national survey of risk factors, protective factors and problem behaviour among young people in England, Scotland and Wales* (2002) Communities that Care.

Department of Health (DH), *United Nations Convention on the Rights of the Child: Second Report to the UN Committee by the United Kingdom 1999* (1999 a) The Stationery Office.

Department of Health (DH), *Unannounced Inspection of Medway Secure Training Centre April 1999* (1999 b) DH.

Department of Health (DH), *Safeguarding Children: A joint Chief Inspectors' Report on Arrangements to Safeguard Children* (2002) DH Publications.

Dignan J, 'The Crime and Disorder Act and the Prospects for Restorative Justice' (1999) Criminal Law Review 48.

Drakeford M and McCarthy K, 'Parents, Responsibility and the New Youth Justice' in B Goldson (ed) *The New Youth Justice* (2000) Russell House Publishing.

ECOTEC, *Report on the Audit of Educational Provision within the Juvenile Secure Estate* (2001) Youth Justice Board.

Evans R, 'Cautioning: Counting the Cost of Retrenchment' (1994) Criminal Law Review 566.

Evans R and Puech K, 'Reprimands and Warnings: Populist Punitiveness or Restorative Justice' (2001) Criminal Law Review 794.

Farrington D, *Understanding and Preventing Youth Crime* (1996) Joseph Rowntree Foundation.

Fionda J, 'New Labour, Old Hat: Youth Justice and the Crime and Disorder Act 1998' (1999) Criminal Law Review 36.

Flood-Page C et al, *Youth Crime: Findings from the 1998/99 Youth Lifestyles Survey* Home Office Research Study 209 (2000).

Gelsthorpe L and Morris A, 'Juvenile Justice 1945–1992' in M Maguire, R Morgan and R Reiner (eds) *The Oxford Handbook of Criminology* (1994) Oxford University Press.

Gelsthorpe L and Morris A, 'Much ado about nothing – a critical comment on key provisions relating to children in the Crime and Disorder Act 1998' (1999) 11 Child and Family Law Quarterly 209.

Ghate D and Ramella M, *Positive Parenting: The National Evaluation of the Youth Justice Board's Parenting Programme* (2002) Youth Justice Board.

Goldson B, 'Wither Diversion? Interventionism and the New Youth Justice' in B Goldson (ed) *The New Youth Justice* (2000) Russell House Publishing.

Goldson B and Jamieson J, 'Youth Crime, the "Parenting Deficit" and State Intervention: A Contextual Critique' (2002) 2 Youth Justice 82.

Goldson B and Peters E, *Tough Justice – Responding to children in trouble* (2000) The Children's Society.

Graham J and Bowling B, *Young People and Crime* Home Office Research Study No 145 (1995).

Grewcock M, 'Judicial Process v Political Whim' (1996) 125 Childright 18.

Hagell A, Hazel N and Shaw C, *Evaluation of Medway Training Centre* Occasional Paper (2000) Home Office.

Haines K, 'Referral Orders and Youth Offender Panels: Restorative Approaches and the New Youth Justice' in B Goldson (ed) *The New Youth Justice* (2000) Russell House Publishing.

Hammarberg T, 'Children, Crime and Society: Perspectives of the UN Convention on the Rights of the Child' in *Child Offenders: UK and International Practice* (1995) The Howard League.

Hayes M and Williams C, 'Offending Behaviour and Children under 10' (1999) Family Law 317.

Hazel N et al, *Detention and Training: Assessment of the Detention and Training Order and its impact on the secure estate across England and Wales* (2002) Youth Justice Board.

Henaghan M, 'New Zealand and the United Nations Convention on the Rights of the Child: A Lack of Balance' in M Freeman (ed) *Children's Rights: A Comparative Perspective* (1996) Dartmouth Publishing.

Hindle D and Leheup R, 'Rethinking provision for delinquents' (1998) 35 Young Minds Magazine 16.

HM Chief Inspector of Prisons, *Young Prisoners: A Thematic Review* (1997) Home Office.

HM Chief Inspector of Prisons, *HM YOI Feltham: Report of an Unannounced Full Inspection 30 November–4 December 1998* (1999) Home Office.

HM Chief Inspector of Prisons, *Unjust Deserts: A Thematic Review by HM Inspector of Prisons of the Treatment and Conditions for Unsentenced Prisoners in England and Wales* (2000 a) Home Office.

HM Chief Inspector of Prisons, *HM YOI Brinsford: Report of an Announced Inspection 19–23 June 2000* (2000 b) Home Office.

HM Chief Inspector of Prisons, *HM YOI/RC Onley: Report of a Full Announced Inspection 9–13 July 2001* (2001 a) Home Office.

HM Chief Inspector of Prisons, *An Unannounced Follow-Up Inspection of HM Prison Eastwood Park 1–3 October 2001* (2001 b) Home Office.

HM Chief Inspector of Prisons, *HM YOI/RC Huntercombe: Report of a Full Announced Inspection 15–19 2001* (2001 c) Home Office.

HM Chief Inspector of Prisons, *HM YOI Feltham: Report of a Full Announced Inspection 14–23 January 2002* (2002 a) Home Office.

HM Chief Inspector of Prisons, *HM YOI Werrington: Report of a Full Announced Inspection 11–15 March 2002* (2002 b) Home Office.

HM Inspectorate of Prisons for England and Wales, *A Second Chance – Review of Education and Supporting Arrangements within Units for Juveniles managed by HM Prison Service* (2001) Home Office.

Home Office (HO) (Chairman Viscount Ingleby), *Report of the Committee on Children and Young Persons* Cmnd 1191 (1960) HMSO.

Home Office (HO), *The Child, the Family and the Young Offender* Cmnd 2742 (1965) HMSO.

Home Office (HO), *Children in Trouble* Cmnd 3601 (1968) HMSO.

Home Office (HO), *The Cautioning of Offenders* Circular 14/85 (1985) HO.

Home Office (HO), *The Cautioning of Offenders* Circular 59/90 (1990 a) HO.

Home Office (HO), *Crime, Justice and Protecting the Public* Cm 965 (1990 b) HMSO.

Home Office (HO), *The Cautioning of Offenders* Circular 18/94 (1994) HO.

Home Office (HO), White Paper *No More Excuses – A New Approach to Tackling Youth Crime in England and Wales* Cm 3809 (1997 a) HMSO.

Home Office (HO), *Tackling Youth Crime* Consultation Paper (1997 b) HO.

Home Office (HO), *New National and Local Focus on Youth Crime: A Consultation Paper* (1997 c) HO.

Home Office (HO), *Preventing Children Offending: A Consultation Document* (1997 d) HO.

Home Office (HO), *The Youth Court 2001: The Changing Culture of the Youth Court, Good Practice Guide* (2001) HO.

Home Office (HO), *Justice for All* Cm 5536 (2002) The Stationery Office.

House of Commons Home Affairs Committee, *Juvenile Offenders* Vol 1, Sixth Report, Session 1992–93.

Howard League, *Banged up, Beaten up, Cutting up: Report of the Howard League Commission of Inquiry into Violence in Penal Institutions for Young People* (1995) Howard League.

Howard League, *Sentenced to Fail – Out of sight, out of mind: Compounding the problems of children in prison* (1998) Howard League.

Howard League, *The Use of Imprisonment for Girls* Howard League Fact Sheet 18 (2000) The Howard League.

Howard League, *Missing the Grade: Education for Children in Prison* (2001) Howard League for Penal Reform.

Howard League, 'Howard League takes Home Secretary to court' (2002) 20 HLM (Issue 3) 13.

Hoyle C et al, *Proceed with caution: An evaluation of the Thames Valley Police initiative in restorative cautioning* (2002) York Publishing Services.

Justice, *Restoring youth justice: New directions in domestic and international law and practice* (2000) Justice.

Lader D et al, *Psychiatric Morbidity among Young Offenders in England and Wales* ONS (2000) The Stationery Office.

Lyon J, Dennison C and Wilson A, *"Tell Them So They Listen": Messages from Young People in Custody* Home Office Research Study 201 (2000) HO.

Mattinson J and Mirrlees-Black C, *Attitudes to Crime and Criminal Justice: Findings from the 1998 British Crime Survey* Home Office Research Study 200 (2000).

Meltzer H and Gatward R, *Mental health of children and adolescents in Great Britain* ONS (2000) The Stationery Office.

Monaghan G, 'The Courts and the New Youth Justice' in B Goldson (ed) *The New Youth Justice* (2000) Russell House Publishing.

Moore S, 'Child Incarceration and the New Youth Justice' in B Goldson (ed) *The New Youth Justice* (2000) Russell House Publishing.

MORI, *Youth Survey 2002: Research Study Conducted for the Youth Justice Board* (2002) Youth Justice Board.

Morris A and Giller H, *Understanding Juvenile Justice* (1987) Croom Helm.

Muncie J, 'Policy Transfers and "What Works": Some Reflections on Comparative Youth Justice' (2002) Youth Justice 27.

Nacro, *A New Three Rs for Young Offenders: Towards a New Strategy for Children Who Offend* (1997) Nacro.

Nacro, *Proportionality in the Youth Justice System* Briefing (2000 a) Nacro.

Nacro, *Facts about Young Offenders* Youth Crime Section factsheet (2000 b) Nacro.

Nacro, *Youth offending teams, race and justice – after the watershed* Youth Crime briefing (2001 a) Nacro.

Nacro, *Some facts about young people who offend* Youth Crime factsheet (2001 b) Nacro.

Nacro, *Young Adult Offenders: A period of transition* A Nacro policy report (2001 c) Nacro.

Nacro, *Girls in the youth justice system* Youth Crime briefing (2001 d) Nacro.

Nacro, *Children who commit grave crimes* (2002 a) Nacro.

Nacro, *Reform of the criminal justice system: implications for youth justice of the White Paper* Nacro Youth Crime briefing (2002 b).

Nacro, *Supervision orders – an overview* Youth Crime briefing (2002 c) Nacro.

Nacro, *Electronic monitoring of children remanded on bail or to local authority accommodation* Youth Crime briefing (2002 d) Nacro.

Nacro, *Electronic monitoring (part two): bail conditions for 17 year olds* Youth Crime briefing (2002 e) Nacro.

Newburn T, 'Young People, Crime, and Youth Justice' in M Maguire, R Morgan and R Reiner (eds) *The Oxford Handbook of Criminology* (2002) Oxford University Press.

Newburn T et al, *The Introduction of Referral Orders into the Youth Justice System: Final Report* Home Office Research Study 242 (2002) HO.

Normand A, 'The Scottish System' in P Cavadino (ed) *Children Who Kill* (1996) Waterside Press.

Pearson G ,'Youth, Crime and Society' in M Maguire, R Morgan and R Reiner (eds) *The Oxford Handbook of Criminology* (1994) Oxford University Press.

Penal Affairs Consortium, *Juveniles on Remand: Recent Trends in the Remanding of Juveniles to Prison Service Custody* (1996) Penal Affairs Consortium.

Phillips C and Bowling B, 'Racism, Ethnicity, Crime and Criminal Justice' in M Maguire, R Morgan and R Reiner (eds) *The Oxford Handbook of Criminology* (2002) Oxford University Press.

Piper C ,'The Crime and Disorder Act 1998: Child and Community "Safety"' (1999) 62 Modern Law Review 397.

Piper C, 'Who are these Youths? Language in the Service of Policy' (2001) 1 Youth Justice 30.

Pitts J, 'Korrectional Karaoke: New Labour and the Zombification of Youth Justice' (2001) 1 Youth Justice 3.

Ramsbotham D, 'Reflections of a Chief Inspector' (2001) 1 Youth Justice 17.

Rutherford A, 'Youth Justice and Social Inclusion' (2002) 2 Youth Justice 100.

Smith D, 'Ethnic Origins, Crime, Criminal Justice' in M Maguire, R Morgan and R Reiner (eds) *The Oxford Handbook of Criminology* (1997) Oxford University Press.

Social Exclusion Unit (SEU), *Bridging the Gap: New Opportunities for 16–18 Year Olds Not in Education, Employment or Training* (1999) .

Social Exclusion Unit (SEU), *Reducing re-offending by ex-prisoners* (2002) .

Social Services Inspectorate, *Inspection of Medway Secure Training Centre, September/October 1998* (1999) Department of Health.

Stone N, 'Legal Commentary "Recommendations for Deportation" and "Shorter Terms of Section 91 Detention"' (2002) 2 Youth Justice 44.

Tutt N (Chairman), *Children and Homicide: Appropriate procedures for juveniles in murder and manslaughter cases* Justice working party report (1996) Justice.

Utting W, *People Like Us: The Report of the Review of the Safeguards for Children Living Away from Home* (1997) The Stationery Office.

Walsh C, 'Imposing order: Child Safety Orders and Local Child Curfew Schemes' (1999) 21 Journal of Social Welfare and Family Law 135.

Walsh C, 'Curfews: No More Hanging Around' (2002) 2 Youth Justice 70.

White P and Woodbridge J, *The Prison Population in 1997* Home Office Statistical Bulletin 5/98 (1998) HO.

Wonnacott C, 'The counterfeit contract – reform, pretence and muddled principles in the new referral order' (1999) 11 Child and Family Law Quarterly 271.

Youth Justice Board, *Delivering Change Youth Justice Board Review 2000/2001* (2001) Youth Justice Board.

Youth Justice Board, *Building on Success Youth Justice Board Review 2001/2002* (2002) Youth Justice Board.

Chapter 19

Conclusion – themes and the way ahead

(1) A GROWING 'RIGHTS CONSCIOUSNESS'

The preceding chapters demonstrate considerable confusion in the law and policy relating to children. A rights-based approach might address at least some of their weaker aspects very effectively if the government and judiciary were prepared to utilise it more wholeheartedly. In particular, such an approach can address the problem experienced by children, alongside other minority groups, of being the focus of various specialised branches of law and policy, all with their own distinctive character, with no coherence or similarity in objectives. By placing the differing aspects of childhood in a framework of rights, rather than, for example, in a medical or educational-based context, the boundaries between the various disciplines start becoming irrelevant, with a far more coherent outcome being possible.

The time is right for such a change in approach, given the greatly increased level of 'rights consciousness' in the country today. The Human Rights Act 1998, by incorporating the ECHR into domestic law, has enhanced public perceptions of the rights enjoyed by all individuals, both against the state and each other. Society is also becoming far more aware of the demands of the CRC, with most public agencies attempting to comply with its broad aims.[1] There appears to be more sympathy with a desire to promote children's rights in more realistic and practical ways. Nevertheless, the developing law does not always reflect such a desire and it would be foolish to ignore the real concerns that many retain over the wisdom of utilising the concept of rights to increase children's well-being. This concluding chapter opens by considering some of these concerns. It then discusses the incoherence underlying the laws and policies affecting children as a class, a problem which, as mentioned above, could be addressed by utilising a rights-based perspective. It proceeds to consider briefly the progress made by the government in ensuring that policies relating to children are initiated and delivered in a more coherent manner. It concludes by setting out the case for the post of a Children's Rights Commissioner for every region within the United Kingdom.

(2) DANGERS OF RIGHTS TALK AND DANGERS OF CAUTION

Adopting the concept of rights in relation to children provokes unease amongst many writers and practitioners. Indeed, this may explain the lack of any widespread

---

1   See the examples of good practice amongst local authorities, cited by V Combe (2002).

enthusiasm for its extensive practical application. In a general context, Wellman urges far greater restraint over employing the language of rights. As he points out, asserting the existence of unreal moral rights discredits the genuine ones and even produces public scepticism over the very existence of such a concept.[2] A failure to distinguish between real and illusory rights undoubtedly plays into the hands of the media, who are only too keen to lampoon the concept of children having rights. The cartoons depicting small children consulting their solicitors over trivial grievances provoke derision. Furthermore, there is a danger that the language of rights can become a form of political correctness used to mask claims made by adults on behalf of children, which might not otherwise escape critical analysis.[3] Thus practitioners from various disciplines tend to assert that children have rights to a range of services, without pausing to reflect on such claims.[4] Are they simply based on their own views of morality, or is the existence of such a 'right' widely acknowledged by society? If so, has it been translated into legal principles? The fact that the law does not acknowledge the existence of such a moral right does not necessarily indicate that it does not exist; it may merely mean that the law is lagging behind public views of morality.

More fundamental are the doubts expressed over the extent to which assertions of rights can really benefit society as a whole. Writers like Archard and Wellman discuss the polarised approaches provoked by such concerns.[5] Defenders of the concept of rights within moral theory argue that appeals to rights can and have produced real improvements in society. Their opponents, however, claim that a rights-based society is 'a cold, hollow one, drained of the sentiments of mutual care and love', where individuals assert their rights *against* each other.[6] Anxiety over the potential destructiveness of 'rights talk' was revived by implementation of the Human Rights Act 1998. Sir John Laws warned of the dangers inherent in the new legislation. In his view:

'... the idea of a *rights-based* society represents an immature stage in the development of a free and just society ... nothing is more important, if we are truly dedicated to freedom and justice, than to see the shortcomings of this fragile pedestal. A society whose values are defined by reference to individual rights is by that very fact already impoverished. Its culture says nothing about individual duty – nothing about *virtue*. We speak of respect for other people's rights. But, crudely at least, this comes more and more to mean only that we should accept that what someone wants to do, he should be allowed to do. Self-discipline, self-restraint, to say nothing of self-sacrifice, are at best regarded as optional extras and at worst (and the worst is too often the reality) as old-fashioned ideas worth nothing but a scoff and a gibe ...'[7]

Like others, Sir John Laws clearly considers that a rights-based society cannot be one characterised by union, intimacy, affection, interdependence and sharing.[8]

Those who oppose extending rights to children use similar arguments. They claim that children's worlds are genuinely different from those of adults, due to their vulnerability and their dependence on their parents and other carers. Loving family

---

2   C Wellman (1999) pp 3 and 176–181.
3   Eg J Ennew's list of 'unwritten rights' which she argues street children are entitled to, including 'the right to control their own sexuality'. See J Ennew (2002) pp 399–401.
4   Eg a health practitioner's enthusiastic assertion to the author that 'babies have a *right* to be breast fed by their mothers'.
5   D Archard (1993) pp 88–91. See also C Wellman (1999) ch 7.
6   D Archard (1993) p 89.
7   J Laws (1998) p 255.
8   D Archard (1993) p 89.

relationships can be damaged by assertions which not only promote individualism but also inhibit and undermine parental authority and family autonomy.[9] This approach, which is continuously returned to in various contexts, would lead to the dubious proposition that even if children are to be deemed rights-holders, they should not be permitted to enforce them against their parents, because of their dependence and inter-dependence. Furthermore, as Archard points out, this type of criticism implies that family relationships can either be based on mutual affection *or* the existence of rights and duties, but not both.[10] This, of course, is far from the truth. For a child to have rights against its parents is not evidence that parental love is not forthcoming. If that love has broken down, it –

> 'is a matter for regret, and recourse to rights may well be second-best. But this is not by itself a reason not to have rights … It merely offers the surety of the minimum which love would provide when that emotion is lacking.'[11]

Underlying many of these concerns appears to be uncertainty over the nature of rights themselves. A recurring concern amongst family lawyers is that by using a rights discourse, those seeking to promote children's well-being are unable to promote their welfare. The suggestion that a rights-based approach to children's interests might even conflict with their welfare has been made by some of those considering the effect of the Human Rights Act 1998 on the principles of child law.[12] As discussed earlier in this work, the argument that a rights-based approach must necessarily be devoid of any element of paternalism or 'welfare' misconstrues the concept of rights.[13] Just as it would be inconceivable to argue that an adult has a right to be treated in a way that fundamentally harms him, the same applies to children. The ECHR represents an attempt to formulate in awkward phraseology some of the rights considered to be essential to civilised society. These are considered to be aspects of the good life, not the bad and should be interpreted in a way that enhances a person's life. A person may certainly suffer a deficit in well-being if his or her rights are displaced by those of another, but the concept of rights cannot guarantee that this will not occur nor that the courts will always balance the rights of one person against another in an entirely equitable fashion.[14]

Articulating children's interests in terms of rights may indeed lead to the behaviour of their caretakers being submitted to far more intensive examination than before, however well intentioned such behaviour is. This, in turn, may risk undermining the relationships through which their needs are usually met. Nevertheless, as Minow asserts, children would not be better off if schools and families were removed from the purview of public scrutiny permitted by rights claims. She suggests that if rights need asserting, conflict has occurred already, and the process of enforcing the right often gives it expression and provides a method of resolution.[15] The validity of Minow's approach is borne out by the case law, particularly that involving children who apply to court for legal authority to reside with an adult other than their parents.[15a] It seems quite unrealistic to argue that, without the prospect of court proceedings, the child and parents would become reconciled. Whilst mediation might avoid the

---

9   M O'Brien Steinfels (1982) p 240.
10   D Archard (1993) p 90.
11   D Archard (1993) p 91.
12   See S Harris-Short (2002) pp 336–337. See also J Herring (1999) esp p 233.
13   See chapter 1, pp 21–22.
14   I am grateful to my colleague, Kenneth Campbell, for his lucid explanation of this point.
15   See M Minow (1987) pp 1890–1891.
15a Under Children Act 1989, s 8. Discussed in chapters 4 and 7.

polarising effect of litigation, in most cases it seems likely that the damage to the relationships between child and parents pre-dates the litigation.

Although Archard and Minow provide answers to a commonly cited concern about the potential destructiveness of rights-talk within families, ideas about rights, if translated into practical contexts, do not always advance children's lives to any significant extent, often because they merely serve adult purposes. King and Piper suggest that the law utilises the concept of children's rights narrowly in order to justify decisions which treat a child in a particular way – for example, as belonging to one parent rather than another.[16] The truth of this criticism can be seen in decision-making on parental contact disputes and on residence disputes between birth parents and third parties. This demonstrates the judiciary enthusiastically adopting the concept of children's rights when reaching decisions which, a century ago, would have been justified by the concept of *parents'* rights.[17]

A recurring concern is that by promoting the rights of children, law and policy will undermine the status and authority of parents. Indeed, this may explain inconsistencies in the extent to which policy makers embrace the notion of children's rights. In situations where there is no apparent conflict between the position of parents and children, the government constantly encourages a greater awareness of children's rights.[18] But in situations where conflict might arise, the remedy adopted is simply to identify children's needs with those of their parents. This thereby avoids the unpopularity which would undoubtedly ensue were the state to adopt a more aggressive stance by promoting children's rights in a way which interfered with their parents' autonomy. For example, the issue of physical punishment within the home continues to be ducked.[19] Similarly, since the theme underlying the whole body of education law is that parents' interests are united with those of their children, parents' choices in all aspects of education are respected, as opposed to children's rights.[20]

Perhaps for the same reason, the judiciary demonstrate a similar ambivalence about promoting children's rights. It had been thought that the Human Rights Act 1998 would provide a much-needed opportunity for them to adjust the principles of law which apply to children and recast them in a rights-based mould.[21] Nevertheless, since incorporation of the ECHR, judicial decision-making in cases involving children has been far from creative. The Court of Appeal shied away from the opportunity to re-evaluate the basis on which children are made the subject of secure accommodation orders.[22] Similarly, the case law dealing with parents' disputes *over* their children reflects a judicial determination not to allow the demands of the ECHR to affect their traditional ad hoc methods of dealing with children's cases through the welfare principle.[23] Whilst it is arguable that a cautious interpretation of the Convention is entirely justified to prevent children's interests being sacrificed to parents' rights, the

16   M King and C Piper (1995) pp 144–145.
17   Discussed in chapters 13 and 14.
18   Eg the Department of Health, through the Quality Protects programme, requires social services departments to consult children on the delivery of children's services. See discussion in chapter 15.
19   Discussed further in chapter 9.
20   See chapters 6, 11 and 12.
21   See J Fortin (1999) p 255.
22   See *Re K (secure accommodation order: right to liberty)* [2001] 1 FLR 526. See discussion in chapter 16, pp 499–500.
23   See *Re B (a child) (adoption by one natural parent)* [2001] UKHL 70, [2002] 1 All ER 641. Discussed further in chapter 8, pp 250–251.

risk is that it may also completely undermine the judiciary's willingness to consider children as independent entities with rights of their own. As Bainham points out:

> '... whereas adult rights are readily acknowledged, the courts are most reluctant to allow any incursions into the traditional process of applying the welfare principle and of regarding the result of this exercise as decisive ... there is a danger that important claims of the child may be overlooked, or understated, unless addressed within a framework of rights.'[24]

Undoubtedly, concerns about embracing the concept of children's rights should be considered seriously but, to a certain extent, they appear slightly dated. The reality is that there is no longer any choice. Since October 2000, when the Human Rights Act 1998 was implemented, we have been living in a rights-based culture. Society must come to terms with the fact that children are as entitled to the practical fulfilment of their rights as anyone else.

(3) THE 'FRAGMENTED' CHILD

One of the most valuable ways in which a rights-based approach can improve the lot of children generally is to encourage a less fragmented approach to childhood. So far as law and policy are concerned, there appear to be at least two groups of children and their treatment is at complete variance.[25] There are the 'sensible', law-abiding children, who as they mature, are deemed perfectly able to take responsibility for their own decision-making. Government policies largely leave this group well alone, trusting their parents to bring them up as they think fit. For these children, the civil law has developed the enlightened and sophisticated concept of *Gillick* competence. The House of Lords in *Gillick v West Norfolk and Wisbech Area Health Authority*[26] saw the wisdom of harnessing the goodwill of sensible adolescents by treating them as individuals fast approaching adulthood. This legal approach promotes the idea that children, when sufficiently mature, can act responsibly if given the legal authority and freedom to do so. They may not only understand their own needs better than their parents, but society needs teenagers who know how to act sensibly without their parents' authority, for example, by taking precautions against unwanted pregnancies. The second group of children are the troubled and the troublesome – those who create the 'headline' problems: youth crime, truancy and school exclusions, social alienation, unemployment and homelessness.

Many of these troubled and troublesome children have the same underlying problems, but the law and policy applied to them depend entirely on the way they first attract adults' attention and whose attention they attract. For example, the children who are disruptive in school, bully others and truant, may end up being excluded, and back at home with little or no attention. Alternatively, their behaviour may be diagnosed as being attributable to their special educational needs (SEN).[27] Their problems, being defined as an educational issue and dealt with under the umbrella of SEN law and policy, gain the attention of educational psychologists, special educational needs co-ordinators and classroom assistants. On the other hand, their disturbed behaviour may suggest mental health problems, with a referral to the

24   See A Bainham (2002) pp 282 and 284.
25   See M King and C Piper (1995).
26   [1986] AC 112.
27   See chapter 12.

CAMHS,[28] with the possibility of ending up as patients in secure psychiatric units under secure accommodation orders.[29]

Some of the troubled children will be identified by social services as requiring protection from abusing or neglectful parents. They may find themselves removed from home and found alternative homes, either through adoption, long-term fostering or in a children's home. A fundamental dilemma is posed by the research indicating that a proportion of the children who need protecting from abuse later become involved in troublesome behaviour themselves. The type of parental behaviour which alerts social workers to the need to intervene under the civil law to protect children from their parents,[30] also correlates with later criminal activity amongst children brought up in such a way.[31] On the one hand, it is recognised that abused children need state protection, but, on the other hand, the law will treat the same children in a particularly punitive way if they become involved in offending behaviour.

The children whose anti-social behaviour attracts the attention of the authorities find themselves in an entirely different environment to that of child protection. Even the principles contained in the civil and criminal legal systems regarding a troublesome child's competence and ability to take responsibility for his or her actions contain utterly opposing viewpoints. The concept of *Gillick* competence not only treats children very liberally, but it also protects them from reaching decisions before they are sufficiently mature to comprehend them. The criminal law treats children in a much more punitive way, expecting them to take responsibility for their actions when they are still extremely immature. The adolescent found guilty of a serious crime may end up in a young offender institution, with little attention to his or her underlying problems.[32] Admittedly, the criminal law has a duty to promote society's needs for protection, whilst the civil law can concentrate on the needs of the individual child. This does not, however, justify the more punitive aspects of criminal law nor explain the internal incoherence of the civil law which becomes so obvious when comparing the opposing principles developed for this second group of children, through various specialised pockets of legal principles.

At present, a child or young person with the same behavioural problem may, depending on the referral, end up in a psychiatric unit, a residential school, a pupil referral unit, a children's home, a secure accommodation unit, or back at home with no support.[33] The extent to which he or she will be able to oppose these actions through separate representation depends entirely on the law relating to the process. If, for example, legal proceedings are mounted to ensure that a young person enters secure accommodation, he or she will be represented by a children's guardian and a solicitor. Equally, if the same young person is required to answer charges in a youth court, he or she gains legal representation. If, however, he or she is excluded from school, the parents alone are entitled to speak on behalf of their offspring, but only if they appeal. If health problems force the young person to seek medical attention, he or she may be treated in a psychiatric unit, on the authority only of the parents. In

---

28   The Child and Adolescent Mental Health Services. For a concise description of the service's functions, see C Sturge (1998) p 17ff. For a lengthy and critical assessment, see Audit Commission (1999).

29   See chapter 5.

30   Discussed in chapter 15.

31   Discussed in chapter 18.

32   See discussion in chapter 18.

33   See, inter alia: R Hodgkin and P Newell (1996) p 35; N Biehal et al (2000) p 76. See generally Social Exclusion Unit (hereafter SEU) (2000) chs 1–4.

each situation, a different set of practitioners with their own specialised training and expertise will see the child's problems and background from an entirely different and sometimes opposing viewpoint.

This fragmented approach to childhood problems encourages practitioners to place children in particular categories of rigidly defined symptoms, rather than to view them as individuals. It not only promotes a simplistic approach to diagnosis and undermines an efficient co-ordination of services, but prevents problems being picked up early in children's lives.[34] More dangerously, it risks alienating the troubled and troublesome against an adult society who appears to see them as little more than nuisances. As Raz has commented in a general context:

> 'The existence within a political society of estranged groups, who do not identify with the state, or the nation, and regard the government as an alien, potentially hostile, government, is destabilizing. Beyond that is the fact that human beings are political animals. That means more than that they can only thrive in political societies which provide the opportunities for the activities which make their lives. It also means that feeling part of a larger community, and being able to identify oneself as a member of such communities is an essential ingredient in people's well-being. Those who are second class citizens are marked by this experience which forces a flawed life on them.'[35]

Raz's comment hints at some of the concerns underlying the heated debates over the existence or otherwise of an 'underclass', composed of individuals who are morally irresponsible, whose behaviour leads them into long-term unemployment, benefit dependency, single parenthood and criminal activity. One of the many weaknesses of the underclass concept is its emphasis on the make-up and behaviour of the members of the underclass, rather than on wider social factors, such as regional unemployment.[36] An off-shoot of the underclass theory is the idea of an anti-social, criminal and feckless youth underclass, distinct from and hostile to wider society.[37] Many authors, like Pearce and Hillman, not only reject the concept of an underclass as being 'simplistic and ideologically motivated' but also the notion of a homogenous group of disaffected young people.[38] Nevertheless, when considering the problems of young people, even the opponents of the underclass theory acknowledge the importance of addressing the growing 'disaffection and disengagement' amongst teenagers.[39]

(4)   THE SOCIALLY EXCLUDED CHILD? A RIGHTS-BASED REMEDY

The government clearly recognises the weakness of a fragmented approach to childhood problems. Its chosen remedy is to adopt 'cross-cutting' policies to address them, using a new label, that of 'social exclusion', to describe their focus. The new term, despite being less pejorative than 'underclass',[40] is directed at similar problems; it is 'a shorthand term for what can happen when people or areas suffer from a combination of linked problems such as unemployment, poor skills, low incomes, poor housing, high crime, bad health and family breakdown'.[41] The government's

---

34   See N Biehal et al (2000) p 87.
35   J Raz (1996) p 125.
36   N Pearce and J Hillman (1998) pp 3–4.
37   See generally R MacDonald (1997).
38   N Pearce and J Hillman (1998) p 4. See also L Johnston et al (2000) pp 2–3.
39   N Pearce and J Hillman (1998) pp 3–6.
40   Discussed above.
41   See SEU (2001) para 1.2.

willingness to review its own mechanisms was triggered by the savage criticisms made by the Social Exclusion Unit (SEU).[42] The SEU drew attention to the lack of coherence in government policy regarding childhood problems, mainly due to lack of departmental co-ordination and liaison.[43] As it observed: 'No single department is in the lead, and the work that departments undertake individually sometimes overlaps confusingly and leaves gaps.'[44] In response, the government established the Cabinet Committee on 'Children and Young People's Services'[45] and the Children and Young People's Unit.[46] Their work, broadly aimed at addressing the two problems considered to be at the root of social exclusion – childhood poverty and disadvantage – is intended to break down traditional departmental boundaries.[47] This infrastructure accompanied new funding streams for children,[48] many of which are designed to support ambitious new programmes with cross-departmental aims, like Sure Start and Connexions.[49]

Despite the government's undoubted enthusiasm for tackling childhood problems with a fresh set of objectives, free of hide-bound territorial ideas, there remain concerns about its ability to achieve any real coherence in strategies for children. Inconsistencies still exist in the aims of the various departmental initiatives, the most obvious lying in their differing approaches towards troubled and troublesome teenagers. For example, the Home Office's 'punitive rhetoric' regarding young offenders is starkly contrasted with the Department of Health's humane attempts to ease the difficulties of care leavers, a proportion of whom swell the youth crime statistics.[50] Furthermore, there is unease over the new services being focused on the 'socially excluded', rather than there being a co-ordinated policy established for all children.[51] Indeed, it is questionable how useful the concept of social exclusion really is. Critics suggest that, like the term 'underclass', social exclusion is merely a rather unsatisfactory shorthand reduction of a complex phenomenon. The government's increasingly common use of the phrase 'social exclusion *and* child poverty' implies the two problems are so closely linked that they are interchangeable, which, of course, is far from the case.[52] Arguably the term has become a 'catch-all' phrase meaning all things to all people,[53] with a potential for increasing the exclusion of those defined as

42 Established to help improve Government action to reduce social exclusion by producing 'joined-up solutions to joined-up problems': phrase used by the Prime Minister in a speech given on 8 December 1997 when explaining the role of the new Social Exclusion Unit.
43 See SEU (2000) esp ch 8, calling for the establishment of cross-departmental strategies. See also SEU (2001) para 3.6.
44 SEU (2000) para 5.7.
45 Chaired by the Chancellor of the Exchequer, with members comprising the Secretaries of State of the various government ministries. The Committee's work is to co-ordinate policies to prevent poverty and underachievement among children and young people and to co-ordinate and monitor the efficiency of their delivery, including work with the voluntary sector.
46 Headed up by the Minister for Young People. Despite being located in the DfES, the Unit operates across departmental boundaries. Its remit is to support the Cabinet Committee in cross-departmental work on child poverty and disadvantage, to co-ordinate the government's strategy on vulnerable children and young people and to administer the Children's Fund.
47 See R Hodgkin and P Newell (2001) pp 20–26 for a useful summary of these projects.
48 Eg the Comprehensive Spending Review 2000 allocated £450m over three years for a new Children's Fund to tackle child poverty and social exclusion.
49 Other initiatives such as the National Child Care Strategy have similar cross-departmental aims. See discussion in chapter 9, pp 289–290.
50 R Hodgkin and P Newell (2001) p 21.
51 R Hodgkin and P Newell (2001) pp 18–19.
52 Emphasis supplied.
53 L Johnston et al (2000) p 3.

socially excluded.[54] By contrast, approaching the needs of all children from a rights-based perspective is *inclusive*, without ruling out targeting the neediest within the group.

Greater coherence would be achieved were the government to develop policies applicable to all children, not just the poor and disadvantaged. The adoption of a rights-based framework, as a basis for a universal strategy for children, would give all children the same entitlements. The CRC would be the best vehicle for such an approach, its scope being far wider than that of the ECHR, which focuses on civil and political rights. Under a rights-based approach, there would be far less temptation to allow the artificial distinctions between children's problems to dominate service design and delivery.[55] Practitioners would be encouraged to consider children as individuals with basic rights, rather than children whose problems fall into certain categories, including 'disadvantage' and 'deprivation'.[56] As Hodgkin and Newell observe:

'The SEU has succeeded in highlighting and setting remedies for the obstacles to the social inclusion of young people, and we recognise that without its policy work on school exclusion this important issue would not have had the attention it deserved. Nonetheless its remit prevents it from celebrating the contribution of all children and thus moving our society on from negative or self-serving attitudes to children.'[57]

A rights-based approach could also address the feelings of disaffection and disengagement that many young people so clearly feel. Rights carry responsibilities. If they were instructed in their status as rights-holders, as envisaged by the CRC, young people might feel more closely engaged in and responsible for the society of which they are members. Concern is growing amongst a number of developed countries throughout Europe over the relative apathy and increasing alienation of teenagers from politics and the democratic process.[58] Indeed, only 46% of females and 60% of males, under 25, voted in the 2001 general election in this country.[59] The Crick report,[60] on whose recommendation citizenship education was made part of the school curriculum, explained that its intention was –

'... to make secure and to increase the knowledge, skills and values relevant to the nature and practices of participative democracy; also to enhance the awareness of rights and duties, and the sense of responsibilities needed for the development of pupils into active citizens; and in so doing to establish the value to individuals, schools and society of involvement in the local and wider community.'[61]

At the very least, citizenship education should achieve an improvement in pupils' knowledge of the democratic process and local and national government structures.[62] But however well designed, educational programmes are not enough on their own.

---

54   R Hodgkin and P Newell (2001) p 18.
55   R Hodgkin and P Newell (2001) pp 18–19.
56   K Tomaševski (1999) para 33.
57   R Hodgkin and P Newell (2001) p 19.
58   R Hodgkin and P Newell (1996) pp 36–38.
59   The turnout in the 2001 election was the lowest since 1918, with those in the younger age groups being less likely to vote than those over 34. See National Statistics (2002) p 220.
60   B Crick (1998).
61   B Crick (1998) para 6.6.
62   See C White et al (2000), whose research indicated (p 44) that the young people interviewed had 'depressingly low levels of political interest and knowledge'. See also Office of National Statistics (2002) reporting (p 220) that only one in three teenagers (aged 12–19) in 1998 expressed an interest in politics.

Currently, many young people do not consider that their views are valued by decision-makers.[63] Indeed, some feel that they are regarded as a 'problem to be solved', not as problem solvers themselves, with the ability to be involved in local and central policies.[64] Attitudes to children and young people need to change, with their competence being fully recognised.[65] Local councils are becoming increasingly aware of the need to involve young people more effectively in local services and initiatives.[66] But, as demonstrated most effectively by other European countries,[67] this process should not be considered merely as an aspect of good practice, but a means of fulfilling young peoples' rights. The existence of the CRC provides ample justification for such an approach. As Newell observes:

> 'The particular task of the Convention is to emphasise that children too are holders of human rights. They are not possessions of their parents or of the state. They are not simply objects of concern. They are not people-in-the-making. They are individuals *now* with views, feelings and rights.'[68]

Increasing numbers of local authorities and health authorities realise this and use the Convention as a framework for developing and auditing many of their services which affect children.[69] It is time central government did the same.

(5)   A CHILDREN'S RIGHTS COMMISSIONER

By passing the Human Rights Act 1998, the government signalled its intention to establish a human rights culture in this country. But as Hodgkin and Newell observe, 'it has been erratic in its commitment to bringing *children's* human rights home in its domestic policies'.[70] Although welcome, the recent structural changes, cross-cutting policy initiatives, and new money for children,[71] are not linked to any general commitment to promoting the rights of all children. Indeed, these initiatives all concentrate on the children who need special help, like the large numbers still living in poverty. Furthermore, the various government departments still retain traditional and hidebound assumptions about children which will be difficult to address without far more radical changes in approach. Thus the Department for Education and Employment, whilst treating parents as the consumers of education, continues to exclude permanently from school many thousands of pupils every year.[72] Meanwhile, the Home Office does little to discourage the public's punitive attitudes towards young offenders, with the United Kingdom locking up higher numbers of young offenders than any other European country.[73]

---

63   See IPPR (2001) pp 17–19.
64   See IPPR (2001) p 12.
65   Save the Children (1997) p 42.
66   See V Combe (2002) which describes numerous examples of impressive local initiatives involving young people.
67   See K Poulsgaard (2001) and M Koebel (2001). Koebel's research focuses on the working of 'children's councils' in France.
68   P Newell (2000) p 18.
69   P Newell (2000) p 33.
70   See R Hodgkin and P Newell (2001) p 13.
71   Discussed above.
72   See chapter 6.
73   See chapter 18.

Lawyers wishing to promote children's rights more effectively are hampered by the way in which the legal principles governing children come into existence. In an uncodified legal system such as our own, changes in law and policy regarding children develop gradually in an entirely haphazard fashion. Pockets of case law reflecting liberal views about children's abilities can only be developed by the judiciary on an ad hoc basis through whatever litigation happens to come before the courts. Indeed, were it not for the zealous enthusiasm of Mrs Gillick to protect her right to family privacy and parental autonomy, the concept of the *Gillick*-competent child might never have emerged.[74] Moreover, as Bainham has pointed out, the essentially discretionary nature of the welfare principle allows the judiciary to duck out of general issues of public policy when dealing with cases, claiming that they are dealing with each on its own merits.[75] Case law develops on an incremental basis, with no underlying policy or cohesion and the opportunities for remedying practical gaps and defects uncovered are very limited. The courts have to wait for further litigation on the same topic or for the government to be sufficiently motivated to deal with the matter through special legislation.

As discussed above, the adoption of a rights-based approach to policy, case law and legislation would produce far greater coherence, particularly if it was firmly harnessed to more effective implementation of the CRC. It has long been recognised that probably one of the most important measures that could be taken to promote children's rights in this country would be to follow the lead taken by Norway in 1981,[76] by appointing a Children's Rights Commissioner, one of whose tasks would be to initiate programmes of law reform. The CRC obliges governments ratifying it to make the principles and provisions of the Convention widely known to adults and children alike,[77] and to produce regular reports to the Committee on the Rights of the Child on their progress towards implementation.[78] Numerous countries, having ratified the Convention, set about promoting these aims by appointing children's ombudsmen or commissioners for children's rights.[79]

Meanwhile despite continued pressure to establish the post of a Children's Rights Commissioner for England,[80] the government maintains that existing structures make such a step unnecessary.[81] In stark contrast, the new executives of Scotland, Wales and Northern Ireland, taking advantage of their devolution from central government in London, are in the process of establishing Children's Rights Commissioners for children within their own regions.[82] The Committee on the Rights of the Child has

74   *Gillick v West Norfolk and Wisbech Area Health Authority* [1986] AC 112.
75   A Bainham (1992) p 554.
76   See M Flekkoy (1991) and (2002).
77   Art 42.
78   Art 44.
79   See P Newell (2000), who (pp 77–79) lists the countries throughout the world who have appointed an ombudsman or commissioner for children. A recent addition to the list is Ireland, who appointed a Children's Ombudsman in 2002.
80   See House of Commons (1998) recommendation 63: a Children's Rights Commissioner should be appointed 'as soon as possible' to act within the United Kingdom. A private member's Bill creating the post of a Children's Rights Commissioner was introduced into the House of Commons in July 1999 under the 'Ten minute Rule'. See text set out by P Newell (2000) ch 4.
81   Department of Health (1998) paras 84–91.
82   In Wales, the Children's Commissioner for Wales Act 2001 established a Children's Commissioner whose remit is to promote the rights and welfare of all children 'ordinarily resident' in Wales. See discussion by K Hollingsworth and G Douglas (2002). In Northern Ireland, the Children's Commissioner Bill 2002 aims to establish a similar post. In Scotland, consultation on the creation of such a post being complete, similar draft legislation was introduced in December 2002.

now twice recommended that the government should establish 'independent mechanisms' to co-ordinate and monitor the implementation of children's rights in this country.[83] More directly, whilst praising developments in Wales, Northern Ireland and Scotland, it stated that it was 'deeply concerned that the State party has not yet established an independent human rights institution for children in England'.[84] Similarly, the Parliamentary Assembly of the Council of Europe not only recommended that all European Council countries should fully implement the CRC, but that they should all also make such appointments.[85]

A refusal to establish a Commissioner for children living in England is regrettable, given that they comprise one of the largest minority groups in the community.[86] Unlike other groups who are represented, for example, by the Commission for Racial Equality, the Equal Opportunities Commission, and the Disability Rights Commission, children do not form a lobby and, without entitlement to vote, have no political voice. The most important aspect of the work of a Children's Rights Commissioner is to persuade policy makers and practitioners to take full account of children's rights and interests. Under current government arrangements, there is no one who can fulfil that role adequately. Like the post of the Children's Rights Director,[87] which relates only to specific children and specific services, the role of the Minister for Young People is far too narrow to take on many of the tasks normally associated with Children's Rights Commissioners abroad, nor is it sufficiently senior.[88] Indeed, there is currently no official in England who can operate independently from government, monitoring its performance and promoting children's human rights at national and local level.

The importance of the office of Children's Rights Commissioner lies in its independence, with an ability to determine its own agenda within a set of broad aims and duties.[89] The government would have no right to direct, control or otherwise interfere with the Commission's work.[90] If the post mirrored that undertaken by similar officials abroad, the Commissioner would highlight, through regular reports, the way in which current laws and policy fail to take children's rights into account. The reports could also draw attention to inconsistencies in emerging case law and identify any amendments needed in law and policy as they arise. Whenever government ministers considered changes in existing legislation, or the introduction of new legislation, they would be obliged to consult the Commissioner and take account of his views, or explain publicly their reasons for failing to do so. Any White Papers,

83   See Committee on the Rights of the Child (1995) paras 8 and 23 and (2002) para 17.
84   Committee on the Rights of the Child (2002) para 16.
85   *Recommendation 1286 (1996) on a European Strategy for Children*, adopted by the Parliamentary Assembly of the Council of Europe, 24 January 1996, para 7(iv).
86   There are over 11 million children in England.
87   Created under the Care Standards Act 2000, with responsibility for the inspection and regulation of residential provision for children living away from home in children's homes, residential family centres, and in foster care.
88   The Minister for Young People is situated in the Home Office, is not a Cabinet minister and has other major responsibilities, not all relating to children.
89   See P Newell (2000) ch 2, for a detailed description of the work that a Children's Rights Commissioner might undertake in this country. See also G Lansdown (2002) and the detailed list of duties required of the Children's Ombudsman for Ireland in the Ombudsman for Children Act 2002.
90   G Lansdown (2002) p 293. Lord Laming's recent suggestion that a newly established National Agency for Children and Families could, in addition to reporting to a Children and Families Board, take on the traditional duties of a children's commissioner for England, appears to overlook this fundamental feature of the commissioner's role. See H Laming (2003) paras 1.34–1.35, p 363 and p 371.

Green Papers, Bills or other policy documents would assist him in such a task by always being accompanied by 'child impact statements' indicating the likely impact of the proposed legislation on children. The Commissioner would also have the power to investigate breaches of rights of children and undertake public inquiries into breaches, in particular child abuse inquiries, with the power to demand documents and examine witnesses.

Those favouring the appointment of a Children's Rights Commissioner for England do not envisage that the work would include taking up complaints on behalf of individual children. Although some children's ombudspersons and commissioners abroad undertake this type of complaint work, they normally do so only in countries with small populations.[91] There is a risk that if such work were undertaken here, it would overwhelm the remainder of the Commissioner's activities.[92] Nevertheless, his remit would include ensuring that all children had effective channels for complaint. He should also have the power to take or support legal action on behalf of groups of children, in circumstances where they were not able to do so on their own behalf. He might, for example, bring class actions on behalf of a group of children claiming their childhood diseases had been caused by industrial pollutants affecting their home environment.[93] His office might also wish to intervene in litigation which potentially has implications for children as a class, despite its origins as a private application in the domestic courts.

One of the principal functions of the office of Children's Rights Commissioner would be to promote the aims of the CRC and a heightened awareness of children's rights under the Convention.[94] At present there appears to be a high level of ignorance about its existence and objectives amongst children in the United Kingdom.[95] The task of a Commissioner would be to follow the example of other countries and ensure that children were made more aware of their rights, perhaps through leaflets and advertising campaigns of various kinds.[96] This would reinforce the citizenship education in schools now providing pupils with instruction about their human rights, as guaranteed both by the CRC and by the ECHR.

There are clearly important tasks waiting to be undertaken by a Children's Rights Commissioner on behalf of children in the United Kingdom. As Lansdown comments, the creation of such a post for every region, including England, 'would serve to demonstrate not only the government's commitment to respect for the human rights of children, but also a willingness to be held to account on that commitment'.[97]

(6)   CONCLUSION

Childhood is not a time that everyone remembers with nostalgia. Since we cannot protect children from suffering a multitude of problems, the 'fragmented' child and the socially excluded child rightly demand our attention. Nevertheless, this should not divert attention from the far larger numbers of children who reach adulthood very

91   Eg Norway, South Australia and Ireland.
92   P Newell (2000) p 55.
93   See E Palmer (1992).
94   See P Newell (2000) pp 51–53.
95   R Bourne et al (1998). This research indicated that whilst only 6% of children in Northern Ireland said they had been told about the CRC in school, 68% of children in India and 53% of children in Zimbabwe said that they had been told about it.
96   Eg the Norwegian ombudsman commissions a regular television slot dealing with issues raised by children about their rights.
97   G Lansdown (2002) p 296.

happily. The advantage of a rights-based perspective is that it avoids categorising the disadvantaged, entitling all to equal respect. Nevertheless, it is not enough for lawyers and policy makers simply to resolve to adopt a rights-based framework for their work, without being clear what children really require to enhance their well-being. Children's rights are not promoted if adults merely deliver a rough approximation of what children need, based on their own prejudices. As this work shows, law and policy can usefully draw on a growing body of research which considers children's needs from a variety of perspectives. Practitioners who are sympathetic to the concept of fulfilling children's rights should bear in mind that to ignore this information produces principles and policies which are devoid of practical utility and which may do more harm than good.

There are, however, those who, as parents, carers or practitioners, come into contact with children every day, but who are not particularly sympathetic with the idea of children's rights. They see it as a concept which not only threatens family stability, but lacks realism, and one which fails to produce ready solutions. They certainly need convincing that it can improve children's lives. This work seeks to show the sceptics how a rights-based approach can be translated into workable policies and legal principles and also that a conscientious attempt to apply these is better than guesswork and intuition. Above all else, the concept of children's rights should be utilised honestly and not as a politically correct tool which only thinly disguises adult caution and narrow-mindedness.

BIBLIOGRAPHY

NB many of these publications can be obtained on the relevant organisation's website.

Archard D, *Children: Rights and Childhood* (1993) Routledge.

Audit Commission, *Children in mind: child and adolescent mental health services* (1999) Audit Commission.

Bainham A, Review note (1992) 14 Journal of Social Welfare and Family Law 552.

Bainham A, 'Can we protect children and protect their rights?' (2002) Family Law 279.

Biehal N et al, *Home or Away? Supporting young people and families* (2000) National Children's Bureau.

Bourne R et al, *School based understanding of human rights in four countries* (1998) Department for International Development.

Combe V, *Up for it: Getting young people involved in local government* (2002) Joseph Rowntree Foundation.

Committee on the Rights of the Child, *Concluding Observations of the Committee on the Rights of the Child: United Kingdom of Great Britain and Northern Ireland* CRC/C/15/Add 34 (1995) Centre for Human Rights, Geneva.

Committee on the Rights of the Child, *Concluding Observations of the Committee on the Rights of the Child: United Kingdom of Great Britain and Northern Ireland* CRC/C/15/Add 188 (2002) Centre for Human Rights, Geneva.

Crick B (Chairman), *Final Report on Education for citizenship and the teaching of democracy in schools* Final Report of the Advisory Group on Citizenship (1998) Qualifications and Curriculum Authority.

Department of Health, *Government Response to the Second Report of the Health Committee on Children Looked After By Local Authorities: Session 1997–98 Children Looked After By Local Authorities* Cm 4175 (1998) The Stationery Office.

Ennew J, 'Outside childhood: Street children's rights' in B Franklin (ed) *The New Handbook of Children's Rights: Comparative Policy and Practice* (2002) Routledge.

Flekkoy M, *A Voice for Children: Speaking out as their Ombudsman* (1991) Jessica Kingsley Publishers.

Flekkoy M, 'The Ombudsman for children: Conception and developments' in B Franklin (ed) *The New Handbook of Children's Rights: Comparative Policy and Practice* (2002) Routledge.

Fortin J, 'The HRA's impact on litigation involving children and their families' (1999) 11 Child and Family Law Quarterly 217.

Harris-Short S, '*Re B (Adoption: Natural Parent)* Putting the child at the heart of adoption?' (2002) 14 Child and Family Law Quarterly 325.

Herring J, 'The Human Rights Act and the welfare principle in family law – conflicting or complementary?' (1999) 11 Child and Family Law Quarterly 223.

Hodgkin R and Newell P, *Effective Government Structures for Children* Report of a Gulbenkian Foundation Inquiry (1996) Calouste Gulbenkian Foundation.

Hodgkin R and Newell P, *UK Review of Effective Government Structures for Children 2001* A Gulbenkian Foundation Report (2001) Calouste Gulbenkian Foundation.

Hollingsworth K and Douglas G, 'Creating a children's champion for Wales? The Care Standards Act (Part V) and the Children's Commissioner for Wales Act 2001' (2002) 65 Modern Law Review 58.

House of Commons, *Select Committee on Health Second Report: Session 1997–98 Children Looked After By Local Authorities* (1998) The Stationery Office.

IPPR, *Politics not Parties: Young people and political engagement* (2001).

Johnston L et al, *Snakes and Ladders: Young people, transitions and social exclusion* (2000) The Policy Press.

King M and Piper C, *How the Law Thinks About Children* (1995) Arena.

Koebel M, 'At what age does one become a citizen?' (2001) 1 Children in Europe 9.

Laming H, *The Victoria Climbié Inquiry: Report of an Inquiry by Lord Laming* Cm 5730 (2003) The Stationery Office.

Lansdown G, 'Children's Rights Commissioners for the UK' in B Franklin (ed) *The New Handbook of Children's Rights: Comparative Policy and Practice* (2002) Routledge.

Laws J, 'The Limitations of Human Rights' (1998) Public Law 254.

MacDonald R, 'Dangerous youth and the dangerous class' in R MacDonald (ed) *Youth, the 'underclass' and social exclusion* (1997) Routledge.

Minow M, 'Interpreting Rights: An Essay for Robert Cover' (1987) 96 Yale Law Journal 1860.

National Statistics, *Social Trends No 32* (2002) The Stationery Office.

Newell P, *Taking Children Seriously: A Proposal for a Children's Rights Commissioner* (2000) Calouste Gulbenkian Foundation.

O'Brien Steinfels M, 'Children's Rights, Parental Rights, Family Privacy, and Family Autonomy' in W Gaylin and R Macklin (eds) *Who Speaks for the Child* (1982) Plenum Press.

Palmer E, 'Children and Toxic Torts' (1992) 4 Journal of Child Law 156.

Pearce N and Hillman J, *Wasted Youth: raising achievement and tackling social exclusion* (1998) IPPR.

Poulsgaard K, 'Children's self-determination and contributory influence: examples from Denmark' (2001) 1 Children in Europe 14.

Raz J, 'Liberty and Trust' in R George (ed) *Natural Law, Liberalism and Morality* (1996) Oxford University Press.

Save the Children, *All together now: Community participation for children and young people* (1997) Save the Children.

Social Exclusion Unit (SEU), *Report of Policy Action Team 12: Young People* (2000) The Stationery Office.

Social Exclusion Unit (SEU), *Preventing Social Exclusion* (2001) SEU.

Sturge C, 'Medical Input to Care Planning: The Contribution of Child and Adolescent Mental Health Services (CAMHS) to the Care Planning Process' in Thorpe LJ and E Clarke (eds) *Divided Duties: Care planning for children within the family justice system* (1998) Family Law.

Tomaševski K, *Report of the Special Rapporteur on the right to education to the UN Economic and Social Council, Mission to the United Kingdom and Northern Ireland (England)* E/CN 4/2000/6/Add 2 (1999).

Wellman C, *The Proliferation of Rights: Moral Progress or Empty Rhetoric?* (1999) Westview Press.

White C et al, *Young people's politics: Political interest and engagement amongst 14 to 24-year-olds* (2000) Joseph Rowntree Foundation.

Appendix I

UN Convention on the Rights of the Child

The Convention on the Rights of the Child was adopted and opened for signature, ratification and accession by General Assembly resolution 44/25 of 20 November 1989. It entered into force 2 September 1990, in accordance with article 49.

Preamble

The States Parties to the present Convention,

Considering that, in accordance with the principles proclaimed in the Charter of the United Nations, recognition of the inherent dignity and of the equal and inalienable rights of all members of the human family is the foundation of freedom, justice and peace in the world,

Bearing in mind that the peoples of the United Nations have, in the Charter, reaffirmed their faith in fundamental human rights and in the dignity and worth of the human person and have determined to promote social progress and better standards of life in larger freedom,

Recognizing that the United Nations has, in the Universal Declaration of Human Rights and in the International Covenants on Human Rights, proclaimed and agreed that everyone is entitled to all the rights and freedoms set forth therein, without distinction of any kind, such as race, colour, sex, language, religion, political or other opinion, national or social origin, property, birth or other status,

Recalling that, in the Universal Declaration of Human Rights, the United Nations has proclaimed that childhood is entitled to special care and assistance,

Convinced that the family, as the fundamental group of society and the natural environment for the growth and well-being of all its members and particularly children, should be afforded the necessary protection and assistance so that it can fully assume its responsibilities within the community,

Recognizing that the child, for the full and harmonious development of his or her personality, should grow up in a family environment, in an atmosphere of happiness, love and understanding,

Considering that the child should be fully prepared to live an individual life in society and brought up in the spirit of the ideals proclaimed in the Charter of the United Nations and in particular in the spirit of peace, dignity, tolerance, freedom, equality and solidarity,

Bearing in mind that the need to extend particular care to the child has been stated in the Geneva Declaration of the Rights of the Child of 1924 and in the Declaration of the Rights of the Child adopted by the General Assembly on 20 November 1959 and recognized in the Universal Declaration of Human Rights, in the International Covenant on Civil and Political Rights (in particular in articles 23 and 24), in the International Covenant on Economic, Social and Cultural Rights (in particular in article 10) and in the statutes and relevant instruments of specialized agencies and international organizations concerned with the welfare of children,

Bearing in mind that, as indicated in the Declaration of the Rights of the Child, "the child, by reason of his physical and mental immaturity, needs special safeguards and care, including appropriate legal protection, before as well as after birth",

Recalling the provisions of the Declaration on Social and Legal Principles relating to the Protection and Welfare of Children, with Special Reference to Foster Placement and Adoption Nationally and Internationally; the United Nations Standard Minimum Rules for the Administration of Juvenile Justice (The Beijing Rules) ; and the Declaration on the Protection of Women and Children in Emergency and Armed Conflict,

Recognizing that, in all countries in the world, there are children living in exceptionally difficult conditions and that such children need special consideration,

Taking due account of the importance of the traditions and cultural values of each people for the protection and harmonious development of the child,

Recognizing the importance of international co-operation for improving the living conditions of children in every country, in particular in the developing countries,

Have agreed as follows:

Part I

Article 1

For the purposes of the present Convention, a child means every human being below the age of eighteen years unless under the law applicable to the child, majority is attained earlier.

Article 2

1. States Parties shall respect and ensure the rights set forth in the present Convention to each child within their jurisdiction without discrimination of any kind, irrespective of the child's or his or her parent's or legal guardian's race, colour, sex, language, religion, political or other opinion, national, ethnic or social origin, property, disability, birth or other status.

2. States Parties shall take all appropriate measures to ensure that the child is protected against all forms of discrimination or punishment on the basis of the status, activities, expressed opinions, or beliefs of the child's parents, legal guardians, or family members.

Article 3

1. In all actions concerning children, whether undertaken by public or private social welfare institutions, courts of law, administrative authorities or legislative bodies, the best interests of the child shall be a primary consideration.

2. States Parties undertake to ensure the child such protection and care as is necessary for his or her well-being, taking into account the rights and duties of his or her parents, legal guardians, or other individuals legally responsible for him or her, and, to this end, shall take all appropriate legislative and administrative measures.

3. States Parties shall ensure that the institutions, services and facilities responsible for the care or protection of children shall conform with the standards established by competent authorities, particularly in the areas of safety, health, in the number and suitability of their staff, as well as competent supervision.

Article 4

States Parties shall undertake all appropriate legislative, administrative and other measures for the implementation of the rights recognized in the present Convention. With regard to economic, social and cultural rights, States Parties shall undertake such measures to the maximum extent of their available resources and, where needed, within the framework of international co-operation.

Article 5

States Parties shall respect the responsibilities, rights and duties of parents or, where applicable, the members of the extended family or community as provided for by local custom, legal guardians or other persons legally responsible for the child, to provide, in a manner consistent with the evolving capacities of the child, appropriate direction and guidance in the exercise by the child of the rights recognized in the present Convention.

Article 6

1. States Parties recognize that every child has the inherent right to life.

2. States Parties shall ensure to the maximum extent possible the survival and development of the child.

Article 7

1. The child shall be registered immediately after birth and shall have the right from birth to a name, the right to acquire a nationality and. as far as possible, the right to know and be cared for by his or her parents.

2. States Parties shall ensure the implementation of these rights in accordance with their national law and their obligations under the relevant international instruments in this field, in particular where the child would otherwise be stateless.

Article 8

1. States Parties undertake to respect the right of the child to preserve his or her identity, including nationality, name and family relations as recognized by law without unlawful interference.

2. Where a child is illegally deprived of some or all of the elements of his or her identity, States Parties shall provide appropriate assistance and protection, with a view to re-establishing speedily his or her identity.

Article 9

1. States Parties shall ensure that a child shall not be separated from his or her parents against their will, except when competent authorities subject to judicial review determine, in accordance with applicable law and procedures, that such separation is necessary for the best interests of the child. Such determination may be necessary in a particular case such as one involving abuse or neglect of the child by the parents, or one where the parents are living separately and a decision must be made as to the child's place of residence.

2. In any proceedings pursuant to paragraph 1 of the present article, all interested parties shall be given an opportunity to participate in the proceedings and make their views known.

3. States Parties shall respect the right of the child who is separated from one or both parents to maintain personal relations and direct contact with both parents on a regular basis, except if it is contrary to the child's best interests. 4. Where such separation results from any action initiated by a State Party, such as the detention, imprisonment, exile, deportation or death (including death arising from any cause while the person is in the custody of the State) of one or both parents or of the child, that State Party shall, upon request, provide the parents, the child or, if appropriate, another member of the family with the essential information concerning the whereabouts of the absent member(s) of the family unless the provision of the information would be detrimental to the well-being of the child. States Parties shall further ensure that the submission of such a request shall of itself entail no adverse consequences for the person(s) concerned.

Article 10

1. In accordance with the obligation of States Parties under article 9, paragraph 1, applications by a child or his or her parents to enter or leave a State Party for the purpose of family reunification shall be dealt with by States Parties in a positive, humane and expeditious manner. States Parties shall further ensure that the submission of such a request shall entail no adverse consequences for the applicants and for the members of their family.

2. A child whose parents reside in different States shall have the right to maintain on a regular basis, save in exceptional circumstances personal relations and direct

contacts with both parents. Towards that end and in accordance with the obligation of States Parties under article 9, paragraph 1, States Parties shall respect the right of the child and his or her parents to leave any country, including their own and to enter their own country. The right to leave any country shall be subject only to such restrictions as are prescribed by law and which are necessary to protect the national security, public order (ordre public), public health or morals or the rights and freedoms of others and are consistent with the other rights recognized in the present Convention.

Article 11

1. States Parties shall take measures to combat the illicit transfer and non-return of children abroad.

2. To this end, States Parties shall promote the conclusion of bilateral or multilateral agreements or accession to existing agreements.

Article 12

1. States Parties shall assure to the child who is capable of forming his or her own views the right to express those views freely in all matters affecting the child, the views of the child being given due weight in accordance with the age and maturity of the child.

2. For this purpose, the child shall in particular be provided the opportunity to be heard in any judicial and administrative proceedings affecting the child, either directly, or through a representative or an appropriate body, in a manner consistent with the procedural rules of national law.

Article 13

1. The child shall have the right to freedom of expression; this right shall include freedom to seek, receive and impart information and ideas of all kinds, regardless of frontiers, either orally, in writing or in print, in the form of art, or through any other media of the child's choice.

2. The exercise of this right may be subject to certain restrictions, but these shall only be such as are provided by law and are necessary:

(a) For respect of the rights or reputations of others; or

(b) For the protection of national security or of public order (ordre public), or of public health or morals.

Article 14

1. States Parties shall respect the right of the child to freedom of thought, conscience and religion.

2. States Parties shall respect the rights and duties of the parents and, when applicable, legal guardians, to provide direction to the child in the exercise of his or her right in a manner consistent with the evolving capacities of the child.

3. Freedom to manifest one's religion or beliefs may be subject only to such limitations as are prescribed by law and are necessary to protect public safety, order, health or morals, or the fundamental rights and freedoms of others.

Article 15

1. States Parties recognize the rights of the child to freedom of association and to freedom of peaceful assembly.

2. No restrictions may be placed on the exercise of these rights other than those imposed in conformity with the law and which are necessary in a democratic society in the interests of national security or public safety, public order (ordre public), the protection of public health or morals or the protection of the rights and freedoms of others.

Article 16

1. No child shall be subjected to arbitrary or unlawful interference with his or her privacy, family, home or correspondence, nor to unlawful attacks on his or her honour and reputation.

2. The child has the right to the protection of the law against such interference or attacks.

Article 17

States Parties recognize the important function performed by the mass media and shall ensure that the child has access to information and material from a diversity of national and international sources, especially those aimed at the promotion of his or her social, spiritual and moral well-being and physical and mental health. To this end, States Parties shall:

(a) Encourage the mass media to disseminate information and material of social and cultural benefit to the child and in accordance with the spirit of article 29;

(b) Encourage international co-operation in the production, exchange and dissemination of such information and material from a diversity of cultural, national and international sources;

(c) Encourage the production and dissemination of children's books;

(d) Encourage the mass media to have particular regard to the linguistic needs of the child who belongs to a minority group or who is indigenous;

(e) Encourage the development of appropriate guidelines for the protection of the child from information and material injurious to his or her well-being, bearing in mind the provisions of articles 13 and 18.

Article 18

1. States Parties shall use their best efforts to ensure recognition of the principle that both parents have common responsibilities for the upbringing and development of

the child. Parents or, as the case may be, legal guardians, have the primary responsibility for the upbringing and development of the child. The best interests of the child will be their basic concern.

2. For the purpose of guaranteeing and promoting the rights set forth in the present Convention, States Parties shall render appropriate assistance to parents and legal guardians in the performance of their child-rearing responsibilities and shall ensure the development of institutions, facilities and services for the care of children.

3. States Parties shall take all appropriate measures to ensure that children of working parents have the right to benefit from child-care services and facilities for which they are eligible.

Article 19

1. States Parties shall take all appropriate legislative, administrative, social and educational measures to protect the child from all forms of physical or mental violence, injury or abuse, neglect or negligent treatment, maltreatment or exploitation, including sexual abuse, while in the care of parent(s), legal guardian(s) or any other person who has the care of the child.

2. Such protective measures should, as appropriate, include effective procedures for the establishment of social programmes to provide necessary support for the child and for those who have the care of the child, as well as for other forms of prevention and for identification, reporting, referral, investigation, treatment and follow-up of instances of child maltreatment described heretofore, and, as appropriate, for judicial involvement.

Article 20

1. A child temporarily or permanently deprived of his or her family environment, or in whose own best interests cannot be allowed to remain in that environment, shall be entitled to special protection and assistance provided by the State.

2. States Parties shall in accordance with their national laws ensure alternative care for such a child.

3. Such care could include, inter alia, foster placement, kafalah of Islamic law, adoption or if necessary placement in suitable institutions for the care of children. When considering solutions, due regard shall be paid to the desirability of continuity in a child's upbringing and to the child's ethnic, religious, cultural and linguistic background.

Article 21

States Parties that recognize and/or permit the system of adoption shall ensure that the best interests of the child shall be the paramount consideration and they shall:

(a) Ensure that the adoption of a child is authorized only by competent authorities who determine, in accordance with applicable law and procedures and on the basis of all pertinent and reliable information, that the adoption is permissible in view of the child's status concerning parents, relatives and legal guardians and that, if required, the persons concerned have given their informed consent to the adoption on the basis of such counselling as may be necessary;

(b) Recognize that inter-country adoption may be considered as an alternative means of child's care, if the child cannot be placed in a foster or an adoptive family or cannot in any suitable manner be cared for in the child's country of origin; (c) Ensure that the child concerned by inter-country adoption enjoys safeguards and standards equivalent to those existing in the case of national adoption;

(d) Take all appropriate measures to ensure that, in inter-country adoption, the placement does not result in improper financial gain for those involved in it;

(e) Promote, where appropriate, the objectives of the present article by concluding bilateral or multilateral arrangements or agreements and endeavour, within this framework, to ensure that the placement of the child in another country is carried out by competent authorities or organs.

Article 22

1. States Parties shall take appropriate measures to ensure that a child who is seeking refugee status or who is considered a refugee in accordance with applicable international or domestic law and procedures shall, whether unaccompanied or accompanied by his or her parents or by any other person, receive appropriate protection and humanitarian assistance in the enjoyment of applicable rights set forth in the present Convention and in other international human rights or humanitarian instruments to which the said States are Parties.

2. For this purpose, States Parties shall provide, as they consider appropriate, co-operation in any efforts by the United Nations and other competent intergovernmental organizations or non-governmental organizations co-operating with the United Nations to protect and assist such a child and to trace the parents or other members of the family of any refugee child in order to obtain information necessary for reunification with his or her family. In cases where no parents or other members of the family can be found, the child shall be accorded the same protection as any other child permanently or temporarily deprived of his or her family environment for any reason, as set forth in the present Convention.

Article 23

1. States Parties recognize that a mentally or physically disabled child should enjoy a full and decent life, in conditions which ensure dignity, promote self-reliance and facilitate the child's active participation in the community.

2. States Parties recognize the right of the disabled child to special care and shall encourage and ensure the extension, subject to available resources, to the eligible child and those responsible for his or her care, of assistance for which application is made and which is appropriate to the child's condition and to the circumstances of the parents or others caring for the child. 3. Recognizing the special needs of a disabled child, assistance extended in accordance with paragraph 2 of the present article shall be provided free of charge, whenever possible, taking into account the financial resources of the parents or others caring for the child and shall be designed to ensure that the disabled child has effective access to and receives education,

training, health care services, rehabilitation services, preparation for employment and recreation opportunities in a manner conducive to the child's achieving the fullest possible social integration and individual development, including his or her cultural and spiritual development

4. States Parties shall promote, in the spirit of international cooperation, the exchange of appropriate information in the field of preventive health care and of medical, psychological and functional treatment of disabled children, including dissemination of and access to information concerning methods of rehabilitation, education and vocational services, with the aim of enabling States Parties to improve their capabilities and skills and to widen their experience in these areas. In this regard, particular account shall be taken of the needs of developing countries.

Article 24

1. States Parties recognize the right of the child to the enjoyment of the highest attainable standard of health and to facilities for the treatment of illness and rehabilitation of health. States Parties shall strive to ensure that no child is deprived of his or her right of access to such health care services.

2. States Parties shall pursue full implementation of this right and, in particular, shall take appropriate measures:

(a) To diminish infant and child mortality;

(b) To ensure the provision of necessary medical assistance and health care to all children with emphasis on the development of primary health care;

(c) To combat disease and malnutrition, including within the framework of primary health care, through, inter alia, the application of readily available technology and through the provision of adequate nutritious foods and clean drinking-water, taking into consideration the dangers and risks of environmental pollution;

(d) To ensure appropriate pre-natal and post-natal health care for mothers;

(e) To ensure that all segments of society, in particular parents and children, are informed, have access to education and are supported in the use of basic knowledge of child health and nutrition, the advantages of breastfeeding, hygiene and environmental sanitation and the prevention of accidents;

(f) To develop preventive health care, guidance for parents and family planning education and services.

3. States Parties shall take all effective and appropriate measures with a view to abolishing traditional practices prejudicial to the health of children.

4. States Parties undertake to promote and encourage international co-operation with a view to achieving progressively the full realization of the right recognized in the present article. In this regard, particular account shall be taken of the needs of developing countries.

Article 25

States Parties recognize the right of a child who has been placed by the competent authorities for the purposes of care, protection or treatment of his or her physical or mental health, to a periodic review of the treatment provided to the child and all other circumstances relevant to his or her placement.

Article 26

1. States Parties shall recognize for every child the right to benefit from social security, including social insurance and shall take the necessary measures to achieve the full realization of this right in accordance with their national law.

2. The benefits should, where appropriate, be granted, taking into account the resources and the circumstances of the child and persons having responsibility for the maintenance of the child, as well as any other consideration relevant to an application for benefits made by or on behalf of the child.

Article 27

1. States Parties recognize the right of every child to a standard of living adequate for the child's physical, mental, spiritual, moral and social development.

2. The parent(s) or others responsible for the child have the primary responsibility to secure, within their abilities and financial capacities, the conditions of living necessary for the child's development.

3. States Parties, in accordance with national conditions and within their means, shall take appropriate measures to assist parents and others responsible for the child to implement this right and shall in case of need provide material assistance and support programmes, particularly with regard to nutrition, clothing and housing.

4. States Parties shall take all appropriate measures to secure the recovery of maintenance for the child from the parents or other persons having financial responsibility for the child, both within the State Party and from abroad. In particular, where the person having financial responsibility for the child lives in a State different from that of the child, States Parties shall promote the accession to international agreements or the conclusion of such agreements, as well as the making of other appropriate arrangements.

Article 28

1. States Parties recognize the right of the child to education and with a view to achieving this right progressively and on the basis of equal opportunity, they shall, in particular:

(a) Make primary education compulsory and available free to all;

(b) Encourage the development of different forms of secondary education, including general and vocational education, make them available and accessible to every child and take appropriate measures such as the introduction of free education and offering financial assistance in case of need;

(c) Make higher education accessible to all on the basis of capacity by every appropriate means;

(d) Make educational and vocational information and guidance available and accessible to all children;

(e) Take measures to encourage regular attendance at schools and the reduction of drop-out rates.

2. States Parties shall take all appropriate measures to ensure that school discipline is administered in a manner consistent with the child's human dignity and in conformity with the present Convention.

3. States Parties shall promote and encourage international cooperation in matters relating to education, in particular with a view to contributing to the elimination of ignorance and illiteracy throughout the world and facilitating access to scientific and technical knowledge and modern teaching methods. In this regard, particular account shall be taken of the needs of developing countries.

Article 29

1. States Parties agree that the education of the child shall be directed to:

(a) The development of the child's personality, talents and mental and physical abilities to their fullest potential;

(b) The development of respect for human rights and fundamental freedoms, and for the principles enshrined in the Charter of the United Nations;

(c) The development of respect for the child's parents, his or her own cultural identity, language and values, for the national values of the country in which the child is living, the country from which he or she may originate, and for civilizations different from his or her own;

(d) The preparation of the child for responsible life in a free society, in the spirit of understanding, peace, tolerance, equality of sexes, and friendship among all peoples, ethnic, national and religious groups and persons of indigenous origin;

(e) The development of respect for the natural environment.

2. No part of the present article or article 28 shall be construed so as to interfere with the liberty of individuals and bodies to establish and direct educational institutions, subject always to the observance of the principle set forth in paragraph 1 of the present article and to the requirements that the education given in such institutions shall conform to such minimum standards as may be laid down by the State.

Article 30

In those States in which ethnic, religious or linguistic minorities or persons of indigenous origin exist, a child belonging to such a minority or who is indigenous shall not be denied the right, in community with other members of his or her group, to enjoy his or her own culture, to profess and practise his or her own religion, or to use his or her own language.

Article 31

1. States Parties recognize the right of the child to rest and leisure, to engage in play and recreational activities appropriate to the age of the child and to participate freely in cultural life and the arts.

2. States Parties shall respect and promote the right of the child to participate fully in cultural and artistic life and shall encourage the provision of appropriate and equal opportunities for cultural, artistic, recreational and leisure activity.

Article 32

1. States Parties recognize the right of the child to be protected from economic exploitation and from performing any work that is likely to be hazardous or to interfere with the child's education, or to be harmful to the child's health or physical, mental, spiritual, moral or social development.

2. States Parties shall take legislative, administrative, social and educational measures to ensure the implementation of the present article. To this end and having regard to the relevant provisions of other international instruments, States Parties shall in particular: (a) Provide for a minimum age or minimum ages for admission to employment;

(b) Provide for appropriate regulation of the hours and conditions of employment;

(c) Provide for appropriate penalties or other sanctions to ensure the effective enforcement of the present article.

Article 33

States Parties shall take all appropriate measures, including legislative, administrative, social and educational measures, to protect children from the illicit use of narcotic drugs and psychotropic substances as defined in the relevant international treaties and to prevent the use of children in the illicit production and trafficking of such substances.

Article 34

States Parties undertake to protect the child from all forms of sexual exploitation and sexual abuse. For these purposes, States Parties shall in particular take all appropriate national, bilateral and multilateral measures to prevent:

(a) The inducement or coercion of a child to engage in any unlawful sexual activity;

(b) The exploitative use of children in prostitution or other unlawful sexual practices;

(c) The exploitative use of children in pornographic performances and materials.

Article 35

States Parties shall take all appropriate national, bilateral and multilateral measures to prevent the abduction of, the sale of or traffic in children for any purpose or in any form.

Article 36

States Parties shall protect the child against all other forms of exploitation prejudicial to any aspects of the child's welfare.

Article 37

States Parties shall ensure that:

(a) No child shall be subjected to torture or other cruel, inhuman or degrading treatment or punishment. Neither capital punishment nor life imprisonment without possibility of release shall be imposed for offences committed by persons below eighteen years of age;

(b) No child shall be deprived of his or her liberty unlawfully or arbitrarily. The arrest, detention or imprisonment of a child shall be in conformity with the law and shall be used only as a measure of last resort and for the shortest appropriate period of time;

(c) Every child deprived of liberty shall be treated with humanity and respect for the inherent dignity of the human person and in a manner which takes into account the needs of persons of his or her age. In particular, every child deprived of liberty shall be separated from adults unless it is considered in the child's best interest not to do so and shall have the right to maintain contact with his or her family through correspondence and visits, save in exceptional circumstances;

(d) Every child deprived of his or her liberty shall have the right to prompt access to legal and other appropriate assistance, as well as the right to challenge the legality of the deprivation of his or her liberty before a court or other competent, independent and impartial authority and to a prompt decision on any such action.

Article 38

1. States Parties undertake to respect and to ensure respect for rules of international humanitarian law applicable to them in armed conflicts which are relevant to the child.

2. States Parties shall take all feasible measures to ensure that persons who have not attained the age of fifteen years do not take a direct part in hostilities.

3. States Parties shall refrain from recruiting any person who has not attained the age of fifteen years into their armed forces. In recruiting among those persons who have attained the age of fifteen years but who have not attained the age of eighteen years, States Parties shall endeavour to give priority to those who are oldest.

4. In accordance with their obligations under international humanitarian law to protect the civilian population in armed conflicts, States Parties shall take all feasible measures to ensure protection and care of children who are affected by an armed conflict.

Article 39

States Parties shall take all appropriate measures to promote physical and psychological recovery and social reintegration of a child victim of: any form of neglect, exploitation, or abuse; torture or any other form of cruel, inhuman or degrading treatment or punishment; or armed conflicts. Such recovery and reintegration shall take place in an environment which fosters the health, self-respect and dignity of the child.

Article 40

1. States Parties recognize the right of every child alleged as, accused of, or recognized as having infringed the penal law to be treated in a manner consistent with the promotion of the child's sense of dignity and worth, which reinforces the child's respect for the human rights and fundamental freedoms of others and which takes into account the child's age and the desirability of promoting the child's reintegration and the child's assuming a constructive role in society.

2. To this end and having regard to the relevant provisions of international instruments, States Parties shall, in particular, ensure that:

(a) No child shall be alleged as, be accused of, or recognized as having infringed the penal law by reason of acts or omissions that were not prohibited by national or international law at the time they were committed;

(b) Every child alleged as or accused of having infringed the penal law has at least the following guarantees:

(i) To be presumed innocent until proven guilty according to law;

(ii) To be informed promptly and directly of the charges against him or her, and, if appropriate, through his or her parents or legal guardians and to have legal or other appropriate assistance in the preparation and presentation of his or her defence;

(iii) To have the matter determined without delay by a competent, independent and impartial authority or judicial body in a fair hearing according to law, in the presence of legal or other appropriate assistance and, unless it is considered not to be in the best interest of the child, in particular, taking into account his or her age or situation, his or her parents or legal guardians;

(iv) Not to be compelled to give testimony or to confess guilt; to examine or have examined adverse witnesses and to obtain the participation and examination of witnesses on his or her behalf under conditions of equality;

(v) If considered to have infringed the penal law, to have this decision and any measures imposed in consequence thereof reviewed by a higher competent, independent and impartial authority or judicial body according to law;

(vi) To have the free assistance of an interpreter if the child cannot understand or speak the language used;

(vii) To have his or her privacy fully respected at all stages of the proceedings. 3. States Parties shall seek to promote the establishment of laws, procedures, authorities and institutions specifically applicable to children alleged as, accused of, or recognized as having infringed the penal law, and, in particular:

(a) The establishment of a minimum age below which children shall be presumed not to have the capacity to infringe the penal law;

(b) Whenever appropriate and desirable, measures for dealing with such children without resorting to judicial proceedings, providing that human rights and legal safeguards are fully respected.

4. A variety of dispositions, such as care, guidance and supervision orders; counselling; probation; foster care; education and vocational training programmes and other alternatives to institutional care shall be available to ensure that children

are dealt with in a manner appropriate to their well-being and proportionate both to their circumstances and the offence.

Article 41

Nothing in the present Convention shall affect any provisions which are more conducive to the realization of the rights of the child and which may be contained in:

(a) The law of a State party; or

(b) International law in force for that State.

Part II

Article 42

States Parties undertake to make the principles and provisions of the Convention widely known, by appropriate and active means, to adults and children alike.

Article 43

1. For the purpose of examining the progress made by States Parties in achieving the realization of the obligations undertaken in the present Convention, there shall be established a Committee on the Rights of the Child, which shall carry out the functions hereinafter provided.

2. The Committee shall consist of ten experts of high moral standing and recognized competence in the field covered by this Convention. The members of the Committee shall be elected by States Parties from among their nationals and shall serve in their personal capacity, consideration being given to equitable geographical distribution, as well as to the principal legal systems.

3. The members of the Committee shall be elected by secret ballot from a list of persons nominated by States Parties. Each State Party may nominate one person from among its own nationals.

4. The initial election to the Committee shall be held no later than six months after the date of the entry into force of the present Convention and thereafter every second year. At least four months before the date of each election, the Secretary-General of the United Nations shall address a letter to States Parties inviting them to submit their nominations within two months. The Secretary-General shall subsequently prepare a list in alphabetical order of all persons thus nominated, indicating States Parties which have nominated them and shall submit it to the States Parties to the present Convention.

5. The elections shall be held at meetings of States Parties convened by the Secretary-General at United Nations Headquarters. At those meetings, for which two thirds of States Parties shall constitute a quorum, the persons elected to the Committee shall be those who obtain the largest number of votes and an absolute majority of the votes of the representatives of States Parties present and voting.

6. The members of the Committee shall be elected for a term of four years. They shall be eligible for re-election if renominated. The term of five of the members elected at

the first election shall expire at the end of two years; immediately after the first election, the names of these five members shall be chosen by lot by the Chairman of the meeting.

7. If a member of the Committee dies or resigns or declares that for any other cause he or she can no longer perform the duties of the Committee, the State Party which nominated the member shall appoint another expert from among its nationals to serve for the remainder of the term, subject to the approval of the Committee.

8. The Committee shall establish its own rules of procedure.

9. The Committee shall elect its officers for a period of two years.

10. The meetings of the Committee shall normally be held at United Nations Headquarters or at any other convenient place as determined by the Committee. The Committee shall normally meet annually. The duration of the meetings of the Committee shall be determined and reviewed, if necessary, by a meeting of the States Parties to the present Convention, subject to the approval of the General Assembly.

11. The Secretary-General of the United Nations shall provide the necessary staff and facilities for the effective performance of the functions of the Committee under the present Convention.

12. With the approval of the General Assembly, the members of the Committee established under the present Convention shall receive emoluments from United Nations resources on such terms and conditions as the Assembly may decide.

Article 44

1. States Parties undertake to submit to the Committee, through the Secretary-General of the United Nations, reports on the measures they have adopted which give effect to the rights recognized herein and on the progress made on the enjoyment of those rights:

(a) Within two years of the entry into force of the Convention for the State Party concerned;

(b) Thereafter every five years.

2. Reports made under the present article shall indicate factors and difficulties, if any, affecting the degree of fulfilment of the obligations under the present Convention. Reports shall also contain sufficient information to provide the Committee with a comprehensive understanding of the implementation of the Convention in the country concerned.

3. A State Party which has submitted a comprehensive initial report to the Committee need not, in its subsequent reports submitted in accordance with paragraph 1 (b) of the present article, repeat basic information previously provided.

4. The Committee may request from States Parties further information relevant to the implementation of the Convention.

5. The Committee shall submit to the General Assembly, through the Economic and Social Council, every two years, reports on its activities.

6. States Parties shall make their reports widely available to the public in their own countries.

Article 45

In order to foster the effective implementation of the Convention and to encourage international co-operation in the field covered by the Convention:

(a) The specialized agencies, the United Nations Children's Fund and other United Nations organs shall be entitled to be represented at the consideration of the implementation of such provisions of the present Convention as fall within the scope of their mandate. The Committee may invite the specialized agencies, the United Nations Children's Fund and other competent bodies as it may consider appropriate to provide expert advice on the implementation of the Convention in areas falling within the scope of their respective mandates. The Committee may invite the specialized agencies, the United Nations Children's Fund and other United Nations organs to submit reports on the implementation of the Convention in areas falling within the scope of their activities;

(b) The Committee shall transmit, as it may consider appropriate, to the specialized agencies, the United Nations Children's Fund and other competent bodies, any reports from States Parties that contain a request, or indicate a need, for technical advice or assistance, along with the Committee's observations and suggestions, if any, on these requests or indications;

(c) The Committee may recommend to the General Assembly to request the Secretary-General to undertake on its behalf studies on specific issues relating to the rights of the child;

(d) The Committee may make suggestions and general recommendations based on information received pursuant to articles 44 and 45 of the present Convention. Such suggestions and general recommendations shall be transmitted to any State Party concerned and reported to the General Assembly, together with comments, if any, from States Parties.

* * *

Appendix II

Human Rights Act 1998

HUMAN RIGHTS ACT 1998

1998 CHAPTER 42

An Act to give further effect to rights and freedoms guaranteed under the European Convention on Human Rights; to make provision with respect to holders of certain judicial offices who become judges of the European Court of Human Rights; and for connected purposes.

9th November 1998

BE IT ENACTED by the Queen's most Excellent Majesty, by and with the advice and consent of the Lords Spiritual and Temporal, and Commons, in this present Parliament assembled, and by the authority of the same, as follows:—

Introduction

1 The Convention Rights

(1)   In this Act 'the Convention rights' means the rights and fundamental freedoms set out in—

(a)   Articles 2 to 12 and 14 of the Convention,

(b)   Articles 1 to 3 of the First Protocol, and

(c)   Articles 1 and 2 of the Sixth Protocol,

as read with Articles 16 to 18 of the Convention.

(2)   Those Articles are to have effect for the purposes of this Act subject to any designated derogation or reservation (as to which see sections 14 and 15).

(3)   The Articles are set out in Schedule 1.

(4)   The Lord Chancellor may by order make such amendments to this Act as he considers appropriate to reflect the effect, in relation to the United Kingdom, of a protocol.

(5)   In subsection (4) 'protocol' means a protocol to the Convention—

(a)   which the United Kingdom has ratified; or

(b)   which the United Kingdom has signed with a view to ratification.

(6)   No amendment may be made by an order under subsection (4) so as to come into force before the protocol concerned is in force in relation to the United Kingdom.

2 Interpretation of Convention rights

(1)   A court or tribunal determining a question which has arisen in connection with a Convention right must take into account any—
- (a)   judgment, decision, declaration or advisory opinion of the European Court of Human Rights,
- (b)   opinion of the Commission given in a report adopted under Article 31 of the Convention,
- (c)   decision of the Commission in connection with Article 26 or 27(2) of the Convention, or
- (d)   decision of the Committee of Ministers taken under Article 46 of the Convention,

whenever made or given, so far as, in the opinion of the court or tribunal, it is relevant to the proceedings in which that question has arisen.

(2)   Evidence of any judgment, decision, declaration or opinion of which account may have to be taken under this section is to be given in proceedings before any court or tribunal in such manner as may be provided by rules.

(3)   In this section 'rules' means rules of court or, in the case of proceedings before a tribunal, rules made for the purposes of this section—
- (a)   by the Lord Chancellor or the Secretary of State, in relation to any proceedings outside Scotland;
- (b)   by the Secretary of State, in relation to proceedings in Scotland; or
- (c)   by a Northern Ireland department, in relation to proceedings before a tribunal in Northern Ireland—
  - (i)   which deals with transferred matters; and
  - (ii)   for which no rules made under paragraph (a) are in force.

Legislation

3 Interpretation of legislation

(1)   So far as it is possible to do so, primary legislation and subordinate legislation must be read and given effect in a way which is compatible with the Convention rights.

(2)   This section—
- (a)   applies to primary legislation and subordinate legislation whenever enacted;
- (b)   does not affect the validity, continuing operation or enforcement of any incompatible primary legislation; and
- (c)   does not affect the validity, continuing operation or enforcement of any incompatible subordinate legislation if (disregarding any possibility of revocation) primary legislation prevents removal of the incompatibility.

4 Declaration of incompatibility

(1)   Subsection (2) applies in any proceedings in which a court determines whether a provision of primary legislation is compatible with a Convention right.

(2)   If the court is satisfied that the provision is incompatible with a Convention right, it may make a declaration of that incompatibility.

(3)   Subsection (4) applies in any proceedings in which a court determines whether a provision of subordinate legislation, made in the exercise of a power conferred by primary legislation, is compatible with a Convention right.

(4)   If the court is satisfied—
    (a)   that the provision is incompatible with a Convention right, and
    (b)   that (disregarding any possibility of revocation) the primary legislation concerned prevents removal of the incompatibility,

it may make a declaration of that incompatibility.

(5)   In this section 'court' means—
    (a)   the House of Lords;
    (b)   the Judicial Committee of the Privy Council;
    (c)   the Courts-Martial Appeal Court;
    (d)   in Scotland, the High Court of Justiciary sitting otherwise than as a trial court or the Court of Session;
    (e)   in England and Wales or Northern Ireland, the High Court or the Court of Appeal.

(6)   A declaration under this section ('a declaration of incompatibility')—
    (a)   does not affect the validity, continuing operation or enforcement of the provision in respect of which it is given; and
    (b)   is not binding on the parties to the proceedings in which it is made.

5 Right of Crown to intervene

(1)   Where a court is considering whether to make a declaration of incompatibility, the Crown is entitled to notice in accordance with rules of court.

(2)   In any case to which subsection (1) applies—
    (a)   a Minister of the Crown (or a person nominated by him),
    (b)   a member of the Scottish Executive,
    (c)   a Northern Ireland Minister,
    (d)   a Northern Ireland department,

is entitled, on giving notice in accordance with rules of court, to be joined as a party to the proceedings.

(3)   Notice under subsection (2) may be given at any time during the proceedings.

(4)   A person who has been made a party to criminal proceedings (other than in Scotland) as the result of a notice under subsection (2) may, with leave, appeal to the House of Lords against any declaration of incompatibility made in the proceedings.

(5)   In subsection (4)—
    'criminal proceedings' includes all proceedings before the Courts-Martial Appeal Court; and
    'leave' means leave granted by the court making the declaration of incompatibility or by the House of Lords.

Public authorities

6 Acts of public authorities

(1)   It is unlawful for a public authority to act in a way which is incompatible with a Convention right.

(2)   Subsection (1) does not apply to an act if—
 (a)   as the result of one or more provisions of primary legislation, the authority could not have acted differently; or
 (b)   in the case of one or more provisions of, or made under, primary legislation which cannot be read or given effect in a way which is compatible with the Convention rights, the authority was acting so as to give effect to or enforce those provisions.

(3)   In this section 'public authority' includes—
 (a)   a court or tribunal, and
 (b)   any person certain of whose functions are functions of a public nature,

but does not include either House of Parliament or a person exercising functions in connection with proceedings in Parliament.

(4)   In subsection (3) 'Parliament' does not include the House of Lords in its judicial capacity.

(5)   In relation to a particular act, a person is not a public authority by virtue only of subsection (3)(b) if the nature of the act is private.

(6)   'An act' includes a failure to act but does not include a failure to—
 (a)   introduce in, or lay before, Parliament a proposal for legislation; or
 (b)   make any primary legislation or remedial order.

7 Proceedings

(1)   A person who claims that a public authority has acted (or proposes to act) in a way which is made unlawful by section 6(1) may—
 (a)   bring proceedings against the authority under this Act in the appropriate court or tribunal, or
 (b)   rely on the Convention right or rights concerned in any legal proceedings,

but only if he is (or would be) a victim of the unlawful act.

(2)   In subsection (1)(a) 'appropriate court or tribunal' means such court or tribunal as may be determined in accordance with rules; and proceedings against an authority include a counterclaim or similar proceeding.

(3)   If the proceedings are brought on an application for judicial review, the applicant is to be taken to have a sufficient interest in relation to the unlawful act only if he is, or would be, a victim of that act.

(4)   If the proceedings are made by way of a petition for judicial review in Scotland, the applicant shall be taken to have title and interest to sue in relation to the unlawful act only if he is, or would be, a victim of that act.

(5)   Proceedings under subsection (1)(a) must be brought before the end of—
 (a)   the period of one year beginning with the date on which the act complained of took place; or

(b) such longer period as the court or tribunal considers equitable having regard to all the circumstances,

but that is subject to any rule imposing a stricter time limit in relation to the procedure in question.

(6) In subsection (1)(b) 'legal proceedings' includes—
  (a) proceedings brought by or at the instigation of a public authority; and
  (b) an appeal against the decision of a court or tribunal.

(7) For the purposes of this section, a person is a victim of an unlawful act only if he would be a victim for the purposes of Article 34 of the Convention if proceedings were brought in the European Court of Human Rights in respect of that act.

(8) Nothing in this Act creates a criminal offence.

(9) In this section 'rules' means—
  (a) in relation to proceedings before a court or tribunal outside Scotland, rules made by the Lord Chancellor or the Secretary of State for the purposes of this section or rules of court,
  (b) in relation to proceedings before a court or tribunal in Scotland, rules made by the Secretary of State for those purposes,
  (c) in relation to proceedings before a tribunal in Northern Ireland—
    (i) which deals with transferred matters; and
    (ii) for which no rules made under paragraph (a) are in force,
    rules made by a Northern Ireland department for those purposes,

and includes provision made by order under section 1 of the Courts and Legal Services Act 1990.

(10) In making rules, regard must be had to section 9.

(11) The Minister who has power to make rules in relation to a particular tribunal may, to the extent he considers it necessary to ensure that the tribunal can provide an appropriate remedy in relation to an act (or proposed act) of a public authority which is (or would be) unlawful as a result of section 6(1), by order add to—
  (a) the relief or remedies which the tribunal may grant; or
  (b) the grounds on which it may grant any of them.

(12) An order made under subsection (11) may contain such incidental, supplemental, consequential or transitional provision as the Minister making it considers appropriate.

(13) 'The Minister' includes the Northern Ireland department concerned.

8 Judicial remedies

(1) In relation to any act (or proposed act) of a public authority which the court finds is (or would be) unlawful, it may grant such relief or remedy, or make such order, within its powers as it considers just and appropriate.

(2) But damages may be awarded only by a court which has power to award damages, or to order the payment of compensation, in civil proceedings.

(3) No award of damages is to be made unless, taking account of all the circumstances of the case, including—
  (a) any other relief or remedy granted, or order made, in relation to the act in question (by that or any other court), and

(b)   the consequences of any decision (of that or any other court) in respect of that act,

the court is satisfied that the award is necessary to afford just satisfaction to the person in whose favour it is made.

(4)   In determining—
(a)   whether to award damages, or
(b)   the amount of an award,

the court must take into account the principles applied by the European Court of Human Rights in relation to the award of compensation under Article 41 of the Convention.

(5)   A public authority against which damages are awarded is to be treated—
(a)   in Scotland, for the purposes of section 3 of the Law Reform (Miscellaneous Provisions) (Scotland) Act 1940 as if the award were made in an action of damages in which the authority has been found liable in respect of loss or damage to the person to whom the award is made;
(b)   for the purposes of the Civil Liability (Contribution) Act 1978 as liable in respect of damage suffered by the person to whom the award is made.

(6)   In this section—
'court' includes a tribunal;
'damages' means damages for an unlawful act of a public authority; and
'unlawful' means unlawful under section 6(1).

9 Judicial acts

(1)   Proceedings under section 7(1)(a) in respect of a judicial act may be brought only—
(a)   by exercising a right of appeal;
(b)   on an application (in Scotland a petition) for judicial review; or
(c)   in such other forum as may be prescribed by rules.

(2)   That does not affect any rule of law which prevents a court from being the subject of judicial review.

(3)   In proceedings under this Act in respect of a judicial act done in good faith, damages may not be awarded otherwise than to compensate a person to the extent required by Article 5(5) of the Convention.

(4)   An award of damages permitted by subsection (3) is to be made against the Crown; but no award may be made unless the appropriate person, if not a party to the proceedings, is joined.

(5)   In this section—
'appropriate person' means the Minister responsible for the court concerned, or a person or government department nominated by him;
'court' includes a tribunal;
'judge' includes a member of a tribunal, a justice of the peace and a clerk or other officer entitled to exercise the jurisdiction of a court;
'judicial act' means a judicial act of a court and includes an act done on the instructions, or on behalf, of a judge; and
'rules' has the same meaning as in section 7(9).

Remedial action

10 Power to take remedial action

(1) This section applies if—
  (a) a provision of legislation has been declared under section 4 to be incompatible with a Convention right and, if an appeal lies—
    (i) all persons who may appeal have stated in writing that they do not intend to do so;
    (ii) the time for bringing an appeal has expired and no appeal has been brought within that time; or
    (iii) an appeal brought within that time has been determined or abandoned; or
  (b) it appears to a Minister of the Crown or Her Majesty in Council that, having regard to a finding of the European Court of Human Rights made after the coming into force of this section in proceedings against the United Kingdom, a provision of legislation is incompatible with an obligation of the United Kingdom arising from the Convention.

(2) If a Minister of the Crown considers that there are compelling reasons for proceeding under this section, he may by order make such amendments to the legislation as he considers necessary to remove the incompatibility.

(3) If, in the case of subordinate legislation, a Minister of the Crown considers—
  (a) that it is necessary to amend the primary legislation under which the subordinate legislation in question was made, in order to enable the incompatibility to be removed, and
  (b) that there are compelling reasons for proceeding under this section,

he may by order make such amendments to the primary legislation as he considers necessary.

(4) This section also applies where the provision in question is in subordinate legislation and has been quashed, or declared invalid, by reason of incompatibility with a Convention right and the Minister proposes to proceed under paragraph 2(b) of Schedule 2.

(5) If the legislation is an Order in Council, the power conferred by subsection (2) or (3) is exercisable by Her Majesty in Council.

(6) In this section 'legislation' does not include a Measure of the Church Assembly or of the General Synod of the Church of England.

(7) Schedule 2 makes further provision about remedial orders.

Other rights and proceedings

11 Safeguard for existing human rights

A person's reliance on a Convention right does not restrict—
  (a) any other right or freedom conferred on him by or under any law having effect in any part of the United Kingdom; or
  (b) his right to make any claim or bring any proceedings which he could make or bring apart from sections 7 to 9.

12 Freedom of expression

(1)   This section applies if a court is considering whether to grant any relief which, if granted, might affect the exercise of the Convention right to freedom of expression.

(2)   If the person against whom the application for relief is made ('the respondent') is neither present nor represented, no such relief is to be granted unless the court is satisfied—
  (a)   that the applicant has taken all practicable steps to notify the respondent; or
  (b)   that there are compelling reasons why the respondent should not be notified.

(3)   No such relief is to be granted so as to restrain publication before trial unless the court is satisfied that the applicant is likely to establish that publication should not be allowed.

(4)   The court must have particular regard to the importance of the Convention right to freedom of expression and, where the proceedings relate to material which the respondent claims, or which appears to the court, to be journalistic, literary or artistic material (or to conduct connected with such material), to—
  (a)   the extent to which—
    (i)   the material has, or is about to, become available to the public; or
    (ii)   it is, or would be, in the public interest for the material to be published;
  (b)   any relevant privacy code.

(5)   In this section—
  'court' includes a tribunal; and
  'relief' includes any remedy or order (other than in criminal proceedings).

13 Freedom of thought, conscience and religion

(1)   If a court's determination of any question arising under this Act might affect the exercise by a religious organisation (itself or its members collectively) of the Convention right to freedom of thought, conscience and religion, it must have particular regard to the importance of that right.

(2)   In this section 'court' includes a tribunal.

Derogations and reservations

14 Derogations

(1)   In this Act 'designated derogation' means—
  . . .
    any derogation by the United Kingdom from an Article of the Convention, or of any protocol to the Convention, which is designated for the purposes of this Act in an order made by the Lord Chancellor.

(2)   . . .

(3)   If a designated derogation is amended or replaced it ceases to be a designated derogation.

(4)   But subsection (3) does not prevent the Lord Chancellor from exercising his power under subsection (1). . . to make a fresh designation order in respect of the Article concerned.

(5)   The Lord Chancellor must by order make such amendments to Schedule 3 as he considers appropriate to reflect—
  (a)   any designation order; or
  (b)   the effect of subsection (3).

(6)   A designation order may be made in anticipation of the making by the United Kingdom of a proposed derogation.

15 Reservations

(1)   In this Act 'designated reservation' means—
  (a)   the United Kingdom's reservation to Article 2 of the First Protocol to the Convention; and
  (b)   any other reservation by the United Kingdom to an Article of the Convention, or of any protocol to the Convention, which is designated for the purposes of this Act in an order made by the Lord Chancellor.

(2)   The text of the reservation referred to in subsection (1)(a) is set out in Part II of Schedule 3.

(3)   If a designated reservation is withdrawn wholly or in part it ceases to be a designated reservation.

(4)   But subsection (3) does not prevent the Lord Chancellor from exercising his power under subsection (1)(b) to make a fresh designation order in respect of the Article concerned.

(5)   The Lord Chancellor must by order make such amendments to this Act as he considers appropriate to reflect—
  (a)   any designation order; or
  (b)   the effect of subsection (3).

16 Period for which designated derogations have effect

(1)   If it has not already been withdrawn by the United Kingdom, a designated derogation ceases to have effect for the purposes of this Act—
    . . .
    at the end of the period of five years beginning with the date on which the order designating it was made.

(2)   At any time before the period—
  (a)   fixed by subsection (1) . . ., or
  (b)   extended by an order under this subsection,

comes to an end, the Lord Chancellor may by order extend it by a further period of five years.

(3)   An order under section 14(1) . . . ceases to have effect at the end of the period for consideration, unless a resolution has been passed by each House approving the order.

(4)   Subsection (3) does not affect—
  (a)   anything done in reliance on the order; or
  (b)   the power to make a fresh order under section 14(1) . . .

(5)   In subsection (3) 'period for consideration' means the period of forty days beginning with the day on which the order was made.

(6)   In calculating the period for consideration, no account is to be taken of any time during which—

    (a)   Parliament is dissolved or prorogued; or

    (b)   both Houses are adjourned for more than four days.

(7)   If a designated derogation is withdrawn by the United Kingdom, the Lord Chancellor must by order make such amendments to this Act as he considers are required to reflect that withdrawal.

17 Periodic review of designated reservations

(1)   The appropriate Minister must review the designated reservation referred to in section 15(1)(a)—

    (a)   before the end of the period of five years beginning with the date on which section 1(2) came into force; and

    (b)   if that designation is still in force, before the end of the period of five years beginning with the date on which the last report relating to it was laid under subsection (3).

(2)   The appropriate Minister must review each of the other designated reservations (if any)—

    (a)   before the end of the period of five years beginning with the date on which the order designating the reservation first came into force; and

    (b)   if the designation is still in force, before the end of the period of five years beginning with the date on which the last report relating to it was laid under subsection (3).

(3)   The Minister conducting a review under this section must prepare a report on the result of the review and lay a copy of it before each House of Parliament.

* * * *

SCHEDULE 1
The Articles

Section 1(3)

Part I
The Convention

Rights and Freedoms

Article 2
Right to life

1

Everyone's right to life shall be protected by law. No one shall be deprived of his life intentionally save in the execution of a sentence of a court following his conviction of a crime for which this penalty is provided by law.

2

Deprivation of life shall not be regarded as inflicted in contravention of this Article when it results from the use of force which is no more than absolutely necessary:

(a)   in defence of any person from unlawful violence;

(b)   in order to effect a lawful arrest or to prevent the escape of a person lawfully detained;

(c)   in action lawfully taken for the purpose of quelling a riot or insurrection.

Article 3
Prohibition of torture

No one shall be subjected to torture or to inhuman or degrading treatment or punishment.

Article 4
Prohibition of slavery and forced labour

1

No one shall be held in slavery or servitude.

2

No one shall be required to perform forced or compulsory labour.

3

For the purpose of this Article the term 'forced or compulsory labour' shall not include:

(a)   any work required to be done in the ordinary course of detention imposed according to the provisions of Article 5 of this Convention or during conditional release from such detention;

(b)   any service of a military character or, in case of conscientious objectors in countries where they are recognised, service exacted instead of compulsory military service;

(c)   any service exacted in case of an emergency or calamity threatening the life or well-being of the community;

(d)   any work or service which forms part of normal civic obligations.

Article 5
Right to liberty and security

1

Everyone has the right to liberty and security of person. No one shall be deprived of his liberty save in the following cases and in accordance with a procedure prescribed by law:

(a)   the lawful detention of a person after conviction by a competent court;

(b)   the lawful arrest or detention of a person for non-compliance with the lawful order of a court or in order to secure the fulfilment of any obligation prescribed by law;

(c)   the lawful arrest or detention of a person effected for the purpose of bringing him before the competent legal authority on reasonable suspicion of having committed an offence or when it is reasonably considered necessary to prevent his committing an offence or fleeing after having done so;

(d)   the detention of a minor by lawful order for the purpose of educational supervision or his lawful detention for the purpose of bringing him before the competent legal authority;

(e)   the lawful detention of persons for the prevention of the spreading of infectious diseases, of persons of unsound mind, alcoholics or drug addicts or vagrants;

(f)   the lawful arrest or detention of a person to prevent his effecting an unauthorised entry into the country or of a person against whom action is being taken with a view to deportation or extradition.

2

Everyone who is arrested shall be informed promptly, in a language which he understands, of the reasons for his arrest and of any charge against him.

3

Everyone arrested or detained in accordance with the provisions of paragraph 1(c) of this Article shall be brought promptly before a judge or other officer authorised by law to exercise judicial power and shall be entitled to trial within a reasonable time or to release pending trial. Release may be conditioned by guarantees to appear for trial.

4

Everyone who is deprived of his liberty by arrest or detention shall be entitled to take proceedings by which the lawfulness of his detention shall be decided speedily by a court and his release ordered if the detention is not lawful.

5

Everyone who has been the victim of arrest or detention in contravention of the provisions of this Article shall have an enforceable right to compensation.

Article 6
Right to a fair trial

1

In the determination of his civil rights and obligations or of any criminal charge against him, everyone is entitled to a fair and public hearing within a reasonable time by an independent and impartial tribunal established by law. Judgment shall be pronounced publicly but the press and public may be excluded from all or part of the trial in the interest of morals, public order or national security in a democratic society, where the interests of juveniles or the protection of the private life of the parties so require, or to the extent strictly necessary in the opinion of the court in special circumstances where publicity would prejudice the interests of justice.

2

Everyone charged with a criminal offence shall be presumed innocent until proved guilty according to law.

3

Everyone charged with a criminal offence has the following minimum rights:

(a) to be informed promptly, in a language which he understands and in detail, of the nature and cause of the accusation against him;

(b) to have adequate time and facilities for the preparation of his defence;

(c) to defend himself in person or through legal assistance of his own choosing or, if he has not sufficient means to pay for legal assistance, to be given it free when the interests of justice so require;

(d) to examine or have examined witnesses against him and to obtain the attendance and examination of witnesses on his behalf under the same conditions as witnesses against him;

(e) to have the free assistance of an interpreter if he cannot understand or speak the language used in court.

Article 7
No punishment without law

1

No one shall be held guilty of any criminal offence on account of any act or omission which did not constitute a criminal offence under national or international law at the time when it was committed. Nor shall a heavier penalty be imposed than the one that was applicable at the time the criminal offence was committed.

2

This Article shall not prejudice the trial and punishment of any person for any act or omission which, at the time when it was committed, was criminal according to the general principles of law recognised by civilised nations.

Article 8
Right to respect for private and family life

1

Everyone has the right to respect for his private and family life, his home and his correspondence.

2

There shall be no interference by a public authority with the exercise of this right except such as is in accordance with the law and is necessary in a democratic society in the interests of national security, public safety or the economic well-being of the country, for the prevention of disorder or crime, for the protection of health or morals, or for the protection of the rights and freedoms of others.

Article 9
Freedom of thought, conscience and religion

1

Everyone has the right to freedom of thought, conscience and religion; this right includes freedom to change his religion or belief and freedom, either alone or in community with others and in public or private, to manifest his religion or belief, in worship, teaching, practice and observance.

2

Freedom to manifest one's religion or beliefs shall be subject only to such limitations as are prescribed by law and are necessary in a democratic society in the interests of public safety, for the protection of public order, health or morals, or for the protection of the rights and freedoms of others.

Article 10
Freedom of expression

1

Everyone has the right to freedom of expression. This right shall include freedom to hold opinions and to receive and impart information and ideas without interference by public authority and regardless of frontiers. This Article shall not prevent States from requiring the licensing of broadcasting, television or cinema enterprises.

2

The exercise of these freedoms, since it carries with it duties and responsibilities, may be subject to such formalities, conditions, restrictions or penalties as are prescribed by law and are necessary in a democratic society, in the interests of national security, territorial integrity or public safety, for the prevention of disorder or crime, for the protection of health or morals, for the protection of the reputation or rights of others, for preventing the disclosure of information received in confidence, or for maintaining the authority and impartiality of the judiciary.

Article 11
Freedom of assembly and association

1

Everyone has the right to freedom of peaceful assembly and to freedom of association with others, including the right to form and to join trade unions for the protection of his interests.

2

No restrictions shall be placed on the exercise of these rights other than such as are prescribed by law and are necessary in a democratic society in the interests of national security or public safety, for the prevention of disorder or crime, for the protection of health or morals or for the protection of the rights and freedoms of others. This Article shall not prevent the imposition of lawful restrictions on the exercise of these rights by members of the armed forces, of the police or of the administration of the State.

Article 12
Right to marry

Men and women of marriageable age have the right to marry and to found a family, according to the national laws governing the exercise of this right.

Article 14
Prohibition of discrimination

The enjoyment of the rights and freedoms set forth in this Convention shall be secured without discrimination on any ground such as sex, race, colour, language, religion, political or other opinion, national or social origin, association with a national minority, property, birth or other status.

Article 16
Restrictions on political activity of aliens

Nothing in Articles 10, 11 and 14 shall be regarded as preventing the High Contracting Parties from imposing restrictions on the political activity of aliens.

Article 17
Prohibition of abuse of rights

Nothing in this Convention may be interpreted as implying for any State, group or person any right to engage in any activity or perform any act aimed at the destruction of any of the rights and freedoms set forth herein or at their limitation to a greater extent than is provided for in the Convention.

Article 18
Limitation on use of restrictions on rights

The restrictions permitted under this Convention to the said rights and freedoms shall not be applied for any purpose other than those for which they have been prescribed.

Part II
The First Protocol

Article 1
Protection of property

Every natural or legal person is entitled to the peaceful enjoyment of his possessions. No one shall be deprived of his possessions except in the public interest and subject to the conditions provided for by law and by the general principles of international law.

The preceding provisions shall not, however, in any way impair the right of a State to enforce such laws as it deems necessary to control the use of property in accordance with the general interest or to secure the payment of taxes or other contributions or penalties.

Article 2
Right to education

No person shall be denied the right to education. In the exercise of any functions which it assumes in relation to education and to teaching, the State shall respect the right of parents to ensure such education and teaching in conformity with their own religious and philosophical convictions.

Article 3
Right to free elections

The High Contracting Parties undertake to hold free elections at reasonable intervals by secret ballot, under conditions which will ensure the free expression of the opinion of the people in the choice of the legislature.

Part III
The Sixth Protocol

Article 1
Abolition of the death penalty

The death penalty shall be abolished. No one shall be condemned to such penalty or executed.

Article 2
Death penalty in time of war

A State may make provision in its law for the death penalty in respect of acts committed in time of war or of imminent threat of war; such penalty shall be applied only in the instances laid down in the law and in accordance with its provisions. The State shall communicate to the Secretary General of the Council of Europe the relevant provisions of that law.

Index